Strategic Management for Decision Making

KENT SERIES IN MANAGEMENT

Strategic Management for Decision Making

MICHAEL J. STAHL
University of Tennessee

DAVID W. GRIGSBY
Clemson University

PWS-KENT PUBLISHING COMPANY
Boston

PWS-KENT
Publishing Company

20 Park Plaza
Boston, Massachusetts 02116

PWS-KENT Publishing Company is a division of Wadsworth, Inc.

Library of Congress Cataloging-in-Publication Data

Stahl, Michael J.
    Strategic management for decision making / Michael J. Stahl and David W. Grigsby.
      p. cm.
    Includes bibliographical references and index.
    ISBN 0–534–92681–9
    1. Strategic planning. 2. Decision-making. I. Grigsby, David W.
II. Title.
HD30.28.S67   1991
658.4′03—dc20

91–19176
CIP

International Student Edition ISBN: 0–534–98579–3
Printed in the United States of America.
91 92 93 94 95 96 -- 10 9 8 7 6 5 4 3 2 1

 This book is printed on recycled, acid-free paper.

Sponsoring Editor: *Rolf A. Janke*
Editorial Assistant: *Marnie Pommett*
Production Editor: *Susan M. C. Caffey*
Manufacturing Coordinator: *Marcia A. Locke*
Interior Designer: *Eve Mendelsohn Lehmann*
Cover Designer and Calligrapher: *Amy S. Veaner*
Interior Illustrator: *Chris Hayden*
Typesetter: *Pine Tree Composition, Inc.*
Cover Printer: *New England Book Components, Inc.*
Printer/Binder: *Arcata Graphics/Halliday*

CONTENTS

9   INTERNATIONAL STRATEGIC DECISIONS   197

PART TWO   STRATEGIC MANAGEMENT APPLICATIONS

CASE ANALYSIS GUIDE   226

CASES

PREFACE

In writing *Strategic Management for Decision Making,* our objectives were three-fold. The first was to offer a comprehensive text that incorporates the latest theory and research in the field. The second was to make it understandable and appealing to a wide audience by incorporating ample illustrations from real organizations and offering interesting and challenging cases. The third was to approach the subject in a way that is unique—examining strategic management as a decision-making process.

The result is a text that can be used in a variety of ways on a number of levels. Its emphasis on practical application, stressing the decision-making aspects of each phase of the strategic management process, makes it ideal for use as a basic text. Our explanations focus on the results of decisions, and numerous examples of real-world strategic decisions are packed into every chapter. Many of these examples are drawn from the popular business press, and a few are listed below in the order in which they appear in the text.

- When Merck and Johnson & Johnson decided to form a joint venture to market over-the-counter drugs, they recognized the changes in the external environment concerning the graying of America with resultant increased demand for drugs.
- The decision by Coca-Cola to divest the Wine Spectrum was in part due to a recognition that producing and marketing wine did not quite fit with its distinctive competence in producing and marketing soft drinks.
- Historically southeastern based, NCNB National Bank's decision to acquire substantial banking assets in Texas and thereby double NCNB's size to approximately $60 billion in assets in 1990 was part of a strategy to concentrate on financial products/services while serving a broader market.
- Wal-Mart's decision to compete partly on the basis of price leadership is reflected in the discounts it demands from its vendors with large volume purchases, its efficient distribution system, and store locations that have usually avoided very high cost areas.

- Motorola's decision to produce and market semiconductors and communications equipment on the basis of extremely high quality was recognized with the Baldrige National Quality Award as an exemplary way to compete and satisfy customers.
- Xerox's decision to implement cross-functional task teams was partly a recognition of the limitations of traditional functional organizational structures.
- General Motors' decision to control profitability in the late 1980s unfortunately occurred at a time when it lost dramatic market share.
- General Electric's decision to build a $1.7 billion manufacturing facility in Spain in the 1990s was associated with growing international opportunities particularly in the European Community.

With its full treatment of theoretical concepts, the inclusion of descriptive research results, and exhaustive references to all of the major work in the field, *Strategic Management for Decision Making* can also support a more intensive investigation of the field by serving as a resource for further study. You will find complete explanations of all of the major theories and recent contributions in strategy, and references to many others. Recent research findings are incorporated into the text of each chapter.

The thread that ties the practical and theoretical aspects of strategic management together is our focus on decision making. This text approaches each aspect of the material from the viewpoint of the decision maker, not solely at the CEO level in large corporations but at all levels and in all types and sizes of organizations. The strategic management process is viewed as a "stream of decisions," each one related to the others. By depicting the process in this way, we believe students will have a better understanding of the total context of the strategic management process.

Specific chapters on international strategic decisions and corporate social responsibility are included. These chapters offer students an appreciation of internationalization and ethics in strategy.

A hierarchical coverage of strategy is included—corporate-level, business-level, and functional-level strategies are covered in sequence in three separate chapters. This hierarchical treatment helps students to understand relationships in strategy and to integrate concepts.

Total quality management concepts are integrated throughout several chapters. This helps the student to understand some linkages between TQM and strategic decisions.

The cases chosen for the book reinforce the concept of a decision-making orientation. They were selected from hundreds of submissions and suggestions. Most of them are new—written in the past three years. Five were written exclusively for this book. A few are classics that have been updated with recent information. They feature an amazing variety of organizations from small family-owned businesses to multinational corporations. They have in common their emphasis on the importance of understanding and mastering the strategic decision process. We think students and instructors alike will enjoy them and learn from them.

To help students learn the case study process, a detailed Case Analysis Guide, one of the most comprehensive in the industry, is included in the text. To help students perform exhaustive financial analysis, sensitivity analysis, and comparative industry analysis, a financial analysis software package (fis-CAL), with financial data from eight of the cases and comparative industry data, accompanies the text.

A comprehensive Instructor's Manual with a testbank (discussion, multiple-choice, and true-false questions), transparency masters, and detailed case teaching notes is also available. This completes a total teaching package.

ACKNOWLEDGMENTS

As with any book of this type, this one represents far more than the efforts of its two authors. Consequently, we have many others to thank for this final product.

We are especially indebted to the case authors. Without them the book could not be a reality. Their willingness to share their work with us is deeply appreciated.

Much of the success of this project is also due to the support and excellent working environments provided us by The University of Tennessee and Clemson University and to our colleagues who unselfishly offered their suggestions, comments, and encouragement. Special thanks are also due to our students who cheerfully endured classroom testing of early drafts of the text and cases.

A number of reviewers deserve a special mention here. They worked long and hard on the manuscript and their comments and suggestions proved to be of immeasurable help in improving our work. They are:

Charles R. Gowen III
Northern Illinois University

Jeffrey S. Harrison
Clemson University

Donald E. Huffmire
University of Connecticut

Daniel F. Jennings
Baylor University

Necmi Karagozoglu
California State University-Sacramento

Rose E. Knotts
University of North Texas

Lynn Neeley
Northern Illinois University

Barbara Spencer
Mississippi State University

A very special thanks goes to Alfreda Bouyer who typed the entire manuscript, never missed a deadline, and kept us organized through it all.

We also thank our families for enduring us during this often difficult (but always interesting) process.

PART ONE

*Strategic
Management
Concepts*

CHAPTER ONE

Strategic Management Decisions

Consider the following events:

- General Motors announced that it would cut its productive capacity of over 5 million automobiles per year to under 4.5 million by 1992.[1]
- IBM Corporation launched the most ambitious software project in its history, one that promised the most sophisticated programs ever designed for IBM mainframe equipment.[2]
- A pharmaceutical joint venture of Johnson & Johnson and Merck agreed to buy the U.S. over-the-counter drug business of ICI Americas (a subsidiary of the giant British firm Imperial Chemical Industries) for over $450 million.[3]
- Japan Broadcasting Company began experimental telecasts of high definition television (HDTV) signals via satellite during the 1988 Olympic games from Seoul.[4]
- JCB Company, Japan's credit card giant, began a major drive to increase the number of its cardholders outside of Japan from 30,000 to over one million.[5]
- The Walt Disney Company announced that Kermit the Frog and Miss Piggy would be moving to the Magic Kingdom as Henson Associates became a part of the Disney empire.[6]

These announcements, all of which were made in a recent year, illustrate the range and scope of high-level activity in some of the world's largest corporations. What do the incidents have in common? They are all *strategic decisions,* and as such, they form the basis for *strategic management.*

STRATEGIC DECISIONS

Strategic decision making is not the exclusive domain of large companies. It is an important activity in all types of organizations—large and small, for profit and not for profit, private and public. Companies of all sizes and all

3

purposes must learn to direct the strategic-management process by engaging in strategic decision making. When your local grocery, bank, or insurance agency decides to offer a new product line or service, it is making a strategic decision. When a hospital or public service agency decides to serve a new clientele, it is making a strategic decision. In short, whenever organizations significantly alter their activities, the strategic-management process is at work.

Three factors distinguish strategic decisions from other business considerations:

1. Strategic decisions deal with concerns that are central to the livelihood and survival of the entire organization and usually involve a large portion of the organization's resources.
2. Strategic decisions represent new activities or areas of concern and typically address issues that are unusual for the organization rather than issues that lend themselves to routine decision making.
3. Strategic decisions have repercussions for the way other, lower-level decisions in the organization are made.

STRATEGIC MANAGEMENT DEFINED

The term *strategic management* is used to refer to the entire scope of strategic decision-making activity in an organization. It may be defined as the set of managerial decisions that relates the organization to its environment, guides internal activities, and determines the long-term performance of the organization.

STRATEGY RELATES THE ORGANIZATION TO ITS ENVIRONMENT

The role that strategic decisions play in relating an organization to its environment may be illustrated by the following two examples:

- Faced with extensive competition from foreign steelmakers, United States Steel Company drastically cut its steel-making capacity in the early 1980s and acquired Marathon Oil Company for $6.4 billion, giving the company a strong foothold in a completely new industry.[7] The result was a very different orientation for the corporation, and that fact was communicated to the public when the company changed its name to USX.
- R. J. Reynolds Industries, a long-time leader in the tobacco industry, went through several changes in its basic business as it responded to its environment. Declining tobacco sales led the company to pursue numerous acquisitions in the consumer foods industry, the largest of which was its merger with Nabisco in 1987, which resulted in the giant consumer goods company RJR-Nabisco.[8]

STRATEGY AS A SERIES OF DECISIONS

A noted theorist in strategy, Henry Mintzberg, described strategy as "a pattern in a stream of decisions."[9] He illustrated this concept by describing the patterns in the many decisions made at Volkswagenwerk over a fifty-four-year period, from which the company's strategy of low priced transportation may be discerned. Mintzberg also described the United States' military strategy of increasing involvement in Vietnam by reporting on the patterns in the many decisions made over two decades.

Mintzberg's view that strategy is "a pattern in a stream of decisions" has at least two implications. First, strategy is not one decision but must be viewed in the context of a number of decisions and the consistency among them.[10] Second, the concept means that the organization must be constantly aware of decision alternatives. Strategy may be viewed as the rationale that governs the organization's choices among its alternatives. For example, a mainframe computer company might ask if it should stay in the mainframe computer business or branch out into personal computers. Should a personal computer company market its products through third-party distributors, or should it have its own sales force? Strategy emerges as a pattern among these smaller decisions and defines the organization's business as a response to its changed environment.

DELIBERATE VS. EMERGENT STRATEGY

If strategy is to be defined as "a pattern in a stream of decisions," one might question whether strategy must always be a purposeful process. Could it also be the result of managers simply "muddling through"—making small decisions on a daily basis—as that can also result in a "pattern in the stream"? Must strategy always be the result of a planned, conscious effort toward goals that result in a pattern?

Mintzberg distinguished between *deliberate strategy* and *emergent strategy*.[11] Traditionally, strategy has been viewed as simply a result of the planning process. A company's goals are set in motion, and its intended strategy is undertaken to achieve them. According to Mintzberg, this view of strategy solely as a deliberate process ignores a wide range of other possibilities.[12] In some cases, a firm may not intentionally set strategy. Its strategy may simply emerge from the grass roots of the organization as a result of its activities. Emergent strategies can also be the result of the implementation process. Alterations in goals and "course corrections" may produce strategies that vary from their original design.

For these reasons, the study of strategy must extend beyond study of the planning process. Kenneth Hatten suggested that we study the decisions themselves and infer strategy from the strategic decisions. "Although quantitative policy research has mostly been descriptive, it has addressed strategic decision making from the preconceived notion of what should be done according to the normative dictates of our theory. But, is that what managers do? Why not work backward from their judgment, explore strategic decision making as a personal and group process and develop new theory?"[13]

THE STRATEGIC MANAGEMENT PROCESS

STRATEGY FORMULATION, IMPLEMENTATION, EVALUATION, AND CONTROL

The strategic management process involves the entire range of decisions an organization makes concerning its central activities. There are three steps in the process. *Strategy formulation* is the set of decisions that determine the organization's mission and establishes its objectives, strategies, and policies. *Strategy implementation* refers to decisions that are made to install new strategy or reinforce existing strategy. These decisions refer to the motivational processes, structure, systems, cross-functional groups, policies, and organizational culture used to make the strategy work. *Evaluation and control* are the activities and decisions that keep the process on track. They include following up on goal accomplishment and feeding back the results to decision makers. Figure 1.1 depicts the steps in the strategic management process.

PLAN OF THE BOOK

This book presents a comprehensive study of the strategic management process and its related areas. The diagram in Figure 1.2 provides a summary of the outline followed in the book. As a prelude to the study of the strategy formulation process, we first consider the individuals who are responsible for strategy and the contexts in which strategy decisions arise. Strategic managers are the focus of the remainder of this first chapter. We consider their relationships and responsibilities as well as their biases, and we look at how strategic consensus is achieved among groups of decision makers. In Chapter 2, we discuss the environment for strategic decision making and its effects on the process. Our study of the environment of organizations includes the external environment, which gives rise to strategic opportunities as well as threats to the organization's goal achievement, and the internal environment, its strengths and weaknesses, and how it is analyzed and audited.

The strategy formulation process encompasses four chapters. The second half of Chapter 2 contains a discussion of the key concepts in strategic decision making. Terms are defined and explained here. We also discuss in this chapter the task of formulating the organization's overall mission and the relationship of that mission to the organization's objectives and strategies.

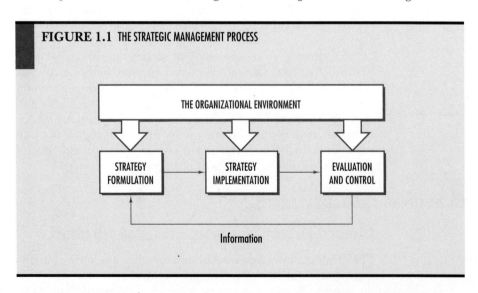

FIGURE 1.1 THE STRATEGIC MANAGEMENT PROCESS

FIGURE 1.2 PLAN OF THE BOOK

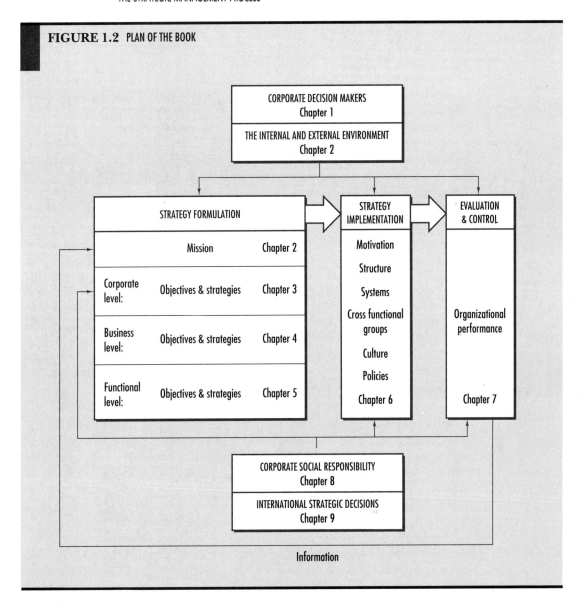

Chapter 3 covers corporate-level strategy—the determination of the organization's primary domain or orientation. The discussion includes concentration, diversification, vertical integration, merger and acquisition, joint ventures, and restructuring strategies.

In Chapter 4, we consider business-level strategies, which are concerned with how the organization will compete within its chosen domain. We discuss the business-level strategies of cost leadership, differentiation, and focus.

Chapter 5 deals with strategies of the organization's various functions.

Strategic decisions concerning production and operations, marketing, finance, human resources, information systems, and research and development are discussed.

Strategy implementation is introduced and discussed in Chapter 6. Here we emphasize the organization's structure, its motivational processes, its systems and processes, cross-functional groups, policies, and the corporate culture as determinants of the successful implementation of strategy.

Chapter 7 deals with the evaluation and control process as it applies to strategic management. We discuss the processes through which the organization's performance is compared to its objectives and the ways in which corrective action is taken to assure goal accomplishment.

The special topic of corporate social responsibility is dealt with in Chapter 8. The role of the organization in society and the organization's responsibility to the various aspects of its environment are subjects of growing concern in both the public and the private sectors. This chapter discusses the role that strategic decisions play in these important areas.

The growing importance of the international arena in business is the topic of Chapter 9, Multinational Strategies and Perspectives. The chapter covers strategic management's role in the global economy and the international implications of strategic decision making.

THE RELATIONSHIP BETWEEN STRATEGY AND PERFORMANCE

The fundamental question "Why should an organization engage in strategic management?" must be answered by looking at the relationship between strategic management and performance. Do companies that have active strategic planning programs fare better than those that do not? Can the adoption of strategic planning actually improve profitability? Given the emphasis on strategic management at the upper levels of most of our largest and most successful corporations, we would expect the answers to these questions to be yes.

Empirical evidence of the relationship of strategic decisions to performance is sometimes difficult to obtain, although a number of researchers have investigated the relationship. In 1986, Lawrence C. Rhyne reviewed fourteen studies that had sought to determine the link between strategic planning and corporate financial performance.[14] He found that eight of the studies generally supported a positive relationship between strategic planning and performance, five studies found no relationship, and one study reported a negative relationship. In a more recent analysis, Pearce, Freeman, and Robinson investigated the strategy-performance relationship by reviewing eighteen independent studies.[15] They found that ten of the eighteen studies supported the notion that formal strategic planning leads to superior performance and eight found no link. The conclusion of both investigations was that although the preponderance of evidence pointed to a positive role for strategic planning in enhancing the financial performance of the firm, conclusive proof was hard to obtain because of the wide variation in formal planning arrangements in the organization studied and in the ways that performance was measured.

Given this general support for the process of strategic planning, the answer to the question "Why should an organization engage in strategic management?" seems to be that, in general, firms engage in strategic decision making in order to enhance their effectiveness and have a better chance of reaching their goals. Moreover, firms that adhere to formal strategic planning are, on the average, better able to obtain positive financial results.

THE STRATEGIC DECISION MAKERS

As with any other important pursuit, the strategic management process requires competent individuals to ensure its success. Responsibility for strategy normally rests with a small number of *strategic managers* within the organization. It is their job to develop competitive responses to a rapidly changing complex environment—a pursuit that requires a wide range of skills and experience. Strategic managers are responsible for the overall performance of the organization; they are often referred to as "general managers" for that reason and are noted for their breadth of experience.[16] *Functional managers,* on the other hand, bear responsibility for specific business functions within the organization. Their expertise lies in one narrow domain such as finance or production.

Because of their overall importance to the success of the organization, it is appropriate to ask, "What are the characteristics of successful strategic managers?" A widely cited article by Edward Wrapp suggested that five essential skills are necessary for strategic managers.[17] Table 1.1 summarizes those skills.

Many of the examples used in this text concerning strategic decision makers are taken from large organizations, primarily because of their familiarity to the reader. This focus is not meant to ignore the strategic decision making that is conducted in existing small businesses or in start-up organizations in an entrepreneurial mode. Many of the strategic tasks conducted by several decision makers in a large organization are often undertaken by one entrepreneur in a start-up organization or an existing small business. Although the strategic processes described in this text and the resulting plans may not be written down in a small organization, they are nevertheless relevant to the individual strategic decision maker who implicitly formulates the strategies and implements them without the benefit of a staff.

CHIEF EXECUTIVE OFFICERS, PRESIDENTS, AND CHAIRMEN

The highest strategic manager in an organization can go by a wide range of titles, but the one most commonly used at the corporate level is that of *chief executive officer* (CEO). As the title implies, that individual has ultimate responsibility for the formulation and implementation of the organization's overall

TABLE 1.1 CHARACTERISTICS OF STRATEGIC MANAGERS

SUCCESSFUL STRATEGIC MANAGERS ARE:

1. **Well informed.** They use a wide range of information sources to keep in touch with activities throughout the organization, and they use information to make more effective decisions.

2. **Skilled at focusing their time and energy.** They delegate effectively and know how to protect their time, yet they know when it is important to make a decision or take action themselves.

3. **Good at playing the power game.** They are sensitive to relationships in the organization's hierarchy, and they know how to build consensus for their ideas and form coalitions for getting their plans accomplished.

4. **Good at being imprecise.** They know how to adapt their goals to changing conditions and avoid committing publicly to detailed plans that may require substantive change.

5. **Accomplished at "muddling with a purpose."** They recognize the difficulty in trying to accomplish complex goals, so they push their programs through piecemeal, dividing objectives into smaller, more easily accomplished parts.

Source: Edward Wrapp, "Good Managers Don't Make Policy Decisions," *Harvard Business Review* 45 (September–October 1967). Reprinted by permission of *Harvard Business Review.* Copyright © 1967 by the President and Fellows of Harvard College; all rights reserved.

strategy. The titles *president* and *chairman of the board* are also commonly used to refer to individuals with responsibility for the overall strategy of the company. Sometimes, all three jobs are vested in one person. In other organizations, the jobs are held by two or three separate executives, and an executive office is formed with the multiple executives.

Because the insights of these executives play such a critical role, a number of writers have stressed the importance of matching the characteristics of these executives with the firm's strategies.[18] For example, in a book aptly titled *The Concept of Corporate Strategy*, K. R. Andrews described the chief executive's role as "Chief Executive as Architect of Purpose."[19] Peter Drucker, one of the most noted authors on management, described effective leadership not in terms of charisma or personality qualities but in the following strategic terms: "The foundation of effective leadership is thinking through the organization's mission, defining it and establishing it, clearly and visibly. The leader sets the goals, sets the priorities, and sets and maintains the standards."[20]

Although the CEO as a leader should articulate the vision of the organization for the future, that vision must be in touch with the vision of the other strategic decision makers, especially that of the board of directors. As the CEO is accountable to the board for corporate performance and direction, the CEO must include the board's input in articulating the corporate vision. A recent article in *Business Week,* "The Quiet Coup at Alcoa: The Untold Story of How the Board Ousted the Chief Executive—and Changed Corporate Strategy," highlighted the importance of CEO-board agreement: "Chief Executive Parry's goal of pursuing his century-old aluminum company into new, Space Age materials showed vision. But Alcoa's customers and employees became confused. Finally, the board went looking for a new CEO."[21] Strategic decision makers must show vision, yet they must also stay in touch.

In pursuing this role as visionary for the organization, CEOs become spokespersons for their organizations. They sometimes become celebrities as well. A mid-1980s issue of *Business Week* contained a cover story entitled "Business Celebrities," with features of Lee Iacocca (CEO, chief salesman and savior of Chrysler), Steve Jobs (founder of Apple Computer and Next, Inc.), T. Boone Pickens (corporate raider and CEO of Mesa Petroleum), Felix Rohatyn (investment banker and rescuer of New York's 1970s financial crisis), and Ted Turner (CEO Of CNN).[22] Another recent article described how John Sculley, as CEO of Apple, spends much of his time articulating his vision of Apple: "Celebrity Chief: Shedding His Shyness, John Sculley Promotes Apple—and Himself: He Gives Resounding Speeches on Plans, Writes a Book."[23]

OTHER MANAGERS AND STAFF MEMBERS

Another strategic manager at the corporate level is the *chief operating officer* (COO), whose role is usually assumed to be one of implementing the strategy decided on by the CEO and the board. Most CEOs solicit the input of the COO, strategic planning staff members, and staff-level vice presidents in strategy formulation.

At the business level, division vice presidents and group vice presidents manage divisions or groups that are usually organized around a group of products or a particular product segment. These decision makers are usually charged with formulating competitive business-level strategies for their businesses. These business-level competitive strategies should be consistent with and flow from the corporate-level strategies.

At the functional level, vice presidents for manufacturing, marketing, finance, human resources, information systems, and research and development are involved with strategic decision making. These strategies need to be consistent with the corporate- and business-level strategic decisions. Indeed, Mintzberg argued that strategic decisions are made at multiple levels in many organizations.[24]

The amount of time and effort these executives spend in planning varies from level to level as the importance of strategic decision making varies with the job and the level of the job. Figure 1.3 indicates how the time horizon for planning varies across levels of management. Top-level executives' time horizon for planning includes years ahead, whereas supervisors typically focus on this week.

BOARD OF DIRECTORS

The *board of directors* represents the interests of the stockholders in the affairs of the corporation. In that capacity, it plays an important role in the strategic management process. Recently, the role of the directors has been growing in

FIGURE 1.3 "IDEAL" ALLOCATIONS OF TIME FOR PLANNING IN THE "AVERAGE" COMPANY

	TODAY	1 WEEK AHEAD	1 MONTH AHEAD	3-6 MONTHS AHEAD	1 YEAR AHEAD	2 YEARS AHEAD	3-4 YEARS AHEAD	5-10 YEARS AHEAD
PRESIDENT	1%	2%	5%	10%	15%	27%	30%	10%
EXECUTIVE VICE-PRESIDENT	2%	4%	10%	29%	20%	18%	13%	4%
VICE-PRESIDENT OF FUNCTIONAL AREA	4%	8%	15%	35%	20%	10%	5%	3%
GENERAL MANAGER OF A MAJOR DIVISION	2%	5%	15%	30%	20%	12%	12%	4%
DEPARTMENT MANAGER	10%	10%	24%	39%	10%	5%	1%	1%
SECTION SUPERVISOR	15%	20%	25%	37%	3%			
GROUP SUPERVISOR	38%	40%	15%	5%	2%			

Source: Reprinted with permission of The Free Press, a Division of Macmillan, Inc. from *Top Management Planning* by George A. Steiner. Copyright © 1969 by The Trustees of Colombia University of the City of New York.

importance because of increasingly vocal stockholders. It is common practice for organizations to have boards of directors consisting of both outsiders and insiders. The inside directors are corporate executives employed by the organization or retired executives of the corporation. They are assumed to be intimately familiar with the firm and are champions of stability, as preserving the status quo is usually to their benefit. As the inside executives all report to the chief executive officer, it is often difficult to depend on them to provide independent direction to the organization. Outside directors, on the other hand, are usually experienced executives from other corporations and other public figures who bring a breadth of perspective and independence to the organization. The outsiders are assumed to be in a better position than insiders to provide counsel to management and to prevent management's strategies from becoming too self-serving or too reckless, and they therefore prevent the board from being a "rubber stamp" for management's ideas.

The articles of incorporation of most corporations place a legal responsibility on the board of directors to represent the interests of the stockholders, whose capital made it possible for the organization to function in the first place. "Stockholder interest" sometimes has been narrowly interpreted to mean maximization of financial returns to the stockholder in the form of dividends and capital gains. Recent increases in the number of lawsuits against board members by stockholders have put board members under increased pressure to maximize stockholder wealth.[25] Some people, however, take a broader view of the role of the board (and management). This role includes many dimensions of corporate social responsibility such as responsibility to employees, the community, and the environment. Whichever view is assumed, many organizational theorists would agree that the role of the board is to protect and further the interests of more than just the entrenched inside executives. As one analyst observed, "From now on, executives will have to be much more accountable for their performance. For the foreseeable future, the corporate balance of power has changed."[26]

Some observers have argued that a board dominated by insiders is akin to having the bear guard the honey jar. In the past two decades, there have been increasing charges of irresponsible management of large corporations— of management representing only its own narrow self-interests and working to the detriment of the stockholders. Corporate raiders have used this situation to argue that they are a force for more responsible management.[27] Proxy fights, in which dissident shareholders attempt to force an action on management, or even to remove management, have become more frequent.[28]

The need for more responsiveness among boards is also reflected in the increasing number of outside members on corporate boards.[29] A recent article reported that 52 percent of directors were outsiders in 1969 and that the percentage had increased to 68 percent in 1985.[30] The percentage of outside directors may be even higher for the important committees on boards (for example, the audit, nominating, compensation, and executive committees). A recent survey of 250 Fortune 500 companies reported that 73 percent of the directors on those important committees were outsiders.[31]

Along with the trend toward a higher percentage of outside representation on the board, more CEOs of other firms are being included among the outside directors. Table 1.2 indicates that the percentages of outside directors who were active CEOs and those who were retired CEOs and other executives have both increased in the sixteen-year period from 1969 to 1985. This trend toward more CEOs from other firms serving on boards has caused increased attention to be paid to the phenomenon of "interlocking directorates."[32] This term refers to the practice of CEOs from other firms serving on multiple boards so that there is a crisscrossing network of CEO board members. The practice of interlocking within the same industry is illegal, but interlocking

TABLE 1.2   CHANGES IN OUTSIDE DIRECTORS (PERCENT)

	1969	1985
Active CEOs	20%	25%
Non-CEO chairmen	12%	6%
Other senior executives	18%	10%
Retired CEOs and other executives	13%	20%
Practicing lawyers	8%	5%
Bankers	5%	2%
Educators	5%	10%
Public officials	1%	4%
All others	18%	18%
TOTAL	100%	100%

Source: Adapted from Exhibit in A. Patton and J. C. Baker, "Why Won't Directors Rock the Boat?" *Harvard Business Review* 65 (November–December 1987): 11. Reprinted by permission of *Harvard Business Review.* Copyright © 1987 by the President and Fellows of Harvard College; all rights reserved.

arrangements across industries are quite common. Interlocking directorates may be beneficial to the firm because other CEOs bring a breadth of experience and knowledge to the board. These outside CEOs may bring knowledge of customers and vendors to the organization. In this way, interlocking directorates may be part of an overall interorganizational strategy or coordination effort.[33]

Both the trend toward greater outside representation and the trend toward a higher percentage of CEOs from other firms among the outsiders seem to be addressing some of the charges aimed at boards. As Kerr and Bettis stated, "Critics have charged that despite their legal responsibility to shareholders, boards seem unable or unwilling to challenge or constrain managements. Boards have been accused of granting automatic increases [in management compensation], regardless of a chief executive's performance, and of taking advantage of their positions to enrich themselves and top managers at shareholders' expense."[34] Because of increased pressure on corporations for financial performance, analysts forecast an increase in the level of accountability both from boards and from the executives the boards are meant to oversee.

AGENCY THEORY

One approach used to reconcile the differing roles of outside directors and inside strategic decision makers is *agency theory.* Several studies have hypothesized that executives pursue personal goals in their strategic decisions, and these goals may conflict with owners' goals. Managerial goals such as growth, smoothed income streams, enhanced power bases, reduced employment risk, and enhanced compensation have been studied.[35] These objectives of executives are frequently seen as being in conflict with organizational goals of profit maximization or increasing shareholder wealth.[36] Agency theory suggests that because of these conflicting goals, owners incur costs associated with executive incentive programs and monitoring activities.[37] These costs are referred to as agency costs.

In a survey of 1988 annual director compensation, some firms were found to be paying substantial compensation to directors. Some of the survey results are shown in Table 1.3. Agency theory suggests that these directors' fees are part of the costs stockholders incur for monitoring and guiding executive actions.

CONSENSUS, BIASES, AND ORIENTATIONS IN STRATEGIC DECISIONS

This book takes the approach that strategy is a pattern in a series of decisions. Therefore, the unit of analysis in studying strategic management should be the strategic decision. Realizing that there are multiple strategic decision makers in an organization, one must pay attention to the issue of consensus among those decision makers. The question of how much insight the strategic decision makers have into their own decisions also assumes importance. In addition, several decision-making biases accompany the strategic decision-making process.

CONSENSUS AND INSIGHT ON STRATEGIC DECISIONS

The issue of consensus among multiple decision makers on strategic decisions has received increased attention of late. As one notes the diversity of background of corporate boards of directors, the differing motivations and roles

TABLE 1.3 HIGHEST AVERAGE ANNUAL TOTAL DIRECTOR COMPENSATION IN 1988

FIRM	COMPENSATION
ITT	$86.400
Sears	63,200
General Motors	58,917
Ford	57,750
Coastal	57,600
Dow Chemical	57,000
USX	55,833
Citicorp	53,759
RJR-Nabisco	53,750

Source: "Where It Pays to be a Director," *Wall Street Journal* (January 11, 1989): B1. Reprinted by permission of the *Wall Street Journal,* © 1989 Dow Jones & Company, Inc. All Rights Reserved Worldwide.

among the decision makers, and the different experiences of the executives as they approach the strategic decision-making process, it becomes evident that consensus may be difficult to achieve. Consensus on strategy formulation decisions may not be critical in a hierarchical organization with a powerful CEO, as many people may defer to the responsibility of the CEO as the fore-most strategy formulator in the firm.[38] Multiple executives in large organizations must implement the decisions, however, so consensus on the implementation of decisions assumes importance. A number of studies have shown that higher consensus on strategy implementation in firms is correlated with higher performance.[39]

Box 1.1 contains an example of the lack of consensus that can occur among executives as they plan a corporation's strategy.

In a broader context, the lack of consensus on strategic issues might explain why strategy is sometimes so controversial and disagreements can become so vehement. For example, a recent article in *Business Week*, "The Family that Hauls Together Brawls Together: Leonard Schoen and His 12 Children Have Split into Two Factions in a Fight for U-Haul's Future,"[40] described how two completely different strategies for expansion were being fought over within the same family. It is easier to understand how proxy fights and battles for corporate control occur when one recognizes that strategic decision makers disagree on the best decisions for the firm to follow. The lack of consensus might also indicate why strategies are usually evolutionary compromises instead of radical departures from past strategies.

Insight into strategic decisions is important because communication problems occur frequently in large organizations with multiple decision makers and many strategic planners on staff. How can the executives communicate with one another if they cannot correctly articulate the important factors in their decision processes? How can the decision makers communicate with the staff to collect and analyze data? Secrecy presents another problem in understanding the phenomenon. Even if executives had perfect insight into how they made strategic decisions, would they reveal those decision processes and models in public interviews? This lack of documented insight is another reason why the unit of analysis in the study of strategy must be the strategic decision and not public pronouncements or published documents.

DECISION-MAKING BIASES

Strategic decision making, like any other type of decision making, is susceptible at many stages to numerous biases. These biases include *simplification,* in which decisions on complex problems are made on the basis of a few simple elements; *hindsight,* in which decisions are made on the basis of improper analogies to past decisions; and *aggregation,* in which decisions are made on the basis of improper grouping of classes or types of information.[41] To simplify the complexity of the strategic decision-making task, executives sometimes employ heuristics, or simple decision-making aids or rules. The simplicity and appropriateness of the particular heuristic are associated with the quality of the strategic decision.[42]

BOX 1.1 STRATEGIC DIFFERENCES AMONG EXECUTIVES WITHIN AN ENGINEERING FIRM

Table 1.4 contains the results of a study of twelve executives who owned and managed a large engineering design firm. The executives were considering whether the firm should merge with or acquire (M&A) a construction firm. Merger or acquisition represented a significant change of strategy for the organization, as it would add construction capability to the firm's already existing design business.

In Table 1.4, the objective weights listed for each executive indicate the importance given to the M&A option by the executives' actual choices as they made decisions on a number of alternatives. These numbers are referred to as objective weights because they were calculated from the executives' *actual* decisions about the company's strategy. The subjective weights listed in the table indicate what the executives *said* was the importance of merger and acquisition to them in reaching their decisions.[a] Both scores were based on 100-point scales. For example, executive #1 said that M&A played a 25-percent role in his decision, but in actuality, M&A accounted for only 11 percent of his decision. Executive #2, on the other hand, attributed much less of his decision (20 percent) to the consideration of merger and acquisition than was actually the case (57 percent).

TABLE 1.4 CONSENSUS AND INSIGHT ON MERGER AND ACQUISITION IN AN ENGINEERING FIRM

EXECUTIVE	OBJECTIVE	SUBJECTIVE
Number	*Weight*	*Weight*
1	11%	25%
2	57	20
3	46	25
4	24	10
5	32	15
6	60	20
7	21	30
8	54	15
9	61	30
10	00	25
11	47	20
12	54	20
Average	39	21
Standard Deviation	21	6

Source: Adapted from Tables 11.1 and 11.2 in M. J. Stahl, *Strategic Executive Decisions* (Westport, Conn.: Quorum Books, 1989).

The range of the numbers and the standard deviations indicate a lack of consensus among the executives. Such low consensus was reflected in the fact that it took years before the firm accomplished a merger, even though the executives had expressed a preference for a merger. This lack of insight into strategic decisions is quite common and has been well documented in the literature. In a series of studies of strategic decision making, Stahl found a lack of insight on decisions concerning acquisition, joint venture, the use of information technology as a strategic weapon, restructuring in a firm, and project selection in many firms.[b]

---

[a] Stahl, M. J. *Strategic Executive Decisions* (Westport, Conn.: Quorum Books, 1989): 4.
[b] Ibid.

The negative effects of various types of biases on the quality of decision making has been well documented by researchers in the field. Studies have also shown that different decision makers do not approach the same decision-making problem in the same way. As Hambrick and Mason stated, "The situation a strategic decision maker faces is complex and made up far more phenomena than he/she can possibly comprehend. The decision maker brings a cognitive base and values to a decision, which create a screen between the situation and his/her eventual perception of it."[43]

Figure 1.4 indicates how the cognitive bases and values of the executives act to screen the situation, impact managerial perceptions, and hence impact the strategic choice. This model explains how the same situation can result in different decisions by different decision makers. Under conditions of bounded rationality, in which a decision maker can intelligently comprehend only a limited amount of information, in a hierarchical organization with a powerful CEO, it is easy to see how the decision-making biases of the CEO can impact the quality of the strategic decision.[44]

STRATEGIC ORIENTATIONS AND DECISION MAKING

In a widely cited typology of organizational orientations, Miles and Snow classified organizations as Defenders, Prospectors, Analyzers, or Reactors.[45] The classification, which has been thoroughly reviewed by a number of other researchers, is helpful in terms of explaining the strategic alternatives that firms choose over time.[46] Miles, Snow, and their colleagues explain the categories in the following way: "Defenders define their entrepreneurial problem as how to seal off a portion of the total market in order to create a stable domain, and

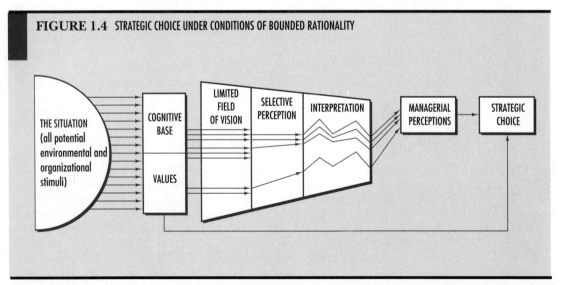

FIGURE 1.4   STRATEGIC CHOICE UNDER CONDITIONS OF BOUNDED RATIONALITY

Source: D. C. Hambrick and P. A. Mason, "Upper Echelons: The Organization as a Reflection of its Top Managers," *Academy of Management Review 9 (1984):* 195.

they do so by producing only a limited set of products directed at a narrow set of the total potential market. Unlike the Defender, whose success comes primarily from efficiently serving a stable domain, the Prospector's prime capability is that of finding and exploiting new product and market opportunities. A true Analyzer is an organization that attempts to minimize risk while maximizing the opportunity for profit—that is, an experienced Analyzer combines the strength of both the Prospector and the Defender."[47] Reactors do not follow a conscious strategy; they "muddle through." Obviously, the Defenders, Prospectors, Analyzers, and Reactors approach strategic decision-making situations very differently.

A good example of an organization that could be called a Prospector is NCNB Corporation. The firm's acquisition history shows how the same situation can be perceived differently with different resultant strategic decisions. Its 1988 acquisition of First Republic Bank of Texas typifies a Prospector at its best. Although other banks analyzed the same situation and apparently concluded that the risks were too large, NCNB Corporation made the acquisition with substantial subsequent praise. As one analyst said, "The recently announced acquisition of First Republic Bank by NCNB Corporation will go down in the annals of bank history as one of the finest transactions ever consummated. The acquisition demonstrates that NCNB's management (which, along with its board of directors, owns nearly 30% of outstanding shares) is dedicated to the on-going creation of shareholder value."[48] Doubling an organization overnight is not the action of either a Defender or an Analyzer. "With its First Republic Bank's assets, NCNB would have, pro forma, nearly $54 billion in assets, making it the eighth largest bank holding concern in the country."[49] Other banks reviewed the risks in the Texas economy, with its disastrous real estate markets and continued softness in the oil industry, and decided to stay away. What caused NCNB to enter? One must know something about the CEO of the firm, Hugh McColl, to understand its Prospector style. *Forbes* described McColl as "the George Patton of Banking" and indicated that his aggressive style may be just what is needed to cause the firm to grow.[50]

The decision-making biases in organizations may be found in their preferences for certain strategies and objectives in formalizing their long-range plans. It is not unusual to find organizations putting in systems and designing organizational structures that are consistent with their biases. Such issues are explored further in our discussion of strategy implementation in Chapter 6.

DEVELOPING THE STRATEGIC MANAGEMENT PROCESS

As we have seen in the foregoing discussion, organizations that practice strategic decision making and implement full-scale strategic planning systems can reap the rewards of improved decision making and enhanced financial success. It is important, therefore, to consider how an organization goes about developing a fully functioning strategic management effort. Research by Gluck, Kaufman, and Wallach suggested that strategic planning in most organizations must evolve through four sequential phases.[51] Phase One is *basic financial planning*, in which the organization simply tries to improve operational control by means of budgetary control. In Phase Two, *forecast-based planning*, the organization extends its time horizon for planning beyond the next year and attempts to predict the impact of future events on its operations. Phase Three, *externally oriented planning*, is reached when the organization begins to plan in terms of its response to market conditions and the anticipated strategies of its competitors. Finally, in Phase Four, *strategic management*, the organization begins to manage all of its resources strategically in order to develop competitive advantages.

Figure 1.5 presents the complete model of the organizational evolution of strategic management. One lesson that may be gathered from this view of the strategy process is that the development of an effective strategic management program within any organization does not occur without a concentrated, pur-

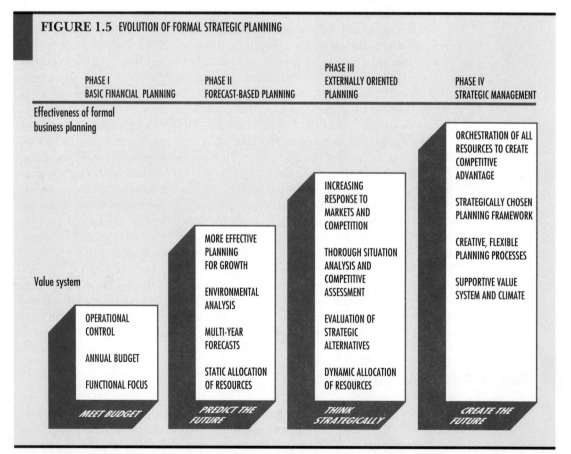

FIGURE 1.5 EVOLUTION OF FORMAL STRATEGIC PLANNING

	PHASE I BASIC FINANCIAL PLANNING	PHASE II FORECAST-BASED PLANNING	PHASE III EXTERNALLY ORIENTED PLANNING	PHASE IV STRATEGIC MANAGEMENT
Effectiveness of formal business planning				ORCHESTRATION OF ALL RESOURCES TO CREATE COMPETITIVE ADVANTAGE STRATEGICALLY CHOSEN PLANNING FRAMEWORK CREATIVE, FLEXIBLE PLANNING PROCESSES SUPPORTIVE VALUE SYSTEM AND CLIMATE
			INCREASING RESPONSE TO MARKETS AND COMPETITION THOROUGH SITUATION ANALYSIS AND COMPETITIVE ASSESSMENT EVALUATION OF STRATEGIC ALTERNATIVES DYNAMIC ALLOCATION OF RESOURCES	
Value system		MORE EFFECTIVE PLANNING FOR GROWTH ENVIRONMENTAL ANALYSIS MULTI-YEAR FORECASTS STATIC ALLOCATION OF RESOURCES		
	OPERATIONAL CONTROL ANNUAL BUDGET FUNCTIONAL FOCUS			
	MEET BUDGET	*PREDICT THE FUTURE*	*THINK STRATEGICALLY*	*CREATE THE FUTURE*

Source: Frederick W. Gluck, Stephen P. Kaufman, and A. Steven Walleck, "Strategic Management for Competitive Advantage," *Harvard Business Review 58*, July–August 1980, pp. 154–161. Reprinted by permission of *Harvard Business Review*. Copyright © 1980 by the President and Fellows of Harvard College; all rights reserved.

poseful development effort aimed at taking the organization through these necessary phases. The remainder of this book presents the wide range of knowledge and skills that an organization's general managers need to acquire in order to develop into a fully functioning strategic management team.

SUMMARY

Following the lead of Mintzberg, we view strategy as a pattern in a series of decisions. The unit of analysis in the study of strategy is the strategic decision rather than a long-range plan, annual report, or public pronouncement.

The relationship of strategy to corporate performance is reviewed. Several studies have documented higher levels of corporate performance associated with formalized strategic planning.

This chapter deals with the role of strategic decision makers in the strategic decision-making process. The strategic decision makers are categorized in terms of the outsiders on the board of directors and the inside executives employed by the organization.

An analysis of the composition of boards of directors reveals two changes in board composition from the past. Today, a higher percentage of board members are outsiders than in the past. In addition, a higher percentage of CEOs of other firms exists on the boards of today relative to the past. This growing phenomenon is labeled as interlocking directorates. Both trends are seen in the context of attempts to require the inside executives to be more accountable to the board and to stockholders. Thus, the role of boards is viewed in the context of agency theory, whereby the owners implement mechanisms to monitor the actions of management.

The inside corporate-level strategic decision makers include the chief executive officer, the president, and usually the chairman of the board. In some organizations, these three jobs are held by one powerful individual. In other organizations, the jobs are split among two or three individuals in an executive office. The chief operating officer, corporate-level planners, and corporate-level vice presidents are also included in the list of corporate-level strategic decision makers. Division and group vice presidents are among the strategic decision makers at the business level. At the functional level, manufacturing vice presidents, marketing vice presidents and other functional vice presidents are typically involved with strategic decision making.

This chapter stresses the importance of consensus among strategic decision makers to help ensure consistent implementation of strategic decisions and higher organizational performance. The need for insight is discussed in the context of communicating the decision criteria to others in the firm.

Decision-making biases, or ways to approach strategic issues, are reviewed in terms of Defenders, Prospectors, Analyzers, and Reactors, as described by Miles and Snow. Corporations approach the same strategic situation differently, partly as a function of their *a priori* strategic decision biases.

DISCUSSION QUESTIONS

1. Explain the concept that strategy is a pattern in a series of decisions.
2. Describe the advantages and disadvantages of increasing outside representation on the board of directors.
3. Describe the advantages and disadvantages of interlocking directorates.
4. Describe the magnitude of agency problems in owner-managed firms.
5. Describe the importance of consensus and consistency in strategic decisions.
6. Give an example of a Defender, a Prospector, an Analyzer, and a Reactor in the computer industry.

ENDNOTES

1. Treece, J. B. and R. Ingersoll, "GM Faces Reality," *Business Week* (May 9, 1989): 114–122.

2. Verity, J. W., "A Bold Move in Mainframes," *Business Week* (May 29, 1989): 72–78.

3. Manges, M., "Drug Firms Set Plan to Acquire Some ICI Assets," *Wall Street Journal* (October 10, 1989): A4.

4. Marbach, W. D. "Super Television," *Business Week* (January 30, 1989): 56–62.

5. Bylinsky, G., "Where Will Japan Strike Next?" *Fortune* (September 25, 1989): 42–52.

6. Katayama, F. H., "The Muppets Sell Out," *Fortune* (September 25, 1989): 8–9.

7. "Oil Would Help: U.S. Steel's Plans for Marathon," *Fortune* (January 25, 1982): 8.

8. Wilson, J. T., "Strategic Planning at R. J. Reynolds Industries," *Journal of Business Strategy* 6 (1985): 22–28.

9. Mintzberg, H., "Patterns in Strategy Formation," *Management Science* 24 (1978): 934–948.

10. Mintzberg, H., "Opening Up the Definition of Strategy," in *The Strategy Process*, ed. J. Quinn, H. Mintzberg, and R. James (Englewood Cliffs, N.J.: Prentice Hall (1988): 13–20; Mintzberg H., and J. A. Waters, "Of Strategies, Deliberate and Emergent," *Strategic Management Journal* 6 (1985): 257–271.

11. Mintzberg, H., and A. McHugh, "Strategy Formation in an Adhocracy," *Administrative Science Quarterly* 30, no. 2 (June 1985): 160–197.

12. Mintzberg, H., "The Design School: Reconsidering the Basic Premises of Strategic Management," *Strategic Management Journal* 11 (March–April 1990): 171–196.

13. Hatten, K., "Quantitative Research Methods in Strategic Management," in *Strategic Management: A New View of Business Policy and Planning* ed. Schendel, D. E. and C. W. Hofer (Boston: Little, Brown and Co., 1979), 448–466.

14. Rhyne, L. C., "The Relationship of Strategic Planning to Financial Performance," *Strategic Management Journal* 7 (September–October 1986): 423–436.

15. Pearce, J. A. II, E. B. Freeman, and R. B. Robinson, Jr., "The Tenuous Link Between Formal Strategic Planning and Financial Performance," *Academy of Management Review* 12, no. 4 (1987): 658–675.

16. Norburn, D., "The Chief Executive: A Breed Apart," *Strategic Management Journal* 10 (1989): 1–15.

17. Wrapp, E., "Good Managers Don't Make Policy Decisions," *Harvard Business Review* 45 (September–October 1967): 91–99.

18. Gerstein, M., and H. Reisman, "Strategic Selection: Matching Executives to Business Conditions," *Sloan Management Review* (Winter 1983): 33–49; Silagyi, A. D., and D. M. Schweiger, "Matching Managers to Strategies: A Review and Suggested Framework," *Academy of Management Review* 9 (1984): 626–637; Miller, D., and J. M. Toulouse, "Chief Executive Personality and Corporate Strategy and Structure in Small Firms," *Management Science* 32 (1986): 1389–1409; Gupta, A. K., and V. Govindarajan, "Business Unit Strategy, Managerial Characteristics, and Business Unit Effectiveness at Strategy Implementation," *Academy of Management Journal* 27 (1984): 25–41; Miller, D., M. Kets de Vries, and J. M. Toulouse, "Top Executive Locus of Control and Its Relationship to Strategy Making, Structure & Environment," *Academy of Management Journal* 25 (1982): 237–253; Quick, J. D., and D. L. Nelson, and J. C. Quick, "Successful Executives: How Independent?" *Academy of Management Executive* 1, no. 2 (May 1987).

19. Andrews, K. R., *The Concept of Corporate Strategy*, rev ed. (Homewood, Ill.: R. D. Irwin & Co., 1980): 11.

20. Drucker, P. F., "Leadership: More Doing Than Dash," *Wall Street Journal* (January 6, 1988): 14.

21. "The Quiet Coup at Alcoa," *Business Week* (June 27, 1988): 58.

22. "Business Celebrities," *Business Week* (June 23, 1986): 100–107.

23. "Celebrity Chief," *Wall Street Journal* (August 18, 1988): 1.

24. Mintzberg, "The Design School."

25. Scheibla, S. H., "A Plague of Lawyers: Being Sued is Still Corporate Directors' No. 1 Worry," *Barron's* (November 17, 1986): 38; Taravella, S., "Corporations Shield Directors," *Business Insurance* 21 (1987): 99–100; Verespej, M. A., "Yet Another Worry: Takeovers, Liabilities, and, Now, Stock Prices," *Industry Week* (November 16, 1987): 18–19.

26. "The Battle for Corporate Control," *Business Week* (May 18, 1987): 102–109.

27. "Power Investors," *Business Week* (June 20, 1988): 116–123.

28. "Evening the Odds in Proxy Fights," *Business Week* (July 4, 1988): 37; Mizruchi, M. "Who Controls Whom? An Examination of the Relationship Between Management and the Boards of Directors in Large American Corporations," *Academy of Management Review* 8 (1983): 426–435.

29. Kesner, I. F., B. Victor, and B. T. Lamont, "Board Composition and the Commission of Illegal Acts: An Investigation of Fortune 500 Companies," *Academy of Management Journal* 29 (1986): 789–799; Kesner, I. F., and R. B. Johnson, "An Investigation of the Relationship Between Board Composition and Stockholder Suits," *Strategic Management Journal* 11 (May–June 1990): 327–336.

30. Patton, A. and J. C. Baker, "Why Won't Directors Rock the Boat?" *Harvard Business Review* 45 (November–December 1987): 10–18.

31. Kesner, I. F., "Director's Characteristics and Committee Membership: An Investigation of Type, Occupation, Tenure, and Gender," *Academy of Management Journal* 31 (March 1988): 66–84.

32. Schoorman, F. D., M. H. Bazerman, and R. S. Atkin, "Interlocking Directorates: A Strategy for Reducing Environmental Uncertainty," *Academy of Management Review* 6 (April 1981): 244; Allen, M. P., "Review of Interlocking Directorates," *American Journal of Sociology* 88 (1983): 1313–1315; Burt, R. S., "Cooptive Corporate Actor Networks: A Reconsideration of Interlocking Directorates Involving American Manufacturing," *Administrative Science Quarterly* 24 (December 1980): 557–582.

33. Zajac, E. J., "Interlocking Directorates as an Interorganizational Strategy: A Test of Critical Assumptions," *Academy of Management Journal* 31 (June 1988): 428–438; Ornstein, M. D., "Interlocking Directorates in Canada: Inter-Corporate Alliance or Class Alliance?" *Administrative Science Quarterly* 29 (1984): 210–231; Palmer, D., R. Friedland, and J. V. Singh, "The Ties That Bind: Organizational and Class Basis of Stability in a Corporate Interlock Network," *American Sociological Review* 15 (1986): 781–796; Palmer, D., "Broken Ties: Interlocking Directorates and Inter-Corporate Coordination," *Administrative Science Quarterly* 28 (1983): 40–55; Kesner and Johnson, "An Investigation of the Relationship. . . ." (1990).

34. Kerr, J. and R. A. Bettis, "Boards of Directors, Top Management Compensation, and Shareholder Returns," *Academy of Management Journal* 30 (December 1987): 645.

35. Aaker, D. A., and R. Jacobson, "The Role of Risk in Explaining Differences in Profitability," *Academy of Management Journal* 30 (1987): 277–296; Amihud, Y., and B. Lev, "Risk Reduction as a Managerial Motive for Conglomerate Mergers," *Bell Journal of Economics* 12 (1981): 605–617; Gomez-Mejia, L. R., H. Tose, and T. Hinkin, "Managerial Control, Performance, and Executive Compensation," *Academy of Management Journal* 30 (1987): 51–70; Jensen, M. C., and W. H. Meckling, "Theory of the Firm: Managerial Behavior, Agency Costs and Ownership Structure," *Journal of Financial Economics* 3 (1976): 305–360; Kamin, J. Y., and J. Ronen, "The Smoothing of Income Numbers: Some Empirical Evidence on Systematic Differences Among Management-Controlled and Owner-Controlled Firms," *Accounting, Organizations and Society* 3 (1978): 141–157; Rhodes, S., *Power, Empire Building and Mergers* (Lexington, Mass.: D. C. Heath, 1983).

36. Jensen and Meckling, "Theory of the Firm", Fruhan, W. E., "How Fast Should Your Company Grow?" *Harvard Business Review* 62 (1984): 84–93.

37. Singh, H., and F. Harianto, "Management-Board Relationships, Takeover Risk, and the Adoption of Golden Parachutes," *Academy of Management Journal* 32 (1989): 7–24; Bentson, G. J., "The Self-Serving Management Hypothesis: Some Evidence," *Journal of Accounting and Economics* 7 (1985): 67–84; Jensen and Meckling, "Theory of the Firm"; Oviatt, B. M. "Agency and Transaction Cost Perspectives on the Manager-Shareholder Relationship: Incentives for Congruent Interests," *Academy of Management Review* 13 (1988): 214–255.

38. Mintzberg, "The Design School": 177.

39. Burgeois, L., "Performance and Consensus," *Strategic Management Journal* 23 (1980): 227–248; Burgeois, L., "Strategic Goals, Perceived Uncertainty, and Economic Performance in Volatile Environments," *Academy of Management Journal* 28 (1985): 548–573; Hrebiniak, L. G. and C. C. Snow, "Top Management Agreement and Organizational Performance," *Human Relations* 35 (1982): 1139–1158; Dess, G. G. "Consensus on Strategic Formulation and Organizational Performance: Competition in a Fragmented Industry," *Strategic Management Journal* 8 (1987): 259–277; Dess, G. G., and N. K. Origer, "Environment, Structure, and Consensus in Strategy Formulation: A Conceptual In-

tegration," *Academy of Management Review* 12 (1987): 313–330.

40. "The Family that Hauls Together Brawls Together," *Business Week* (August 29, 1988): 64–66.

41. Bukszar, E., and T. Connolly, "Hindsight Bias and Strategic Choice: Some Problems in Learning From Experience," *Academy of Management Journal* 31, no. 3 (1988): 628–641; Duhaime, I. M., and C. R. Schwenk, "Conjectures on Cognitive Simplification in Acquisition and Divestment Decision Making," *Academy of Mangement Review* 10 (1985): 287–295; Lang, J. R., M. J. Dollinger, and K. E. Marino, "Aggregation Bias in Strategic Decision-Making Research," *Journal of Management* 13, no. 4 (1987): 689–702; Barnes, J. H., "Cognitive Biases and Their Impact on Strategic Planning," *Strategic Management Journal* 5 (1984): 129–137; Bateman, T. S., and C. P. Zeithaml, "The Psychological Context of Strategic Decisions," *Strategic Management Journal* 10 (1989): 587–592.

42. Abulsamb, R., B. Carlin, and R. R. McDaniel, "Problem Structuring Heuristics in Strategic Decision Making," *Organizational Behavior and Human Decision Processes* 45, no. 1 (1990): 28–39; Thomas, J. B., and R. McDaniel, "Interpreting Strategic Issues: Effects of Strategy and the Information Processing Structure of Top Management Teams," *Academy of Management Journal* 33 (1990): 286–306.

43. Hambrick, D. C. and P. A. Mason, "Upper Echelons: The Organization as a Reflection of its Top Managers," *Academy of Management Review* 9 (April 1984): 195.

44. Mintzberg, "The Design School": 190.

45. Miles, R. E. and C. C. Snow, *Organizational Strategy, Structure, and Process* (New York: McGraw-Hill, 1978).

46. Hambrick, D. C., "Some Tests of the Effectiveness and Functional Attributes of Miles and Snow's Strategic Types," *Academy of Management Journal* 26 (1983): 5–26; Hambrick, D. C., "Taxonomic Approaches to Studying Strategy: Some Conceptual and Methodological Issues," *Journal of Management* 10 (1984): 27–43; Smith, K. G., J. P. Guthrie, and M. J. Chen, "Miles and Snow's Typology of Strategy, Organizational Size, and Organizational Performance," *Academy of Management Best Papers Proceedings* (1986): 45–49; Zahra, S. A., "Corporate Strategic Types, Environmental Perceptions, Managerial Philosophies, and Goals: An Empirical Study," *Akron Business and Economic Review* 18 (Summer 1987): 64–77.

47. Miles, R. E., et al., "Organizational Strategy, Structure and Process," *Academy of Management Review* 3 (July 1978): 550.

48. "NCNB Corporation—The Right Bank, The Right People, The Right Deal," *Salamon Brothers Stock Research* (August 17, 1988): 1.

49. "Hard-Charging NCNB Seizes a Large Share of Banking in Texas: Bailout of First Republic Bank Will Make CEO McColl Seem 'a Hero or a Bum,'" *Wall Street Journal* (August 1, 1988): 1.

50. "The George Patton of Banking," *Forbes* (January 25, 1988): 44.

51. Gluck, F. W., S. P. Kaufman, and S. Wallach, "Strategic Management for Competitive Advantage," *Harvard Business Review* 58 (July–August 1980): 154–161.

 ## ADDITIONAL READINGS

Aakar, D. A. "How to Select a Business Strategy." *California Management Review* 26, no. 3 (1984): 167–175.

Chaganti, R. S., V. Mahajan, and S. Sharma. "Corporate Board Size, Composition, and Corporate Failures in Retaining Industry." *Journal of Management Studies* 22 (1985): 400–417.

Chung, K. H., M. Lubatkin, R. C. Rogers, and J. E. Owers. "Do Insiders Make Better CEO's than Outsiders?" *Academy of Management Executive* 1, no. 3. (1987).

Coughlan, A. T., and R. M. Schmidt, "Executive Compensation, Management Turnover, and Firm Performance." *Journal of Accounting and Economics* 7 (1985): 43–66.

Dalton, D. R., and I. F. Kesner. "Inside/Outside Succession and Organizational Size: The Pragmatics of Executive Replacement." *Academy of Management Journal* 26, no. 4 (December 1983): 736–742.

Eisenhardt, K. M. "Making Fast Strategic Decisions in

High-Velocity Environments." *Academy of Management Journal* 32 (1989): 543–576.

Eisenhardt, K. M., and L. J. Bourgeois. "Politics of Strategic Decision Making in High-Velocity Environments." *Academy of Management Journal* 31 (1988): 737–770.

Elgart, L. D. "Women on Fortune 500 Boards." *California Management Review* 24, no. 4 (1983): 121–127.

Finney, M., and I. I. Mitroff. "Strategic Plan Failures." Pp. 317–335 in *The Thinking Organization,* edited by H. P. Sims and D. E. Fioia. San Francisco: Jossey-Bass, 1986.

Heidrick & Struggles, Inc. *The Changing Board.* Chicago: Heidrick & Struggles, 1986.

Jackofsky, E. F., J. W. Slocum, Jr., and S. J. McQuaid. "Cultural Values and the CEO: Alluring Companions?" *Academy of Management Executive* 2, no. 1 (1988): 39–49.

Jonas, H. S., R. E. Fry, and S. Srivastiva. "The Office of

the CEO: Understanding the Executive Experience." *Academy of Management Executive* 4 (August 1990): 36–48.

Jones, T. M. "Corporate Board Structure and Performance: Variations in the Incidence of Shareholder Suits." Pp. 345–359 in *Research in Corporate Social Performance and Policy*, edited by J. E. Post. Greenwich, Conn.: JAI Press, 1986.

Kerr, J., and R. A. Bettis. "Boards of Directors, Top Management Compensation, and Shareholder Returns." *Academy of Management Journal* 30, no. 4 (1987): 645–664.

Kesner, I. F. "Directors' Stock Ownership and Organizational Performance: An Investigation of Fortune 500 Companies." *Journal of Management* 13, no. 3 (1987): 499–507.

Kohls, J. "Corporate Board Structure, Social Reporting, and Social Performance." Pp. 165–189 in *Research in Corporate Social Performance and Policy*, edited by L. E. Preston. Greenwich, Conn.: JAI Press, 1985.

Korn/Ferry International. *Board of Directors: 14th Annual Study.* New York: Korn/Ferry International, 1987.

Levinson, H. "You Won't Recognize Me: Predictions About Changes in Top-Management Characteristics." *Academy of Management Executive* 2, no. 2 (1988): 119–125.

Matlins, S., and G. Knisely. "Update: Profile of the Corporate Planners." *Journal of Business Strategy* 2 (Spring 1981): 75–77.

Mattar, E., and M. Ball. *Handbook for Corporate Directors.* New York: McGraw-Hill, 1985.

Mintzberg, J. *Power In and Around Organizations.* Englewood Cliffs, N.J.: Prentice-Hall, 1983.

Norburn, D. "GOGOs, YOYOs, and DODOs: Company Directors and Industry Performance." *Strategic Management Journal* 7 (1986): 101–117.

Rechner, P. L., and D. R. Dalton. "The Impact of CEO as Board Chairperson on Corporate Performance." *Academy of Management Executive* 3 (1989): 141–143.

Reinganum, M. R. "The Effect of Executive Succession on Stockholder Wealth." *Administrative Science Quarterly* 30 (1985): 46–60.

Waldo, C. N. *Boards of Directors: Their Changing Roles, Structure and Information Needs.* Westport, Conn.: Quorum Books, 1985.

Zojac, E. "CEO Selection, Succession, Compensation and Firm Performance." *Strategic Management Journal* 11 (1990): 217–230.

CHAPTER TWO

The Strategic Decision Making Process

INTRODUCTION

As indicated in Chapter 1, there are usually a number of strategic decision makers who are charged with formulating the strategic plan for an organization that will be used to guide its actions for years into the future. This chapter and the next three chapters deal primarily with the strategy formulation process. A hierarchy of strategic decisions exists in the strategy formulation process in which corporate-level strategic decisions influence business-level strategic decisions that influence functional-level strategic decisions.

Common elements of a strategic plan are a mission statement; a list of corporate objectives, including long-, medium-, and short-range objectives; and corporate-level strategies. Each of these terms is defined later in this chapter. The strategic plan may be viewed as a framework for strategic decision making. Indeed, a series of strategic decisions is made as the strategic plan is formulated.

The strategic decision makers have their own sets of decision-making biases or preferences for action. The biases or preferences for action shape the decision makers' view of the situation.[1] In spite of these decision-making biases, there are some common elements in the environment that decision makers analyze in their strategic decision making processes. In addition, there are some common relationships between the strategic choices and the environment, common terms and concepts used in a strategic plan, and common strategic planning tools employed as strategic decision making aids.

Box 2.1 shows that even one of the world's largest and most respected

BOX 2.1 IBM PLANS FOR A CHANGED ENVIRONMENT

In every one of the first four years (1983–1986) of *Fortune*'s annual survey of the most admired companies in America, IBM was ranked at the top of the list. In the 1987 survey, IBM slipped to seventh most admired. In the 1988 survey, IBM dropped out of the top ten and fell all the way to number 32.[a] What happened?

IBM found itself in a changed environment and was slow to respond. A 1986 article noted that mainframe computer sales were in a stall, and IBM's historical strength had been in mainframe sales. The computer industry's growth was occurring in minicomputer and microcomputer sales. The article also noted that IBM suffered severe networking problems. The company had at least nine major computer architectures or internal designs, which were labeled "IBM's Tower of Babel."[b] Customers were demanding networking at the time so that applications software and databases could be used on a variety of computers in their organizations. "Amazingly, Chairman John Akers says the quintessential marketing company lost touch with the buyers," *Fortune* reported.[c] Akers did not want that to happen again. He wanted IBM "to become the world's champion in meeting the needs of customers."[d] IBM's market valuation had been the largest in the world by far in 1986 as it approached $100 billion. But even a company of that size and power found that it could not ignore its changed environment. Its profits were down, its stock was down, and the firm was losing customers. Indeed, IBM's market valuation shrank by nearly 24 billion in 1986.[e]

Because it is not easy to turn a ship the size of an aircraft carrier around in a short period of time, IBM vacillated for awhile but finally decided to fight back. "To reignite growth, [IBM is] undergoing its toughest self-scrutiny in years," reported *Business Week*. "THE PLAN: Aware that its problems are not all external, IBM is starting to make changes that are affecting every corner of the company, from research and development to marketing and senior management."[f] The plan includes cost cutting, new products with an emphasis on networking, streamlined management, more aggressive marketing, and long-term strategic changes, with more emphasis on software and less emphasis on hardware. As it sometimes takes years to implement a changed strategy in an organization the size of IBM, some stock market analysts forecasted that IBM's profits would not resume meaningful long-term growth before 1989.[g]

---

[a] "America's Most Admired Corporations," *Fortune* (January 19, 1987): 18–33, "America's Most Admired Corporations," *Fortune* (January 18, 1988): 32.

[b] "IBM: Trying to Put All the Pieces Together," *Business Week* (April 21, 1986): 62–63.

[c] "IBM's Big Blues: A Legend Tries to Remake Itself," *Fortune* (January 19, 1987): 34–53.

[d] "The New IBM," *Fortune* (August 14, 1989): 31.

[e] "Whatever Happened to that Old Rip Van Winkle Stock?" *Fortune* (January 19, 1987): 54.

[f] "How IBM is Fighting Back," *Business Week* (November 17, 1986): 152–157.

[g] *Value Line Investment Survey* (New York: Value Line, 1988).

firms is not immune to its external environment and must decide how to respond to a changed environment.

ANALYZING THE ENVIRONMENT: SWOT ANALYSIS

In formulating a strategic plan, the strategic decision makers must analyze conditions internal to the organization as well as conditions in the external environment.[2] This analysis is so pervasive in strategic analysis that it is referred to as analysis of internal *Strengths* and *Weaknesses* and external *Opportunities* and *Threats*—"SWOT."

INTERNAL STRENGTHS AND WEAKNESSES

Issues that are internal to the organization and usually under the direct control of management are referred to as internal strengths and weaknesses. A strength is defined as anything internal to the company that may lead to an advantage relative to competitors and a benefit relative to customers. Conversely, a weakness is defined as anything internal that may lead to a disadvantage relative to competitors and customers. Many of these internal items are the result of prior management decisions and are usually found within the confines of the organization.[3]

Good examples of internal strengths may be found in a *Business Week* article in which America's most competitive companies were highlighted. For example, the "best of the best," in terms of the "use of labor," was Marion Laboratories with a 37-percent annual rate of increase in inflation-adjusted operating income per employee for the period 1981–1986. The company's labor productivity is a definite strength.[4]

Examples of weakness may be found in *Fortune*'s annual ranking of most- and least-admired corporations. Among the least admired, in terms of "quality of management," was Bank of America, which had suffered huge loan losses. In terms of "quality of products or services," "innovativeness," "long-term investment value," and "ability to attract, develop, and keep talented people," American Motors was among the least admired.[5] To say that there were substantial internal weaknesses in these two firms is an understatement. American Motors had consistently lost market share and was acquired by the Chrysler Corporation in 1988.

Table 2.1 shows some typical internal and external issues examined in a SWOT analysis. (The Case Analysis Outline presented immediately before the cases in this text explores these issues in much greater detail.)

A flexible organizational structure and a "can do" corporate culture are obvious internal strengths. These strengths can be contrasted to bureaucratically oriented organizations such as some federal agencies in which work is organized the way it has always been organized, and no one assumes responsibility to get the job done. Disparate corporate cultures and organizational structures can be definite weaknesses, as many firms have learned after a merger.

TABLE 2.1 *TYPICAL SWOT ANALYSIS ISSUES*

INTERNAL ENVIRONMENT: STRENGTHS
AND WEAKNESSES
Top management and the board of directors
Financial position
Operations
Marketing
Human resources
Research and development
Information systems
Organizational structure and corporate culture

EXTERNAL ENVIRONMENT: OPPORTUNITIES
AND THREATS
Economic trends
Technological trends
Regulatory trends
Physical trends
Social/demographic trends
Competitive trends

Experienced, competent top management is a definite internal asset, particularly if the firm is in a rapidly changing or fiercely competitive environment. A board of directors that brings a fresh perspective to strategic issues, as opposed to rubber-stamping management's preferences, is also an internal strength.

Financial management is an area in which a strong position can facilitate almost any decision management cares to implement. But a sickly financial position with disastrous debt levels can weaken almost any organization. For example, the Chrysler Corporation was in such bad shape financially in the early 1980s that the best intentions of their new chairman, Lee Iacocca, would have led nowhere if the federal government had not provided loan guarantees. A weak financial position can prohibit an organization from responding to the best of external opportunities.

Typically, strong operations and strong marketing are the core elements that brought a strong organization to its current position. Modern plants and equipment, good plant locations, state-of-the-art technology, and the capability to produce quality products or services are the operation's strengths. A strong distribution system, products or services that are demanded by the customer, competitive prices, and effective advertising are the ingredients of a strong marketing program. IBM had been noted as a very strong operations and marketing combination before it lost touch with its customers both for the networking need and for the nonmainframe computer need.

Obvious strengths in human resources refer to the level of energy and training of the firm's personnel. The true potential of a highly trained work force is not realized if work rules are very restrictive, as General Motors learned in the 1970s. The company spent considerable effort in the 1980s negotiating less restrictive work rules so that the contributions of its human resources could be more fully realized.

Information systems (collections of hardware, software, data, and means to access them) are being used as competitive weapons more frequently. A growing number of firms are providing products and services to their customers through the firm's information system. For those firms, strength in information systems is much more than efficient internal processing of payroll records.

A research and development program that continually turns out new and valuable products is a definite corporate asset, in contrast to a program funded for widow dressing only. Merck, the largest domestic pharmaceutical company, is credited with having a very productive R&D program. Merck also topped the list of *Fortune*'s most-admired companies for 1987, 1988, 1989, and 1990.[6]

Since by definition internal strengths and weaknesses are within the confines of the organization, it is assumed that they can be changed. Perhaps an exception to this notion is a severely weakened financial condition in which the firm is so weak that no additional financing can be obtained. With that exception, internal strengths and weaknesses are assumed to be not as problematic as external opportunities and threats, as the external conditions are usually not under the direct control of the corporate decision makers.

EXTERNAL OPPORTUNITIES AND THREATS

An opportunity is anything in the external environment that may help a firm reach its goals. A threat is anything in the external environment that may prevent a firm from reaching its goals. Some opportunities are so strong that they may cause the firm to evolve its goals.

An organization ignores the external environment at its own great peril, as IBM will testify. There are opportunities and threats in the external environment that are not under the direct control of the organization's decision makers but nevertheless must be responded to if the firm wishes to remain healthy. Paying attention to the external environment has been labeled environmental scanning.[7] The frequency and breadth of environmental scanning are positively related to organizational performance.[8]

Many studies support the concept that there needs to be a link between the organization's strategic decisions and its environment.[9] This concept has led to the evolution of a contingency view, which holds that the strategic choices are contingent on the external environment.[10] This attention to the external environment is a characteristic of healthy companies. According to *Business Week*, "Renewing companies comprehend uncertainty. The dilemma is that strategy is needed, but the future is uncertain. In response to that, the renewing companies treat information as their main competitive advantage and flexibility as their main strategic weapon. Their ability is to sense opportunity where others can't, see it where others can't, act while others hesitate, and demur when others plunge."[11]

Two good examples of firms that pay attention to external opportunities are Squibb and J. P. Morgan. In an issue describing America's most competitive firms, *Business Week* described how the pharmaceutical firm constantly looks for new needs for prescription drugs ("Squibb's Rx for Success: Find a Need and Fill it") and told how the banking firm, by paying attention to its customers, found that there was an opportunity to enter investment banking ("How J. P. Morgan Keeps Its Ear to the Ground").[12]

Each of the items in Table 2.1 listed under "External Environment" may be an opportunity or a threat, depending on the nature of the trend at the time. Unlike the trends listed under "Internal Environment," these items are not under the direct control of management. Management, however, can obviously respond to them with adequate strategic planning.

The creation of "blush" wines, or White Zinfandel, is a good example of the way some American wineries transformed a threat into an opportunity. "White Zinfandel is a marketing masterpiece and a monument to American ingenuity," commented one writer. "Just when things looked bleakest for that most 'American' of grape varieties, a group of canny California vintners turned certain economic disaster into a resounding triumph. This phenomenon should be a case study in every graduate school of business across the land."[13] There was a massive shift in American consumer tastes away from red wines to white wines in the later 1970s and early 1980s. This social trend was a serious threat to many American wineries that had planted substantial quantities of Zinfandel grapes, a variety used to make a very dark red wine. Rather than destroy all those vineyards and suffer staggering losses some vintners found that if they just left the Zinfandel grape skin out of the fermentation process, a very light pink wine resulted. They labelled the wine "blush" or White Zinfandel. Rather than suffer losses because of a threat, they came up with a new product to create an opportunity.

In order to at least recognize the changing economic environment, firms typically spend millions of dollars on economic forecasts performed by both in-house economists and external economic consultants. Forecasts of the length and severity of recessions and other environmental changes can obviously aid strategic decision makers as they evaluate mergers, joint ventures, and other long-term strategic moves involving substantial financial resources.[14] It almost appears that a number of firms ignored this type of forecasting during the late 1980s. Interest charges as a percentage of pretax profits of nonfinancial corporations rose from about 10 percent in the mid-1960s to about 50 percent in 1987.[15] Such debt burdens are not easy to cover in economic downturns. (As this was being written, many analysts were concerned that the relatively high debt levels in corporate America would magnify the severity of a recession as bankruptcies and defaults increased in 1990–91.)

Firms also spend substantial resources on technological forecasting. The effect that changing technology can have upon the competition in an industry is dealt with in Chapter 4. Here, we will mention as an example the impact of the technological change from mainframe computers to personal computers on the computer industry and on computer users.

One of the changes in the external environment that can have the most profound effect is a change in government regulation. Depending on the nature of the change and the firm's status as an incumbent in the industry or a potential entrant, changes in government regulation can have a revolutionary impact because the rules of the game are changed, sometimes abruptly, with the stroke of a pen. For example, deregulation of the airline industry changed the nature of competition from non-price to price competition. Some observers claimed that this change, along with the assumption by Braniff Airlines that the government would reregulate, caused the bankruptcy of that airline.[16] Recognizing the profound sudden impact of changes in government regulation, firms usually pay very close attention to potential regulatory changes. Firms frequently employ lobbyists and join industry associations to monitor potential changes and to influence the nature of the regulation.

Changes in the physical environment, such as a depletion of a natural resource, are sometimes relatively easier for the firm to deal with than some of the other environmental dimensions, as such physical changes usually occur at a slower rate and the firm is better able to plan a strategic response. For example, assumed depletion of primary petroleum supplies in this country allows firms to explore alternatives ranging from foreign supplies to alternative energy supplies and secondary methods of petroleum extraction such as coal liquefaction.

Social and demographic changes can have either a sudden or a slowly developing impact on the organization. If the changes are due to a change in consumer tastes that may cause a substitution effect, the change can be brutally sudden. If the changes are due to a demographic development, the impact may be years in the making. For example, as average life expectancy increases in the latter part of the twentieth century, and as the "baby boom" generation born after World War II ages, it is expected that an aging population will demand more health services and prescription drugs. Such an evolutionary change can be planned for years in advance by health care and pharmaceutical firms. On the other hand, a change in consumer tastes in the mid-1970s from gas-guzzling cars to economical cars associated with the OPEC oil embargo had a much faster impact.

Pragmatically, firms are constantly paying attention to the actions of their competitors. Theoretically, some argue that competitive strategic decisions, like corporate strategic decisions, should be contingent on external conditions.[17] Changes in competition such as the entrance of a new competitor in the industry or the exit of an old competitor can be either a dramatic threat or a once-in-a-decade opportunity. For example, Japanese competitive moves to produce more autos in this country in the late 1980s and into the 1990s may be a bigger threat than the import of Japanese autos were in the early 1980s. "Will the Auto Glut Choke Detroit? By 1990, the Japanese may be building some 1.8 million vehicles a year in the U.S.—more than the current car output of Chrysler," warned *Business Week*.[18] In response to such a competitive threat, GM decided to shrink: "GM Faces Reality: Soon the World's Largest Auto Maker Will be Smaller. Much Smaller."[19] According to this article, the firm planned to implement a number of internal changes to meet the external threat. Changes were planned in manufacturing, to produce higher-quality and more differentiated products; marketing, including product innovations and more aggressive pricing; human resources as the firm shrank; and organizational structure as the number of plants was reduced.

Such far-reaching changes due to competitive threats underline the importance of the competition and why competitive strategy and competitor analysis are treated in a separate chapter in this text (Chapter 4). Impacts on functional-area strategies in areas such as manufacturing, marketing, and human resources receive specific treatment in Chapter 5. The point is that external environmental threats and opportunities can shake up many functions in the organization for many years. Sometimes the organization's very survival is threatened.

THE STRATEGIC PLAN

Once the internal strengths and weaknesses and the external opportunities and threats have been assessed, the strategic decision makers are in a position to formulate the strategic plan. Ideally, the plan should be formulated in such a way as to capitalize on external opportunities, avoid or work around external threats, build on internal strengths, and avoid or work around internal weaknesses. Indeed, many organizations try to maximize the number of situations in which they can capitalize on external opportunities with internal strengths; these are grow-and-invest situations. Similarly, many firms try to minimize the number of situations that emphasize external threats and internal weaknesses. Such situations suggest shrinkage or withdrawal. We will return to the strategy implications of these SWOT combinations after the following discussion of the concepts of the strategic plan.

MISSION

The corporate mission refers to a statement of the business(es) conducted by the firm or a statement of corporate purpose. The statement indicates *why* the organization exists.[20] As a mission statement refers to the entire organization, there is only one mission per firm.

The mission statement is usually written from the perspective of the customers rather than the stockholders, the employees, the managers, or any other constituency. Thus, although a statement such as "The XYZ Company is in the business of making money" may be true, it is not a mission statement. Some argue that the customer perspective, or attention to customer value, is the primary characteristic of Total Quality Management. "The first and *THE* central function of management should be the determination, creation, enhancement, and delivery of net value to the customer."[21]

Mission statements usually contain descriptions of the primary products or services offered by the firm; the market or customers served, including their geographic domain; the value provided to the customers; and the activities or functions performed by the firm. An example of a mission statement is the following one:

> Standard Oil Company (Indiana) is in business to find and produce crude oil, natural gas and natural gas liquids; to manufacture high quality products useful to society from these raw materials; and to distribute and market those products and to provide dependable related services to the consuming public at reasonable prices.[22]

Another good example is contained in the Warner-Lambert Creed:

> Our mission is to achieve leadership in advancing the health and wellbeing of people throughout the world. We are committed to providing high-quality health care and consumer products of real value that meet customer needs.[23]

There appear to be two sources of mission statements, one from organizational statements and the other from resource allocation decisions of the strategic decision makers. The second reflection of mission may be referred to as the operative, or real, mission. Annual reports and long-range planning documents are usually sources for statements of mission. Capital budgets can be a source for determining the operative mission statements. For example, in the mid-1970s, after the OPEC oil embargo, some petroleum companies, in an effort to be popular with various constituents, decided to change their mission statements to indicate that they were "diversified energy companies." The new statements indicated that the companies were involved with oil, coal, geothermal, nuclear, and solar energy; they were not just petroleum companies. Yet some firms continued to spend nearly all of their capital budgets on petroleum exploration. With trivial commitments to the other energy forms, they were not really diversified energy companies. Did investors prefer a more diversified company? One can only speculate why the difference existed between the stated and the real or operative mission statement.

OBJECTIVES

Once the business has been defined, or the *why* has been decided, it is appropriate to turn to the *what*. Objectives refer to the specific kinds of results the organization seeks to achieve.[24] Objectives can refer to results desired for the entire corporation; these are corporate objectives. Objectives can also exist at the business level, the functional-area level, or even lower levels in the organization.

Objectives should be specific, measurable, time phased, and achievable. The last characteristic explains why objectives are considered *after* the mission. The mission can broadly determine what is achievable. For example, a 24-percent compounded rate of growth in sales may be appropriate and achievable in a rapidly growing biotechnology company. Such an objective may be inappropriate, however, in a major steel company in a stagnant market. Objectives are quantitatively expressed. Some analysts are forecasting that increasing attention will be paid to market share and sales growth objectives in the 1990s, as these two measures indicate relative changes in value realized by customers. A growing number of companies are refocusing on providing customer value in the 1990s as a competitive mandate.[25]

Objectives may be short, medium, or long term. Although there is no precise definition of the dividing point among the three classes of objectives, many would agree that one year or less refers to a short-term objective and five years or more refers to a long-term objective. For the purposes of this book, the time in between refers to a medium-term objective.

Objectives may be written in many areas of company activities. It is not uncommon, however, to see corporate objectives expressed in the areas of growth, profitability, debt structure, market share, stockholder/owner welfare, employee welfare, and social responsibility. Table 2.2 contains several examples of objectives in these areas for varying time periods.

STRATEGIES

Once the objectives have been decided, the strategic decision makers are in a position to decide *how* to achieve them. This is a choice of strategy. The choice of strategy is so central to the study and understanding of strategic management and decision making that three separate chapters are devoted to strategy in this text. Strategy exists at several levels in the organization, just as objectives are found at multiple levels. Chapter 3 covers corporate-level strategic decisions. It includes the corporate-level strategies of concentration (single product and market), horizontal diversification (related and unrelated), vertical integration (backward and forward), merger and acquisition (friendly and hostile), joint venture (domestic and international), and restructuring (retrenchment, divestiture, bankruptcy, and liquidation). Chapter 4 deals with business-level strategic decisions and covers cost leadership, differentiation, and focus in detail. Chapter 5 is about functional-level strategic decisions,

TABLE 2.2   EXAMPLES OF OBJECTIVES

		SHORT TERM	LONG TERM
Result	*Indicator*	*One Year*	*Five Years*
Marketshare	Percent	30%	35%
Growth	$ Sales	$400,000,000	$600,000,000
Profitability	ROI	.12	.15
Debt	D/E ratio	.40	.30
Stockholder	EPS	$2.40	$4.80
Employee	Turnover	<12%	<8%
Society	Charitable gift	$5,000,000	$10,000,000

including financial, marketing, production/operations, human resources, information systems, and research and development strategies. These strategies at the various levels indicate how the firm and its various units will achieve the respective objectives.

STRATEGIC DECISION MAKING AIDS

As the strategic decision makers evaluate several alternatives in their decision-making process, there are some commonly accepted tools or concepts available for their use. These tools may be viewed as strategic decision making aids. Although the data for the models may be gathered by other officers or members of the strategic planning staff, the executives use the data in the models to help formulate strategic decisions.

PRODUCT/MARKET/INDUSTRY LIFE CYCLES

One of the most widely used and commonly understood strategic planning tools is the Life Cycle Concept. The concept has been around for so long and is so widely used that it is difficult to trace its originator.[26] The concept holds that products and markets and entire industries develop, grow rapidly, mature, saturate, and decline in a somewhat predictable fashion.[27] If sales are plotted as a function of time, this predictable pattern is a lazy-S curve. Figure 2.1 is an example.

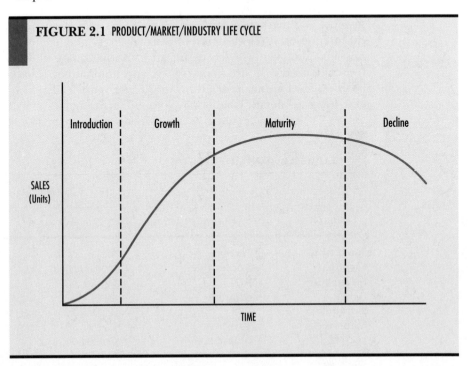

FIGURE 2.1 PRODUCT/MARKET/INDUSTRY LIFE CYCLE

In the introduction/development phase, the product is initially offered to the customers, and sales are slowly built up as more customers become aware of the product. After a certain critical mass of demand has been established, sales take off in an exponential growth rate as increasingly large numbers of new customers demand the product for the first time. Such sales attract entrants into the industry with resulting competitive turbulence and shakeout of the weaker competitors. As initial demand is satisfied and sales become replacement sales, the industry reaches maturity. At this stage, further sales gains for one firm come at the expense of another firm rather than from first-time customers. As technology makes the product obsolete, or as substitute products arrive, sales decline. Some firms leave the industry, and the remaining firms "milk" the product for profitability with little new investment.

There are problems with using the Life Cycle Concept as a precise strategic decision making tool. It is almost impossible to predict how long a certain phase of the life cycle will last or know the height of the curve (units sold). Thus, the concept's use as a forecasting tool is very limited. Even so, if a firm can determine what stage it is in at the time, it can pursue certain strategic actions to lengthen the phase (for example, product modification) or increase its profitability (for example, process improvement). Indeed, helping executives decide what strategic and competitive moves are appropriate as a function of what phase the product or industry is in at the time may be the most important advantage of the Life Cycle Concept.[28] One may grow, invest, and market aggressively in the early stages, but it appears that harvesting profits and decreasing financial commitments are more appropriate in the later stages.[29]

Most large companies are diversified to a degree. Typically, they have businesses and/or products at different stages of the life cycle. Indeed, an implication of the Life Cycle Concept is that a firm should have new products at various early stages to provide for the future growth of the firm as older products mature and decline.

BCG MATRIX

Recognizing that some firms have multiple products of varying strength, the Boston Consulting Group is credited with developing the concept of a matrix that portrays the strength of the various products or activities.[30] As one of the BCG Matrix's original purposes was to help firms decide which businesses should grow and which businesses should exit, the matrix has been used in corporate strategic decisions.[31] The matrix is sometimes used at the business level to help firms decide if they need different products within a given business. Indeed, the term "strategic business unit" (SBU) is often used to describe the product groupings or activities. The BCG Matrix is one of the simplest of the business portfolio matrix approaches to strategic planning. It has only four cells (with rather catchy labels) uses two simple variables on the two dimensions.

The horizontal dimension is Relative Market Share, the ratio of the firm's market share to the market share of the largest rival firm. The vertical dimension is Market (or Industry) Growth Rate, preferably in constant dollars. Each product is represented by a circle. The area of each circle is in accordance with the relative importance of that product to the firm typically in terms of sales. Figure 2.2 contains an example of a BCG Matrix for the James River Corporation in 1986. The corporation was involved in a number of different paper products.

The cell labels and the conditions behind them have obvious strategic implications.[32] The "Cash Cows" (that is, the positions in sanitary paper, communication papers, pulp, and specialty papers) can be used to generate cash flow to grow other products. The "Stars" (the packaging and the disposable food and beverage products) are well positioned with relatively high market share and are in markets with high growth rates. Those products could use some of the cash generated from the "Cash Cows" as investments in order to grow. The one "Question Mark" (the nonwovens product group) needs careful scrutiny to see which way it will go. Sometimes "Question Marks" are divested, and sometimes they are heavily invested in and transformed into "Stars." The matrix indicates that the firm has only one "Dog"—custom coated film. Typically, "Dogs" are divested or liquidated. As a lesson for the future, firms usually try to determine how a product became a "Dog" prior to divestiture or liquidation.

Another example of "Cash Cow" was the Lotus 1-2-3 Spreadsheet from the

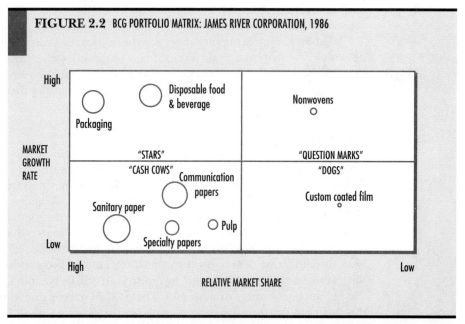

FIGURE 2.2   BCG PORTFOLIO MATRIX: JAMES RIVER CORPORATION, 1986

Sources: James River Corporation Annual Report, 1986; "Fortune 500 Largest Industrial Corporations," *Fortune* (April 27, 1987); 364–387; "Outlook '87," *Pulp and Paper* (January 1987); 48–68; "Paper and Forest Products Industry," *Value Line Investment Survey* (April 30, 1987).

Lotus Development Corporation in the late 1980s. The Lotus 1-2-3 Spreadsheet was expected to generate 73 percent of Lotus's revenue in 1988. Meanwhile, other competitors were aggressively stepping up their sales of spreadsheets, and Lotus was having trouble introducing new products. This case demonstrates that it is difficult to make consistent strategic decisions when a firm has one very strong "Cash Cow," which may be in its mature life-cycle stage, and when it has no other apparent "Star" products.[33]

Although the BCG Matrix is intuitively appealing and instructive in its strategic implications, there are strong criticisms of its use. Some analysts argue that a four-cell matrix is too simple because strategic competitive positions are more complicated than "high" and "low." Others argue that the two dimensions are simplistic proxies of complex variables. Specifically, market growth rate is only one factor involved in industry attractiveness, and relative market share is only one factor in a computation of competitive position.[34] Because of its relative simplicity, the BCG Matrix has limited use. In some firms it is used primarily for forecasting cash flows.

GE BUSINESS SCREEN

Another and more complex business portfolio planning approach to strategy is the General Electric Business Screen.[35] There are nine cells in the GE Business Screen. The two variables plotted in this approach are Industry Attractiveness and Business Strength/Competitive Position.

Calculation of a score for Industry Attractiveness per product or strategic business unit is a five-step process. First, select the criteria used to evaluate the industry. Criteria such as market size, market growth rate, industry profitability, competitive intensity, cyclicity, technological requirements, capital requirements, threats, and opportunities are used. Second, weight each criterion in accordance with the strategic decision makers' judgment of the importance of the criterion to the firm's objectives. Third, rate the industry on each of the criteria selected in the first step, usually with a scale ranging from 1 to 5. Fourth, multiply the weights from the second step by the ratings from the third step to achieve a weighted score per criterion. Fifth, sum the weighted scores to find a total attractiveness score for the industry. An example of this calculation is found in Table 2.3. With an overall weighted value that theoretically ranges from 1.00 to 5.00 in this example, a computed value of 3.9 indicates that this particular industry is quite attractive.

Business Strength/Competitive Position is mathematically computed in a similar fashion. Each business is rated on such criteria as relative market share, size, growth rate, profitability, strengths and weaknesses, competitiveness, and match between business's strengths and industry's requirements. Weights are assigned to each criterion, a rating is assigned to each criterion, and a composite value is calculated. The two composite values of Competitive Position and Industry Attractiveness are then plotted to locate that business's position in the matrix. To complete the GE Business Screen, similar calculations are then conducted for all the other businesses in which the firm is involved.

TABLE 2.3 CALCULATING INDUSTRY ATTRACTIVENESS: AN EXAMPLE

INDUSTRY ATTRACTIVENESS FACTOR	WEIGHT	RATING	VALUE
Market size	0.15	3	0.45
Market growth rate	0.20	5	1.00
Industry profitability	0.20	4	0.80
Competitive intensity	0.15	4	0.60
Cyclicity	0.05	3	0.15
Tecnological requirements	0.05	2	0.10
Capital requirements	0.10	4	0.40
Threats and opportunities	0.10	4	0.40
	1.00		3.90

Figure 2.3 shows a GE Business Screen for the Kerr-McGee Corporation for 1985. At the time, Kerr-McGee was a diversified energy company with operations primarily in the Southwest. The area of each circle is proportional to the size of the industry, and the size of the pie slice within each circle reflects the business's market share. The matrix was constructed by using equal weights with a number of the criteria listed above.

The strategic implications of the matrix are to build those businesses that are in the three cells in the upper-left corner, hold those that occur on the three diagonal cells, and harvest or divest those that fall in the three in the lower-right corner. For Kerr-McGee, the matrix indicates that the petroleum business could be further built up and invested in, the coal and chemical businesses are in holding patterns, and the uranium business is a candidate for harvesting or divestiture. Indeed, the uranium and nuclear fuel industries were not exactly growth industries in the mid-1980s, a fact indicated by a number of highly publicized cancellations of nuclear power plants.

Kerr-McGee's uranium business had received much unfavorable publicity due to the Karen Silkwood incident. Silkwood was a Kerr-McGee employee who died in an automobile accident as she allegedly was traveling to give documents to reporters with evidence of improper operations and unsafe working conditions at her place of work.[36] The unfavorable publicity (a book and a movie) and prolonged litigation caused some experts to suggest that Kerr-McGee leave the uranium industry. The implication is that Kerr-McGee's competitive position in the uranium industry was not expected to improve in the short to medium term.

The GE Business Screen is not without controversy. Some observers argue that there is too much subjectivity in the construction of the matrix. Some argue that it is a much better tool than the BCG Matrix because the GE Screen considers much more information, involves the judgment of the strategic decision makers, and focuses on competitive position. This focus on competitive position may be considered a forerunner of a considerable strategic emphasis on competitive strategy at the business level in American industry (and in this book; see Chapter 4). Others argue that the GE Screen does not give adequate

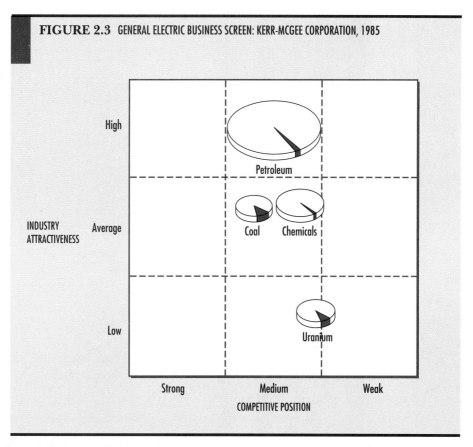

FIGURE 2.3 GENERAL ELECTRIC BUSINESS SCREEN: KERR-MCGEE CORPORATION, 1985

Sources: Smith, G., D. Arnold, and B. Bizzell, *Strategy and Business Policy: Cases.* (Boston: Houghton Mifflin Co., 1986), pp. 225–245; Kerr-McGee Annual Report, 1985; *Moody's Industrial Manual*, 1986, pp. 3206–3218.

consideration to growth. According to Hofer and Schendel, "The principal difficulty with the GE Business Screen is that it does not depict as effectively as it might the positions of new businesses that are just starting to grow in new industries. In such instances, it may be preferable to use a fifteen-cell matrix in which businesses are plotted in terms of their competitive position and their stage of product/market evolution."[37] Thus, Hofer developed the Product/Market Evolution Portfolio Matrix, or Life Cycle Matrix. An example is shown in Figure 2.4. It marries the Life Cycle Concept introduced earlier in this chapter with the Competitive Position dimension of the GE Business Screen. A disadvantage of this approach is that by including the Life Cycle Concept, the matrix substitutes a one-variable definition of growth for a detailed consideration of industry attractiveness. Because of this one-variable definition, the Life Cycle Matrix is not widely used.

Which matrix should one use? Each matrix has its strengths and weak-

FIGURE 2.4 A PRODUCT EVOLUTION PORTFOLIO MATRIX: IBM, 1990

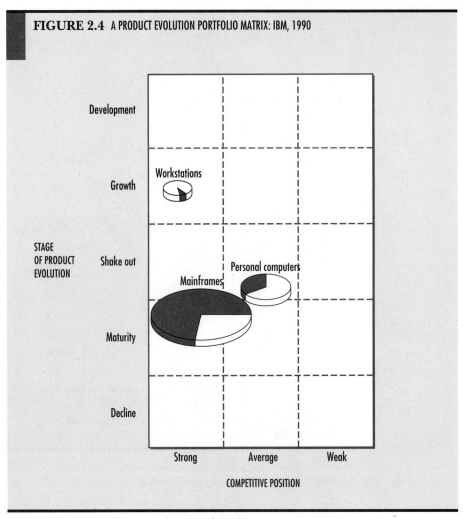

Source: Standard and Poor's Industry Surveys (January 1990); C75–C87.

nesses. In the case of single-product or single-business firms, such complexity is not required. In the case of multiproduct or multibusiness organizations, one might start with the GE Business Screen. It is preferred to the BCG Matrix in many situations because the GE Screen forces the decision makers to think through and calculate competitive position. In contrast, the BCG Matrix focuses attention on financial implications. As Chapter 4 argues, consideration of competitive position is an activity that more American firms need to do on a regular basis. The GE Screen also forces the decision makers to think through and calculate industry attractiveness. Thus, the GE Screen requires a detailed strategic planning process in itself. If certain products or businesses are highlighted as needing further attention because they are on the transition line between life-cycle phases, one might also use the Life Cycle Matrix to highlight developing winners or potential losers.

   None of these portfolios is meant to be a substitute for strategic decision making. They are strategic decision making aids. For example, the BCG Matrix gives a quick idea of cash generation and cash uses, but it is far from being a detailed capital budget. These matrices are meant to focus on some issues for further exploration and consideration.

LEARNING/EXPERIENCE CURVES

Another powerful decision-making tool used in the strategy formulation process is the learning curve or experience curve. The curve is frequently used to justify aggressive pricing decisions of new products and to discourage new

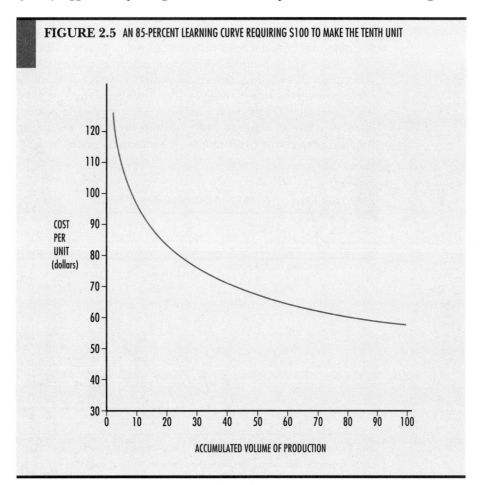

FIGURE 2.5 AN 85-PERCENT LEARNING CURVE REQUIRING $100 TO MAKE THE TENTH UNIT

COST PER UNIT (dollars)

ACCUMULATED VOLUME OF PRODUCTION

entrants into the business.[38] The learning curve is based on the constant decline in the deflated marginal cost of production with increasing cumulative volume of production. Increased labor, management, and material productivity are associated with learning-curve effects. The learning-curve slope refers to the percentage of learning. This is the percentage level to which marginal costs fall each time cumulative output doubles. For example, an 85-percent learning curve means that marginal costs fall to 85 percent of their previous level each time cumulative output doubles.[39]

Figure 2.5 (see page 43) is a graph of an 85-percent learning curve. Progressively higher and higher cumulative output levels are required to realize the same percentage marginal cost reduction because the volume must double. The percentage reduction in deflated marginal cost is constant.

Typical learning curve slopes are 90 percent, 85 percent, and 80 percent. Different slopes are realized in different firms as a function of management's willingness to incorporate suggestions for improvement, increased efficiencies in material usage, increased efficiencies in labor usage, and other cumulative experience factors. Table 2.4 shows the costs for cumulative volume and different learning percentages. The table contains at least two messages. First, the marginal cost declines dramatically with higher cumulative volume. Second, there is a substantial difference in marginal cost as a function of the percentage of learning, especially at higher cumulative volumes.

A principal strategic implication of the learning curve is in terms of pricing decisions.[40] There are at least two different pricing strategies based on the learning curve. A firm can follow a short-run profit pricing strategy, in which the firm reaps large profits early by keeping its prices high while its marginal

TABLE 2.4 THREE DIFFERENT LEARNING CURVES

CUMULATIVE NUMBER OF UNITS MADE	90% L-C	85% L-C	80% L-C
1	$10.00	$10.00	$10.00
2	9.00	8.50	8.00
4	8.10	7.22	6.40
8	7.29	6.14	5.12
16	6.56	5.22	4.10
32	5.90	4.44	3.28
64	5.31	3.77	2.62
1,000	3.50	1.98	1.08
10,000	2.47	1:15	0.52
100,000	1.74	0.67	0.24
1,000,000	1.22	0.39	0.12

Note: The marginal costs are for a specific unit with all units having a first-unit deflated cost of $10.00.

Source: Reprinted by permission of the publisher from "Industrial Life Cycles and Learning Curves: Interaction of Marketing and Production" by Louis E. Yelle, *Industrial Marketing Management* vol. 9, p. 314. Copyright 1980 by Elsevier Science Publishing Co., Inc.

cost of production declines with increased volume. This is shown as Period A in the left part of Figure 2.6. If held too long, such a strategy encourages competitors to enter the market, which may result in a steep price decline or a competitive shakeout. Such a pattern is depicted in Period B in the left part of Figure 2.6. As a result of the competition, profit margins remain thin in Period C.

Alternatively, the firm may follow a barrier pricing strategy in which it aggressively lowers prices as its costs decline with increased cumulative volume. Such lowered prices act as a barrier to market entry and keep the firm's market share high—another strategic implication. The firm's profit margins may be modest, but long-term profits tend to be relatively stable. Such a pricing strategy is shown in the right half of Figure 2.6.

Whichever pricing strategy is followed, there are strong reasons for the firm to enter the market early and build cumulative volume so that its costs decline. The subject of market entry barriers is dealt with in much greater detail in Chapter 4.

RELATING THE PLAN TO THE ENVIRONMENT

This chapter has spent considerable effort analyzing the environment, discussing the essential elements of a strategic plan, and reviewing some strategic decision making tools. This section attempts to show some relationships among these factors.

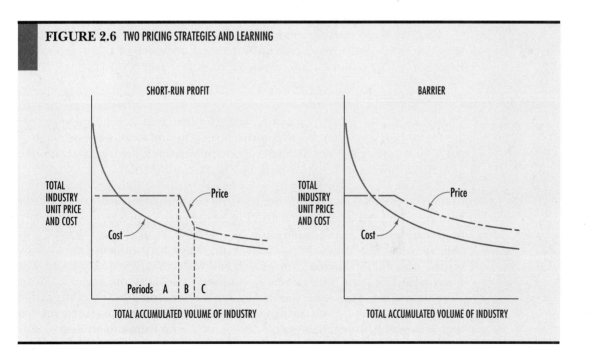

FIGURE 2.6 TWO PRICING STRATEGIES AND LEARNING

CONSISTENCY AND FIT

In relating the strategic decisions to the environment, there are at least two important characteristics to consider. The first is internal consistency. The decisions on mission, objectives, and strategies must be consistent with each other. Some analysts prefer to label this the need for congruence, as opposed to a need for consistency: "For an organization to really pull together strategically, there must be congruence between the corporate strategy and the strategies of the other units in the organization. Strategic business units or product/market groups require their own strategies, but these strategies must complement one another and be supportive of the corporate strategy."[41] For example, failure of the plan is almost guaranteed if a firm's corporate mission statement proposes to design, develop, produce, and market the world's most advanced supercomputers, yet the financial and research and development strategies allot only 1 percent of sales to the R&D budget and a personnel policy contains a temporary hiring freeze prohibiting the hiring of new computer scientists because of temporary revenue shortfalls.

Some people view internal consistency of the plan as a necessary but not sufficient condition for success of the strategic plan. A sufficient condition for success is viewed as external fit of the plan with the environment. External fit refers to how well the internal elements of the strategic plan relate to the external environment.[42] How well do the internal strengths and weaknesses and the strategic plan relate the organization to the opportunities and threats in the external environment? Some view this alignment of the organization and its resources with external opportunities and threats as the essence of strategic management.[43] Chapter 3 discusses this external dimension of strategic fit in detail.

Chapter 3 also discusses an internal dimension of strategic fit—the extent to which the various products and functional activities of the organization share some common activities or resources so that synergy occurs.

SWOT AND STRATEGIES

There are certain generic corporate strategies that tend to be more appropriate for certain combinations of internal strengths and weaknesses with external opportunities and threats than other combinations. Figure 2.7 relates the generic corporate strategies to various SWOT combinations.

The "Grow" quadrant is the most enviable of the four quadrants. With numerous environmental opportunities and substantial internal strengths, the firm can grow and invest. Concentrating on the current products and markets or pursuing merger and acquisition as a growth strategy are relevant. The "Shrink" quadrant is just the opposite. With major environmental threats and critical internal weaknesses, downsizing and withdrawal are appropriate. The lower-right quadrant, with substantial internal strengths and major environmental threats, suggests that the firm should use its strengths in slightly different arenas. Therefore, diversifying into related areas and pursuing merger and acquisition with others in related areas are appropriate strategies. The

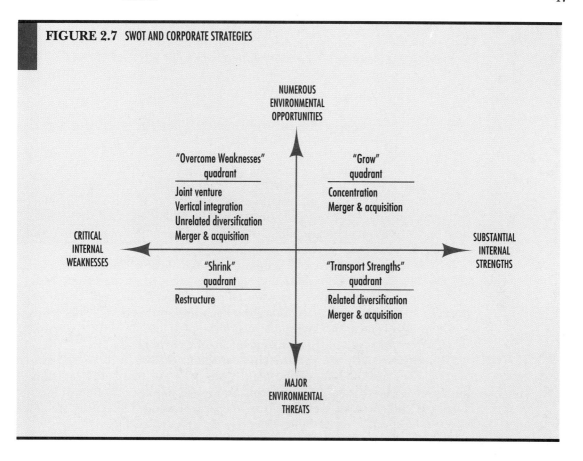

FIGURE 2.7 SWOT AND CORPORATE STRATEGIES

NUMEROUS
ENVIRONMENTAL
OPPORTUNITIES

"Overcome Weaknesses"
quadrant
_____
Joint venture
Vertical integration
Unrelated diversification
Merger & acquisition

"Grow"
quadrant
_____
Concentration
Merger & acquisition

CRITICAL
INTERNAL
WEAKNESSES

SUBSTANTIAL
INTERNAL
STRENGTHS

"Shrink"
quadrant
_____
Restructure

"Transport Strengths"
quadrant
_____
Related diversification
Merger & acquisition

MAJOR
ENVIRONMENTAL
THREATS

upper-left quadrant, with numerous environmental opportunities and critical internal weaknesses, suggests that the firm take strategic actions to overcome or avoid the weaknesses. Temporary (joint venture) or long-term partnerships (merger and acquisition) with others, integration back to the source of raw material or forward to the end-use customer, or diversification into other areas that avoid the weaknesses may be appropriate strategies. The existence of merger and acquisition in three of the four quadrants indicates that the M&A strategy can be used as a complement to several different objectives. The next chapter is devoted to exploring these corporate strategies in much greater detail.

SUMMARY

This chapter describes an overall corporate strategic decision making process. An analysis of internal strengths and weaknesses and external opportunities and threats, known as a SWOT analysis, is a prelude to deciding on the strategic plan.

The chapter attempts to show how all organizations interact with and are affected by the external environment in which they function. There are environmental opportunities to be capitalized on and external threats to be avoided or minimized. Indeed, many theorists argue that the essence of strategic decision making is to navigate the organization in such a fashion that the opportunities are realized and the threats are avoided. These external environmental dimensions include economic, technological, regulatory, physical, social/demographic, and competitive factors.

Similarly, there are dimensions of the internal environment that must be considered in formulating a strategic plan. These dimensions include top management and the board of directors, financial position, operations, marketing, human resources, information systems, research and development, and organizational structure and corporate culture. The internal strengths in these dimensions must be capitalized on in formulating the strategic plan, and the internal weaknesses must be overcome or avoided.

The corporate strategic plan contains at least three elements: *why, what,* and *how.* The main, all-encompassing, element is the mission statement. It describes what business(es) the firm is in. This definitional statement is the *why* of the firm. Decisions on mission are the most important strategic decisions, as the mission is meant to guide the rest of the plan and the entire organization. There is only one mission statement for the corporation.

Objectives refer to the specific kinds of results the organization hopes to achieve. They are the *what* of the plan. Objectives can be of different time duration (short, medium, or long term), and they can exist at different levels (corporate, business, or functional) in the organization. Objectives should, however, be specific, measurable, time phased, and achievable.

Strategies refer to the *how* of the plan. Strategies are so fundamental to the formulation of the strategic plan that three separate chapters are devoted to the study of strategies in this book. Chapter 3 covers the corporate-level strategies of concentration, horizontal diversification, vertical integration, merger and acquisition, joint venture, and restructuring. Chapter 4 deals with the business-level strategies of cost leadership, differentiation, and focus. Chapter 5 covers the functional-level strategies of finance, marketing, production/operations, human resources, information systems, and research and development.

The chapter reviews four commonly accepted strategic decision making tools. The Product/Market/Industry Life Cycle Concept indicates that products, markets, and entire industries develop, grow rapidly, mature, saturate, and decline in a somewhat predictable fashion. The position of the firm on this lazy-S–shaped curve has implications for the formulation of the strategic plan.

The BCG Matrix is one of the simplest of the business portfolio matrix approaches to strategic planning. The BCG Matrix is a four-cell matrix with the two dimensions of Relative Market Share and Market Growth Rate.

The General Electric Business Screen is a more complex business portfolio planning approach. Its nine cells are described in terms of Industry Attractiveness and Competitive Position. Calculation of each dimension requires considerable judgment from the strategic decision makers concerning the underlying variables comprising the dimension and values on each variable. Because of some perceived weaknesses with the GE Screen, the Life Cycle Concept has been combined with the GE Screen to yield the Life Cycle Matrix. These business portfolio matrices offer prescriptions for growing, holding, or divesting certain businesses.

The Learning/Experience Curve is used to justify aggressive pricing decisions of new products and to discourage new entrants into the business. These curves are based on the constant decline in the marginal cost of production each time cumulative output doubles.

Certain generic corporate strategies seem to be appropriate for certain SWOT conditions. These combinations are described in Figure 2.7. The generic corporate strategies are described in detail in Chapter 3.

DISCUSSION QUESTIONS

1. Describe strengths, weaknesses, opportunities, and threats as they relate to the strategic management process.

2. Define mission, objectives, and strategies, and tell how they relate to each other.

3. Describe the uses and limitations of the Product/Market/Industry Life Cycle Concept.

4. Describe the General Motors Corporation on the BCG Matrix.

5. Describe the General Motors Corporation on the GE Screen.

6. Compare and contrast the strengths and weaknesses of the BCG Matrix and the GE Screen as portfolio planning tools.

7. How would you use the learning-curve concept in market entry and pricing decisions in the personal computer industry?

ENDNOTES

1. Lord, R. G., and K. Maher, "Alternative Information-Processing Models and Their Implications for Theory, Research, and Practice," *Academy of Management Review* 5, no. 1 (1990): 9–28.

2. Ireland, R. D., et al., "Strategy Formulation Processes: Differences in Perceptions of Strength and Weaknesses Indicators and Environmental Uncertainty by Managerial Level," *Strategic Management Journal* 8, no. 5 (September–October 1987): 469–486.

3. Stevenson, H. H., "Defining Corporate Strengths and Weaknesses," *Sloan Management Review* 17, no. 3 (1976): 51–68; Snow, C. C., and L. G. Hrebiniak, "Strategy, Distinctive Competence and Organizational Performance," *Administrative Science Quarterly* 25, no. 2 (1980): 317–337.

4. "America's Leanest and Meanest: Companies that are Rising to the Challenge of Tougher Competition," *Business Week* (October 5, 1987): 78–84.

5. *Fortune* (January 19, 1987): 20–21.

6. Ibid., p. 19; *Fortune* (January 18, 1988): 32; *Fortune* (January 30, 1989): 68; *Fortune* (January 29, 1990): 59.

7. Hambrick, D. C., "Environmental Scanning and Organizational Strategy," *Strategic Management Journal* 3 (1982): 159–174; Thomas, P. S., "Environmental Scanning, the State of the Art," *Long Range Planning* 13, no. 1 (1980): 20–28.

8. Daft, R. L., J. Sormunen, and D. Parks, "Chief Executive Scanning, Environmental Characteristics, and Company Performance: An Empirical Study," *Strategic Management Journal* 9 (March–April 1988): 123–139.

9. Boulton, W. R., et al., "Strategic Planning: Determin-

ing the Impact of Environmental Characteristics and Uncertainty," *Academy of Management Journal* 25 (1982): 500–509; Javidan, M., "The Impact of Environmental Uncertainty on Long Range Planning Practices of the U.S. Savings and Loan Industry," *Strategic Management Journal* 5 (1984): 381–392; Miller, D., and P. H. Friesen, "Strategy Making and the Environment: The Third Link," *Strategic Management Journal* 4 (1983): 221–235; Andrews, K. R., *The Concept of Corporate Strategy,* 3rd ed. (Homewood, Ill.: Irwin, 1987); Bourgeois, L. J., III, "Strategy and Environment: A Conceptual Integration," *Academy of Management Journal* 5 (1980): 25–39; Hambrick, D. C., "Environment, Strategy, and Power Within Top Management Teams," *Administrative Science Quarterly* 26 (1981): 253–276; Jauch, L. R., R. W. Oxborn, and W. F. Glueck, "Short-Term Success in Large Business Organizations: The Environment-Strategy Connection," *Strategic Management Journal* 1 (1980): 49–63.

10. Fredrickson, J. W., and T. R. Mitchell, "Strategic Decision Processes: Comprehensiveness and Performance in an Industry with an Unstable Environment," *Academy of Management Journal* 2 (1984): 399–423; Lindsay, W. M., and L. W. Rue, "Impact of the Organization Environment on the Long-Range Planning Process: A Contingency View," *Academy of Management Journal* 23 (1980): 385–404; Hambrick, D. C., "High Profit Strategies in Mature Capital Goods Industries: A Contingency Approach," *Academy of Management Journal* 26, no. 4 (1983): 87–107.

11. "Corporate Renewal: How America's Best Companies Get Better," *Business Week* (September 14, 1987): 101.

12. *Business Week* (October 5, 1987): 80–81.

13. Blue, A. D., "White Zinfandel," *Bon Appetit* (August 1988): 24.

14. Armstrong, J. S., "The Value of Formal Planning for Strategic Decisions: Review of Empirical Research," *Strategic Management Journal* (1982): 197–211; Robinson, R. B., Jr., and J. A. Pearce II, "The Impact of Formalized Strategic Planning on Financial Performance in Small Organizations," *Strategic Management Journal* 3 (1983): 197–207.

15. "Borrowing Binge: Takeover Trend Helps Push Corporate Debt and Defaults Upward: Analysts Worry that Load Will Worsen Downturn in the Next U.S. Recession," *Wall Street Journal* (March 15, 1988): 1.

16. Bailey, E. E., D. R. Graham, and D. P. Kaplan, *Deregulating the Airlines* (Cambridge, Mass.: MIT Press, 1986).

17. Murray, A. I., "A Contingency View of Porter's Generic Strategies," *Academy of Management Review* 13 (1988): 390–400.

18. "The Auto Glut," *Business Week* (March 7, 1988): 54–55.

19. "GM Faces Reality," *Business Week* (May 9, 1988): 114.

20. Cochran, D. S., F. R. David, and C. K. Gibson, "A Framework for Developing an Effective Mission Statement," *Journal of Business Strategies* 2 (1985): 4–17; MacGinnis, S., "The Mission Statement: A Key Step in Strategic Planning," *Business* (November–December 1981): 39–43; Pearce, J. A., II, "The Company Mission as a Strategic Goal," *Sloan Management Review* (Spring 1982): 15–24; Staples, W. A., and K. U. Black, "Defining Your Business Mission: A Strategic Perspective," *Journal of Business Strategies* 1 (1984): 33–39.

21. Carothers, H. C., G. M. Bounds, and M. J. Stahl, "Managerial-Leadership," in *Competing Globally Through Customer Value: The Management of Strategic Suprasystems.* ed. Stahl, M. J., and G. M. Bounds (Westport, Conn.: Quorum Books, 1991).

22. Pearce, J. A., and F. David, "Corporate Mission Statements: The Bottom Line," *Academy of Management Executive* 1 (1987): 110.

23. Warner-Lambert Creed, Warner-Lambert Company, 1990.

24. McCaskey, M. B., "A Contingency Approach to Planning: Planning With Goals and Planning Without Goals," *Academy of Management Journal* 17, no. 2 (1974): 281–291.

25. Stahl and Bounds, *Competing Globally Through Customer Value;* "King Customer," *Business Week* (March 12, 1990): 88–94; "What Customers Really Want," *Fortune* (June 4, 1990): 58–68; Kearns, D. A., "Leadership Through Quality," *Academy of Management Executive* (May 1990): 86–89.

26. Clifford, D. K., Jr., "Leverage in the Product Life Cycle," *Dun's Review* (May 1965); Levitt, T., "Exploit the Product Life Cycle," *Harvard Business Review* (November–December 1965): 81–94.

27. Thorelli, H. B., and S. C. Burnett, "The Nature of Product Life Cycles for Industrial Goods Businesses," *Journal of Marketing* 45, no. 4 (1981): 97–108.

28. Anderson, C. R., and C. P. Zeithaml, "Stage of the Product Life Cycle, Business Strategy, and Business Performance," *Academy of Management Journal* 27, no. 1 (March 1984).

29. Wasson, C. R., *Dynamic Competitive Strategy and Product Life Cycles,* 3rd ed. (Austin: University of Texas Press, 1978).

30. Hedley, B., "Strategy and the Business Portfolio," *Long Range Planning* (February 1977): 2–12.

31. Hax, A. C., and N. S. Majluf, "The Use of the Growth-Share Matrix in Strategic Planning," *Interfaces* 13, no. 1 (February 1983): 46–60.

32. MacMillan, I. C., D. C. Hambrick, and D. L. Day, "Strategic Attributes and Performance in the BCG Matrix—A PIMS-based Analysis of Industrial Product Businesses,"

Academy of Management Journal 25 (December 1982): 510–531.

33. "After Years of Glory, Lotus is Stumbling in Software Market: Milking a Sick Cash Cow?" *Wall Street Journal* (August 30, 1988): 1.

34. Hofer, C. W., and D. Schendel, *Strategy Formulation: Analytical Concepts* (St. Paul: West Publishing Co., 1978): 31–32.

35. Hall, W. K., "SBU's: Hot New Topic in the Management of Diversification," *Business Horizons* (February 1978): 20.

36. Ezell, J. S., *Innovations in Energy: The Story of Kerr-McGee* (Norman: University of Oklahoma Press, 1979); "Kerr-McGee Settles Contamination Suit with the Family of Karen Silkwood," *Wall Street Journal* (August 25, 1986): 40; Rashke, R., *The Killing of Karen Silkwood* (Boston: Houghton Mifflin Co., 1981).

37. Hofer and Schendel, *Strategy Formulation*, p. 33.

38. Day, G. S., and D. Montgomery, "Diagnosing the Experience Curve," *Journal of Marketing* 47 (Spring 1983): 44–58; Dolan, R. J., and A. P. Jeuland, "Experience Curves and Dynamic Demand Models," *Journal of Marketing* 45 (Winter 1981): 52–62; Ghemawat, P., and A. M. Spence, "Learning Curve Spillovers and Market Performance," *Quarterly Journal of Economics* 100 (1985): 839–852; Lieberman, M. B., "The Learning Curve, Diffusion, and Competitive Strategy," *Strategic Management Journal*, 8, no. 5 (September–October 1987): 441–452; Alberts, W. W., "The Experience Curve Doctrine Reconsidered," *Journal of Marketing* 53 (1989): 36–49.

39. Rapping, L., "Learning and World War II Production Functions," *Review of Economics and Statistics* 48 (1965): 81–86; Spence, A. M., "The Learning-Curve and Competition," *Bell Journal of Economics* 12 (Spring 1981): 49–70.

40. Clarke, R. H., M. W. Darrough, and J. M. Heineke, "Optional Pricing Policy in the Presence of Experience Effects," *Journal of Business* 55 (1982): 517–530; Lieberman, M. B., "The Learning Curve and Pricing in the Chemical Processing Industries," *Rand Journal of Economics* 15 (Summer 1984): 213–228.

41. Tregoe, B. B., and J. W. Zimmerman, *Top Management Strategy* (New York: Simon and Schuster, 1980); 31.

42. Venkatraman, R., and J. Camillus, "Explaining the Concept of 'Fit' in Strategic Management," *Academy of Management Review* 9, no. 3 (1984): 513–525.

43. Ginsberg, A., and N. Venkatraman, "Contingency Perspectives of Organizational Strategy: A Critical Review of Empirical Research," *Academy of Management Review* 10, no. 3 (1985): 421–434; Mintzberg, H., "The Design School: Reconsidering the Basic Premises of Strategic Management," *Strategic Management Journal* (March–April 1990): 192; Venkatraman, N., and J. Prescott, "Environment-Strategy Coalignment," *Strategic Management Journal* (January 1990): 1–24.

■ ADDITIONAL READINGS

Ackoff, R. L. *A Concept of Corporate Planning*. New York: John Wiley and Sons, 1970.

Bresser, R. K., and R. C. Bishop. "Dysfunctional Effects of Formal Planning: Two Theoretical Explanations." *Academy of Management Review* 8 (1983): 588–599.

Chandler, A. D. *Strategy and Structure: Chapters in the History of American Enterprise*. Cambridge, Mass.: MIT Press, 1962.

Duncan, R. "Characteristics of Organizational Environment and Perceived Environmental Uncertainty." *Administrative Science Quarterly* 17 (1972): 313–327.

Gray, D. H. "Uses and Misuses of Strategic Planning." *Harvard Business Review* 64 (1986): 89–97.

Hofer, C. S., and D. Schendel. *Strategy Formulations: Analytical Concepts*. St. Paul: West Publishing Co., 1978.

Keats, B. W., and M. A. Hitt. "A Causal Model of Linkages Among Environmental Dimensions, Macro Organizational Characteristics and Performance." *Academy of Management Journal* 31 (1988): 570–598.

King, W. R. "Evaluating Strategic Planning Systems." *Strategic Management Journal* 4 (1983): 263–277.

Lawrence, P., and J. Lorsch. *Organization and Environment*. Boston: Division of Research, Harvard Business School, 1967.

Lenz, R. T. "Environment, Strategy, Organization Structure and Performance: Patterns in One Industry." *Strategic Management Journal* 1 (1980): 209–226.

Lorange, P., and R. F. Vancil. *Strategic Planning Systems*. Englewood Cliffs, N.J.: Prentice-Hall, 1977.

MacMillan, I. C., D. C. Hambrick, and D. L. Day. "The Product Portfolio and Profitability—a PIMS-Based Analysis of Industrial Product Businesses." *Academy of Management Journal* 25 (December 1982): 733–755.

Miles, R. E., C. C. Snow, and J. Pfeffer. "Organization-Environment: Concepts and Issues." *Industrial Relations* 13 (1974): 244–264.

Schendel, D. E., and C. W. Hofer. *Strategic Management: A New View of Business Policy and Planning*. Boston: Little, Brown, 1979.

CHAPTER THREE

Corporate-Level Strategic Decisions

CHOICES AMONG STRATEGIES

Corporate-level strategic decisions deal with the question "What business(es) should we be in?" By definition, a decision implies that a choice is made among alternatives. In the case of corporate strategy, that decision may be made *formally* as a result of an explicit long-range planning process involving external consultants and sophisticated planning models. Alternatively, the decision may be made *informally* based on the insight and intuition of the firm's executive(s), or it may be made *haphazardly* and *randomly* because of the failure to make such strategic decisions explicit. In the third mode, the firm implicitly settles for the status quo.

However the corporate-level strategic decision is made, all organizations are faced with choices among possible businesses or industries. These decisions may result in an overall mission statement such as "The mission of Apple Computer is to design, manufacture, and market personal computers to the business, educational, and professional user." Once such a mission statement has been decided on, the organization is left with the decision of how to enter, improve, or exit the chosen business(es). This stage usually involves choices among new alternative activities. These decisions may be further classified as the six separate corporate-level strategies shown in Table 3.1. Each of these strategies is discussed in detail later in this chapter.

Box 3.1 describes how one major corporation decided on several of these strategies including concentric diversification, acquisition, and divestiture. It also describes a famous merger that ended up as a divestiture due to a lack of fit with its core business.

To say that there has been much controversy over the issue of how the

TABLE 3.1   CORPORATE-LEVEL STRATEGIES

GENERAL	SPECIFIC
Concentration	Single product and/or market
Horizontal diversification	Related/concentric, unrelated/conglomerate
Vertical integration	Backward or forward
Merger and acquisition	Friendly or hostile
Joint venture	Domestic or international
Restructuring	Retrenchment, divestiture, bankruptcy, liquidation

BOX 3.1   COCA-COLA'S ACQUISITION AND DIVESTITURE OF TAYLOR WINES: HOW GOOD WAS THE FIT?

In the 1970s, some changes were occurring in the wine industry that caught the attention of decision makers at Coca-Cola. First, a beverage industry analysis reported that wine consumption was growing in the United States, both in absolute terms and per capita. "Wine sales in the foreseeable future should grow 8% a year, versus less than 3% for distilled spirits, according to Marvin Shanken, editor of *Impact,* a widely respected liquor industry newsletter. By 1980, says Shanken, wines will overtake distilled spirits in gallons."[a] Second, the distribution channel was changing. "Wine is increasingly purchased by women right along with groceries. Thirty-five percent of all wine is sold in supermarkets."[b]

Such growth and distribution channels were quite attractive to Coca-Cola. After all, a beverage is a beverage, isn't it? Production and marketing strategies that work so well with soft drinks should work with other beverages, shouldn't they?

Apparently attracted to the growth, familiar distribution channels, and expected production and marketing fit between soft drinks and wine, Coca-Cola acquired Taylor Wine Company in January 1977.[c] Coca-Cola chose Taylor, specifically, because Taylor had maintained its premium prices while others were cutting prices, and it had an upscale image.[d]

Coca-Cola went so far to protect the name "Taylor" and prevent its use and possible confusion in the minds of the consumer that Coca-Cola sued to keep a Taylor family member from using his own name on his wine. "Walter S. Taylor, a grandson of the founder of the giant Taylor Wine Company, must take his name off the labels of bottles containing wine produced by his own company, Bully Hill," reported the *New York Times.* A judge upheld a request by the Coca-Cola Company of Atlanta, for an injunction forbidding Mr. Taylor to use the name because of confusion over the wine made by the Taylor Wine Company, which Coca-Cola purchased last year."[e]

After the acquisition, Coca-Cola found itself in an industry in which the competition was somewhat respectful of others' territory. Apparently thinking that it could accomplish with advertising in the wine industry what it had accomplished with advertising in the soft drink industry, Coke went on the attack with its advertising muscle. It launched a series of comparative taste tests in which it identified the names of its competitors.[f] This bold move infuriated Gallo, Taylor's largest competitor, and strengthened competition on the basis of price. Such price competition lowered Taylor's margins and hurt its upscale image.

Coke also had problems on the production side. "Because wine has to be aged, inventory costs run a lot higher than in soft drinks. Coke added to its woes by vastly overestimating the amount of grapes it needed in inventory. Coke decided to get rid of the grapes by coming out with Vivante, an inexpensive wine that competed head-to-head with Gallo's Carlo Rossi brand. Coke, instead of breaking even, swallowed an $8 million loss."[g]

After encountering both marketing and production problems in a business that did not seem to fit very well with its expertise and other operations, Coca-Cola divested. It sold its wine operations in 1983 to Seagram Company for $210 million—the amount Coke paid for the purchases.[h]

Maybe a beverage is not a beverage.

---

[a] "Beverages: Basic Analysis," *Standard and Poor's Industry Surveys* (October 19, 1989): B-71.

[b] "Coke Takes a Champagne Chaser," *Forbes* (October 15, 1976): 66.

[c] Boulton W. R., and P. G. Holland, "Coca-Cola Wine Spectrum," in *Business Policy: The Art of Strategic Management,* ed. W. R. Boulton (New York: Macmillan Publishing Co., 1984): 430.

[d] Ibid., p. 437.

[e] "People and Business," *New York Times* (August 16, 1977): 58.

[f] R. C. Gordon, "Try Taste Test Ads, Taylor Told, But U.S. Won't Give Prior OK," *Advertising Age* (August 21, 1978): 1.

[g] "Coca-Cola: A Sobering Lesson From Its Journey Into Wine," *Business Week* (June 3, 1985): 97.

[h] Ibid., p. 96.

CEO and the board of a company decide on corporate strategy is an understatement. Organizations are constantly faced with difficult questions such as "Should we concentrate, diversify, vertically integrate, acquire, temporize, or refocus?" Contradictory answers to many of their questions may be found in two well-known theoretical approaches to corporate strategy: the Capital Asset Pricing Model (CAPM) and the concept of strategic fit.

STRATEGIC FIT AND CAPM AS STRATEGIC DECISION MAKING TOOLS

STRATEGIC FIT

Strategic fit relies on the concept of relatedness in making decisions concerning the appropriateness of the various operating divisions of a company.[1] It assumes that a corporation should pursue only those strategic alternatives in which it has some distinctive competence. Naylor and Tapon and Mullins proposed that in contrast to strategic fit, the theories of modern finance, which stress unrelatedness and contracyclicity, might be useful strategic planning tools.[2] Both of these two approaches are discussed in detail because of their implications for corporate strategic decisions.

A theory for concentric diversification and relatedness has been developed in the strategic fit literature. This approach promotes the concept of concentric/related diversification, which maintains a common thread throughout the business activities. A company builds on the activities that it is already competent at doing and operates in a core area. The result of strategic fit is synergy in some fashion. The advantage of strategic fit is that it provides a common focus for a relatedly diversified organization.

Thompson and Strickland identified three types of strategic fit.[3] *Product-market* fit can be achieved when distribution channels, sales forces, promotion techniques, or customers can be handled at the same time for more than one product or service. A good example is Anheuser Busch's decision to use its beer distribution channels and marketing techniques to market a line of Eagle Brand snack foods. The prior Coke example is another example of product-market fit. *Operating* fit involves economies being realized in areas such as purchasing, warehousing, production and operations, research and development, or personnel from more than one product or service. For example, Levi Strauss has capitalized on its production expertise in the manufacture of denim jeans and extended the expertise to other fashion goods, dresses, and other apparel. *Management* fit occurs when managers are given responsibility over areas in which they have experience. This strategy allows the company to tap years of accumulated exposure from one line of business to another. For example, a successful insurance company might decide to enter real estate sales.

Of the three dimensions of fit, management fit has been the least supported. After an extensive analysis of failed acquisitions that subsequently resulted in divestiture, Porter questioned the importance of management fit. "The best portfolio managers generally limit their range of business in some way, in part to limit the specific expertise needed by top management."[4] After another recent analysis of failed mergers, the importance of management fit in mergers was questioned. "One of the most common blunders is an assumption by executives that the skills honed in one business can be readily applied to another."[5] A more recent analysis of mergers stressed operating fit. "Most managers realize that they must bring operational expertise to an acquisition—not just financial skills."[6] Because of the limited value of management fit as a guiding concept, this book sticks with product-market fit and operating fit in its discussion of strategic fit.

CAPM IMPLICATIONS

As described in Appendix 3.1, the Capital Asset Pricing Model opposes the concept of strategic fit. A CAPM-designed portfolio of unrelated earnings streams stresses unrelated businesses. In accord with the CAPM, concentration is out of the question, horizontal diversification is emphasized to its limits, vertical integration across the entire spectrum is pushed, merger and acquisition is a very frequently used corporate strategy, and little corporate focus is sought.

THE PARADOX: STRATEGIC FIT OR THE CAPM?

The use of strategic fit as a decision guideline for corporate strategy contrasts with the CAPM. Adherents of strategic fit in a relatedly diversified company looking at acquisition candidates want a high *positive* correlation between the business candidate and the rest of its portfolio. The CAPM tells us that a very low or even *negative* correlation represents the optimum candidate for acquisition, with other factors constant.

Bettis expressed concern over this conflict between the two theories.[7] The value of a firm as measured by the CAPM does not include a provision for firm-specific risk, as it can be diversified away. The conclusion, then, is that managers should not be concerned with managing firm-specific risks as such behavior will not be rewarded by investors. But Bettis pointed out that the managing of firm-specific risk is at the very heart of strategic management. The matching of firm-specific resources with opportunities in the environment involves the management of such risks. This type of strategic adaptation has been depicted in organizational theory as the determining factor for the survival of the organization (see Chapter 2).

Bettis used the example of managing entry barriers, which might be used to deter the entrance of new competitors making essentially the same product. This is certainly a firm-specific type of risk. Modern financial theory would not be concerned with the management of this firm-specific risk, as the firm would not be rewarded for doing so. But many of the prominent writings in strategic management consider the building of entry barriers to be of primary importance.[8] The management of entry barriers is discussed in great detail in Chapter 4.

In the area of acquisitions, Salter and Weinhold criticized the idea that unrelated diversification offers shareholders a superior means of reducing their investment risk.[9] Empirical research provides little support for unrelated corporate diversification over a diversified portfolio of comparable securities with respect to risk reduction. If so, diversified companies represent no more to the shareholder than a mutual fund. In fact, these companies may be less valuable because of higher overhead costs and lower liquidity.

Another misconception, according to Salter and Weinhold, is that adding countercyclical businesses to a company's portfolio leads to a stabilized earnings stream and a heightened valuation by the marketplace. In other words, the correlation between the earnings of the acquisition candidate and the existing portfolio should be negative, if possible, as prescribed by the CAPM. This is merely an extension of the first misconception: The goal is to enhance the "safety" of the portfolio's income stream through unrelated diversification. The difficulty with implementation is that finding countercyclical businesses is virtually impossible. Similar to stocks, companies move in conjunction to some degree.

Salter and Weinhold suggested several ways for actually creating value for the shareholder, two of which relate to strategic fit. One suggestion is essentially product-market fit: Investments in markets closely related to current fields of operation can reduce long-run average costs. The second describes operating fit: Business expansion in an area of competence can lead to the generation of a "critical mass" of resources necessary to outperform the competition.

Recent evidence supports the notion of strategic fit with its concept of core business relatedness versus the unrelated conglomerate diversification message of the CAPM. Concern for knowing the customer and providing customer value in a Total Quality Management approach suggest that more attention will be paid to strategic fit. In his 1987 analysis of mergers that subsequently resulted in divestiture, Porter found that most of the acquisitions based on unrelated diversification resulted in subsequent divestiture because the hoped-for value never materialized. After extensive analysis of the acquisition and divestiture decisions of 497 executives, Stahl noted that the executives did not make either acquisition or divestiture decisions in accord with the conglomeration dictates of the CAPM.[10] Indeed, their acquisition decisions supported the importance of the strategic fit concepts of marketing fit and operating fit. Stahl also noted higher profitability, higher sales growth, and lower financial risk for relatedly diversified firms relative to conglomerates.

Business Week provided further evidence in support of the strategic fit concepts in strategic decisions with three recent analyses. One of "the seven deadly sins in mergers and acquisitions" is "Straying Too Far Afield," it said.[11] The article described a few famous mergers that failed due to lack of fit and stressed the importance of maintaining a focus on core operations through divestiture. "Rather than simply dumping dogs, companies are making moves to spin off and scale down healthy businesses to concentrate on what they do best."[12] Wall Street seemed to be stressing the importance of fit via the pricing mechanism. "Partly because Wall Street discounts the stock of conglomerates, 'focus' is the word on the lips of most CEO's."[13]

A HYBRID BUSINESS VALUATION MODEL

Based on these empirical findings, the reviewed literature, and Appendix 3.1, it is possible to suggest a number of potential revisions to the CAPM as a strategic decision making tool. Perhaps the most obvious of these would be to drop the interaction term from the model entirely. Certainly, based on Stahl's research and decision makers' limitations in processing interactions, little insight is gained with use of the interaction. Second, it may be reasonable to include components of strategic fit in a proposed model. Two factors, marketing fit and production fit, are certainly major considerations in the determination of how well a business unit works with the rest of the firm.

Stahl proposed the model shown as Equation 3.1:

$$V_j = R_j - s_j + MF_j + PF_j \tag{3.1}$$

where

V_j = expected value of business unit j;
R_j = expected profit for business unit j;

$$s_j = \text{variability for } R_j;$$
$$MF_j = \text{marketing fit with the other business units;}$$
$$PF_j = \text{production fit with the other business units.}$$

"Marketing fit and production fit could be based on actual or estimated costs or benefits that the overall firm derives from the inclusion of the business candidate in its portfolio. Costs (or a lack of fit) would be negative and thus discourage the business unit's inclusion unless its returns were very high."[14] This hybrid model argues that marketing fit and production fit should be considered when making acquisition and divestiture decisions.

Based on this theoretical background, the weight of empirical evidence, and current practice on the side of strategic fit, the corporate-level strategic decision alternatives open to the strategic decision makers can now be reviewed.

CONCENTRATION

Why do some firms choose to concentrate on a single product and/or a single market? Are they passing up growth opportunities? Are they risking extreme volatility, or even demise, associated with such narrow businesses?

The combination of product and market considered in these concentration strategies can be visualized in the product-market matrix as depicted in Figure 3.1. The three upper and left cells in Figure 3.1 are concentration or

FIGURE 3.1 PRODUCT-MARKET MATRIX

	PRODUCT/SERVICE	
	Similar	Differentiated
Narrow	CONCENTRATION	CONCENTRIC MARKETING
MARKET		
Broad	CONCENTRIC OPERATIONS	CONGLOMERATE DIVERSIFICATION

related/concentric diversification strategies. As the figure indicates, concentric diversification strategies are broader or more differentiated than concentration strategies. The Differentiated Products/Services–Broad Markets cell is considered a conglomerate diversification strategy. There are several decision rationales for choosing concentration strategies. The strategic decision makers may feel comfortable with the markets and products/services with which they are familiar and may shun the unfamiliarity of other markets or products/services. Even if they are willing to consider alternatives, there may be little economy of scale due to expansion primarily because of the technology employed. Reduced costs associated with learning effects may not be possible in other markets or other products/services. Both of these reasons may be relevant in service industries in which the service may be produced at the point of delivery. There may be little marketing fit or operating fit with other products/services or other markets.

There are three forms of concentration. *Penetration* strategies simply seek to increase market share. A good example is the cola wars between Coke and Pepsi. *Product development* strategies slightly modify basic product lines to capture more of the market. Kellogg's introduction of a new cereal is a good example. *Market development* seeks to expand the customer base for present product lines. For example, an airline discount fare targeted at college students might try to draw new customers.

Hair styling salons, banks, car repair shops, and other service organizations can be characterized by the matrix in Figure 3.1. Most styling salons are multiple-product yet narrow market organizations. Their expertise or distinctive competence is in the delivery of their services to a local clientele. Although they may start as single product/service firms offering only services dealing with hair, they may grow into other personal appearance services/products. Some offer retail hair care products, some offer tanning facilities, and some offer manicures. As there is little marketing fit to enter broader markets and few economies of scale to expand geographic coverage, such firms usually stay local.

Historically, banks have been narrow market firms that specialized in offering personalized services to local customers. Under times of government regulation limiting interstate banking, such concentration was logical. Yet even under such regulation, Banker's Trust of South Carolina engaged in a consistent merger and acquisition strategy throughout the state of South Carolina in the 1970s.[15] The bank had found that there were substantial economies of scale by spreading certain fixed costs such as computer operations over a larger business base. Thus, it lowered its overall cost structure. When the banking laws were changed to allow interstate banking in the early 1980s, several superregional banks were formed to lower their cost structures. Examples that come to mind are NCNB National Bank and First Union, both headquartered in Charlotte, North Carolina. Both had branches in several southeastern states and asset bases approaching $30 billion in 1988.[16] Although both had grown dramatically through merger and acquisition activity since banking deregulation, few expected them to diversify from financial products/services. With its subsequent acquisitions in Texas, NCNB continued to concentrate on financial products/services while serving a broader market. After the acquisitions in Texas, the assets of NCNB National Bank reached about $60 billion in 1990.

A third example of concentration is the retail auto repair industry. Shops that specialize in the services they offer tend to be local firms. They may specialize in similar kinds of autos or certain levels of repair. Other firms have decided due to a distinctive competence in a specific product or a specific service to concentrate on that specific product/service in a national market. Midas (mufflers) and Jiffy Lube (oil change) are two national examples. Although their market is broader, their products/services are few. Such concentration allows them to "stick to their knitting" and develop a distinctive competence, as suggested in the popular book *In Search of Excellence*.[17] In so doing, they may even lower their cost structure through familiarity with national purchasing trends, economies of scale, standardization, advertising, and the spread of fixed costs over a large business base.

There are costs and risks associated with concentration, however. As the CAPM indicates, variability in earnings may be high. The concentrator may be subject to survival threats due to the formation of competitors or the development of substitute products/services.

Some decision makers hold the view that big is better. If the strategic decision makers at the executive level are compensated in part on the basis of the size of the firm (for example, annual sales volume or growth), it is easy to imagine a built-in bias for dramatic growth, which frequently implies diversification.

HORIZONTAL DIVERSIFICATION

There are few topics in corporate-level strategic decision analysis that have received as much attention from strategy researchers as the issue of corporate diversification.[18] Should we concentrate on a core area in which we have built distinctive competence, as advised in the best seller *In Search of Excellence*?[19] To insulate our firm from risk of downturns in one product or market, should we diversify horizontally into products or markets that are related to our core business?[20] To further spread financial risk, as suggested by the Capital Asset Pricing Model, should we diversify into unrelated products and markets and transform the corporation into a conglomerate?[21]

This question of diversification can be viewed as an expansion of the Differentiated Products/Services–Broad Market cell from the Product-Market Matrix in Figure 3.1. This diversification dimension is shown in Table 3.2.

The reader may wish to think of conglomerate diversification as the logical extreme of the Capital Asset Planning Model applied to the design of organizations. In order to diversify risk, the strategic decision makers enter many unrelated or even contracyclical markets with different earnings streams. In the CAPM theory, this evens out the fluctuations in the corporate earnings by reducing the variability of the total return stream. Such a firm also finds itself in totally unrelated industries in which there is little or no strategic fit. For

TABLE 3.2 THE RELATEDNESS DIMENSION

CONGLOMERATE DIVERSIFICATION	CONCENTRIC DIVERSIFICATION	CONCENTRATION
Very Low Relatedness		Very High Relatedness

example, ITT, under the direction of Harold Geneen, was in businesses as diverse as telecommunications and insurance during the 1970s. LTV (Ling-Temco-Vought), under the strategic direction of Jim Ling, was in industries ranging from aerospace to steel making. TRW (Thompson-Ramo-Woolridge) was in industries as diverse as aerospace, auto parts, and water meters. (It is worth noting that conglomerates frequently have multiple letters or names in their corporate titles, which reflect the history of the merger of several corporate entities.)

Conglomerates were in vogue in the 1960s during a merger boom as a growth strategy. Many CEOs liked conglomerates if their compensation was tied to growth or the size of the firm. As investors began to see that the profitability of conglomerates was less than the earnings of other forms of organizations, the stocks of conglomerates were being discounted by Wall Street by the late 1980s.[22]

Concentrically or relatedly diversified firms follow the dictates of strategic fit and stick to a distinctive competence principally in terms of operating fit or marketing fit. Good examples include Champion International, which is focused around the concept of producing forest products that include paper products and wood building supply products. Similarly, Procter and Gamble builds on marketing fit and is focused around the concept of marketing many consumer products directly to the end-use consumer. Merrill Lynch, by building on operating and marketing fit, offers a number of related financial services.

As competition heated up internationally in the 1980s, many firms spun off businesses in which they had little distinctive competence and refocused on core areas, as the concentric conglomeration model suggests.[23] If investors wished to diversify their financial risk in their investments in the late 1980s, many bought common stock mutual funds. The low price-earnings multiples attached to the stocks of conglomerates in the late 1980s indicated that investors were not bidding up the prices of conglomerately diversified firms.

VERTICAL INTEGRATION

Vertical integration refers to how close the firm is to the end-use consumer or the source of raw material in the stage of production/delivery. Backward vertical integration refers to the concentration of efforts at the stage of raw materials production. Forward vertical integration refers to a shift in the firm's activities closer to retailing the product/service directly to the consumer. Table 3.3 depicts the concept of vertical integration.

Backward vertical integration is associated with upstream companies. Such firms are frequently characterized by commodity products, standardization, low-cost production, process improvements, capital intensity, and technological skills. Alternatively, forward vertical integration is associated with downstream companies. They are characterized by proprietary products, customization, high-margined marketing, product innovation, people intensity, and marketing expertise.

Some firms seek upstream activities to protect a source of supply or to insulate the parent firm from price fluctuations in the raw material. An example is the Ford Motor Company's production of steel to be used in the production of automobiles. Another is the ownership and growth of forests by firms in the paper industry. Champion International owned a large part of the trees that were used in its production of paper in the late 1980s. In contrast, the James River Corporation owned a small fraction of the trees used in its paper production and sought its distinctive competence in the paper production process itself.[24]

Others seek forward vertical integration so that the customer will identify with the firm and demand its product by name. For example, in the textile and apparel industries, the fabric producers (textile firms) are frequently different from the garment cutters/assemblers (apparel firms). Milliken and Company, one of the country's largest textile producers, had an agreement with some of its apparel customers to identify garments made from Milliken's material. In the summer of 1988, a pair of men's shorts retailed by the J. C. Penney Co. under the label Par Four® had an additional label on the garment indicating that the garment was made of material from Milliken. It is left to the reader to decide how much the addition of Milliken and Company's name to the garment helped sales of the product. It does seem that the Made in America/Buy American Campaign, conducted by a number of firms in the textile and apparel industries in the late 1980s, had the effect of increased sales of domestically manufactured textile products.

Some forward vertical integration attempts might backfire for some of the same reasons the textile example seemed to work.[25] For example, much of the gasoline Americans pumped into their automobiles in 1990 was refined from

TABLE 3.3   THE VERTICAL INTEGRATION DIMENSION

RAW MATERIALS	PRIMARY MANUFACTURING	FINISHED PRODUCTS	WHOLESALING	RETAILING
Backward Vertical Integration				Forward Vertical Integration

OPEC crude oil, but it was nearly impossible for the consumer to identify which gallon originated in Texas and which gallon originated in the Middle East. If OPEC owned the gasoline and the retail outlet (gasoline station) where the gasoline was pumped into the automobile, it is hard to imagine that the identification would help sales, given many Americans' misgivings about OPEC and the Middle Eastern situation in 1990. Iraq's invasion of Kuwait in the summer of 1990 did not help. Forward vertical integration is not advised if the producer does not wish to be visible to the customer.

Firms that are integrated across the entire vertical integration dimension depicted in Table 3.3 are known as "fully integrated" companies. A good example is the Shell Oil Company. The firm has operations ranging from exploration for crude oil and oil drilling and refining to wholesaling and retailing petroleum products under its name in its own retail outlets.

Increased vertical integration from the position on the vertical integration dimension where the firm currently operates is a form of diversification. Such a move to become more integrated in addition to one's current position spreads risk and leads to areas in which management has limited competence. This is conceptually similar to increased horizontal diversification.

Harrison, Hall, and Caldwell tested the profitability of a sample of firms that were highly vertically integrated and found that they had lackluster performance.[26] Apparently, the diversification activities required of increased vertical integration detract attention and resources from the firm's core of distinctive competence. This yields lower profitability just as unrelated horizontal diversification does. One step away from current operations on the vertical integration dimension may be analogous to related diversification. Several steps away from current operations is conceptually similar to conglomerate diversification.

MERGER AND ACQUISITION

The single most controversial and newsworthy corporate strategy in the late 1980s was merger and acquisition, commonly referred to as M&A. As the abbreviation implies, the terms are usually used together in reference to the joining of two separate corporations or organizational entities. The term may also imply the purchase by firm X of one division or strategic business unit that is being divested by firm Y. Separately, the two words—merger and acquisition—have different connotations. *Merger* refers to a friendly joining together of two organizations as in a corporate marriage, usually with the sanction of both firms' top strategic decision makers. *Acquisition* usually implies an unfriendly or hostile takeover without the sanction of the acquired firm.

Whether friendly or not, M&A is controversial and newsworthy for several reasons. First, the sums of money involved are typically huge, reaching into several billions of dollars.[27] Second, the very survival of the firm as currently known to management, workers, and other vested interests is at stake. Third, the control and management of the firm are in question, particularly in a hostile takeover. Top executives typically lose their jobs after a hostile take-over.[28] The M&A area is so controversial and newsworthy that it has spawned some of its own language, as indicated in Table 3.4.

A good example of a proposed raid to acquire a major firm was Carl Icahn's attempt to acquire Texaco in 1988. As the business news media reported, "Carl Icahn proposed to acquire Texaco for $60 a share, or $14.5 billion, after truce talks between the two sides collapsed. But the offer depends on several factors, including Texaco's willingness to present the bid to holders and Icahn's ability to obtain financing. Texaco officials were skeptical that such an offer, which could lead to history's biggest takeover, would ever be completed."[29] Indeed, Icahn seemed to be so sure of the profit potential that on May 27, 1988, he published an open letter to the Board of Directors of Texaco. "While this offer is subject to financing, I am so confident that my financing will be in place by the time of the meeting that we are prepared to place $100 million in cash or cash equivalents in an escrow account. This $100 million will be forfeited if at the time of the stockholder's meeting the financing is not in place."[30] Although the raid was foiled, such sums of money and such drama make for good reading in the business press! When he sold his

TABLE 3.4   MERGER AND ACQUISITION TERMS

RAIDER   Usually a wealthy individual who attempts to take over corporations for near-term profit. Due to either the receipt of "greenmail" or profits through subsequent piecemeal divestiture, the raider's primary interest is usually short-term profit rather than long-term management of the corporation.

GOLDEN PARACHUTES   A severance package for the top-level executives of the purchased company. As a way to encourage them to leave, the packages are usually lucrative, reaching into seven figures.

GREENMAIL   The corporate purchase of stock from a corporate raider at a premium. The raider is paid an above-market price not paid to other stockholders. Greenmail is outlawed in many states as it does not serve the best interests of all stockholders.

CAMOUMAIL   Camouflaged greenmail. The purchase of stock from a corporate raider by a corporate friend at a premium. The corporation can argue that it did not pay greenmail.

JUNK BONDS   Corporate bonds with very low ratings and high interest rates. Such risky financial instruments were often used to finance hostile takeovers.

LEVERAGED BUYOUT (LBO)   Using or pledging the assets of the acquired firm to repay or secure the debt from the purchase. Frequently used by top management to maintain control of a firm by taking it private.

POISON PILL   Measures implemented to deter a hostile takeover. An example is the assumption of onerous debt in the event of a takeover.

WHITE KNIGHT   A company, organization, or individual that rescues a company involved in a hostile takeover by buying the company on more friendly terms. White knights typically offer higher prices than the corporate raider and/or promise not to fire top management.

stock in Texaco in 1989 after the unsuccessful bid, Icahn received a $600 million pretax profit on a $1.4 billion investment![31]

Such high sums also imply that there are few firms that are safe from the corporate raider. Some observers have argued that the best way to defend from raiders is to keep the firm's stock price high through consistent, healthy quarterly profits.

Other than short-term profit, why would firms be involved in M&A activity? There are several reasons. Merger and acquisition can be a way to implement other strategies. In pursuit of concentration, a firm might try to buy its competitor, although this type of acquisition is controlled by the Justice Department. Merger and acquisition is a way to pursue either concentric or conglomerate diversification. It is used extensively by conglomerate firms, which typically do not develop their own products/services as a way to enter new markets. Merger and acquisition may also be used by a firm to vertically integrate. Instant market share can be achieved with M&A activity, whereas internal product development activity may take several years before substantial market share is realized. If executives are compensated on the basis of market share growth or the firm's size, there may be a built-in bias toward merger and acquisition.

The corporate world contains many examples of failed acquisitions.[32] One article gave examples of several failed mergers and offered "The Seven Deadly Sins in Mergers and Acquisitions":

1. Paying too much.
2. Assuming a boom market won't crash.
3. Leaping before looking.
4. Straying too far afield.
5. Swallowing something too big.
6. Marrying disparate corporate cultures.
7. Counting on key managers staying.[33]

The failed merger of Coca-Cola and the Taylor Wine Company, discussed in Box 3.1, is an example of "straying too far afield."

In an examination of the relationship between business-level competitive advantage and corporate strategy, Porter reported on the acquisition and subsequent divestiture history of "33 large, prestigious U.S. companies over the 1950–1986 period and found that most of them had divested many more acquisitions than they had kept."[34] Although M&A is a glamorous, high-stakes game, perhaps the size of the game and the failure rate should send up warning signs about its dangers. Far too many of today's corporate marriages end up in the divorce courts of tomorrow's divestitures. (Divestiture is discussed later in this chapter under "Restructuring.")

JOINT VENTURE

Sometimes the dangers of merger and acquisition are recognized, but the firm needs a temporary partner for a variety of reasons. These reasons might include the amount of capital involved, a desire to share the financial risk, a lack of technical expertise, and a need to penetrate a market rapidly. Rather than pursuing M&A as a long-term marriage of two corporations, firms sometimes pursue a temporary partnership, referred to as a joint venture.[35]

Joint ventures are typically more involved than supplier-customer contractual business transactions (although contracts are involved due to the size of joint ventures, sometimes running into billions of dollars). There may also be a pooling of personnel, plants, equipment, management expertise, and technical expertise.

Stahl recently asked 184 executives from large corporations to indicate the importance they placed on five criteria for entering into joint ventures.[36] The five criteria were derived from other joint venture studies.[37] The data Stahl reported were divided into three groups: the 27 firms that were primarily regional in scope, the 35 firms that were primarily national in scope, and the 122 firms that were international in the scope of their operations. Table 3.5 contains the relative importance of the criteria calculated from the executives' joint venture decisions. The points for all of the criteria add up to 100.

The data from the table indicate that among these 184 executives there were three important reasons for entering into joint ventures. These decision makers decided to pursue joint ventures primarily for technology/knowledge acquisition. This reason is especially true for the international firms, which placed 36 points out of 100 on this criterion on the average. The other two important criteria for entering into joint ventures were market penetration and financial risk minimization. Indeed, market penetration assumed increased importance as the scope of its operations ranged from regional to national to international. The more geographically widespread the firm, the more important it became to gain instant market penetration through joint ventures. Backward integration and financial return were not very important reasons for entering into joint ventures.

A recent example of a joint venture for the apparent sake of technology/knowledge acquisition was the General Motors–Toyota joint venture in California to manufacture Chevrolet Nova automobiles. It appeared that GM entered into that joint venture because it wished to know more about Toyota's managerial and quality control programs. This joint venture, however, empha-

TABLE 3.5   RELATIVE IMPORTANCE OF JOINT VENTURE CRITERIA

SCOPE	MARKET PENETRATION	TECHNOLOGY/ KNOWLEDGE ACQUISTION	BACKWARD INTEGRATION	FINANCIAL RISK MINIMIZATION	FINANCIAL RETURN
Regional (N = 27)	18	32	6	31	13
National (N = 35)	25	29	6	31	9
International (N = 122)	28	36	6	23	7

Source: Porterfield, R. I., and M. J. Stahl, "Joint Venture Decisions," in *Strategic Executive Decisions: An Analysis of the Difference Between Theory and Practice,* ed. M. J. Stahl (Westport Conn.: Quorum Books, a division of Greenwood Press, 1989), p. 87. Used by permission.

sized the potential problems of joint ventures between competitors. The *Wall Street Journal* reported, "General Motors is quietly weighing a tricky call on whether to allow Toyota Motor Corp to build trucks at the companies' joint venture plant in California. If GM says yes, the profitability of the company— New United Motor Manufacturing, Inc., generally called Nummi—would be greatly enhanced. But GM could hurt its own truck sales by handing Toyota a quick way around the 25% tariff on imported trucks. The situation illustrates the dilemmas that will increasingly confront auto makers in managing the intercompany alliances that are the hottest fad in their industry."[38]

It also appears that technology/knowledge acquisition was instrumental in the joint venture between Hewlett-Packard and Canon to produce and market laser printers for microcomputers. During the joint venture, most of the production of the laser printers was done by Canon and the marketing was done by H-P under H-P's label. After the joint venture, Hewlett-Packard did both.

The Alaska pipeline construction project was a joint venture for the apparent sake of financial risk minimization. As billions of dollars were involved and as there were technical risks, several petroleum companies shared the project.

Many of our international trading partners understand the importance of technology acquisition as a reason for joint ventures. A three-week lecture tour to the People's Republic of China by this book's senior author in late 1987 included interviews, lectures, and discussions with many Chinese managers, educators, and graduate students in Beijing, Shanghai, and Wuxi. It was apparent that the Chinese understood the importance of technology acquisition, as they knew that they were technologically behind other world competitors in many industries. They also understood that joint ventures were a way to acquire that technology. They were not bashful about entering into such temporary business arrangements for the sake of acquiring the technology. Examples range from automobile production with Germans to hotel construction with Americans. As world trade assumes increasing importance, we can expect an increased number of international joint ventures.

RESTRUCTURING

There are four separate substrategies under the label of restructuring strategies: retrenchment, divestiture, bankruptcy, and liquidation. They are listed in the order from least to most severe in terms of impact upon the organization. They all have in common the concept that the organization is being made smaller for a changed market.

RETRENCHMENT

Retrenchment refers to downsizing and cost cutting to meet a marketplace with reduced demand for the firm's products or services. The retrenchment may include layoffs, cuts in salary, hiring freezes, and plant closings. Because of the hardships associated with some of these approaches, retrenchments are usually controversial, and it is not unusual for firms to delay restructuring past the point at which it is needed. By that time, the restructuring is more painful because the corporate fat and waste have become more ingrained.

It is not uncommon to see firms retrench during a business contraction or recession. If a firm retrenches during a healthy business expansion, one wonders if it was suffering from severe competition in its markets.

A good example of retrenchment is the American automobile industry of the 1980s and early 1990s. Chrysler almost went bankrupt before undergoing a massive restructuring under the leadership of chairman Lee Iacocca. His decisions (combined with federal loan guarantees) to restructure, slim down, cut back, and refocus a bloated company that was out of control and out of touch are credited with the survival of the company. Partly because of his restructuring success, Iacocca became an American folk hero.[39]

The Ford Motor Company restructured shortly after losing nearly two billion dollars in 1980. It emerged in the late 1980s to report the highest profits of the American auto firms, even surpassing GM for the first time in several decades. Indeed, Ford earned nearly $5 billion in 1987.

GM delayed restructuring until after its competitors restructured. It finally took the bitter medicine in the late 1980s. Forecasters predicted that GM would close six factories and lay off 100,000 workers between 1988 and 1992.[40] There was some evidence that GM did not restructure in time to prevent serious erosion of its market share to the Japanese. "Japanese companies captured a record 26% of U.S. auto sales last year [1989]," said the *Wall Street Journal*. "By the mid-1990s, their combined share could top one-third of the market and exceed that of GM."[41]

The securities industry is another good example of restructuring. After the stock market crash of October 1987, the industry found itself bloated and facing a dramatic decline in revenues. After advising many firms in other industries to restructure, Wall Street found it hard to follow its own advice.[42] Layoffs, salary cuts, branch closings, and shrinkage are never pleasant.

DIVESTITURE

Divestiture refers to selling a division or business unit of the firm. The recent trend in corporate divestiture represents a remarkable turnaround from the 1960s, when it was thought that acquisitions were the key to the continued success of the firm. A significant amount of research and attention has been given to the strategic option of acquisition, but relatively little light has been shed on the alternate issue of divestiture. This situation stems in part from the perception that a divestment represented a failure on the part of the management team that was involved. Consequently, prior to the early 1970s, few divestments took place, and the executives who were involved were somewhat reluctant to discuss their parts in the decision process.[43]

As many firms have reevaluated the divestment process and its impact on the company's overall performance (particularly its impact on stock prices), more divestments have taken place.[44] Thus, it is reasonable to consider divestment a management tool that will be used more frequently in the future.[45]

Hayes suggested that many managers see divestiture as simply the reverse side of the acquisition coin.[46] When considered from a corporate strategy perspective, however, divestiture is quite different from acquisition, and decisions regarding the act of divestiture must be made in that light. Specifically, the manager cannot simply take acquisition decision processes and do the reverse to accommodate divestiture decisions.[47]

A fundamental reason for a divestment is to clarify the divesting firm's image as perceived by the stock market. Potential investors cannot fully value a conglomerate firm's many, diverse business units. That is, the conglomerate's overall strategy and resulting direction are unclear to the stock buyer. As a result, Brooks noted, the stock price of the conglomerate firm is priced artificially low.[48] Seely suggested that "investors prefer companies that are easy to understand and are willing to pay for them."[49] Slater suggested that the investor, *not* the company, perform any diversification of a portfolio.[50] In this way, the investor can understand each business as it relates to his or her private portfolio. This entire concept is summarized by Weinger, who stated, "The thicker the annual report, the lower the price earnings multiples."[51] Indeed, a number of researchers have noted the tendency for share prices to rise after a divestiture announcement.[52]

Increased attention was given to divestiture as a way for strategic decision makers to shape the firm in the late 1980s. Conglomerates have taken the lead in jettisoning assets. Their goal is to stay ahead of the raiders and get their businesses in focus.[53]

A good example of a recent large divestiture decision was the divestiture of its farm equipment operations by the former International Harvester. The divestiture was part of an overall restructuring and refocusing on heavy truck operations under the new label of Navistar. "The most painful decision and one with traumatic consequences involved the announcement in November 1984 that the agricultural equipment operations would be sold. Navistar International Corporation stands as an example of an American company that managed to avoid bankruptcy and to revitalize itself. It has successfully transformed itself from a sluggish bureaucracy to a streamlined, world class manufacturer with a growing reputation for being a superfast innovator."[54]

The decision to divest is not only a way to refocus the firm. It contains an element of power for a new strategic decision maker who attempts to assert independence from past policies. Stahl examined the divestiture decisions of 339 executives and found that nearly all of their decisions were influenced by the absence of the executive who had made the acquisition earlier.[55] For example, in Pillsbury's sale of Godfather's Pizza, one wonders if the planned divestiture so soon after the departure of the prior CEO was a coincidence. As the *Wall Street Journal* noted, "Godfather's Pizza was one of Mr. Stafford's first acquisitions. John Stafford resigned under fire February 29, 1988."[56]

BANKRUPTCY

Some strategic decision makers use a declaration of bankruptcy under Chapter 11 of the bankruptcy laws as a temporary way to seek legal protection from their creditors. The time gained is usually used to restructure the firm and its debts. The firm typically emerges in a leaner form from bankruptcy and resumes operations. Examples are Continental Airlines, which used bankruptcy to void a union contract, and Braniff Airlines, which used bankruptcy to restructure. The John Manville Corporation filed for protection of the courts under the bankruptcy laws while deciding how to handle its asbestos-related lawsuits. In early 1989, Eastern Airlines used bankruptcy as a way to stop negative cash flow during a labor strike. If a firm is unable to restructure while in bankruptcy, it may liquidate the entire firm or at least divest major parts.

For a retailer, bankruptcy may have particular risks. In early 1990, as part of the largest retailing bankruptcy in history, the Campeau Corporation used Chapter 11 as a way to seek protection from its creditors.[57] As retailer B. Altman & Co. found out earlier, however, liquidation may be inevitable due to the unwillingness of suppliers to ship inventory.[58]

LIQUIDATION

Perhaps the most dramatic admission of failure of all the restructuring strategies is liquidation, when the firm's assets are sold, usually under the supervision of the courts, to satisfy the firm's out-of-control indebtness. The firm ceases to exist as an entity. A highly visible example is Eastern Airline's liquidation in early 1991. Seeing grounded Eastern aircraft awaiting sale and empty Eastern departure gates in the Atlanta airport in early 1991 was a reminder that even large corporations can fail and suffer liquidation.

SUMMARY

This chapter explores the corporate-level strategic decisions associated with the question "What business(es) should we be in?" As a theoretical background for the question, the unrelated diversification precepts of the Capital Asset Pricing Model are reviewed in contrast to the related diversification precepts of the strategic fit concept. Total Quality Management concepts, many studies, acquisition decisions, divestiture decisions, and current practice support the concept of relatedness, strategic focus, or distinctive competence in corporate-level strategic decisions. The chapter proposes a model of the value of a business unit to the firm, including marketing fit and production fit.

Six different corporate-level strategies are covered in this chapter. Concentration strategies include both similar product/service and narrow market focus firms. Such concentrated firms stay closest to their specialized competence but suffer the risk of variability in earnings more than many other firms.

Partly to address those risks, diversification strategies are formulated. Horizontal diversification strategies include both related/concentric diversification and unrelated/conglomerate diversification. In the related category, there is some form of corporate synergy, fit, or focus related to distinctive competence that ties the business units together. In the conglomerate mode, there is no common theme tying the unrelated businesses together; ideally, the unrelatedness itself insulates the firm from variability in earnings. Considerable evidence supports concentric fit as a way to diversify and stick to a profitable core competence.

Forward vertical integration, as a corporate strategy, involves integrating the firm forward or downstream to move closer to the end-use customer. Alternatively, backward integration is an upstream move closer to raw material sources. Company operations along many stages of the vertical integration dimension can be viewed as a form of vertical diversification.

The strategic world of mergers and acquisition is a world unto itself with its own language (Table 3.4). With high-stakes games ranging into the billions of dollars, M&A is pursued for a variety of reasons. If there is a lack of fit between the two organizations it is not unusual for the merger or acquisition to fail and be dissolved in a subsequent divestiture.

Joint ventures are an increasingly popular form of temporary corporate strategic linkage. Due to the need to acquire the technological expertise of another or the need to gain access to markets, a number of firms, particularly those with international operations, are pursuing such temporary corporate marriages.

Partly due to intense international competition, there was a wave of corporate restructuring in the United States in the mid- and late 1980s. As companies attempted to refocus on what they did best, there was much retrenchment activity, including plant closings, layoffs, salary cuts, and corporate slimming exercises. The chapter explains divestitures as a strategic decision tool to help a firm refocus and increase its profitability by shedding business units unrelated to its core distinctive competence.

Once the corporate-level decisions are made, firms can concentrate on the business-level competitive decisions described in the next chapter.

APPENDIX 3.1

The CAPM as a Strategic Decision Making Tool[59]

A financial model for evaluating potential businesses for inclusion in a port-folio of business was proposed by Naylor and Tapon.[60] Their model company is a decentralized conglomerate that currently owns m different businesses. Risk is measured by the product of the standard deviation of a particular business's rate of return s and the correlation coefficient between the business's rate of return and the rate of return on the portfolio of all m businesses, de-noted by r_m. Naylor and Tapon chose this measure of risk because a company's risk is measured by its contribution to the standard deviation of the rate of return of the entire market portfolio.

If one were considering only a particular business, a high s might be unde-sirable. Yet an r_m of zero would make business more attractive, as virtually all firm-specific risk could be eliminated through diversification. Any $r_m > 0$ im-plies there is systemic risk associated with a firm that cannot be diversified away. This product, $r_m s$, can be used as a measure of risk in discounting a projected earnings stream.

By subtracting a risk premium from the expected rate of return R for a business, the certainty equivalent rate of return is determined. The certainty equivalent rate is a return that equates a risky income flow to a guaranteed income flow. For risk averters, this guaranteed income flow is less than the expected return for a project. Risk premium is defined as $r_m s$ multiplied by p, the market price of risk. The coefficient measures the tradeoff the market is willing to make for extra risk when increased returns are desired. Thus, the certainty equivalent rate of return required by the market for a specific com-pany is equal to $R \text{-} p r_m s$. In a perfectly competitive market, p is a constant. The risk premium implies that for every additional unit of risk $r_m s$ borne by inves-tors, the rate of required return increases by $p r_m s$. Assuming the expected re-turn will continue indefinitely, the expected value of firm V was expressed by Sharpe:[61]

$$V = \frac{R - pr_m s}{i} \qquad (3.2)$$

where i is the risk-free interest rate. Investment in the parent company is desirable as long as the expected value V is greater than the amount invested I.

This same analysis is extended to the divisions of a company. For each division j,

$$V_j = \frac{R_j - pr_{jm}s_j}{i} \qquad (3.3)$$

where

V_j = expected value of business j;
R_j = expected rate of return of business j;
s_j = standard deviation of rate of return of business j;
r_{jm} = correlation coefficient between rate of return for business j and rate of return for the portfolio of businesses.[62]

The goal is to choose a portfolio of businesses that maximizes the value V of the company.

Brownlee corrected the definition of value in Equation 3.3; the difference between two interest rates divided by a third interest rate cannot produce a dollar value.[63] Naylor acknowledged his error and stated that R should have been defined as expected profit rather than expected rate of return.[64] Boardman and Carruthers[65] question the conclusions drawn by Naylor and Tapon, but their reformulation of Equation 3.3 contains the same variables. No conflict was posed for this book, where implications for corporate strategy from CAPM concepts were sought.

After introducing the model, Naylor and Tapon then showed its usefulness for managing a portfolio of businesses.[66] The risk-free rate i and the risk premium p cannot be influenced by management, but managers do have some control over the other three parameters. A strategic decision maker relying on the CAPM would like to plan a strategy to increase the company's rate of return R and decrease s and r_m. Naylor and Tapon dismiss the management of R, noting that there are too many uncontrollable factors considering the company's many divisions. The proposed CAPM management of r_m consists of designing a portfolio of businesses so that r_m is as close to zero as possible or even negative. The model stresses a widely diversified portfolio of businesses with negatively correlated or uncorrelated earnings streams.

DISCUSSION QUESTIONS

1. How do the concepts of strategic fit and related diversification relate to one another?

2. How do the concepts of the Capital Asset Pricing Model (CAPM) and conglomerate diversification relate to one another?

3. Discuss the advantages and the risks of concentration strategies.

4. Compare and contrast the concepts of horizontal diversification and vertical integration. Describe the advantages and disadvantages of each.

5. Why do so many mergers and acquisitions fail?

6. Describe the advantages and the risks of pursuing a joint venture versus a merger.

7. Describe the advantages and the risks of restructuring.

ENDNOTES

1. Bettis, R. A., "Modern Financial Theory, Corporate Strategy, and Public Policy: Three Conundrums," *Academy of Management Review* 3, no. 8 (1983): 406–415; Venkatraman, N., and J. Camillus, "Exploring the Concept of Fit in Strategic Management," *Academy of Management Review* 9 (1984): 513–525.

2. Naylor, T. H., and F. Tapon, "The Capital Asset Pricing Model: An Evaluation of Its Potential as a Strategic Planning Tool," *Management Science* 10, no. 28 (1982): 1166–1173; Mullins, D. W., Jr., "Does the Capital Asset Pricing Model Work?" *Harvard Business Review* 60 (1982): 105–114.

3. Thompson, A. A., Jr., and A. J. Strickland III, *Strategy and Policy: Concepts and Casts* (Plano, Texas: Business Publications, 1981).

4. Porter, M. E., "From Competitive Advantage to Corporate Strategy," *Harvard Business Review* (May–June, 1987): 51.

5. "Do Mergers Really Work," *Business Week* (June 3, 1985): 89.

6. "Merger Mania," *Business Week* (March 21, 1988): 126.

7. Bettis, "Modern Financial Theory, Corporate Strategy, and Public Policy."

8. Porter, M. E., *Competitive Strategy* (New York: The Free Press, 1980).

9. Salter, M. S., and W. A. Weinhold, "Diversification via Acquisition: Creating Value," *Harvard Business Review* 56 (1978): 166–176.

10. Stahl, M. J., *Strategic Executive Decisions: An Analysis of the Difference Between Theory and Practice* (New York: Quorum Books, 1989).

11. "Do Mergers Really Work," p. 90.

12. "Splitting Up: The Other Side of Merger Mania," *Business Week* (July 1, 1985): 50.

13. "Merger Mania," p. 126.

14. Stahl, *Strategic Executive Decisions,* p. 52.

15. Boulton, W. R., *Business Policy: The Art of Strategic Management* (New York: MacMillan, 1984).

16. *Value Line Investment Survey* (New York: Value Line, 1988): 2033.

17. Peters, T. J., and R. N. Waterman, *In Search of Excellence* (New York: Harper and Row, 1982).

18. Bettis, R. A., and W. K. Hall, "Diversification Strategy: Accounting Determined Risk and Accounting Determined Return," *Academy of Management Journal* 25, no. 2 (1982): 254–264; Biggadike, R., "The Risky Business of Diversification," *Harvard Business Review* (July–August 1979): 99–110; Montgomery, C. A., "The Measurement of Firm Diversification: Some New Empirical Evidence," *Academy of Management Journal* (1982): 299–307; Palepu, K., "Diversification Strategy, Profit Performance, and the Entropy Measure," *Strategic Management Journal* 6 (1985): 239–255; Pitts, R. A., and R. Hopkins, "Firm Diversity: Conceptualization and Measurement," *Academy of Management Review* 7 (1984): 620–629.

19. Peters and Waterman, *In Search of Excellence.*

20. Haugen, R. A., and T. C. Langetieg, "An Empirical Test for Synergism in Mergers," *Journal of Finance* (September 1975): 1003–1014; Montgomery, C. A., and H. Singh, "Diversification Strategy and Systematic Risk," *Strategic Management Journal* (1982): 181–191; Rumelt, R. P., "Diversification Strategy and Profitability," *Strategic Management Journal* 3, no. 4 (1979): 359–369; Varadarajan, P. R., and V. Ramanujam, "Diversification and Performance: A Reexamination Using a New Two-Dimensional Conceptualization of Diversity in Firms," *Academy of Management Journal* 30, no. 2 (1987): 380–393.

21. Amit, R., and B. Wernerfelt, "Why do Firms Reduce Business Risk?" *Academy of Management Journal* 33 (1990): 520–533; Marshall, W. J., J. B. Yauritz, and E. Greenberg, "Incentives for Diversification and the Structure of the Conglomerate Firm," *Southern Economic Journal* 51, no. 1 (1984): 1–23; Mason, H. R., and M. Goudzward, "Performance of Conglomerate Firms: A Portfolio Approach," *Jour-*

nal of Finance 31 (1976): 39–48; Reinhardt, U. E., "Conglomerate EPS: Immediate and Post Merger Effects," *Accounting Review* 47, no. 2 (April 1972): 360–370.

22. "Merger Mania," p. 126; "De-Diversification: Aid to Productivity," *Wall Street Journal* (May 14, 1990): 1.

23. "Splitting Up," p. 5; Porter, "From Competitive Advantage to Corporate Strategy."

24. Smith, G. D., D. R. Arnold, and B. G. Bizzell, *Strategy and Business Policy: Cases* (Boston: Houghton Mifflin, 1986).

25. "OPEC Nations Move to Market Gasoline Directly to Consumers," *Wall Street Journal* (April 20, 1988): 1.

26. Harrison, J. S., E. H. Hall, Jr., and L. G. Caldwell, "Assessing Strategy Relatedness in Highly Diversified Firms," *Journal of Business Strategies* 7, no. 1 (Spring 1990): 34–46.

27. Cameron, D., "Appraising Companies for Acquisition," *Long Range Planning* 10 (August, 1977): 21–28; Kumar, P., "Corporate Growth Through Acquisitions," *Managerial Planning* 39 (July–August 1977): 9–12; Lev, B., and G. Mandelker, "The Microeconomic Consequences of Corporate Mergers," *Journal of Finance* 25, no. 4 (September 1970): 791–802.

28. Siehl, C., D. Smith, and A. Omura, "After the Merger: Should Executives Stay or Go?" *Academy of Management Executive* 4, no. 1 (1990): 50–60.

29. "Texaco, Icahn End Talks: Investor Plans Bid for Firm," *Wall Street Journal* (May 26, 1988): 1.

30. "An Open Letter to the Board of Directors of Texaco," *Wall Street Journal* (May 27, 1988): 29.

31. "Icahn Sells Stake in Texaco Inc. in Surprise Move," *Wall Street Journal* (June 2, 1989): 3.

32. Duhaime, I. M., and C. R. Schwenk, "Consequences of Cognitive Simplification in Acquisition and Divestment Decision Making," *Academy of Business Management Review* 10 (April 1985): 287–295; Hunt, J. W., "Changing Pattern of Acquisition Behaviour in Takeovers and the Consequences for Acquisition Processes," *Strategic Management Journal* 11 (January 1990): 69–77.

33. "Do Mergers Really Work," p. 90.

34. Porter, "From Competitive Advantage to Corporate Strategy," p. 43.

35. Berg, S., and P. Friedman, "Corporate Courtship and Successful Joint Ventures," *California Management Review* 22 (1980): 85–91.

36. Stahl, *Strategic Executive Decisions.*

37. Berg, S., and P. Friedman, "Joint Ventures in American Industry," *Mergers and Acquisitions* 13, no. 2 (1978): 28–41; Berg, S., and P. Friedman, "Impacts of Domestic Venture on Industry," *Review of Economic Statistics* 63 (1981): 293–298; Berg, S., and P. Friedman, "Joint Venture Competition, and Technological Complementaries from

Chemicals," *Southern Economic Journal* 43 (1977): 133–137; Roulac, S., "Structuring the Joint Venture," *Mergers and Acquisitions* 15, no. 1 (1980): 4–14; Harrigan, K. R., *Strategies for Joint Ventures* (Lexington, Mass.: Lexington Books, 1985).

38. "GM Mulls Tough Call in Toyota Venture," *Wall Street Journal* (June 10, 1988): 1.

39. Iacocca, L., *Iacocca: An Autobiography* (New York: Bantam Books, 1984).

40. "Shrinking Giant: The New-Model GM Will Be More Compact But More Profitable: Over Next Five Years, Firm May Close Six Factories, Lay Off 100,000 Workers," *Wall Street Journal* (June 6, 1988): 1.

41. "Auto Industry in U.S. is Sliding Relentlessly Into Japanese Hands," *Wall Street Journal* (February 16, 1990): 1.

42. "The Splintering of Wall Street: Now It's the Street's Turn to be Restructured," *Business Week* (March 21, 1988): 1.

43. Hayes, R., "New Emphasis on Divestment Opportunities," *Harvard Business Review* (July–August, 1972); Alder, H. S., "The Thorough Way to Approach Divestment," *Management Focus* (May–June, 1981): 3–7; Lynch, M., "Many Firms are Selling Off Acquisitions to Clarify Their Images, Lift Their Stocks," *Wall Street Journal* (December 4, 1980): 54.

44. Boudreaux, K. J., "Divestiture and Share Price," *Journal of Financial and Quantitative Analysis* (November, 1975): 619–626.

45. Nees, D., "Increase Your Divestment Effectiveness," *Strategic Management Journal* 2 (April–June, 1981): 119–130.

46. Hayes, "New Emphasis on Divestment Opportunities."

47. Alder "The Thorough Way to Approach Divestment"; Cohen, R., and S. Slatter, "How to Divest," *Management Today* (May 1983): 92–95; Donaldson, G., *Managing Corporate Wealth: The Operation of a Comprehensive Financial Goals System* (New York: Praeger Publishers, 1984).

48. Brooks, B., "Some Concerns Find that the Push to Diversity Was a Costly Mistake," *Wall Street Journal* (October 2, 1984): 37.

49. Seely, M., as quoted in M. Greenebaum, "Making the Most of Unnoticed Assets," *Fortune* (June 15, 1981): 241–242.

50. Slater, M., as quoted in B. Brooks, "Some Concerns Find that the Push to Diversify Was a Costly Mistake," p. 37.

51. Quoted in Lynch, "Many Firms are Selling Off Acquisitions," p. 54.

52. Hearth, D. P., and J. K. Zaima, "Voluntary Divestitures and Value," *Financial Management* (Spring 1984): 10–16; Jain, P. C., "The Effect of Voluntary Selloff Announcements on Shareholder Wealth," *Journal of Finance* (March 1985): 209–224; Miles, J. A., and J. D. Rosenfeld, "The Effect of Spinoff Announcements on Shareholder Wealth," *Journal of Finance* (December 1983): 1597–1606; Rosenfeld, J. S., "Additional Evidence on the Relation Between Divestiture Announcements and Shareholder Wealth," *Journal of Finance* (December 1984): 1437–1448; Zaima, J. K., and D. P. Hearth, "The Wealth Effects of Voluntary Selloffs: Implications for Divesting and Acquiring Firms," *Journal of Financial Research* (Fall 1985): 227–236.

53. "Splitting Up," p. 50; "De-Diversification: Aid to Productivity," p. 1.

54. Baruchi, C., and C. Barnett, "Restructuring for Self-Renewal: Navistar International Corporation," *Academy of Management Executive* (February 1990): 36–37.

55. Stahl, *Strategic Executive Decisions.*

56. "Pillsbury Sale of Godfather's Expected Soon," *Wall Street Journal* (May 25, 1988): 3.

57. "It'll Be a Hard Sell: Getting Campeau's Creditors to Agree Could Take Years," *Business Week* (January 29, 1990): 30.

58. "Lessons for Campeau: It's Not Easy Being a Chapter 11 Retailer," *Wall Street Journal* (January 30, 1990): 1.

59. This section is adapted from Chapters 3, 4, 5, and 6 of Stahl, *Strategic Executive Decisions;* and from Naylor and Tapon, "The Capital Asset Pricing Model."

60. Naylor and Tapon, "The Capital Asset Pricing Model."

61. Sharpe, W. R., "Capital Asset Prices: A Theory of Market Equilibrium Under Conditions of Risk," *Journal of Finance* 19 (1964): 425–442.

62. Naylor and Tapon, "The Capital Asset Pricing Model," p. 1168.

63. Brownlee, B. J., "Erratum to 'The Capital Asset Pricing Model: An Evaluation.of Its Potential as a Strategic Planning Tool,' by Naylor, T. H., and F. Tapon," *Management Science* 29 (1983): 633.

64. Naylor, T. H., "Reply to Brownlee Erratum," *Management Science* 29 (1983): 633.

65. Boardman, A. E., and N. E. Carruthers, "A Note on the Use of the CAPM as a Strategic Planning Tool," *Management Science* 31 (1985): 1589–1592.

66. Naylor and Tapon, "The Capital Asset Pricing Model."

ADDITIONAL READINGS

Baron, D. "Investment Policy, Optimality, and Mean Variance Model." *Journal of Finance* 32 (March 1979): 207.

Berg, S., and P. Friedman. "Joint Venture in American Industry Part III—Public Policy Issues." *Mergers and Acquisitions* 13, no. 4 (1979): 18–29.

Brodley, J. "Joint Ventures and Antitrust Policy." *Harvard Law Review* 95, no. 7 (1982): 1521–1590.

Cozzolino, J. "Joint Venture Risk—How to Determine Your Share." *Mergers and Acquisitions* 16, no. 3 (1981): 35–39.

Donaldson, G. "Financial Goals & Strategic Consequences." *Harvard Business Review* (May–June, 1985): 57–66.

Duncan, J. "Impacts of New Entry and Horizontal Joint Ventures on Industrial Rates of Return." *Review of Economics and Statistics* 64 (1982): 339–343.

Hamermesh, R. G., and R. E. White. "Manage Beyond Portfolio Analysis." *Harvard Business Review* (January–February 1984): 103–109.

Markowitz, N. "Nonnegative or Not Negative: A Question About CAPMs." *Journal of Finance* (May 1983): 283–295.

Kanter, R. M. *When Giants Learn to Dance: Mastering the Challenge of Strategy, Management, and Careers in the 1990s.* New York: Simon and Schuster, 1989.

Peterson, R., and J. Shimada. "Sources of Management Problems in Japanese-American Joint Venture." *Academy of Management Journal* 1, no. 3 (978): 796–804.

Rappaport, A. "A Critique of Capital Budgeting Questionnaires." *Interfaces* (May 1979): 100–102.

Roberts, E. "New Ventures for Corporate Growth." *Harvard Business Review* (July–August, 1980): 134–142.

Stiglitz, J. "On the Irrelevance of Corporate Financial Policy." Pp. 136–151 in *Modern Developments in Financial Management,* edited by S. C. Myers. New York: Praeger, 1976.

Sullivan, J., and Peterson, R. "Trust in Japanese-American Joint Ventures." *Management International Review* 22 (1982): 30–40.

Sutton, R. I., and D'Aunno, T. "Decreasing Organizational Size: Untangling the Effects of Money and People." *Academy of Management Review* 14, no. 2, (1989): 194–212.

Walter, G. A., and J. B. Barney. "Management Objectives in Mergers and Acquisitions." *Strategic Management Journal* 11 (1990): 79–86.

CHAPTER FOUR

Business-Level Strategic Decisions

This chapter examines the most important business-level strategic decision: how the firm competes in its chosen business. Should the firm compete on the basis of cost leadership? Should the firm compete on the basis of quality? Should the firm compete on the basis of image? Should the firm compete by focusing on a narrow customer segment? This level of strategy has received increasing and much-deserved attention recently in a number of American industries, due in part to intense global competition.

THE CONCEPT OF BUSINESS-LEVEL STRATEGIES

Once the firm has decided at the corporate level in which businesses it wishes to operate, and has decided how to enter the business, it must decide how to compete in that business. Even if it has operated in that industry for a long time, the firm must address the question of how to compete now and in the future. Most companies compete by virtue of their daily operations, but their success is left to chance if they do not understand the competitive forces shaping their industry and explicitly chart a course to deal with the competition.

Unfortunately, the concept of competitive business-level strategy is somewhat confusing, as several writers have tried to articulate dimensions of strategy using different labels. Some of those strategic competitive dimensions are listed in Table 4.1. The reader may observe from the dates listed next to the authors' names that considerable attention has been given to this subject recently.[1]

Although the labels connote slightly different meanings, there is considerable agreement on at least two generic business-level strategic dimensions. Whether it is labeled efficiency, low delivered cost, or cost leadership, one of these dimensions is business-level competition on the basis of low cost/price. The other dimension is business-level competition on the basis of differenti-

TABLE 4.1 BUSINESS-LEVEL STRATEGIC DIMENSIONS

AUTHORS	STRATEGIC COMPETITIVE ALTERNATIVES	
Hofer and Schendel (1978)	Efficiency	Effectiveness
Hall (1980)	Low delivered cost	High differentiation
Porter (1980, 1985)	Cost leadership	Differentiation

Source: Stahl, M. J., M. D. Hanna, and D. M. Parks, "Competitive Strategic Decisions: Is Focus a Separate Strategy?" in *Strategic Executive Decisions: An Analysis of the Difference Between Theory and Practice,* ed. M. J. Stahl (Westport Conn.: Quorum Books, a division of Greenwood Press, 1989), p. 96. Used by permission.

ated products/services. This dimension has been titled effectiveness, high differentiation, and, simply, differentiation.

A third dimension (focus) was recently added by Porter.[2] Firms employing a focus strategy choose a specific market segment for their business-level activities. Focus as a way to compete in an industry is described in more detail later in this chapter.

It is obviously an oversimplification to say that the only ways to compete in all industries are cost leadership, differentiation, or focus. Recognition of generic competitive business-level strategies, however, allows one to analyze the competition and the competitive forces in an industry with a common model. One of the most widely cited models for analyzing competition in an industry is Porter's Five Forces Model.

PORTER'S FIVE FORCES MODEL

Certainly the most influential writer on the subject of competitive business-level strategy during the 1980s was Michael E. Porter.[3] During a time of fierce foreign competition on a scale never before witnessed by American industry, Porter reminded industry that strategy boils down to how the firm competes against other firms in the marketplace.

Strategy is not merely an abstraction of models and concepts at the corporate level. Strategy includes an analysis of potential entrants, suppliers, buyers, substitutes, and competitors. Based on his work in industrial economics, Porter categorized the competitive forces shaping an industry in his Five Forces Model of Industrial Competition. The model, reproduced in Figure 4.1, has been one of the most widely used and often cited models in strategic management. By examining each of the five forces, one can assess the forces that drive competition in an industry and evaluate the probability of successfully competing in an industry prior to entry. In such a fashion, one can rate the industry's attractiveness for entry, analyze competitive trends, and plot future strategy.

FIGURE 4.1 FORCES DRIVING INDUSTRY COMPETITION

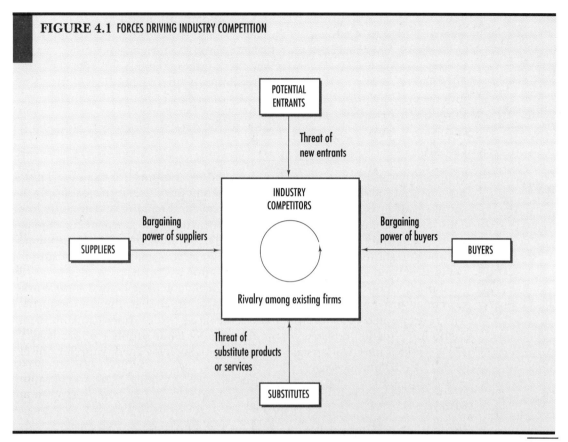

Source: Reprinted with permission of The Free Press, a division of Macmillan, Inc. from *Competitive Strategy: Techniques for Analyzing Industries and Competitors* by Michael E. Porter. Copyright © 1980 by The Free Press.

POTENTIAL ENTRANTS

The power of firms in an industry to influence prices, control resources, and shape the nature of competition within the industry is inversely proportional to the threat of new entrants. Indeed, the maintenance of entry barriers is such an important topic that it is treated as a separate section later in this chapter.

The American automobile industry offers an example of the effect of potential entrants. In the 1960s, many auto executives in Detroit thought that the barriers to entry into the American auto industry were too high because of the capital requirements. Consequently, they viewed the competition in terms only of other American firms. It is an understatement to say that they were unprepared and did not regard the Japanese auto companies as serious competitors until those firms had made dramatic inroads into the American market.

Incumbent firms frequently spend substantial resources building market entry barriers. High entry barriers limit the competition and tend to be associated with high profitability. The reverse is also true. In the apparel industry, for instance, entry barriers tend to be low and profit margins limited. Entry barriers are low because there are few cost advantages to incumbents, the capital required to buy or lease sewing machines is limited, and it is difficult to differentiate the product. As competitors can enter rather readily, the competition limits prices and profits.

SUPPLIERS

Supplier power refers to the ability of providers of inputs (for example, labor, raw materials, and machinery) to determine the price and terms of supply. If supplier power is high, profit margins of firms in the industry tend to be low. This lower margin makes an industry less attractive to strategic decision makers who are evaluating an entry decision. The number of different suppliers is a rough indication of supplier power. In general, a small number of suppliers is associated with high supplier power, and vice versa.

Supplier power in the auto industry is formidable. The United Auto Workers Union has a near monopoly on the supply of labor to the auto industry. The concentrated supplier power keeps the labor cost of American auto firms high. In the textile industry, on the other hand, labor supplier power is relatively weak, as most workers are not unionized. Such low labor supplier power is associated with low wages.

BUYERS

Buyer power refers to the ability of customers of the industry to influence the price and terms of the purchase. If buyer power is high due to the existence of only a few buyers or well-organized buyers, the industry is not particularly attractive to the strategic decision makers considering entry.

As the buyers are so disparate in both the automobile and textile industries, their buyer power is limited. In the concentrated airline industry, however, buyer power is formidable relative to the purchase of aircraft. A major airline can be quite effective in obtaining price concessions from Boeing, McDonnell-Douglas, or Airbus Industries.

SUBSTITUTES

The relative availability of substitutes for an industry's products or services directly affects the power of incumbent firms. As the number of substitutes rises and as the ease of substitution increases, the power of incumbent firms to control prices and shape competition decreases.

A good example of competitive forces arising from substitutes is the development and production of synthetic fibers in the textile industry. Textile firms that dealt only with natural fibers discovered a new source of competition as synthetic fibers became widely accepted.

RIVALRY

Rivalry refers to the degree to which firms respond to competitive moves of other firms in the industry. In some industries, firms respect one another's market niches and collection of customers and pursue a "live and let live" strategy. In other industries, cutthroat competition is the rule, and all competitive moves are countered.

A great example of competitive forces shaped by the rivalry among firms is the domestic wine industry. As described in Box 3.1 in the previous chapter on the acquisition of Taylor Wine by Coca-Cola, the wine industry had been a "gentlemen's" industry in which the competitors respected each other's turf and concentrated on making good wine. When Coca-Cola attacked Gallo, Coke changed the rules of the game and forced Gallo to retaliate with intensive advertising and aggressive pricing.

ENTRY BARRIERS[4]

A major force shaping competition within an industry is the threat of new entrants. To keep potential entrants out of the chosen industry, firms often spend considerable resources erecting or maintaining barriers to entry.[5] Indeed, some argue that the development and maintenance of entry barriers is one of the prime strategic management functions in an industry and is deserving of special attention. This competitive force has been discussed since the mid-1950s.[6]

Barriers to market entry are crucial environmental factors that influence incumbent firms' market shares and profits. In markets in which strong barriers to entry exist, potential entrant firms have difficulty entering the market early, or they enter the market as late entrants.

Late market entry is usually disadvantageous as it requires substantial resource commitments to overcome the lead of early entrants. Late entry can have some benefits, however. A latecomer might enter the market with improved or more technologically advanced products or without the need to create primary demand for the products. Risk is sometimes lower because demand has already been demonstrated. IBM's entry into the personal computer industry in 1982, years after the Apple Computer Company had established and dominated the market for personal computers, is a good example of late market entry. Although Apple claimed the market early by being first, IBM brought its considerable resources to the industry and quickly overcame the late start.

Barriers to entry were described by Shepherd[7] as anything that decreases the likelihood, scope, or speed of the entry of potential competitors into the market. Similarly, Porter defined entry barriers as "features of an industry that give incumbents inherent advantages over potential entrants".[8] Barriers embrace all kinds of specific legal devices, such as patents, mineral rights, and franchises, as well as more general economic barriers.

Porter's entry barrier proposals include and combine the most important entry barriers that have been discussed in previous literature. Porter's entry barriers include cost advantages of the incumbents, capital requirements, product differentiation, customer switching costs, access to distribution channels, and government policy.[9]

COST ADVANTAGES OF INCUMBENTS

Economies of scale and experience/learning curve are the two major sources of cost advantages that serve as market entry barriers if used appropriately. Other cost advantages may include those that cannot be copied by potential entrants, such as proprietary product technology, favorable access to raw materials, favorable location, and government subsidies.

DuPont's construction of large plants to produce chemical pigments is a good example of the use of economies of scale as an entry barrier.[10] The aerospace industry is noted for using learning curves in aircraft pricing to keep potential competitors out. Once the Hughes Aircraft Company had built the first batch of communications satellites, Hughes was able to lower its costs on subsequent batches and thus keep potential competitors out.

CAPITAL REQUIREMENTS

Capital requirements constitute a traditional form of economic market entry barrier, which was first delineated over three decades ago.[11] More recently, Porter argued that the need to invest large financial resources in order to compete creates a barrier to market entry, whether those resources must be raised in capital markets or not. Expanding on Porter's arguments, Harrigan claimed that if the capital requirements for market entry are high, the likelihood of entry will be lower and the technological scale will be higher.[12]

Eaton and Lipsey recently studied the strategic use of capital by firms to create market entry barriers.[13] They concluded that the useful economic life of capital, as well as the amount of capital, acted as a barrier to market entry in certain markets.

The automobile industry presents a good example of huge capital requirements as an entry barrier. Who could raise the billions of dollars needed to mass-produce large numbers of cars to compete with GM, Ford, or Chrysler? When both the Bricklin Vehicle Corporation and the DeLorean Motor Corporation were formed, they produced small quantities of specialized sports cars that could be hand assembled. Therefore, they both avoided considerable capital requirements and sidestepped that entry barrier.[14]

PRODUCT DIFFERENTIATION

Product differentiation was first regarded as a market entry barrier by Bain in 1956. According to Porter, product differentiation means that established firms have brand identification and customer loyalties stemming from past advertising, customer service, and product differences or simply longevity in the industry.[15] In addition, Porter pointed out that technology changes also play an important role in the pattern of product differentiation.[16] This is especially true if technology is proprietary or if technology diffuses unevenly in the industry.

According to Schmalensee, early market entrants gain product differentiation advantage over later entrants when customers become convinced that the first brand in any product class performs satisfactorily.[17] The first brand becomes the standard against which subsequent entrants are rationally judged, and it is harder for later entrants to convince consumers to invest in learning about their products.

A good example of product differentiation as a market entry barrier is a BMW automobile. Because of BMW's reputation as one of the world's most highly engineered sports sedans, few firms historically competed with BMW in that arena. Recently, with previously unheard-of levels of quality and new technology, including antilock brake systems and powerful multivalve engines, the Japanese have attacked BMW's product differentiation barrier of highly engineered sports sedans. The Infiniti and Lexus models are aimed to attack that barrier with technology and quality. Thus, quality and technology can be used to attack a product differentiation market entry barrier.

CUSTOMER SWITCHING COSTS

Switching costs lock the buyer to particular sellers. Usually, technological changes can raise or lower these costs. Porter argued that there are six major sources of switching costs:[18]

1. cost of modifying a product to match a new supplier's product
2. cost of testing or certifying a new supplier's product to ensure substitutability
3. investment required in new accessory equipment necessary to use a new supplier's product
4. investment in retraining of employees
5. cost of establishing new logistical arrangements
6. psychic cost of severing a relationship with present suppliers

A good example of customer switching costs as a market entry barrier is the purchase of aircraft by the major airlines. If an airline has repeatedly used only Boeing aircraft, the airline's costs in retraining pilots and maintenance personnel, buying new spare parts, modifying service facilities, and making other changes would present formidable switching costs. Another example is IBM's dominance of the mainframe computer industry. The costs to customers are substantial to switch to competing mainframes in terms of retraining computer operators and users, buying new software, funding new maintenance agreements, and buying new peripherals.

ACCESS TO DISTRIBUTION CHANNELS

A barrier to market entry can be created by the new entrant's need to secure distribution channels for its product.[19] Unless firms can develop their own distribution channels or acquire other firms to employ as their distributors (in a forward vertical integration move), access to distribution channels remains as an important barrier to market entry. Often, the first or early entrants use intensive distribution strategies to limit potential market entrants' access to distributors.

In the mid-1980s, access to distribution channels was a critical factor for the personal computer clone manufacturers. If they could not negotiate shelf space with Computerland or some other major distributor of personal computers, they were forced to either maintain their own distribution network, as Tandy did with its Radio Shack stores, or accept limited market share.

GOVERNMENT POLICY

Government policy can limit the number of firms in a market through licensing requirements and other controls.[20] Although limiting the number of firms in an industry usually decreases competition, such controls are often claimed to protect the public and the environment.

In the interstate motor carrier market, regulatory reforms have had an important impact on the number of firms and on the number of applications filed before the Interstate Commerce Commission to enter the market. Despite the increases in the number, Moore claimed that because the operating authorities (permits) were so narrowly drawn, the entry into the motor carrier industry was limited and competition hindered.[21] Pustay empirically compared the impact of different administrative and legislative reforms on entry into the motor carrier industry.[22] His conclusions indicated that the effect of the Motor Carrier Act of 1980, which deregulated the industry, was far broader than most reforms, impacting entry into markets of all sizes, especially the largest. However, the administrative reforms had the effect of reducing some of the regulatory burdens placed on carriers.

Recently, the federal product and geographic barriers to entry have been reduced in the banking industry.[23] Modification of the Bank Holding Company Act in 1970, the Depository Institutions Deregulation and Monetary Control Act of 1980, and the Garnst Germain Depository Institutions Act of 1982 are the most recent examples of deregulation. Several superregional banks were subsequently formed. For example, through aggressive acquisitions, NCNB National Bank and First Union National Bank both expanded to conduct operations in many southeastern states and to grow their asset bases to nearly $30 billion each. NCNB subsequently acquired banks in Texas and approached $60 billion in assets in the late 1980s. Before the reduction in barriers to interstate banking, each company had focused on North Carolina with much smaller asset bases.

RELATIVE IMPORTANCE OF SIX BARRIERS

What is the relative importance of each of the six market entry barriers? Stahl asked 137 executives of Fortune 500 firms to indicate the importance they placed on each of the six barriers in making market entry decisions.[24] The executives were asked to make separate decisions for early market entry and

TABLE 4.2   RELATIVE IMPORTANCE OF SIX MARKET ENTRY BARRIERS

ENTRY BARRIER	EARLY ENTRY	LATE ENTRY
Cost advantages of incumbents	21	22
Product differentiation of incumbents	20	19
Capital requirements	21	20
Customer switching costs	13	15
Access to distribution channels	14	13
Government policy	11	11

Source: Karakaya, F., and M. J. Stahl, "Market Entry Barriers and Market Entry Decisions," in *Strategic Executive Decisions: An Analysis of the Difference Between Theory and Practice*, ed. M. J. Stahl (Westport Conn.: Quorum Books, a division of Greenwood Press, 1989), p. 115. Used by permission.

for late market entry. The importance they attributed to each of the six market entry barriers is indicated in Table 4.2. Higher importance was indicated by higher points in their market entry decisions. The points add up to 100.

The first message from the data in Table 4.2 is that the relative importance of the six barriers is approximately the same for late as well as for early market entry. Second, there appear to be two classes of variable in terms of importance for executives' market entry decisions. Cost advantages of incumbents, product differentiation of incumbents, and capital requirements are each quite important in shaping market entry decisions. Of lesser importance are customer switching costs, access to distribution channels, and government policy. It is interesting to note that cost advantages of incumbents and product differentiation of incumbents are to of the most important market entry barriers. Cost leadership and differentiation are two of the three generic competitive strategies described by Porter.[25]

PORTER'S GENERIC COMPETITIVE STRATEGIES

COST LEADERSHIP

Cost leadership refers to the absolute lowest cost of manufacture in the industry. Although many firms strive for a low-cost position, obviously only one can be the lowest-cost producer. Please note that the reference is to cost, not price, leadership. A firm could be the lowest-cost producer yet not charge the lowest price; such a firm would enjoy a profit margin well above the average in the industry. Cost leaders can compete on price more effectively than their higher-cost rivals, and they often do so.

How is cost leadership achieved? There must be a pervasive commitment throughout the organization to achieving a low-cost structure without ignoring quality and other features desired by the customer in order to lower the costs. Cost savings are sought through economies of scale, learning/experience curve effects, low wages, buyer power in purchasing, and so on.

A good example of cost leadership through economies of scale is Anheuser-Busch. By building huge breweries with large productive capacity, which spread fixed costs over large quantities of production, the marginal cost of production is lowered due to economies of scale in water processing, refrigeration, and packaging equipment.

The aerospace industry, especially the Boeing Company, is expert at achieving lost costs through successful application of learning-curve concepts. Recognizing that the variable cost of production declines with increasing volume, Boeing is noted for assuming such lowered costs into its cost estimates. In such a fashion, the company is able to price aggressively and still maintain adequate profit margins.

Wal-Mart has achieved cost leadership in the discount retail market through buyer power from large volume purchases, an efficient distribution system that includes extremely large strategically located distribution centers, and careful attention to store location. Such cost leadership has allowed Wal-Mart to become the price leader and beat the competition.

Several American apparel companies have lowered their wage structure by sewing garments in the Caribbean, where wages are dramatically lower than in this country. Under a special government provision known as Section 807 of the Tariff Code, which was meant to foster economic development in the Caribbean, tariffs are assessed only on the value added in the sewing if the cloth is manufactured and cut in the United States.

There is a danger in pursuing cost leadership through economies of scale. Such a move implies substantial capital investment. If demand for the product declines dramatically, the excess capital investment could become a substantial "white elephant." Dramatic declines in demand in a short time period are often associated with a substitution effect. For example, the synthetic fiber production industry expanded productive capacity dramatically in the 1970s to produce polyester fiber for men's polyester leisure suits. After the fad passed, demand for polyester yarn production plummeted. Several large plants costing tens of millions of dollars, which had been constructed a few years earlier solely to produce polyester fibers, were closed.

Demand for a firm's product at its historical price can decline if a competitor devises a new technology to produce the item at a lower cost. Genentech, a bioengineering company, estimated that by using a new genetic engineering process, it could produce insulin at a thousandth of the cost of the old insulin production process.[26] Genentech then had to make a major pricing decision: It could price its product near the historical price in the industry and reap a phenomenal profit margin, or it could price its product closer to the cost of production and dramatically grow its market share. Genentech did not have its own distribution channel in 1982 and chose to license its insulin to Eli Lilly & Co., which held over 80 percent of the domestic insulin market at the time.

Lilly was eager to license Genentech's low-cost production process and at the same time remove the threat of Genentech entering its market.

DIFFERENTIATION

Differentiation refers to a product or service that is perceived by the customer as somehow unique. Differentiation frequently consists of building a brand image through extensive advertising, putting extra features or options in the product to make it different from competing products, providing extra customer service with the product, staffing an extensive dealer network for repair and distribution, or distributing only very high quality items.

Differentiation relies on the concept that customers will pay more for an item if they perceive that it is different and if the basis for the difference is valued by the customer. In theory, the extra price justifies the extra marketing and production costs, although the price is not ignored. There is often a limit to how much extra the customer will pay for a differentiated product.

Note the use of the word "perception" in the description of differentiation. The task is to convince the customer that there is something unique about the product, so advertising frequently plays a huge role in differentiation strategies. For example, many blind taste tests of beer have indicated that there is little identifiable difference in the taste of beer within the same class of beer (such as premium or light). Yet brewing companies spend millions of dollars in advertising campaigns to convince consumers that there are differences. Similar comments have been made about soft drinks; indeed, the "cola wars" of the 1980s are infamous for their claims.

It is not unusual for differentiators to employ substantial consumer research efforts. If the firms can identify changing consumer tastes, they can be the first to offer a new differentiated product. Procter and Gamble and the Coca-Cola Company are two examples of differentiators with substantial consumer research efforts. In addition, both companies heavily advertise to convince the consumer that the products are different.

A good example of differentiation associated with brand image was the Izod Company in 1986. Their knit shirts with the alligator logo on the chest demanded a price premium even though a knit shirt of virtually the same cloth, the same style, and the same fit, but without a logo, could be purchased for substantially less at the time.

In the major home appliance industry, the Maytag Company has differentiated itself with a perception of very high reliability in their products. Their famous television commercials showed a Maytag repairman who was bored due to a lack of service calls. The reliability theme supported the price.

The Caterpillar Company has differentiated itself with an extensive dealer network for parts and repair. Many construction firms know that if their "Cat" breaks, they can get it fixed quickly. Many construction firms will pay a premium price for such a service because of the high cost of a delayed project if the equipment is idle.

The most obvious danger to pursuing differentiation as a generic strategy is that the customer might no longer demand the basis of differentiation. A good example is the Izod knit shirt mentioned earlier. After the rage thrived for a while, sales declined as consumers became less willing to pay the premium for a product that had become commonplace.

FOCUS

As a generic competitive strategy, focus is an attempt to serve a particular target group, segment, or market niche and serve it well. The first pursuing focus as a strategy pays strict attention to the needs of the target segment, even more so than the cost leader or differentiator, because the niche pursued by the focuser is so small. Focus refers to the narrowness of the market served rather than the characteristics of the product/service, as with the generic strategies of cost leadership and differentiation. In serving the market niche, one usually refers to cost focus or differentiation focus. In cost focus, the firm is able to offer a product to a very narrow market segment more cheaply than competitors. In differentiation focus, the firm offers a product/service to a specific market segment more differentiated than any competitor's product/service.

A good example of differentiation focus is a Rolls Royce automobile. The extreme attention to luxury and detail, with a correspondingly very high price, caters to a very narrow market segment. Another example is Cray supercomputers, with their enormous unequaled number-crunching computational power. Although Cray's products were sold to less than a few dozen customers in 1989, the prices ranged into the many millions of dollars at a time when computer prices were falling. Revco's senior citizen discounts on prescription drugs is an example of cost focus.

Just as there are dangers in pursuing the two other generic strategies, there are risks in pursuing focus as a competitive strategy. One danger is that a competitor could offer a product even more attuned to the needs of the target segment. At the time of this writing, the Japanese were widely rumored to be developing the next generation of supercomputers to sell to Cray's customers. Another danger is that customer needs and tastes could change. If there were a severe worldwide depression, the forecasted sales of Rolls Royce autos could plummet.

A good example of the pursuit of focus as a competitive strategy came from Campbell Soup in the late 1980s. According to *Business Week*, "Campbell Soup is cooking up a strategy that may revolutionize mass marketing in the U.S. The once-stodgy food giant has begun to tailor its products, advertising and sales efforts to fit different regions of the country—even different neighborhoods within a city."[27] Such a focused strategy, however, for large national firms can have disadvantages as local firms retaliate on their turf, as the *Wall Street Journal* reported. "But even if the product is right for the region, national marketers can encounter strong retaliation from local competitors, who have more at stake. That happened when Campbell introduced its spicy Ranchero beans in the Southwest. The local biggie, Ranch Style Beans, now owned by American Home Products Inc., suddenly sprang to life with heavy advertising and promotion, blunting the Campbell rollout."[28]

Wright argued that focus is more relevant for smaller firms who can pay better attention to a market niche's specific needs.[29] The size of the cost disadvantage associated with a focused strategy for a national firm was noted by General Foods. "General Foods figures that regionally oriented promotion of its Maxwell House coffee cost two to three times more than a single national campaign."[30]

COST LEADERSHIP AND DIFFERENTIATION THROUGH QUALITY

Recently, two different analyses of Porter's strategies argued that both cost leadership and differentiation are simultaneously achievable and may be needed for sustained competitive advantage. Conditions of quality, innovation, commitment of users to products of rival firms, learning effects, economies of scale, and economies of scope were mentioned as some conditions for achieving both strategies.[31]

A growing number of writers have argued that superior quality is the principal way to achieve both low cost and differentiation.[32] Indeed, this is a primary concept of Total Quality Management. This strategy seems to have been employed by the Japanese in a number of industries, including consumer electronics and automobiles. P&G, Xerox, and Warner-Lambert are three firms who have used quality as a way to achieve both low cost and differentiation.[33] Quality, as a critical component of manufacturing strategy and as a near necessity of customer value, is discussed at length in Chapter 5. Various ways and examples to implement strategies based on quality are discussed in Chapter 6.

RELATIVE IMPORTANCE OF THREE STRATEGIES

In order to test the relative importance attributed to each of the three generic business-level competitive strategies, and to test Wright's concept that focus is more relevant for smaller firms, Stahl examined the competitive strategic decisions of thirty-five executives in the textile industry and thirteen executives in the printing industry.[34] The executives in the textile industry made separate decisions for industrial fabrics, home fabrics, and apparel fabrics. Table 4.3 indicates the relative importance they attributed to each of the three strategies. The points for the three strategies total 100.

The executives from the printing industry placed significantly more weight on focus than did the executives from the textile industry. The printing executives were from smaller companies, many with less than 100 employees. The textile executives were from larger companies, some with more than 10,000 employees. Thus, Wright's proposition that focus is a more relevant strategy for smaller firms was supported.

TABLE 4.3   RELATIVE IMPORTANCE OF THREE GENERIC STRATEGIES

| STRATEGY | TEXTILE INDUSTRY | | | PRINTING INDUSTRY |
	INDUSTRIAL	HOME	APPAREL	
Cost	58	45	48	25
Differentiation	13	30	33	42
Focus	29	25	19	33

Note: There were 35 executives in the textile industry sample and 13 executives in the printing industry sample.

Source: Stahl, M. J., M. D. Hanna, and D. M. Parks, "Competitive Strategic Decisions: Is Focus a Separate Strategy?" in *Strategic Executive Decisions: An Analysis of the Difference Between Theory and Practice,* ed. M. J. Stahl (Westport Conn.: Quorum Books, a division of Greenwood Press, 1989), p. 102. Used by permission.

STUCK IN THE MIDDLE

Porter argued that there is a fourth state of affairs in business-level competitive strategy; he labeled it "stuck in the middle."[35] It is not a deliberate strategy per se. Rather, it is the result of not being able to successfully pursue any of the three generic strategies. Sometimes the firm is not sure if cost leadership, differentiation, or focus is the best strategy for an industry. Sometimes the firm is unwilling or unable to make the necessary financial commitments to a market to achieve the lowest cost structure with economy of scale. Sometimes the firm is not willing or able to achieve the highest differentiation with unequaled quality or dealer networks. Sometimes the firm is not able to achieve regional identification in many regions with separate products and separate advertising campaigns. The result of not having the lowest costs, not being really differentiated in the minds of the consumer, or not successfully targeting a market segment results in a weak profitability and market picture. Being "stuck in the middle" is almost always associated with lower profitability and mediocre market share.

In the early 1980s, it appeared that the J. C. Penney Co. was stuck in the middle. Penney's was not a low-price discount retailer; nor was it an upscale department store. It certainly was not focused on a narrow market segment. In the mid-1980s, it attempted to differentiate itself by deleting most hard goods and major appliances from its offerings and concentrated on more upscale soft goods. Penney's performance slowly improved. In the late 1980s, Sears seemed to recognize that it had been stuck in the middle and lowered prices across the board in a national campaign emphasizing its new lower prices. Sears was still stuck in the middle in 1990, as the company was having difficulty lowering its costs. Usually, it takes much work and time for large organizations to change competitive strategies and images in the minds of consumers.

COMPETITIVE GROUP ANALYSIS

Another very useful concept in the analysis of competitors and the development of competitive business-level strategy is the analysis of strategic groups within an industry.[36] The concept of strategic group analysis, originated by Porter, has been extended by several academic researchers who have empirically and statistically defined groups of competitors in an industry.[37]

Conceptually, the first step is to identify the important competitive dimensions. In other words, on what specific factors are the firms competing within the industry? This description of competitive dimensions is more specific than the generic competitive strategies. For example, instead of describing competition in the airline industry as differentiation, a specific description of differentiation through distribution network or number of markets served is required. Once the competitive dimensions are described, two dimensional plots of the dimensions with the positions of the competitors are developed. Next, analysis of the firm's position relative to the competitors and to customers' needs is performed. This competitive group analysis indicates the soundness of current strategy, the need for corrective action in that industry, or the wisdom of entering a market if the firm is not already in that market.

Examples of competitive groups from the airline industry are contained in Figures 4.2 and 4.3. The relevant competitive dimensions are defined as cost position and size of the carrier. Cost position is measured by operating expense per available seat mile (ASM). Operating expense per ASM is a commonly used measure of airline cost structure.[38] Size of the carrier is measured by ASM.

In 1981, the major competitors operated with a similar cost position that reflected the government's regulation of prices and provided little incentive for the airlines to reduce costs. Indeed, regulation of prices encouraged competition on bases other than price. After the industry was deregulated, price competition became relevant. Thus, cost structure became very relevant. The 1986 plot in Figure 4.3 shows the different alignment of the competitors once cost position assumed importance.

It is not unusual to see such a diagonal pattern in a strategic group map if one of the dimensions is cost or price and the other dimension is differentiation. In general, the higher the price or cost, the more of the differentiated quality or feature the customer demands. A firm can decide where on the diagonal to position itself and anticipate reasonable profitability. If by using different or proprietary technology or a high quality level the firm can significantly lower its cost structure, or deliver a more differentiated product at the same cost, an off-diagonal position may also be possible and carry with it substantially higher-than-average profitability. The particular role that technology, especially information technology, can play in competitive strategy is described in the next section.

Once the firm knows exactly who its competitors are, and on what basis

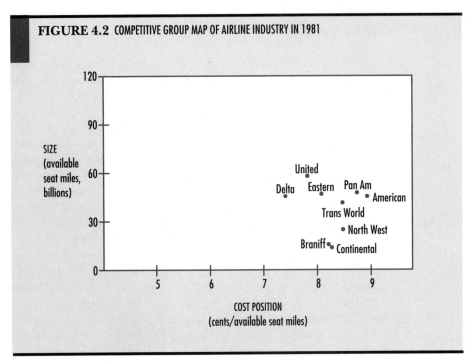

FIGURE 4.2 COMPETITIVE GROUP MAP OF AIRLINE INDUSTRY IN 1981

Source: Moody's Transportation Manual (New York: Moody's Investor's Services, 1982).

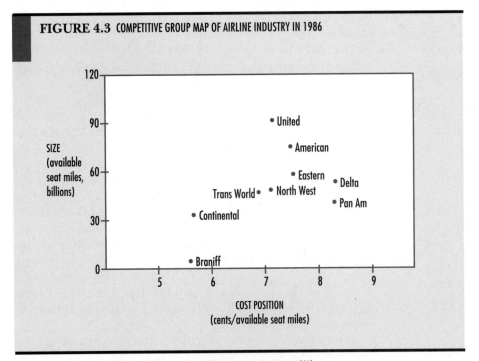

FIGURE 4.3 COMPETITIVE GROUP MAP OF AIRLINE INDUSTRY IN 1986

Source: Moody's Transportation Manual (New York: Moody's Investor's Services, 1987).

they are competing, it becomes important to anticipate their competitive moves. Figure 4.4 is used as a guide to competitor analysis with the use of conjectures. The figure indicates that the firm must know something about the rival's decision-making process and consider that knowledge in the firm's own decisions. If nothing else, the use of conjectures forces attention on the competitors and on contingency plans.

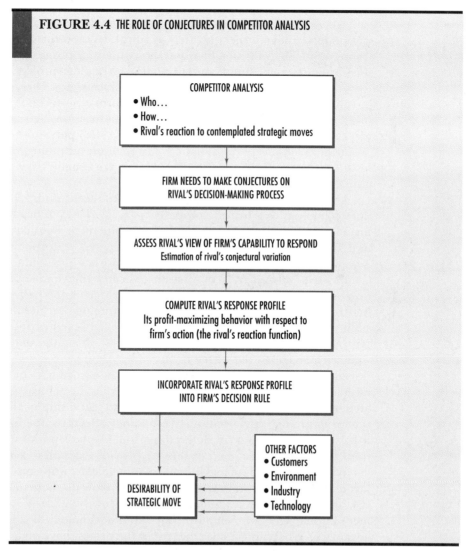

FIGURE 4.4 THE ROLE OF CONJECTURES IN COMPETITOR ANALYSIS

Source: Amit, R., I. Domowitz, and C. Fershtman, "Thinking One Step Ahead: The Use of Conjectures in Competitor Analysis," *Strategic Management Journal* 9 (September–October 1988): 434. Copyright © 1988 by John Wiley & Sons, Ltd. Reprinted by permission of John Wiley & Sons, Ltd.

94

INFORMATION TECHNOLOGY AND COMPETITIVE STRATEGY[39]

According to Porter, "Technological change is one of the principal drivers of competition. Of all the things that can change the rules of competition, technological change is among the most prominent."[40] Information technology was chosen for this discussion relative to competitive strategy because of its widespread impact, several great examples, and some relevant research. In more general terms, information systems strategy is reviewed in Chapter 5.

Many firms have used information technology to gain a competitive advantage within their respective industries. The decision to invest in an information technology project is often a critical decision that can determine the long-term profitability of a firm and its competitive position within the industry. Ideally, the selection of an information technology project ought to evolve from the overall corporate- and business-level strategies. There must be a clear integration between the selection of an information technology project and the company's strategy. Unfortunately, communications between top management and management information systems (MIS) personnel are often poor. To further complicate the situation, information technology projects that offer the potential for competitive advantage are usually risky, long-term commitments.[41]

The management literature is replete with recent studies linking information technology to a firm's competitive strategy. Titles indicative of this trend include "Information Systems Redraw Competitive Boundaries," "Information Technology Changes the Way You Compete," "Information Technology: A New Competitive Weapon," and "How Information Technology Gives You Competitive Advantage."[42] Why has there been so much interest in the integration of information technology with strategy during the past five years? Alan Kantrow noted, "This link exists because technology defines the range of possibilities and oftentimes provides the means of implementing the strategy. A critical link between technology and strategy exists, the only real choice is whether managers want to see it."[43]

Examples of companies that have been able to gain a competitive advantage using information technology are numerous. Porter argues, however, that all have gained their competitive edge due to increasing product differentiation or improving cost position. "Technology affects competitive advantage if it has a significant role in determining relative cost position or differentiation."[44] The firms described in Box 4.1 provide examples of both situations.

What is the decision-making policy of managers who employ information technology to gain a competitive advantage? How do these managers balance risk and competitive advantage potential? How relevant is return on investment for managers who employ information technology to gain a competitive advantage? What impact does the cost of the project have on a manager's decision to invest? Stahl modeled the decisions of 281 executives from a nationwide sample who were members of the International Society for Planning and Strategic Management.[45] These executives made decisions concerning new in-

BOX 4.1   THREE EXAMPLES OF INFORMATION TECHNOLOGY AS A COMPETITIVE WEAPON

American Airlines   An often-cited example of a company gaining a competitive advantage through differentiation achieved with information technology is American Airlines' Sabre reservation system. American started designing Sabre when United Airlines announced plans for its own reservation system for travel agents. United's system was exclusively for its own flights. American made the decision to provide all airline's schedules so that agents would use their system all the time. By creating total dependence on its system, American Airlines gained market share. It listed its own flights first and many agents never looked farther. Max Hooper, executive vice president of American Airlines, said "We saw it as a marketing tool from day one."[a] American Airlines leased reservations and ticketing terminals to travel agents. The Sabre reservation system allowed American Airlines to gain a competitive advantage through differentiation of its services.

American Hospital Supply Company   A classic example of a company gaining a competitive edge by using information technology to reduce its relative cost position is provided by American Hospital Supply Company (AHSC), whose customers consist of purchasing agents for hospitals and clinics. A market survey revealed that ASHC's current and potential customers wanted a central distributor of medical supplies that could meet most of a hospital's needs. AHSC decided to implement a full-line product distribution strategy. A computer terminal was placed in each customer's office. AHSC's system provided order entry, invoicing and billing, inventory control, and shipping—automatically and with a high degree of timeliness, responsiveness, and accuracy. This supply company could now meet a twenty-four-hour delivery schedule. Customers were able to reduce their inventory stock levels from seventy-five to thirty days, and the customers' purchasing and inventory financing costs went down. Since 1978, when AHSC embarked on this strategy, its sales have grown at an approximate compounded rate of 17 percent per year. It enjoyed pre-tax profit margins of about four times the industry average and a market share of nearly 50 percent during the mid-1980s.[b]

Avis   Another example of a company using information technology to reduce its relative cost position is Avis car rental. Avis car rental used the Wizard system to improve its service to customers. Wizard provided Avis with information about the location, cost, and performance of its fleet, which helped Avis bargain more effectively with its suppliers. Thus, Avis gained a competitive advantage over Hertz, National, and other car rental agencies. "The national network and the service levels it established 'upped the ante' for getting into the business and served as a barrier to entry."[c] In addition, Wizard improved the cost/performance ratios and forestalled the development of substitutes.

Did these three companies achieve their competitive edge through luck, as Barney argued,[d] or by utilizing some conceptual process or framework to translate the potential competitive advantage of information technology into corporate strategy? In a 1986 poll of the Society for Information Management (mostly MIS directors), King found that 59 percent of the companies had either an irregular process or no formal approach at all for identifying strategic uses of information technology.[e] It appears that luck and randomness are still factors some of the time.

---

[a] Harris, C., "Information Power—How Companies Are Using New Technolgies to Gain a Competitive Edge," *Business Week* (October 14, 1985).

[b] McFarlan, W. F., "Information Technology Changes the Way You Compete," *Harvard Business Review* (May–June 1984).

[c] Janulaitis, M. W., "Gaining Competitive Advantage," *InfoSystems* (Octover 1984): 56–58.

[d] Barney, J. B., "Strategic Factor Markets: Expectations, Luck, and Business Strategy," *Management Science* 32 (1986): 1231–1241.

[e] Buday, R. S., "Quicksand—What Kills Strategic Systems," *InformationWEEK* 116 (1987).

formation technology projects as a function of competitive advantage potential, cost, risk, and return on investment. The results are shown in Table 4.4.

On the average, these 281 executives from a variety of industries placed 30 percent of their weight in making a decision to fund a new information technology project on the competitive advantage potential of the project. This was separate from the weight they placed on traditional measures such as return on investment and risk. For the sake of gaining a competitive advantage through the use of new information technologies, they were willing to experience a more modest return on investment. It seems that their decisions agreed with Porter[46] concerning the importance of technology as a strategic competitive weapon independent of traditional financial decision rules.

TABLE 4.4   RELATIVE IMPORTANCE OF FOUR FACTOR FOR INFORMATION TECHNOLOGY PROJECTS

FACTOR	RELATIVE IMPORTANCE
Cost	11
Risk	34
Information system competitive advantage potential	30
Return on investment	25

Note: There were 281 executives in this sample.

Source: Holmes, J. D., and M. J. Stahl, "Information Strategy as a Competitive Weapon," in *Strategic Executive Decisions: An Analysis of the Difference Between Theory and Practice,* ed, M. J. Stahl (Westport Conn.: Quorum Books, a division of Greenwood Press, 1989), p. 133. Used by permission.

RELATIONSHIP OF BUSINESS AND CORPORATE STRATEGIES

Chapter 3 described corporate strategy in terms of "What business(es) do we want to be in?" Business-level strategy is described in this chapter in terms of "How do we compete in the chosen business(es)" Now we must ask, "How are the two questions related?"

The overall model of the strategic planning process discussed in Chapter 2 argues for consistency in the plan as a necessary condition for its implementation and success. Porter presented compelling evidence that a prime difference between successful acquisitions and failed acquisitions resulting in subsequent divestiture is the consistency between the two levels of strategy.[47] He argued that if a firm has developed expertise as a cost leader at the business level, it should enter future businesses in which cost leadership is important. The firm should not pursue future businesses in which differentiation or focus are required because the firm does not have the expertise to implement those strategies.

For example, if a firm in the chemical industry is experienced at competing through economies of scale in designing and operating large capital-intensive chemical plants that produce huge quantities of a standardized chemical, that firm should stick to competition on the basis of cost leadership. The firm probably does not have the expertise to compete in a business in which advertising and distribution on the basis of a differentiated product is required. Therefore, the firm should choose to enter and compete only in those businesses in which it can compete on the basis of cost leadership. Thus, experience in business-level strategy helps to determine the choice of businesses to enter. This point argues that business-level strategy influences corporate-level strategy.

This view also presents another argument for the corporate-level strategies of concentration or concentric diversification. Strategic fit may be described in terms of competence in a particular kind of competition. The sustainability of that competence must also be considered.[48] Sustained competitive advantage is more likely if the firm is dedicated to that kind of competition throughout its operations. For example, Wal-Mart is likely to maintain its cost leadership strategy for some time, as nearly all of its operations are geared to that form of competition.

SUMMARY

This chapter deals with the issue of how a firm competes in its chosen business(es). This question has assumed increased importance in the past decade due, in part, to intense foreign competition.

Porter is credited with clarifying the issue of how firms compete with his Five Forces Model of Industry Competition. Part of the model stresses the importance of entry barriers as a way to shape competition in an industry. Six entry barriers are reviewed. The most important (according to a sample of executives' decision) are cost advantage of incumbents, product differentiation of incumbents, and capital requirements. Two of these entry barriers are noteworthy because cost leadership and differentiation are contained in Porter's articulation of three generic competitive strategies. Cost leadership as a generic business-level competitive strategy refers to production of the product or service at the lowest cost of manufacture in the industry. Differentiation refers to the offer of a product or service that is perceived by the customer as somehow unique. Focus is an attempt to serve a particular target group, segment, or market niche and serve it well. Data from a group of executives supported the concept that focusing on a market niche or segment is more relevant for smaller firms.

Analysis of strategic groups in an industry is also seen as an important way to analyze the competitive structure in an industry. By plotting how the major firms in an industry compete along two competitive dimensions important to the customer, a decision maker can decide how to competitively position the firm.

This chapter also reviews the importance of technology, especially information technology, in shaping competitive position in an industry. Data from a group of executives indicate that the executives understand the importance of pursuing new information technology projects to gain competitive advantage, even if the payoff is not fully obvious in return on investment calculations.

The relationship between corporate- and business-level strategies is reviewed. The idea of strategic fit assumes that the two levels of strategy are consistent and that the firm competes at the business level in ways that it has expertise. Thus, an argument is advanced in favor of concentration or concentric diversification as a corporate-level strategy.

DISCUSSION QUESTIONS

1. What is the difference between corporate and business levels of strategy?
2. How are the two levels of strategy related?
3. What is the implication of the relationship between corporate- and business-level strategies for diversification strategies?
4. Analyze the personal computer industry with the Five Forces Model of Industry Competition.
5. Analyze entry into the U.S. brewing industry in terms of the six market entry barriers discussed in the text.
6. Give one example each of a college or university that primarily follows one of the three generic competitive strategies.
7. Conduct a strategic group analysis of the automobile industry.
8. How does information technology shape competitive strategy?

ENDNOTES

1. Hall, W. K., "Survival Strategies in a Hostile Environment," *Harvard Business Review* 58 (1980): 75–85; Hofer, C. W., and D. Schendel, *Strategy Formulation: Analytical Concepts* (St. Paul: West Publishing Co., 1978); Porter, M. E., *Competitive Strategy* (New York: Free Press, 1980 and 1985).

2. Porter, *Competitive Strategy* (1980, 1985).

3. Ibid.; Porter, M. E., "From Competitive Advantage to Corporate Strategy," *Harvard Business Review* (May–June 1987): 43–59.

4. This section is adapted from Stahl, M. J., *Strategic Executive Decisions: An Analysis of the Difference Between Theory and Practice* (Westport, Conn.: Quorum Books, 1989), Chapter 9; and Porter, *Competitive Strategy* (1980), Chapter 1.

5. Karakaya, F., and M. J. Stahl, *Market Entry and Exit Barriers* (Westport, Conn.: Quorum Books, 1991).

6. Ibid.

7. Shepherd, W., *The Economies of Industrial Organization* (Englewood Cliffs, N.J.: Prentice Hall, 1979).

8. Porter, *Competitive Strategy* (1980), p. 14.

9. Ibid., p. 7.

10. Boulton, W. R., *Business Policy: The Art of Strategic Management* (New York: Macmillan, 1984): 470.

11. Karakaya, F., and M. J. Stahl, "Barriers to Entry and Market Entry Decisions in Consumer and Industrial Goods Markets," *Journal of Marketing* 53 (April 1989): 80–91.

12. Harrigan, K. R., "Barriers to Entry and Competitive Strategies," *Strategic Management Journal* 2, no. 4 (1981): 395–412.

13. Eaton, C. B., and R. G. Lipsey, "Exit Barriers and Entry Barriers: The Durability of Capital as a Barrier to Entry," *Bell Journal of Economics* 11, no. 2 (1980): 721–729.

14. Hosmer, L. T., *Strategic Management: Text and Cases on Business Policy* (Englewood Cliffs, N.J.: Prentice Hall, 1982): 122.

15. Porter, *Competitive Strategy* (1980).

16. Porter, *Competitive Strategy* (1985).

17. Schmalensee, R., "Product Differentiation Advantages of Pioneering Brands," *American Economic Review* 72, no. 3 (June 1982): 350–371.

18. Porter, *Competitive Strategy* (1980), p. 10.

19. Ibid.

20. Ibid.

21. Moore, T. G., "The Beneficiaries of Trucking Regulation," *Journal of Law and Economics* 21, no. 2 (1978): 327–334.

22. Pustay, M. W., "Reform of Entry into Motor Carrier Act of 1980 Necessary?" *Transportation Journal* 25 (1985): 11–24.

23. Beatty, R. P., J. F. Reim, and R. F. Schapperie, "The Effect of Entry on Bank Shareholder Wealth: Implications for Interstate Banking," *Journal of Banking Research* 16 (Spring 1985): 8–15.

24. Stahl, *Strategic Executive Decisions*.

25. Porter, *Competitive Strategy* (1980, 1985).

26. Smith, G. D., D. R. Arnold, and B. G. Bizzell, *Strategy and Business Policy: Cases* (Boston: Houghton Mifflin, 1986).

27. "Marketing's New Look," *Business Week* (January 26, 1987): 64.

28. "National Firms Find that Selling to Local Tastes is Costly, Complex," *Wall Street Journal* (9 February 1987): 3.

29. Wright, P., "A Refinement of Porter's Strategies," *Strategic Management Journal* 8 (1987): 93–101.

30. "National Firms Find . . . ," p. 3.

31. Murray, A. I., "A Contingency View of Porter's 'Generic Strategies,'" *Academy of Management Review* 13, no. 3 (1988): 390; Hill, C. W., "Differentiation Versus Low Cost or Differentiation and Low Cost: A Contingency Framework," *Academy of Management Review* 13, no. 3 (1988): 401.

32. Deming, W. E., *Out of the Crisis* (Cambridge, Mass.: MIT Press, (1986); Garwin, D. A. *Managing Quality: The Strategic and Competitive Edge* (New York: Free Press, 1988); Ishikawa, K., *What is Total Quality Control? The Japanese Way* (Englewood Cliffs, N.J.: Prentice-Hall, 1985); Stahl, M. J., and G. M. Bounds, eds. *Competing Globally Through Customer Value: The Management of Strategic Suprasystems.* (Westport, Conn.: Quorum Books, 1991).

33. Kearns, D. T., "Leadership Through Quality," *Academy of Management Executive* 4 (May 1990): 86–89. See also Locander, W., and W. Saxton, "Application to P&G"; and Judge, W. et al., "Application to Capsugel," both in Stahl and Bounds, *Competing Globally Through Customer Value.*

34. Stahl, *Strategic Executive Decisions.*

35. Porter, *Competitive Strategy* (1980, 1985).

36. Ibid.

37. Harrigan, K. R., "An Application of Clustering for Strategic Group Analysis," *Strategic Management Journal* 6 (1985): 55–73; Dess, G. G., and P. S. Davis, "Porter's Generic Strategies as Determinants of Strategic Group Membership and Organizational Performance," *Academy of Management Journal* 27 (1984); 467–488; Cool, K. O., and D. Schendel, "Strategic Group Formation and Performance: The Case of the U.S. Pharmaceutical Industry,

1963–1982," *Management Science* 33, no. 9 (1987): 1102–1124; McGee, J., and H. Thomas, "Strategic Groups: Theory, Research and Taxonomy," *Strategic Management Journal* 7 no. 2 (1986): 141–160; Oliva, T., D. Day, and W. DeSarbo, "Selecting Competitive Tactics: Try a Strategy Map," *Sloan Management Review* 28, no. 3 (1987): 5–15; Primeaux, W. J., Jr., "A Method for Determining Strategic Groups and Life Cycle Stages of an Industry," in *Strategic Marketing Management,* ed. H. Thomas and M. Gardner (New York: John Wiley, 1985).

38. Bailey, E. E., D. R. Graham, and D. P. Kaplan, *Deregulating the Airlines* (Cambridge, Mass.: MIT Press, 1986).

39. This section is adapted from Stahl, *Strategic Executive Decisions,* Chapter 10, and Porter, *Competitive Strategy* (1985), Chapter 5.

40. Porter, *Competitive Strategy* (1985), p. 164.

41. Buday, R. S., "Quicksand—What Kills Strategic Systems," *InformationWEEK* 116 (1987).

42. Cash, J. I., Jr., and B. R. Konsynski, "Information Systems Redraw Competitive Boundaries," *Harvard Business Review* (March–April 1985);   McFarlan, W. F., "Information Technology Changes the Way You Compete," *Harvard Business Review* (May–June 1984); Parsons, G. L., "Information Technology: A New Competitive Weapon," *Sloan Management Review* (Fall 1983); Porter, M. E., and V. E. Miller, "How Information Technology Gives you Competitive Advantage," *Harvard Business Review* (July–August 1985).

43. Kantrow, A., "The Strategy-Technology Connection," *Harvard Business Review* (July–August 1980): 6–21.

44. Porter, *Competitive Strategy* (1985), p. 169.

45. Stahl, *Strategic Executive Decisions.*

46. Porter, *Competitive Strategy* (1985).

47. Porter, "From Competitive Advantage to Corporate Strategy."

48. Coyne, K. P., "Sustainable Competitive Advantage—What It Is, What It Isn't," *Business Horizons* (January–February 1986): 54–61; Ghemawat, P., "Sustainable Advantage," *Harvard Business Review* 64, no. 5 (1986): 53–58.

ADDITIONAL READINGS

Anderson, C. R., and C. P. Zeithaml. "Stage of the Product Life Cycle, Business Strategy, and Business Performance." *Academy Management Journal* 1 (1984): 5–24.

Dillon, W. R., R. Calantore, and P. Worthing. "The New Product Problem: An Approach for Investigating Product Failures." *Management Science* 25 (December 1979): 1184–1196.

Gale, B. T. "Market Share and Return on Investment." *Review of Economics and Statistics* 54 (November 1982): 412–423.

Glazer, A. "The Advantages of Being First." *American Economic Review* 75, no. 3 (June 1985): 473–480.

Holloway, C. "Strategic Management and Artificial Intelligence." *Long Range Planning* (October 1983).

Karnani, A. "Generic Competitive Strategies." *Strategic Management Journal* 5 (1984): 367–380.

Miller, D., and P. H. Friesen. "Strategy Making in Context: Ten Empirical Archetypes." *Journal of Management Studies* (1977): 253–280.

McKenney, J. L., and W. F. McFarlan. "The Information Archipelago—Maps and Bridges." *Harvard Business Review* (September–October 1982).

McLean, E. R., and J. V. Soden. *Strategic Planning for MIS.* New York: John Wiley and Sons, 1977.

Phillips, L. W., D. R. Chang, and R. D. Buzzell. "Product Quality, Cost Position and Business Performance: A Test of Some Key Hypotheses." *Journal of Marketing* 47, no. 2 (1983): 26–43.

Robinson, W. T., and C. Fornell. "Sources of Market Pioneering Advantages in Consumer Goods Industries." *Journal of Marketing Research* 22 (August 1985): 305–317.

Samli, C., and J. Wills. "Strategies for Marketing Computers and Related Products." *Industrial Marketing Management* 15 (1986): 23–32.

Schnaars, S. T. "When Entering Growth Markets, Are Pioneers Better than Poachers?" *Business Horizons* (March–April 1986): 27–36.

Smiley, R. H., and A. S. Ravid. "The Importance of Being First: Learning, Price and Strategy." *Quarterly Journal of Economics* (May 1983): 353–362.

Urban, G. L., T. Carter, S. Gaskin, and Z. Mucha. "Market Share Rewards to Pioneering Brands: An Empirical Analysis and Strategic Implications." *Management Science* 32, no. 6 (June 1986): 645–659.

Waverly, R. G. "PIMS: A Tool for Developing Competitive Strategy." *Long Range Planning* 17 (June 1984): 92–97.

Yip, G. S. *Barriers to Entry: A Corporate Strategy Perspective.* Lexington, Mass.: D.C. Heath and Company, 1982.

CHAPTER FIVE

Functional-Level Strategic Decisions

INTRODUCTION

This chapter deals with the strategic decisions made within each of the business functions used to complement and support the competitive advantage sought by the business-level strategy. These strategic decisions made within the functions of production/operations, marketing, finance/accounting, human resources, research and development, and information systems are referred to as functional-level strategic decisions.

The nature of functional strategy in terms of the pattern of decisions made in that function, along with the necessary consistency of functional strategy with business strategy, was recently highlighted in a manufacturing strategy text.

> To be effective, each functional strategy must support, through a specific and consistent pattern of decisions, the competitive advantage being sought by the business strategy. For example, decisions in such areas as pricing, packaging, distribution, and field service—all subparts of the marketing functional strategy—would be very different if the desired competitive advantage were high volume/low cost rather than, say, unique features/customized service. It cannot be overemphasized that it is the pattern of decisions actually made, and the degree to which that pattern supports the business strategy, that constitutes a function's strategy, not what is said or written in annual reports or planning documents.[1]

These two themes of consistency—between the business level and the functional level of strategy and among functional strategies—were reflected recently in the business press. "American manufacturers have boosted productivity for several years now, largely by closing old plants and laying off workers. But the U.S. still lags behind Japan and other countries in productivity growth.

The problem: We focus on capital investment as a way to reduce labor—ignoring the huge benefits to be gained from improved quality, reduced inventories, and faster introduction of new products."[2] The article described how some firms were moving to change the way decisions were made in manufacturing and accounting. Two objectives were to ensure consistency between the business level and functional levels of strategy and to ensure consistency between the two functional areas.

Box 5.1 describes some of the changes. By using life-cycle accounting and considering the benefits of quality, flexibility, and faster cycles, which add value for the customer, some of the newer accounting procedures are better able to justify new technology.

Another way to depict the desired consistency among the corporate, business, and functional levels of strategy and among the various functions is shown in Figure 5.1. Although the figure is drawn like a traditional, hierarchical organizational diagram (as discussed in Chapter 6), there are both similarities and differences between this figure and the traditional diagram. The similarity is the hierarchical notion that the strategic decisions at the higher level are meant to determine and shape the decisions at the lower level(s). The difference is that the scalar chain concept (that is, a lower level reporting to only one upper level) is not followed. Specifically, the same marketing strategic decisions could be employed in more than one business strategy (indicated by the solid line from marketing strategic decisions to three different business strategic decisions).

The literature has shown that firms that have built a "distinctive competence" have higher organizational performance (as discussed in Chapter 2). The desirability of building and communicating a "distinctive competence" to its customers in its functional areas suggests that the same functional strategies should be employed in all of a firm's business strategies. This idea presents another argument against conglomerate diversification, in which different functional strategies may be employed in different businesses.

If a firm employs different functional strategies in all of its businesses, as in a conglomerately diversified firm, Figure 5.1 would change shape and be extremely complicated. In a conglomerate organization, for example, there would be different blocks for marketing strategic decisions flowing from different business strategic decisions. With different marketing strategies in the

---

BOX 5.1   NEW COST-MANAGEMENT SYSTEMS FOR VALUE-ADDED MANUFACTURING

Many cost-accounting systems used in American manufacturing allocate overhead costs on the basis of the direct labor hours required to produce a product. Computer-aided manufacturing and other technologies, however, have dramatically reduced the labor content of many products. With invalid overhead allocation, many manufacturing and marketing managers do not know the accurate cost of producing a product, and with fallacious production costs, their pricing decisions may be divorced from reality. This situation may present their competitors with an opportunity to better position competing products. "In the face of so many maddening problems, a small but growing number of companies are retooling their cost-accounting systems," *Fortune* reported. "Some thirty manufacturers, including Rockwell, Eastman Kodak, and General Electric, are part of an organization called Computer Aided Manufacturing International, which has been at work for two years developing a conceptual framework to update cost management systems."[a]

Thomas Pryor, when head of CAM-I's cost-management project, castigated traditional cost-accounting principles, as reported by *Business Week*. "Man-hour analysis fails to justify new technology, he insists. Automation has already wrung out labor costs. Thumping the table, he declares: 'Cost accounting is wrecking American business. If we're going to remain competitive, we've got to change.' Pryor outlines an accounting system that would justify more investment through quantifiable improvements in such 'intangibles' as quality, flexibility, and turnaround time."[b]

The cost model of CAM-I's system consists of five elements:

- ***Product focus.*** Costs are charged directly to the product as opposed to allocating them to the product on the basis of direct labor.
- ***Value orientation.*** Instead of examining fixed vs. variable costs or direct vs. indirect labor, costs are measured that add value and those that do not add value.
- ***Operational measurements.*** Pre-production, production and post-production costs are measured.
- ***Strategic information.*** A main goal is to provide information to support strategic decisions.
- ***Simplification.*** Fewer allocations, fewer cost centers and fewer data collection points must be part of new cost-management systems.[c]

The cost-accounting systems at many firms are not based on the preceding five tenets. Thus, many current systems may be providing misleading information to decision makers plotting competitive moves in the marketplace. According to *Fortune*, "Most large companies seem to recognize that their costs systems are not responsive to today's competitive environment. But few companies have seized the opportunity that awaits those that modernize their accounting practices. Quite simply, accurate cost information can give a company a competitive advantage."[d]

A competitive advantage is gained with more accurate cost information, which is associated with precise pricing decisions. In addition, there is competitive advantage in a cost-management system that more precisely recognizes the benefits of quality, flexibility, and faster cycles. Such new cost-management systems help the decision makers justify more investment in manufacturing to yield customer value.

---

[a] "Accounting Bores You? Wake Up," *Fortune* (October 12, 1987): 48.
[b] "That Old Time Accounting Isn't Good Enough Anymore," *Business Week* (June 6, 1988): 112.
[c] "New Accounting for Integrated Manufacturing," *Manufacturing Week* (March 9, 1987): 19.
[d] "Accounting Bores You?" p. 49.

FIGURE 5.1 THE HIERARCHY OF STRATEGIC DECISIONS

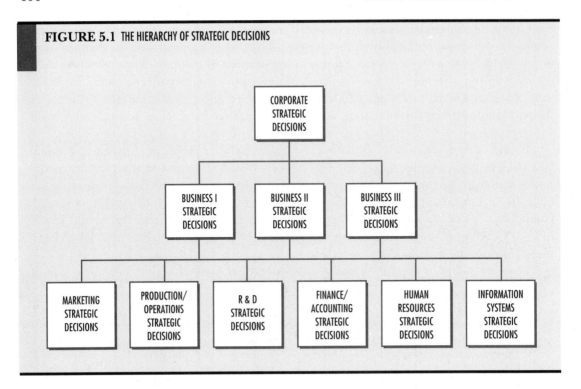

same firm, it would be hard to build a distinctive competence in marketing. Both customers and stockholders could easily become confused concerning the firm's competence and focus in marketing. Indeed, in a conglomerate, there may be little or no focus in marketing.

Many firms have attempted to optimize decisions in production/operations, or marketing, or finance/accounting, or human resources, or research and development, or information systems. In optimizing decisions in one functional area, firms sometimes ignore the impact on the other functional areas. For example, in the 1960s and 1970s, the Chrysler Corporation was noted for product engineering. By the late 1970s, marketing and finance were weak sisters, and near bankruptcy followed. This chapter repeatedly emphasizes the importance of consistency among the functional strategic decisions as each of the functions is reviewed.

PRODUCTION/OPERATIONS

Production and operations strategy has received considerable attention in the recent past. Much of the attention is due to the competitive challenge of international manufacturers, notably the Japanese. Partly in response to the competitive challenge, some writers have stressed the importance of linking manufacturing strategy with corporate- and business-level strategy to ensure consistent decisions.[3] Some authors have argued that manufacturing is the way to compete.[4] Others have forecasted increased strategic advantage due to manufacturing strategy in the future.[5]

One of the most widely cited books dealing with the subject of competition through manufacturing strategy is *Restoring Our Competitive Edge*, by Hayes and Wheelwright. The book's second chapter describes the characteristics of manufacturing strategy and lists the criteria for evaluating a manufacturing strategy. These criteria are shown in Table 5.1. These two themes of consistency (both internal and external) and of contribution (to competitive advantage) should be stressed repeatedly in evaluating the soundness of the manufacturing strategy. In a broader sense, these two themes should be used to evaluate the soundness of any functional strategy.

TECHNICAL CORE

One of the first decisions that must be made in formulating a manufacturing strategy concerns the technical core of the business. Are the technical core and the distinctive competence primarily in terms of manufacturing, assembly, service, or marketing? This question is a more detailed examination of the generalized corporate strategic question of what business(es) the firm is in. The technical core decision has obvious implications for the other decisions that must be made in the manufacturing strategy arena. For example, in the early 1980s when the Chrysler Corporation was at the brink of bankruptcy, the firm nearly became an assembler of parts manufactured by others and a distributor of Japanese-manufactured autos. That model was in sharp contrast

TABLE 5.1   CRITERIA FOR EVALUATING A MANUFACTURING STRATEGY

CONSISTENCY (INTERNAL AND EXTERNAL)
- Between the manufacturing strategy and the overall business strategy
- Between the manufacturing strategy and the other functional strategies
- Among the decision categories that make up the manufacturing strategy
- Between the manufacturing strategy and the business environment

CONTRIBUTION (TO COMPETITIVE ADVANTAGE)
- Making tradeoffs explicit, enabling manufacturing to set priorities that enhance the competitive advantage
- Directing attention to opportunitites that complement the business strategy
- Promoting clarity regarding the manufacturing strategy throughout the business unit so its potential can be fully realized
- Providing the manufacturing capabilities that will be required by the business in the future

to the Ford Motor Company, which historically has manufactured its own parts and components, including some of the basic steel used in its autos.

This issue of a technical core in manufacturing, assembly, service, or marketing has received considerable interest in corporate America. The formation of the "hollow" corporation, the decline of U.S. manufacturing, the threat to the U.S. economy, and some disturbing trends in American manufacturing have been noted. "From autos to semiconductors, many U.S. manufacturers are turning into marketers for foreign producers," noted *Business Week* in 1986. "A new type of company is emerging—one that may design or distribute but doesn't actually make anything. A hollow corporation. It is a phenomenon our economy cannot afford."[6] As this book went to press, there was some evidence that the trend was being reversed, but the phenomenon continues to deserve special attention in corporate America. Some firms may retain their technical core or distinctive competence in marketing, but our industry will not be severely threatened unless American firms completely exit manufacturing.

QUALITY

Few issues have received as much attention in discussions of manufacturing strategy as the issue of quality.[7] American managers have been accused of not paying enough attention to quality as a competitive weapon, especially relative to international competitors such as the Japanese.[8] Experts forecast that increasing attention will be paid to quality in American industry, at least until no major quality differences are perceived between American and Japanese manufacturers.

It may take years before the efforts to improve quality pay off in the perception of quality. As Thurston indicated, "The relevant measure of quality does not reside in the product. It resides between the customer's ears."[9] Efforts in this direction are starting to pay off. For example, America's successful high technology companies were following some important rules at the dawn of 1990 to improve their world competitiveness. One of the rules focused on "QUALITY, QUALITY, QUALITY." The message was that even high technology won't get far in the marketplace if it isn't produced with high quality. *Fortune* reported, "The Malcolm Baldridge National Quality Award administered by the U.S. Commerce Department signals government recognition that American companies need a push to match the competition. In November, President Bush handed out awards to the 1989 winners, Xerox and Milliken."[10]

In another example, Motorola was recently recognized for regaining market share from its Japanese rivals. One of Motorola's secrets was described by *Business Week* as "Built-In Quality. CEO George Fisher's mission has been distilled into a handful of key goals, capped by attaining Six Sigma quality. That's statistical jargon for near-perfect manufacturing—a rate of just 3.4 defects per million products. Only relatively simple products, such as calculators, have reached this level, but Motorola expects to do so across the board by 1992."[11] Likewise, Michelin was recently recognized in the business press for its successes, including its unrelenting pursuit of quality. "One of Michelin's secrets is a business style remarkably similar to that of a Japanese company. It consistently sacrifices all short-term concerns for the pursuit of just two objectives: quality and market share."[12]

Many companies, however, continue to define quality relative to the *company* rather than to the *customer*. Such an approach misses the point of this book concerning a firm's mission relative to the customer, not the company. "Though managers increasingly acknowledge the importance of quality, many continue to define and measure it from the company's perspective," said one analyst. "Closing the gap between objective and perceived quality requires that the company view quality the way the consumer does."[13] The functional-level manufacturing strategy concerning quality should be consistent with, and flow from, the corporate-level decision concerning the customer. This is a characteristic of Total Quality Management.

It may be some time before American consumers associate high quality with many American products. A recent nationwide poll dealing with quality perceptions found that "most Americans don't pin the blame for the country's competitive woes on foreigners but on the U.S. itself. Fifty-four percent say the problems are mostly the result of U.S. management and labor falling behind in productivity and in the quality of goods."[14]

Unlike the firms cited earlier that have integrated quality into their corporate fabric, a number of companies still view quality as just another program. As one analyst noted, "more than 80 percent of the Fortune 500 companies have made some type of in-house quality and productivity improvement effort. Unfortunately, in many instances, these improvement efforts have not been tightly interwoven with the organization's strategic management practices. When quality improvement is not linked to the organization's key strategies, employees will perceive it as just another faddish program."[15]

Table 5.2 indicates that American CEOs viewed quality as a top priority in manufacturing. Their ideas, however, were not matched by American manufacturing managers.

Noted authority and writer W. Edwards Deming has captured the attention of corporate America with his emphasis on quality. Figure 5.2, a reproduction

TABLE 5.2   RANKINGS OF MANUFACTURING CRITERIA BY CEOs AND MANUFACTURING MANAGERS

CRITERIA	CEO RANK	MM RANK
Improving & maintaining quality	1	3
Maintaining/lowering manufacturing costs	2	2
Keeping delivery promises	3	1
Maintaining flexibility for changeovers	4	4
Introducing new products	5	5

Source: Swamidass, P. M., "Manufacturing Strategy: Its Assessment and Practice," *Journal of Operations Management* (August 1986): 479. Used by permission.

FIGURE 5.2 THE PERVASIVE ROLE OF QUALITY

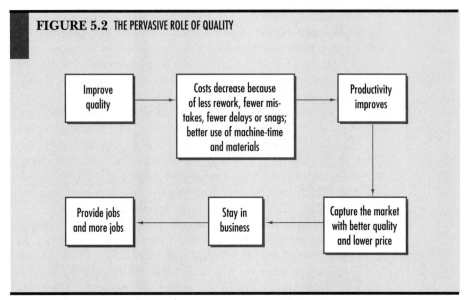

Source: Reprinted from *Out of the Crisis* (p. 3) by W. E. Deming, by permission of MIT and W. E. Deming. Published by MIT, Center for Advanced Engineering Study, Cambridge, MA 02139. Copyright © 1986 by W. E. Deming.

of a diagram from his book, indicates the pervasive nature of quality to the corporate enterprise. Deming argued that high quality and low cost are found together. Thus, quality is a key to differentiation and cost leadership as simultaneous business-level competitive strategies. According to Deming, quality is not an afterthought that is inspected for at the end of the production process. Rather, quality is a philosophy that must pervade an organization in its approach to doing business. "Cease dependence on inspection to achieve quality," he wrote. "Eliminate the need for inspection on a mass basis by building quality into the product in the first place."[16]

CAPACITY

A manufacturing strategy question that needs almost constant attention by the firm is the issue of capacity. How much capacity does the firm require? When should the capacity be made available? What type of capacity is needed? The amount of capacity can be a dual-edged sword. Porter tells us that a high capacity can help create a market entry barrier by keeping the cost of manufacture low. He also reminds us that the same high capacity can create market exit barriers, as a firm may be unwilling to scrap facilities even if demand falters.[17]

There seems to be a bias in manufacturing to build more capacity than is economically optimal because production managers do not wish to lose sales through an inability to meet demand. With delays in building new capacity, however, it is not unusual to see the new capacity become available *after* the peak in demand. Perhaps due to concern with cost cutting, there is also a built-in bias within production/operations to produce only one or a few items to simplify the manufacturing process. These biases must be examined carefully in light of the corporate and business strategies to determine the capacity decisions best for the firm.

FACILITIES

The size of the facilities is not independent of the amount of the capacity, nor is the specialization of the facilities independent of the type of the capacity, but there are some separate issues to be decided concerning facilities. Location can be a strategic competitive weapon if the location decision is viewed in terms of servicing the customer, as in a differentiation strategy, or in terms of lowering the cost of doing business, as in a cost-leadership strategy. For example, a major manufacturing firm described in one of the cases in this book has many more plants per dollar of sales than its competitors. This advantage is due in part to the firm's strategy of locating smaller plants near its many customers to better service the customers rather than building a few gigantic, centrally located plants to achieve the greatest economy of scale.

Over the past decade, there has been a continuing shift in manufacturing facilities to the Sun Belt in this country. The shift may continue for some time due to its causes: a large population pool, favorable labor costs, and an attractive quality of life.[18]

TECHNOLOGY

Few subjects in manufacturing strategy have received as much attention recently as the use of technology, specifically automation and computers, as a way to gain a competitive advantage in manufacturing. Factory automation and computerized factories have been hailed as ways to make the U.S. competitive, but a wholesale commitment remains to be seen.[19]

Factory automation is more than a question of adding a few robots. Indeed, there are new ways of thinking associated with automation. According to *Industry Week,* automation used to mean updating an operation or process, with little effect on management practices. Computer-integrated manufacturing (CIM), however, "embraces broader policies, standards, and people in addition to computer hardware and machinery. The challenge for manufacturers is to accep' CIM and to think in strategic dimensions."[20] Box 5.1 indicates some of the changed thinking that must occur if automation is to be successful.

Factory automation also has been referred to by the broader term "computer-enabled enterprise" rather than CIM. "Companies will need to change their thinking," said the *Wall Street Journal.* "If you use old-fashioned assumptions about, say, inventory costs and parts rejects in making return-on-investment calculations, CEE will often appear to be uneconomic. The whole point is to have no inventory or rejects."[21] With CEE, inventory, quality rejects, and direct labor dollars decrease. There is usually an increase in quality, flexibility, and timeliness.

PRODUCTION PLANNING AND CONTROL

Production planning and control concerns most production/operations organizations on a daily basis and has strategic implications in terms of the output being controlled. Control on the basis of material or inventory alone implies a strategy of cost leadership. Control on the basis of delivery dates alone, which may imply a higher inventory level, implies a strategy of differentiation through customer service.

There is a sophisticated, computer-oriented production planning and control system that can reduce inventory level as well as speed up delivery times. A material requirements planning (MRP) system is also expensive: Two recent surveys indicate that the total cost of implementation is between $600,000 and $800,000, but there are potential benefits in both reduced inventory and improved delivery times.[22] Table 5.3 presents figures from the two separate studies of the benefits of MRP systems. In both studies, the average amount of inventory was reduced and delivery performance was improved.

MRP systems, with reduced inventory levels, are consistent with a low-cost competitive strategy. With their improved delivery dates, they are also consistent with a differentiation competitive strategy. The two studies indicate that between one-third and two-thirds of American manufacturers use MRP systems.[23] As more firms use MRP systems, other firms may need to introduce such production planning and control systems in order to compete. The above-mentioned implementation costs may be small prices to pay for improved operating costs in addition to improved delivery performance. The reader may note that this strategy is another example of using information

TABLE 5.3   AVERAGE OPERATING BENEFITS OF MRP FIRMS

	LAFORGE & STURR STUDY (107 COMPANIES)		ANDERSON ET AL. STUDY (679 COMPANIES)	
	Pre-MRP Estimate	*Current Estimate*	*Pre-MRP Estimate*	*Current Estimate*
Inventory turnover (turns)	4.5	7.9	3.2	4.3
Delivery lead time (days)	55.6	41.7	71.4	58.9
Percentage of time (meeting delivery promises)	73.9	88.6	61.4	76.6

Source: LaForge, R. L., and V. L. Sturr, "MRP Practices in a Random Sample of Manufacturing Firms," *Production and Inventory Management* (3rd Quarter 1986): 134 (Table 5). Reprinted with permission from the American Production and Inventory Control Society, Inc.

systems to gain a competitive advantage, as discussed in Chapter 4 and in the last section of this chapter.

MARKETING

Another functional strategy that has received considerable attention is marketing. Indeed, a separate body of literature has been developed concerning marketing strategy, marketing management, and strategic marketing.[24] Much of the literature points out the need for marketing decisions to be consistent with corporate- and business-level strategic decisions and with the other functional decisions. Consistency among the functional areas, particularly between manufacturing and marketing, seems to be a necessary condition for continued corporate success. Firms that also pay attention to implementation issues seem to be laying the groundwork for continued success. These twin issues—consistency among functional strategies and attention to implementation details—are being addressed in the marketing world by trendsetter Procter & Gamble. Box 5.2 indicates that P&G's switch from a brand-management system to a category-management system is nothing short of a marketing revolution.

There are four separate decision areas in marketing strategy. The familiar "4 P's" are product/service, price, place/distribution, and promotion/advertising.

PRODUCT/SERVICE

In answering the question "What is the product/service?" the firm needs to consider the product mix, product life-cycle stages, the target customers, and the product mission philosophy.

BOX 5.2   CONSISTENCY AND CATEGORY MANAGEMENT AT PROCTER & GAMBLE

ADVERTISING. P&G advertised Tide as the best detergent for tough dirt. Brand managers for Cheer made the same claim. Now a category manager decides positioning for Tide as well as Cheer to avoid conflicts.

PACKAGING. Brand managers demanded new packages simultaneously. Designers complained that the projects were hurried. Now the category manager decides which brand needs a new package first.

MANUFACTURING. Previously, Dreft had the same claim on P&G's plant as Tide, even if Tide needed more supplies for a big promotion. Now a manufacturing staffer reports to the category manager, which helps to coordinate production.

Source: "The Marketing Revolution at Proctor & Gamble," *Business Week* (July 25, 1988): 72; "P&G Rewrites the Marketing Rules," *Fortune* (November 6, 1989): 34–48.

Sometimes attempts to suboptimize in marketing by building market share, or increasing sales volume, independent of other strategies causes the firm to lose sight of these other strategies, particularly the product mission philosophy. Figure 5.3 shows one model of ways to improve performance in strategic marketing. Some of the market penetration, product development, and market development decisions can cause the firm to lose sight of the mission as well as the corporate- and business-level competitive strategies. Consistency with the other functional-level strategies sometimes can also be ignored.

There is increasing evidence that many firms are paying attention to product/service in their product design efforts. After spending more than a decade in the "backseat," product design is now being considered from both manufacturing and marketing perspectives, according to *Business Week*. "U.S. manufacturers are once again discovering that it is key to industrial competitiveness. . . . It's at the very heart of a product. A good design appeals to the eye, but it must also be reliable, easy, and economical to operate and service. It should also be simple to manufacture."[25]

Who are the target customers? That is a question that every firm should be able to answer without hesitation. Just as important, who are the targeted customers of the future? Different answers to the two questions can have profound implications for changes in marketing strategy and changes in the entire firm. For example, a so-called megatrend in this country is the "graying" of America as the post–World War II baby boomers reach maturity and senior citizen status. Different products need to be designed and marketed to meet such a trend. As *Business Week* reported, "By 2020 almost one-third of the U.S. population will be 55 or older. Most will be entering a period of physical decline, with brittle bones and diminished strength and senses. Other companies are beginning to realize that doors can have latches instead of knobs, labels can have big print, and household staples can come in easy-to-open packages. The field of designing products to meet the needs of an aging population is about to explode."[26]

PRICE

Some analysts argue that pricing decisions are the least understood and least consistent strategic decisions made in organizations.[27] Indeed, pricing decisions are strategic because they communicate to the firm's competitors and customers whether the firm is competing on the basis of price leadership or differentiation. The firm needs to determine if it wishes to communicate that it is offering a nondifferentiated commodity-like product that should be purchased because of its low price or a differentiated product that deserves to be purchased at a premium price.

Figure 5.3 indicates how a firm wishing to increase sales volume and penetrate markets might lower its prices. But the firm must ask itself if such price cuts would be consistent with a differentiation strategy. The figure also indicates that if the firm wishes to improve profitability, it might increase price. Again, the firm must ask itself if such price hikes would be consistent with a price-leadership strategy.

FIGURE 5.3 GENERIC PERFORMANCE IMPROVEMENT STRATEGIES

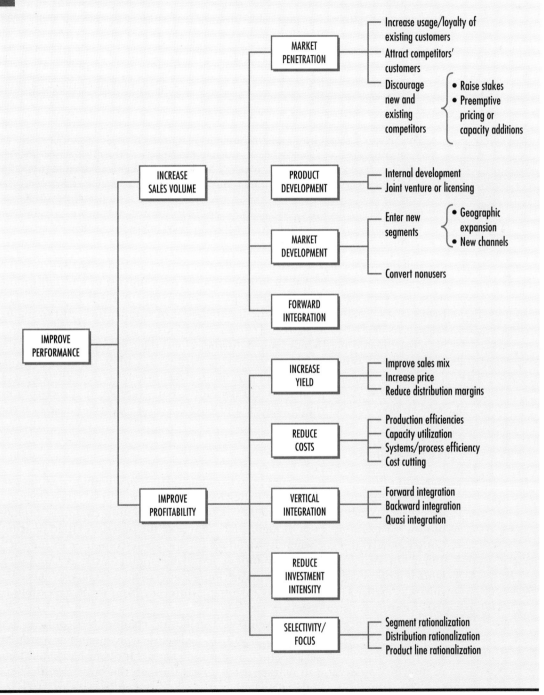

Two different articles concerning personal computers from the same business publication demonstrate the importance of pricing relative to strategy. One article, "Clone-Computer Business is Booming: Low Prices Help IBM Knockoffs Win New Fans," describes the marketing of clones to IBM's personal computer at low prices by copycat personal computer manufacturers.[28] The article also describes customers' wariness about the reliability and peace of mind associated with the clones. The other article describes the premium prices IBM was charging for its second-generation personal computers partly because of its "Micro Channel Architecture."

> The Micro Channel isn't mere technology. It is IBM's mystery ingredient: an electronic version of the "MFP" in Colgate toothpaste or the "Chlorinol" inside Comet cleanser, intended to give IBM's PC extra zing in a crowd of look-alikes. As such, the Micro Channel is one of IBM's most audacious marketing gambits ever. Its mission is to create a premium image, and preferably command a premium price, that will rebuild IBM's prowess and profit margins in a business that is starting to resemble the hawking of the lowliest of commodities.[29]

Pricing on the basis of cost-plus (that is, a fixed add-on to actual cost) is a strategy that can cause a firm to lose sight of its competition and ignore the messages sent to customers about price leadership or differentiation. The firm's cost of manufacture may be independent of competitors' cost of manufacture, as described by learning curves or the existence of market entry barriers. Distribution inefficiencies may further cloud the cost picture. Pricing decisions should not be made on the basis of cost-plus. Rather, pricing decisions should be strategic decisions that reinforce business-level competitive decisions and corporate-level strategic decisions. For example, if the corporate level stresses market share growth, a pricing decision might be biased on the low side to encourage sales.

PLACE/DISTRIBUTION

In terms of distribution strategy, the firm must consider whether it will use its own distribution channels or outside channels. Firms must make this decision on every product they offer, whether they have distribution channels in place or not. For example, even though IBM had one of the best-developed distribution channels in place when it introduced its personal computer in the early 1980s, the firm decided to use independent distributors such as Computerland and other computer stores to distribute its personal computers. This decision was made in part to reach customers different from those accessible to IBM's existing distribution system.

The existence of a well-developed distribution channel is a considerable corporate asset that helps a firm decide to market new products. For example, it appears that Anheuser-Busch's distribution channel for beer had something to do with its decision to market snack foods through the same channel.

The firm also must decide whether the proper incentives are in place for its own channels. This problem occurs sometimes when new products or classes of products are introduced. For example, what kind of incentive could IBM offer its sales force to sell personal computers compared to the incentive it offers to sell mainframe computers?

Place also includes the geographic distribution of facilities. A firm must have distribution facilities in place to serve the customers alluded to in its mission statement. For example, in the 1970s, the Coors Brewing Company was concentrating primarily on the western United States. After Coors decided to become a national firm in the 1980s, it took years to open distribution facilities throughout the rest of the country.

The firm must also question whether distribution is adequate. No matter what system is used, if the distribution channels are empty or inadequate the customer cannot buy the product. It is only a matter of time before the customer goes elsewhere and brands the inadequate distributor as an unreliable supplier.

PROMOTION/ADVERTISING

Few areas in marketing receive as much attention as promotion or advertising. Questions of ethics or truth in advertising, method of promotion, effectiveness, and use of in-house or outside promotional forces must be considered.

The issues of method and effectiveness are especially important in attempting to create an image for a product that may not be a differentiated product to start with. For example, the many blind taste tests of beer that have been conducted seriously question whether there are identifiable taste differences within a class of beers. Nonetheless, beverage firms spend millions of dollars on advertising per year to convince consumers that there are differences. Some of the comparisons of advertising budgets and sales suggest that the consumers are indeed convinced that there are differences. Table 5.4 shows the advertising spending and market shares of the top brewers for 1987. Although the relationship is not perfect, it does indicate that for beer, higher ad spending means higher market share. A firm must ask itself if there is a

TABLE 5.4   BREWERS' MARKET SHARE AND AD SPENDING IN 1987

BREWER	AD SPENDING (IN MILLIONS)	MARKET SHARE
Anheuser Busch	$304.4	39.8%
Miller	171.4	20.5
Stroh	45.7	11.3
Coors	84.7	8.2
Heileman	15.6	8.1

Source: "Second String: In a World of Millers and Buds, Coors Beer Has to Play Catch-Up," *Wall Street Journal* (November 3, 1988): 1; "Heileman's Happy Hour is Still a Long Way Off," *Business Week* (November 7, 1988): 108.

relationship between advertising spending and sales in its industry and its products/services.

Some firms prefer to contract out their promotional activities rather than conduct them with in-house resources. If the firm decides on such an approach, it must be careful to ensure that the resultant promotional campaign fits the firm's competitive business strategies and the targeted market. There is a story about Procter & Gamble's ad campaign for marketing Camay soap in Japan. After sales flopped, P&G discovered that the translation of the television ads indicated "bad manners" between the man and woman in the ad due to cultural differences in interpreting a bath scene.[30] After that experience, the firm decided to hire foreign nationals to work in marketing and other areas in order to understand cultural differences.

 FINANCE

OBJECTIVES/STRATEGIES

Finance is a functional level of strategy in which the consistency of the functional strategy with the corporate- and business-level strategies *and* the consistency of the decisions within the functional strategy are critical. There are few other functional-level strategies in which decisions can be as counterproductive and dysfunctional for the entire corporation if they do not mesh.[31] For example, decisions on profitability can run counter to decisions on sales growth, which in turn can run counter to decisions on leverage. A firm may decide on massive doses of leverage as a takeover defense, thereby incurring such large-debt service payments as to hurt profitability. Or a firm may accept marginal credit risks as customers to accomplish a sales target but hurt profitability due to some poor credit risks.

There is a critical need in the financial area for the objectives and strategies to be clearly stated. An objective of "improved profitability" is dramatically different from an objective of "improved return on equity by at least one-half of 1 percent per year for each of the next five years." The Case Analysis Guide, which accompanies the cases for this text, presents the formulas for the ratios discussed in this section on financial strategy.

Some industries prefer one ratio or group of ratios to others. The industry nature of the business may suggest the kinds of ratios that are preferable. For example, capital-intensive industries such as steel-making may prefer return on investment as a profitability ratio. Wholesalers such as grocers may prefer sales-based measures such as return on sales as a profitability ratio. The firm's objectives should be quantitative enough to suggest the choice of ratios. Whichever ratio or ratios the firm prefers, it should clearly and consistently indicate over time which ratio or ratios it is using.

In each of the following four areas of discussion the ratios or objectives should always be compared with the firm's own past experience and with industry averages, where such comparisons are available. This relative comparison should be undertaken both in the strategy formulation phase to indicate what is possible and in the evaluation and control stage to indicate possible reasons for differences between planned and actual numbers.

PROFITABILITY

In the area of profitability, there are at least six different ratios that may be of interest: return on investment (ROI), return on stockholder's equity (ROE), earnings per share (EPS), gross profit margin, operating profit margin, or net profit margin. Whichever of these ratios the firm prefers, it should clearly and consistently indicate which ratios it is using.

Many analysts have asserted that an emphasis on maintaining stock value leads to short-term decision making on the part of management. That is, management fails to undertake long-term projects due to a focus on short-term profitability. This assertion, however, is not supported by empirical evidence. Woolridge documented the positive response of stock prices to long-term strategic decisions, even if the strategic decisions have a small short-term profit.[32] Recently, Kaplan argued that the value of a firm depends largely on its future cash flows.[33] Making the long-term profitability decisions is a sign of a strong, mature management team.

There is a large and growing percentage of executives who feel that cash flow is a more important measure of a company's financial performance than profitability. In a recent *Business Week* survey, 602 top executives responded to the question "Which is a more important measure of your company's financial performance—earnings per share or cash flow per share?" Fifty-four percent indicated EPS, 44 percent indicated cash flow per share, and 2 percent were "not sure."[34] Cash flow is associated with the viability of leveraged buy-outs (LBOs). As leveraged buy-outs become more controversial, and as the battle for corporate control intensifies, even more executives, analysts, and strategic planners will view cash flow per share as the more important measure of corporate performance.

LIQUIDITY AND CASH MANAGEMENT

There are at least three liquidity ratios that may be of interest to a firm. The current ratio, the quick (acid-test) ratio, and the inventory to net working capital ratio are frequently examined. Whatever number(s) the firm prefers based on industry averages and the firm's own past history, stability is important in and of itself. Substantial variance in these numbers questions the firm's ability to meet its short-term financial obligations.

Cash management usually refers to the balancing of cash inflows with cash outflows. Many firms prepare a cash budget or a cash-flow budget to insure that there will be adequate amounts of cash for short-term needs. Some firms have been known to speed up accounts receivables and to slow down accounts payable in order to improve their cash position. When cash flow becomes that critical, one must ask how soon before the bankruptcy or the divestiture occurs.

LEVERAGE AND CAPITAL MANAGEMENT

Few financial strategic decisions have received as much attention in the recent past as leverage.[35] *Business Week* made the following criticism of growing American debt: "No, it's not Las Vegas or Atlantic City. It's the U.S. financial system. The volume of transactions has boomed far beyond anything needed to support the economy. Borrowing—politely called leverage—is getting out of hand. The result: The system is tilting from investment to speculation."[36] Given the rash of leveraged buy-outs in 1988 and the accompanying debt loads, some analysts warned of the risks associated with the high debt loads, claiming that some executives believed LBOs damaged the economy.[37] In the 1988 survey of corporate executives described in the profitability section, 11 percent responded that they expected their company to sell stock over the next year, and 17 percent responded that they expected their company's debt load to increase over the next year. Yet 47 percent also responded that they felt that American companies are carrying too much debt.[38]

If the amount of leverage is too high, why are firms planning to further increase their debt loads? This leverage question must be addressed in the broader context of corporate strategy and corporate control. As *Business Week* pointed out, "The driving force behind most increases in leverage is management's desire to stay in charge."[39] In an interesting analysis of equity financing, the opposite of debt financing, one analyst wrote, "Selling new shares dilutes ownership. And a smaller—not larger—shareholder base is often deemed desirable in an era of gargantuan battles for corporate control."[40]

Like the other financial decisions, there are several different ratios to choose from. Common ratios include debt to assets, debt to equity, long-term debt to equity, times interest earned, and fixed-charge coverage. Because of LBOs, with their bias toward debt, and corporate raiders, who indirectly encourage corporations to keep their debt levels high, we predict that it will be some time before leverage ratios in this country return to the levels of the early 1970s. Maybe the junk bond debacle and the bankruptcy of Drexel Burnham will help foster a return to former leverage levels.

ASSET MANAGEMENT

Asset management, which is usually measured by activity ratios, is an area of financial strategy in which there is little disagreement concerning the appropriate levels of the measures. As long as the firm is protected against inventory stock-outs, most people would agree that the more intensely the assets are worked the better. Whereas some of the other financial decisions discussed in this section on financial strategy have advantages and disadvantages relative to the corporate- and business-level objectives, there are few drawbacks to working the firm's assets or inventory more intensely. Perhaps the only limits are company history and industry comparisons.

The typical activity ratios used as measures of asset management are total asset turnover, fixed-asset turnover, net working capital turnover, inventory turnover, and collection period for receivables. The last measure may be the only one in which higher-level strategy may indicate that more is not better. As the ratio is formed by a division of accounts receivables by annual credit sales, the measure could be reduced by shrinking the numerator of accounts receivables. Shrinking accounts receivables to the extreme would result in potentially lost sales. If other strategies are aimed at a dramatic increase in sales, such a suboptimization of the collection period would be counterproductive. This is another case in which other strategies need to be addressed for the sake of consistency among strategies.

INVESTMENT RATIOS

Typical investment ratios are the price-earnings ratio, dividend payout, and common stock dividend yield. Management of these ratios is definitely an area in which the other relevant strategies, and even the issues of corporate control and ownership, must be considered.

Low price-earnings ratios have been known to encourage corporate raiders. The firm may wish to keep the ratio high through stock buybacks or through a series of decisions to reduce the volatility of earnings.

Low or volatile dividend payouts or common stock dividend yields have been known to anger investors. The result may be a lower stock price than otherwise due to investors' sales of stock or investors' attempts to terminate the firm's top executives. Therefore, the executives may pursue a series of decisions to stabilize the dividend stream. Indeed, dividend policy is a serious matter at many directors' meetings, as considerable information concerning future profitability is inherent in dividend decisions.[41] Stable or growing dividends communicate confidence in future profitability. Volatile dividends communicate uncertainty and risk concerning future profitability.

HUMAN RESOURCES

HUMAN RESOURCE PLANNING

An increasing body of literature in the arena of human resource strategy has argued that human resource planning should be included in strategy formulation.[42] Because of two significant trends in human resources—the "graying" of America and decreased skill and educational levels—a strategic plan that does not include a human resource plan could be impossible to implement. For example, it would be absurd for a firm to develop a strategy of cost leadership if the firm's operations are labor intensive and it deals with a strong union that demands high wages and implements restrictive work rules.

Figure 5.4 attempts to describe the relationship between competitive strategy and human resource strategy. The figure logically argues that considerations of competitive strategy, including competitive advantage and distinctive competence, need to be reflected in human resource strategy—and vice versa.

A significant human resource issue that will confront American firms in

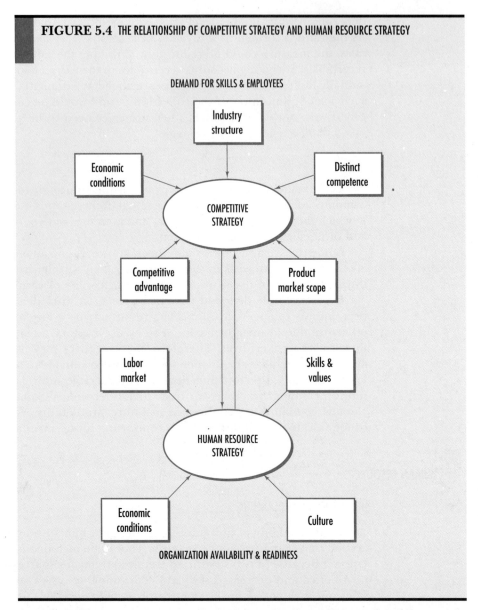

FIGURE 5.4 THE RELATIONSHIP OF COMPETITIVE STRATEGY AND HUMAN RESOURCE STRATEGY

Source: Lengnick-Hall, C. A., and M. L. Lengnick-Hall, "Strategic Human Resource Management," *Academy of Management Review* 13 (1988): 467. Used by permission.

the future, and impact most of the human resource strategies discussed in this section, is the problem of labor shortages. The "help wanted" sign may be a fixture across the country during the 1990s. "America faces an era of worker scarcity that may last to the year 2000," predicts the business press.[43] As a measure of the labor shortage, Figure 5.5 forecasts the declining number

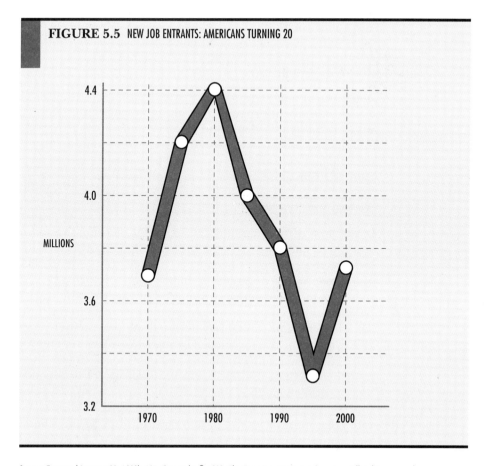

FIGURE 5.5 NEW JOB ENTRANTS: AMERICANS TURNING 20

Source: Fortune (January 30, 1989): 187. Copyright © 1989, The Time Inc. Magazine Company. All rights reserved.

of new job entrants to the year 2000. One of the reasons for the labor short-ages is the aging of America. As medicine, nutrition, and life-styles improve, Americans are living longer. The median age of the U.S. population is ex-pected to increase from about 28 in 1970 to approximately 36 in the year 2000.[44] One recent article described programs businesses were implementing to better utilize senior workers: "With the ranks of younger employees thin-ning, smart corporations are realizing that their best recruits may be over 55. To hold onto them longer and keep them motivated, employers have started so-called phased retirement programs, offered paid sabbaticals, and even awarded new job titles with higher pay. In such companies, older employees are thriving."[45]

In the future, more firms may be implementing human resource strate-gies and policies to deal with these twin issues of labor shortages and an aging population. The labor shortages may even shape some competitive business-level strategies. Some firms may decide not to compete in labor-intensive operations where there are labor shortages, or they may decide to make massive capital investments to automate historically labor-intensive processes.

RECRUITMENT AND SELECTION

In the recruitment and selection area, a firm must ask itself if it employs adequate recruitment programs and processes so that it selects the right personnel with the right skill mix and in the right numbers for its operations. "Right" means those who fit with the strategies.[46] If the answer to the question is no, the firm may consider using external human resource search firms as a supplement to its in-house human resource office.

TRAINING AND DEVELOPMENT

In the area of training and development, the organization must ask itself at least three questions: What is the effectiveness of its activities? To what skill level do the employees need to be trained and developed? Will the training and development programs be in-house or conducted by outsiders? These issues have received increased attention in American industry because, as some people have argued, a primary competitive resource is human capital, and America's human capital has declined. As one analyst stated, "The nation's ability to compete is threatened by inadequate investment in our most important resource: people. Put simply, too many workers lack the skills to perform more demanding jobs. And as the economy comes to depend more on women and minorities, we face a massive job of education and training—starting before kindergarten. Can we afford it? We have no choice."[47] The article indicated that more firms are becoming substitute teachers because of inadequacies in our educational system. We can expect to see American firms spending more money on training and development and becoming more involved in the American educational system in the future.[48]

COMPENSATION AND REWARDS

There are two primary issues in the area of compensation and rewards. First, is there a link between performance and compensation?[49] Second, are the wages and fringe benefits competitive?

There are some firms for whom the link between performance and compensation—and the performance of the firm itself—is legendary. Examples include Lincoln Electric and Nucor Steel. At Nucor, even nonsupervisory hourly employees receive bonuses tied to performance. The above-average performance of Nucor, as a minimill in the steel industry, and the above-average performance of Lincoln Electric, as the world's largest manufacturer of welding machines, are both well documented.[50]

As this book was being written, a growing number of companies were using profit-sharing plans as incentive programs. The evidence on the corporate use of profit-sharing plans indicated that employees perform better and are more in touch with corporate performance and the impact of the marketplace upon the health of the firm, turnover rates decline, and compensation costs become more flexible.[51] The costs become more flexible because in years of decreasing corporate profitability, compensation decreases. The decreased compensation costs may make it easier to avoid layoffs, a result desired by socially responsible corporations (as discussed in Chapter 8). For all of these reasons there may be an increased use of profit-sharing plans in American industry.

The competitiveness of wages and fringe benefits is an important issue on two accounts. First, competitiveness is frequently associated with the success of the recruiting program. It is difficult to attract talent with below-market compensation. Second, turnover is frequently associated with the competitiveness. If substantially higher compensation can be found elsewhere, turnover is usually a problem. Because of the importance of competitive compensation and fringes, firms typically spend substantial resources on wage and fringe benefit surveys.

EMPLOYMENT SECURITY

Employment security has received increased attention recently as many firms have restructured, divested, and slimmed down. The most important concern in this area involves the link to corporate strategy. If a firm is in an industry with few downturns or with uninterrupted growth, is dominant in that industry, and is committed to growth, the firm can almost guarantee employment security. The no-layoff policy of IBM is famous. In difficult times, the firm will retrain and transfer employees rather than lay them off. Alternatively, a firm in a highly volatile industry, especially one in a nondominant position, may need to use layoffs to meet the vagaries of the marketplace.

The second decision in this area concerns the level to which employment security is extended. Does the policy extend to all employees or only to executives, managers, certain skilled employees, or professionals? A policy extended to all is easier to communicate, implement, and defend on the basis of equity but costly to maintain in case of a business slowdown.

LABOR RELATIONS

A company's decisions in the labor relations area are obviously affected by the existence of a union. Indeed, many firms that are not unionized will go to great lengths, including relocating to the South, to avoid unions. For example, Mack Truck moved from Allentown, Pennsylvania, where it dealt with a very strong union, to South Carolina, which has one of the strongest nonunion traditions in this country.

The union issue may become less of an issue as unions continue to lose strength in this country. That decline, however, has created a vacuum in the settlement of labor issues. The vacuum has caused confusion in many firms, which cannot find answers to their pressing labor questions and are searching for a replacement for the bargaining table. "Until a few years ago, most of the nation's work-related problems got resolved, for better or worse, by Darwinian struggles between labor and management," reported *Business Week*. Today, "with unions representing less than 13% of the private-industry work force, down from more than 20% in the 1970s, more and more nonunion employees are looking to the courts for protection."[52]

Companies also need to ask if their labor relations have a history of being congenial or combative. Congenial relations are a definite asset if a firm needs to implement a new strategy. Combative labor relations can all but kill attempts to restructure. A move into other industries, or a move into other technologies partly to save costs by eliminating jobs, can be difficult to implement in the face of combative labor relations.

RESEARCH AND DEVELOPMENT (R&D)

RELATIONSHIP TO CORPORATE STRATEGY

What is the relationship of R&D to corporate strategy? Is the purpose of R&D aggressive new product development or process improvement?[53] Different corporate strategies imply different answers to these questions. For example, a pharmaceutical firm like Merck, with its growth philosophy, invests considerable financial resources in R&D for the purpose of aggressive new product development. Alternatively, a textile firm, with more limited growth possibility, may use R&D primarily for modest manufacturing process improvement.

A firm also must address the structure and placement of research and development in the corporate hierarchy. Placement of R&D as a major corporate resource at the same level as other functions is consistent with a strong tie between R&D and corporate strategy. Placement of R&D within the manufacturing world is consistent with the role of R&D primarily for process improvement.

LEVEL OF EFFORT

What is the level of effort associated with R&D? Expenditures in this area must be considered as a percentage of sales, relative to the past, and relative to industry averages. The relative comparisons are consistent with the notion of R&D expenditures as a competitive weapon from which future products will be derived. For example, the prescription drug industry is adept at using large R&D programs, whose budgets may be 10–12 percent of corporate sales, as a way to derive tomorrow's products. Research and development programs that are formulated solely on the basis of a fixed amount, independent of sales or industry averages, are not consistent with a competitive-weapon mentality.

PROJECT SELECTION

One way to determine whether managers are thinking strategically in their R&D program is to examine how project selection decisions are made. If the

TABLE 5.5 IMPORTANCE OF PRODUCT DEVELOPMENT CRITERIA BY GROUP

CRITERION	STRATEGIC MANAGEMENT	INTRODUCTORY MANAGEMENT	MANAGERS
Long-term profitability	37	32	43
Short-term profitability	23	28	24
Technical risk	10	13	10
Market risk	6	12	15
Resource availability	23	13	7
Market pressure	1	2	1

Source: Stahl, M.J., and T. W. Zimmerer, "Modeling Product Development Decision Policies of Managers and Management Students," *IEEE Transactions on Engineering Management* (February 1983): 21. Copyright © 1983 IEEE. Used by permission.

criteria used for the decisions are long term and are oriented toward customers or profitability, the managers are thinking in strategic terms. If the criteria used are short term or are resource dependent, the managers are not thinking strategically. For example, Stahl and Zimmerer examined how fifty manufacturing managers, twenty-nine senior undergraduate students in a strategic management course, thirty-six sophomore and junior students in an introductory principles of management course made product development decisions. On the basis of thirty-two simulated decisions per individual, the weights in Table 5.5 were observed from their decisions. Notice that the managers placed more importance on long-term profitability and less importance on resource availability than the students and thus were thinking more strategically than the students. The weights were based on 100 total points for all criteria.

CONTROL

When discussing research and development, sometimes the terms "customer pull" or "R&D push" are used. The former denotes projects undertaken because customers want certain products; the latter denotes projects approved because someone in R&D wants them. This latter category of projects, if it becomes too large, can cause R&D to lose touch with the customer and lose its relationship to corporate strategy. Thus, the issues of the corporate objectives for R&D and control of R&D need to be addressed. These topics are covered later in Chapter 7, Control and Evaluation.

INFORMATION SYSTEMS

Mason argued that information can play three different roles relative to strategy.[54] First, information can be used to record and report transactions. In this way, information serves a bookkeeping role. Second, information can be used to track and describe the state of the market, competitors' moves, and other useful external conditions. Here, information serves a strategic planning role. Third, information and information systems (IS) can be used as integral parts of the firm's operations. In this mode, it may be hard to distinguish the information or the information systems from the firm's products or services. Thus, information and information systems serve as competitive weapons. This realization of the competitive role of information systems is relatively recent and deserves special attention.

TRANSACTION/BOOKKEEPING ROLE

This historical role of IS may be the least exciting and least imaginative use of IS. The power of computer hardware and software is used to record, track, and report transactions. This particular role views IS in the cost-center mentality, as expenditures are to be controlled and costs are to be avoided.[55] As the IS in this mode does not have a direct bearing on strategy or competitive weapons, this historical role is frequently covered under the subject of implementation systems in many strategic management texts.

STRATEGIC PLANNING ROLE

In this role, information systems are used as an integral part of the strategic planning process. The IS is used to collect, interpret, and report information concerning market and competitor moves that aid in strategic planning. Some authors have described use of the IS as a strategic decision support system or as a strategic intelligence system.[56] For example, Camillus and Lederer focused an entire article on "the importance of selecting a Computer Information System whose design is in keeping with the strategic management processes of the organization."[57] It is not unusual to find corporate computers tied into many large external data bases concerning industry, market, and demographic trends. These data bases may be used as external intelligence in strategy formulation. Furthermore, it is not unusual to find large computers doing large simulations to help the executives model the results of alternative strategic decisions. Some forecasters argued that information technology will dramatically reshape the functions of managers: "Top management will have centralized control *and* decentralized decision making."[58]

COMPETITIVE WEAPON ROLE

Peter Drucker, one of the most frequently cited management theorists, argued that businesses have little choice but to become information based. He maintained that the use of information and information systems will influence the way businesses conduct their operations and compete.[59] This view of IS as a competitive weapon that provides value for the customer or helps the firm compete is a relatively new viewpoint that has received special attention as a functional-area strategy.[60] For example, in documenting the value of computer integrated manufacturing, Avishai noted, "For some U.S. companies, computer integrated manufacturing is the only way to justify staying in a business."[61]

A recent article described four ways that information technology was used as a competitive weapon in marketing: (1) as salesperson productivity tools, (2) in direct mail and fulfillment, (3) in telemarketing, and (4) in sales and marketing management. "By automating the sales and marketing functions, companies have increased sales anywhere from 10% to more than 30%."[62]

A financial publication documented the use of expert systems, which use information systems to emulate the decisions of human experts, in financial management. Table 5.6 from that article presents examples of the use of various expert systems for various financial applications. In some of these applications, the expert system becomes an integral part of the product/service offered to the customer. In such cases, the IS is serving a competitive weapon role.

Information systems are being used by some wholesalers to electronically link suppliers to customers for automatic ordering and distribution to gain a competitive advantage. "Food and drug wholesalers are leading the way," reported *Business Week.* "Some are tying their computers into buyers' inventory systems with custom software that will soon permit automatic reordering. Experimental systems are being used to predict the hour when drugstores will sell out. That way wholesalers can resupply them in time, but not too early."[63]

TABLE 5.6 EXPERT SYSTEMS FOR FINANCIAL APPLICATIONS

EXPERT SYSTEM	COMPANY	FUNCTION
Authorizer's Assistant	American Express	Credit authorization
Broker Monitoring System	Bear, Stearns & Co.	Account monitoring
Capital Expert System	Texas Instruments	Capital expense proposals
ExMarine	Coopers & Lybrand	Marine underwriting
ExperTax	Coopers & Lybrand	Tax advising
Financial Advisor	Palladian	Corporate strategy planning
Financial Analyzer	Athena Group	Commercial loan approval
Financial Statement Analyzer	SEC	Financial statement analysis
Lending Advisor	Syntelligence	Credit analysis
Letter of Credit Advisor	Bank of America	Letters of credit validation
Mortgage Loan Analyzer	Arthur Anderson	Mortgage loans evaluation
Plan Power	APEX	Financial planning
Portfolio Advisor	Athena Group	Portfolio management
Trader's Assistant	Arthur D. Little	Security broker selection
Underwriting Advisor	Syntelligence	Commercial underwriting

Source: Holsapple, C. W., K. Tam, and A. B. Whinston, "Adapting Expert System Technology to Financial Management," *Financial Management* (Autumn 1988): 16. Used by permission.

SUMMARY

This chapter deals with functional strategies as the pattern of decisions actually made in the respective function. The degree to which that pattern supports the business strategy and the consistency among the various functional strategies are repeatedly stressed as necessary characteristics of successful strategy.

The major decisions in the production/operations strategy area concern the technical core, quality, capacity, facilities, technology, and production planning and control. The need for consistency among these six decisions is highlighted.

The major decisions in marketing strategy concern the product/service, price, place/distribution, and promotion/advertising. These elements must be consistent with each other and with what production/operations can deliver.

Financial strategies concern objectives, profitability, liquidity and cash management, leverage and capital management, asset management, investment ratios, and financial planning and control. Financial strategies have received a great deal of attention recently because of the apparent inconsistency among some of the decision areas. For example, some firms have inordinately leveraged themselves to protect against hostile takeovers, but they have done so at the expense of profitability.

Human resource strategies concern human resource planning, recruitment and selection, training and development, compensation and rewards, employment security, and labor relations. As a labor shortage becomes more pronounced in this country in the 1990s, firms will probably devote more resources to human resource planning. The firms will also spend more resources scrutinizing the other decisions for consistency among themselves and in support of the competitive strategies.

The most important research and development strategy issue concerns the relationship of R&D to corporate strategy. If R&D is part of an aggressive new product development strategy, a series of decisions logically follow from such a link, including funding levels, project selection decisions, and the structure for R&D. If R&D is used primarily for process improvement, the decisions are more conservative.

Information systems strategy is a relatively recent topic in the study of functional-level strategies. Information systems are used for transactions/bookkeeping, for strategic planning, or as competitive weapons. Increasing numbers of organizations are using information systems for the two latter reasons.

DISCUSSION QUESTIONS

1. Define functional-level strategies.
2. Explain the desired relationship among corporate-level, business-level, and functional-level strategies.

3. Explain the desired relationship among the different functional strategies.

4. Explain the relationship between technology and quality.

5. Describe the two different bases for pricing decisions.

6. Why is consistency among the financial strategy decisions important?

7. Why is human resources planning assuming increased importance?

8. Describe two different roles for R&D in an organization.

9. Describe the three different roles information systems can play.

ENDNOTES

1. Hayes, R. H., and S. C. Wheelwright, *Restoring Our Competitive Edge: Competing Through Manufacturing* (New York: Wiley, 1984): 29.

2. "The Productivity Paradox," *Business Week* (June 6, 1988): 100.

3. Shroeder, R. G., J. G. Anderson, and G. Cleveland, "The Content of Manufacturing Strategy: An Empirical Study," *Journal of Operations Management* 6, no. 4 (August 1986): 405–415; Skinner, W., *Manufacturing in Corporate Strategy* (New York: John Wiley & Sons, 1978); Wheelwright, S. C., "Manufacturing Strategy: Defining the Missing Link," *Strategic Management Journal* 5 (1984): 77–91; Wheelwright, S. C., et al., "Integration of Manufacturing Strategy and Business Strategy," in *Manufacturing Trends in the 1980's* (New York: Booz, Allen, and Hamilton, 1981); Nemetz, R., and L. Fry "Flexible Manufacturing Organizations: Implications for Strategy Formulation and Organization," *Academy of Management Review* 13, no. 4 (1988): 627–638.

4. Buffa, E. S., *Meeting the Competitive Challenge: Manufacturing Strategy for U.S. Companies* (Homewood, Ill: Dow Jones-Irwin, 1984); Buffa, E. S., "Making American Manufacturing Competitive," *California Management Review* (Spring 1984): 29–46; Skinner, W., "Getting Physical: New Strategic Leverage from Operations," *Journal of Business Strategy* 3, no. 4 (Spring 1984): 74–79; Skinner, W., *Manufacturing: The Formidable Competitive Weapon* (New York: Wiley, 1985); Wheelwright, S. C., and R. H. Hayes, "Competing Through Manufacturing," *Harvard Business Review* 64, no. 1 (1985): 99–109.

5. Jelinek, M., and J. D. Goldhar, "The Strategic Implications of the Factory of the Future," *Sloan Management Review* 25, no. 4 (1984): 29–37; Meredith, J. R., "The Strategic Advantages of the Factory of the Future," *California Management Review* 29, no. 3 (1987): 27–41; Billatos, S., "Guidelines for Productivity and Manufacturing Strategy," *Manufacturing Review* 1 (1988): 164–167.

6. "The Hollow Corporation: The Decline of Manufacturing Threatens the Entire U.S. Economy," *Business Week* (March 3, 1986): 57.

7. "Auto Quality," *Business Week* (October 22, 1990): 84; Garvin, D. A., *Managing Quality: The Strategic and Competitive Edge* (New York: The Free Press, 1988); Phillips, L. W., D. R. Chang, and R. D. Buzzell, "Product Quality, Cost Position and Business Performance: A Test of Some Key Hypotheses," *Journal of Marketing* 47 (Spring 1983); Zeithaml, V., "Consumer Perceptions of Price, Quality and Value: A Means-End Model and Synthesis of Evidence," *Journal of Marketing* 52 (July 1988): 2–22; *Quality: Executive Priority or Afterthought? Executive Perceptions on Quality in a Competitive World* (Milwaukee: American Society for Quality Control, 1989): 1–30.

8. Stahl, M. J., and G. B. Bounds, "Global Competition," in *Competing Globally Through Customer Value: The Management of Strategic Suprasystems,* ed. M. J. Stahl and G. B. Bounds, (Westport, Conn.: Quorum Press, 1991): 3–13.

9. Thurston, W. R., "Quality is Between the Customer's Ears," *Across the Board* (January 1985): 99.

10. "Getting High Tech Back on Track," *Fortune* (January 1, 1990): 74; Ishikawa, K. *What is Total Quality Control? The Japanese Way,* (Englewood Cliffs, N.J.: Prentice-Hall, 1985).

11. "The Rival Japan Respects," *Business Week* (November 13, 1989): 108–118.

12. "Long-Term Thinking and Paternalistic Ways Carry Michelin to Top," *Wall Street Journal* (January 5, 1990): 1.

13. Zeithaml, V. A., "Consumer Perceptions of Price, Quality, and Value," *Journal of Marketing* (July 1988): 2–22.

14. "Americans Have Uses for 'Peace Dividend' That Aren't Selfish: Japan's Perceived Supremacy," *Wall Street Journal* (January 19, 1990): 1.

15. Bremer, M. S., "Linking Strategic Management and Ongoing Quality Improvement," *National Productivity Review* 8, no. 1 (Winter 1988–1989): 11–22.

16. Deming, W. E., *Out of the Crisis* (Cambridge, Mass.: MIT Press, 1986): 23.

17. Porter, M. E., *Competitive Strategy* (New York: The Free Press, 1980): 7 and 259.

18. "The Sun Belt Gains Manufacturing Jobs as Nation

Loses Them: Population Pool, Labor Costs and the Quality of Life Help Region Lure Firms," *Wall Street Journal* (April 1, 1988): 1.

19. "High Tech to the Rescue: More Than Ever, Industry is Pinning its Hopes on Factory Automation," *Business Week* (June 16, 1986): 100–108; "How Automation Could Save the Day: Computerized Factories Might Make the U.S. Competitive, But a Commitment is Lacking," *Business Week* (March 3, 1987): 72–74; Ayers, R., "Future Trends in Factory Automation," *Manufacturing Review* 1, no. 2 (1988): 93–103.

20. "CIM: Much More Than Adding Computers," *Industry Week* (February 9, 1987): 47.

21. "Manufacturing's New Window of Opportunity," *Wall Street Journal* (April 19, 1988): 35.

22. Anderson, J. C., et al., "Material Requirements Planning Systems: The State of the Art," *Production and Inventory Management* (Fourth Quarter 1982): 51–66; LaForge, R. L. and V. L. Sturr, "MRP Practices in a Random Sample of Manufacturing Firms," *Production and Inventory Management* (Third Quarter 1986): 127–139.

23. LaForge and Sturr, "MRP Practices," p. 130.

24. Biggadike, E. R. "The Contribution of Marketing to Strategic Management," *Academy of Management Review* 6 (1981): 621–632; Day, G., *Strategic Market Planning: The Pursuit of Competitive Advantage* (St. Paul: West Publishing, 1984); Day, G., "Strategic Market Analysis and Definition: An Integrated Approach," *Strategic Management Journal* 2 (1981): 281–299.

25. "Smart Design: Quality is the New Style," *Business Week* (April 11, 1988): 102–103.

26. "Gray Expectations: A New Force in Design," *Business Week* (April 11, 1988): 108.

27. Dean, J., "Pricing Policies for New Products," *Harvard Business Review* 54 (November–December 1976): 141–153; Gross, I., "Insights From Pricing Research," in *Pricing Practices and Strategies* (New York: Conference Board, 1979); Rao, R. C., and F. M. Bass, "Competition, Strategy, and Price Dynamics: A Theoretical and Empirical Investigation," *Journal of Marketing Research* 22 (1985): 283–296.

28. *Wall Street Journal* (October 7, 1988): B1.

29. "Mystery Machine: IBM Computer Buyers Are Bewildered by PCs with Secret Ingredient: With a New 'Micro Channel', Firm Uses Marketing Ploy to Charge Premium Price," *Wall Street Journal* (March 22, 1988): 1.

30. "After Early Stumbles, P&G is Making Inroads Overseas," *Wall Street Journal* (February 6, 1989): B1.

31. Cornell, B., and A. C. Shapiro, "Corporate Stakeholders and Corporate Finance," *Financial Management* (Spring 1987): 5–14; Donaldson, G., "Financial Goals and Strategic Consequences," *Harvard Business Review* (May–June 1985): 57–66; Donaldson, G., *Managing Corporate Wealth: The Operation of a Comprehensive Financial Goals System* (New York: Praeger Publishers, 1984).

32. Woolridge, J. R., "Competitive Decline and Corporate Restructuring: Is a Myopic Stock Market to Blame?" *Journal of Applied Corporate Finance* 1 (1988): 26–36.

33. Kaplan, R., "Does the Financial Plan Match the Strategic Plan?" *Financial Executive* (July–August 1989): 42–43.

34. "The View From the Executive Suite," *Business Week* (November 7, 1988): 143.

35. Mandelker, G., and S. G. Rhee, "The Impact of the Degrees of Operating and Financial Leverage on Systematic Risk of Common Stock," *Journal of Financial and Quantitative Analysis* (March 1983): 45–57; Prezas, A. P., "Effects of Debt on the Degrees of Operating and Financial Leverage," *Financial Management* (Summer 1987): 39–44; Sandberg, C. M., W. G. Lewellen, and K. L. Stanley, "Financial Strategy: Planning and Managing the Corporate Leverage Position," *Strategic Management Journal* 8 (1987): 15–24.

36. "The Casino Society," *Business Week* (September 16, 1985): 78.

37. "The LBO Binge," *Wall Street Journal* (October 27, 1988): 1.

38. "View From the Executive Suite," p. 143.

39. "Learning to Live with Leverage," *Business Week* (November 7, 1988): 141.

40. "What Does Equity Financing Really Cost," *Business Week* (November 7, 1988): 146.

41. Ang, J. S., "Do Dividends Matter: A Review of Corporate Dividend Theories and Evidence," *Monograph Series in Finance and Economics* 2 (1987).

42. Baird, L., I. Meshoulam, and G. DeGive, "Meshing Human Resources Planning with Strategic Business Planning: A Model Approach," *Personnel* 60, no. 5 (1983): 14–25; Dyer, L., "Bringing Human Resources into the Strategy Formulation Process," *Human Resource Management* 22, no. 3 (1983): 257–271; Schweiger, D. M., J. M. Ivancevich, and F. R. Power, "Executive Actions for Managing Human Resources Before and After Acquisition," *Academy of Management Executive* 1, no. 2 (1987): 127–138; Schweiger, D. M., and J. M. Ivancevich, "Human Resources: The Forgotten Factor in Mergers and Acquisitions," *Personnel Administrator* 30 (1985): 47; Schuler, R. S., "Repositioning the Human Resource Function: Transformation or Demise?" *Academy of Management Executive* 4 (1990): 49–60; Pucik, V., "Strategic Alliances, Organizational Learning, and Competitive Advantage: The HRM Agenda," *Human Resource Management* (1988): 77–93.

43. "The Coming Labor Shortage: Help Wanted," *Business Week* (August 10, 1987): 48.

44. "Making Better Use of Older Workers," *Fortune* (January 30, 1989): 184.

45. *Fortune* (January 30, 1989): 179.

46. DeSanto, J. F., "Work Force Planning and Corporate Strategy," *Personnel Administrator* 28, no. 10 (1983): 33–42; Olian, J. D., and S. L. Rynes, "Organizational Staffing: Integrating Practice with Strategy," *Industrial Relations* 23, no. 2 (1984): 170–183; Schuler, R. S., and S. E. Jackson, "Linking Competitive Strategies with Human Resource Management Practices," *Academy of Management Executive* 1 (1987): 207–219; Schuler, R. S., and I. C. MacMillan, "Gaining Competitive Advantage Through Human Resource Management Practices," *Human Resource Management* 23, no. 3 (1984): 241–256.

47. "Human Capital: The Decline of America's Work Force," *Business Week* (September 19, 1988): 100.

48. "Saving Our Schools," *Fortune* (Special Issue, Spring 1990).

49. Migliore, R. H., "Linking Strategy, Performance and Pay," *Journal of Business Strategy* 3, no. 1 (1982): 90–94; Hambrick, D. C., and C. C. Snow, "Strategic Reward Systems," in *Strategy, Organization Design and Human Resource Management*, ed. C. C. Snow (Greenwich, Conn.: JAI Press, 1989): 333–368.

50. "Nucor," in *Strategy and Business Policy: Cases*, G. D. Smith, A. R. Arnold, and B. G. Bizzell (Boston: Houghton Mifflin Co., 1986): 322–347; "The Lincoln Electric Company," in *Cases for Strategic Management*, ed. J. H. Barnett and W. D. Wilsted (Boston: PWS-KENT, 1989): 415–437.

51. "Watching the Bottom Line Instead of the Clock," *Business Week* (November 7, 1988): 134–135.

52. "Needed: A Replacement for the Bargaining Table," *Business Week* (January 9, 1989): 38.

53. Kiczmarski, T. D., and S. J. Silver, "Strategy: The Key to Successful New Product Development," *Management Review* (July 1982): 26–40; Pappas, C., "Strategic Management of Technology," *Journal of Product Innovation Management* 1 (January 1984): 30–35; Fryxell, G. E., "Multiple Outcomes from Product R&D: Profitability Under Different Strategic Orientations," *Journal of Management* 16 (1990): 633–646.

54. Mason, R., "Information System Technology and Corporate Strategy," in *The Information Systems Research Challenge, Proceedings*, ed. F. W. McFarlan (Boston: Harvard Business School Press, 1984).

55. King, W. R., "Strategic Planning for Information Resources: The Evolution of Concepts and Practice," *Information Resources Management Journal* (Fall 1988): 2–3.

56. Bakos, J. Y., and M. E. Treacy, "Information Technology and Corporate Strategy: A Research Perspective," *MIS Quarterly* (June 1986): 107–119; Fredericks, P., and N.

Venkatraman, "The Rise of Strategy Support Systems," *Sloan Management Review* 29 (Spring 1988): 47–54; Henderson, J. C., J. F. Rockard, and J. G. Sifonis, "Integrating Management Support Systems into Strategic Information Systems Planning," *Journal of Management Information Systems* 4, no. 1 (Summer 1987): 5–24; Holloway, C., and J. A. Pearce, "Computer Assisted Strategic Planning," *Long Range Planning* 15 (1982): 56–63; Pyburn, P. J., "Linking the MIS Plan with Corporate Strategy: An Exploratory Study," *MIS Quarterly* 7, no. 2 (1983): 1–14; Sabherwal, R., and V. Grover, "Computer Support for Strategic Decision-Making Processes: Review and Analysis," *Decision Sciences* 20 (1989): 54–76; Scott, M. M., "The Role of Decision Support Systems in Corporate Strategy," in *Corporate Strategy*, ed. T. H. Naylor (New York: North Holland Publishing Co., 1982): 97–112.

57. Camillus, J. C., and A. L. Lederer, "Corporate Strategy and the Design of Computerized Information Systems," *Sloan Management Review* (Spring 1985): 35.

58. Applegate, L. M., J. I. Cash, and D. Q. Mills, "Information Technology and Tomorrow's Manager," *Harvard Business Review* (November–December 1988): 128.

59. Drucker, P. F., "The Coming of the New Organization," *Harvard Business Review* (January–February 1988): 45–53.

60. Gerstein, M., and H. Reisman, "Creating Competitive Advantage with Computer Power," *Journal of Business Strategy* 3 (Summer 1982): 53–60; Ives, B., and G. P. Learmonth, "The Information System as a Competitive Weapon," *Communications of the ACM* (December 1984): 1193–1201; Johnston, H. R., and M. R. Vitale, "Creating Competitive Advantage with Interorganizational Information Systems," *MIS Quarterly* 12 (June 1988): 153–165; McFarlan, F. W., "Information Technology Changes the Way You Compete," *Harvard Business Review* (May–June, 1984): 35–47; Parsons, G. L., "Information Technology: A New Competitive Weapon," *Sloan Management Review* (Fall 1983): 3–14; Porter, M. E., and V. E. Millar, "How Information Gives You Competitive Advantage," *Harvard Business Review* 63, no. 4 (1985): 149–159; Weisman, C., *Strategy and Computers: Information Systems as Competitive Weapons* (Homewood, Ill.: Dow Jones-Irwin, 1985); Lederer, A., and R. Nath, "Making Strategic Information Systems Happen," *Academy of Management Executive* 4 (1990): 76–83.

61. Avishai, B., "A CEO's Common Sense of CIM," *Harvard Business Review* (January–February 1988): 110–117.

62. Moriarty, R. T., and Swartz, G. S., "Automation to Boost Sales and Marketing," *Harvard Business Review* (January–February 1989): 100.

63. "Mom and Pop Move Out of Wholesaling," *Business Week* (January 9, 1989): 91.

ADDITIONAL READINGS

Blois, K. J. "The Structure of Service Firms and Their Marketing Policies. *Strategic Management Journal* 4 (1983): 251–261.

Bowen, D. W., C. Siehl, and B. Schneider. "A Framework for Analyzing Customer Service Orientations in Manufacturing." *Academy of Management Review* 14, no. 1 (1989): 75–95.

Buzzell, R. D., and F. D. Wiersema. "Modeling Changes in Market Share: A Cross-Sectional Analysis." *Strategic Management Journal* 2 (January–March 1981): 27–42.

Cady, J. F. "Marketing Strategies in the Information Industry." In *Marketing in an Electronic Age,* edited by R. D. Buzzell. Cambridge, Mass.: Harvard Business School Press, 1985.

Collins, P. D., J. Hage, and F. Hull. "Organizational and Technological Predictors of Change in Automaticity." *Academy of Management Journal* 31, no. 3 (1988): 512–543.

Crosby, P. B. *Quality is Free: The Art of Making Quality Certain.* New York: McGraw-Hill, 1979.

———. *Quality Without Tears: The Art of Hassle-Free Management.* New York: McGraw-Hill, 1984.

Dyer, L. "Studying Human Resource Strategy: An Approach and an Agenda." *Industrial Relations* 23, no. 2 (1984): 156–169.

———. "Strategic Human Resource Management and Planning." Pp. 1–30 in *Research in Personnel and Human Resource Management,* edited by K. M. Rowland and G. R. Ferris. Greenwich, Conn.: JAI Press, 1984.

Hayes, R. H., S. C. Wheelwright, and K. B. Clark. *Dynamic Manufacturing: Creating the Learning Organization.* New York: The Free Press, 1988.

Houston, F. S. "The Marketing Concept: What It Is and What It Is Not. *Journal of Marketing* 50, no. 2 (1986): 81–87.

Jaikumar, R. "Post-Industrial Manufacturing." *Harvard Business Review* 86, no. 6 (1986): 69–76.

Juran, J. M. *Juran on Planning for Quality.* New York: The Free Press, 1988

———. *Juran's Quality Control Handbook.* New York: McGraw-Hill, 1988.

King, W. R. "Evaluating Strategic Planning Systems." *Strategic Management Journal* 4, no. 3 (1983): 263–277.

———. "How Effective is Your Information Systems Planning?" *Long Range Planning* (August 1988).

Kotha, S., and D. Orne. "Generic Manufacturing Strategies: A Conceptual Synthesis." *Strategic Management Journal* (May–June 1989): 211–232.

Larreche, J. C., and V. Srinivasan. "STRATPORT: A Decision Support System for Strategic Planning." *Journal of Marketing* 45, no. 4 (Fall 1981): 39–52.

———. "STRATPORT: A Model for the Evaluation and Formulation of Business Portfolio Strategies." *Management Science* 28, no. 9 (September 1982): 979–1001.

McLean, E. R., and J. V. Soden, eds. *Strategic Planning for MIS.* New York: Wiley-Interscience, 1977.

Montgomery, D. B. "Toward Decision Support Systems for Strategic Marketing." In *Strategic Marketing and Strategic Management,* edited by D. Gardner and H. Thomas. New York: John Wiley & Sons, 1985.

Montgomery, D. B., and C. B. Weinberg. "Toward Strategic Intelligence Systems." *Journal of Marketing* 43, no. 4 (Fall 1979): 41–52.

Richardson, P. R., A. J. Taylor, and J.R.M. Gordon. "A Strategic Approach to Evaluating Manufacturing Performance." *Interfaces* 15, no. 6 (November–December 1985): 15–27.

Skinner, W. "Operations Technology: Blind Spot in Strategic Management." *Interfaces* 14, no. 1 (January–February 1984): 116–125.

Swamidass, P. M., and W. J. Newell. "Manufacturing Strategy, Environmental Uncertainty, and Performance: A Path-Analytic Model." *Management Science* 33 (1987): 509–524.

Warner, T. N. "Information Technology as a Competitive Burden." *Sloan Management Review* 55 (Fall 1987): 59–60.

Young, L. F. "A Corporate Strategy for Decision Support Systems." *Journal of Information Systems Management* 1, no. 1 (Winter 1984): 58–62.

Zygmont, J. "Manufacturers Move Toward Computer Integration." *High Technology* 7, no. 2 (1987): 28–33.

CHAPTER SIX

Strategy Implementation

THE IMPORTANCE OF IMPLEMENTATION

Some theorists argue that a principal role of management is to implement or install strategy. According to this view, strategic leaders should design and continuously improve the motivational processes, policies, cross-functional groups, organizational systems, structures, and corporate culture that focus on discovering, creating, improving, and delivering value to the user or customer.[1] This chapter argues that no strategic plan, no matter how brilliantly formulated, is worth even the paper on which it is written if it cannot be implemented.

Mintzberg maintained that an increasingly important determinant of organizational effectiveness is the organization's ability to implement new strategies.[2] Conceptually, implementation has been defined as "a procedure directed by a manager to install planned change in an organization."[3] For purposes of this book, a slightly broader definition is used to include any device (such as systems, policy, structure, or culture) used by a manager to install new strategy or reinforce existing strategy.

Organizational structure, systems, policies, motivational processes, cross-functional groups, and culture are viewed as means to implement the strategic plan. Inconsistencies among the formulated strategic plan and these implementation devices can prevent successful implementation of the best plan.

Unfortunately, little attention is paid to the implementation side of the strategy equation. Implementation is usually not very visible. It frequently consists of day-to-day attention to operational details by many managers and usually is played out in the long term. This approach is contrasted with the very visible, high-energy, intensely focused activity of strategy formulation. Formulation is frequently written up in the popular business press, as noted in earlier chapters. Formulation can be exciting when multibillion dollar deals are offered and countered. Formulation also can be concentrated in short time periods when merger offers, counter offers, threatened lawsuits, and final buyouts all occur in a matter of days.

"The Seven Deadly Sins in Mergers and Acquisitions," outlined by *Business Week* in 1985, include "Marrying Disparate Corporate Cultures" and "Counting on Key Managers Staying."[4] Box 6.1 describes both sins in the merger of Fluor Corporation and St. Joe Minerals Corporation. Some might argue that this merger is an example of first, a bad acquisition and second, poor implementation. That is not the point of the example or of this chapter. Brilliantly conceived strategy formulation that is appropriate for external opportunities and threats, appropriate for internal strengths and weaknesses, and internally consistent is viewed as a necessary, but not sufficient, condition for organizational success. Organizational success requires brilliant strategy formulation as well as implementation of the strategy. Box 6.1 clearly demonstrates that the meshing of two different corporate cultures is easier said than done. A

BOX 6.1   FLUOR AND ST. JOE MINERALS: THE PERILS OF MERGING DIFFERENT CORPORATE CULTURES

Fluor Corporation had amassed $200 million in cash from its very successful engineering and construction business and decided to seek a merger partner outside its traditional field. The minerals business looked like a natural fit. Fluor had built mines and knew the mining business firsthand. Furthermore, metal prices typically ran countercyclical to ups and downs in the construction industry. When St. Joe Minerals Company faced a hostile takeover threat, Fluor decided to play the "white knight" and merged the two businesses in a stock trade.[a]

Managing the merged company proved more difficult than creating it would have been. The cultures of the two companies were at oppostie ends of the spectrum. St. Joe's headquarters ruled with a light hand. "We had a small, tight, almost partnership operation," said John C. Harned, a former St. Joe official. "Decisions could be made very quickly; it was just the reverse at Fluor."[b] Power at Fluor resided with a huge staff, and centralized decision making was the rule.

At first, Fluor allowed the mining company to operate autonomously, but Fluor's centrally controlled style eventually led it to tighten the reins. Rampant executive turnover resulted at St. Joe. Of the twenty-two officers who managed the company in 1981, only seven remained in 1985.[c]

---

[a] Shao, M., "Fluor and St. Joe Uncork Toast to Merger: Spurned Seagram Seeks Another Partner," *Wall Street Journal* (April 9, 1981): 4.
[b] *Business Week* (June 3, 1985): 92–93.
[c] "Top St. Joe Minerals Post is Changing," *New York Times* (December 8, 1982): D2.

recent analysis of mergers, corporate cultures, and executive turnover revealed many situations in which there were cultural mismatches and high resultant executive turnover. That analysis indicated that 75 percent of the executives of acquired companies are gone in five years.[5]

Making the corporate culture work and retaining the right personnel are not the only strategy implementation issues. This chapter deals with motivation, structure, systems and processes, cross-functional groups, policies, and culture as implementation devices. Several examples are offered concerning the implementation of strategies to compete on the basis of quality, as quality promises to be a competitive battleground through most of the 1990s.

MOTIVATION

MANAGERIAL MOTIVATION

Simply because the top-level strategic decision makers decide to implement a certain strategy does not necessarily mean that functional-level managers will actively and enthusiastically comply. Inertia, failure to perceive strategic significance, bounded rationality, and a host of other reasons may cause the functional managers to continue to allocate their efforts in established ways. Inertia (habit, or the way things have been done in the past) may be especially problematic in large organizations with an established history or pattern of behavior.

The Expectancy Theory of motivation has been used to describe strategy implementation efforts by functional managers.[6] One study found three distinct determinants of functional manager effort to implement strategic changes. First, the middle manager's assessment of his or her ability to implement the required program affected his or her effort. This factor was referred to as the *ability factor*. The second reported factor was the manager's assessment of the probability of success of the proposed strategy; this was the *probability factor*. The third factor was the association between the strategic-change goals and the individual manager's goals—the *instrumentality factor*.

Judge and Stahl recently investigated the importance of each of these three motivational factors to the managerial motivation to implement a quality improvement program in a pharmaceutical firm with plants in five countries.[7] Table 6.1 indicates the relative importance of the three factors and managerial motivation to implement the new strategies for thirty-four managers from plants in all five countries. Although there are significant differences among the five countries, the most important conclusion is that the managers' implementation effort is most closely linked to instrumentality. In other words, the managers' own goals had to be linked to the new strategic goals if they were to forcefully implement the new strategy. Therefore, organizations should consider such an instrumentality factor when attempting to implement new strategies in the design of managerial compensation, incentive, reward, recognition, and other systems affecting managers' goals.

TABLE 6.1   RELATIVE IMPORTANCE OF FACTORS IN MANAGERIAL IMPLEMENTATION EFFORT

COUNTRY	ABILITY	PROBABILITY	INSTRUMENTALITY
United States	9.6%	39.3%	51.1%
Japan	23.0	0.7	76.3
Belgium	16.3	22.9	60.8
France	2.8	7.5	89.7
United Kingdom	9.7	48.4	41.9
Overall Sample:	5.8	21.5	72.7

Source: Judge, W., and M. J. Stahl, "Decision Modeling Managerial Effort in Strategy Implementation: A Multinational Test," *Proceedings of the National Decision Sciences Institute* (November 1990).

EMPLOYEE MOTIVATION

Similarly, it is extremely important to consider and strengthen the motivation of nonmanagerial employees to implement new strategies or reinforce existing strategies. Table 6.2 contains the responses to a recent survey conducted by the American Society for Quality Control concerning the importance of methods of improving quality. The 601 responding senior executives indicated that the most important method of improving quality throughout American business was employee motivation.[8]

An example of the importance of motivation and strategy implementation

TABLE 6.2   IMPORTANCE OF METHODS OF IMPROVING QUALITY

RANK ORDER	METHOD
1	Employee motivation
2	Actively involved corporate leader
3	Employee education
4	Process control
5	Quality improvement teams
6	Expenditures on capital equipment
7	More control over suppliers
8	Improved administration support group output
9	More inspection

Source: Adapted from data found in *Quality: Executive Priority or Afterthought?* (Milwaukee: American Society for Quality Control, 1989): 11.

concerns General Motors and its new Saturn complex. General Motors has gone to previously unheard-of lengths to pay attention to employee motivational issues in the implementation of the Saturn project. The United Auto Workers and GM view each other as partners in the relationship. From the president on down, all employees are salaried. Everyone eats in the same cafeterias. New hires receive five days of training and may get 750 additional hours.[9] Such policies, which more closely treat all employees as colleagues, are attempts to motivate workers.

TRAINING

A number of firms are listing training as a strategy implementation device. Although some would argue that training is skill based rather than motivation based, there may be elements of both. In many training programs associated with the implementation of new strategies, it appears that there is a heavy dose of motivation through building commitment and signaling of important issues. For example, Xerox described the way it implemented a quality strategy. "Our first step in implementing the Leadership-Through-Quality process was to train management with their family work groups. To assure the commitment of management at every level, Leadership-Through-Quality training began with our top tier family work group—my direct reports and me. It then cascaded through the organizations led by senior staff, gradually spreading worldwide to some 10,000 employees."[10]

Education was listed as the third most important implementation device by the 601 executives in Table 6.2. At the Capsugel Division of Warner-Lambert, the significant investment of time and money in a multiweek training program attended by managers from worldwide operations signaled that the organization was serious about a quality improvement program.[11]

▪ STRUCTURE

Chandler offered the following definition of structure and hypothesized the relationship between structure and strategy.

> Structure can be defined as the design of organization through which the organization is administered. The design, whether formally or informally defined, has two aspects. It includes, first, the lines of authority and communication between the different administrative offices and officers, and, second, the information and data that flow through these lines of communication and authority. Such lines and data are essential to assure the effective coordination, appraisal, and planning so necessary in carrying out the basic goals and policies and in knitting together the total resources of the enterprise.[12]

Although few would quibble with Chandler's definition of structure, there is a substantial disagreement among organizational scholars over whether Chandler's implication that strategy (goals) determines and causes structure or whether structure causes strategy. Those in the latter camp hold that a given structure, with its hierarchy, established bureaucracy, and formalized systems, is prone to establish only certain kinds of strategies. Hall and Saias argued that the organizational structure acts as an information filter and therefore shapes the strategic decisions.[13] Their concept is depicted in Figure 6.1. The concept of structure acting as an information filter and shaping the strategic decisions fits well with the imperfect nature of the strategic decision making process described in Chapter 1.

The purpose of this section is not to settle the debate concerning whether strategy causes structure or structure causes strategy. A major point must be made, however, that strategy and structure must be consistent with one another if there is to be successful implementation of the chosen strategy. A logical corollary of this notion is that one should be able to design structure once the strategy is known. Conversely, one should be able to infer strategy by examining structure.

A good example of consistency between strategy and structure may be found in the acquisition of Eastern Airlines by Frank Lorenzo and Texas Air. The risk in the acquisition was described by *Business Week:* "Frank Lorenzo's bid for Eastern Airlines is the latest and most daring move in the restructuring of the airline industry. Will it work? For Frank Lorenzo, buying Eastern may prove far easier than running it."[14] The subsequent strike, bankruptcy, and liquidation indicate how difficult it was.

The innovative, complex structure that Lorenzo had built to insulate himself and Texas Air from the risk of the Eastern Airlines acquisition was de-

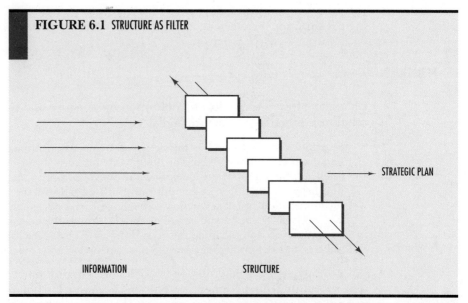

FIGURE 6.1 STRUCTURE AS FILTER

INFORMATION   STRUCTURE

STRATEGIC PLAN

Source: Hall, D. J., and M. A. Saias, "Strategy Follows Structure," *Strategic Management Journal* (1980): 156. Copyright © 1980 by John Wiley & Sons, Ltd. Reprinted by permission of John Wiley & Sons, Ltd.

scribed as a "House of Mirrors" by the *Wall Street Journal.* "Thanks to Mr. Lorenzo's masterly corporate architecture, huge losses at subsidiaries don't stop cash from moving to the top. While the airlines' public debt holders anxiously watch the deficits close in on half a billion dollars, the parent company keeps raking in from the airlines an assortment of management fees, airplane rents, airport-gate rents, fuel-purchase commissions and other payments. 'Upstreaming' of cash, company officials call this, and it totaled more than $150 million for the parent last year."[15]

Figure 6.2 contains a diagram of Lorenzo's structure, which implements the strategy of insulation from risk. The insulation was not total, however. In 1990, thee was speculation that Eastern's creditors would force either a merger with Continental, a liquidation, or a sale.[16] Again the *Wall Street Journal* reported: "Frank Lorenzo, who used debt, bankruptcy law and an iron will to transform a fly-speck Texas carrier into one of the nation's largest concerns, is leaving the company that he built. And according to people familiar with the details, he will be $17 million richer for his troubles."[17] In 1991, Eastern Airlines was liquidated.

The structure depicted in Figure 6.2 is very complex. There are several other organizational forms for the strategist to choose from in attempting to implement a chosen strategy. Before presenting the various structural forms, it is useful to place the alternative structures in perspective.

Figure 6.3 lists various structures in terms of complexity. In general, the lower the relatedness becomes in the corporate strategy, the higher the structural complexity becomes. Thus, one could reverse the relatedness dimension of Figure 3.2 and lay it on top of Figure 6.3. In such a fashion, there would be consistency between strategy and structure.[18]

Another way to examine the consistency between strategy and structure is to observe evolutions in structure as organizations grow and change. In their book concerning the role of structure in implementation, Galbraith and Nathanson presented a stages-of-growth model (Figure 6.4) as a way to describe concurrent changes in structure and strategy. The more complex the strategy becomes, the more complex the structure becomes.[19]

With both Figures 6.3 and 6.4 as overall models of alternative structures, it is now appropriate to review the alternatives in detail.

FUNCTIONAL

The functional organizational form is one of the most common organizational structures found in firms pursuing a strategy of concentration or very high relatedness. In a functional structure, like activities or functions are grouped together. Figure 6.5 is an example of a functional structure, that of the Dictaphone Corporation. Sales and service activities are grouped together; engineering and production activities are grouped together; and financial, accounting, and budget activities are grouped together. Other firms pursuing the functional form may have a substantial corporate staff reporting directly to the chief executive officer in an advisory capacity.[20]

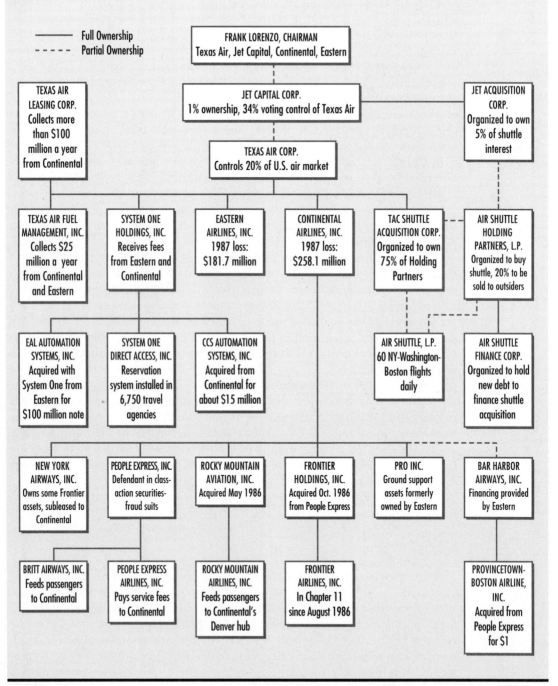

FIGURE 6.2 THE HOUSE THAT FRANK LORENZO BUILT

——— Full Ownership
‑ ‑ ‑ ‑ Partial Ownership

FRANK LORENZO, CHAIRMAN
Texas Air, Jet Capital, Continental, Eastern

TEXAS AIR LEASING CORP.
Collects more than $100 million a year from Continental

JET CAPITAL CORP.
1% ownership, 34% voting control of Texas Air

JET ACQUISITION CORP.
Organized to own 5% of shuttle interest

TEXAS AIR CORP.
Controls 20% of U.S. air market

TEXAS AIR FUEL MANAGEMENT, INC.
Collects $25 million a year from Continental and Eastern

SYSTEM ONE HOLDINGS, INC.
Receives fees from Eastern and Continental

EASTERN AIRLINES, INC.
1987 loss: $181.7 million

CONTINENTAL AIRLINES, INC.
1987 loss: $258.1 million

TAC SHUTTLE ACQUISITION CORP.
Organized to own 75% of Holding Partners

AIR SHUTTLE HOLDING PARTNERS, L.P.
Organized to buy shuttle, 20% to be sold to outsiders

EAL AUTOMATION SYSTEMS, INC.
Acquired with System One from Eastern for $100 million note

SYSTEM ONE DIRECT ACCESS, INC.
Reservation system installed in 6,750 travel agencies

CCS AUTOMATION SYSTEMS, INC.
Acquired from Continental for about $15 million

AIR SHUTTLE, L.P.
60 NY-Washington-Boston flights daily

AIR SHUTTLE FINANCE CORP.
Organized to hold new debt to finance shuttle acquisition

NEW YORK AIRWAYS, INC.
Owns some Frontier assets, subleased to Continental

PEOPLE EXPRESS, INC.
Defendant in class-action securities-fraud suits

ROCKY MOUNTAIN AVIATION, INC.
Acquired May 1986

FRONTIER HOLDINGS, INC.
Acquired Oct. 1986 from People Express

PRO INC.
Ground support assets formerly owned by Eastern

BAR HARBOR AIRWAYS, INC.
Financing provided by Eastern

BRITT AIRWAYS, INC.
Feeds passengers to Continental

PEOPLE EXPRESS AIRLINES, INC.
Pays service fees to Continental

ROCKY MOUNTAIN AIRLINES, INC.
Feeds passengers to Continental's Denver hub

FRONTIER AIRLINES, INC.
In Chapter 11 since August 1986

PROVINCETOWN-BOSTON AIRLINE, INC.
Acquired from People Express for $1

Source: "House of Mirrors," *Wall Street Journal* (April 7, 1988): 1. Reprinted by permission of the *Wall Street Journal,* © 1988 Dow Jones & Company, Inc. All Rights Reserved Worldwide.

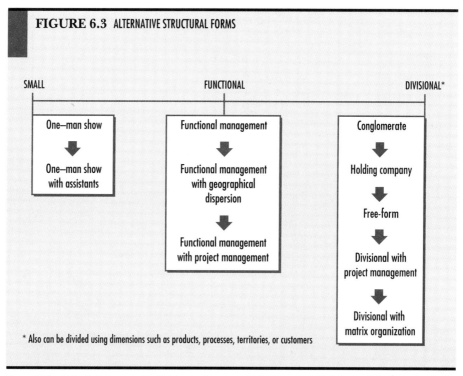

FIGURE 6.3 ALTERNATIVE STRUCTURAL FORMS

SMALL	FUNCTIONAL	DIVISIONAL*
One–man show ⬇ One–man show with assistants	Functional management ⬇ Functional management with geographical dispersion ⬇ Functional management with project management	Conglomerate ⬇ Holding company ⬇ Free-form ⬇ Divisional with project management ⬇ Divisional with matrix organization

* Also can be divided using dimensions such as products, processes, territories, or customers

Source: Shirley, R. C., M. H. Peters, and A. I. El-Ansary, *Strategy and Policy Formation: A Multifunctional Orientation* (New York: John Wiley & Sons, 1981), p. 239. Copyright © 1981 by John Wiley & Sons. Used by permission.

Strategic advantages. It is most appropriate to implement the functional form when the firm is pursuing a concentration or very high relatedness strategy. When the firm has a single product or only a few products, the functional structure is appropriate. Such a structure allows for maximum economy of scale and specialization of effort.

Strategic disadvantages. As the number of products, kinds of customers, or markets grow, coordination becomes increasingly difficult in the functional organization. In such a situation, a more complex organization is more appropriate.

GEOGRAPHIC

As the firm's markets become geographically diverse, even while the firm continues with closely related products aimed at similar kinds of customers, it is not unusual for the simple functional form to evolve into a geographic structure. Common functions continue to be grouped together within each geographic segment but not across segments. Figure 6.6 is an example of a generic geographic form.

FIGURE 6.4 A STAGES-OF-GROWTH MODEL

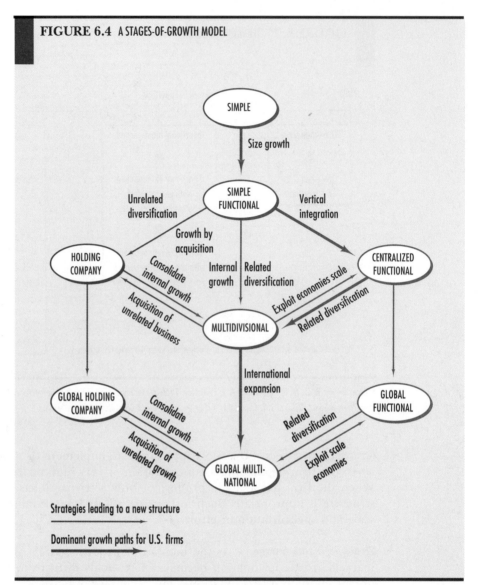

Strategic advantages.   A principal advantage of such a structure from a strategy implementation viewpoint is that the organization can focus on the needs of the customers in each geographic segment. Functional coordination within each geographic segment is relatively easy.

Strategic disadvantages.   A disadvantage from a strategy implementation viewpoint is that the firm's image in the minds of customers may become blurred

FIGURE 6.5 A FUNCTIONAL ORGANIZATION (THE DICTAPHONE CORPORATION)

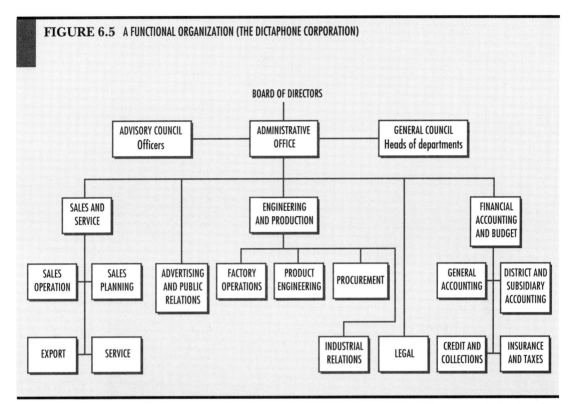

Source: J. A. Litterer, *Organizations: Structure and Behavior.* Copyright © 1963 by John Wiley & Sons, Inc. Reprinted by permission of John Wiley & Sons, Inc.

FIGURE 6.6 A GEOGRAPHIC ORGANIZATION

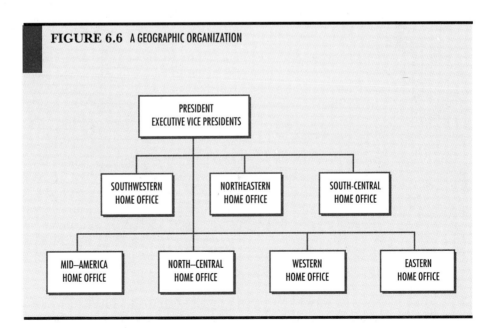

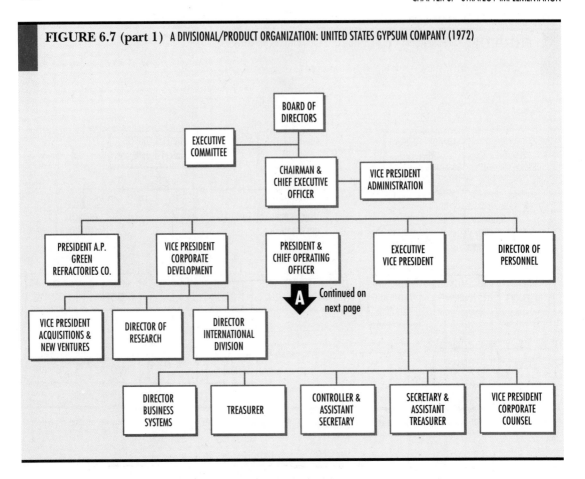

FIGURE 6.7 (part 1) A DIVISIONAL/PRODUCT ORGANIZATION: UNITED STATES GYPSUM COMPANY (1972)

if each geographic segment tailors itself. Coordination of a specific function such as production across geographic segments can become difficult. The structure can also be expensive because there is a duplication of functions across the various geographic segments and an added layer of management.[21]

DIVISIONAL/PRODUCT

As the firm further pursues related diversification, and as the number of products and number of customer segments grow, it is not unusual for the firm to evolve to a divisional or product structure. Figure 6.7 shows an example of this type of structure. Each product group is like a minicompany in itself, even though there are several functional specialties centralized at the corporate level. Some refer to such a structure as a product structure or a decentralized business structure with separate focus on a separate set of products or businesses.[22]

Strategic advantages. The primary strategic advantage of a divisional structure is that most of the resources associated with a specific group of products

FIGURE 6.7 (part 2)

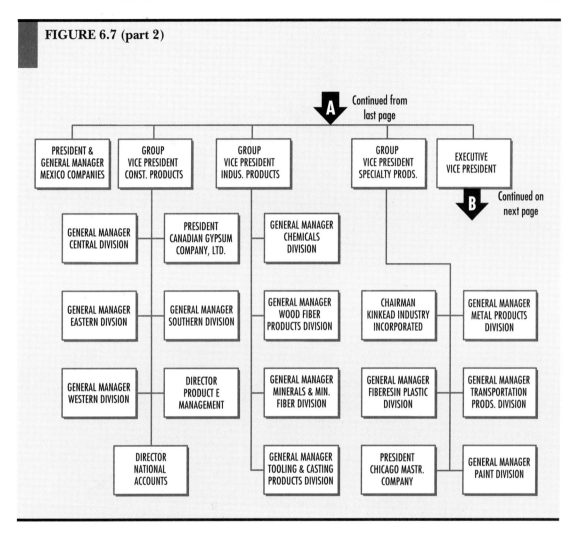

or businesses are grouped together, which allows for easier coordination within the division. Thus, it is assumed that the customers of the groups of products are better served.

Strategic disadvantages. Disadvantages of a divisional/product structure include the cost and duplication of functions within the division and more difficult coordination among divisions. Economies of scale are sometimes difficult to achieve in such a structure.

STRATEGIC BUSINESS UNIT/HOLDING COMPANY

If a firm pursues unrelated or conglomerate diversification as a strategy, it will frequently evolve into a strategic business unit/holding company organizational form. An SBU may be defined as a grouping of businesses or divisions

FIGURE 6.7 (part 3)

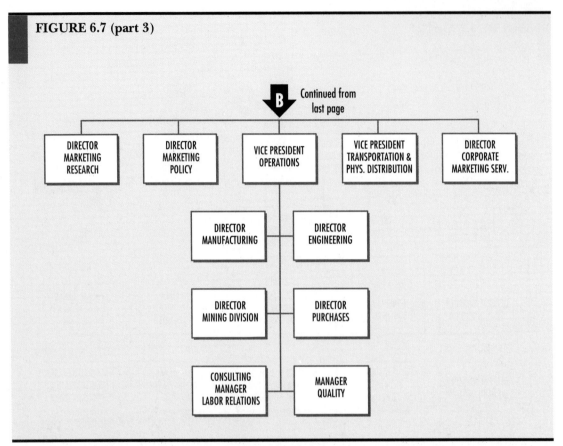

Source: Janger, A. R., *Corporate Oranization Structures: Manufacturing.* Copyright © 1973. Reprinted by permission of The Conference Board, Inc., New York.

based on important common strategic dimensions. An SBU organization is like a multiple divisional organization with an added layer of management. In such an organization, there is almost no strategic commonality among the SBUs within the firm. It is as if the parent firm is loosely overseeing a number of nearly autonomous companies. The term "holding company" is often used with such a structure. Figure 6.8 is a generic example of an SBU structure. Unlike the divisional/product structure, there are few functional specialists centralized at the corporate level.

Strategic advantages.   From a strategy viewpoint, such a structure is consistent with and mandated by a conglomerate or unrelated diversification strategy. A recognition that completely different products or services are offered to different markets or customer groups is consistent with such a structure.

Strategic disadvantages.   The SBU structure has several disadvantages. Coordinating the various SBUs into the overall firm can be very difficult. Resource

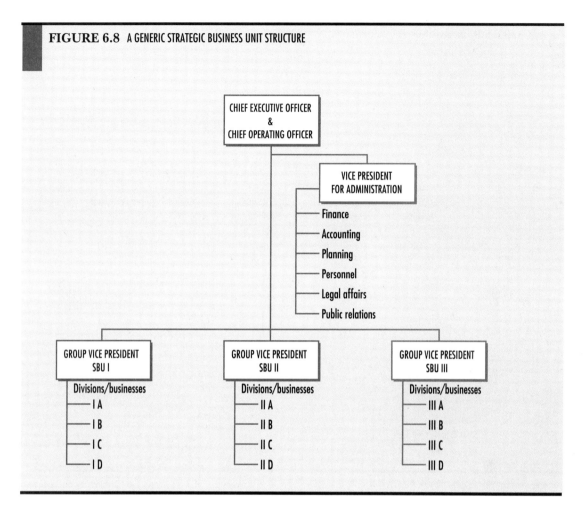

FIGURE 6.8 A GENERIC STRATEGIC BUSINESS UNIT STRUCTURE

allocation and control from the corporate level to the various SBUs is problematic, and duplication of staffs and functions at the various levels is also an issue.[23]

MATRIX

Partly as an attempt to deal with the coordination issues across various product/business lines while retaining functional specialization and economy of scale, some firms employ a matrix organizational structure. Figure 6.9, showing the Dow-Corning Company is an example. Various businesses do not completely "own" the functional resources as in a divisional or SBU structure. Rather, the businesses or product lines "borrow" the functional resources from the functional home offices.[24] Such a form evolved in the aerospace industry due to the growth, development, and subsequent completion of discrete projects in that industry.[25]

FIGURE 6.9 THE MATRIX OR GRID ORGANIZATION: DOW-CORNING 1973

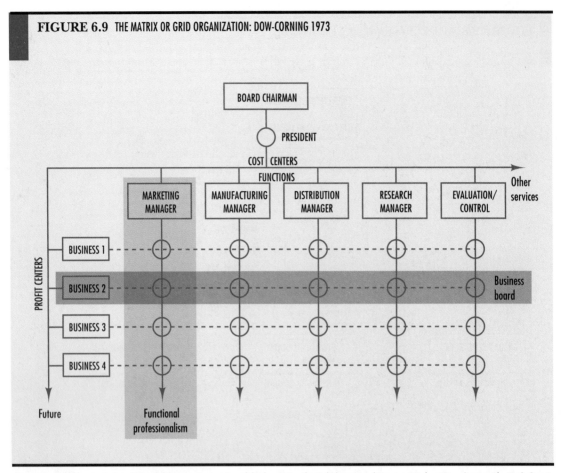

Strategic advantages.   A strategic advantage of such a form is the ability to deal with a number of new or constantly changing products or projects. Thus, a matrix structure may be appropriate in high-technology industries such as aerospace, computers, and electronics with streams of new products as part of their competitive strategy.

Strategic disadvantages.   Although increased coordination is the desired goal, matrix forms have had their share of coordination problems.[26] Matrices are very expensive and even dysfunctional in stable organizations with few products. Communications may become garbled. Finally, some people have trouble reporting to more than one individual.

MULTINATIONAL

As a firm's strategy becomes global, the organizational form can become quite complex. As Figure 6.4 indicates, a global strategy may be associated with a global holding company, a global multinational, or a global functional structure. The decision of whether to use a global functional structure or a global multinational structure is partly a function of whether the parent decides to place the primary profit centers at the function or at the region.[27]

Strategic advantages.   From a strategic viewpoint, there must be an ability to focus on the various countries or geographic segments in a multinational structure. The duplication in functions and staff is frequently recognized as a necessary price to pay for the ability to better serve the target markets.[28]

Strategic disadvantages.   Coordination may be difficult, but many firms have recognized that they do not have many choices in the era of intense foreign competition. (Partly because of the intensity of this competition, Chapter 9 is devoted exclusively to the issue of international strategy.)

MERGER, ACQUISITION, AND STRUCTURAL FIT

This section on alternative organizational structures has highlighted one of the reasons why many acquisitions fail. Each structural form has its strengths and weaknesses and seems to be appropriate for specific strategies. Attempts to merge together two or more different companies with different structures resulting from slightly different strategies have been associated with the subsequent failure of many acquisitions. If one adds different corporate cultures to the equation, the deck seems to be stacked against the merger of unrelated companies. (Chapter 3 discusses mergers and acquisitions in terms of strategic fit in detail.)

SYSTEMS/PROCESSES

BUDGETS

Budgets serve several functions: planning, communication, and control, to name a few. In the area of planning or formulation, the amount of resources required for a strategy is frequently associated with the decision to pursue the strategy. The risk of the plan, in terms of the probability of the payoff, also is considered. Once those strategic and financial decisions and a commitment to allocate the resources have been made, however, the budget serves a communication function in the organization as the strategy is implemented. Allocation of financial resources in a budget signals or communicates the real strategic priorities.

There are two categories of budgets: performance or operational and resource.[29] Performance or operational budgets are targets or expected results associated with levels of activity such as sales and production. Resource budgets typically consist of capital budgets and plan the amount of resources needed to accomplish the operational budget. As the strategy is implemented, these budgets communicate the formulated strategy. Indeed, some analysts argue that there are two kinds of strategies: the stated strategy found in public statements like annual reports and the real or operative strategy found in the capital budget. For example, the real or operative strategy of some oil companies in the late 1970s indicated that they were primarily oil companies, as over 90 percent of their capital budget was petroleum related. Their stated strategies, however, indicated that they were diversified energy companies.

The budgeting system must be consistent with the strategy for successful implementation. For example, if the strategy assumes conglomeration and a holding-company kind of structure is implemented, the budgeting system should be much more decentralized than in a centralized structure with a more concentrated strategy and functional structure.

Govindarajan argued for separate systems to implement separate strategies in multibusiness organizations. His study focused on "what is perhaps the most crucial aspect of strategy implementation in large, multibusiness organizations: recognizing that different business units within the same corporation often pursue different strategies and that the administrative mechanisms that corporate headquarters use to manage those businesses should differ."[30] If Govindarajan is correct, the added complexity of multiple administrative implementation systems may be another reason why conglomerates are hard to fathom and manage.

PROCEDURES

Like budgets and structures, the detailed procedures an organization uses—"the way we do business" at the operating level—must be consistent with the strategy for successful implementation. For example, the procedure used to deal with customer returns at a major mail order business like Land's End or L. L. Bean must be consistent with the overall strategy of customer satisfaction and sales growth. Such procedures, which allow unlimited, unquestioned returns, are usually different from those used by some discount chains, which seem to follow the rule, "Let the buyer beware" or "Once the customer has bought the item, it is the customer's problem." Likewise, procedures concerning when to shut down a production line due to quality problems must be consistent with the firm's strategy on quality.

INFORMATION SYSTEMS

Historically, many strategists studied information systems under the heading of implementation systems. The concern was whether the information system, in its budgeting and accounting modes, and in its record-keeping function for sales and production, could produce the correct information in a timely fashion for internal consumption. In such a mode, a concern was to control the cost of the information system. According to one analyst, "Because the then-current view was that of a 'cost center' or expense, the Information System budget was generally established on the basis of the prior years' budgets."[31]

This book takes the view that information systems have advanced to the stage of technological evolution that they can be used as strategic competitive weapons in many industries. In this role, information systems may be indistinguishable from a firm's products, services, or other competitive assets.[32] Thus, information systems are covered in greater detail in Chapters 4 and 5 as components of competitive business-level and functional-level strategy.

Some people have asked if information systems produce the right kind of information for strategic decisions.[33] A company might ask, does our system routinely collect and process needed information on market trends, customer preferences and demand, competitor moves, and other environmental changes so that effective strategic decisions can be made? Grigsby, Stahl, and Barman hypothesized different information needs and different strategic decision models as functions of organizational centrality and formality when an organization contemplates acquisition.[34] Figure 6.10 shows the relationship

FIGURE 6.10 ORGANIZATIONAL DETERMINANTS OF STRATEGIC DECISION MODELS

ORGANIZATIONAL CENTRALITY	ORGANIZATIONAL FORMALITY	
	Formal	Informal
Centralized	Systematic bureaucracy (hierarchical decision making)	Managerial autocracy (individual decision making)
Decentralized	Adaptive planning (group decision making)	Political expediency (coalition decision making)

Source: Grigsby, D. J., M. J. Stahl. and S. Barman. "The Structure and Process of Corporate Acquisition Decisions," *Business Insights* (Fall–Winter, 1989): 41.

between two dimensions of organizational structure and type of strategic decision making.

CROSS-FUNCTIONAL GROUPS/TASK FORCES

In implementing a new strategy, some firms bring together temporary groups
of high-profile personnel to start the implementation. Such groups typically
are drawn from every major function throughout the organization to signal
to the entire organization that the new strategy affects all. Typically, the new
strategy cuts horizontally across the vertical functions.[35] Rather than reorganizing the structure, such cross-functional groups or task forces are usually temporary. Rather than replacing the structure, such teams usually help the structure implement a new strategy. For example, in the Capsugel Division of
Warner-Lambert, "Qualitivity" teams were installed with representatives from
the major functions to cut across the major functions and systems to improve
quality.[36] In implementing its organizational change focusing on quality, Xerox refers to the implementation of "special, cross-organizational, task
teams."[37]

BOX 6.2   CAPSUGEL-GREENWOOD QUALITY POLICY

Capsugel is the leader in the production of high quality, two-piece, hard gelatin capsules
and related services to our customers. To continue our position, we must:

Work with and assist our suppliers to provide us with products that meet or exceed our
needs. Our product's quality is only as good as our own quality systems and those of our
suppliers.

Continually strive to understand, control, and improve our processes and procedures
through participation in problem solving teams.

Do it right the first time. Never forget that you, no matter what job you perform, are
responsible for the quality of your work.

Focus on the needs of the customer by providing more and better products and services
than our competitors. Routine assessment of our capability and our customers' needs will
help maintain Capsugel as the market leader.

Never compromise our values regardless of time pressures or workload.

The Greenwood operation will embrace a restless discontent for the status quo, and
thereby strive for improvement in the way we operate for the benefit of our customers,
suppliers, and our employees.

Source: Capsugel/Warner-Lambert Quality Steering Committee, Greenwood, S.C. (1989), reprinted with permission.

■ POLICIES

Policies, or guides for action, are represented by the collection of methods, rules, and practices the organization uses to implement strategy and administer or operate the organization. Policies are more detailed statements than strategies. The choice of policies is meant to flow from and be consistent with the choice of mission, objectives, and strategies.

Just as strategies exist at several levels, so do policies. An example of a corporate-level policy is IBM's "no layoff" policy. In good and bad times, the company has tenaciously stuck to its policy of not laying off employees. K-Mart, Cadillac, and Chevrolet all have customer service policies—probably very different from one another.

A good example of a detailed policy on quality is found in the Capsugel-Greenwood Quality Policy (Box 6.2). Capsugel is a division of Warner-Lambert Pharmaceutical Company. Such a divisional quality policy is consistent with the flows from Warner-Lambert's creed (see Chapter 2) of "providing high-quality health care."

The number of firms with quality policies has been growing as many more firms on a worldwide basis have been competing with strategies based on quality. Garvin found that the success of the quality strategy is based in part on the thoroughness or soundness of the quality policies and the understanding of those policies by both management and the work force.[38]

■ CULTURE/SHARED VALUES

THE NATURE AND IMPORTANCE OF CULTURE

A major implementation variable is corporate culture, known as "shared values" by some.[39] Many organizational theorists today write of the importance of corporate culture in implementation and argue that culture needs to be considered in the formulation of strategy.[40] The title of an article on corporate culture from the popular business press is directly tied to the theme of this section: "What Corporate Culture Is and How Shared Values Contribute to the Success or Failure of Strategy."[41]

Steiner and Steiner introduced the concept of culture in a broad sociological perspective. "In a society, the term *culture* refers to a predictable set of values transmitted across generations. When embodied in institutions and rituals, these values direct social behavior toward essential goals."[42] Daft described organizational culture in a more specific organizational context and indicated the ways managers reinforce culture. "Culture is the set of key values, beliefs and understandings that are shared by members of an organization. Managers can design ceremonies and slogans, devise symbols, and repeat stories to disseminate the underlying values and philosophy that are consistent with organizational strategy. These devices are means through which organizational members can reach a shared understanding about these values."[43] For example, Ford used the slogan "Quality is Job 1" to communicate the value of quality to employees and customers. Genentech held elaborate beer bashes on Fridays to communicate the value of openness among its scientists and managers. Box 6.3 describes three examples of corporate culture from the Fortune 500.

How important is corporate culture? Ott argued that organizational decision patterns can be predicted from the values inherent in the corporate culture of a firm.[44] The potential for analyzing competitors and predicting their decisions in such a fashion (as discussed in Chapter 4) should not be minimized.

In their best seller on America's best-run companies, *In Search of Excellence*, Peters and Waterman directly addressed the importance of corporate culture in one of their eight basic principles. The eighth and summary principle of excellent companies is "simultaneous loose-tight properties—fostering a climate where there is dedication to the central values of the company combined with tolerance for all employees who accept those values."[45] Values seem to be as important for a corporation as they are for a society in shaping behavior.

CHANGING CORPORATE CULTURE

Corporate cultures tend to be enduring; they change slowly and only with great effort.[46] In an appropriately titled article, "The Corporate Culture at IBM: How It Reinforces Strategy," a business publication described the rigid bureaucracy and concern for rules at IBM.[47] Six years later, the same periodi-

---

BOX 6.3   CORPORATE CULTURE IN THREE ORGANIZATIONS

- **International Business Machines Corporation,** where marketing drives a service philosophy that is almost unparalleled. The company keeps a hot line open twenty-four hours a day, seven days a week, to service IBM products.

- **Digital Equipment Corporation,** where an emphasis on innovation creates freedom with responsibility. Employees can set their own hours and working style, but they are expected to articulate and support their activities with evidence of progress.

- **Delta Airlines, Inc.,** where a focus on customer service produces a high degree of teamwork. Employees will substitute in other jobs to keep planes flying and baggage moving.

Source: "What Corporate Culture Is and How Shared Values Contribute to the Success or Failure of Strategy," *Business Week* (October 27, 1980): 43.

cal reported that IBM's culture had yielded to new values and shed some of its bureaucracy.[48] The more recent article described how the corporate culture had been slowly changing to accommodate a different competitive market.

Although corporate culture is not easy to change, and the process of change takes much time, a number of firms have recognized the importance of changing culture as they embark on new competitive strategies. New strategies based on quality require special cultural change because the old culture may have valued throughput and schedules. Xerox, Procter & Gamble, and the Capsugel Division of Warner-Lambert are three examples of firms that have invested years to change corporate cultures toward greater emphasis on quality.[49]

Cultural change is effected with a variety of implementation techniques discussed in this chapter including training, motivational programs, new structures, new systems, cross-functional groups, and new stories or symbols spread by management. For example, P&G circulates stories about how its production-line workers get close to the customer to help the customer resolve quality complaints. A story is told of a P&G production-line worker who, in an attempt to resolve a quality issue, called a customer and investigated the length of time and the temperature at which the customer had baked a Duncan Hines angel food cake.[50]

SUMMARY

This chapter studies some of the issues in strategy implementation, the less-visible, longer-term phase of the strategy process. Implementation consists of the issues involved in putting the formulated strategy to work. No strategy, no matter how brilliantly formulated, will succeed if it cannot be implemented.

The major implementation issues studied in this chapter are motivation, structure, systems/processes, cross-functional groups/task forces, policies, and corporate culture/shared values.

Although some take the position that strategy determines structure, and others argue that structure limits and determines strategy, this chapter holds that issue to be moot. The real issue is whether the strategy and the structure are consistent. Several failed mergers attest to the problems of inconsistency between strategy and structure.

The motivation of both managers and nonmanagers to implement new strategy needs to be considered in the strategy implementation program. Training and the alignment of individual goals with the new strategic goals are used to address motivation. Several organizational structures are reviewed. In general, as the strategy evolves away from concentration and relatedness, the structure becomes more complex. The functional form has like activities grouped together. It is consistent with a concentration or very high relatedness strategy. In the geographic form, all of the corporate activities in a defined geographic/territorial area are grouped together. This form is consistent with a geographically dispersed organization that wishes to focus its activities on the various geographic markets. The divisional form groups all corporate activities associated with a group of products or businesses. It is consistent with a strategy of an increased number of products or different markets. The strategic business unit form groups all corporate activities that are strategically linked together but different from other corporate strategies. The SBU form is consistent with a conglomerate or unrelated strategy. The matrix form consists of businesses overlaid, or cutting across, the various functions and is consistent with a strategy consisting of many products/programs/projects, each of finite duration. The multinational form consists of a global matrix or holding company structure. It is consistent with a global strategy.

Systems/processes are viewed as an important issue in implementation. Budgets communicate the importance of strategies by the resources they command. Procedures communicate strategies and put them into practice at the operating level.

Cross-functional groups/task forces are frequently used in the implementation of new strategy. Such groups, typically drawn from the entire organization, communicate the cross-functional nature and the importance of the new strategy.

Policies are guides for action that are more detailed than strategies. Corporate culture consists of shared corporate values that guide action throughout the firm. Such values, if consistently implemented, are characteristic of successful firms. Although changing corporate culture is not easy, many firms recognize the importance of such a change if a major new strategy is to be implemented.

DISCUSSION QUESTIONS

1. Describe the link between middle-management motivation and strategy implementation.
2. Why is the subject of corporate structure important in a merger?
3. Why is the subject of corporate culture important in a merger?
4. Does strategy determine structure, or does structure determine strategy? Defend your answer.
5. Explain the association between the relatedness dimension in corporate strategy and structural complexity.
6. What kinds of strategies are consistent with functional, geographic, divisional, SBU, and matrix structures?
7. Describe at least one advantage and disadvantage of each of the five structural forms in the preceding question.
8. How do cross-functional groups/task forces help strategy implementation?
9. How does corporate culture reinforce strategy?

ENDNOTES

1. Stahl, M. J., and G. M. Bounds, eds. *Competing Globally Through Customer Value: The Management of Strategic Supra-systems.* (Westport, Conn.: Quorum Books, 1991): xv.

2. Mintzberg, H., *Mintzberg on Management* (New York: The Free Press, 1989).

3. Nutt, P. C., "Tactics of Implementation," *Academy of Management Journal* (1986): 231.

4. "Do Mergers Really Work," *Business Week* (June 3, 1985): 92.

5. Siehl, C., D. Smith, and A. Omura, "After the Merger: Should Executives Stay or Go?" *Academy of Management Executive* (February 1990): 50–60.

6. Guth, W. D., and I. C. MacMillan, "Strategy Implementation versus Middle Management Self-Interest," *Strategic Management Journal* (1986): 313–327; Vroom, V., *Work and Motivation* (New York: John Wiley & Sons, 1964).

7. Judge, W., and M. J. Stahl, "Decision Modeling Managerial Effort in Strategy Implementation: A Multinational Test," *Proceedings of the National Decision Sciences Institute* (November 1990).

8. American Society for Quality Control, *Quality: Executive Priority or Afterthought?* (Milwaukee: American Society for Quality Control, 1989): 11.

9. "Here Comes GM's Saturn: More Than a Car, It's GM's Hope for Reinventing Itself," *Business Week* (April 9, 1990): 56–62.

10. Kearns, D. T., "Leadership Through Quality," *Academy of Management Executive* (May 1990): 87.

11. Judge, W., et al., "Application to Capsugel/Warner-Lambert," in Stahl and Bounds, *The New Competitive Mandate.*

12. Chandler, A. D., Jr., *Strategy and Structure* (Cambridge, Mass.: MIT Press, 1962): 16.

13. Hall, D. J., and M. A. Saias, "Strategy Follows Structure," *Strategic Management Journal* (1980): 149–163.

14. "The High Flier," *Business Week* (March 10, 1986): 104.

15. "House of Mirrors," *Wall Street Journal* (April 7, 1988): 1.

16. "Lorenzo May Land a Little Short of the Runway," *Business Week* (February 5, 1990): 46.

17. "Lorenzo Plans to Sell Continental Air Stake to Scandinavian Air," *Wall Street Journal* (August 9, 1990): 1.

18. Shirley, R. C., M. H. Peters, and A. I. El-Ansary, *Strategy and Policy Formation: A Multifunctional Orientation,* 2d ed. (New York: John Wiley & Sons, 1981): 238–250.

19. Galbraith, J. R., and D. A. Nathanson, *Strategy Implementation: The Role of Structure and Process* (St. Paul: West Publishing Co., 1978): Chapter 8.

20. Ibid., pp. 7–10.

21. Shirley, Peters, and El-Ansary, *Strategic and Policy Formation,* pp. 238–250.

22. Hax, A. C., and N. C. Majluf, *Strategic Management: An Integrative Perspective* (Englewood Cliffs, N.J.: Prentice-Hall, 1984): 383–399.

23. Ibid., pp. 383–399.

24. Galbraith and Nathanson, *Strategy Implementation,* pp. 7–10.

25. Cleland, D. I., and W. R. King, *Systems Analysis and Project Management,* 3d ed. (New York: McGraw-Hill, 1983).

26. Cleland, D. I., and W. R. King, eds., *Project Management Handbook,* 2d ed. (New York: Van-Nostrand Reinhold, 1988); Davis, S. M., and P. R. Lawrence, "Problems of Matrix Organizations," *Harvard Business Review* (May–June 1978): 131–142.

27. Galbraith and Nathanson, *Strategy Implementation,* p. 110.

28. Lorange, P., *Implementation of Strategic Planning* (Englewood Cliffs, N.J.: Prentice-Hall, 1982): 198.

29. Gray, J., and K. S. Johnston, *Accounting for Management Action* (New York: McGraw-Hill, 1973): 26–27.

30. Govindarajan, V., "A Contingency Approach to Strategy Implementation at the Business-Unit Level: Integrating Administrative Mechanisms with Strategy," *Academy of Management Journal* 31 (December 1988): 828–853.

31. King, W. R., "Strategic Planning for Information Resources: The Evolution of Concepts and Practice," *Information Resources Management Journal* (Fall 1988): 1–9.

32. Mason, R., "Information System Technology and Corporate Strategy," in *The Information Systems Research Challenge, Proceedings,* ed. F. W. McFarlan (Boston: Harvard Business School Press, 1984).

33. Radford, K., *Information Systems for Strategic Decisions* (Reston, Va.: Reston Publishing Co., 1978); Rinaldi, D., and T. Jastrgembski, "Executive Information Systems: Put Strategic Data at your CEO's Fingertips," *Computerworld* 20 (October 27, 1986): 37–51.

34. Grigsby, D. J., M. J. Stahl, and S. Barman, "The Structure and Process of Corporate Acquisition Decisions," *Business Insights* (Fall–Winter 1989): 40–45.

35. Sirkin, H., and G. Stalk, Jr., "Fix the Process, Not the

Problem," *Harvard Business Review* (July–August 1990): 26–33; Langley, C. J., and M. C. Holcomb, "Achieving Customer Value Through Logistics Management," in Stahl and Bounds, *The New Competitive Mandate.*

36. Judge et al., "Application to Capsugel-Warner-Lambert."

37. Kearns, "Leadership Through Quality."

38. Garvin, D. A., "Quality Problems, Policies, and Attitudes and the United States and Japan," *Academy of Management Journal* 29, no. 4 (1986): 653–673.

39. Barney, J., "Organizational Culture: Can it be a Source of Sustained Competitive Advantage?" *Academy of Management Review* 11 (1986): 656–665; Saffold, G., "Culture Traits, Strength, and Organizational Performance," *Academy of Management Review* 13 (1988): 546–558; Schien, E., *Organizational Culture and Leadership* (San Francisco: Josey-Bass, 1985); Weiner, Y., "Forms of Value Systems: A Focus on Organizational Effectiveness and Cultural Change and Maintenance," *Academy of Management Review* 13 (1988): 534–545.

40. Sapienza, A. M., "Believing is Seeing: How Culture Influences the Decisions Top Managers Make," in *Gaining Control of the Corporate Culture,* ed. R. H. Kilman, M. J. Saxton, R. Serpa & Associates (San Francisco: Josey-Bass, 1985): 66–83; Shrivastava, P. "Integrating Strategy Formulation with Organization Culture," *Journal of Business Strategy* 5, no. 3 (1985): 103–111; Walsh, J. P., and L. Fahey, "The Role of Negotiated Belief Structures in Strategy Making," *Journal of Management* 12 (1986): 325–338.

41. *Business Week* (October 27, 1980): 42–48.

42. Steiner, G. A., and J. F. Steiner, *Business, Government, and Society,* 5th ed. (New York: Random House, 1988): 504.

43. Daft, R. L., *Organization Theory and Design,* 2d. ed. (St. Paul: West Publishing Co., 1986): 488.

44. Ott, J. S., *The Organizational Culture Perspective.* (Chicago: R. D. Irwin, 1989): 197.

45. Peters, T. J., and R. H. Waterman, Jr., *In Search of Excellence* (New York: Harper and Row, 1982): 10.

46. Lorsch, J., "Managing Culture: The Invisible Barrier to Strategic Change," *California Management Review* 28 (1986): 95–109; Miller, D., C. Droge, and J. M. Toulouse, "Strategic Process and Content as Mediators Between Organizational Context and Structure," *Academy of Management Journal* 31 (September 1988): 544–569; "The Difficult Task of Changing Corporate Culture: The Case of Corning Glass," *Wall Street Journal* (April 22, 1983): 1; Kilmann, Saxton, Serpa & Associates, *Gaining Control of the Corporate Culture.*

47. *Wall Street Journal* (April 8,1982): 1.

48. "Vaunted IBM Culture Yields to New Values: One Less Layer of Bureaucracy" *Wall Street Journal* (November 11, 1988): 1.

49. Judge et al., "Application to Capsugel/Warner-Lambert"; Locander, W., and R. Saxton, "Application to Procter & Gamble"; Locander, W., G. B. Bounds, and W. Osterhoff, "Application to Xerox"; all in Stahl and Bounds, *Competing Globally Through Customer Value.*

50. "Procter & Gamble Rewrites the Marketing Rules," *Fortune* (November 6, 1989): 91.

ADDITIONAL READINGS

Ansoff, H. I. *Implanting Strategic Management.* Englewood Cliffs, N.J.: Prentice-Hall, 1984.

Baker, E. "Managing Organizational Culture." *Management Review* 20 (1980): 8–13.

Bourgeois, L. J., and D. R. Brodwin. "Strategic Implementation." *Strategic Management Journal* (1984): 241–264.

Channon, D. *Strategy and Structure in British Enterprise.* Boston: Harvard Business School, Division of Research, 1973.

Child, J. "Organization Structure, Environment and Performance: The Role of Strategic Choice." *Sociology* 6 (1972): 1–22.

Fredericks, P., and Venkatraman, N. "The Rise of Strategy Support Systems." *Sloan Management Review* 29 (Spring 1988): 47–54.

Fredrickson, J. W. "The Strategic Decision Process and Organization Structure." *Academy of Management Review* 11 (1986): 280–297.

Govindarajan, V. "Implementing Competitive Strategies at the Business-Unit Level." *Strategic Management Journal* 10, no. 3 (May–June 1989): 251–269.

Gupta, A. K., and V. Govindarajan. "Business Unit Strategy, Managerial Characteristics, and Business Unit Effectiveness at Strategy Implementation." *Academy of Management Journal* 27 (March 1984): 25–41.

Miller, D. "Strategy Making and Structure: Analysis and Implications for Performance." *Academy of Management Journal* 30 (1987): 7–32.

———. "Relating Porter's Business Strategies to Environment and Structure: Analysis and Performance Implications." *Academy of Management Journal* 31 (1988): 280–308.

Miller, D., and J. Toulouse. "Chief Executive Personality and Corporate Strategy and Structure." *Management Science* 32 (1986): 1389–1409.

Miles, R., and C. Snow. *Organizational Strategy, Structure and Process.* New York: McGraw-Hill, 1978.

Mintzberg, H. "Strategy Making in Three Modes." *California Management Review* 16, no. 2 (1973): 44–58.

Mintzberg, J. *The Structuring of Organizations.* Englewood Cliffs, N.J.: Prentice-Hall, 1979.

Nath, R., ed. *Comparative Management: A Regional View.* Cambridge, Mass.: Ballinger, 1988.

Rumelt, R. *Strategy, Structure, and Economic Performance.* Cambridge, Mass.: Harvard Univesity Press, 1974.

Westley, F. R. "Middle Managers and Stragegy: Micro-dynamics of Inclusion." *Strategic Management Journal* 11, no. 5 (September 1990): 337–351.

CHAPTER SEVEN

Evaluation and Control

Once the strategic choice decisions have been made, the strategic plan has been formulated, and the strategy has been implemented, there is still a crucial decision needed to ensure long-term success. A strategic evaluation and control process needs to be decided on and installed so that the organization can monitor performance and take corrective action if needed. Strategic evaluation and control is defined as the process of evaluating strategic plans and monitoring organizational performance so that actual performance can be compared with desired performance and corrective action taken if needed.

An organization that does not control its activities may find itself threatened with its very survival. As Box 7.1 indicates, SmithKline Beckman became a takeover candidate partly because it lost control of its sales and other activities.

THE IMPORTANCE OF STRATEGIC CONTROL

Why does actual performance sometimes not match the performance desired in the strategic objectives? Was the strategic plan severely flawed in its formulation? Did management's implementation of the plan fall short? Were there uncontrollable factors external to the organization that prevented achievement of the plan? These questions suggest the importance of evaluation and control and a need to understand how the plan can go awry.

INTENDED AND REALIZED STRATEGIES

Henry Mintzberg, one of the foremost theorists in the area of strategic management, tells us that no matter how well the organization plans its strategy, a different strategy may emerge. He coined the terms "intended strategies" and "realized strategies" and related them to deliberate, unrealized, and emergent strategies, shown in Figure 7.1. Starting with the intended or

---

BOX 7.1 FALLING SALES ENDANGERED SURVIVAL OF SMITHKLINE BECKMAN

For years, SmithKline Beckman, the pharmaceutical giant with annual sales of nearly $5 billion, rode the success of the ulcer medication Tagamet. For a while, Tagamet had the distinction of being the biggest-selling prescription drug of all time. In the words of CEO Henry Wendt, "It was 'a pharmaceutical gusher,' and for years his biggest worry was meeting demand. 'Make as much as you can,' he told production executives in a SmithKline magazine. 'As much as you can!' "[a]

The euphoria induced by Tagamet's success unfortunately obscured management's view of the changing market. A painful period in SmithKline's history resulted during which the company experienced declining sales of Tagamet, saw its president resign, suffered a stock price drop, and became the target of takeover speculation. "The shakeup goes on at SmithKline Beckman," *Business Week* reported. "Citing 'policy differences' with Chairman Henry Wendt, President George Ebright resigned on Jan. 25. On the same day, SKB announced dismal 1988 earnings. With declining sales of ulcer-fighter Tagamet and a big third-quarter writie-off, SKB's 1988 operating income plunged nearly 56%, to $364 million."[b] While producing as much as the company could, SmithKline seemed to lose sight of competitor's moves in the area. According to one source, "Management was slow to respond to the influx of competition in the anti-ulcer market. As a result, Tagamet has lost—and continues to lose—significant market share."[c]

Some knowledgeable individuals attribute many of SmithKline's woes to a loss of control. "SmithKline lost track of Tagamet's rate of sales," said the *Wall Street Journal*. "Mr. Wendt, acknowledging that he shares responsibility for the surprise, adds, 'The management of this business lost control of this extremely important product in the largest market.' "[d] Partly as a result of its weakened condition, SmithKline Beckman remained the subject of takeover speculation in early 1989[e] In July of that year, SmithKline Beckman merged with Beecham PLC of Great Britain.[f]

---

[a] "Drop in Tagamet Sales is Putting SmithKline in Danger of Takeover," *Wall Street Journal* (January 13, 1989): 1.
[b] "SmithKline Beckman: Developing an Ulcer?" *Business Week* (February 6, 1989): 43.
[c] "SmithKline Beckman," *Value Line Investment Survey* (February 10, 1989): 1270.
[d] *Wall Street Journal* (January 13, 1989): 1.
[e] *Value Line Investment Survey* (February 10, 1989); *Wall Street Journal* (January 13, 1989).
[f] "The Drug Industry," *Value Line Investment Survey* (August 11, 1989): 1254.

---

planned strategies, he related the five types of strategies in the following manner: "(1) Intended strategies that get realized; these may be called *deliberate* strategies. (2) Intended strategies that do not get realized; these may be called *unrealized* strategies. (3) Realized strategies that were never intended; these may be called *emergent* strategies."[1]

There are a number of ways in which the realized strategy can become

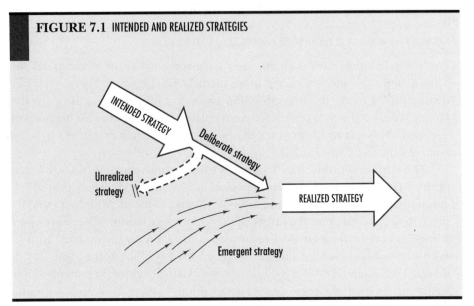

FIGURE 7.1 INTENDED AND REALIZED STRATEGIES

Source: Mintzberg, H., "The Strategy Concept I: Five P's for Strategy," *California Management Review* (Fall 1987): 14. Copyright 1987 by The Regents of the University of California. Reprinted from the *California Management Review*, Vol. 30, No. 3. By permission of The Regents.

different from the planned or intended strategy. The intended and realized strategies may differ because of unrealistic strategic decisions, poor judgments about the external environment, managerial incompetence in implementing the strategic decisions, uncontrollable changes in the external environment, or a failure in leadership to motivate individuals to pursue the intended strategy. Recognizing the number of different ways that intended and realized strategies may differ underscores the importance of evaluation and control systems so that the firm can monitor its performance and take corrective action if the actual performance differs from the intended strategies and planned results.

THE RENEWAL FACTOR

The importance of strategic controls was underscored in a recent book by Robert Waterman (of *In Search of Excellence* fame). In the more recent book, *The Renewal Factor: How the Best Get and Keep the Competitive Edge*, Waterman described the characteristics of organizations that effectively manage change and adapt their strategies, systems, products, and operations so that they prosper from the forces shaping the competition.[2] One of Waterman's renewal factors is "friendly facts and congenial controls."

The renewing companies treat facts as friends and financial controls as liberating. Morgan Guaranty and Wells Fargo not only survive but thrive all through the troubled waters of bank deregulation because their control systems are sound, their risk is contained, and they know themselves and the competitive situation so well. Meanwhile, the renewers maintain tight, accurate financial controls. Their people don't regard controls as an imposition of autocracy, but as the benign checks and balances that allow them to be creative and free.[3]

If people know where the control limits are, they have the freedom to operate within the limits. If limits are not known, people can only wait until a manager autocratically tells them they have gone too far in the manager's opinion.

CHARACTERISTICS OF CONTROL AND THE ENVIRONMENT

In designing evaluation and control activities, an organization must consider both controllable and uncontrollable phenomena. Attention must also be paid to the kinds of changes that exist in the external environment.

CONTROL TYPES

Lorange, Morton, and Ghoshal argued that organizations face situations with different degrees of control.[4] Each situation is a different control type. Figure 7.2 describes the alignment of degrees of control and control types. It is important for the organization to classify the situations in terms of degrees of control so that it can implement appropriate corrective action. Even uncon-

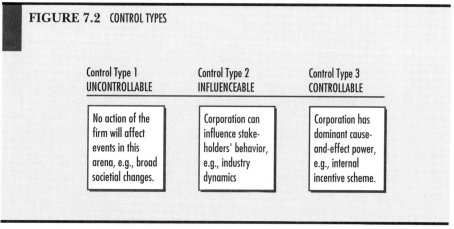

FIGURE 7.2   CONTROL TYPES

Control Type 1 UNCONTROLLABLE	Control Type 2 INFLUENCEABLE	Control Type 3 CONTROLLABLE
No action of the firm will affect events in this arena, e.g., broad societial changes.	Corporation can influence stake-holders' behavior, e.g., industry dynamics	Corporation has dominant cause-and-effect power, e.g., internal incentive scheme.

Source: Reprinted by permission from p. 9 of *Strategic Control Systems* by P. Lorange, M. Morton, and S. Ghoshal. Copyright © 1986 by West Publishing Company. All rights reserved.

trollable situations require a response from the organization if they affect the firm's strategies and objectives. For example, in the 1980s, organizations could not control the increasing numbers of dual-career families, but employers could respond by instituting liberal child-care policies to accommodate working couples with children. An example of a controllable situation is one of declining sales due to a change in sales commissions. The employer has the power to institute a more powerful commission structure to revitalize sales.

ENVIRONMENTAL CHANGES

The concept of organizational slack offers another way to view the type of control system that may be appropriate for the situation or type of change facing an organization.[5] Proponents of organizational slack argue that an organization should leave some slack in the utilization of its resources or maintain some unused capacity so that the organization can respond to changes in its environment. Thompson hypothesized that the principal corporate purpose of slack is to protect and insulate the organization from volatility in its external environment.[6] If dramatic unforeseen competitive threats arise, or external opportunities develop, the theory suggests that the organization needs some underutilized resources or potential in order to capitalize on the opportunities or counter the threats. Slack is not a substitute for controls; rather, it allows for dramatic, uncontrollable, unplanned changes in the environment.

Sharfman et al. presented an analysis of environmental changes classified by their speed and extent (Figure 7.3). Their classification serves as a prelude to understanding the amount of organizational slack appropriate for a situation. A firm operating in the upper-left quadrant of Figure 7.3, faced with slow and small environmental changes, does not need to possess much slack. On the other hand, an organization operating in an environment with fast and large changes (lower-right quadrant) must consider significant amounts of organizational slack if it is to respond to those external environmental changes. The kinds of environmental changes and the amount of slack should be reflected in the width of the tolerances around the standards or in the deviations in organizational performance permitted before corrective action is pursued in a control sense. For example, some petroleum companies maintain a presence in several forms of energy in case there is another dramatic change in the worldwide oil situation.

EXTENT OF EVALUATION AND CONTROL

There is a difference between strategic evaluation and control systems and operational control systems. Strategic evaluation and control systems include evaluation of the appropriateness of the objectives and the strategies as well as subsequent control of performance in accord with the plan. Operational control accepts the objectives and attempts to control operations in accord with the plan. For example, reformulation of profit objectives due to increased costs associated with the OPEC oil embargo can be classified under strategic evaluation and control. In contrast, adherence to manufacturing cost-control

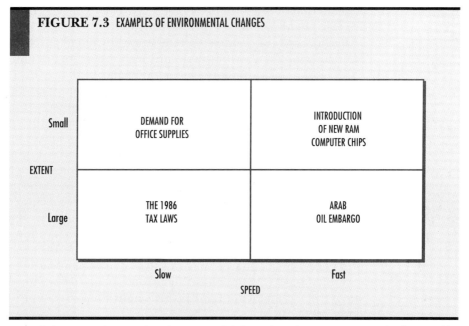

FIGURE 7.3 EXAMPLES OF ENVIRONMENTAL CHANGES

Source: Sharfman, M., et al., "Antecedents of Organizational Slack," *Academy of Management Review* 13 (1988): 605. Used by permission.

objectives in spite of inflationary pressures can be classified under operational control.

Schendel and Hofer offered a comprehensive five-step approach to evaluate strategy. Their steps "involve the assessment of : (1) the internal consistency of the organization's goal structure; (2) the quality of the process(es) and underlying analysis used to formulate the strategy; (3) the content of the strategy; (4) whether the organization can implement or execute the strategy effectively and efficiently; and (5) early performance results indicators."[7] Such assessment of the goals is part of the definition of evaluation and control used in this text.

In stressing the control aspect, Lorange, Morton, and Ghoshal offered description of control; "The system necessary to exercise control is defined as that combination of components which act together to maintain actual performance close to a desired set of performance specifications."[8] This second aspect of maintaining actual performance close to the desired level is also part of the definition of strategic evaluation and control used here. Lorange, Morton, and Ghoshal developed the concept further by describing three kinds of control: strategic, tactical, and operational. They described strategic control in terms of the strategic direction of the organization in relation to its environment. Tactical control deals more with the implementation of the strategic plan. Operational control deals with near-term achievement of goals.[9]

The same three theorists described the importance of control categories as a function of organizational hierarchy. Their configuration is shown in Figure 7.4. The discussion in this text focuses on strategic and tactical control, as our interest is in evaluation of the strategies and objectives as well as control of organizational activities in accord with the strategies and objectives. This text does not focus on short-run operational control activities that blindly control performance in accordance with earlier established objectives, despite changes in environment. Operational control should flow from and be consistent with strategic and tactical control. For example, if the corporation has a goal of a 5-percent reduction in costs for the year, it makes sense for a department to decrease overtime authorizations by 20 percent in one month.

Like Lorange, Daft described major control systems as a function of organizational hierarchy. Additionally, Daft included the kinds of plans and reports associated with the various control systems. For example, organizational control systems deal with strategic plans, overall objectives, and profit goals and involve systemwide, long–time-period (quarterly, annual) reports. Management control systems deal with departmental performance, subobjectives, programs, and budgets and involve departmentwide, periodic (weekly, monthly) reports. Supervisory control systems deal with operation plans, schedules, and activities and involve individual, frequent (daily, weekly) reports.[10]

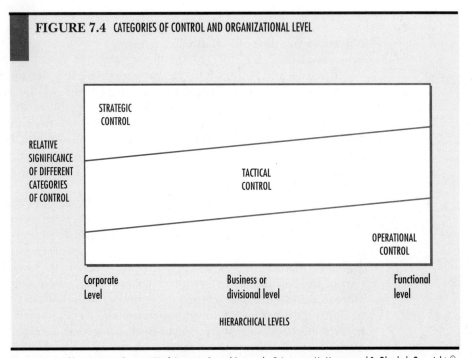

FIGURE 7.4 CATEGORIES OF CONTROL AND ORGANIZATIONAL LEVEL

RELATIVE SIGNIFICANCE OF DIFFERENT CATEGORIES OF CONTROL

STRATEGIC CONTROL

TACTICAL CONTROL

OPERATIONAL CONTROL

Corporate Level

Business or divisional level

Functional level

HIERARCHICAL LEVELS

Source: Reprinted by permission from p. 125 of *Strategic Control Systems* by P. Lorange, M. Morton, and S. Ghoshal. Copyright © 1986 by West Publishing Company. All rights reserved.

SIX EVALUATION AND CONTROL PROCESS STEPS

The evaluation and control process described here contains six steps. The six steps are described below and in Figure 7.5.

1. Determine what to control. What are the objectives the organization hopes to accomplish?
2. Set control standards. What are the targets and tolerances?
3. Measure performance. What are the actual results?
4. Compare the performance to the standards. How well does the actual match the plan?
5. Determine the reasons for the deviations. Are the deviations due to internal shortcomings or due to external changes beyond the control of the organization?
6. Take corrective action. Are corrections needed in internal activities to

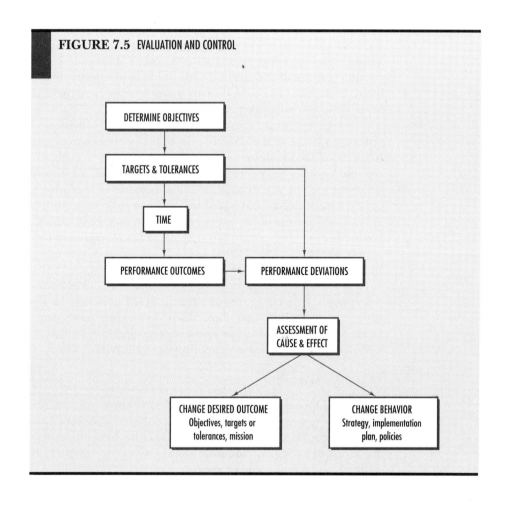

FIGURE 7.5 EVALUATION AND CONTROL

correct organizational shortcomings, or are changes needed in objectives due to external events?

DETERMINE WHAT TO CONTROL

This is the first decision the organization faces in the control arena. In deciding what to control, the organization must communicate through the actions of its executives that strategic control is a needed activity.[11] Without top management's commitment to controlling activities, the control system could be useless.

What objectives does the organization really hope to accomplish? In focusing on the planned objectives, which form the basis of the control system, it is useful to review the characteristics of objectives outlined in Chapter 2. Well-formulated objectives meet the first test in the evaluation process. Objectives refer to the specific kinds of results the organization seeks to achieve. Objectives should be specific, measurable, time-phased, and achievable. Table 2.2 contains examples of time-phased, specific objectives. If the objectives do not meet these characteristics, it is nearly impossible to control subsequent activities and performance, as the organization will not know when it has achieved the amorphous goal. For example, if the objective is stated as "increase profitability," how will the organization know if it has increased profitability by enough, and by what date, and with which profitability measure? On the other hand, a goal to "increase ROI by 1 percent by next year" gives managers a more concrete measurement.

Objectives should also be consistent. Lack of consistency will almost guarantee that some of the objectives will not be met. For example, if one goal is to increase market share by 5 percent in two years in highly competitive industry, and another goal is to increase return on sales by 4 percent in two years, one goal may be achieved only at the expense of the other goal.

In determining what to control, there should be a control point, or a measurement for control for every objective. Conversely, one must ask if the behavior needs to be controlled if there is no objective. Without the objective, it may not be clear to all that control is needed. Some may need to infer the objectives from the actual behavior.

One should recognize biases in decision making and their implications for control. Are the biases of executives influencing the decisions on which objectives to control? Are those decision-making biases causing certain objectives or control points to be ignored? For example, in Box 7.2, it appears that GM decided to control profitability but not market share.

SET CONTROL STANDARDS

In setting the control standards, an organization must identify the targets, determine the tolerances around those targets, and specify the timing of the specific standards. In setting the targets, the firm must deal with the issue of the exact behaviors or organizationally relevant measures it is attempting to control.[12] The behaviors or measures of the organizational outcomes must be

BOX 7.2   WAS GM CONTROLLING PROFITABILITY BUT NOT MARKET SHARE?

GM pleasantly surprised Wall Street with record earnings in 1988 and a stock split. "Earnings for all of 1988 hit a record of $4.86 billion," the *Wall Street Journal* reported. "But amid all the hoopla sits a striking dichotomy between the company's financial performance and its market performance. Last year produced GM's best earnings ever, but also its worst car-market share in the U.S. since 1930—36:1%. GM is fighting a two-front war, and winning on one front but not the other."[a] Figure 7.6 shows GM's rich earnings in contrast to its disappointing market share trend. Increasing market share and increasing net income appear to have been two inconsistent goals for GM.

Some analysts argue that GM has turned the corner and will start to regain market

FIGURE 7.6 GM'S EARNINGS REBOUND, BUT NOT ITS MARKET SHARE

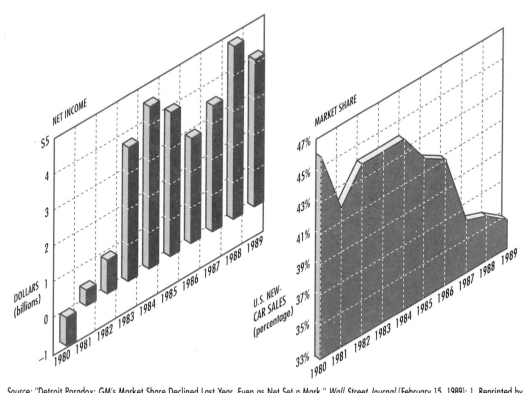

share, but disagreement over the quality of the earnings remains. Therefore, if the firm continues to control costs, market share may suffer. "Yet some members of the financial community remain unimpressed. The fatter profits are not the result of a dramatic improvement in GM's basic U.S. auto business. A reduction in capital spending of more than 15% from 1987's level was partly responsible. GM's profit margins continue to trail Ford's substantially, implying that GM has a long way to go before it's as efficient a money-maker as its smaller rival."[b] GM's productivity also trailed Ford's: In 1989, GM used thirty-nine hours per vehicle to build a car in North America versus twenty-six hours per vehicle for Ford.[c]

Much of the background of GM's CEO Roger Smith is in finance. The business press has questioned if that background is a roadblock to GM's success: "The finance men hold the high ground, but their analyses, which tend to follow trends rather than anticipate them, helped keep GM from deploying the minivan that its designers developed in the 1970s. Their caution has also delayed the four-door versions of the GM-10 cars and the Blazer sport-utility vehicle. More recently, some GM product people say privately that the pressure to increase short-term profits is causing short-sighted scrimping on their programs."[d]

This tug-of-war between profits and market share could be resolved in the near future in a dramatic way. If GM closes four assembly plants, the issue will be resolved for years to come in favor of profits. According to *Business Week,* "First, GM has yet to recognize that it has only 35% of the market, not the 45% it is geared up to handle. Last April, President Stempel promised that GM's North American factories 'will approach 100% capacity utilization' by 1992. It was a startling announcement since, barring an unlikely huge gain in market share, it would mean shutting up to four assembly plants."[e]

Some investment analysts feel that the giant auto maker can improve both profits and market share: "We think the company's efforts to reduce costs, reduce capacity, and develop successful new models, combined with its marketing and distribution muscle, may well lead to a larger and more profitable share of the worldwide vehicle market 3 to 5 years hence."[f] CEO Roger Smith is not quite so sure. In an interview, he stressed GM's success in improving quality and restructuring for the future, but he was a little vague about market share: "I just don't know whether we'll recapture the near-50% market share we had ten years ago."[g]

GM's market share continued to erode in 1989.[h] By late 1989, its new car market share had slid to 34.7 percent and its new truck market share to 34.9 percent.[i]

---

[a] "Detroit Paradox: GM's Market Share Declined Last Year, Even as Net Set a Mark," *Wall Street Journal* (February 15, 1989): 1.
[b] "GM's Bumpy Ride on the Long Road Back," *Business Week* (February 13, 1989): 74.
[c] "The New Drive to Revive GM," *Fortune* (April 9, 1990): 54.
[d] *Wall Street Journal* (February 15, 1989): 1.
[e] *Business Week* (February 13, 1989): 74.
[f] "General Motors," *Value Line Investment Survey* (December 23, 1988): 105.
[g] "The U.S. Must Do as GM Has Done," *Fortune* (February 13, 1989): 73.
[h] "With Its Market Share Sliding, GM Scrambles to Avoid a Calamity," *Wall Street Journal* (December 14, 1989): 1.
[i] "The New Drive to Revive GM," *Fortune* (April 9, 1990): 54.

tied directly to the goal defined in the first step of determining what to control. Otherwise, the control system may reinforce behavior that makes individuals or parts of the organization look good on the control system's measures to the detriment of the organization's actual goals.[13] For example, if the goal is to increase sales by 5 percent for the next year, the standard should be set in terms of net sales after customer returns, cancelled orders, and provisions for uncreditworthy customers. The organization does not benefit if items are shipped to customers who cannot pay for them, but a salesperson could look good temporarily on the standard of increased sales if the control system was not measuring net sales. This issue is particularly important as one views the three categories of control described in Figure 7.4—strategic, tactical, and operational. The target should be stated in broader terms at the strategic level and more specific terms at the operational level.

Tolerances are often thought of as statistical confidence intervals. Actual performance anywhere within the tolerance band does not risk corrective behavior. For example, an inventory target may be stated as "reduce inventory by $2 million within six months." If the tolerance is plus or minus 10 percent, the target could be viewed as accomplished if the actual performance is a reduction of $1.8 million to $2.2 million.

Setting the timing associated with the standards is a problem for many organizations. It is not unusual for short-term objectives to be met at the expense of long-term objectives.[14] For example, sales incentives and special advertising campaigns sometimes artificially boost sales in the current quarter at the expense of future sales. The auto industry was notorious for this problem as the 1990s began.

MEASURE PERFORMANCE

In recording actual results, an organization must measure the performance in time for management to take corrective action.[15] For example, if the goal is to increase market share by 5 percent this year, the organization must measure its sales and the sales of its competitors. Measurement of competitors' sales could be time consuming, but it must be done in a timely enough fashion so that management can take corrective action before the year is over.

Many types of measurements taken for control purposes are based on some form of historical standard.[16] For example, automobile companies use ten-day sales figures, which are compared with the same ten-day sales figures from the previous year. The organization must ensure that it is measuring only those outcomes that it wishes to control at the time and not measuring items just because it has measured them in the past. Many organizational members may infer intent to control by management if management measures certain outcomes. This perception may distract from the important organizational priorities. For example, a pharmaceutical company may have as a goal aggressive new product development. Yet it may be measuring and reporting the hiring of new research scientists because of an old campaign to control personnel costs. Some may interpret the reporting as an attempt to control personnel costs and a desire to keep personnel costs down. Such a move could be dysfunctional for the goal of aggressive new product development.

COMPARE PERFORMANCE TO STANDARDS

The actual performance must be compared to the standards. This step may seem obvious, but some organizations collect reams and reams of actual performance data and results from their ongoing operations without comparing the actual with the standard. Government agencies are noted for collecting all kinds of data but not using them to control operations.

Is this the step missed in the SmithKline Beckman case? Did the organization collect data on sales of Tagamet, but not compare the actual sales data with the sales objective in a timely fashion? It appears that data on Tagamet's sales were collected, but the comparison of the actual sales with the objective was not immediately made public.

DETERMINE THE REASONS FOR THE DEVIATIONS

In this step, the organization needs to ask if the deviations are due to internal shortcomings or external changes beyond the control of the organization. What is the cause and what is the effect? This is a step in which there is a substantial difference between strategic control and operational control. In operational control, concern is focused on finding the internal cause that needs to be changed. In strategic control, the organization also asks if the cause is external to the organization. The locus of the cause, either internal or external, has different implications for the kinds of corrective action.

The organization needs to ask which control type situation (see Figure 7.2) is operative. An uncontrollable situation such as the Arab oil embargo described in Figure 7.3 or Iraq's invasion of Kuwait in 1990 implies there is almost nothing the organization can do in the short term to control the situation. In the second control type situation, described in Figure 7.2 as influenceable, the organization may be able to influence events external to itself. For example, in the situation shown in Figure 7.3 as the 1986 tax laws, the organization may be able to influence the pending legislation through lobbying activities. In the controllable situation, as described in Figure 7.2, the organization needs only the commitment to take corrective action, as the cause is internal.

TAKE CORRECTIVE ACTION

Taking corrective action may be easier said than done. For internal changes, strength of conviction is needed. The organization may need to commit some slack resources in other areas to correct the situation.[17] Alternatively, the organization may need to abandon some capital resources because they are no longer needed due to quality deficiencies, process deficiencies, or excessive cost. Such capital facilities may serve as an exit barrier, however, and executives may be reluctant to admit that the facilities are no longer needed and should be abandoned.[18]

Deciding on internal changes and taking corrective action may involve changes in objectives, targets, tolerances, strategies, or implementation plans. Such changes obviously cause a reexamination of why the original plans were formulated and implemented the way they were. Such changes may also cause a reexamination of the biases and the judgment of the decision maker who decided in favor of the original plans. In the situation described in Box 7.2, were GM decision makers reluctant to take corrective action on market share because they were biased toward controlling profitability? Sometimes, maintaining the status quo is a politically safer alternative. It is also easier for large organizations because redirecting organizational inertia may be time and resource consuming. Aircraft carriers and organizations change directions slowly. Just as there are physical forces at work to keep an aircraft carrier moving in the same direction, there are financial, social, and bureaucratic forces at work to keep an organization moving in the same direction. Some people have speculated that IBM relied on its mainframe-centered strategy too long simply because it had prior substantial success with that strategy.

For external changes, care is needed in taking corrective action. If the organization attempts to influence events or trends external to itself through lobbying, advertising, or other public awareness programs, the organization may run the risk of such efforts backfiring. There are unresolved corporate responsibility issues (see Chapter 8) regarding the proper role of organizations in influencing events external to themselves. For example, what is the proper role, if any, of American oil companies in influencing governments in the Middle East? What is the proper role of political action committees and lobbying organizations? What is the proper boundary between a business organization trying to influence events or trends external to itself for favorable business conditions and the role of the government in engineering social and political change?[19]

If changes in the external environment are so severe that changes in objectives or even in the corporate mission are mandated, the changes should be made only after the most intense scrutiny. For example, in 1990, many analysts were forecasting that tobacco products and smoking would be nonexistent in this country by the year 2000. Unable to meet sales objectives in such an external environment and partly in response to that forecast, some tobacco firms have been diversifying their business interests. Examples include Philip Morris, which acquired Miller Beer, and RJR, which acquired Nabisco. Some tobacco companies are also expanding their international sales. As Chapter 9 discusses, sales growth for some products in the United States had fallen to near zero due to saturated domestic markets. Simultaneously, growing economies in other countries were associated with exploding sales growth. Increasingly, firms will need to be extremely attentive to international changes as part of their strategic evaluation and control activities.

■ SUMMARY

This chapter deals with the decisions needed to evaluate and control the strategic plan and corporate performance of a company. Once the strategic choice decisions have been made and the decisions have been implemented, the organization needs to take steps to ensure that the actual performance is corrected in accord with the plan.

Mintzberg tells us that frequently there are differences between intended and realized strategies. For a variety of reasons, including managerial shortcomings in formulation and implementation, there may be unrealized strategies. Due to external events beyond the control of management, there may also be emergent strategies. As these all may combine to yield a realized strategy different from the intended strategy, the organization needs to evaluate and control its strategic decisions.

In implementing a strategic control system, the organization must distinguish between various control types, including uncontrollable, influenceable, and controllable. Controllable situations are under the direct cause-and-effect power of the organization to correct. Uncontrollable situations imply that no action of the firm will affect the situation because the firm is powerless in this arena. Influenceable situations may in some cases be controlled indirectly. These control types are viewed relative to the speed and extent of environmental changes. Fast, large changes leave the organization almost powerless to control in the short term. Slow, small changes leave the organization room to effect control action.

Three categories of control are described: strategic, tactical, and operational. Strategic control is usually implemented at the top of the organization and implies evaluation of the strategic plan as well as corrective action. Operational control is implemented primarily at lower organizational levels and implies strictly corrective action. Tactical control primarily focuses on corrective action with some evaluation of the strategic plan.

A comprehensive strategic control system requires the organization to sequentially engage in six control process steps. First, determine what to control. Second, set control standards. Third, measure performance. Fourth, compare the performance to the standards. Fifth, determine the reasons for the deviations. Sixth, take corrective action.

■ DISCUSSION QUESTIONS

1. How are planning, evaluation, and control linked?
2. Describe the importance of the strategic control process.
3. Describe the primary difference between strategic control and operational control.
4. Define and relate intended, deliberate, unrealized, emergent, and realized strategies.

5. How do different control types affect strategic evaluation and control activities?

6. Describe the six strategic control process steps in the case of a computer manufacturer who just introduced a new personal computer.

 ENDNOTES

1. Mintzberg, H., "Patterns in Strategy Formulation," *Management Science* 24 (1978): 945.

2. Waterman, R. H., Jr., *The Renewal Factor: How the Best Get and Keep the Competitive Edge* (New York: Bantam Books, 1987).

3. "The Renewal Factor," *Business Week* (September 14, 1987): 105.

4. Lorange, P., M. Morton, and S. Ghoshal, *Strategic Control Systems* (St. Paul: West Publishing Co. 1986).

5. Sharfman, M., et al. "Antecedents of Organizational Slack," *Academy of Management Review* 13 (1988): 601–614; Singh, J., "Performance, Slack and Risk taking in Organizational Decision Making," *Academy of Management Journal* 29 (1986): 562–585.

6. Thompson, J. D., *Organizations in Action* (New York: Mc-Graw-Hill, 1967).

7. Schendel, D., and C. Hofer, *Strategic Management: A New View of Business Policy and Planning* (Boston: Little, Brown and Company, 1979): 190.

8. Lorange, Morton, and Ghoshal, *Strategic Control Systems*, p. 10.

9. Ibid., pp. 11–14.

10. Daft, R. L., *Organization Theory and Design*, 3d ed. (St. Paul: West Publishing Co., 1989): 318.

11. Bales, C. F., "Strategic Control: The President's Paradox," *Business Horizons* (August 1977): 17–28; Horovitz, J. H., "Strategic Control: A New Task for Top Manage-

ment," *Long Range Planning* 12 (June 1979): 28–37; Melville, D. R., "Top Management's Role in Strategic Planning," *Journal of Business Strategy* (Spring 1981): 57–65.

12. Govindarajan, V., and J. Fisher, "Strategy Control Systems, and Resource Sharing: Effects on Business-Unit Performance," *Academy of Management Journal* 33 (1990): 259–285.

13. Hirst, M. K., "Reliance on Accounting Performance Measures, Task Uncertainty, and Dysfunctional Behavior: Some Extensions," *Journal of Accounting Research* 21 (1983): 596–605; Lawler, E., and J. Rhode, *Information and Control in Organizations* (Menlo Park, Calif.: Goodyear, 1976): 83–94.

14. Horovitz, "Strategic Control," pp. 28–37.

15. Daft, R., and N. Macintosh, "The Nature and Use of Formal Control Systems for Management Control and Strategy Implementation," *Journal of Management* 10 (Fall 1984); 43–66.

16. Anthony, R., J. Dearden, and N. Bedford, *Management Control Systems* (Homewood, Ill., Irwin, 1984): 158–159.

17. Singh, "Performance, Slack and Risk Taking," p. 563.

18. Porter, M., *Competitive Strategy: Techniques for Analyzing Industries and Competitors* (New York: The Free Press, 1980): 259.

19. Friedman, M., *Capitalism and Freedom* (Chicago: University of Chicago Press, l962).

ADDITIONAL READINGS

Churchill, N. "Budget Choice: Planning vs. Control." *Harvard Business Review* 62 (July-August 1984); 150–164.

Eisenhardt, K. M. "Control: Organizational and Economic Approaches." *Management Science* 31 (1985): 134–139.

Flamholtz, E. "Accounting, Budgeting, and Control Systems in Their Organizations Context: Theoretical and Empirical Perspectives." *Accounting, Organizations and Society* 8 (1983): 153–169.

Giglioni, G. B., and A. G. Bedeian. "A Conspectus of Management Control Theory: 1900-1972." *Academy of Management Journal* 17 (1974): 292–305.

Gomez-Mejia, L., H. Tosi, and T. Hinkin. "Managerial Control, Performance, and Executive Compensation." *Academy of Management Journal* (March 1987): 51–70.

Govindarajan, V., and A. Gupta. "Linking Control Systems to Business Unit Strategy: Impact on Performance." *Accounting, Organizations and Society* 10 (1985): 51–66.

Hoskisson, R. E., and M. A. Hitt. "Strategic Control Systems and Relative R&D Investment in Large Multiproduct Firms." *Strategic Management Journal* 9 (1988): 605–621.

Lorange, P. "Strategic Control: Some Issues in Making it Operationally More Useful." pp. 247–271 *Competitive Strategic Management*, edited by R. B. Lamb. Englewood Cliffs, N.J.: Prentice-Hall, 1984.

Lorange, P., and D. Murphy. "Considerations in Implementing Strategic Control." *Journal of Business Strategy* 4, no. 4 (1984): 27–35.

Lucas, H. D., and J. A. Turner. "A Corporate Strategy for the Control of Information Processing." *Sloan Management Review* (Spring 1982): 25–36

McEachern, W. A. *Managerial Control and Performance.* Lexington, Mass.: D. C. Heath, 1975.

Oballe, N. "Organizational/Managerial Control Processes: A Reconceptualization of the Linkage Between Technology and Performance." *Human Relations* 37 (1984): 1047–1062.

Pfeffer, J., and G. R. Salancik. *The External Control of Organizations.* New York: Harper & Row, 1978.

Roush, C. H., Jr. "Strategic Resource Allocation and Control." In *Handbook of Business Strategy*, edited by W. D. Guth Boston: Warren, Gorham and Lamont, 1985.

Ruefli, T., and J. Sarrazin. "Strategic Control of Corporate Development Under Ambiguous Circumstances." *Management Science* 27 (1981): 1158–1170.

CHAPTER EIGHT

Corporate Social Responsibility

The 500 largest companies in the United States control assets of over $6 trillion, the equivalent of $25,000 for every man, woman, and child in the country. General Motors Corporation's annual sales, in excess of $100 billion, are larger than the gross national products of all but twenty-five countries in the world. GM's employees number over 800,000, the equivalent of a good-sized city. IBM's profits totalled nearly $6.5 billion in a recent year, a record for corporate earnings. *Fortune* magazine recently reported that twenty-six international companies, nineteen of them Japanese, each had net cash and marketable securities of over $1 billion.[1]

With their enormous size and power, modern corporations have the potential to affect people's lives dramatically, in both positive and negative ways. Given this potential for both harm and good, it is not surprising that the view that businesses, whether large or small, should act in socially responsible ways has many adherents inside and outside the business world.

Social responsibility is defined as decisions made and actions taken by executives that are not necessarily in the direct economic interests of the company but are desirable in terms of the broader values or objectives of our society. The focus of social responsibility is therefore on the voluntary actions of business executives to utilize the resources of their organizations in improving society.

The abstract concept of social responsibility is, understandably, easier to deal with than the reality. To whom should business be responsible? The answer, of course, depends on one's own interests and point of view. Corporate decision makers are legally obligated to pursue primarily the interests of the company's owners. Most corporations' actions, however, affect a wider range of individuals, groups, and other organizations. Should those affected have a voice in controlling the activities of businesses? If so, to what extent?

THE MULTIPLE-STAKEHOLDER VIEW OF SOCIAL RESPONSIBILITY

The individuals, groups, and organizations that have an interest in the activities of a corporation are generally referred to as stakeholders. The company affects, and is affected by, various stakeholders as it pursues its objectives, and strategic decision makers must take into account the actions of one or more of them when making practically any decision. The range of stakeholder interest in a company's activities has been depicted by Freeman on a two-dimensional grid, shown in Figure 8.1. The vertical dimension shows the type of "stake" a group has in the company—an equity interest in the company as a member of the ownership group; an economic stake due to direct market influence exercised by the company's actions; or an "influencer" stake, such as that of groups affected by a firm's activities, although not in marketplace terms.[2] The horizontal dimension depicts the type of power the stakeholder exercises over the company. Formal power is the ability to control the actions of the firm directly. Economic power is the ability to influence the company's

---

FIGURE 8.1 A "REAL WORLD" STAKEHOLDER GRID

	Formal or voting	Economic	Political
Equity	STOCKHOLDERS DIRECTORS MINORITY INTERESTS	EMPLOYEE/OWNERS	DISSIDENT STOCKHOLDERS
STAKE Economic	PREFERRED DEBT HOLDERS	SUPPLIERS DEBT HOLDERS CUSTOMERS EMPLOYEES COMPETITORS	LOCAL GOVERNMENTS FOREIGN GOVERNMENTS CONSUMER LOBBIES UNIONS
Influencers	OUTSIDE DIRECTORS LICENSING BODIES	REGULATORY AGENCIES	FEDERAL AND STATE GOV'T TRADE ASSOCIATIONS ENVIRONMENTAL GROUPS

POWER

Note: Grid location denotes primary, but not necessarily sole, orientation of stakeholder.

Source: Adapted from *Strategic Management: A Stakeholder Approach* by R. E. Freeman. Copyright © 1984 by Pitman Publishing Co.

actions through market forces. Political power is the ability to influence the firm's actions through regulations, legislation, or litigation.

Various stakeholders groups depicted in Figure 8.1 could, of course, be placed in more than one cell. The intention is to show the primary orientation of each group. For example, outside directors often hold stock in the company they serve and therefore could be represented in the Equity Stake/Formal Power cell also. Their primary involvement as stakeholders, however, is to provide an outside "influencer" role on the corporation's board, so they are listed in the Influencer Stake/Formal Power cell. These various roles of stakeholders highlight the importance to an organization of having an accurate view of the stakes and power of its various stakeholders. For instance, a firm may treat its union purely as an economic interest group, only to be surprised when the union exercises its political power to get a bill introduced in the legislature to prevent a planned plant closing.[3]

Each stakeholder group uses its own set of criteria to judge the actions of the corporation; thus, the strategic decision makers deal with a "multiple constituency" model of performance. Owners and stockholders are interested in increased stock value and a fair distribution of profits. Customers and consumer groups equate the success of a company to its demonstrated ability to deliver safe, affordable products. Employees and their unions judge a firm by its wages and benefits and by the working conditions and job security it provides. Competitors expect a firm to engage in fair competitive practices. Suppliers want fair dealings and prompt payments. Local communities judge a company by how well it protects the environment while providing jobs and contributing tax benefits. Society at large may have other criteria, such as minority hiring, charitable giving, or sponsorship of the arts, for good corporate performance.

Stakeholders sometimes play roles that support each other. For example, government agencies such as the Federal Trade Commission often respond to and support consumer groups in their attempts to influence corporate decisions. State and local government and civic groups often work in concert to attract new industries to their areas. Given the wide range of concerns among various stakeholders, the potential for conflict over strategic decisions is inevitable when different stakeholders hold conflicting views about what actions a corporation should take. The two incidents described in Box 8.1 illustrate the complexity of conflicts among stakeholders.

In cases of stakeholder conflict, questions of priority inevitably arise. How do decision makers respond to the demands of the various stakeholder groups? Whose concerns take precedence? A 1984 nationwide survey sponsored by the American Management Association investigated management's responsiveness to various stakeholder groups.[4] Executive, middle, and supervisory managers, 1,460 in all, were asked to rate the importance of various stakeholder groups on a scale of 1 to 7, with 7 representing a "very important" stakeholder. As shown in Table 8.1, customers rated highest in importance among executives, followed by employees and majority owners. Supervisory and middle levels managers' rankings agreed with those of the executives, ex-

BOX 8.1   TWO CASES OF STAKEHOLDER CONFLICT

Champion International Paper Co.   As the Pigeon River winds through the mountains of North Carolina, its waters are filled with bass and trout. About twenty-five miles before crossing into Tennessee, the river turns the color of coffee, and the only fish found in it are bottom-dwelling carp. In 1988, the Environmental Protection Agency determined that a process used to bleach wood pulp at the Canton, North Carolina, plant of Champion International Paper Company was responsible for the pollution.

Environmental groups and the state of Tennessee appealed to the EPA to force Champion to treat the 45 million gallons of water per day it cycled out of and back into the river. The state of North Carolina, which had earlier approved the company's operating permit, entered the dispute on the side of Champion, claiming that the discharges affected only the color and not the quality of the water. The company claimed that the technology necessary to meet the EPA's standards did not exist and that enforcement would result in closure of the plant. Shutting down would mean the loss of 2,200 jobs and $160 million in economic impact in the local economy.

Environmental groups appealed to citizens of both states to support the EPA standard, citing the benefits of scenic beauty and the economic impact of recreation and tourism in the area. An opposing grass-roots organization called "Save Champion" was formed in the Canton area, and it enlisted thousands of volunteers in its fight against the EPA. Newspaper and television ads were used to notify its supporters of the times and locations of public hearings on the EPA permit, thereby ensuring packed houses of pro-Champion supporters. Letter-writing campaigns and door-to-door solicitation brought further pressure on the EPA and environmental groups. The result was a compromise agreement in which Champion agreed to work within existing technology to improve the water quality under strict monitoring by the EPA. Under the compromise agreement, up to 1,000 Champion workers may lose their jobs as the mill is modernized and production is cut back.

General Motors Corporation   General Motors Corporation and the city of Detroit have a long-standing relationship. As the leading employer in the "Motor City," GM plays a large role in economic, civic, and cultural activities. In 1980, the corporation announced that it would close two of its older plants in the Detroit area by 1983. City officials, fearful of the negative impact the closing would have on the already-depressed local economy, urged GM to find a solution that would allow the company to keep these operations in Detroit. GM suggested that if the city could find an appropriate site, consisting of about 500 acres with access to transportation lines, the company would build its new plant within the city.

Detroit officials, working with the town of Hamtramack, suggested locating the plant on the site of an abandoned Chrysler plant. The site, which became known as the "Poletown" location, met GM criteria but would require extensive expansion. Homes, businesses, and churches would have to be condemned and bulldozed to make way for the new facility. As the city began to appropriate the land, protests developed in the community and soon drew national attention. Citizen groups claimed that their community was being destroyed by GM and the city of Detroit. Ralph Nader, longtime nemesis of GM, brought his organization into the dispute on the side of the local residents.

The Poletown incident placed GM in the unenviable position of being criticized for callousness and insensitivity to human needs whether it left Detroit or stayed. GM stood by its promise to build the plant. The result was the displacement of 1,600 families.

Sources: Smothers, P., "Industry and River Form a Gulf Between Two States," *New York Times* (January 31, 1988): 1. Satchell, M., "Fight for Pigeon River," *U.S. News and World Report* (December 4, 1989): 27–32. "Pushing the Boundaries of Eminent Domain," *Business Week* (May 4, 1981): 174. "Last Days of Poletown," *Time* (March 30, 1981): 29.

cept that these two groups rated employees slightly higher in importance than customers. Supervisory managers rated the general public as more important than owners and public officials as more important than stockholders.

Although there is, as this study shows, some agreement among managers on the importance of certain stakeholders, the degree to which strategic decision makers are responsive to the concerns and demands of various groups is influenced by a multitude of factors in the environment. Decision makers have different points of view, come from different backgrounds, work in different corporate cultures, and must comply with different community standards—all of which influence the corporation's social responsiveness.

TABLE 8.1   IMPORTANCE OF VARIOUS STAKEHOLDER GROUPS

	EXECUTIVE MANAGERS: (n = 889)	MIDDLE MANAGERS: (n = 422)	SUPERVISORY MANAGERS: (n = 149)
Customers	6.40	6.10	5.57
Employees	6.01	6.11	5.93
Owners (majority)	5.30	4.51	4.07
General public	4.52	4.49	4.38
Stockholders	4.51	3.79	3.35
Elected public officials	3.79	3.54	3.81
Government bureaucrats	2.90	2.05	3.09

Scores are based on a scale of 7 (very important) to 1 (not important).

Source: Posner, B. Z., and W. H. Schmidt, "Values and the American Manager: An Update," *California Management Review* 26, no. 3 (1984): 206. Copyright © 1984 by the Regents of the University of California. Reprinted from the *California Management Review*, Vol. 26, No. 3. By permission of the Regents.

INFLUENCES ON SOCIAL RESPONSIBILITY

Although the critics of corporate decision making sometimes characterize business leaders as "robber barons" who operate only to serve their own interests in an unfettered environment, this view ignores a considerable number of actual constraining factors. These constraints can be summarized under four categories: government and regulatory influences, ethical influences, societal influences, and competitive influences. Figure 8.2 illustrates these influences, which together act to inhibit the inappropriate use of corporate power.

GOVERNMENT AND REGULATORY INFLUENCES

Although American business operates in what we know as a "free enterprise" system, the powers of the federal government and state governments to regulate that system are considerable. Under its authority to regulate interstate commerce, as granted by Article 1, Section 8 of the United States Constitution, Congress controls a very wide range of business activity. Some of the more important regulatory agencies and their responsibilities are listed in Table 8.2.

The 1970s and 1980s witnessed significant reductions in federal regulation. Airline deregulation was accomplished during the Carter administration. During the Reagan years, the railroads and the trucking industry were deregulated, as were natural gas distributors, financial institutions, oil pipeline companies, intercity buses, and parts of the communications industry.[5]

Some analysts have predicted that the 1990s will see a return to regulation. The U.S. airline industry, which has been reduced, through consolidation, from more than twenty major carriers to just six that control over 90 percent

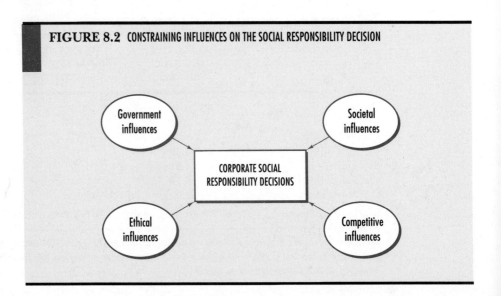

FIGURE 8.2 CONSTRAINING INFLUENCES ON THE SOCIAL RESPONSIBILITY DECISION

TABLE 8.2   SOME FEDERAL REGULATORY AGENCIES AND THEIR RESPONSIBILITIES

CONSUMER PRODUCT SAFETY COMMISSION (CPSC)	Develops and enforces safety standards for consumer products.
ENVIRONMENTAL PROTECTION AGENCY (EPA)	Develops and enforces standards for air, water, and noise pollution.
EQUAL EMPLOYMENT OPPORTUNITY COMMISSION (EEOC)	Investigates, and conciliates, and prosecutes employment discrimination complaints based on race, sex, religion, creed, or national origin.
FEDERAL COMMUNICATIONS COMMISSION (FCC)	Grants licenses and regulates interstate wire, radio, and television systems.
FEDERAL TRADE COMMISSION (FTC)	Enforces laws and develops guidelines dealing with unfair business practices.
FOOD AND DRUG ADMINISTRATION (FDA)	Develops and enforces standards for the purity and labeling of foods, drugs, cosmetics, and hazardous consumer products.
INTERSTATE COMMERCE COMMISSION (ICC)	Grants operating licenses and regulates interstate rail, bus, truck, and water carriers.
OCCUPATIONAL SAFETY AND HEALTH ADMINISTRATION (OSHA)	Regulates safety and health conditions in the workplace.
SECURITIES AND EXCHANGE COMMISSION (SEC)	Regulates the buying and selling of corporate stocks and bonds and requires public disclosure of the financial conditions of publicly held corporations.

of the traffic, is likely to be the first industry to feel the effects of the reregulation movement.[6] As this book went to press, the House of Representatives had passed its version of a bill that would give the secretary of transportation the authority to delay for fifty days any attempt to acquire 15 percent or more of an airline.[7] Congress was also considering the Airline Consumer Rights Bill, which would bar airlines from cancelling flights with low bookings.[8]

In addition to maintaining regulatory control, government affects strategic decisions in a number of other significant ways. Government is a major customer of American business. Total purchases by federal, state, and local governments amounted to almost 20 percent of 1989 GNP, a total dollar value of $1,022.1 billion.[9] Government contracting procedures also affect business practices. Businesses that seek government contracts must comply with additional regulations that cover prevailing wage rates, subcontracting with minority businesses, affirmative action goals, and health and safety rules.

The government also affects strategic decisions by actually subsidizing and promoting certain businesses. Direct price subsides for farm commodities, tax incentives for capital investment, foreign trade protection, and exclusive licensing are all ways that the federal government intervenes in the free market process in order to aid certain industries and segments of the economy. Al-

though the impact of these programs is usually quite subtle, government actions to rescue troubled companies have occasionally been headline news. A
good example occurred in 1979, when Congress granted $1.5 billion in loan
guarantees to prevent the collapse of the Chrysler Corporation.[10]

The government is also a major owner of productive resources in our
economy. Federal agencies control vast stockpiles of raw materials such as oil
reserves and timber lands. In addition, the government competes directly with
private business in a number of markets, such as shipbuilding, dam and road
construction, and delivery of packages.

Finally, the government acts as a regulator of capital markets. Through
monetary policy, the government controls the cost of capital for business expansion. By making loan guarantees such as those in the housing industry,
government agencies tend to lower the overall cost of doing business for
lenders and thereby affect lending rates.

Should the United States have a national policy concerning the roles of
business and government? If so, what should that policy include? According
to some observers, the federal government's role as a regulator of business
activity has led to an unnecessary and counterproductive "adversarial" relationship between the government and the business community. As the market
for American goods and services becomes increasingly an international one,
U.S. corporations have found themselves competing with firms in the Far East
and in Europe that benefit from the supportive policies, and sometimes outright sponsorship, of their national governments. In *The Next American Frontier,*
Reich suggested that the U.S. should develop a national policy aimed at helping its industries adapt to world competition.[11] In the opinion of its advocates,
a system of incentives designed to ensure the changeover from high-volume
standardized production to more flexible manufacturing, along with subsidies
to firms entering new world markets, could help U.S. firms compete on an
equal basis.

ETHICAL INFLUENCES

The ethical standards of strategic decision makers act as a self-regulating force
in the decision process by helping to assure that corporations act in socially
responsible ways. The ethics of business leaders are often criticized by the
press and the public, and much recent attention has been focused on ethical
questions in the business world. In 1988, *Business Week* reported that interest in
corporate ethics had increased in the wake of scandals in the financial world
involving insider trading.[12] Authorities in the field of business ethics report
that interest in the field is greater than it has ever been and that ethical standards are becoming increasingly important criteria for evaluating the performance of managers.[13]

A number of ethical standards, or criteria for judging the ethicality of
decisions, have been proposed. For example, the *utilitarian principle* proposes
that one should act in ways that result in the greatest good for the greatest
number of people. The decision maker attempts to satisfy the interests of the

largest number of those affected by ethical questions. *Rule-based ethics* hold that one should adopt a set of general principles, or rules, that may be applied to guide one's actions. The "Golden Rule" is often cited as a decision aid. *Kant's categorical imperative* proposes that one should always act in such a way that one's actions would be acceptable if applied to all. If a decision maker would be unwilling for the entire business community to act in a certain way, that act must be considered unethical. *Motive-based (deontological) ethics* hold that one's duty is the guiding principle in the determination of right and wrong. This view would lead decision makers to value the sanctity of contracts very highly and to consider motives as important determinants of behavior.[14]

The personal ethical standards of managers are often based on more than one of these criteria. An executive might, for example, adhere to a strong set of rules for behavior but also consider utilitarian principles in some circumstances. Differences in orientation can lead to very different decisions on ethical questions, as the fictitious incident in Box 8.2 illustrates.

As this example illustrates, applying personal ethical standards to business decisions can be a very ambiguous undertaking. Further contradictions occur in applying ethical standards in strategic decisions. Even though an individual may be quite clear in terms of his or her own personal conduct, being called on to act on behalf of a corporation that must satisfy multiple stakeholder interests is never simple. For that reason, corporations often develop codes of ethics in order to remove some of the ambiguity. According to a 1987 poll, 93 percent of the largest U.S. companies had ethics codes.[15]

BOX 8.2 AN ETHICAL DILEMMA

The general manager of a restaurant chain discovers that his best supplier of fresh seafood, one that had been providing exceptional quality and very good prices, makes extensive use of illegal immigrant labor in its seafood processing operations. Acting on utilitarian principle, the restaurant manager might continue to contract with the supplier, since his customers, his employees, and the owners of both firms benefit from this relationship. In addition, any harm done might be considered minimal and widely diffused in the economy. Acting on rule-based ethics might lead to a very different conclusion, however, especially if a guiding principle in the manager's ethical standard is never to act illegally or to contribute to illegal activities in any way. Applying Kant's categorical imperative might also cause the manager to rethink his relationship with the supplier. If all restaurants dealt with illegal employers, the effect might be to drive legal employers out of business, an unacceptable result. Finally, motive-based ethics applied to this situation might result in continuing the relationship. As the restaurant manager's motive is to provide the best fresh seafood at the lowest price to his customers, and he did not intend harm to anyone, his relationship with the supplier might be viewed as acceptable.

Developing codes for ethical conduct and making them work effectively are, unfortunately, two different things. A study reported in the *Wall Street Journal* found that companies having written standards of conduct for executives were cited for infractions by federal agencies more often than organizations that did not have written codes.[16] According to Robert Albanese, two conditions are necessary if ethics codes are to encourage more values-driven behavior. First, the codes should be developed through a process that involves line managers and others who will be directly affected by the code's tenets. The development process should therefore involve as many of the firm's relevant stakeholders as is possible and practical. Second, ethics codes will be implemented more successfully if they receive the ongoing, active support of top management.[17] In a study conducted by the Conference Board, 80 percent of companies having ethics codes said that top management participated directly in drafting them.[18]

Communicating the basic philosophy of top management to lower-level managers in the corporation can be a powerful force in instilling ethical values. At Hewlett-Packard, the corporate policy is "to honor our obligations to society by being an economic, intellectual, and social asset to each nation and each community in which we operate."[19] General Motors managers carry with them a card containing the "General Motors Guiding Principles," eleven statements of corporate ethical and social responsibility standards.[20]

One of the best-known corporate codes is the corporate credo developed by Johnson and Johnson Corporation. This credo, featured in Box 8.3, was originally developed by the company's founder, Robert Wood Johnson, to provide guidance to employees in prioritizing various stakeholder concerns. It has been credited with giving company officials a basis for acting quickly during the company's Tylenol tainting crises in 1983 and 1986, and it plays a key role in Johnson and Johnson's rating as America's most admired corporation in the area of community and environmental responsibility.[21]

The ethical standards of decision makers within the organization ultimately play a key role in determining a wide range of strategic decisions. Freeman and Gilbert proposed the concept of "enterprise strategy" to denote the conjunction of ethical and strategic thinking. They posed the question, "What do we stand for?" as one that must be answered along with "What business are we in?"[22] The corporation's commitment to a set of values and ethical principles must be communicated to members of the organization and to its relevant stakeholders. Likewise, the actions of the firm must be consistent with its articulated enterprise strategy.

SOCIETAL INFLUENCES

Society's influence on strategic decisions takes several forms. The most powerful way that society exercises its control over the strategic decisions of corporations is through market forces. Society's tastes and preferences are communicated through the aggregate effects of the individual buying decisions of

BOX 8.3 JOHNSON AND JOHNSON'S CORPORATE CREDO

Our Credo

We believe our first responsibility is to the doctors, nurses and patients,
to mothers and fathers and all others who use our products and services.
In meeting their needs everything we do must be of high quality.
We must constantly strive to reduce our costs
in order to maintain reasonable prices.
Customers' orders must be serviced promptly and accurately.
Our suppliers and distributors must have an opportunity
to make a fair profit.

We are responsible to our employees,
the men and women who work with us throughout the world.
Everyone must be considered as an individual.
We must respect their dignity and recognize their merit.
They must have a sense of security in their jobs.
Compensation must be fair and adequate,
and working conditions clean, orderly and safe.
We must be mindful of ways to help our employees fulfill
their family responsibilities.
Employees must feel free to make suggestions and complaints.
There must be equal opportunity for employment, development
and advancement for those qualified.
We must provide competent management,
and their actions must be just and ethical.

We are responsible to the communities in which we live and work
and to the world community as well.
We must be good citizens — support good works and charities
and bear our fair share of taxes.
We must encourage civic improvements and better health and education.
We must maintain in good order
the property we are privileged to use,
protecting the environment and natural resources.

Our final responsibility is to our stockholders.
Business must make a sound profit.
We must experiment with new ideas.
Research must be carried on, innovative programs developed
and mistakes paid for.
New equipment must be purchased, new facilities provided
and new products launched.
Reserves must be created to provide for adverse times.
When we operate according to these principles,
the stockholders should realize a fair return.

Johnson & Johnson

Source: Johnson and Johnson Corp. Reprinted with permission.

customers. Another important way that society affects strategy is in the political arena. By making known its priorities through the electoral process, the public communicates its desires for increased (or decreased) regulation of business, its alternatives for government purchases of social programs or national defense, and other societal concerns.

Although the aggregate effects of *individual* decisions have a powerful influence over corporate- and business-level strategy, *collective* action in both the marketplace and the political arena has increased substantially over the past three decades. The rise of increasingly powerful influence groups has become an issue that strategic decision makers must face. Table 8.3 lists examples of groups that attempt to influence strategic decisions. These organizations operate through the political process by pressuring public officials to support their positions and sponsor legislation favorable to their goals and through the marketplace by attempting to influence consumer behavior with informational campaigns and, at times, boycotts of certain products.

COMPETITIVE INFLUENCES

The actions of competing firms directly affect the strategic decisions of corporations in the area of social responsibility. Perhaps the most obvious benefit to society from competitive actions is that of better, safer, and more economical products that come about through competitive improvements. For example, the much-heralded improvement in the quality of American automobiles in the late 1980s was brought about primarily through competition with Japanese

 TABLE 8.3   GROUPS THAT AFFECT THE STRATEGIC DECISIONS OF CORPORATIONS

CONSUMER ORGANIZATIONS
- Common Cause
- Consumer Federation of America
- National Consumers League
- Ralph Nader's Public Citizen

ENVIRONMENTAL ORGANIZATIONS
- Greenpeace International
- National Wildlife Federation
- The Nature Conservancy
- Sierra Club

SPECIAL INTEREST ORGANIZATIONS
- Action for Children's Television
- American Association of Retired Persons
- Group Against Smoking and Pollution
- Mothers Against Drunk Driving

automakers. Competitive actions also improve the flow of information to consumers. By offering product comparisons and conflicting claims, competitors dilute one another's power in the marketplace, thereby ensuring that a single firm cannot take unfair advantage.

In addition to improvements in consumer prices and product quality, there are other ways that the actions of competitors affect the social responsibility decisions of businesses. Group pressure to act responsibly is often levied against firms that violate industry norms for behavior. Firms that make excessive claims for their products, engage in deceptive advertising, or violate industry taboos by using competitors' products in advertising often find themselves special targets of increased competition.

Cooperative pressures to act responsibly can also be positive. Through their trade associations, competitors often come together to take responsibility for a social concern in the industry. For example, in the toy industry, voluntary product safety standards have been developed that go beyond the normal restrictions placed on toys by the Consumer Product Safety Commission. Member firms of the Toy Manufacturers of America are strongly urged to adopt the guidelines.[23]

THE SOCIAL RESPONSIBILITY DEBATE

Many corporations have made decisions to use their resources to improve the world outside the firm. (A number of other terms are often used to describe corporate social responsibility: social policy, community responsiveness, public affairs, and social concerns, for example.) Activities include programs in education, civil rights and equal opportunity, urban development and renewal, sponsorship of the arts and cultural events, natural resource conservation, environmental protection, health and medicine, and government affairs.

The question of whether or not it is proper for a corporation to pursue social responsibility objectives has long been a subject of controversy among managers. Both sides of this issue are examined in the following paragraphs.

ARGUMENTS FOR VOLUNTARY ACTIONS BY CORPORATIONS

According to Steiner and Steiner, there are three major ideas in the argument that business should assume social responsibilities. First, society expects business to do so. Second, the long-run self-interests of business are best served when business assumes responsibilities. Finally, the assumption of social responsibilities serves to reduce government regulation and public criticism.[24]

Society Expects It. Corporations are creatures of society. They are chartered by the states and therefore exist only by the consent of the people. It can be argued, then, that business incurs a social responsibility that arises from this social power. If corporations do not remain responsible to society through their actions, the public will demand either that restrictions be placed on the corporations' power or that their existence no longer be guaranteed. This view also implies that, as the needs of society grow and change, corporations must keep up by changing their actions. S. P. Sethi has pointed out that there exists a "legitimacy gap" between corporate responsibility and public expectation. In other words, businesses can rarely perform all of the societal functions the public would like them to. If this gap grows too wide, the public will demand that business be forced to assume a greater role.[25]

It Is In the Long-Run Best Interest of the Firm.   In 1981, the Committee for Economic Development, a group composed of some of the nation's top business leaders, issued its statement on corporate responsibility: "It is in the enlightened self-interest of corporations to promote the public welfare in a positive way. . . . Indeed, the corporate interest broadly defined by management can support involvement in helping to solve virtually any social problem, because people who have a good environment, education, and opportunity make better employees, customers, and neighbors for business than those who are poor, ignorant, and oppressed."[26] This "enlightened self-interest" justification is, to many, simply a long-range view of profitability. It recognizes the vast complex of interconnections in modern society that link the fate of the corporation to the fate of society as a whole. The logic is that if a company serves society and is a "good corporate citizen," its actions will result in increased public esteem. It will be rewarded through increased purchases of its products and services by an appreciative public.

Researchers have been interested in the relationship between a corporation's social responsiveness and its financial performance. Of fifteen studies conducted between 1972 and 1985, nine showed a positive link between corporate responsibility and profits; the other six did not find a relationship between the two. The results, therefore, are not conclusive. One problem in the research has been the lack of agreement over how to measure corporate social performance.[27]

The Firm Will Avoid Future Regulation.   Much of the vast body of government regulation has arisen as a response to stakeholder concerns over business practice. Consumer complaints over widespread deceptive advertising led to the formation of the Federal Trade Commission and its broad powers to regulate the content of advertising. Likewise, public concern over water and air pollution in the 1970s led to the founding of the Environmental Protection Agency. It follows, therefore, that the assumption by business of increased responsibility for social concerns may reduce the pressure for future regulatory efforts.

By taking the initiative for social responsibility and thereby avoiding regulation, corporations may be able to mitigate the increased concentration of power in government and thereby enhance their own relative power. Corporations can also achieve lower operating costs, as voluntary measures are generally less expensive than programs for compliance with regulations. Finally, corporations will benefit by retaining the flexibility and freedom to make decisions unhampered by cumbersome regulatory oversight and thus will be better able to react competitively to changing conditions in world markets.[28]

ARGUMENTS AGAINST VOLUNTARY ACTIONS BY CORPORATIONS

A more conservative approach to the assumption of social responsibilities by the modern business corporation simply states that the most responsible action a company can engage in is to maximize its profits. This view is founded on four related ideas: First, the only legitimate purpose of business is to maximize the profits of its owners. Second, social responsibility programs act to disrupt normal market forces. Third, there is potential for the roles of government and business to become confused. Finally, the pursuit of social programs as well as economic goals could make corporations too powerful.

Profit Maximizing Is the Only Legitimate Purpose of Business.   This view holds that businesses are single-purpose entities. They exist in order to return profits to their owners, the stockholders. Managers are hired by the stockholders to maximize profits and are held accountable for how well they do that. If managers pursue other goals, such as the betterment of society, they do so without any authority, either explicit or implicit. Nobel laureate Milton Friedman expressed this view in his classic work, *Capitalism and Freedom:*

> There is one and only one social responsibility of business—to use its resources and engage in activities designed to increase its profits so long as it stays within the rules of the game, which is to say, engages in open and free competition, without deception or fraud. . . . Few trends could so thoroughly undermine the very foundations of our free society as the acceptance by corporate officials of a social responsibility other than to make as much money for their stockholders as possible. This is a fundamentally subversive doctrine.[29]

Social Responsibility Subverts the Market System.   Friedman also argued that when business executives pursue social goals, they incur costs that must eventually be passed on to consumers. According to Friedman, if market prices of goods and services contain added costs for social action, the relative costs of producing them are distorted and the allocative mechanisms of the market will therefore be distorted.[30]

In a highly competitive business environment, socially responsible firms would be priced out of the market. Social action programs will therefore tend to be concentrated in industries where firms already have monopolistic positions, and such a situation would serve only to compound market inefficiencies.

The Roles of Government and Business Will Be Confused.   When the costs of social programs must be incorporated into market prices, the public is being required to pay for the social goal without having had the opportunity to express its desire for it. In the view of classic economics, this amounts to "taxation without representation" and can lead to a dangerous mixture of public and private concerns. Interestingly, this view agrees with that of some advocates of the increased pursuit of social goals through regulation. Their view is that the only legitimate way to pursue social goals is through our elected representatives. If the public wants, say, cleaner air, it will vote for representatives who will impose tighter pollution emissions standards upon industry. In that way, the people are saying, "We want cleaner air, and we are willing to pay for it through increased prices of consumer goods."

Business Can Become Too Powerful.   This view simply holds that the economic power of corporations, if brought to bear on social problems, could be a double-edged sword. The potential exists for doing good, but that power could also be used in ways that might shape the social system for a corporation's own purposes. In other words, if the corporations become the main force for social change, the values of business might drive our social system as well as our economic system. This concern over the possibility of corporations overstepping their traditional roles has been voiced by members of the business community. According to Irving Shapiro, former Dupont executive, "Unless they are careful, executives can get sucked into controversial areas where they don't have any particular competence, and in extreme cases their efforts to help could amount to unwarranted meddling."[31]

There is evidence that corporate leaders recognize and struggle with arguments on both sides of the corporate responsibility debate. In a 1984 study, Ford and McLaughlin asked CEOs to respond to statements taken from Keith Davis's classic article on corporate social responsibility. The 116 CEOs indicated their general agreement with eleven arguments for the acceptance of social responsibility and disagreement with eleven arguments against the corporation's assumption of social responsibility. These results indicate that CEOs may be aware of, and agree with, the notion of corporate social responsibility, but their actions lag behind their beliefs.[32]

A SOCIAL RESPONSIBILITY CONTINUUM

Although there are no objective guidelines for determining the proper strategy in the realm of corporate social responsibility, social response alternatives can be arrayed on a continuum, as shown in Figure 8.3. This Figure shows four positions that reflect differing strategic management decisions. At one extreme, "minimum compliance," the firm simply complies with social issues that are required by law and limits its responses to its legal requirements.

Farther along the continuum is the position of the "good corporate citizen." Corporations that adopt this strategy are concerned about complying with the public's standards on issues. This strategy could include going beyond the required legal standards in areas covered by the law, if the public views this action as something that responsible corporations do. For example, a com-

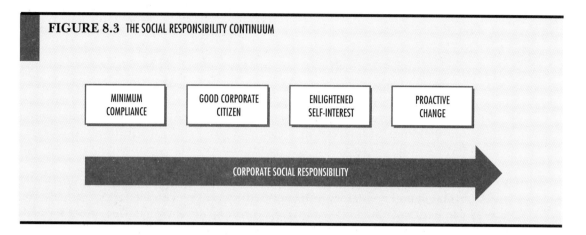

FIGURE 8.3 THE SOCIAL RESPONSIBILITY CONTINUUM

pany might provide fully paid medical plans for all employees or improve employee safety beyond minimal standards.

A more active role in social responsibility would be taken by firms adopting an "enlightened self-interest" approach. This position involves the use of social programs as a strategic advantage, usually by initiating innovative or highly visible programs. The idea is to set the organization apart from others in the area of corporate social concern. IBM's Community Service Assignment Program and Mobil Oil Company's contributions to public television are examples of how companies can enhance their public esteem in ways that may increase profits in the long run.

A few firms go beyond the "enlightened self-interest" position and attempt to actively use the corporation's assets to improve society. This is the "proactive" position. For example, a firm might decide to contribute to the war on poverty by locating a new facility in an inner-city area and training hard-core unemployed people for jobs there in spite of more economical alternatives elsewhere. Strategic managers in proactive firms must be very careful. In their zeal, they could adopt positions that are too far out of the mainstream of public opinion and in doing so risk possible stockholder uprisings or public censure in the marketplace.

Most firms adopt positions ranging from "good corporate citizen" to "enlightened self-interest." The good corporate citizens attempt to comply with the public's consensus on social issues. They ordinarily adopt this position not in order to use corporate social responsibility as a competitive weapon but to avoid negative public sanctions. Firms taking the "enlightened self-interest" approach seek to create competitive advantages through their public image. For them, social responsibility programs are an added weapon in their strategic arsenals. Firms adopting the "minimum compliance" usually do so out of fiscal necessity. These are typically firms with meager profit margins whose primary concern is short-term survival.

SUMMARY

This chapter deals with the relationship of the corporation to society. The recognition that the vast powers of the modern corporation carry with it an equally large responsibility to use that power responsibly in an important message for managers. A multiple-stakeholder view of social responsibility points out the range of interests in society that are tied to the fortunes of corporations. Conflict between the viewpoints and expectations of these various stakeholders requires management to balance these interests skillfully.

A discussion of the four constraining forces on corporate decisions—government and regulatory influences, ethical influences, societal influences, and competitive influences—revealed a constantly changing environment for making social responsibility decisions. Increasing deregulation offers challenges as well as opportunities for strategic decision makers. Growing concern over ethics and morality is reflected in new approaches to social responsibility and increased demand for ethical codes of behavior. Changing societal influences call for flexible policies to keep up with rapidly shifting tastes and preferences and to keep abreast of social concerns. Competitive influences on social responsibility are also growing, and industry groups have stepped up their efforts at self-regulation in order to avoid unwanted government regulation.

The social responsibility debate is an ongoing controversy. The arguments in favor of increased assumption of social responsibility on the part of business are (1) society expects business to assume social responsibilities, (2) the long-run self-interests of business are best served when it does so, and (3) the assumption of social responsibilities serves to reduce government regulation and public criticism. The arguments presented against the assumption of social responsibilities by business are (1) pursuit of social programs is not a legitimate purpose of business, (2) it subverts normal market influences, (3) it leads to a confusion of the roles of business and government, and (4) it ultimately can lead to too powerful a role for business in society.

A continuum of social responsibility positions ranges from minimum compliance with the law to proactive social change through corporate strategic decisions. Corporations generally use the social responsibility decision moderately. They adopt positions in the middle range, adhering either to "good corporate citizenship" or "enlightened self-interest."

DISCUSSION QUESTIONS

1. Define the concept of social responsibility. Is this definition a static or a dynamic one? In what ways do you think the area of social responsibility has changed in the past five years?
2. Using the Freeman model of "real world" stakeholder groups, give an example of a group with an equity stake, a group with an economic stake, and a group with an

influencer stake in a corporation. Explain how the interests of these groups might come into conflict and how those conflicts could be resolved.

3. How would each of the groups you identified in Question 2 evaluate the performance of the firm?

4. Comment on the advisability of the adoption of national policy of cooperation between business and the federal government to replace the present system of regulatory control. Should this be done? If so, what should the most important features of such a policy be?

5. Does the management profession need a standard "code of ethics" such as that of the medical and legal professions? What are the possible benefits and shortcomings of such a code?

6. Summarize the basic arguments for and against the assumption of social responsibilities by business. Which side, in your opinion, has the better case? Explain.

ENDNOTES

1. "The Forbes 500," *Forbes* (April 25, 1988): 136, 180; Rapoport, C., "How Japan Will Spend Its Cash," *Fortune* (November 21, 1988): 195.

2. Freeman, R. E., *Strategic Management: A Stakeholder Approach* (Boston: Pitman Publishing Co., 1984): 58.

3. Ibid., p. 61.

4. Posner, B. Z., and W. H. Schmidt, "Values and the American Manager: An Update," *California Management Review* 26, no. 3 (1984): 206.

5. Steiner, G. A., and J. F. Steiner, *Business, Government, and Society* (New York: Random House, 1988): 182.

6. LaBich, K., "Should Airlines be Reregulated?" *Fortune* (June 19, 1989): 82; Kuttner, R., "Plane Truth: The Case for Reregulating Airlines," *New Republic* (July 17, 1989): 21.

7. Payne, S., "Memo to Airlines: Deregulation's Days are Numbered," *Business Week* (November 13, 1989): 59; "Close the Gate on Airline LBOs," *Aviation Week and Space Technology* (January 22, 1990): 15.

8. Poling, B., "Bill to Propose Tougher Rules on Air Delays, Discount Seats," *Travel Weekly* (April 2, 1987): 2.

9. "National Income and Product Accounts," *Survey of Current Business* (May, 1990): 4.

10. "Big Loss, Bigger Bailout," *Time* (November 12, 1979): 98–100; "Will 3 Billion Be Enough?" *U.S. News and World Report* (November 12, 1979): 78–79.

11. Reich, R. B., *The Next American Frontier* (New York: Times Books, 1983).

12. "Businesses Are Signing Up for Ethics 101," *Business Week* (February 15, 1988): 56.

13. Bennett, A., "Ethics Codes Spread Despite Skepticism," *Wall Street Journal* (July 15, 1988): 17.

14. Beauchamp, T. L., and N. E. Bowie, *Ethical Theory and Business* (Englewood Cliffs, N.J.: Prentice-Hall, 1983); Hoffman, W. M., and J. M. Moore, *Business Ethics* (New York: McGraw-Hill, 1984).

15. Murray, T. J., "Ethics Programs: Just a Pretty Face," *Business Month* (September, 1987): 30.

16. Albanese, R., "Spotlight on Managerial Ethics," *Management Update* (Fall 1988): 1.

17. Ibid., p. 2.

18. Bennett, "Ethics Codes Spread," p. 17.

19. Hewlett-Packard Corporation, *1985 Annual Report*, p. 5.

20. Steiner and Steiner, *Business, Government, and Society*, p. 280.

21. Kiechel, W., III, "Unfuzzing Ethics for Managers," *Fortune* (November 23, 1987): 229–234; Schulta, E., "America's Most Admired Corporations," *Fortune* (January 18, 1988): 32–52.

22. Freeman, R. E., and D. R. Gilbert, Jr., *Corporate Strategy and the Search for Ethics* (Englewood Cliffs, N.J.: Prentice-Hall, 1988).

23. *The Toy Industry Fact Book* (New York: Toy Manufacturers of America, 1989): 8–12.

24. Steiner and Steiner, *Business, Government, and Society*, pp. 252–254.

25. Sethi, S. P., "A Conceptual Framework for Environmental Analysis of Social Issues and Evaluation of Busi-

ness Response Patterns," *Academy of Management Review* (January, 1979): 65.

26. Committee for Economic Development, *Social Responsibilities of Business Corporations* (New York: CED, 1981): 25–26.

27. For examples of these studies see the following: Moskowitz, M., "Choosing Socially Responsible Stocks," *Business and Society Review* 1 (1972): 71–75; Bowman, E. H., and M. Haire, "A Strategic Posture Toward Corporate Social Responsibility," *California Management Review* (Winter 1975): 49–58; Sturdivant, F. D., and J. L. Ginter, "Corporate Social Responsiveness: Management Attitudes and Economic Performance," *California Management Review* (Spring 1977): 30–39; Cochran, P. L., and R. A. Wood, "Corporate Social Responsibility and Corporate Performance," *Academy of Management Journal* (March 1984); Aupperle, K. E., A. B. Carroll, and J. D. Hatfield, "An Empiri-

cal Examination of the Relationship Between Corporate Social Responsibility and Profitability," *Academy of Management Journal* (June 1986): 446–463.

28. Steiner, G. A., and J. B. Miner, *Management Policy and Strategy* (New York: Macmillan, 1986): 40–41.

29. Friedman, M., *Capitalism and Freedom* (Chicago: University of Chicago Press, 1962).

30. Friedman, M., "The Social Responsibility of Business is to Increase Its Profits," *New York Times Magazine* (September 13, 1970).

31. Steckmest, F. W., *Corporate Performance: The Key to Public Trust* (New York: McGraw-Hill, 1982).

32. Ford, R., and F. McLaughlin, "Perceptions of Socially Responsible Actions and Attitudes: A Comparison of Business School Deans and Corporate Chief Executives," *Academy of Management Journal* (September 1984): 666–674.

 ADDITIONAL READINGS

Aaker, D. A., and G. S. Day. *Consumerism: Search for the Consumer Interest.* 4th ed. New York: The Free Press, 1982.

Andrews, K. A., and D. K. David, eds. *Ethics in Practice: Managing the Moral Corporation.* Boston: Harvard Business School Press, 1989.

Bick, P. A. *Business Ethics and Responsibility: An Information Sourcebook.* Phoenix: Oryx Press, 1988.

Brady, F. N. *Ethical Managing: Rules and Results.* New York: Macmillan, 1990.

Business and Professional Ethics Journal (any issue). Troy, N.Y.: Human Dimensions Center, Rensselaer Polytechnic Institute.

Business and Society Review (any issue). New York: Warren, Gorham and Lamont.

Chamberlain, N. W. *The Limits of Corporate Responsibility.* New York: Basic Books, 1973.

Donaldson, T. *The Ethics of International Business.* New York: Oxford University Press, 1989.

Ewing, D. W. *Freedom Inside the Organization.* New York: McGraw-Hill, 1977.

Farmer, R. N., and W. D. Hogue. *Corporate Social Responsibility.* 2d ed. Lexington, Mass.: Lexington Books, 1985.

Frederick, W. C., K. Davis, and J. E. Post. *Business and Society: Corporate Strategy, Public Policy, Ethics.* 6th ed. New York: McGraw-Hill, 1988.

Jones, D. G. *A Bibliography of Business Ethics.* Lewiston, N.Y.: E. Millen Press, 1986.

Journal of Business Ethics (any issue). Boston, Mass.: D. Riedel Publishing Co.

Pastin, M. *The Hard Problems of Management: Gaining the Ethics Edge.* San Francisco: Jossey-Bass, 1986.

Paul, K., ed. *Business Environment and Business Ethics: The Social, Moral and Political Dimensions of Management.* Cambridge, Mass.: Ballinger, 1987.

Sawyer, G. C. *Business and Society: Managing Corporate Social Impact.* Boston: Houghton-Mifflin, 1979.

Sturdivant, F. D. *Business and Society: A Managerial Approach.* Homewood, Ill.: R. D. Irwin, 1985.

CHAPTER NINE

International Strategic Decisions

Today, one of the most discussed topics in the area of strategic decisions concerns global, international, or multinational strategy.[1] How does a firm in the United States counter increasing international competitiveness? How can industry reverse the decline of American competitiveness? Should an American firm close down domestic production and produce offshore? How should a firm raise capital in international financial markets? What resources should be allocated to multinational marketing versus domestic markets? These questions and others like them concerning international strategic decisions force strategists to broaden the scope of strategic planning to the international arena. Box 9.1 discusses the shift to international activities by several American firms.

CHANGES IN THE INTERNATIONAL ARENA

DECLINE OF U.S. COMPETITIVENESS

Much has been written about the decline of American competitiveness in the international arena. The U.S. merchandise trade deficit skyrocketed from about $22 billion in 1980 to nearly $160 billion in 1987. About one in three automobiles purchased in this country in the late 1980s was foreign made. Most consumer electronics products purchased in this country, including televisions and stereos, were produced by international competitors. Semiconductors and shoes have been hit by intense foreign inroads. The United States' share of world markets shrank in a number of different products. For example, from 1978 to 1988, the U.S. share of world markets in autos shrank from 19 percent to 18.2 percent, in floppy disks from 66 percent to 4 percent, and in machine tools from 14 percent to 7 percent.[2]

In trying to analyze reasons for the decline of American competitiveness,

BOX 9.1   MARKETS AND PROFITS ARE GROWING ACROSS INTERNATIONAL BORDERS

Increasingly, firms in the United States are finding that markets and the profits associated with those markets are growing faster outside of this country than within it. As the 1980s gave way to the 1990s, a growing number of American firms across a variety of industries were heavily involved in an international trend. They were increasing their production overseas, increasing their investment in plant and equipment in other countries, experiencing more rapid growth in international markets than in domestic markets, and enjoying better profit margins internationally than domestically. The magnitude of some of the international investments suggests that the corporate decision makers expect growth in international markets to continue.

For example, in December 1988, General Electric announced a major manufacturing capital investment in Spain: "General Electric Co. has completed a wide-ranging European site search by announcing plans to build a $1.7 billion plastics and silicones manufacturing facility at the port city of Cartagena on the southeast coast of Spain. The project will be built in phases over a 15-year period."[a] About one year later, as communism was undergoing wrenching changes in eastern Europe, General Electric bought just over 50 percent of Tungsram, a state-owned lighting manufacturer in Hungary, for $150 million.[b]

Examples abound in the auto industry of increased manufacturing outside of the United States by American firms, as reported in *Industry Week*.

> Ford Motor, for example, is planning to import minicars built in South Korea, will produce cars for the Canadian market in a 70% owned affiliate plant in Taiwan, and is building a plant in Mexico to export cars to the U.S. Chrysler Corp. is selling autos built by Mitsubishi Motors Corp. in Japan. General Motors Co. takes cars from Suzuki Motor Co., its Japanese affiliate, and from Daewoo Group, GM's Korean affiliate. A study by Arthur Andersen & Co. predicts that by the year 1995, some 25% of the auto parts that go into American-built cars will be produced in U.S. owned plants abroad, up from the current level of 15%.[c]

Examples abound as well in the consumer electronics industry—at least in those parts of the consumer electronics industry in which any American firms still have a manufacturing presence. *Industry Week* reported on Motorola's buying or building of semiconductor and telecommunications equipment plants in Taiwan, Japan, Hong Kong, Singapore, and Mexico. "The growing reliance on production by overseas affiliates is a major reason for the American Electronics Association's estimate of a $12 billion U.S. trade deficit in electronics in 1985."[d]

The profitability in the international markets is frequently superior to domestic profitability. According to the *Wall Street Journal* in 1989, "This year, 80% of Coke's operating earnings will come from abroad, up from 50% just four years ago. Coke may seem as American as apple pie, but the company now makes more money in Japan than in the U.S."[e] And in *Business Week:* "Coke earns about 37 cents for every gallon of soda that it sells in Japan vs. about 7 cents in the U.S. H. J. Heinz enjoys profit margins of up to 20% on its baby food sales in Italy, compared with 5% in the U.S."[f] Although GM's profits in North America left much to be desired in 1988, GM yielded net income of nearly $2 billion in Europe.[g]

Thanks to intense market competition and affluent consumers who have been bombarded with advertising throughout their lives, many American markets are saturated. Conversely, many markets in other countries are relatively untapped, especially in consumer goods. Thus, the relative growth opportunities are apparent, as the business press noted: "The real future in soft drinks is overseas, where on the whole people consume only 14% as much soda pop as Americans do. Overseas consultants and even competitors concede that Coke is in a better position than anybody else to take advantage of the potential market growth."[h] And: "Colgate is building a toothpaste factory in India and other plants in Thailand and Malaysia, where increasingly affluent consumers want Palmolive soap, shampoo, and dishwashing products."[i]

---

[a] "General Electric Investing $1.7 Billion in Manufacturing Facility in Spain," *Site Selection* (December 1988): 1382.

[b] "Who Gains from the New Europe?" *Fortune* (December 18, 1989): 84.

[c] "Exodus: Where is U.S. Industry Going? It's Heading Where Many American Manufacturers Have Already Gone—Offshore," *Industry Week* (January 6, 1986): 29.

[d] *Industry Week* (January 6, 1986): 29.

[e] "As a Global Marketer, Coke Excels by Being Tough and Consistent," *Wall Street Journal* (December 19, 1989): 1.

[f] "The Action is Abroad," *Business Week* (May 1, 1989): 29.

[g] "With Its Market Share Sliding, GM Scrambles to Avoid a Calamity," *Wall Street Journal* (December 14, 1989): 1.

[h] *Wall Street Journal* (December 19, 1989): 1.

[i] *Business Week* (May 1, 1989): 29.

Mitroff and Mohrman identified several factors: the growth of the modern large corporation, which stressed mass production for mass markets; the roles of government and organized labor, which stressed consumption and increasing wages for unions; an overdependency on slack; the emergence of the world economy; and short-term myopia, which stressed attention to quarterly profits.[3] Mitroff and Mohrman offered three lessons to be learned by American business.

> First, America had used up all its strategic reserves, or slack. The only slack still remaining is the boundless energy, creativity, and self-confidence of the American people, if only we could harness those resources to our advantage once again. Second, the age of unrefined mass production and mass consumption is over. This is the age of highly refined, specialized niche markets, paradoxically mass niche markets. Third, every strategy that created success in times of stability and plenty now produces failure in these times of severe worldwide competition.[4]

Tom Peters, coauthor of *In Search of Excellence,* echoed some of the above themes in a recent article.[5] He described a number of dramatic changes between the "old" way of doing business and the "new" way. One of the areas he stressed was the international area. He described the international operations of "old" as an adjunct activity in which "global brands" were managed from the United States. In the "new" way, international operations were described as a primary activity. "The focus is new market creation, not just lagging follow-up use of U.S. products including extensive off-shore product development, and tailoring of all products."[6]

By the mid-1980s, the changes had become so profound, and America had lost so much of its competitiveness in the international arena, especially to the Japanese, that one analyst suggested a merger between Japan and the U.S. That merger proposal, as a way to solve America's international competitiveness problems, is reproduced in Box 9.2.

The information in Box 9.2 documents and underscores the magnitude of the changes that have occurred in the international strategic arena. Immedi-

---

BOX 9.2   MARRIAGE: AN ACCEPTABLE SOLUTION?

The White House should investigate a simpler supply-side solution to the nation's monetary and fiscal problems—merger between the United States and Japan. An American-Nippon union would vastly increase the supply of savings in the U.S. financial markets. Like all insecure nations, modern Japan has a great propensity to work and save. Like all imperial powers in transition to humbler status, the United States has a great compulsion to borrow and spend in order to maintain a lifestyle that it can no longer really afford.

It was once fashionable to argue that capitalist countries had to pursue expansionary foreign policies in order to find new markets. But Japan and the United States have turned traditional theories about imperialism upside down.

The U.S. has solved the old problem of underconsumption by creating a welfare state and military industrial complex. It no longer needs a reserve army of consumers, but a reserve army of savers. In Japan, by contrast, the financial system discourages consumption and the constitution prohibits rearmament. Japan has thus evolved into a natural saver of last resort for the U.S.

Why solemnize the relationship in a formal union when the current dalliance is so satisfactory? First, the United States boom is maturing. As inflationary wrinkles appear in 1985, even the Japanese will begin to wonder if they should recycle their dollars as freely as they have so far. Second, if the U.S. would eliminate the fiction of having a financial system autonomous from Japan's, dollar interest rates could collapse and alleviate Latin America's debt servicing problem. Third, union with Japan will permit the U.S. to continue looking after the defense needs of its older relatives in Europe. The final argument is that the U.S. Treasury may accidentally destroy the unique trans-Pacific financial equilibrium now sustaining U.S. recovery and rearmament.

Source: Adapted from Hale, D., "A Modest Proposal for Marriage," *Financial Times* (October 17, 1984): 8. Used by permission of Kemper Financial Services, Chicago.

ately after World War II, the United States was the unquestioned world economic power; today, it is no longer an island unto itself. Indeed, the U.S. must compete economically with some of the same countries it defeated militarily in World War II.

CHANGING CURRENTS, CROSS-CURRENTS, AND THEMES

Michael Porter, the strategist associated with much of the competitive business-level strategy discussed in Chapter 4, has recently extended his writings to international competitive strategy. He has discussed several changing currents in international competition that have become quite strong since World War II. These changing currents serve as a background to an understanding of international competitive strategy. They are

1. Growing similarity of countries
2. Fluid global capital markets
3. Falling tariff barriers
4. Technological restructuring
5. Integrating role of technology
6. New global competitors[7]

The net result of these changing currents has been to make the international arena a fiercely competitive marketplace in which the standards of competitive success have risen dramatically in the last few decades. In dealing with international competitive forces, Ghoshal extended the concepts of production fit and marketing fit (Chapter 3) to the international arena. He offered specific examples of "factory automation with flexibility to produce multiple products at Ford and servicing multinational customers world-wide at Citibank."[8] Some analysts predict that large firms will increasingly extend production fit and marketing fit across international arenas to deal with international competitive currents.

Henzler and Rall reinforced the forces associated with increasing trends toward international strategic competition in their discussion of responses to the globalization challenge.[9] Their Factors Favoring Globalization are shown in Figure 9.1. They used a straightforward analysis of supply and demand to come to the same conclusion as Porter that there has been increasing international competition. They also determined that the forces responsible for the increased international competition will most likely be long-lived forces.

Several of these changes are reflected in the data on international competitiveness. Table 9.1 documents worker productivity in the U.S., Japan, West Germany, and South Korea from 1950 to 1987. In that time period, the United States had gone from a position of unquestioned superiority in worker productivity to a position of a slim lead. Such small productivity differences indicate a reason for fierce international competitiveness among the four countries.

Just as the level of international competition has risen, there have been some cross-currents that have made the patterns of international competition

FIGURE 9.1 FACTORS FAVORING GLOBALIZATION

DEMAND	Homogeneous requirements of industrial customers operating worldwide (e.g., machine tools, plant construction)
	Uniform technical standards
	Homogeneous demand from consumer levels (consumer electronics, small cars, prestige goods, etc.)
SUPPLY	Significant economies of scale: • R & D • Purchasing • Manufacturing • Distribution Advantages in access to resources Opportunity for positive differentiation through special skills/features of business system
ECONOMIC ENVIRONMENT	Low/no customs barriers Free movement of capital

Source: Henzler, H., and W. Rall, "Facing Up to the Globalization Challenge," *McKinsey Quarterly* (Winter 1986): 52–68. Used by permission.

TABLE 9.1   AMERICA'S SHRINKING LEAD IN WORKER PRODUCTIVITY

	1950	1970	1987
United States	$23.3	$34.5	$39.2
Japan	3.5	15.8	27.6
West Germany	8.0	21.4	31.6
South Korea	N.A.	5.6	13.3

Note: Figures are output per worker in thousands of 1987 dollars. Dollar amounts were translated from foreign currencies using purchasing power parities.
N.A. = Not Available.

Source: "Many Americans Fear U.S. Living Standards Have Stopped Rising: Nagging Lag in Productivity," *Wall Street Journal* (May 1, 1989): 1. Reprinted by permission of the *Wall Street Journal,* © 1989 Dow Jones & Company, Inc. All Rights Reserved Worldwide.

very complex and different from earlier competitive strategies of the 1950s. Due to the cross-currents, it is no longer adequate to have a standardized, global strategy in which an American firm manufactures standardized products in the United States and distributes them worldwide. These cross-currents are:

1. Slowing rates of economic growth
2. Eroding types of comparative advantage
3. New forms of protectionism
4. New types of government inducement
5. Proliferating coalitions among firms from different countries
6. Growing ability to tailor to local conditions[10]

Because of the currents and cross-currents, many more firms have become international in their strategies and operations. These strategies are complicated relative to the strategies employed in the era shortly after World War II. The recent strategies revolve around several themes described by Porter:

1. There is no one pattern of international competition nor one type of global strategy.
2. The globalization of competition has become the rule rather than the exception by 1986.
3. The nature of international competition has changed markedly in the last two decades.
4. Implementing a global approach to strategy requires a difficult organizational reorientation for many firms.[11]

The forces for increased international economic competition and international strategies were well entrenched as this book was being written in 1990. It appeared that the forces in favor of increased competition were becoming stronger. Trade barriers were scheduled to be lowered so dramatically in Europe in 1992 that some spoke of the "United States of Europe." The U.S. and Canada were in the process of lowering trade barriers. Japan was locating a number of automobile manufacturing plants in this country. Korea was competing internationally and taking market share from Japan in the same way that Japan took market share from the U.S., namely price leadership.[12] The People's Republic of China was entering the international competitive arena as it strengthened its internal economy. It appeared that international strategic decisions would only take on increased importance as the United States entered the 1990s.

INTERNATIONAL STRATEGIC OPTIONS

TYPES OF INTERNATIONAL STRATEGY

After discussing the forces in favor of globalization, Henzler and Rall presented the four major global decision alternatives facing a firm. These four alternatives are a function of the advantages of global business systems versus the advantages or importance of local adaptation. The advantages of global business systems may arise from economic advantages associated with economies of scale or learning curve effects or from other worldwide efficiency or competitive advantages. Advantages of local adaptation may arise from cultural, regulatory, economic, or competitive bases. Henzler and Rall's Global/ Local Tradeoff is shown in Figure 9.2.

Examples of global businesses include computers and consumer electronics, in which there were few advantages of local adaptation and strong advantages of globalization. Local/national businesses were defined as those in which high local adaptation is important for national success and there are few arguments in favor of globalization. Examples include food processing and basic chemicals. "Blocked" local businesses are those that might be global from a purely economic advantage viewpoint, but government restraints prevent such globalization and encourage local businesses. Examples include regional telephone networks and parts of the weapons industry. Multinational/ multimarket businesses are those that require some degree of local adaptation and in which globalization of all functions offers little competitive advantage. Electrical equipment is one example.[13] These two dimensions, Advantages of Global Business System and Advantages of Local Adaptation, are two powerful strategic dimensions for a firm to consider as it makes decisions on international strategy.

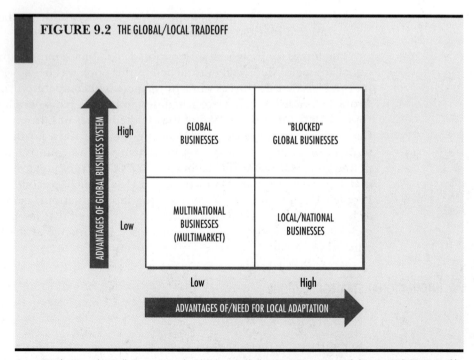

FIGURE 9.2 THE GLOBAL/LOCAL TRADEOFF

Source: Henzler, H., and W. Rall, "Facing Up to the Globalization Challenge," *McKinsey Quarterly* (Winter 1986): 52–68. Used by permission.

INTERNATIONAL MARKETS AND PRODUCTS

Once the firm has decided to pursue a degree of international activities, a more discrete listing of decision alternatives is needed. Using a familiar treatment of Market Scope and Product Scope, and borrowing a growth vector analysis from J. Daniels, Sheth and Eshghi developed a grid designed to produce nine strategic decision alternatives (Figure 9.3).

A good example in the Present Products/Existing Market cell is the apparel industry, which uses offshore sewing of garments as a way to lower costs for apparel. Ford and Chrysler have provided examples for the Existing Market/Improved Products cell: Chrysler licensed an Italian-designed body for one of its autos, and Ford licensed Japanese engine parts for its Super High Output engine in a Ford Taurus. Chevrolet provided examples in the Existing Market/New Products cell by distributing a Geo line of small low-priced cars. In the Expanded Market/Present Products cell, Colgate-Palmolive was building a toothpaste manufacturing capability in Southeast Asia at the time of this writing. As personal-care practices change in increasingly affluent Asian coun-

FIGURE 9.3 INTERNATIONAL STRATEGIC DECISION ALTERNATIVES

		Present products	Improved products	New products
	Existing market	1. Reduce cost by offshore procurement or production	2. License product technology from abroad to differentiate present products	3. Add complementary products by distributing for foreign manufacturers
MARKET SCOPE	Expanded market	4. Seek foreign markets with higher product usage rates	5. Seek foreign markets by differentiated product stragegy	6. Acquire foreign products and integrate them forward
	New market	7. Transfer of technology through licensing or joint venture	8. Transfer of technology product, which is differentiated through R & D	9. Acquire foreign companies in foreign markets

PRODUCT SCOPE

tries, we should expect to see increasing activities of this type. In the New Market/Present Products cell, an example occurred between the People's Republic of China and Volkswagen when the PRC entered into a joint venture to produce VW autos in the PRC. In the Expanded Market/Improved Products category, an example occurred when a popular word-processing software package (WordPerfect) was modified to include spell checkers in foreign languages. A good example in the New Products/New Markets cell occurred when Grand Met of England acquired Pillsbury, including its Burger King subsidiary. The management of Grand Met acknowledged that they had no experience in the fast-food industry.

The nine different strategic alternatives have different implications for international operations. Daniels presented a growth vector analysis (Figure 9.4) as a way to understand the operational implications of the nine different international strategic decisions described in Figure 9.3. The process of loosening trade barriers among the western European nations, known as Europe 1992, should create a large, lucrative, loosely organized, multinational market in Europe. As Europe loosens its trade barriers, we can expect to see American firms pursuing more of the operations listed in Figure 9.4 in Europe.[14]

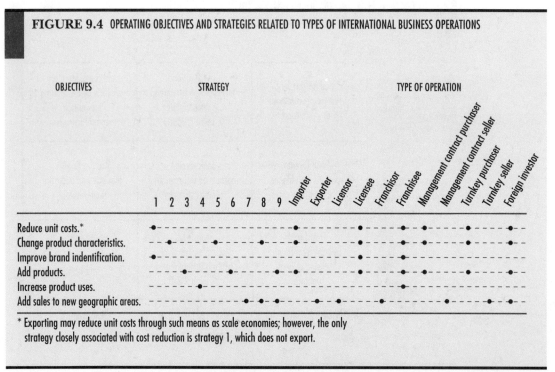

FIGURE 9.4 OPERATING OBJECTIVES AND STRATEGIES RELATED TO TYPES OF INTERNATIONAL BUSINESS OPERATIONS

* Exporting may reduce unit costs through such means as scale economies; however, the only strategy closely associated with cost reduction is strategy 1, which does not export.

Source: Daniels, J., "Combining Strategic and International Business Approaches Through Growth Vector Analysis." *Management International Review* 23, no. 2 (1983): 4–15. Used by permission of Gabler Publishers, Wiesbaden, Germany.

In international operations, Kogut argued that the firm should confront "the decision of what activities and technologies along the value-added chain a firm should concentrate its investment and managerial resources in, relative to other firms in its industry."[15] Kogut described an international value-added analysis with data from Panasonic and Radio Shack (Figure 9.5). As Panasonic adds most of its value in manufacturing and wholesaling, it should concentrate on those activities in its international operations. Conversely, as Radio Shack adds most of its value in its marketing activities, it should concentrate on those activities in its international operation.

FIGURE 9.5 VALUE-ADDED ANALYSIS FOR CONSUMER ELECTRONIC PRODUCTS

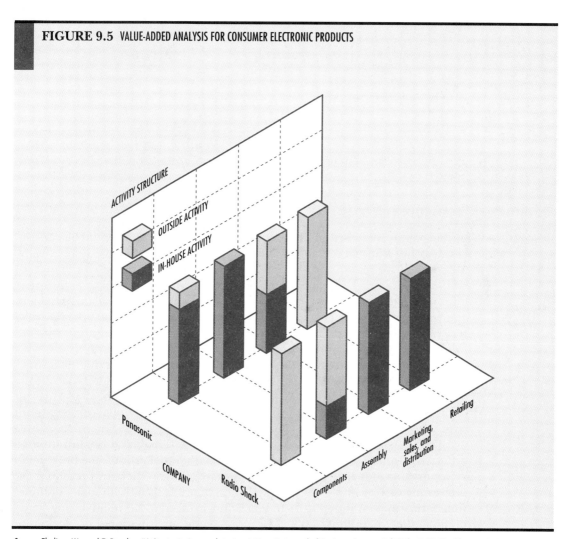

Source: Ebeling, W., and T. Doorley, "A Strategic Approach to Acquisitions," *Journal of Business Strategy* 3 (1983): 44–55. Used by permission.

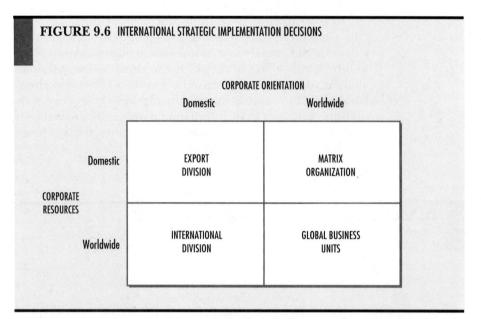

FIGURE 9.6 INTERNATIONAL STRATEGIC IMPLEMENTATION DECISIONS

Source: Reproduced from Sheth, J., and Eshghi, G., *Global Strategic Management Perspectives* (Cincinnati: South-Western Publishing Co., 1989): xii, with the permission of South-Western Publishing Co. Copyright 1989 by South-Western Publishing Co. All rights reserved.

IMPLEMENTATION DECISIONS

As thoroughly discussed in Chapter 6, strategy and structure should be consistent. It is not unusual for an organization to change its strategy dramatically for competitive reasons. Just as it takes time to turn a ship the size of an aircraft carrier, however, it takes time for a firm to change its structure, for organizational inertia reasons. As indicated in the first section of this chapter, many of the forces favoring international economic competition are relatively recent yet quite strong. Thus, it is not unusual to find an organization with an international strategy and a domestic structure.

In an attempt to stress the desired consistency between international strategy and structure, Sheth and Eshghi developed a grid of global strategic management perspectives, shown in Figure 9.6. The figure is instructive in understanding the desired consistency between international strategy and structure.[16]

The transition from a domestic firm to an international organization is not a trivial one. The transition requires changes in operations, the functional areas, organizational structure, and corporate culture. Dickson presented an interesting case example of an organization that was faced with many of these transformations. Although the organization preferred the relative simplicity of domestic operations, it became a reluctant multinational to maintain growth.[17] Sheth and Eshghi described the haphazard evolution of some firms into "reluctant multinationals":

Many companies become multinational reluctantly. They start off as export houses, and as international business grows and becomes a significant part of corporate revenues, they become more involved in foreign operations. However, the corporate culture still remains domestic, and the international division is treated as a stepchild. The situation becomes one of them vs. us. Although they may be resolved by a matrix organization, what is lacking is a true worldwide orientation in product design, manufacturing, and marketing functions.[18]

Although a matrix organization is not a panacea, it has been used in a number of international situations. A matrix allows a firm's domestic operations to integrate across functions and business units. A good example of a multinational matrix organization is shown in Figure 9.7 on page 210.

Egelhoff recently reviewed the literature on strategy and structure in multinational corporations. He concluded that there is a new element of strategy—the relative size of foreign manufacturing—that is an important predictor of structure.[19] International manufacturing and operations strategy is reviewed in the next section.

INTERNATIONAL FUNCTIONAL STRATEGIC DECISIONS

INTERNATIONAL OPERATIONS STRATEGY

Few functional areas have received as much attention from writers in international strategy as international production and operations strategy. Several recent articles have pointed out the severity of the international challenge facing U.S. manufacturing, production, and operations and have discussed some needed changes if American industry is to remain competitive in this area.[20]

A good example of the heralded competitive advantage of Japanese manufacturers relative to American manufacturers is shown in Figure 9.8. Bower and Hout documented the shorter time Toyota took to complete most manufacturing operations relative to Detroit, with the net result that Toyota needed three years to develop a new car versus five years for Detroit. The authors argued, however, that some American firms were starting to recognize fast-cycle capability as a competitive weapon. "People in fast-cycle companies think of themselves as part of an integrated system, a linked chain of operations and decision-making points that continuously delivers value to the company's customers."[21]

One of the most scathing criticisms of American manufacturing was offered by one of the most noted writers in the field of operations strategy, S. Wheelwright. "U.S. manufacturing competitiveness has slipped in a broad range of industries," Wheelright wrote. "The decline of U.S. manufacturing competitiveness has not been due primarily to labor costs. The single most important explanation for the worldwide decline in U.S. manufacturing competitiveness is management's view of the manufacturing function, its role, and

FIGURE 9.7 A MULTINATIONAL MATRIX ORGANIZATION

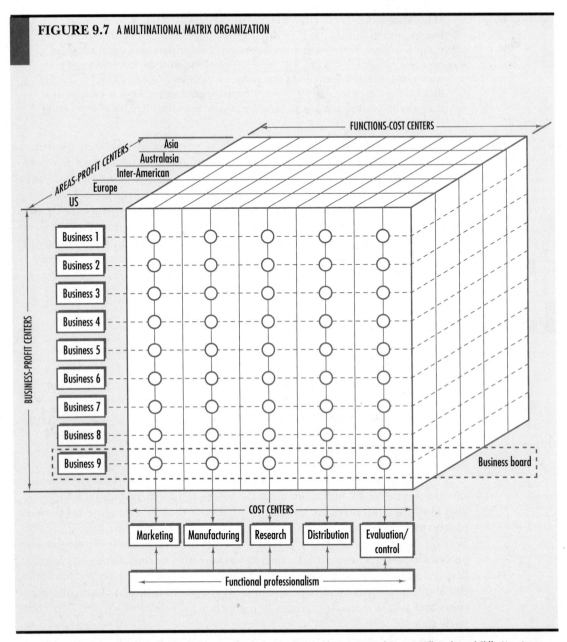

Source: Peter Lorange, *Implementation of Strategic Planning,* © 1982, p. 199. Reprinted by permission of Prentice-Hall, Englewood Cliffs, New Jersey.

FIGURE 9.8 FAST-CYCLE CAPABILITY

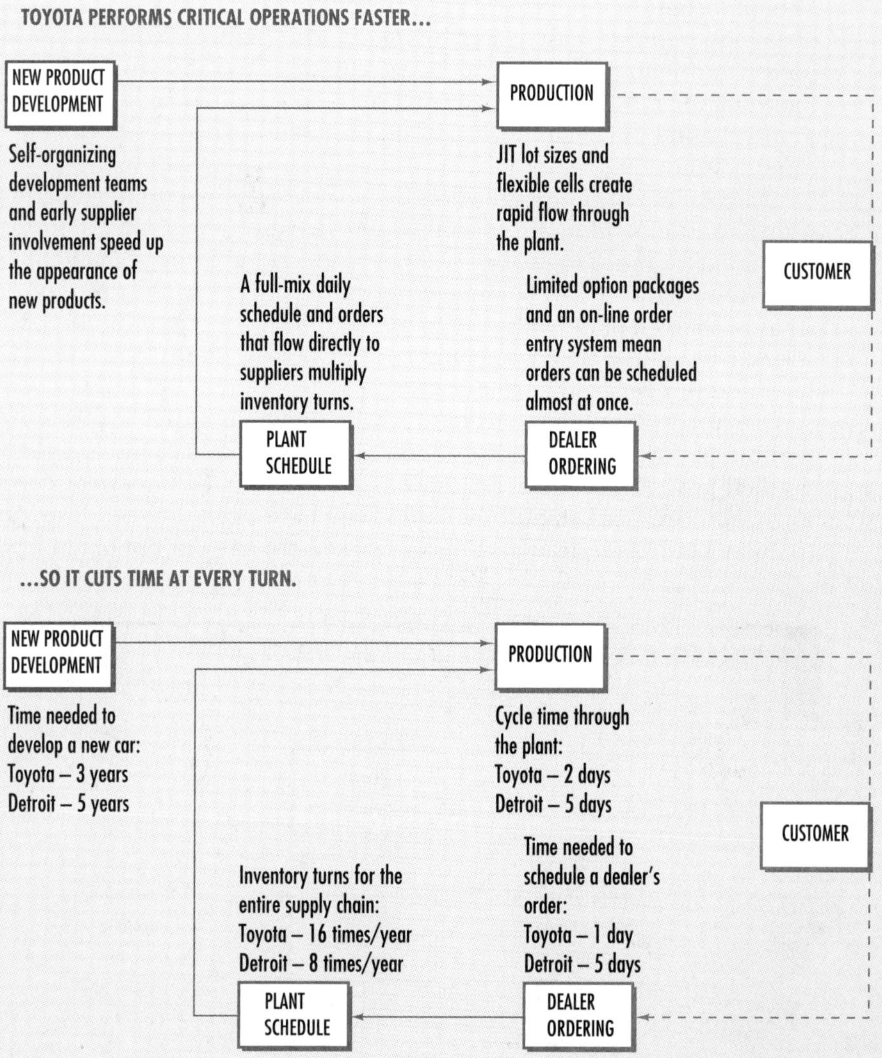

TOYOTA PERFORMS CRITICAL OPERATIONS FASTER...

| NEW PRODUCT DEVELOPMENT | → | PRODUCTION |

NEW PRODUCT DEVELOPMENT

Self-organizing development teams and early supplier involvement speed up the appearance of new products.

A full-mix daily schedule and orders that flow directly to suppliers multiply inventory turns.

PRODUCTION

JIT lot sizes and flexible cells create rapid flow through the plant.

Limited option packages and an on-line order entry system mean orders can be scheduled almost at once.

CUSTOMER

PLANT SCHEDULE

DEALER ORDERING

...SO IT CUTS TIME AT EVERY TURN.

NEW PRODUCT DEVELOPMENT

Time needed to develop a new car:
Toyota – 3 years
Detroit – 5 years

Inventory turns for the entire supply chain:
Toyota – 16 times/year
Detroit – 8 times/year

PRODUCTION

Cycle time through the plant:
Toyota – 2 days
Detroit – 5 days

Time needed to schedule a dealer's order:
Toyota – 1 day
Detroit – 5 days

CUSTOMER

PLANT SCHEDULE

DEALER ORDERING

Source: Reprinted by permission of *Harvard Business Review.* An exhibit from "Fast-Cycle Capability for Competitive Power" by J. Bower and T. Hout (November-December 1988). Copyright © 1988 by the President and Fellows of Harvard College; all rights reserved.

how that ought to be carried out. Thus, restoring that competitive edge requires a basic change in philosophy, perspective, and approach."[22]

In 1985, when Wheelwright wrote his critique of the American mind-set concerning manufacturing, many U.S. firms had not yet realized the severity of the changes facing American production due to international competition. The important forces influencing a firm's decision to pursue global manufacturing operations—cost competitiveness, competitive markets, government policy, and manufacturing processes—are depicted in Figure 9.9. Several of the changing cross-currents, currents, and themes discussed in the first section of this chapter impact quite heavily on production and manufacturing, as indicated in Figure 9.9.

Factors in cost competitiveness include the relative cost of labor, materials, transportation, and, more recently, exchange rates. Some decisions to manufacture in Taiwan, Korea, the Caribbean, and Hong Kong seemed to be associated with relatively low labor costs in those countries. The more recent decisions by many Japanese firms to locate manufacturing facilities in this country seemed to be associated with the cost advantage due to the strength of the Japanese yen versus the American dollar.

Competitive markets become a reason to pursue global manufacturing operations as foreign competitors enter American markets and as international markets grow. The former may have been a reason for Goodyear to enter the European tire market, and the latter may have been a reason for Whirlpool to enter Latin American and Asian markets for growth opportunities.

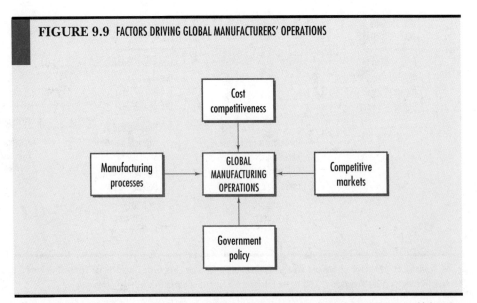

FIGURE 9.9 FACTORS DRIVING GLOBAL MANUFACTURERS' OPERATIONS

Source: Reproduced from Sheth, J., and Eshghi, G., *Global Operations Perspectives* (Cincinnati: South-Western Publishing Co., 1989): viii, with the permission of South-Western Publishing Co. Copyright 1989 by South-Western Publishing Co. All rights reserved.

Government policy that lowers trade barriers encourages global manufacturing operations. Sometimes fear of import restrictions from a host government causes a firm to decide to locate manufacturing facilities in the host country so that the manufactured items escape the feared import restrictions. This reasoning may explain the decisions of several Japanese firms to locate automobile plants in the United States.

Improved manufacturing technologies have been associated with the decision to pursue global manufacturing operations. Automation and the extensive use of information technologies permit many firms to pursue worldwide operations with efficiency.

As Figure 9.2 suggests, international operations decisions may take several different forms. Export operations seem to be appropriate for generic products such as agriculture products, diamonds, and strategic metals. Specialty chemicals, telecommunications, and processed foods are examples in which localization of operations is important. Therefore, licenses, subsidiary operations, or joint ventures may be appropriate. In the appliance industry, customization by country is desirable. "Americans make free-standing behemoths; Europeans prefer smaller build-ins. In France, 80% of washing machines are top-loaders; elsewhere, 90% are front-loaders. Nine out of ten German ranges are electric; elsewhere, gas is the rule."[23] With customization by country and scale economies with regard to interchangeable parts, multinational operations or a subsidiary structure are appropriate. Consumer electronics and office equipment are two examples in which localization of operations is unimportant and global operations or integrated manufacturing are appropriate.[24]

Global manufacturing will be an international competitive battleground at least through the 1990s. There is hope for the U.S. manufacturing industry. After Wheelwright's criticism of 1985, a growing number of American firms seemed to have recognized the challenge and were in the process of implementing some of the needed changes in 1990.[25] According to *Business Week,* "A new vision of tomorrow's manufacturing enterprise is emerging. This time, automation won't just get slapped on top of the same old structure, which simply produces more bad results quicker. Instead, reorganization will take place from the ground up. The goal isn't just to work faster, but smarter—with the help of lots of artificial intelligence (AI) buried in a new generation of manufacturing systems. The Japanese may outclass the U.S. in manufacturing skills, but these few ultra-advanced plants are so far an all-American thrust."[26]

INTERNATIONAL MARKETING STRATEGY

International marketing strategy has received almost as much attention in the literature as the area of international operations strategy. The decision to market globally, the decision to pursue either standardized or focused international marketing programs, cross-cultural differences affecting advertising and packaging programs, and some classic international marketing errors have all been well documented.[27]

The international marketing errors described in Box 9.3 are enlightening.

BOX 9.3   SOME PROBLEMS IN IMPLEMENTING GLOBAL MARKETING DECISIONS

Ignorance of language differences sometimes causes products to be shunned by consumers in other countries. For example, Chevrolet's "Nova" was spoken as "no va" in Spanish, which means "it doesn't go." Coca-Cola in Chinese characters became "bite the wax tadpole" or "a wax-flattened mare." Ford's "Fiera" meant "ugly old woman" in Spanish.[a]

Initially, Campbell's canned soups did not catch on in soup-loving Brazil. A study indicated that most Brazilian housewives felt they were not fulfilling their responsibilities if they served soup they could not call their own. The Brazilian housewives, however, had few problems using dehydrated products, which they could use as a soup starter and still add their own ingredients.[b] Campbell's Soup tried to sell condensed soup in Great Britain, but the British were convinced that they were receiving half as much soup as before. The company was obliged to modify the product by adding water to conform to the accepted mode of purchase.[c]

Johnson and Johnson had problems selling baby powder in its original package in Japan. Japanese mothers feared that powder would fly around their small homes and enter their immaculate kitchens when sprinkled from the plastic bottle. Sales picked up after Johnson and Johnson repackaged the powder in a flat box with a powder puff, which allowed the Japanese mothers to apply the powder sparingly.[d]

Tandy Corporation planned its first Christmas promotion of Radio Shack stores in Holland in anticipation of December 25, as is the custom in this country. After experiencing disappointing sales, the company discovered that the Dutch exchange gifts on December 6, St. Nicholas Day.[e]

---

[a] Ricks, D., *Big Business Blunders: Mistakes in Multinational Marketing* (Homewood, Ill.: Dow Jones-Irwin, 1983): 37–47.

[b] "Brazil: Campbell Soup Fails to Make it to the Table," *Business Week* (October 21, 1981): 66.

[c] Hardy, K., "Add Value, Boost Margins," *Business Quarterly* (Summer 1989): 63.

[d] Kraar, L., "Inside Japan's 'Open' Market," *Fortune* (October 5, 1981): 122.

[e] "Radio Shack's Rough Trip," *Business Week* (May 30, 1977): 55.

Some companies have discovered that something as simple as a product's name can prove to be insulting when translated. The errors indicate the importance of careful, detailed planning, including awareness of cultural and language differences, before implementing the decision to market products or services in other countries.

There are several reasons why a firm may decide to launch an international marketing program. The most important reasons are summarized in Figure 9.10. The lack of growth in domestic markets is one of the most common decision criteria for pursuing an international marketing program. For example, in the U.S. appliance industry, lack of growth in the American mar-

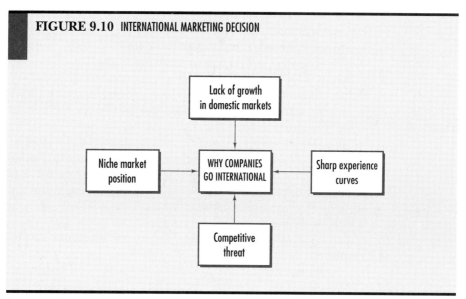

FIGURE 9.10 INTERNATIONAL MARKETING DECISION

Source: Reproduced from Sheth, J., and Eshghi, G., *Global Marketing Perspectives* (Cincinnati: South-Western Publishing Co., 1989): viii, with the permission of South-Western Publishing Co. Copyright 1989 by South-Western Publishing Co. All rights reserved.

kets seems to have been associated with decisions to launch international marketing programs. As *Fortune* noted, "Why go global? Simple: After four decades of rising sales and relentless consolidation, the American white-goods business is no place to make serious money. The market is as mature as your great-aunt Maude. Unit sales plateaued at 28 million in 1987 and are expected to fall more than 2% in 1990."[28]

Sharp experience curves associated with high volume and dramatically lowered production costs seem to be another decision criterion for launching international marketing programs. The electronics and semiconductor industries are two good examples. Competition is another strong reason to market internationally. Sometimes international marketing is an offensive move to prevent competitor inroads or a semioffensive move in response to a competitive threat. Sometimes the move is defensive and in retaliation to actual competitor moves. As this book was being written, U.S. automobile companies were trying to build sales programs in Japan, partly in response to Japanese inroads in the American automobile market. Some firms have positioned themselves in niche markets and can become global niche marketers. Rolls Royce and Mercedes are two good examples.[29]

INTERNATIONAL FINANCE STRATEGY

The international financial picture has received almost as much attention in the recent past as the subjects of international operations and marketing strategies. Various authors have dealt with the issues of incentives for international investments, international investment decisions, international cost of capital, capital structure, and the extreme volatility in exchange rates.[30]

Since it became the largest stock market in the world in the 1980s and thereby influenced other stock exchanges, the Tokyo Stock Market is now of great interest to many Americans.[31] Several global financial forces are highlighted in Box 9.4, which concerns the shortening of Japanese horizons.

Many analysts have presented the notion that the volatility in international finance is a major issue in itself. According to Lessard, "The emergence of global competition, coupled with both increased integration of financial markets and continued exchange rate volatility represents a major threat and challenge to U.S. firms that have been accustomed to world market leadership under multidomestic competition."[32] This exchange rate volatility may continue partly because of increased use of debt financing by multinationals on a worldwide basis.[33]

In an attempt to model the volatility of international finance, Figure 9.11 is offered. As more and more foreign financial markets become linked electronically to each other on a real-time basis, the volatility can increase. The

BOX 9.4   THE SHORTENING OF JAPANESE HORIZONS

One of the most powerful yet least celebrated forces driving commerce toward global standardization is the monetary system, along with the international investment process.

Today money is simply electronic impulses. With the speed of light it moves effortlessly between distant centers (and even more distant places). A change of ten basis points in the price of a bond causes an instant and massive shift of money from London to Tokyo. The system has profound impact on the way companies operate throughout the world.

Take Japan, where high debt-to-equity balance sheets are "guaranteed" by various societal presumptions about the virtue of "a long view," or by government policy in other ways. Even here, upward shifts in interest rates in other parts of the world attract capital out of the country in powerful proportions. In recent years more and more Japanese global corporations have gone to the world's equity markets for funds. Debt is too remunerative in high-yielding countries to keep capital at home to feed the Japanese need. As interest rates rise, equity becomes a more attractive option for the issuer.

The long-term impact on Japanese enterprise will be transforming. As the equity proportion of Japanese corporate capitalization rises, companies will respond to the shorter term investment horizons of the equity markets. Thus the much-vaunted Japanese corporate practice to taking the long view will gradually disappear.

Source: Modified and reprinted by permission of *Harvard Business Review*. An excerpt from "The Globalization of Markets," by T. Levitt (May–June 1983): 92–102. Copyright © 1983 by the President and Fellows of Harvard College; all rights reserved.

FIGURE 9.11 DIVERSITY AND VOLATILITY OF INTERNATIONAL FINANCE

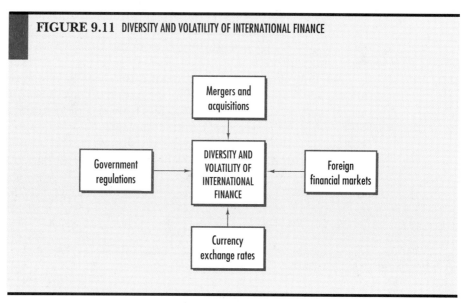

electronic speed with which the world's stock markets crashed in unison in October 1987 is a telling example of how foreign financial markets affect the volatility of international finance. The floating currency exchange rates in operation since the late 1970s have increased volatility since the fixed exchange rate era. In the time of fixed exchange rates, government regulations may have dampened volatility. In the era of floating exchange rates, new government regulations may increase volatility as funds seek market levels independent of government restraints. The Federal Reserve Board has seen some of its power to control U.S. interest rates diminished due to the size of the Japanese and German financial markets.[34] International mergers and acquisitions add to diversity and complexity in international finance. For example, in the recent acquisition of Pillsbury by Grand Met, should the financing calculations be done on the basis of cost-of-capital calculations from Great Britain or from the United States?

INTERNATIONAL HUMAN RESOURCE MANAGEMENT STRATEGY

As many firms have decided to pursue international production, marketing, and financial opportunities, an increasing amount of attention has been focused on the subject of international human resource management (HRM) strategy. Many recent articles have pursued the concept of cultural differences that must be addressed in international HRM activities.[35] Some theorists have explored specific cultural differences in areas such as training procedures and have studied different HRM practices in the United States, Korea, Japan, Europe, and China.[36]

A telling description of national differences in managerial assumptions about supervision is contained in the data in Figure 9.12. The data are from a 1986 survey by Laurent of managers from several countries. Such dramatic differences in the perceived role of management might explain different international HRM practices such as the disparate degrees of participation in corporate governance between management and workers.

FIGURE 9.12 NATIONAL DIFFERENCES IN MANAGERIAL ASSUMPTIONS

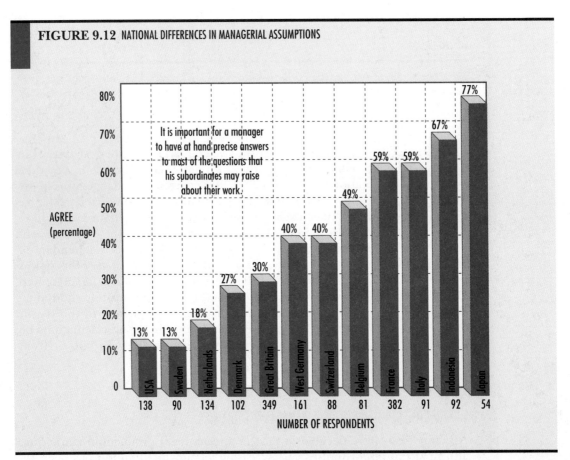

Source: Laurant, A., "The Cross-Cultural Puzzle of International Human Resource Management," *Human Resource Management* 25, no. 1 (Spring 1986): 93. Copyright © 1986 by John Wiley & Sons, Inc. Used by permission of John Wiley & Sons, Inc.

INTERNATIONAL R&D STRATEGY

It appears that R&D has become a potent international competitive weapon.[37] "Now, R&D is Corporate America's answer to Japan Inc.," said *Business Week* in 1986. "Call it Science Inc. In less than a decade, as U.S. companies have struggled against the wave of competition from abroad, they have reshaped the way new products and processes are developed. Company scientists are working shoulder-to-shoulder with academic researchers. Arch-competitors are forging alliances with one another. And research spending is soaring."[38] American nondefense R&D spending as a percent of gross national product increased from 1.6 percent to 1.9 percent between 1979 and 1987. That increase followed the period from 1972 to 1979 in which the percentage was unchanged at 1.6 percent.[39]

Not only are American firms spending more on R&D as part of an international strategy, but they are also protecting those investments in R&D more aggressively. Patent-infringement litigation has increasingly been used as part of a firm's international R&D strategy. The *Wall Street Journal* reported in 1988 that Texas Instruments "earned $191 million last year—nearly half its pretax profit—from successful patent-infringement litigation against nine rivals in Japan and South Korea." Other semiconductor companies, as well as biotechnology companies, computer makers, and software houses, were doing the same as part of a "stiffening resolve to protect their secrets."[40]

Some analysts forecast that corporate America will make increasing use of R&D as an international competitive weapon.[41] A firm must also be able to produce what it invents, however.[42] Thus, the strength of R&D and operations programs becomes important in assessing a firm's international competitive strength.

INTERNATIONAL INFORMATION SYSTEMS STRATEGY

Like R&D, information systems will increasingly become an international competitive weapon. Examples include computer-integrated manufacturing and airline computerized worldwide reservation systems.[43] The strength of a firm's information systems could assume importance in assessing the firm's international competitive strength. Few models exist to describe international R&D strategy or international information systems strategy, as they are both relatively new areas of international functional strategy.

SUMMARY

International economic competition has increased dramatically in the past few decades. Associated with that increased competition is a relative decline in America's competitiveness. As international competition is expected to intensify in the years ahead, associated partly with worldwide declining trade barriers, the subject of international strategy assumes increased importance.

The advantages of global business systems must be weighed relative to the advantages of local adaptation in deciding on international strategy. That tradeoff may yield either global businesses, multinational/multimarket businesses, "blocked" global business, or local/national businesses.

There are at least nine different international strategic decision alternatives, which may be explained in terms of market scope and product scope. The alternatives in existing markets are to reduce cost by offshore procurement or production, license product technology from abroad to differentiate present products, and add complementary foreign products by distributing for foreign manufacturers. In expanded markets, alternatives include seeking foreign markets with higher product usage rates, seeking foreign markets by differentiated product strategy, and acquiring foreign products to integrate them forward. In the new market category, alternatives are to transfer technology through licensing or joint venture, transfer technology product differentiated through R&D, and acquire foreign companies in foreign markets.

The preceding nine different international strategic decision alternatives are associated with varying degrees of international operations. The operations range from importer to foreign investor. In pursuing international operations, firms should analyze their activities to determine where and how they add value.

International structural implementation decision alternatives are functions of corporate resources and corporate orientation. The alternatives include export division, international division, matrix organization, and global business units. Decisions on global manufacturing operations are functions of manufacturing processes, cost competitiveness, competitive markets, and government policy. The strategic alternatives for international operations include global operations (integrated manufacturing), export operations, multinational operations (subsidiary structure), and localized operations (licenses and joint ventures). Firms frequently pursue international marketing programs because of competitors threats, a lack of growth in domestic markets, cost advantages due to sharp experience curves, or their own niche market position.

The diversity and volatility of international finance have increased due to the growth in foreign financial markets, international mergers and acquisitions, floating exchange rates, and variable government regulations.

International human resource management strategies are complicated by cultural differences and differing assumptions among managers from different countries concerning the role of management versus the role of nonmanagers. Both international R&D strategy and international information systems strategy are growing in use as international competitive weapons.

DISCUSSION QUESTIONS

1. Describe some of the forces favoring globalization.
2. Differentiate between global and multinational strategies.

3. Describe the international strategic decision alternatives.

4. Does cost competitiveness promote or hinder international manufacturing? How?

5. Is an international marketing program an offensive or a defensive competitive move? Explain.

6. How is the growth of foreign financial markets related to the diversity and volatility of international finance?

■ ENDNOTES

1. Chatravarty, B. S., "Strategic Planning for a Global Business," *Columbia Journal of World Business* 20 (Summer 1985): 3–10;   Farin, W. R., and C. B. Gilmore, "Developing a Strategy for International Business," *Long Range Planning* 19 (June 1985): 81–85; Garland, J., R. Farmer, and M. Taylor, *International Dimensions of Business Policy and Strategy,* 2d ed. (Boston: PWS-KENT Publishing Co., 1990); Kefalas, A. G., *Global Business Strategy* (Cincinnati: South-Western Publishing Co., 1990); Godiwalla, Y. H., "Multinational Planning—Developing a Global Approach," *Long Range Planning* 19 (April 1986): 110–116; Leontiades, J. C., *Multinational Corporate Strategy* (Lexington, Mass.: D. C. Heath, 1985); Ricks, D. A., B. Toyne, and Z. Martinez, "Recent Developments in International Management Research," *Journal of Management* 16 (1990): 219–253; Phatak, A., *International Dimensions of Management,* 2d ed. (Boston: PWS-KENT Publishing Co., 1989); Porter, M. E., "Changing Patterns of International Competition," *California Management Review* 27 (Winter 1986): 9–40.

2. "Getting High Tech Back on Track," *Fortune* (January 1, 1990): 74.

3. Mitroff, I., and S. Mohrman, "The Slack is Gone: How the United States Lost Its Competitive Edge in the World Economy," *Academy of Management Executive* 1 (February 1987): 65–70.

4. Ibid., p. 69.

5. Peters, T., "A World Turned Upside Down," *Academy of Management Executive* 1 (August 1987): 233–243.

6. Ibid., p. 234.

7. Porter, M. E., ed., *Competition in Global Industries* (Boston: Harvard Business School Press, 1986): 2–3.

8. Ghoshal, S., "Global Strategy: An Organizing Framework," *Strategic Management Journal* 8 (September–October 1987): 435.

9. Henzler, H., and W. Rall, "Facing Up to the Globalization Challenge," *McKinsey Quarterly* (Winter 1986): 52–68.

10. Porter, *Competition in Global Industries,* pp. 3–4.

11. Ibid., pp. 5–7.

12. "Japan is Getting a Dose of What It Gave U.S.: Low-Priced Imports," *Wall Street Journal* (July 20, 1988): 1.

13. Henzler and Rall, "Facing Up to the Globalization Challenge," pp. 71–72.

14. "Reshaping Europe: 1992 and Beyond," *Business Week* (December 12, 1988): 48–73; "Writing the New Rules for Europe's Merger Game," *Business Week* (February 6, 1989): 48–49; Weihrich, H., "Europe 1992: What the Future May Hold," *Academy of Management Executive* 4 (May 1990): 7–18; Yon, E., "Corporate Strategy and the New Europe," *Academy of Management Executive* 4 (August 1990): 61–65.

15. Kogut, B., "Designing Global Strategies: Comparative and Competitive Value-Added Chains," *Sloan Management Review* 26 (Summer 1985): 15–28.

16. Sheth, J., and G. Eshghi, *Global Strategic Management Perspectives* (Cincinnati: South-Western Publishing Co., 1989): xii.

17. Dickson, D., "Case of the Reluctant Multinational," *Harvard Business Review* (January–February 1983): 6–16.

18. Sheth and Eshghi, *Global Strategic Management Perspectives,* p. xiii.

19. Egelhoff, W., "Strategy and Structure in Multinational Corporations: A Revision of the Stopford and Wells Model," *Strategic Management Journal* 9 (January–February 1988): 1–14.

20. Bocker, H., et al., "The Factory of Tomorrow: Challenges of the Future," *Management International Review* 26 (1986): 36–49; Ferdows, K., et al., "Evolving Global Manufacturing Strategies: Projections into the 1990's," *International Journal of Operations and Production Management* 6 (1985): 5–14; Flaherty, M., "Coordinating International Manufacturing and Technology," in Porter, *Competition in Global Industries,* pp. 83–110; Starr, M., "Global Production and Operations Strategy," *Columbia Journal of World Business* 19 (Winter 1984): 17–22; Sheth, J., and G. Eshghi, *Global Operations Perspectives* (Cincinnati: South-Western Publishing Co., 1989).

21. Bower, J., and T. Hout, "Fast-Cycle Capability for Competitive Power," *Harvard Business Review* (November–December 1988): 110–118.

22. Wheelwright, S., "Restoring the Competitive Edge in

U.S. Manufacturing," *California Management Review* 27, no. 3 (1985): 26–42.

23. "A Heartland Industry Takes on the World," *Fortune* (March 12, 1990): 110–112.

24. Sheth and Eshghi, *Global Operations Perspectives,* p. xi.

25. "Made in the U.S.A.: Manufacturers Start to Do It Right," *Fortune* (May 21, 1990): 54–64.

26. "Smart Factories: America's Turn?" *Business Week* (May 8, 1989): 142.

27. Levitt, T., "The Globalization of Markets," *Harvard Business Review* (May–June 1983): 92–102; Quelch, J., and E. Hoff, "Customizing Global Marketing," *Harvard Business Review* (May–June 1986): 59–68; Barksdale, H., et al., "A Cross-National Survey of Consumer Attitudes Towards Marketing Practices, Consumerism and Government Regulations," *Columbia Journal of World Business* 17, no. 2 (Summer 1982): 71–85; Sethi, S., and J. Post, "Public Consequences of Private Action: The Marketing of Infant Formula in Less Developed Countries," *California Management Review* 21, no. 4 (1979): 35–48; Terpstra, V., *International Dimensions of Marketing,* 2d ed. (Boston: PWS-KENT Publishing Co., 1988): 185; Jatusripitak, S., L. Fahey, and P. Kotler, "Strategic Global Marketing: Lessons from the Japanese," *Columbia Journal of World Business* 20, no. 1 (Spring 1985): 47–53.

28. *Fortune* (March 12, 1990): 110.

29. Sheth, J., and G. Eshghi, *Global Marketing Perspectives* (Cincinnati: South-Western Publishing Co., 1989): vi.

30. Dymsza, W., "Trends in Multinational Business and Global Environments: A Perspective," *Journal of International Business Studies* (Winter 1984): 25–46; Weigand, R., "International Investments: Weighing the Incentives," *Harvard Business Review* (July–August 1983): 146–152; Folks, W. R., and R. Aggarwal, *International Dimensions of Financial Management* (Boston: PWS-KENT Publishing Co., 1988); Alhashin, D., and J. Arpan, *International Dimensions of Accounting,* 2d ed. (Boston: PWS-KENT Publishing Co., 1988); Stanley, M., "Capital Structure and Cost-of-Capital for the Multinational Firm," *Journal of International Business Studies* 12, no. 1 (Spring–Summer 1981): 103–120.

31. "The Tokyo Stock Market: And How Its Swings Affect You," *Business Week* (February 12, 1990): 74–84.

32. Lessard, D., "Finance and Global Competition: Exploiting Financial Scope and Coping with Volatile Exchange Rates," in Porter, *Competition in Global Industries,* pp. 147–148.

33. Collins, J., and W. Sekely, "The Relationship of Headquarters Country and Industry Classification to Financial Structure," *Financial Management* 12, no. 3 (Autumn 1983): 45–51.

34. "Fed Has Lost Much of Its Power to Sway U.S. Interest Rates," *Wall Street Journal* (March 12, 1990): 1.

35. Dowling, P. J., and R. S. Schuler, *International Dimensions of Human Resource Management* (Boston: PWS-KENT Publishing Co., 1990); Blocklyn, P. L., "Developing the International Executive," *Personnel* (March 1989): 44–48; Earley, P. C., "Intercultural Training for Managers," *Academy of Management Journal* 30, no. 4 (1987): 685–698; Adler, N. J., *International Dimensions of Organizational Behavior,* 2d ed. (Boston: PWS-KENT Publishing Co., 1991); Hofstede, G., "The Cultural Relativity of Organizational Practices and Theories," *Journal of International Business Studies* 14, no. 2 (1983): 75–90; Miller, E., et al., "The Relationship Between the Global Strategic Planning Process and the Human Resource Management Function," *Human Resource Planning* 9, no. 1 (1986): 9–23; Punnett, B. J., "International Human Resource Management," in *Canadian Dimensions in International Business,* ed. A. Rugmon (Toronto: Prentice-Hall Canada, 1989).

36. Tung, R., "Selection and Training Procedures of U.S., European, and Japanese Multinationals," *California Management Review* 25, no. 1 (1982): 57–71; Munchus, G., "Employer-Employee Based Quality Circles in Japan: Human Resource Policy Implications for American Firms," *Academy of Management Review* 8, no. 2 (1983): 255–261; Helburn, I., and J. Shearer, "Human Resources and Industrial Relations in China: A Time of Ferment," *Industrial and Labor Relations Review* 38, no. 1 (1984): 3–15; Kim, K., H. Park, and N. Suzuki, "Reward Allocations in the United States, Japan and Korea," *Academy of Management Journal* 33, no. 1 (1990): 188–198.

37. Johnson, S., "Comparing R&D Strategies of Japanese and U.S. Firms," *Sloan Management Review* 25 (Spring 1984): 25–34; "Innovation: The Global Race," *Business Week* (June 15, 1990).

38. *Business Week* (June 23, 1986): 134.

39. "Missed Opportunities," *Wall Street Journal* (November 14, 1988): R21.

40. "Going on the Offense," ibid., p. R37.

41. Keller, R., and R. Chinta, "International Technology Transfer: Strategies for Success," *Academy of Management Executive* (May 1990): 33–43.

42. "What U.S. Scientists Discover, the Japanese Convert Into Profit," *Wall Street Journal* (June 25, 1990): 1.

43. De Meyer, A., and K. Ferdows, "Integration of Information Systems in Manufacturing," *International Journal of Operations and Production Management* 5, no. 2 (1985): 5–12; "Smart Factories: America's Turn?" *Business Week* (May 8, 1989): 142; "Race for Computerized Booking Systems is Heating Up Among European Airlines," *Wall Street Journal* (December 1, 1988): B3.

ADDITIONAL READINGS

Bartlett, C. A. and S. Ghoshal. "Managing Across Borders: New Strategic Requirements." *Sloan Management Review* 28 (1987): 7–17.

Crawford, M., and J. Poole. *Ten Years of Multinational Business.* Cambridge, Mass.: Abt Books, 1982.

Daniels, J. D., R. A. Pitts, and M. J. Tretter, "Organizing for Duel Strategies of Product Diversity and International Expansion." *Strategic Management Journal* 6 (Summer 1985): 223–237.

Davidson, W. H., and D. G. McFetridge. "Recent Directions in International Strategies: Production Rationalization or Portfolio Adjustment?" *Columbia Journal of World Business* 19 (Summer 1984): 95–101.

Doz, Y. L., and C. K. Prahalad. "Headquarters Influence and Strategic Control in MNCs." *Sloan Management Review* 23 (Fall 1981): 15–30.

———."How MNCs Cope With Host Country Intervention." *Harvard Business Review* 58 (March–April 1980): 149–157.

Egelhoff, W. G. "Strategy and Structure in Multinational Corporations: An Information-Processing Approach." *Administrative Science Quarterly* 27 (September 1982): 435–458.

Geringer, J. M., P. W. Bearzish, and R. C. daCosta. "Diversification Strategy and Internationalization: Implications for MNE Performance." *Strategic Management Journal* 10 (1989): 109–119.

Goehle, D. G. *Decision Making in Multinational Corporations.* Ann Arbor, Mich.: UMI Research Press, 1980.

Gotcher, J. W. "Strategic Planning for Multinationals—The Views of Governments and Scientists." *Long Range Planning* 14 (February 1981): 23–31.

Grinyer, P., S. Al-Bazzaz, and M. Yasai-Ardekani. "Strategy, Structure, the Environment, and Financial Performance in 48 United Kingdom Companies." *Academy of Management Journal* 23 (June 1980): 193–220.

Hamel, G., and C. K. Prahalad. "Managing Strategic Responsibility in the MNC." *Strategic Management Journal* 4 (October–December 1983): 341–351.

Haner, F. T. *Global Business Strategy for the 1980s.* New York: Praeger, 1980.

Herbert, I. J. "Strategy and Multinational Organization Structure: An Interorganizational Relationships Perspective." *Academy of Management Review* 9 (1984): 259–271.

Iverstine, J., D. Townsend, and P. Wright, "The Developing World to 1990—Trends and Implications for Multinational Business." *Long Range Planning* 15 (August 1982): 116–125.

Jaeger, A. M. "The Transfer of Organizational Culture Overseas: An Approach to Control in the Multinational Corporation." *Journal of International Business Studies* 14 (Fall 1983): 91–114.

Jaeger, A. M., and B. R. Baliga. "Control Systems and Strategic Adaptation: Lessons From the Japanese Experience." *Strategic Management Journal* 6 (1985): 115–134.

Miller, E. L., S. Beechler, B. Bhatt, and R. Nath. "The Relationship Between the Global Strategic Planning Process and the Human Resource Management Function." *Human Resource Planning* 9 (1986): 9–23.

Ohmae, K. *The Mind of the Strategist: The Art of Japanese Business.* New York: McGraw-Hill, 1982.

Punnett, B. F. *Experiencing International Management.* Boston: PWS-KENT Publishing Co., 1989.

Robinson, J. *Multinationals and Political Control.* New York: St. Martin's Press, 1983.

Sethi, N. K. "Strategic Planning system for Multinational Companies." *Long Range Planning* 15 (June 1982): 80–89.

Starr, M. K. "Global Production and Operations Strategy." *Columbia Journal of World Business* 19 (Winter 1984): 17–22.

Takamiya, M. "Japanese Multinationals in Europe: Internal Operations and Their Public Policy Implications." *Columbia Journal of World Business* 26 (Summer 1981): 5–17.

Thorelli, H. B., and H. Becker. "The Information Seekers: Multinational Strategy Target." *California Management Review* 23 (Fall 1980): 46–52.

PART TWO

Strategic Management Applications

Case Analysis Guide

INTRODUCTION

If your strategic management course is like most, the instructor will make extensive use of case analysis. You will study business strategy cases, which are accounts of actual business situations, and be placed in the role of a top-level decision maker. By introducing a variety of situations, the case method provides a wide range of opportunities for you to apply the skills learned in this course and other business courses and to begin building confidence in your decision-making ability.

Although case study may be a new experience for you and therefore confusing at first, you will quickly see that it can increase your understanding of the complex world of strategic decision making and sharpen your analytical skills. Case study will also enhance your knowledge of the strategic conditions in different industries. Although there is no substitute for real-world management experience, case study is "the next best thing to being there."

This case study guide is offered to familiarize you with the expectations of you as a student. It will help guide you through your first cases and will show you how to prepare the analyses that will be required. The cases represent a broad range of strategic decisions, all taken from real life. There are large and small businesses; for-profit and not-for-profit organizations; and companies engaged in manufacturing, service industries, and distribution activities. There are successful organizations as well as organizations that are struggling. In some, the company and the names of managers have been disguised, but many of the organizations are ones that you will readily recognize. The majority deal with recent events, but there are also a few classic business strategy cases.

READING AND STUDYING THE CASE

Because you are expected not only to read cases as they are assigned, but to analyze them and develop sound, reasoned judgments that will lead to recommendations, the case method requires a level of preparation that often goes well beyond that required in a traditional lecture course. It is important, therefore, that you devote plenty of time to studying and analyzing each case.

To get the most out of a case, read it at least two times and, if possible, separate the two readings in time. On the first reading, go through the case rather quickly, without trying to take notes or underline. Read it as you would a magazine article or short story. Get a general idea of the situation the company is in—its industry, its position within the industry, and its competition. Note the date of the latest case information. Treat the tables and financial statements merely as illustrations rather than try to analyze them at this time.

Before your second reading, stop and think about the case. Ask yourself, "What are the central issues?" and "What do I need to try and uncover in my analysis?" All business strategy cases revolve around one or, at most, two or three major problems or decision points. The earlier you can identify these the better, as they will guide your analysis. During your second reading of the case, take notes on the case facts that are important for analysis.

There will undoubtedly be instances when you feel that you do not have all the information you need to make the best decision. The information provided in case reports is often incomplete by design. Just as real-world managers are often called on to make decisions without extensive information, this aspect of the case method is not unlike real experience. One of the most important steps toward becoming an effective strategic decision maker is knowing how to make the most of the limited amounts of information the environment provides.

The time frame for decisions is an important element in any case. That is, you should make decisions based only on information that was available to the managers at the time of the case date, although it may seem a bit artificial at times. You may even be required to ignore some information you may have about the company or its situation. For instance, if you are analyzing a 1986 case, your knowledge of the stock market crash of October 1987 should not affect your handling of the case. Although you are encouraged to do outside research, you should resist the temptation to second-guess the decision makers on the basis of information they could not have had.

Your professor may assign you or other class members the responsibility of updating a case by researching recent information on the company. Later information about the strategies that firms actually adopted and their subsequent outcomes often proves to be an interesting way to complete the study of a case. Appendix B of this guide contains information that can assist you in doing outside research on companies. A company's actual strategy should not be taken as the "right" answer, however, even if it proved to be a very profitable one for the company, as any number of other recommended strategies might also have been successful.

DOING THE ANALYSIS

ORGANIZE THE CASE FACTS

Cases sometimes present a bewildering number of names, titles, dates and other facts that are hard to keep straight. Before proceeding with an in-depth analysis of the case, make sure you have a sufficient grasp of the facts. Sometimes it may be necessary to construct a chronology to help you keep in mind the sequence of significant case events and their relationships. To keep names, organizational titles, and relationships in focus, you may need to sketch a rough organization chart if one is not provided in the case. Once you have an adequate grasp of the case facts and the central issues, you are ready to begin an in-depth analysis.

START WITH FINANCIAL ANALYSIS

"Number crunching" is nearly always the best way to begin a case analysis, as it gives you an objective assessment of the company's performance and can help identify problem areas for further analysis. Key financial ratios must be calculated so that you can get a reading on the company's financial performance and condition. Exhibit 1 provides a review of the most often used financial ratios (in case your ratio analysis skills are a bit rusty). Keep in mind that ratios should be interpreted only in light of the organization's situation, and remember that trends are always important. For that reason, two or more years of financial statements are usually included in the cases so that any trends in the ratios can be discerned. Industry averages with which to compare the key ratios are also helpful; if not contained in the case, these averages are available from a number of reporting services (see Appendix B).

Converting the financial statements to "common-size" ones is also helpful. The balance sheet is common-sized by setting total assets equal to 100 percent and then calculating each balance sheet account as a percentage of total assets. Income statements are common-sized by setting net sales equal to 100 percent and then calculating each item as a percentage of net sales. With common-size statements, relative relationships among the various accounts can readily be seen and trends noted over time. These relationships and trends can indicate other problems to be investigated. Common-size statement information is best used in combination with other information. For example, a steadily increasing cost of goods sold as a percentage of net sales may indicate waste, loss of efficiencies in production, increased raw materials prices that have not been passed on to buyers, or some combination of these factors.

Financial analysis can be one of the most time-consuming parts of your preparation. You can save yourself a lot of time if you do only those analyses

EXHIBIT 1   KEY FINANCIAL RATIOS

RATIO	FORMULA	EXPRESSED AS
PROFITABILITY RATIOS		
Return on investment	$\dfrac{\text{Net income after taxes}}{\text{Total assets}}$	percentage
Return on stockholders equity	$\dfrac{\text{Net income after taxes}}{\text{Total stockholder's equity}}$	percentage
Earnings per share	$\dfrac{\text{NIAT-preferred dividends}}{\text{No. common shares outstanding}}$	dollars
Gross profit margin	$\dfrac{\text{Sales—CGS}}{\text{Sales}}$	percentage
Operating profit margin	$\dfrac{\text{Net income before taxes and interest}}{\text{Sales}}$	percentage
Net profit margin	$\dfrac{\text{Net income after taxes}}{\text{Sales}}$	percentage
LIQUIDITY RATIOS		
Current ratio	$\dfrac{\text{Current assets}}{\text{Current liabilities}}$	decimal
Quick (acid-test) ratio	$\dfrac{\text{Current assest—inventories}}{\text{Current liabilities}}$	decimal
Inventories to net working capital	$\dfrac{\text{Inventories}}{\text{Current assets—current liabilities}}$	decimal
LEVERAGE RATIOS		
Debt to assets	$\dfrac{\text{Total debt}}{\text{Total assets}}$	percentage
Debt to equity	$\dfrac{\text{Total debt}}{\text{Total stockholders equity}}$	percentage
Long-term debt to equity	$\dfrac{\text{Long-term debt}}{\text{Total stockholders equity}}$	percentage
Times-interest earned	$\dfrac{\text{NI before taxes and interest}}{\text{Interest expenses}}$	decimal
Fixed-charge coverage	$\dfrac{\text{NI before taxes and interest + lease obligations}}{\text{Interest expenses + lease expenses}}$	decimal

(*continued*)

EXHIBIT 1 (continued)

RATIO	FORMULA	EXPRESSED AS
ACTIVITY RATIOS		
Total asset turnover	$\dfrac{\text{Sales}}{\text{Total assets}}$	decimal
Fixed asset turnover	$\dfrac{\text{Sales}}{\text{Fixed assets}}$	decimal
Net working capital turnover	$\dfrac{\text{Sales}}{\text{Current assets—Current liabilities}}$	decimal
Inventory turnover	$\dfrac{\text{Sales}}{\text{Average inventory of finished goods}}$	decimal
Collection period for receivables	$\dfrac{\text{Average accounts receivable}}{\text{Annual credit sales/365}}$	days
INVESTMENT RATIOS		
Price-earnings ratio	$\dfrac{\text{Market price per share}}{\text{EPS}}$	decimal
Dividend payout	$\dfrac{\text{Annual dividends per share}}{\text{EPS}}$	percentage
Common stock dividend yield	$\dfrac{\text{Annual dividends per share}}{\text{Market price per share}}$	percentage

that you need rather than using the same standard analyses for every case. Thus, you need to use your head at least as much as your calculator or computer spreadsheet. The focus should be on developing information to help you understand the company and to provide the basis for recommendations to solve its problems.

FOCUS YOUR ANALYSIS

Effective case analysis must include both an internal analysis of the firm and an external analysis of the firm's operating environment. Internal analysis is usually handled by taking a functional approach, first making sure you understand the organization's top management and its corporate- and business-level objectives and strategies, and then moving on to analyze each of the company's functional-level objectives and strategies. Part II of the Case Analysis Outline (Appendix A) contains a step-by step internal analysis plan.

External analysis can best be accomplished by breaking the environment down into sectors and analyzing the influence of each sector separately. Consider the possible effects of the economy, demographics, and social change. Analyze the regulatory environment, resource availability, and technological change. Above all, do a thorough analysis of the competitive environment. Part III of the Case Analysis Outline (Appendix A) lists some questions to consider in external analysis.

The analysis process can be very time consuming if one tries to analyze every aspect in detail. For that reason, you should let the key issues in each case indicate which aspects of the case you will treat in detail. The Case Analysis Outline (Appendix A) can help you through the analytical process. Keep in mind that it is intended as comprehensive resource rather than a structured checklist. You will probably want to emphasize different aspects of analysis for each individual case, as the focal points in each case are different.

MAKE RECOMMENDATIONS

The end result of your analyses will be your recommendations. These should be based solely on the findings of your analysis and should include supporting evidence for any judgmental elements included. Although real-world business decisions are often subject to intuitive processes, more analytical processes are always preferred unless the decision makers have a great deal of firsthand experience with the type of strategic problems encountered in the case. Therefore, a statement such as "My analysis shows the following . . ." is always better than "I believe the company should . . . ."

Most professors prefer that you prepare a list of several feasible alternatives to the case problems. This process allows you to compare competing solutions from which you select your recommendations. In drafting the solution, implementation issues should not be ignored, especially financial ones. A recommendation is always strengthened considerably if you can show that the company has the resources to accomplish it and if you present well–laid-out implementation scheme including as much detail as facts allow. If you recommend a strategic change, include a timetable and budget for accomplishing the new strategy, assign specific managers the responsibility for carrying it out, and tell how the company should follow up to make sure the new strategy is successful.

Perhaps one of the hardest adjustments to make to the case method is the realization that there is no such thing as the "right" answer or even the "right" approach. After all the work you put in, there is a natural tendency to wonder, "Did I get it right?" Remember that strategic decision making is not an exact science. Just as two businesses that adopt completely different courses of action while competing in the same markets are often both successful, different approaches and solutions to the same case also are often both "right." (It is exactly that quality that makes strategic management a challenging and interesting field.) Although no single solution or approach is the only "right" one, there are always some decisions that are better than others and some ways to approach a decision situation that are superior to other approaches. As you develop and refine your case analysis skills, you will also increase your ability to identify the conditions under which different approaches and solutions may be successful. The important thing to remember in case analysis is to justify and support your recommendations with thorough analysis.

CLASS DISCUSSIONS

Instructors have a number of ways of handling case discussions in class. These range from structured discussion, in which specific questions about the case are asked and sometimes distributed in advance, to unstructured discussions, in which the students are given some latitude in identifying the important issues in the case and in presenting their analyses and recommendations. As most business strategy courses utilize the unstructured approach, and few students have encountered it before, we discuss it here.

A good case discussion can be a very rewarding class experience for everyone, but its success depends on good preparation by you and the right set of expectations. Keep the following points in mind:

1. Before class, reduce your analysis to two or three pages of notes. Your notes should include your list of the key issues in the case, a SWOT summary (identifying strengths, weaknesses, opportunities, and threats), key financial ratios, a list of two or three feasible alternatives, and your recommendations. Refer to these notes often during the discussion, and add any new ideas that come up.

2. One of the most important things to bring to class with you is an open mind. Once the discussion starts, you will undoubtedly find that there are nearly as many approaches to the case as there are class members. Although there is merit in standing by your convictions, keep in mind that most complicated management problems can best be approached by the refinement process, which requires decision makers to be open to a variety of views.

3. Make the classroom time count by not rehashing case facts. Assume that everyone is familiar with the facts and get right into identifying key issues and problems and analyzing them. Strive to reach the decision-making level of participation (see Exhibit 2).

4. Remember that you cannot test your ideas if you remain silent. In an active class, that may mean that you have to assert yourself to get the floor. Be careful not to equate "air time" with participation, however. Do not dominate the conversation, especially if you have little to add.

5. If a class discussion is going well, you will discover that the professor has done very little of the talking. His or her role in the discussion is to keep the flow of ideas coming, challenge opinions that are offered, insist on reasons behind your statements, and occasionally summarize the analysis.

EXHIBIT 2   FOUR LEVELS OF CASE DISCUSSION

FACT SHARING
The lowest level of discussion. The class simply goes over case facts without really analyzing them. Symptoms of underlying problems are discussed without uncovering the problems themselves.

PROBLEM FINDING
A step above fact sharing. The class goes through a structured analysis of the company. Strengths, weaknesses, opportunities, and threats are uncovered, and the problems underlying the symptoms are identified.

PROBLEM SOLVING
The third level of class discussion. Attention is directed to the problem areas, problems are prioritized, and recommended solutions are developed for each problem area.

DECISION MAKING
The highest level of class discussion. Organizational problems are seen as a whole. Solutions are merged into an overall strategic plan, and implementation considerations are included.

ORAL PRESENTATIONS

Students are sometimes assigned cases to present orally, usually in teams of three or four students. The degree of formality in the presentation is up to the professor, but regardless of the formality, preparation for the presentation and the actual conduct of the case in class will differ markedly from informal class discussion. Thorough preparation will naturally be important, as the entire presentation of issues, analysis, and decision may be up to you and the other members of your team. Here are some points to keep in mind if you are assigned an oral case presentation:

1. Make sure the audience knows the case facts. If the case has not been assigned to the rest of the class to read, the first part of the presentation will have to be devoted to factual material. Although this step is important, keep it brief to allow time for your analysis. Handing out fact sheets is a good way to move this step along quickly.

2. It often helps to identify a role for yourself. The role of outside analyst or consultant is usually preferable to the role of corporate official, as it allows you to speak more objectively.

3. Organization is important, and communicating the organization of your talk early in the presentation is a good idea. Identify the issues early in the presentation so you can focus on them throughout the analysis. Summarize at several points to remind the audience of where you are in the talk.

4. Visual aids can significantly improve a presentation, but they also can be overdone. Prepare a few good charts and graphs to help tell the story, but don't bury the audience in needless detail.

5. Make your recommendations as thorough as you can. Always include financial and staffing plans for the implementation of your recommendations and provide for evaluation and follow-up.

6. Take questions from the floor if allowed. They are a good way to demonstrate your knowledge of the case and depth of thinking. You should set up ground rules for questions at the beginning, however, so you won't be interrupted at unwanted times.

▌ WRITTEN CASE ASSIGNMENTS

A written case analysis may be assigned, either as a structured paper in which you are asked to address specific issues or topics in the case, or as a comprehensive analysis. To prepare a written analysis, you should go through much the same preparation as for class discussions, but here your analysis would probably need to be more thorough.

The written format of your paper will vary according to the particular case and the wishes of your professor. If the assignment is a structured one, you may want to address the questions one by one and present your recommendations. If the unstructured approach is taken, you may need some suggestions as to how you should organize the contents of the paper. The outline in Exhibit 3 is offered as an example that applies to most business strategy cases in your textbook.

▌ DOING ADDITIONAL RESEARCH

Case analysis sometimes requires research to find additional information about the firm or its industry in order to recommend a course of action. You may, for example, want to update the information in a case that is several years old or to investigate more thoroughly the firm's environment or competition. You may also use the library to develop your own business strategy case from secondary sources.

Fortunately, most college and university libraries and public libraries are well equipped to provide the necessary resources. The companies themselves also can be important source of current information, and many of them will willingly provide you with copies of their quarterly and annual reports as well as other information. Company sources should not be relied on exclusively, however, as information that is unfavorable to the company is unlikely to be obtained that way. Whatever your approach, Appendix B contains a listing of the most frequently used resources for case research.

EXHIBIT 3   SUGGESTED OUTLINE FOR WRITTEN CASES

I. Introduction. Give a brief statement of the purpose of the report and how the report is organized. You might also include some basic facts about the company as a way of introduction.

II. Internal Analysis.
   A. Present situation. Discuss the firm's present strategy. Describe its markets, products or services; its competitive orientation; and the scope of its activities. What is being attempted, and how? How well is it working?
   B. Financial resources. Describe the financial condition of the company and assess its ability to meet the demands of its environment and to provide for future growth.
   C. Strengths and weaknesses. Discuss the company's strong and weak points as uncovered in your analysis of the various functional areas.

III. External Analysis.
   A. General environment. Describe any feature of the economic, technological, regulatory, physical, and social environments that is relevant to the organization's future.
   B. Operating environment. Describe the competitive environment. Who are the competitors? What are their strengths and weaknesses?
   C. Opportunities and threats. Summarize all of the relevant issues uncovered by your external analysis.

IV. Key Decisions. Identify the main points at issue in the case. What are the problems and decisions the company faces? What should be the focus of the recommendations?

V. Alternatives. Describe each of the possible strategies the firm could adopt. Discuss each one and include its strong and weak points.

VI. Recommended Decisions. Tell what you think the company should do. What should its strategy be? Justify your choice on the basis of analysis. Discuss implementation, evaluation, and follow-up. Include time estimates for implementation and financial staffing plans where appropriate.

VII. Appendices, Tables, and Graphs.

Keep in mind that sometimes the cases use disguised company names and are therefore impossible to research directly. Also, most privately held companies do not make it a practice to share financial information with the public, as publicly held companies are required to do. This limitation can make it difficult to obtain the latest information on some companies, although you can usually obtain information about their industries. The major financial reporting services often report estimates of the sales, profits, and key ratios for private companies, and their estimates are considered quite accurate.

It is generally true that the larger the company is, the more information you will find. Most of the Fortune 500–size companies discussed in the cases are the subjects of many news articles, industry analyses, and trade reports and therefore make excellent subjects for secondary case research.

WORKING IN TEAMS

Just as strategic decisions in real businesses are often the products of teams of managers working together, professors frequently assign class members to teams for the preparation of case reports in order to provide a more realistic experience in the decision-making process. Teamwork may be a new experience for you and the other members of your team. The following points may make your team experience a more successful and satisfying one:

1. Determine the relative strengths and skills of team members and divide the work to take advantage of them. Breaking the analysis down into distinctive parts will avoid duplication of effort.

2. Meet often and work as a team. Remember that your performance on the assignment depends on each other. Make sure that meetings are scheduled when all members can attend and that meetings are planned ahead of time.

3. Use consensus processes and make decisions jointly. Make sure the final product is consistent throughout. Teams often make the mistake of presenting a final paper or presentation that is simply an accumulation of parts instead of a single analysis with a unified set of recommendations.

SUMMARY

This chapter presents a general framework for analyzing strategic management cases and developing case reports. These guidelines may seem long to you now, but as you become more familiar with the process, much of it will become automatic. The purpose is to get you started on the road to formulating effective strategic decisions and communicating the results of your analyses.

Case analysis, like any other valuable skill, takes time to develop and requires concentration and hard work. The rewards are plentiful, however. In addition, case analysis is very personal. Every successful decision maker eventually adopts a style that is his or her own. For that reason, you will probably find it necessary to modify the framework presented in this chapter to fit your own work habits and decision style. We suggest that you follow this guide closely until you feel comfortable with the process, and then use it only occasionally to review your own procedure and analyses.

APPENDIX A

Case Analysis Outline

I. The Present Situation
  A. Mission, objectives, strategies, policies
      1. Mission: What business(es) is the company in? Is the mission relatively stable or undergoing change?
      2. Objectives: What is the company trying to accomplish? Are corporate-level, business-level, and functional objectives consistent with the corporate mission and with each other? Are objectives written down, or must they be inferred from performance?
      3. Strategies: How is the company attempting to achieve its objectives? Are the strategies consistent with the mission and objectives? Are strategies coordinated, or do they appear to be developed piecemeal?
      4. Policies: Does the corporation have well-developed guidelines for carrying out its strategies? Do they seem to enhance or hinder goal accomplishment?
  B. Corporate performance
      1. Financial performance: Is the company's financial performance adequate? What is its net profit margin, its return on investment, and earnings per share? What are the trends in these overall measures of performance?
      2. Goals: How well is the organization meeting its objectives? Does present performance match expectations?
      3. Competitive stance: Is the company remaining competitive in its industry? Is it maintaining or enhancing its market share?

II. Internal Analysis—Strengths and Weaknesses
  A. Organizational structure and corporate culture
      1. Type: What type of organizational structure does the firm have: simple, functional, divisional, or matrix?

   2. Centralization: Is decision making centralized at top management levels, or decentralized throughout the organization?
   3. Culture: Is there a well-defined culture? Is the culture market oriented, product oriented, or technology oriented?
   4. Consistency: Are the company's structure and culture consistent with the firm's objectives and strategies?
B. Top management and board of directors
   1. The CEO: How would you rate the CEO in terms of knowledge, skills, and abilities? Is his/her overall management style autocratic or participative?
   2. The board: Is the board of directors directly involved in the strategic management process, or is it a "rubber-stamp" board?
   3. Top managers: How would you rate the overall capability of the top management team? Is there an adequate plan for executive succession and training for top management positions?
C. Financial management
   1. Functional objectives and strategies: Does the company have clearly stated financial objectives and strategies? Are they consistent with the company's overall objectives?
   2. Profitability: How is the company performing in terms of profitability ratios? How does this performance compare with past performance and industry averages? Does a common-sized income statement reveal any discrepancies in the components of net income?
   3. Liquidity and cash management: How is the firm performing in terms of its liquidity ratios? Are cash-flow problems indicated? How do the ratios compare with past performance and industry averages?
   4. Leverage and capital management: Is the firm's leverage appropriate, as evidenced by its leverage ratios? Is the amount of leverage in keeping with the industry and the company's strategies for expansion?
   5. Asset management: Are inventories, fixed assets, and other resources being effectively managed as indicated by the activity ratios? How do these ratios compare with the firm's past performance and other firms in the industry?
   6. Financial planning and control: What individuals are involved in the firm's financial planning? How often are budgets prepared? How closely are spending decisions monitored, and who has the authority to control financial resources? How sophisticated are the financial and asset management systems of the firm?
D. Operations management
   1. Technical core: Does the technical core of the organization center around production, service, or merchandising?
   2. Capacity: Is the productive capacity of the firm adequate for present needs and for future growth in operations?

  3. Quality: Is the quality of the product or service adequate and in keeping with the company's goals? Are quality assurance systems in place and functioning properly?
  4. Efficiency: Is operating efficiency adequate? Can it be improved?
E. Marketing management
  1. Product: What is the company's present mix of products and/or services? At what stages in their product life cycles are they? Who are the firm's target customers? Is there a readily identifiable product-mission philosophy?
  2. Price: Are prices competitive and in keeping with product quality and the target market? Is price determination demand based, competitive, or on a cost-plus basis?
  3. Place: Is the distribution system adequate? Does the company maintain its own sales team or depend on outside firms? Is it an integrated part of the company or separately controlled? Are relations with the sales force and distributors good? Do compensation systems provide the right amount of incentives?
  4. Promotion: How does the company advertise and promote its products or services? Is the promotion effort effective? Is promotion designed in-house or by outside firms?
  5. Marketing information systems: How does the company identify new markets or target groups? Is the marketing department involved in the development of new products? How does the company exchange information with the distribution system?
F. Human resources management
  1. Human resources planning: Is there an effective human resources planning effort? Are personnel requirements included in strategy formulation and facilities planning?
  2. Obtaining personnel: Are adequate processes in place for obtaining qualified personnel? How are personnel recruited and selected?
  3. Retaining and improving human resources: Are training programs effective? Are performance evaluation and improvement managed effectively? Are grievances handled well?
  4. Compensation: Is the compensation system effective and fair? Is pay generally competitive or above competitive levels? Are fringe benefits high or low for the industry? Does the firm have a profit-sharing plan?
  5. Labor relations: If the company is unionized, are relations with labor organizations congenial or combative?
G. Research and development
  1. Organization: Is there one centralized R&D department, or is R&D decentralized?
  2. Level of R&D effort: What percentage of the firm's resources are devoted to the R&D effort? How does this compare with competitors?

      3. Control: How is the R&D effort controlled? Where in the organization is policy established for R&D?

  H. Management information systems

      1. Is a management information system in use at all levels—operational, middle management, and top management?

      2. Is the system adequate to meet information needs at each level?

      3. Does the organization use a centralized MIS or independent decentralized systems for various departments and functions?

      4. Is the MIS cost effective?

      5. Does the strategic management process make use of a decision support system (DSS) to aid in strategic analysis?

III. External Analysis—Opportunities and Threats

  A. Economic environment. What is forecast for the industry, and how are economic events likely to affect this firm? How would an inflationary period or a recession affect product demand?

  B. Technological environment. What innovations are likely to occur that will affect either products and services or production processes? Is the rate of change in technology increasing or slowing?

  C. Regulatory environment. Are there any present or expected government and/or industry regulations that present either threats or opportunities? Are there ongoing efforts to monitor or actively participate in the regulatory process?

  D. Physical environment. Can we expect any significant depletion of needed resources? Will there be any changes in the physical surroundings of the organization that might affect the accomplishment of its goals or present opportunities?

  E. Social/demographic environment. Are any important demographic changes in customers, suppliers, or the labor pool expected? Are tastes and preferences changing in a way that might affect this firm?

  F. Competitive environment. Who are the firm's competitors? What are their market shares? How effective are they? How likely is the entrance of new competition? Are there close substitutes for the company's products or services?

A P P E N D I X B

Resources for Case Research

▮ COMPUTERIZED DATA BASES

CD/Corporate: U.S. Public Companies [formerly DATEXT]
Cambridge, Mass.: Lotus Development Corporation. Updated quarterly.
A menu-driven CD-ROM data base of financial and business information on
nearly 12,000 U.S. publicly held companies, 50 industry groups, all Standard
Industrial Classification (SIC) business groups, and top corporate executives.
The information, which is primarily from the Disclosure II data base (Disclosure, Inc.), provides financial data and textual information extracted from Securities and Exchange Commission (SEC) filings of public companies. Material
from six other sources provides selected Wall Street security analysts reports,
abstracts and citations to journal articles, biographical information, and stock
transaction information.

Corporate and Industry Research Reports (CIRR)
Wellesley Hills, Mass.: Silver Platter Information. Updated monthly.
A CD-ROM data base indexing research reports and periodicals published by
Wall Street analysts and economists from major security and investment firms.
Information can be searched by company, industry, or keyword terms.

InfoTrac
Belmont, Calif.: Information Access Company.
InfoTrac is a microcomputer-based index on CD-ROM. Information included
in the InfoTrac data base comprises a general, comprehensive, research-
oriented data source. It provides general interest topics, business information,
and technical data as well as current data from the *New York Times* and the *Wall
Street Journal.* InfoTrac can be searched by subject, personal name, corporate
name, geographic place name, title or book, and other classifications. Book
and movie reviews are also included.

Adapted from Siler, F. B., and M. L. Moon, *Reference Guide No. 3: Information on Companies and Industries* (Clemson, S.C.: Clemson University Libraries, 1990).

HANDBOOKS AND GUIDES

Business Researchers Handbook, 2nd ed.
Washington, D.C.: Washington Researchers. 1983.
A how-to guide to working with information requesters, getting the best research results, and putting together cogent research reports. Appendices include a listing of federal centers, a list of toll-free hotlines to call for business information, a listing of government offices that offer free market studies, a list of who has what in terms of company information, and federal sources of information on private and public companies.

Competitor Intelligence: How to Get It, How to Use It
By Leonard M. Fuld. New York: Wiley. 1985.
Provides a basic understanding of intelligence-gathering techniques and practices. It also provides an extensive listing of basic sources of intelligence such as federal, state, and local sources; corporate intelligence in print; sources for specific industries; statistical sources, directories, and associations; data bases for corporate intelligence; and sources of foreign intelligence.

Company Information: A Model Investigation, 2nd ed.
By Wendy Law-Yone. Washington, D.C.: Washington Researchers. 1983.
This model investigation of a closely held private company reveals the depth of information that can be uncovered in company research. It describes methodology, techniques, and sources for finding facts about a company's structure, marketing, finances, philosophies, and labor situation.

Finding Company Intelligence: A Case Study
By Howard John Endean, Jr. Washington, D.C.: Washington Researchers. 1984.
Provides a candid account of the complex task of piecing together a company profile. MCI Airsignal, a wholly owned subsidiary of MCI Communications Corporation, is used as a model for this investigation of a business enterprise. Biographical references are included.

GENERAL INFORMATION SOURCES

Business Information Sources, rev. ed.
By Lorna M. Daniells. Berkeley: University of California Press. 1985.
A basic, annotated guide to important reference sources such as indexes, directories, financial manuals, and statistical publications as well as selected books, periodicals, and reference works pertaining to specific companies and industries.

Encyclopedia of Business Information Sources, 8th rev. ed.
Detroit: Gale Research. 1990.
Lists books, periodicals, organizations, bibliographies, data bases, and other

sources of information on a wide variety of business-related topics. A good source to use for information on specific industries.

How to Find Information About Companies: The Corporate Intelligence Sourcebook, 7th ed.
Lorna M. Daniells, Elizabeth M. Williams, and Beth Gibber, eds. Washington, D.C.: Washington Researchers. 1988.
A guide to facts and figures about public and private companies, domestic or foreign. It also provides a list of annotated sources such as directories, investment services, indexes, and abstracts.

Business Information: How to Find It. How to Use It, 2nd ed.
By Michael R. Lavin. Phoenix: Oryx Press. 1991.
This text is organized into four parts. Part I introduces concepts important to business and discusses basic forms of published information, major sources of unpublished information, and basic finding tools. Part II provides sources of information on companies. Part III provides sources of information such as demographic data, statistics and industries, and general economic indicators. Part IV provides information on specific areas of business such as marketing information, business law sources, and tax law publications. Title and subject indexes are included.

Business Firms Master Index
Jennifer Mossman and Donna Wood, ed. Detroit: Gale Research. 1985.
A guide to sources of information about companies in the United States and Canada and foreign firms with offices in the U.S. Indexes specialized and general sources such as directories, dictionaries, encyclopedias, buying guides, and special issues of leading magazines.

Small Business Sourcebook
Detroit: Gale Research. Published biennially and updated between editions by supplements.
Part I provides profiles of 100 popular small businesses, describing sources and services for each particular business. Included are information sources such as associations, educational programs, reference works, sources of supply, statistical sources, trade periodicals, and consultants. Part II identifies general types of organizations and publications of interest to small business owners such as government agencies, associations, and venture capital firms.

Guide to U.S. Government Publications
J. L. Andriot, ed. McLean, Va.: Documents Index. Published annually with updating supplements issued quarterly.
An annotated guide to the important series of periodicals currently being published by various U.S. government agencies. Agency and title indexes are included. This is an excellent source for serial publications published by the Department of Commerce.

Source of State Information on Corporations
Washington, D.C.: Washington Researchers. 1984.
Describes documents that are available through nineteen state offices within all fifty states. Documents available from the state offices include financial statements, environmental impact studies, uniform commercial code documents, and reports of inspections and investigations of businesses.

 DIRECTORIES

U.S. BUSINESSES

Million Dollar Directory
New York: Dun & Bradstreeet, Marketing Services Division. Published annually.
Lists businesses whose net worth is $500,000 or more. This source is composed of four volumes, one of which is a master index for all volumes containing an alphabetical listing of businesses, businesses listed geographically, and businesses grouped by industry classification. For each form it gives officers and directors, line of business, Standard Industrial Classification (SIC) codes, approximate sales, number of employees, stock exchange abbreviation, stock ticker symbol, division names and functions, principal bank, accounting firm, and other information.

Standard & Poor's Register of Corporations, Directors, and Executives
New York: Standard & Poor's. Published annually and includes supplements for U.S. and Canadian corporations and executives.
This register covers more than 37,000 corporations and over 405,000 corporate executives in all areas of U.S. business and industry. Volume I is an alphabetical listing of corporations and includes information such as principal directors and personnel, SIC codes, address and telephone number, sales volume, and number of employees for each company. Volume II contains biographical data. Volume III provides the four-digit codes for over 900 industries, groups companies by their SIC codes, and arranges companies geographically by state and city.

The Facts on File Directory of Major Public Corporations
Stanley R. Greenfield, ed. New York: Facts on File. Updated annually.
Contains key statistical and personnel data on 6,000 American public corporations. Includes the following information for each corporation: name, address, telephone number, SIC code, number of employees, corporate officers, selected financial information, and more. The following indexes are provided: directors by company, a geographical list of corporations, corporations by primary four-digit SIC code, and an alphabetical listing of all officers and directors.

Everybody's Business: An Almanac, the Irreverent Guide to Corporate America
Milton Moskowitz, Michael Katz, and Robert Levering, eds. San Francisco: Harper & Row. 1980.
A profile of about 317 large companies, including such information as address, history and background, sales, profits, number of employees, stock performance, and consumer brands.

Directory of American Research and Technology
Jaques Cattell Press, ed. New York: Bowker. Updated annually.
Alphabetical listing of public and private businesses in the United States performing research and development activities. This source includes 6,040 parent organizations with the 4,951 subsidiaries. Information given for each company includes name, address, telephone number, telex numbers, cable address, fields of research and development, and more. Includes a geographical, personnel, and subject classification index.

Directory of American Firms Operating in Foreign Countries
New York: Simon & Schuster. Updated annually.
Volume I lists over 4,000 American corporations controlling more than 16,000 foreign business enterprises. Gives name, address, officer in charge, products, services, and number of employees. Volumes II and III list businesses by country of operation, giving address, products, and home office in the U.S.

CORPORATE AFFILIATIONS

Directory of Corporate Affiliations
Skokie, Ill. National Register Publishing. Published annually with supplements issued as *Corporate Action.*
Section I is a cross-reference index for all subsidiaries, divisions, and affiliates. Section II lists over 4,000 major American parent companies, giving line of business; approximate sales; number of employees; ticker symbol; top officers; and subsidiaries, divisions, or affiliates. Includes a geographic and SIC index.

America's Corporate Families
Parsippany, N.J.: Dun's Marketing Services. Published annually. Also known as *The Billion Dollar Directory.*
Contains information on more than 8,000 U.S. parent companies and their 44,000 domestic divisions and subsidiaries. An essential tool for tracking nationwide corporate linkage and ownership. Companies are listed alphabetically, by ultimate parent, geographically, and by industry classification. A cross-reference of divisions and subsidiaries is included.

America's Corporate Families and International Affiliates
Parsippany, N.J.: Dun's Marketing Services. Published annually.
Section I lists companies alphabetically by U.S. ultimate parent and their Canadian and other foreign subsidiaries, alphabetically by Canadian ultimate parent and their U.S. subsidiaries, and alphabetically by foreign ultimate parent and their U.S. subsidiaries. Section II lists multinational businesses geo-

graphically. Section III lists multinational businesses by industry SIC. A sub-sidiary–to–ultimate parent cross-reference is provided.

INTERNATIONAL BUSINESSES

Principal International Businesses
New York: Dun & Bradstreet. Published annually. Subtitled "The World Marketing Directory."
Contains detailed data on 55,000 leading firms in 133 countries. Includes name, address, cable or telex number, sales volume, number of employees, SIC number, description of activities, name of chief executive, and more. The businesses are arranged alphabetically, geographically, and by industry classification.

The China Directory of Industry and Commerce and Economic Annual
New York: Van Nostrand Reinhold.
Lists 10,000 Chinese industrial and commercial enterprises, industry by industry, giving their name, address, major products and business lines, and other information. Also included is an economic annual providing information on trade with China; the general economic situation; the economic situations of municipalities, provinces, and autonomous regions; economic laws and regulations; and a chronicle of major events in China from 1978 to 1982.

Europe's 15,000 Largest Companies
London: Europe's Largest Companies.
Published annually.
This source pinpoints the profit makers and money losers; the largest companies by country and by industry; the largest banks, insurance companies by country and by industry; the largest banks, insurance companies, and advertising companies; and hotels and restaurants.

Canadian Trade Index
Toronto: Canadian Manufacturers' Association. Published annually.
A comprehensive directory listing over 13,000 Canadian manufacturing firms. The firms are listed alphabetically with address, telephone number, branch and sales offices, senior operating executive, parent and subsidiary companies, products, brand names, export contacts, Telex/TWX, and more. Also lists head offices and plants alphabetically by municipality and province and lists companies alphabetically by 10,000 product classifications.

The French Company Handbook
Paris: International Business Development, published with the *International Herald Tribune.*
A blue-chip guide for evaluating French companies. Gives key company profiles of French companies, industry evaluations, history and structure of the Paris Stock Market, and other information.

Japan Trade Directory
Tokyo: Japan External Trade Organization. Also known as *Nihon Boeki Shinko-kai.* Updated periodically.

Provides information on about 2,200 Japanese companies and 10,000 prod-ucts and services. Part I, Products and Services, contains alphabetical export and import indexes to companies listed in Part II. Part II, Prefectures and Companies, gives business and tourist information on each prefecture, includ-ing main products, crafts, industries, and tourists attractions, in an attractive color layout. In addition, detailed information is provided on each company operating within the prefecture. Part II also contains a listing of trade and industrial associations, an alphabetical company index, and a trade name in-dex. Part III, Advertising, contains additional information on products and companies, along with photographs or illustrations of featured products.

How to Find Information About Japanese Companies and Industries
Washington, D.C. Washington Researchers. 1984.
Describes sources of information such as international organizations; Japa-nese government agencies; U.S. federal and state organizations in Japan; pri-vate sector organizations such as banks, accounting firms, and consultants that maintain offices in Japan; and sources of published information.

Directory of Foreign Manufacturers in the United States, 4th ed.
By Jeffrey S. Arpan and David Ricks. Atlanta: Georgia State University, College of Business Administration, Business Publications Division. 1990.
Contains a list of foreign manufacturers in the United States, giving the par-ent company, product, and SIC code. Includes the following indexes: U.S. com-panies by state location, parent companies by name, parent companies by country, and products by Standard Industrial Classification.

MINORITY BUSINESSES

National Directory of Minority and Women-Owned Business Firms
Oak Brook, Ill. Business Research Services. Published annually and supple-mented by *Update.*
Lists 30,000 minority-owned business firms and 10,000 women-owned business firms. Each business listing is grouped first by SIC code and business descrip-tion and then by geographic area.

MERCHANTS AND MANUFACTURERS

Thomas Register of American Manufacturers and Thomas Register Catalog File
New York: Thomas Publishing. Published annually with some volumes accom-panied by supplements entitled "Important Addenda."
A comprehensive directory of American manufacturing firms. Volumes 1–12 list over 115,000 U.S. manufacturers by specific product or service. Volumes 13–14 list the companies alphabetically, giving address, branch offices, subsidi-aries, production asset classification, and principal offers. Volumes 15–21 are "Catalogs and Companies."

Kelly's Manufacturers and Merchants Directory
Kingston upon Thames (U.K.): Kelly's Directories. Published annually.
Merchants, manufacturers, wholesalers, and firms are listed by trade and pro-

fession, brand and trade name, and alphabetically in this world directory. Other sections include Products and Services Showcase and International Exporters and Services.

Brandnames: Who Owns What
By Diane Waxer Frankenstein (in consultation with George Frankenstein). New York: Facts on File. 1986.
A guide to the corporation that ultimately owns each product. Divided into four sections: Section 1 is an alphabetical list of brand names arranged by product category. Section 2 is an alphabetical list of consumer companies giving a brief history, a description of all consumer brands, address, telephone number, chief officer, and more. Section 3 is an alphabetical list giving brand names, of the largest foreign consumer companies selling in the U.S. Section 4 is an index by company and brand name.

BUSINESS ASSOCIATIONS AND ORGANIZATIONS

Encyclopedia of Associations
Detroit: Gale Research. Published annually in four volumes.
Volumes I and II contain a listing of over 25,000 national and international associations arranged by broad classification. Gives the following information for each association: the name of the chief officer, a brief statement of activities, number of members, names of publications, and more. Volume III is a Names and Key Word index, and Volume IV is a Geographic and Executive index.

Business Organizations, Agencies and Publications Directory
Detroit: Gale Research. (Continues *Business Organizations and Agencies Directory.*) Updated annually.
A guide to trade, business, and commercial organizations, government agencies, stock exchanges, labor unions, chambers of commerce, diplomatic representation, trade and convention centers, trade fairs, publishers, data banks and computerized services, educational institutions, business libraries and information centers, and research centers.

National Directory of Addresses and Telephone Numbers
New York: Bantam Books. Updated annually.
Contains a listing of 150,000 hard-to-find business names, addresses, and telephone numbers. Includes special sections on accounting, advertising, banks, law firms, travel, and other categories and a classified listing of private and public corporations. All entries are listed alphabetically and by category.

The Directory of Directories
Detroit: Information Enterprises, distributed by Gale Research. Published biennially.
An annotated guide to business and industrial directories, professional and scientific rosters, and other lists and guides of various kinds.

BIOGRAPHICAL

Reference Book of Corporate Management
New York: Dun & Bradstreet. Published annually.
Contains biographical data on 200,00 principal officers and directors of more than 13,000 leading U.S. companies. Entries included the following data: name and title, year of birth, marital status, education, military service, and career information.

The Corporate 1000: A Directory of Who Runs the Top 1000 U.S. Corporations
Washington, D.C.: The Washington Monitor.
A guide to the men and women who direct and manage America's largest corporations. The individual companies are listed alphabetically with a brief business description and an approximation of sales or assets. Includes a name index, a company index, an index of companies by industry classification, and a geographical index.

Who's Who in America
Chicago: Marquis Who's in America. Published as part of *Who's Who in American History.* Published biennially.
Presents biographical data on prominent living Americans, including the most important business executives.

INDUSTRY INFORMATION

INDUSTRY INFORMATION SOURCES

Standard Industrial Classification Manual
Washington, D.C.: Office of Management and Budget. Available from the U.S. Government Printing Office. Some volumes accompanied by supplements.
The SIC manual is a guide to one of the most extensive classification systems in use in the United States. It divides U.S. industries by type of activity and assigns an industry code number that is determined by the product or service rendered. The entire field of economic activity (agriculture, forestry, construction, manufacturing, wholesale and retail trade, finance real estate, and so on) is covered. Classifies to a maximum of four digits. An alphabetical index is included.

Standard & Poor's Industry Surveys
New York: Standard & Poor's. Published quarterly.
Provides economic and investment analyses of 65 major industries divided into 34 surveys. Operating and financial data is given for leading companies (approximately 1,500) in each industry, allowing for comparison. For each survey a basic analysis giving an in-depth description of the industry's performance and forecasting short- and long-term prospects for sales and earnings is published yearly. Three "Current Analyses," which report on late developments and estimate results for the period immediately ahead, are also published annually.

Moody's Investors Industry Review
New York: Moody's Investors Service. Published biweekly. Also known as
Moody's Investors Fact Sheets Industry Review.
Provides a ranked list of the leading companies in over 140 industry groups
according to 12 key financial, operating, and investment criteria. Includes
comparative financial statistics such as stock price range and earnings per
share for the 5 or so leaders. About 4,000 companies are included in all.

U.S. Industrial Outlook
Washington, D.C.: Business and Defense Services Administration. Available
from the U.S. Government Printing Office. Published annually.
Gives information on recent trends and outlook for about five years in over
200 individual industries. The short narratives with statistics usually contain
discussions of changes in supply and demand for each industry, developments
in domestic and overseas markets, price changes, employment trends, capital
investment, and other measures.

Current Industrial Reports
Washington, D.C.: U.S. Department of Commerce, Bureau of the Census.
Available from the U.S. Government Printing Office. Published monthly.
Gives current statistics on commodity production and shipments for approximately 5,000 products accounting for more than one-third of all U.S. manufacturing. The series includes monthly, quarterly, and semiquarterly reports. Publication schedules vary for individual industries. All monthly and quarterly
series include annual summaries.

INDUSTRY FINANCIAL STATISTICS

Industry Norms and Key Business Ratios
New York: Dun & Bradstreet Credit Services. Subseries of *Dun's Financial Profiles.* Published annually.
Contains financial ratios for 125 retailing, wholesaling, manufacturing, and
construction lines of business.

RMA Annual Statement Studies
Philadelphia: Robert Morris Associates. (Continues *Annual Statement Studies.*)
Gives financial and operating ratios for about 300 lines of business including
manufacturers, wholesalers, retailers, services, and contractors. Contains six
parts: Parts 1–4 cover balance sheet and profit and loss composites, with selected ratios, all by company size and groups; Part 5 contains additional profit
and loss data; and Part 6 contains a finance industry supplement for small
loan and sales finance ratios.

Almanac of Business and Industrial Financial Ratios
Englewood Cliffs, N.J.: Prentice-Hall. Published annually.
Gives financial and operating ratios for about 160 industries, including banks
and financial industries as well as manufacturing, wholesaling, and retailing
industries.

Quarterly Financial Report for Manufacturing, Mining, and Trade Corporations.
Washington, D.C.: U.S. Department of Commerce, Bureau of the Census.
Available from the U.S. Government Printing Office.
Gives estimated statements of income and retained earnings, balance sheets,
and related financial and operating ratios for all manufacturing, mining, and
trade corporations. The statistical data are classified by industry and by asset
size.

SPECIAL ISSUES GUIDES FOR INDUSTRY TRADE JOURNALS

Guides to Special Issues and Indexes of Periodicals, 3rd ed.
Miriam Uhlan, ed. New York: Special Libraries Association. 1985.
Designed to facilitate rapid location of specialized data published in consumer, trade, and technical periodicals. Also provides a classified listing of
periodicals and a subject index of special issues. It gives details on over 1,200
periodicals that publish special features or indexes on a regular basis.

*Special Issues Index: Specialized Contents on Business, Industrial, and Consumer Jour-
nals*
Compiled by Robert Sicignano and Doris Prichard. Westport, Conn.: Greenwood Press. 1982.
An alphabetical list of over 1,300 periodicals, giving for each the names of the
special issues (and dates) in four categories: buyer's guides/directories, statistical summaries, convention and show reports, and review/preview issues. A subject index is included.

Guide to Industry Special Issues.
Cambridge, Mass.: Ballinger Publishing. Published annually. Also known as
Harfax Guide to Industry Special Issues.
Lists special issues and regular features of trade, business, and economic journals. The articles identified by this guide all contain marketing and financial
statistics or directory information on 65 industries. Entries include articles
showing market shares of particular products; production statistics for, or financial analysis of an industry; and lists of products or companies.

CORPORATE FINANCIAL INFORMATION

CORPORATE ANNUAL REPORTS AND 10-K REPORTS

Perhaps the most commonly cited source of information about a company is
the annual report to stockholders. The annual report contains two basic types
of information: an explanation of the company's operations during the prior
year and developments that may affect operations in succeeding years and
financial reports, usually in the four basic forms of income statement, balance
sheet, statement of retained earnings, and statement of change in financial
position.

Similar information is filed annually in 10-K reports to the Securities and

Exchange Commission. Submitted in standard form by all corporations, the 10-K report includes a narrative description of the business, management decisions and analysis, financial statements, legal proceedings, and several other categories of information.

Annual reports are readily available from the issuing corporation. Many annual and 10-K reports are available through subscription services such as Q-FILE, a microfiche collection from Q-DATA Corporation, St. Petersburg, Florida. Q-FILE provides annual reports, 10K reports, and proxy statements since 1983 for companies listed on the New York Stock Exchange.

Company Profile Resources
New York, N.Y.: R. R. Bowker.
This source consists of a printed catalog and company profiles on microfiche. It provides profiles of over 1,200 publicly owned corporations, private companies, government agencies, and educational institutions. The profiles contain directory information such as name of company, address, city and state, zip code, telephone number, industry code, date founded, number of employees, subsidiaries or parentage, sales and assets, date of fiscal year ended, and inclusion in the Fortune 500 list of major U.S. corporations. Indexes to the printed catalog include employer, industry, and geographic guide. The documents on microfiche contain information such as the annual report, the company's overview, product description, research activities, 10K annual report, 10Q quarterly report, career opportunity information, benefits, and a research analyst report.

Directory of Companies Required to File Annual Reports with the Securities and Exchange Commission
Washington, D.C.: U.S. Securities and Exchange Commission. Available from the U.S. Government Printing Office. Published annually.
Contains a listing of companies required to file annual reports under the Securities Act of 1934. Includes companies with securities listed on national securities exchanges as well as companies with securities traded over the counter. Companies are listed alphabetically and by industry group.

MOODY'S INVESTOR SERVICE

Moody's publishes a series of seven manuals that collectively provide information on more than 20,000 domestic and foreign corporations and over 15,000 municipal governments and government entities. Information includes company histories, financial performance, industry norms and trends, and comparative statistics. All seven Moody's manuals, which are listed below, are published annually and are kept up to date by frequent new reports.
Banking and Finance Manual
Industrial Manual
International Manual
Municipal Government Manual
OTC Industrial Manual

Public Utility Manual
Transportation Manual

In addition, Moody's publishes surveys and reviews that are issued fre-
quently and on a regular basis:
Bond Review
Bond Survey
Dividend Record
Handbook of Common Stock
Investors Industry Review

CORPORATE/BUSINESS RANKINGS

Dun's Business Rankings
Parsippany, N.J.: Dun's Marketing Services. Published annually.
Ranks 7,500 top U.S. public and privately owned businesses by sales volume
and by employee size within state and industry category. Separate sections
rank public and private companies individually by number of employees and
by sales. Other useful features include a numeric and alphabetical SIC code
index; a stock ticker symbol cross-reference; a division cross-reference (alphabetical index); and Selected Business Executives, listed by function.

Ward's Business Directory of Largest U.S. Companies
Belmont, Calif.: Information Access Co. Published annually.
This directory is divided into three sections. In Section A, Part 1 ranks 8,000
public companies by sales within SIC industry classification and displays up
to 30 fields of financial data taken from annual reports and 10-K reports. Part
2 ranks public and private companies according to sales volume within SIC
industry classifications. Section B lists public and private companies in zip
code order by states and cities. Section C lists companies in alphabetical order.
A special feature includes "top 1,000" listings in several categories: most profitable U.S. corporations, publicly held companies ranked by sales volume, privately held companies ranked by sales volume, and others.

Ward's Business Directory of Major U.S. Private Companies
Belmont, Calif.: Information Access Co. Published annually.
Lists major U.S. private companies with sales ranging from $500,000 to $11
million per year. Section A ranks private companies according to annual sales
within SIC industry classifications. Section B lists major U.S. private companies in zip code order by states and cities. Section C identifies companies
alphabetically by company name. Section M is a master index of 100,000 companies listed in all three volumes of *Ward's Business Directory*. Special features
include listings of U.S. companies with sales of $10 million, companies with
200–500 employees analysis of private companies by SIC industries, and analysis of private companies by state.

The 101 Best-Performing Companies in America
By Ronald N. Paul and James W. Taylor. Chicago: Probus Publishing. 1986.
Ranks the 101 best-performing companies by sales volume, labor productivity, capital productivity, number of employees, growth in stockholder equity, year-end stock price, and longevity. Also profiles the 101 companies, giving a brief business description, officers, and financial data for each.

Dow Jones–Irwin Business and Investment Almanac
Homewood, Ill.: Dow Jones–Irwin. Published annually.
Includes a section entitled Largest Companies, which provides rankings for U.S. and international industrial and service companies.

What's What in American Business: Facts and Figures on the Biggest and the Best
By George Kurian. Chicago: Probus Publishing. 1986.
Provides a comprehensive ranking of companies and industries in numerous categories.

The Almanac of American Employers: A Guide to America's 500 Most Successful Large Corporations
By Jack W. Plunkett. Chicago: Contemporary Books. 1985.
Companies from all parts of the United States and from all industry segments are profiled and ranked by salaries, benefits, financial stability, and advancement opportunities. Alphabetical, geographical, and industry indexes are included.

The 100 Best Companies to Work For in America
By Robert Levering, Milton Moskowitz, and Michael Katz. Reading, Mass. Addison-Wesley. 1984.
100 companies are rated in the following areas: pay, benefits, job security, chance to move up, and ambience. Also provides information on work environment, number of employees, headquarters, and location of headquarters and main employment centers for each company.

CORPORATE/BUSINESS PERFORMANCE STATISTICS

Value Line Investment Survey
New York: A. Bernhard. Published weekly.
Analyzes and reports on about 1,700 stocks in 80 industries. The statistics, charts, and brief explanatory text are reviewed and updated industry by industry on a rotating basis every thirteen weeks. Data includes a ten-year history on 23 key investment factors plus future estimates for the next three to five years. Quarterly sales, earnings, dividends, Value Line ratings, reviews of late developments, and future prospects also are reported. This service includes a weekly letter called "Selection & Opinion," which gives views on business, economic outlook, advice on investment policy, Value Line's stock price averages, and other information.

NEWSPAPERS AND NEWSPAPER INDEXES

National Newspaper Index
Belmont, Calif.: Information Access Company. Available on microfile.
Lists articles from the *New York Times,* the *Wall Street Journal,* the *Christian Science Monitor,* the *Los Angeles Times,* and the *Washington Post* from 1984 to the present.

Wall Street Journal Index
Wooster, Ohio: Newspaper Industry Center, MicroPhoto Division, Bell & Howell. Published monthly.
A monthly index, cumulated yearly, listing all articles published in the *Wall Street Journal.* Articles are organized by subject and then listed chronologically.

The Wall Street Journal
New York: Dow Jones. Published daily except Saturday and Sunday.
The leading U.S. daily financial newspaper, indispensable for business people. It includes business and financial news, numerous informative articles, company news and digest of earnings, commodity prices, stock market price quotations, P/E ratios, and sales for the NYSE, AMEX, OTC, CBOE, and so on. Dow Jones, Value Line, Standard & Poor's, and other averages are given as well.

Barron's National Business and Financial Weekly
Chicopee, Mass.: Dow Jones & Co.
Excellent articles on prospects for industries and individual companies, new regulations, and other business and financial topics of interest to investors. Includes weekly stock and bond prices for the NYSE, AMEX, OTC, CBOE and for mutual funds. Quotes current Dow Jones averages and other market indicators, basic economic and financial indicators, foreign exchange rates, and more.

Journal of Commerce and Commercial
New York: Journal of Commerce and Commercial Bulletin. Published daily, except Saturday and Sunday.
Contains general business and industrial news, but is especially important for its coverage of commodities, commerce, and shipping.

INDEXES AND ABSTRACTS

Predicast's F & S Index: United States
Cleveland, Ohio: Predicasts. Formerly *F & S Index of Corporations & Industries.* Published weekly with monthly, quarterly, and annual cumulations.
Best source for periodical information on specific companies or specific industries. Indexes the *Wall Street Journal* and the financial pages from the *New York Times.* Each issue has two sections: citations arranged alphabetically by company name and a section arranged numerically by SIC code number.

Business Periodicals Index
New York: H. W. Wilson Co. Published monthly with a cumulative annual edition.
A cumulative subject index to periodicals in the fields of accounting, advertising, banking and finance, general business, insurance, labor and management, marketing and purchasing, office management, public administration, taxation, and others. Entries include personal names and companies.

Magazine Index
Belmont, Calif.: Information Access Company. Distributed on microfilm.
Computer-produced cumulative indexing (May 1983 to the present) of more than 400 magazines covering a wide variety of subject fields including business, economics, and related topics. Also includes product reviews and book reviews.

Index to U.S. Government Periodicals
Chicago: Infordata International. Issued quarterly; fourth-quarter edition is cumulative for the year.
Indexes by author and subject articles published in over 170 periodicals published by the federal government. A good source for information on national and international business and economic conditions.

Monthly Catalog of U.S. Government Publications
Washington, D.C.: Superintendent of Documents, U.S. Government Printing Office. With semiannual and annual indexes.
Provides "official" access to U.S. government documents. The format has varied in the past several years, but usually has indexes by author, title, and subject. Indexes provide short titles and accession number. With accession number, user locates full descriptions of documents and SuDoc numbers. A good source for access to publications of the Department of Commerce.

Congressional Information Service Index (CIS)
Washington, D.C.: Congressional Information Service. Issued monthly, cumulating quarterly.
A comprehensive subject index and abstract to the working papers of Congress, consisting of committee hearings, reports, and prints as well as publications of joint committees and subcommittees, executive documents, and special publications. Good source for tracing legislation pertaining to business and industry.

SELECTED JOURNALS AND PERIODICALS

Business and Society Review
New York: Warren, Gorhan & Lamont. Published quarterly.
Contains articles covering a wide range of topics on the role of business in a free society. The Company Performance Roundup in each issue briefly reviews notable achievements or failures of specific companies in areas of public

concern. An annual list of African-American corporate directors is included in the fall issue.

Business Week
New York: McGraw-Hill. Published weekly.
An excellent source for information on the business outlook and economic developments as well as information on specific companies and industries. Special features include Corporate Scoreboard (quarterly—third issue in March, May, August, and November), Bank Scoreboard (annual—mid-April issue), International Scoreboard (annual—mid-July issue), and Investment Outlook Scoreboard (annual—last December issue).

Dun's Business Month
New York: Dun & Bradstreet Publications. Formerly *Dun's Review*. Published monthly.
Contains short, readable articles on a wide range of topics of interest to business persons, including management, company news, money and markets, communications, industries, and more. Special features include an annual article on the five "best-managed companies" (December issue) and a list of current job offerings (November issue).

Economist
London: The Economist Newspaper. Published weekly.
Contains information on world business and finance, world politics, and current affairs. Also gives state of the economy for various countries and stock market indexes for major exchanges.

Forbes
New York: Forbes. Published biweekly.
Special features include Special Report on International Business, consisting of ranked lists of the 100 largest foreign investments, U.S. multinationals, and foreign companies (July, first issue); Earnings Forecast for the Forbes 500 Companies (November, last issue); and the Annual Forbes 400, with brief data on the richest Americans (mid-September issue).

Fortune
Chicago: Time-Life, Inc. Published biweekly.
Excellent source for information on U.S. and international companies, economic and financial trends, industries, new products, government regulations, and other news. Special features include First 500 Largest Industrial Corporations (May, first issue); Second Largest 500 Industrial Commercial Banks, Life Insurance Companies, Diversified-Financial, Retailing, Transportation and Utility Companies (July, second issue).

Harvard Business Review
Boston: Harvard University, Graduate School of Business Administration. Published biweekly.
One of the most outstanding professional management journals, with practical articles by recognized authorities on all aspects of general management

policy. Topics of special interest include business policy, ethics for executives, executive compensation, human relations, marketing, planning and strategy, and mergers and acquisitions.

Journal of Business Strategy
Boston: Warren, Gorham & Lamont. Published quarterly.
Contains scholarly, in-depth articles on both theory and application of corporate strategy. The articles focus on such topics as acquisitions, competition, market share, and other areas of interest in the field of strategic management.

Journal of Small Business Management
Morgantown, W.V.: International Council for Small Business. Formerly *JSB. Journal of Small Business.* Published quarterly.
Each issue contains about eight articles on a special theme such as financial management, computerization, or small business and society of interest to members of the International Council for Small Business. Also includes book reviews, a Resources section on the theme topic, and small business news notes.

Mergers and Acquisitions
Philadelphia: Information for Industry. Publication frequency varies.
Contains articles on the state of the art in merger, acquisition, and divestiture methodology. Also contains a roster of U.S. mergers and acquisitions, joint ventures, and cooperation agreements in each issue. It includes reports on corporate sell-offs, a Washington update, information on the world scene, and other business news.

Nation's Business
Washington, D.C.: Chamber of Commerce of the United States. Published monthly.
Publishes the Economic Outlook each January forecasting markets and business. Contains popular articles on business, economics, finance, politics, government activity, and so on. Best features include interviews with business and government officials.

Strategic Management Journal
New York: Wiley. Published bimonthly.
Publishes articles on all aspects of strategic management theory and practice. Topics covered include strategic resource allocation, organization structure, leadership, entrepreneurship and organization purpose and processes, and strategic decision processes.

ECONOMIC AND BUSINESS STATISTICS

Statistical Abstract of the United States
Washington, D.C.: U.S. Department of Commerce, Bureau of the Census. Available from the U.S. Government Printing Office.

The most comprehensive compilation of industrial, social, political, and economic statistics of the United States. This source is divided into subject sections, each of which is preceded by a brief summary giving an explanation of terms used, major source, and origin of data used. Most of the tables are on an annual basis with data for preceding years included for historical comparisons. Numerous specialized supplements are also published (for example *State and Metropolitan Area Data Book*).

Handbook of Basic Economic Statistics
Washington, D.C.: Bureau of Economic Statistics. Issued monthly.
A compilation of current and historical statistics condensed from federal government data on American industry, commerce, labor, and agriculture. More than 1,800 statistical series are included, with some data going as far back as 1913 or to the first year when the statistics were published. Cumulates monthly with the previous year appearing in the January issue.

American Statistics Index (ASI)
Washington, D.C.: Congressional Information Service. Published annually.
A comprehensive, descriptive guide and index to the statistics published by all government agencies, congressional committees, and statistics-producing programs. Each issue is composed of two parts: The Index section provides access by detailed subjects and names, by categories, by titles, and by report numbers; the Abstract section is arranged by issuing agency and gives full descriptions of statistics in each publication, including time period covered, geographical breakdown, and other indicators.

Business Statistics
Washington, D.C.: U.S. Department of Commerce, Bureau of Economic Analysis. Available from the U.S. Government Printing Office. Published biennially.
A supplement to the monthly *Survey of Current Business* providing a historical record of approximately 2,500 statistical series appearing currently in the S-pages of the *Survey.* Tables give annual data beginning with 1947, quarterly beginning with 1966, and monthly beginning with 1973.

Survey of Current Business
Washington, D.C.: U.S. Department of Commerce, Bureau of Economic Analysis. Available from the U.S. Government Printing Office. Published monthly.
A comprehensive statistical summary of national income and product account of the United States, including national income by industry, personal consumption expenditures by major type, government expenditures by type of function, foreign transactions, savings and investment, income and employment by industry, and more. Statistics usually cover the past four years. A supplement, *Business Statistics,* is issued biennially.

Federal Reserve Bulletin
Washington, D.C.: Board of Governors of the Federal Reserve System. Published monthly.
Presents current articles on economics, money and banking, policy, and other

"official" statements issued by the U.S. Board of Governors of the Federal Reserve System. The Financial and Business Statistics section, the second half of each issue, is composed of current U.S. banking and monetary statistics.

Economic Indicators
Washington, D.C.: U.S. Government Printing Office. Available from the Superintendent of Documents. Prepared for the Joint Economic Committee by the Council of Economic Advisers.
Gives the state of the economy and the business outlook. Presents statistical tables and charts for basic U.S. economic indicators such as total output, income, and spending; employment, unemployment, and wages; production and business activity; and currency, credit, security markets, and federal finance.

LIZ CLAIBORNE, INC.

DAVID W. GRIGSBY

"We like to think of ourselves as the IBM of the garment district," stated Jay Margolis, president of Liz Claiborne, Inc.'s women's sportswear division in a 1989 interview.[1] If financial success and industry dominance were the criteria, the comparison was an apt one for the thirteen-year-old company. Liz Claiborne, Inc., led by its glamorous namesake, had topped $1 billion in sales for the second year in a row, a remarkable feat in the apparel industry. Since going public in 1981, the company had become the largest U.S. industrial firm headed by a woman and, in 1985, had been declared the second-most-admired corporation in America by *Fortune* magazine. By 1989, Liz Claiborne controlled an estimated one-third of the $2 billion better women's sportswear market and had added a line of men's sportswear and the company's own cologne label. With her clothes selling in over 3,500 stores across the country, Liz Claiborne had become a household name.

ELISABETH CLAIBORNE ORTENBERG

The company's founder and namesake was the daughter of a European banker and, as such, spent much of her early childhood in Europe. Her family later moved from Brussels to New Orleans and then to Baltimore, giving the young Claiborne a wide exposure to culturally diverse societies and experiences, which had a lasting affect on her sense of style. Before finishing her high school education, Claiborne left the United States and returned to Brussels to pursue her interests in the fine arts. At the age of 20, she won a *Harper's Bazaar* design contest that fueled her ambition to become a leading designer. Against the wishes of her parents, she continued to pursue this interest and went to work as a sketcher and model in a New York design firm. Discovering her self-

---

Source: **Prepared by Professor David W. Grigsby, Clemson University, as a basis for classroom discussion and not to illustrate either effective or ineffective handling of administrative situations. © David W. Grigsby, 1990.**

identity, Claiborne decided to change her image and cut her long dark hair into the shorter style that became her trademark.

In the mid 1950s, Claiborne became a designer for a large women's sportswear company. Shortly thereafter, she and her boss, Arthur Ortenberg, were married. Claiborne's success in design eventually landed her the position of chief designer at Youth Guild, a junior dress division of Jonathan Logan, Inc. She remained at Logan until Liz Claiborne, Inc. was born in 1976.

Liz Claiborne is not an open, gregarious person. Her associates see her as very private and shy, yet friendly to those around her. As Arthur Lefkowitz, her old boss at Jonathan Logan, stated: She was a "very private girl, low key, not pushy, and a hard worker." She "wasn't a playgirl." [2] Despite her retiring personality, Liz Claiborne has adjusted well to the celebrity that accompanied her firm's meteoric rise. By 1988, her popularity had surpassed that of all other American designers. Few chief executives were as recognizable as Liz Claiborne, whose appearance at the age of 59 reflected her success and personality. The image was a familiar one in the fashion world: close-cropped black hair, strong, sculptured face, and a voice that was firm, low, and very precise. Wearing her trademark oversized glasses, she appeared slim, tanned—a vigorous personality. On one occasion in 1988, she made a personal appearance at Macy's New York store on Herald Square and was greeted by crowd of 600 women who behaved as if she were a rock star.

FROM START-UP TO INDUSTRY LEADERSHIP: 1976–1983

Liz Claiborne, Inc. was founded in 1976 by Claiborne, her husband Arthur Ortenberg, and manufacturing expert Leonard Boxer. Marketing specialist Jerome Chazen was added to the firm a year later. Launched with an investment of $255,000 the company's mission was to provide an alternative to the stuffy business suits career women were wearing to the office. Designers had looked on businesswomen as "mini-men" dressed in female versions of men's suits, complete with bows for ties. Claiborne perceived a more casual trend in women's business wear and advocated leaving the structured suit-and-tie outfit to the high-powered law and business firms. She designed a classic line of related components both for business and for leisure that were designed around a "more feminine look" concept, and she offered them at affordable prices.

With experienced management and some of the best designers in the business, the company's presence in the apparel industry had an immediate impact. Its headquarters building, featuring clean lines and lots of white, was located one block off of Times Square, in the heart of New York's Garment district. By September of the first year, the firm was already running in the black.

Claiborne's initial designs were in sportswear, divided into four lines—Spectator, Casual, Lizwear, and Lizsport—all of which were priced in the "better" price range. Pricing was targeted to be just below other well-known designers such as Ralph Lauren and just above mass-market designers such as

Bernard Chaus. A Petites Division was also created to offer fashions designed for the smaller figure. Each division was run by separate management staffs, but all lines were coordinated at the corporate level to assure a consistent image for the company's various products.

The company grew rapidly over the first five years. In 1981 the firm decided to go public with an offering at $19 a share and raised $6.5 million. At the time of the stock offering, earnings had increased tenfold since 1976 and the company boasted an average compounded annual rate of sales growth of more than 40 percent. In 1982 a new dresses line was added to the sportswear segment. Claiborne was hesitant at first to move into this line, but Ortenberg persuaded her to do so. The line turned out to be one of the company's most successful segments, grossing $10 million in its first year. That same year, the company licensed its name for the production of accessories, including belts, scarves, and gloves. In 1983 the company added the new label Lizkids, a better sportswear line for children. Liz Claiborne's product categories are summarized in Exhibit 1.

FURTHER GROWTH AND CONSOLIDATION, 1984–1988

In 1984, the company concentrated on building its reputation as a fashion merchandiser and solidifying its markets. Closer relationships with retailers were cultivated, and plans for expanding the company still further were laid.

In 1985, sales rose to over $550 million, and the company earned a 10.9-percent return on sales, which turned out to be one of the highest net profit margins in the industry. The apparel industry was experiencing a number of problems at the time. For most companies, production costs were skyrocketing while sales levels fell or remained relatively stable. Contributing to Claiborne's success in spite of flat industry sales were several changes initiated during

EXHIBIT 1   LIZ CLAIBORNE, INC.: PRODUCT CATEGORIES AS A PERCENTAGE OF SALES

	1987	1986	1985
Misses Sportswear	53%	54%	64%
Petite Sportswear	12	13	16
Dresses	14	16	16
Accessories	13	10	—
Menswear	7	5	2
Girls	1	2	2
Total	100%	100%	100%

Source: Liz Claiborne, Inc., 1987 Form 10–K.

the year. The accessories line, which had previously been licensed to outside companies, was bought outright in an effort to gain more control over the company's products. It brought in an additional $50 million in sales revenue. Claiborne realized that accessories have greater appeal during down cycles in their basic clothing lines. Accessories allow women to purchase fewer individual pieces of clothing, yet ultimately have more outfits by using accessories as interchangeable accents.

A new line, Claiborne fashions for men, was added to the company's collection in 1985. The line was composed of sweaters, shirts, and slacks designed to be worn as complete outfits. According to Jerome Chazen, "We discovered that 70% of our women customers also bought clothes for their husbands."[3] Claiborne began shipping men's clothing to retailers at the close of 1985. Plans were also being made at that time to enter into a joint venture with Avon for the distribution of a new fragrance the following year.

1986 brought more success to Liz Claiborne, Inc. The new Claiborne men's line hit the market in the early part of the year and earned $40 million in sales its first year. The accessories line brought in $82 million only one year after being acquired from its licensees. Total revenues for 1986 jumped up to $813 million, $100 million over projections. Liz Claiborne led all firms in the apparel industry on net profit margin (10.6 percent), return on equity (34.8 percent), and return on investment (25.7 percent). The firm was listed on the Fortune 500 for the first time (#437), at only eleven years of age. It led all Fortune 500 firms that year in return on investment.

In 1986, Claiborne debuted its joint venture with Avon as planned. The first product, the fragrance, hit the market in September. The company undertook the first national advertising campaign in its history to promote this product as a light, "workday" scent. The campaign was a straightforward, honest sell, costing approximately $5 million, with no sexual motifs apparent. In some circles the firm was criticized for its lackluster ad campaign with no "glitz."

In the apparel industry, 1987 will not be remembered with fondness. There was a general problem of overstocking in the stores, and too many stores carried similar items, which caused customers simply to stop buying. In addition, most designers misread the consumer market and offered much shorter hemlines, similar to the miniskirts of the 1960s. Liz Claiborne, along with her competitors, fell prey to a rebellion against the shorter skirts. A company spokesman noted that this might have been an indication that the firm was losing touch with its customers, who were "a bit older and more conservative than was previously thought."[4]

Claiborne's stated objectives in 1987 were twofold: to improve the product and to train sales personnel in the "Claiborne way," which was to understand the customer and "see the clothing through Claiborne eyes."[5] While other apparel firms in the industry suffered through an unfortunate year, Liz Claiborne, Inc. posted remarkable sales gains in spite of its misreading of hemline preferences. Total sales for the year were up 29.5 percent over 1986 to $1.05 billion, making Liz Claiborne, Inc. a billion-dollar sales company for the first time.

The Petites Division strengthened its position over the year by making changes in its operations. A new designer was hired, and the division's offices and showroom space were expanded. Reporting patterns were restructured so the Petites Division would report directly to the Sportswear Group. Claiborne, the menswear segment, posted a sales increase of 79 percent in 1987, its second full year of production, bringing in $75 million. Encouraged by the line's early success, Claiborne decided to expand it to include men's furnishings—dress shirts, hosiery, ties, and underwear. The accessories line also did well in 1987, posting a 66-percent increase over 1986 sales, at $136 million. Handbags proved to be the best seller. Dresses posted an 11-percent increase over 1986 and brought in $141 million. Liz Claiborne Cosmetics Division had sales of $26 million for the year and gained significant market share. Its product was one of the top five fragrances sold in the U.S. Claiborne planned to continue this line, but because of unusual acquisitions made by Avon decided to discontinue the joint venture and seek another supplier for the product.

In September 1987, Claiborne introduced a new line of bridge sportswear under the Dana Buchman label. This merchandise was priced to capture a niche just above Liz Claiborne's better-priced lines and just below designer sportswear. Although it recognized this venture as somewhat risky, the firm felt confident that it could capture a reasonable market share in this niche. Projections were for the new line to bring in approximately $5 million in sales for the first four months and then steadily build market share.

A number of problems were corrected in 1987. The Claiborne men's line experienced problems when customers complained that the men's pants fit poorly and were basically too baggy. New pants designs were tried for the following season. Lizkids sales, at $15 million, were disappointing. The company determined that the Lizkids problem was twofold. First, the fashions were merely scaled-downed versions of womens' styles and, as such, were too sophisticated for children. Second, retail stores had no system for effectively displaying "better" children's fashions. The most common means of display was to separate by size, not price. Claiborne found her "better" childrens sportswear hanging next to lower-quality and lower-priced styles. To correct this problem, Claiborne began working directly with retailers to set up Lizkids boutiques.

In 1988, the company continued to experience some fallout from the apparel industry's slump. In spite of that, 1988 brought moderate (by Claiborne standards) financial success. Sales rose 13.2 percent over 1987 levels, to a total of over $1.18 billion. The company rose from #312 to #299 on the Fortune 500 listing. Profits, however, declined 3.6 percent, from $114.4 to $110.3 million. (Selected financial data for the company are presented in Exhibit 2.) A number of factors were behind the decline in profitability. Women's sportswear sales, which accounted for 60 percent of Claiborne's total revenue, had increased by only 3 percent, in contrast to the usual 20 percent annual rate. Many analysts thought that the firm's size was making it increasingly unable to respond to the market's needs and that Liz Claiborne would never again grow at its past rate. Liz Claiborne's management, on the other hand, felt confident that, with the support of new ventures, the company could rebound. Plans were

EXHIBIT 2 LIZ CLAIBORNE, INC.: SELECTED CONSOLIDATED FINANCIAL HIGHLIGHTS, 1983–1988

	1988	1987	1986	1985	1984	1983
Net sales	$1,184,229	$1,053,324	$813,497	$556,553	$391,272	$228,722
Gross profit	425,944	397,755	311,250	214,853	147,517	84,064
Net income	110,341	114,414	86,194	60,580	41,938	22,398
Earnings per common share	1.26	1.32	1.00	.71	.50	.27
Working capital	402,069	320,802	213,171	151,950	97,299	57,887
Total assets	629,082	482,369	247,787	225,910	142,826	91,320
Long-term debt	14,107	14,464	–0–	10,000	–0–	–0–
Stockholders' equity	457,826	356,956	247,787	162,729	104,417	64,498
Dividends per common share	.18	.16	.12	.08	.05	–0–
Weighted average common shares	87,484,695	86,933,364	86,270,552	85,395,824	84,577,140	84,013,344

Note: All dollar amounts are in thousands except per-share data.

All common-share data has been adjusted to reflect all stock dividends previously paid.

Source: Liz Claiborne, Inc., *1988 Annual Report.*

already in the works to open its own stores and to offer a new line of clothes for larger women. Wall Street, however, was not that optimistic. Claiborne's stock price fell from $35 to $17 during the year.

The general malaise in the apparel industry was expected to continue into 1989. Most industry analysts believed that sales would rock along at their present levels unless some new fashion trend emerged to create some excitement in the stores. Liz Claiborne's sales were expected to incr~ se by only 4 percent in 1989.

Despite its somewhat disappointing showing for the year, further recognition was bestowed on the company in 1988. When *Fortune* magazine asked 8,000 executives, outside directors, and financial analysts to rate the ten largest firms in their respective industries on eight attributes for its list of "America's Most Admired Corporations," Liz Claiborne, Inc. once again scored at the top of its industry. The company was rated second in quality of management and innovation. Later that year, *Fortune* also named the company one of "America's Fastest-Growing Companies" for 1988.

TOP MANAGEMENT AND ORGANIZATION

The mission of management, as seen through Liz Claiborne's eyes, was to "generate meaningful work by creating products of integrity—to share the rewards of success amply, at all levels."[6]

Brenda Gall, vice-president at Merrill Lynch, attributed Liz Claiborne's success to the fact that it had four key individuals with complementary strengths in different areas of the business. "Usually when you get a start-up, you have a strength in one or two areas—design and sales, or design and finance—you don't have all the bases covered. These people *had* all the bases covered. They've planned their business from day one, and they're still planning."[7]

From its inception, Claiborne has embodied the concept of team management. Liz Claiborne herself was responsible for the designing function; Arthur Ortenberg's strengths were finance, administration, and organization; Jerome Chazen was the sales and marketing expert; and Leonard Boxer was in charge of production and operations. These four individuals shared responsibility for long-range planning and strategic decisions.

By 1986, however, the top management team had become aware of the need to train successors for their jobs. Liz Claiborne began to delegate more and more of her own designing duties to staff members and by 1988 had stepped back to perform only editing functions. Part of the reason for that change was the changing nature of the design trade. What had been a "sketch, take a long lunch, leave at 5:00 and go to parties" type of a day had become a twelve-hour-a-day job because of competitive pressures for larger, more coordinated lines of products. As the demands of managing her rapidly growing company increased, Claiborne found less and less time for actual designing. Ortenberg, continuing his team approach to management, spent much time training a new group of managers to take over the business after his retirement.

Some organizational restructuring took place in 1987. The company's three sportswear divisions—Collections, Lizwear, and Lizsport—were combined into the Sportswear Group, and Jay Margolis was put in charge of this segment. He was given the title executive vice-president, Women's Sportswear Group. Girls sportswear was moved to the Lizwear label. The executive committee, which had been in control of the firm since its founding, was replaced by the policy committee, which reported directly to the board of directors. Its functions were to monitor market share and identify and evaluate business opportunities. Its major objective was to maintain the spirit of Claiborne and Ortenberg after they left the company.

Three new positions were created during 1987. An executive vice-president of operations and corporate planning was added whose primary functions were to oversee production planning, resource acquisition, and manufacturing distribution. Harvey Falk, who succeeded Leonard Boxer, assumed this title. Falk, a certified public accountant, had been with the company since 1982. His previous position was executive vice-president, finance. In addition, a senior vice-president of corporate sales and marketing, responsible for coordinating marketing efforts among the nine divisions, was created. Robert Bernard was appointed to fill this position. Bernard, who had left R. H. Macy's to join Liz Claiborne in 1985, previously served as head of sportswear sales. As noted earlier, Jay Margolis assumed the titles of executive vice-president and president of the Women's Sportswear Group. Margolis had been at Claiborne since 1984, serving in various management capacities in the Sportswear Division. Before coming to Liz Claiborne, Margolis had been a division president at Ron Chereskin, Inc., a sportswear manufacturer. Exhibit 3 lists the corporate officers of Liz Claiborne, Inc.

MARKETING STRATEGY

The Claiborne marketing strategy is straightforward: Know your customer. Claiborne's customer is "about 35 years old and not a perfect size 8."[8] Capitalizing on the trend of increasing numbers of women entering the work force,

EXHIBIT 3   LIZ CLAIBORNE, INC.: CORPORATE OFFICERS (JANUARY 1, 1989)

NAME	AGE	POSITION(S)
Elisabeth Claiborne Ortenberg	59	Chairman of the board, president and chief executive officer
Arthur Ortenberg	62	Vice-chairman of the board and secretary
Jerome A. Chazen*	62	Vice-chairman of the board and, effective June 1989, chairman of the board
Harvey L. Falk*	54	Executive vice-president, Operations and Corporate Planning and, effective June 1989, president and vice-chairman
Jay Margolis*	40	Executive vice-president; president, Women's Sportswear Group and, effective June 1989, vice-chairman and president, Women's Sportswear Group
Robert Abajian	57	Senior vice-president, Women's Sportswear, design
Robert Bernard	38	Senior vice-president, corporate sales and marketing
Ellen Daniel	53	Senior vice-president; Collections Division
Kenneth Ganz	54	Senior vice-president, corporate distribution
Matthew Langweber	37	Senior vice-president; president, Retail Division
Jack Listanowsky	41	Senior vice-president, operations
Alois J. Lohn	54	Senior vice-president, manufacturing
Larry McDonald	54	Senior vice-president, corporate textile engineering
Nina E. McLemore*	43	Senior vice-president; president, Accessories Division
Allen McNeary*	41	Senior vice-president; president, Dress Division
Jo Miller	38	Senior vice-president; First Issue, Retail Division
Samuel M. Miller	51	Senior vice-president, finance
Hank Sinkel	43	Senior vice-president, sportswear, sales
Kathry D. Connors		Vice-president, human resources
Roberta Schuhalter Karp		Vice-president, corporate counsel
Walter L. Krieger		Vice-president, financial operations
Jeffrey H. Shendell		Vice-president, allocations and sales support
Claudia Wong		Vice-president, corporate Far East operations
Elaine H. Goodell		Controller
Robert P. McKean		Treasurer

*Member, policy committee

Sources: Liz Claiborne, Inc., *1988 Annual Report;* 1988 Form 10-K.

Claiborne offers stylish, classic clothes tailored for the working woman. Its marketing strategy is to sell clothes through leading department stores and specialty stores. The selections must be designed with consistent highly individual styling—a "designer line," but at prices a working woman can afford. The working woman, said Liz Claiborne, "isn't going to spend $2,000 on a suit."[9]

Claiborne's vision for her corporation has always been to "create, identify and act upon opportunities for ourselves and our customers." Specifically, the objective is to "provide all needs except formal evening wear, coats, nightwear and bathing suits." Chazen identifies the Claiborne customer as the "executive, professional career woman who is updated in her taste level, as opposed to the traditional customer who wears structured suits." Jack Schultz, general merchandise manager for Sanger Harris, concurs: The fashions are "up-to-date, not avant-garde."[10]

The company prides itself on its close working relationship with its retailers, which is considered to be the best in the industry. Despite the fact that Claiborne refuses to provide them with "markdown money" (funds to cover retailers when they are forced to hold a clearance of slow-selling goods), the relationships hold. Different from other firms in the industry, Claiborne's marketing technique centers around the New York showroom. Refusing to operate a road sales force, Claiborne forces retailers to make initial contact with her in her own showroom. As the stores' top managers usually arrive for the season's showing, the relationship begins at a much higher level than at her competitors. Costs are also reduced by eliminating unnecessary travel.

Mark Shulman, senior vice-president and general merchandising manager for I. Magnin in San Francisco, called it the "best run apparel company on Seventh Avenue today." Other retailers such as Jack Schultz, general merchandise manager for Sanger Harris stores in Texas, stated that Claiborne was the largest and most successful of their accounts. Carol Greer, senior vice-president and general merchandise manager of Rich's in Atlanta, said that "what Claiborne does best is thoroughly understand the customer, her lifestyle, and the price she's willing to pay."[11]

Claiborne provides a great deal of on-site support to its retailers. Fashion specialists travel to all the stores, talking to customers, taking photographs of displays, and giving seminars to the sales people. They take time to discuss the company's goals and fashion point of view. According to Chazen, "The most important thing they get across is that we care about them and we expect them to care in return."[12] In addition, all retailers receive copies of the "Claiboard Receiving Guide," which categorizes names and style numbers by style group and provides buyers with a management tool for keeping up with orders and shipments. Claiborne personnel also help organize the in-store boutiques so that items that go together are displayed properly.

Store displays and groupings are important in the Liz Claiborne marketing system. Within each of the company's seven lines, clothes are grouped by the use of common fabrics and colors. A typical group might consist of a sweater, skirt, pants, and two or more coordinated blouses and T-shirts. Retailers are encouraged to show the items together, as Claiborne representatives believe their clothing sells better that way. Sometimes a single customer will buy an entire coordinated group.

There are six seasons in a Claiborne year: Pre-Spring, Spring One, Spring Two, Fall One, Fall Two, and Holiday. In a recent *New Yorker* article, James Lardner described Liz Claiborne's seasonal planning as follows: "Claiborne bases its production on the number of garments it expects to sell in the two-month period that each season, typically, stays in the stores. Most items are sellouts, and sometimes they sell out very quickly, but there is no provision for increasing output in response to demand; nor is a garment ever repeated in a subsequent season, although its success might inspire something similar."[13] Marketing efforts and sales growth are monitored by a system called SURF (systematic updated retail feedback). Data is gathered on a cross-section of stores representative of size and geographic location. By manipulating the data received weekly, managers can get a good feel of consumer spending habits.

The marketing efforts of the firm reflect both Claiborne and Ortenberg's personalities: intense and somewhat arrogant, driven by a mission of product quality and service. Claiborne herself has always expressed a willingness to be involved with her customer. When preparing clothes for market, she always tries to ask herself, "How much would I pay for that piece?" She frequently travels across the country, stopping in her boutiques, chatting with customers, trying to pick up on the smallest of trends in their buying behavior.

One important part of the winning formula has been the way Liz Claiborne's clothes fit her customers, whose figures often deviate from the ideal image presented by fashion models. Claiborne has said that she has no desire to lead a fashion parade. She prefers "seeing women walking along the streets dressed in my clothes, or coming up to me and saying, 'I love your clothes. Once I start wearing them, that's all I want to buy.' I think that's terrific."[14]

PRODUCTION AND OPERATIONS

Although the company employs over 2,200 workers, it has no manufacturing facilities. Its entire production is contracted out. Claiborne has found that by manufacturing overseas, primarily in the Far East, it can significantly reduce overhead and, by keeping its capital investments low, can post returns on equity of close to 50 percent.

Claiborne's production administration staff, headquartered in the North Bergen, New Jersey, plant, is primarily responsible for maintaining cost and quality among the contractors. Staff members' duties range from production engineering and supplier allocation to quality control. Most of the suppliers to the firm are located in Hong Kong, South Korea, Taiwan, the Philippines, and China. Purchases are made through short-term purchase orders rather than formal long-term contracts. Approximately one-half of the supply of raw materials comes from overseas, specifically Hong Kong, Taiwan, and Japan.

Production lead times in the apparel industry from the time the order is placed to the time the piece arrives for sale can be quite long. Claiborne often makes manufacturing commitments later in the production cycle than some if its competitors in order to assure that the product reflects up-to-date consumer tastes. These constraints understandably can cause problems with some suppliers. It is necessary, therefore, to maintain good relationships with the overseas suppliers that one has found to be reliable. At Claiborne, domestic suppliers' activities are monitored by staff specialists at the North Bergen plant while overseas offices monitor its foreign suppliers. They are located in Hong Kong, Taipei, Tel Aviv, Singapore, Shanghai, Manila, and Florence. Claiborne also works through independent agents located in Korea, Portugal, and Brazil.

Concerns over political and economic conditions abroad were prominent during the 1980s. All incoming merchandise is subject to U.S. Customs duties, and import quotas apply to certain classifications of merchandise, a result of bilateral agreements between the U.S. and exporting countries. Recognizing that escalation of these restrictions could significantly harm the firm, Claiborne tried to allocate as much merchandise as possible to categories not covered by quota regulations. The company's efforts and worries were not unfounded. In 1985 Congress passed legislation calling for tighter restrictions on textile and apparel imports. President Reagan, however, vetoed the referendum. Nevertheless, the danger signals were apparent. Should tighter controls be enforced to protect American jobs, Liz Claiborne, Inc. would suffer repercussions.

DIVERSIFICATION AND STRATEGIC ISSUES

As the company's growth in its primary markets began to level off in the late 1980s, concerns were aired over the level of diversification the company had accomplished and the amount that might be necessary to sustain success in this very volatile industry. Jay Meltzer, industrial analyst at Goldman Sachs & Co., noted that if the firm were to continue to grow, "they'll have to diversify." Yet he also noted that there is an inherent risk in diversification, as management could get farther and farther away from doing what they know best.[15]

Diversification plans were announced in 1988. Liz Claiborne introduced a new sportswear label, sold exclusively through the company's own stores under the First Issue trademark. Stores were located in high-traffic shopping mall locations in major cities. The line was priced just below Liz Claiborne Collections, placing it in direct competition with The Limited, The Gap, and Banana Republic. The first stores were opened in the northeastern U.S. in February 1988, and expansion continued during the year. A total of thirteen stores were opened in 1988, and thirty more were planned to be in operation by the end of 1989. Claiborne estimates the cost of opening one of these stores to be $150,000, with no projected profit until 1990. The possibility of expanding the chain overseas was also being considered.

In 1988, the company assumed full ownership of its fragrance line, thus ending its stormy three-year relationship with Avon. A men's fragrance was being developed and would be introduced in the fall of 1989. The company also expanded its Canadian operations in 1988 and established a jewelry division in 1989.

Another expansion of the Claiborne fashion empire occurred in 1988, when a new line of fashions for larger women was introduced at the end of the year. Called Elizabeth, it offered traditional Liz Claiborne styling at prices comparable to the company's main sportswear lines in a full range of large sizes. It was estimated that between 35 and 40 million women wear size 14 or above, representing a $10 billion market. Claiborne's primary competition in this market is Geoffrey Beane.

A program to expand the company's presence in the marketplace was initiated in 1987. "Project Consumer" was designed to reinforce ties to Claiborne buyers. There were two major thrusts. The first was to increase the number of Claiborne's in-store product specialists, who help train retail sales personnel and display merchandise. The second was to initiate larger in-store boutiques for Liz Claiborne lines in leading department stores. The first boutique was opened in Jordan Marsh's downtown Boston store. This personalized selling space offered the consumer a choice of shopping for dresses, misses sportswear, hosiery, accessories, and fragrances all in one location.

LIZ CLAIBORNE WITHOUT LIZ?

Liz Claiborne and her husband, Arthur Ortenberg, announced in February 1989 that they intended to retire at the end of the year. Although they had scaled back their roles in the firm over the previous few years, their announcement came as something of a surprise to the industry. The couple stated that they wanted to devote more time to environmental projects and personal interests. They planned to remain as board members of the firm. In preparation for their impending retirement, they sold 900,000 shares of stock during 1989, reducing their investment to $82 million.

Leonard Boxer had retired in 1988, and his responsibilities had been assumed by Harvey L. Falk, executive vice-president for operations and corporate planning. Of the four founders, only Jerome Chazen would remain.

Initial response to the retirement announcement was pessimistic, and stock prices dropped by over $1, with 2 million shares changing hands. Although most analysts felt that investors were overreacting, others voiced real concern. In the apparel industry, where products are often very closely identified with the founder's image, firms often face difficult transition periods after their founders retire. Top management at Liz Claiborne is confident, however, that the organization they built will continue to prosper without them, and some in the industry agree. As designer Bill Blass said, "There is a tendency in our business to overstay your welcome. I love the idea of stepping down. I like the idea they know when to do it."[16]

According to a 1988 article in *Fortune,* the quality that makes companies like Liz Claiborne and the other so-called billion dollar kids distinct is the presence of an entrepreneurial atmosphere. The founders frequently have their own strong visions of the future and are very determined to have a piece of action out in the market. Cofounder and vice-chairman Jerome Chazen reflected "We knew we wanted to clothe women in the work force. We saw a niche where no pure player existed. What we didn't know was how many customers were out there."[17]

Given its past dependence on that level of entrepreneurial spirit, the future of Liz Claiborne, Inc. in 1989 was uncertain. Had the company reached the limits of its growth potential, or would the plans made for management succession provide a smooth transition and continued success for Liz Claiborne, Inc. without Liz? Exhibit 4 contains Liz Claiborne's farewell to the stockholders, published in the 1988 Annual Report.

EXHIBIT 4   LIZ CLAIBORNE, INC.: PRESIDENT'S LETTER, 1988 ANNUAL REPORT

As I get ready to close the door behind myself, I find myself compelled to look once more over my shoulder and let my eyes and mind inventory the company I leave. There's Bob Abajian, the new Liz of sportswear, an extraordinary amalgam of talent, integrity, and professional know-how. There's Jay Margolis, the merchant supreme who perfectly synthesizes within himself who we are and what we stand for. There's Harvey Falk, who Jerry, Art, and I feel privileged to have worked with, whose knowledge of operations and whose unsurpassed credibility assures me that our supply base and engineering capabilities will only get better. I am reassured as I bring up mental pictures of our extraordinary team, so many players we love and respect. So many players I owe so much to.

These are the things that are important to me, the things I urge my colleagues to engrave deeply in their memories — that product and engineering are primary; that we are dedicated to coherent, consistent design; that we have the character to bypass fad and trend and live or die by a taste level we can be proud of; that we all learn and relearn the fundamentals of the game —fit, stitching, color matching, fabric evaluation; that top quality makes us proud and shoddy quality is intolerable.

I want all of us to remember that this company was started with pennies and a vision. And respect for our craft. And respect for our suppliers. And a firm regard for the intelligence and good discriminating sense of our ultimate consumer. And let's never forget that what we have demonstrated is that individuals working as a team can bring elegance and vitality to any endeavor.

I have done what I set out to do. I have participated in the building of a company that is certain of successful perpetuation. I thank you for having been, with me, part of a grand adventure.

Signed,
Liz Claiborne
Chairman, President and Chief Executive Officer

Source: Liz Claiborne, Inc., *1988 Annual Report.*

THE APPAREL INDUSTRY

The following statement by Fred Wenzel, chief executive officer of Kellwood Co., a large U.S. apparel manufacturing firm, sums up the state of the industry in early 1989:

> Apparel manufacturing in the U.S. will always be present, but certain . . . apparel can best be made in newly industrialized countries. Not only is their direct labor cost substantially lower, but all other costs [as well], resulting in prices that this country cannot meet. Therefore, we must look to design, style, and service as our major weapons against imports.[18]

The U.S. apparel manufacturing industry is a very fragmented, labor-intensive business. The American Association of Apparel Manufacturers estimates that there are over 12,000 firms, only half of which employ twenty or more workers. This top half accounts for over 80 percent of the jobs and most of the business. Competition among U.S. firms and with foreign competitors is, in a word, fierce. Intense price pressure has historically kept prices, operating margins, and wage rates low compared with other manufacturing industries. Most of the smaller companies produce a very narrow range of products, often under contract for a larger firm or a retailer.

The industry is geographically concentrated in the northeastern states. Sixty percent of U.S. apparel is manufactured in New York, California, Pennsylvania, and New Jersey. Practically all of the high-fashion and tailored clothing comes from these states, while factories in the South and Southeast specialize in items amenable to large-volume production runs such as jeans, slacks, and underwear.

Three types of manufacturing operations predominate in the industry: manufacturers, jobbers, and contractors. Manufacturers purchase the material from textile companies and then cut, sew, and sell the finished product to retailers. Jobbers typically buy material and sell the finished product but "job out" the manufacture to outside factory operations, or contractors, who receive the material and make the product according to specifications.

OVERSEAS PRODUCTION

In recent years, production of apparel goods in the United States has declined significantly in real terms as apparel sales companies have sought the cost advantages available through overseas production. U.S. companies have contracted with offshore producers and in a growing number of cases have opened their own production facilities overseas. Apparel imports grew from $5.8 billion in 1980 to $15.8 billion in 1986 while exports of U.S. apparel products actually declined. Exhibit 5 shows import and export totals for textile and apparel goods for the years 1980, 1985, and 1986, the latest year available as of the case date.

Offshore sourcing can be accomplished in two ways. Apparel may be imported under a quota system or under Item 807 of the U.S. Tariff Schedule. Under the quota system, U.S. companies design and market clothing in the

EXHIBIT 5   U.S. EXPORTS AND IMPORTS OF TEXTILES AND APPAREL PRODUCTS, 1980–1986

	1980	1985	1986
EXPORTS			
Textile Mill Products	3,457	2,112	2,347
Apparel	1,001	600	727
Total	4,458	2,712	3,074
IMPORTS			
Textile Mill Products	2,372	4,714	5,517
Apparel	5,767	13,595	15,836
Total	8,139	18,309	21,353
TRADE BALANCE	−3,681	−15,597	−18,279

Source: U.S. Department of Commerce, Bureau of the Census, *Statistical Abstract of the United States, 1988* (Washington, D.C.: Government Printing Office, 1988).

U.S. but contract for their materials and manufacture according to company specifications. Goods are shipped to the U.S. in accordance with quota agreements negotiated with those countries under the Multi-Fiber Agreement, a pact involving fifty-four countries. The quotas are based on a number of variables, including past levels of imports from that country. Liz Claiborne, along with most of its close competitors, manufactures almost all of its clothing in the Far East under this quota system. Although sharp declines in the dollar against other world currencies in the 1980s had a significant effect on world trade, they had little effect on the price of goods purchased abroad by American apparel companies. Most imports come from Asian countries whose currencies are pegged to the dollar.

The quota system of importation, although very economical for outsourcing American production, has some inherent problems. Long lead times are necessary to process orders offshore, so companies must plan their lines far in advance. The advance time often proves to be a hindrance in the rapidly changing world of fashion goods. Another problem is that quotas are sometimes poorly managed by officials in the source countries. If quotas are oversubscribed, even by mistake, U.S. Customs officials may seize the excess. Bernard Chaus, a competitor of Liz Claiborne, had merchandise worth $11.6 million embargoed in 1986 because of inaccurate record keeping in the People's Republic of China. The result was unfilled orders at the retail level and a substantial loss of profits for the company. Manufacturers and labor unions in the U.S. have openly criticized the liberal quota allotments handed out by the U.S. Customs officials in the 1980s, especially those granted to nations in the Far East.

Under Item 807, apparel firms ship cut fabrics to be finished overseas. When the goods are shipped back to the U.S., duty is paid only on the value added. Because the cost of transporting cut fabric is a factor, most of the Item 807 arrangements have been made with factories in Mexico and the Caribbean. Imports of textiles, apparel, and footwear manufactured under Item 807 increased 80 percent between 1980 and 1985. Fashion goods companies such as Claiborne have not used Item 807 sourcing to the extent that other apparel companies, such as Farah Manufacturing, a maker of men's pants, have.

EMPLOYMENT

Increased production abroad has led to loss of jobs in U.S. apparel manufacturing and has kept wage levels below other manufacturing wages. Exhibit 6 details employment and earnings figures for the industry compared to all manufacturing. Although the average wage of apparel workers in 1986, at $5.81, was nearly $4.00 per hour below the average manufacturing wage, comparative wages in the Far East ranged from as little as $0.20 per hour in China to around $2.00 in Hong Kong.

More than half of all production workers in the apparel industry are unionized. The two major unions are the Amalgamated Clothing and Textile Workers Union (ACTWU) and the International Ladies Garment Workers (ILGWU). Both major unions actively support and lobby for increased quota restrictions on imported goods.

The incentive to outsource is not all due to wage differentials. Apparel importers have stated that they cannot get the quality and reliability from domestic sources that is available overseas.

EXHIBIT 6   EMPLOYMENT AND EARNINGS IN U.S. APPAREL INDUSTRY

	APPAREL AND OTHER TEXTILE PRODUCTS		TOTAL MANUFACTURING	
Year	No. Employed (thousands)	Ave. Wage ($)	No. Employed (thousands)	Ave. Wage ($)
1986	1,115	5.81	19,186	9.73
1985	1,162	5.73	19,426	9.52
1984	1,202	5.53	19,590	9.17
1983	1,169	5.37	18,687	8.84
1982	1,158	5.18	18,848	8.50
1981	1,256	4.98	20,281	7.98
1980	1,297	4.57	20,361	7.27
1979	1,313	4.23	21,062	6.69
1978	1,332	3.94	20,505	6.17
1977	1,316	3.62	19,682	5.68

Source: U.S. Bureau of Labor Statistics.

THE MARKET

Estimated at over $166 billion in 1987, the market for apparel goods continued to be one of the largest consumer segments in the U.S. economy in the late 1980s. Although personal consumption expenditures for clothing and related articles had grown each year, the rate of increase had moderated. Furthermore, as a percent of disposable income, apparel expenditures had declined from around 5.6 percent in 1973 to approximately 4.75 percent in 1986. Exhibit 7 shows apparel expenditures for this fourteen-year period. The slowed rate of growth was attributed to a combination of several factors, including the reluctance of consumers to increase their debt loads and the relative lack of big-selling "trendy" goods during the previous few years. Expectations were for the market to remain strong through the late 1980s and early 1990s but for annual increases to be at a more modest level than in the early 1980s.

EXHIBIT 7   CONSUMER APPAREL EXPENDITURES, 1973-1986

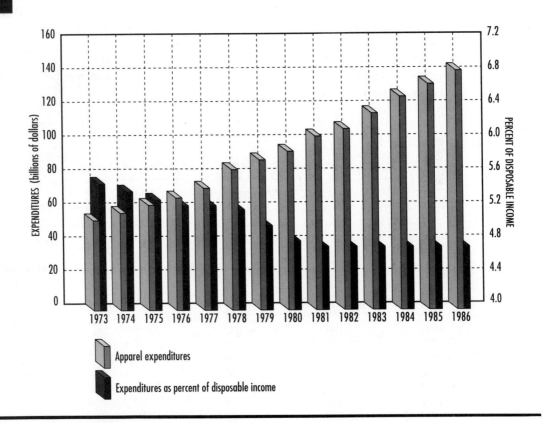

Note: Expenditure amounts represent the seasonally adjusted annual rate.

Source: U.S. Department of Commerce.

Earnings growth was also expected to continue, but also at modest levels. The general outlook was for a quite healthy apparel market in the United States.

THE COMPETITORS

Liz Claiborne's success in designing clothes that appeal to the professional woman attracted a number of significant competitors, including Evan Picone, Donna Karan, Ralph Lauren, and Adrienne Vittadini. Most of them were priced above Claiborne, however. Competition for Liz Claiborne's other lines ranged from designer lines competing with Dana Buchman offerings to specialty lines such as those competing with Claiborne's larger sizes. Surveys of Liz Claiborne customers indicated that they also shopped specialty stores such as Benetton. The competition is therefore hard to specifically identify. In 1989 Liz Claiborne had succeeded in defining and defending a rather unique niche in the market, which could be summarized as "designer clothing at nondesigner prices." The company could legitimately claim to be the "largest women's sportswear manufacturer in the United States" and "the largest better dress company in America."[19]

COMPETITIVE STRATEGIES

As growth stabilized in the industry, manufacturing was further deemphasized in favor of foreign outsourcing. Many companies, such as Kellwood, divested their old manufacturing facilities and looked for acquisitions of other marketing-oriented companies with brand-name products. Competition in the apparel sales industry had come to revolve almost exclusively around design, styling, and service. Another significant marketing innovation of the 1980s was the inclusion of apparel maker and retailer under the same corporate umbrella. Benetton Corp. and The Gap are two companies that have successfully integrated their operations. Liz Claiborne inaugurated its own retail outlets in 1987.

Keener competition among apparel firms also caused more pressure to be placed on manufacturers to tighten their lead times. Designs must be approved and coordinated with the company's other seasonal offerings, a process that can take several months. After samples of goods are shown to buyers in, for instance, a large department store chain and their orders are placed for the company's line, fabrics are ordered for delivery in six to eight weeks. After the fabric is received, the manufacturer typically needs four to six months to finish and ship the goods. In all, the manufacturing part of the cycle can take up to nine months. Adding in design lead times often brings the whole apparel pipeline to around 66 weeks.

One marketing innovation has made lead times even more critical. Traditionally, there have been five seasons for women's wear (summer, early fall, late fall/winter, resort season, and spring). Buying cycles for these seasons have often meant that buyers were placing orders for up to three seasons in the future. Liz Claiborne introduced the six-season fashion year, which increased the number and frequency of seasonal orders to fill at the factory level. Several of Claiborne's competitors followed suit with their own six- and seven-season fashion years.

In the fashion goods segment, a variety of quick response alternatives are being sought to counter long manufacturing lead times. Greater cooperation and communication between retailers and manufacturers has helped some. Large buyers such as Bloomingdale's and Macy's have direct access to the design staffs of such firms as Liz Claiborne and Ralph Lauren. Point-of-sale technology has helped reduce lead times on certain replacement items during the seasonal run.

A number of contractors in the United States have attempted to lure back the apparel business with promises of reduced lead times. Ralph Lauren increased its domestic sourcing in 1987 over previous levels in an attempt to gain a quicker response to the market. Industry analysts predicted that domestic sourcing would also regain favor as sentiment for protectionism grew in Washington. In 1986, The Limited, an integrated manufacturer, announced that it was actively seeking more domestic sources for its contracts. U.S. producers also attempted to be more competitive with foreign contractors through improved technology. Innovations that sought to reduce high-cost labor input were being developed rapidly. Computer-aided garment design was refined through the introduction of improved software packages. Automated marker-making systems and improved water-jet and laser fabric cutting systems were reducing scrap costs as well as labor costs. Programmable sewing units, based on microprocessor technology, were on-line by 1987 in a few plants, although these and most other high-tech innovations were prohibitively expensive for most of the smaller producers.

ENDNOTES

1. Deveny, K., "Can Ms. Fashion Bounce Back?" *Business Week* (January 16, 1989): 64–70.

2. Oberlink, P., "Liz is Big Biz," *Madison Avenue* (October 1986): 29–31.

3. Gannes, S., "America's Fastest-Growing Companies," *Fortune* (May 23, 1988): 28–40.

4. Denveny, "Can Ms. Fashion Bounce Back?" p. 66.

5. Liz Claiborne, Inc., *1987 Annual Report,* p. 6.

6. Ibid.

7. Oberlink, "Liz is Big Biz," p. 29.

8. Deveny, "Can Ms. Fashion Bounce Back?" p. 64.

9. Ibid.

10. Skolnik, R., "Liz the Wiz," *Sales and Marketing Management* (September 9, 1985): 173–176.

11. Ibid., p. 173.

12. Ibid, p. 174.

13. Lardner, J., "Annals of Business: The Sweater Trade—I," *New Yorker* (January 11, 1988): 45.

14. Oberlink, "Liz is Big Biz," p. 30.

15. Skolnik, "Liz the Wiz," p. 176.

16. Trachtenberg, J. A., and T. Agins, "Can Liz Claiborne Continue to Thrive When She is Gone?" *Wall Street Journal* (February 28, 1989): A1.

17. Gannes, "America's Fastest-Growing Companies," p. 30.

18. "Textile, Apparel, and Home Furnishings: Current Analysis," *Standard & Poor's Industry Surveys* (August 27, 1987): T82.

19. Liz Claiborne, Inc., *1987 Annual Report,* p. 4.

ADDITIONAL REFERENCES

"Fortune 500 Largest Industrial Corporations." *Fortune* (April 24, 1989): 346–401.

Lardner, James. "Annals of Business: Global Clothing Industry—Part I." *New Yorker* (January 11, 1988): 39–73.

"Annals of Business: Global Clothing Industry—Part II." *New Yorker* (January 18, 1988): 57–73.

Liz Claiborne, Inc. *1988 Annual Report.*

Liz Claiborne, Inc. *SEC Form 10-K, 1987.*

Schultz, Ellen. "America's Most Admired Corporations." *Fortune* (January 18, 1988).

Sellers, Patricia. "The Rag Trade's Reluctant Revolutionary." *Fortune* (January 5, 1987): 36–38.

Smith, Adam. "How Liz Claiborne Designed an Empire." *Esquire* (January 1986): 78–79.

"Textile, Apparel, and Home Furnishings: Current Analysis." *Standard & Poor's Industry Surveys* (December 11, 1986): T61–T62.

U.S. Department of Commerce. *Statistical Abstract of the United States,* 108th ed. Washington, D.C.: Government Printing Office, 1988.

CASE 2

CARMIKE CINEMAS, INC.　　　　　MARILYN L. TAYLOR

Mike Patrick, president of Carmike Cinemas, Inc., put the September 1986 month-end reports in his drawer. He glanced at the pile of notes he had hand-written as he went through the reports. He would ask his secretary, Jo, to dis-tribute them to various company managers. For the most part, the notes asked for the reasons behind specific expenditures in September or gave directions regarding expense reduction.

In half an hour Mike planned to join Carl Patrick, his father, chairman of Carmike. The father and son team had purchased Carmike, then named Mar-tin Theatres, in 1982. At the time of the purchase Martin was the seventh largest U.S. theatre circuit and had been a Fuqua Industries Inc. subsidiary for over 12 years. Fuqua was a large diversified company. The equity in Carmike was held entirely by Carmike, Inc., a private Georgia company owned by the Patrick family and a New York investment company.

Mike knew his father would spend some time on the issue of taking the company public. There were a number of issues to be considered before mak-ing the decision. Jay Jordan and others at the investment company wanted to withdraw all or a major part of their investment. His own family would likely be able to reduce their investment in Carmike by offering some of their stock in a secondary issue. However, the Patrick family owned 51% of Carmike's stock and Mike felt strongly that he wanted to be clearly in charge of the com-pany. Mike wondered how the broader investment community would view the various strategic and operational moves undertaken at Carmike over the pre-vious four years. He thought briefly of the acquisition of the video movie chain. An infusion of cash and reduction of debt would position Carmike to take advantage of other potential acquisitions on a timely basis. Mike also realized that resiliency was important as the company faced numerous chal-lenges including difficult industry conditions and continuing capital require-

Source: **Prepared by Professor Marilyn L. Taylor, University of Kansas, as a basis for classroom discussion. The research for the case was partially supported by the Univer-sity of Kansas School of Business Research Fund provided by the Fourth National Bank and Trust Company, Wichita, Kansas.** © **Marilyn L. Taylor, 1989.**

ments. However, going public entailed some costs including potentially more scrutiny by shareholders, public disclosure of company moves, and the costs of required reports and public relations with shareholders, the investment community, and the general public.

Whether to go public was a dilemma. He began to jot some notes under the heading "Pros and Cons of Going Public in Fall, 1986."

HISTORY OF THE COMPANY

Carmike Theatres was originally founded as the Martin Theatres circuit in 1912. Mr. C. L. Patrick, the company's chairman of the board, joined Martin Theatres in 1945 and became the general manager and director in 1948. Fuqua Industries, Inc. purchased the Martin family business holdings including Martin Theatres in 1969. Mr. Patrick served as president of Fuqua from 1970 to 1978 and as vice chairman of the board of directors of Fuqua from 1978 to 1982.

During the 13 years that Martin was a part of Fuqua the subsidiary had been a cash generator for its parent company. Fuqua sold a number of the Martin properties. In 1981 Fuqua completed the sale of three TV stations which had come with the original purchase. Only the theatre circuit remained.

Mike strongly felt that the executives at Martin had largely kept the theatre chain in a holding pattern during its time as a Fuqua subsidiary. The treasurer, for example, had been promoted because he was "sort of in the right place at the right time . . . when the previous treasurer, a brilliant man," had a stroke in 1969. Further, Mike explained that when Carl Patrick moved to Atlanta in 1970 as president of the parent company Fuqua, Ron Baldwin as next Martin president was "good in real estate but very poor in accounting."

The purchase price for Martin Theatres was $25M. Financing arrangements for purchasing Martin Theatres were very favorable. The total investment by the Patrick family was less than $250,000. However, the purchase of the theatres was highly leveraged (see financial statements in Exhibit 1). Early efforts were directed toward improving the company's cash flow in order to reduce the debt. At the same time the company had significant capital improvement requirements. To make the venture viable, the Patricks undertook a number of changes in operations which are described in the ensuing sections of this case. Success was by no means assured, as Mike Patrick explained:

> When we bought Martin, Martin was going downhill. It looked bad. And I want you to know that it looked pretty bad for us for a while. I mean it really did. For a while there we were asking ourselves, "Why are we in this mess?" Not only were we leveraged 100%, but we realized that we had to spend somewhere in the neighborhood of $25M more dollars to renew the company.

At the time of Carmike's acquisition of Martin Theatres, the circuit had 265 screens (excluding 26 drive-in theatre screens) located in 128 theatres.

EXHIBIT 1   CARMIKE CINEMAS, INC.: FINANCIAL STATEMENTS 1982–1986

	FISCAL YEARS ENDED				
	March 25, 1982	*March 31, 1983*	*March 29, 1984*	*March 28, 1985*	*March 27, 1986*
INCOME STATEMENT DATA					
Revenues					
Admissions	$33,622	$40,077	$43,778	$49,040	$42,828
Concessions and other	13,595	15,490	16,886	19,917	18,150
	47,217	55,567	60,664	68,957	60,978
Costs and expenses					
Cost of operations (exclusive of concession merchandise)	36,436	39,981	44,760	50,267	45,902
Cost of concession merchandise	2,695	2,703	3,117	3,566	3,004
General and administrative	2,522	2,878	3,008	2,702	2,760
Depreciation and amortization	2,348	1,964	2,868	3,140	3,385
	44,001	47,526	53,753	59,675	55,051
Operating income	3,216	8,041	6,911	9,282	5,927
Interest expense	380	2,569	2,703	2,337	2,018
Income before income taxes	2,836	5,472	4,208	6,945	3,909
Income taxes	1,323	2,702	1,615	3,054	1,745
Net income	$ 1,513	$ 2,770	$ 2,593	$ 3,891	$ 2,164
Earnings per common share	—	$ .65	$ .61	$ .92	$ .51
Weighted average common shares outstanding	—	4,200	4,200	4,200	4,200
BALANCE SHEET DATA					
(at end of period)					
Cash and cash equivalents	$(1,317)	$ 433	$ 767	$ 770	$ 786
Total assets	34,742	27,754	35,324	34,953	40,665
Total long-term debt	3,656	18,853	22,125	16,969	18,843
Redeemable preferred stock	—	405	405	405	405
Common shareholders' equity	27,752	2,829	5,382	9,233	11,357

Carmike had acquired or constructed an additional 215 screens and closed or disposed of 44 screens since 1982.

MIKE PATRICK'S BACKGROUND

Mike Patrick had worked in Martin Theatres first as a high school student in Columbus, Georgia, later in Atlanta as a student at Georgia State University, and still later back in Columbus as he finished his studies in economics at

Columbus College. He explained these time periods in his life and how he became acquainted with the company:

> Movie theatres was the only business in which I wanted really to work . . . it's a fun business. If you are in construction, no one cares about your business. But if you tell someone that you are in the theater business, then everybody has seen a movie. Everyone has something they want to talk about. So it's an entertaining industry. Plus when I got into it, I was in the night end of it. I wasn't into administrative. So I got captured, as I called it. If you have never worked at night, then you don't understand. I really went to work at 8 a.m. and got off at 10 a.m. and then went back at 2 p.m. and got off at 11 p.m. at night. So your whole group of friends is a total flip flop. You have nighttime friends. Before you know it, you are trapped into this life. All your friends work at night. So your job becomes a little more important to you because that's where you spend all your time. Working in a theater . . . is a lot of fun. It really is, especially when you are 19 and you get to handle the cash. A theatre is a cash business.
>
> My father was president of Martin. In 1970 he became president of Fuqua and moved to Atlanta. My father wanted to sell the house in Columbus and my mother did not want to. I was very homesick for Columbus. . . . So I said, "I will go to Columbus College and I will live in the house." I moved back here in the summer of 1970 and worked in the accounting department because I wanted to understand the reports, why I filled out all these forms, and where they went. I learned then that the treasurer of the accounting department did not understand the paper flow at all.

The Patrick family and a limited number of investors acquired Martin Theatres in April 1982 in a leveraged buy-out for $20M in cash and a 10% note in the principal amount of $5M. Mike Patrick became president of Carmike Theatres, as the new company was called. He explained the advantage of working so long in the company.

> I had done every job in this company except that of Marion Jones, our attorney. But my brother is an attorney, so I have someone in the family to talk to if I have a question. No one can put one over on me. . . . I've fired them too, and I want to tell you something—I do my own firing . . . and firing a man who is incompetent when he doesn't know it is hard. He breaks down because he thinks he's good. When I first became president there was a member of my family who had to go. The other management noticed that.

POST-BUYOUT—STREAMLINING THE ORGANIZATION

In considering the purchase of Martin, Mike Patrick had described the firm to his father as "fat." Mike described what he did after purchase of the firm:

> It appeared that each layer of management got rid of their responsibilities to the next echelon down. For example, I could not figure out what the president did. . . . I kept looking at senior management trying to figure out what they did. I sort of took an approach like you call zero budgeting. Instead of saying my budget was $40,000 last year and I need 10% more this year, I required that each individual justify everything he did. For example, there is now only

one person in our financial department. The young man in there makes less than the guy that had the job as vice president of finance three years ago, and the current guy does not have a subordinate. The advertising department went from a senior level vice president level to a clerk. You are talking about the difference between $80K and a $19K salary.

When we got hold of the company, we let go the president, the financial vice president, and the senior vice president. At the same time the film procurement people retired, because they were over 65. So I have streamlined the organization tremendously. When we got Martin, Martin had 2,100 employees. Since then we bought a circuit called Video out in Oklahoma. They had 900 employees. Today I have 1,600 employees. Let me double check that number. As of October 31, I had 1,687 and the year before I had 1,607. So I actually have 80 more employees than I had last year. But when I got the company, it had 2,100 and the other company had 900.

Of the employees approximately 65% were paid minimum wage. Another 9% were paid sub-minimum wage. About 8% of the employees were in a managerial capacity and the company was totally non-union. Employee relationships were generally good. Initially, however, there were difficulties. Mike Patrick recalled the initial time period.

Management was not well disciplined when we came into Martin. I had to almost totally clean house: I eliminated all of top management but it took about six months to get second-level management to where it felt secure and at the same time develop a more aggressive attitude. I call it a predator attitude. But that first year we had some great hits, such as "E.T." We did so well that first year breaking all previous records so that the management team, even though it was new, became really confident, maybe too confident. Today they don't believe we can lose. Here's a list of the directors and key employees (see Exhibit 2).

The company also implemented improved technology in order to trim the number of employees. Mike Patrick explained what happened in one city when he wanted to replace the projectionists with totally automated projec-

EXHIBIT 2   CARMIKE CINEMAS, INC.: BACKGROUNDS OF DIRECTORS, OFFICERS AND KEY EMPLOYEES

C. L. Patrick (61), who has served as chairman of the board of directors of the company since April 1982, joined the company in 1945, became its general manager in 1948, and served as president of the company from 1969 to 1970. He served as president of Fuqua from 1970 to 1978, and as vice chairman of the board of directors of Fuqua from 1978 to 1982. Mr. Patrick is a director of Columbus Bank & Trust Company and Burnham Service Corporation.

Michael W. Patrick (36) has served as president of the company since October 1981 and as a director of the company since April 1982. He joined the company in 1970 and served in a number of operational and film booking and buying capacities prior to becoming president.

EXHIBIT 2 (continued)

Carl L. Patrick, Jr. (39) has served as a director of the company since April 1982. He was the director of taxes for the Atlanta, Georgia, office of Arthur Young & Co. from October 1984 to September 1986, and is currently self-employed. Previously, he was a certified public accountant with Arthur Andersen & Co. from 1976 to October 1984.

John W. Jordan, II (38) has been a director of the company since April 1982. He is a co-founder and managing partner of The Jordan Company, which was founded in 1982, and a managing partner of Jordan/Zalaznick Capital Company. From 1973 until 1982, he was vice president at Carl Marks & Company, a New York investment banking company. Mr. Jordan is a director of Bench Craft, Inc. and Leucadia National Corporation, as well as the companies in which The Jordan Company holds investments. Mr. Jordan is a director and executive officer of a privately held company which in November 1985 filed for protection under Chapter 11 of the Federal Bankruptcy Code.

Carl E. Sanders (60) has been a director of the company since April 1982. He is engaged in the private practice of law as chief partner of Troutman, Sanders, Lockerman & Ashmore, an Atlanta, Georgia, law firm. Mr. Sanders is a director and chairman of the board of First Georgia Bank and a director of First Railroad & Banking Company of Georgia, Fuqua Industries, Inc., Advanced Telecommunications, Inc., and Healthdyne, Inc. and a former governor of Georgia.

David W. Zalaznick (32) has served as a director of the company since April 1982. He is a co-founder and general partner of The Jordan Company, and a managing partner of Jordan/Zalaznick Capital Company. From 1978 to 1980, he worked as an investment banker with Merrill Lynch White Weld Capital Markets Group, and from 1980 until the formation of The Jordan Company in 1982, Mr. Zalaznick was a vice president of Carl Marks & Company, a New York investment banking company. Mr. Zalaznick is a director of Bench Craft, Inc. as well as the companies in which The Jordan Company holds investments. He is a director and executive officer of a privately held company which in November 1985 filed for protection under Chapter 11 of the Federal Bankruptcy Code.

John O. Barwick, III (36) joined the company as controller in July 1977 and was elected treasurer in August 1981. In August 1982 he became vice president–finance of the company. Prior to joining the company, Mr. Barwick was an accountant with the accounting firm of Ernst & Whinney from 1973 to 1977.

Anthony J. Rhead (45) joined the company in June 1981 as manager of the film office in Charlotte, North Carolina. Since July 1983, Mr. Rhead has been vice president–film of the company. Prior to joining the company he worked as a film booker for Plitt Theatres from 1973 to 1981.

Lloyd E. Riddish (58) has been employed by the company since 1948. He served as a district manager from 1971 to 1982 and as eastern division manager from 1982 to 1984, when he was elected to his present position as vice president–General Manager.

Marion Nelson Jones (39) joined the company as its general counsel in December 1984 and was elected secretary of the company in March 1985. Prior to joining the company, Mr. Jones was a partner in the law firm of Evert & Jones in Columbus, Georgia, from 1979 to 1984.

tion booths. He consulted with the company attorney regarding action the projectionists could take in retaliation:

> I called our attorney in and I asked him "What is the worst that could happen?" The attorney said, "You might have to reinstate the projectionists and pay them the back pay." I said, "You mean there is no million dollar fine?" He replied "No, you just got to worry about reinstatement and back pay." He went on to say, "Well, why are you going to get rid of the projectionists?" I said, "There is automated projectionist equipment for showing movies that will work very similar to an eight-track player. If we convert the theatres, we won't need projectionists." And he said, "Well, you can do it."
>
> However, the city had a code which said to be a projectionist you must take a test from the city electrical board to be certified. That law was put in about 1913 because back in the old days, they didn't have light bulbs. A projector then used two carbon arcs and it was a safety issue because back then film was made out of something that burned. That was before my time that film burned like that. Often they had fires in the lamp house. Now we have Zenith bulbs. The projectionists hadn't gone and gotten their certification from the electrical board for years. But the rule was on the books. So I figured the only problem we had was the city. As soon as we fired the projectionists, they went to the Council. They complained that the managers were doing the projectionist job without certification from the electrical board. The police raided my theater. I sued the City of Nashville.... In the meantime we sent an engineer up from Columbus and started teaching all our managers how to pass the electrical board test. As they began to pass the board, the rule became a moot question.

Martin had already leased and installed all the needed equipment except an automatic lens turn. The cost of $15,000 per projector was not justified when it took only a few seconds to change the lens. The new equipment eliminated the position of projectionist. The theatre managers took over the job of changing the lens. Mike explained how he was able to get the theatre managers to cooperate.

> I told our managers that once the automated projectionist booth was in operation and the job of projectionist eliminated I would give them a raise consisting of 40% of whatever the projectionists had made. So all of a sudden the manager went from being against the program of converting to automated projectionist booths to where I got a flood of letters from managers saying, "I passed the projectionist test. I'm now certified by the electrical board. Fire my projectionist."

IMPROVING THEATRE PROFITABILITY

At the time they purchased the Martin Theatre circuit, the Patricks were well aware that some of the theatres were losing money and that much of Martin's facilities were quickly becoming outmoded. A 1981 consulting report on Martin underscored that during the 1970s Martin had not aggressively moved to multiplexing. In addition, one of the previous presidents had put a number of theatres into "B-locations" where according to Mike Patrick there were "great

leases . . . but the theatres were off the beaten track." Mike explained his approach for handling the situation:

> I looked at all the markets we were in, the big markets where the money was
> to be made, and I said, "Here's what we will do. First, let's take the losers and
> make them profitable. At the time the losing theaters were a $1.2M deficit on
> the bottom line. So I decided to experiment. . . . Phenix City is a perfect exam-
> ple. I took the admission price from $3.75 to $.99. Everybody said I was a fool.
> The first year it made $70K which I thought was a great increase over the
> $26K it had been making. The next year what happened was the people in
> Phenix City are poor, very poor blue collar workers, but the theater is as nice
> as anything I have over here (in Columbus). So as word of mouth got going
> that theater kept getting better, and better. Now it almost sells out every Fri-
> day, Saturday, and Sunday. And I still charge $.99. That theatre will make over
> $200K this year.

As Mike put it, the conversion to "dollar theatres" was "a new concept.
No one else is doing that." By 1986, Carmike had twenty "99 theatres." The
company also offered a discount in admission prices on Tuesdays and discount ticket plans to groups. Two facilities called "Flick 'n' Foam" had restaurants and bar services in the theatre.

In addition, Mike Patrick continued to consider potential acquisitions.

> I'm looking at a circuit of theaters in a major metropolitan area. Now the
> owner hasn't told me that it is for sale yet. He wants me to make him an offer
> and I won't do it. I want him to make me the first offer. He has no new facili-
> ties. All his theatres are twins except one and that's a triple. He's getting killed.
> A large chain is coming against him with a twelve-plex. He's located all around
> the metro area and he's getting killed. He had that town for years and now
> he's almost knocked out of it. His circuit is going to be worthless. I've been
> up there. There are no 99 or dollar theaters anywhere. His locations are good
> for that. You see for a 99 theater, the location must not be a deterrent. It
> cannot be downtown, because downtown cannot support a night life so that's
> a deterrent. In the south, you don't want to be in a black area. White people
> won't go there. In Port Arthur you don't want to be in the Vietnamese area.
> Basically you don't want to be anywhere there is a minority.

FACILITY UPGRADING

When the Patricks purchased Martin Theatres in 1982, its facilities were
quickly becoming outmoded. As Mike put it, "We were basically non-competitive . . . we were just getting hit left and right in our big markets . . . the biggest
thing we had was a twin and we had competitors dropping four and six-plexes
on us." One reason for Martin's earlier reticence to convert to multi-screen
theatres was the tendency to put emphasis on the number of theatres rather
than screens. In addition, management of the theatre company, although not
so required by the parent company, had managed the circuit for its cash flow.
Patrick explained, "Ron (Baldwin) really never understood working for a $2B
company. He still managed the firm as though it were privately owned."

Mike Patrick explained the difficulties in the early 1980s:

> Oh, we were just outclassed everywhere you went. Ron Baldwin told me that
> Columbus Square was doomed. It was going black. I made it an eight-plex.
> With our nice theater, the Peachtree, I added one screen but I didn't have any
> more room. But I took the theater no one liked and made it an eight-plex. It
> is also one of our most profitable theaters we have today.

New theatres, either replacements or additions, were undertaken usually
through build, sale, and leaseback arrangements. Carl Patrick explained that
in 1985 the theatres were about 75% leased and about 25% company owned.

By 1986 the company had become the fifth largest motion picture exhibitor in the United States and the leading exhibitor in the southern United
States in terms of number of theatres and screens operated. The company
operated 156 theatres with an aggregate of 436 screens located in 94 cities in
11 southern states with a total seating capacity of 125,758 (see Exhibit 3).

All but 22 theatres were multi-screen. Approximately 95% of the company's screens were located in multi-screen theatres, with over 62% of the
company's screens located in theatres having three or more screens. The company had an average of 2.79 screens per theatre. The company's strategy was
designed to maximize utilization of theatre facilities and enhance operating
efficiencies. In the fiscal year ending March 27, 1986, aggregate attendance at
the company's theatres was approximately 15.3 million people.

The company owned the theatre and land for 37 of its 156 theatres. The

EXHIBIT 3 CARMIKE CINEMAS, INC.: THEATRES AND SCREENS, 1986

State	NUMBER OF SCREENS PER THEATRE						Total	Percent of Total Screens
	1	2	3	4	5	6–8		
Alabama	1	16	9	12	0	15	53	12.2%
Florida	1	0	3	0	0	0	4	0.9%
Georgia	3	12	15	4	10	16	60	13.8%
Kentucky	0	2	0	4	5	6	17	3.9%
New Mexico	0	2	0	0	0	0	2	0.4%
North Carolina	0	28	9	4	0	0	41	9.4%
Oklahoma	9	24	3	12	10	18	76	17.4%
South Carolina	0	10	6	0	0	0	16	3.7%
Tennessee	6	24	12	32	0	18	92	21.1%
Texas	2	16	3	28	0	18	67	15.4%
Virginia	0	8	0	0	0	0	4	1.8%
	22	142	60	96	25	91	436	100.00%
Percent of total screens	5.0%	32.6%	13.8%	22.0%	5.7%	20.9%	100.0%	

company owned 30 other theatres which were built on leased land. Another 78 theatres were leased. In addition, Carmike shared an ownership or leasehold interest in 11 of its theatres with various unrelated third parties.

Exhibit 4 describes the scope of the company's theatre operations at the end of five fiscal years.

Carmike's screens were located principally in smaller communities, typically with populations of 40,000 to 100,000 people, where the company was the sole or leading exhibitor. The company was the sole operator of motion picture theatres in 55% of the cities in which it operated, including Montgomery, Alabama; Albany, Georgia; and Longview, Texas. The company's screens constituted a majority of the screens operated in another 22% of such cities, including Nashville and Chattanooga in Tennessee and Columbus, Georgia. The locations of the company's theatres are indicated in Exhibit 5.

Carmike gave close attention to cost control in construction, as Mike Patrick explained:

> Under Fuqua Martin usually owned the theatre. In some instances the land was also owned; in others the company had a ground lease. Since theatres were basically the same from one site to another, the cost of construction of the building was fairly standardized once the site, or pad, was ready.

Mike Patrick built his first theatre in 1982 at a cost of $26/s.f. At the time the usual price in the industry was $31/s.f. He explained that even his insurance company had questioned him when he turned in his replacement cost estimate. In order to reduce his costs Mike Patrick had examined every element of cost. Initially the Patricks worked with the E&W architectural firm as Martin theatres had done for years. Mike Patrick explained that their costs were so favorable that other theatre companies began to use E&W. Eventually E&W costs went up. In 1985 Mike employed a firm of recent University of Alabama graduates to be the architects on a new theater in Georgia.

Costs were also carefully controlled when a shopping center firm built a theatre Carmike would lease. The lease specified that if construction costs would exceed a certain amount, Carmike had the option of building the theatre. Without that specification there was, as Mike Patrick explained, no incen-

EXHIBIT 4 CARMIKE CINEMAS, INC.: OPERATIONS, 1982–1986

DATE	THEATRES	SCREENS
March 25, 1982	128	265
March 31, 1983	126	283
March 29, 1984	158	375
March 28, 1985	160	407
March 27, 1986	156	415

EXHIBIT 5 CARMIKE CINEMAS, INC.: THEATRE LOCATIONS

The Company currently operates 156 theaters with an aggregate of 436 screens in 11 southern states. Those communities in which the Company operates theaters are indicated on the map below.

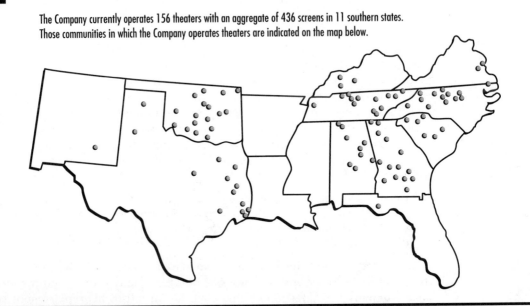

tive for the development firm to contain costs. Carmike's lease payment was based on a return on investment to the development firm. On a recent theatre the estimated costs had come in at $39/s.f. versus the $31/s.f. that the lease specified. Mike Patrick convinced the development company to use one of his experienced contractors in order to reduce the $39/s.f.

ZONE STRATEGY

The orientation under Martin management in the 1970's had been a system wide operations approach. Mike Patrick's approach to theatre location and number of screens was zone by zone and theatre by theatre.

Mike explained that the basic strategic unit in a theatre chain was a geographic area called a zone. A small town would usually be one zone. Larger cities usually had two or more zones. Considering competitive activity in a zone was critical. Mike explained what happened over a period of two years in one major metropolitan area (see Exhibit 6).

> This city has a river which divides it in two. There is only one main bridge and so there are automatically two zones. There is also a third zone which is isolated somewhat. When we first bought Martin there were seven theatres and fourteen screens.
>
> Let me tell you what happened in that Zone A. A strong competitor came in and built a six-plex against me in a shopping center. [See #1 in Exhibit 6.] I leased land, built a six-plex theater [#2], and did a sale lease-back. I built the

EXHIBIT 6 CARMIKE CINEMAS, INC.: MAP OF THE CITY WITH THREE ZONES

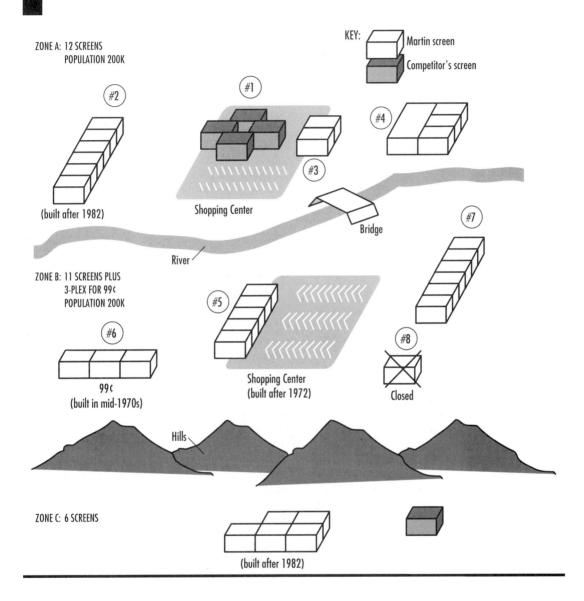

KEY:
Martin screen
Competitor's screen

ZONE A: 12 SCREENS
POPULATION 200K

#2
(built after 1982)

#1

#3

#4

Shopping Center

Bridge

#7

River

ZONE B: 11 SCREENS PLUS
3-PLEX FOR 99¢
POPULATION 200K

#6
99¢
(built in mid-1970s)

#5
Shopping Center
(built after 1972)

#8
Closed

Hills

ZONE C: 6 SCREENS

(built after 1982)

six-plex here right off one of the two shopping centers. I leased the equipment and I leased the building. I actually have no investment. Last year that theater made $79K. Think about the return you have with no investment!

I took the single theater in the shopping center [#3] and put a wall down the middle of it. That cost me $30K. I added an auditorium to a triple [#4]. Both of these theatres are near the competitor's six-plex. Now it's six—four here and two here. So that is six against his six. So now I have twelve screens in Zone A. That's about the number of screens the population in Zone A can support. So no one else can come in. My competitor has no advantage over me in negotiations with Warner Brothers and Paramount. In fact, I have an advantage over him. He's only here in one location and I am in three.

In the other zone I took a twin and added three auditoriums [#5]. Then I took a triple theater and made it a dollar house, $.99 discount. . . . It was way off the beaten track, way off [#6]. So I had eight screens against the competitor theatres [#7]. There was an opposition single screen, but he closed [#8]. We now have twenty screens in those two zones.

If you are playing Rocky, you can sell three prints to this town. If you choose your theatres carefully as to where you show it, you can make a lot more money. That's something the previous president (of Martin) never understood.

EXPANSION

In May 1983 Carmike acquired the outstanding stock of Video Independent Theatres, Inc. The purchase price included $1.1M cash and $2.7M in a note. The note was at 11% payable in three equal installments. Mike talked about the acquisition:

During the 1970s Martin had not been aggressive. In our industry if you are not on the attack you are being attacked. Then you are subject to what the industry does. We believe in making things happen.

Video was owned by a company which had bought Video for its cable rights. In the mid 1970s the management was killed in an air crash. I went up and talked to the guy in charge of Video. He said he told me the parent company wasn't interested in theatres.

The circuit had a lot of singles and a lot of profitable drive-ins. We borrowed $1M as a down payment and the parent accepted a note for the remainder due in three equal yearly installments.

We immediately looked at all the drive-ins and sold two drive-ins for about $1.5M. So immediately we paid back the down payment. We planned to use the cash flow to meet the installment payments and the depreciation to rebuild the circuit. Today Video is completely paid for.

In some of the towns we went into a tremendous aggressive buying program for film which was very successful. In another we bought out an independent who was building a five-plex. In others we converted twins into four-plexes. We closed singles and in some instances over-built with four, five, or six-plexes. Our revenue per screen as a result is low.

In one town we went in with a new six-plex which cost $620K. We had used basic cement block construction and furnished the facility beautifully. An independent had put in a four-plex, about the same size facility, which has cost $1.1M. A large circuit also had a twin. I attacked with a six-plex during a time when the state economy was down. In addition, there was a lot of bad pictures. The two companies really beat each other up during the period bidding up what pictures were available. The independent went under. We'll pick up that theatre from the bank. The circuit was bought by a larger company which wants to concentrate on larger cities. They've offered us their twin.

CONTROL SYSTEMS

The company also put considerable emphasis on budgeting and cost control. As Mike Patrick explained, "I was brought up on theatre P&L's." The systems he set in place for Carmike theatres were straightforward. "Every theatre had what Mike called "a PL . . . I call them a Profit or Loss Statement." Results came across Patrick's desk monthly and results for the theatres were printed out in descending order of amount of profit generated for that month. No overhead was charged to the theatres. As Mike explained, "if you can charge something to an overhead [account], then no one cares, no one is responsible." Rather, each administrative department had a monthly statement. Mike Patrick explained his approach:

> I used something like zero budgeting on every department. For example, here's the Martin Building. It cost me $18,700 for the month. The report for the Martin Building even has every person's name. . . . What they made last year, what they made this year, what they made current month, every expense they have. . . . For example I know what my dad's office cost me each month and mine also.
>
> Everyone must answer, be responsible, for everything they spend. They can't come to me and say, "Well, we've done it every year this way." Since 1982 we have become more efficient and more efficient each year.

Every department head received a recap each week. Mike noted that in a recent weekly report he had a charge for $2,000 for new theatre passes reading Carmike instead of Martin. Charges for business lunches appeared on the statement of the person who signed the bill. Mike checked the reports and required explanations for anything out of line. Theatre expenses also received close scrutiny, as he explained.

> Then I go a step beyond that. All district managers have a pet peeve. They all want their facilities to look brand new. You can write them letters, you can swear, you can cuss. It makes no difference. They are in that theater and that's the only thing they see. It's their world. They want new carpet every week. They want a new roof every week. They want a new projector and a new ticket machine every week. . . . the government says you have to capitalize those expenditures [but] I hate to capitalize on expenses. The government says if the air conditioning breaks, you capitalize it. Bullshit. I wrote the check for $18K. The money is gone.
>
> So, now I give every district manager a repair report. It shows anything charged to repairs. Yes, I could probably accomplish the same thing with a cash flow statement, but they wouldn't understand it.

MANAGING THE THEATRES

The company did not have a nepotism policy. Indeed, Mike Patrick encouraged the hiring of family. Especially in smaller towns where there might be several family members in visible positions, hiring family was seen as a deterrent to theft. As Mike Patrick explained:

I will let them hire family for two reasons: One, they don't want to quit me. They're married to me as much as they are the family. Second, you get people who just would not steal. They have more to lose than just the job. None of the family will steal from me because it would have a direct bearing on the father, the uncle, the whole family. I am in a lot of little towns and in a small town a son is either going to work on a farm, a grocery store, a filling station, or a theater, cause there is no industry there. The cleanest job in town is the theater manager. Also, in a small town we allow the manager to look like he owns the theatre. Cause I don't go in and act like "Here's the boss" and all that.

Theater managers are paid straight salary. Under Fuqua ownership the manager's salary was linked to theatre performance. But changes in company operations led to the change. Theater managers don't make the theater profit; the movie does. Theatre managers used to select the movies. But now they don't have anything to do with selection. I am the only theater chain in the United States in which the booking and buying for the circuit is done by computer from right here on my desk. This computer is hooked to Atlanta and Dallas, which are my two booking offices.

Mike Patrick had hired both booking managers after retirements of the previous incumbents. He explained how one came to work for Carmike:

Let me tell you how I got Tony Reed. Tony Reed was the biggest SOB I went against. He was the booker in a small city and that circuit was the best in town. He used to give me fits. And I used to spend more time trying to figure out how to get prints away from him than anybody else. So what did I do? I hired him. He made $19K/year working for a competitor and he makes $65K working for me. That's a lot of difference.

The planning system for booking films was set up so that past, current, and future bookings could be called up by theatre, zone, or film. In addition, competitors' bookings were also available. The system allowed interaction between home office and the two booking offices, one in Atlanta and the other in Dallas.

THE OUTLOOK IN 1986

As the 1985 year came to close, Carmike, like much of the industry, faced disappointing year-end results. Part of the problem was attributed to the number of executive turnovers in the movie production companies. Mike explained:

A number of production executives changed jobs within a 90-day period. That meant that production stopped. Production is like developing a shopping center. It takes 18 months from the time you decide to do it to the time it opens. This year is off because there were no pictures out there. I believe that it will get better . . . Rocky IV has just come out so we will end the year on an upbeat.

The industry faced a number of challenges that affected Carmike. Lack of films was a negative factor. However, the increase in ancillary markets for films, such as video purchase and rental, was viewed as a positive factor, as Mike explained:

> By 1979–80 the ancillary market became very big. I understand the ancillary market is now about $3B and our side is $4B ... [but] I talked to a man in Home Box Office when he first started. He told me that they could not figure a way to sell a movie on its first run at all. If it was a bad movie, he couldn't give it away. If it was a good movie, he had all the attendance watching it he needed. He told me, "Mike, I want you to do better every year. The more blockbusters you get, the more demand I have. If you get 'Who Shot Mary' and it dies in your theater, no one will watch it on Home Box Office." The theatre is where you go to preview a movie. That establishes the value. So I realized then that CBS will pay more for a big movie than they will a lousy one so anything that comes through the tube, is no problem with me. I love it because [the revenues] help create more new movies.

An increase in films might be offset by the unabated increase in number of screens. However, the Patricks did not, as did others, foresee the demise of the movie theatre. Mike especially felt that the difficult times offered opportunities to those who were prepared:

> There is more opportunity in bad times than in good times. The reason is that no one wants to sell when business is good and if they do the multiples are too high. So you want to buy when business is bad [and] ... you got to plan for those times.
>
> I have to know where my capital is. I run this company through this set of reports. This is every financial thing you want to know about Carmike Theaters—construction coming up, everything we are going to spend, source of cash, where it's going to go, everything. One of the critical things we are thinking about is how to expand. I know that if industry business goes bad, within 90 days, three or four more circuits are going to come up for sale. I must be in a position to buy them and I must have the knowledge to do it with. I will not bet the store on any deal.
>
> I am trying to buy a theatre circuit right now [it's priced] at $16M. At $16M I am paying a premium for that circuit, a big premium because it loses money every year, but I am going to fire its management. I could buy it as part of Martin [but] if Martin would buy it then Martin would be liable for the money, so I don't want to do that. So what's my alternative? ... I will take $2 or $3M out of Carmike or have Carmike borrow $13M and purchase the theatre circuit. Then we expect that the cash flow from the purchased circuit will pay back the $13M.

Mike Patrick was on the continuous outlook for new opportunities. One of those opportunities was outside the theatre industry, as he explained:

> Our new office building is 100% financed with an Industrial Revenue 20-year bond issue. In case the theater business goes bad, I want to own an asset that is not a theater.

APPLIED CAD KNOWLEDGE, INC. PART A: THE "BOOM/SPLAT" SYNDROME

**JOHN A. SEEGER
AND RAYMOND M.
KINNUNEN**

Something is seriously wrong with this planet. Look at us. I'm working a hundred and twenty hours a week or more, and not catching up. I've got these
two friends—both recently divorced, like me—who aren't working at all:
they're living off their girl friends, and loving it. One of them is basking in
Hawaii. But here I am, busting my ass and giving my customers problems
anyhow.

Some guys go on television and say, "Send money now," and people *do*. I
ask my best customer to send $30,000, and he goes bankrupt instead. What's
wrong with this picture?

Jeff Stevens, president and 90 percent owner of Applied CAD Knowledge,
Inc., was reporting on current sales and production levels to the two business
school professors who comprised his board of directors. It was late August of
1987, and the three men sat in a booth at Bogie's restaurant. The waitress,
Patty, was accustomed to these monthly meetings; she offered another round
of Lite Beer. "Make mine cyanide," said Stevens. "On the rocks, please."

Applied CAD, a small service bureau which designed electronic circuit
boards, was experiencing the highest sales levels in its three-year history. June
sales had reached $50,000—leaving a backlog of $90,000; July shipments had
set a record at $58,000; August would be nearly as high. The problem facing
Stevens through the summer of 1987 was a shortage of good designers to work
as part-time freelancers. The surge in business saw Stevens sitting at the computer consoles himself, doing design work on second and third shifts, six or
seven days a week. After eight weeks of this schedule, the strain was showing.
One director asked about the longer-range sales picture, and Stevens summed
it up:

Source: Prepared by Professor John A. Seeger, Bentley College, and Professor Raymond M. Kinnunen, Northeastern University, as a basis for class discussion. Distributed by the North American Case Research Association. © John A. Seeger and Raymond M. Kinnunen, 1990.

There's nothing on the books at all for late fall, and not much likely. Every major customer we have is in "busy phase" right now. When these designs are finished, it will be another four to six months before their next generation of product revisions. In the meantime, everybody is burned out. All I'm hoping for right now is a front porch, a rocking chair, a lobotomy, and a drool cup.

THE ELECTRONICS INDUSTRY AND CIRCUIT BOARD DESIGN

The United States electronics industry in 1987 was a sprawling giant, some of whose sectors were growing while others remained in a protracted slump. In 1986, total industry size was variously estimated as $100 billion to $182 billion.

A basic part of nearly every electronic product was the printed circuit board (PCB) to which a variety of electronic components were attached. These components ranged from old-fashioned resistors and capacitors to transistors and the most modern integrated circuit chips. All components needed some sort of platform to sit on, and some way to make connection with other components.

In the 1930s and '40s, circuit boards were made from thin, non-conducting fiberboard with metal pins and sockets attached. Assembly operators wound the wire leads of the circuit's resistors, capacitors, etc. around the proper pins and soldered them in place. By the 1960s, this technology had become highly automated. Numerically controlled machines positioned the components and connected the pins to one another with wires. By the 1980s both the pins and the wires had disappeared, replaced by electrically conductive lines which were "printed" or plated onto (or under) the surface of the board itself. Wire leads from electrical components are inserted through small holes in the board and soldered on the underside.

The increasing complexity of electronic circuits presented a problem for PCB technology. When connections were made with wires, assemblers simply attached one end, routed the wire over the top of everything between the two pins involved, and attached the other end where it belonged. With printed circuits, however, designers are constrained to two dimensions on a flat board; they must route the line between two pins without touching any other lines. Furthermore, efficient design calls for the components to be tightly packed together, grouped by function. Designers frequently find situations where they cannot lay out a trace from one point to another without interfering with other traces.

"Multilayer" PCBs (see Exhibit 1) ease this problem by providing "upstairs" layers on the board, allowing the designer to "go over the top." Multilayer boards contain at least three layers of traces, and sometimes more than twenty layers. Skilled designers seek to minimize the number of layers required for a given circuit, in order to reduce manufacturing costs: multilayer PCBs are far more expensive to manufacture.

Board design was made more complicated by increasing density of compo-

EXHIBIT 1   MULTILAYER PRINTED CIRCUIT BOARD

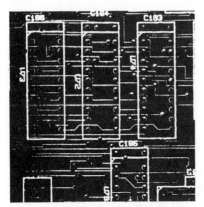 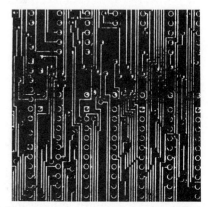

Sections of the top surface (left) and the bottom surface (right) of a four-level circuit board designed by Applied CAD Knowledge for the maker of a communications controller. The entire board measures 10½ by 15 inches.

nents, by sensitivity of components to heat (some threw off large amounts of heat, while others would go haywire if their operating temperature was disturbed), and by radio-frequency interference (some components generated static, while others might "hear" the noise and try to process it). The layout of components on the board had tremendous impact on how well the finished product worked, as well as on its manufacturing cost.

In 1983, according to *Electronic Business* magazine, multilayer boards had sales of $900 million, or 25 percent of the PCB market. By 1993, multilayer boards were forecast to reach sales of $5.6 billion, or 41 percent market share. Exhibit 2 shows PCB sales and projections by type of board.

Frost and Sullivan, Inc., a New York market research firm, estimated (in *The Printed Circuit Board Market in the U.S.,* July 1986, quoted by permission) that the total U.S. PCB market reached $3.7 billion in sales in 1985, a decrease of 12 percent from 1984's production. PCBs were projected to grow to a likely $6.5 billion by 1990 and to $10.8 billion in 1995. Multilayer PCBs were expected to be the fastest-growing type, averaging 15.7 percent per year annual growth. A little over half the market was served in 1985 by independent PCB fabricators, as opposed to captive suppliers, Frost and Sullivan said.

TRENDS IN CIRCUIT BOARD DESIGN EQUIPMENT

Originally (and still, for simple circuits), an engineer or technician worked from a "schematic" drawing of the circuit, which showed how the various components were connected. On a large layout table, the PCB designer manually

EXHIBIT 2   SALES AND PROJECTIONS FOR PCBs BY TYPE OF BOARD

PCB Type	1983		Annual Growth Rate	1993	
	Sales in $ Millions	Market Share		Sales in $ Millions	Market Share
Multilayer	900	25%	20%	$5,600	41%
Double-sided	2,000	56	13%	6,700	49
Flexible	353	10	10%	916	7
Single-sided	307	9	4%	454	3
	$3,560	100%		$13,670	100%

Source: *Electronic Business* (February 1, 1985): 87.

drew in the components and linked them with black tape (or ink), to produce a "photo master" film which was in turn used to manufacture the circuit board. As circuits became more complex, the manual process bogged down.

By the mid 1970s, computer-aided design (CAD) vendors began to offer computer systems specifically for PCB designing. Racal-Redac, Inc., a British firm, was the first to offer a system which permitted PCB designers to interact with the computer, trying various routings of traces to see how they looked on the graphic display. This approach, based on the moderate-price DEC PDP-11, competed well against established CAD systems such as those made by Gerber Scientific or Computervision, whose equipment was priced in the $500,000 class and still lacked interactive design capability.

By 1982, prices for PCB design systems had fallen below $100,000. New CAD equipment makers entered the field with automated routing or documentation features which carried substantial advantages over the established Redac software. Calay and Cadnetix, as examples, introduced strong entries—neither being compatible with the Redac or Sci-Cards or Telesis equipment already in the field. Racal-Redac Ltd. had perhaps taken the greatest strides to tailor its software to run on a variety of computers. Said Ian Orrock, chief executive of Redac's CAD division in England, "We're all going to end up being software houses."

Another important feature of the new CAD equipment was ease of use; the older systems might require months of learning time before a designer became proficient.

SERVICE BUREAU OPERATIONS

In the late 70s, with high equipment costs and low availability of trained designers, only the largest electronics firms designed and produced their own PCBs. Service bureaus took advantage of the market opportunity, acting as the primary design resource for smaller clients and as peak load designers for firms with in-house capacity. These small service firms specialized in design, working for electronics companies in the same way an architect works for real estate developers. Exhibit 3 shows the relationship between firms in the PCB production process.

When the design phase of a job was finished, the computer tape or disk containing the final output would be carried to a photoplotting service bureau for creation of the precision film needed for manufacturing. The equipment for photoplotting was far more complex and expensive than the computer systems needed for design. Only a few design shops in the New England area had their own photoplotting capability; they performed this work for other service bureaus and for electronics firms' in-house design departments as well as for their own design clients.

The actual production of PCBs might be done by the electronics company itself or by a fabrication shop which specialized in the work. The New England area was home to some 80 to 100 fab shops, many of which offered design as well as manufacturing services. A few large firms (Hadco at $125 million in sales) were equipped to service very large orders—100,000 or more boards of a design—but most fab shops fell in the $1 to $2 million size range, with an average order size of 25 to 30 relatively small boards. One such fabricator estimated its average low-tech PCB was priced at $22 each, with a setup charge of $150. For the most difficult boards, in small quantities with rigid testing requirements, Applied CAD's customers might pay as much as $1,000 each for fabrication.

As electronics firms purchased and began to use the newer CAD systems, they wanted service bureaus to be equipped with similar or compatible machines. A firm with its own Telesis equipment, for example, would favor Telesis-equipped service bureaus for its overload work. Service bureaus felt the

EXHIBIT 3 WORK FLOW BETWEEN FIRMS IN PRODUCTION OF PRINTED CIRCUIT BOARDS

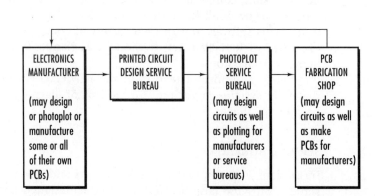

pressure to acquire the most up-to-date hardware and software available, in order to qualify as bidders.

When a service bureau invested in CAD equipment, the sheer size of the investment created pressure to use the equipment intensively. Multi-shift operations were common, but the supply of designers to staff them was severely limited. Typically, a service bureau did not hire permanent staff for all three shifts: the work load was too unpredictable. Service bureaus generally hired moonlighting designers from established electronics firms to staff their second and third shifts.

Printed circuit board design requires a peculiar combination of human skills, primarily in spatial geometry, circuit insight, memory, and persistence. A talented designer—perhaps capable of completing a complex design in three weeks of console time—might be several times more productive than a "journeyman." In the early 1980s, talented designers willing to work odd shifts were earning over $100,000 per year; few of them had college educations.

Most customers requested separate quotations for each board; often, customers asked for bids from several service bureaus. Design clients always ran on tight schedules, Jeff Stevens observed, wanting their work to be delivered "yesterday":

> Circuit board design is usually one of the last steps before a new product goes into production. Our design time may be the customer's time-to-market. It's natural for them to be in a hurry.

For the design of a large, complex, four-layered PCB a client might pay between $10,000 to $15,000. Such a project might require five to six man weeks of labor input (two-thirds of which might be designer's time); it might involve extensive communication between Applied CAD and a wide variety of the client's technical personnel, and it would often require the designer to work through the night at various project stages to make deadlines. Much of the time would be spent sorting out and coordinating conflicting information and directions from different technical people in the client company. Stevens noted,

> Even our clients themselves won't always know completely what they want. When we take their directions to their logical conclusions, problems often occur. Then we have to show them what developed. You spend a lot of time on the phone with clients, sometimes at 3:00 A.M. Often, I make decisions for the client, so the work can go ahead; later, I have to convince the client the decision was right.

Clients were inclined to stay with their existing service bureaus, unless they were severely burned. Good relationships between service staff and engineering personnel helped minimize communication errors, and availability of the data base from the original job allowed for revisions or modifications at much lower cost. Design reliability remained a key attribute of a service bureau's reputation, since whole product lines (or engineers' jobs) might depend on the PCB design's working properly, and on its prompt delivery:

We had one job, in the old days, where a satellite was literally sitting on the launch pad, waiting for a corrected module design. The engineers had discovered a design flaw. They flew into town with the specs, and then took turns sitting behind the designer at the scope, or sitting beside their hotel room telephone, waiting to answer any questions that might come up. In this business, you have to deliver.

FUTURE TRENDS IN PCB DESIGN

By the end of 1986, a number of vendors had developed PCB designed packages to run on personal computers—primarily the IBM XT or AT machines. These software systems, some including automatic routing, were priced as low as a few hundred dollars or as high as $13,000, and varied widely in their features and capabilities. In-house design capability thus became practical for most electronics firms, although many lacked the PCB expertise that still marked the better service bureaus. Free-lance designers, too, could now acquire their own equipment. Exhibit 4 compares the features and prices of 24 such software packages.

In the 1980s, as the cost of entering the service bureau business dropped, many new firms appeared. Jeff Stevens observed, "When I started at Redac in 1978, there were three service bureaus in New England. By 1983 there were maybe a dozen. Now there might be seventy-five, and it could reach 100 in another year." In 1987, several competing service bureaus in the area were owned by former employees of Racal-Redac, where Jeff himself had learned the business. Exhibit 5 lists the major competitors in the northeastern United States in 1986. The small firms in this listing were design specialists like Applied CAD, Stevens noted; the larger firms all supplied finished boards to their customers.

For the longer run, some industry analysts speculated that constant advances in miniaturizing electronic circuits might permit semiconductor technology to reduce certain whole PCBs (such as those developed for computer memory) into a single integrated circuit chip.

APPLIED CAD KNOWLEDGE, INC.: HISTORY

Jeff Stevens had learned the rudiments of circuit board design in his first job after high school graduation, as a technician in a five-person product development laboratory. Here, in 1975, one of his duties was to prepare enlarged prints of circuits, using black tape on white mylar. In another, concurrent job as a technician in an electronics manufacturing firm, he learned how the circuits themselves worked.

In 1977, Stevens left his two technician jobs for an entry-level design position with Racal-Redac in Littleton, Massachusetts. Redac operated a service bureau to complement its sales of DEC hardware and British software. As a pioneer in the field, Redac at the time boasted a near-monopoly in powerful

EXHIBIT 4   LOW-COST PC BOARD DESIGN SOFTWARE AVAILABLE, SPRING 1987

COMPANY	PRODUCT	BASE PRICE	REQUIRED HARDWARE	OPERATING SYSTEM	AUTO-ROUTER	AUTO-ROUTER PRICE	AUTO-PLACEMENT	COMPATIBLE NET LISTS	MAXIMUM NUMBER OF COLORS	MAXIMUM NUMBER OF TRACES	MAXIMUM NUMBER OF COMPONENTS	MAXIMUM NUMBER OF LAYERS	PACKAGING TECHNOLOGIES
ABACUS SOFTWARE	PC BOARD DESIGNER	$195	ATARI 520ST OR 1040ST	GEM	•				2	1100 LINES	250	2	SMD
ACCEL TECHNOLOGIES	TANGO-PCB	$495	IBM PCXT OR PCAT	MS-DOS	•			ACCEL, OMATION, ORCAD	16	26,000 LINES	1000	9	SMD
APTOS SYSTEMS	CRITERION II	$4000	ARTIST 1 CARD AND IBM PCXT OR PCAT	MS-DOS	•	$5000	•	APTOS, FUTURENET, P-CAD	16	2000 NETS	1000	50	SMD, ECL, ANALOG
AUTOMATED IMAGES	PERSONAL 970	$8000	IBM PCXT OR PCAT	MS-DOS				APPLICON, FUTURENET, ORCAD	16			16	SMD, HYBRID
B&C MICROSYSTEMS	PCB/OE	$395	IBM PCXT OR PCAT	MS-DOS (AND THE AUTOCAD DRAFTING PACKAGE)				B&C	16				
CAD SOFTWARE	PADS-PCB	$975	IBM PCXT OR PCAT	MS-DOS	•	$750	•	FUTURENET	16	4511 NETS	784	30	SMD, FINE-LINE
CASE TECHNOLOGY	VANGUARD PCB	$4250	IBM PCAT, SUN-1 OR DEC MICROVAX	MS-DOS, UNIX, OR VMS	•	$5500	•	CASE	16	2000 NETS	1000	256	SMD
DAISY SYSTEMS	PERSONAL BOARDMASTER	$8000	IBM PCXT OR DAISY PL388	DNIX				DAISY	7	14,000 LINES	14,000	255	SMD
DASOFT DESIGN	PROJECT: PCB	$950	IBM PCXT OR PCAT	MS-DOS	•	$2450	•	DASOFT	6			4	SMD
DESIGN COMPUTATION	DRAFTSMAN-EE	$1147	IBM PCXT OR PCAT	MS-DOS	•				16	4000 NETS	300	20	FINE-LINE
DOUGLAS ELECTRONICS	DOUGLAS CADCAM	$395	APPLE MACINTOSH	MACINTOSH					2				SMD, ANALOG
ELECTRONIC DESIGN TOOLS	PROCAD	$2495	IBM PCXT OR PCAT AND 80000 COPROCESSOR	MS-DOS	•	$2495	•	ELECTRONIC DESIGN TOOLS	16	10,000 NETS	3000	56	SMD, CONSTANT-IMPEDANCE
ELECTRONIC INDUSTRIAL EQUIPMENT	EXECUTIVE CAD	$11,000	IBM PCXT OR PCAT	MS-DOS	•		•	ELECTRONIC INDUSTRIAL EQUIPMENT	16			4	SMD, ECL
FUTURENET	DASH-PCB	$13,000	IBM PCAT AND 32032 COPROCESSOR	UNIX	•			FUTURENET	4			10	FINE-LINE
HEWLETT-PACKARD	EGS	$7000	HP 9000	HP-UX				HP	15			255	HYBRID
KONTRON	KAD-286	$10,400	IBM PCAT	MS-DOS	•			KONTRON	64	5000 LINES	3200	256	ECL, SMD, HYBRID
PERSONAL CAD SYSTEMS	PCB-1	$6000	IBM PCXT OR PCAT	MS-DOS	•	$6000	•	P-CAD, FUTURENET	16	1000 LINES	300	50	SMD
RACAL-REDAC	REDBOARD	$12,000	IBM PCXT OR PCAT	MS-DOS	•		•	RACAL-REDAC	16	1900 NETS	511	16	SMD
SEETRAX (IN US, CIRCUITS AND SYSTEMS)	RANGER	$5000	IBM PCAT	MS-DOS	•	$2000	•	SEETRAX	16	10,000 NETS	1400	16	SMD
SOFTCIRCUITS	POLOPLUS	$1024	COMMODORE AMIGA 1000	AMIGADOS	•				16				
VAMP	MCCAD	$395	APPLE MACINTOSH	MACINTOSH	•	$995	•	VAMP	2	32,000 LINES	32,000	6	SMD, METRIC
VISIONICS	EE DESIGNER II	$1875	IBM PCXT OR PCAT	MS-DOS	•	$1475	•		16		999	26	SMD
WINTEK	SMARTWORK	$895	IBM PCXT OR PCAT	MS-DOS	•			WINTEK	3			6	SMD
ZIEGLER INSTRUMENTS (IN US, CADDY)	CADDY ELECTRONIC SYSTEM	$2495	IBM PCXT OR PCAT	MS-DOS	•	$2500	•	ZIEGLER	16			128	ANALOG

Source: EDN (March 18, 1987): 140–141. Used by permission.

EXHIBIT 5   PC DESIGN SERVICE BUREAUS IN NEW ENGLAND

SALES VOLUME OF 0–1 MILLION DOLLARS/YEAR
ABINGTON LABS.
BERKSHIRE DESIGN
CAD TEC
CADTRONIX, LTD.
COMPUTER AIDED CIRCUITS, INC.
DATALINE PCB CORP.
DESIGN SERVICES
ENERGRAPHICS
GRAPHICS TECHNOLOGY CORP.
HERBERTONS, INC.
HET PRINTED CIRCUIT DESIGN
HIGH TECH CAD SERVICE CO.
JETTE FABRICATION
LSI ENGINEERING
P C DESIGN COMPANY
PAC-LAB, INC.
PACKAGING FOR ELECTRONICS
PC DESIGN SERVICES
POINT DESIGN, INC.
POWER PROCESSING, INC.
PRODUCT DEVELOPMENT CO.
QUALITRON CORP.
QUALITY CIRCUIT DESIGN, INC.
RESEARCH LABS, INC.
SCIENTIFIC CALCULATIONS, INC.
TRACOR ELECTRO-ASSEMBLY INC.
WINTER DESIGN

SALES VOLUME OF 1–2 MILLION DOLLARS/YEAR
AUTOMATED IMAGES, INC.
AUTOMATED DESIGN, INC.

CAD SERVICES, INC.
ANTAL ASSOCIATES
MULTIWIRE OF NEW ENGLAND
TECCON
TECH SYSTEMS & DESIGN
KENEX, INC.
ALTERNATE CIRCUIT DESIGN TECH-NOLOGY
PHOTOFABRICATION TECHNOL-OGY INC.

SALES VOLUME OF 2–5 MILLION DOLLARS/YEAR
TEK-ART ASSOCIATES
STRATCO REPROGRAPHIX
ALTEK CO.
EASTERN ELECTRONICS MFG. CORP.
DATACUBE, INC.
OWL ELECTRONIC LABORATORIES

SALES VOLUME OF 5–10 MILLION DOLLARS/YEAR
TRIAD ENGINEERING CO.
PHOTRONIC LABS, INC.

SALES VOLUME OF 10+ MILLION DOLLARS/YEAR
ALGOREX CORP.
ASI AUTOMATED SYSTEMS, INC.
AUGAT INTERCONNECTION GROUP
RACAL-REDAC SERVICE BUREAU
SYNERMATION, INC.

Source: Beacon Technology, *New England Printed Circuit Directory.* Copyright © 1985. Reprinted by permission.

systems dedicated to PCB design. Jeff Stevens, in a training rotation, joined Redac's service bureau as a data-entry technician.

> We had three computer systems—about 20 people altogether. A system then cost about $200,000 and a lot of companies didn't have enough design work to justify buying one.
>
> In data entry, you prepare code to represent all the terminals and components on the board. I refused to code the first job they gave me, and nearly

got fired. Finally I convinced them that the job *shouldn't* be coded: the turkey who engineered it had the diodes in backward, and the circuit wasn't going to work. About a week later, they put me in charge of data entry, supervising the guy who had wanted to fire me.

Stevens became a designer, then a lead designer, then operations manager of the service bureau. Under his leadership, the operation dramatically improved its reputation for quality and on-time delivery, as well as its financial performance:

> When I took over in October of 1981, monthly sales were $50,000 and monthly expenses were $110,000. In six months we turned it around: monthly sales were $110,000 and expenses were $50,000. There was a tremendous amount of dead wood. We had a big bonfire with it, and went from 26 people to 16. In some ways, it was a brutal campaign, I guess.

In June 1983, Stevens left Racal-Redac to work as a consulting designer, helping electronics firms with their CAD decisions as well as doing freelance design work. He had developed design and management expertise and established a reputation in industry circles which he could now broker directly to clients who were familiar with his previous work.

In December 1983, Jeff established Applied CAD while still working from his home in Pepperell, Massachusetts. By purchasing used computer equipment and installing it himself in his living room, Stevens was able to hold his initial investment to $35,000; the largest cost element was $28,000 for the software purchased from his former employer. Financial data on Applied CAD's latest three years of operation are shown in Exhibit 6.

> The equipment pretty well filled up the living room, and through the summer I couldn't run it during the daytime: we didn't have enough electricity to cool it down. Winter solved that problem, though; the PDP-11 heated the house.

Jeff had sought the help of a business school professor who lived in Littleton to negotiate the purchase of software from his former employer. This professor and another, also from a well-known Boston area school, purchased small stock interests as Applied CAD was incorporated and became members of the board of directors. By the fall of 1985, the board met monthly for three to four hours, usually during the first week of the month. At most meetings the board first discussed the previous month's sales and current levels of cash, accounts receivable, backlog and payables. (Exhibit 7 shows the data recorded in these talks.) Other typical agenda items ranged from the purchase of new equipment and/or software, to marketing, to personnel problems and bank relationships.

In late 1984, Applied CAD leased a 1,000 square foot office suite on the ground floor of a new building near the Merrimack River in Tyngsboro, Massachusetts. Jeff Stevens designed the interior space to hold a central computer room (with special air conditioning), a darkened "console room" for the actual design work, and a large front office. By January of 1985, the computing equipment was installed and operating. The console room was furnished with two Recaro

EXHIBIT 6   FINANCIAL STATEMENTS OF APPLIED CAD KNOWLEDGE, INC., 1985–1987

BALANCE SHEET

	1985	1986	1987
ASSETS			
Current assets:			
Cash	$128,568	$ 14,148	$ 33,074
Accounts receivable, trade	18,865	15,375	14,250
Prepaid taxes and other current assets	4,853	1,200	5,074
Total current assets	152,286	30,723	52,398
Property and equipment	174,079	190,079	203,079
Less accumulated depreciation	48,697	86,357	124,062
Total Property and Equipment	125,382	103,722	79,017
Total Assets	$277,668	$134,445	$131,415
LIABILITIES AND STOCKHOLDERS' EQUITY			
Current liabilities:			
Accounts payable, trade	$127,685	$ 9,025	$ 21,823
Current maturities of long-term debt	13,300		
Income taxes payable	4,008		2,303
Other current liabilities	5,000	5,373	70
Total current liabilities	149,993	14,398	24,196
Long-term debt, less current maturities	41,121	83,247	53,663
Stockholder's equity:			
Common stock, no par value; authorized 15,000 shares, issued and outstanding 1,000 shares	25,000	25,000	25,000
Retained earnings	61,554	11,800	28,556
Total stockholder's equity	86,554	36,800	53,556
Total Liabilities and Stockholders' Equity	$277,668	$134,445	$131,415
STATEMENT OF INCOME AND RETAINED EARNINGS			
Net Revenues	$328,262	$232,540	$346,627
Cost of revenue:			
Salaries, wages, and outside services	134,686	116,835	209,998
Research and development	14,154	7,551	13,731
Software costs	65,131	18,864	
Total cost of revenue	$213,971	$143,250	$223,729
Gross profit	114,291	89,290	122,898
Selling, general, and administrative expenses	72,320	143,051	77,732
Operating profit	41,971	(53,761)	45,166
Bad debt expense			(28,660)
Interest income (expense), net	2,331	3,176	(10,103)

EXHIBIT 6   (continued)

STATEMENT OF INCOME & RETAINED EARNINGS

	1985	1986	1987
Income before income taxes	44,302	(50,185)	6,403
Income taxes	4,508	0	0
Net income	39,794	(50,185)	6,403
Retained earnings, beginning of year	21,760	62,385	22,154
Retained earnings, end of year	$ 61,554	$ 11,800	$ 28,557

EXHIBIT 7   APPLIED CAD KNOWLEDGE, INC.: MONTHLY SALES AND MONTH-END RECEIVABLES, BACKLOGS, CASH LEVELS

	A/R	SALES	BACKLOG	CASH
January 1986	$18	$20	$20	$98
February	*	10	*	*
March	18	10	12	62
April	18	10	20	28
May	24	20	26	26
June	*	10	*	*
July	14	25	*	18
August	70	50	30	15
September	90	40	*	8
October	50	30	*	26
November	19	5	10	17
December	24	10	18	14
January 1987	13	3	*	7
February	40	21	*	8
March	35	28	22	6
April	32	22	23	11
May	25	22	50	5
June	50	50	90	10
July	90	58	30	10

Amounts shown in thousands of dollars.

*Information not available.

ergonometric chairs (at $1,100 each) for the designers' use; the front office held a large receptionist's desk and a sparse collection of work tables, file cabinets, and spare hardware.

HARDWARE AND SOFTWARE

After moving into his new quarters, Jeff Stevens located another PDP-11/34 computer—this one for sale at $7,000. Adding it to his shop required purchase of another Redac software package, but the added capacity was needed. Other, competing CAD systems were now available, but the decision to stick with Redac seemed straightforward to Jeff:

> Redac systems had several advantages. They were specifically dedicated to PCB design work and they had software that were brutally efficient. They were familiar to most of the freelance designers in the area. Wide acceptance of Redac's software makes it easier to get overflow work from companies who demanded compatibility with their own equipment. Not to mention that I know this gear backward and forward, and could keep several machines busy at once.

The Redac software was originally developed in 1972, which made it very old by industry standards. Jeff pointed out, however, that because machines were slower in 1972 and had much less memory, their software *had* to be extremely efficient. Having used this software for a long time, he said, "I've been able to make process modifications to improve its efficiency, and I know all its intricacies." Jeff had developed some proprietary software for PCB design work which he believed kept him at the cutting edge of the competition. At times, he wondered about the possibilities of licensing his proprietary software to other PCB design firms. He concluded, however, that the small market for this type of software product would probably not justify the necessary marketing and additional product development costs.

In addition to the original equipment purchased by Jeff in 1983, the company purchased a VAX Model 11/751 and a Calay Version 03 in December of 1985 at cost of approximately $170,000. (See Exhibit 8 for the cash flow statements prepared for the bank to obtain a loan). The VAX was intended to be used as a communications and networking device and for developing new software. The Calay was a dedicated hardware system that included an automatic router which could completely design certain less complex boards without an operator. On more complex boards it could complete a major percentage of the board, leaving a designer to do the remainder. Jeff and the board felt that this automatic routing capability might open a new market for the company for less complex boards. They also felt that the manufacturer of the Calay, as well as the Calay user group, would supply new customer leads. Some of these expectations had been met.

In September of 1986, a software upgrade to the Calay was purchased for approximately $28,000. Although bank financing was available, Jeff decided

EXHIBIT 8 APPLIED CAD KNOWLEDGE, INC.: CASH FLOW PROJECTIONS AS OF DECEMBER 16, 1985

	DEC 1985	JAN 1986	FEB 1986	MAR 1986	APR 1986	MAY 1986	JUN 1986	JUL 1986	AUG 1986	SEP 1986	OCT 1986	NOV 1986	DEC 1986	TOTAL $(000S)
SALES	25	30	30	30	30	30	30	30	30	30	30	30	30	360
EXPENSES[1]	20	24	29.5	29.5	29.5	29.5	29.5	29.5	29.5	29.5	29.5	29.5	29.5	348.5
PROFIT	.5	6	.5	.5	.5	.5	.5	.5	.5	.5	.5	.5	.5	11.5
OPENING CASH	141	148	102	102.5	88	88.5	89	89.5	90	90.5	91	91	91.5	
RECEIVABLES	37	17	30	30	30	30	30	30	30	30	30	30	30	
DISBURSEMENTS[2]	30	24[3]	29.5[4]	29.5	29.5	29.5	29.5	29.5	29.5	29.5	29.5	29.5	29.5	
TAXES[5]		29[6]		15										
CLOSING CASH	148	102	102.5	88	89	89	90	90.5	91	91	91.5	92		

1. Expenses include rent, heat, light, power, salaries, contract work, telephone, etc. This level of expenses will support sales double those projected.
2. Figures do not include depreciation which would only influence total profit.
3. Includes loan payment of 4K/mth.
4. Includes new employees at 66K/yr.
5. Taxes based on the following assumptions: 1985 profit of 150K; 50K software expense on new equipment; 20K depreciation on new equipment; 10K misc. expenses; investment tax credit of 15K.
6. 25% of equipment costing 156K.

to pay cash for this purchase, to avoid raising his monthly fixed expenses. The new purchases gave Applied CAD enough machine capacity to support some $2 million in annual sales.

The VAX, however, was not being fully used as originally intended—to allow hands-off automation of the firm's varied pieces of computing equipment, as well as providing batch data processing capacity. In its ultimate form, the VAX might actually operate the older, more cumbersome systems. It would be able to juggle dozens of design tasks between work stations and autorouters, queuing and evaluating each job and calling for human intervention when needed. One director, visualizing robots sitting in Applied CAD's Recaro chairs, called this the "Robo-Router plan." To carry it out would require an additional investment of approximately $15,000 in hardware and another $10,000 to $20,000 in programming, along with a significant amount of Jeff's time. The investment would result in very substantial cost reductions and reduced dependence on freelance designers, but it would only pay for itself under high volume conditions.

APPLIED CAD'S ORGANIZATION

Jeff oversaw all operations in his company, did all the high level marketing/ sales contact work with clients, and did much of the technical design work as well. Another full-time designer was hired in May of 1985 put had to be terminated in September of 1986 due to persistent personal problems. Steve Jones, Jeff's data manager and former assistant at Redac, became a full-time employee in January 1986. Among other duties, Steve covered the telephone, coordinated technical work done by freelance contractors in Jeff's absence, and performed various administrative duties. Steve had a B.S. in engineering and, before Redac, had worked for other PCB electronics companies. In April of 1987 Jeff hired John MacNamara, a former subcontract designer, on a full-time, salaried basis.

In May of 1987 Jeff also hired a part-time person to keep the books, write checks, and handle other office related matters. For this first three months, she focused on straightening out the books and tax-related items. She was also trying to find time to set up an accounting package on the personal computer. The package had been purchased in August of 1986 (at the request of board members), for the purpose of generating accurate monthly statements. Since the company's founding, the board had been asking for accurate end-of-month data on sales, accounts receivable, cash balance, backlog, and accounts payable. They also wanted monthly financial statements, although Stevens himself saw little point in them: cash flow projections served his immediate needs. The accounting package was chosen by one of the board members, based partly on its broad capabilities. For example, it could assist in invoicing and aging receivables.

Jeff had other capable designers "on call"—available for freelance project work when the company needed them. Depending upon the market, there were time periods when Jeff could obtain the services of several contractors to meet peak work loads. In general, design contractors worked on a negotiated fixed-fee basis for completing a specific portion of a design project. In July of 1987, however (after sales in June reached approximately $50 thousand and the backlog reached $90 thousand), Jeff found it hard to attract contract designers with free time. The backlog consisted of about 15 boards ranging in price from $800 to $15,000. The electronics industry had turned upward and in busy times everyone was busy. Consequently, freelance designers were committed to their own customers or employers who were also busy. Jeff attempted to fill the production gap by working as a third-shift designer.

At most of its meetings, the board of directors spent considerable time discussing the current business climate and the future sales outlook. This usually led to a discussion of hiring someone to take over the marketing and sales function. It was generally agreed that such a person could not only contribute to the company's growth in sales but also free up a considerable amount of Jeff's time that could be devoted to design and operational matters. When Applied CAD was busy, however, Jeff had very little time to devote to finding, hiring, and working with such a person. Even if one were hired, a salesperson would require Jeff's time for introductions to the present customers and for responding to questions about new sales potentials.

When Applied CAD was *not* busy, Jeff's concern over the reliability of future cash flows made him hesitant to make the major salary commitment that a marketing professional would require. He was aware of the contrary pressures: "I can't get out of the 'boom-splat' syndrome," he said.

To Jeff, the "splat" came when backlogs and cash balances fell. The winter of 1987, for example, had felt to him like hitting a wall. See Exhibit 7 for monthly totals of sales, backlogs, etc. as estimated by Jeff at monthly board meetings.

BUSINESS OPTIONS

In August of 1987, Jeff was contemplating the current business climate, his accomplishments with Applied CAD over the past three years, and where the company was headed. His major objective—agreed with the board—was growth. Jeff had discussed many times with his board the needs for a marketing person and a promotional brochure for the company. He hoped to attract someone with top management credentials who could work with him as a peer. On occasion, he had talked with marketing people about the job, but most of these prospective employees lacked the level of skills and PCB experience Jeff hoped to acquire. He had also talked with commercial artists about design of a brochure. Jeff and his board felt that a "first class" brochure would cost between $5 and $10 thousand.

Marketing in the PCB business, especially among companies with sales of under $1 million, was characterized as informal. Very few companies had full-time people devoted to the marketing task; in most cases it was the owner-president who handled marketing and sales. Most small companies had their own list of faithful customers and new customers tended to come by word of mouth. In the under $1 million segment it was not uncommon for a company when extremely overloaded with work to farm out a board to a competitor. Also, certain other services, such as photoplotting, were done by shops that also did design work. Consequently, there was considerable communication among the competitors; the players seemed to know who got what jobs.

The marketing job at a company like Applied CAD would consist mainly of coordinating the advertising and a sales brochure, calling on present customers, and attempting to find new customers. Such a person needed a working knowledge of PCB design which required experience in the industry. People with these qualifications normally made a $40–50,000 base salary plus commissions; frequently their total compensation exceeded $100,000 per year. Of major concern to Jeff were Applied CAD's erratic history of sales and cash balances and the difficulty of predicting sales volume any further than two months in advance. He balked at taking on responsibility for an executive-level salary, lacking confidence in the future. "This would probably be somebody with kids to feed or send to college," Jeff said. "How could I pay them, in slow times?"

Still, marketing appeared to be the function most critical to achieving the growth rates Jeff Stevens and his Board hoped for. It was key, also, in meeting the major potential threat posed by the recent availability of inexpensive software which could enable personal computers (PCs) to design printed circuit boards (see Exhibit 4). Jeff had heard that some of that new software could perform almost as well as the more expensive equipment used by Applied CAD. He wondered how the advent of low-cost software might be turned into an opportunity, not a threat.

Four possible responses had occurred to Jeff and his board: Applied CAD could ignore the PC software, adopt it, distribute it, or sell its own software to the PC users. Ignoring the new technology might work in the short run, since the complex boards designed by Applied CAD would not be the first affected; in the long run, however, failure to keep up with technology would leave more and more jobs subject to low-cost competition.

By adopting the new software for his next equipment expansion, Applied CAD could take a proactive stance. Jeff could buy a system or two to see how good they were, and hire people to work on the new systems on a freelance basis. Of course, he would need a flow of jobs to experiment with. A variation of this alternative was to sit back and wait while ready to move quickly if he saw something developing.

A third alternative, acting as a distributor for the PC software, would give Applied CAD a product to sell to prospects who insisted on doing their own design. This could establish relationships with people who might later need overload capacity.

Fourth, Applied CAD could proceed with development of its proprietary software, creating a product to sell to PC users. Jeff estimated that his Automated Design Review System could save both time and grief for other designers. In some tasks, it could cut the required design time in half. In all jobs, the capability to check the finished design against the original input automatically and completely could improve quality. ADRS already existed in rough form; it was one of the elements which would make up the "Robo-Router" system, if that were implemented.

Many of these options seemed to require significant marketing skills—strengths—where the company was presently weak. The technical questions could be answered, if Jeff had the time to work on them. But the marketing questions called for a person with extensive industry experience, broad contacts, a creative imagination, and the ability to make things happen.

Amid all the other problems facing him as owner of a small business, Jeff was trying to figure out how to shape his business for the long-range future, and how to attract the kind of person he could work with to assure growth—and survival. He looked across the table at Bogie's restaurant, caught the eye of one director, and yawned. Tonight, after this meeting, he hoped to finish the design of a particularly complicated board. His best customer was desperate for this job.

APPLIED CAD KNOWLEDGE, INC.
PART B: THE NEW
MARKETING DIRECTOR

RAYMOND M. KINNUNEN
AND JOHN A. SEEGER

· In September of 1987, as the summer rush slowed, Jeff Stevens began to talk seriously with Jerry King, regional sales manager of Calay Systems, Inc., about the marketing problems of Applied CAD Knowledge, Inc. Stevens wanted someone to become in effect a co-owner and officer of the small firm. King had been a principal in his own service bureau in the very early days of auto-mated PCB design, and retained friendships and contacts with high level per-sonnel in many electronics firms. Exhibit 1 shows King's resume.

After a month of conversations and negotiations, including a meeting with the board of directors, the two men reached tentative agreement on employ-ment terms which would give King a 3% commission on all company sales, a car allowance, and a base salary of $40,000 per year. Since the marketing per-son would be influential in pricing many jobs, it was important to preserve his regard for profitability; King was offered a stock interest in Applied CAD, contingent on the bottom line at the end of 1988. With a handshake of agree-ment, Stevens set out to reduce the terms to an employment contract letter.

The following night, Jerry King called Stevens to express his regret that he would be unable to accept the marketing VP position, after all: he had just received an offer from AT&T to set up Australian operations for a new ven-ture. It was simply too good an offer to refuse, King said. A dejected Jeff Ste-vens reported the development at the next board meeting; "We're back to square one," he said. "And the next 'splat' is just about to arrive."

Applied CAD's monthly sales dropped to half their mid-1987 level, and the backlog dropped to near zero. On December 8, however, Jerry King called

---

Prepared by Raymond M. Kinnunen, Northeastern University, and John A. Seeger, Bentley College, as a basis for class discussion. Distributed by the North American Case Research Association. All rights reserved to the authors and the North American Case Research Association. © Raymond M. Kinnunen and John A. Seeger, 1988.

EXHIBIT 1   RESUME OF JERRY KING

Jerry King

Married
Four Children
Excellent Health

EDUCATION:

FAIRLEIGH DICKENSON UNIVERSITY, Madison, New Jersey
Major: Business Administration

U.S. NAVY, Electronics "A" School, Pearl Harbor, Hawaii

CONTINUING EDUCATION, including numerous seminars and workshops in Corporate Finance, Power Base Selling, Territory Time Management, The Art of Negotiating, Computer Graphics in Electronics, Sales Management and Marketing Techniques.

EXPERIENCE:

GENERAL BUSINESS MANAGEMENT: Establishing policies and procedures for high volume cost efficient business operations, planning promotions for new business development, hiring, training and supervising personnel, including management level, designing and conducting management, sales, marketing and CAD/CAM training seminars internationally.

TECHNICAL BACKGROUND: Twenty-one years of direct Printed Circuit Design, Fabrication and Electronics CAD/CAM marketing experience. Helped to create detailed business plans for three start-up companies including a high volume printed circuit design service bureau and raised five million dollars in venture capital used to purchase state-of-the-art CAD/CAM systems and other related equipment. Managed the development and marketing of a PCB Design Automation turn-key system which was sold exclusively to Calma/GE in 1977 and integrated with their GDS1 TRI-DESIGN system. Very strong market knowledge in Computer Aided Engineering (CAE), Computer Aided Design (CAD), Computer Aided Test (CAT), and Computer Aided Manufacturing (CAM).

ACCOMPLISHMENTS:

Particularly effective in areas of personnel management, motivation and training, thereby increasing sales volume production flow, productivity and employee morale. Significant career accomplishments in customer relations, marketing, and sales leadership and management.

EMPLOYMENT HISTORY:

1986–Present   Calay Systems Incorporated, Waltham, Massachusetts
                  SENIOR ACCOUNT MANAGER
    Responsible for a direct territory consisting of Northern Massachusetts, Vermont, New Hampshire, Maine and Quebec.

1985–1986   Automated Systems Incorporated, Nashua, N.H.
                  EASTERN REGIONAL SALES MANAGER
    Responsible for regional design and fabrication service sales with a regional quota in excess of $5 million.

1981–1985   Engineering Automation Systems, Inc., San Jose, California

(continued)

EXHIBIT 1 (continued)

WESTERN REGIONAL SALES MANAGER

Responsible for new Printed Circuit Design CAD/CAM system. Set up regional office, hired and trained sales and support staff of twelve people. Western regional sales were in excess of fifty percent of the company's business.

September 1984 PROMOTED TO NATIONAL SALES MANAGER

1978–1981   Computervision Corporation, Bedford, Massachusetts
                   NATIONAL PRODUCT SALES MANAGER

Responsible for all electronic CAD/CAM system sales and related products. Provided direct sales management and training to the national field sales team, conducted sales training internationally, assisted in developing competitive strategy, technical support and new product development. Reported to the Vice President of North American Division.

March 1980 PROMOTED TO MANAGER, CORPORATE DEMONSTRATION and BENCHMARK CENTER

Managed team of 38 people who performed all corporate level demonstrations and benchmarks. Supported field offices with technical information and people worldwide. Reported to the Vice President of Marketing Operations. THIS WAS A KEY MANAGEMENT POSITION FOR THE COMPANY.

1966–1978   King Systems, Inc., San Diego, California (a Printed Circuit Design
                   CAD/CAM and NC Drilling Service Bureau) FOUNDER, PRESI-
                   DENT, CHAIRMAN and MAJOR STOCKHOLDER

Served as Chief Executive Officer in charge of all aspects of the operation. Primary activities in sales management, direct field sales and customer relations. Responsible for financial administration, production operations and personnel administration. Assessed future needs and created business planning for increasing market share, facilities capability and penetrating new market opportunity. Developed a new concept in contract services for blanket sales to large government and commercial prime contractors.

Jeff to say he had just decided against Australia, and would like to apply again for the marketing vice-president position, if it was still open. Jeff agreed, and the next day Jerry presented to Jeff and the board a plan for reaching $1 million in sales in 1988, and for growing by $1 million per year in the following two years. This plan is partially reproduced in Exhibits 2, 3, and 4. Concerned with the timing of cash flows, one of the directors asked how long it would take to generate enough new sales to cover their added marketing expenses. King responded, "If I couldn't provide more than enough sales to cover my pay, I wouldn't take the job."

Although not officially joining Applied CAD until January 4, Jerry spent the rest of December in joint calling, with Jeff, on customers where Calay and Applied CAD shared some interests. In these first weeks, the "chemistry" Jeff

EXHIBIT 2   EXCERPTS FROM JERRY KING'S DECEMBER 9, 1987, BOARD PRESENTATION

INTRODUCTION

The plan is a detailed road map for taking Applied CAD Knowledge, Incorporated (ACK) from the current sales volume to more than three million annual sales volume over the next three years. It identifies target markets, competitive environment, and sales tactics which will be used for achieving the sales projections during the plan period from January 1st 1988 through December 31st 1990. The projections show a monthly breakdown for 1988 and a yearly number for 1989 and 1990. The monthly projections were created on Lotus and provide for projected, forecasted and actual sales bookings for each month. As each month passes the actual numbers are entered and a goal status report is generated as part of the end of month reporting. At the end of each quarter a new quarter will be added so that there will always be four consecutive quarters of monthly projections.

The aggressive growth which is outlined will require significant expansion of facilities, personnel and equipment in order to maintain consistent QUALITY and ON TIME deliveries and insure REPEAT BUSINESS from established customers. It is required that the management and the Board of Directors of ACK provide the necessary production controls and capital/operating budgets to support expansion commensurate with sales volume increases over the term of the plan.

The PCB design service market can be divided into three major segments. Each of these segments will include companies who design and manufacture electronic equipment for Commercial, Industrial, Aerospace and Military vertical market areas.

MAJOR ACCOUNTS & GOVERNMENT SUB-CONTRACTORS (MA)

Major Accounts are Fortune 1000 companies. They present a significant opportunity for multiple board contracts and blanket purchase agreements. Any one company could fill ACK's capacity.

PRIMARY ACCOUNTS (PA)

Primary accounts are companies who have been doing business for more than three years (not a start-up) and typically do between 5-500 million in annual sales. These companies represent the most consistent level of business. The type of contracts available from this market segment are usually on the level of one to four board designs per month. Typically, each board or project has to be sold separately at the project engineering level.

VENTURE START-UP ACCOUNTS (VA)

Venture start-up companies usually are operating on stringent budgets. They typically have no internal CAD capability and therefore must rely on outside service. The business potential for this market segment is very significant. This market represents a high risk and therefore is avoided by the major competitors leaving more opportunity for the smaller operation. It is not unusual to obtain sole source product level contracts from companies in this market.

EXHIBIT 3 BOOKINGS PROJECTIONS FOR APPLIED CAD KNOWLEDGE, INC.

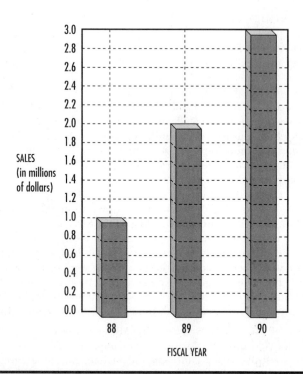

EXHIBIT 4 PCB DESIGN MARKET

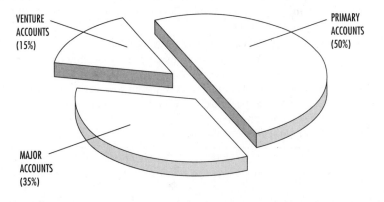

Source: Frost and Sullivan, 1985.

EXHIBIT 5   APPLIED CAD KNOWLEDGE, INC.: SALES PROJECTIONS PRESENTED TO THE BOARD, JANUARY 8, 1988

FORECAST Q1 1988: SALES BY CUSTOMER

ACCOUNT NAME	JAN 50%	90%	FEB 50%	90%	MAR 50%	90%	TOT 50%	TOT 90%	GRAND TOTAL
CUSTOMER A	0.0	20.0	0.0	8.0	20.0	0.0	20.0	28.0	48.0
PROSPECT I	0.0	7.0	0.0	0.0	0.0	0.0	0.0	7.0	7.0
PROSPECT II	5.0	0.0	2.0	0.0	2.0	0.0	9.0	0.0	9.0
CUSTOMER B	0.0	0.0	12.0	0.0	0.0	0.0	12.0	0.0	12.0
CUSTOMER C	12.0	0.0	0.0	0.0	0.0	0.0	12.0	0.0	12.0
CUSTOMER D	0.0	0.0	12.0	0.0	0.0	0.0	12.0	0.0	12.0
CUSTOMER E	0.0	30.0	0.0	0.0	20.0	0.0	20.0	30.0	50.0
PROSPECT III	0.0	0.0	15.0	0.0	20.0	0.0	35.0	0.0	35.0
PROSPECT IV	0.0	0.0	15.0	0.0	20.0	0.0	35.0	0.0	35.0
PROSPECT V	0.0	6.5	0.0	0.8	0.0	3.8	0.0	11.1	11.1
CUSTOMER F	0.0	0.0	0.0	7.0	0.0	0.0	0.0	7.0	7.0
TOTAL	17.0	63.5	56.0	15.8	82.0	3.8	155.0	83.1	238.1

FORECAST FY 1988: BOOKINGS BY PRODUCT TYPE

	SERVICE	SOFTWARE	TOTAL	ACCUM. TOTAL
January	33	15	48	48
February	48	5	53	101
March	53	15	68	169
Quarter 1	124	35	169	
April	60	5	65	234
May	68	15	83	317
June	75	5	80	397
Quarter 2	203	25	228	
July	80	15	95	492
August	85		85	577
September	88	15	103	680
Quarter 3	253	30	283	
October	90	8	98	778
November	95	15	110	888
December	98	15	113	1001
Quarter 4	283	38	321	

Stevens had hoped for became readily apparent. The two men's skills complemented each other well: this would be a highly effective team, Stevens felt.

As 1988 began, King and Stevens continued to work closely together. Since Applied CAD's office layout did not provide the privacy needed for telephone prospecting, Jerry worked out of his home, joining Jeff several times per week

EXHIBIT 6 APPLIED CAD KNOWLEDGE, INC.: SALES PROJECTIONS, 1988

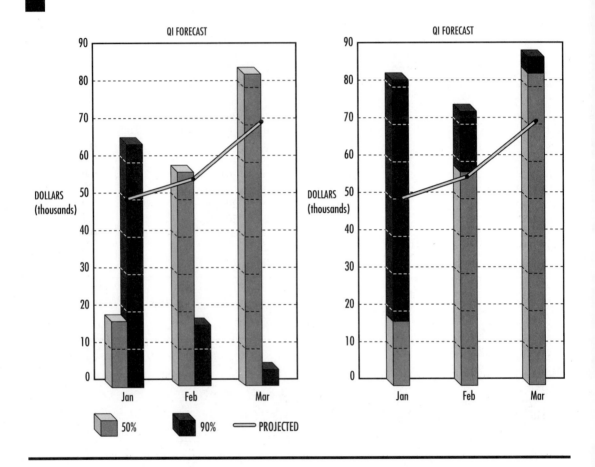

on joint sales calls. At the January 8 meeting of the board of directors, the two men presented detailed sales projections for the first quarter and broader estimates for the entire year (see Exhibits 5 and 6). One account alone—California PrinCo—held the promise of some $250,000 in sales over the next four months. An old and steady customer of Applied CAD, PrinCo was nearing a decision on a major expansion in their use of circuit boards.

January sales totalled only $6,000 but many prospects seemed close to signing for large orders. At the February 19 board meeting, Jeff and Jerry predicted sales of $100,000 per month for February and March; it appeared a 1988 sales goal of $1,000,000 might still be reachable. Exhibit 7 shows monthly sales and backlogs through January 1988.

EXHIBIT 7   APPLIED CAD KNOWLEDGE, INC.: MONTHLY SALES AND MONTH-END RECEIVABLES, BACKLOGS, AND CASH LEVELS

	A/R	SALES	BACKLOG	CASH
January 1986	18	20	20	$98
February	*	10	*	*
March	18	10	12	62
April	18	10	20	28
May	24	20	26	26
June	*	10	*	*
July	14	25	*	18
August	70	50	30	15
September	90	40	*	8
October	50	30	*	26
November	19	5	10	17
December	24	10	18	14
January 1987	13	3	*	7
February	40	21	*	8
March	35	28	22	6
April	32	22	37	11
May	25	22	50	5
June	50	50	90	10
July	90	58	30	10
August	*	25	*	10
September	34	25	50	21
October	62	48	9	8
November	50	24	*	*
December	14	34	9	33
January 1988	8	6	*	19

Amounts shown in thousands of dollars.
*Information not available.

CHOCOLATE EMPORIUM, INC.

ALAN AIDIFF AND
MARILYN L. TAYLOR

Paul Scott, a small business counselor, put down the receiver after speaking with Jon Lewis, a new client. Lewis was scheduled to come into the office in two hours to discuss his new business venture. Jon Lewis was referred to Scott by a mutual friend. Lewis' new business, Chocolate Emporium, Inc., was experiencing some difficulty. The situation wasn't unusual; most new businesses experience some early difficulties. Paul Scott agreed to perform an analysis of Chocolate Emporium, Inc., and its market. As Paul reviewed the information he had gathered on Jon's business, he realized a two-prong attack was needed in order to make a go of the business: a) increase revenues and b) decrease costs. He also realized that abandonment was an alternative.

BACKGROUND INFORMATION

Jon Lewis worked for $15\frac{1}{2}$ years in insurance (sales and agency management) before deciding to engage in his present venture, Chocolate Emporium, Inc. His insurance job, which required extensive traveling throughout the Midwest, restricted his family life. Jon chose a medium-sized (population 53,000) Midwestern college town as the location of his business. This type of environment closely resembled that of his youth. Jon liked the schools and the accessibility to a larger metropolitan area 35 miles away. Of greater importance though, was the fact that the location Jon chose had *no* major chocolate specialty shop. Jon began researching the idea of chocolate store approximately two years before he actually opened the doors of Chocolate Emporium, Inc. The initial idea of a chocolate store was based on two successful examples that had been operating in his hometown. One of these chocolate stores in particular was appealing to Jon. Jon was attracted to the "sit down," "family" image the store

Source: **Prepared by Alan Aidiff and Professor Marilyn L. Taylor, University of Kansas, as a basis for class discussion. Distributed by the North American Case Research Association.** © **Marilyn L. Taylor, 1990.**

portrayed. It was this image that Jon hoped to replicate in his own chocolate store. With this image in mind, Jon prepared to start up his business.

SITE ANALYSIS

Jon was aware that pedestrian traffic would be an important element in future success of his venture. He contacted the local Chamber of Commerce to get information on shopping areas and pedestrian traffic patterns. After observing several areas of the city, Jon decided the downtown area was his best bet. From the start, however, he encountered problems of high rent, long leases, and dilapidated premises. All available downtown sites were eliminated for one or more of these reasons.

Jon then considered alternatives to the downtown area. The alternatives included several free-standing buildings which housed one or more shops/stores. After six months of searching for a site, Jon identified a new shopping mall under construction along a major trafficway. The mall was the only one in the city and was located in the southern part of the city. Jon viewed this location favorably since much of the city's growth had been in that direction for the last five years. Jon ultimately selected a corner location in the mall (see Exhibit 1, #205) due to favorable lease provisions, year-round access, and new physical facilities. In addition, Jon anticipated that the other stores would draw customers thus enhancing customer traffic around his store.

EXHIBIT 1 MALL LAYOUT

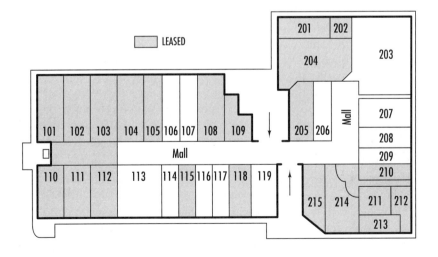

COMPETITION

Jon wanted the Chocolate Emporium to be a retail store for high-quality chocolates and candy. As Jon's market research progressed, he became more convinced that chocolate and candy sales were seasonal and that he could expect
sales peaks primarily during the holiday seasons. He decided to extend his
product line to include soda fountain items. This aspect of the business was
not initiated, however, until after the shop opened. Thus the product lines of
the Chocolate Emporium eventually included chocolates, candy, and fountain
items, e.g., ice cream and carbonated beverage items. A factor underlying Jon's
decision to choose the Midwestern college town was the lack of direct competition in the local chocolate market. However, there were several competitors in
the candy and soda fountain markets (see Exhibit 2). Jon felt that his primary
competition would be:

- *The Candy Store* (See CS on Exhibit 2.) · The Candy Store carried very
  few chocolates and sold mostly candies. The store was located in the
  downtown area and was privately owned and managed. The Candy
  Store was probably the only direct competition in candy sales for Chocolate Emporium.
- *Dairy Queen* (DQ) · Dairy Queen was long known primarily for its fountain operations and had recently increased its efforts in the restaurant
  segment of its operation. DQ had a long tradition in the area of fountain operations. The stores were located east and south of Chocolate
  Emporium and were franchise operations.
- *Baskin-Robbins* (BR) · Baskin-Robbins was solely a fountain operation.
  The name Baskin-Robbins was associated with 31 flavors of ice cream
  and was likely to have repeat customers. The store was located east of
  Chocolate Emporium on the same trafficway and was a franchise operation.
- *Zarda Dairy* (ZD) · Zarda Dairy had extended its market segment to include convenience stores with ice cream and fountain items provided
  by the dairy operation. Zarda Dairy was located in a nearby metropolitan area and was privately owned/managed. The store was located west
  of Chocolate Emporium on the same trafficway.
- *Perkins* (P) · Although Perkins was primarily a restaurant operation, it
  did carry a limited selection of ice cream and fountain items. In addition, Perkins had recently promoted a market campaign highlighting
  the variety of desserts on their menu. Perkins was a franchise operation
  located across the parking lot from Chocolate Emporium.

There was also indirect competition from the local grocery stores. All the
local grocery stores carried a variety of candies and chocolates, although the
chocolate lines were not as widely varied as those at Chocolate Emporium.
The major difference in the candy is that the grocery stores sold pre-packaged
candies whereas Chocolate Emporium weighed out what the customer wanted
to buy. Jon preferred this personal touch.

EXHIBIT 2 LOCAL COMPETITION FOR CHOCOLATE EMPORIUM, INC.

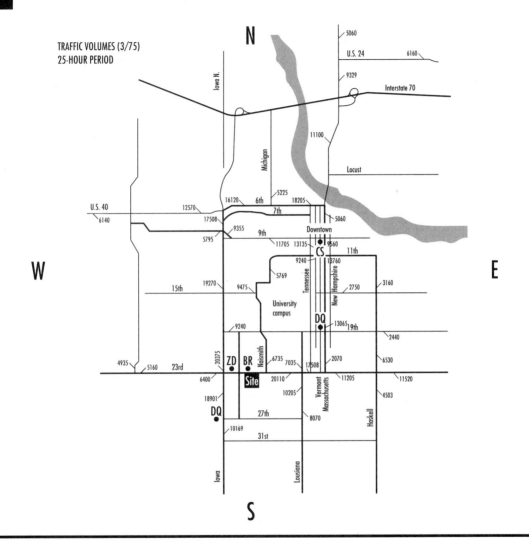

TRAFFIC VOLUMES (3/75)
25-HOUR PERIOD

MARKET AND RETAIL PREPARATION

Jon had no previous retail experience. He felt "very good about his ideas and their prospects" but realized a positive attitude alone was insufficient. Before deciding to start an independent operation, he searched for franchise opportunities (see Exhibit 3). After investigating several options, Jon decided to remain an independent operator and explore the chocolate market on his own. He contacted suppliers of various chocolates and candies. During this time

EXHIBIT 3   POTENTIAL FRANCHISES EXPLORED BY JON LEWIS

NAME OF OPERATION	RESULTS OF INVESTIGATION
1. Godiva	— very expensive chocolates (specialized in box chocolates). — did not have a bona fide franchise arrangement. — would have had minimum space and inventory requirements. — cost prohibitive (@ $14/lb.).
2. Russell Stover	— were not providing for franchise arrangements at time of investigation. — anticipating change in near future and willing to discuss franchise arrangements at that time.
3. Hershey's	— did not provide franchises for retail operations. — was willing to sell carload quantities for retail sales.
4. Swenson's	— originally Jon wanted access to ice cream vs. bona fide franchise. — price negotiations fell through. — had to withdraw and see other sources.
5. Hagen Daas	— wanted to provide exclusive ice cream dealership; no chocolates or candies — withdrew due to above restrictions.

Jon became closely acquainted with the manager of a chocolate retailer in a nearby metropolitan area. This particular retailer was owned by a chocolate factory in the same area. Ultimately this factory became Jon's major supplier of chocolates. He arranged to work at the retail outlet 2-3 days per week for six months. During this time he learned as much about the retail operation as possible.

The retail outlet that Jon worked with was located in a large shopping mall which had opened in the heart of the metro area (population about 2M) about five years prior. Pedestrian traffic in the mall was brisk all year. Jon noticed that frequently people would "browse" the different candy and chocolate counters. The retail outlet also had many repeat customers. The manager told Jon that some of their customers had been regular patrons as long as she had managed the store. It was Jon's hope that he could replicate this type of business in his small retail store.

During this six-month period, Jon attended several chocolate and candy conventions. He enjoyed "discussing products with the suppliers and prospects for the future." Jon became very knowledgeable about the chocolate industry. He arranged to receive specialty items not available through his major supplier. Eventually his sources of supply included chocolate and candy producers located across the U.S. He prided himself in the ability to locate suppliers and expanded the types of chocolates and candies he carried in stock. In the case of the fountain and ice cream product line, Jon relied solely upon one supplier. His rationale was that these items are refrigerated and the closer the proximity of his supplier the less problem with shortages and spoilage. Jon had had no problem with back orders from any of his suppliers.

Jon could usually rely upon delivery of goods within a week of when they were ordered. Given the close proximity of his major chocolate and dairy suppliers, he would receive goods sooner if he personally picked them up. The terms were cash on delivery. Since Jon was a newer small retailer, his suppliers were hesitant to extend credit. Jon hoped these suppliers' terms would change over time.

FINANCING OF THE BUSINESS

Jon was able to acquire a bank loan of $66K through a local bank. This loan was collateralized by Jon's personal portfolio of stocks and bonds. In addition, Jon contributed about $32K of the initial outlay costs from personal funds. A $19K loan from a relative provided the remainder of the financing for initial asset expenditures and the early months of operating the business.

CURRENT SITUATION

In talking with Jon Lewis, Paul Scott was impressed with his knowledge of the chocolate industry. The history and refinement of the cocoa bean frequently entered the discussion. This entrepreneur was fascinated with the industry and market he chose to enter. Jon Lewis was the epitome of the entrepreneur: enthusiastic about his product and energetic. Indeed, he usually worked 60 or more hours a week.

SHOPPING MALL STATUS

The shopping mall Jon chose had been vacant for two years prior to his lease arrangement. In discussing this fact with the developer, Paul received no apparent explanation. The developer simply explained "the retail interest originally anticipated never surfaced." At the time of Paul's analysis, the mall was about two-thirds occupied (see Exhibit 1). The occupants included the following:

- 4 small specialty shops (Locations #118, 115, 104, 105)
- an electronics store (109)
- a video game center (108)
- a large nightclub (210–215)
- a travel agent (201)
- a flower shop (202)

- a fitness center (204)
- Jon's chocolate/fountain shop (205)
- clothing store (101-103, 110-112)

In addition, a cafeteria was under construction in the east end of the mall (see Exhibit 1, #203, 207–209). The increase in occupancy was partly due to the efforts of the older occupants. In fact, Jon chaired a committee of current occupants that actively promoted the mall to enlist new retail interest. When asked, Jon knew of no advertising campaign by the developers to promote the mall.

Paul spoke with a colleague about the mall advertising and his colleague related the findings of a demographic study performed by the developers. Paul's colleague made the following comment on the findings of the study:

- The study was geared toward supply of labor rather than toward customers (e.g., can you hire enough workers for your store?).
- A study of customer potential was included but did not include customer flow.
- Future projections from the study were unrealistically high.
- The center/mall went into operation with little customer data.

The shopping mall was located adjacent to one of the busier traffic intersections in the city (see Exhibit 2). To the west of the mall was a major department store and to the cast a vacant lot. Behind the mall, to the south, were single- and multiple-family dwellings. The entire area south of the mall was zoned for residential use. Across from the mall, to the north, were several fast food restaurants. The area north of these businesses, though, was zoned for residential use. Essentially, the mall was part of "strip development" along a major trafficway.

Paul Scott had visited the shopping mall on a number of occasions. He observed that there were few (if any) people browsing in the mall itself, i.e., between the shops. Jon agreed with Paul's observation. Jon expressed concern about the cafeteria being constructed next to him on the east side of the mall. He was fearful that people might enter the cafeteria from outside (on the north) and thus eliminate any location advantage he might have (see Exhibit 1).

FACILITIES

A major advantage of the mall location was its new facilities. The mall had handicap access and restrooms. At the time of Paul's analysis, one end of the mall was vacant (see Exhibit 1). The other end of the mall was occupied by a clothing retailer (101-103 and 110-112, Exhibit 1). Because new occupants were still entering the mall much construction was in progress.

Jon did not provide carryout service. He felt strongly about maintaining the "sit down" image. Since the fountain area was a later addition to the business, Jon admitted that it might require redesigning to facilitate an efficient workflow. For example, he had over 30 flavors of ice cream but could only display nine flavors at any one time. Jon planned to remedy this problem by the next peak fountain season.

Jon also wanted to ensure that he had adequate storage space. Consequently, he had a 10′ x 12′ walk-in freezer installed (see Exhibit 4 for store layout). Paul noticed that the freezer was two-thirds empty and discussed the freezer capacity with Jon. Jon stated that he anticipated a monthly sales level of approximately $25,000 and felt that a 10′ x 12′ freezer would be the amount of storage space necessary to accommodate that level of business. Paul discovered later that a nearby Baskin-Robbins had a 10′ x 6′ freezer.

Jon purchased a van truck in order to provide special deliveries for chocolate orders. Jon charged $1 for delivery. He recounted a delivery incident to

EXHIBIT 4 CHOCOLATE EMPORIUM LAYOUT

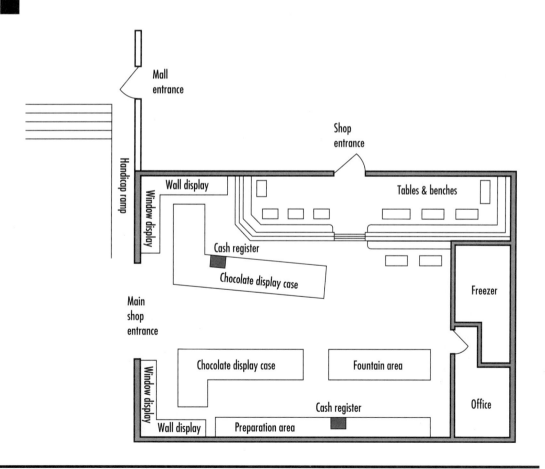

Paul Scott. On Valentine's Day he had advertised giving candy instead of the traditional flowers. He received a request from a sorority house and when he arrived in the van, several of the sorority women questioned him about Chocolate Emporium and quizzed him about who was getting the candy. Jon felt that incidents like these provided visibility for the business.

MARKETING FACTORS

In analyzing Chocolate Emporium, Paul made efforts to focus upon the market area. The city in which Chocolate Emporium was located had a population of approximately 53,000. There was no predominant industry. The business community and the Chamber of Commerce actively promoted the town as an attractive location for businesses to locate. Several Fortune 500 companies had located smaller branches in the area; however, none had over 300 to 400 employees. There was a large rural population and many of the rural inhabitants used the city for shopping on weekends. A twenty-year city plan called for improvement of the downtown shopping area to cope with retail traffic. In fact, the City Commission rejected a proposal for a new shopping mall in favor of promoting the downtown improvement plan.

The primary employer in the area was the university which had about 25,000 students. (About one third of these were considered residents of the town.) There were definite seasonal trends in sales. During the fall, the football games created a high potential for business volume. In the summer, however, most of the students returned home. The student population had grown steadily during the 1970s but in the last two years there had been almost no increase in the number of students.

EXHIBIT 5   NEWSPAPER ADVERTISING FOR CHOCOLATE EMPORIUM, INC.

THE ULTIMATE GIFT FOR DAD
For the Dad who has everything . . . a box made of milk chocolate. Fill it with Jelly Bellies, Almond Toffee, White Chocolate Pretzels, Raspberry Creams, Sour Balls, or a combination of your Dad's favorites. We're restocked and ready to surprise your dad with the Ultimate Gift from the Chocolate Emporium.

Note: University daily newspaper — $1/column inch ($5/day)

TASTE APPEAL
Recapture the flavor of honest-to-goodness soda fountain treats. You'll find all your favorites, made with our delicious ice cream and luscious toppings. Savor the richness of a creamy Soda, Malt, Sundae, or New York Egg Creme . . . or try an old-fashioned Phosphate. Not to be missed are our delicious Banana Splits and our special Pink Panther.

Note: Local daily newspaper — $3/column inch ($12/day)

Jon was aware of the importance of advertising and was actively experimenting to find "the answer to his market woes." He advertised in both the university and local newspapers as well as radio commercials (see Exhibits 5 and 6). He wanted to design an advertisement that promoted a "sit-down" and "family" image. The shopping center had one large central sign which had space only for the shopping center name. Each of the businesses had been given permission to hang a banner below the sign for the 30 days following their grand opening. To partially overcome this situation, Jon parked the van every day so that the Chocolate Emporium logo faced the traffic. As previously

EXHIBIT 6   RADIO ADVERTISEMENTS FOR CHOCOLATE EMPORIUM, INC.

(1)
Narrator:
Are you burning the midnight oil?
Do you have three exams tomorrow?
Did your roommate leave last week?
Are you lonely?

Well, wake up! Take a study break! Chocolate Emporium is pulling for you too, with an "all nighter" tonight only. The coffee pot's hot, the ice cream's cold, and they have lots of nibbles for you!

They'll be open all night! Tonight only! So, wake up at Chocolate Emporium in the Southern Hills Mall, 23rd and Ousdahl.

Chocolate Emporium! Chocolate Emporium! Chocolate Emporium!

(2)
(S)   Jonsey!
(J)   What? Who said that?
(S)   It's me, you're sweet tooth!
(J)   My what?
(S)   Your sweet tooth. You're not going to get another box of that pre-packaged junk that passes for candy, are you?
(J)   Well, what else is there?
(S)   Fresh chocolate candy. Or wickedly rich fudge. An ice cream cone or a delicious soda from Chocolate Emporium in _____.
(J)   Where?
(S)   Chocolate Emporium in _____. They have everything to satisfy your sweet tooth, and a satisfied sweet tooth is a <u>quiet</u> sweet tooth, Jonsey.

      That's Chocolate Emporium at _____.

PRICE/30 SEC. (AM)	PRICE/30 SEC. (FM)
$14.25 (prime time)	$12.30 (prime)
11.65 (regular time/19 spots per wk.)	11.00 (regular time/11 spots per wk.)
10.70 (regular time/20–29 spots per wk.)	11.65 (prime time/12–17 spots per wk.)
10.00 (regular time/30–39 spots per wk.)	9.70 (regular time/12–17 spots per wk.)

EXHIBIT 7 CHOCOLATE EMPORIUM, INC. FINANCIAL STATEMENTS

BALANCE SHEET 9/25/8_

ASSETS— CURRENT
Cash—Petty	$ 195.00	
Savings	371.84	
Deposits	35.00	
		$ 601.84

INVENTORY
Merchandise	6,075.94	
Office Supplies	901.77	
	6,977.71	
		$ 7,579.55

LONG-TERM ASSETS
Van	8,493.75	
Moveable	39.807.92	
Leashold	21,922.50	
Cash Value of Insurance	26,319.00	
	96,549.17	
		104,128.72

LIABILITIES
Current—Bills	5,297.26	
Rent	4,661.07	
Sales Tax	396.57	
F.I.C.A.	400.00	
	10,754.90	
Bank	66,451.50	

LONG TERM
Owner's Contribution	58,122.50	
Family Loan	19,000.00	
Loans Against Insurance	5,198.70	
Contract Labor	6,394.74	
		165,922.34
Retained Earnings		61,793.38
Total Liabilities and R/E		104,128.96

INCOME STATEMENT 2/10/8_ to 9/25/8_

Total Revenues		$42,689
Cost of Goods Sold	31,012	
Other Variables Operating Expenses	33,028	
Fixed Operating Expenses	27,927	
Total Operating Expenses		92,012
Net Income (Loss) Before Interest, Depreciation, Taxes		(49,323)
Depreciation		7,087
Net Income (Loss) Before Interest and Taxes		(56,410)
Interest		5,383
Net Income (Loss)		($61,793)

EXHIBIT 8 CHOCOLATE EMPORIUM, INC.: MAJOR OPERATING EXPENSES

	TOTAL TO DATE (9/24)
Contract Labor	$ 8,118
Rent (Accrued, not paid)	4,550
Education & Training	95
Utilities	2,202
Insurance	2,059
Machine Rental	578
Advertising	11,268
Car Expense (Van included; 90% is fuel cost)	972
Entertainment	65
Office Supplies	371
Telephone	521
Misc. Expense Items	74
Legal Expenses (Articles of Incorporation in 1980 Cost $680)	960
Dues & Publications	176
Travel	237
Bank Fees (In. origination, ckg. acct.)	58
Overdraft Expenses	38
Employee Benefits	102
Salaries for Officers	7,385
Freight	1,113
Postage	90
Wages	15,289
FICA	2,074
Life Insurance	475
Licenses & Permits	613
Other Misc. Taxes (mostly sales tax)	1,521
Property Tax (Accrued)	N/A
TOTAL	$61,000

mentioned, Jon also used the van for occasional deliveries. This aspect of the business was a minor contributor to sales and the van usually "remained parked in its usual spot." Paul felt that this method of advertising was innovative but questioned its effectiveness. Jon was also experimenting with using the classified ads in the local newspapers and the coupon books which were sold by local service clubs.

FINANCIAL AND INVENTORY STATUS

Paul found that Jon kept accurate records but that no summaries, income statement, or balance sheet had been prepared. One of Paul's first tasks was to provide an Income Statement and Balance Sheet (see Exhibit 7). Paul also provided a detailed list of operating expenses (Exhibit 8) and charted revenue by product line (Exhibit 9) and percentage of revenue by product line (Exhibit 10). Paul discovered that Jon was four months behind in his rent. In discussing the mall with the developer, Paul learned that roughly one-half of the occupants were behind in their rent. The developer did not view late rents as a severe problem since his major concern was to increase the mall's occupancy.

Paul was curious about the direct expenses/revenues associated with the van purchase. He was able to summarize them as follows:

Direct Expenses
- original cost $12,231 w/3 yr. S. L. depreciation schedule
- direct expenses: $3,737 (depreciation)
  $971 (mostly fuel)
- van financing: $62.50/month loan package

EXHIBIT 9 CHOCOLATE EMPORIUM, INC.: SALES BY PRODUCT LINE

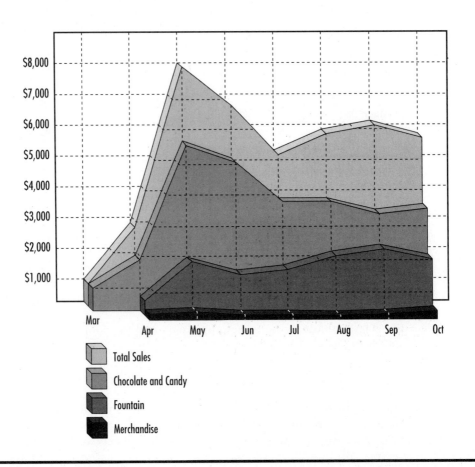

EXHIBIT 10 CHOCOLATE EMPORIUM, INC.: PERCENTAGE GROSS SALES BY PRODUCT LINE

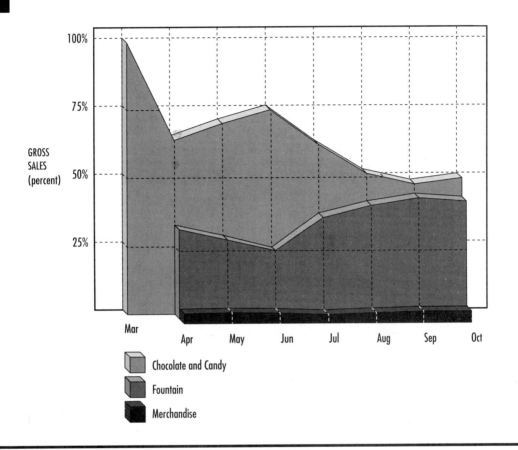

Direct Revenues

- $15-20/month on the average
- $150-170 for Easter

The ice cream and chocolates were stored in the walk-in freezer. When reviewing inventory control procedures, Paul noted that orders were based on a stock tally sheet placed on the freezer. Whoever took a container of ice cream or a quantity of chocolate from the freezer made a notation on the sheet.[1] Paul could not help but notice that Jon had a large volume of ice cream in stock. In fact,, he discovered later that Jon had three weeks' stock on hand. When discussing ice cream inventory with a nearby competitor, Paul learned that the competitor never kept more than a one-week stock of ice cream on hand at any one time. The competition said the inventory level might vary slightly during the summer months. Paul discussed inventory with Jon and discovered that Jon had over 53 suppliers (see Exhibit 11 for summary of the six most active). Further probing by Paul revealed that over one-half of the cost of goods was to regional suppliers (see Exhibit 11).

PERSONNEL

Jon was the only full-time employee at Chocolate Emporium. His only hiring requirement was that each employee must work more than 10 hours/week. When working, the employees could help themselves to whatever they wanted in the store. Jon had no formal training program for new employees. His turnover was very low, and, in fact, only one person had quit in 10 months of operation. All of Jon's help were students who received minimum wage with the exception of his assistant manager who received $3.65/hour. As Jon put it,

EXHIBIT 11   CHOCOLATE EMPORIUM, INC.: MAJOR SUPPLIES

DISTANCE FROM CHOCOLATE EMPORIUM	COMMENTS	% OF PURCHASES 2/81–10/81
(80 miles)	1. Prices — bulk chocolate candies for fudge: 100–200 lb. order has 8% freight charge 200–500 lb. order has 5% freight charge over 500 lb. order is freight free	(direct) 22%
(35 miles)	2. Bittermens — hard candy and misc. pre-wrapped candies: all freight UPS	(wholesaler) 9%
(150 miles)	3. Blum's of San Francisco (order came from distribution center) — cocoa and specialty chocolates: less than 50 lb. order delivered by UPS; greater than 50 lb. order by truck	(direct) 1%
(25 miles)	4. Meadow Gold — ice cream and other dairy products: all freight delivered by truck	(direct) 28%
(35 miles)	5. Regal Distributor — sundae toppings: all freight UPS	(direct) 1.5%
	6. A.B. Colver — carbonated beverages and paper products: no delivery charge	(direct) 1.5%
	TOTAL	63%

EXHIBIT 12   CHOCOLATE EMPORIUM, INC.: MANNING SCHEDULE

Time	Monday	Tuesday	Wednesday	Thursday	Friday	Saturday	Sunday
a.m.							
9:30	—	1	1	1	1	1	
10:00	—	1	1	1	1	1	
11:00	1	2	1	1	1	2	
p.m.							
12:00	1	2	1	1	1	2	1
1:00	2	2	1	1	1	2	2
2:00	2	2	2	2	2	2	2
3:00	2	2	2	2	2	2	2
4:00	2	2	2	2	2	2	2
5:00	2	2	2	2	2	2	2
6:00	2	2	2	2	2	2	2
7:00	2	2	2	2	3	3	2
8:00	2	2	2	2	3	3	2
9:00	2	2	2	2	3	3	2
10:00	2	2	2	2	3	3	2
	1	1		1			1

Note: Mall is open 10:00 a.m. to 8:30 p.m. Figures include assistant manager but not Jon.

"I don't like to underpay people, I found out that (a nearby ice cream competitor) pays as little as $2.00 an hour!" The store was manned by at least two people during most hours of operation (see Exhibit 12). In addition, Jon helped out if customer traffic was heavy.

ENDNOTES

1. Inventory break-down:

   a. Ice Cream $1,538
   b. Chocolate/Candy $4,525
   c. Soda Products $ 169
   d. Merchandise $ 150
   e. Packing Materials $ 901

C A S E 5

PIZZA DELIGHTS

JAY HORNE, CHRISTINE
PERKINS, KIM GOATES,
PETER ASP, KEN SARRIS,
JOHN LESLIE, AND
JAMES J. CHRISMAN

On the night of April 5, 1986, Earnest Outbanks, manager of the St. George Street Pizza Delights, located in a suburb of Spartanburg, South Carolina, hung up the phone after a two-hour conversation with Leonard Lloyd, owner of three Pizza Delights franchise restaurants in Greer, South Carolina. Outbanks glanced at the clock and noticed that it was almost 11 P.M. There was still a lot of work to be done before closing, and the conversation with Lloyd had put him behind schedule. Although Outbanks tried to concentrate on the job at hand his thoughts kept returning to Lloyd's proposal to purchase the franchise in partnership with him from the Pizza Delights Corporation.

Since assuming control of the company-owned restaurant on St. George Street in 1981, Outbanks had managed to change a sluggish, break-even operation into the second most profitable Pizza Delights in the Greater Spartanburg area (see Exhibit 1 for a map of the area and Exhibit 2 for 1983–1985 income statements). Outbanks' success attracted the attention of Leonard Lloyd, who was interested in acquiring a Pizza Delights franchise in the Spartanburg market. In early 1986, Lloyd contacted Outbanks to discuss the possibility of forming a partnership to purchase the restaurant. Although the two men met on several occasions nothing had yet been resolved. Outbanks had dreamed of owning his own franchise for several years and Lloyd's idea sounded quite attractive. Outbanks was reluctant to give an immediate answer, though. His career with Pizza Delights had been quite successful and he believed that his future with the firm was bright. However, he knew that Lloyd was impatient and that a decision had to be made in the near future.

The remainder of this case describes the history of Pizza Delights, the competitive environment and operations of the St. George Street restaurant, and Leonard Lloyd's business activities and franchise proposal.

Source: **Prepared under the direction of Professor James J. Chrisman, University of South Carolina. The case was prepared for classroom discussion and not to illustrate either effective or ineffective handling of administrative situations. Names and places have been disguised at the request of case subjects. Distributed by the North American Case Research Association.** © **James J. Chrisman, 1989.**

EXHIBIT 1 AREA MAP

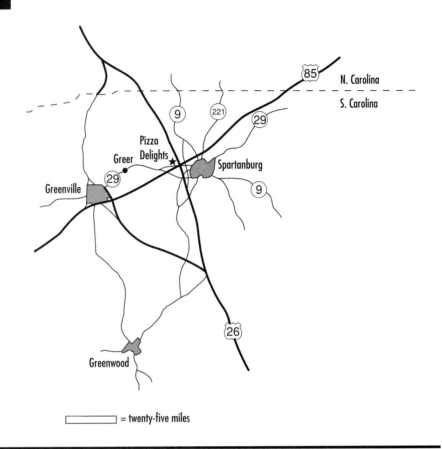

= twenty-five miles

PIZZA DELIGHTS, INC.: COMPANY BACKGROUND AND STRUCTURE

The Pizza Delights chain was established in the greater Omaha, Nebraska, area in the late 1960s. Pizza Delights was one of the first chains to offer customers a limited range of strictly Italian dishes such as pizza and spaghetti. The restaurants enjoyed immediate success because they offered the public a quality pizza with a high level of personal service.

Pizza Delights' early successes caught the attention of a large food manufacturing corporation which, in the late 1970s, purchased the company as well as the rights to their exclusive recipes. With the corporation's financial backing, Pizza Delights restaurants began to appear all over the U.S. Through-

INCOME STATEMENTS

	1985	1984	1983
GROSS FOOD SALES	557,278	478,603	422,375
Less allowances	7,869	7,547	7,038
Less sales promotions	34,394	32,982	31,651
NET FOOD SALES	515,015	438,074	383,686
Plus vending machines	1,734	2,103	1,923
Plus game machine	1,582	1,661	1,843
TOTAL REVENUE	518,331	441,838	387,452
COST OF GOODS SOLD	144,406	133,225	117,486
GROSS PROFIT	373,925	308,613	269,966
OPERATING COSTS			
Management Salary	54,373		
Crew labor	56,445	111,391	108,476
Other labor	12,979		
National advertising	7,544		5,637
Coop advertising	12,652	22,880	7,629
Local advertising	9,001		8,538
Operating expenses	12,795		13,330
Utilities cost	19,531		16,343
Maintenance	9,749	40,464	9,019
Uniforms	349		1,113
Other	2,474		2,110
Premiums	5	1,110	210
OPERATING PROFIT	176,028	132,778	97,981
Plus TJTC Credit	4,435	0	0
Less Fixed Costs	47,467*	33,985*	35,647
TOTAL PROFIT	132,996	98,793	62,334

*See Fixed Cost Schedule below.

FIXED COST SCHEDULE FOR 1984–1985 INCOME STATEMENTS

	1985	1984
FIXED COSTS	$47,466	$33,985
T.J.T.C. Expense	161	54
Bank charges	570	615
Personal property tax	221	254
Real estate taxes	3,939	3,939
Licenses & fees	269	289
Equipment depreciation	10,149	7,774
Leasehold amortization	2,618	2,768
Building rental	17,417	15,813
Contigent lease rent	8,442	502
Insurance	2,441	1,909
Abandonment & property	1,236	65
Goodwill amortization	3	0

out this period of rapid expansion, the high degree of quality and service that was Pizza Delights' trademark was maintained.

In the 1980s Pizza Delights introduced several new products including the small pan pizza (1983), the double decker pizza (1984), and the Italian turnover pizza (1985). All of these products met with considerable success in the market-place.

By 1986 the chain had grown to nearly 1,500 restaurants. Management planned to open 100–200 new restaurants per year over the next decade. Six regional offices, located in major population centers across the United States, had been added since the 1970s in order to accommodate this growth. These regions were subdivided into areas, which were further subdivided into districts (see Exhibit 3). Each region, area, and district had a full-time staff of managers, accountants, inspectors, and other personnel to insure that each individual restaurant fulfilled its duties to the corporation.

HISTORY OF THE ST. GEORGE STREET RESTAURANT

The St. George Street Pizza Delights was built in 1974 primarily to serve customers in the Greater Spartanburg area. It also served commuters and vacationers traveling on Interstate 26 and Interstate 85. In its first few years the restaurant had shown low to moderate profits. The population growth of the Greater Spartanburg area led to increased sales and profits for the restaurant. The growth in population, however, also led to increased competition in the St. George Street restaurant's trade area. By 1981, when Outbanks became manager, the restaurant's net profits before taxes had dipped to $42,680, their lowest level since 1975.

Outbanks inherited a restaurant crew that had been described by the dis-

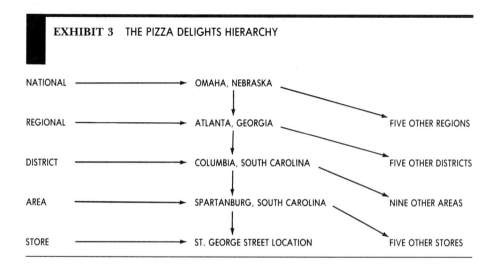

EXHIBIT 3   THE PIZZA DELIGHTS HIERARCHY

trict manager as probably the "most lazy and inhospitable bunch he had ever met." In addition, food costs at the restaurant had been astronomical. Cooks were not preparing the pizzas according to Pizza Delights standards. None of the ingredients were weighed, and Outbanks also suspected that employees were taking pizzas home and giving them away to their friends.

By 1986 most of the obvious problems had been solved and the restaurant's profits had risen steadily under Outbanks' stewardship. His emphasis had been on new policies to improve the efficiency of operations. Although only 20 years old in 1981, Outbanks felt his extensive experience in the pizza business had helped him handle the restaurant's problems. In addition, he had been able to deal effectively with high school and college age employees. Most of the 1986 staff were replacements whom Outbanks had personally selected and trained.

THE GREATER SPARTANBURG ENVIRONMENT

Located in northern South Carolina, Spartanburg was a city of approximately 45,000 people. Situated in an agricultural region that produced cotton, peaches, melons, and feed crops, the city was the seat of Spartanburg County and was part of the tri-county region (Spartanburg, Greenville, and Pickens counties) that made up the Greenville-Spartanburg SMA (Standard Metropolitan Area). A variety of manufacturing businesses in industries such as textiles, metals, rubber, paper, chemicals, clothing, and plumbing supplies were located in the Spartanburg area. The city was also the site for several colleges and universities (see Exhibit 4).

The population of the city of Spartanburg declined by 6.2 percent between 1978 and 1984 (see Exhibit 5). During the same time period the populations of the surrounding county and SMA increased by 8.5 percent and 11.7 percent, respectively. At the same time, the population of the United States grew 8.4 percent.

EXHIBIT 4   COLLEGES & UNIVERSITIES IN SPARTANBURG COUNTY: ENROLLMENTS

INSTITUTION	ENROLLMENT
University of South Carolina — Spartanburg	2,778
Spartanburg Technical College	1,813
Converse College	1,078
Spartanburg Methodist College	1,067
Wofford College	1,034
Rutledge College — Spartanburg	447
TOTAL ENROLLMENT	8,217

Source: South Carolina Statistical Abstract — 1984.

EXHIBIT 5 1978 & 1984 POPULATION STATISTICS FOR SPARTANBURG, SPARTANBURG COUNTY, GREENVILLE-SPARTANBURG SMA, SOUTH CAROLINA, SOUTH ATLANTIC REGION, AND UNITED STATES

Year	Total Population (thousands)	% of U.S.	Total Households (thousands)	% of U.S.	Median Age	% OF POPULATION BY AGE GROUP				
						0–17	18–24	25–34	35–49	≥ 50
SPARTANBURG										
1978	46.9	.02%	16.7	.02%	31.2	26.8%	14.2%	14.6%	16.3%	28.1%
1984	44.9	.02%	17.4	.02%	32.2	24.5%	13.3%	17.0%	16.0%	29.2%
% Change	−6.2%		+4.2%							
SPARTANBURG COUNTY										
1978	196.7	.09%	67.8	.09%	30.6	28.0%	12.6%	16.7%	17.2%	25.5%
1984	213.5	.09%	78.3	.09%	32.1	26.6%	11.1%	17.2%	19.6%	25.5%
% Change	+8.5%		+15.5%							
GREENVILLE-SPARTANBURG SMA										
1978	541.4	.25%	184.5	.24%	29.8	27.9%	13.9%	17.1%	17.1%	24.0%
1984	605.0	.25%	222.1	.26%	31.3	26.2%	12.6%	17.8%	19.5%	23.9%
% Change	+11.7%		+20.4%							
SOUTH CAROLINA										
1978	2,934.8	1.3%	933.8	1.2%	27.7	31.2%	14.5%	15.9%	16.0%	22.5%
1984	3,353.4	1.4%	1,172.0	1.4%	29.8	28.2%	13.3%	17.6%	18.1%	22.7%
% Change	+14.3%		+25.5%							
SOUTH ATLANTIC REGION*										
1978	34,981.7	15.9%	12,186.8	15.9%	30.3	28.2%	13.4%	15.7%	16.3%	26.4%
1984	39,904.5	16.8%	14,612.2	16.8%	32.3	25.4%	12.1%	17.2%	18.5%	26.8%
% Change	+14.1%		+19.9%							
UNITED STATES										
1978	219,768.5	100%	76,904.7	100%	30.1	28.8%	13.2%	15.7%	16.4%	26.0%
1984	238,274.7	100%	86,926.6	100%	31.7	26.3%	12.2%	17.4%	18.3%	25.9%
% Change	+8.4%		+13.0%							

* Includes: Delaware, District of Columbia, Florida, Georgia, Maryland, North Carolina, South Carolina, Virginia, and West Virginia.
Source: "Survey of Buying Power," *Sales & Marketing Management,* 1979 and 1985.

Between 1978 and 1984 per capita incomes increased by about 40 percent in the city of Spartanburg and by more than 50 percent in both Spartanburg county and the Greenville-Spartanburg SMA. By contrast, per capita incomes rose over 60 percent in South Carolina, the South Atlantic region, and the United States during the same period. In 1984, effective per capita buying incomes in the Spartanburg area were approximately $9,000 compared to about $8,500 for the rest of South Carolina (see Exhibit 6).

Sales of eating and drinking places in the city had increased by 5 percent since 1978 (see Exhibit 7). There appeared to be greater opportunities for

EXHIBIT 6 EFFECTIVE BUYING INCOMES IN 1978 & 1984: SPARTANBURG, SPARTANBURG COUNTY GREENVILLE-SPARTANBURG SMA, SOUTH CAROLINA, SOUTH ATLANTIC REGION, AND UNITED STATES

	TOTAL EBI (IN THOUSANDS)	PER CAPITA EBI	AVERAGE HOUSEHOLD EBI	MEDIAN HOUSEHOLD EBI
SPARTANBURG				
1978	$308,625	$ 6,580	$18,481	$14,721
1984	$410,214	$ 9,136	$23,576	$18,782
% Change	+32.9%	+38.8%	+27.6%	+27.6
SPARTANBURG COUNTY				
1978	$1,127,798	$ 5,734	$16,634	$14,702
1984	$1,943,381	$ 9,102	$24,820	$21,828
% Change	+72.3%	+58.7%	+49.2%	+48.5%
GREENVILLE-SPARTANBURG SMA				
1978	$3,203,011	$ 5,916	$17,360	$15,349
1984	$5,434,481	$8,983	$24,469	$21,540
% Change	+69.7%	+51.8%	+41.0%	+40.3%
SOUTH CAROLINA				
1978	$15,425,876	$ 5,256	$16,519	$14,047
1984	$28,550,182	$ 8,514	$24,360	$20,969
% Change	+85.1%	+62.0%	+47.5%	+49.3%
SOUTH ATLANTIC REGION				
1978	$212,961,331	$ 6,088	$17,475	$14,681
1984	$408,218,168	$10,230	$27,937	$23,576
% Change	+91.7%	+68.0%	+59.9%	+60.6%
UNITED STATES				
1978	$1,439,815,449	$6,552	$18,722	$16,231
1984	$2,576,533,480	$10,813	$29,640	$25,496
% Change	+78.9%	+65.0%	+58.3%	+57.1%

Source: "Survey of Buying Power," *Sales & Marketing Management,* 1979 and 1985.

growth outside the city, as the migration to the suburbs provided increased demand for restaurants in these locations. Between 1978 and 1984 sales for eating and drinking establishments increased by 35 percent in Spartanburg county and by 47 percent in the Greenville-Spartanburg SMA.

COMPETITION IN THE SPARTANBURG AREA

The pizza industry had rapidly expanded in the 1980s. In 1986, the St. George Street restaurant competed with seventeen local and nationally owned pizza restaurants in the Greater Spartanburg area, several other Pizza Delights restaurants, and 170 restaurants of other types. Exhibits 8–10 provide common-

EXHIBIT 7 TOTAL RETAIL AND EATING AND DRINKING PLACES SALES IN 1978 & 1984: SPARTANBURG, SPARTANBURG COUNTY, GREENVILLE-SPARTANBURG SMA, SOUTH CAROLINA, SOUTH ATLANTIC REGION, AND UNITED STATES

	Total Retail Sales	Sales per Capita	EATING & DRINKING PLACES		
			Total Sales	Sales per Capita	% of Total Retail
SPARTANBURG					
1978	$417,207	$ 8,896*	$41,507	$885*	9.9%
1984	$526,485	$11,725*	$43,625	$972*	8.3%
% Change	+26.2%	+31.8%	+5.1%	+9.8%	
SPARTANBURG COUNTY					
1978	$ 635,084	$3,229	$58,911	$299	9.3%
1984	$1,015,451	$4,756	$79,688	$373	7.8%
% Change	+59.9%	+47.3%	+35.3%	+24.7%	
GREENVILLE-SPARTANBURG SMA					
1978	$1,911,506	$3,531	$175,057	$323	9.2%
1984	$3,117,321	$5,153	$257,667	$426	8.3%
% Change	+63.1%	+45.9%	+47.2%	+31.9%	
SOUTH CAROLINA					
1978	$ 9,243,104	$3,149	$ 670,142	$228	7.3%
1984	$15,484,516	$4,618	$1,343,043	$401	8.7%
% Change	+67.5%	+46.6%	+100.4%	+75.9%	
SOUTH ATLANTIC REGION					
1978	$129,343,686	$3,697	$11,434,037	$327	8.8%
1984	$220,144,917	$5,517	$19,950,436	$500	9.1%
% Change	+70.2%	+49.2%	+74.5%	+52.9%	
UNITED STATES					
1978	$ 817,461,457	$3,720	$ 71,602,628	$326	8.8%
1984	$1,296,659,715	$5,442	$124,035,013	$564	9.6%
% Change	+58.6%	+46.3%	+73.2%	+73.0%	

*Retail sales per capita for the city are higher than for the county, SMA, state, region, and nation due to the large number of non-city resident sales.

Source: "Survey of Buying Power," *Sales & Marketing Management,* 1979 and 1985.

size income statements, balance sheets, and financial ratios, respectively, for traditional and fast food restaurants with assets of less than $1 million in 1985. Exhibit 11 shows the locations of competitors in the St. George Street area. Exhibit 12 summarizes the product, service, and pricing strategies of Pizza Delights and its major competitors.

Domino's. Domino's, Inc. was the leading competitor for delivered pizza. The company's strategy was to offer its customers fast delivery (usually less than

EXHIBIT 8 AVERAGE COMMON-SIZE INCOME STATEMENTS FOR TRADITIONAL & FAST FOOD RESTAURANTS IN THE U.S. WITH ASSETS OF LESS THAN $1 MILLION IN 1985

	TRADITIONAL* (N = 481)	FAST FOODS** (N = 301)
Sales	100.0%	100.0%
Cost of Goods Sold	43.8%	39.3%
Gross Profit	56.2%	60.7%
Operating Expenses	52.6%	55.0%
Other Expenses	1.6%	2.7%
Net Profit Before Taxes	2.1%	3.0%

*Includes restaurants selling prepared foods and drinks for consumption on the premises. Caterers and industrial and institutional food service establishments are also included (SIC 5812).

**Includes franchise operations (SIC 5812).

Source: Robert Morris Associates, *'86 Annual Statement Studies.*

EXHIBIT 9 AVERAGE COMMON-SIZE BALANCE SHEETS FOR TRADITIONAL & FAST FOOD RESTARANTS IN THE U.S. WITH ASSETS OF LESS THAN $1 MILLION IN 1985

	TRADITIONAL* (N = 481)	FAST FOODS** (N = 301)
ASSETS		
Cash & Equivalents	12.1%	14.9%
Trade Receivables (Net)	4.3%	1.9%
Inventory	7.6%	4.8%
All Other Current Assets	2.6%	2.6%
Total Current Assets	26.6%	24.2%
Fixed Assets (Net)	56.3%	53.0%
Intangibles (Net)	4.5%	6.2%
All Other Non-Current Assets	12.6%	16.6%
Total Assets	100.0%	100.0%
LIABILITIES & OWNERS' EQUITY		
Current Liabilities	40.0%	38.6%
Long-Term Debt	32.8%	35.6%
All Other Non-Current Liabilities	2.9%	2.1%
Total Liabilities	75.7%	76.3%
Owners' Equity (Net Worth)	24.3%	23.7%
Total Liabilities + Owners' Equity	100.0%	100.0%

*Includes restaurants selling prepared foods and drinks for consumption on the premises. Caterers and industrial and institutional food service establishments are also included (SIC 5812).

**Includes franchise operations (SIC 5812).

Source: Robert Morris Associates, *'86 Annual Statement Studies.*

EXHIBIT 10   FINANCIAL RATIOS FOR TRADITIONAL & FAST FOOD RESTAURANTS IN THE U.S. WITH ASSETS OF LESS THAN $1 MILLION IN 1985

Ratios	TRADITIONAL RESTAURANTS*			FAST FOOD RESTAURANTS**		
	Upper Quartile	Median	Lower Quartile	Upper Quartile	Median	Lower Quartile
Current	1.3	0.7	0.3	1.2	0.6	0.3
Quick	0.8	0.4	0.2	0.9	0.4	0.1
Sales/Receivables	INF	451.0	74.9	INF	INF	507.1
Cost of Sales/Inventory	46.1	27.4	16.1	59.6	42.7	28.2
Sales/Working Capital	51.0	−38.5	−12.1	56.2	−31.4	−11.8
Times Interest Earned	4.9	2.0	0.4	5.9	2.5	1.0
Cash Flow/Current Portion of LT Debt	4.5	1.6	0.7	5.4	2.4	1.2
Debt/Equity Ratio	1.0	3.2	−26.2	1.2	3.8	−14.5
Asset Turnover	5.2	3.5	2.2	5.1	3.3	2.4
Return on Equity (%)	62.1%	23.1%	4.6%	81.6%	36.7%	15.9%
Return on Assets (%)	17.1%	5.3%	−3.1%	20.0%	9.6%	1.0%

INF = Infinite.

*Includes restaurants selling prepared foods and drinks for consumption on the premises. Caterers and industrial and institutional food service establishments are also included (SIC 5812). 481 establishments were studied.

**Includes franchise operations (SIC 5812). 301 establishments were studied.

Source: Robert Morris Associates, '86 Annual Statment Studies.

30 minutes) and medium priced pizza. Domino's sold only pizza; the firm did not include other Italian dishes on its menu. Domino's pizza was considered low to medium quality.

Little Caesar's.   Little Caesar's was a chain restaurant which catered to the take-out customer; it did not make deliveries or provide facilities for eat-in dining. Its pizza was considered average quality and was priced accordingly. The chain also offered special Greek and Italian salads, sandwiches, and sliced pizza. Little Caesar's frequently placed two-for-one coupons in local newspapers.

Pizza Factory.   Located in the nearby Stephenson Plaza, this national chain restaurant provided take out services as well as eat-in dining facilities. Customer service was low, however, as the restaurant did not employ waitresses. Pizza Factory offered low priced, medium quality pizza, a variety of sandwiches, a salad bar, and alcoholic beverages.

EXHIBIT 11 LOCATIONS OF THE ST. GEORGE STREET PIZZA DELIGHTS AND ITS COMPETITORS

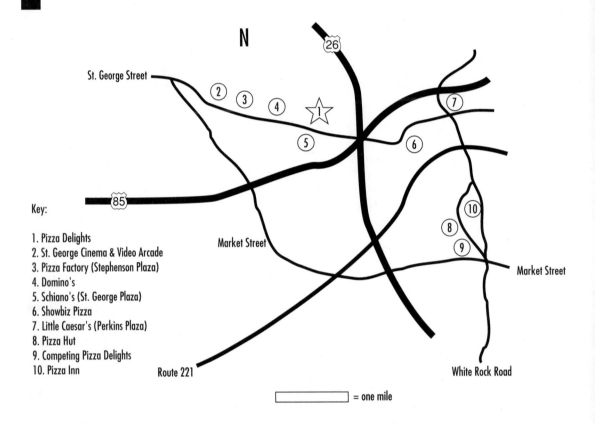

Key:

1. Pizza Delights
2. St. George Cinema & Video Arcade
3. Pizza Factory (Stephenson Plaza)
4. Domino's
5. Schiano's (St. George Plaza)
6. Showbiz Pizza
7. Little Caesar's (Perkins Plaza)
8. Pizza Hut
9. Competing Pizza Delights
10. Pizza Inn

= one mile

Showbiz Pizza.   Showbiz Pizza was a national chain restaurant catering to children. Its dining room decor included dancing bears, games, and other attractions. Showbiz offered a medium quality pizza at a medium to high price.

Pizza Hut.   Pizza Hut was Pizza Delights' largest competitor. Pizza Hut was a full-service pizza restaurant, offering high levels of service and a quality product at a medium to high price. In the 1980s the company successfully introduced several new pizza products, each of which it advertised heavily.

Pizza Hut's White Rock Road location was only a few miles to the east of the St. George Pizza Delights. This Pizza Hut was more successful than the other Pizza Delights restaurant located nearby. Because of the growing population in the area, the Pizza Hut Corporation had considered building a new restaurant on St. George Street. These plans had concerned Outbanks because 30–35% of his customers were from the immediate area. After conducting a

EXHIBIT 12 COMPARISONS OF PRODUCT, SERVICE AND PRICING STRATEGIES OF PIZZA COMPETITORS

	PIZZA DELIGHTS	DOMINO'S	LITTLE CAESAR'S	PIZZA FACTORY	SHOWBIZ	PIZZA HUT	PIZZA INN	SCHIANO'S
Services								
Eat-In	yes	no	no	yes	yes	yes	yes	yes
Take-Out	yes	yes	yes	yes	no	yes	yes	yes
Delivery	no	yes	no	no	no	no	yes	no
Buffet	no	no	no	no	no	no	yes	no
Luncheon Menu	yes	no	no	yes	yes	yes	yes	no
Salad Bar	yes	no	no	yes	no	yes	yes	no
Service Level	high	high (delivery only)	low	low	high	high	high	high
Products (Dinner only)								
Quality	med/high	low/med	medium	medium	medium	med/high	low/med	high
# of Pizzas on Menu	6	2	6	6	5	10	12	6
Types of Pizzas	2	1	1	1	1	3	2	2
Sizes	3	2	3	3	3	3	4	3
Slices	no	no	yes	no	no	no	no	no
Meat/Fish Toppings	6	4	6	9	4	7	6	5
Vegetable Toppings	6	7	7	10	6	8	7	6
Italian Dishes	spaghetti	no	no	no	no	spaghetti, cavatini	spaghetti, lasagna	parmigiana, calzone, lasagna
Sandwiches (# × sizes)	4	0	3 × 2 / 3 × 3	4	5	3 × 2	4	6 × 2
Salads (exc. Bar)	no	no	no	no	1	no	1	2
Alcoholic Beverages	beer	no	no	beer	beer	beer	beer, wine	beer, wine
Other Beverages	soft drinks, tea, milk, coffee	coke	soft drinks	soft drinks, tea	soft drinks, tea, milk, coffee	soft drinks, tea, milk, coffee	soft drinks, tea, milk, coffee	soft drinks

(continued)

EXHIBIT 12 (continued)

	PIZZA DELIGHTS	DOMINO'S	LITTLE CAESAR'S	PIZZA FACTORY	SHOWBIZ	PIZZA HUT	PIZZA INN	SCHIANO'S
Prices								
Med. Cheese Pizza	$ 7.45	$ 6.02	$ 6.78	$ 6.70	$ 8.09	$7.05–7.25	$5.80–7.80	$4.95–6.45
Med. 5–7 Toppings (#)	$10.00 (6)	—	$10.29 (5)	$ 9.55 (6)	$10.99 (6)	$ 9.80 (6)	$9.35–9.75 (7)	$9.20–10.70 (6)
Med. 8–11 Toppings (#)	$10.80 (9)	$11.12 (9)	—	$11.25 (11)	—	$10.60 (9)	$10.20–10.70 (9)	$10.20–11.70 (8)
Lg. Cheese Pizza	$ 9.85	$ 8.17	$ 9.28	$ 8.00	$ 9.99	$9.45–9.65	$9.00–9.50	$7.20–8.70
Lg. 5–7 Toppings (#)	$12.70 (6)	—	$13.52 (5)	$10.95 (6)	$12.99 (6)	$12.50 (6)	$11.85–12.35 (7)	$12.20–13.70 (6)
Lg. 8–11 Toppings (#)	$13.55 (9)	$15.42 (9)	—	$13.25 (11)	—	$13.35 (9)	$12.80–13.40 (9)	$13.20–14.70 (8)
Toppings — Med./Lg.	$.85/.95	$1.02/1.45	$.77/.96	$.85/.95	$.90/1.00	$.90/1.00	$.85/.95	$.85/1.00
Italian Dishes	$1.99–3.39	—	—	—	$1.39–2.59	$2.09–4.49	$1.89–3.89	$3.29–6.95
Sandwiches	$ 2.89	—	$2.25–2.69	$ 2.49	$ 2.29	$2.79–3.79	$0.79–2.59	$2.15–4.55
Salads	$ 2.49	—	$1.20–4.69	$ 2.59	$ .99	$ 2.79	$ 1.99	$1.79–3.49
Alcohol (Glass)	$ .95	—	—	$ .75		$ 1.00	$ 1.00	$.95–1.60
Other Beverages	$.50–$.75	$0.65	$.48–$.87	$.55–$.75	$.50–$.79	$.50–$.80	$.45–$.80	$.65

market survey Pizza Hut decided against building the new restaurant in 1986. The project, however, was still under consideration for the future.

Pizza Inn.   Besides Pizza Hut, Pizza Inn was Pizza Delights' most formidable competitor. Pizza Inn offered a variety of services including eat-in dining, take-outs, home delivery (started in early 1986), a salad bar, a luncheon buffet during the weekdays, and a dinner buffet every Tuesday. Its pizza was low to medium quality and was priced accordingly.

Schiano's.   Schiano's was part of a chain which offered high quality, high priced "New York" style pizza and extensive service. This restaurant was still under construction but was scheduled to open in late 1986. The site was located directly across the street from Outbanks' restaurant in the new St. George Street Plaza.

Grocery Stores.   The grocery stores in the area stocked a diverse line of pizzas and pizza products including microwave pizzas, store-made pizzas, and national brands of frozen pizzas. For the do-it-yourself customers, grocers also offered pre-packaged pizza ingredients such as instant pizza crust, sauces, grated pizza cheese, and sliced pepperoni. These products were generally of lower quality than the pizzas served in restaurants. Prices for store-bought and do-it-yourself pizzas generally ranged from $.79 to $4.00.

DELIVERY

In the 1980s several pizza delivery stores, such as Domino's, were opened in the Greater Spartanburg area. To penetrate this segment of the market, Pizza Delights had opened a delivery store in August 1984 in the northeastern section of Spartanburg. This store produced pizzas for delivery only to households within a ten-mile radius of the store. This delivery area included about 70 percent of Greater Spartanburg but excluded most of the area served by the St. George Street restaurant.

In order to save transportation and delivery costs, the delivery store held orders until a large number of pizzas could be delivered to one area. As a result, delivery times sometimes exceeded one hour, and pizzas were frequently delivered cold. According to market research, approximately 75 percent of the customers surveyed were dissatisfied with the Pizza Delights delivery service.

THE ST. GEORGE STREET RESTAURANT

Although pizza was the primary product, the St. George Street restaurant also offered other items such as sandwiches, spaghetti, and a salad bar. Menu items and prices at the St. George Street restaurant are listed in Exhibit 13.

EXHIBIT 13   THE ST. GEORGE STREET LOCATION: MENU ITEMS & PRICES

	SMALL	MEDIUM	LARGE*
Pizza			
Double Decker (3 varieties)	$8.00	$10.80	$13.55
Pan Pizzas:			
—Cheese	$5.05	$ 7.45	$ 9.85
—Delight (6 toppings)	$7.30	$10.00	$12.70
—Super Delight (9 toppings)	$8.00	$10.80	$13.55
Additional toppings	$ .75	$ .85	$ .95

(Pepperoni, Ham, Pork, Beef, Italian Sausage, Mushroom, Onion, Green Pepper, Black Olive, Jalapeno Pepper, Anchovy, Extra Cheese)

	SMALL	REGULAR
Spaghetti		
w/ Meat sauce	$1.99	$3.19
w/ Meatballs	$2.39	$3.39
Salad bar		
as a meal	$2.49	
with a meal	$1.99	
children under 12	$ .99	
Sandwiches (4 varieties)	$2.89	

Drinks	Soft Drinks:				
	Pitcher $2.25	Coffee	$.50	Beer: Glass	$ .95
	Large $ .75	Milk	$.55	Pitcher	$3.95
	Medium $ .70	Ice Tea	$.65		
	Small $ .65				

LUNCHEON SPECIALS: MONDAY–FRIDAY

	ONLY	W/SALAD BAR (ONE TRIP)
Italian Turnover**		
Cheese	$2.49	$3.88
Sausage	$2.49	$3.88
Small Pan Pizza		
Pepperoni	$1.79	$3.18
Supreme		$3.58
(6 toppings)	$2.19	

*Small pizzas served 1–2 persons; medium 3–4 persons; large 5–6 persons.

**Guaranteed to be ready in 10 minutes or the lunch is free.

Exhibit 14 provides a per-item breakdown of food and beverage sales and costs for 1984–1985.

According to Outbanks, the restaurant did not have a specific target market; all types of people frequented the restaurant. The store was convenient to area residents, shoppers of the two nearby plazas, commuters, and theater-goers. Almost 50% of the St. George Street restaurant's customers drove between three and five miles to the restaurant. Market research sponsored by the corporation indicated that regular customers composed 58% of the cus-

EXHIBIT 14   THE ST. GEORGE STREET LOCATION: GROSS PROFIT BY PRODUCT LINE

	1985	1984
Pizza		
Eat-in Pizza	$204,886	$168,174
Carry-Out Pizza	215,806	181,774
Net Pizza	$420,692	$349,948
Plus: Pizza Allowances	5,772	4,806
Coupon Sales	31,213	30,241
Total Prom/Adv Sales	36,985	35,047
Gross Pizza Sales	$457,677	$384,995
Cost of Pizza Dough	20,530	17,793
Cost of Toppings	38,066	30,666
Cost of Cheese	47,944	41,698
Cost of Paper-Pizza	6,580	5,663
Freight	99	1,157
Total Pizza Cost	$113,219	$ 96,977
GROSS PROFIT ON PIZZA	$344,458	$288,018
Beer: Sales	$ 13,747	$ 13,236
Costs	4,453	4,004
GROSS PROFIT ON BEER	$ 9,294	$ 9,232
Drinks: Sales	$ 39,599	$ 33,200
Costs	8,162	6,584
GROSS PROFIT ON SOFT DRINKS	$ 31,437	$ 26,616
Other: Salad Sales	26,295	27,012
Pasta Sales	9,069	9,873
Sandwich Sales	5,615	4,805
Other Prom/Adv. Reven.	5,278	5,482
Total Other Sales	$ 46,257	$ 47,172
Cost of Other Sales	18,572	20,649
GROSS PROFIT ON OTHER SALES	$ 27,685	$ 26,523

tomer base and that they ate at the restaurant once a month on average. Quality and service were the two most frequently cited reasons why customers visited the St. George Street location.

SALES PATTERNS

Sales at the St. George Street restaurant were seasonal. The winter months of January, February, and March accounted for only 13% of yearly revenues. The months of April through June accounted for 24% of sales while 31% of sales occurred between October and December. The peak season for sales was in the months of July to September with 32% of sales. September was typically the best month for the restaurant (18% of annual sales) because of the weekly football games at the nearby high school. After the games spectators and students often met for a evening snack at Pizza Delights.

Average weekly sales were approximately $10,500. As shown in Exhibit 15 the slowest day of the week was Monday, which accounted for only about 8.5% of sales. Friday was the busiest day, accounting for 23.4% of weekly revenues.

Lunch sales were always low. The best day for lunchtime sales was Friday, but even on this day lunch sales averaged only 3.3% of weekly revenues. The slowest day for lunch was Tuesday, which accounted for only 1.8% of weekly sales. The Pizza Delights Corporation had introduced the Italian turnover pizza as a strictly lunchtime item to boost lunch sales at its restaurants. Lunch sales had not increased at the St. George Street location, however; sales had simply shifted from the small pan pizzas to the Italian turnovers.

ADVERTISING AND SALES PROMOTION

The St. George Street restaurant spent over $29,000 on national, co-op, and local advertising in 1985 (see Exhibit 2). All national and co-op advertising for

EXHIBIT 15   DAILY SALES BREAKDOWNS

	LUNCH		DINNER	
	$	%	$	%
Monday	198	1.9	692	6.6
Tuesday	186	1.8	716	6.8
Wednesday	191	1.8	874	8.3
Thursday	260	2.5	1,390	13.3
Friday	350	3.3	2,105	20.0
Saturday	308	2.9	1,761	16.8
Sunday	205	1.9	1,277	12.1

Average sales per week: $10,513

the Pizza Delights chain restaurants was coordinated by an advertising firm in Washington, D.C., and was financed by the restaurants on a percentage-of-sales basis. This policy applied to both company-owned and franchised restaurants, neither of which had any input into these decisions. A sample announcement of a new promotional campaign for the Italian turnover is provided in Exhibit 16.

National advertising was arranged by the corporation, to familiarize people with the Pizza Delights name and products. It consisted primarily of commercials aired on national television during prime-time and the weekends.

Co-op advertising was done on a district-by-district basis to promote individual restaurants and products. The bulk of the Greater Spartanburg area co-op advertising was done in the peak fall season. The main component of the co-op advertising was a monthly four-color, free-standing insert in the city

 EXHIBIT 16   PROMOTIONAL ANNOUNCEMENT TO SPARTANBURG PIZZA DELIGHTS

HOT NEWS FROM YOUR FRIENDS AT BEAUMONT GREEN ADVERTISING

TO: Pizza Delights Managers & Employees/Spartanburg
DATE: February 26, 1986
SUBJECT: Advertising for the Italian Turnover

Background
Many of you will recall the tremendous success that the introduction of the small pan pizza had on our business in 1983. In 1986, the opportunity to stimulate both trial and frequency at lunch lies mainly in the area of menu expansion. Therefore, the Italian Turnover has been developed. This new product will increase your sales and profits at lunch. You have all shown your operational strength with the Double Decker Pizza introduced in 1984. Let's make the Italian Turnover the success story of 1986!

Television
Starting March 14, 1986 and running through May 1, 1986 three new TV commercials focusing on the Italian Turnover will be run.

Radio Promotions
A radio promotion has been developed and implemented. This promotion is provided free of charge in exchange for Italian Turnovers for giveaways. Details of the promotion are provided below:
WASQ-FM will encourage listeners to be the "X" number caller that spotted the WASQ logo on one of the Italian Turnover outdoor billboards. Winners receive two Italian Turnovers and two medium soft drinks. There are to be three giveaways per day, Monday thru Friday, for a total of 60 giveaways.

Outdoor
There will be outdoor boards strategically placed in the area. The message will be "Turn over a new lunch with the Italian Turnover," which is the main print advertising theme for the introduction of the Italian Turnover. These boards will be posted from March 26, 1986 to May 10, 1986.

newspaper. This ad usually was accompanied by coupons which allowed customers a 15–20% discount off regular prices.

Local ads were paid by the individual restaurants and placed in local papers. Franchise owners had greater discretion than managers of company-
owned restaurants concerning the types and amounts of local promotions
used.

Outbanks had tried a variety of promotional techniques to increase sales.
For example, if a child read five books in one month he or she would receive
a free small pan pizza. During birthday parties at the restaurant participants
were given the opportunity to create their own pizzas in the kitchen. Two
other past promotions were "family night" and "football night." Family night
was a dinner promotion in which a family could buy a large pizza and a
pitcher of soft drinks for $9.95. According to Outbanks this promotion was a
huge success at the St. George Street restaurant but was discontinued by the
corporation because of low response on a national level. On "football night"
small pan pizzas and soft drinks were sold at high school football games for
99 cents. This promotion was also discontinued because the district office felt
that it would ruin Pizza Delights' high quality/high service image. Despite the
district office's concerns, Outbanks noted that the football night promotion
generated additional sales of around $800 per game.

PURCHASING

According to Outbanks, all the supplies used at company-owned restaurants
had to be obtained from the parent company. These items included everything from straws and napkins to pizza dough and pepperoni. If an emergency
situation occurred, such as a shortage of green peppers, the restaurants were
allowed to make purchases from outside suppliers as long as these purchases,
in total, did not exceed one percent of yearly sales for the individual restaurant. However, the practice of outside buying was not encouraged by the corporation.

All purchases at company-owned restaurants in excess of $500 had to be
approved by the area supervisor, the district manager, and the regional vice-
president before the restaurant manager could proceed with the investment.
The lag between requests and approvals sometimes created problems for Outbanks. For example, the new small pan pizzas, double decker pizzas, and Italian turnover pizzas required a great deal of refrigerator space for storage.
According to Outbanks, however, Pizza Delights had not provided his restaurant with the additional freezer capacity needed to store these items.

Franchised restaurants had more flexibility in purchasing than company-
owned restaurants. To insure standardization, items such as printed napkins
and pizza ingredients still had to be purchased from the parent corporation
but other items, such as pizza cutters, could be purchased from outside
sources. Outbanks believed that certain items such as sauce ladies (an $8 item)
could be purchased from outside suppliers at prices that were 10–20% less
than the prices charged by the corporation.

EXHIBIT 17 THE ST. GEORGE STREET LOCATION: RESTAURANT LAYOUT

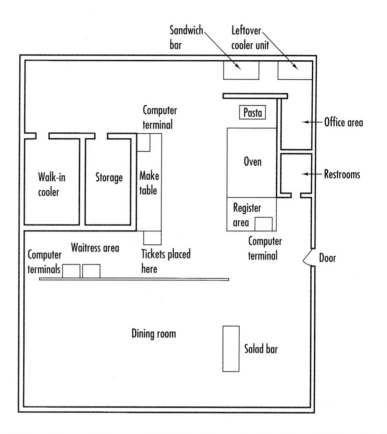

OPERATIONS

Order Processing. The layout of the St. George Street restaurant is shown in Exhibit 17. Orders were processed as follows:

After taking an order the waitress punched it into one of the computer terminals located near her station or the cash register. Tickets were printed out on printers located over the cook's make table and at the waitress station. If the order was for a pan pizza, the cook had to walk twenty feet to the walk-in cooler and get a dough shell. If the order was for a double decker pizza, the dough was rolled out on the table at that time. The pizza, whether it was double decker or pan, was then made on the table and placed in the oven. Next, the ticket was moved to an order stand at the end of the make table where an employee-in-charge would place it on a ticket holder. During busy nights tickets were often misplaced.

Pizzas were cooked on a conveyor oven which was two years old and in good repair. The oven had two conveyors. The upper conveyor was kept in operation at all times; the lower conveyor was used only during peak periods. Both conveyors were ten feet long. Uncooked pizzas were loaded on the first two feet of each conveyor. The oven was six feet long and could accommodate up to six pizzas at a time, per conveyor. The last two feet of the conveyors were used to allow the pizzas to cool off before serving.

After the pizza was cooked, it was given to take-out customers at the cash register where payment was made. Waitresses took the pizza and ticket to the tables of dine-in customers who made payment after they finished dining.

Operating Concerns.   Outbanks realized that there were several capacity problems that needed to be resolved if sales and profits at the restaurant were to increase. For example, oven capacity was limited by the speed of the conveyors and this constrained sales on busy nights. Even though the conveyor-type oven cooked pizzas faster (eight minutes for cooking and one minute for cooling) than traditional pizza ovens under normal circumstances, the speed of the conveyors could not be adjusted up or down. With traditional ovens it was possible to "stack" cook the pizzas. Although this procedure sometimes lowered the quality of the final product (e.g. burnt pizzas) and created confusion among the workers, it did allow many more pizzas to be cooked during the course of an evening. Furthermore, while the conveyor oven produced a more uniform quality pizza, the traditional oven was better for cooking items such as spaghetti and hot sandwiches. Outbanks had considered purchasing another conveyor oven at an installed price of $12,500 but had not discussed this idea with the area supervisor. Outbanks estimated that a traditional oven would cost $8,200 installed.

Cooler space was another problem. Outbanks stated that the constant traffic in and out of the cooler made it difficult to keep items cold. For example, customers consistently complained that the beer was too warm. Outbanks speculated that this was one reason why beer sales had not increased as rapidly as the sales of other items. Warm beer was not the only concern, however. According to Outbanks, because pizza ingredients and other foods were not kept cold enough, inventory spoilage, which amounted to about $175–$200 per month, was increasing. The problem was especially noticeable on the peak nights of Friday and Saturday. On these nights employees had to shuffle items around in the walk-in freezer to make room for the dough shells. This situation often caused older stock to be used last.

Outbanks had spoken to the district manager about purchasing a new walk-in cooler for the restaurant but had no idea how long it would take for the Pizza Delights hierarchy to approve the purchase. The new walk-in cooler was estimated to cost approximately $11,000.

Outbanks also noted that dining room seating and parking capacity at the restaurant was limited. The dining room consisted of 22 tables which could seat 88 customers. During busy nights customers were forced to form a line out the door, waiting for an empty table. Furthermore, the parking lot had only thirty spaces, which created havoc on Friday and Saturday nights as take-out and dine-in customers tried to find a place to park. Due to the limited parking, employees were required to park in a dirt field behind the restaurant. Outbanks estimated that it would $8,000 to pave the field and that this area would provide 15 additional parking spaces.

EMPLOYEES

Outbanks' staff included two assistant managers, Pete Gorman and Betty Franks, who were responsible for supervising the restaurant when Outbanks was not working and for helping him with other managerial chores such as purchasing, inventory, and scheduling. Both assistant managers were required to work a minimum of 55 hours per week for which they were paid $5.80 per hour. Assistant managers were paid time-and-one-half for any additional hours worked.

Gorman was a 36-year old ex-high school teacher. He had been an assistant manager at another Pizza Delights for several years prior to joining Outbanks' staff. Gorman was characterized by one employee as a stringent, rule-oriented manager who was actively seeking a promotion. Franks was a recent graduate of Clemson University. According to Outbanks she had brought many innovative ideas to the restaurant, including the idea to weigh out the cheese instead of using cheese cups. Although Outbanks had not yet tried this idea, he knew of a manager in another location who had cut his cheese costs by 10% using this technique.

In addition to Outbanks, Gorman, and Franks, the St. George Street restaurant employed 17 hourly workers, including six waitresses, seven cooks, two dishwashers, and two "employees-in-charge" (EICs). Most of these employees worked on a part-time basis. All employees were evaluated twice each year and received an automatic ten-cent raise regardless of performance.

The waitresses were responsible for seating customers, taking orders, and serving the meal to the customer. Although their base pay was below the minimum wage, after tips waitresses usually earned well above the minimum wage of $3.35 per hour. Cooks were hired to do prep-work, cook the food, and maintain the cleanliness of the facility. Their starting pay was at or slightly above the minimum wage. Besides washing dishes, dishwashers were responsible for keeping the dining room and other work areas clean. They were usually hired at minimum wage and promoted to cook after a few months. The EICs were cooks or waitresses who, through experience and expertise, had shown that they could handle additional responsibilities. Paid in excess of $4.00 per hour, they were responsible for the supervision of the cooking and the daily book-keeping.

Commenting on his staff Outbanks said, "The St. George Street Pizza Delights is a quality restaurant because everyone from me to the dishwashers work as a team to provide the best product, with the best service, to our customers." The cooks and waitresses, however, were generally young and often had conflicting responsibilities, such as school or another job. Consequently, Outbanks realized that maintaining a high level of commitment among them would be difficult.

LABOR COSTS

In accordance with company policy, all labor costs were computed daily. Pizza Delights had established a labor grid which stipulated how many employees were needed each day during lunch and dinner (see Exhibit 18). Outbanks used these labor grids and the average break times given to employees to calculate his daily labor needs and prepare the work schedule. At the end of each

EXHIBIT 18   PIZZA DELIGHTS PROJECTED LABOR SCHEDULE: LUNCH & DINNER

LUNCH		DINNER	
Projected Sales per hour 11 AM–4 PM	Projected Labor Needs (# of workers)	Projected Sales per hour 4 PM–Closing	Projected Labor Needs (# of workers)
$ 0– 41	2	$ 0– 95	2
42– 61	3	96–143	3
62– 87	4	144–190	4
88–119	5	191–211	5
120–156	6	212–255	6
157–180	8	256–295	8
181–202	9	296–338	9
203–245	10	339–379	10
246–298	11	380–423	11
299–342	12	424–461	12
343–387	13	462–507	13
388–450	14	508–547	14
451–519	15	548–589	15
520–614	16	590–631	16
615–695	17	632–673	17

Average total hours of breaktime per week:

Monday	Tuesday	Wednesday	Thursday	Friday	Saturday	Sunday
2.6	2.6	2.9	3.5	4.6	4.2	1.9

Average hourly pay scale per position:

Assistant Managers	$5.80
Employees-in-charge	$4.10
Cook	$3.45
Waitresses	$2.30 plus tips
Dishwasher	$3.35

day, the actual number of employee hours were compared to the suggested labor grid hours, given the daily sales volume. All variances had to be explained to the district manager.

The number of employees needed per sales dollar was higher during lunch hours because of the lower per item price of lunchtime products, and because of the extra demands in providing a ten-minute guarantee for serving the small pan and Italian turnover pizzas.

Since the introduction of the Italian turnover pizza, each Pizza Delights restaurant was required to have a minimum of ten employees present during the guaranteed hours of 11 A.M. to 1:30 P.M., Monday thru Friday, in order to better promote the new product. As a result, an average of 55 employee hours were needed on the weekdays between 8 A.M. and 4 P.M. No minimum was specified for the weekends, however. Before the Italian turnover was introduced, the St. George Street restaurant operated with a total of 28 employee hours between 8 A.M. and 4 P.M. on Monday, Tuesday, Wednesday, Saturday, and Sunday, 33 total employee hours on Thursdays, and 38 total employee hours on Fridays.

LLOYD'S GREER AREA PIZZA DELIGHTS FRANCHISE OPERATIONS

Leonard Lloyd had been involved in the pizza business for five years prior to his interest in the St. George Street Pizza Delights. In 1986 he owned three Pizza Delights franchises, all of which were profitable. The first Pizza Delights franchise Lloyd acquired was built in 1978 in Greer, South Carolina, a small rural town of about 10,000 people. The restaurant was company-owned during its first three years of operation. Recognizing the potential of the restaurant, Lloyd, an area businessman, purchased the franchise from Pizza Delights in 1981 for $375,000, plus $1.2 million for the right to use the company's brand name.

In his first year of operation Lloyd increased the seating capacity at the restaurant from 65 to 150 people. He felt that the demand for pizza in the Greer area could easily accommodate a dining area of that size. Sales revenues increased 7 percent that year.

In 1982, disenchanted by the slow growth in sales, Lloyd decided to offer customers more specials and new dining options. Two-for-one coupons were placed in the local newspapers on a regular basis. Taking advantage of his two ovens and massive dining area, Lloyd also began to offer a lunch buffet during the weekdays to attract students from a nearby community college. Sales revenues increased by 10 percent almost immediately, and many customers began inquiring about the possibility of a Sunday buffet. Lloyd's decision to extend the buffet to Sundays allowed him to capture a larger share of the after-church market, increasing sales during a time of the week that had traditionally been slow.

According to Lloyd, the Greer franchise was very successful and the outlook for the future was bright. Restaurant sales had increased by about 33 percent since 1982. Its only direct pizza competitor, Papa Joe's, offered relatively little service and relied almost entirely on take-out business.

In 1983 and 1984 Lloyd purchased the franchises to two additional Pizza Delights restaurants in two small rural communities, both approximately 5–10 miles outside of Greer. Both of these restaurants followed the same strategy as the Greer restaurant and both were profitable. Lloyd had been able to retain the managers of these restaurants by giving them minority ownership positions in the business.

THE FRANCHISING PLAN

Although neither Outbanks nor Lloyd had worked out all the details of the franchising plan, Lloyd expected that many of the same strategies he had used at the Greer restaurants would be feasible at the St. George Street location. Lloyd wanted to offer a buffet-style dinner or lunch to customers at least once or twice a week. He also wanted to use more coupons and promotions to increase sales during slow periods. Outbanks had considered these options in the past, but company policy had prevented him from implementing them.

Lloyd was also considering setting up a delivery service at the St. George Street location. Spartanburg was the home of six colleges, and Lloyd expected that such a service would be welcomed by students in the area. A delivery operation would require two half-time employees paid at the minimum wage, plus the purchase of two used cars for approximately $5,000 apiece. Gas, maintenance, depreciation, and other related operating expenses associated with the vehicle were estimated at 20 cents per mile.

FRANCHISE FINANCING ARRANGEMENTS

Lloyd had some initial inquiries at the Pizza Delights' district office in Columbia, South Carolina, to determine if purchasing the restaurant would be feasible. The district office quoted Lloyd a price of $725,000 for the physical facilities plus an annual payment amounting to 12% of the restaurant's net profits before taxes. The Pizza Delights brand name was valued at over $1 million. However, Lloyd knew he would not have to pay this fee since he had already purchased the brand rights for the Greer restaurants.

Lloyd was prepared to invest $250,000 in the restaurant. Outbanks' financial commitment would be considerably less as he had only around $25,000 to $30,000 to invest. Lloyd planned to borrow the balance of the funds from one of the financial institutions in the area.

A Spartanburg banker stated that for a commercial loan her bank would require Lloyd and Outbanks to provide at least 25 percent of the total funds needed to purchase the franchise. In addition, both Lloyd and Outbanks would be required to give the bank a first mortgage on the restaurant, as well as pledge all their personal assets as security. The loan itself would probably be a term loan amortized over 15 years with a balloon payment after 3–5 years. In 1986 the prime rate for commercial borrowing was 7.5%. Lloyd realized that he would probably have to pay at least 1.5–2.5% over prime. Lloyd figured that payments for a straight 15 year amortized loan of $500,000 at 10% interest would amount to $5,373 per month or almost $65,000 per year.

The Spartanburg banker also informed Lloyd that franchise loans were not frequently approved by her bank, citing an example of another Pizza Delights franchise in Greenwood, South Carolina (population approximately 20,000), that was recently denied a loan. Exhibits 19 and 20 provide the 1985 income statement and balance sheet for the Greenwood Pizza Delights

 EXHIBIT 19   1985 INCOME STATEMENT FOR THE GREENWOOD PIZZA DELIGHTS

SALES		$638,284
Food In	$322,928	
Food Out	239,260	
Food Delivery	14,064	
Food Sub-Total	$576,252	
Beverages In	$ 61,612	
Beverages Delivery	120	
Beverages Sub-Total	$ 61,732	
Premiums	300	
COST OF GOODS SOLD		$184,400
Food Cost	$167,600	
Beverage Cost	$ 16,800	
Premiums	0	
GROSS PROFIT		$453,884
OPERATING EXPENSES		$303,560
Advertising	$ 22,000	
Auto & Delivery Expenses	600	
Payroll	198,325	
Repairs	19,403	
Utilities & Telephone	30,504	
Operating Supplies	10,320	
Other Operating Expenses	22,408	
OPERATING PROFIT		$150,324
ADMINISTRATIVE EXPENSES		$131,080
Royalty Fee	$ 19,000	
Insurance	12,450	
Interest	7,770	
Depreciation	27,250	
Rent	42,000	
Taxes & Licenses	4,000	
Other Administrative Expenses	18,610	
NET PROFIT BEFORE TAXES		$ 19,244

EXHIBIT 20   1985 BALANCE SHEET FOR THE GREENWOOD PIZZA DELIGHTS

ASSETS		$119,820
Cash in Bank	− $14,200	
Cash on Hand	1,000	
Investments	2,700	
Accounts Receivable	1,500	
Inventory	7,500	
Total Current Assets	− $ 1,500	
Automobiles	$17,500	
less Depreciation	− 9,500	
Net Automobiles	$ 8,000	
Equipment	$150,000	
less Depreciation	− 70,000	
Net Equipment	$ 80,000	
Leasehold Improvements	$10,200	
less Depreciation	− 3,000	
Net Leasehold	$ 7,200	
Total Fixed Assets	$95,200	
Deposits	$ 220	
Insurance Reserve Fund	1,700	
Prepaid Insurance	3,000	
Prepaid Rent	4,200	
Franchise Fees	17,000	
Total Other Non-Current Assets	$26,120	
LIABILITIES		$ 63,950
Accounts Payable	$ 650	
Other Current Liabilities	13,300	
Total Current Liabilities	$13,950	
Long-Term Liabilities	$50,000	
EQUITY		$ 55,870
LIABILITIES + EQUITY		$119,820

franchise. Lloyd was not particularly worried by the banker's pessimism, however. He had a successful track record in business and had never experienced problems obtaining financing in the past. He saw no reason why it would be different this time.

FRANCHISE OWNERSHIP AND MANAGEMENT

Based on his conversations with Lloyd, Outbanks anticipated that he would receive a one-quarter to one-third interest in the business, plus his normal salary, for managing the restaurant. Outbanks also expected to have complete control over day-to-day operations. With respect to strategy and policy matters, Outbanks believed that both he and Lloyd would have an equal voice, an arrangement Outbanks felt was similar to the deal Lloyd had made with the other franchise managers.

OUTBANKS' DILEMMA

After weighing the pros and cons of the situation in his mind, Outbanks still was not sure whether he should join Lloyd in the franchising venture or try to advance in the company. Outbanks felt that he was responsible for most of the restaurant's current success and deserved a share of the profits. Yet he admired Lloyd for his success with the Greer Pizza Delights franchises. On the other hand, Outbanks wondered if Lloyd's plans, which had worked so well in Greer, would be successful at the St. George Street restaurant. He also knew the Pizza Delights was growing rapidly and that there might soon be an area supervisor position open for a young, energetic manager with a proven track record.

Personal problems also caused Outbanks to wonder whether he would continue to have the time, money, and motivation to devote to such a venture. A major dispute with his recently estranged wife had greatly taxed Outbanks' mental and physical endurance. This dispute, which Outbanks expected to end in divorce, was also likely to deplete his financial resources once it had been settled.

Despite all of his problems, as Outbanks prepared for closing time he resolved to give Lloyd an answer before the end of the following week.

BRITHINEE ELECTRIC, INC.

SUE GREENFELD

Wallace, Jr. and Don Brithinee are identical twin brothers in their early forties. Wallace, Jr. (also known as Wally) holds the title of President while Don is the company's vice president and controller. As teenagers, they started Brithinee Electric Company with their parents. The senior Wallace Brithinee was the firm's first president and major stockholder. The Brithinee twins worked for the company while they entered U.C. Riverside at the age of 16. They graduated with highest honors at 19, and by 23, both had earned. Ph.D.s in mathematics from U.C. Riverside. By 1988, Brithinee Electric company had twenty-three employees, and was commemorating twenty-five years in business. A celebration called for an elaborate dinner to be held upon a chartered boat with important Brithinee Electric customers and friends.

The company appears to be financially successful both from appearance of physical facilities and from remarks made by employees. A 16,750 sq. ft. Mediterranean-styled structure houses the firm. Constructed primarily during the years of 1971 and 1972, the building was expanded later in 1979. The Brithinee facility is located in an industrial area of Colton, California, a region of southern California expected to have high population growth. Outside on the lawn rests an industrial motor on a small pedestal surrounded by a bed of petunias. Inside, the facility is attractive with original oil paintings hung in the office sections of the building. Some pictures depict European settings. On the walls are displayed various awards given to them for outstanding service or distribution. One is from Toshiba, another from Baldor.

The company has been changing, especially in the eighties. The core business of Brithinee is directed fundamentally toward large industrial electrical motors, both as a distributor and as a firm which undertakes the rewinding of the motors. When insulation breaks down in a motor and the bearings need service or replacement, this company offers its service to rewind and rebuild

Source: Prepared by Professor Sue Greenfeld, California State University, San Bernardino as a basis for classroom discussion and not to illustrate either effective or ineffective handling of administrative situations. © Sue Greenfeld, 1990.

the motor. Part of the service includes free pick-up and delivery of motors for their customers.

The company's primary industry (large-scale motors) declined significantly up through 1984. Wally felt this decline could not be attributed only to the imports of competitive products, but rather U.S. businesses require fewer large motors than before. The increased usage of smaller motors has been an important industry trend and Brithinee watched a number of their competitors go out of business. Even though the overall industry has "shrunk," Brithinee Electric still grew in sales and revenues throughout the eighties.

The most pressing issue facing this company at the initial write-up of the case is one of employee development and job rotation. With the desire to have the company flexible to opportunities, Wally expressed the need to have employees with a broad range of talents and skills, but this need for job rotation was not universal at their company. Wally wondered about the employees of Brithinee: What are their personal goals? Is there room for them to be fulfilled at Brithinee Electric? Don wondered: How can we get our employees to be more independent so that the firm is not totally dependent upon the 100% involvement of the Brithinee "boys"?

COMPANY HISTORY

Zora and Wallace Brithinee, Sr. came to the southern California area from Detroit shortly after WWII. Wallace Brithinee, Sr. was primarily a "motorman," an individual who specializes in the repair and maintenance of electrical motors. He received his training primarily through vocational programs while in high school and by fixing motors during his service in the U.S. Navy prior to his relocation to California.

The Brithinees' first business began in 1946 but only lasted about nine years. It was never considered very successful. Wally, Jr. described these lean days as "a form of starvation." Wallace Brithinee, Sr. abandoned his business, took the equipment home and began working for someone else. However, this early experience would prove helpful in the later development of the current business. In the interim, the senior Brithinee helped set up another shop for a man in Ontario, California.

Then in about 1961 or 1962, Wallace Brithinee, Sr. formed another organization called Brithinee and Coleman with a local contractor named Bill Coleman. At that time, the Brithinee twins started working in the business. However, after a year, there was a falling out of the partners. In October of 1963, Brithinee, Sr. initiated the current business with his family. The twins were 15 at the time.

In the early days, everything was done "the hard way." The work was back-breaking. Electric motors are heavy, and the business had no cranes to facilitate the moving of equipment. Customers have critical needs and frequently their motors need fixing immediately. Wally, Jr. described the situation as "working around the clock." Back in the sixties, the entire business consisted of repair work. Don elaborated that one major element contributing to Brithinee Electric's survival in those days was the "sweat and muscle" of himself and his brother to get the emergency repair work out. This he viewed as a contribution to capital because their work was performed mostly without financial compensation.

Then around 1970, Lincoln Electric came out with an appealing low price motor. This made Brithinee consider that rather than get involved in one of "these midnight rushes" to repair an old motor, they might be able to sell their customers a new motor instead. They then instigated the stocking of new motors which represented the first major change in direction for the company.

Next came the construction of 10,000 sq. ft. of the current facility taking about one and a half years to build. Primarily this was the responsibility of Wallace Brithinee, Sr. but after completion of the building, Wallace, Sr. became less involved with the business. His two sons increasingly took over. At this time, the company began hiring more people. The mid-seventies witnessed a growth spurt. The number of employees increased from seven or eight in the early seventies to twenty-three by 1980. Wally described the construction of the current facility as a very bold step in the Brithinees' history, but in 1972 they were very optimistic about the future of the company.

In the late seventies, problems arose on the home front. In 1978 Zora Brithinee was diagnosed as having multiple cancer starting as hip pain. This meant that Wallace Brithinee's time and attention was devoted to her care and he was quite distraught over her death briefly afterwards. A short time later he suffered a heart attack. Luckily he recovered quite well, but this created transition problems. There was no real place for the senior Brithinee after he returned to the business in 1980. He eventually "retired" from the business.

In the eighties, the firm started to get into "big ticket" items where an order might call for a single piece of equipment selling for $40,000 or $100,000. This strategy replaced relying on repairs and the sales of smaller items. By 1987, the shop did approximately $1 million in repairs, a figure that has been relatively flat since 1980. Sales, on the other hand, showed constant upward growth and were approximately $4 million in 1987. The latter also included development of custom-made equipment, one of Brithinee's newer areas.

COMPANY FACILITY

The front part of the facility is devoted to offices where proposal development and engineering design is conducted (see Exhibit 1). One project includes a graphic display of a water system which they were developing for the Eisenhower Medical Center. The firm also does its own in-house brochures. The office staff wears many different hats, answering the telephone, taking an order, making a purchase, or doing research and design. The coffee room is

EXHIBIT 1 FLOOR PLAN OF BRITHINEE ELECTRIC

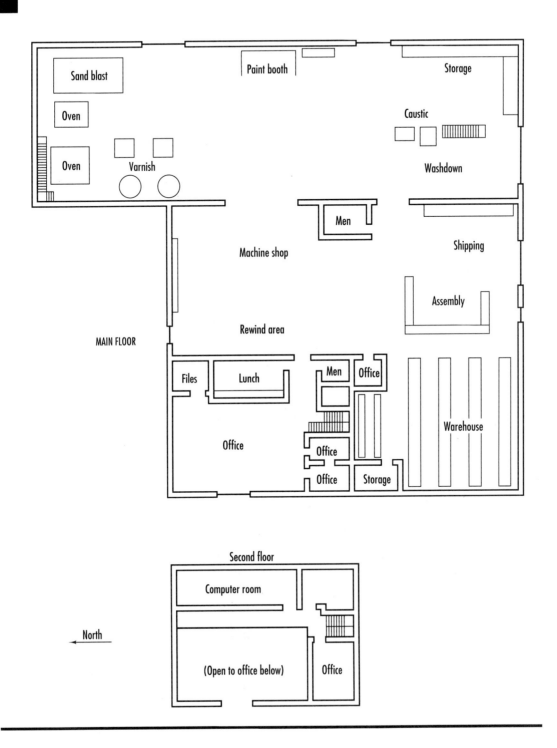

Sand blast

Oven

Oven

Varnish

Paint booth

Storage

Caustic

Washdown

Men

Machine shop

Shipping

Assembly

Rewind area

MAIN FLOOR

Files

Lunch

Men

Office

Office

Office

Storage

Office

Office

Warehouse

Second floor

Computer room

North

(Open to office below)

Office

small but serves multiple purposes as a combination conference and lunch center. A white board lists the day's assignment for the shop workers.

The back of the facility is large. Here motors are repaired and rewound. In 1979 the facility's back area was expanded by 6,750 sq. ft. At the entry door is a panel for testing equipment as a motor enters or leaves. On the north end of the facility are two industrial ovens: one for bonding the wiring in the motor, another for "cleaning" a motor. In the latter case, the 700° F temperatures burn off the bonding material to allow the motor to be rebuilt and rewound. Other shop areas are used to create the wiring, "impregnate" the wiring, perform vibration analysis, and rebuild old motors or build new customized equipment for their customers. The entire shop area appears clean and orderly.

Throughout the ceiling is an elaborate set of cranes and steel frames. This allows for the ease of moving large equipment and motors. Brithinee Electric has the ability to move a piece of equipment from one corner to another without expending a tremendous amount of energy or time. "Swamp coolers" also have been installed in the ceiling. This draws hot air out of the shop area and keeps this part of the facility relatively comfortable in the hot summers of southern California, where temperatures often reach 100° during the day. The office areas are air-conditioned.

A foreman's office is located near the entrance to the shop floor as one enters from the coffee room. A time clock is attached to the outside of the foreman's office. Inside, on the foreman's desk sits a Macintosh computer. This permits the foreman, Rod Samples, to keep a record on each customer job.

Due to a security problem and a desire not to construct high density fencing around the perimeter of the property, Brithinee parks ten vehicles inside the building at night. They have been doing this since the mid-seventies. Their rationale for not building a fence was their desire to keep the outside of the firm looking aesthetically pleasing.

CHANGING INDUSTRY CHARACTERISTICS

The motor repair industry is one of shrinkage. In the sixties, many larger firms such as Siemens A. G. of Germany and General Electric bought up repair and service shops. Exxon for one wanted to diversify strategically out of oil when they purchased Reliance Electric. Yet realized profits throughout the industry were lower than expected and many organizations floundered during that time period. Exxon also left this industry by selling off Reliance Electric.

This industry shrinkage was one reason Brithinee Electric made the decision to enter the market of state-of-the-art electronic motor controls. They also made the decision to investigate artificial turf systems and have done some work in this area. They want to stay flexible in case opportunities develop where they have some expertise. They consider their primary customers to be the food industry, water pump facilities, sand and gravel industry, and grass turf businesses. Customers are located throughout California, but are primarily focused in the high desert (up through the middle of California), low desert (Coachella and Imperial Valley), San Diego, San Bernardino, Riverside, and Ontario.

In terms of forecasting sales or repairs, their industry is unpredictable. The summer months tend to be a little slower than other times, but not always. The weather is a big factor. Rain causes high levels of demand as motors fail or need servicing. Many sales and repairs are "one-of-a-kind." A repair job can take anywhere from 6 to 120 hours. Inside their casing, motors differ significantly from manufacturer to manufacturer.

Dick Marino, the outside salesman, indicated that in the area of repairing motors, Brithinee has about 75 competitors, many of them "mom and pop" operations. Another employee noted that some customers were becoming more price conscious in the recent economy. Brithinee's prices are considered above the industry norm. According to Don, Brithinee Electric Works to distinguish itself by providing high quality service, and that most of Brithinee's customers are not that price sensitive.

COMPUTERIZATION

The early 1980s was the time that Brithinee's major supplier of electrical hardware (Toshiba International Corporation of Houston, Texas) first introduced a line of microprocessor-based motor control hardware and later a line of small-scale programmable controllers. Although Brithinee Electric had occasionally sold electric drive hardware from other manufacturers, there was a reluctance on the part of Wally and Don to sell this more complex hardware until they felt it could be offered with the "great reliability and support they were accustomed to giving" their customers.

Yet these new systems could be a promising sales opportunity if the firm could master the complexities of this new "smart" machinery. According to Wally, the underlying philosophy of "smart" machinery implies more complete control of a piece of machinery. The machine, for example, only uses as much energy as is needed to produce the desired outcome. Since the machine only uses as much power as is absolutely necessary, the machine's components can be reduced in size, helping to conserve materials as well as energy.

While "smart machinery" is relatively new for industrial motors in the United States, the Brithinees discovered this philosophy in place for some time by their European suppliers. In particular, their German gearmotor suppliers long have produced what are, in appearance, "undersized" gearmotors for their power ratings. Yet these same products are among the most reliable products the Brithinees offer.

By providing the combination of hardware, application engineering, and software needed, Wally stated an overall systematic application is required.

This means being familiar with how the customer uses motors in a total systems approach. In some cases, this includes working with the customer's engineering staff to find solutions.

This also suggests how essential a knowledge of programming and electrical controls is to Brithinee Electric. Wally mentioned the main issue is providing both system reliability and the complete service backup necessary to maintain the software and the systems that customers had come to expect from Brithinee Electric. Customers had told Don and Wally a great many horror stories of equipment that never worked correctly, and for which the service was sadly lacking. Wally affirmed that the Brithinee company is "determined not to enter a market where they could not properly support their product."

Wally and Don very much want to be in the business of "smart machinery," but finding talented help continues to be a problem. One employee, George Rainey, had been very instrumental in building the control-panel assembly operation at Brithinee, but he recently retired. In his place, Brithinee Electric hired a young electronic technician familiar with Toshiba electronic drive products. Like everyone else, this person wears many hats: he makes presentations to customers, he develops prices on system hardware, and he services equipment built by Brithinee Electric and by some of its competitors.

Still, Wally Brithinee expressed concern that the firm is too thinly staffed in the area of high-technology products. Furthermore, Wally has been unable to motivate his programmer/technician, or to make him sense the team spirit that Wally feels the others have. Consequently, Wally feels the need to develop a backup for the programmer/technician should he decide to leave.

INVENTORY AND OFFICE STAFF

Brithinee Electric has an inventory philosophy of "completeness" where they attempt to maintain at least one of every part they might need to help a customer out of a "midnight jam." They also have a contract with a friendly customer in Coachella Valley, California, to carry certain items of their inventory. Coachella Valley is in the low desert approximately 75 miles away from their main facility. A separate record is maintained for that stock. Thus Brithinee carries one of the largest inventories of motor equipment in southern California.

They also have a philosophy for the office staff where all ten people including Wally and Don sell to customers, and buy parts to service their customers. This means no separate sales or purchasing department exist. For example, if a customer needs a certain type of part and Brithinee Electric does not have it in stock, the person will then call the manufacturer directly and order the part. The part will then be invoiced and reshipped to their customer.

One employee wondered whether eventually this would have to be changed, but for the time being, she seemed to think it was working. Don disagreed. He wants to develop a better system. He feels there is a definite lack of control and this is bothersome. It causes a duplication of paperwork with so many people capable of producing forms on their own desk computer. According to Don, the main culprit of this process is Wally. Don said, "I haven't been able to reach him on that point yet." Purchasing worries Don because the "process is too disseminated" over different individuals. The only office person not selling to customers is Kathy. She buys bearings, windings, and parts for the shop.

FINANCES AT BRITHINEE

Finances are tightly watched by Don. Before any invoices are paid, Don's red stamp of approval has to appear. All checks bear his signature, but Don laughingly stated that signing all the checks "doesn't mean you know the numbers." Don said Brithinee Electric is on sound financial footing. (See Exhibit 2.) Recently the company has been able to line up a $200,000 unsecured credit line. This will relieve pressure on cash flow if for some reason a major customer is unreasonably slow in paying the account to Brithinee or if the company needs additional working capital for expansion or equipment. To illustrate, one major customer in North Hollywood purchases approximately $80,000 of product per month from Brithinee. Thus, Brithinee is highly dependent upon that customer to pay their bills on time. Prior to 1984, Brithinee had some cash flow problems but this area Don worked very hard to correct. Brithinee keeps three sets of records: one for repairs, one for sales, and one consolidated for both repairs and sales. (Exhibit 3 shows income from repairs and sales.)

According to Don, the firm has a good credit rating. Each year they replace two or three of their vehicles. The company pays cash for such purchases. Don feels this is cheaper than borrowing. Brithinee Electric's philosophy regarding long-term debt is to have none. Don realized that some in business school might advocate leverage, but for them, he feels more "comfortable" having zero debt. Don calls the company financially conservative.

In this industry, average terms are net 30 days meaning that customers have thirty days to pay. Don thought most competitors have an average collection period of 60 days. Brithinee Electric's ranges from 31 to 33 days. Don stated, "that is no accident. That has been planned." Some accounts earn cash discounts such as 1/10, n/30. If an account seriously abuses the credit extended to them, then Brithinee just changes the terms.

According to Madeleine, who is in charge of accounts receivable, Brithinee Electric gives credit very cautiously. A new customer might get only 10 days before the bill is due. For new customers or those who changed their paying habits (e.g., one who stopped taking cash discounts), Madeleine might have them checked through Dun & Bradstreet's credit service. For very large account receivables, she might call a customer's accounts payable personnel to find out when Brithinee Electric was scheduled to be paid and/or to verify the invoice had been received. Each month a certain amount of excess cash

EXHIBIT 2 BRITHINEE ELECTRIC, INC.: HISTORICAL REVENUES, 1969–1987

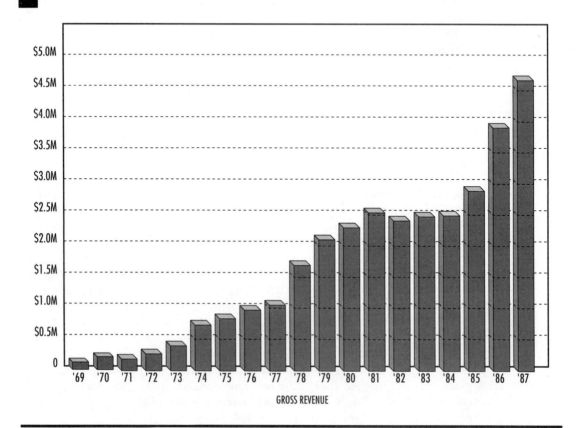

GROSS REVENUE

accumulates. Don stated he likes to keep a cash cushion in the bank, but wondered if the company could turn some cash into a more productive asset. (Exhibit 4 on page 380 shows the company's balance sheet.)

SAFETY ISSUES

One challenge is to keep the facility clean. Another is to avoid physical injuries, especially those to one's back. For this reason, Brithinee Electric emphasizes keeping the work areas clutter free and stresses the correct use of cranes. Proper lifting and proper handling is top priority. One person, Linda Butek, had been assigned as an assistant to top management to oversee safety related issues. Her position had been created two years previously. If someone on the

EXHIBIT 3   BRITHINEE ELECTRIC, INC.: STATEMENT OF INCOME

	1986	1987
REPAIRS		
INCOME		
Rewinds	$210,340.21	$224,095.95
Rewind Labor	210,340.10	223,095.91
Parts	221,033.78	247,770.66
Labor	267,436.34	297,213.64
Machine Repair	80,307.50	105,603.83
Balancing	43,255.39	50,481.24
Restack	4,274.00	1,944.00
Repair Disc. Stator	(1,539.98)	(2,277.02)
Repair Disc. Resale	(430.79)	(549.90)
Misc. Income — Repairs	5,479.86	5,059.54
MFG Investment — Repairs	384.95	120.42
Interest Income — Repairs	2,882.19	4,057.57
Total Income	$1,043,763.55	$1,156,615.84
COST OF REPAIRS		
Repair Materials	$95,646.98	$103,306.38
Parts	109,458.20	99,955.25
Outside Services	14,370.43	22,168.25
Office Vacation	3,052.88	0.00
Shop Salaries	408,845.43	463,869.98
Total Cost Repairs	631,373.92	689,299.86
GROSS PROFIT	$412,389.63	$467,315.98
OPERATING EXPENSES		
Accounting & Legal	$737.50	$1,169.13
Advertising	1,599.74	2,318.77
Auto — Gas & Parking	4,805.56	6,509.71
Auto Lease & Truck Rent.	303.71	488.01
Auto Repair/Maint — Parts	19,520.61	16,205.34
Bank Charges	4.97	250.00
Business Promotion	6,103.08	5,452.30
Over/Shorts	0.08	21.89
Coffee Room Supplies	1,636.60	1,776.35
Computer Supplies	5,398.75	15,467.34
Depreciation — Repairs	27,502.13	32,866.72
Donations	880.48	1,261.97
Dues & Subscriptions	1,848.41	1,138.74
Employee Welfare — Repairs	1,500.87	1,812.36
Equipment Rental — Repairs	589.50	1,148.75
Meetings & Conventions	3,473.37	4,052.74
Insurance	43,906.86	51,729.39
Interest	353.58	0.22
Maintenance Supplies	2,033.17	2,755.60

(continued)

EXHIBIT 3 (continued)

	1986	1987
Office Supplies	5,809.04	7,475.03
Postage	1,698.16	1,769.09
Outside Services	6,541.82	7,379.56
Profit Sharing	43,139.49	48,343.37
Rent	31,020.00	43,458.00
Repair & Maint. Shop	11,084.61	23,178.69
Salaries, Clerical	41,981.74	44,619.52
Officers Salaries	83,060.00	74,914.00
Salaries, Sales	28,366.95	29,325.77
Shop Expense — Repairs	13,709.10	2,052.65
Uniforms	3,162.54	3,310.75
Taxes — Licenses	10,406.70	7,016.96
Taxes — Payroll	48,034.37	53,919.57
Accrued Payroll Taxes	——	1,364.06
Telephone	15,461.60	17,044.21
Travel	2,337.79	1,504.02
Utilities	35,296.98	43,228.50
Total Operating Expenses	$503,309.86	$556,329.08
NET INCOME (LOSS)	($90,919.93)	($89,013.10)
SALES		
INCOME		
3 Phase 1 Phase Motors	$1,063,876.95	$1,186,831.37
Gear Motors	212,124.79	177,569.48
DC Motors	39,938.09	24,892.96
Controls	427,822.49	366,251.16
Inverters	970,344.74	1,654,893.67
Programmable Controllers	14,605.47	14,265.15
Parts	80,874.30	62,180.63
Labor, Sales	5,671.01	3,165.00
Labor, Inverter Service	16,162.08	16,106.66
Restock	407.85	50.00
Freight	13,748.99	14,050.44
Customer Purchases (Other)	2,127.44	840.75
Interest Income — Sales	3,204.92	4,057.63
Misc. Income	7,554.61	5,059.58
MFG Investment	384.94	120.44
Total Income	$2,858,848.67	$3,530,334.92
COST OF SALES		
Purchases	$350.45	$33.60
Accounts Payable — Discount	(25,053.35)	(25,192.42)
3 Phase Motors	778,354.25	827,859.34
DC & Gear Motors	182,018.16	139,098.20
Controls	271,061.28	299,136.39
Inverters	823,397.63	1,336,496.44
Programmable Controllers	15,151.22	25,553.84

EXHIBIT 3   (continued)

	1986	1987
Parts	66,201.84	47,004.86
Sales — Commissions	1,602.65	1,048.66
Inventory Variance	(90,073.32)	(88,766.10)
Total Cost of Sales	$2,023,010.81	$2,562,272.81
GROSS PROFIT	$835,837.86	$968,062.11
OPERATING EXPENSES		
Accounting & Legal	$737.50	$1,530.11
Advertising	1,599.74	2,318.78
Auto — Gas & Parking	4,805.51	6,511.00
Auto Lease & Truck Rent.	303.72	487.99
Auto Repair/Maint — Parts	19,522.18	16,207.00
Bank Charges	9.28	250.00
Business Promotion	6,142.50	5,469.59
Cash Discounts	26,711.32	27,477.85
Over/Shorts	0.49	20.64
Coffeeroom Supplies	1,636.63	1,776.47
Depreciation — Sales	27,502.13	32,866.73
Computer Supplies	6,043.74	15,467.42
Donations	880.47	1,261.98
Dues & Subscriptions	1,880.19	1,138.75
Employee Welfare — Sales	1,500.88	1,812.38
Equipment Rental — Sales	589.50	714.14
Meetings & Conventions	3,473.38	4,052.78
Freight	41,977.78	40,832.11
Insurance	40,788.75	49,351.73
Interest	353.60	0.23
Maintenance Supplies	2,033.20	2,884.22
Office Supplies	5,807.03	7,349.74
Postage	1,682.49	1,757.41
Outside Services	6,479.29	8,167.57
Profit Sharing	43,139.50	48,343.38
Rent	31,020.00	43,458.00
Repair & Maint. Shop	2,320.93	135.79
Salaries, Clerical	59,217.33	85,582.40
Officers Salaries	114,140.00	139,126.00
Salaries, Sales	29,942.19	40,291.35
Shop Expense — Sales	6,573.31	528.94
Taxes — Licenses	9,673.71	7,092.62
Taxes — Payroll	318.82	1,303.23
Accrued Payroll Taxes	0.00	1,364.06
Telephone	15,455.75	17,044.29
Travel	2,337.80	1,428.42
Total Operating Expenses	$516,600.64	$615,405.10
NET INCOME (LOSS)	$319,237.22	$352,657.01

EXHIBIT 4 BRITHINEE ELECTRIC, INC.: BALANCE SHEET (AS OF DECEMBER 31)

	1986	1987
CURRENT ASSETS		
Petty Cash Fund	$645.28	$1,654.19
Cash in Bank — SPNB	23,146.60	14,290.72
Intercapital Liquid Fund	1.36	1.36
U.S. Securities Trust (ILAF)	22,348.19	23,156.57
SPNB — Money Market Account	110,966.26	121,372.03
Accounts Receivable	391,910.94	414,851.06
Inventory	479,193.19	567,959.29
Prepaid Income Taxes	42,000.00	94,186.00
Total Current Assets	1,070,211.82	1,237,471.22
FIXED ASSETS		
Shop Equipment	268,921.58	299,423.08
Auto & Trucks	214,148.14	229,492.76
Office Equipment	76,140.39	100,986.04
Leasehold Improvement	32,221.74	32,221.74
Total Fixed Assets at Cost	591,431.85	662,123.62
Accum Deprec — Schedule 1	(477,014.10)	(542,747.55)
Net Depreciable Fixed Assets	114,417.75	119,376.07
OTHER ASSETS		
Sales Tax Deposit	2,150.00	2,150.00
Deposits — Schedule 2 — Note 5	7,820.00	7,820.00
Oil & Tax Investment	4,746.10	4,746.10
Organizational Cost	920.90	920.90
Amortization	(920.90)	(920.90)
Total Other Assets	14,716.10	14,716.10
TOTAL ASSETS	$1,199,345.67	$1,371,563.39
CURRENT LIABILITIES		
Accounts Payable	360,403.12	385,913.07
SUI Payable	(4.20)	10.23
FUI Payable	38.69	11.29
Sales Tax Payable	8,320.12	11,253.90
Accrued Payroll Liability	0.00	27,281.15
Accrued Payroll Taxes	0.00	2,728.12
Total Current Liabilities	368,757.73	427,197.76
LONG-TERM LIABILITIES		
Total Long-Term Liabilities	0.00	0.00
SHAREHOLDER'S EQUITY		
Capital Stock Note 4	13,000.00	13,000.00
Treasury Stock	(80,072.30)	(123,748.10)
Retained Earnings	669,342.95	791,469.82
Net Income (Loss)	228,317.29	263,643.91
Total Shareholders' Equity	830,587.94	944,365.63
TOTAL LIAB. & SHAREHOLDERS' EQTY	1,199,345.67	1,371,563.39

shop floor sees anything needing safety attention, he or she fills out a form. This would be submitted to Linda. The company has also been spending time on earthquake preparedness. This includes securing and bracing shelving. In an earthquake, shelving could shake and fall over. Earthquake preparedness is a recurring issue for California. Scientists have been predicting a 50-50 chance that a major quake will occur in California within the next 50 years. In 1988 many Californians panicked when reminded that Nostradamus, a 16th century astrologer, predicted a city in the new world would rupture and fall into the sea. Some believed he was referring to either San Francisco or Los Angeles.

For other safety questions, one unresolved matter deals with the health of Brithinee's employees. One motor rewinder had acquired carpal tunnel syndrome. This is a numbness or pain of the thumb and first two fingers which occurs from their overuse. This is a common problem for people who use their hands for extended periods of time, such as workers in textile manufacturing, upholstering, and assembly line work. In the motor rewinder's hands, the pain and numbness lasted nearly five months. During that time she could not work for the company. Brithinee Electric held the position open for the individual, but the firm does not appear active in educating their employees about this type of occupational illness.

However, the company was taking very positive steps in the area of waste disposal. Virtually anything coming into the shop might be considered a hazardous material. Customers' motors are dirty. They have to be washed off so they are clean for repair. That water needs treatment and/or disposal. Brithinee Electric, then, is considered a "hazardous waste generator." Linda Butek attends seminars all the time to help reduce the company's waste. Keeping up is constantly a challenge. New legislation in hazardous waste disposal recently passed but was not yet really enforced. New legislation is also in the making in the state of California. In 1988, California had greater restrictions concerning hazardous waste than did the federal government. For example, one bill calls for counties to develop a hazardous waste management plan and reduce or minimize hazardous waste in their area. Another bill mandates that each company in an area must have a hazardous waste reduction plan as well. Neither bill had passed at the time the case was written, but there existed an expectation that these bills might be voted into law in the near future.

Brithinee is very interested in reducing the amount of water they need for their operation. This means they would become a "hazardous waste treatment" facility and this raises an entirely new set of regulations that need attention. Linda presented this question: Is it better for Brithinee to have more waste lower in hazardous content, or is it better to have a smaller, but more concentrated hazardous waste? Brithinee Electric has already taken a position on this question, but they are still concerned whether their decision was the right one. As of 1988, Linda felt guidance from San Bernardino County and other government agencies has been inadequate in this regard. This is an area of major future expense.

In addition, Brithinee Electric has other hazardous products on the premises: propane to run the fork-lifts, greases for motors, plus paints and varnishes. The paint area and the ovens generate fumes. There is also a sandblast area to clean off certain types of motors. Therefore, Brithinee is also considered a "hazardous material handler." All areas must have permits and this means annual site visitations at different times from different government agencies: the city of Colton, the county of San Bernardino, the state of California, and the Air Quality Management District (AQMD).

To illustrate, both the paint booth and the ovens are required to have permits from the AQMD. This agency wants to see the type of equipment used, how the area is being ventilated, and make sure that not too much smoke or pollutants are being released into the air. The fire department has increasing responsibility as related to hazardous materials and frequently checks. The fire department wants to know the exact location of hazardous products in order to protect their fire personnel and to use the appropriate fire extinguishing techniques when necessary. The Department of Health Services of San Bernardino County has the responsibility for overseeing the hazardous waste generators. The Environmental Protection Agency from the state of California is also interested in looking over the permits of Brithinee Electric. In none of the site visitation cases will Brithinee be notified prior to the agency's visit. Inspection agencies have the right to turn up on any day in order to see the operation.

QUALITY CIRCLES AND JOB ROTATION

In the late 1970s and 1980s, many U.S. firms experimented with quality circles where ten to twelve people meet once a week. In these circles, people discuss how they can do the job better and attain more quality in the product or service. Westinghouse and Lockheed both used quality circles extensively during that time for certain major projects. Brithinee Electric also attempted to institute quality circles in the early eighties, but their experiment lasted only two or three months. One employee thought the idea was good and questioned why the circles were abandoned, but two other employees complained that the circles degenerated into gripe sessions.

Contrary to the expressed hopes of Wally, many shop personnel do not feel job rotation or job enrichment exists at Brithinee. Only the office staff expressed a sense that enough job variety prevails. On the other hand, almost universally the shop personnel said they wanted more variety in their jobs. They often feel "bored" at times, but these statements were followed by the same people saying "there is too much work to allow for job rotation."

Many shop personnel attribute the lack of job rotation to the shop foreman, Rod Samples, who makes all the work assignments for the shop and posts them on the coffee room board. Rod is characterized as "a bright guy," "sharp," "knows his stuff," "intuitive," but also as "moody," "abrasive," "aloof" and "does not communicate" with everyone as he should. At the encouragement of Wally and Don, Rod has participated in various supervisory training programs, but no employee interviewed referenced any improvement in Rod's interpersonal skills. Wally expressed both his appreciation and frustration in

Rod's behavior. One problem is the lack of a suitable alternative. Rod is methodical; he does the paperwork correctly and gets the work done, but he at times seems to demean the contributions of the shop workers. For example, when Wally would ask a shop worker a question, Rod would sometimes intercede and answer for the worker. Wally wanted the worker to answer for himself or herself. Wally identifies Rod as a "bottleneck" to the implementation of his and his brother's philosophy concerning job rotation. Wally wondered: How should the company handle Rod?

Although many shop personnel indicated they are very happy to be working at Brithinee, a constant thread emerged throughout the interviews. Many feel that they somehow want more recognition and/or feedback for the job they do. They need to hear they are doing a good job. Some feel positive feedback through the handsome bonuses they receive in their paycheck, but even so they also want the verbal praise as well.

ORGANIZATIONAL CULTURE

There appears to be a high degree of family sentiment within the organization. Yet, this opinion was more frequently vocalized by Wally, Don, and by members of the office staff than by individuals from the shop. Employees in the shop tend to have less overall formal education and to be less self-motivated in attending seminars and learning than the office personnel. Although not apparent in the first round of interviews, this pattern began to emerge as more individuals were questioned. Members of the office staff mention the company in terms of "we" more often than did the thirteen members of the shop. Office staff expressed the notion that Brithinee is very good about allowing their employees to grow into different jobs (i.e., permitting the person's job to change as the person gains new or different skills).

However, this is not a universal sentiment even in the office. A few mentioned a slight friction exists between the personalities of the office versus those in the shop. One individual said the office personnel think they are "la-dee-da" (or better than the shop employees). Another employee revealed that he was surprised to see so many "cliques" in such a small organization. He indicated five "cliques" at Brithinee exist. Don responded that Brithinee has some groups of people who are more comfortable with each other than outside the group, but he did not consider this abnormal. No one in the organization felt that these groupings harm the productivity of the organization. Overall the morale of the shop personnel appears lower than the morale of the office staff.

PERSONNEL PRACTICES

According to Don and Wally, people hired after 1972 tended not to have backgrounds in building motors. Instead people were hired who exhibited a "good work attitude." Rod Samples, the production manager, stated that people were trained for their job at Brithinee Electric. Turnover was low. Few employees ever left Brithinee. Reasons cited include: good benefits, nice atmosphere, clean organization. One employee who had worked in another shop prior to Brithinee Electric described the experience as "going from the dungeon to Disneyland." Yet, a fair number of employees in the shop were disgruntled. One major issue for some is lack of job rotation.

In addition, Don and Wally were known for not firing anyone. Only one employee was ever mentioned as "being fired" and this individual had been caught for stealing copper wire and reselling it. A couple of employees did point out instances where some employees had been "encouraged" to leave. Don indicated only three individuals had ever been "fired" from Brithinee. He had been responsible for firing two of them. In the latter cases, a lack of personality agreement was cited as the cause. With turnover so low, this means in the past three years only five new people had been hired. Of these five individuals, the jobs had been essentially created for three of them.

The following comments by Wally highlight the personnel policies at Brithinee:

> We are not anxious to hire and fire people. We aren't one to say we have a job so let's go out and hire five more people. We just don't believe in it. We add people slowly. We try to bring them into the culture (not so easy to do sometimes), and [we] try to make them feel that they are part of the family so to speak. People don't accept new people very easily. Depends. Very hard to fit people in without creating friction, without creating hard feelings from the older folk who are already there. It's tough to find people who are non-threatening to others. It's a tough situation and that's a problem. We haven't figured out how to solve all of that just yet. . . . We don't want prima donnas here. . . . Our customers view us as having high quality people throughout.

All employees except Wally and Don Brithinee are paid on an hourly basis. This even includes the outside salesman, Dick Merino, who stated he prefers it that way. Almost all the employees like being paid hourly because they frequently can earn more money by working overtime. To illustrate, the production manager, Rod Samples, often works from 7:00 A.M. to 5:00 P.M. six days a week. He does this by choice, but he appreciates being well-compensated for his time. Overtime is frequent, but according to Don, not enough to justify hiring more people.

Most of the employees feel they are well-paid. However, there are exceptions. Two employees indicated that individuals are not paid fairly. (The lowest paid made approximately four times the minimum wage or approximately the average starting salary of a college graduate in accounting. The highest paid shop person made about twice that.) Although the casewriter pursued the issue of pay equity, the individuals who complained could not actually explain their rationale for why they perceived this pay inequity. It just exists in their eyes. In a different instance, one employee thought most people for what they do are overpaid at Brithinee. Others thought pay at Brithinee is a mystery. Don said individuals are rewarded on the basis of "effort" to the extent that pay increases are based 85% to 90% on effort in meeting the needs of the customer, and 10%–15% on skill.

Ideally Don and Wally would like to stagger the evaluations such that two employees would be evaluated every month, but in actuality, half the employees are evaluated at a time. Don asserted "trying to put a dollar sign on a human being . . . that's the toughest job an employer has—to put a value on another person's time and effort."

Many of the employees complimented Don and Wally Brithinee for being "first-class" guys. If an employee wants a new piece of equipment because (1) the old piece of equipment was old or dangerous, or (2) a new piece of equipment would allow the person to do his or her job better, Don and Wally would buy the equipment regardless of the price. The only question asked: Would this help to do the job better with higher quality?

PROFIT SHARING

Profits are pooled from all areas and shared by the employees regardless of how the profits are generated, either by repairs or sales. To encourage a philosophy of meeting the customer needs, the company does not pay more to repair people if they fit more motors nor do they pay salespeople on commission. The Brithinee profit sharing program was described by many employees as "generous." Employees of the company are unaware, however, that new changes in the tax reform package might have an impact on how Brithinee handles their profit sharing in the future.

BENEFITS

New employees receive one week vacation after one year, two weeks after two years, three weeks after five years, and four weeks plus one day after ten years. There is no allotment for sick leave. Don feels strongly that their system eliminated sick leave abuse, which has been problematic for other companies. Brithinee's industry typically does not have a widespread use of sick leave. Don stated, "the goal is to reward people for being here." He also added that employees could accumulate vacation allotment and then use it for other occasions such as illness or personal leave.

FUTURE CHALLENGES FOR BRITHINEE

Almost universally Brithinee employees responded favorably about Brithinee's future, but there are concerns. One person asked: How can Brithinee compete in a very price conscious environment? There was also an acknowledgment that the industry is very competitive and has become even more competitive in the past few years. Customer loyalty to Brithinee is not as strong as it had once been because so many people are very price conscious.

One of the persons involved in inside sales plainly stated: "(I)t is just harder to make a sale than it was before."

Employees appear to have a strong sense of what the company stands for, i.e., quality service, but no one remembered the company having a formal written mission statement. Don said the following:

> We never crystallized our mission ... but I guess it would be to provide first class or highest quality service for industrial clients to their rotating electrical apparatus and to provide very dependable service in the distribution of electrical motor controls and electronic control devices.

Don added that Brithinee Electric wants to be known for their good service. They would not just take any job. They would turn down jobs which they felt unequipped to handle. Don stated they want to give the highest value to their customers.

By the year 1993, Don wants to see a Brithinee Electric expansion beyond their current location. Plus he wants to see a more independent work force (one less dependent on his brother and himself). He feels this would make the business more valuable and "more tolerable." This would be a "great accomplishment." He also hopes to see a better developed sales effort with a broadening of the sales products. He wants to achieve more sophisticated systems than they now sell. Don admitted they do not have a formal planning system at the current time to help them achieve these objectives. However, he seemed confident taking these items slowly one step at time would be the way to accomplish them.

Don expressed the sentiment that he works day-in and day-out to create an independent work force. He attempts to push decisions on to other people, force them to be less dependent on himself and his brother, train people so they have the tools to make decisions. Then day-in and day-out, he stresses the philosophy of Brithinee Electric which is "service to the customer first over quick profits or any other short-term goals." He stated "devotion to the customers adds to the permanence of our business." Later, he commented "our motor business was built up on—if it was in our grasp to do the job, we said 'yes, we will do it' and we made ourselves available even if that meant canceling our plans to do something else ... but we did it and that's how we built up this business. ... we have always been willing to put ourselves out. Even at three in the morning."

In terms of broadening beyond the local location, Don and Wally have been in discussion with other businesses. In the past couple of months, another business in Oxnard, California, had been offered to them as a possible purchase, but no steps have been taken in this area. They were still evaluating it. The most likely type of purchase would be another business similar to their own, but possibly in the San Diego area where they already have a few customers. They want to be able to clone most of their business but cover another area. Don wondered: Is it more cost effective to set up a location in San Diego which is 100 miles south, or is it better to attempt to handle those customers from the current location using their own trucks and delivery service? Could they handle all their work from Colton and still be properly represented in San Diego?

PLAN FOR SUCCESSION

They have no plan for eventual succession of the company. Wally is single and has no children. Don has one child, a daughter five months old. In 1980, they already experienced one crisis over transition which occurred when the twins' father returned to the business after his wife's death. After the senior Brithinee recovered from his heart attack, he positioned himself out of the company. Currently, Wally reflected that Brithinee Electric has no plans to sell out. Personally he is having "too much fun."

THE GOLDEN GATE BREWING COMPANY

**BRENT CALLINICOS
AND RICHARD I. LEVIN**

At a booth in Harry's, a bar overlooking the San Francisco Bay, James Cook poured a fresh glass of amber-colored Golden Gate Lager and dropped a bottle cap onto the beer's head. The cap floated like a lily pad on the foam. "That's what you get from using all malt, no rices or corn—a very firm head," he said. "It looks like whipped cream and acts like egg whites, as my father used to say." When Cook's glass was finished, the inside was coated with strips of foam, *Belgian lace* in brewer's jargon, and a sign of a beer's purity. "People usually think of a local beer as crummy, cheap beer. I plan to change the way they think," Cook said.

Cook is apt to talk this way, because (1) he is president of the fledgling Golden Gate Brewing Company, (2) he is the brewer of Golden Gate Lager, and (3) he is the sixth consecutive eldest son to become a brewer.

Cook, 36, is a former high-paid, high-powered management consultant with the Boston Consulting Group; he holds a Harvard B.A., M.B.A., and J.D. In 1984, Cook's idea of brewing and distributing a high-quality beer, capable of luring discerning beer drinkers away from European and Canadian imports, was just an idea. Golden Gate Lager was introduced in San Francisco on July 4, an appropriate day, but accidental timing according to Cook. The Golden Gate Brewing Company was incorporated in 1984.

Cook's goal is clear: "I intend to go head to head against imported beers. Nowhere in the world but America do they drink so much imported beer. Here, imported beer is popular because our domestic beer is so bad. My work is to give Americans an alternative to drinking foreign beers. I want to start a revolution in the way people think about American beer. There is nothing

Source: **Prepared by Brent Callinicos, research assistant, under the direction of Professor Richard I. Levin, University of North Carolina—Chapel Hill as a basis for classroom discussion and not to illustrate either effective or ineffective handling of administrative situations.** © **Richard L. Levin, 1988.**

wrong with standard domestic beers, for what they are. They are clean, consistent and cheap. But they are also bland and mediocre. They are mass market products. People can recall, off the top of their heads, the advertising, the slogans and the music for most beers, but they can't remember the taste."

For years, small local breweries have been swallowed up by the giants like Anheuser-Busch. The advent of small boutique breweries, in California, Colorado, and New York, making limited quantities of quality beer, has opposed this trend. Analogous to David confronting Goliath, Cook acknowledges that the odds and the history are against small regional breweries. But Cook is betting on a combination of his family brewing background, his own management training, and a limited target market to create long-term Golden Gate Lager drinkers.

Golden Gate Lager is currently sold in two locations. San Francisco and Munich. As of November 1985, the current sales volume of 6,000 cases per month represents less than one minute of production for Anheuser-Busch. Cook reports that he has sold as much beer in the past 6 months as Anheuser-Busch makes in about six minutes: "They spill more beer every hour than I make in a month." In six months, the Golden Gate Brewing Company has sold 25,000 cases in California. His more than 200 accounts range from liquor stores to exclusive hotels to neighborhood bars, such as Harry's. Exhibits 1–3 provide information regarding the population demographics of the San Francisco SCSA (Standard Consolidated Statistical Area) and general demographics of U.S. beer drinkers.

"By my standards I have been very successful," said Cook. Demand had been strong, but he wondered if it would last. "People who drink imports will try it because it's new, but will Golden Gate Lager be just a flash?" Cook is hoping there are enough beer aficionados in San Francisco, but he is wondering if he should try to expand in Europe, or if he should concentrate on the west coast, the east coast, or selected cities throughout the country. How fast should he expand? Can Cook sustain his momentum as regionals, such as Coors, expand distribution nationwide? With several comparable local brews being sold in the area, will his marketing strategy have to change? Given the complex issues facing the beer industry, how should he proceed? What are the risks involved? Cook realized he needed to make some strategic decisions.

THE BEER INDUSTRY IN THE UNITED STATES

DIMENSIONS OF THE INDUSTRY

The annual retail value of the brewing industry's products is near $3.7 billion. Total employment in the industry is close to 40,000 persons. The average hourly earnings of a brewing industry employee was $18.27 in 1985, a 3.2% increase over 1984. In a recent typical year, the industry's gross assets amounted to $6,639,979,000. Its net worth, computed from income tax returns, was $3,377,780,000.

EXHIBIT 1 SAN FRANCISCO BAY AREA

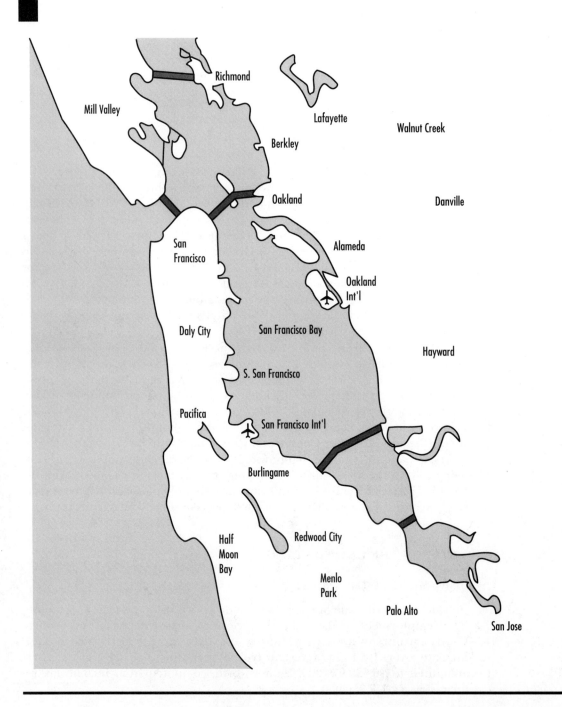

EXHIBIT 2   POPULATION CHARACTERISTICS, SAN FRANCISCO/OAKLAND SCSA, 1980

During the decade 1970 to 1980, the population of San Francisco/Oakland SCSA (Standard Consolidated Statistical Area) increased by 142,000 people, or 4.5%.

NUMBER OF PEOPLE

Year	SF/Oakland SCSA*	Percent Change
1960	2,649,000	N/A
1970	3,109,000	17.37
1980	3,251,000	4.57

*SCSA = Standard Consolidated Statistical Area

AGE COMPOSITION

Age	# People	Percent of SCSA
Under 18	1,296,000	25.02
18–24	666,000	12.86
25–34	989,000	19.10
35–44	668,000	12.90
45–54	536,000	10.35
55–64	491,000	9.48
65–over	533,000	10.29
Under 21	1,571,000	30.33

ETHNIC DATA

Race	Percent of SF/Oakland SCSA
White	62.37
Black	10.71
Spanish	9.64
Indian	10.93
Eskimo	.47
Other**	5.88

**Includes Japanese, Chinese, Filipino, Korean, Asian Indian, Vietnamese, Hawaiian, Samoan, etc.

EDUCATION, PERSONS 25 YEARS OLD AND OVER

Years of Education	Percent of SCSA
Less than 5	3
High School Only	71
Four year college or more	26
Median school years completed	13

Of the persons 16 years old and over, 66.5% were in the labor force. (This includes those in armed forces.) Of these 43.4% were females and 56.6% were males.

OCCUPATION

Group	Percent of SCSA
Managerial and Professional	28.28
Technical and Sales-related	35.43
Service Occupations	11.84
Farming/Forestry/Fishing	1.15
Craft/Repair Group	11.12
Operators/Laborers	12.18

INCOME BREAKDOWN

Income	Households	Percent of SCSA
Under $5,000	199,763	10.12
$5,000–$9,999	243,278	12.32
$10,000–$19,999	511,225	25.90
$20,000–$34,999	611,279	30.97
$35,000–$49,999	258,758	13.11
$50,000–Over	149,577	7.58
Total households	1,973,880	
Median income	$20,607	

EXHIBIT 3 1983 U.S. BEER DRINKER DEMOGRAPHICS

PERCENTAGE OF THE POPULATION DRINKING

	Domestic	Light	Imported	Malt	Ale	Draft
All Adults	39.6%	24.4%	15.8%	8.3%	8.6%	26.2%
Males	54.0	28.6	22.0	11.0	12.0	35.6
Females	26.6	20.6	10.3	5.9	5.5	17.7
Age:						
18–24	51.2	29.1	26.6	14.8	14.0	36.5
25–34	49.0	30.8	20.8	10.9	10.9	36.1
35–44	39.3	27.8	15.8	7.3	7.8	26.8
45–54	35.5	23.5	13.5	5.6	7.0	22.8
55–64	30.9	16.7	8.5	4.1	5.6	16.9
65 or older	23.4	13.0	4.6	4.3	3.8	9.8
Grad. college	47.5	32.2	28.0	6.0	12.4	36.3
Attended college	45.3	30.0	22.0	8.9	11.9	33.5
Grad. high school	38.4	23.9	13.6	8.4	7.8	25.8
Not grad. high school	23.6	17.4	8.5	9.2	5.6	16.7
Employed full time	46.2	30.2	20.4	9.0	10.5	33.2
Part time	36.7	24.9	17.7	8.0	9.0	26.5
Not employed	32.1	17.3	10.1	7.6	6.2	17.7
Professional	48.2	32.8	27.1	7.4	12.8	37.0
Clerical/Sales	38.6	29.8	17.6	7.3	9.2	29.2
Craftsman/Foreman	52.9	30.7	17.7	9.1	8.4	36.3
Other employed	44.3	25.5	16.2	11.5	9.6	28.9
Single	50.8	28.5	29.0	14.9	14.5	36.5
Married	38.3	24.1	12.9	6.1	7.1	24.6
Divorced	30.7	20.2	11.0	8.7	6.7	19.6
Parents	41.0	26.5	14.5	8.8	7.7	27.9
White	39.8	24.9	15.8	6.1	8.4	27.4
Black	36.8	19.3	14.4	25.4	9.8	16.4
Other	42.0	27.6	25.6	12.7	7.5	27.6
Geographic location:						
Northeast	42.9	22.0	22.3	7.2	13.5	27.7
East central	39.1	24.2	11.6	7.5	9.3	27.2
West central	42.3	29.0	13.1	7.4	5.6	30.3
South	32.7	22.8	11.1	9.6	6.4	21.0
Pacific	45.1	26.1	22.3	9.5	7.8	28.4
Household income:						
$40,000 +	45.6	29.7	24.1	6.0	11.8	32.7
$30,000 +	44.2	28.8	22.5	6.0	10.7	32.0
$25,000 +	44.1	28.4	21.3	6.4	10.3	31.4
$20–24,999	38.1	26.0	14.0	6.8	7.7	27.5
$15–19,999	42.5	26.7	14.5	10.0	8.7	28.8
$10–14,999	36.0	20.9	11.2	9.1	7.1	21.7
under $10,000	32.3	16.5	9.5	11.3	6.5	16.6

WHAT THE INDUSTRY BUYS

Agricultural commodities, the output of more than four million acres of farm land worth over $700 million, are used annually by the brewing industry. These include

- 4.9 billion pounds or 143.8 million bushels of choice malt—worth $380M;
- other select grains, chiefly corn and rice—worth $221 million; and
- hops—value to the grower of $80 million.

Some 86.9% of all beer sold is packaged in cans or bottles. In one year, the brewing industry uses more than

- 33.1 billion steel and aluminum cans;
- 19.2 billion bottles in returnable and non-returnable form; and
- $525 million for interest, rentals, repairs, maintenance, etc.

The industry's annual bill for containers—cans, bottles, kegs, and related packaging materials purchased from other American industries—is close to $4.5 billion. Supplies and services of numerous kinds are also required in brewing and distributing malt beverages. Annual average outlays for these include

- fuel, power, and water, $420 million;
- wholesale payroll, $1.8 billion; and
- brewery equipment and improvements, $550 million.

THE INDUSTRY'S PRODUCTS
AND TERMINOLOGY

Beers fall into two broad categories—those that are top-fermented and those that are bottom-fermented.

Bottom-fermented

Pilsner/Pilsener. The world's most famous beer style, it was named after the excellent beer brewed in Pilsen, Czechoslovakia, for the past 700 years. The term became generic, but the finest example remains Pilsner Urqueil from Pilsen. It is a pale, golden-colored, distinctly hoppy beer.

Lager. All bottom-fermented beers are lagers. This is a generic term, though it is sometimes applied to the most basic bottom-fermented brew produced by a brewery. In Britain and the United States, the majority of lagers are very loose, local interpretations of the Pilsner style.

Bock. Bock Beer is a special springtime brew, made like lager beer, but of a somewhat deeper color and more pronounced flavor.

Top-fermented

Ale. Generic term for English-style top-fermented beers. Usually copper-colored, but sometimes darker. It is usually paler in color and differs in flavor from lager beer.

Porter. Originally a local London beer made with roasted, unmalted barley, well hopped, and blended. Dark brown, it is as heavy as most ales.

Stout. Darker in color and sweeter or maltier than ale. The darkest, richest, maltiest of all regularly produced beers.

"Malt Liquor." This is a term conjured up to describe beers that exceed the legal alcohol levels—5% in the United States—of that nation. They are most often made as lagers, but the American version can be sweetish or more bitter than the traditional lagers.

Barrel. This refers to a full barrel, which has a volume of 31 gallons.

INDUSTRY OVERVIEW

Historically, the U.S. beer industry had many small regional producers, but now it is emerging as an oligopoly—a market structure dominated by only a few firms. In 1876, there were 2,685 breweries and in 1947 there were only 500. The number of operating breweries declined from more than 350 in 1952 to fewer than 80 in 1982 (see Exhibit 4). Acquisition, consolidation, and standardization has characterized this industry. While this trend has been mirrored in each of the four census regions, it was least pronounced in the South and the West, where the overall demand for beer grew rapidly. Major national firms were more willing to purchase struggling regional producers or construct new facilities in the South and West. Today there are six major national brewers which control over 90% of the domestic sales. The companies are Anheuser-Busch, Miller, Stroh, Heileman, Coors, and Pabst (see Exhibit 5).

After several years of flat or nearly flat sales, beer consumption declined about 0.7% in 1984. This represents the first decline in twenty-seven years. The year 1984 also closed with a decline in production of approximately 1.2%. Per capita consumption of beer has also declined, and for 1985, per capita consumption is estimated to remain at the 1984 level—24 gallons. The long-term outlook for the industry is less encouraging. Chris Lole of the Stroh Brewery Co. believes beer sales will remain flat for the next ten, possibly twenty, years (see Exhibits 6–9).

EXHIBIT 4   NUMBER OF OPERATING BREWERIES BY CENSUS REGION

REGION	1952	1960	1970	1982	PERCENT OF TOTAL 1952	PERCENT OF TOTAL 1982
Northeast	100	62	45	18	28.0	22.8
North central	164	99	61	25	45.9	31.6
South	42	33	26	20	11.8	25.3
West	51	35	22	16	14.3	20.3
Total U.S.	357	229	154	79	100.0	100.0

EXHIBIT 5   LEADING U.S. BREWERS' DOMESTIC BEER MARKET SHARE (In %)

BREWER	1970	1975	1980	1982	1983	1984
Anheuser-Busch	18.2	23.7	28.9	33.5	34.1	34.6
Miller	4.2	8.7	21.5	22.3	21.1	22.1
Stroh[1]	2.7	3.5	3.6	13.0	13.7	13.5
G. Heileman	2.5	3.1	7.7	8.2	9.9	9.3
Adolph Coors	6.0	8.0	8.0	6.8	7.7	7.2
Pabst	8.6	10.5	8.7	6.8	7.2	6.8
Genesee	1.2	1.5	2.1	1.9	1.8	1.9
C. Schmidt	2.5	2.2	2.1	1.8	1.8	1.7
Falstaff	5.4	5.0	2.3	1.8	1.5	1.8
Pittsburgh			.6	.6	.6	.5
Other	48.7	33.8	14.5	3.3	.6	.6
Total	100.0	100.0	100.0	100.0	100.0	100.0

[1]Stroh acquired F.M. Schaefer Brewing and Jos. Schlitz Brewing in 1981 and 1982, respectively.

However, there is one segment of growth in this troubled industry—imports. Imported brands have grown from 0.7% of total consumption in 1970 to 3.4% in 1983 (aided somewhat over the years by a strong U.S. dollar). Imports occupy the highground in terms of quality in consumers' perception; and trading up continues to benefit imports. As import volume has grown, an increasing number of brands have appeared, and many more are now being advertised. The continued growth in this segment, coupled with the decline in domestic sales, meant an increase in imports' share to almost 4% in 1984.

For regional and smaller brewers, it is becoming increasingly difficult to move a product that is falling in demand and cannot be backed by the advertis-

EXHIBIT 6   U.S. BEER SALES—DOMESTIC AND IMPORTED, 1984 AND 1983

	31-GALLON BARRELS (IN MILLIONS)		% OF TOTAL		% GAIN/ LOSS
	1984	*1983*	*1984*	*1983*	*1984*
Domestic beer	175.3	177.5	96.1	96.6	− 1.2
Imported beer	7.2	6.3	3.9	3.4	14.3
Total sales	182.5	183.8	100.0	100.0	− 0.7

Note: Total does not include exports.

EXHIBIT 7   PRODUCTION OF MALT BEVERAGES IN THE UNITED STATES, SELECTED YEARS (IN THOUSANDS)

YEAR	BARRELS	YEAR	BARRELS
1904	48,265	1977	172,229
1914	66,189	1978	171,639
1924	4,891	1979	183,515
1934	37,679	1980	188,374
1944	81,726	1981	194,542
1954	92,561	1982	193,984
1964	103,018	1983	195,664
1974	153,053	1984	193,416

ing revenues of the large national breweries. Interestingly, the microbrewer/ brew pub trend continues. More and more entrepreneurs are allured by the prospects of concocting their own distinctive beer and operating their own business.

Some explain the disappointing sales trends by pointing to the 7% price hike many brewers took at the beginning of 1983. This put beer prices well ahead of the inflation rate. However, there was no discernible improvement in sales when prices were discounted and income and employment levels improved.

EXTERNAL FACTORS: THREATS TO THE INDUSTRY

The beer industry must operate in a changing environment, where the name of the game is survival for some domestic breweries. There are several external threats that affect the beer industry. First is that the U.S. population is increasingly interested in healthier lifestyles, which could reduce beer consumption. Consumption and purchase-pattern preference of 25–40-year-olds have changed dramatically in recent years. This group, because of interests in appearance, exercise, and career advancement, exhibits a preference for drinks with fewer calories and lower alcohol content. Over-40 drinkers are also increasingly health and diet conscious.

EXHIBIT 8   U.S. PER CAPITA CONSUMPTION OF MALT BEVERAGES, 1974–1984 (YEARS IN GALLONS)

1974	20.9	1978	23.1	1982	24.4
1975	21.3	1979	23.8	1983	24.2
1976	21.5	1980	24.3	1984	24.0
1977	22.4	1981	24.6		

EXHIBIT 9 BARRELAGE OF TOP TEN BREWERS, 1984 VS. 1983 (IN 31-GALLON BARRELS)

	1984	1983	GAIN/LOSS (BARRELS)	GAIN/LOSS (%)
Anheuser-Busch	64,000,000	60,500,000	3,500,000	5.8
Miller	37,520,000	37,470,000	50,000	0.1
Stroh	23,900,000	24,300,000	(400,000)	−1.6
G. Heileman	16,760,000	17,549,000	(789,000)	−4.5
Adolph Corrs	13,187,000	13,719,000	(532,000)	−3.9
Pabst	11,562,000	12,804,000	(1,242,000)	−9.7
Genesee	3,000,000	3,200,000	(200,000)	−6.3
C. Schmidt	2,500,000	2,800,000	(300,000)	−10.7
Falstaff	2,338,000	2,705,000	(367,000)	−13.6
Pittsburgh	950,000	1,000,000	(50,000)	−5.0
All others	2,134,000	3,597,000	(1,463,000)	−40.7
Total	177,851,000	179,644,000	(1,793,000)	−1.0

Note: Total includes exports but no imports.

An important negative factor for future beer sales is demographics. Growth of the 18–34-year-old age group is winding down. Beer sales have closely tracked the baby boom age bulge in the population. Domestic industry sales grew at only a 0.6% compounded rate in the 1950s and 3.5% in the 1960s and 1970s. Exhibit 10 shows that the teenage population (the source of most new drinkers) has been decreasing and is forecast to continue its decline. Brewers, therefore, confront a decline in potential new users. In addition, the young adult population (20–29 years) is also declining. The beer industry relies on this segment to replace sales lost due to attrition in the future drinking population. Finally, people between the ages of 30 and 49 will increase substantially and by 1990 will constitute 30% of the population. Historically, this group has been an important age group. However, industry analysts say this group is the one most concerned about alcohol abuse and drunk driving. This category has been nicknamed the neo-prohibitionists.

The beer industry faces another demographic change that will create problems. Blue collar workers have traditionally been the heaviest consumers of beer. Today, the economy is shifting toward the service sector and the blue collar work force is declining.

The emergence of wine coolers is also taking a toll on the beer industry. Wine coolers appeal to beer drinkers and to non-beer drinkers. Coolers are, to some extent, a beer substitute. Introduced five years ago, there are about 50 cooler brands now available, which contain 6% alcohol. Retail sales in 1984 were $360 million and in 1985 approached $700 million. However, cooler sales for 1986 are projected at 35 million cases, versus the 2.5 billion cases of

EXHIBIT 10   U.S. POPULATION BY SELECTED AGE GROUPS, 1983–1990

	POPULATION			COMPOUND ANNUAL CHANGE
AGE GROUP	*1983*	*1985*	*1990*	1983–90
Young children				
Under 15 Years	22.0%	21.7%	21.9%	0.8%
Teens,				
15–19	8.2	7.7	6.8	−1.7
Young adults,				
20–29	18.3	18.1	16.0	−0.3
Middle years				
30–39	15.1	15.9	16.8	2.5
40–49	10.4	10.8	12.7	3.9
Older adults,				
50–64	14.3	13.8	13.1	−0.3
Senior citizens,				
65 and older	11.7	12.0	12.7	2.2
Total population				
(millions)	243.3	238.6	249.8	0.9

the beer market. Some analysts believe that wine coolers are firmly established, while others contend that coolers are just a fad.

The market will shrink further due to the enforcement of drunk driving laws and the rise of the national drinking age to 21. The growing awareness of the need for responsible drinking habits has been fostered by groups such as Mothers Against Drunk Drivers (MADD). According to MADD, about 55% of all highway fatalities in 1983 were drinking related; 1984 figures indicated a small decline to 54%. The sobering truth has brought attention to the dangers of alcohol abuse and has resulted in stiffer penalties for drunk drivers and new laws to combat alcohol abuse.

In July 1984, President Reagan signed into law the National Minimum Drinking Age Act, which grants the federal government the authority to withhold federal highway funds from states that fail to raise their legal drinking age to 21 by 1987. When the law was enacted there were 27 states and the District of Columbia with a minimum age below 21, but many have introduced legislation to raise the age, or are expected to.

Some 360 new drunk driving laws have been passed nationwide since 1981, and many states and municipalities have banned "happy hour," which encourages increased alcohol consumption through discount prices. Also, there are 37 states with statutes holding the establishments and hosts liable for the subsequent behavior of intoxicated patrons or guests. These could also serve to reduce been consumption.

The Industry's Reaction. Faced with these problems, many other industries would retrench, concentrate on keeping primary profit-making brands afloat, and try to ride out the storm. The brewery industry's response has been almost the opposite. New brands and extensions have appeared on retailers' shelves at a record pace. Beers that had been available only regionally are being moved into broader distribution. New light beers, low-alcohol beers, low-priced beers, super-premium beers, and malt liquors have emerged. Exhibit 11 lists the brands introduced in 1984 by both national and regional brewers.

The major U.S. brewers introduced twenty-one new products or line extensions in 1984. Two-thirds of these new product introductions were low-alcohol or low-calorie products. Anheuser-Busch (A-B) was the first major brewer to unveil its low-alcohol entry, LA; and regional brewers soon got into

EXHIBIT 11 DOMESTIC BEER BRANDS INTRODUCED IN 1984

BRAND	BREWER
Black Label 11-11 Malt Liquor	Heileman
Black Label LA[1]	Heileman
Blatz LA[1]	Heileman
Big Man Malt Liquor	Eastern Brewing
Choice[1]	F.X. Malt
Golden Hawk	Schmidt
Ice Man Malt Liquor	Pabst
I.C. Golden Lager	Pittsburgh
King Cobra Malt Liquor	Anheuser-Busch
LA[2]	Anheuser-Busch
Light-N-Lo[1]	Latrobe
Little Kings Premium	Schoenling
Lone Star LA[1]	Heileman
Low Alcohol Gold[1,2]	Pabst
Low Alcohol Pabst Extra Light[1,2]	Pabst
Meister Brau Light	Miller
Milwaukee's Best	Miller
Old Style LA[1]	Heileman
Oscar Wildes's	Pearl
Plank Road Original Draft	Miller
Rainier LA[1]	Heileman
Schaefer Low Alcohol[1]	Stroh
Schmidt LA[1]	Heileman
Select Special 50 Low Alcohol[1]	Pearl
Sharpe's LA[1]	Miller
Silver Thunder Malt Liquor	Stroh

[1]Low in alcohol.
[2]Repositioned brand.

the act. To date, however, the low- and no-alcohol products have not worked out well. They are viewed as weak with no zing. They seem to appeal to the drinker who does not drink very much beer to begin with, in contrast to light beer, which appeal to the heavy beer drinker.

Although new product introductions slowed in 1985, the beer industry is doing everything possible to attract new customers. A shrinking market means brewers must steal share from competitors. Large brewers generally desire to have something for everyone. Today, brewers do not want to be underrepresented. The lower-price/lower-profit beer category has also seen introduction. Traditionally, in the low-price segment, price is supposed to move the product, and no advertising is performed due to the thin margins. National firms are now doing away with tradition by expanding marketing budgets.

Taxes.   The brewing industry confronts another problem, the ever-present threat of a federal excise tax increase. In 1984, Congress enacted legislation to increase the excise tax on distilled spirits. This increase is most likely an indication of what is almost certain to follow. Increases in the rate have accompanied each national emergency since the first dollar-a-barrel tax was applied during the Civil War. Federal legislators look at the excise tax as part of the solution to the nation's huge deficit. The anti-alcohol movement seeks to link the excise tax to a Medicare/Medicaid bailout. The distillers are seeking tax equity with beer and wine. An increase in this tax, however, would squeeze profit margins even more.

Beer is one of the most highly taxed consumer products. Taxes constitute the largest individual item in the price of beer. The federal excise tax is $9 a barrel, and state taxes average approximately $5.41 a barrel. (Effective February 1977, a brewer who produces not more than 2 million barrels of beer in a year has a $7 a barrel federal tax rate on the first $60,000 sold or consumed.) In addition, there are federal and state occupational taxes on brewers, wholesalers, and retailers, as well as local taxes in some states.

In 1983, the United States government received $1.6 billion in excise taxes on malt beverages. Combined annual federal, state, and local taxes equal almost three billion dollars. The government earns over $14 for each barrel of beer or ale sold; the brewing industry's average profit rate per barrel after taxes is estimated between two and three dollars.

INTERNAL: INDUSTRY FACTORS

The major causes of the national beer industry oligopoly appear to be economies of scale and product differentiation. Economies of scale, which occur when large plants produce at lower unit costs than smaller ones, appear to exist in the beer industry in which brewing and bottling processes have become increasingly mechanized. The increased capacity attained by many individual breweries over the past twenty years has forced the closing or sale of numerous regional producers. Industry experts contend that the wave of consolidation has not ended. Additional economies of scale in volume and production are necessary. Currently there is excess capacity and certain plants are inefficient (see Exhibit 12). Except for A-B, the industry is operating between 75% and 85% of capacity. If plants are consolidated, resulting in increased volumes, profitability can be increased.

Even though the U.S. beer industry is suffering from overcapacity, two brewers announced expansion plans during 1985. The Adolph Coors Company intends to build a $70 million beer packaging plant in Virginia, and, if sales justify it, the facility will be expanded to include full brewing facilities. The G. Heileman Brewing Company plans to construct a new brewery in Milwaukee. The facility will specialize in more costly imported-style beers. The industry's overcapacity was accentuated by Miller Brewing's decision to write-down $140 million of its $450 million new plant and Stroh Brewery Company's decision to close its older, underutilized Detroit plant.

Successful product differentiation occurs when a firm convinces customers that real or imagined differences in its beer render it preferable to that of the competitors. Larger brewers, with national sales and multi-plant operations, can often more easily attain this "high-quality" image than local or regional brewers. There also appear to be economies of scale in brand proliferation and product extensions. Large brewers can more easily (and cost-effectively) segment all price and product categories. The high fixed costs associated with advertising new brands can be spread over a large sales volume that smaller brewers do not have. Large firms can realize lower advertising costs on each barrel than can small firms. If the larger brewers can induce their smaller competitors to expend huge amounts on media advertising, the former are better able to withstand the resulting cost-price squeeze.

EXHIBIT 12   U.S. BREWING INDUSTRY CAPACITY AND USAGE, 1983

BREWER	NUMBER OF PLANTS	TOTAL CAPACITY	SHIPMENTS	% OF CAPACITY
Anheuser-Busch	11	66.5	60.5	91.0
Miller	7	54.0	37.5	69.4
Stroh	7	32.6	24.3	74.5
G. Heileman	12	25.5	17.5	68.6
Adolph Coors	1	15.5	13.7	88.4
Pabst	4	15.0	12.8	85.3
Genesee	1	4.0	3.2	80.0
C. Schmidt	2	5.0	3.2	64.0
Falstaff	5	5.0	2.7	54.0
Pittsburgh	1	1.2	1.0	83.3
All others	34	7.4	3.7	50.0
Domestic total	85	231.7	180.1	77.7

Note: Total capacity and shipments are given in millions of barrels.

Advertising has grown considerably in importance and in expense. In 1984, brewers spent an estimated $780 million. Advertising expenditures in 1983 averaged $2.74 per barrel. The evidence that high advertising expenditures and high-profit levels are positively correlated is, however, somewhat mixed. At Schlitz, for example, advertising expenditures on each barrel rose dramatically at a time when sales and operating profit per barrel both fell. Similarly, Coors had higher profit figures when advertising expenditure levels were extremely low and lower profits when advertising outlays accelerated. However, A-B and Miller have increased both profit on each barrel and market share, at a time when advertising expenditures increased.

Imports. To the dismay of domestic brewers, imports are expected to perform well throughout the remainder of the 1980s. Between 1980–1984, the quantity of beer imported increased about 12% annually. Five countries, the Netherlands, Canada, West Germany, Mexico, and the United Kingdom, account for about 90% of all U.S. imports, but over forty other countries also ship beer to the United States. The imports' share of the U.S. beer market has grown from 1.1% in 1975 to 3.9% in 1984. A New York based research firm projects a 15% increase in import shipments for 1986. By 1990, it predicts the import market will almost double in worth. Of the 120 beer wholesalers that the firm interviewed, 68% felt imports would capture at least 10% of the total U.S. beer market by the end of the decade.

Ten years ago, imported beers were esoteric products consumed by a small elite, in a handful of markets. Since then the industry has exploded, with beer drinker's desire, taste, and imagery fueling this growth. According to industry analyst Emanuel Goldman. "The imports have image. We live in a self-indulgent age that's getting more and more self-indulgent, and people want something different. They can get something different, upscale and feel good about it with imports. There is tremendous selection, too. The consumer seems to feel that imports are superior beers."

The top ten imported brands dominate about 87% of import sales. Heineken maintains the lead with an estimated 34% of the market, while Molson holds second place with 13.4%. Fortifying the Canadian segment is Moosehead in the number four spot and Labatt in the fifth place with 6% and 4.5% of the market, respectively. Beck's is in third place with 8.9% of the market and its closest German competitor, St. Pauli Girl, ranks seventh. Rounding out the top ten is Mexico's Dos Equis in sixth place; Australia's Foster's Lager, eighth; Amstel, the leading imported light beer, number nine; and Corona from Mexico in tenth place. (See Exhibit 13.)

Favorable demographics and an improving economy have aided this segment. The rise of the Hispanic population and the popularity of Mexican cuisine have fared well for Mexican beers, while the growing oriental population has given rise to a host of Chinese and Japanese brews. Most significant has been the appeal of imported beer to status-conscious consumers. A prime market eager for imported beers has been the young urban professionals, with a desire for unusual and different products, especially those of a foreign bent.

EXHIBIT 13 IMPORTED BRANDS (BY SALES)

TOP TEN	SECOND TEN (ALPHABETICALLY)
1. Heineken (Netherlands)	Carta Blanca (Mexico)
2. Molson (Canada)	Dinkelacker (Germany)
3. Beck's (Germany)	Dortmunder (Germany)
4. Moosehead (Canada)	Grolsch (Netherlands)
5. Labatt (Canada)	Guinness (U.K.)
6. St. Pauli Girl (Germany)	Kirin (Japan)
7. Dos Equis (Mexico)	Kronenbourg (France)
8. Foster's Lager (Australia)	O'Keefe (Canada)
9. Amstel Light (Netherlands)	San Miquel (Philippines)
10. Corona (Mexico)	Tecate (Mexico)

In addition, imports have seen only two price increases in the last five years, and as long as imported beer prices stay close to the superpremium domestic brews, they will remain a good buy for the consumer. With the domestic category remaining relatively flat. Americans looking for full-flavored beers are trading up to the imports.

The strong U.S. dollar has encouraged importation. An estimated ten new imported beers entered the U.S. every month in 1984. Exhibit 14 provides a partial list of the imported brands introduced in 1984. If the dollar becomes weaker, many of these beers may disappear, because they will be unable to pay the price of admission.

There are two major obstacles in trying to capture American market share. The first is Van Munching & Company, which distributes Heineken. Heineken, with its commanding market share, essentially sets the benchmark pricing level for much of the import category. Many feel you cannot enter the U.S. market if you are above Heineken in price. The second major problem is a paradox created by the very success of the category, namely brand proliferation and the resulting market dilution.

Success hinges on the ability to come up with the "unique selling proposition" to cut through the multitude of brands competing for available market share. One technique used by imports is a unique packaging profile. The theory behind this is that the consumer knows none of the beers, but he will try the one that looks a little different. This is supported by the number of American beer drinkers who first bought Grolsch, if for no other reason than to see what sort of brew was in its distinctive bottle with the old-fashioned wire closure and ceramic stopper. More imports are also moving to a green bottle for their products. Consumer research shows that Americans feel green glass is more appealing for a light-colored beer.

Although beer tasting and tavern promotion nights are the most cost-effective ways to promote public awareness, reliance on heavy advertising is in-

EXHIBIT 14   IMPORTED BEER BRANDS INTRODUCED IN 1984

BRAND	COUNTRY	BRAND	COUNTRY
ABC Stout	Singapore	Hombre	Mexico
Affligem	Belgium	John Peel Export	Britain
Alfa Beer	Holland	Jever Pilsner	West Germany
Anchor Pilsener	Singapore	Kaiser	Germany
Bamburger Hofbau	Germany	Koff Stout	Finland
Brador	Canada	Kronenhaler[1]	Austria
Broken Hill	Australia	Lindener	West Germany
Castillio Beer	Italy	Lorimer	Britain
Castle St.	Britain	Maes Pils	Belgium
China Beer	Taiwan	Oktober Beer	West Germany
China Clipper	China	Orangebloom	Holland
Danish Light	Denmark	Pacifico	Mexico
De Koninck	Belgium	Rolland Light	Germany
Dempseys	Ireland	Scandia Gold	Denmark
Elan[1]	Switzerland	Tientan	China
Feingold Pils	Austria	Vaux	Britain
Felinfoel	Britain	Vienna Lager	Austria
Festive Ale	Britain	Warteck[1]	Switzerland
Glacier	Sweden	Wolfbrau	Germany
Golden Ox	Germany	Yuchan Beer	China
Grizzly Beer	Canada	Zero[1]	Germany

[1]Denotes low or non-alcoholic brand.

creasing. In 1985, Van Munching spent an estimated $22 million advertising and promoting Heineken. For Molson $15 million was spent. St. Pauli Girl had a $14 million budget, and Mexican Tecate plans regional advertising at $4 million in 1986. Although imports account for less than 4% of the beer market, the category held 10% of all beer advertising in 1984. About five imported beers represent 78.9% of all imported beer advertising. Heineken leads the list of import advertisers with 33.9%, Molson has 20.5%, Amstel Light follows with 15.8%, Moosehead and St. Pauli Girl trail with 4.5% and 4.2%, respectively. However, some importers are not marketing at all and some import companies have ten to twenty restaurants and delicatessens to whom they sell beer.

Exports.   Confronted with a static-to-declining domestic market, beer producers are being forced to seek new markets abroad. A-B sees the international market, which is more than twice as large as the U.S. market, as critical to U.S. brewers' long-term success. Miller's vice-president Alan Easton echoes this view. "Anybody who is really serious about being in the beer industry is going to have to consider participating in non-U.S. markets." Because substantial foreign opposition exists, brewers are seeking to expand government efforts to negotiate for trade barrier reductions. Exhibit 15 illustrates 1983 U.S. beer exports and imports by continent of destination and origin respectively.

During the first seven months of 1985, Canadian imports of U.S. beer increased more than 250%, to about $10 million. The major cause behind this increased export activity occurred because some Canadian brewery workers went on strike, and Canadian retailers turned to the U.S. brewers for supplies. Immediately following settlement of the labor dispute, U.S. sales to Canada fell to the prestrike levels. Under normal conditions, Canadian provinces protect local producers by severely limiting beer imports.

Currently, the U.S. is Canada's major export customer for beer. In contrast, the U.S. is a residual supplier of beer to Canada. This may change, making Canada a promising market. Some provinces, particularly in Western Canada, are insisting that foreign beers be imported freely. The new Liberal government in Ontario (37% of Canada's beer drinkers reside in Ontario) is promising to break up the Ontario brewers' retail monopoly.

Anheuser-Busch provides an example of how domestic producers can develop overseas markets. Anheuser is relying on licensees to brew regular Budweiser for its overseas production, marketing, and distribution. To meet A-B standards, the licensees import ingredients from the U.S. and their production must be approved by Anheuser's four international brewmasters, as well as chairman August A. Busch, III. Licensees are brewing Bud in Britain, Japan, and Israel. Negotiations are being conducted in Australia, Korea, and Philippines. Anheuser is also considering the purchase of foreign breweries and exports to about ten other countries. Budweiser has failed, however, to crack the West Germany market, and France has been a disappointment.

EXHIBIT 15 U.S. BEER IMPORTS AND EXPORTS

1983 EXPORTS BY CONTINENT OF DESTINATION		1983 IMPORTS BY CONTINENT OF ORIGIN	
Continent	*Percentage*	*Continent*	*Percentage*
North America	28.9	North America	35.1
Europe	2.8	Europe	59.9
Asia	33.1	Asia	2.8
Caribbean	20.8	Caribbean, Central	
Central America	1.0	America, South America,	
South America	2.3	Africa, Australia/Oceania	2.2
Africa	1.7		
Australia/Oceania	9.4		

NATIONAL BREWERS

Anheuser-Busch, Inc. The St. Louis-based "King of Beers" has the most profit-able product mix in the industry and is least in need of price increases. The key to its growth has been the world's best-selling beer, Budweiser. Bud has taken a big part of the youth market from Miller High Life and now commands a 24% market share (see Exhibits 16 and 17). A good product reputation and a powerful distribution network of virtually exclusive distributors contributes to A-B's success. A-B has marketing muscle and the average wholesaler does a 50% greater volume than his counterpart at Miller. A-B also has exposure; advertising expenditures in 1985 were $440 million. A-B has created the ability to outspend its competitors, because its gross margin and gross profits are growing while others are not. Moreover, A-B is in the driver's seat as far as pricing goes.

Miller Brewing Company. Acquired in 1970 by Philip Morris, Inc., Miller surged during the 1970s and continues to be in the number two position. Unfortunately, the premium-priced High Life brand has been losing momentum and its luster as sales erode. However, the Lite brand is doing well, but faces more competition. The strategy of introducing two low-priced, low-profit beers, Meister Brau and Milwaukee's Best, is questioned by analysts. They believe this maneuver, coupled with a large advertising budget, cannot succeed. Miller is innovating at the higher segment with Plank Road and Miller High Life Genuine Draft. It is trying to reposition Lowenbrau as a brand with world-

EXHIBIT 16   TOP FIVE NATIONAL BREWERS

1984 RANK	COMPANY NAME	PRINCIPAL BRANDS
1.	Anheuser-Busch, Inc. St. Louis, MO	Budweiser, Bud Light, Michelob, Michelob Light, Busch, Natural Light, LA, King Cobra Malt Liquor
2.	Miller Brewing Co. Milwaukee, WI	Miller High Life, Miller Lite, Plank Road, Milwaukee's Best, Meister Brau, Sharpe's LA, Lowenbrau, Genuine Draft
3.	The Stroh Brewery Co. Detroit, MI	Stroh's, Stroh's Light, Old Milwaukee, Piels, Schlitz, Signature, Schaefer, Goebel, Silver Thunder Malt Liquor
4.	G. Heileman Brewing Co. La Crosse, WI	Old Style, Old Style LA, Special Export, Blatz, Rainer, Black Label, Lone Star, 11-11 Malt Liquor
5.	Adolph Coors Company Golden, CO	Coors, Coors Light, Herman Josephs, George Killian's Irish Red

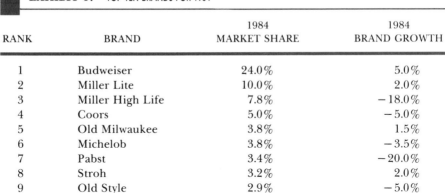

EXHIBIT 17 TOP TEN BRANDS FOR 1984

RANK	BRAND	1984 MARKET SHARE	1984 BRAND GROWTH
1	Budweiser	24.0%	5.0%
2	Miller Lite	10.0%	2.0%
3	Miller High Life	7.8%	−18.0%
4	Coors	5.0%	−5.0%
5	Old Milwaukee	3.8%	1.5%
6	Michelob	3.8%	−3.5%
7	Pabst	3.4%	−20.0%
8	Stroh	3.2%	2.0%
9	Old Style	2.9%	−5.0%
10	Bud Light	2.3%	10.5%
Top 10 Total		66.2%	−30.5%

wide image. Because the beer is brewed in Milwaukee, not Munich, this campaign has failed in the past. Miller remains hopeful about its future.

The Stroh Brewery Company. Until 1981, this family-owned brewery, founded in 1849, was primarily a regional brewer. Since acquiring F&M Schaefer Brewing Co. in 1981 and Jos. Schlitz Brewing Co. in 1982, Stroh has carved a comfortable lead over its nearest competitor, G. Heileman. The acquisition of Schlitz gave Stroh a strong national wholesalers' network to distribute the rest of its products. Stroh's national rollout had some bad introductions in the Northeast, but it has a solid product line—Stroh's, Old Milwaukee, Schaefer, and superpremium Signature. A company with good management, Stroh will be a difficult force to contend with: it has minimized unit costs and is operating at full capacity. Moreover, because it is a private company, it does not have to show good quarterly returns; it just has to generate enough cash flow to cover the family's needs.

G. Heileman Brewing Company. The G. Heileman Brewing Co. entered 1984 leading the industry in five-year profitability and growth. The return on equity averaged 31.7%. It has eleven breweries—five in the Midwest and two each in the South, Southwest, and Northwest. Heileman's growth is a result of acquisition, and it has expanded its own distribution network by acquiring companies with well-established distribution systems. Despite excellent, street fighting management and good marketing, Heileman lacks a national image for its brands. This makes competing with A-B difficult. Heileman is, however, competing with the imports by building a new small plant exclusively for the production of a specialty beer. It does not want to mix the new beer with its domestic brands.

Adolph Coors Company.   Famous for its mountain spring water, Coors is expanding from its regional mystique to become a national brewery. The rollout has worked very well, especially in New England, where it now advertises at the rate of one TV commercial per resident per second. Also, Coors seems to have stemmed the market share erosion in its core territories out west and hopes to regain the lost ground. Coors Light is doing very well, and in 1985 accounted for 40% of Coors' total barrelage. The success of Coors Light is helping to elevate the confidence that both the consumers and the wholesalers have in the Coors brand name. The imported superpremium George Killian's Irish Red is also making strong headway.

THE REGIONAL, SMALL BREWERS

In an industry increasingly dominated by a few firms, several regional brewers have endured and continue to flourish. Some are large, nearly "Big-Six" status, while others are small-scale. Some have 150-year histories and others have only recently emerged. All stand as evidence that hometown loyalties and the strength of the regional market can be cornerstones of success.

This distinctive group must grapple with the issues confronting their specific markets while trying to find ways to survive. Some of the strategies being used include (1) the specialty brewer serving the moderate beer drinker and catering to the growing market of image-enhanced goods in select markets, (2) the dual-purpose brewer who wants to serve his loyal and home market while developing more prestigious and distinctive beers for select markets, and (3) the more traditional regional brewer whose markets are blue-collar and whose customers are more loyal than those in the more transient metropolitan areas.

The Genesee Brewing Company, Rochester, NY.   Founded just after Prohibition's demise, Genesee is now the seventh largest brewery in America. Genesee's territory has been expanding and now includes all of the East Coast, Ohio, Indiana, Kentucky, West Virginia, and the province of Ontario. For a brewery considered to be a regional, Genesee has also implemented major advertising campaigns. Genesee had an impressive growth rate throughout the 1970s, with sales increasing at an average annual rate of 10.3%.

The F.X. Matt Brewing Company, Utica, NY.   The F.X. Matt Brewing Co. reflects the tradition of family involvement that characterizes the industry. F.X. Matt, II understands both the romance and the realities of the industry. He realizes the necessity of an economical operation. Therefore, he constantly upgrades equipment not justified for a brewery this size. Besides the strategy of capital improvements, three other factors have been keys to success: consistent quality, loyal personnel and a "hands-on" management philosophy. The extensive product line includes Utica Club, Utica Club Light, Utica Club Cream Ale, Matt's Premium, Matt's Premium Light Choice (a low-alcohol beer), Maximus Super Beer (with 6.5% alcohol content), and Saranac 1888, the newest product. Approximately 125 distributors carry Matt products throughout New

York, Pennsylvania, parts of New England, and north-central Colorado. Distributors must have a good game plan, ability to cover the market, competence, and a particular way of doing business.

The newest product, Saranac 1888, an ultrapremium all-malt lager, was created in response to the phenomenal growth of imported beers. This is not a mass-produced/mass-promoted product. It is sold with a combination of point-of-purchase materials and placement in proper places.

Dixie Brewing Company, New Orleans, LA. Neal Kaye, Jr., president of Dixie, bought the company in June of 1983. The brewery was founded by the Merz family in 1907. It produces Dixie and Dixie Light, Coy International Private Reserve (a superpremium), and Rhinoceros (a malt liquor). The company also imports two French beers, Panache and 33. Dixie's advertising dollars go into national cable television spots and distribution is handled through their own subsidiary. Kaye points out that there is no other brewery like it in the Deep South, so unless one is built, he is confident Dixie will survive.

Anchor Brewing Company, San Francisco, CA. In 1965, Fritz Maytag, heir to part of the Maytag appliance fortune, bought this bankrupt brewery. Using his personal finances, he embarked on an extensive capital investment plan to renovate and replace equipment. Anchor, operating at a loss for ten years, went into the black in 1975. Anchor's initial annual capacity of 600 barrels has been expanded to 50,000 barrels. In 1984, Anchor produced over 37,000 barrels. The brewery's flagship, Anchor Steam Beer, accounts for 80% of sales, and Anchor Porter and Anchor Liberty constitute 7% of total sales. The remaining sales volume is made up by a barley ale, wheat beer, and its Christmas ale.

The brewery initially self-distributed its products, but it now uses two distributors on the West Coast. With over 100 total distributors, Anchor is available on the West Coast, in parts of Maryland, Delaware, Virginia, Washington, D.C., New Jersey, Connecticut, and Massachusetts. The company has done almost no advertising, but relies instead on distinctive packaging.

A quasi-market research study provided the following buyer profile: The buyers are young adults, upscale, predominately college-educated and very knowledgeable about beer. Many drink a variety of beers and consider themselves aficionados. They drink primarily imported brands and enjoy a rich, distinctive taste in the beer they consume.

Maytag explains Anchor's success: "We start with a respect for the brewing tradition and a reputation for integrity. It's a concept that starts with the product. Our brew is low-key, high-quality and non-establishment. We actually try to make a beer that most people don't like—heavy, hoppy, and flavorful. It's traditional and distinctive, not designed for high volume, but for rapid growth, with relatively high margins, on a small scale."

Walter Brewing Company, Eau Claire, WI. Mike Healy, Jr. recently purchased this brewery for $1 million. He will transform it, with the help of Alan Dikty, a brewing consultant and managing editor of *New Brewer,* into a specialty brewery, to capture a part of the lucrative import market. "Selling a standard beer is the road to disaster," says Dikty. "You can't beat the big boys at their own game."

THE MICROBREWERS

The American brewing industry has one small, dedicated group of mavericks. These are the microbrewers, with annual production under 15,000 barrels. Microbreweries are as individual as the personalities of their owners, yet all share an attitude of respect and enthusiasm for the brewer's art.

The majority of microbrews represent a historic genus of malt beverage that was common in pioneer America and until shortly after World War II in Great Britain. By the 1940s this had disappeared from the U.S., and by 1960 was difficult to find in Great Britain. During the 1970s, this traditional mode of brewing was renewed in England, primarily due to the country's "real ale" partisans. Brewed by top-fermentation, the generic term for this type of beer is *ale.*

Jack McAuliffe, an unemployed sailor who started the first microbrewery in 1976 in Sonoma, California, reintroduced this English-type brew in the U.S. His New Albion Brewery survived only a few years, but others have followed. Today there are about twenty-five micros and another thirty are set to begin production in 1986. Exhibit 18 provides a comprehensive list of American microbreweries.

The "real ale" is not the only style produced by microbreweries. A new American style—"nouveau lager"—has emerged on the market. This bottom-fermented beer is decidedly more hoppy and is brewed in the German Reinheitsgebot tradition. Reinheitsgebot dates from 1516, when the Bavarian ruler of that day, Wilhelm IV, limited the ingredients in beer to water, malted barley, hops, and yeast. This edict may be the oldest consumer protection law still on the books. In West Germany, Norway, and a few other countries, all beer produced for local consumption must be "Reinheitsgebot Pure," with only those four ingredients, no cereals, no additives, and no enzymes. This new wave of American beers are nearly all made to these specifications.

The West Coast is a hotbed of microbrewery activity. The area is an ideal geographic market for these niche beers, because of the generally high personal incomes, coupled with a widespread awareness and appreciation of small wineries. The classic flavor and quality these breweries achieve, combined with their anti-establishment stance, has resulted in attractive alternatives for the price-inelastic, high-end beer drinker.

Microbrewing, however, is not ironclad. In 1982, in the San Francisco Bay area, there were five micros in business. Only two are still brewing. With a failure rate of more than 40%, this business is not for amateurs. Micro success is often unattainable, because of competition from imported labels and the inescapable economies of scale involved. Microbreweries are faced with the dilemma of needing to increase production in order to sell more aggressively

EXHIBIT 18   AMERICAN MICROBREWERIES

NAME	LOCATION
Riley-Lyon Brewing Co.	Little Rock, AR
Palo Alto Brewing Co.	Mountain View, CA
Sierra Nevada Brewing Co.	Chico, CA
Stanislaus Brewing Co.	Modesto, CA
Thousand Oaks Brewing Co.	Berkeley, CA
Golden Gate Brewing Co.	Berkeley, CA
Boulder Brewing Co.	Boulder, CO
Snake River Brewing Co.	Caldwell, ID
Millstream Brewing Co.	Amana, IA
Boston Beer Co.	Boston, MA
Montana Beverage Co.	Helena, MT
The Manhattan Brewing Co.	NY, NY
Old New York Brewing Co.	NY, NY
Wm. S. Newman Brewing Co.	Albany, NY
Columbia River Brewing Co.	Portland, OR
Widmer Brewing Co.	Portland, OR
Reinheitsgebot Brewing Co.	Plano, TX
Chesapeake Bay Brewing Co.	Virginia Beach, VA
Hart Brewing Co.	Kalama, WA
Hales Ales Ltd.	Coleville, WA
Independent Ale Brewing Inc.	Seattle, WA
Kemper Brewing Co.	Rolling Bay, WA
Kuefner Brewing and Malt Co.	Monroe, WA
Yakima Brewing and Malt Co.	Yakima, WA
BREW PUBS:	
Buffalo Bill's Microbrewery & Pub	Hayward, CA
Mendocino Brewing Co.	Hopeland, CA
Hopeland Brewery	Hopeland, CA

and to exploit economies of scale. At the same time, they must contend with a mature and oversaturated market that simply does not justify scaling up.

Because of their low volume, it is also difficult for them to find a distributor. The few distributors that are receptive are normally attracted by label graphics and by superlative quality. Electric labels offset the generic identity of many of their primary products. Most distributors cannot, or will not, distribute a label that represents such small numbers. Therefore, most micro-brewers must rely on personalized pre-selling of their brew to retailers. First-hand contact is essential for success. It is also invaluable for gauging a constantly changing marketplace. Furthermore, even if one can attract a regional distributor, personal calling regularly outsells the distributor.

Another marketing device used by micros in point-of-purchase materials.

Microbreweries need to cut through the array of labels confronting the consumer in the import and specialty segment. The volume does not warrant a comprehensive advertising campaign, so point-of-purchase materials are the most cost-effective.

Micros are surviving for now, by charging a little more, by maintaining a rigorous quality-conscious image, and by providing more and more beer drinkers with the joys of fresh, wholesome, handmade brews. *Premium* is again becoming an adjective that means something.

PROFILES OF SEVERAL MICROBREWERIES

Sierra Nevada Brewing Company, Chico, CA. Located in a farming and college town near Sacramento, this ale brewery has a current production of 3,000 barrels. Started in 1979, the first brew was sold in 1981. Sierra Nevada produces pale ale, porter, and stout, which all retail for about $18 a case. The firm also sells full and half kegs of draft ale and a Christmas ale. Operating efficiency and a steadily growing reputation among serious beer lovers have proven to be keys for survival. But owner/brewer, Camusi, predicts a shakeout among microbrewers, a direct result of dilution in the specialty market. The critical areas of size and capacity may be the deciding factors in its long-term success. Sierra Nevada has added to its capacity every year and now approaches an annual capacity of 7,500 barrels. Its draft beer, accounting for a large percentage of its volume, enables the brewery to avoid the crowded single bottle market. Camusi believes growth is essential for survival. He must exploit economies of scale and achieve efficiency. According to Camusi. "The really small brewery is just not a viable business anymore."

Mendocino Brewing Company, Hopeland, CA. Situated 100 miles north of San Francisco, this brewery was formed from the equipment and staff of the defunct New Albion Brewery. This micro has overcome many of the economic viability issues of distribution and scale by operating a "brew pub." Approximately 660 barrels a year of ale, porter, and stout are sold through the pub under the name of the Hopeland Brewery. Mendocino produces a wide variety of products, with Red Tail Ale its mainstay.

This amber, heavy bodied, English-style brew sells in a one-and-a-half-liter magnum bottle for $6. Its Black Hawk Stout, pale ale, and Christmas, summer, and spring ales sell on draft at the pub. The owners describe the Mendocino Brewing Co. as a "domestic alternative" which provides a small group of beer drinkers with a fresh, premium product. By selling exclusively to a local market, this micro has overcome the problem of finding distributors. Because of the vagaries of foreign exchange, and the cost of glass and brewing materials, the brew pub may be the solution to running a small brewery.

Boulder Brewing Company, Boulder, CO. Founded in 1979 by a small group of home brewers, this brewery sold its first beer on July 3, 1980. Boulder's products are unpasteurized. English-type brews. The two products, Boulder Extra Pale Ale and Boulder Stout, are sold in 12-ounce non-returnable bottles. No draft is produced. Accounts are served by those wholesale distributors who approached the company.

Distribution is confined to the state of Colorado, with a network of twelve outlets currently handling the brewery's products. Although the company enjoys considerable free publicity, word-of-mouth advertising serves as its primary source of demand. Marketing resources are focused on upgrading packaging graphics. These are products consumers drink for taste. A public stock offering in September 1983 financed the company's capitalization and construction of its recently completed $1.1 million brewery. Forty million common shares were issued at 5 cents a share, raising a total of $2 million. The new facility covers about 14,000 square feet and annual capacity now stands at 15,000 barrels.

The Old New York Beer Company, New York, NY. The first of the nouveau lagers came from New York in 1982, when Matthew Reich introduced New Amsterdam Amber, a rich, hoppy, full-bodied, all malt lager beer. Reich invested his life's savings, $10,000, and hired Dr. Joseph Owades, an international brewing consultant and director of the Center for Brewing Studies in San Francisco, to design a lager beer similar to Anchor Steam.

Reich had always dreamed of being a brewer. While working as the director of operations at Hearst Magazine, he often wished he was out creating his own beer. He believed there was room for a connoisseur's beer, the kind that poured from kegs, without rice or corn—a "pure" beer. For two years Reich and Owades slaved over the beer's body, color, and taste, during which time Reich still worked at Hearst.

Basing their decision on a fifteen-page business plan, twenty-two private investors invested $255,000 to form a limited partnership. In the summer of 1982, Reich left Hearst, and that August he began buying brewing time at F.X. Matt Brewing Company in Utica, NY. New Amsterdam Amber ferments for one week and ages for twenty-six days before being bottled or kegged and shipped to Manhattan.

In 1983, Old New York Beer Co. sold 44,000 cases for $600,000. Sales doubled to $1.2 million in 1984, with earnings of $50,000 (after taxes). Reich expects to reach a sales level of $1.8 million in 1985 on 100,000 cases. The average retail price for a six-pack is $6.

Like other micros, Reich personally sold his brew, first approaching trendy restaurants and bars in Manhattan. While he originally intended to target only NY, his beer is now available in 21 states, including the West Coast. Reich's initial success has enabled him to raise an additional $2.2 million from two venture capital firms. He is using the money to construct a new brewery in Manhattan that will also have a restaurant, a tap room, and a visitors' center. Although this action dilutes Reich's holding in the company to 25%, it improved Old New York's image and increased its annual production capacity to 30,000 barrels. When the brewery is completed late in 1986, he will be able to triple 1985's expected production.

THE GOLDEN GATE BREWING COMPANY

BACKGROUND

With a Cambridge home, an office overlooking the Boston Harbor from the thirty-first floor of a prestigious downtown address, and a quarter-million-dollar annual salary, James Cook was the picture of yuppie success. But something was missing.

James Cook, christened Charles James, attended Harvard College, where he majored in government and graduated with honors in 1971. For the next three years, he was a mountaineering instructor with Outward Bound. In 1974, he returned to Harvard to study law and business administration. In 1977, Cook climbed to the snow-covered peak of Alaska's 20,320 ft. Mount McKinley. "After traveling for weeks and seeing nothing but white," he recalls, "I wondered what magic sight awaited me at the summit. And when I got to the top, there it was, glowing in the light, an empty beer can, planted like somebody's flag. Ah," he exclaims, "the power of beer is transcendent!"

With a J.D. and an M.B.A. James joined the renowned Boston Consulting Group (BCG). He never took the bar exam, as he had no desire to practice law. He spent seven years honing his management skills and advising industrial, primarily international, managers. After six years he got tired of telling other people how to run their company and decided to start his own. "I wanted to create something, I wanted to make something of my own," said Cook. As noted in BCG's annual report, 30% of those who leave go on to start new businesses. Another 46% join small companies in top executive positions. BCG's corporate structure encourages many consultants to start their own companies and it is a training ground for some of the brightest, most successful risk-takers in the country. James' choices boiled down to either brewing beer or building a chain of for-profit medical clinics in Seattle.

The consultant in Cook voted for the doc-in-the-box set-up. But as the eldest son of a fifth generation brewer, he figured he really did not have a choice.

Cook's family has the longest line of brewmasters in the U.S. The first Cook brewmaster immigrated in the 1840s from Bohemia, near what is now Pilsen, Czechoslovakia. Cook's great-great-grandfather, Louis, operated a tiny brewery (the Louis Cook Brewery) in St. Louis, not far from the original A-B brewery and used a lager recipe he inherited from his fathers. Louis brewed beer when Eberhard Anheuser was still selling soap and Budweiser was a European beer. James' father, Charles Joseph, Jr., worked as a brewmaster at several breweries in Cincinnati. However, this was the time when all the local breweries were going belly-up. After four breweries fell out from under him, his father abandoned the family trade, moved to California, and opened an industrial chemical distributorship.

James vividly remembers the smell of fermenting beer on days he visited his father at work. "I liked it. I never liked hard liquor and never understood wine. Even now I drink two–three beers a day, rarely less, rarely more. Breweries are neat places and the brewmaster has the best job. He walks around, tastes beer and makes changes. It's almost like playing God," notes Cook. Cook believes he was put on earth for one thing—"to make the greatest beer in the U.S."

James' father discouraged his idea. He was proud of the fact that, after generations of brewers, James was the first to go to college. He said, "James, it took us 150 years to get the smell of the brewery out of our clothes, and you want to go back there?" He thought James was out of his mind. But as James points out, "On the surface it was an insane thing to do, but I was convinced there was a small emerging market for what I wanted to do. It was the time for microbreweries and hand-crafted beers, and it seemed tragic that I was ending a line of five generations of brewers. I realized Americans had begun to appreciate premium beers in recent years, especially on the West Coast, but I felt they relied too heavily on imported beers, which are inherently inferior. I think that the American appreciation of beer is very much in its infancy. We're in the Blue Nun stage of beer drinking. There was a time when people thought that Blue Nun was a great wine, just as now there are people who think Heineken and Beck's are great beers. In fact, they're the Schlitz of Europe. They have a certain mystique, but it's a phony mystique. These beers aren't fresh. Beer has a shelf life that's not a whole lot longer than orange juice. And you'd never think of buying orange juice from Germany. In Germany, they don't drink Beck's. They drink the local beer. Americans have this notion that the farther away a beer is made, the better it is. But the imports we get in America not only have preservatives, which are illegal in Germany, but by the time they arrive here, they are almost always spoiled, stale and/or skunked. Beer must be fresh. It deteriorates the instant you put it in a bottle. The day it leaves the brewery, it goes downhill. The travel time in importing beer and use of green bottles that expose beer to damaging light can often mean the expensive imported beer is not what it claims to be."

THE START-UP

Although Cook has no formal education in brewing, he studied notes and material his father had saved from the Siebel Institute of Brewing in Chicago where he learned to be a brewmaster. Although American tastes in mass marketed beers has drifted toward light, paler versions, Cook decided to buck the tide, go with family tradition, and brew a full-bodied lager. He wanted a connoisseur's beer, brewed in an "old world" tradition.

His father suggested he revive the old family formula. After searching his father's attic in Cincinnati, Cook found his great-great-grandfather's original recipe, first developed by his ancestor in the 1870s. With his family's formula, Cook hired biochemist and brewery consultant Joseph L. Owades to aid in devising the final formula. In the summer of 1984, Cook traveled to the fermentation lab at the University of California at Davis and worked with Owades on translating Louis Cook's Midwestern American lager into a 1980s West Coast superpremium beer.

The formula is water, malt, hops, and a special yeast strain developed by Owades. The hops are the best in the world, Tettnang and Hallertau Mittlelfreuh hops, imported from Bavaria at a cost of $4.50 per pound. A pound of ordinary hops costs $.55. The hops, according to Cook, are key, as they give the beer its flavor. Two-row summer malted barley and some caramel malt are used for color and body. Although many people think that water is the most important ingredient that goes into beer, it is, in fact, the least important. The quality of the yeast strain is much more important, but is seldom talked about as it lacks advertising appeal. Cook points out, "When you listen to what people advertise about their beers, it's things that have real macho appeal—fire brewing, beechwood aging, mountain spring water. What matters are things like hops, malt, and yeast. Unfortunately, they don't have the advertising appeal of cool mountain streams."

To make this beer formula a reality Cook needed to raise capital. He tossed in all his personal savings, $100,000, and raised an additional $300,000 from friends, business associates, clients, and even his father. "While you can start a small boutique brewery with $400,000, a good lager is difficult to produce in a microbrewery. A lager requires more sophisticated brewing equipment and more careful handling than the ale produced by most micros. I was forced to find an existing brewery, and luckily, I was able to find a brewery in Berkeley that was perfect for my purposes," relates Cook. The Berkeley Brewery, by contract and federal regulation, becomes the Golden Gate Brewing Company while James' beer is being produced there.

THE BREWING PROCESS

This 100-year-old recipe requires a craft brewing process not used by American brewers in this century. The sweetness is drawn from the malt through a decoction mash, a process traditional in Germany, but rarely used any more by American brewers. Fresh hops are added in six stages during the brewing process to give the beer its complex hop character. (The usual process is to add hops only during the cooking stage of production, when boiling extracts the greatest amount of bitterness; this process, therefore, is more economical.) Cook's beer is then *krausened* (a second fermentation that carbonates the beer and also removes some of its impurities) for a smoother taste and a natural carbonation. A final addition of fresh hops is made to the beer as it ages to impart the striking aroma. This is a labor-intensive technique.

Molded after Czechoslovakia's Pilsener Urqueil and the original Lowenbrau, this time-consuming brewing process requires a level of personal attention that would be difficult to maintain in a modern mass-production brewery. Golden Gate takes 40–45 days to make—one day to "cook," seven days to ferment, and about two weeks to krausen. The rest of the time is lagering, or aging. These efforts in the brewing process create the full-bodied flavor, rich with coppery color.

The beer is produced in batches, between 250–300 barrels per batch. Cook was not pleased with the first batch, some of which was used to pitch prospective accounts. The problem was over-filtration. "The technician tried to get it to look like Budweiser," said Cook. "I am more interested in flavor than clarity, and the over-filtration removed some of the subtle flavors and hops bouquet." Cook currently travels to Berkeley every one to two weeks to oversee the brewing of a new batch. He follows the process step by step to ensure that his recipe is followed precisely.

PACKAGING

All Golden Gate beer is currently bottled; no draft beer is produced. The classic American beer bottle, the 12-ounce longneck, or bar bottle, that requires an opener, is used. This shape and the cap offer the most protection from light and oxidation. The bottle is also a dark brown, because a dark bottle protects beer from light, a deadly enemy of beer. Beer left in light for more than ten minutes begins to spoil.

Because of U.S. consumers' perceptions of quality, many imported beers come in green bottles. All the research focus groups show that Americans believe they're getting a better product in a green bottle. According to Cook, "That's why Heineken, Beck's, and Molson come in green bottles—which is a shame. Nobody in the world drinks beer out of green bottles except Americans. In Canada, Molson is sold in a brown bottle."

After being bottled in Berkeley, the beer arrives in San Francisco four hours later. Cook has hired two truck drivers and leases trucks. Each trip to San Francisco costs about $800 per truck. Initially, 500 cases per week were delivered, but this has grown to about 1,500 cases per week. (Each truck has a maximum capacity of 2,500 cases.) The beer is delivered to an old San Francisco brewery, where Cook rents office and warehouse space, prior to distribution.

ORGANIZATION

The employment roster of the Golden Gate Brewing Co. numbers five people, including James Cook—the brewer and chief salesman. In addition to two truck drivers, there are a part-time bookkeeper and an accounts manager, Rhonda Kallman, who was James' secretary at BCG. Her numerous and varied duties include selling and even delivering when necessary. To keep overhead as low as possible, the business has no secretary, no typewriter, and no computer. Cook also took a 75% pay cut from his BCG salary.

FINANCIAL INFORMATION

According to Cook, the Golden Gate Brewing Co. stopped losing money around July or August. "It is still in the red, but we're getting back toward recovering our losses. The business after six months is doing remarkably well," reports Cook. Exhibit 19 shows the Golden Gate Brewing Company's income statement for the first six months of operations.

Golden Gate sells for about $0.25 more per bottle than Heineken, or $1.75–$3.50 per bottle retail. A six-pack retails for about $6.50 and a case varies from $20 to $24. Asked if he thought the high price might limit sales, Cook said, "I don't drink wine, but I understand a good bottle of wine costs about $30. Well, for the price of a mediocre bottle of wine, you can go out and buy a six-pack of the best beer in America." Golden Gate wholesales for about $16 a case.

This fresh, smooth brew with strong overtones of fruit and honey and a creamy head costs two to three times what it costs to brew the popular imported beers. The delivered cost into San Francisco was initially listed at $12 a case, but, because of increased volume, it is now down to $10.50 a case. Other

EXHIBIT 19   1985 INCOME STATEMENT, GOLDEN GATE BREWING COMPANY

Sales	$408,000[1]
Cost of goods sold	273,000[2]
Gross margin	$135,000
Less:	
Shipping	840[3]
Salaries & wages	101,003[4]
Office/warehouse rent	4,800[5]
Truck leasing	20,800[6]
Marketing and promotion	55,000[7]
Repairs	1,000[8]
Depreciation	7,500[9]
Gen. sell/admin & other exp.	9,057[10]
Net income (loss) before taxes	($65,000)

[1] Includes 25,000 cases sold in California and 500 in Munich.

[2] The first 3,500 cases cost $12/case, the rest cost $10.50/case.

[3] Includes shipping costs of $.07/bottle for 500 cases shipped. (Larger shipments would decrease the per bottle cost.)

[4] Includes Cook's salary of $25,000 for July–December and average hourly earnings of his four employees of $18.27/hr. (Another 4% increase is expected in 1986.)

[5] Office and Warehouse rent totals $800/month.

[6] 26 truck trips were made into San Francisco in the first six months.

[7] Includes $35,000 for booklet and $10,000 for placards used in July and August.

[8] Cost of incidental repairs, including labor and supplies, which do not add materially to the value of the property.

[9] Depreciation is on the straight-line basis, assuming a 20 yr. useful life, no salvage value, one-half year's depreciation taken in the first year and $300,000 of assets acquired.

[10] Included are salaries and wages not deducted elsewhere, amounts not otherwise reported, such as administrative, general and office expenses, bonuses and commissions, delivery charges, research expenses, sales discounts, travel expenses, etc.

expenses include salaries, office and warehouse rent, truck leasing, marketing and promotion, public relations, general selling, and administrative expenses and taxes.

ADVERTISING AND MARKETING

Golden Gate Lager is an unadvertised beer in a business in which advertising dominates the consumer's purchase decision. It is primarily a locally marketed beer in a business in which the national brands have driven out many small breweries. And Golden Gate is a beer whose flavor Americans have rarely tasted in the popular domestic, or even imported, beers.

Even though his strategy has been to create a brand identity without advertising, one of the first things Cook did was to hire an advertising agency and a public relations firm. James stated, "I looked for companies that were enthusiastic about this venture. I needed people who could start at the beginning with me, help with name selection, product positioning, packaging, and promotional material. I needed an intelligent sounding board for what I was doing."

All the marketing and promotion has been done with a budget that would not begin to pay for one 30-second spot on Monday Night Football. The main marketing element is quality and freshness, and the main marketing tool is personal selling and word-of-mouth. Tabletop display cards are also placed in bars and restaurants in and around San Francisco. In addition, a little blue miniature booklet, each hand-applied, dangles from each long-stem bottle. The booklet is entitled "Why Is This Special Beer Different?" and describes the beer, brewing process, and flavor. The first order alone cost $35,000.

There is no advertising budget, but during the summer of 1985 Cook experimented with advertising. Placards were placed on the sides of San Francisco's tour buses. While it was relatively cheap advertising at $5,000 per month, Cook is not sure it was worth it. "I don't think we generated enough sales to pay for it." This experience confirmed his gut feeling that small, specialized companies do better relying on word-of-mouth advertising and publicity. "The first thing you must have in business is a solid, substantial advantage over the alternatives. Somehow you've got to have a reason for people to buy your product, and it's got to be more solid than anything advertising can create. There are very few products that have really lasted long-term on marketing alone," says Cook. "However, nothing is so good that it automatically sells itself. You have to go out and hustle."

He links the logistics of introducing this beer to those of a fine wine, with the best advertising being word-of-mouth, but Cook was fortunate to gain a credible third-party endorsement. Less than two months after the introduction of Golden Gate Lager, this superpremium, full-bodied, amber brew was crowned the Best Beer in America at the annual Great American Beer Festival in Denver. One beer is selected the best by the 4,000 attendees. This year's contest had over 102 entries. The resulting publicity played a major role in boosting sales. Cook, thrilled by the victory, said, "For a family that has been making beer for 150 years to suddenly get recognized as making the best beer in the country—that is the ultimate accolade."

James Cook also conducts his own market research and studies. Three nights per week he visits local pubs and restaurants. He questions patrons as to why they drink imports when they can have Golden Gate. He asks what they like about imported brands. He asks beer drinkers for their opinion of Golden Gate. If they have not tasted Golden Gate, he describes the flavor and suggests they try it. After a short conversation, he identifies himself as the brewer. Aside from polling patrons, Cook chats with bartenders and questions waitresses and waiters about sales. According to Cook, "The neatest thing is to come into a bar and see people drinking my beer. The second neatest thing is to take the empty cases out."

DISTRIBUTION

"Getting the beer on the market boils down to a door-to-door campaign with restaurants, bar managers, and liquor store owners," says Cook. Cook converts his BCG briefcase into a cooler by adding cold packs, places four or five bottles of Golden Gate in it, and asks potential carriers to taste the beer. "The response is incredible." boasts Cook. "Bar managers and owners like the personal attention. It shows them how much you believe in your product."

Beer is sold today through massive advertising. Beer salespeople today are primarily order takers. They do not sell the beer—the advertising does. The distribution system of large wholesalers often provides retailers with indifferent service on popular brands with marketing power. The outlet has no choice. Even if the delivery service is poor, there are brands an establishment has to carry. Because Golden Gate requires an amount of personal attention and credibility that the normal beer sales and distribution channels cannot give, Cook has set up his own distribution company. He even goes as far as making deliveries, pinstriped suit and all, out of his station wagon. Normally, his drivers will handle this.

Cook realizes all this costs money, probably twice what traditional distributors pay. Cook is currently negotiating with a major regional beer distributor. Affiliation with a large distributor provides access to numerous, established accounts that Cook would otherwise have to pursue one by one. He wonders if this is a sound strategy.

TARGET MARKET

The Golden Gate Company's Golden Gate Lager is trying to reach less than 4% of all beer drinkers. The target is the beer drinker who knows how to distinguish a well-made from an average to below-average one, and who cares more about quality and taste than advertising appeal. Cook believes the typical Golden Gate drinker could be anyone, from gourmets to yuppies to construction workers, who likes a good beer. The current diverse cross-section of drinkers cuts across traditional demographics.

EXPORT PLUNGE

In October 1985, James Cook performed an unusual feat. He shipped 12,000 bottles (500 cases) of Golden Gate Lager to Munich, West Germany, a city with the most finicky beer drinkers in the world. Golden Gate is the first U.S. brewed beer to be sold in West Germany outside U.S. military bases. Good taste is not enough in Germany. The beer must pass the strict Reinheitsgebot, or German Beer Purity Law. It took four weeks before the Wiehenstathan, or beer institute, gave his beer their seal of approval. Obtaining an import license was the next task. The 500 cases were sent to George Thaler, a business consultant friend and now part-time beer distributor, who attempts to get Germans to try, and then order, Golden Gate. Thaler explains his sales techniques as follows, "I bring three cold bottles with me, then I tell them what has happened to beer in America and then discuss the brewing process. Then we taste." Thaler says Germans like the beer, which helps both sales of Golden Gate and the image American products have. "It's a quality image for a U.S. product."

The Munich market is not without problems. In Munich, six breweries own 90% of all pubs and they will only serve their brand of beer. Therefore, Golden Gate is locked out of all but a few of Munich's restaurants, delicatessens, and hotels (the so-called "free bars"). In addition, although shipping costs add only $.07 to the price of a bottle of Golden Gate, the beer costs 30%–50% more than German draft beers, or about 5 1/2 marks more per beer. But Thaler explains that this is consistent with the product positioning. "We don't want student beer drinkers to get drunk on Golden Gate. We want the beer connoisseur to drink Golden Gate." Thaler presently has five accounts taking seventy cases per week, which he delivers in the trunk of his Mercedes-Benz. The accounts range from a high-class delicatessen to a New York style bar.

Cook's plunge into West Germany is designed primarily to demonstrate his product's quality; he is now considering expansion. Thaler hopes to soon expand to Dusseldorf and Austria. Cook wonders what other markets he should pursue, how fast he should expand, and how much time he should devote to export possibilities. He is confident that his time-consuming brewing process and choice ingredients make Golden Gate competitive with the best of European brews.

CAPITAL EXPANSION

Cook formed his company with two goals initially: (1) to brew the best lager in the U.S.—"an answer to the best Europe has to offer, a beer with absolutely no compromises" and (2) to brew the beer in San Francisco. Cook has achieved his first goal, but his second has yet to be realized. "The beer is as good as I thought," says Cook. "But I guess it will take longer than I wanted to get it brewed in San Francisco. Maybe next summer."

The Golden Gate Brewing Co. currently rents office and warehouse space at an old San Francisco brewery. This brewery, with three feet thick walls, was abandoned in 1965. It was cheaper to abandon than tear down. It is now owned by the nonprofit Neighborhood Development Corporation, but Cook has an option on about one-fourth of the building's 170,000 square feet. He hopes to be able to buy the building, renovate it, and brew Golden Gate in 40,000 square feet, after funding completion. Cook estimates his needs at $3.75 million, with $1.1 million going for renovations and $2.1 million for new tanks and bottling gear. His goal is an annual capacity of 30,000 barrels. The project is initially expected to create twelve to fifteen new jobs and has the potential to create fifty-five to sixty. Actual renovation and equipment installation is estimated to take four to ten months. Cook says it would be cheaper to build a brewery in the suburbs, but "romance" led him to the old SF brewery. "I could save $800,000 if I moved to a suburban industrial park, but I don't want to make California, or West Coast Lager Beer. I want to make Golden Gate Lager."

Cook has explored several financing possibilities—Industrial Revenue Financing, Urban Development Action Grants, and market rate financing. Are there other sources that he should consider? He needs to evaluate the pros and cons of each source and determine if proceeding with his second goal is viable at this time.

Industrial Revenue Financing.   Industrial Revenue Bonds (IRB) are vehicles that developers and corporations use to raise low interest financing for construction projects. They are issued by a municipality only to achieve tax exempt status, and are not guaranteed by the full faith and credit of the government. IRB's are backed by the future revenue of the project. IRB's were originally designed to attract industry into communities for employment and economic benefits through the use of tax exempt financing. IRB loans in San Francisco generally carry interest rates of 70% of prime with a 15-year balloon and a 30-year amortization.

The San Francisco Industrial Development Financing Authority (SFIDFA) must give initial approval to an application by Cook's Golden Gate Brewing Company. The revenue bonds must then gain city council and mayoral approval. Cook is confident that the mayor will bestow enthusiastic support; he campaigned or revitalizing San Francisco neighborhoods. Once the IRB's are approved, a bank must agree to loan the funds. Most banks require the IRB loans to be secured by the personal guarantees of the principals.

Urban Development Action Grants.   The UDAG is another possibility. By financing projects that otherwise would not be feasible, the UDAG program is designed to create jobs and expand the city's real estate tax base.

The UDAG is a flexible program which offers a source of cheap money. The maturity and interest rate are negotiated between the city and the borrower. The collateral is normally limited to the assets being financed (and personal guarantees). The UDAG can be used for fixed assets whose life expectancy exceeds seven years. The terms and conditions negotiated between the city and the borrower must be approved by the city council and the U.S. Department of Housing and Urban Development. The UDAG process averages three to four months. Another important advantage of this subsidy is that the UDAG can be mixed with IRB's and other federal programs. Exhibits 20, 21, and 22 highlight other criteria of this program.

The UDAG subsidy does have one drawback. To raise money for future projects, the local program shares in the profits of the subsidized projects. This can restrict profit potential. Cook was not excited about sharing profits and/or giving up control or ownership.

EXHIBIT 20   UDAG CRITERIA FOR SELECTION

The following criteria have been developed by the central office staff for the review, rating, and ultimate selection of UDAG applications, for approval:

1. Relative distress of the applicant.
2. Private leverage: the ratio of private investment to UDAG funds. The national average is now 6.2 to 1, and the ratio should be at least 5 to 1 to insure competitiveness. A ratio below 5 to 1 must be strongly supported by other factors and less than 2.5 to 1 will not be considered.
3. Repayment of action grant recipient. At least a portion of the grant should be returned to the city for recycling. The repayment may be structured as a "soft" second mortgage or lease so the developer virtually has a grant if the project is not successful.
4. Permanent jobs. Weight is given to the total number of jobs created, the number of low/moderate income jobs created, and the ratio of UDAG funds to jobs created. Currently, a cost of $5,000 or less per job created is considered competitive. Retained jobs are also important.
5. New taxes. New taxes created and the ratio of new taxes to Action Grants dollars. A return of $.10 per dollar is competitive.
6. Commitment to minority participation. The creation of minority jobs and the inclusion of minority entrepreneurs is weighted heavily.
7. Commitment to hire and train hard-core unemployed is a plus factor.
8. Other public participation. Investment of funds by the state and/or city is a good measure of their support of the project.
9. Feasibility. The project must be feasible socially and economically, and the participants should be capable of starting within one year of preliminary approval and completing the project within four years of that date.

The program seeks to fund an equal number of commercial, industrial and neighborhood projects. To date, approvals have been 36% industrial, 34% commercial, and 30% neighborhood.

EXHIBIT 21   TEN QUESTIONS CORPORATIONS ASK ABOUT UDAG

1. Why does the federal government help businesses finance plant and equipment? Creating jobs in distressed cities is a national goal. UDAG will help companies finance fixed assets that create jobs.
2. Is it free money? What's the catch?
   - UDAG won't finance the whole project. At least 72% of the project's cost must come from private sources.
   - Businesses reimburse the city for use of Action Grand funds.
   - UDAG won't finance working capital/assets with useful lives under 5 years.
3. If the funds must be repaid, what's the rate?
   Terms are negotiable. Repayments are tailored to the project's economics and allow a fair return to the owner. UDAG may ask for a share of cash flow as an equity kicker.
4. Which cities are eligible?
   Almost half the cities and towns in the United States meet HUD's distress criteria, ranging from New York, NY (population—7,800,000) to Woodlawn, ID (population 321). Call Frank Ridenour, (202) 755–6784, to find out if a city is eligible.
5. Do successful companies qualify?
   UDAG has made awards for projects involving large and profitable companies. UDAG looks for a financing short-fall in a single project's economics.
6. How bad is the red tape?
   UDAG's requirements are similar to those of private lenders. The application is not short, but the city prepares most of it with information you provide. UDAG guarantees an answer in two months.
7. Is there a loan ceiling?
   There are no ceilings on Action Grants; awards have ranged from $35,000 to $30,000,000. UDAG can lend up to 28% of project costs when sufficient private capital cannot be raised.
8. Can action grants be combined with other government programs?
   UDAG encourages developers and cities to seek other public funds. Action Grants can facilitate tax-free bond financing on projects up to $20,000,000.
9. Do my competitors know about this program?
   Absolutely! UDAG has participated in over 900 industrial and commercial ventures in over 80 different industries.
10. What are my chances of getting a UDAG?
   UDAG's are awarded competitively. Chances are excellent, if you have
   - A project which creates jobs and increases city tax revenues.
   - Private funding for about 80% or more of the project cost.
   - Firm, private financing commitments.
   - Evidence the project needs the Grant.
   - A project ready to proceed.

EXHIBIT 22   HOW THE FUNDS FLOW IN A UDAG FUNDING

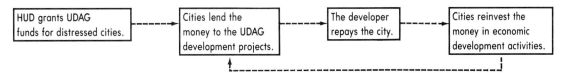

Action Grant Funds Have a Range of Uses
Site Improvements
New construction
Industrial/Commercial rehabilitation
Water mains & sewers
Machinery & fixed equipment

UDAG Can Provide Various Kinds of Financing
Loans
Interest Subsidies
Leasing Financing
Equity Investments

The Action Grant Program Is Flexible and Can Be Tailored to Fit Your Needs
UDAG finances large & small projects
Terms are negotiable
Response is quick
Technical assistance is available from HUD

What Do You Need, To Get An Action Grant?
A project that creates jobs
At least $2.50 of private funds for each $1 of UDAG
Evidence that the project needs the grant
Firm, private financing commitments
A project that increases tax revenues
A project that is ready to proceed

Market Rate Financing.   Another option for capital, explored by Cook, is market rate financing from local commercial banks. San Francisco has five major banks, one of which, the Bank of San Francisco, has already solicited the Golden Gate Brewing Company. Cook has yet to supply necessary financial statements or projections, however. The loan would be a mortgage, used to cover all the expenses associated with the completed property. The interest rate would be based on the prime rate. Cook feels that the rate on a commercial mortgage would be prime +1% for a 15-year balloon with a 30-year amortization.

EXPANSION/GROWTH STRATEGY

Winning America's Best Beer Award, and the resulting publicity, caused many distributors from other states to solicit the Golden Gate Brewing Co. and Golden Gate Lager. Cook has put several possible new accounts temporarily on hold and has turned down requests from distributors in Washington, Colorado, Kentucky, and Alaska. Cook's current agreement with the Berkeley Brewery limits production and Cook felt it was important to penetrate and service

San Francisco first. Renovating the old San Francisco brewery, however, would provide a much higher production capacity level. Exhibits 23 and 24 illustrate beer-consumption trends in various states and regions. Cook also realized that beer is regulated in fifty different ways in the U.S. The bureaucratic red tape is complicated and time-consuming. Cook sometimes thinks it is easier to sell Golden Gate in Munich than in the U.S. Germany requires only that the beer be pure.

EXHIBIT 23   BEER CONSUMPTION STATISTICS FOR SEVERAL U.S. STATES*

	PACKAGED GALLONS	DRAFT GALLONS	TOTAL GALLONS	WHOLESALE DOLLARS	RETAIL DOLLARS
New England					
Maine	22,402	3,200	25,602	$102,409	$159,758
New Hampshire	28,903	5,920	34,822	144,513	226,885
Vermont	12,306	1,637	13,943	55,492	86,012
Massachusetts	117,321	24,030	141,351	572,471	858,707
Rhode Island	20,930	3,225	24,155	96,619	140,097
Connecticut	54,138	9,824	63,962	259,047	375,619
Middle Atlantic					
New York	305,532	62,579	368,111	1,472,444	2,282,289
New Jersey	138,460	23,482	161,942	644,528	999,018
Pennsylvania	221,903	74,871	296,774	1,142,579	1,770,998
E.N. Central					
Ohio	234,138	33,390	267,528	1,070,111	1,626,568
Indiana	107,096	14,068	121,164	502,829	769,328
Illinois	249,523	34,026	283,549	1,091,662	1,735,742
Michigan	176,066	34,408	210,473	837,684	1,315,164
Wisconsin	128,732	28,258	156,991	627,962	954,502
South Atlantic					
Delaware	4,247	2,051	6,298	65,517	87,792
Maryland	90,898	13,724	104,622	276,363	403,490
Wash, D.C.	16,366	1,819	18,185	73,102	97,226
Virginia	113,741	12,638	126,379	502,990	674,006
Florida	289,779	28,982	318,761	1,198,540	1,594,058
West S. Central					
Louisiana	95,670	10,630	106,300	430,515	576,891
Texas	442,226	33,797	476,023	1,785,086	2,374,164
Pacific					
Washington	75,910	18,884	94,794	364,956	481,742
Oregon	46,397	13,964	60,361	240,238	319,517
California	575,622	63,958	639,580	2,398,424	3,213,888

*Gallon and dollar amounts in thousands

EXHIBIT 24 U.S. BEER CONSUMPTION, 1985 GALLONS*

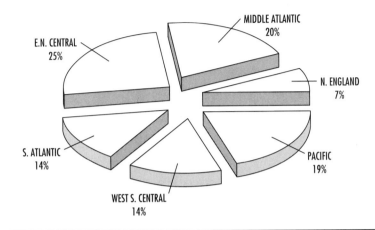

*Includes both packaged and draft.

Regardless, Cook wonders, should I expand, how quickly should I expand, and where? Cook concedes that he will never slay the major domestic giants. "I don't compete with them. I make a different product and sell it for a different price. I compete with foreign beers." But he is uncertain of the strategy he should use. Should he just pursue California, or should be select particular cities? (Los Angeles, for example, contains the third largest market for imported beer, after New York and Chicago.) Or should he go for West Coast states, the East Coast, the country? Should he pursue the foreign markets? Should he approach distributors and, if so, how should he screen them? Is his marketing strategy satisfactory, or are changes necessary? Should the product line be extended? Should be proceed with plans to brew Golden Gate in San Francisco? If so, how should he finance that project? Are there other sources of financing available which he needs to evaluate? What volume would be necessary to break even? Are there other decisions he needs to make to insure a viable brewing company?

Cook understands that success hinges on moving Golden Gate out of the trial/novelty category and making it a regular, if not exclusive, choice for the customers. Cook realizes that brand loyalties changes slowly in the beer market and, even with strong initial sales, a small brewer faces long odds. Cook, a divorced father of two, Megan, six, and Charlie, five, is determined to produce a first-rate beer and have a brewery to pass on to his son or daughter. He hopes there will be a seventh generation of brewers.

CASE **8**

THE RISE AND FALL
OF YUGO AMERICA, INC.

**CAROLYN SILLIMAN
AND JEFFREY S.
HARRISON**

> The five years that I invested in the Yugo project were rewarding and matur-
> ing for me, although I had a modest financial equity and a large amount of
> sweat equity invested in the company. In hindsight, there were areas where
> we failed, but I feel as though it all made a significant impact on the product
> and pricing aspect of the automobile industry.

William E. Prior, cofounder, former chief executive, and president of Yugo
America, Inc. collected his thoughts and reflected on the past five years as he
glanced across a crowded airport. It was June 1989, only five months after his
company had declared bankruptcy. Looking back, he noted that the privately
held company had traveled a rocky road, yet made the most significant impact
on the automobile industry in the decade.

It was 1983 when Prior and his two partners, Malcolm Bricklin and Ira
Edelson, stumbled upon the idea of a company featuring a low-priced import.
Bricklin, who was probably best known for the flashy sports car prototype that
bears his name, was heading up the project as its main financial backer. Prior
was the former president and general manager of Automobile Importers from
Subaru, the nation's second largest Subaru distributor, a company Bricklin
had founded after the collapse of his sports car project. Edelson was Briklin's
accountant and financial advisor. The three men had been researching the
automobile industry, looking for a niche in the already crowded new car market. From their research, the men came to the conclusion that there was no
"entry level car"; that is, there was not a new automobile inexpensive enough
for the average first-time buyer. Bricklin, Prior, and Edelson concluded that
they had discovered "a market in search of a product."

Once the concept was conceived, the three entrepreneurs began their

Source: **Prepared by Carolyn Silliman and Professor Jeffrey S. Harrison, Clemson University, as a basis for classroom discussion and not to illustrate either effective or
ineffective handling of administrative situations.** © **Jeffrey S. Harrison, 1990.**

search for a low-priced, "no frills" mode of basic transportation. They determined that production costs would be too high in the United States, so they began evaluating the possibility of importing. In looking for a country which manufactured such a product, they wanted to meet three requirements:

1. The foreign company was not presently exporting to the United States, but desired to do so.
2. The overall quality of the car would be inferior to American and Japanese cars but could meet United States standards and consumer requirements.
3. The foreign company would be able to sell the cars at a low enough price for the new company to make marginal profits.

Bricklin, Prior, and Edelson spent four months investigating and traveling to countries in pursuit of the "right" country and product that met the three requirements. They researched manufacturing plants in Brazil, Japan, Mexico, Poland, France, Rumania, Czechoslovakia, England, and the Soviet Union before they discovered the Zastava car factory in Yugoslavia. Zavodi Crvena Zastava, Yugoslavia's leading automobile manufacturer, had been producing the Yugo GV model for five years and was quite receptive to Bricklin's proposal. Bricklin, Prior, and Edelson toured the Yugoslavian plant in May 1984 and began discussing the terms of a contract that same month.

Yugoslavian officials were eager to hear of the Yugo America venture. The country's economy was weak, and it owed (in 1985) approximately $19 billion to the Western world. In order to purchase goods from the West, such as oil, steel, and electronics, Yugoslavia had to have "hard" currency (a universal currency of choice). The dinar, Yugoslavia's monetary unit, was not considered hard currency, so the country had to earn dollars by exporting. Yugoslavia's modest exports, including jewelry, tourism, furniture, leather, and sporting guns, did not contribute a significant sum in terms of national debt. Since cars are an expensive item, Yugoslavian officials saw the venture as a profitable method of increasing the supply of hard currency in their monetary economy.

Bricklin and Zastava agreed that 500 Yugos should be shipped to a Baltimore port in early August 1985, so that the cars would be in showrooms and ready to sell later that month. In addition, technicians would be trained at the Zastava's plant prior to the launch in America, in order to guarantee customer satisfaction when the cars were sold and serviced. Bricklin and his partners returned to the United States in late May 1984 and began setting up operations.

COMPETITIVE STRATEGY

Competitive maneuvering among car manufacturers revolves around such factors as innovative options and styles, pricing, and brand name/reputation. Of these factors, Yugo's strategy focused on pricing. Innovative options and styles were not considered important, since the car was an older model and had no fancy options included in the base price. The company could not rely on reputation, since the company did not have an established name.

Yugo America took advantage of a pricing scheme which set it apart from other automobile manufacturers. At $3,995, it was the lowest priced car in America. Because price is important to most car buyers, Yugo felt that its low price strategy gave the company an advantage over other small cars. Major price competitors included the Toyota Tercel, Volkswagen Fox, Chevrolet Sprint, and, later, the Hyundai Excel; however, the Yugo GV was priced below all of these competitors. Instead of targeting families or status-conscious individuals, Yugo America made its car appealing to the first-time buyer looking for an economical subcompact.

OPERATIONS BEGIN

Four strategic decisions were made at the onset of operations:

1. The cars would be sold through "dual dealerships"; that is, Yugo would be a partner to an established retailer, such as Ford or Subaru. In this manner, Yugo America's executives hoped the public would associate its name with another successful manufacturer's name and reputation.
2. Prior, Bricklin, and Edelson decided that the company would import regionally rather than nationally. More specifically, Yugo America, with a home base in Upper Saddle River, New Jersey, would establish itself among Northeastern dealers. Approximately 23% of all import cars are sold in this region, and the Northeastern coast is the closest to Yugoslavia.
3. There would be a small number of dealers selling a large number of Yugos. The idea behind this decision was that the dealers would be making a substantial profit from the large number of cars, which would motivate them and encourage them to sell more.
4. The price of the car would be low, but the company would stress the fact that the car was of acceptable quality.

The first task to accomplish before announcing the introduction of the Yugo GV in America was to set up a management hierarchy. As mentioned previously, Malcolm Bricklin was Yugo America's chief financial backer. As chairman, he owned 75% of the company. William Prior, who would act as president and head of operations, owned 1%. Ira Edelson owned 2% of the company and held the title of financial administrator. The remaining 22% was held by investors who were not involved in the management of the company.

In February 1985, the company began recruiting automobile dealers. (The company's founders had been reviewing dealers for over four months, but the actual signing did not take place until February.) Tony Cappadona was hired as dealer development manager and given the responsibility of locating established dealers who were interested in selling the Yugo. In addition, extensive surveys helped Mr. Cappadona determine the best area placement of Yugo franchises. By the end of July, the first 50 dealers were contracted in Pennsylvania, Massachusetts, New York, New Jersey, Connecticut, Rhode Island, Delaware, Maryland, and Washington, D.C.

Some dealers were hesitant to sign because of the financial commitment involved. Pressure from Manufacturers Hanover Trust Company required that Yugo America produce 50 letters of credit by December 1985. By the terms of agreement, dealers had to produce a $400,000 stand-by letter of credit to cover at least two months of vehicle shipments. The dealer also had to pay $37,000 for a start-up kit and arrange financing for a floor plan. A floor plan is an agreement between a financial institution and an auto dealership to finance the vehicles that are on the lot. The financial institution retains title to the automobiles until they are sold, which allows the financial institution to offer extremely attractive rates to the dealership, usually one to two percentage points above the prime lending rate. A typical floor plan would only require $600,000 of credit. However, the commitment of funds was excessive for such a risky operation. In response to these concerns, Yugo executives assured dealers that the Yugo GV would sell itself.

Bricklin contacted Leonard Sirowitz, a New York advertiser, to write and launch a $10 million campaign prior to the debut of the Yugo GV. Sirowitz, who helped to create the Volkswagen Beetle advertisements during the 1960s, expected the Yugo ads to reach a potential one million buyers via newspapers, magazines, and television. He hoped to convince Americans that, despite their views of Communist Yugoslavia, the $3,995 car was of sound quality.[1] Yugo's first slogan intended to catch the consumer's eye by asking, "The Road Back to Sanity: Why Pay Higher Prices?"

In addition to trained technicians, Yugo's support system of quality parts and service was comprehensive. The company received 180 tons of spare parts to distribute among dealers during the summer of 1985. The company implemented the industry's first Universal Product Code inventory system, which enhanced the accuracy and efficiency of inventory processing. In addition, service schools were developed so that technicians would have no problems or questions when repairing the cars. For the "do-it-yourself" consumers, Yugo America published its own repair manuals and included a toll-free telephone number for assistance.

THE YUGO ARRIVES IN AMERICA

The first shipment of 500 cars from the Zastava plant arrived in mid-August 1985 (a picture of the Yugo is found in Exhibit 1 and its features are listed in Exhibit 2). Ten cars were sent to each of the fifty dealers in the Northeast. Each dealer was instructed to reserve two cars as demonstration vehicles and to uphold this condition at all times. By the end of August, the cars were polished and ready for their national debut.

Yugo's official entry into the automobile industry was announced on August 26, 1985. It was a long-awaited moment, and consumers were equally as

EXHIBIT 1   THE YUGO GV

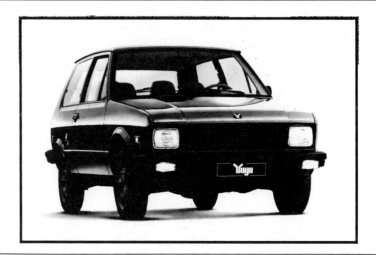

excited about the car as the Yugo employees. The Yugo frenzy spread so quickly that thirty-three dealerships were added and 3,000 orders were taken for cars by September 9. Customers paid deposits in order to reserve their cars, and by the end of 1985, a six-month waiting list was tallied. Indeed, Yugo's founders had discovered "a market in search of a product."[2]

During its first year of operations, which ended July 31, 1986, Yugo America, Inc. grossed $122 million from the sale of 27,000 automobiles and parts and accessories. The Yugo was hailed as the "fastest selling import car in the history of the U.S."[3] The company employed 220 dealers throughout the Southeast and East Coast, and it was estimated that the consumer credit divisions of Chrysler, Ford, and General Motors financed one-third of the Yugo retail sales.[4] At the end of July, Prior announced the expansion of the New Jersey home office to include a corporate planning department. He also informed reporters of Yugo's new slogan, "Everybody Needs a Yugo Sometime."[5]

PROBLEMS BEGIN

In February 1986, *Consumer Reports* published the first of two articles criticizing the Yugo GV. Reporters mocked Malcolm Bricklin for his other car ventures (the Subaru 360 and the Fiat Spider) which had recently failed. The writers pointed out that, after adding destination charges, dealer preparation fees, and a stereo, the price of the car exceeded $4,600. The magazine's personal test evaluation was also published. It stated that the transmission was "sloppy," the steering was "heavy," the ride was "jerky," and the heating system was "weak and obtrusive."[6]

EXHIBIT 2   YUGO GV STANDARD FEATURES

VEHICLE TYPE
Front-engine, front-wheel drive, four passenger, three-door hatchback.

DIMENSIONS AND CAPACITIES
Wheelbase: 84.6 inches
Overall Length: 139.0 inches
Overall Height: 54.7 inches
Overall Width: 60.7 inches
Headroom: Front: 37.0 inches
              Rear: 36.0 inches
Legroom: Front: 39.0 inches
            Rear: 39.0 inches
Ground Clearance: 4.8 inches

Luggage Capacity: 18.5 + 9.0 cubic feet
Fuel Capacity: 8.4 gallons
Curb Weight: 1,832 pounds

ENGINE
Type: Single overhead cam, 1.1 liter 4-cylinder with aluminum cyl. head. Dual barrel
      carburetor
Bore & Stroke: 80 × 55.5 mm.
Displacement: 1116 cc.
Compression Ratio: 9.2:1
Horsepower: 54hp at 5,000 rpm.
Torque: 52 lbs. at 4,000 rpm.

DRIVE TRAIN
Transmission: 4-speed Manual
Final Drive Ratio: 3.7
Gear Ratios: 1st-3.5, 2nd-2.2, 3rd-1.4, 4th-1.0, Reverse-3.7

SUSPENSION
Front: Independent, MacPherson struts, anti-sway bar.
Rear: Independent, transverse leaf spring with lower control arms

BRAKES
Front: 8.0″ disc, power-assisted
Rear: 7.2″ drum, power-assisted
Rear brake proportioning valve

WHEELS AND TIRES
Wheels: Steel
Tires: Tigar 145SR-13, steel-belted radials with all-weather tread design.

ELECTRICAL
Bosch electronic ignition
Alternator: 55 amp
Battery: 12 volt, 45 amp

(*continued*)

EXHIBIT 2   (continued)

ECONOMY
City: 28 mpg
Highway: 31 mpg

STANDARD EQUIPMENT
1.1 liter 4-cylinder overhead cam engine
Front-wheel drive
4-wheel independent suspension
Power assisted brakes, disc front, drum rear
Front anti-sway bar
Rack and pinion steering
Color-coordinated fabric upholstery
Full carpeting, including carpeted luggage compartment
Reclining front seats
Folding rear seats—27.5 cu. ft. luggage space
3 grab handles
2 dome lights
Visor vanity mirror
Analog instrument gauges
Low fuel warning light
Steel-belted radial tires (145 × 13)
Lexan bumpers
Plastic inner front fender shields
Bosch electronic ignition
Rear brake proportioning valve
Full-size spare tire
Front spoiler
Hood scoop
Hub caps
PVC undercoating
Opening rear quarter windows
Rear window electric defroster
Quartz halogen headlights
Body side molding
Special owner's tool kit
Cigarette lighter
Locking gas cap
Dual storage pockets
Concealed radio antenna
Spare fuse and bulb kit
Night/day rear-view mirror
Electric cooling fan
Console

Source: Yugo America, Inc. promotional materials.

The writers continued by criticizing almost every aspect of the car, from seat coverings to the "not-so-spacious" trunk. The safety of the car was questioned, but could not be verified by government crash tests. It was noted, however, that the impact of a collision at 3 mph and 5 mph severely twisted and crushed the bumpers. It was estimated that repairing the damage to the front and rear bumpers was $620 and $461, respectively.[7] Twenty-one other defects were discovered, ranging from oil leaks to squealing brakes. A survey by J. D. Power and Associates (included in the article) concerning customer satisfaction revealed that over 80% of Yugo buyers had reported problems. In short, the writers did not recommend the Yugo GV at *any* price.

The Yugo was facing increasing competition as well. In late 1985 Hyundai Motor America, a subsidiary of the giant South Korean industrial company, announced the American introduction of the Hyundai Excel for $4,995. The Excel was a hatchback model that included standard features which were comparable to the Yugo GV. Therefore, the Excel posed a direct threat to the Yugo GV in the lower priced automobile market.

By mid-October 1986, Yugo America responded to the *Consumer Reports* article and increasing consumer complaints by making 176 improvements to the car without raising its price.[8] Prior stated that Yugo spent between $2.5 and $3 million to improve its image through advertisements and national incentives. Independent dealers offered additional rebates, as well, in an effort to boost sagging sales.

Looking ahead, Yugo America had hoped to introduce some new models, all within the lower price range. For 1987, the Yugo GV would be given a "face lift" to take on an aerodynamic look, and a convertible GV would be available later in the year. In order to meet the needs of couples and small families, Yugo anticipated the 1988 debut of a five-door hatchback, which would compete with the Honda Accord. A four-door sedan would be added to the line between 1989 and 1990, and a two-seater sports car named "TCX" would be the highlight of 1990.[9]

During 1986, there were rumors that Yugo America was considering a move to "go public" by issuing common stock, since the company was beginning to experience financial tension. The proposal was later cancelled for two reasons. First, Bricklin did not want to surrender any of his equity (75%). Second, the company was starting to feel the effects of negative publicity, and financial consultants felt that the stock would not bring a fair price. For the time being, Yugo would remain a private company.

MORE TROUBLE

In April 1987, *Consumer Reports* released its annual survey of domestic and foreign cars, and once again, Yugo's image was tainted. The writers criticized the Yugo GV from bumper to bumper, stating that "the manual transmission was very imprecise . . . the worst we've tried in years." As for comfort, "small, insufficiently contoured front seats" contributed to an "awkward driving position." In addition, the ride of the car was described as "noisy" and "harsh."[10]

Besides the negative description of the car's driving performance, the article publicized the results of an independent crash test. This test, which was not mandated by law, disclosed the results of a crash at 35 miles per hour among domestic and foreign automobiles. (The National Highway Traffic Safety Administration requires that all cars pass the national standard impact at 30 miles per hour.) The Yugo GV was among the 40% which did not pass the test. In fact, it received the lowest possible ranking with respect to driver and passenger protection. The report indicated that the steering column "moved up and back into the path of the driver's head," and the seats "moved forward during the crash, increasing the load on occupants."[11]

Consumer Reports also reported that damage to the front and rear bumpers when hit at an impact of 3 and 5 mph was $1,081, the highest in its class. This was particularly embarrassing to Yugo America, since many of its foreign competitors (including Toyota, Mazda, and Saab) escaped the collisions without a scratch.[12]

Before the second *Consumer Reports* articles, Yugo sold every car coming into its ports every month. Sales in 1987 were the highest to date. From there, Yugo's problems started to catch up with the company. The negative image of the Yugo was apparent, and dealers were forced to offer $500–750 rebates as an incentive to buy. In addition, several new programs and extended warranties were offered to entice customers. Monthly sales levels started to decline, and waiting lists became virtually obsolete.

Through all of these problems, William Prior remained an exemplary figure for all of the Yugo-Global employees. As Tony Cappadona stated, "Bill added a lot of charisma and dedication to the company. He let the employees know that everyone was working to achieve a mission. They (the employees) didn't mind working 10 or 12 hours a day, because they saw Bill putting in twice as much."

CHANGES IN OWNERSHIP

The 1987 year was marked by the acquisition of Yugo America, Inc. by Global Motors, Inc., a company founded by Malcolm Bricklin. Bricklin established Global Motors as an umbrella corporation for importing cars worldwide. Gaining 91% of Yugo America, Global became its parent, distributor, and holding company, and it helped with the coordination and distribution of Yugos as they arrived at the Baltimore port.

By 1988, Yugo America and Global Motors began contemplating the sale of a substantial portion of the company in an effort to avoid bankruptcy. In April, Mabon Nugent and Company, a New York investment firm, purchased Global Motors for $40 million.[13] Bricklin sold 70% of his equity for $20 million, and a debenture was purchased from Global for an additional $20 million. A management group headed by Prior and Edelson agreed to contribute

$2.1 million to obtain 5.5% of the company. The management group would be awarded stock options periodically over the following three years, to bring the group's total ownership to 22%. Prior was named chief executive officer during the acquisition.[14]

THE FINAL YEAR

By April 1988, the company's operating problems had also increased. Not only had the *Consumer Reports* articles thrashed the Yugo GV again, but dealers were beginning to undermine the company as well. William Prior stated that dealers would often persuade buyers to purchase one of their other brands instead of a Yugo. To make things worse, Consumers could only receive 36-month financing with the purchase of a Yugo. Conversely, Ford Motor Credit and other financiers offered 60-month plans on their own cars, which resulted in lower payments. The thought of lower monthly payments was incentive enough for a prospective Yugo buyer to change his decision to purchase. If the former tactic did not persuade the buyer, the salesperson would criticize the Yugo directly and accentuate the features of the other line. Higher commissions on more costly brands increased the motivation of salespeople to move away from the Yugo.

Even after deciding to buy a Yugo, many consumers ran into additional difficulties when they tried to obtain financing. Because the typical Yugo customer was a young, low-income, first-time buyer, lending institutions were hesitant to make high-risk loans to persons in this segment of the market. It was estimated that as many as 70% of all Yugo customers were declined for credit, since the majority had no previous credit history and a debt-income ratio of over 50%. This common scenario was discouraging for both the customers and dealers. Enticing advertisements lured customers in, and yet many could not obtain financing. The dealers became frustrated because of the amount of time and effort contributed to "put the deal together." Prior described the situation as "an inefficiency in the market."

In an effort to hurdle these financing roadblocks, Yugo America announced in June 1988 that it would design its own program for financing. The first-time buyer plan was administered through Imperial Savings Association, a $10-billion institution based in San Diego. Yugo and Imperial intended to protect themselves by charging a higher annual percentage rate—as much as four percentage points higher than those of other finance companies. In doing so, Yugo America could establish a "higher-than-average" reserve for loan defaults. Though the annual percentage rate was higher, buyers could finance the loan over 60 months so that monthly payments remained low.[15]

Approximately 50 dealers were enrolled in the program. Imperial was hesitant to allow all of the dealers to take advantage of Yugo Credit, since there were still some "bugs" in the system. Also, each state required separate licensing, and Yugo did not have the time to wait for acceptance in each state.

The financing program was terminated after 90 days. One of the provisions of the plan required Yugo America to be "in good standing" financially. Bills were accumulating at Yugo and company debt was becoming unmanageable. Imperial Savings had to pull out.

In November 1988, William Prior and 71 other employees were released from the company, leaving a skeleton crew of 71 remaining. Mabon Nugent's intentions were to cut costs in an effort to relieve cash-flow pressures and generate additional funds for product development. Marcel Kole, senior vice president and chief financial officer of Global Motors, temporarily replaced

EXHIBIT 3   GLOBAL MOTORS, INC. BALANCE SHEET, DECEMBER 31, 1988 (UNAUDITED)

ASSETS

Cash	0
Due to/from subsidiaries	27,145
Due from manufacturer	15
Inventories	0
Prepaid and other current assets	48
	27,208
Property, plant and equipment (at cost)	8
Less: Accumulated depreciation	(1)
	7
Investment in subsidiaries	223
Deferred charges	
Total Assets	27,438

LIABILITIES AND EQUITY

Acceptances payable	0
Accounts payable and accrued expenses	1,429
Notes payable	11,825
Due to/from subsidiaries	0
Estimated warranty (current)	0
	13,254
Estimated warranty (long-term)	0
Long-term debt	11,000
Minority interest	0
Shareholders' deficiency	3,184
Total Liabilities and Equity	27,438
	0

Note: Amounts are given in thousands of dollars.

Source: Bankruptcy Docket Number 89 00680, filed January 30, 1989, United States Bankruptcy Court, District of New Jersey.

Prior as president and chief executive of Yugo America. Turnover within the company was high, and national advertising was brought to a halt.[16] Norauto LP of Ohio agreed to finance two shipments of Yugos backed by letters of credit. Norauto, a firm which aids bankrupt, terminated, or distressed companies, took possession of the cars until Yugo America could repay the $14.3 million letter of credit.[17]

Mabon Nugent and Company had written off $10.5 million as a loss in Global Motors by January 30, 1989. It was estimated that Global would need $10 million to get back on its feet, but Mabon Nugent did not feel that contributing more money to a dying company was a worthy investment. The firm's partners considered selling the company to Zastava or private investors, but neither of the ideas were pursued.[18] Global officially filed for Chapter 11 bankruptcy on January 30, 1989.[19] Global's unaudited balance sheet reported in the petition for bankruptcy is contained in Exhibit 3.

A HAZY FUTURE FOR YUGO AMERICA

After declaring bankruptcy in January 1989, parent company Global Motors, Inc. discharged 250 (of 300) Yugo America employees. Zastava, honoring the warranty of the cars, began seeking financial backing so that the company could remain afloat. By February 1989, three lawsuits had been filed against Global Motors and Mabon Nugent and Company. William Prior sued the companies for breach of contract and Turner Broadcasting System in Atlanta filed suit demanding $182,000 for unpaid bills. A third lawsuit, by Imperial Savings, alleged that Mabon Nugent was "involved in the day-to-day operations of the company (Global)" before it (Mabon Nugent) actually took control of Yugo-Global in 1988. Mabon Nugent denied the charge.[20]

John A. Spiech became Yugo's new president and chief executive, succeeding Marcel Kole. Spiech, a veteran of the automobile industry, had full confidence in the company and its product, stating, "Whatever happened wasn't the car's fault. It is still good, low-cost, reliable transportation."[21] He intended to take the company to the top, even though he was starting from the very bottom.

ENDNOTES

Much of the information in this case is based on personal interviews with William Prior and Tony Cappadona, conducted in June 1989.

1. J. Fierman, "Can A Beetle Brain Stir a Yearning For Yugos?" *Fortune* (May 13, 1985): 73.

2. "The Price is Right," *Time* (September 9, 1985): 58.

3. J. L. Kovach, "We Don't Overpromise," *Industry Week* (October 13, 1986): 73.

4. Ibid.

5. J. A. Russell, "Yugo Grosses $122 Million in First Year," *Automotive News* (September 1, 1986): 42.

6. "How Much Car for $3990?" *Consumer Reports* (February 1986): 84–86.

7. Ibid.

8. Kovach, "We Don't Overpromise."

9. J. A. Russell, "Zastava to Construct Plant For U.S. Yugos," *Automotive News* (May 20, 1985): 2.

10. "The 1987 Cars," *Consumer Reports* (April 1987): 200–215.

11. Ibid., p. 200.

12. Ibid., p. 208.

13. J. A. Russell, "Bricklin's Import Firm Sold in $40 Million Deal," *Automotive News* (April 18, 1988): 1, 56.

14. Ibid.

15. J. Henry, "Low Finance: Yugo Offers Loans to Spur Buyers," *Automotive News* (August 1, 1988): 1, 51.

16. C. Thomas, "Prior Ousted: Shaky Global Trims Ranks," *Automotive News* (November 14, 1988): 1, 58.

17. J. Henry, "Yugo, Liquidator in Accord," *Automotive News* (March 27, 1989): 1.

18. J. Henry, "Global Struggles to Remain Afloat," *Automotive News* (January 30, 1989): 1, 257.

19. Henry, "Yugo, Liquidator in Accord."

20. J. Henry, "More Yugo Grief—Maker Plans Termination," *Automotive News* (February 20, 1989): 1, 51.

21. D. Cuff, "A Car Industry Veteran Will Try to Revive Yugo," *New York Times* (March 17, 1989): D4.

SONOCO PRODUCTS, INC.

MYRA REGISTER, LISA
SCOTT, SHERYL WEST,
AND DAVID W. GRIGSBY

In early 1988, Charles W. Coker, president and CEO of Sonoco Products Company, had reason for celebration. The previous year had seen his company set records in sales growth and profits, with sales reaching over $1 billion for the first time and profits reaching an all-time high of over $60 million. The future also looked good for Sonoco. The company was becoming a worldwide leader in the consumer packaging industry and held a commanding share of the fast-growing plastic grocery bag market. Sonoco's April 1987 acquisition of the Consumer Packaging Division of Boise Cascade had been the largest in its history. Coker also had reason to be a bit more apprehensive about the future than ever before. To finance the Boise Cascade purchase, Sonoco had increased its long-term debt by 4.5 times. Although Sonoco's basic markets looked strong, industry analysts had begun to wonder if this traditionally conservative company, still led by descendants of its founder, could assimilate its recent growth and continue to expand.

HISTORY OF THE COMPANY

After the Civil War, Major James Lide Coker came home to Hartsville, South Carolina, from a Union prison with a shattered hip and a determination to help rebuild the war-torn South. Over time, he opened a country store, a bank, a cotton mill, and a college, but he was convinced that the South's future hinged on scientific farming and the development of industry. In the 1890s, Coker's eldest son, James, became interested in the processes of pulping and paper making, using the region's abundant pine forests. The major soon became involved in the development of this idea and raised $20,000 to begin a

Source: **Prepared under the direction of Professor David W. Grigsby, Clemson University, as a basis for classroom discussion and not to illustrate either effective or ineffective handling of administrative situations. The authors acknowledge the assistance and cooperation of officials of Sonoco Products Company, but take full responsibility for the accuracy of information contained in the case. © David W. Grigsby, 1990.**

pulp and paper venture. They hoped to market the pulp commercially, but this idea soon had to be abandoned. Instead, they decided to focus their efforts on making paper. Their first machine turned out between five and eight tons of paper per twenty-four-hour day. This first mill became known as the Carolina Fibre Company. Shortly thereafter, an agreement was reached to form a company to use the paper manufactured by the Carolina Fibre Company to produce paper cones for the textile industry. These cones, made of a thick cardboard-like paper, were used to wind yarns in the manufacturing process of various fabrics. Paper cones would gradually replace the heavier and more costly wooden cones used in the textile industry. The new company was designated the Southern Novelty Company, a name that was later abbreviated to Sonoco.[1]

Through the early 1900s, the textile industry grew rapidly and Sonoco grew with it. After Major Coker's death in 1918, his son Charles was named President. Under his leadership, Sonoco grew from a one-product company to be a leading supplier of textile-related manufacturing supplies. When Charles Coker died in 1931, he left a solid foundation for the future growth of Sonoco. Charles's two sons, James Lide Coker and Charles Westfield Coker, had grown up in Sonoco, working for the company in the summers during high school and college. After their father's death, James Coker, the eldest of the two, was named president. Under James Coker's leadership, Sonoco began yet another period of growth. The introduction of manmade fibers spurred rapid growth in the textile industry, increasing the demand for Sonoco's products. Sonoco began expanding, opening eight plants in new locations outside of Hartsville. After James Coker's death in 1961, his younger brother, Charles, took over the presidency and served until 1970, when he stepped aside to become honorary chairman of the board. His son, Charles W. Coker, then became the fourth generation of the Coker family to head Sonoco.[2] In 1988, Charles W. was beginning his nineteenth year as president and CEO. The directors and executive officers of Sonoco are listed in Exhibit 1.

In the 1960s, Sonoco's composite paper core process, which had been used to produce wound paper tubes for rolls of cloth and carpet and other industrial applications, was adapted to produce composite paper cans for concentrated fruit juices, motor oils, refrigerated dough, and dozens of other applications. This entry into the packaging industry began a diversification program that, by the 1980s, had taken Sonoco into virtually every area of consumer packaging, including plastic bottles and grocery bags.

Sonoco's growth and diversification in the 1970s and 1980s was accomplished through a combination of internal innovation and strategic acquisition. By acquiring key companies in critical new technological areas to supplement its own internal research and development in new packaging processes, Sonoco managed to position itself among the top two or three competitors in several segments of the consumer packaging industry while maintaining its leadership in specialized industrial products. Until the Boise Cascade merger, however, Sonoco's acquisitions, although numerous, had been relatively small ones.

In 1988, Sonoco was ranked 240th in the Fortune 500[3] and employed more

EXHIBIT 1   THE OFFICERS OF SONOCO PRODUCTS COMPANY, 1988

CORPORATE OFFICERS
Charles W. Coker, 55, President
Thomas C. Coxe, III, 58, Executive Vice President
Russell C. King, Jr., 54, Senior Vice President
F. Bennett Williams, 58, Senior Vice President
J. Gary Caudle, 51, Vice President-Corporate Development
Peter C. Coggeshall, Jr., 45, Group Vice President
C. William Claypool, 53, Vice President-Paper Division
H. Gordon Dancy, 49, Vice President-High Density Film Products Division
Harris E. DeLoach, Jr., 44, Vice President-Administration and General Counsel
Robert C. Elmers, 41, Vice President-Human Resources
F. Trent Hill, Jr., 36, Vice President-Finance
Ronald E. Holley, 46, Vice President-Industrial Products Division
Harry J. Moran, 56, Vice President-Consumer Products Division
Earl P. Norman, Jr., 52, Vice President-Technology and Planning
John R. Tinnell, 49, Vice President-Drum Operations
James L. Coker, 48, Secretary
Charles J. Hupfer, 42, Treasurer

Source: Sonoco Products Company, *1988 Annual Report*

than 14,000 workers in 200 operations in the U.S. and abroad. Some 150 branch plants were strategically located throughout the U.S. in order to take advantage of transportation efficiencies and to provide services to its wide range of customers. Internationally, Sonoco operated in 20 foreign countries.[4]

Despite its size and dominance in several of its markets, Sonoco is far from being a household word. Adding to its relative obscurity is the company's frequent confusion with Sun Oil Company, which is often referred to as "Sunoco." Nevertheless, millions of consumers unknowingly come in contact with Sonoco products every day as they pull aluminum foil from a Sonoco tube, open a Sonoco composite can of orange juice, refill their car's crankcase from a Sonoco plastic oil bottle, or carry their groceries home in a Sonoco Polysack bag.

Sonoco is the largest producer of spiral tubes in the world. The company is also a major manufacturer of paperboard, producing over 800,000 tons annually in some 300 grades of paper. Sonoco is also one of the largest users of recycled wastepaper in the country, an accomplishment that has earned the company praise from several environmental groups.

ORGANIZATION

Sonoco is organized into seven distinct operating groups and divisions: Industrial Products Division, Consumer Packaging Group, Drum Operations, Paper Group, International Division, High Density Film Products Division, and Special Products Operations. According to Peter Coggeshall, senior executive vice-president, Sonoco can be considered "almost completely integrated, producing its own paper, adhesives, lacquers, and varnishes; and designing and building its converting machinery." Russell King, senior vice-president, says, "The company is no longer considered just a paper company that also makes some packaging products. This perception is gradually changing and Sonoco is becoming known as a packaging company that happens to make a lot of its own paper." Sonoco, in essence, can be described as a "packaging job shop."

INDUSTRIAL PRODUCTS DIVISION

The Industrial Products Division is Sonoco's traditional business. This division produces paper and plastic tubes and cones, which are used by a variety of industries for winding products such as paper, film, foil, textiles, and tape. Sonoco tubes are also used as shipping and storage containers and for certain operations in the construction industry such as forms for casting large concrete columns. Sonoco is the only national manufacturer of products of this type, with a network of more than forty plants in twenty-eight states. Primary competition for the division is from numerous regional producers. Besides its national network of plants, Sonoco's vertical integration and strong technology base are two other major competitive advantages. Sonoco has excellent relationships with almost every major textile, paper, film, and tape manufacturer in the United States.[5]

The Industrial Products Division produces its products according to customer specifications and therefore carries no inventory of finished goods. Depending on the grade of paper, special coatings, and the build-up of the tube or core, the customers' orders can be manufactured to resist heat, certain chemicals, and moisture.

A guiding principle of the Industrial Products Division is to help its customers reduce their manufacturing costs. Much of Sonoco's success can be attributed to its ability to create a paper or plastic product that does the same job as an existing one, but at a lower cost. For instance, cones used in the textile industry for winding yarn were originally heavy, expensive, wooden ones. With Sonoco's paper cones, the customer got a lightweight, less expensive cone. Likewise, when plastics became a more economical solution for certain industrial applications, Sonoco shifted some of its products to plastic. This same principle has been applied in other Sonoco divisions. The Fibre Drum Division, for example, promotes its products as replacements for steel drums in some markets, and has begun shifting many of its customers to plastic drums. The IPD sales force is trained to look for possibilities of improvement in a customer's operation and focuses on innovative ways of improving a customer's product or production system.

The IPD is organized geographically in order to keep a local focus on competition. Since plants in different regions of the country often concentrate on a single product or group of products, there is also an underlying departmentalization by process. IPD departments at the home plant in Hartsville—spiral department, parallel department, convolute department, and cone department—supply technical expertise to plants in other localities. All salespeople, however, are responsible for generating orders of all the division's products. Sales territories are divided geographically throughout the U.S. Account representatives in the field are supported by an inside sales force. The Industrial Products Division's largest customers include DuPont, Hoechst-Celanese, 3M, International Paper, and Burlington Industries.

With its fourty-four plants, Sonoco's Industrial Products Division is able to meet its customers' needs on a timely basis, often on a just-in-time basis. Some customers, such as DuPont or 3M, can call in an order for a truckload of tubes and have it the next day. Quality is also an important consideration. For example, the spiral paper cores used to wind plastic film are required to fit very precise specifications, to thousandths of an inch. Sonoco has improved the reliability of this technology to the point that 3M has "officially certified" Sonoco as a supplier. This means that 3M will not inspect any of the cores shipped to its Greenville, South Carolina, plant from Sonoco's spiral tube plant located in nearby Fountain Inn.[6] Although the Industrial Products Division could be considered to be operating in a mature market, by applying innovative solutions to customers' problems its business has continued to increase. Sonoco estimated that in 1988 it had "over 80% of the cone market, and over 50% of the tube and core market."[7]

CONSUMER PACKAGING GROUP

The Consumer Packaging Group consists of the Consumer Products Division, Petroleum Products Division, and the business development and technology area. Among the division's customers in 1988 were practically every major food and oil company, including Proctor & Gamble, General Foods, Coca Cola, Pillsbury, Pennzoil, and Kraft. Primary products produced by the Consumer Products Division are composite and plastic cans and fiber and plastic caulking cartridges. The Petroleum Products Division's main products are one-quart plastic oil bottles. Both of these operations are clear industry leaders in their markets. According to the Sonoco's 1987 annual report, "A major strategy of this group is to develop long-term relationships with customers which allow for innovative package development. Such innovation is a key to successful competition in the packaged goods marketplace".[8]

Many of the Consumer Packaging Group's innovations come out of its research facility located at Sonoco headquarters in Hartsville, South Carolina. The Packaging Development Center was established in 1987 as a separate facility to respond to customers' needs for more innovative packaging. A major thrust of the facility has been to increase Sonoco's technological strength in plastics so that it will match the company's expertise in paperboard technology. Plastic products accounted for 15 percent of Sonoco's total sales in 1987. Company officials expect this percentage to rise significantly in the 1990s.

An example of a packaging innovation developed by Sonoco is its new TablePak™ product line developed in 1987 for the frozen foods industry. TablePak containers are made from a new combination of paper and plastics. The containers are made to be taken directly from the freezer and placed in either conventional or microwave ovens.

Overall, the Consumer Packaging Group has been the fastest growing division of the company, with most of the growth coming in the 1980s. By 1988, its total revenues equalled that of the Industrial Products Division, and it was estimated that consumer packaging and industrial products each represented 40 percent of Sonoco's total operations. Paper production and other products comprised the remaining 20 percent.

General sales manager Ray McGowan explains that a disruption in the packaging industry resulted when companies such as American Can and Continental Can began shifting their focus toward financial services and making acquisitions outside of packaging. "Sonoco saw a void in the overall marketplace for somebody who was *just* a packaging company. The growth took place, with the composite can business as the base, through acquisitions to a large degree." Composite cans are basically paper tubes that have been sealed airtight with some type of metal or plastic ends.

Many of Sonoco's most recent acquisitions have been in this area of the business. Some of these include the can division of Container Corporation of America, General Can Corporation, certain Owens-Illinois plants, and Continental Fibre Drum. The largest acquisition, on April 1, 1987, was that of the Consumer Packaging Division of Boise Cascade Corporation. Boise Cascade apparently wanted to leave the packaging industry and return to being strictly a paper company. Although the purchase cost Sonoco over $170 million in cash plus the assumption of $6.6 million in long-term debt, the company considered it an excellent opportunity to increase its share of the consumer packaging industry. The acquired operations manufacture composite cans and/or plastic bottles used in packaging motor oil, frozen juice concentrate, snack foods, refrigerated dough, and other products.

Sonoco was able to make the transition to consumer packaging by taking the winding technology used for making tubes and cones and applying it to the manufacture of composite cans. In 1963, Coker recognized a movement from metal cans to the lighter weight, less expensive composite cans and decided to enter what he saw as an emerging business. Sonoco's first composite can plant was built in Charleston, South Carolina, for the purpose of making motor oil cans. From there, Sonoco moved into other consumer packaging areas that were beginning to use composite cans. For over twenty years, composite cans afforded Sonoco a stable product with little technological change.

By the 1980s, however, packaging technology had become far more volatile, with packages changing every three to four years. As McGowan acknowledged, "The growth will come with the new packages—not what is currently being made." It has been estimated that over 22,000 new products are introduced every year—2000 in the grocery area alone. Approximately one-third of them will require new packages. Dick Puffer, director of public relations and corporate advertising, voiced a similar view: "If we are going to be a vital force in the packaging industry, we have to be ready to give the customer a package in whatever material a customer wants that package—in a very short span of time."

McGowan explained that Sonoco's objective for this division "is not to be known as a composite can manufacturer, but as a package supplier for consumer products." It is willing to grow and change as long as there continues to be a demand for different types of packages.

HIGH DENSITY FILM PRODUCTS DIVISION

One of Sonoco's most promising new ventures is its High Density Film Products Division, which changed its name in 1988 from the Polysack Division. This division is responsible for the manufacture and distribution of plastic bags for the grocery and retail sales industries. Its most successful product has been grocery bags sold under the trade name QuickMate. As of 1988, more than 60 percent of all U.S. grocery chains were using plastic bags, and industry reports noted that plastic held a 50% percent share of the market. Sonoco held a leading share of the national market in 1988 and was by far the dominant supplier in the Southeast. Of the top twenty-five grocery operators in America, Sonoco's Polysack bags were in twenty-one of the chains. The company opened its fourth and fifth Polysack plants in 1987 and its sixth plant in 1988.

Sonoco plastic bags are promoted in the grocery industry as a way to reduce costs and increase productivity for the grocery chains. The bag has proven to be valuable in several ways. Grocers benefit from lower per-unit cost per bag, as compared to paper bags. In addition, the shipping, handling, and storage costs for bags is reduced because Polysack bags require only one-eight the space of paper bags. The actual number of bags used in a store can also be reduced because the stronger plastic bag eliminates the need for double-bagging heavy items.

Despite these obvious advantages, the acceptance of plastic grocery bags has been slow. In fact, the battle with traditional paper grocery bags resulted in Polysack Division losses in its first four years.[9] Sonoco did not expect the transition to plastic to take as long as it did. In a 1987 interview, Charles W. Coker said, "We knew we had an excellent product that was cost advantageous. What we did not anticipate is we had to sell each individual store on the concept and had to sell it store by store."[10]

Sonoco's studies indicated that use of its plastic bags, if properly implemented, could result in a significant reduction in the number of bag set-up motions required of a store employee. This translates into quicker packing of groceries and therefore shorter checkout lines for the store. The Polysack Division's marketing effort was extended to include a total redesign service for a customer's check-out lines. Switching to the QuikMate system has improved front-end productivity as much as 25 percent for some stores.[11] Sonoco also provides training for stores making the change from traditional paper bags. Sonoco teams teach the store's employees how to set up and pack the new bags properly. In an additional effort to further the acceptance of the new bags, Sonoco experts have also assisted a manufacturer of store equipment in designing checkout counters especially made for the new bags.[12]

Sonoco's dominance in the plastic grocery bag segment has been attributed to its early decision to use high-density, high-molecular plastic, which has proven to be the preferred material. According to Rick Brown, marketing manager for the division, of all grocery chains using plastic bags, 84 percent were using high-density plastic bags in 1988.

In 1987, the Polysack Division more than doubled its 1985 profits as a result of volume increases and high capacity utilization. According to industry sources, Sonoco held 35% percent of the plastic grocery bag market in 1988 and was the industry leader. Mobil Corp. occupied second place, but the gap between the companies was widening dramatically. As for the future of the Polysack Division, management projected that it would account for 10 percent of Sonoco's total profits by 1990.[13]

Building on its success in the grocery industry, the Polysack Division introduced a line of plastic bags for department and discount stores in 1987. Marketed under the label Rollmate, these bags come in several sizes in the familiar "t-shirt" shape and are wound on Sonoco paper cores and dispensed through a counter system developed by the division. According to Sonoco Polysack executives, retail sales represent a potential market that could be as large as the market for grocery bags.[14]

DRUM OPERATIONS

In 1985, Sonoco acquired Continental Fibre Drum as an entry into the semi-bulk packaging market. In 1987, the operation changed its name to Sonoco Fibre Drum. By 1988, Sonoco Fibre Drum operated thirteen plants around the country. The company expanded its role in semi-bulk packaging with the addition of plastic drum operations in 1986, and by 1988 it operated three plants under the name Sonoco Plastic Drum.[15]

Primary markets for Sonoco drums are the chemical, pharmaceutical, and food industries. Besides general economic and market share growth, the division seeks growth from conversions of steel drum users to fiber and plastic. Sonoco is seen as the technology leader in the fibre drum industry, which is a competitive advantage in markets having special requirements.

Sonoco competes with one other national fibre drum manufacturer and several smaller, regional firms. Besides its recognized technological leadership, its complete lines of fibre and plastic drums and its reputation for quality are some of its competitive advantages.[16]

An example of product innovation in the fibre drum division is the ResponsePak, a nest of five heavy-duty drums that range in size from seven to fifty-five gallons. The drums were developed to withstand the ravages of almost anything that can be shoveled into them. They provide safe, temporary containment of spilled hazardous waste materials until final disposal is possible. ResponsePak drums are being marketed to local fire departments, which, under new federal guidelines, are required to have emergency toxic waste disposal capability.[17]

PAPER GROUP

The Paper Group consists of Sonoco's U.S. paper mills, which produce paperboard from recycled wastepaper; the company's corrugating medium production operation; Paper Stock Dealers, a wastepaper packing subsidiary; and Sonoco's relatively small forest products operations.

One of the world's largest producers of uncoated cylinderboard, Sonoco generates approximately 565,000 tons annually when its eleven U.S. paperboard mills operate to capacity. Cylinderboard is sold mostly to internal operations for conversion into paperboard packaging products. The division benefits from long, cost-effective production runs, made possible by this "captive" market. Cylinderboard capacity has grown in step with the company's consumer products growth. In 1988 Sonoco added 6 percent additional tonnage to its capacity through new manufacturing strategies and capital improvement at its existing mills.

The corrugating medium operation is a joint venture with Georgia-Pacific, which takes all the output, approximately 15,000 tons of corrugated paperboard, from the machines for use in its cardboard carton facility. Wastepaper, mainly from old corrugated containers, is one of Sonoco's primary raw materials. The company collects about 85 percent of its supply through its wastepaper subsidiary. Sonoco annually consumes more than one million tons of wastepaper in its operations, making it one of the largest users of recycled materials in the world.[18]

SPECIAL PRODUCTS OPERATIONS

Sonoco's smaller activities are grouped together under the Special Products Operations umbrella. The Baker Division is a major producer of nailed wood, plywood, and metal reels for the wire and cable industry. The Fibre Partitions Division produces solid fiber and corrugated partitions for shipping cartons. Sonoco produces aluminum and steel beams for the textile industry and a variety of castings for a multitude of other industries through its Briggs-Shaffner Division. The Adhesives Division and Machinery Manufacturing Operations are part of the company's vertical integration, although both have some outside sales as well.

INTERNATIONAL DIVISION

Mike Bullington, director of international staff at Sonoco, describes the company, with its operations located in twenty countries, as a "multidomestic" company. It is multidomestic in the sense that its international operations are replicas of the company's U.S. operations rather than support activities.

Sonoco's first international extension came about in the 1920s and was an effort to follow Sonoco's traditional customers to other parts of the world. In time, the company's international operations were extended to include overseas counterparts to practically every market that the company serves in the U.S.

Sonoco's international operations are organized according to four world regions: Europe, Canada, Latin America, and the Pacific. Most of the company's foreign operations are carried out through wholly owned subsidiaries. European operations are the oldest and largest segment. There are six converting plants and three major paper-making facilities in England producing both industrial and packaging products. There are also three converting plants in the Netherlands, one in Norway, and one in Spain, and a paper mill in Germany.

Until 1987, European profits were not as high as Sonoco desired. The year .ended, however, with sales of $31.4 million, a 53.2-percent gain over 1986. Operating profits for 1987 were over $2 million. The European group moved its headquarters to Brussels in 1988 in order to have better access to Sonoco's continental customers and to place more emphasis on continental European opportunities (the headquarters of the European Community (EC) are located in that city). Although the company held a leading share of the converted paper market in England, its presence on the continent was minimal prior to 1988. Sonoco's plans at that time were to expand its European activities through acquisitions.

The International Division's second largest operation is in Canada. Canadian operations stretch from Newfoundland to Vancouver Island. Its major customers are paper mills. Sonoco makes packaging materials for the Canadian paper mills and supplies Canadian textile firms with paper tubes and cones. Sonoco also holds a 49-percent share in Domtar Sonoco Containers, Inc., a company that makes composite cans and other products.

Latin America is the third largest of Sonoco's international operations. The company has five plants in Mexico: two paper mills, two converting plants, and a fibre drum plant. Operations in Columbia include a small paper mill, several converting plants, and a major composite can operation. The composite oil can business is attractive in Colombia. Because unscrupulous dealers often resell used oil to unsuspecting customers, Colombians are leery of plastic bottles or any other package that can be refilled. Sonoco solved this problem by offering composite oil cans with easy-open tops similar to potato chip cans. Sonoco also has small operations in Venezuela and Puerto Rico.

Sonoco's newest international group is the Pacific region. Although it is the smallest international operation, it is one with great potential for growth. It is estimated that half of the world's population is in this area. Sonoco has three plants in New Zealand, six plants in Australia, and one plant in Singapore. Until recently, Sonoco had a 45-percent share in a major packaging company in Australia. It was sold in order to buy 100 percent of the company's industrial packaging division. Sonoco has plans to increase its presence in the Pacific Rim and is conducting market surveys in Korea, Thailand, and Indonesia.

Each of the International Division's four regions—Europe, Canada, Latin America, and the Pacific—has its own president, who reports to Jim McGee, Sonoco's group vice-president for international operations, who is located at corporate headquarters in Hartsville. A support group under the direction of Mike Bullington is also located in Hartsville. It is comprised of four major groups: an operations support group, consisting of engineers whose job is to make sure that technology is exchanged between the U.S. and the foreign operations and vice versa; a marketing group, which is responsible for market surveys and various worldwide trade shows; a project manager, who is in charge of organizing and implementing an entire special project such as a new plant installation; and a financial group, which handles all of the budgeting, forecasting, capital analysis, and consolidations of earnings for the international operations.

To combat language and cultural barriers, Sonoco prefers to manage its international operations with local personnel wherever possible. Two of the four group presidents are natives of host countries, as are all second-line managerial personnel.

Sonoco's basic philosophy of business extends to the international arena. Mike Bullington explains that Sonoco is basically trying to do two things internationally. The first is "to leverage Sonoco's capabilities worldwide." All of the many products, the new markets, and the methods of satisfying customers that are developed in the U.S. are spread throughout the world. By spreading the development costs over a much larger base, a cost reduction occurs. Also, as many of the countries in which Sonoco operates are not as economically developed or technologically integrated as the U.S., Sonoco can often use obsolete equipment or machinery in many of the foreign operations where much lower labor costs offset any productivity gains that are realized with much of the company's modern equipment used in the U.S.

The second goal that Sonoco is trying to accomplish by operating internationally is to stay abreast of new developments in other countries. For instance, the world's leaders in high-performance and high-speed paper-making machinery happen to be in the Scandinavian countries. Sonoco can learn about the technologies of the machinery in each country while satisfying the customers' needs. Sonoco capitalizes on what it learns overseas by transferring the new technology to its domestic operations.

COMPETITION

Sonoco's competition lies in several directions. The company is simultaneously involved in the paper, packaging, plastics, partitions, and corrugated products industries, as well as several others. Its focus since 1986, however, has been in the packaging industry. The packaging industry can be divided into four segments, categorized by materials:

1. Metal Containers (cans). Sonoco is not involved in this segment. The largest metal container producer in the U.S. market is Triangle Industries.

2. Glass Containers. Sonoco does not compete in this segment, either. The glass industry has recently undergone much restructuring and consolidation. Ball Corporation is the leader in glass containers.

3. Paperboard Products. This segment includes corrugated boxes, folding cartons, tubes, cores, and cans. It is Sonoco's traditional business and remains the company's strongest area. Sonoco is the industry leader in terms of tubes, cores, and cans, but it does not compete in the carton and box areas, except through one joint venture with Georgia-Pacific. The largest competitor for paperboard products is Jefferson-Smurfit Corporation.

4. Plastics. Sonoco considers plastics the wave of the future in packaging and strives to be well positioned for new technology and opportunities for alternative packaging forms. There are many competitors in the plastic packaging business, which has no clear leader. In the Polysack business, Sonoco competes primarily with Mobil Corporation and Surrey Industries.

According to Warren Hayslip, director of planning, all of these areas—metal, glass, and paper—are converging rapidly on plastics. Traditional packaging materials in each of the first three segments are being replaced by plastic products. For this reason, Sonoco's competition for new business can be considered dispersed across the entire packaging industry.

As Sonoco is among the dominant competitors in most of its present markets, much of the company's competition has sought to imitate Sonoco. As Hayslip put it, "The competitors in many markets tend to be smaller, less well capitalized, and often not as advanced in their manufacturing and quality." Overall, Sonoco places more emphasis on its customers than its competition. Dick Puffer stated, "We worry about competition in that Sonoco doesn't want to be surprised. This often means monitoring all segments of the packaging industry. In many of its markets, but especially in converted paper products, Sonoco could end up competing with a company in the metal or glass industry simply because both companies are converging on plastics."

Acknowledging the fact that the $60 billion packaging industry has many players in it, Sonoco strives to compete by differentiating its products. According to Puffer, Sonoco sells value, not just a package. Sonoco attempts to set itself apart from its competition by constantly seeking new and better ways of producing both its industrial and its consumer packages.

Sonoco is the only international producer of paper and industrial packaging products. Consequently, international competition basically comes from local producers within the various countries. This local competition is one of the main reasons that the international operations are set up autonomously.

Sonoco's goal to be in the number one or two position in each of its markets holds true for the international arena as well. Sonoco holds leading market positions in England, Australia, Canada, and Mexico and has good positions in several other countries.

MARKETING

Although Sonoco's products are used in a wide array of packaging and industrial applications, the company name is not well known. Sonoco executives do not consider this lack of identity a problem, however. Increasing the general public's awareness of Sonoco would not generate more sales. It would only inform people about, for example, who manufactures the can in which their Pillsbury biscuits are packaged. Marketing efforts are therefore geared exclusively toward industrial buyers. The primary marketing vehicles used in that effort are industry journals, trade show presentations, brochures, and direct mail campaigns. Following a recent reorganization, each division has its own marketing staff with total responsibility for the division's marketing program.

As a result of its focused diversification within the packaging industry, Sonoco enjoys a remarkable degree of independence and stability in relation to its customer base. No segment of its business is dependent, to any material degree, on a single or few customers, and none of the company's products are seasonal.[19]

A concept shared by the marketing staffs of all divisions is the idea of selling not just a product, but an entire service package. For the most part, the products will sell themselves; especially industrial products, as they are necessary to the manufacturing process and are manufactured to the customer's specifications. The primary task of the marketing force is to persuade and reassure customers that Sonoco is the best company from which to purchase the products. This is done by promoting the company's unique service assets, two of which are just-in-time delivery and statistical process control. The customer is assured that Sonoco will deliver the highest quality products on a dependable delivery schedule. Just-in-time delivery can eliminate expensive inventory carrying costs as well.

With over 200 branch plants worldwide, Sonoco is considered to have an abnormally high number of plants per dollar volume of sales. Having such a great many plants increases overhead, but Sonoco's management believes the advantages of lower transportation costs far outweigh these increases. An important benefit is that the branch plants are located near some of their large customers, enabling Sonoco to quickly meet customers' needs. Few competitors can match Sonoco's just-in-time delivery system. Although expensive in terms of increased scheduling and labor costs, this system has significantly improved Sonoco's reputation for reliable delivery and service.

With its highly trained staff of packaging scientists, Sonoco offers customers a commitment to insuring their products' success. Engineers work with customers to adapt their packing equipment to new packages. The Consumer

Packaging Division runs field checks in the marketplace to discover consumer response to new packages. The Polysack Division offers training programs to increase the efficiency of those using the new grocery bags. Sonoco sells a complete package of services because, as Ray McGowan, general sales manager in consumer products, states, "If we don't, our competitors will." As of 1988, the company had 238 employees engaged in new product development and technical support for existing products. Sonoco's new packaging research facility in Hartsville, which became operational in 1988, added significantly to the customer support effort.

FINANCIAL MANAGEMENT

Through the 1970s and 1980s, Sonoco's growth rate varied between 10 and 15 percent, with prospects for future growth considered excellent. Sonoco passed the $1 billion sales mark in 1987 for the first time. One of management's primary goals is to achieve $3 billion in sales by the mid-1990s. The company's growth history is detailed in Exhibit 2. In 1988, Sonoco's net income was $96,277,000, compared with $61,482,000 in 1987, $54,676,000 in 1986, and $49,409,000 in 1985. This represents an average increase of over 19 percent. Current assets in 1988 totaled nearly $378 million, and Sonoco had over $533 million in property, plant, and equipment. Current liabilities totaled $189.8 million, while long-term debt totalled $275.5 million after quadrupling to $263.5 million the year before. Sonoco's consolidated statements of income for the year ended December 31, 1988, are presented in Exhibit 3, and its consolidated balance sheets for the same period are presented in Exhibit 4 (page 457). Consolidated changes in shareholders' equity are shown in Exhibit 5 (page 458) and cash flows in Exhibit 6 (page 459).

The huge increase in long-term debt was due to the 1987 acquisition of the Consumer Packaging Division of Boise Cascade. The purchase price was $175 million, almost all of which was financed through long-term debt. While the acquisition strengthened Sonoco's position as a major packaging company and increased the size of the company by one-third, a side effect was that substantial cost reductions had to be made. These reductions involved closing eight plants, consolidating activities, and eliminating over 400 jobs. Adjustments also included a $10 million pretax write-off in the fourth quarter of 1987, which translated to almost 13 cents per share.[20]

In the past, debt related to acquisitions had been absorbed by the company's rapid growth in sales. For example, Sonoco's 1985 acquisition of Continental Fibre Drum, for $72 million, was also debt financed. Sonoco generated enough cash, however, to pay off over half the loan within the first year. Absorption of the much larger Boise Cascade acquisition will be more difficult.

The Tax Reform Act of 1986 had no significant effect on Sonoco. Lower tax rates were offset by changes in international tax provisions and by the loss of the Investment Tax Credit. In the future, however, Sonoco expects its overall effective tax rate to drop approximately 40 percent.

EXHIBIT 2   SONOCO'S GROWTH

YEAR	NET SALES	NET INCOME
1900	$17,000	$2,000
1910	132,000	29,000
1920	908,000	304,000
1930	1,598,000	200,000
1940	5,018,000	540,000
1950	18,895,000	1,635,000
1960	38,200,000	2,460,000
1970	125,027,000	6,600,000
1971	135,808,000	8,140,000
1972	154,820,000	8,729,000
1973	188,559,000	11,188,000
1974	225,669,000	13,588,000
1975	199,550,000	14,524,000
1976	242,425,000	18,881,000
1977	270,634,000	20,910,000
1978	344,204,000	23,263,000
1979	421,480,000	27,238,000
1980	490,397,000	32,511,000
1981	533,349,000	38,716,000
1982	538,617,000	29,070,000
1983	668,628,000	37,274,000
1984	740,869,000	42,535,000
1985	869,598,000	49,409,000
1986	963,796,000	54,676,000
1987	1,312,052,000	61,482,000
1988	1,599,751,000	96,277,000

Sources: *The Story of Sonoco* (company publication) and Sonoco Products Company, 1988 Annual Report.

HUMAN RESOURCE MANAGEMENT

A unique aspect of Sonoco is that its personnel department does not measure turnover. According to Jack Westmoreland, director of corporate personnel, "If we ever start having turnover, we'll know it." He went on to explain that when he previously measured personnel turnover, the numbers were almost insignificant. Gradually he reduced the number of times per year it was measured until now it is not reported at all. "Our people stay with us," says Westmoreland.

Traditionally, Sonoco's policy has been to promote from within. The majority of its personnel are hired to fill entry-level positions. Rarely is an experienced manager hired from outside the company and, if so, only for higher-level

EXHIBIT 3   SONOCO PRODUCTS COMPANY CONSOLIDATED BALANCE SHEETS

	1988	1987
ASSETS		
Current Assets		
Cash and cash equivalents	$ 20,375	$ 14,447
Receivables	164,252	140,046
Inventories	163,706	134,427
Prepaid expenses	29,514	32,585
	377,847	321,505
Property, Plant and Equipment	533,427	482,357
Cost in Excess of Fair Value of Assets Purchased	45,809	42,714
Investments in Affiliates	6,642	15,143
Other Assets	13,734	15,906
	$977,459	$877,625
LIABILITIES AND SHAREHOLDERS' EQUITY		
Current Liabilities		
Payable to suppliers and others	$154,013	$160,074
Notes payable and current portion of long-term debt	22,465	10,850
Taxes on income	13,284	6,609
	189,762	177,533
Long-Term Debt	275,535	263,489
Deferred Income Taxes	57,676	56,691
Shareholders' Equity		
Common shares, no par value		
Authorized 75,000,000 shares		
Issued 45,920,440 shares	7,175	7,175
Capital in excess of stated value	45,982	45,847
Translation of foreign currencies	(3,516)	(9,137)
Retained earnings	417,115	348,884
Treasury shares at cost (1988–2,059,607, 1987–2,154,779)	(12,270)	(12,857)
	454,486	379,912
	$997,459	$877,625

Note: Amounts are in thousands.

Source: Sonoco Products Company, *1988 Annual Report.*

EXHIBIT 4   SONOCO PRODUCTS COMPANY CONSOLIDATED INCOME STATEMENTS

	1988	1987	1986
Sales	$1,599,751	$1,312,052	$963,796
Cost and expenses			
Cost of products sold	1,263,978	1,044,556	761,121
Selling, general and administrative expenses	148,417	129,176	96,957
Interest expense	25,175	18,593	8,552
Acquisition consolidation charges		10,000	
Income from operations before income taxes	162,181	109,727	97,166
Taxes on income	67,029	48,714	44,435
Income from operations before equity in earnings of affiliates	95,152	61,013	52,731
Equity in earnings of affiliates	1,125	469	1,945
Net income	$ 96,277	$ 61,482	$ 54,676
Average shares outstanding	43,816,224	43,865,245	43,806,380
Net income per share	$2.20	$1.40	$1.25
Dividends per share	$.64	$.50	$.41

Note: Dollars in thousands except per share.

Source: Sonoco Products Company, *1988 Annual Report.*

positions. In recent years, however, rapid growth has forced Sonoco to depend more on outside hiring, especially in new technical areas such as plastics. When interviewing for a salaried position, a prospective employee meets and talks to eight to ten people during the first visit, estimates Westmoreland. Upon being hired, every new salaried employee meets individually with the president, vice-presidents, and chief officers of the company.

Sonoco communicates with its employees through posted notices and through *Sonoco News,* published monthly by the public relations department. The company also encourages feedback from its employees. By using the "Sonofone" system, employees can complain or ask questions. A secretary takes the calls and, if the caller chooses to be identified, will receive a personal response that day from an executive who is qualified to answer. If the employee does not wish to be identified, a response to the question or complaint will be posted in each department, Sonoco's open door policy, which is printed in the company's policy manual, states that employees can approach any manager—even the president—with a problem or inquiry.

Sonoco's employee benefits package includes fully paid health and dental plans. A thrift and savings plan is also offered, in which the company will match a percentage of each dollar saved in Sonoco's credit union. The credit

EXHIBIT 5   SONOCO PRODUCTS COMPANY CONSOLIDATED STATEMENTS OF CHANGES IN SHAREHOLDERS' EQUITY

	COMMON SHARES	CAPITAL IN EXCESS OF STATED VALUE	TRANSLATION OF FOREIGN CURRENCIES	RETAINED EARNINGS	TREASURY SHARES
January 1, 1986	$7,175	$45,802	$(19,428)	$272,631	$(10,437)
Net income				54,676	
Dividends, $.41 per share				(17,963)	
Translation gain (net of $631 in taxes)			427		
Issuance of treasury shares under stock option plan.		(127)			134
December 31, 1986	7,175	45,675	(19,001)	309,344	(10,303)
Net income				61,482	
Dividends, $.50 per share				(21,942)	
Translation gain (net of $879 in taxes)			9,864		
Issuance of treasury shares under stock option plan.		172			475
Treasury shares acquired					(3,029)
December 31, 1987	7,175	45,847	(9,137)	348,884	(12,857)
Net income				96,277	
Dividends, $.64 per share				(28,046)	
Translation gain (net of $171 in taxes)			5,621		
Issuance of treasury shares under stock option plan.		135			587
December 31, 1988	$7,175	$45,982	$ (3,516)	$417,115	$(12,270)

Note: Dollars in thousands.

Source: Sonoco Products Company, *1988 Annual Report.*

union also extends loans to employees at low rates of interest. An employee stock ownership plan is offered to key employees. At the end of 1987, some 4,808 employees participated in the plan.[21]

Sonoco's relations with organized labor have always been placid. The company's main plant at Hartsville is nonunion. Sonoco's approach to preventive labor relations is straightforward: "If we treat employees right—give them fair pay, good benefits—they won't need a union," says Westmoreland. Although its main plant has remained nonunion, employees at many of the subsidiaries acquired in expansion are represented by collective bargaining contracts. In 1988, approximately half of Sonoco's eligible employees were unionized. The

EXHIBIT 6 CONSOLIDATED STATEMENTS OF CASH FLOWS

	1988	1987	1986
Cash Flows From Operating Activities			
Net income...	$ 96,277	$ 61,482	$ 54,676
Adjustments to reconcile net income to net cash provided by operating activities:			
Depreciation, depletion and amortization........................	69,055	57,086	35,654
Gain on sale of stock of affiliated companies	(3,980)	(1,224)	
Loss on assets retired..	340	1,540	1,259
Dividends from affiliates	807	1,437	312
Equity in earnings of affiliates..	(1,125)	(469)	(1,945)
Exchange (gain) loss..	(62)	713	(1,961)
Increase in deferred taxes......................................	413	1,945	7,284
Provision for losses on accounts receivable	962	1,908	774
Changes in assets and liabilities net of effects from acquisitions and foreign currency adjustments:			
(Increase) in accounts receivable...............................	(17,270)	(29,401)	(8,127)
(Increase) decrease in inventory................................	(24,530)	(14,901)	2,196
(Increase) in prepaid expenses	(62)	(13,582)	(15,735)
Increase in payables and taxes....................................	5,685	28,041	16,846
(Increase) in other assets and liabilities	(2,777)	(4,440)	(304)
Net cash provided by operating activities.................................	123,733	90,135	90,929
Cash Flows From Investing Activities			
Purchase of property, plant and equipment	(93,599)	(104,757)	(45,072)
Cost of acquisitions, exclusive of cash	(35,266)	(170,517)	(22,217)
Sale (purchase) of stock of affiliated companies.....................	16,275	3,995	(969)
Proceeds from the sale of assets	4,583	2,166	2,201
Net cash used by investing activities..	(108,007)	(269,113)	(66,057)
Cash Flows From Financing Activities			
Proceeds from issuance of debt	51,171	214,971	25,010
Principal repayment of debt...	(32,642)	(22,781)	(27,585)
Cash dividends...	(30,243)	(20,841)	(16,868)
Treasury shares acquired		(3,029)	
Other	710	713	(1,961)
Net cash (used) provided by financing activities....................	(11,004)	169,033	(21,404)
Effects of exchange rate changes on cash	1,206	4,083	(2,230)
Increase (decrease) in Cash and Cash Equivalents......................	5,928	(5,862)	1,238
Cash and Cash Equivalents at beginning of year........................	14,447	20,309	19,071
Cash and Cash Equivalents at end of year	$ 20,375	$ 14,447	$ 20,309
Supplemental cash flow disclosure			
Interest paid	$ 24,185	$ 17,373	$ 5,836
Income taxes paid...	$ 63,086	$ 48,110	$ 28,337

Note: Dollars in thousands.

Source: Sonoco Products Company, *1988 Annual Report.*

company has a good reputation of getting along well with these unions, stressing cooperation instead of confrontation.

CORPORATE CULTURE AT SONOCO

In an address to the operations committee on July 20, 1987, P. C. Coggeshall, Sr., former senior executive vice-president, presented a list of words he felt described the culture at Sonoco. Included in this list were, of course, such ideas as honesty, integrity, and fairness. Coggeshall also mentioned other characteristics that, although not unique to Sonoco, have been instrumental in the company's success. One of these terms is "family control." Through the years the Coker sons have not only been willing to be involved in the family business, but have also been fully capable of managing this ever-growing company. Although each man had his own particular insights, this handing down of leadership has kept individual talents focused on the company's primary goals and has lent stability to the overall operation.

Another characteristic is the "organizational pride" that Sonoco instills in its employees. Ever since its beginnings during the Reconstruction period, the company has been forced to deal with adverse and changing conditions. According to Coggeshall, "This history and pride allows teamwork to flourish. . . . Performance stimulating pride, stimulating performance."[22] Employees at Sonoco "work hard but enjoy what they're doing," explains Westmoreland. "This is true at every level."

The concept of teamwork is a guiding principle at Sonoco. Evidence of this idea appears in *Sonoco News,* where headlines read, "Teamwork Makes a Good Idea Work," and "To Build the Championship Team."[23] Company president C. W. Coker has expressed to the shareholders the importance of having employees who are committed to achieving the goals of both their specific division and the company as a whole. "We believe that our mission and our goals are understood by our employees. This is important, because our chances of success are enhanced as our employees all pull in the same direction." As Coker explains, one of the goals at Sonoco "is to foster an atmosphere of teamwork . . . and maintain the loyalty and dedication that is tradition among all Sonoco employees."[24] It is the recognition of this fact that has led the company to be people oriented. Westmoreland claims that although many businesses say they have a people orientation, at Sonoco this is not simply a philosophy but a "genuine, sincere approach" to operating the business. Management practices are based on treating every individual with respect and consideration.

From its inception, Sonoco has had strong ties with its people. It started as a family-run business, and early employees, growing up in the small town of Hartsville, knew the Coker family personally. The company has tried to hold on to this relationship with its people in spite of its growth and success. While tradition remains important, the company is also aware of the benefits of embracing new attitudes. Coggeshall points out that after the acquisition of another company, the plan is not to make new employees into traditional Sonoco workers. Instead, an attempt is made to merge the new cultures, drawing on the strengths of each possibly very different way of corporate life.

Employees are encouraged to develop their talents and ideas through Sonoco's program of incentive compensation. Employees are given monetary awards for suggestions adopted by the company. In December 1986, the second-largest award ever earned ($19,118) was received by a worker in the cone department. The employee commented that his supervisors had been very cooperative in working on the idea. "I was proud to be able to help the company as well as myself. I am fortunate to work for a company that has such a fine suggestion system."[25]

Another form of incentive compensation is the company's program for educational reimbursement. Under Sonoco's educational policy, the company will reimburse an employee for 75 percent of the expenses involved in job-related training. Safety is also an important part of employee development. Prizes are awarded for having a perfect safety record. Loyalty and faithful service are recognized in a unique way. After working for the company for twenty-five years, employees can become members of the "Old Timers Club," which allows them to participate in special company-sponsored events. The team spirit concept is supplemented through the company's sponsorship of bowling teams and both men's and women's softball teams.

The team concept at Sonoco goes beyond the workers and the company and extends to its customers. "Giving them what they have a right to expect and a little more" defines Sonoco's "customer orientation." "We will focus on our customers," claims Coker. "We exist to help them achieve their goals, and only if they grow profitably will we have the opportunity to do likewise. It is absolutely essential that we provide products and services which are responsive to present and longer term needs of our customers."[26] Sonoco personnel often work with customers to develop new products and applications. Says Coker, "Change is a way of life with us and, if anything, the rate of change will only accelerate in the future."[27]

STRATEGY

By focusing its growth in activities with which it is familiar, Sonoco has maintained a first- or second-place market share in all of its markets. Starting with paper cores in 1899 and moving gradually into other areas (such as packaging), the company has grown consistently at a rate of 15 percent in recent years. Maintaining this growth, however, has not been without problems. Until 1985, the company's marketing, engineering, and personnel functions were staffed at the corporate level. Each division would "pay" the company for the use of these services. With growth and the addition of new divisions such as Polysack and Consumer Packaging, the demand for these services became greater and more diverse. The task of coordinating the services in order to meet the needs for various departments became increasingly cumbersome. In

1985, it was decided that many of the divisions had grown large enough to be responsible for staffing these functions on their own. The process of "divisionalization" was begun.

At first it was a struggle for those working in corporate offices to start new departments in these areas. People were forced to become very specialized in areas they barely had been exposed to previously. Toby Reynolds, manager of marketing services for IPD, explained that he had never developed an ad or created a brochure before the divisionalization took place. Although in 1988 his department was still in what he called a "learning mode," he predicted that by the following year the transition would be complete.

In spite of the difficulty of adjustment, Sonoco management feels that the new system will be of great benefit to the company. According to Ray McGowan, each division will be able to "manage business more clearly and be more focused on what our needs are rather than fit into a mode that has to meet everyone's needs." Having these skills more readily available has made it easier to accomplish many tasks that formerly required a few feet of red tape.

The staffing aspects of implementing a rapid growth strategy can be very problematic. Sonoco believes that the key to effective hiring is to find the right type of management talent first, and then allow the managers to staff their own departments. In a rapid growth situation, this process can be prohibitively time consuming. Fortunately for Sonoco, much of its growth has come through acquisitions that happened to have very talented managers. McGowan, who came to the company in its acquisition of Container Corporation of America, estimates that three-fourths of the people in the Consumer Packaging sales department came to Sonoco via acquisitions.

With most acquisitions there is a period of adjustment in which to discover how the strengths of the two companies can best be combined to achieve the company's overall strategy. Customers' expectation of "business as usual" from the day of the purchase can cause frustrations for all involved. The management at Sonoco feels that its strategy of balanced growth—combining acquisitions such as Boise Cascade with internal growth, such as its Polysack Division—is the most effective one for lessening these effects while capitalizing on acquisition opportunities.

Sonoco's growth pattern has changed through the years. Initially, the company was known as a paper company that also made a few packaging products. In 1986, senior management decided to refocus the strategy of Sonoco to a "packaging company that happens to be vertically integrated." Much of Sonoco's business in the 1970s was still concentrated in the textile industry; if this had not changed, it is questionable where the company would be today. By focusing on the packaging industry, especially consumer packaging, Sonoco's competitive position has improved greatly. In addition, as one industry analyst has noted, as many of the consumer packaging products are linked to lower-cost or staple items such as food and cleaning agents, economically troubled times should not affect Sonoco as dramatically as they will some companies.[28]

The term "focused diversification" has been used to describe Sonoco's strategy. All of its products are either directly in the packaging industry or are packaging related. While plastic packaging products are, for example, different from the company's typical products, the commonality of their end use is the same. Sonoco's decision to focus on packaging meant divesting some of its subsidiaries. A metal building subsidiary, although very profitable, was divested in 1985. A common carrier trucking subsidiary was also sold.

In addition to Sonoco's diversification strategy, the company seeks to be a low-cost producer. This strategy is apparent through the many branch plants located throughout the U.S. and overseas. The plants are often located near major customers, allowing for just-in-time delivery. Sonoco also has what are called "focused factories" that produce only one product, thus providing increased efficiency and decreased complexity in the manufacturing process.

Even though "responsiveness" is one of the driving forces in Sonoco's plants, it can cause problems. With very short lead times, methods for predicting the future demands of customers are not much help. Therefore, when a sudden influx of orders occurs, scheduling work can be difficult. Certain customers have priority, and when one of them calls in an order to be delivered the next day, not only are other orders pushed behind, but overhead costs are increased due to overtime. Just-in-time delivery is a distinct advantage for Sonoco and its customers and its customers is an important means of differentiating Sonoco's products, but in 1988 its implementation had not yet included long enough lead times for production processes to be scheduled efficiently.

There are three main determining factors in the company's strategic decision making process. The first is the concept of leadership. According to Dick Puffer, "Sonoco wants to be the top producer in the market if it can be." A second-place position in the market is also acceptable, and third place will be reluctantly accepted if the business is a profitable one. If Sonoco's position is any lower, it will sell the business. Sonoco bases this objective on an analysis of the PIMS database, which indicates that in order to accumulate reasonable returns, a company must be among its market's top three competitors. Puffer says that the second factor in the company's decision to venture into a business is whether or not it can "become the low-cost producer or one of the low-cost producers." As mentioned earlier, Sonoco operates at very high efficiency levels. The company prides itself on producing a quality product at a low cost. The third determining factor in the decision-making process is value. Top executives ask themselves "what kind of value can Sonoco offer to the customer to make it worth the customer's while to buy from a new person entering the market." Basically, the question of what new business to enter goes back to the customer.

The formal strategic planning process at Sonoco also has been decentralized along division lines. Each of twelve operating groups is responsible for planning its own future and making its own business-level strategic decisions. A corporate planning group looks at the overall company and considers issues that cannot be addressed by the operating groups. The corporate planning department decides both what businesses to enter and which to avoid or divest. Warren Hayslip, director of planning, says that strategic thinking must take place throughout the organization, for every decision. "It is not simply, 'we want to be bigger or we would like to make these products'; there is an in-depth justification of capital and in-depth analysis."

As the company operates in a global economy, its strategy also has an international dimension. The International Division of Sonoco expects continued growth. Hayslip states that "Sonoco's worldwide strategy is multidomestic in the sense that we have separate operations that are linked together by technology, by know-how, by financial resources, etc., but the operations are autonomous to a large extent in that they have their own marketing team, their own manufacturing team, their own plants, and they function as a separate operating unit." The International Division's strategy basically is to leverage what Sonoco has in the U.S. According to Mike Bullington, International Operations are expected to grow geographically at a "10–12 percent compounded growth rate for the next 5 years." In many of the countries, Sonoco will attack a specific niche in a market. For example, surveys have shown that in Taiwan Sonoco could not be a broad-line producer of products. Consequently, Sonoco will try to segment this market by focusing on products that cannot be made by local producers. The niche will be high-quality, specialty products such as sophisticated film cores.

CONCLUSION

From its beginnings as a small producer of paper tubes and cones for the southeastern textile industry at the dawn of the twentieth century, Sonoco has become a supplier of industrial products, consumer packages, and plastic containers for corporations throughout the U.S. and overseas. With Sonoco's goal of becoming the leading U.S. packaging company, one would expect its management to be one that gambles, jumping at every opportunity for expansion. Sonoco's management has, however, traditionally chosen to let the company grow slowly, concentrating on the products and technologies most familiar to the company.

Sonoco's focus has undergone a series of related shifts over the years. The first was the step from industrial products to consumer packaging, primarily the manufacture of composite cans. The company used its technological expertise in converted paper products to enter this new market. Once it was established in the new industry, Sonoco began acquiring expertise to enter new segments of the packaging arena, such as plastic oil containers.

Sonoco's acquisition of Boise Cascade's consumer packaging activities in 1987 represents a departure from the company's slow-growth policy. The merger will potentially place Sonoco at the top of several of its most important business segments, but at a high cost. The company has taken on more debt than it has ever had. Although Sonoco officials feel that the company has sufficient resources for much more growth, the restrictions that increased debt places on top management are significant. Higher fixed obligations for debt service will necessitate more attention to cash flow and may restrict the amount of capital the company can invest in new packaging technology. Further strategic expansion may be limited as a result of the company's higher leverage position.

It took Sonoco eighty-seven years to reach the billion-dollar sales mark. Coker expects the company's sales to reach $3 billion by the mid-1990s and states that the company will continue to grow because a growing company provides the best security for employees, customers, and suppliers. This is not the goal of a complacent, inward-looking company. In 1988 the question remained as to whether or not this family-run corporation can continue to absorb its newly initiated rapid growth while maintaining its reputation for quality and service.

ENDNOTES

Much of the information for this case was derived from interviews conducted in March 1988 with the following Sonoco personnel:

- Rick Brown, marketing manager, Polysack Division
- Mike Bullington, director of international staff
- P. C. Coggeshall, senior executive vice-president
- Warren Hayslip, director of planning
- Charlie Hupfer, director of tax and audit
- Ray McGowan, general sales manager, Consumer Products Division
- Dick Puffer, director of public relations and corporate advertising
- Toby Reynolds, manager of marketing services, Industrial Products Division
- J. E. Westmoreland, director of corporate personnel

1. *The Story of Sonoco Paper Products Since 1899* (Hartsville, S.C.: Sonoco Products Company, 1977): 3.

2. Ibid., pp. 4–5.

3. "The Fortune 500," *Fortune* (April 24, 1989): 362.

4. Sonoco Products Company, *Form 10-K, 1987.*

5. Sonoco Products Company, *1987 Annual Report,* p. 5.

6. "Sonoco Named Certified Supplier for 3M," *Sonoco News* (January 1988): 7.

7. *Investment Research* (Hartsville, S.C.: Sonoco Products Company, 1988.)

8. Sonoco Products Company, *1987 Annual Report,* p. 5.

9. "NYC Grocer Cuts Operating Costs 10% with Sonoco Plastic Sacks," *Sonoco Solutions* (Hartsville, S.C.: Sonoco Products Company, 1988): 1.

10. Fladung, Thom. "Sonoco on Front Line in Battle to Woo Customers," *The State* (Columbia, S.C.) (December 21, 1987): B1.

11. *You Get More Out of Packaging with Sonoco.* Sonoco publication no. SP1212, 1987.

12. "Oklahoma Grocer Increases Front-end Productivity, Frees Up Labor with New Express Lane Check-out and Plastic Sacks," *Sonoco Solutions* (Hartsville, S.C.: Sonoco Products Company, 1988): 1.

13. "Sonoco Products Company," *NCNB Investment Research* (November 16, 1987): 3.

14. Sonoco Products Company, *1987 Annual Report,* p. 7.

15. Ibid., p. 6.

16. Ibid.

17. Sonoco Products Company, *1985 Annual Report,* inside cover.

18. Sonoco Products Company, *1987 Annual Report,* pp. 6–7.

19. Sonoco Products Company, *Form 10-K, 1987.*

20. Sonoco Products Company, *1987 Annual Report,* p. 13.

21. Sonoco Products Company, *Form 10-K 1987*.

22. Matthews, R. W., "To Build the Championship Team," *Sonoco News* (February, 1988): 3.

23. *Sonoco News* (February 1988).

24. "Coker Credits Company Success to Loyal, Dedicated, Employees," *Sonoco News* (May 1987): 5.

25. "Teamwork Makes a Good Idea Work," *Sonoco News* (February, 1988): 7.

26. *Sonoco News* (January, 1987).

27. "Coker Credits Company Success to Loyal, Dedicated, Employees."

28. Fladung, "Sonoco on Front Line."

CHRYSLER ACQUIRES AMERICAN MOTORS

JOSEPH WOLFE

On March 9, 1987, Chrysler Corporation and Renault of France (a major holder of American Motors stock) signed a letter of intent under which Chrysler would buy American Motors Corporation (AMC) in a deal initially valued at $1.11 billion involving stocks, bonds, and cash. Under the terms of the original agreement, Chrysler would trade $522 million in its stock for AMC's outstanding shares, give Renault a $200 million ten-year note at 8 percent for its AMC interest, and pay Renault $35 million in cash. Wall Street's reaction was immediate: Chrysler's stock rose $1.50 per share to $53.875 and AMC's stock rose 75 cents to $4.25. Soon after this initial increase, Chrysler's stock experienced a serious decline: during the week of April 13 its stock fell from $54.50 to $36.375 per share. Standard & Poor put Chrysler and AMC on its credit watch, while stating, "Chrysler is paying roughly $2 billion in common stock, assumed debt and other obligations, including unfunded pensions and legal contingencies. In return, it's receiving a business with questionable prospects."[1]

The acquisition was ultimately approved by AMC's board of directors after Chrysler "sweetened" the offer by increasing the initial offer of $4.00 of Chrysler stock for each share of AMC stock to $4.50 a share (resulting in an exchange of $595 million rather than the initial $522 million). Wall Street's reaction was again immediate: Chrysler's stock fell $1.25 to $34.125 and AMC's stock rose 12.5 cents to $4.25. On August 5, 1987, AMC's stockholders unanimously agreed to Chrysler's terms thus ending the turbulent and often frustrated career of American Motors and the joining of that organization to an equally crisis-ridden automobile manufacturer.

Cash-rich Chrysler had been looking for an acquisition for quite a while.

Source: **Prepared by Professor Joseph Wolfe, University of Tulsa, as a basis for classroom discussion and not to illustrate either effective or ineffective handling of administrative situations. Joel Garrot and Tisha Rohr assisted in the preparation of this case, which employs both public and privately obtained materials. © Joseph Wolfe, 1989.**

In commenting on the AMC move. Chrysler chairman Lee A. Iacocca said. "We believe our decision to acquire American Motors is right for both companies—not just for the immediate future, but even more so for the long haul. ... It'll strengthen both of us in what's already a tough market." Whenever doubts about the advisability of making the acquisition were raised. Chrysler vice-president Bennett Bidwell stated, "Iacocca kept banging us over the head saying. 'This is for the long haul. This is a once-in-a-lifetime opportunity to broaden the distribution network, get a brand and a new plant and go forward. You take the pimples and the warts along with the beauty marks.'"[2]

CHRYSLER'S HISTORY

The Chrysler Corporation was founded by Walter P. Chrysler in 1921 with the purchase of the ailing Maxwell Motor Company. The first car to bear his name, the six-cylinder "70" of 1924, was something of a sensation with its four-wheel contracting hydraulic brakes and 70-mph performance. Sales of 43,000 units were reported in 1925. By 1928 Chrysler had laid the foundations to rival Ford in its total volume, and General Motors in the number of models and cars it produced. The firm acquired the Dodge Brothers and launched two new makes, the Plymouth Four in the low price field and the DeSoto Six at the higher end of the price spectrum. The Chrysler Corporation sold 98,000 cars in 1929, and by 1936 the firm was selling more cars than the once-mighty Ford Motor Company. The path to sales success, however, was not without its mishaps.

In 1934 Chrysler brought out its Airflow designs for both its DeSoto and Chrysler cars. Though the cars featured a welded unitary body that was 40 times more rigid than conventional designs, headlights mounted flush in the body, and a completely aerodynamic shape, they were commercial failures, and they were hurriedly supplemented by the Airstream line in 1935. For the next 20 years the company's styling policy was basically cautious and conservative, and the firm emphasized a car's engineering over its appearance. Despite Chrysler's conservative styling approach, one of its major competitors had problems of its own. The Ford Motor Company was still basically a one-car company, even though it had acquired the Lincoln motorcar in 1922 and had introduced the Mercury in 1939, and it was racked by internal management strife and external union problems. By 1946 Chrysler had over 25 percent of the American automobile market and was number two (behind General Motors) in both 1947 and 1948. But by 1949 Ford had usurped Chrysler's spot behind GM.

Over the next two and a half decades Chrysler's overall market share generally deteriorated and slipped to as low as 9.6 percent of the market in 1962 and to 8.5 percent in 1981.[3] (See Exhibit 1.) At this time the firm instituted two financial policies: it employed debt to cushion itself against more violent swings in demand, and it maintained a GM-type dividend policy to sustain its attractiveness to investors.

EXHIBIT 1   AMERICAN MARKET SHARES BY CORPORATION

YEAR	GM	FORD	CHRYSLER	INDEPENDENTS[a]	IMPORTS[b]
1946	37.7%	21.9%	25.7%	14.5%	—
1947	41.8	21.0	21.7	15.2	—
1948	40.6	18.8	21.4	18.6	0.4
1949	42.8	21.3	21.4	14.2	0.2
1950	45.4	24.0	17.6	12.8	0.2
1951	42.8	22.1	21.8	12.8	0.4
1952	41.7	22.7	21.2	13.4	0.7
1953	45.0	25.1	20.3	9.0	0.5
1954	50.7	30.8	12.9	5.0	0.5
1955	50.7	27.6	16.8	4.0	0.8
1956	50.7	28.4	15.4	3.6	1.6
1957	44.8	30.3	18.3	3.0	3.4
1958	46.3	26.4	13.9	5.2	8.1
1959	42.1	28.1	11.3	8.3	10.1
1960	43.6	26.6	14.0	8.2	7.5
1961	46.5	28.5	10.7	7.7	6.4
1962	51.8	26.3	9.6	7.3	4.8
1963	51.0	24.8	12.3	6.6	5.1
1964	49.0	26.0	13.8	5.1	6.0
1965	50.0	25.4	14.6	3.7	6.1
1966	48.1	26.0	15.3	3.1	7.3
1967	49.5	22.1	16.0	3.0	9.3
1968	46.7	23.7	16.2	2.9	10.4
1969	46.7	24.2	15.1	2.6	11.2
1970	39.7	26.4	16.0	3.1	14.6
1971	45.1	23.5	13.7	2.6	15.0
1972	44.4	24.3	13.8	3.0	14.5
1973	44.3	23.5	13.3	3.5	15.1
1974	41.8	24.9	13.5	3.9	15.7
1975	43.3	23.0	11.7	3.8	18.1
1976	47.2	22.4	12.9	2.6	14.8
1977	46.3	22.6	10.9	1.7	18.2
1978	47.6	22.9	10.1	1.5	17.7
1979	46.4	20.3	9.0	1.6	22.6
1980	45.9	17.2	8.8	2.0	26.1
1981	44.5	16.2	8.5	1.6	27.2
1982	44.0	16.9	8.6	1.4	27.8
1983	44.1	17.1	9.2	2.1	25.9
1984	44.2	19.0	9.5	1.8	23.5
1985	42.8	19.0	11.3	1.2	25.7
1986	41.2	18.2	11.5	0.7	28.4

[a]Includes Crosley, Hudson, Nash, Studebaker, Packard, Kaiser-Frazer until early 1960s; AMC alone thereafter.

[b]Includes Austin, Bantam, Fiat, Renault, and Volkswagen in the 1950s; changed to Datsun/Nissan, Toyota, Honda, Mercedes-Benz, Volvo, Saab, and Volkswagen in the 1960s.

Source: Automotive News, April 30, 1980, p. 15 for 1946–1979 data; Motor Vehicle Manufacturers Association of the U.S., Inc. and Ward's Automotive Yearbooks for 1980–1986 data.

In the 1960s, under the guidance of Lynn Townsend, a former accountant with Touche, Ross, Chrysler expanded worldwide with plants in Australia, South Africa, South America, and Europe. Two acquisitions, Simca in France and Rootes Motors Ltd. in Great Britain, were failing companies when they were acquired, and Chrysler was unable to turn them around. Additionally, they continued to siphon needed funds from American operations which were beginning to be inefficient producers in their major market. One consultant at the time estimated that Chrysler's production costs were 10 percent per car higher than Ford's, and Ford itself was inferior to GM in its production efficiencies.

Chrysler also began to suffer an image problem. Although the firm attracted the more conservative customer, Chrysler executive Eugene Cafiero noted that its buyers were a little older and they had less income. Accordingly they purchased fewer options and they kept their cars longer. To remedy this situation, Townsend offered "hot" cars such as the Dodge Charger and Coronet, and the Plymouth Road Runner, Satellite, Barracuda, and 'Cuda, and launched its "Dodge Rebellion" advertising campaign, while featuring cowgirls and hoopla. Unfortunately the average Chrysler-product customer was not rebellious and felt abandoned or scorned by the company that had courted them so vigorously in earlier years.

By the 1970s Townsend was still emphasizing large cars, although there were indications that Americans could no longer afford to own and operate them. Chrysler spent $450 million to restyle its full-size line while GM was introducing its small-sized Vega in 1971. Ford was launching the Pinto, and AMC was ushering in the Gremlin. Accordingly, Chrysler possessed no small cars when the Arab oil embargo began in 1973. With sales falling to unprofitable levels, Townsend lowered Chrysler's break-even point by firing or laying off thousands of designers and engineers. Despite these economy moves, the firm lost $260 million in 1975 and Townsend was replaced by John Riccardo, another ex-accountant from Touche, Ross.

Riccardo created a $5.5 billion program designed to move Chrysler into the small car market, but his plan was destined for problems and delays. New models experienced production snafus and quality control problems, and product recalls were frequent thus destroying the firm's hard-earned reputation for engineering excellence. By 1978 Chrysler's rebuilding program appeared to be on track as its new subcompact, front-wheel-driven Omnis and Horizons were named *Motor Trend* magazine's 1978 Car of the Year. Unfortunately, *Consumer Reports* labeled the same products "not acceptable" and stated so on the front cover of its July 1978 issue. These cars possessed what the magazine stated was an alarming directional instability at speeds greater than 50 mph. This same steering problem caused Canadian authorities to refuse the purchase of these vehicles for government use.

Riccardo's building program escalated an additional $2.2 billion and sales for all Chrysler products fell drastically. Losses amounted to $204.6 million and the company found its financial resources dwindling. To cover long-term financial operations Chrysler prepared to issue a block of preferred stock even though both Moody's and Standard & Poor rated the issue speculative. Merrill Lynch completed the offering with an 11 percent dividend yield while Chrysler continued to borrow heavily from both insurance companies and banks.

With the arrival, in December 1978, of Lee Iacocca, who had been fired by Henry Ford over policy differences, Chrysler began another turnaround. During the next two years many of the firm's foreign operations were sold off for cash to keep the firm afloat until it could design and launch a new fleet of more saleable cars. In August 1978 Peugeot-Citroen purchased Chrysler's European subsidiaries for $230 million in cash and Peugeot stock representing approximately 12.5 percent of its equity. In February 1979 GM purchased Chrysler's Venezuelan assembly plants, and the following year brought the acquisition of Chrysler's equity in Chrysler Fevre Argentine and the purchase of Chrysler do Brasil by Volkswagen.

With sales falling and losses increasing, it appeared that time would run out before Chrysler could bring its new, highly touted K cars (Aries and Reliant) to market in 1981. Both Riccardo and Iacocca immediately began to lobby for government assistance. In late December 1979 Congress passed its famous Chrysler Motors loan guarantee bill, which called for contributions of $462.5 and $125.0 million from union and nonunion employees respectively. Additionally, Chrysler would issue $162.5 million in stock to its workers, and the federal government would waive its status as senior creditor on $400 million of new bank loans, on loans from state and local governments, and on loans of $100,000 or less from small suppliers. The government would also establish a board to monitor the aid package and set a 0.5 to 1.0 percent fee on loan guarantees of $1.5 billion.

Although the government had stepped in to help Chrysler, the government's aid imposed a number of strategic restrictions on the firm's operations. Chrysler had to narrow the variety and assortment of its lineup of cars, could produce only four-cylinder, front-wheel-drive cars, and had to withdraw from the heavy-duty truck industry; additionally, the firm had to use all of its funds for internal operations. With these restrictions on Chrysler's strategic flexibility, Iacocca accelerated the repayment of the firm's debt as soon as increased sales and profits made it possible.

In April 1985 Chrysler increased its holdings in Mitsubishi Motors from 15 percent to 24 percent and announced a joint venture in which it would market a Maserati sports car built in Italy. Ford and GM were also courting European manufacturers and were buying up the stock of Alfa Romeo and Lotus. One year later, Chrysler announced its intention to acquire 51 percent of Maserati while construction was started in Bloomington-Normal, Illinois, for a joint Chrysler-Mitsubishi assembly plant. In 1987 Chrysler announced that it would acquire Lamborghini in an attempt to compete with Mercedes and Porsche in the superluxury sports car market. Exhibit 2 presents a list of selected significant dates in the firm's history.

EXHIBIT 2   SIGNIFICANT EVENTS IN CHRYSLER'S HISTORY

YEAR	EVENT
1921	Company founded by Walter P. Chrysler
1924	Chrysler car introduced
1928	Firm acquires Dodge Brothers; introduces Plymouth and DeSoto automobiles
1934	Airflow designs introduced
1936	Chrysler Motors outsells Ford Motors for first time
1946	Chrysler market share climbs to 25.7 percent
1948	Independents obtain 18.6 percent of the American automobile market
1949	Ford outsells Chrysler Motors
1954	Ford obtains its peak market share of 30.8 percent
1959	Imported cars obtain 10.1 percent of the American market
1962	General Motors reaches its highest market share of 51.8 percent; Chrysler's market share falls to 9.6 percent
1964	Ford Mustang introduced; imported cars take 6.1 percent of the market
1966	U.S. government institutes strict automobile safety regulations, mandatory recall announcements, and emissions regulations
1967	Air Quality Act passed by Congress
1973	Imported cars take 15.1 percent of the market; OPEC cartel created
1974	Chrysler loses $52 million
1975	Lynn Townsend replaced by John Riccardo; firm loses $260 million
1976	$7.5 billion downsizing plan initiated; Chrysler loses $206 million; independents obtain 2.6 percent of American sales; 12.6 million American cars recalled
1978	Lee Iaccoca hired; Chrysler loses money for next three years
1979	Chrysler obtains a $1.5 billion loan guarantee package; firm loses $1.1 billion; Japanese cars take 22.6 percent of the American market
1980	250,000 American automobile workers on layoff; GM loses $763 million, Ford loses $1.5 billion, and Chrysler loses $1.7 billion; GM budgets $40–$75 billion for capital investment until 1985
1983	Honda opens a plant in Ohio; Nissan opens a truck manufacturing plant in Tennessee—cars to be produced there in 1985; Chrysler repays all guaranteed loans
1986	Acquires Gulfstream Aerospace Corporation with sales of $634.7 million
1987	Commits $12.5 billion to a five-year product and capital spending program in core automobile business

AMERICAN MOTORS' HISTORY

Chrysler's acquisition of AMC marks the demise of a firm whose origins date back to 1902 and the production of the one-cylinder Rambler by the Thomas B. Jeffery Company at Kenosha, Wisconsin. As the American automobile industry began to mature in the early 1950s, the remaining independents that had been able to survive the Great Depression sought to merge with one another as a way to salvage or forestall their dwindling fortunes. Packard merged with Studebaker in 1954, but that combination failed by 1963, although the Packard itself was not discontinued until 1968; Willys merged with Kaiser-Frazer in 1952, but they folded in 1955. American Motors was created in 1954 through the merger of the Nash-Kelvinator Corporation and the Hudson Motor Company. AMC was an innovator from its inception. By design or default it did not wish to follow the "Big Three." Bill Chapin, grandson of Roy Chapin, the founder of Hudson Motors, and son of Roy Chapin, Jr., AMC chairman from 1967 to 1978, described AMC's philosophy accordingly:

> AMC made a very valiant attempt to separate themselves from General Motors and Ford and Chrysler and give themselves an identity that people would recognize in the marketplace.[4]

In the late 1950s, in a last-ditch effort to save the company, AMC dropped its large Nash and Hudson cars and focused its attention on the Rambler, which had been resurrected as a nameplate in 1950 as a 100-inch-wheelbased economy car selling for $1,808. George Romney, a past AMC chairman and the major force behind the company's switch to compact cars, recalls how the Rambler forced the other American automakers to build compacts of their own.

> It was successful. That was before any foreign cars penetrated the market. I talked about competitors' cars as being gas-guzzling dinosaurs and we ran very newsworthy advertisements selling the cars.[4]

After Romney left AMC in 1962 to pursue a political career, the firm began to abandon its small-car strategy when it introduced a series of large cars and a sports car called the Javelin. In 1970, trying to escape the perception that it built boring cars for older, equally boring motorists, AMC dropped the Rambler and replaced it with an unsuccessful line of small cars featuring cute names and unique shapes—the Pacer (fishbowl), the Gremlin (triangular), and the Hornet (square).

The idea of differentiating themselves from the Big Three may have been sound, but problems accompanied the execution of the stand-alone strategy. AMC had planned to put GM's rotary engine in the Pacer but GM dropped the engine and AMC had to use one of its older six-cylinder engines instead. Accordingly, the Pacer lost the fuel efficiency it was designed to deliver, and it also had to undergo front-end design changes to accommodate its replacement engine. Additionally, the fishbowl-shaped, large-windowed Pacer was an interesting design concept but many people thought it was ugly as well as difficult to air condition. The triangular-shaped Gremlin also had its problems. Although the name "Gremlin" was supposed to conjure images of fun and impish delight, gremlin was also a mechanic's term for describing a troublesome engine. The era was not all bad luck for AMC, however, as it acquired the Kaiser Jeep Corporation in 1970, and the Jeep proved to be the company's only real moneymaker.

In 1979 Regie Nationale des Usines Renault (Renault) began to acquire a stake in AMC as a method for securing a stronger foothold in the huge Ameri-

EXHIBIT 3   SIGNIFICANT EVENTS IN AMERICAN MOTORS' HISTORY

YEAR	EVENT
1954	American Motors created from merger of the Hudson Motor Company and Nash-Kelvinator; Nash sells 62,911 cars while Hudson sells 50,660 units
1955	AMC sells 194,175 cars of which 83,852 were Ramblers and 45,535 were Hudsons
1957	Nash and Hudson cars taken out of production; Rambler only car made by AMC
1958	186,227 Ramblers sold, ranked seventh in American automobile sales
1959	Record profits of $60.3 million on 401,446 units
1962	George Romney leaves AMC
1967	Roy Chapin, Jr. becomes chairman of the board
1970	Rambler taken out of production; Pacer, Gremlin, and Hornet introduced; acquires Kaiser Jeep Corporation
1978	W. Paul Trippett becomes chairman of the board
1979	Renault of France acquires 22.5 percent of the AMC stock for $150 million
1980	Renault invests $310 million more in AMC stocks—has five of 16 seats on the board of directors
1983	AMC sells 226,580 cars
1984	Records first profit after 14 consecutive quarters of losses; Jose J. Dedeurwaerder named AMC president—Renault officials occupy the three most important positions in AMC
1986	AMC sells 77,005 cars; Jeep sales are 207,514, up to 14.4 percent over 1985 sales; Joseph E. Cappy becomes president and CEO; Renault chairman Georges Besse assasinated by a French terrorist group
1987	New Renault chairman, Raymond Levy, says profitability to be the holding company's main goal; Chrysler buys out AMC

can automobile market. Renault would ultimately buy up 46.1 percent of AMC's common stock, although the venture accumulated losses of $839 million from 1979 to 1986. Although many people said Renault was wise to unload the perennially money-losing AMC, others believed that Renault/AMC was about to have its best year in 1987/1988 with the introduction in 1987 of three new models—the Alpine sports car and the Medallion compact both made in France, and the Premier, a family-sized car built in AMC's ultramodern Bramalea, Ontario facility. Exhibit 3 traces AMC's history since its creation in 1954.

THE AMC ACQUISITION

TERMS

Chrysler's acquisition plan calls for the purchase of 50.5 million shares of AMC common stock for the equivalent of $4.50 a share, or approximately

$226 million, with a new issue of ten-year, 8 percent Chrysler bonds. Other holders of AMC common (59.3 million shares) and convertible preferred (71.3 million shares) stock would receive Chrysler common stock, with a market value of about $4, for each share of AMC stock. The price was to be based on the value of Chrysler stock shortly before the transaction was closed. Chrysler, however, said it would give AMC stockholders at least 0.0687 shares of Chrysler stock for each share of AMC stock. This could have the effect of pushing the value of the proposal above $4.50 per share of AMC stock provided Chrysler stock rose above $65.50 a share. (See Exhibit 4.) The cost of these AMC

EXHIBIT 4 END-OF-WEEK PRICES OF CHRYSLER AND AMERICAN MOTORS STOCK, DECEMBER 1986-AUGUST 1987

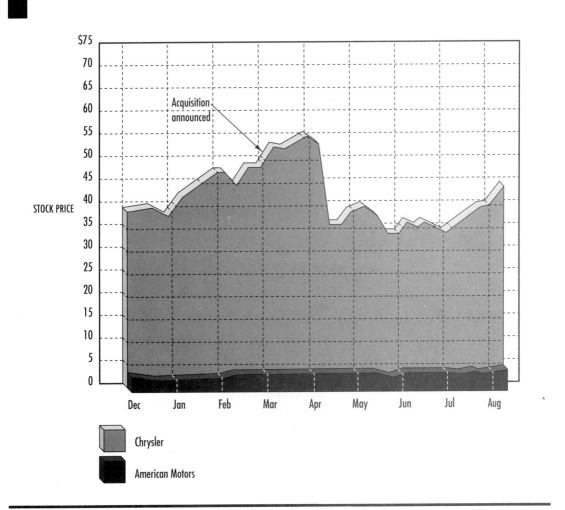

shares would total approximately $590 million, with an additional $35 million in cash going to Renault for its interest in AMC's finance subsidiary.

With the acquisition of American Motors, Chrysler must assume AMC's unfunded pension liabilities (somewhere in the area of $330 to $400 million) as well as its $767 million long-term debt. With about $25 million in transaction costs minus AMC's $120 million cash on hand, Chrysler will pay a minimum of about $2 billion for AMC. Additionally, Chrysler will agree to a profit-sharing arrangement with Renault, the percentage to be tied to AMC's performance. If AMC's operations show a profit Renault could ultimately receive an additional $350 million, which would result in a purchase price of more than $2.3 billion. However, in the words of Robert Miller, Jr. who con-

EXHIBIT 5 CHRYSLER ASSEMBLY, SUBASSEMBLY, AND DISTRIBUTION FACILITIES

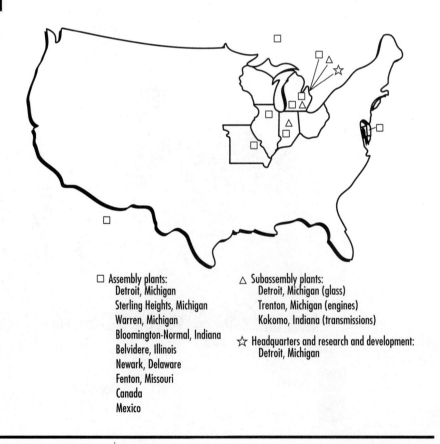

☐ Assembly plants:
   Detroit, Michigan
   Sterling Heights, Michigan
   Warren, Michigan
   Bloomington-Normal, Indiana
   Belvidere, Illinois
   Newark, Delaware
   Fenton, Missouri
   Canada
   Mexico

△ Subassembly plants:
   Detroit, Michigan (glass)
   Trenton, Michigan (engines)
   Kokomo, Indiana (transmissions)

☆ Headquarters and research and development:
   Detroit, Michigan

ducted the final negotiations for Chrysler, "The day we have to write a check for $350 million is the day we'll be laughing . . . all the way to the bank."

CAPACITY

Chrysler currently has nine assembly plants with a total capacity of 1.8 to 2.1 million vehicles per year. Because they have been running at about 100 percent of capacity, Chrysler has been using AMC's Kenosha plant to assemble its Chrysler Fifth Avenue, Dodge Diplomat, and Plymouth Gran Fury, all full-sized passenger cars. Even with this subcontracted production, AMC was operating at only about 49.0 percent of its own full-time capacity. With the acquisition of AMC Chrysler obtains 15 manufacturing facilities, four of which are assembly plants, which add the capability of producing 796,000 vehicles to Chrysler's overtaxed production capability. One of the acquired assembly plants is AMC's state-of-the-art $675 million facility in Bramalea—the most efficient automobile plant in North America. AMC's plants in Kenosha, Wis-

EXHIBIT 6 AMERICAN MOTORS ASSEMBLY, SUBASSEMBLY, AND DISTRIBUTION FACILITIES

☐ Assembly plants:
   Kenosha, Wisconsin
   Toledo, Ohio
   Brampton, Ontario, Canada
   Bramalea, Ontario, Canada

☆ Administrative offices and research and development:
   Southfield, Michigan
   Detroit, Michigan
   Burlington, Wisconsin

consin, Brampton, Ontario, and Toledo, Ohio, are considered antiquated, and some analysts believe that at least parts of them will ultimately have to be shut down. Exhibits 5 and 6 present the locations of both Chrysler's and AMC's major North American facilities.

Along with AMC's physical facilities, Chrysler inherits its work force, which has been rather demoralized by the firm's dwindling profits and the continuous pressure of imminent layoffs and an unfunded retirement plan. United Auto Workers (UAW) locals at the Kenosha and Toledo plants used the threat of strikes as a lever to obtain the most lucrative contracts in the industry, including more paid vacations and a larger number of union officials on the AMC payroll. While workers at Chrysler and AMC receive approximately the same hourly wage rate, AMC's labor costs are higher because of differences in local union agreements and a relatively inefficient plant in Kenosha. In the two months preceding the acquisition, union members repeatedly resisted AMC's demands to slash wages and to make other work-rules concessions,

EXHIBIT 7   AMERICAN MOTORS' 1987 PRODUCT LINE

AMC EAGLE
  4-door, $11,485
  4-door wagon, $12,301
  Limited, $13,033

RENAULT
  Alliance
  2-door, $6,399–$7,625
  2-door hatchback, $6,399–8,499
  2-door convertible, $11,099–$12,099
  4-door, $6,599–7,900
  4-door hatchback, $7,250–$7,950

GTA
  2-door, $8,999
  2-door convertible, $12,899

ENCORE
  base price, $6,710

MEDALLION
  4-door DL, $9,965
  4-door LX, $10,479
  4-door wagon, $10,693

PREMIER
  $14,000 (approx.)

ALPINE
  $30,000 (approx.)

JEEP
  Comanche
  4 wheel drive, short bed, $9,877
  4 wheel drive, long bed, $10,244
  2 wheel drive, short bed, $6,995
  2 wheel drive, long bed, $7,787

WRANGLER
  Sahara, $11,995
  Laredo, $13,395
  Base price, $10,595

CHEROKEE
  2 wheel drive, 2-door $10,441
  2 wheel drive, 4-door $11,675
  4 wheel drive, 2-door $12,415
  4 wheel drive, 4-door $13,270

WAGONEER
  Grand Wagoneer, $24,623
  Limited, $21,926

even though the firm said refusal would mean plant closings. When AMC received concessions in 1985, Toledo workers sabotaged Jeeps on the assembly line.

Most of AMC's 19,500 workers were delighted by the news of the buyout and felt that management was the cause of their problems. Cliff Shively, a worker at the Jeep plant, expects great things to come from the merger. "Whatever Iacocca touches turns to gold." The UAW's officialdom, which has had a long, stormy relationship with AMC in the past, is basically positive about the deal. As UAW president Owen Bieber stated, the acquisition "creates a good match that potentially points the way to a more secure future for workers at both companies."[6]

EXHIBIT 8   CHRYSLER'S 1987 PRODUCT LINE

CHRYSLER
   Lebaron, GTS
      Highline, $10,577
      Premium, $12,192
   Lebaron Formal
      Sedan, $11,121
      Wagon, $12,669
   Lebaron Coupe
      Highline, $11,720
      Premium, $12,713
   Lebaron Convertible
      Base, $13,974
   New Yorker
      4-door only, $14,876
   5th Avenue
      4-door only, $16,446

SPECIAL INTEREST VEHICLE
   Voyager Passenger Wagon
      Standard Series, $10,876
      Grand series, $12,216

PLYMOUTH
   Horizon America
      5-door, $6,107
   Sundance
      Subcompact 2- or 4-door, $7,999
   Reliant
      2-door, $8,778–$9,222
      4-door, $8,778–$9,222
      4-door wagon, $8,778–$9,222

   Caravell
      4 door sedan, $10,238–10,952
   Gran Fury
      4-door, $11,780

DODGE
   Shadow, $7,875
   Daytona, $10,025
   Diplomat, $11,407
   Lancer, $10,482
   Ram Wagon, $12,469
   Mini Ram Van (FWD), $9,717
   Ram Van (RWD), $10,047
   Ram 50 Pickup, $6,845
   Colt, $5,899
   Charger, N/A
   Omni, $6,200*
   Aries, $6,995
   Dodge 6000, $10,659
   Caravan, $10,887
   Dakota, $8,244
   Ram Pickup, $8,793
   Ram Charger, $11,549
   Vista, $11,122

*Estimated

PRODUCT LINES

Chrysler acquires AMC's current product line, which, as Exhibit 7 shows, includes AMC's Eagle, the Renault Alliance/Encore subcompact line, the newly introduced Renault Medallion, and the Jeep line, consisting of the Comanche, Wrangler, Cherokee, and Wagoneer. Additionally, Chrysler will market the Renault Alpine, a $30,000 sports car, and the Premier, both due for introduction in the fall of 1987. Chrysler's own product line is shown in Exhibit 8. Exhibit 9 provides excerpts from test reports on three of AMC's products as published by *Consumer Reports.*

Sales of the Alliance have been falling since its introduction in 1982 and

EXHIBIT 9   SELECTED TEST REPORTS ON AMC PRODUCTS

AMC EAGLE
Car features full-time four-wheel drive. Its old body design lacks interior room, especially in the cargo area of the wagon.[1]

RENAULT ALLIANCE/ENCORE
The optional 1.7-liter 4 started easily and ran well. The 5-speed manual transmission shifted smoothly into the first four gears but awkwardly into fifth and reverse. The automatic transmission shifted smoothly. Weak acceleration with automatic and 1.4-liter 4. This front-wheel-drive car handled very well in normal driving, somewhat imprecisely at the track. Excellent braking. The front seats were very comfortable except for tall people, who needed more leg room. Most drivers wanted to sit higher; the steering wheel was too high and too horizontal. The *Alliance's* rear seat was uncomfortable for two or three; the *Encore's* rear seat was tighter and very uncomfortable for two or three. Fairly comfortable ride. Moderate noise level. Effective air-conditioning and ample ventilation, but slow, hard-to-modulate heating. Poorly designed horn control, not on steering wheel. Clear displays. Predicted reliability—much worse than average.[2]

RENAULT/EAGLE MEDALLION
The *Eagle Medallion* offers comfort, conveniences, and performance far more impressive than those of Renault products we've tested in the past. However, every Renault model sold in this country has turned out to be relatively trouble-prone. People who have owned *Renaults* probably wouldn't leap at the chance to buy another—even under another name. Although Chrysler, in its agreement with AMC, has pledged to sell and service the car for five years, buyers considering the *Eagle Medallion* must come to grips with the possibility that the car could have a short future in this country.

BEST CHOICES
The best choices in the compact class remain the *Toyota Camry,* the *Mitsubishi Galant,* the *Mazda 626,* and the *Nissan Stanza.* Domestic models that have scored quite well in our tests include GM's *Buick Skylark, Oldsmobile Calais,* and *Pontiac Grand AM.*[3]

---

[1]"Summary Judgments of the 1987 Cars," (*Consumer Reports* 52, no. 4 (April 1987): 218.

[2]"Buying a Used Car," *1987 Buying Guide Issue* 51, no. 12 (1987): 62–63.

[3]"Road Tests: Eagle Medallion, Chevrolet Corsica," *Consumer Reports* 52, no. 11 (November 1987): 708–711.

the Encore's sales performance has also been disappointing (see Exhibit 10); Chrysler officials have stated that these models will be discontinued. The Medallion, priced at about $11,000, and the $14,000 Premier, both modern front-wheel-drive mid-size cars similar to models in the Chrysler fleet, are designed to compete against Ford's Taurus and Mercury Sable, Honda's Accord, and Toyota's Camry; *Consumer Reports'* evaluations of these four cars are excerpted in Exhibit 11. In the short time since the introduction of the Medallion, dealers have been satisfied with its sales, and they hope the Premier's sales will be an improvement over those of the Alliance. Chrysler itself is also concerned about sales of the Premier, as the terms of the acquisition call for a commitment by Chrysler to sell 300,000 Premiers between 1988 and 1992 or pay a penalty to Renault.

The Jeep line, which Iacocca calls "the best-known automotive brand name in the world," sold a record 207,514 units in 1986, capturing 4.5 percent of the American truck market. This accounts for over one-fourth of the U.S. sport-utility segment of the truck market, which includes the Ford Bronco, Chevrolet Blazer, and such Japanese imports as those made by Suzuki and Toyota. Although Chrysler has been highly successful with its innovative minivans, the company is not represented in the sport-utility segment of the truck market. Robust growth is forecast for this segment, with sales expected to increase from 732,000 in 1986 to 1.15 million in 1991. Exhibit 12 shows the market shares obtained by the major manufacturers that participated in the utility and recreational vehicle market in the United States from 1984 to 1986.

EXHIBIT 10   UNIT SALES OF AMC PRODUCT LINE

MAKE/MODEL	1985	1984	1983
AMC Eagle	12,776	20,654	31,207
Renault:			
Alliance	71,494	100,366	126,008
Encore	39,179	69,235	20,182
Jeep*	234,973	188,272	111,950

WORLD WHOLESALE UNIT SALES

	1986	1985	1984	1983
Automobiles	66,372	151,481	248,955	270,019
Jeep vehicles	221,362	240,769	193,428	113,443
Totals	287,734	391,769	442,383	383,462

*Production figures rather than unit sales

Source: 10K Reports

EXHIBIT 11   SELECTED TEST REPORTS ON MEDALLION AND PREMIER COMPETITION

FORD TAURUS/MERCURY SABLE

Both the 3-liter V6 and the 2.5-liter 4 started and ran well. With the V6, the overdrive automatic transmission usually shifted very smoothly. With the 4, the automatic transmission shifted smoothly, but acceleration was not more than adequate. This front-wheel-drive model handled very well; the wagon version was especially competent. Fairly long stopping distances and considerable brake fade, but stops were straight. Exceptionally comfortable front seats. Excellent driving position with power seat; but without the power adjustment, the seat was too low and the steering wheel too high. Rear seat fairly comfortable for two or three. Quiet inside. Stable, tightly controlled ride on all but the bumpiest roads. Excellent climate-control system. Excellent controls and displays. Predicted reliability—Worse than average, but not specific trouble spots have shown up in the first partial year.

HONDA ACCORD

The 2-liter 4 sometimes stalled once after a cold start and occasionally hesitated while warming up. The 4-speed automatic transmission usually shifted smoothly. This front-wheel-drive car handled very well. Very good brakes. Very comfortable front seats; low, sporty-car driving position. Rear seat uncomfortable for two or three. Moderate noise level. Firm ride with good control. Excellent climate-control system. Excellent controls and displays. Predicted reliability—much better than average.

TOYOTA CAMRY

The 2-liter 4 started and ran very well. The automatic overdrive transmission shifted smoothly; it provides a choice of Power or Normal range. This front-wheel-drive model handled steadily and accurately. Excellent brakes. Exceptionally comfortable front seats. Excellent driving position, with plenty of adjustment. Rear seat very comfortable for two, comfortable for three. Moderate noise level. Smooth, soft ride. Excellent climate-control system. Excellent controls and displays. Predicted reliability—no data; new model. Previous *Camry* models have been much better than average.

Source: "Summary Judgments of the 1987 Cars." *Consumer Reports* 52, no. 4 (April 1987): 225, 220, 222.

Chrysler could have developed a new vehicle of its own comparable to the Jeep, but the investment would have ranged from $1.1 to $2.0 billion and would have taken several years' time.

Although a number of its subassemblies have been manufactured by General Motors in the past, Jeep has problems with long-term consequences. Exhibit 13 provides relevant information. Over $1.7 billion in product-liability suits have been filed against AMC for turnover accidents in Jeeps. The injured persons claim that, among other problems, the vehicle's roll bar offers inadequate protection. Under the acquisition agreement, Chrysler assumes liability for any damages assessed up to an undisclosed ceiling, and Renault will help make any payments above that undisclosed amount.

EXHIBIT 12 UTILITY AND RECREATIONAL VEHICLE MARKET SHARES

	1986	1985	1984
General Motors	31.2%	35.9%	36.1%
Ford	27.6	29.3	29.9
American Motors	12.9	12.9	13.5
Toyota	11.6	9.8	8.7
Chrysler	4.8	4.3	5.3
Nissan	4.1	4.9	4.6
Suzuki	3.5	—	—
Isuzu	3.2	2.4	1.1
All others	1.1	0.5	0.8
All manufacturers	100%	100%	100%

SHARE OF U.S. LIGHT TRUCK MARKET, 1986

Chrysler	12.8%
American Motors	4.5%
(Includes utility vehicles)	

EXHIBIT 13 SELECTED TEST REPORTS ON JEEP AND SIMILAR VEHICLES

The Yugo GV, the Hyundai Excel, and the American Motors Corporation's Jeep Comanche received the lowest scores in the latest round of government frontal crash tests at 35 miles per hour, suggesting an increased likelihood of head injuries to occupants of those automobiles....

The government permits a vehicle a maximum score of 1,000 in the head-injury category for a 30-mph crash, but it does not set a requirement for 35-mph crashes. It is generally agreed a score exceeding 1,000 indicates a higher risk of head injury, with the potential for injury rising as the score increases.

In the safety agency's latest crash tests, which involved eight vehicles, the Jeep Comanche pickup scored 2,700 in the head-injury category on the passenger side of the vehicle. This is the highest head-injury score posted for either the driver or passenger side by any of eleven vehicles tested so far this year. The Comanche's driver-side score was 1,052....

The Comanche also scored above the level thought to indicate an increased risk of chest injury to the driver. The Hyundai and Yugo had better scores on the chest-injury test.

Source: Wall Street Journal, June 12, 1987, p. 40.

EXHIBIT 14   DOMESTIC DEALERSHIPS BY MANUFACTURER

	1986	1978	1977	1976
General Motors	11,570*	11,565	11,610	11,670
Ford	6,745*	6,723	6,722	6,712
Chrysler	4,026	4,786	4,822	4,811
American Motors	1,472	1,661	1,612	1,690

DOMESTIC DEALERSHIPS

	1987	1986	1985	1984	1983
Chrysler	4,038*	4,026	4,007	3,994	3,872
American Motors	1,500*	1,472	1,562	1,624	1,709

*Estimated

Source: 10K and stockholders' reports.

DISTRIBUTION

Chrysler's network of 4,026 dealers would expand by about one-fourth with the addition of 1,472 AMC dealerships. Exhibit 14 itemizes the number of franchised dealers existing in the United States by manufacturer. Chrysler executives say they will operate the AMC dealer network as a third distribution system, separate from Dodge and Chrysler-Plymouth, at least temporarily, while working to eventually integrate their product development teams. Given AMC's past sales records, however, the strength of its dealerships is questionable. Christopher Cedergren, of J. D. Powers & Associates, a company that studies consumers' perceptions of the quality and image of cars sold in the American market, addresses Chrysler's challenge in attempting to improve AMC's dealerships:

> What [Chrysler's] got to do is to weed out the weaker dealers and bring in the stronger ones. Attracting good dealers shouldn't be all that hard now, however, I'd say that the value of a Jeep/Renault dealership is considerably higher now than it was [before the acquisition].

Chrysler and AMC dealers have differing views on the benefits of the merger. James Kelel, part owner of a Renault/Jeep dealership in Detroit says, "I see more products coming down the road in the future for us. We haven't had many products to sell for a long time."[7] Ian Steedman, a sales representative with a Tulsa Jeep/Renault dealership, concurs. "Iacocca's riding high right now—I don't see how we can lose. We'll have more stability with Chrysler backing us financially. Plus, the Fifth Avenues will be shipped for us to sell here and we need a car like that in this market." On the other hand, Joel Beja, sales manager at a Dodge dealership in Hempstead, Long Island, saw things differently: "Right now, I have ten Chrysler, Dodge, and Plymouth dealers within 15 minutes' drive from me. I'm not thrilled about AMC dealers selling Chrysler cars. We're already saturated here."[8]

ENDNOTES

1. "Chrysler Buyout of AMC Pleases Analysts," *Tulsa Tribune* (March 10, 1987): B1

2. Schlesinger, Jacob M., and Amal Kumar Naj, "Chrysler to Buy Renault's Stake in AMC; Seeks Rest of Company," *Wall Street Journal* (March 10, 1987): 3.

3. *Automotive News* (April 30, 1980): 15.

4. "Decline of AMC Started in 1960s," *Tulsa Tribune* (March 10, 1987): B2.

5. Ibid.

6. Schlesinger and Naj, "Chrysler to Buy Renault's Stake in AMC," p. 24.

7. Ibid.

8. Ibid.

ADDITIONAL REFERENCES

"AMC Turning Over Retail Financing Line to Chrysler Corp." *Wall Street Journal* (June 16, 1987): 48.

"Buying a Used Car." 1987 *Buying Guide, Consumer Reports* 51, no. 12 (1987): 56–89.

Jeffreys, Steve. *Management and Managed: Fifty Years of Crisis at Chrysler.* New York: Cambridge University Press, 1986.

MVMA Motor Vehicle Facts and Figures. Detroit: Motor Vehicle Manufacturers Association, 1987.

1986–87 Industry Norms and Key Business Ratios. New York: Dun & Bradstreet, 1987.

1987 Almanac of Business and Industry Financial Ratios. Englewood Cliffs, N.J.: Prentice-Hall, 1987.

"Road Tests: Eagle Medallion, Chevrolet Corsica." *Consumer Reports* 52, no. 11 (November 1987): 708–711.

Schlesinger, Jacob M. "AMC Accepts Sweetened Bid from Chrysler." *Wall Street Journal* (May 21, 1987): 8.

Standard NYSE Stock Reports, June 5, 1987. New York: Standard & Poor, 1987.

Standard NYSE Stock Reports, July 21, 1987. New York: Standard & Poor, 1987.

"Summary Judgments of the 1987 Cars." *Consumer Reports* 52, no. 4 (April 1987): 210–229.

Ward's Automotive Yearbook. Detroit: Ward's Communications Inc., 1984.

"Yugo, Hyundai and Jeep Model Vehicles Fare Poorly in Safety Agency Crash Test." *Wall Street Journal* (June 12, 1987): 40.

Zammuto, Raymond F. *Assessing Organizational Effectiveness.* Albany: State University of New York Press, 1982.

SELECTED FINANCIAL RESULTS FOR CHRYSLER MOTORS (THOUSANDS OF DOLLARS)

	FISCAL YEAR ENDING		
	12/31/86	12/31/85	12/31/84
ASSETS			
Cash	$ 285,100	$ 147,600	$ 75,200
Marketable securities	$ 2,394,300	2,649,900	1,624,900
Receivables	372,500	207,500	332,200
Inventories	1,699,600	1,862,700	1,625,900
Other current assets	612,500	445,800	321,700
Total current assets	$ 5,364,000	$ 5,313,500	$3,979,900
Property, plant and equipment	$ 8,885,300	$ 7,304,400	$6,247,700
Accumulated depreciation	(2,767,500)	(2,664,800)	(2,534,500)
Net plant and equipment	$ 6,117,800	$ 4,639,600	$3,713,200
Investments and advances to subsidiaries	$ 2,307,300	$ 2,070,400	$1,240,900
Other noncurrent assets	674,100	-0-	-0-
Deposits and other assets	-0-	581,800	128,700
Total assets	$14,463,200	$12,605,300	$9,062,700
LIABILITIES			
Notes payable	$ 119,800	$ 195,300	$ 6,700
Accounts payable	2,958,300	2,504,500	2,323,000
Curent long-term debt	82,200	101,600	42,800
Accrued expenses	1,960,700	1,927,800	1,698,900
Income taxes	-0-	-0-	13,600
Other current liabilities	-0-	-0-	30,700
Total current liabilities	$ 5,121,000	$ 4,729,200	$4,115,700
Deferred charges	$ 712,400	$ 690,200	$ 21,700
Long-term debt	2,334,100	2,366,100	760,100
Other long-term liabilities	950,900	604,500	859,300
Total liabilities	$ 9,118,400	$ 8,390,000	$5,756,800
Net common stock	$ 229,800	$ 153,200	$ 123,900
Capital surplus	1,866,600	1,943,200	2,325,300
Retained earnings	3,567,500	2,153,300	921,200
Treasury stock	319,100	34,400	64,500
Shareholder equity	$ 5,344,800	$ 4,215,300	$3,305,900
Total liabilities and net worth	$14,463,200	$12,605,300	$9,062,700

Source: 10K reports.

CHRYSLER INCOME STATEMENT

	FISCAL YEAR ENDING		
	12/31/86	12/31/85	12/31/84
Net sales	$22,586,300	$21,255,550	$19,572,700
Costs of goods sold	18,635,200	17,467,700	15,528,200
Gross profit	$ 3,951,100	$ 3,787,700	$ 4,044,500
Selling, general and administrative expenses	$ 1,613,100	$ 1,576,800	$ 1,255,000
Depreciation and amortization	543,600	263,700	554,400
Nonoperating income	563,600	422,500	195,200
Interest expense	32,700	—	—
Pretax income	$ 2,325,300	$ 2,369,800	$ 2,430,300
Provision for income taxes	921,700	734,600	934,200
Extraordinary items	—	—	883,900
Net income	$ 1,403,600	$ 1,635,200	$ 2,380,000

RATIO ANALYSIS

	FISCAL YEAR ENDING		
	12/31/86	12/31/85	12/31/84
Quick ratio	0.60%	0.64%	0.49%
Current ratio	1.05	1.12	0.97
Receivables turnover	60.63	102.44	58.92
Inventories turnover	13.29	11.41	12.04
Inventories days sales	27.09	31.55	29.91
Current debt/equity	0.02	0.02	0.01
Total debt/equity	0.45	0.59	0.24
Net income on sales	0.06	0.08	0.12
ROA	0.10	0.13	0.26
ROE	0.26	0.39	0.72

STOCK INFORAMTION, WEEK ENDING 7/16/87

Outstanding shares (thousands)	214,052
Volume	4,140,300
High	39.125
Average	38.750
Low	36.000
Market value (thousands of dollars)	$8,294,515
EPS	5.98
Price/earnings ratio	6.40

Source: 10K reports and Value Line reports.

487

A P P E N D I X   B

	FISCAL YEAR ENDING		
	12/31/86	12/31/85	12/31/84
ASSETS			
Cash	$ 145,198	$ 143,324	$ 92,641
Receivables	230,620	224,954	154,828
Inventories	369,358	413,441	468,986
Other current assets	43,491	37,843	65,020
Total current assets	$ 788,667	$ 819,562	$ 781,475
Property, plant and equipment	$1,659,092	$1,398,602	$1,272,252
Accumulated depreciation	(412,015)	(371,052)	(341,808)
Net plant and equipment	$1,247,077	$1,027,550	$ 930,444
Investments and advances to subsidiaries	$ 129,512	$ 90,007	$ 73,471
Deposits and other assets	60,086	63,825	44,770
Total assets	$2,225,342	$2,000,944	$1,830,160
LIABILITIES			
Notes, payable	$ 9,349	$ 2,000	$ -0-
Accounts payable	303,462	275,676	236,665
Current long-term debt	16,951	155,559	200,973
Accrued expenses	289,599	323,920	286,222
Income taxes	-0-	-0-	-0-
Other current liabilities	136,712	59,355	73,788
Total current liabilities	$ 756,073	$ 816,510	$ 797,648
Long-term debt	$ 105,123	$ 561,403	$ 429,092
Other long-term liabilities	985,608	400,072	252,153
Total liabilities	$1,846,804	$1,777,985	$ 681,245
Preferred stock	$ 145	$ 73,744	$ 72,508
Net common stock	1,167	183,461	183,460
Capital surplus	993,537	482,632	482,631
Retained earnings	(596,055)	(498,235)	(371,694)
Treasury stock	(20,256)	(18,643)	(15,638)
Shareholder equity	$ 378,538	$ 222,959	$ 351,267
Total liabilities and net worth	2,225,342	2,000,944	1,830,160

Source: 10K reports and Value Line reports.

AMERICAN MOTORS INCOME STATEMENT

	FISCAL YEAR ENDING		
	12/31/86	12/31/85	12/31/84
Net Sales	$3,462,504	$4,039,901	$4,215,191
Cost of goods sold	2,858,284	3,504,791	3,594,229
Gross profit	$ 604,220	$ 535,110	$ 620,962
Selling, general and administrative expenses	$ 480,047	$ 445,265	$ 425,501
Depreciation and amortization	155,108	136,879	114,034
Nonoperating income	23,968	12,712	28,064
Interest expense	84,352	90,941	94,022
Pretax income	$ (91,319)	$ (125,263)	$ 15,469
Provision for income taxes	-0-	-0-	-0-
Extraordinary items	-0-	-0-	4,500
Net income	$ (91,319)	$ (125,263)	$ 19,969

RATIO ANALYSIS

	FISCAL YEAR ENDING		
	12/31/86	12/31/85	12/31/84
Quick ratio	0.50%	0.45%	0.31%
Current ratio	1.04	1.00	0.98
Receivables turnover	15.01	17.96	27.22
Inventories turnover	9.37	9.77	8.99
Inventories days sales	38.40	36.84	40.05
Current debt/equity	0.04	0.70	0.57
Total debt/equity	0.32	3.22	2.19
Net income on sales	(0.03)	(0.03)	0.00
ROA	(0.04)	(0.06)	0.01
ROE	(0.24)	(0.84)	0.06

STOCK INFORMATION, WEEK ENDING 7/16/87

Outstanding shares (thousands)	139,122
Volume	2,844,000
High	4.750
Average	4.250
Low	4.125
Market value (thousands of dollars)	$591,268
EPS	−0.67
Price/earnings ratio	−6.30

Source: 10K reports and Value Line reports.

A P P E N D I X   C

1986 RATIO ANALYSIS OF FORD AND GENERAL MOTORS

	FORD	GM
Quick ratio	0.77%	0.67%
Current ratio	1.18	1.17
Receivables turnover	17.98	9.10
Inventories turnover	10.83	11.65
Inventories days sales	33.25	30.90
Current debt/equity	0.09	-0-
Total debt/equity	0.23	0.13
Net income on sales	0.05	0.03
ROA	0.09	0.04
ROE	0.22	0.10

STOCK INFORMATION FOR FORD AND GENERAL MOTORS, WEEK ENDING: 7/16/87

	FORD	GM
Outstanding shares (thousands)	268,400	317,810
Volume	5,073,700	4,072,900
High	107.250	85.375
Average	107.000	83.250
Low	101.000	80.500
Market value (thousands of dollars)	$28,718,800	$26,457,682
EPS	15.350	7.310
Price/earnings ratio	6.900	11.300

Source: 10K reports.

A P P E N D I X   D

 CONSOLIDATED POST-ACQUISITION PRO FORMA RESULTS, 1986 (IN THOUSANDS OF DOLLARS)

ASSETS	
Cash	$ 395,298
Marketable securities	2,394,300
Receivables	603,120
Inventories	2,068,958
Other current assets	655,991
Total current assets	$ 6,117,667
Property, plant and equipment	$10,544,392
Accumulated depreciation	(3,179,515)
Net plant and equipment	$ 7,364,877
Investments and advances to subsidiaries	$ 2,436,812
Other noncurrent assets	674,100
Deposits and other assets	60,086
Total assets	$16,653,542
LIABILITIES	
Notes payable	$ 129,149
Accounts payable	3,261,762
Current long-term debt	99,151
Accrued expenses	2,250,299
Income taxes	—
Other curerent liabilities	136,712
Total current liabilities	$ 5,877,073
Deferred charges	$ 712,400
Long-term debt	2,639,223
Other long-term liabilities	1,936,508
Total liabilities	$11,165,204
Net common stock	$ 230,419
Capital surplus	1,798,175
Retained earnings	3,151,380
Treasury stock	308,364
Shareholder equity	$5,723,338
Total liabilities and net worth	$16,653,542

(continued)

(continued)

ESTIMATED POST-ACQUISITION INCOME STATEMENT

Net sales	$26,048,804
Cost of goods sold	21,493,484
Gross profit	$ 4,555,320
Selling, general and administrative expenses	$ 2,093,147
Depreciation and amortization	698,708
Nonoperating income	587,568
Interest expense	117,052
Pretax income	$ 2,233,981
Provision for income taxes	$ 921,700
Extraordinary items	$ -0-
Net income	$ 1,312,281

A P P E N D I X   E

 INDUSTRY NORMS S.I.C. 3710, MANUFACTURING: MOTOR VEHICLES AND EQUIPMENT

AGGREGATE CORPORATION AVERAGES

Number of enterprises	2,972
Total receipts (in millions)	171,175.6

SELECTED OPERATING FACTORS AS A PERCENT OF NET SALES

Cost of operations	70.6
Compensation of officers	0.2
Repairs	0.7
Bad debts	0.4
Rent on business property	1.1
Taxes (exclusive of federal tax)	2.6
Interest	5.7
Depreciation/depletion/amortization	4.9
Advertising	1.0
Other expenses	9.5
Net profit before tax	3.3

SELECTED FINANCIAL RATIOS

Current ratio	1.5%
Quick ratio	1.3
Net sales to net working capital	4.1
Coverage ratio	1.6
Total liability to net worth	2.7

SELECTED FINANCIAL FACTORS IN PERCENTAGES

Debt ratio	73.1%
Return on assets	3.1
Return on equity	5.7
Retained earnings to net income	43.7

Source: 1987 Almanac of Business and Industry Financial Ratios.

LAUREN ADER,
SUZANNE BRAGG,
TIM CUNNINGHAM,
ROB RIEMENSCHNEIDER,
TIM SCHORR,
CHARLES WILLIAMS,
SEXTON ADAMS, AND
ADELAIDE GRIFFIN

CASE 11

NCNB TEXAS NATIONAL BANK

They say that everything is big in Texas! The July 1988 acquisition of the insolvent First RepublicBank Corporation sure fits the statement. The new era in Dallas banking was the result of a $4 billion bailout by the Federal Deposit Insurance Corporation, the largest to date, along with a sweetheart deal for North Carolina National Bank (NCNB) of Charlotte, N.C. NCNB is picking up 20 percent of the failing operation for a mere $210 million.

NCNB is one of the healthiest banking operations in the country with $28.6 billion in assets and will now be the nation's tenth largest banking firm. Experts said that NCNB's southern way of looking at business and the people it associates with would help soften the blow to Texas pride that the deal represented. Texans such as Trammell Crow and Ross Perot, who have done business with NCNB, have given it high marks. Perot has gone as far as to personally tell NCNB chairman, Hugh McColl, that he will pitch in if NCNB cannot raise all the money.[1]

Even though the stockholders of the First Republic holding companies lost their investments, this transaction offered a new beginning in three ways. First, it should help restore the morale of the First Republic employees who have been subject to all the inconveniences of a failing bank. Second, it will help to restore the faith of depositors which was part of the problem causing a run on deposits at First Republic, and third, it will pump in new capital allowing the new bank to begin making new loans and developing new income.[2]

INDUSTRY SITUATION: BANKING IN TEXAS

The problems with the Texas banking industry in the latter part of 1988 were as much a result of a boom as a bust. At this time, the problems plaguing Texan

Source: Prepared under the direction of Professor Sexton Adams, University of North Texas, and Professor Adelaide Griffin, Texas Woman's University, as a basis for classroom discussion and not to illustrate either effective or ineffective handling of administrative situations. © Sexton Adams and Adelaide Griffin, 1990.

banks were predominantly the result of boom and then bust in the oil industry and consequently the real estate market. Bad real estate and energy loans were the major problems.[3] In the early 1980s, Texas oil was selling at $34 a barrel up from $9 in 1978.[4] Homes and offices were being built at a rapid rate. The damand for and supply of funds was high. Oil companies, petroleum service and supply companies, developers, construction companies, and certainly banks were making money. The relative ease with which this money was being made created an environment conducive to risk taking on the part of banks.

TEXAS BANKS THOUGHT BIG

Until 1987, banks in Texas were not allowed to have branches and out-of-state banks could not buy Texas banks. This encouraged Texas banks to think big rather than in terms of retail banking. A very small part of the average loan portfolio was devoted to individuals. The assets of larger banks were predominantly devoted to energy and large-scale construction loans.[5]

RISKY OIL LOANS

Although loans to oil production companies were profitable, the real high-return was being made in loans to oil field service and supply companies which supplied drilling rigs and tools. Unfortunately, these loans were also more risky.[6] A 65% plunge in oil prices through the period of the early to mid-1980s had its initial effects on the oil companies and companies in related industries and their ability to service their debt.[7] Non-performing loans, those loans on which payments were not being made but had not yet been written off as bad debt, increased drastically. By the end of 1986, Texas' nine largest banks held $6 billion in non-performing assets. This figure had increased to $7.2 billion by mid 1987.[8] Reserves to non-performing assets averaged only 36% in Texas banks. Additionally, the restructuring within oil companies affected jobs, spending, and personal and commercial real estate.[9]

REAL ESTATE LOANS

For some time after the initial decline of oil prices, real estate was still viewed as a relatively safe area in which to loan money. In fact the flight of funds from energy loans caused an increase in the activity of real estate loans. Many banks were trying to loan their way out of their oil problems.[10] The previous high demand for real estate had inflated its price. The demand for office space and the prices paid for office space were both inflated. The strength of consumer spending made commercial development for shopping areas strong. Additionally, the high employment rate and the relatively healthy salaries being paid made the market for homes strong. During the 1985 San Antonio building boom, many of the loans being made were for raw land. The value of this land was inflated, perhaps intentionally, through "flip" deals in which land is sold between developers, each time at a profit, but never actually developed.[11] This was not a unique phenomenon and is typical of what was happening in this market. A change in federal regulatory policy in 1982 allowed savings and loans into the commercial real estate business. These relative newcomers not only made bad investments, but also increased competition in this area and helped fuel the boom which was to be the downfall.[12] Although delayed somewhat, the demand for real estate followed the price of oil down. The demand for office space, shopping center lease space, and houses came down drastically from 1984 to 1988.[13]

The problems in the energy and real estate industries not only affected banks directly by loan defaults, but also indirectly when the property used as collateral or acquired by the banks by foreclosure lost much of its value. The value of collateral pledged on energy loans followed the price of oil down. At year end 1986, insolvent savings and loans in Texas also held $6.7 billion in foreclosed real estate.[14] The real estate held by S&Ls and other lending institutions had a pledged collateral value which was much greater than the current market value. For example, a 34-story office building in Houston became the property of a bank through foreclosure. This building was constructed in 1984 at a cost of $90 million. It was sold by the bank for $30 million.[15] These foreclosures were the result of empty office buildings not producing adequate lease payment cash flow to service the mortgage.[16]

In the fall of 1986, the Federal Home Loan Bank Board issued a guideline which stated that thrifts were to write down assets to their true market value. This rule was obviously aimed at the Southwest, especially Dallas. The Dallas Area Board of Examiners was increased by 250 members. In response to this action, Texas S&L commissioner Linton L. Bowman III said that there was not an S&L in Texas which could withstand classification of its assets and remain solvent.[17]

POOR BANKING PRACTICES

Some argue that bad banking was as much to blame for the trouble of some Texas banks as the recession. American State Bank in Lubbock offers some evidence in support of this statement. This institution attributes its two consecutive profitable quarters in 1987 to its conservative lending policy. American State has almost no energy loans in its portfolio and a smaller than Texas average in real estate and construction.[18] Conversely, Panhandle Bank and Trust Co. in the north Texas oil country had a loan portfolio which was 96% energy loans. This bank has subsequently been closed.[19]

All this led to growing losses, closed banks, and mergers. In 1987, the seven largest Texas banks had losses of $2.6 billion.[20] Of the $7.5 billion in real estate loans that First Republic held prior to its closing, $2.1 billion were paying no interest because of forced renegotiation of loan contracts. Much of this was to developers for raw land, one of the most volatile forms of real estate in terms of market value.[21] In early 1988, the Federal Bank of Dallas accounted for 73% of loans to banks. The average for 1987 was less than 50%.[22] Texas banks accounted for 21 of 59 bank failures through May of 1988 and 50 of 184 in 1987. It is estimated by C. J. Lawrence, a New York brokerage house, that as of May 1988, the federal government had spent about $6 billion shoring up Texas banks. During the first quarter of 1988, First Republic had the second biggest loss in American banking history.[23]

WARY INVESTORS

The conditions in the Texas banking industry also made it difficult for banks to keep the funds they had or to attract new funds by gaining depositors or issuing stock. The stock of many Texas banks was trading for a fraction of its book value. This devaluation lessened the pure equity that a bank had to offset bad debts.[24] Although it was possible for some banks to paint a picture of relative health, investors were aware of the inflated value of assets held by most Texas banks. Investors generally avoid areas in which the risk factor is unclear or deceptively understated. Not only were new investors scarce, but old depositors were making an exodus out of Texas banks. Foreign investors seem to be the most easily frightened.[25] First Republic lost $1.5 billion in deposits during the first quarter of 1988.[26] Rising interest rates and the relative scarcity of depositors were making funds more expensive for banks who were unable to pass this on to their barely solvent debtors.[27]

Texas politicians and bankers argued for forbearance, deferral of interest to governmental lenders, or exceptions to the FDIC rules for determination of insolvency, on the grounds that the economy would bounce back. They also argued that the FDIC and FSLIC could not afford to rescue all the institutions that were technically insolvent or that would be before there was a turnaround. Those opposed to forbearance argued that it would just allow lending institutions to dig a deeper hole by trying to lure depositors with higher interest rates.[28] Ned Eichler of the University of California, Berkeley, says, "Only by liquidating, not merging or selling, a substantial number of institutions can the survivors have any chance to operate" at sustained profit levels.[29]

SIGNS OF AN IMPROVING TEXAS ECONOMY

Leading economic indicators in Texas, especially employment, were showing improvement in 1988; but oil and real estate had not yet shown significant recovery.[30] Experts say that banks do not recover as soon as the economy does. The devalued assets on its books have to inflate up to a reasonable price level before significant recovery can be made.[31] However, competition for deposits was waning and thus the cost of debt for Texas banks was coming down.[32]

HISTORY

FIRST REPUBLICBANK CORPORATION

The history of NCNB Texas Bank must begin with a look at the ill-fated birth of First RepublicBank Corporation. Sources close to the facts say it is a story of misguided decisions and looking the other way. The "bankers" said that the government O.K. of the merger between RepublicBank and InterFirst in June 1987 that created First RepublicBank was the correct response to the prolonged Texas banking crisis, but it did not turn out that way.

The fact that RepublicBank wanted to merge with InterFirst is no surprise even though their being allowed to shocked most bankers. The two banks had been rivals for seventy years. They shared the feeling of "being the leader" over the years as different markets peeked and slumped.

InterFirst Bank built its business on the high-risk, high-return oil field service business being quick to loan money to wild-cat operations that could either hit it big or lose it all. When crude oil prices rose more than four-fold between 1978 and 1981, InterFirst ran over RepublicBank in the earnings game. InterFirst made $207 million in 1982, about $63 million more than Republic.[33]

RepublicBank, on the other hand, had always operated conservatively, historically favoring the production side of the energy business. They leaned toward loaning money to oilmen who could tap already proven reserves. In fact, Republic was the first bank to make loans using oil reserves as collateral. But the loss of the market lead in 1982 and the blow to the Republic ego by InterFirst led to changes in the conservative Republic way of doing business.

RIVALRY BETWEEN REPUBLIC AND INTERFIRST

In 1982, Republic announced it would overhaul its management structure by creating six lines of business (LOB) in an effort to flatten its management structure and get back on track to compete with its "rocketing" rivals. These six departments were: General Banking, Real Estate, Energy, Corporate Banking, Funds Management and Operations, and Multinational.[34]

Initially, the separate lines of businesses (LOBs) seemed to be providing the recovery for Republic that they were designed for. Each LOB had a high degree of autonomy and were looked on as "Banks within the Bank." The Real Estate LOB in particular blossomed into multiple departments and a growing portfolio. But trouble lurked among the ranks. Some long-time Republic people were fearful that "fiefdoms"' would occur and that the different departments would become so competitive that the rigid spine of the bank would be broken by competing loyalties; they were right.

The Real Estate LOB provided renewed confidence throughout the bank in 1983 and 1984. At the same time, InterFirst experienced humiliation when they were devastated by a combination of slumping oil prices and being overextended to strapped members of the oil-service industry. Suddenly, Republic was back on top and InterFirst was faced with working out millions of dollars in bad loans.[35]

The same fate eventually fell upon Republic with its large real estate portfolio. The difference is that InterFirst was honest with itself about the books. Republic was slow to change loans to non-performing status when the market fell soft. Several large development firms heavily debted to Republic had to ask for re-structuring of their loans. But the atmosphere at Republic forced loan officers to report figures that upper management wanted to hear and not the correct answers.[36] Was this the result of the extreme competition between the LOBs?

MERGER BETWEEN REPUBLIC AND INTERFIRST

By the time Republic and InterFirst merged, Republic had $22.6 billion in assets and 41 subsidiary banks. InterFirst had $18.5 billion in assets and 68 subsidiaries. Their merger created the 12th largest bank company in the U.S. Just two months after the announcement, banking misfortune lashed out at Republic. Brazil, heavily debted to Republic, declared a moratorium on interest payments. Close to $300 million in Republic loans to Brazil were classified as non-performing.

PROBLEMS AFTER THE MERGER

The merger finally took place in June of 1987. That same month, one of Republic's biggest real estate clients, Southland Financial, announced that it had $300 million in burdensome bank notes. Three months later, Vantage Company said it needed to restructure $2.1 billion in debt, a large part of which was owed to Republic.[37]

In December, just six months after the merger, First Republic announced an end-of-the-year total net loss of $657 million. The year before Republic had made $54 million; two years earlier, $140 million. Non-performing assets soared from $2.4 billion to $3.9 billion. The RepublicBank Tower was put up for sale. Real estate losses continued to soar in the early 1988 and then, the kiss of death; a run on deposits. In January and February alone First Republic lost $990 million from worried depositors withdrawing funds. Finally in March, First RepublicBank went to the FDIC for a $1 billion infusion. That was the end of the line for top management. As part of the bailout, the FDIC wanted new leaders.[38]

FIRST REPUBLIC FAILED

The infusion did not help to stop the obvious. Finally, on July 29, 1988, the once proud house of Republic (now First RepublicBank) was sold to outsiders.

ANALYSIS OF THE FAILED "SUPERBANK"— FIRST REPUBLICBANK

While creditors tried to cope with the loss of hundreds of millions of dollars, others were trying to understand what led to possibly the most expensive bank bailout in the nation's history. With the help of extensive government documentation and interviews with regulatory officials and other sources, some of the story began to come out and show its ugly side.

OTHER OFFERS WERE REJECTED

First of all, federal banking regulators rejected an acquisition offer for one of the two banks merged to form First RepublicBank that would have saved the government substantial expense. Security Pacific National Bank of California offered to *pay* the government $50 million as an "insurance premium" on the health of the new bank. They also offered to pay the first $1 billion in loan losses over five years.[39]

FULL REVIEW WAS NOT CONDUCTED PRIOR TO MERGER

Industry analysts point out that the Office of the Comptroller of the Currency failed to conduct a full review of the troubled banks' records. The merger of InterFirst and RepublicBank was recommended by senior officials even though the banks' books were a year old when reviewed. The Office of the Comptroller of the Currency relied instead on information provided by bank executives.[40]

The next fiasco occurred when the bank examiners that were assigned to evaluate the merger proposal were told even before the examination that the deal would be approved. A banking source said,

> There was no doubt that the decision had been made to approve it. [The Examiners] did not see how the deal was going to work, but others in the organization did.[41]

POLITICAL INVOLVEMENT

It would appear that the political arena was buzzing over this deal. Some of the most politically influential people in Dallas advocated a "Texas solution" and opposed InterFirst or RepublicBank being purchased by an outside bank. Vice President George Bush and Texas Senator Lloyd Bentsen were briefed by bank officials on the status of the merger application along with Treasury Secretary James Baker. All three say, through spokesmen, that they made no attempt to influence the decision on the merger even though all three had close ties to senior officials at both InterFirst and RepublicBank.[42]

Out of all this, the real question revolves around regulators' decision to approve the merger of two failing banks, rivals, into one gigantic bank. That decision, according to expert sources, ultimately led to a bigger disaster. In fact, at least one source believes it accelerated the event.[43]

Senior officials in the Comptroller's Office of the Federal Reserve concede that their staff expressed "a great deal of reservation" about the merger.[44] Comptroller Robert Clarke admits to knowing that both institutions were in trouble. He passed the buck by stating that the senior officials concurred that there was a "reasonable chance" that the merger would work.[45]

NORTH CAROLINA NATIONAL BANK

North Carolina National Bank was formed in 1960 from a merger of American Commercial Bank of Charlotte, N.C., and Security National Bank of Greensboro, N.C., creating the nation's 65th largest bank with 51 offices and assets of $500 million. Since then, it has expanded steadily to a business with a national reputation known for aggressively capitalizing on opportunities and opening new markets.

In 1974, NCNB Plaza was completed. As a 40 story building, it was Charlotte's tallest building at the time. From then on, NCNB grew in financial strength more than with buildings.

In 1982, NCNB bought National Bank of Lake City, Florida. This move helped open the door to interstate banking. That successful move possibly was the catalyst for a five year buying spree that tripled NCNB's assets to $29 billion. It was during that time in 1983 that the current Chairman, Mr. Hugh McColl, Jr., was elected to succeed Thomas Storrs, 24 years after joining the bank as a management trainee.[46]

NCNB'S PAST PROBLEM EXPERIENCE

Life at NCNB was not always rosy. In 1975, NCNB earned the distinction of being named a "problem bank." The scenario sounds familiar to Texas bankers; a close to $200 million loss in bad loans was generated on total assets of $5 billion due to over-involvement in real estate loans. Jim Thompson, vice-chairman of NCNB, admits, "quite candidly, we got over involved in real estate at precisely the time the market fell out from under us." NCNB pulled back on the balance sheet, almost exiting the real estate lending business entirely. In 1981, NCNB sold its unprofitable NCNB Mortgage Corporation to Bankers Trust of South Carolina for $31.5 million.[47]

Is NCNB making the same mistake in Texas? Thompson feels that "it was one of the best learning experiences this company could ever have." After the crisis for NCNB, the firm concentrated on paying off many of the loans it had used to grow to over $6 billion in assets from its original $500 million. It has since grown to assets of $28.6 billion and seems poised and ready to overcome the pitfalls of a sluggish Texas economy.[48] However, the question remains: Is Texas ready for NCNB?

OTHER CONTENDERS FOR FIRST REPUBLIC

In July of 1988, NCNB awaited the decision of the FDIC along with other bidders including Citicorp and Wells, Fargo & Co. First Republic's chairman, Albert Casey, had also submitted a plan that would keep them independent. First Republic had already borrowed $3 billion from the Fed just to stay alive after the devastating run on deposits in the spring of 1988. Other options to the FDIC included asking the Fed to recall its loan that would throw the bank into insolvency. This move would also wipe out the interest of investors in

First Republic's bonds and stock. One last option would be for the FDIC to operate the corporation on its own.[49]

While the FDIC agonized over whether NCNB was the clear cut choice to take control of First Republic Bank, NCNB was not wasting time in getting ready. Since April 1988, Senior V.P. of marketing, Brad Iversen and his staff in North Carolina were working to create a campaign to sell Texans on NCNB.[50]

Exhibit 1 is a copy of the press release distributed on Friday, July 29, 1988, announcing that NCNB had won the race. This was the first of many pieces

EXHIBIT 1   ANNOUNCEMENT OF NCNB'S ACQUISITION OF FIRST REPUBLICBANK CORP.

FIRST REPUBLICBANK BECOMES NCNB TEXAS NATIONAL BANK

CHARLOTTE—NCNB Corp. reported today it has entered into a management agreement with the Federal Deposit Insurance Corporation (FDIC) through which NCNB will manage a single, newly established bank, NCNB Texas National Bank, which has acquired the assets and assumed certain liabilities (including all deposit liabilities) of the subsidiary banks of First RepublicBank Corp.

NCNB also entered into an agreement in principle which provides that NCNB will make a 20-percent equity investment in the new bank and that NCNB will obtain a five-year option to purchase the remaining 80 percent from the FDIC. NCNB stressed it will have no exposure to First Republic's asset quality problems, and that the transaction will not be dilutive to NCNB's shareholders. Further, both NCNB and NCNB Texas National Bank have been indemnified by the FDIC from liability to creditors of First RepublicBank Corp. and its nonbank subsidiaries.

"This transaction is very much in the best interest of all concerned," said NCNB Chairman Hugh L. McColl Jr. "Obviously, NCNB brings to Texas a wealth of experience in operating statewide banks. The FDIC retains significant participation in NCNB Texas National Bank's profitable growth going forward. Furthermore, customers and employees of the former First Republic banks and others throughout Texas will benefit from the revitalization of the largest bank in the state.

"We look forward to working with the people in the former First Republic team in revitalizing the premier banking franchise in Texas," McColl said. "Despite their recent problems, First Republic's banks have maintained many of their historic strengths, including the quality of their people and their corporate, retail and trust operations."

NCNB Texas National Bank will open for business on a normal schedule at former First Republic locations. The former personnel will continue to staff the offices. All deposits in the new bank are fully insured by the FDIC.

"As for NCNB, this transaction is another major step in the expansion strategy we've followed over the years and takes advantage of our skill and experience in consolidating and enhancing bank operations. In addition, we are optimistic about the future growth and success of the Texas economy. This transaction allows us to establish a significant presence in the Texas market in association with a major banking firm there," McColl continued.

Under the transaction with the FDIC, NCNB will have a $210 million, 20-percent equity ownership position in the new bank. The FDIC will own the remaining 80 percent and NCNB will have an exclusive five-year option to purchase these shares.

"The structure of this arrangement poses minimal financial risk to NCNB shareholders," McColl said. Under terms of the agreement, the FDIC assumed the financial

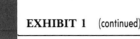

EXHIBIT 1   (continued)

risk of existing credit problems in the former First Republic subsidiary banks. A separate pool of written-down, troubled assets will be created in the new bank, the cost of which will be borne by the FDIC. The FDIC and NCNB will share, proportionate to their ownership, in the earnings of the new bank.

Francis (Buddy) Kemp, president of NCNB Corp., will be chairman of the new bank. Timothy P. Hartman, chief financial officer of NCNB Corp., will become vice chairman and chief financial officer of NCNB Texas National Bank. Each will report to Hugh L. McColl, chairman of NCNB Corp. and CEO of the corporation and of the new bank.

Charlotte-based NCNB Corp. is a $28.6 billion bank holding company that owns full-service banks in six Southeastern states.

A FEW WORDS FROM AL CASEY

Naturally, I am disappointed that the recapitalization plan we submitted was not accepted. But NCNB is an outstanding banking organization with proven leadership, and we wish them every success.

I have pledged my complete cooperation, and I know that I can count on yours as well. This action brings resolution to a situation that, for some of you, has lasted almost five years. It lifts the cloud that has hung over this organization and will allow former First Republic Bankers, now NCNB Texas National bankers, the opportunity to once again aggressively compete in this great banking market.

I deeply appreciate the efforts you have made and the spirit in which you have made them. One era is over, but another is just beginning, a future filled with bright prospects for all of us—and for our customers. You now are part of a super-regional banking organization that stretches from Maryland to Florida and now includes Texas.

Please join me in welcoming Hugh McColl, Buddy Kemp, Tim Hartman and the other members of the NCNB team. I know you will prove to them, as you did to me, what a group of talented people we have in this company.

A NOTE TO EMPLOYEES FROM BUDDY KEMP, CHAIRMAN OF NCNB TEXAS NATIONAL BANK

Dear Fellow Employees:

My name is Buddy Kemp, and I'm president of NCNB Corporation. More important to you, I'm also chairman of NCNB Texas National Bank—your bank—the successor to First Republic banks. I look forward to meeting you personally.

As you know, our NCNB management team will be working with you to rebuild a strong, healthy and powerful bank in Texas. My associates from NCNB will be visiting all former First Republic locations to help introduce us to you. They will go back to their regular assignments in a few days, but we wanted to have someone available to you to answer questions—and to assure you that we understand how important you are to the future of the bank. We need you.

We want you to come to work on your regular schedule and be prepared to take care of your customers. Your pay and benefits and other conditions of employment will continue as they were before. We hope you will quickly see that the changes caused by the FDIC actions will be healthy and positive for you and for your customers.

I am looking forward to working with you.—Francis B. Kemp

Source: First Source 1, no. 13 (August 1, 1988). Published by Corporate Public Affairs for employees of NCNB Texas National Bank; used with permission.

of information distributed to employees, customers, and others to help them understand what was involved in this transaction and how it affects them. It was re-produced through the bank's internal publication, *First Source.*

OPERATIONS

NCNB TAKES OVER

NCNB Texas National Bank was formed with the acquisition of First Republic-Bank Corporation's 134 banking facilities located in 39 counties throughout Texas.[51] This represents a Texas presence in the major market areas of Dallas, Fort Worth, Houston, Austin, and San Antonio.

NCNB Corp. was already the largest bank holding company in the Southeast, with full-service banks in North Carolina, South Carolina, Georgia, Florida, Maryland, and Virginia. Emerging as one of the 10 largest branch systems in the nation, NCNB's greatest presence was in the three Southeastern Atlantic Coast states of North Carolina, South Carolina, and Florida. Within this area, NCNB maintained 659 offices in 11 states as well as in Australia, the Cayman Islands, Germany, and the United Kingdom.[52] (For more NCNB facts see Exhibit 2.)

OPERATING PROBLEMS FOR NCNB TEXAS

NCNB may indeed have gotten a sweetheart of a deal when they purchased First Republic, but the trade-off for this financial dream may have been an operating nightmare. Exhibit 3 depicts one of the biggest of their problems.

CREDIT CARD BUSINESS

NCNB operated the credit card business of First RepublicBank Corporation since August 2, 1988, in an agreement with the FDIC, in hopes of acquiring the credit bank as part of its takeover.[53] However, Citicorp, one of the largest issuers of credit cards in the country, outbid the NCNB Corporation. NCNB

EXHIBIT 2   NCNB CORPORATION FACT SHEET

- NCNB Corporation is a multi-bank holding company based in Charlotte.
- As of June 30, 1988, NCNB Corporation had assets of $28.6 billion, making it the largest bank holding company in the Southwest.
- NCNB Corporation was the sixth most profitable among the 25 largest U.S. banks in 1987, a year in which it ranked 18th in size.
- NCNB Corporation manages full-service offices through banks in seven states.
- Other subsidiaries include NCNB Leasing Corporation, NCNB Mortgage Corporation, NCNB Securities Inc., Panmure Gordon Bankers Ltd. of London, and Panmure Gordon & Co. Ltd. (a stockbrokerage) in London.

EXHIBIT 2   (continued)

NCNB'S BANKS

Bank	NCNB Texas National Bank
Headquarters	Dallas
Locations	134 offices in 39 counties
Assets	$26.8 billion
Employees	15,000
Loan Production Offices	Denver, New Orleans
International Branches and	London, Nassau, Singapore, Caracas, Mexico
Representative Offices	City, Sao Paulo, Seoul, Taipei, Paris, Tokyo
Bank	NCNB National Bank of North Carolina
Headquarters	Charlotte
Locations	225 in 103 communities
Assets	$16.1 billion
Employees	6,600
Loan Production Offices	New York City, Chicago, Nashville, Rockville (Md.), Baltimore, Los Angeles, Dallas
International Branches and	London, Georgetown (Cayman Islands), Guernsey
Representative Offices	(Channel Islands), Sydney, Frankfurt
Wholly Owned Merchant Bank	NCNB Australia Ltd.
Bank	NCNB National Bank of Florida
Headquarters	Tampa
Locations	197 in 27 counties
Assets	$9.8 billion
Employees	3,500
Bank	NCNB South Carolina
Headquarters	Columbia
Locations	113 in 23 counties
Assets	$3.2 billion
Employees	1,300
Bank	CentraBank
Headquarters	Baltimore
Locations	8 in Baltimore
Assets	$277 million
Employees	136
Bank	NCNB National Bank, Georgia
Headquarters	Atlanta
Locations	6 in DeKalb County
Assets	$210 million
Employees	79
Bank	NCNB Virginia
Headquarters	Dumfries
Locations	2 in Prince William County
Assets	$19.7 million
Employees	27

EXHIBIT 3   ANNOUNCEMENT OF NCNB'S OPERATIONS PROBLEMS

BANK TO RESUME HANDLING OPERATIONS FUNCTIONS

The following article was written by Darwin Smith, corporate executive vice-president, support, for NCNB Texas:

In August, NCNB Texas entered into an Interim Management Agreement with First RepublicBank Corp. to manage the operations of First RepublicBank Services Corp. and Republic Bank Integrated Processing Corp., which provide a number of critical bank operations for the bank. This agreement expires Oct. 31, 1988.

The employees of the two services companies are an integral part of the NCNB Texas team. Unfortunately, however, efforts to date to reach an agreement with First RepublicBank Corp. to acquire the services companies or to transfer their employees to NCNB Texas have been unsuccessful. As a result, and as a matter of safe and sound banking practices, we have determined that NCNB Texas must re-establish within our own organization the critical bank operations functions currently handled by the services companies.

We intend that the bank will resume handling those functions after Oct. 31. Functions under written contracts with the former First Republic banks, such as data processing, will continue to be provided by the services company.

Plans for the anticipated transition are well under way. NCNB Texas intends to continue providing our customers with the same level of high-quality service throughout this period.

Significant contributions have been made by all employees on the NCNB Texas team—from bank and services companies alike—towards achieving and maintaining this high level of service. Your continued cooperation and patience are requested during this transition time.

We will announce further details regarding NCNB Texas' operations and staffing plans through *FirstSource* next week.

Source: First Source 1, no. 25 (Ocfober 18, 1988). Published by Public Affairs for employees of NCNB Texas; used with permission.

officials were disappointed they did not acquire this operation, because they viewed the cardholders as customers of NCNB Texas. In mid-1988, NCNB Corporation had 1.2 million cardholders nationwide, with outstanding balances of $800 million, and they vowed that they would win back the Texas market lost to Citibank.[54]

MANAGEMENT: THEN AND NOW

KEY PLAYERS FROM FIRST REPUBLICBANK CORPORATION

The key players in the birth of First Republic, and its funeral, were Gerald Fronterhouse, H.R. "Bum" Bright, and Robert Stewert.

Gerald Fronterhouse was the chairman and CEO of RepublicBank before the merger. He pushed hard for approval of the acquisition of cross-town rival InterFirst bank.[55]

H. R. "Bum" Bright was the largest shareholder in RepublicBank. He initially proposed the merger with InterFirst, calling it a Texas solution to the protracted banking crisis in the state.[56]

Robert Stewart was the chairman and CEO of InterFirst. He contacted George Bush, James Baker, and Lloyd Bentsen to ask their support for the merger.[57]

FDIC APPOINTS AL CASEY

Albert V. Casey, a former chairman of American Airlines with social and business ties to the Dallas-Fort Worth area, was named to the First Republic post by the FDIC the day that the bank projected a $1.5 billion first-quarter loss in April 1987.[58]

In business circles, Casey was known as a turnaround artist, a gambler, a bottom-line manager and a survivor of corporate mine fields.[59]

Coming out of retirement for the task, Casey's role grew from caretaker to active bidder on behalf of the bank-holding company's management and existing shareholders. Casey proposed a plan that would keep the bank "Texas owned." However, when NCNB Corp. won the bid for the troubled bank, Casey's tenure was cut short.[60]

"Casey was brought in for a short term, and he served his purpose well," said Frank Anderson, a Dallas-based banking analyst. "But I think that he honestly believed the First Republic plan would be approved. I think he believed that to the end."[61]

NCNB TEXAS: DIRECTORS NAMED TO BOARD OF NEW BANK

NCNB Texas had five members on the board of directors in 1988. Buddy Kemp, who was appointed chairman of NCNB Texas, served as chairman of the board. Also on the board were Hugh McColl, chairman and chief executive officer of parent NCNB Corporation in addition to being chief executive officer of NCNB Texas; Tim Hartman, vice-chairman and chief financial officer of NCNB Texas; W. W. Johnson, chairman of NCNB South Carolina; and Ken Lewis, president of NCNB Texas.[62]

NCNB Brought Strong Management to Dallas. On August 9, 1988, NCNB Texas Chairman Buddy Kemp announced a six-member corporate management team comprised of former NCNB Corporation executives and former First RepublicBank competition executives. Kemp was quoted to say:

> We are fortunate to be able to draw upon the expertise and experience of the Texas bank and the NCNB Corp.; it offers the best of both worlds. This blend of management talents provides us the dynamic leadership necessary to achieve our goal of revitalizing the state's largest bank.[63]

Kemp believed that due to the dedication of all NCNB Texas employees a strong sense of commitment and team work became evident at the bank.

Hugh McColl

NCNB Corp.'s chairman has been described as aggressive, strong willed, intensely competitive. He's also been lauded as a generous visionary, a socially conscious chief executive who looks out for his people and doesn't hesitate to throw his company's clout behind good works.

McColl describes himself as having drive, energy and a determination to succeed that sometimes comes close to too much competitiveness.[64]

Others have described McColl as "aggressive, brash, swashbuckling." Chief lieutenants in company headquarters were known to plot strategy in an office they lovingly refer to as the "war room."[65]

Francis "Buddy" Kemp.   Buddy Kemp is the Chairman of the new NCNB Texas National Bank.

Francis "Buddy" Kemp was raised around financial institutions. His father, and later his mother, managed a savings and loan in a small North Carolina town. He worked there, too, between stints at college.[66]

Kemp has an MBA from Harvard Business School. Co-workers have described him as "intense, energetic and dedicated."[67] However, Kemp finds time to enjoy activities other than banking. He spends time on civic and cultural projects from the Symphony to Chamber of Commerce activities to the United Way.

Tim Hartman.   Tim Hartman, vice-chairman and CFO of the new bank, is a certified public accountant who has been depicted as having a talent for making results of intricate number crunching "easy to understand." "He uses a professional approach, without talking down to his listeners. . ." Hartman began working for NCNB in 1982. The following year he became a NCNB corporate vice-president.[68]

It was Tim Hartman who guided NCNB's negotiations with the FDIC through weeks of torturous meetings. "He grabbed hold of it in April and never let it go," McColl said. "He stayed with the project and negotiated endless hours with the FDIC patiently explaining the tax benefit over and over and over again."[69] The only advantage that NCNB had that could be quantified was the tax benefit. The other bidders did not have the courage to go after the tax benefit, but Tim Hartman did. Chuck Cooley, NCNB's head of personnel stated:

We are where we are because of many people. But if you had to pick one single indispensable individual, it would be Tim Hartman.[70]

Ken Lewis.   Ken Lewis is the 41-year-old president of NCNB Texas. He is responsible for the banks' 134 offices throughout the state as well as Trust, Multinational, and Corporate banking activities.[71] He says of himself, "I don't come

with a lot of frills. It's not difficult to understand me." He has been described as tough, demanding, and popular to work for.[72]

Ralph Carestro.   Ralph Carestro is responsible for all real estate and energy lending. He joined NCNB in 1978. He was a National Science Foundation Fellow at Ohio State University.[73] "There's no room for emotions when it comes to making banking decisions in real estate," he says.[74] As for the Texas challenge that lies ahead, Carestro acknowledges that getting to the point of leadership in Southwest and national real estate lending that he desires will be his greatest career challenge to date. "I'm up to it," he says.[75]

Jim Erwin.   Jim Erwin was the previous vice-chairman of First RepublicBank. He began his banking career as a credit trainee. Erwin holds a masters degree from the University of Texas. He began working for NCNB Texas (after the takeover) as president of the special asset bank.[76]

Raleigh Hortenstine.   Hortenstine is another employee who came to NCNB after the takeover. He is responsible for all fund management activities for NCNB Texas. He held the same position at First RepublicBank.[77]

For reference to the other "key players," refer to Exhibit 4.

EMPLOYEE RELATIONS

When RepublicBank and Interfirst merged, employees of the new bank experienced uncertain futures as there were shock waves of multiple layoffs and management changes. Then there continued to be anxiety as the fate of First Republic became evident. But, when NCNB Corp. came to Dallas, employees were assured that their jobs would remain intact, and they were greeted with southern warmth. A Dallas employee, working for the new bank, recalls that during the first week a rose was placed on everyone's desk with a note attached from Buddy Kemp. A few weeks later, all employees received an NCNB coffee mug, with a note enclosed that read "the coffee is on," to coincide with the television ad with the same theme.

Much attention was given to employees. They wore NCNB name tags the first week—for the benefit of NCNB representatives who were on hand to talk to them and answer their questions.[78]

NCNB wholeheartedly believes that people bank with people, not a building. And that's why they go to great lengths to hire, train, and retain the best and brightest people.[79]

Seeking new talent, NCNB selects approximately 250 promising young people from colleges and universities to join one of several NCNB management training programs.[80]

NCNB holds each job within the corporation in high esteem. And because having knowledgeable, well-equipped people in place is critical to their service level, NCNB views training as a process, not an event.[81]

EXHIBIT 4 NCNB ORGANIZATIONAL CHART (SEPTEMBER 1988)

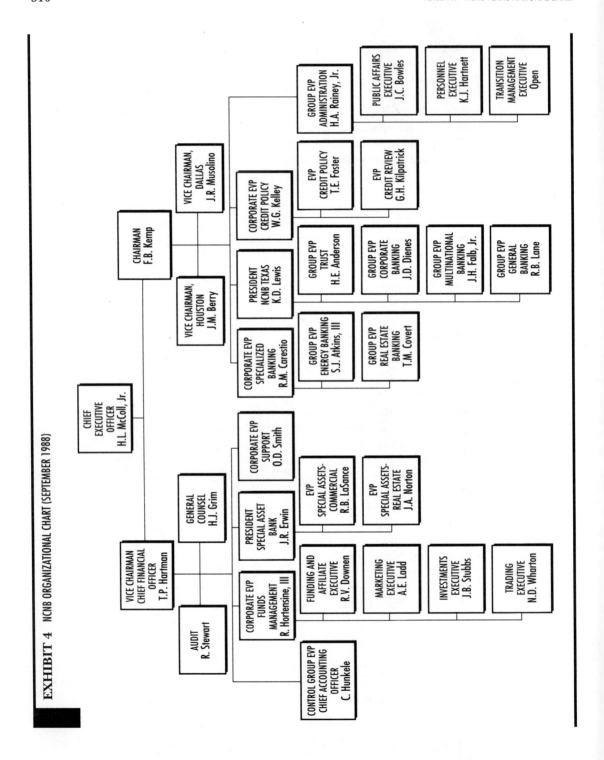

NCNB gives careful attention to its people's concerns. They realize that offices must be pleasant places to work and visit. An awareness that personal concerns affect professional endeavors led them to survey employees about family issues. They identified two primary concerns: child care and wellness. NCNB has been recognized as a corporate trendsetter in addressing these social issues. A child care referral service has been instituted, maternity leaves extended to six months and to include time-off for fathers, and a phased-in return to work option for new mothers introduced. In addition, NCNB is involved in efforts to expand the availability of child care in several communities. To aid employees with personal problems, NCNB provides an assistance program which makes counseling services available on a confidential basis.[82]

MARKETING

FIRST REPUBLICBANK CORPORATION

When Republic and Interfirst merged, there was publicity surrounding the event. But after the dust settled, industry observers recall that marketing efforts by the new "superbank" were minimal.

NCNB TEXAS

NCNB began plastering its name all over Texas immediately upon its entrance into the Texas market.

For months, the senior vice-president–marketing for NCNB Corporation and his staff in North Carolina could not tell anyone what they were doing, but they were preparing a campaign in hopes of NCNB winning the bid for First RepublicBank. The day before NCNB was told that their deal had been secured, 1,600 posters and 1,600 flyers, 80,000 customer letters, newspaper ads, radio spots, and monthly statement notes were shipped Thursday by Federal Express to Dallas.[83]

"The deal" was announced on Friday. By Sunday, the efforts of NCNB and First RepublicBank marketing staff was strategically plastered all over the state: "There's a new star in Texas and the sky's the limit," the posters proclaim.[84]

Dallas–Fort Worth radio listeners were immediately addressed by a catchy 60-second spot featuring a man and woman discussing a trip to the bank.[85]

ADVERTISING CAMPAIGN

The fall 1988 advertising campaign for NCNB Texas was a three-pronged approach. The focus was on attracting and retaining customers.[86] The campaign strategy included two-page newspaper ads and television commercials which ran in all NCNB Texas markets. The campaign was aimed at both individual consumers and commercial decision-makers, emphasizing the bank's commitment to customer service and reinforcing the strength of the new banking organization

> The trio of approaches were image/positioning ads, which focused on business philosophy and customer relationships, ongoing product ads and business-to-business white papers, which provided factual information about the bank.

The three types of advertising ran simultaneously throughout the rest of 1988.

TYPE OF AD	MEDIUM
Image/Positioning	television
	newspaper
	consumer magazines
	billboards
Product	television
	newspapers
White Papers	southwest edition of *Wall Street Journal*

The ads were used for different purposes. The image/positioning ads spoke primarily to individual customers. They were designed to communicate what NCNB stands for and how they could help the individual customer. These ads pushed the stability, service, and safety of NCNB.[87] These ads featured Buddy Kemp in different settings "chatting" in a friendly, helpful manner. The ads spoke to opportunity.

Observers say NCNB Texas' television advertising was warm and straightforward. Buddy Kemp began each ad by saying, "Hi, I'm Buddy Kemp." The first ad, which ran soon after the takeover, introduced Buddy Kemp as he sat in an executive chair. He talks about how NCNB is glad to be in the neighborhood. The second ad, which began running in late September 1988, shows Buddy Kemp sitting at a table with a pot of coffee. He invites the listener to come on in, have a cup of coffee, and "let's talk." In yet a third ad the focus is a conference table, and the focus is still "come on in and we'll listen to you." Observers say that by the second or third time they hear this newcomer, he comes across like the friend down the street that you've known for years.

The product ads were closer to traditional bank advertising. They featured the different products available to customers at NCNB. The aim was to depict NCNB as responsive to customer needs and desires.[88]

The white paper ads were directed specifically at upscale consumers and commercial decision makers. The idea was to displace any skeptics of NCNB's strength and safety. These ads contained detailed information on the NCNB-FDIC agreement, rankings and other information as it became available.[89]

COMPETITION

The Texas banking industry encountered very turbulent times in the mid- to late 1980s. First RepublicBank's competitors (now NCNB Texas' competitors) also struggled in this Texas economy.

Texas Commerce BancShares, Inc. of Houston was acquired by Chemical New York in May of 1987. Chemical then cut about 10 percent of its work force of 21,000 and shed assets in a move to boost flagging profits. In January of 1988, Chemical reported a $853.7 million loss for 1987, which included a $122 million deficit at Texas Commerce for the first eight months after it was acquired by the giant New York bank.[90]

Allied BancShares Inc. of Houston was acquired by First Interstate Bancorp of Los Angeles in January of 1988. On January 20, 1988, First Interstate reported a $95 million loss in the fourth quarter as it made a special addition to its reserve to cover troubled loans to less-developed countries. This contributed to a loss for the full year of $556.2 million.[91]

First City Bancorporation, Inc. of Houston was the fourth-largest bank-holding company in Texas. In September of 1987, federal officials announced a $1.5 billion rescue plan led by former Chicago banker A. Robert Abboud. In March of 1988, First City shareholders approved the government-assisted bailout and reorganization plan.[92]

Texas American BancShares, Inc. used layoffs in 1986 to cut costs. Like other banks, Texas American had been plagued by financial problems stemming from bad loans and the general downturn in the state economy. In January of 1988, TAB announced the previous year's shortfall to be $78 million.[93]

MCorp of Dallas announced in 1987 that the Dallas bank-holding company would be able to compete on its own and would not seek a merger partner. MCorp, the second-largest bank company in Texas (following NCNB Texas) reported a $258.3 million loss for 1987. In February of 1988, MCorp sold its majority-owned MTech computer services unit to Electronic Data Systems Corp. of Dallas for $281 million in cash and securities.[94]

Exhibits 5, 6, and 7 graphically explain the standings of the major banks in Texas by comparing total assets, loans, and total deposits. Keep in mind that Texas Commerce Bancshares, Inc. is part of Chemical Banking and includes business in New York as well as Texas. It is interesting that Chemical Banking is the only institution represented without significant losses in all categories. Likewise, Allied Bancshares, Inc. is a part of First Interstate Bancorp and includes business in California.

Total company assets were used to compare financial strength of Texas banking institutions (see Exhibit 5). This was felt appropriate since future banking efforts by Texas based banks will have to compete with the financial strength of those banks with out-of-state corporate bases. This effort more accurately describes NCNB's future competition. Exhibits 6 and 7 reflect only Texas business to accurately compare Texas market position.

LEGAL

As of the *1987 Annual Report* for First RepublicBank, a suit was pending in the U.S. District Court brought by a group of plaintiffs against twenty-two banks, including First RepublicBank Dallas.

EXHIBIT 5 TEXAS BANKS ASSETS

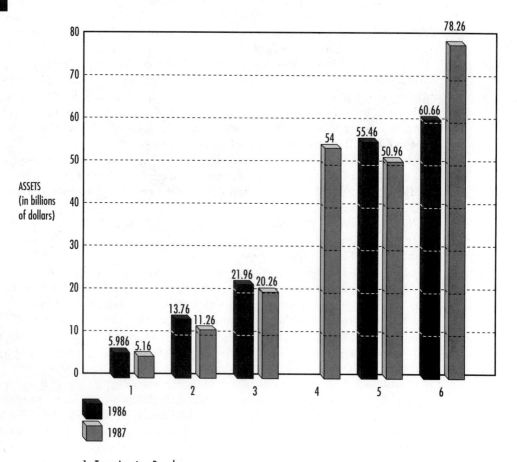

1 - Texas American Bancshares
2 - First City Bancorp. of Texas
3 - MCorp
4 - NCNB Texas (formerly First RepublicBank Corp.*)
5 - First Interstate Bancorp
6 - Chemical Banking (formerly Texas Commerce BancShares, Inc.)

*Based on 1987 Annual Report
Source: Standard & Poor's Corp. Stock-Exchange Reports

EXHIBIT 6   TEXAS BANKS LOANS (TEXAS ONLY)

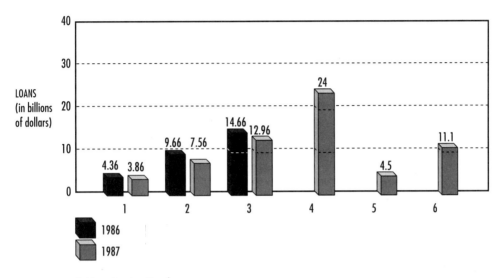

1 - Texas American Bancshares
2 - First City Bancorp. of Texas
3 - MCorp
4 - NCNB Texas (formerly First RepublicBank Corp.*)
5 - First Interstate Bancorp
6 - Chemical Banking (formerly Texas Commerce BancShares, Inc.)

*Based on 1987 Annual Report
Source: Standard & Poor's Corp. Stock Exchange Reports

EXHIBIT 7 TEXAS BANKS DEPOSITS (TEXAS ONLY)

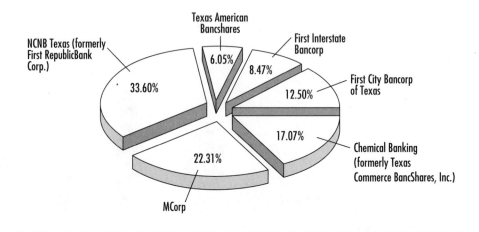

The suit alleges that the banks have engaged in improper conduct in failing to restructure credit agreements on terms the plaintiffs consider reasonable and makes many other allegations, including wrongful control, domination, economic coercion, bad faith, breach of fiduciary duty, breach of contract, violation of the Sherman Act, violation of the Bank Holding Company Act and violation of the Racketeer Influenced and Corrupt Organizations Act.[95]

Although the plaintiffs in this case were seeking damages of at least $1.2 billion, First RepublicBank was contesting the suit and believes that the suit will be without merit.

Another class action suit was inherited by First RepublicBank from Inter-First. The suit was filed against certain InterFirst directors and senior officers for "alleged violations of the federal securities law, based on alleged past misrepresentations about InterFirst's financial condition and operations."[96] No discovery has been conducted in connection with this suit, but management believes that ultimate liability, if any, will not have a material effect on the financial position of First RepublicBank.

In addition to the above mentioned cases that NCNB Texas inherited when they took over First RepublicBank, they also ran into legal problems by choosing the new name NCNB Texas National Bank. In the case, the El Paso–based Texas National Bank claimed that NCNB Texas National Bank was an infringement on its name. The common name to be used in marketing and advertising, however, will be NCNB Texas, the bank said in a release. NCNB said it will use the "Texas National" part of the name in contractual and legal documents only. Lawyers for El Paso's Texas National Bank and newcomer NCNB Texas National Bank say they will settle their differences out of court.[97]

There are sure to be additional lawsuits resulting from the many stockholders in the First Republic holding companies who will lose their investments as a result of the NCNB takeover.

FINANCIAL

FIRST REPUBLIC'S FINANCIAL STRUGGLES

When the June 1987 merger of RepublicBank Corporation and InterFirst Bank Corporation took place, it was treated as a purchase transaction on the books. It provided a financial service franchise throughout Texas with $33 billion in assets, 24 billion in loans, and 25 billion in deposits at year end. The new First RepublicBank Corporation achieved increased operating efficiencies during the year due to combined overhead savings of 9 percent.[98] Unfortunately, this success was more than offset by the rest of the story.

In 1987, the company suffered record losses and there was concern about the uncertainty of repayment of loans to 18 lesser developed countries. The year 1988 did not offer improvement. The real estate fallout continued to take its toll. Loan loss provisions amounted to $1.4 billion in the first quarter alone. Non-performing assets increased $543 million during the same three months bringing the non-performing assets ratio to 19 percent—well above the industry. Finally, net interest income fell tremendously over 1987 and the first quarter of 1988. This decline resulted from the increase in non-performing assets which in turn caused the net interest rate margin to decrease by 47 basis points.[99] Other key financial figures are shown in Exhibits 8, 9, 10, and 11.

So what does all this mean? Well, First RepublicBank could not receive enough through loan repayment, principal as well as interest, to make interest payments on deposits, much less invest in loans in more profitable areas. The bank desperately needed funds to make these loans and regain cash inflows in the form of interest income; that is how banks stay in business.

NCNB'S ACQUISITION OF FIRST REPUBLICBANK

Before First RepublicBank went under Chapter 11, common stock prices fell from $19 in 1986 to $.75 at June 30, 1988. Stockholders lost their investments, but NCNB was ready to rebuild. To get things started, NCNB obtained a favorable tax ruling from the Internal Revenue Service which enabled the bank to use the losses from bad loans to shelter taxes. NCNB would benefit from a roughly $700 million tax break.[100]

EXHIBIT 8   FIRST REPUBLICBANK EARNINGS SUMMARY

| | DECEMBER 31 | | | | |
	1983	1984	1985	1986	1987
Net interest income	$479.6	$553.1	$600.4	$509.6	$681.7
Net interest income[1]	581.8	655.8	693.0	612.1	743.4
Provision for loan losses	116.6	130.5	117.9	229.1	885.4
Non-interest income	132.1	159.4	165.8	207.8	254.2
Non-interest expenses	367.2	436.3	487.9	487.9	746.2
Income (loss) before income taxes	127.9	145.7	160.4	.4	(695.7)
Provision (benefit) for income taxes	(2.3)	8.4	20.2	(53.6)	(38.9)
Net income (loss)	130.2	137.3	140.2	54.0	(656.8)

Note: Amounts given in millions.

[1] Net interest is presented on a tax equivalent basis using the incremental federal tax rate of 46% for years through 1986 and 40% for 1987.

Source: First Republic, *1987 Annual Statement.*

EXHIBIT 9   FIRST REPUBLICBANK FINANCIAL SUMMARY (INCOME STATEMENT)

| | THREE MONTHS ENDED MARCH 31 | |
	1987	1988
Net interest income	$108,799	$ 159,278
Provision for loan losses	55,029	1,391,456
Non-interest income (loss)	57,338	(23,904)
Non-interest expenses	107,112	244,844
Income (loss) before income taxes	3,996	(1,500,926)
Provision (benefit) for income taxes	(6,400)	758
Net income (loss)	10,396	(1,501,684)
Net income (loss) per common share:		
Primary	$ .30	$ (45.99)
Fully diluted	$ .30	$ (45.99)

Note: Amounts given in thousands, except per common share.

Source: First Republic, *1988 Quarterly Report.*

EXHIBIT 10 FIRST REPUBLIC BALANCE SHEET DATA

	AT MARCH 31	
	1987	1988
Loans, net of unearned income	$14,678	$22,657
Earning assets	17,810	26,149
Total asset	20,288	28,367
Deposits	15,300	21,882
Stockholders' equity	1,223	(344)
Stockholders' equity per common share	$ 40.25	$ (19.48)

Note: Amounts given in millions, except per common share.

Source: First RepublicBank, *1988 Quarterly Report.*

Before the Texas acquisition, NCNB held assets of over $28 billion. (For additional NCNB financial information, refer to Exhibit 12.) After adding NCNB Texas, the corporation held over $54 billion in assets. It certainly seemed that NCNB could withstand loan losses which are estimated at $5.1 billion as a worst-case scenario.[101] President of NCNB Texas, Buddy Kemp, believes that the bank can initially operate with a mere 5-percent loan growth.[102] NCNB not only expects to stabilize and rebuild the old First Republic, but also to bring the bottom line back in the black soon. Worst-case financial projections forecast net income in 1989 of over $140 million (see Exhibit 13).[103]

In order to bring about such a positive change, NCNB chairman, Hugh McColl, Jr., says that NCNB Texas will be making new loans, not collecting bad ones. The task ahead is to determine the market which NCNB Texas will target.

EXHIBIT 11 FIRST REPUBLICBANK CORP.'S ROAD TO FAILURE

	1986	1987	1988
Net Income (in millions)	$54.4	($656.8)	($2,259.7)
Non-Performing loans (in millions)	$853	$3,922	$5,135
Common stock price	$19.00	$3.75	$0.75

Source: First RepublicBank documents.

EXHIBIT 12   FINANCIAL SUMMARY: NCNB CORPORATION AND SUBSIDIARIES

	1988	1987	CHANGE
For the Three Months Ended June 30			
Net income	$ 59,267	$ 54,471	8.8%
Per common share	.70	.68	2.9
Cash dividends paid on common shares	19,516	16,771	16.4
Per common share	.23	.21	9.5
Return on average total assets	.84%	.88%	(4.5)
Return on average shareholders' equity	15.16	16.00	(5.3)
For the Six Months Ended June 30			
Net income	$129,292	$108,361	19.3%
Per common share	1.53	1.36	12.5
Cash dividends paid on common shares	38,965	33,512	16.3
Per common share	.46	.42	9.5
Return on average total assets	.90%	.85%	5.9
Return on average shareholders' equity	16.81	16.29	3.2
At June 30			
Assets	$28,609,620	$24,624,128	16.2%
Deposits	19,659,046	17,742,694	10.8
Loans and leases, net of unearned income	17,882,530	16,576,215	7.9
Investment securities	5,670,620	3,167,942	79.0
Earning assets	25,481,925	20,831,771	22.3
Shareholders' equity	1,609,363	1,490,390	8.0
Per common share	18.91	17.74	6.6
Common shares outstanding	85,095,915	83,997,886	1.3
Capital ratios:			
Primary	6.76%	7.41%	
Total	7.92	8.70	
Daily Average for the Three Months Ended June 30			
Assets	$28,472,036	$24,876,178	14.5%
Deposits	19,092,306	17,710,204	7.8
Loans and leases, net of unearned income	17,582,169	16,177,734	8.7
Investment securities	5,687,653	3,704,070	53.6
Earning assets	25,189,372	21,887,974	15.1
Shareholders' equity	1,572,731	1,365,663	15.2
Per common share	18.53	17.05	8.7
Common shares outstanding	84,854,059	80,085,498	6.0

EXHIBIT 12 (continued)

	1988	1987	CHANGE
Daily Average for the Six Months Ended June 30			
Assets	$28,833,113	$25,688,444	12.2%
Deposits	18,969,814	17,534,357	8.2
Loans and leases, net of unearned income	17,345,119	15,919,529	9.0
Investment securities	6,213,639	4,372,156	42.1
Earning assets	25,547,960	22,677,011	12.7
Shareholders' equity	1,547,173	1,341,388	15.3
Per common share	18.26	16.79	8.8
Common shares outstanding	84,710,522	79,903,700	6.0

Note: Dollars in thousands except per-share information.

TARGET MARKETS

"Texas clearly has a future. It is a dynamic economy, it is diversifying and it is growing," says Don Griffith of Interstate Bancorp.[104] Restoring Texas financial institutions means restoring the Texas economy and a restored Texas economy means new business for NCNB Texas. Kemp's plan is to seek loans to small and medium size businesses—businesses which should spring from the revived economy. In addition, Kemp plans to take a larger share of the con-

EXHIBIT 13 NCNB TEXAS NATIONAL BANK: WORST-CASE FINANCIAL PROJECTIONS

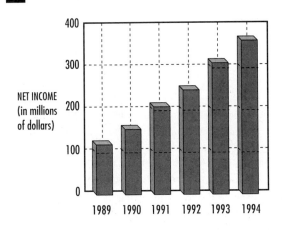

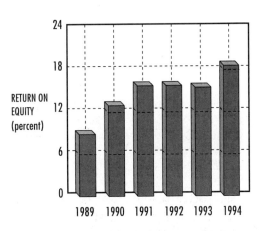

Source: NCNB Corp.

sumer market. NCNB believes that "retail banking initiatives aimed at attracting more consumer accounts should take hold."[105]

Another idea of NCNB was that if cities can be revitalized, the banking
business will grow. Investing in the cities of Texas may be another target market.[106] NCNB may concentrate in small business, consumers, and cities, but the
overall idea will be to diversify as much as possible.

FUTURE OUTLOOK

Beyond the short-term goals of establishing a presence for the 134-office Texas
affiliate of Charlotte, N.C.–based NCNB Corporation, Buddy Kemp faced the
more difficult task of building a long-term business in a state whose financial-
services industry is in disarray.[107] Kemp had announced a strategy of seeking
loans to small- and medium-size businesses and grabbing a larger share of the
consumer market. But the state's still sluggish economy could make that difficult, industry officials said.[108]

However, NCNB officials were optimistic about NCNB's opportunities in
Texas. As relative newcomers to Texas, they believed they had a more objective
view, and believed that Texas was in a lot better shape than many Texans realized. In a presentation to the North Texas chapter of the National Association
of Industrial and Office Parks, Hugh L. McColl, Jr., chairman and CEO of
NCNB Corporation, cited some encouraging signs that the Texas economy
had begun to move again. in fact, McColl believed the economic turnaround
had already happened as evidenced by the increase in total employment in
Texas as a rate exceeding the national employment growth rate.[109]

Officials from NCNB Texas believed their bank had the strength to stabilize and rebuild First Republic. The optimism of these officials was obvious,
and their message comes out loud and clear; "NCNB & Texas: A Promising
Alliance."

ENDNOTES

1. Liz Galtney, "Anatomy of a Bank Disaster," *U.S. News and World Report* (August 15, 1988): 38.

2. "Welcome, NCNB," *Dallas Morning News* (August 1, 1988): 12A.

3. John H. Taylor, "Battered but Still Afloat," *Forbes* (May 2, 1988): 49–50.

4. Bill Minutaglio, "The Pride and Fall of Republic Bank," *Dallas Life Mazazine* (September 4, 1988): 8–18.

5. Empty Building, Crumbling Banks: Turmoil in Texas Banking," *Economist* (January 23, 1988): 73–75.

6. Minutaglio, "Pride and Fall."

7. William G. Smith, "The Good, the Bad, and the Closed," *Texas Business* (October 1987): 37–41.

8. Toni Mack, "The Unloved Ones," *Forbes* (November 2, 1987): 34–37.

9. Smith, "The Good, the Bad, and the Closed."

10. "Empty Building, "Crumbling Banks."

11. Taylor, "Battered but Still Afloat."

12. "Bad Banking Deserves Penalties," *Wall Street Journal* (March 30, 1988): 18.

13. "Empty Building, Crumbling Banks."

14. Mack, "The Unloved Ones."

15. Todd Vogel, "Texas Banks: Who Wants 'Em?" *Business Week* (June 8, 1987): 120.

16. Mack, "The Unloved Ones."

17. Todd Vogel, "Oil Patch Thrifts Are Deep in Gloom," *Business Week* (February 23, 1987): 47–49.

18. Smith, "The Good, the Bad, and the Closed."

19. Ibid.

20. Taylor, "Battered but Still Afloat."

21. "On the Run," *Economist* (February 27, 1988): 68–70.

22. Ibid.

23. "Texas Banks Over the Brink," *Economist* (May 7, 1988): 74–77.

24. "Calling For Help," *Economist* (March 19, 1988): 87–89.

25. "On the Run."

26. "Calling For Help."

27. Mack, "The Unloved Ones."

28. Vogel, "Oil Patch Thrifts."

29. Hayes, Jack M. "The Gravity of Texas Bank Problems Underscores and Extent of FDIC's Woes," *Savings Institution* (May 1988): 33–35.

30. "On the Run."

31. Vogel, "Texas Banks."

32. "On the Run."

33. Minutaglio, "Pride and Fall," p. 8.

34. Ibid., p. 11.

35. Ibid., p. 12.

36. Ibid., p. 13.

37. Ibid., p. 17.

38. Ibid., p. 18.

39. Galtney, "Anatomy of a Bank Disaster," p. 38.

40. Ibid.

41. Ibid.

42. Ibid.

43. Ibid., p. 39.

44. Ibid.

45. Ibid.

46. John Cleghorn, "Texas Venture Continues NCNB's Grow-To-Survive Regional Strategy," *Dallas Morning News* (July 30, 1988): 19A.

47. Tom Steinert-Threlkeld, "NCNB Endured '75 Crisis," *Dallas Morning News* (August 2, 1988): 1A, 6A.

48. Ibid.

49. David LaGesse, "First Republic Decision Awaited," *Dallas Morning News* (July 28, 1988): 1D.

50. Maria Halkias, "NCNB Staffers Get the Feel of Dallas," *Dallas Morning News* (August 1, 1988): 10A.

51. First RepublicBank Corporation, *1988 Annual Report*, p. 1.

52. NCNB Corporation documents.

53. Nina Andrews, "Citicorp to Buy Texas Credit Card Business," *New York Times* (September 12, 1988): 25.

54. Ibid., pp. 25, 29.

55. Galtney, "Anatomy of a Bank Disaster," p. 38.

56. Ibid.

57. Ibid.

58. Jim Mitchell, "Casey Battled to Keep Bank in Texas Hands," *Dallas Morning News* (July 31, 1988): 26A.

59. Ibid.

60. Ibid.

61. Ibid.

62. *Prime Times* (August 1988).

63. *First Source* (August 9, 1988).

64. *Prime Times* (August 1988).

65. John Taylor, "The George Patton of Banking," *Forbes* (January 25, 1988): 44.

66. *Prime Times* (August 1988).

67. Ibid.

68. Ibid.

69. *Prime Times* (December 1988): 4.

70. Ibid.

71. *First Source* (August 9, 1988).

72. *Prime Times* (October 1988): 2.

73. *First Source* (August 9, 1988).

74. *Prime Times* (December 1988): 3.

75. Ibid.

76. *First Source* (August 9, 1988).

77. Ibid.

78. Halkias, "NCNB Staffers Get the Feel of Dallas," p. 10A.

79. NCNB documents.

80. Ibid.

81. Ibid.

82. Ibid.

83. Halkias, "NCNB Staffers Get the Feel of Dallas," p. 10A.

84. Ibid.

85. Ibid.

86. *First Source* (September 9, 1988).

87. Ibid.

88. Ibid.

89. Ibid.

90. "Upheaval For Texas Bank-Holding Companies," *Dallas Morning News* (March 16, 1988): 12A.

91. Ibid.

92. Ibid.

93. Ibid.

94. Ibid.

95. First RepublicBank, 1987 Annual Report, p. 41.

96. Ibid.

97. "Newcomer Bank to Shorten Name,' *Dallas Morning News* (August 11, 1988): 5D.

98. *First RepublicBank, 1987 Annual Report,* p. 3.

99. *First RepublicBank, Quarterly Report,* March 31, 1988, p. 10.

100. *Wall Street Journal* (August 1, 1988).

101. "Bank Upbeat About Future," *Dallas Morning News* (July 31, 1988).

102. *Dallas Morning News* (August 11, 1988).

103. *Dallas Morning News* (July 31, 1988).

104. "Deal Seen as Boost for State," *Dallas Morning News* (July 30, 1988).

105. Michael Weiss, "Kemp on Stump for NCNB Texas," *Dallas Morning News* (August 11, 1988): 1D.

106. "NCNB Comes to Texas With Crises Experience," *Dallas Morning News* (August 2, 1988).

107. Weiss, "Kemp on Stump."

108. Ibid.

109. Kenneth D. Lewis, "The Outlook for Banking in Texas," Speech given on October 5, 1988.

NORTHERN TELECOM

LEW G. BROWN AND
RICHARD SHARPE

Hall Miller, vice-president of marketing for the Central Office Switching Division of Northern Telecom, Inc., looked up from the magazine on his desk to a picture of a single, snow-covered log cabin with stately mountains rising in the background. The picture reminded him of his childhood in British Columbia.

His eyes moved from the picture to the window, where he could see traffic already starting to pile up on the portion of Interstate 40 which ran through Research Triangle Park, North Carolina, between Durham, Chapel Hill, and Raleigh. It was mid-afternoon in March 1988, and the traffic would be bumper-to-bumper in another hour.

Hall smiled as he realized that the picture on the wall represented his perception of Northern's performance in the U.S. while the impending traffic jam reminded him of the changing market conditions he felt the company would soon be facing.

Hall had been reviewing the results of a survey conducted by *Communications Week* in the fourth quarter of 1987. The purpose of the study was to identify purchase trends and priorities in the selection of central office telephone switching equipment. The survey respondents were primarily telephone company planners who were directly involved with selecting and purchasing central office switches.

Hall was interested in the results of the *Communications Week* survey since he wanted to use the information to prepare for the quarterly meeting of the regional marketing managers which would be held in early April. These managers were assigned to each of the seven regions into which Norther Telecom had divided the U.S. for marketing purposes. It was these managers' responsibility to work with the sales force in each region to develop overall mar-

Source: **Prepared by Professor Lew G. Brown, University of North Carolina–Greensboro, and Richard Sharpe as a basis for classroom discussion and not to illustrate either effective or ineffective handling of administrative situations.** © **Lew G. Brown, 1990.**

keting strategies. They also worked on quotations and new business development in their regions.

Hall felt the time had come to get the group to step back and assess the overall market situation faced by the Central Office Switching Division and to identify potential changes in the division's marketing strategy.

HISTORY

Northern Telecom, Inc. (NTI), the U.S. subsidiary of Canadian-based Northern Telecom, Ltd. (NTL), was originally part of the Bell System. Bell Canada, the parent company of NTL, was a subsidiary of AT&T until the late 1950s when AT&T was ordered to divest its foreign subsidiaries. Prior to that divestiture and for some time afterwards, Northern Telecom was known as Northern Electric, the Canadian counterpart of AT&T's U.S. manufacturing arm, Western Electric.

Despite the divestiture, Northern Telecom still had a captive customer in its parent, Bell Canada; and this relationship gave it roughly 80% of the Canadian market. However, Northern's management realized that if it were to survive it would have to design its own equipment. Previously, Northern had made copies of telephone equipment manufactured by Western Electric. To make its own equipment, Northern would have to be able to afford the massive research and development budgets required in the telecommunications equipment industry. The Canadian market alone would not support the required level of investment. Therefore, Northern broadened its market by establishing its presence in the U.S. in the 1960s and 1970s as a supplier of telephone switches.

A telephone switch is a device that routes individual calls from the person making the call to and through the telephone network. Once in the network, the call is routed from switch to switch until reaching the person being called. Initially, Northern Telecom had sold switches known as "private branch exchanges." These private branch exchanges were switches which were owned by the customer, such as a manufacturing company or a university, and were housed in the customer's facilities. Northern also sold the telephone sets which went with its systems.

Manufacturing and support facilities were established in West Palm Beach, Florida; Atlanta, Georgia; Richardson, Texas; Minnetonka, Minnesota; San Ramon, California; and Nashville, Tennessee, the U.S. headquarters of NTI. Northern's first facility in North Carolina opened in the early 1970s in Creedmoor, a small community north of Durham. It still amazed Hall to think that Northern had grown from 300 people at Creedmoor to 10,000 employees in the Raleigh area in less than a decade.

DEVELOPMENT OF THE DIGITAL SWITCH

Throughout the 1970s, Northern Telecom, in conjunction with Bell-Northern Research (BNR), Northern's R&D equivalent to Bell Labs, developed a process known as digital switching. Unlike *analog* signals—a continuous wave of electrical signals varying in amplitude and frequency in response to changes in sound—*digital* signals involve sampling the human voice at a rate of 8,000 times per second and breaking it into a stream of thousands of bits of electrical pulses in a binary code. As the pulses are routed through the network, they are multiplexed, which involves coding each pulse and sending them together in streams. Because each pulse is coded, it can be sent immediately and followed by other pulses from other conversations. This allows transmission of multiple conversations simultaneously on the same line. At each telephone switch, the pulses are either routed to another switch or are multiplexed (put back together) into voice signals and sent to the appropriate terminating party for the call.

Digital technology offered a number of advantages over analog switching, including faster and "cleaner" transmission, lower costs per line, and decreased floor space requirements for switching equipment (a digital switch required less than 50% the space of an analog switch).

In 1970, Northern developed the SP-1, a hybrid electro-mechanical switch whose functions were digitally controlled. In 1975, it introduced the first completely computerized telephone switch, the SL-1. The SL-1 was a significant technological advance over the analog and hybrid switches then in use and became a platform for a high-performance product line that allowed businesses to significantly reduce their telecommunications costs.

With its development of the digital switch, Northern entered the central office switch market. As opposed to private branch exchanges, central office switches are located in the telephone company's facilities. The customer's telephone sets are connected directly to the telephone company's switch rather than to its own switch located in its facilities. Thus, Northern's customer became the telephone company rather than individual businesses. Northern installed its first digital central office switch in 1979.

THE BREAKUP OF AT&T AND EQUAL ACCESS

Until the early 1980s, AT&T had a monopoly in the U.S. telephone market, providing local and long distance telephone service through the Bell System to more than 85% of the U.S. Western Electric was the only supplier of telecommunications equipment to AT&T. The remaining 15% of the telephone service market was served by 1,200 "independent" telephone companies. Northern Telecom, along with other equipment vendors, sold its products to these independent telephone companies.

In 1982, through the provisions of the Modification of Final Judgment which ordered the breakup of AT&T, AT&T divested the 22 local operating companies comprising the Bell System. Although the "new" AT&T retained the long distance portion of the business (called AT&T Communications), the newly formed Bell operating companies provided local telephone service and became distinct entities which were no longer tied to AT&T. As such, the Bell operating companies were now free to buy telecommunications equipment

EXHIBIT 1 BELL REGIONAL HOLDING COMPANIES

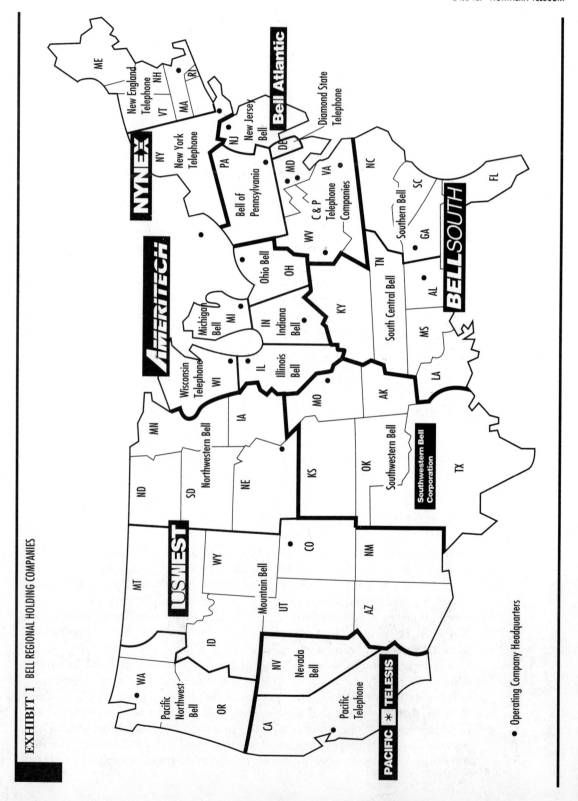

• Operating Company Headquarters

from suppliers other than Western Electric (renamed AT&T Technologies). For Northern Telecom and other vendors, divestiture was the end of a monopoly and the beginning of a highly competitive marketplace. Exhibit 1 shows how the 22 Bell operating companies, such as Southern Bell and South Central Bell, were grouped to form seven regional holding companies, such as Bell-South.

The Modification of Final Judgment also included the provision that the local telephone companies must provide exchange access to all long distance carries (such as MCI and United States Sprint) "equal in type, quality, and price to that provided to AT&T and its affiliates." In order to provide "equal access," many telephone exchanges (central office switches) had to be replaced with digital technology switches. Northern Telecom was well positioned at that time for success in the U.S. central office switching market, having a product lead in digital switching and being able to compete in an open market driven by equal access.

Thus began an era for Northern known to some observers in the industry as "one of the great marketing successes of recent times." Northern's sales went from $2.7 billion U.S. in 1983 to $4.2 billion in 1985, and it ranked second only to AT&T.

NORTHERN'S PRODUCTS

HARDWARE

Northern Telecom's digital central office switching components fell into four categories: systems, remotes, extensions, and lines. "Systems" equated to digital central office switches. Northern had three versions collectively known as the DMS Family (Digital Multiplex System)—the DMS-100, the DMS-100/200, and the DMS-200. The DMS-100 handled local lines only, the DMS-100/200 handled both local lines and toll trunks (trunks were lines between offices carrying long distance traffic), and the DMS-200 handled toll trunks only. Each DMS system had a maximum capacity of 100,000 lines.

Exhibit 2 presents a picture of a DMS-100 switch and a line card. The switch contains numbers of these line cards, one per subscriber line. The software resident in the switch and each line card allows the "programming" of each telephone served by the switch to determine which centrex features that telephone will have.

Exhibits 3 and 4 show Northern Telecom's U.S. installed equipment base by customer type, by product category, and sales by year.

"Remotes" were digital switching units that extended central office features to remote areas. Northern's remotes ranged in size from 600 to 5,000 lines. Unlike central office systems which were housed in buildings, remotes were often constructed in environmentally controlled cabinets and placed outside on concrete platforms in areas away from central offices. In addition to extending central office features and services, most remotes had some "stand-

EXHIBIT 2   A NORTHERN TELECOM DMS-100 CENTRAL OFFICE SWITCH (TOP) AND A LINE CARD (BOTTOM)

Note: Each line card serves one telephone line.

EXHIBIT 3   NORTHERN TELECOM, INC.: DMS-100 FAMILY INSTALLED BASE BY CUSTOMER TYPE, AS OF YEAR-END 1987

CUSTOMER	SYSTEMS	REMOTES	EXTENSIONS	LINES (000'S)
Bell operating companies	658	248	1,106	9,841
Independent operating companies	434	1,303	1,120	5,686
Total U.S.	1,092	1,551	2,226	15,527

EXHIBIT 4   DMS-100 FAMILY U.S. SALES BY YEAR

YEAR	SYSTEM	REMOTES	EXTENSIONS	LINES (000'S)
1979	5			2
1980	13			75
1981	69	31	19	453
1982	51	86	41	492
1983	83	130	58	798
1984	116	210	152	1,379
1985	266	304	332	3,665
1986	235	359	604	3,962
1987	254	431	1,015	4,701
Total	1,092	1,551	2,226	15,527

Source: Northern Telecom data.

alone" capability (i.e., if the host central office switch went out of service for some reason, calls could still be made between customers being served by the same remote). Remotes also provided a cost savings in lines by performing a line concentrating function since all the subscribers who were served by a remote in a particular location were wired to the remote rather than to the central office. Thus, all the customers on the remote were served by a single pair of wires extending from the remote to the central office. Remotes could be located up to 150 miles away from their hosts.

"Extensions" represented hardware additions and software upgrades to existing Northern switches.

"Lines" were reported in thousands; thus, as of year-end 1987, NTI had over 15.5 million lines in service. A line represented the ability to serve one customer.

SOFTWARE

In addition to hardware, an important portion of Northern Telecom's product line was software. Northern Telecom's DMS switches were driven by both operating software (similar to DOS in a PC environment) and applications software performing specific functions (such as an accounting program to log and bill long distance calls). Centrex (originally an AT&T brand name) had become a generic term describing any central-office-based applications software package combining business-oriented voice, data networking, and control features bundled with intercom calling and offered to end users as a package. As a shared central-office-based service, centrex was designed to replace applications served by equipment located at the customer's premises, such as key telephone systems and private branch exchanges. As opposed to investing in telephone switching equipment, the customer simply paid the telephone company a monthly fee per centrex line for access to a multitude of sophisticated business voice and high-speed data features. Call Forwarding and Call Waiting were examples of centrex basic voice features that had been offered to the residential market. Contrex (as an AT&T brand offering) was widespread throughout the 22 local Bell System telephone companies prior to divestiture. Centrex (as a generic product) was a major source of revenue for the telephone operating companies. The companies billed the customers each month for the features they had selected for use in their telephone systems.

AT&T STRATEGY

In the late 1970s, AT&T began what was known as a "migration" strategy, urging business customers to a private branch exchange (on-site) solution for their telecommunications needs as opposed to a central-office-based solution. Implementation of this strategy, which was designed to "bypass" the local telephone companies, intensified during and following divestiture. Telephone companies were directly affected by this strategy, for end users began purchasing their own private branch exchanges directly from AT&T and other vendors, rather than paying the telephone company's monthly per-line fees for central-office-based business services. Telephone companies did not like this migration strategy since it threatened their revenues.

Northern Telecom introduced its digital centrex applications software and was able to capitalize on the resentment telephone companies felt towards AT&T. Meridian Digital Centrex (MDC), Northern's centrex software offering, was introduced in 1982, and sales grew significantly from 1985 to 1987. Exhibit 5 shows NTI's MDC statistics by customer type.

EXHIBIT 5   MERIDIAN DIGITAL CENTREX STATUS—USA, AS OF MARCH 26, 1988 (1Q88)

	IN-SERVICE		SHIPPED & IN-SERVICE		IN-SERVICE, SHIPPED, & FIRM ORDERS		
	Systems	*Lines*	*Systems*	*Lines*	*Systems*	*Lines*	*SRs*
Bell operating companies	594	1,610,166	696	1,956,973	757	2,087,921	44
Independent operating companies	265	292,633	280	387,810	288	401,299	6
Total U.S.	859	1,902,799	976	2,344,783	1,045	2,489,220	50

Numbers are cumulative across the page.

"SRs" = schedule requests; jobs not yet firm orders

Source: Northern Telecom data.

Telephone companies purchased Northern's MDC software for their DMS switches for the purpose of reselling to end users the business services features the applications software provided. The telephone companies often renamed the service for the purpose of developing brand identity and loyalty (much as in the same way Sears bought appliances made by Whirlpool and sold them under the Kenmore label). BellSouth, for example, used John Naismith, the author of *Megatrends,* to advertise centrex as ESSX service. Exhibit 6 provides a profile of some of the major MDC software end users by vertical markets served. Exhibit 7 provides a breakdown by line size of Northern's DMS systems that had MDC software.

FINANCIAL PERFORMANCE

Exhibit 8 is a consolidated review of the financial performance of Northern Telecom Limited and its subsidiaries during the period 1977–1987. As indicated, revenues for 1987 were $4.8 billion, up 11% from 1986. Net earnings for 1987 rose 15% to $329 million, up from $287 million in 1986.

As noted in the bottom portion of Exhibit 8, Northern Telecom Limited had five principal business areas, central office switching, integrated business systems and terminals, transmission, cable and outside plant, and other. Central office switching, Hall's division, accounted for $2.6 billion or 53% of total revenues in 1987.

The integrated business systems and terminals group sold on-premises customer equipment such as private branch exchanges, local area networks, data terminals, electronic and key telephone systems, residential telephones, and special applications telephone systems. Many of the products sold by the

EXHIBIT 6   MERIDIAN DIGITAL CENTREX MAJOR END USERS

VERTICAL MARKETS	# OF MAJOR MDC END USERS	EXAMPLE
Universities	35	Indiana University
Government		
Municipal	30	City of Las Vegas
State	20	Suncom (Florida)
Federal	11	Senate/White House
Major businesses	50	Ford Motor Company
Airports	15	Los Angeles Airport
Banks	27	Citicorp
Hospitals	16	Marquette Hospital
Telephone companies	11	NYNEX Headquarters

Source: Northern Telecom data.

EXHIBIT 7   MERIDIAN DIGITAL CENTREX LINE SIZE DISTRIBUTION

NUMBER OF MDC LINES	NUMBER OF INSTALLED SYSTEMS OF THIS SIZE
1–1,999	658
2,000–9,999	241
10,000+	71
MDC software, no lines	75
Total in-service, shipped, and on order through 1Q88	1,045

Source: Northern Telecom data.

business systems and terminals group were offered under the Meridian product line name.

The transmission group and cable and outside plant group sold digital subscriber carrier systems, microwave radio transmission systems, fiber optic systems and cable, and network management systems.

Exhibit 9 presents a summary of Northern's income statements by geographic area for the 1985 to 1987 period. Although sales outside of the U.S. and Canada represented only a small percentage of total sales, Northern had scored a major breakthrough in 1985 by landing a five-year, $250 million contract with Nippon Telegraph and Telephone (NTT) and becoming the first foreign company to sell switches to NTT.

NTL had 48,778 employees as of year-end 1987, and 1987 earnings per share were $1.39.

THE CHANGING MARKETPLACE

Hall felt that Northern's success through the 1980s had been driven by five major factors:

- a sustained product development lead in digital central office switching technology (AT&T did not introduce a digital central office switch until 1983);
- access to a huge market which had previously been restricted due to monopolistic constraints;
- a willingness in that new market to be served by a vendor other than AT&T (AT&T had moved from the position of supplier and parent organization to that of a competitor);
- equal access legislation requiring product replacement of old technology exchanges with new digital switches; and
- the ability to dilute the effect of AT&T's migration strategy on the Bell

operating companies by providing them with revenue-generating features in MDC applications software for the DMS.

Despite Northern's success, however, Hall realized that the marketplace was changing and that Northern needed to reconsider its strategy to respond to these changes.

AT&T's 5ESS

Demand for digital switches had exceeded supply in the early 1980s, and AT&T had not entered the digital switching marketplace until 1983 with the 5ESS switch. As a result, Northern Telecom had a substantial competitive lead in both product/feature development and in marketing its products to the telephone companies. AT&T had found itself in the unusual position of being an industry technology "follower" rather than the industry leader. Moreover, because of its monopoly position, AT&T had not been concerned previously with having to market its products.

Exhibit 10 compares Northern's DMS and AT&T's 5ESS shipments in half-year increments starting in 1985. Although only 13 of AT&T's 5ESS units were in service by the end of 1983, with an additional 72 being placed in service in 1984, pent-up demand in the telephone companies for additional products to help satisfy equal access requirements and the desire to have multiple suppliers helped sales of the 5ESS grow rapidly. Moreover, Northern experienced delivery problems in 1985 with one of its remote switch products and performance problems with a particular release of operating system software. Combined with the strong market demand for digital technology, these events helped to assure that AT&T's 5ESS would be a successful product. The U.S. telephone digital switching market became a two-supplier arena.

AT&T claimed to have 800 5ESS systems, 660 remotes, and 15 million lines in service as of September 1987 (these figures included some switches located outside the U.S. and some within the AT&T system itself). Northern Telecom had 1,092 systems, 1,551 remotes, and 15.5 million lines in service as of the end of 1987.

PRICING

Due to equal access, demand for digital switches exceeded supply from 1982 to 1986. During this period, delivery was the primary determinant of which vendor would be chosen. Volume sales agreements negotiated with each regional or local telephone company for multiple changeouts of old technology switches were the norm rather than the exception. Price was not a key selection criteria.

However, with supply exceeding the demand for digital switches from 1986 onward, the situation had become one of competitive bidding for each switch replacement, with bidding parties offering aggressive discounts. The objective was to win the initial system even at the sake of short-term profits,

EXHIBIT 8   CONSOLIDATED 11-YEAR REVIEW

NORTHERN TELECOM LTD. AND SUBSIDIARIES (MILLIONS OF DOLLARS)		1987
	EARNINGS AND RELATED DATA	
	Revenues	$4,853.5
	Cost of Revenues	2,895.8
	Selling, general, and administrative expense	917.8
	Research and development expense	587.5
	Depreciation on plant and equipment	264.1
	Provision for income taxes	141.5
	Earnings before extraordinary items	347.2
	Net earnings applicable to common shares	328.8
	Earnings per revenue dollar (cents)	6.8
	Earnings per common share (dollars)	
	—before extraordinary items	1.39
	—after extraordinary items	1.39
	Dividends per share (dollars)	0.23
	FINANCIAL POSITION AT DECEMBER 31	
	Working capital	570.7
	Plant and equipment (at cost)	2,345.6
	Accumulated depreciation	1,084.2
	Total assets	4,869.0
	Long-term debt	224.8
	Redeemable retractable preferred shares	153.9
	Redeemable preferred shares	73.3
	Common shareholders' equity	2,333.3
	Return on common shareholders' equity	15.6%
	Capital expenditures	416.7
	EMPLOYEES AT DECEMBER 31	48,778

QUARTERLY FINANCIAL DATA (UNAUDITED) (MILLIONS OF DOLLARS EXCEPT PER SHARE FIGURES)		1987
	Revenues	$1,299.1
	Gross Profit	584.9
	Net earnings	140.0
	Net earnings applicable to common shares	136.0
	Earnings per common share	0.57
	Weighted average number of common shares outstanding (thousands)	236,444

REVENUES BY PRINCIPAL PRODUCT LINES (MILLIONS OF DOLLARS)		1987
	Central office switching	$2,577.2
	Integrated business systems and terminals	1,302.0
	Transmission	498.6
	Cable and outside plant	408.2
	Other telecommunications	67.5
	Total	$4,853.5

EXHIBIT 8 (continued)

1986	1985	1984	1983	1981	1979	1977
$4,383.6	$4,262.9	$3,374.0	$2,680.2	$2,146.1	$1,625.5	$1,149.7
2,730.5	2,078.9	2,074.1	1,713.3	1,542.5	1,117.0	821.4
764.6	701.9	603.2	454.8	300.1	234.9	149.1
474.5	430.0	333.1	263.2	151.8	117.6	64.2
247.3	203.3	162.8	126.6	100.8	77.9	29.1
127.9	132.8	120.3	79.3	29.8	30.3	45.5
313.2	299.2	255.8	183.2	92.1	97.4	76.3
286.6	273.8	243.2	216.7	105.4	97.4	80.2
6.5	6.4	7.2	8.1	4.9	6.0	7.0
1.23	1.18	1.06	0.83	0.45	0.53	0.48
1.23	1.18	1.06	0.98	0.50	0.53	0.51
0.20	0.18	0.16	0.16	0.14	0.12	0.11
1,188.7	933.9	859.0	563.4	421.6	477.4	307.3
1,975.2	1,737.5	1,458.0	1,152.2	829.8	602.4	356.9
877.3	672.4	591.5	506.4	355.0	237.8	184.3
3,961.1	3,490.0	3,072.9	2,309.4	1,809.4	1,620.8	698.8
101.1	107.6	100.2	102.3	207.5	165.0	48.0
281.0	277.5	293.6	—	—	—	—
73.3	73.3	—	—	—	—	—
1,894.9	1,614.6	1,379.8	1,178.3	719.5	793.5	431.0
16.3%	18.3%	19.0%	21.7%	15.7%	14.6%	19.4%
303.8	457.3	437.3	305.7	174.9	148.4	42.1
46,202	46,549	46,993	39,318	35,444	33,301	24,962

4th QTR		3rd QTR		2nd QTR		1st QTR
1986	1987	1986	1987	1986	1987	1986
$1,314.4	$1,158.1	$1,032.2	$1,253.0	$1,067.4	$1,143.3	$969.6
536.1	479.1	404.5	489.9	389.4	403.8	323.1
132.2	69.5	66.0	77.6	64.9	60.1	50.1
125.9	66.2	59.4	72.9	58.0	53.7	43.3
0.54	0.28	0.25	0.31	0.25	0.23	0.19
234,767	236,024	234.199	235,573	223,650	235,237	233,154

1986	1985	1984	1983
$2,230.9	$2,141.3	$1,452.9	$981.9
1,284.7	1,256.6	1,162.9	985.8
468.1	431.2	385.1	376.3
348.4	373.4	314.9	275.5
51.5	60.4	58.9	60.7
$4,383.6	$4,262.9	$3,374.0	$2,680.2

EXHIBIT 9   NORTHERN TELECOM, LIMITED INCOME BY GEOGRAPHIC AREA, 1985–1987

	1987	1986	1985
Total Revenues			
United States	$3,103.0	$2,965.6	$2,967.3
Canada	2,140.3	1,771.1	1,792.8
Other	272.1	245.9	215.2
Less, inter-area transfers	(661.9)	(599.0)	(712.4)
Total Revenues	$4,853.5	$4,383.6	$4,262.9
Operating Earnings			
United States	$787.0	$674.2	$699.6
Canada	491.6	383.8	319.8
Other	(11.1)	18.8	12.0
Total Operating Earnings	$1,267.5	$1,076.8	$1,031.4
Less: Research and Development	($587.5)	($474.5)	($430.0)
Less: General Corporate Expenses	($227.6)	($188.3)	($179.3)
Net Operating Earnings	$452.4	$414.0	$422.1
Plus: Other Income	36.3	27.1	9.9
Earnings Before Tax	$488.7	$441.1	$432.0
Identifiable Assets			
United States	$1,807.2	$1,749.6	$1,868.2
Canada	1,297.5	1,189.3	1,389.8
Other	181.1	210.1	264.2
Corporate Assets*	332.4	460.3	204.6

Note: Dollars in millions.

*Corporate Assets are principally cash and short-term investments and corporate plant and equipment.

Source: Northern Telecom, Limited, *1987 Annual Report.*

EXHIBIT 10   NORTHERN DMS AND AT&T 5ESS SYSTEM SHIPMENTS BY HALF-YEAR

	NORTHERN	AT&T
1H85	144	169
2H85	145	141
1H86	108	152
2H86	139	144
1H87	128	135
2H87	127	130

Source: Northern Telecom data; AT&T estimates.

for winning the switch meant additional opportunities for revenue through software and hardware upgrades and extensions.

In 1987, the industry average price of a digital switch was estimated at $326 per line of capacity. However, discounts of up to 30% on this price were not uncommon. A switch with a 20,000 line capacity might be bid in the $4.5 million range. Switch prices ranged from $1 million to $10 million, with an average price of $2.5 million.

Hall had concerns that the discounts the vendors were offering often resulted in the winner leaving large sums of money on the table (e.g., coming in with a bid at $500,000 less than the next lowest competitor, when all that would have been necessary to win the switch was a $100,000 discount). Moreover, Hall did not want bids to be so low that the telephone companies would refuse to accept higher bids.

THE END OF EQUAL ACCESS

In addition to increased competition and pricing pressures from AT&T, other factors were affecting the market. With the completion of the equal access process, telephone company construction budgets were declining 3–4% annually. Along with the decline in capital budgets was a corresponding increase in the expense budgets. As a result of this shift, telephone companies were expected to allocate more budget dollars towards upgrading equipment and less towards the purchase of new switches.

THE ANALOG SWITCH REPLACEMENT MARKET

Following equal access, the next major determinant of growth in the U.S. telecommunications market was replacement of analog switches. These switches were analog stored program control (software driven) AT&T switches that were installed in the late 1960s and the 1970s. Exhibit 11 shows historical information and projections of the central office switch market by technology from 1986 through 1991. As indicated in Exhibit 11, analog switches accounted for 57 million lines of the total installed base in 1987, or 46% of the market, compared to a total of 36 million digital lines. The "Other" category represents older analog switches which were electro-mechanical switches (no software).

Numerous factors were involved in analog replacement, which was estimated to be a $30 billion market over the next 30 years. Unlike other switches that had to be replaced, analog switches had been upgraded to support equal access requirements since they were software driven. With depreciation service lives of 15–20 years, they would remain in the network until the early 1990s, assuming that the depreciation rates and regulatory positions did not change (switch replacement required approval from the appropriate state public utility commission). The latest versions of these switches offered a comprehensive set of centrex features, and they were large in terms of line size (30,000–55,000 lines). As such, a digital replacement switch would require both sufficient capacity and an equivalent set of centrex features.

EXHIBIT 11   CENTRAL OFFICE EQUIPMENT MARKET BY TECHNOLOGY TOTAL MARKET (THOUSANDS OF LINES)

	1986	1987	PROJECTED 1988	1989	1990	1991
Installed Base						
Digital	27,048	36,560	45,230	54,072	62,693	72,057
Analog	56,143	57,022	57,426	57,854	56,750	54,800
Other	38,175	31,322	25,613	19,826	15,933	12,293
Total	121,366	124,904	128,269	131,752	135,376	139,150
Percent						
Digital	22.3	29.3	35.3	41.0	46.3	51.8
Analog	46.3	45.6	44.8	43.9	41.9	39.4
Other	31.4	25.1	19.9	15.1	11.8	8.8
Demand						
Digital	10,066	9,508	8,670	8,844	8,620	9,365
Analog	1,591	881	417	429	36	0
Total	11,657	10,389	9,087	9,273	8,656	9,365
TOTAL BELL OPERATING COMPANIES						
Installed Base						
Digital	14,509	21,341	27,389	33,553	39,997	46,966
Analog	53,899	54,729	55,114	55,451	54,317	52,379
Other	25,246	20,114	15,998	11,891	9,077	6,648
Total	93,654	96,184	98,501	100,895	103,391	105,993
Percent						
Digital	15.5	22.2	27.8	33.3	38.7	44.3
Analog	57.6	56.9	56.0	55.0	52.5	49.4
Other	27.0	20.9	17.2	11.8	8.8	6.2
Demand						
Digital	6,904	6,832	6,048	6,165	6,443	6,969
Analog	1,530	830	385	338	0	0
Total	8,434	7,662	6,432	6,502	6,443	6,969
TOTAL DEPENDENT OPERATING COMPANIES						
Installed Base						
Digital	12,539	15,219	17,841	20,519	22,696	25,091
Analog	2,244	2,293	2,312	2,403	2,433	2,421
Other	12,929	11,208	9,615	7,935	6,856	5,645
Total	27,712	28,720	29,768	30,857	31,895	33,157
Percent						
Digital	45.2	53.0	59.9	66.5	71.0	75.7
Analog	8.1	7.9	7.8	7.8	7.6	7.3
Other	46.7	39.1	32.3	25.7	21.4	17.0
Demand						
Digital	3,162	2,676	2,622	2,679	2,177	2,396
Analog	61	51	32	91	36	0
Total	3,223	2,727	2.654	2,770	2,213	2,396

Source: Northern Business Information, *Central Office Equipment Market* (1987 edition).

540

These analog switches were usually housed in "wire centers," which were simply buildings that housed more than one type of central office switch and were typically located in high-growth metropolitan areas. Northern had a number of strategies to establish a presence in these wire centers in the hope that this initial presence would provide a competitive advantage when an analog switch became available for digital replacement. Other vendors were marketing adjuncts for the analog switches, which were enhancements designed to prolong their life, while these same vendors worked to develop competitive digital switches. As such, these adjuncts were basically "stopgap" measures designed to meet a particular need and to buy additional time for R&D switch development.

ISDN

Beyond the replacement of analog switches, the next phase of telecommunications technology was called ISDN (Integrated Services Digital Network). ISDN would allow the transmission of voice, data, and video simultaneously over the same facilities. With existing technology, voice, high-speed data, and video had to be transmitted separately or over separate lines. While business telecommunications in 1988 were 90% voice and 10% data, this ratio was predicted to move to 50%/50%. Cost, space, and time constraints would require that voice and data be integrated over one network.

ISDN would also allow standard interfaces between different pieces of equipment, such as computers; and it would free end users from concerns as to whether new equipment from one vendor would interface with equipment made by another vendor which an end user might already own.

Although universal standards for ISDN had yet to be resolved, useful applications were already apparent. Since ISDN phones were designed to display the calling number and the name assigned to the number on a small screen simultaneous with ringing, the party being called would be able to know where the call was coming from prior to answering. This call screening ability would provide opportunities to enhance 911 services (police, fire department, rescue squad, etc.) by immediately identifying the calling party's location and other useful information (such as a known medical condition or the location of the nearest fire hydrant) and by efficiently routing both the call and the information to all parties involved. A person served by ISDN could talk to her banker while looking at her account information on a computer terminal and send data instructions to move funds, simultaneously on the same line.

ISDN was flexible in that from any ISDN telephone jack, one could connect a computer terminal, personal computer, file server, printer, facsimile or telex machine, or video camera. Equipment could be moved to any location without having to worry if a specific kind of cable were available. The various pieces of equipment could share a common ISDN loop for data and voice transmission, reducing or eliminating the need for modems and multiplexers. Data on an ISDN network could be transmitted at a rate up to six times faster than standard analog networks but at a comparable cost.

Northern was positioning ISDN as its premier Meridian Digital Centrex software offering, since it offered both business voice features and high-speed data capabilities over a single line. Northern's strategy was to "migrate" end users from MDC to ISDN, stressing that existing MDC feature capabilities could serve customer needs today while ISDN standards and applications were being developed by industry regulatory organizations and other telecommunications equipment and computer vendors. In addition, MDC integrated with ISDN, with ISDN combining existing voice and data services while adding additional new features and sophisticated applications.

AT&T, on the other hand, had been advertising ISDN heavily to end users and was attempting to position it as a technologically superior *replacement* to centrex, rather than as a centrex enhancement. AT&T was pursuing this strategy since BRCS, its digital centrex offering, was perceived as being much less "feature-rich" than its analog centrex systems or Northern's Meridian Digital Centrex.

Northern Telecom placed the first successful ISDN phone call in the U.S. in November 1987, and had a number of DMS sites in service offering ISDN capabilities. In addition, both Northern Telecom and AT&T had numerous ISDN field trials and commercial applications scheduled with telephone companies and business end users throughout the country at specific sites during the 1988–1990 time frame.

COMPETITION

In addition to the changing market and technological environments, Northern faced a number of strong competitors. Replacement of analog switches and ISDN were two potential markets attracting other equipment companies into the U.S. digital central office telecommunications market. Also, most of the telephone companies were interested in having a third equipment supplier in addition to AT&T and Northern Telecom to ensure that pricing and product development remained highly competitive.

Another potential opportunity/threat for Northern was that the seven regional holding companies (RHCs) had petitioned Judge Green to lift the restrictions barring them from providing information services, going into the long distance business, and manufacturing terminals and central office switches through direct subsidiaries and/or joint ventures.

Finally, although the level of competition was increasing the number of competitors was actually decreasing. In 1979, there had been 30 major telecommunications equipment manufacturing companies in the developed world. Estimates were, however, that this number would decrease to 15 by 1989. Some experts estimated that a firm needed a 10% worldwide market share to survive. The worldwide telecommunications construction market was estimated to be $109 billion for 1988, up from $100 billion in 1987, with the U.S. accounting for 22% of this market.

Following is a discussion of some of Northern's competitors and the inroads each had made into the Bell operating companies.

SIEMENS

Siemens, a West German conglomerate, had sales of 8 billion DMs for its tele-communications segment in 1987 (sales for the entire company in 1987 were $20 billion U.S.). Seventy-three percent of Siemens' total sales for the year were from Germany and Europe, with 10% from North America.

The headquarters for Siemens' U.S. telecommunications division was in Boca Raton, Florida. An R&D facility was also located at Boca Raton, while manufacturing sites were located at Cherry Hill, New Jersey, and Hauppauge, New York. Siemens had 25,000 employees in the U.S.

Siemens' digital central office offering was the EWSD. It was available in three versions: DE3, with a maximum capacity of 7,500 lines; DE4, with a maximum capacity of 30,000 lines; and DE5, with a maximum capacity of 100,000 lines.

Siemens had announced ambitious feature roll-out plans for its offerings, promising both Centrex and ISDN feature parity with both AT&T and Northern Telecom. However, whether it could effectively leapfrog the software development intervals incurred by the industry leaders remained to be seen.

Siemens had made inroads with five of the seven RHCs: Ameritech, Bell-South, Bell Atlantic, NYNEX, and Southwestern Bell. Siemen's progress had been based primarily on both competitive pricing and the desire of the Bell Operating Companies to increase competition in the central office switch market.

In spite of its recent success, industry consultants cited operational/maintenance problems with the EWSD regarding system reliability, architecture, and compliance to Bellcore standards (Bell Communications Research, or "Bellcore," was a standards organization jointly owned by the seven RHCs.) However, heavy R&D efforts were under way to resolve these issues at Boca Raton, and Siemens was fully committed to adapting its products to U.S. market specifications.

Siemens had a $2.1 million contract with West Virginia University to develop computer-based training courses in the operation of EWSD central office equipment. In terms of joint ventures and acquisitions, the company purchased 80% of GTE's foreign transmissions operations in 1986.

ERICSSON

Ericsson, a Swedish-based telecommunications company, had consolidated international sales of $5.5 billion U.S. in 1987. Europe and Sweden accounted for 84% of the geographic distribution of total sales for the year, with the U.S. and Canada contributing 7%. Like Siemens, Ericsson was attempting to crack the hold that Northern Telecom and AT&T shared on the U.S. central office switch market. Ericsson had targeted the Bell Operating Company market in BellSouth, NYNEX, Southwestern Bell, and US West.

Ericsson's digital central office offering was the AXE 10. Ericsson had already installed the AXE in 64 countries, had a worldwide installed base of over 11 million lines, and dominated markets in the developing world. Like Siemens, Ericsson had announced aggressive feature roll-out plans (bypassing years of software development by AT&T Technologies and Bell-Northern Research) which it might not be able to deliver.

The AXE was manufactured in 16 countries and was being made available by Ericsson's Network Systems Division in Richardson, Texas. No plans were under way to construct manufacturing facilities for the AXE in the U.S., although Ericsson was considered to have superior skills in setting up manufacturing plants in foreign countries and training local workers for skilled jobs.

Ericsson had made a number of recent strategic moves intended to strengthen its position in the U.S. The company had reorganized by regions to serve more effectively the RHC markets; moreover, it had reorganized marketing for the division into the functional areas of market development, marketing communications, systems engineering, and marketing systems. Plans had been announced for a technical training center at the company's U.S. headquarters in Richardson, Texas. In addition, Ericsson had announced that it would be working with IBM to develop private networking capabilities.

NEC

NEC had $13 billion in sales in U.S. dollars for 1987, $4 billion of which was from its "communications" segment. Geographic sales distribution percentages were classified as "domestic" (Japan) at 67% and "overseas" at 33%.

NEC's digital central office offering was the NEAX61E. The switch was primarily an ISDN adjunct that interfaced analog systems and grew into a full central office. As such, it was basically an interim offering that was designed to extend the life of analog switches while buying time to improve the product in the hopes of having a competitive offering ready when analog replacement began. NEC claimed that the NEAX61 was serving 4.8 million lines in over 250 sites in 40 countries.

NEC's U.S. headquarters was located in Irving, Texas, where production of the system was scheduled to begin by mid-1988. NEC had made inroads with four of the seven RHCs—Bell Atlantic, NYNEX, Pacific Telesis, and US West.

The company had recently announced plans for a switching technology center in Irving, Texas, dedicated to developing software for central office switches and customer premises equipment. A second facility in San Jose, California, would develop software for intelligent transport networks, transmission systems, data communications, and network management systems. NEC claimed that it was moving its software development closer to its customers.

A major problem that NEC had to overcome was one of perception. NEC's first attempt to enter the U.S. market with the NEAX61 in the early 1980s met with little success. The product was highly touted, launched, and subsequently withdrawn due to numerous performance issues. Many industry experts felt that NEC was again entering the market prematurely with a product that was not powerful enough to meet U.S. requirements to support advanced business features or large capacities.

STROMBERG-CARLSON

Stromberg-Carlson was a division of Plessy, a British telecommunications corporation. Plessy had 1987 revenues of $2.45 billion from all product lines. Because Stromberg was a division, reliable data on its 1987 financial performance was not available. Stromberg-Carlson's product offering was the DCO (Digital Central Office). It was available in three versions: the DCO-CS, which was a toll version of the DCO (7,000 trunks maximum); the DCO-SE (a 1,080 line switch designed to serve as a rural central office); and the DCO (32,000 lines maximum). In addition, Stromberg-Carlson offered a full line of remotes, ranging in size from 90 lines to 10,000 lines.

Unlike Siemens, Ericsson, and NEC, Stromberg-Carlson had been a player in the U.S. telecommunications marketplace for a number of years. Stromberg was a primary supplier to the independent operating companies and was committed to maintaining strong ties with them. Stromberg's strategy was to target small-to-mid-size central offices (5,000–12,000 lines), focusing on rural applications. While Stromberg's lack of a large switch limited the market it could address, its niche strategy had served it well over the years in that it could economically provide digital central capabilities in small line sizes.

However, Stromberg was now trying to crack the Bell Operating Company market as well. The company had made inroads with BellSouth and Pacific Telesis and had recently signed a volume supply agreement with South Central Bell for the 1989–1990 time frame.

Stromberg-Carlson's U.S. headquarters and DCO manufacturing facility were located in Lake Mary, Florida (a suburb of Orlando). While Stromberg stated that it had a manufacturing capacity of 1 million lines per year at the Lake Mary facility, less than half of this capability was being used.

In response to its agreement with South Central Bell, Stromberg-Carlson had recently opened sales offices in Birmingham, Alabama. The company had a small installation force and was negotiating with AT&T to arrange to install some of its switches in South Central Bell.

Stromberg-Carlson shipped its 1,000th remote in December 1987, and placed its two millionth line in service in January 1988. Two hundred switches, 400 remotes, and 400,000 lines were shipped by Stromberg-Carlson to the U.S. market in 1987.

ALCATEL N.V.

Alcatel was established in France in 1985 as a subsidiary of Alcatel S.A. In December 1986, the firm's present name was adopted with the transfer of assets from its parent, Compagnie General d'Electricité (CGE). At the same time, CGE and International Telephone and Telegraph (ITT) combined their telecommunications activities with ITT assuming 37% ownership of Alcatel. Alcatel offered digital switches, cable and fiber optic transmission networks, and radio and satellite transmission systems. 1986 sales were 10.6 million French francs.

The ITT deal allowed Alcatel to gain a position in West Germany, Italy, and Spain. While Alcatel had been insignificant in the world telecommunications market, the arrangement with ITT set the stage for it to become a major equipment manufacturer. Alcatel's strengths in transmission facilities offset ITT's weakness in this area. ITT contributed a dominant position in switching in the European market. Although the acquisition introduced Alcatel to the U.S. market due to ITT's presence, it was not clear what effect this would have on the U.S. market. ITT had been working unsuccessfully for several years to develop a switch for the U.S. market.

CONCLUSION

Musing over the status of Northern's potential competitors, Hall Miller's gaze returned to the magazine on his desk. Overall, the *Communications Week* study

EXHIBIT 12   SUMMARY OF VENDOR PERFORMANCE RANKINGS BY BELL OPERATING COMPANY RESPONDENTS (N = 497)

	AT&T	ERICSSON	NEC	NORTHERN TELECOM	SIEMENS	STROMBERG-CARLSON
Initial Cost	3.12	3.37	3.42	3.83	3.51	3.76
Life Cycle Cost	3.55	3.26	3.29	3.53	3.48	3.26
Strength of Financial Backing	4.66	3.48	3.74	4.24	4.05	3.05
Availability	3.90	3.36	3.29	4.17	3.40	3.56
Service/Support	4.07	3.21	2.97	3.39	3.22	3.50
Reliability	4.06	3.31	3.08	3.52	3.47	3.24
Delivery	3.76	3.18	2.80	3.71	3.21	3.39
Experience in Industry	4.88	3.97	3.34	4.29	3.78	3.91
High Technology Company	4.63	3.77	3.69	4.28	4.08	3.23
Sound Technical Documentation	4.32	3.24	2.67	3.50	3.37	3.10
Breadth of Product Line	4.07	3.24	3.14	3.90	3.33	2.80
International Experience	3.19	4.08	3.83	3.58	4.20	2.64
Long-Term Commitment to R&D	4.44	3.81	3.83	3.99	3.91	3.04

Scale of 1–5; 5 = excellent, 1 = poor

Source: "The Central Office Switch Study," *Communications Week*, April 1987.

EXHIBIT 13   SUMMARY OF VENDOR PERFORMANCE RANKINGS BY INDEPENDENT OPERATING COMPANY RESPONDENTS (N = 1,047)

	AT&T	ERICSSON	NEC	NORTHERN TELECOM	SIEMENS	STROMBERG-CARLSON
Initial Cost	2.40	2.67	3.70	3.67	3.12	3.96
Life Cycle Cost	3.24	2.74	3.17	3.71	3.04	3.61
Strength of Financial Backing	4.65	3.31	3.69	4.34	3.65	3.50
Availability	3.56	2.61	3.22	4.06	2.93	4.03
Service/Support	3.79	2.81	2.98	3.81	3.02	3.75
Reliability	4.23	2.80	3.41	4.08	3.25	3.63
Delivery	3.46	2.61	3.16	3.83	2.91	3.80
Experience in Industry	4.74	3.27	3.55	4.58	3.62	4.19
High Technology Company	4.72	3.35	3.93	4.45	3.84	3.72
Sound Technical Documentation	4.47	2.78	2.95	4.08	3.32	3.63
Breadth of Product Line	4.16	2.83	3.43	4.12	3.27	3.47
International Experience	3.84	3.48	4.04	3.84	4.03	3.27
Long-Term Commitment to R&D	4.67	3.21	3.80	4.29	3.69	3.57

Scale of 1–5; 5 = excellent, 1 = poor

Source: "The Central Office Switch Study," *Communications Week,* April 1987.

had given Northern high marks relative to most of the competitors. However, there were shortcomings in particular areas he wanted to address. (Exhibits 12 and 13 contain the results of the study, segmented by Bell and independent operating company respondents.

In terms of the changing market and increased competition, Hall felt Northern had a competitive advantage in that the company had the largest installed base of digital switches of any vendor. This would help generate revenue through hardware and software extensions and new features prior to the replacement of analog switches. However, Hall had seen AT&T's 5ESS shipments reach parity in a relatively short period of time, and it seemed that competitors were popping up everywhere. In addition, 1988 MDC sales had been sluggish. Hall felt this was largely due to customer confusion resulting from AT&T's hype of ISDN.

Hall glanced out the window towards the Raleigh-Durham Airport. It was 5:20 P.M., and the highway was packed with traffic. He decided that he would develop a presentation for the regional marketing managers which outlined the division's position and presented a number of possible changes in the marketing strategy that the division could consider. This would generate discussion and help the group focus on the options that needed more in-depth study before a decision could be made.

Hall closed the magazine and placed it, along with several other pieces of information that had been gathered for him, in his briefcase. Despite the traffic and the work, he had to get home in time for his daughter's 6 P.M. soccer game. Perhaps he would be able to work on his analysis after supper.

TEXAS AIR CORPORATION

BOBBY G. BIZZELL AND
ROBERT L. ANDERSON

It was early April 1988. Under government regulatory pressure from Congress, the Transportation Department began a safety investigation of Texas Air Corporation. The Federal Aviation Administration (FAA) and the Transportation Department began a maintenance inspection of Texas Air's Continental Airline unit as part of an overall "fitness" study of Texas Air, including its financial and management practices. This inspection followed the FAA's fining of Eastern Air Lines, another subsidiary of Texas Air, $863,000 for maintenance and safety violations. Eastern and Continental together account for roughly 20 percent of the nation's available airline seats.[1]

Apart from the concerns about safety, the Transportation Department also investigated Texas Air's complex financial structure. Monetary transactions between Texas Air, Eastern, and Continental raised questions whether substantial funds and other resources were being diverted from the air carrier subsidiaries. The Transportation Department order said Texas Air may have siphoned so much cash from its airline subsidiaries that it ran the risk of leaving the carriers without the financial resources necessary for assuring safe and adequate air transportation.[2]

The regulator's investigation of Texas Air's financial structure followed a lawsuit in which Texas Air Corporation accused two labor unions (Air Line Pilots Association and International Association of Machinists) of leading an illegal conspiracy to destroy its Eastern Air Lines subsidiary. Texas Air Corporation sought $1.5 billion in damages.

Texas Air Corporation is a traditional holding company with 40 employees, very similar to holding companies of other airlines and other United States corporations. The company has grown through expansion of its subsidiaries in the constantly changing environment brought about by airline deregulation. The chief executive officer and chairman of the board of Texas Air

---

Source: **Prepared by Professor Bobby G. Bizzell, University of Houston–Downtown, and Professor Robert L. Anderson, College of Charleston, as a basis for classroom discussion and not to illustrate either effective or ineffective handling of administrative situation.** © **Bobby G. Bizzell, 1990.**

Corporation is 48-year-old Francisco A. Lorenzo. Lorenzo and his company have always maintained that they conduct internal transactions at arm's length, and that their overriding goal is to build airlines.[3]

HISTORY OF THE FIRM

Texas Air Corporation was incorporated on June 11, 1980, in Delaware as a holding company to acquire Texas International Airlines, Inc. Its present title was adopted on May 28, 1981.

Francisco A. Lorenzo is the founder of Texas Air Corporation. His first job in the airline industry was as a financial analyst for Trans World Airlines in 1963. Six years later, he was running his own acquisition firm, looking for an airline to buy. By 1972 Lorenzo acquired a small airline called Texas International which served primarily the Southwest region of the United States.

In 1978, after Lorenzo stemmed the losses at Texas International (TI), he surprised the airline industry by trying to acquire National Airlines, a company ten times the size of TI. As of June 1979, TI held an aggregate of 2,100,000 shares (24.6 percent) of National Airlines stock at an aggregate cost of $59,211,501. In August 1979 Pan American Airlines agreed to various proposals to acquire the entire 24.6 percent interest. The final sale was completed on December 31, 1979, for a transaction total of $108 million.

On October 31, 1982, the operations of Continental Air Lines, Inc. and Texas International Airlines, Inc. were combined under the name "Continental Airlines." Less than a year later, Continental Airlines temporarily suspended domestic operations and filed voluntary petitions for reorganization under Chapter 11 of the Federal Bankruptcy Code in Bankruptcy Court. Continental's plan of reorganization was confirmed by Bankruptcy Court and became effective on September 2, 1986. In the same year while Texas Air operated Continental Airlines and New York Air, it began pursuing other acquisitions including Frontier Airlines, People's Express, and Eastern. On February 1, 1987, Texas Air merged New York Air, Frontier Airlines, and People's Express into Continental. This overnight merger was not free of difficulties. There were too many aircraft types, crews were unfamiliar with the equipment on which they were flying, and scheduling problems resulting in flights sitting on the ground because they did not have a full flight crew.[4] At this time, Continental led the industry in complaints (see Exhibit 1), and its competitors began running advertisements similar to one of American Airlines', which featured a drawing of a flying garbage can.

On November 25, 1986, Eastern Air Lines, Inc. became a wholly owned subsidiary of Texas Air Corp. Lorenzo acquired Eastern for $600 million and then brought its profitable operations closer to Miami, Florida, its home base. The first divestment was Eastern's computer-reservation subsidiary, System One Direct Access, Inc., which in 1986 generated $225 million in cash profits. System One manages and coordinates the marketing and computer processing system owned by System One Direct Access, Inc., EAR Automation Systems,

EXHIBIT 1 COMPLAINTS AGAINST MAJOR AIR CARRIERS

AIRLINES	COMPLAINTS IN 1987 (PER 100,000 PASSENGERS)
Continental	27.32
Northwest	15.70
Pan Am	12.39
Eastern	11.77
TWA	11.75
Hawaiian	7.25
United	6.35
Braniff	5.18
Midway	4.86
American	3.83
American West	3.32
USAir	3.10
Piedmont	2.62
Delta	2.07
Pacific Southwest	1.60
Alaska	1.57
Southwest	1.43
Aloha	0.54

Source: *Dallas Times Herald* (October 7, 1989): A-15.

Inc. (which are wholly owned subsidiaries of Eastern), and CCS Automation System (a wholly owned subsidiary of System One). This reservation system was installed in over 6,750 travel agencies nationwide. Eastern's own investment bankers had valued part of the system at between $200 million to $320 million, but Texas Air paid Eastern $100 million for the entire system. Texas Air paid with a note bearing interest of 6.5 percent, payable in 2001. The $100 million valuation and method of payment were approved by one appraisal firm and two major investment houses. The Texas Air note was convertible upon issuance into Texas Air stock. This issue was similar to securities that had previously been issued publicly and were routinely traded on the public market.

Texas Air combined System One with CCS Automation System, a system it had picked up from Continental a year earlier for $15 million. CCS provided computer reservations, flight planning, weather, and related services to domestic and international airlines and others in the travel industry. It also provided computerized support of aircraft maintenance, parts inventory, accounting, and frequent traveler programs. As a direct unit of Texas Air, System One became the third-ranked and fastest-growing reservation system in the travel-agent market.

In 1988, System One drew funds from Continental and Eastern that the airlines used to pay to themselves. These included a fee of $1.65 for each airline reservation plus other fees, totalling about $120 million a year in Eastern's case alone. A Texas Air spokesman declined to say what income, if any, the parent company drew from this unit, and the financial statements fail to reveal any additions of capital by the parent.[5] System One accumulated $64 million of its own debt. In the short period it had been owned by Texas Air, its net income was $2 million. This income was welcomed by Lorenzo's subsidiary companies. (See Exhibit 2.)

In September 1983 Lorenzo placed the company in Chapter 11 bankruptcy, in order to revoke all the carrier's expensive union contracts and cut salaries by as much as 70 percent.[6] As the acquirer of financially troubled Eastern, he began a showdown with the union that represents its mechanics and ground crews. In current contracts with Eastern machinists, he is looking at wage cuts of as much as 60 percent.[7]

CURRENT CONDITIONS

Mr. Lorenzo has maintained control of his $8-billion-a-year enterprise through a special class of supervoting stock held by his personal holding company, Jet Capital Corporation. With only one percent of the equity of Texas Air, it has 34 percent voting control. Nevertheless, Lorenzo is inclined to believe that the goal of the current leadership of the International Association of Machinists (IAM) has been to take over the company. In the most recent suit, the machinists union sued Eastern and Texas Air Corp. claiming they had begun a campaign to strip Eastern of valuable assets.[8] The suit alleges that certain stock that Eastern employee trusts owned (acquired in exchange for wage concessions in 1984) gave them standing as shareholders to block the transfer of assets. The lawsuit also cited the sale of Eastern's reservation system (System One) to another Texas Air unit, arguing that the transaction deprived the company of future revenue and also charged that the price Texas Air paid was significantly below fair market value. Since Texas Air acquired Eastern in 1986, Eastern unions have been locked in a war over wages and costs. Eastern had been scaling down in size and shuffling assets until two recent, significant union victories in court. One decision blocked the sale of Eastern's East Coast Shuttle Service to a new unit of Texas Air, and the other undercut strike preparations under way at Eastern by barring the airline from contracting with outside pilots until a strike occurs.

Meanwhile, with support from the unions and encouragement from the rival carriers, some 150 congressmen called for an investigation of Texas Air.[9] The Transportation Department agreed to the investigation only after the Federal Aviation Administration fined Eastern $863,000 for safety violations. These FAA violations did not put lives at risk though, because after inspecting all of Eastern's 267 planes, 43 were temporarily ordered out of service for reasons ranging from fuel leaks to cut tires to a brake problem. No serious maintenance errors were cited, in fact in Mr. Lorenzo's 17 years as an airline

EXHIBIT 2 THE HOUSE THAT FRANK LORENZO BUILT

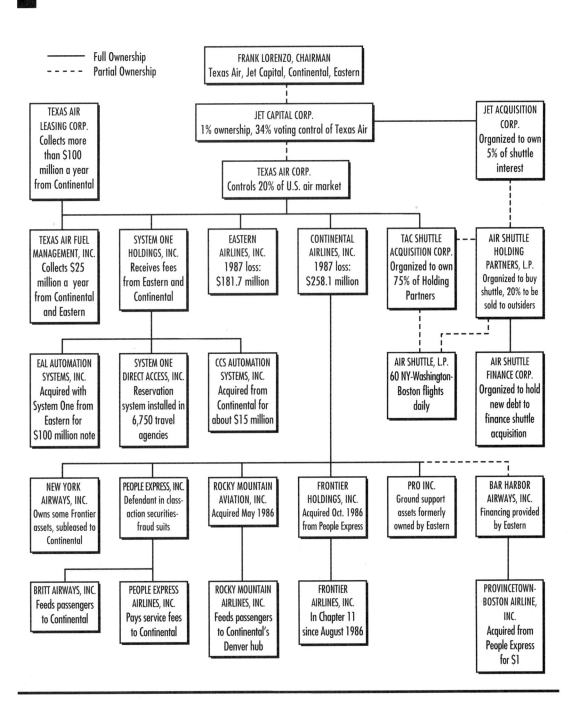

EXHIBIT 3   TEXAS AIR CORPORATION: COMPARATIVE BALANCE SHEET

	1986	1985	1984	1983	1982	1981	1980
				YEARS ENDED DECEMBER 31			
ASSETS							
Cash & Cash Investments	1,211,053	656,879	223,098	151,800	106,271	132,317	154,431
Receivables	715,685	225,756	189,890	99,154	157,335	160,911	29,481
Inventories	284,729	52,516	32,794	28,629	34,625	43,484	7,121
Other Current	99,098	42,350	40,305	24,872	28,160	15,837	4,457
Total Current Assets	2,310,565	977,501	486,087	304,455	326,391	352,549	195,490
Net Property Value & Equip.	5,383,790	887,404	801,517	848,051	928,358	936,496	158,507
Other Assets	500,256	71,433	36,759	25,453	20,409	12,271	58,420
Total Assets	8,194,611	1,936,338	1,324,363	1,177,959	1,275,158	1,301,316	412,417
LIABILITIES							
Current Liabilities	2,275,894	404,582	252,425	135,832	415,956	405,002	82,871
Long Term Debt	3,337,901	545,435	217,518	259,212	515,948	605,001	196,238
Other Liability	1,776,947	811,164	881,241	855,116	279,777	250,860	48,304
Total Liabilities	7,090,742	1,821,181	1,351,184	1,250,160	1,211,681	1,260,863	327,413
EQUITY							
Retained Earnings	(55,399)	(118,719)	(204,154)	(246,112)	(58,758)	(8,419)	40,145
Other Equity	859,268	233,876	177,333	173,911	122,235	48,872	44,859
Total Equity	803,869	115,157	(26,821)	(72,201)	63,477	40,453	85,004
Total Liability & Equity	8,194,611	1,936,338	1,324,363	1,177,959	1,275,158	1,301,316	412,417

Note: Amounts given in thousands.

EXHIBIT 4 INCOME STATEMENT OF TEXAS AIR CORPORATION

	YEARS ENDED DECEMBER 31						
	1986	1985	1984	1983	1982	1981	1980
INCOME							
Operating Revenues	4,406,897	1,944,190	1,371,702	1,246,215	1,516,320	719,400	291,496
Operating Expenses	3,891,936	1,691,140	1,182,726	1,297,723	1,467,870	716,083	269,421
Depreciation & Amortization	277,583	88,087	81,776	84,364	94,419	44,163	15,528
Total Operating Expenses	4,169,519	1,779,487	1,264,502	1,382,087	1,562,289	760,246	284,949
Operating Income (Loss)	237,378	164,703	107,200	(135,872)	(45,969)	(40,846)	6,547
Other Income & Expense:							
Debt Expense	306,996	106,515	91,393	78,104	97,833	60,579	19,650
Interest Income	77,373	34,200	19,370	10,319	10,726	19,615	15,412
Equity in Losses of Eastern & People	(29,316)	—	—	—	—	—	—
Other Income (Net)	42,262	11	15,160	25,793	80,968	29,832	4,311
Total Other Expenses (or Income)	158,045	72,326	56,863	41,992	6,139	11,132	(73)
Net Income Before Taxes	79,333	92,377	50,337	(177,864)	(52,108)	(51,978)	6,620
Income Tax less Credits	6,630	1,396	-0-	-0-	(3,133)	(4,793)	2,630
Net Income	72,703	90,981	50,337	(177,864)	(48,975)	(47,185)	3,990

Note: Amounts given in thousands.

chief executive, his carriers have suffered just one fatal accident. Nevertheless, the publicity surrounding the FAA's special safety inspection of the airline caused a drop in Eastern's bookings between April 15–20, 1988.[10]

Texas Air Corporation reported a consolidated first quarter (1988) net loss of $124.3 million, the holding company's fifth consecutive unprofitable quarter. The company reported an operating profit of $1 million for the quarter on revenues on $2.1 billion. These results include Continental, Eastern, and System One.

In the first quarter of 1987, Texas Air reported a loss of $100.7 million on revenues of $2 billion. The company reported an operating profit of $51.8 million in the first quarter of 1986.

Although Texas Air made small profits on its operations, the cost servicing the company's $5 billion debt has kept them in the red. (See Exhibits 3 and 4.)

On May 6, 1988, the same day that Eastern announced it suffered an operating loss in the first quarter, Texas Air Corp. along with Eastern filed suit against the unions representing the airline's pilots, mechanics, and baggage handlers. The lawsuit, filed in federal court in Miami, Florida, alleged that the Air Line Pilots Association (ALPA) and the International Association of Machinists (IAM) were attempting to gain ownership and control of Eastern and in the process damage the company's reputation. The unions had been trying to buy Eastern since before Texas Air acquired Eastern. The IAM represents about 12,000 Eastern employees, including mechanics, baggage handlers, aircraft cleaners, and other ground service personnel. ALPA represents 3,600 pilots at Eastern. The lawsuit sought $1.5 billion in damages.

When asked to describe his vision of Texas Air five years from now, Lorenzo said: "I foresee a company that is very responsive to its customers and its employees—one of the most competitive companies in the business. I also see a company that will be profitable. It's not going to have its debt levels vanish overnight, however. It will still be substantially leveraged."[11]

INDUSTRY NOTES

The flying public has agreed on the need for the government to ensure that travelers are safe when they fly. The allegations of safety deficiencies at Eastern and Continental have implanted fear and uncertainty in the traveling public. Until the allegations were resolved, a few travelers decided to avoid flying on Eastern or Continental which imposed a financial hardship on Texas Air.

It is important for the flying public to understand the circumstances that surround the questions raised regarding the safety and efficiency of not only Eastern and Continental, but of all major U.S. airlines. The question of air safety stems from 1978 when the government deregulated the airline industry. The purpose of deregulating the airlines was to get the government out of the business of protecting the industry from competition. Deregulation brought air travelers the benefits of price competition, offered travelers a wider range of price and quality options, forced the airlines to achieve improvements in efficiency, and exerted downward pressure on inflated wages. At the same time however, congestion and delays clearly increased and travelers complaints rose. (See Exhibit 5.) Many industry critics claim deregulation was a failure.[12] On the contrary, the enormous response of travelers to the availability of these new options is a justification, not a condemnation, of deregulation.

When Congress deregulated the industry in 1978, the airlines carried only 275 million domestic passengers per year—a number that the nation's airports, airlines, and air-traffic control system could easily handle. In 1988, U.S. airlines will carry about 475 million travelers, and by 1995, the number will soar to over 600 million.[13] The crowding has contributed to service problems ranging from late departures to lost baggage. At the same time, the crowded skies have put a heavy strain on the air-traffic control system which was not built to handle such volume. While some critics say airline safety has eroded and travelers are subjected to delays and inconveniences due to deregulation, if the airlines were regulated there would not be discount fares or the service that has allowed millions of people to fly more often.[14]

The U.S. Department of Transportation requires all airlines to provide "report cards" showing how well or how poorly they serve the public. Carriers must report how often their flights depart late, how frequently they mishandle baggage, and other similar information. This information, with the assistance of the government could provide the flying public the facts needed to make choices in carriers.

Before airline deregulation, airline labor contracts were easy to negotiate. Air carriers consented to most union demands and passed the costs of those demands along to travelers in the form of higher air fares. Now that the days of the regulated industry are over, new competitive pressures have causes industry and labor to collide.[15] In the course of the Eastern dispute, labor leaders have depicted Lorenzo as a "union buster" and enemy of organized labor.[16] Much rides on the outcome at Eastern. A Lorenzo victory might break the

EXHIBIT 5   WHAT MAKES AIR PASSENGERS MAD

Flight delays	45.5%
Lost or delayed baggage	15.6%
Bad service	12.2%
Refunds for lost tickets	6.7%
Ticketing mistakes	6.0%
Overbooking	4.9%
Fares	2.0%
Smoking	1.9%
Other	5.2%

Source: Dallas Times Herald (October 7, 1989): A-15.

arrangements in which major airlines have been able to pass on to travelers the mounting costs of baggage handlers and pilots. Would a Lorenzo defeat preserve organized labor's ability to maintain wage patterns set before deregulation? Would it prevent Texas Air from serving as the industry price leader, looking for market share by keeping fares low?

While the dispute and investigation of Texas Air continues, major competitors are taking advantage of the situation. In New York, Pan Am's East Coast Shuttle Service, which competes directly with Eastern, had record traffic during Eastern's safety inspection. In fact, Pan Am's share of the East Coast Shuttle market grew, hitting a record 47 percent. Carl Icahn, CEO of Trans World Airlines announced a major thrust into Florida and expansion of international routes. This announcement was triggered by Eastern cutting its international routes from Florida. Delta Air Lines, Inc. and United Airlines, Inc. recorded impressive profits during the first quarter of 1988. Delta earned $56.1 million for the quarter ended March 31, 1988, or $1.15 a share, a 113-percent increase over the $26.4 million it earned in the same quarter in 1987. United Airlines had a first quarter profit of $27.9 million or 58 cents per share, compared with a loss of $54.5 million or $1.07 per share in the same period a year earlier. The impact of the investigation of Texas Air may have contributed to this significant increase in profits. In Denver where United and Continental compete head-to-head, United's market share rose sharply. As Hartsfield International Airport in Atlanta where Delta is based, Eastern announced a reduction by 29 flights which will leave it with 282 flights beginning June 1, 1988. Delta anticipated an increase in traffic as a result. Of course Texas Air is competing fiercely for its market share. Continental offered low off-peak fares on certain days and also reduced the advance purchase requirements from fourteen days to three days. These fare reductions were matched by American Airlines, Delta Air Lines, and United Airlines in markets in which they compete with Continental.

In conclusion, the 30-day federal investigation of Texas Air ended with the Department of Transportation's final report stating that Eastern and Continental both considered safety and reliability essential to succeed in business. The FAA inspected each aircraft an average of five times each, and not a single plane was grounded. In efforts to publicize the investigation, Texas Air featured full-page advertisements welcoming the inspection. Now that the investigation is over, Texas Air is eager to let the public know that they passed the safety and performance tests with flying colors.

ENDNOTES

1. Bock, Gordon, "Air Follies," *Time* (April 25, 1988): 60.

2. Davis, Bob, "U.S. Regulators Are Investigating Texas Air's Fitness to Run Carriers," *Wall Street Journal* (April 14, 1988): 3.

3. Ibid.

4. Hamilton, Martha M., "A Tale of Two Airlines: Texas Air, USAir Survive at Different Speeds," *Washington Post* (May 22, 1988): H7.

5. Petzinger, Thomas, and Paulette Thomas, "Lorenzo's Texas Air Keeps Collecting Fees From Its Ailing Units," *Wall Street Journal* (April 7, 1988): 14.

6. DeMott, John S., "Kind Words for Continental," *Time* (January 12, 1987): 30.

7. Bock, "Air Follies.

8. Thomas, Paulette "Texas Air Unit Sued by Union Over Eastern Assets," *Wall Street Journal* (April 1, 1988): 25.

9. Bushwhacking Texas Air," *New York Times* (April 15, 1988): 10.

10. McGinley, Laurie, and Paulette Thomas, "Eastern Air Says FAA Safety Checks Have Caused 'Slight Drop' in Bookings," *Wall Street Journal* (April 20,1988): 6.

11. Lorenzo, Frank, "Lorenzo Holds His Course for Texas Air," *Wall Street Journal* (May 12, 1988): 6.

12. Crandall, Robert, "Bringing Back Federal Restraints Would Be a Giant Step Backward," *Dallas Times Herald* (October 7, 1987): A13.

13. Ibid.

14. Kahn, Alfred, "The Effect of Deregulation is Precisely as Intended," *Dallas Times Herald* (October 7, 1987): A13.

15. Magnuson, Ed, "Be Careful Out There," *Time* (January 12. 1987): 25.

16. Fields, Jack, "Unfair to Texas Air and Houston," *Houston Chronicle* (May 13, 1988): 31.

EASTMAN KODAK COMPANY: THE STERLING DRUG ACQUISITION

DAVID W. GRIGSBY AND
CHARLES G. CARTER

By any measure one cares to choose, Eastman Kodak Company is one of the premier success stories of American business. Begun in 1877 as a part-time venture by the photographic pioneer and inventor, George W. Eastman, the company quickly became the foremost producer of photographic equipment and supplies in the world, a position it has held ever since. By 1989, Eastman Kodak had diversified into a wide range of high-technology products and services. Its sales in 1988 were over $17 billion, and it was listed as #18 on the Fortune 500.

Eastman Kodak's story has not been without its ups and downs, however, and the 1980s proved to be especially troubling times for the photographic giant. Competitive challenges in Kodak's basic product markets and new technological challenges to its dominance of the industry caused top executives to rethink the company's basic mission and objectives. The result was a number of important changes at Eastman Kodak, some of which have significantly altered the way the company does business. These changes include the complete reorganization of the company's operating divisions, the repositioning of many of Kodak's product lines, and the multibillion-dollar acquisition of Sterling Drug Co., a major producer of pharmaceuticals and household products.

Early in 1989, as the company entered its 100th year of incorporation, Colby Chandler, Kodak's CEO and chairman of the board, had reason to be pleased with the way these changes were going. He also knew, however, that the once-complacent giant company would face even greater challenges in its next 100 years.

Source: **Prepared by Professor David W. Grigsby and Research Assistant Charles G. Carter, Clemson University, as a basis for classroom discussion and not to illustrate either effective or ineffective handling of administrative situations. © David W. Grigsby, 1990.**

HISTORY OF THE COMPANY

Eastman Kodak's founder, George Washington Eastman, was born in Waterville, New York, on July 12, 1854.[1] His family moved to Rochester in 1860, where his father had established the city's first commercial college. George's father died two years later, leaving his mother to take in boarders to supplement the family's modest income. The deprivation of his childhood impressed upon Eastman the importance of thrift, which, in time, came to be one of his most notable characteristics. After seven years in the public schools, Eastman took a job in a Rochester insurance office. At the age of 20 he secured a position as junior bookkeeper at the Rochester Savings Bank, where he advanced rapidly. By age 21, Eastman had managed to save over $3,000, which was over twice his annual salary.

At the age of 23, Eastman became fascinated with photography and spent ninety-four of his carefully saved dollars on photographic equipment. He began developing his own prints and soon was experimenting with new methods of reducing the weight and size of photographic equipment in use at the time. By 1879 Eastman had obtained patents on a coating machine, which he used to begin a part-time business preparing photographic plates. In 1880, Eastman left his job with the bank to devote all of his time to the business.

In 1884, Eastman began experimenting with various substitutes for the bulky glass "dry plates" in widespread use at the time. That year he developed a paper-backed flexible film that could be cut into strips and wound on rollers. He renamed his company the Eastern Dry Plate and Film Company and raised new capital of $200,000 to market his inventions. The company introduced its first camera the following year, 1885. Film rolls for 100 pictures were mounted inside a small box camera called the Kodak, which sold for $25. The camera had to be returned to the company for developing. National advertising was launched featuring the slogan "You push the button, we do the rest." The age of amateur photography had begun, although photography was still a relatively expensive hobby.

Further research at the Eastman Company resulted in rapid advances in film and photographic equipment. At the request of Thomas A. Edison, a transparent film was developed in 1887 to be used in his then-experimental motion picture camera. The Eastman Company was incorporated in 1890 with a capital stock issue of $1 million and reorganized two years later as Eastman Kodak Company with capital of $5 million. Expansion continued despite the financial panics of the 1890s, and a second reorganization occurred in 1898, with capital stock of $8 million.

In 1891 a daylight-loading film, which eliminated the necessity of sending cameras back to the company for developing, was introduced. Cheap pocket Kodaks priced as low as $5 put photography within every person's reach by 1895, and photography then became a mass-market hobby. The company continued to expand through the first three decades of the twentieth century, with capital doubling every few years.

By 1900, Eastman Kodak employed 3,000 workers. The original factory on State Street in Rochester was expanded, and a new facility known as Kodak Park was developed north of the city. A branch plant was opened in Harrow, England, to manufacture equipment and film for the rapidly growing European market.

At times, Eastman had difficulty exercising control over his greatly expanded business. He made decisions independently on the board of directors and summarily fired anyone who disagreed with his views. Eastman sought loyalty among his employees, however, through liberal employee benefit programs and some of the most progressive wage bonus plans in existence. Although he refused to allow collective bargaining, Eastman sought to reduce turnover with up-to-date medical facilities, social programs, improved lunchroom facilities, and shorter working hours. Loyalty was high among Eastman Kodak employees, who numbered 15,000 by 1920.

Instrumental in the early growth of Eastman Kodak were a number of successful battles fought for dominance of the photographic equipment market. From the earliest days of the company, George Eastman had been fiercely protective of his position in the industry. In 1892, he discharged Henry Reichenbach, one of his closest assistants, along with two others, when it was disclosed that the three were planning to form a rival company. A number of other rival companies were simply bought out, usually at premium prices. In 1898, Eastman bought out all the photographic paper producers in the United States and contracted with a European cartel to buy all of its product shipped to the U.S. Photographic equipment dealers were required to sign exclusive contracts with Kodak. An arrangement with Edison also assured Eastman of exclusive access to the burgeoning motion picture film market. The result of these dealings was a 75- to 80-percent share of the home photography market and virtually all of the photographic paper and motion picture film markets. Eastman Kodak's profit margin in 1912, averaged across all product lines, was over 71 percent.

Antitrust sentiment began to grow, and in 1915 the firm was found to be in violation of several antitrust regulations by a federal court. Upon appeal, Eastman agreed to sell off several subsidiaries and modify his business practices. In return, the Justice Department agreed to drop the case.

Eastman, who was a lifelong bachelor, became one of the country's leading philanthropists, dispensing most of his vast fortune during his lifetime. His gifts added substantially to the endowments of M.I.T., the University of Rochester, and a number of other institutions.

At the time of Eastman's death, the company he founded had grown to enormous size. In addition to the Rochester and Harrow facilities, there were manufacturing plants in Kingsport, Tennessee, and in France, Germany, Australia, and Hungary. The main plant at Kodak Park covered 240 acres and held 120 buildings. Over 9,500 workers were employed in the Rochester area alone. Eastman committed suicide on March 12, 1932, at the age of 77. He left a note that read, "My work is done, why wait?"

Kodak continued to grow and prosper after Eastman's death, and became, in every sense of the word, the giant of the photographic industry. The company enjoyed a virtual monopoly from the time the silver halide photographic imaging process became a manufacturing reality. So invincible was the company that employees within the company referred to Kodak as "The Great Yellow Father."

A significant milestone in photography, as well as in the growth of the company, was the advent of reliable color processing, which put color photography within the budgets of advertisers, magazine publishers, and amateur photographers. In the 1940s, Eastman Kodak scientists invented and patented the Kodacolor process, which quickly became the standard color film processing system. Following the advent of Kodacolor, the vast majority of all color processing in the U.S. was done in Kodak's labs. In the mid-1950s, Eastman Kodak was ordered to divest much of its photoprocessing capacity under an antitrust consent decree handed down in the federal courts. Kodak then began licensing the process to independent photoprocessing firms throughout the country and selling them photographic paper and supplies to use in the process.

Kodak continued to grow throughout the 1950s and 1960s despite a number of other unfavorable antitrust rulings. Its Instamatic and Pocket Instamatic cameras made higher-quality amateur photography easier for millions of consumers, and the company's professional products maintained their reputation for high quality and dependability. A series of incidents beginning in the late 1960's, however, rocked the company to its very foundation.

COMPETITION WITH JAPAN

Around 1967, the two Japanese photographic companies Konishiroko and Fuji began targeting the United States photographic market. Their first target was the very profitable photographic paper market, in which Kodak held a virtual monopoly. Kodak, with its hold on the market, had concentrated on high product quality, developing the best papers for true color representation in finished photographs. The Japanese entered the market with lower-quality papers and began competing for the photofinishers' paper business on the basis of lower price. In most cases, the amateur photographers served by the photofinisher could not discern a difference in the end product (their Christmas pictures of Aunt Jane and the family still looked like Aunt Jane and the family). Meanwhile, the profit margins of the photofinishers increased as they bought larger and larger amounts of the cheaper Japanese papers.

Konishiroka and Fuji concentrated their quality control efforts on improving the batch-to-batch consistency of their product. This innovation reduced set-up costs for the photofinisher. Kodak continued to stress the overall quality of its papers, ignoring the batch-to-batch consistency dimension. Kodak's share of the photographic paper market continued to decline. In the early 1970s, Konishiroka acquired Photomat Corporation, a chain of photofinishers, to further solidify its share of the U.S. photographic paper industry.

On another front, Fuji Photo Film Corporation, which was a familiar company in the Far East but not well known in the U.S., concluded from market studies in the early 1970s that Kodak had diverted its attention from the retail photo film business. According to Fuji, Kodak spent little time and effort merchandising film at retail locations. Sensing this as a weakness, Fuji launched a drive to gain placement of its film in the same stores that carried Kodak. To gain retail acceptance, Fuji merchandised its products in multiroll packages using colorful point-of-sale displays. The strategy worked. Fuji Photo Film USA, Inc. quickly grabbed nearly 10 percent of the retail film business. Kodak countered the measures, but never fully recaptured the market share loss.

At the same time, Kodak, lulled to sleep by its dominance in the industry, allowed manufacturing costs to increase. Suppliers were recruited out of provincialism and convenience to plants rather than low cost/quality bidding. Since gross margins were near 70 percent for film and photographic paper, cost considerations were not of the utmost importance and the high mark-up covered many unfortunate choices.

Kodak also was vulnerable in its foreign markets. International sales, which accounted for a substantial portion of Kodak's revenue, dropped as Agfa, a West German Film manufacturer, aggressively pushed for shelf space in Europe and South America.

Other product lines within Kodak suffered as well. In the early 1970s the company elected not to develop a 35mm camera line, only to see Japanese 35mm cameras replace the Pocket Instamatic as the amateur camera of choice. In an attempt to reestablish its dominance in the camera market, Kodak introduced its disk-format camera in 1982. Kodak also allowed Polaroid to develop the instant photo concept without challenge until 1983. When Kodak did release its own version of the instant-picture camera, Polaroid sued Kodak for patent infringement.

Kodak has always seen quality as an essential product ingredient. This rigid adherence to high quality has sometimes cost the company dearly, however. For example, Kodak, targeting the high end of the photocopier market, continued to make copier parts from metal rather than the less expensive molded plastic while Xerox, Sharp, Canon, and others found that profits were much higher at the lower end of the market, where lower manufacturing costs were important to stay competitive. Kodak's refusal to shift its focus and sacrifice quality cost it competitive position by pricing its product out of the largest and most profitable segment of the photocopier market.

Kodak's woes were exacerbated by two unforeseen economic events. In the 1960s and 1970s, silver, one of the main ingredients in photographic film, sold in the twenty- to thirty-dollar range per ounce. By 1980, silver had risen to just over fifty dollars per ounce, due in large part to a scheme by the Hunt brothers of Texas to control the silver market. This high price persisted for nearly a year. Eventually, shortages of silver eased and prices began to return to historic levels. Just as silver prices adjusted downward and gross margins were returning to former levels, however, the dollar rose relative to foreign currency making foreign goods cheaper in the U.S. and U.S. goods more expensive overseas. Fuji, recognizing this unique opportunity, sharply reduced prices of its basic consumer film. Kodak was forced to compete in price with Fuji, but at a staggering cost. The *New York Times* estimated that the combined effects of the silver shortage plus the dollar value fluctuation cost Kodak in the neighborhood of $3.5 billion over a five-year period.

Kodak's problems were not limited to product considerations. The company's management style reflected the culture of a slow-moving, lumbering giant. As the mainstay of the product line had remained stable for over a quarter of a century, there had been little incentive to innovate, take risk, or move quickly. At best, Kodak's cradle-to-grave, paternalistic, insular attitudes generated loyalty and stability in the work force. At worst, this management style stifled entrepreneurial spirit, a desire to compete, and the ability to respond to market changes quickly.

As Kodak had grown in the post–World War II economy, the company had added layers to the management organization. What resulted was the classic deep and tall organization structure. Much of the power within the organization resided in top management and staff positions, however. Corporate planning and research managers controlled the flow of information within the organization and authorized spending for new products. The financial staff determined product prices, and research staffs often had the final say as to whether and when new products were to be released. These managers often forced product decisions through the chain of command all the way up to the corporate management committee. Exhibit 1 illustrates the company's organizational structure up to 1981.

Even with the thoroughness of Kodak's approach to manufacturing and quality control and an army of corporate managers, some important business functions were not being done. Robert Murray, a corporate financial executive in 1976, noticed that no one had the responsibility to track corporate market share and competitive activity.

KODAK IN THE 1970s AND 1980s

Two major threats faced the company in the late 1970s. The first was a threat to its technological dominance in the photographic industry, and the second was the introduction of electronic imaging as a replacement for traditional chemical imaging processes. In terms of the first threat, Kodak had long been the leader in silver halide processes, but the Japanese had made significant strides in the last few years. Fuji had successfully developed the first commercially viable 1000-speed film, and there had been other breakthroughs that suggested that Kodak's technological leadership might be questioned.

A more significant threat was the replacement of silver halide photography with electronics. In the early 1970s, Kodak's management become convinced that electronic imaging would someday replace traditional chemical imaging. Although electronic photography still had a long way to go, in terms of resolution and color rendering, before it matched the quality available in

EXHIBIT 1 EASTMAN KODAK, 1981

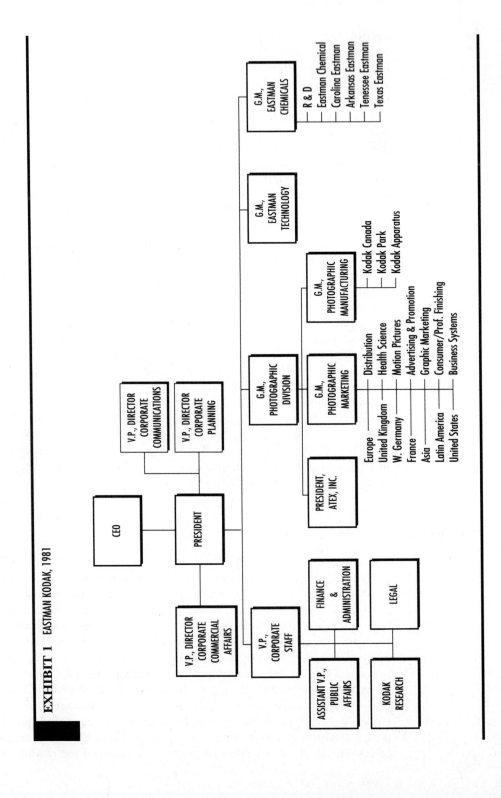

chemical imaging, advances were being made rapidly. Electronic imaging, when fully developed, would have advantages over chemical processes. Electronic images would be available for use instantaneously (no chemical processing), and they could be transmitted electronically in digital format over telephone lines and computer networks. The advantages, moreover, were significant to heavy users of Kodak products, such as the print journalism industry. It was clear to Kodak's management that if the company wanted to remain in the imaging business, it would have to acquire an expertise in electronics.

Accompanying this anticipated redefinition of the company's principal business were a multitude of other reasons for expanding the technological base of the company. One of the most compelling was the opportunity to draw on Kodak's considerable expertise in organic chemicals, an area that could be applied in a number of businesses.

In 1972, Kodak management adopted a plan for expanding the company's range of activities into other areas. Three industries were targeted for expansion: (1) electronic imaging and computer mass storage devices, (2) pharmaceuticals and biotechnology, and (3) photofinishing. To provide a vehicle for the purchase of enterprises within these three targeted industries, Eastman Kodak organized Eastman Technology, Inc.

The Technology Group's first purchase was Spin Physics of San Diego, California, in 1972. Spin Physics developed and manufactured high-technology magnetic recording disks for computer technology. In 1981, Eastman Kodak purchased Atex, Inc., a developer of computer-based text and graphics equipment. Along with Eikonix, purchased in 1985, these two companies served the newspaper printing business and expanded into desktop publishing and word processing equipment and software. Recognizing the tremendous growth of personal computers and the mass storage needed to store data within computers, Kodak purchased Verbatim Corporation, makers of the well-known Data-Life floppy disks for $175 million in 1985.

Several acquisitions were made in the pharmaceutical and biotechnology industries. BioImage Corporation, a maker of analytical equipment for medical and biotechnology applications, was acquired in 1986. Genecor, an industrial biotechnology research and development company, and International Biotechnologies, a manufacturer of biological agents and molecular instrumentation for universities, hospitals, and research firms, were both acquired in 1987. To supplement internal development of pharmaceutical products, Eastman Kodak also entered into joint ventures with Halcon International, ICN Pharmaceuticals, and Immunex Corporation to develop pharmaceuticals for the heart and immune systems and radiographic diagnostic dyes.

The photofinishing industry, closest to Eastman Kodak's original core photographic film business, received perhaps the most noticeable attention. Fox Photo Labs was acquired in 1986 for $91 million. Fox was a large photofinisher with wholesale and mini–photo labs in twenty-three states. That same year, Kodak purchased American Photographic Group for $43 million. This company was a privately held photofinishing firm operating in seventeen states. Joint ventures with Fuqua Industries and Magese KK of Japan, announced in 1987, further expanded photofinishing capabilities and technology in both the U.S. and Japan. The grouping of Fox's Ektra photofinishing labs, Fuqua's Colorcraft, American Photographic Group, and Kodak's own processing labs provided the company with a dominant position in this fast-growing segment of the industry.

ORGANIZATIONAL AND MANAGEMENT CHANGES

Colby H. Chandler became chief executive officer and chairman of the board at Eastman Kodak in 1983. Chandler's career at Kodak had begun in 1950, when he joined the company after serving as a Marine in World War II and completing a degree in engineering physics at the University of Maine. Starting in the Quality Control Division, Chandler was steadily promoted through the ranks. In the early 1970s, he served as project manager for Kodak's foray into office copiers. So successful was this venture that in 1977, Chandler was made president of the company.

Chandler has been described by his colleagues as a "corporate visionary." He recommended that Kodak reshape its organization structure to emphasize the uniqueness of each product group. Another key to Chandler's vision was to replace old-guard executives with more vigorous and aggressive line managers. Enter J. Phillip Samper.

Like Chandler, Samper was a career Kodak employee. He rose through the marketing and international ranks. Samper spent fourteen years overseas, mostly in Latin America. On his return to Rochester, Samper recognized the effects bureaucracy and lack of response had had on the organization. In 1980, Samper went on a campaign to shake up the organization and remove the complacent attitude. The silver market cooperated with Samper, and line managers began to get the message. Samper is quoted as saying that "it is easier to get people to sign onto a culture change in bad times."

Faced with a falling stock price, a devaluation of both Moody's and Standard & Poor's debt rating, heated competition in the film industry, and spiraling costs, Chandler and Samper orchestrated a revolutionary reorganization of the company in 1984. The first action was to split the company into twenty-four separate operating units. (See Exhibit 2.) At the head of each unit was a manager charged with the responsibility to make decisions. This process often involved promoting managers over the heads of previous supervisors. For instance, W. J. Prezzano moved from a middle manager position in international marketing to head Kodak's Photographic Products Group. Charles Trowbridge, also a middle manager in marketing, moved to the general manager's position in the Commercial and Information Systems Division. Bill Fowle, previously far down the manufacturing hierarchy, was named to head manufacturing. These moves signalled a change in promotion policy from the old seniority system to one stressing performance and vision.

Another departure from the Kodak of old was the building of entrepreneurial spirit within the divisions, starting with the general manager's posi-

EXHIBIT 2 EASTMAN KODAK, 1986

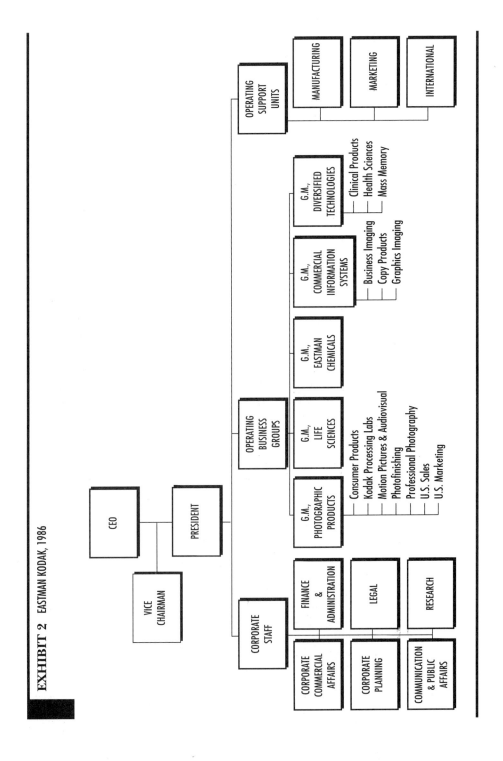

tion. Chandler wanted the new general managers to think small. Each GM would be responsible for both costs and quality. He wanted them to be "fast on their feet." Risk taking would now be acceptable. A team approach to product development would be used instead of chain-of-command decision making. To assist the development of new products, Kodak set up a New Ventures Division to provide seed money and technical assistance. Part of this division was a technology assessment department to help new product champions incorporate the latest technology into designs.

The results of the new plan manifested themselves quickly. New products hit the market much faster than before. For instance, in 1986 and 1987, 250 new products were introduced. Kodak's newest color copier took only two and a half years from conception to delivery of the first model. The lithium battery took only three to four years to develop and was promised to last ten years. The previous management structure would have taken more than ten years to develop the product. Finally, the Fling 35, Kodak's new disposable camera, was completely designed by CAD (computer aided design) at substantial time savings.

Perhaps most traumatic were the personnel changes instituted by Chandler and Samper. Gone were the employee bowling alley, guarantees of life-time employment, and nearly 25,000 jobs from 1984. The large corporate staffs that had dominated the organization before Chandler and Samper took over were reassigned to the operating units. Samper admits the changes were not easy. He says, "There's been an enormous amount of pain and trauma. And the culture's not completely changed yet."

Other elements in the reorganization included a significant reduction in slow-moving or highly specialized products; the buying back of 22 million shares of stock; divestiture of a textile dye company; and the assumption of $1.1 billion dollars of additional debt.

After completing the reorganization phase, Chandler shifted emphasis to a repositioning phase. A significant move toward repositioning the company was the acquisition of Sterling Drug Company in 1988.

LIFE SCIENCE DIVISION AND THE STERLING
DRUG ACQUISITION

Kodak's expansion into pharmaceuticals and biotechnology seemed to many to take the company far afield from its traditional business of photography. There are, however, very close technological ties between the two industries. The foundation of the silver halide photographic process is chemical transformation. Over the years, Kodak has made substantial improvements to the technique, nearly to the point of perfection.

Photographic chemicals are, by nature, highly unstable; the slightest light, heat, or moisture variation will affect the film emulsion. To control the film-making process Kodak produces and mixes most of its own raw chemicals. Additionally, Kodak researchers have aggressively sought new methods to record images on a chemical film emulsion. These same researchers look for not only innovative photographic imagery products, but also new chemical compounds and processes to improve current technology. In sum, Kodak's expertise in chemicals and chemical processes extends substantially beyond the photographic film product category. Success in the chemical film process led Kodak to pursue the manufacture of other chemicals basic to American industry. In 1988, for instance, sales of Kodel, a synthetic textile fiber, and other plastics and chemicals accounted for over 18 percent of all Kodak sales.

An outgrowth of this expertise in chemicals was Kodak's desire to pursue products in the pharmaceutical industry. Most proprietary drugs are synthetic chemical products. In 1984, Kodak started its Life Science Division with the express charter to broaden the company's product mix beyond basic manufacturing chemicals and photographic chemicals. Leo J. Thomas, a leading Kodak researcher, was selected to head the unit. To supplement research from Kodak's other divisions, Thomas hired top managers from Ciba-Geigy and Merck.

Thomas pursued a strategy of modest growth by joint venture and equity investments in small, undercapitalized, start-up biotechnology firms. As Kodak had ample resources for this type of investment, the strategy was sound. Thomas's major criteria for joint venture was a firm that was small and had products nearly ready for chemical trials. More specifically, Kodak targeted companies developing products in the immune system, cardiovascular system, and central nervous system.

Kodak's Life Science Division, however, remained mostly a research unit with very little in the way of commercial products to show for its efforts. In 1985, Kodak's board made a strategic decision to diversify into pharmaceuticals. CFO Paul Smith led a discreet search for suitable pharmaceutical companies to acquire. Sterling was high on the list. Kodak, however, felt that Sterling Drug was unavailable and did not pursue the company at that time.

On January 4, 1988, Kodak's acquisition search priority changed drastically. On that day, Hoffman-LaRoche, a large Swiss drug company, made a hostile bid for Sterling Drug at $72.00 per share. Hoffman-LaRoche would eventually sweeten the bid to $81.00 per share as Sterling fought the takeover attempt. Kodak reacted to Hoffman-LaRoche's move by focusing total attention on the company. Knowing that Sterling was now on the "available" list, Chandler called John M. Pietruski, its CEO, to discuss a potential merger. Pietruski reacted favorably to Kodak's courting because Sterling was looking for a "white knight" to fend off the unwanted attack from Hoffman-LaRoche.

Sterling Drug seems to be a good fit for Kodak. It manufactures ethical drugs (25 percent of sales); household products, cosmetics, and toiletries (48 percent of sales); and proprietary drugs (27 percent of sales). Within the ethical drug group, Sterling sells Bayer, Panadol, Phillips Milk of Magnesia, Haley's M-O, and Midol. Lysol, Mop & Glo, and d-Con are well-known household products. In the proprietary drug market, Sterling Drug offers the well-known analgesics Talwin and Demerol as well as other products such as pHiso-Hex and NegGram. When questioned later why he pursued Sterling Drug so aggressively, Chandler said, "The merger will accelerate our entry into the $100 billion per year pharmaceutical industry."

During the 1984–1987 period, the proprietary drug group had a higher growth rate, at 33.6 percent, than any other division in Sterling Drug. The ethical drug business, however, had the highest gross margin of all divisions, ranging from 20.5 percent in 1984 to 23.3 percent in 1985. In addition, Sterling is aggressively seeking new proprietary drugs. Milrinone, an ACE inhibitor that could challenge Squibb's leading drug Capoten, may be successful in the treatment of congestive heart failure. Omnipaque iohexal is a new low-ionic imaging agent for radiodiagnostic procedures. Sterling Drug will provide Kodak's credibility and expertise in applying for a federal Food and Drug Agency (FDA) license for new products.

On January 22, 1988, after the stock market had closed, Kodak offered $89.50 per share for Sterling Drug. This amount represents $8.50 per share, or a 10.5 percent increase, over Hoffman-LaRoche's second offer of $81.00 per share. Furthermore, Chandler pledged to keep Sterling Drug intact, ending speculation that the household products division would be sold. Sterling Drug closed at $78.75, down $0.125 on Friday, January 22, 1988.

At the bid price, Kodak had to raise $5.1 billion to purchase all of the outstanding shares of Sterling Drug stock. To raise this amount in cash, Kodak approached Banker's Trust Co. to work out a three-year revolving credit arrangement. Banker's Trust, in turn, syndicated the loan to a many as thirty different banks. The problem with the $5.1 billion loan was not the credit worthiness of Kodak or the "business judgment" of this acquisition, but the first year's interest payment, calculated to be nearly $330 million. To obtain the best possible interest rate, Kodak negotiated with Banker's Trust several alternatives for the interest rate. According to the agreement, Kodak can choose one of these options:

1. As base rate, Banker's Trust prime rate or the Federal Funds rate, whichever is higher, plus 0.25 percent
2. The reserve adjusted London Interbank offered rate plus 10 points
3. Competitive bid by another bank, with Banker's Trust Co. acting as broker/agent

Financial analysts reacted with mixed feelings to the Kodak–Sterling Drug merger. On the one hand, many though it was a wise acquisition on Kodak's part because Sterling's businesses fit with Kodak's and filled in some strategic gaps. On the other hand, many felt that Kodak overpaid. Analysts are concerned about stock dilution as Kodak amortizes $4.07 billion in good will. At a thirty-year rate, this amortization results in a dilution of $0.31 per share. The acquisition also changes Kodak's capital structure so that Kodak's debt-to-capital ratio would be around 57 percent. Accordingly, both Moody's and Standard & Poor's lowered their investment rating of Kodak.

EASTMAN KODAK IN 1988

Kodak made significant progress during 1988 in fulfilling its goal to expand into related markets. The purchase of Sterling Drug on February 23, 1988, dramatically added to net sales, which were up 28 percent to $17.034 billion, and profits, which rose 39 percent to $2.938 billion. A summary of Kodak's financial statements for the years 1981 through 1988 are shown in Exhibit 3. Sterling Drug Company's sales and gross margins, by division, are shown in Exhibit 4.

In addition to the Sterling Drug purchase, Kodak also acquired IBM's copier service business for an undisclosed amount in 1988. This acquisition was consistent with Kodak's goals for its existing copier business and, in essence, eliminated a competitor at the high end of the copier equipment market, a segment Kodak pursues vigorously.

Kodak's worldwide employment increased in 1988 to 145,300, up 17 percent from the previous year. Most of the increase in employment was attributed to the Sterling Drug acquisition.

Kodak also continued its expansion in photofinishing laboratories. It gained twenty-five photofinishing labs in France by acquiring Les Laboratoires Associés. Also, Kodak solidified business in a joint venture with Fuqua Industries and others by forming an independent company known as Qualex, Inc.

On a per-share basis, Eastman Kodak's profit performance increased from $3.52 per share to $4.31 per share, a 22.4 percent increase. Total consumer spending for photographic equipment, supplies, and services was estimated at approximately $10 billion in 1987. According to *Standard & Poor's Industry Surveys*, recent growth in the industry was attributable to two factors: "new and improved products and services, and a population mix that has increasingly shifted toward a relatively affluent and free-spending 25- to 40-year-old age group."[2]

THE PHOTOGRAPHY INDUSTRY

Total consumer spending for photographic equipment, supplies, and services was estimated at approximately $10 billion in 1987. According to *Standard & Poor's Industry Surveys*, recent growth in the industry was attributable to two factors: "new and improved products and services, and a population mix that has increasingly shifted toward a relatively affluent and free-spending 25- to 40-year-old age group."[2]

An estimated 13.3 billion pictures are taken each year by amateur photographers, 97 percent of which are color photographs. A large proportion of them (65 percent) are taken using 35mm equipment. The largest share of consumer spending, some 39 percent, goes for photofinishing—chemically processing exposed film and printing slides and prints. Expenditures for photography are detailed by segment in Exhibit 5. Although retail innovations such as "minilabs," which offer speedy on-site film processing, account for a growing percentage of the market, traditional retail outlets still predominate in the industry. Exhibit 6 shows the relative shares of various retail outlets in a recent year.

One of the most significant trends in the industry in recent years has been the shift toward 35mm cameras and equipment. The 35mm market is

EXHIBIT 3   EASTMAN KODAK COMPANY AND SUBSIDIARIES: FINANCIAL SUMMARY, 1981–1988

	1988	1987
Sales	$ 17,034	$ 13,305
Earnings from operations	2,938	2,111
Earnings before income taxes	2,236	1,984
Net earnings	1,397	1,178
EARNINGS AND DIVIDENDS		
Net earnings—percent of sales	8.2%	8.9%
—percent return on avg. shareowner's equity	21.8%	19.0%
—per common share	4.31	3.52
Cash dividends declared—on common shares	616	572
—per common share	1.90	1.71
Common shares outstanding at close of year	324.2	324.1
Shareowners at close of year	174,110	168,517
Earnings retained	781	606
BALANCE SHEET DATA		
Current assets	$ 8,684	$ 6,791
Properties at cost	15,667	13,789
Accumulated depreciation	7,654	7,126
Total assets	22,964	14,698
Current liabilities	5,850	4,140
Long-term obligations	7,779	2,382
Total liabilities and deferred credits	16,184	8,685
Total net assets (shareowners' equity)	6,780	6,013
SUPPLEMENTAL INFORMATION		
Sales—Imaging	$ 10,575	$ 9,711
—Chemicals	3,033	2,600
—Health	3,691	1,230
Research and development expenditures	1,147	992
Additions to properties	1,914	1,652
Depreciation	1,057	962
Taxes (excludes payroll, sales, and excise taxes)	973	911
Wages, salaries and employee benefits	5,469	4,645
Employees at close of year—in the United States	87,900	81,800
—worldwide	145,300	124,400
SUBSIDIARY COMPANIES OUTSIDE THE U.S.		
Sales	$ 7,748	$ 5,572
Earnings from operations	997	797
Eastman Kodak Company equity in net earnings (loss)	661	439

Note: Dollar amounts and shares given in millions, except per-share figures.

Source: 1988 Annual Report.

EXHIBIT 3 (continued)

1986	1985	1984	1983	1982	1981
$11,550	$10,631	$10,600	$10,170	$10,815	$10,337
724	561	1,547	1,027	1,860	2,060
598	530	1,624	1,020	1,872	2,183
374	332	923	565	1,162	1,239
3.2%	3.1%	8.7%	5.6%	10.7%	12.0%
5.8%	4.8%	12.6%	7.5%	16.2%	19.4%
1.10	.97	2.54	1.52	3.17	3.41
551	553	578	587	581	566
1.63	1.62	1.60	1.58	1.58	1.55
338.7	338.5	350.0	372.5	372.5	365.6
172,713	184,231	189,972	200,005	203,788	220,513
(177)	(221)	345	(22)	581	673
$ 5,857	$ 5,677	5,131	$ 5,420	$ 5,289	$ 5,063
12,919	12,047	10,775	10,049	9,344	7,963
6,643	6,070	5,386	4,801	4,286	3,806
12,994	12,142	10,778	10,928	10,622	9,446
3,811	3,325	2,306	2,172	2,146	2,119
981	988	409	416	350	93
6,606	5,580	3,641	3,408	3,081	2,676
6,388	6,562	7,137	7,520	7,541	6,770
$ 8,352	$ 8,531	$ 8,380	$ 8,097	$ 8,935	$ 8,258
2,378	2,348	2,464	2,285	2,151	2,349
1,056	...	...	...	...	...
1,059	976	838	746	710	615
1,438	1,495	970	889	1,500	1,190
956	831	758	652	575	452
329	297	793	543	801	1,026
4,912	4,482	4,148	4,340	4,446	4,099
83,600	89,200	85,600	86,000	93,300	91,900
121,450	128,950	123,900	125,500	136,500	136,400
$ 4,387	$ 3,429	$3,367	$ 3,410	$4,279	$ 4,017
400	169	113	60	302	450
167	(9)	25	(65)	72	188

EXHIBIT 4   STERLING DRUG: SALES AND GROSS MARGINS, 1984–1987

	1984		1985		1986		1987	
	Sales (mill.)	Gross Marg.	Sales (mill.)	Gross Marg.	Sales (mill.)	Gross Marg.	Sales (mill.)	Gross Marg.
Proprietary Drug	269.4	(10.4%)	280.0	(15.0%)	326.5	(16.8%)	360	(17.0%)
Household	509.6	(17.9%)	566.4	(18.0%)	588.7	(16.5%)	640	(16.5%)
Foreign	681.9	(11.9%)	656.6	(10.8%)	774.1	(10.6%)	900	(10.5%)
Ethical Drug	267.7	(20.5%)	268.8	(23.3%)	301.1	(21.9%)	340	(22.0%)

Source: *Value Line* (1988).

EXHIBIT 5 U.S. CONSUMER EXPENDITURES IN PHOTOGRAPHY

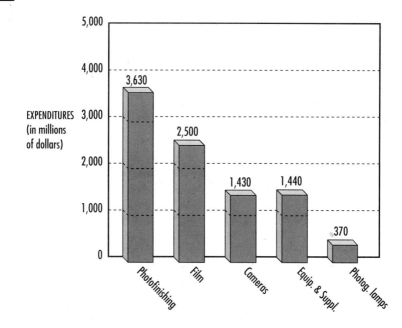

Source: 1985 Wolfman Report.

composed of both the lens/shutter rangefinder ("point-and-shoot") cameras and the more sophisticated single-lens reflex (SLR) cameras favored by professionals and advanced hobbyists. Although SLR sales were sluggish in the late 1980s, technological improvements in "point-and-shoot" cameras such as automatic film loading, built-in flash units, and autowinding caused sales for those cameras to mushroom. By 1987, sales of the once-popular disk camera had declined precipitously, as had those of cartridge film cameras. Polaroid's introduction of its "Spectra" line, with its improved picture quality, breathed new life into the instant camera market. Exhibit 7 shows relative market shares in 1985 and 1987 by camera type.

A number of technological advances in photography and related products were made in the late 1980s. Videocassette recorders (camcorders) grew rapidly during the 1980s and by 1987 had virtually replaced 8mm home movies in the marketplace. Camcorder sales had little impact on the conventional "still" camera business, however. According to *Standard & Poor's Industry Surveys*, "This is likely due to the familiarity, portability, and permanent images provided by still cameras, as well as improvements in products and services for still camera users."[3] Recent development in electronic still-picture imaging may prove to be a threat to traditional chemically processed photography, however. In 1986 several companies introduced electronic still cameras that record and store images on a two-inch diameter magnetic video disk. Images

EXHIBIT 6 U.S. RETAIL SPENDING IN PHOTOGRAPHY

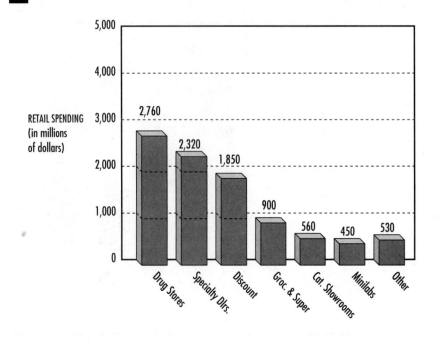

Source: 1985 Wolfman Report.

may be viewed on a television set, enchanced electronically, and then reproduced using special printers, or they may be transmitted over telephone lines.
At around $40,000, the systems were targeted for professional and publishing
markets. As new developments in still-imaging technology in the 1990s bring
about reduced costs, the new electronic still cameras could become competitive with traditional photographic processes.

The introduction of simpler-to-use 35mm cameras and improved film accounted for significant increases in the photofinishing segment in the 1980s.
Between 1981 and 1985, retail photofinishing grew at a compound annual
rate of 11 percent, reaching $3.63 billion in 1985. Estimates placed total retail
photofinishing sales at over $4 billion in 1986 and at nearly $4.5 billion in
1987. The new minilabs, most of which are located in shopping malls, were
the fastest-growing part of this segment and by 1987 accounted for nearly $1
billion in sales. Leading chains of minilabs include MotoPhoto, CPI Corp.,
and Fox Photo, each with around 200 to 300 locations. The total number of
minilabs in operation stood at about 12,000 in 1986.

The majority of all photographs are still developed by large wholesale
labs, which receive exposed film from drug and discount stores and by direct
mail. A large amount of consolidation took place among the wholesale labs in
the late 1980s, with Eastman Kodak leading the way. In December 1986, Kodak
acquired Fox Photo for $91 million, divesting Fox's minilab business but keep-

EXHIBIT 7 U.S. CAMERA SALES, 1985 AND 1987

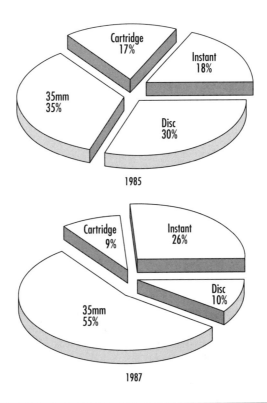

1985

1987

Source: Photographic Trade News, 1986 and 1988.

ing its large wholesale photofinishing operations. American Photographic Group, another large wholesale photofinisher, was purchased by Eastman Kodak for $43 million in October 1987. Kodak also announced in December 1987 that it planned to launch a joint venture with Fuqua Industries' Colorcraft wholesale photofinishers. The combination would have given the two companies over $600 million in photofinishing business. This announcement caused Phototron Corp., a California photofinisher, to raise antitrust objections, claiming that the joint venture, combined with Kodak's 80-percent share of the retail film business, gave it too powerful a hold on amateur photography. A federal district court in Ft. Worth, Texas, ordered a preliminary injunction against the joint venture.

ENDNOTES

1. Most of the information in this section is taken from Ingham, J. N., *Biographical Dictionary of American Business Leaders* (Westport, Conn.: Greenwood Press, 1983).

2. "Photography," *Standard & Poor's Industry Survey* (March 10, 1988): L48.

3. Ibid., p. L46.

LANDS' END, INC.

CARON H. ST. JOHN

In 1963, Gary Comer ended his successful 10-year career as a copywriter for Young & Rubicam to found a mail order company specializing in sailing equipment and fittings. Comer and his sailing partner, Dick Stearns, opened a small catalog outlet store in Chicago's old tannery district and called it Lands' End Yacht Stores. The misplaced apostrophe in "Lands' End" was a typographical error in their first printed publicity that they could not afford to correct—so the name stayed with them. Their first catalog was titled "The Racing Sailor's Equipment Guide." Comer explains: "There were a lot of changes taking place [in the sailing industry]—new companies, new ideas, no one really understood them. We set out to not only supply the fittings but show how to use them, so there was a lot of editorial in those books [early Lands' End catalogs]."[1]

After five years of limited success, Comer bought out Stearns and three other partners who had joined the company. He gradually began adding products to the catalog that would appeal to the weekend sailor, such as luggage and clothing. In 1976 Comer pulled out of the intensely competitive sailing equipment segment and focused exclusively on luggage and clothing. He then moved the executive offices to a new location in Chicago and relocated the warehouse and customer service departments to Dodgeville, Wisconsin. In 1981, Lands' End began a national advertising program to describe the company's business philosophy and build a reputation for quality, value, and service. That advertising campaign introduced the phrase "direct merchant" as a way of describing the company's approach to business.

Between January 1984 and January 1986, Lands' End's sales increased by 84% and income increased by 73%. In October of 1986, after 23 years of successfully selling sailing equipment, clothing, and related items as a Sub-

---

Source: **Prepared by Professor Caron H. St. John, Clemson University, with the assistance of Stephen H. Meeker as a basis for classroom discussion and not to illustrate either effective or ineffective handling of administrative situations. © Caron H. St. John, 1990.**

chapter S firm, Lands' End sold 14% of its shares to the public. For the fiscal year that ended January 31, 1987—its first year to pay corporate income tax—Lands' End reported a net income of $18.6 million on sales of $265 million. After 11 months the stock split 2 for 1.

When Lands' End went public in 1986, some analysts criticized Comer for making the move too late. Gene Mueller, a broker with Blunt Ellis & Loewi said, "It would have been better for them to go public five or six years ago, when they were recording seven and eight-fold increases in sales. The problem with such growth is that it reaches a plateau. It's going to be much harder to double sales from $230 million to $500 million than growing from $30 million to $100 million."[2] However, by fiscal year ended January 1989, sales were $456 million, income was 32.3 million, and earnings per share were $1.61—up from $0.56 in 1986. In early 1989, Gary Comer made the cover of *Fortune* magazine as part of a story titled "Getting Customers To Love You."[3]

By late 1989 problems were beginning to surface. In November, Lands' End announced that profits for the first nine months of its fiscal year had fallen 23% from the nine-month period the year before. Sales projection for the 1989 Christmas season were expected to be up by a meager 4% over the 1988 season. One month later, in December 1989, Lands' End announced that profits for the fiscal year ending 1990 would be down by 13% from 1989. When the announcement was made, the company's stock fell $4.62 to $23.75 in one day. A company spokesman commented, "There's no question we've had some slowdown in response to our catalogs. We're not convinced at this point that we know whether its because of macroeconomic factors or something that's related to Lands' End or the way we're marketing the products or the products themselves."[4]

THE MAIL ORDER INDUSTRY

Although many people view catalog shopping as a 20th century phenomenon, shopping by mail can be traced back to the mid-18th century. In 1744, Benjamin Franklin published a catalog of close to 600 books and promised, "Those persons who live remote, by sending their orders and money to said B. Franklin may depend on the same justice as if present."[5] Throughout the 1800s, mail order companies offered the practical product needs of the time such as seeds, sewing machines, and dry goods. In 1872, Aaron Montgomery Ward published his first multi-product catalog. With 163 items, most priced at $1.00, the catalog became a wish book—and the modern era of mail order shopping was under way.

The mail order industry of the late 1980s and 1990s includes a wide array of products and services. Clothing, sports equipment, craft supplies, housewares, gardening products, magazine subscriptions, book and record clubs, auto clubs, insurance, prescription drugs, and film processing are among the many products and services available by mail.

MAIL ORDER INDUSTRY TRENDS

During the early and mid-eighties, catalog retailing experienced 10–12% annual growth with the number of Americans who shopped by phone or mail increasing from 57.4 million in 1983 to 88.5 million in 1988. During those years, technological developments contributed substantially to the growth trend. Catalog companies made use of computerized databases that allowed them to profile names on mailing lists and select those that met certain demographic characteristics. This ability to segment buyers and focus product and marketing efforts spurred the development of specialty catalogs that were marketed to customer niches.

The convenience of mail order was enhanced by improved computer and communication systems. Toll-free 24-hour 800 numbers and readily available bank cards made catalog shopping easy. Integrated order placement and inventory systems allowed catalog companies to take orders, monitor inventory levels in real time, check a customer's credit, and fill orders quickly.

According to industry observers, the improved service and convenience offered by catalog companies could not have come at a better time. With more women entering the work force, household incomes increased as time available for shopping decreased. As Elsa Gustafson of Lands' End noted, Lands' End management believes families with two working parents and small children are more interested in using their discretionary time to do things together rather than shop. The mail order purchase of gifts, clothing, toys, and books takes pressure off of harried working parents.

The mail order industry attributes much of its growth in the 1980s to the prevalence of these two wage-earner families. For many catalog retailers, the target market is households headed by 25–44-year-old adults with three or more family members and household incomes of more than $30,000 per year. Since 1980, the number of households headed by 35–44 year old adults has increased by 38%—the largest gains of any other age group. (Exhibits 1 and 2 give demographic information on families.)

Studies have indicated that people who use mail order services are generally satisfied with the experience. A Direct Marketing Association–sponsored survey of 2,300 catalog customers revealed that people prefer catalog shopping because they feel they are getting more complete product information.[6] Once a customer has had a positive experience with mail order he or she is more likely to order again—and to try different kinds of products from different companies. However, if a customer's first experience with mail order is unsatisfactory, he or she may be reluctant to try again and may generalize that experience to include all mail order companies.

In 1988, approximately 58% of mail order purchases were made by women (Exhibit 3). As shown in Exhibit 4, clothing, non-food gifts, and gardening supplies are the items customers are most likely to purchase through mail order.

As the decade of the 1980s closed, there were several disturbing trends on the horizon. In 1988, 88.5 million Americans shopped by mail or phone—only

EXHIBIT 1   AGE AND INCOME STATISTICS FOR HOUSEHOLDS BY TYPE IN 1988 AND MEDIAN INCOME IN 1987

	HOUSEHOLDERS AGED 25–34			HOUSEHOLDERS AGED 35–44			HOUSEHOLDERS AGED 45–54		
	Households No. (000)	Median Income	Percent of Type	Households No. (000)	Median Income	Percent of Type	Households No. (000)	Median Income	Percent of Type
Total	20,000	$26,923	100.0	19,323	$34,929	100.0	13,630	$37,250	100.0
% change 1980–1988	11.0	−5.0		36.0	1.0		8.0	3.0	
Families	15,008	28,813	72.9	15,852	36,836	82.0	11,138	37,250	81.7
Married couples with children*	8,665	31,111	42.1	10,121	40,372	52.4	3,980	44,785	29.2
Nonfamily	5,575	22,694	27.1	3,471	24,586	18.0	2,492	20,001	18.3

*(with children under 18 living at home)

Source: Waldrop, Judith, "Inside America's Households," *American Demographics* 11, No. 3 (March 1989): 20–27.

EXHIBIT 2   PAST AND FUTURE DEMOGRAPHIC TRENDS

DEMOGRAPHIC TRENDS—1980 TO 1988

1. In 1988, there were 91 million households in America, a 13-percent increase over 1980.
2. The number of households headed by people aged 35–44 increased by 38 percent between 1980 and 1988, making it the fastest growing population segment.
3. The number of households headed by people under age 25 fell by 20 percent between 1980–1988.
4. Married couples declined as a share of all households from 61% in 1980 to 57% in 1988.
5. Although the number of married couples with children was predicted to grow during the 1980s, that segment fell from 31% of households in 1980 to 27% in 1988.
6. The median income of younger householders still lags behind what it was in 1979, but the over age 65 segment is gaining in median income faster than any other age group.

FUTURE DEMOGRAPHIC TRENDS
There are three fundamental trends:

1. The number of households headed by 45–54 year olds will increase as the baby boomers enter their mid-forties.
2. The composition of households will continue to change with fewer described as "married couples with children."
3. Household incomes are separating into two categories: those that keep up with inflation and those that do not.

Source: Waldrop, Judith, "Inside America's Households," *American Demographics* 11, No. 3 (March 1989); 20–27.

EXHIBIT 3   NUMBER OF AMERICAN ADULTS WHO SHOPPED BY PHONE OR MAIL

YEAR	MILLION	% MALE	% FEMALE
1988	88.5	42.0	58.0
1987	88.0	46.9	54.1
1986	87.7	41.9	58.1
1985	76.2	41.3	58.7
1984	64.4	40.7	59.3
1983	57.4	40.6	59.4

Source: "Study of Media and Markets, 1983–1988," Simmons Market Research, New York.

EXHIBIT 4   PRODUCT PURCHASES BY CATALOG CUSTOMERS

	% OF CATALOG CUSTOMERS WHO PURCHASED THESE ITEMS
Clothing	93
Non-Food Gifts	80
Gardening	71
Home Furnishings	70
Housewares	66
Food	62
Hardware	61
Sporting Goods	49

Source: "DMA Survey Uncovers Consumers' Attitudes on Catalog Shopping," Press Release, Direct Marketing Association, Inc., New York.

.5 million more than in 1987 and .8 million more than in 1986. This slowdown in the number of new catalog customers suggests a slowdown in mail order shopping and is in sharp contrast to the 10–12% increases that were evident in the early and mid-1980s.

At the same time that market demand seems to be leveling, costs of operating a mail order business are on the rise. In 1991, the U.S. Post Office is expected to increase rates on third-class mail by roughly 17%—which will add millions of dollars to the cost structures of mail order firms and make it much more risky for a company to mail catalogs to customers who do not order. Rising costs will make mailing list management practices more important to the cost control efforts of firms and will further encourage development of specialty catalogs targeted to particular types of customers.

As of now, few states require sales tax on mail order purchases but in 1989 momentum began to gather nationwide to require mail order companies to collect sales taxes. Catalog companies are concerned that the addition of sales tax will price their products out of the market. Purchasing a product by mail order has always required that either the buyer or the catalog company pay for postage and handling. Many customers have rationalized that the postage and handling has not substantially affected the price of the items purchased because in the stores they would have to pay sales tax. If customers are required to pay both, then they may feel they can get equivalent items for a better price at the mall.

COMPETITION

In the past 10 years, thousands of people have started mail order businesses. Estimates of the total number of companies that sell via mail order range from 10,000 to over 13,000.[7] So many new catalog businesses have started up that there is widespread concern in the industry that consumers are becoming overwhelmed by the sheer number of catalogs in their mailboxes. The number of new catalogs is increasing by more than 16% per year. The Direct Marketing Association estimates that catalog retailers mailed more than 12.4 billion catalogs in 1988—which translates into 50 catalogs for every man, woman, and child in America.

The amount of capital required to start up a mail order business is usually much less than that required to open a retail store. Products may be purchased from vendors rather than produced by the company, and the services and supplies required to prepare, print, and mail catalogs are available from list brokers, photographers, and printing houses. In addition to its product inventories and computer system, one of the most valuable assets a mail order company will own is its mailing list. Since mailing lists are frequently valued in the accounting records at $0.00, returns on investments tend to be very high for mail order firms.

With so many companies vying for a position, competition in the mail order industry is intense. Many are small, private companies that specialize in one unique product such as smoked salmon or office calendars. At the other end of the spectrum are large retailers and wholesalers with multi-product mail order divisions such as Bloomingdales and J. C. Penney.

In recent years, large general merchandise catalogs have been replaced by specialized catalogs for very specific customer groups. The trend toward specialty catalog marketing has influenced the planning of the large general merchandise catalog companies. Montgomery Ward discontinued its general merchandise catalog altogether. Spiegel and Bloomingdales, among others, have developed their own specialty catalog groups. As part of a major revamping of its catalog business, Sears is planning to issue six apparel catalogs and one catalog of durable home products called "Home" in 1989.

Most mail order companies deal with two sets of competitors—other comparable mail order companies and retail stores. Mail order companies try to compete with retail stores by offering hard-to-get items, a wider selection than a store can offer, the convenience of shopping from home, and, in some cases, discount prices. To encourage potential customers to try mail order, some companies have begun advertising their products and their shop-at-home convenience in the newspapers and magazines that are purchased by the customers they hope to target. Retailers have begun to take notice. The *Direct Marketing* trade publication quotes Donald Zale, chairman of the Zale's jewelry chain, as saying, "Catalogs are public enemy number one. They are a threat to the existence of retail stores. They are in existence to take customers out of your stores. We must band together to begin to formulate the kinds of strategies to insure our survival!"[8]

Once a customer has been won over to mail order, the company must convince the customer to buy from it rather than one of the many other mail order companies. The techniques that mail order companies use to get the attention of customers are often very creative. Virtually all companies have easy-return policies and toll-free numbers for customers to use when placing orders—but some companies accept telephone orders 24 hours a day, seven days a week, some pay all of the postage required to deliver merchandise, and others provide toll-free numbers for customers to use to check on the status of an order. In the apparel and gift areas, catalogs are mailed out very frequently—almost like the sales fliers that come from local department stores. Most catalogs have full product descriptions and many use loss leaders and free gifts to encourage customers to buy.

Many companies are developing catalogs with more of a "magazine" look. High quality photography and glossy, heavy weight paper are combined with anecdotes and stories to draw potential customers to the catalog as they would be drawn to a magazine. To offset the cost of printing these expensive catalogs, some companies carry advertisements for non-competitive products. Some companies offset costs by charging customers a fee for their catalogs.

COMPETITION IN THE CASUAL APPAREL SEGMENT

The Robinson-Humphrey Company investment firm estimates that consumers spent $2.7 billion on men's and women's apparel from specialty mail order catalogs in 1986—almost twice the amount spent in 1980.[9] In casual apparel, there are four dominant companies: L. L. Bean, Eddie Bauer, J. Crew, and Lands' End.

L. L. Bean is a privately held mail order marketer of outdoor sporting apparel and footwear. Founded in 1912 as a hunting shoe manufacturer, L. L. Bean now manufactures tote bags and a full line of sailing and hunting footwear. As the largest shareholder in this industry segment, the company generates 85% of its sales from mail order with the remaining 15% from its one retail store in Freeport, Maine.[10] In 1989, the company reported a small 3% increase in sales over the previous year.

Excluding its specialty areas, L. L. Bean mails 10 catalogs to its prospective

EXHIBIT 5   CATALOGS AND MAILINGS IN 1987

	NUMBER OF DIFFERENT CATALOGS PRODUCED ANNUALLY	MILLIONS OF COPIES MAILED
Lands' End	13	64
L. L. Bean	22*	85
Spiegel	42	150
J. Crew	12	15

*Includes a variety of specialty camping and equipment catalogs, some of which have very small circulation.

Source: Addis, Ronit, "Big Picture Strategy," *Forbes* (January 9, 1989); 70–89.

customers each year for a total of 60 million catalogs. The product line carried in the catalog includes very traditional denim and khaki pants and skirts, oxford cloth shirts, jackets and overcoats, and boots—with a heavy emphasis on plaids, stripes, all-cotton fabrics, and little fashion influence. Items are priced competitively with the products of other casual apparel mail order firms plus L. L. Bean pays all postage and handling.

Although competition in the casual apparel segment has increased substantially in recent years, L. L. Bean has made very few changes in the way it designs and develops its catalogs. Clothes models look like average people between 30 and 50 years of age. Most clothing items are shown without models. Very few scenic "location shots" are used in the catalogs. While L. L. Bean issues a small, special catalog of casual women's apparel, the primary catalog carries many more items for men. The results of a focus group of non-customers suggested that the L. L. Bean catalog is directed toward serious outdoor sportspeople, particularly older men, while the Lands' End catalog has more fashionable clothing and is targeted toward men and women who enjoy the outdoors.[11]

In addition to its reputation for excellent quality and service, L. L. Bean has developed an image with its catalog that helps it sell merchandise. Many of the items in the catalog do not make money for the company but are there to support the image. A customer browsing through an L. L. Bean catalog sees casual clothing positioned among the axes, sleeping bags, duck decoys, and bird feeders—and the clothing takes on a more rugged, outdoor aura. As one of their senior officers noted, "We would not sell the casual clothing if we didn't have duck decoys in the book."[12] When asked by a team of marketing analysts what she thought about when someone said "L. L. Bean," one customer said, "I see a small log cabin. There's a light in the window. The snow is falling. It is beautiful and calm."[13]

Another strong competitor in casual apparel is Eddie Bauer. Eddie Bauer was started as a family business many years ago and was subsequently sold to General Mills. In 1988, as part of a restructuring at General Mills, Eddie Bauer was sold to Spiegel, the largest U.S. catalog retailer with 1989 revenues of $1.7 billion. Eddie Bauer offers merchandise that is comparable in quality and price to that offered by L. L. Bean but with a higher percentage of items for women and more fashion-conscious styling. The Eddie Bauer catalog has a sleek, magazine appearance. The layouts are beautifully photographed with attractive models dressed in Eddie Bauer fashions surrounded by mountains or sail boats—depending on the season. The clothing receives almost secondary treatment to the upscale, sporting Northern Pacific lifestyle that is portrayed.

Eddie Bauer has successfully operated Eddie Bauer retail stores for several years. The stores offer much of the same merchandise that is in the catalogs including over-stocks. While Eddie Bauer is smaller (less than $200 million in sales) than L. L. Bean, it has been growing rapidly over the last several years through its catalog and retail store sales and is expected to benefit a great deal from its alliance with Spiegel. According to one source,[14] Eddie Bauer has increased its share of market at the expense of Lands' End in recent years. Spiegel experienced a 21% increase in sales, a 29% increase in profits, and a 7.5% gross margin in fiscal year 1989. Exhibit 6 compares prices for selected clothing items at Lands' End, L. L. Bean, and Eddie Bauer.

A third major competitor in the casual apparel mail order segment is J. Crew, a division of the privately held J. Crew, Inc. J. Crew mailed its first catalog in 1983 and since then sales have risen from $3 million to more than $100 million, making it the fourth largest company in the casual apparel mail order segment. J. Crew offers a product mix focused on t-shirts, rugby shirts, sweaters, skirts, pants, and shorts in all-natural fabrics. The company characterizes the image it portrays in its catalogs as "a sports oriented life-style" and uses beautiful location shots and youthful, active models. J. Crew targets college students as well as young adults and families with its catalogs.

As the smallest of the four major casual apparel companies, J. Crew is trying to sustain growth in a maturing market. In 1989, the company cut back some staff positions, was late with payments to some suppliers, and failed in an attempt to sell off a division of the company that was not in mail order. J. Crew recently made an expansion move that concerned some industry observers. Facing the slower expected growth in catalog retailing, J. Crew opened its first retail store in New York City in 1989 and announced plans to open 40 more stores over the next five years. The company says it plans to take advantage of its retail stores to add women's career apparel to its product line. The company's move into store retailing was met with much skepticism because of the troubles other catalog companies have had making a similar move. Last year, Royal Silk, a very successful catalog retailer, was forced to declare Chapter 11 bankruptcy when its attempts to move into store retailing failed.

EXHIBIT 6   SAMPLE MERCHANDISE AND PRICE RANGES—SPRING 1989

	LANDS' END	L. L. BEAN	EDDIE BAUER
Solid, Long Sleeve 100% Cotton Oxford Shirt	$19.50–33.50	$24.50	NA
Madras, Plaid, Gingham Long Sleeve Shirts	21.00–29.00	21.00–37.00	25.00–30.00
100% Cotton Denim Full Skirt	34.50	35.00	36.00
Men's Swim Trunks	14.00–28.00	22.50–28.00	20.00–24.00
Sport Shorts	10.50–28.00	14.00–33.00	15.00
Knit Shirts	12.00–20.00	16.50–23.00	17.00–22.00
Cotton Pullover Sweaters (Crew, Shaker, Fatigue)	29.50–44.50	29.00–39.00	28.00–65.00

Note: Price ranges reflect different weights and styles within product categories.

Source: Prepared by the casewriters from 1989 Spring/Summer catalogs for each of the three companies.

LANDS' END

Lands' End concentrates on traditional, unbranded, high quality clothing such as oxford cloth dress shirts, khaki trousers, heavy-weight sweats, and knit sports shirts and sweaters that are sometimes lower priced than comparable regular-priced items in department and specialty stores. At the request of customers, the company has recently introduced a line of children's clothing and is venturing into some domestic items such as sheets and comforters. Analysts and managers have credited Lands' End's past success to its quality merchandise, commitment to value pricing, and its high level of service to customers. The Lands' End Principles of Doing Business are shown in Exhibit 7.

 EXHIBIT 7 THE LANDS' END PRINCIPLES OF DOING BUSINESS

Principle 1: We do everything we can to make our products better. We improve material, and add back features and construction details that others have taken out over the years. We never reduce the quality of a product to make it cheaper.

Principle 2: We price our products fairly and honestly. We do not, have not, and will not participate in the common retailing practice of inflating mark-ups to set up a future phony sale.

Principle 3: We accept any return, for any reason, at any time. Our products are guaranteed. No fine print. No arguments. We mean exactly what we say: GUARANTEED. PERIOD.

Principle 4: We ship faster than anyone we know of. We ship items in stock the day after we receive the order. At the height of the last Christmas season the longest time an order was in the house was 36 hours, excepting monograms which took another 12 hours.

Principle 5: We believe that what is best for our customer is best for all of us. Everyone here understands that concept. Our sales and service people are trained to know our products, and to be friendly and helpful. They are urged to take all the time necessary to take care of you. We even pay for your call, for whatever reason you call.

Principle 6: We are able to sell at lower prices because we have eliminated middlemen; because we don't buy branded merchandise with high protected mark-ups; and because we have placed our contracts with manufacturers who have proved that they are cost conscious and efficient.

Principle 7: We are able to sell at lower prices because we operate efficiently. Our people are hard working, intelligent, and share in the success of the company.

Principle 8: We are able to sell at lower prices because we support no fancy emporiums with their high overhead. Our main location is in the middle of a 40-acre cornfield in rural Wisconsin. We still operate our first location in Chicago's Near North tannery district.

Source: Lands' End, Inc., *1987 Annual Report.*

MARKETING

Instead of following the common practice of renting mailing lists from other companies, Lands' End has developed its own proprietary mailing list through a national "space advertising" program. Lands' End advertises in the *Wall Street Journal* and *USA Today* as well as 30 magazines which appeal to the more affluent, "upscale" subscriber. The ads are not used to sell the company's products—instead they are supposed to create an image for the name "Lands' End." The advertisements portray Lands' End as a good neighbor, someone you can count on. At the bottom of the advertisements is a toll-free number to call to get a free "subscription" to the Lands' End catalog. Competitors L. L. Bean and Spiegel also use advertising but the ad focus is on promoting sales and catalogs rather than the company image. Lands' End has used these advertisements to help increase the size of its mailing list in the last three years. In 1989, the company tried national television advertising for a short time.

When a customer receives his or her first catalog from Lands' End, a pamphlet is enclosed that describes the history of the company. The photograph on the front page of the pamphlet is of a country road with old rural mail boxes. It says, "It was really good to hear from you, and have the opportunity to send our catalog and tell you how things are out our way." The pamphlet is filled with photographs of the small town of Dodgeville, Wisconsin, and of employees with their families. The purpose of the pamphlet is to convey a sense of traditional small town values of integrity and service.

The company updates and refines its proprietary mailing list of approximately 10 million names before each catalog mailing. Lands' End monitors the recency, frequency, and dollar amount of purchases by customers as a way of gauging customer interest. The company actively manages its list in this way in an attempt to avoid wasting money mailing catalogs to customers who are unlikely to make a purchase. Of the ten million people who receive catalogs each month, 45% have made purchases within the past 36 months. In 1988 the company mailed 76 million of its 115 page catalogs. The best customers received approximately 13 catalogs during the year—at least one per month.

Lands' End uses its space advertising and list management practices to reach a select target market. Research studies have shown that approximately 40% of Lands' End's customers are in the 35–49 age group with 29% in the 25–34 age group. Median annual income for Lands' End households is almost twice that of the U.S. population, 70% of customers are professionals or managers, and 88% attended college.[15]

Lands' End catalogs have a distinct magazine appearance. One 1989 catalog looked like an old issue of the *Saturday Evening Post*—with a Norman Rockwell cover, volume and issue numbers printed at the top, and a boldface listing of the "features" inside. The catalogs make use of other magazine techniques such as background stories and monthly publication to stimulate the interest of readers. The first eight pages of one catalog was devoted to the "story of cotton" while another profiled a trip through the Sahara desert. The catalogs describe products in detail and offer the company's views about the benefits of the merchandise.

Management at Lands' End feels strongly that the company's major competitors are department and specialty stores—not other mail order companies. There are some inherent disadvantages associated with shopping by mail that the company tries to overcome. To make catalog shopping more like the service customers get in a store, Lands' End included a tear-out guide for matching shirts and ties in a recent catalog. Since customers cannot drape a tie across a shirt like they can in a store, the company developed a template of shirts of different colors with a cut-out opening for the tie. All of the ties described in the catalog were of the correct size to view under the template. This system allowed the customer to compare shirts and ties for color and style.

Lands' End tries to be responsive to the requests of customers. Company volunteers respond personally to the approximately 50,000 letters the company receives from customers each year. When customers wrote in and complained that knit shirts did not have breast pockets, the company added a pocket to its standard knit shirt. Customers protested when a 100% cotton twill skirt was dropped from the catalog so the company brought the skirt back. After receiving several requests, Lands' End added turtlenecks in a sweatshirt fabric to its product line. The company is so proud of its responsiveness to customers that it featured letters from customers in its 1989 annual report.

OPERATIONS

Lands' End owns a 100,000 square foot office building, a 277,000 square foot warehouse, and 78 acres of undeveloped land in Dodgeville, Wisconsin, as well as a 10,000 square foot soft-side luggage manufacturing operation in West Union, Iowa. The company also leases office space and operates seven outlet stores in the Chicago area.

Lands' End provides a toll-free number that may be used 24 hours a day, seven days a week to place orders or request a catalog. Orders are entered on-line into a computerized inventory control system which updates the company's mailing list and provides a database for tracking product demand and response to mailings.

Lands' End boasts of a 24-hour turnaround time on orders. To achieve this, operators use the real-time inventory data to immediately tell the caller if a product is in stock. If it is not, the screen will tell the operator when the next shipment is expected and show a variety of alternatives including, in some cases, the name of another retailer. If the merchandise is in stock, the order is placed and the inventory files are updated in real time. The system simultaneously checks the credit of the customer through data links with American Express and, for MasterCard and VISA purchases, National Data Corporation.

The processing of orders takes place at night. At midnight, high speed laser printers print two sets of bar-coded tickets for each order—one for picking and one for packing. Warehouse workers use the picking tickets to determine which items must be pulled from storage bins. The warehouse worker affixes the bar-coded picking ticket to the package and places it in a tray on a conveyor belt. A laser scanner reads the bar-codes so that items are automatically sorted by customer order.

With the exception of soft luggage, Lands' End purchases all of its products from approximately 250 independent manufacturers. Nearly 80% of its merchandise is purchased from vendors in the United States with the remainder purchased from Europe and Asia through two trading companies, Mitsubishi Textiles and British Isles Buying Agency. Lands' End management feels that using U.S. vendors when possible gives the company an advantage over its competitors that purchase goods from the Far East. Having production facilities so close by allows them to exercise some control over design, quality, and delivery speed.

Lands' End maintains an extensive quality control group including three airplanes and pilots. Buyers and quality assurance personnel develop the company's own product specifications. Before agreeing to use a vendor, the staff puts garments through rugged quality testing. Inspectors make frequent inspection visits to vendors' plants and if vendors do not uphold the Lands' End commitment to quality, they are dropped. "We don't go two streets over because its a nickel cheaper," Comer says, "If a manufacturer meets our standards, we'll stick with him. Otherwise we move on."[16]

MERCHANDISE MIX

Gary Comer has resisted allowing Lands' End to become fashion driven. In 1983, the company introduced a line of dress clothing for men and women called the Charter Collection. The garments were made from expensive Italian silks with trendier styling than typically found in a Lands' End catalog. Although Charter was spun off into its own catalog and was making money, Comer was uncomfortable with the potential for a diluted company image. He said, "It was developing into this fashion business, and I knew I didn't want that. When they started shooting photographs of models in London, I said, 'That's it, enough.'"[17]

At the specific request of customers, Lands' End has added selected new products to its line such as swimsuits and extra-large and petite sizes. Recently, at the request of customers, Lands' End added a line of children's clothing that met with considerable success—$15 million in sales in 1988. Similar to Eddie Bauer and L. L. Bean, the company has added a line of high quality domestic items such as sheets and comforters that it feels will appeal to its existing customer base.

1989—A YEAR OF CHANGE

Effective January 1, 1989, Richard C. Anderson replaced Gary Comer as president and chief operating officer of Lands' End. Anderson, a director of the company since 1978 and vice-chairman since 1984, was promoted as part of a planned management succession designed to allow Comer to spend more of his time on the broad issues affecting the company's long-range direction. Comer continued as chairman and chief executive officer. As part of the reorganization, Comer became chairman of the company's executive committee which is responsible for strategic and financial planning. Anderson was put in charge of the company's policy committee which is responsible for operations planning.

At the beginning of 1989, management at Lands' End was advocating a conservative approach to growth. The company estimated that its potential market would be about 13.5 million households by 1990 and it planned to use two approaches to further penetrate that market.[18] One approach was to increase the size of its mailing list by using its space advertising techniques to reach more of its target market. A second approach was to add new products that would be of interest to the traditional Lands' End customer—so that they would rely on Lands' End for a larger portion of their household purchases. Movement into retail outlets was not a growth alternative. Comer has indicated for some time that he is not interested in opening retail stores such as the ones operated by Eddie Bauer and others. He sees retail store management as a completely different business.

In 1989 (the fiscal year that ended January 31, 1990) Lands' End added some higher-priced merchandise to its product mix including $200-plus cashmere sweaters. With children's clothing, domestics, and higher-end apparel added to the product line, the catalog grew from an average of 115 pages in 1988 to about 149 pages in 1989. The company mailed 91 million catalogs—15 million more than in 1988.

EXHIBIT 8   LANDS' END STATEMENT OF OPERATIONS

| | FOR THE YEAR ENDED JANUARY 31 | | | |
	1990	1989	1988	1987
Net Sales	$545,201	$455,806	$336,291	$265,058
Cost of Sales	313,573	261,671	190,348	152,959
Gross Profit	231,628	194,135	145,943	112,099
Selling, G&A	184,910	143,486	107,699	83,454
Income from Operations	46,718	50,649	38,244	28,645
Net interest and other	552	1,493	84	(159)
Income before Income Tax	47,270	52,142	38,328	28,486
Tax Provision	18,199	19,860	16,208	9,836
Adj. for change in accounting			685	
Net Income	$ 29,071	$ 32,282	$ 22,805	$ 18,650
Net income per share	$ 1.45	$ 1.61	$ 1.14	$ 0.73

Note: Dollars in thousands, except per-share amounts.

EXHIBIT 9   LANDS' END INC. BALANCE SHEETS

	JANUARY 31		
	1990	1989	1988
ASSETS			
Current assets:			
Cash and cash equivalents	$ 8,254	$ 32,139	$ 28,175
Receivables	348	755	274
Inventory	85,709	66,820	46,444
Prepaid expenses	5,403	3,967	3,363
Total current expenses	99,714	103,681	78,256
Property, plant & equip. at cost:			
Land and buildings	38,335	31,267	15,114
Fixtures and equipment	41,123	25,192	21,974
Leasehold improvements	1,512	1,234	908
Construction in progress	4,637	3,280	674
Total property, plant and equipment	85,607	60,973	38,670
Less depreciation/amortization	18,389	13,502	9,947
Property, plant and equipment, net	67,218	47,471	28,723
Total assets	$166,932	$151,152	$106,979
LIABILITIES AND SHAREHOLDERS' INVESTMENT			
Current liabilities:			
Current maturities of long term debt	$ 1,775	$ 1,860	$ 1,918
Accounts payable	24,415	25,904	21,223
Advance payment orders	203	350	453
Accrued liabilities	10,568	9,734	7,226
Accrued profit sharing	1,652	3,285	2,646
Income taxes payable	5,302	10,397	5,394
Total current liabilities	43,915	51,530	38,860
Long term debt, less current mat.	5,031	6,806	8,667
Deferred income taxes	3,382	868	2,778
Shareholders' investment:			
Common stock, 19, 881, 394 (1990)			
and 20,040,294 (1989, 1988) outstnd.	201	200	200
Donated capital	8,400	7,000	—
Paid-in capital	23,340	22,308	22,308
Deferred compensation	(959)	—	—
Retained earnings	87,516	62,440	34,166
Treasury stock, 194,900 shares	(3,894)	—	—
Total shareholders' investment	114,604	91,948	56,674
Total liabilities and shareholders' investment	$166,932	$151,152	$196,979

Note: Dollars are given in thousands.

Expecting an excellent sales year in 1989, the company entered 1989 with a record $66.8 million invested in inventory. When sales volume did not meet expectations, the company mailed four million special mailers to keep sales up and inventories in balance. The sales push increased selling expenses which were not then offset by higher sales volume. In the summer of 1989, employees praised the company as a wonderful place to work but were well aware of increasing pressures to keep down costs. In late fall 1989, customers received catalogs from Lands' End with many of the newer items marked "Sorry, Not Available" across the picture layouts. While there had been an occasional two-page section in the catalog showing "clear the decks" specials (overstocks) in 1988, in late 1989 the overstock sale section of the catalog grew much larger and was included in every catalog.

In early 1990, Lands' End's stock traded around $19 per share compared to its high of $35 per share in April 1989. When the company compiled its performance for fiscal year ended January 31, 1990, sales for the year were $545 million—20% greater than the previous year's sales. Net income for the year was $29.1 million—10% less than what the company earned the year before. For the first time in four years, Lands' End had failed to exceed its goal of 10% pretax return on sales. (Lands' End financial statements are shown in Exhibits 8 and 9.)

Several factors were identified by management and industry analysts as contributing to the problems at Lands' End: an overall slowdown in consumer spending in 1989 and price discounts at department stores of up to 25% which made store purchase more attractive than catalog purchase. Some analysts criticized Lands' End's product mix as "tired" and pointed to the threat of the Spiegel-backed Eddie Bauer. Faced with increasing competition from stores and other catalogers as well as increasing sales and catalog costs, Lands' End entered fiscal 1991 with some very difficult decisions to make.

ENDNOTES

1. Addis, Ronit, "Big Picture Strategy," *Forbes* (January 9, 1989): 72.

2. Freeman, Laurie, "Lands' End a Beacon for Mail-Order Market," *Advertising Age* (December 8, 1986): 74.

3. Sellers, Patricia, "Getting Customers To Love You," *Fortune* (March 13, 1989): 38–49.

4. "Lands' End Says Profit for Fiscal 1990 is Likely to Fall About 13% From 1989," *Wall Street Journal* (December 12, 1989): A5.

5. Ross, Nat, "A History of Direct Marketing," in *Fact Book: An Overview of Direct Marketing and Direct Response Advertising* (New York: Direct Marketing Association, 1986).

6. "DMA Survey Uncovers Consumers' Attitudes on Catalog Shopping," Press Release, Direct Marketing Association, Inc., New York (September 1988).

7. Sroge, Maxwell, "Mail Order Industry Overview," in *Inside the Leading Mail Order Houses*, 3rd ed. (Lincolnwood, Ill.: NTC Business Books, 1987): viii.

8. Raphel, Murray, "Which Came First, the Chicken or the Egg?" *Direct Marketing* (June 1986): 99.

9. Wewer, Dan R., "Lands' End, Inc.," Investment Report, Robinson-Humphrey Company, Inc. (March 1988).

10. Sroge, "Mail Order Industry Overview," p. 51.

11. Takeuchi, Hirotaka, and Merliss, Penny Pittman, 'L. L. Bean.: Corporate Strategy," *Harvard Business School Case: 9-581-159* (Boston, Mass: Harvard Business School, Publishing Division, 1981); rev. 5/88.

12. Raphel, "Which Came First," p. 98.

13. Ibid.

14. Bremner, Brian, and Hammonds, Keith H., "Lands' End Looks a Bit Frayed at the Edges," *Business Week* (March 19, 1990): 42.

15. "Lands' End, Inc.: Our Market," Press Release, Lands' End Research, Lands' End, Inc., Chicago, Ill.

16. Caminiti, Susan, "A Mail Order Romance: Lands' End Courts Unseen Customers," *Fortune* (March 13, 1989): 45.

17. Ibid.

18. Interview with Elsa Gustafson, Lands' End Public Relations, spring 1990.

DIEMOLDING CORPORATION

L. RICHARD OLIKER

INTRODUCTION

Diemolding Corporation began operations in 1920 as a molder of custom plastic products, headquartered in Canastota, New York. It started as a typical, small, family manufacturing firm whose shareholders were also the original management team. In its early days, both management and labor worked for wages. No dividends were paid and all of the firm's net profits were reinvested in the business. Being economically conservative, management grew the firm using internally generated capital. Very little leveraging was employed (a feature of its financial operation which worked to the firm's advantage during the 1929–1939 period).

Diemolding's founder, Donald Hicks Dew, was born in Canastota and was an engineering graduate of Cornell University. He worked for typewriter companies in both Syracuse and Ilion, New York, as well as serving in the Corps of Engineers during World War I. While working for Remington Rand Typewriter Company, he decided to go into business for himself, being encouraged by that firm's works manager to "look into plastics." He returned to Canastota and developed a plastic space bar and platen knob which he sold to his old employer—Remington Rand. After a two year start-up period, and with the financial backing of his father, he constructed the first building of the present company—which is still being used. The site for this plant was on land owned by his grandfather.

Top management was engineering-oriented. Consequently, the firm specialized in custom molding, working closely with its industrial customers in the design and maintenance of the molds used in its manufacturing operations. The firm also developed an in-house capability to re-tool and re-build the molds sent to it by some of its customers. In addition, it also designed and constructed molds on site to fit specific customer needs. The corporation

Source: **Prepared by Professor L. Richard Oliker, Syracuse University, as a basis for classroom discussion and not to illustrate either effective or ineffective handling of administrative situations.** © **L. Richard Oliker, 1990.**

established definitive operating relationships with its key customers by emphasizing its engineering know-how as a distinguishing trade mark. This particular operating approach served the firm well in its first 55 years of operation.

Diemolding initially employed a single technological capability. Its presses were oriented toward and limited to the thermoset process, whereby dense plastic materials are molded under high pressure and great heat to fit the engineering specifications of individual customers. Most of the firm's initial sales were generated from successful bidding on contracts from companies which were much larger than Diemolding. While competition was fierce, management was successful in developing a reputation for a high quality product which met all customer requirements and was delivered on time and within budget. During World War II, sales, relative to previous years, rose sharply, reaching the $2 million level in 1944.

MOVING TOWARD CORPORATE MATURITY

During the 1950s, a second generation of the Dew family gradually took over the direct management of the firm. In 1959, the family incorporated Hubbard Industries in a new plant in Wampsville, New York (a small village located three miles from the first manufacturing facility). This plant initially operated as a completely separate strategic business unit, dedicated to molding thermoplastic products for custom markets. This move represented the introduction of a new technological process to Diemolding's production capabilities and increased its potential to more fully meet the overall molding needs of its larger customers. It was also a move which ended the era in which the firm could be described as a "typical small family business."

The second generation of owner/managers in the Dew family (Donald and Jarvis) completed college educations interrupted by World War II, took positions with other companies to gain professional managerial experience, and then returned to Diemolding. Jarvis joined the firm in 1949. Donald returned two years later. The former recognized that the war had dramatically expanded both plastics technology and the markets which could utilize molded plastic parts. He took over the firm's marketing program and initiated an aggressive sales campaign. Donald took over the operations end of the business, as well as its financial affairs.

In 1962, the tool and die making operations were shifted to the Wampsville location and the Dietooling Division was started. It was a unit designed for the manufacture and repair of tools and molds for both the firm and its competitors. Within two years, this division commenced to perform these same operations for non-plastic companies, and also enlarged its capacity to include the design and manufacture of new machines for other non-plastic markets. It had its own general manager and was directly responsible for developing its own markets. This was the first step toward what eventually was to become a management strategy of decentralization.

In 1964, following a long and debilitating union strike at the Canastota plant, management decided to create a new thermosetting operation—which was eventually located in Victoria, Virginia. This non-union plant became a general purpose operation which catered to a wide variety of customized product needs. At the same time, its sister thermoset division in Canastota began to seek new customers in different market segments. This diversification move allowed Diemolding to penetrate markets which had been untapped up to that time. Hubbard, Virginia, and Dietooling all grew during the late 1960s and early 1970s, but all three units suffered from relatively low profitability during this period—generally related to the inexperience of their managers.

ORGANIZATIONAL RESTRUCTURING

During the mid-1970s, top management concluded that it was both expensive and cumbersome to continue Hubbard Industries as a completely separate company with different auditors, pension plan, banking relationships, board of directors, and all of the other requirements of an independent subsidiary. The Dew family bought out the single outside stockholder and reorganized Hubbard as another division of the Corporation. The three molding divisions (Canastota, Virginia and Hubbard) were all controlled from the Canastota location. This centralized structure continued until the end of the decade.

Between 1974 and 1979, Diemolding continued a slow growth pattern, reaching a total sales level of $15 million at the end of that period. However, after-tax profits continued to average less than 5 percent. Management reinvested most of its working capital back into the business, at a rate which usually exceeded annual depreciation. Centralization, however, was not working as a viable business strategy. Operational responsibilities had become blurred, as had the ability of the firm to successfully determine separate markets for its three molding divisions. Customer specialization on the part of each division was becoming increasingly more difficult to maintain, as new domestic competitors entered these markets, as foreign manufacturers invaded other market segments, and as raw material prices rose sharply.

In the first half of 1979, top management believed that the corporation had reached the weakest point in its history, relative to its fundamental business definition as a custom molding company. The firm had become non-competitive in terms of pricing effectiveness, the efficiency of its marketing efforts, and the quality of its engineering capabilities. Its manufacturing and sales personnel appeared to be operating at cross-purposes. Customer dissatisfaction was on the rise. And low profitability continued to characterize the corporation's financial operations.

During the second half of 1979, management decided that a fundamental organization change was needed in order to more closely identify the corporation's basic problems, realign operating responsibilities, and provide a means to test managerial capabilities on the division level. Manufacturing and marketing operations were decentralized. Two new divisions were created, bringing the total to six (See Exhibit 1):

Division	Business Definition
Canastota	Custom Thermoset Molder (specialized)
Dietooling	Custom Engineering (tool & die)
Hubbard	Custom Thermoplastic Molder
Virginia	Custom Thermoset Molder (general)
DMC Sales	Marketing of Thermoset Product Lines
DHD Medical Products	Marketing of Thermoplastic Products

EXHIBIT 1 DIEMOLDING CORPORATION: 1985 ORGANIZATION CHART

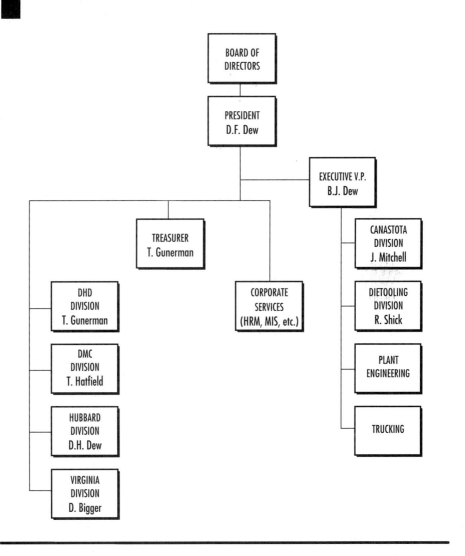

A general manager headed each division and reported directly to one of the family members at the Canastota headquarters unit. These division mangers had profitability responsibilities, as well as those associated with markets and resources. A three-year period—1980, 1981, and 1982—was devoted to the conversion of the corporation from its centralized structure to the new decentralized decision format. By the end of that period, the process was considered to be essentially complete for the Canastota, Hubbard, and Virginia divisions. The DMC Sales Division was interdependent with the Canastota Division, since its role was limited to the marketing of that division's output. In like manner, the DHD Division sold the output of Hubbard—which had (in 1982) developed the firm's first proprietary products. While its basic business still centered upon its custom molding operations, management was cautiously optimistic concerning the profit potential of the proprietary products being developed for the medical marketplace.

Using its two existing technologies, Diemolding attempted to expand its capacity to design, manufacture, assemble, package, sell, and distribute its own products—as well as meeting the custom molding needs of a wide range of industrial customers. It had identified the following areas as targets of opportunity, as it moved out of the 1981–82 recession period: process engineering, product development, process innovation, and marketing creativity. The first two areas had already given Diemolding a superior reputation, relative to the "shoot and ship" molder who characterized the average firm in the industry.

Given the advent of Diemolding's product development capability, management decided to consider a product-market matrix (see Exhibit 2) which would be tailored to the corporation's size, financial strength, and managerial capability. The latter area was a major concern, given the marketing problems which the firm had already experienced. The profit-centered responsibilities of each division manager called for a broader range of competencies than had been the case under the firm's former centralized organization structure.

Early in 1983, another three-year plan was initiated. Its goal was to provide individual division managers time to determine their specific markets and/or manufacturing capabilities, and, ultimately, to decide whether or not their markets and management teams could meet corporate profit objectives. It was during this period that top management realized that attracting and retaining good general managers had become one of its major problems. The Corporate Policy Statement for 1984 (See Exhibit 3) indicates top management's expectations for that period.

INDUSTRY NOTE

Diemolding management viewed the plastic molding industry as one easily characterized as "fragmented"; i.e., one in which no single firm had a significant market share or could strongly influence industry outcomes. Many of the

EXHIBIT 2 DIEMOLDING CORPORATION: 1989 ORGANIZATION CHART (EFFECTIVE 1/1/89)

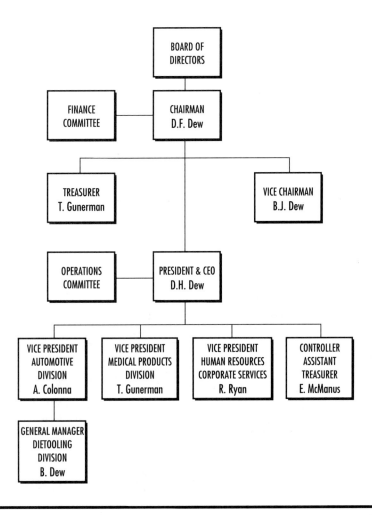

firms (like Diemolding) were privately held, offered both differentiated and undifferentiated products, and had a broad range of technological sophistication. It was an industry identified by:

1. Low barriers to entry.
2. An absence of economies of scale, in that there were many firms with roughly equal cost structures.
3. Fairly high inventory carrying costs (specifically for goods in process).
4. Erratic sales fluctuations, which, in spite of the fact that small-scale

EXHIBIT 3   DIEMOLDING CORPORATION: 1984 CORPORATE POLICIES

Individual division managers and corporate department heads are responsible for having annual and quarterly objectives which implement these policies for their respective areas of responsibility.

1. Each division manager and corporate department head is responsible for meeting the following basic management requirements:
   a. have divisional or departmental objectives available to all appropriate personnel.
   b. clearly indicate priorities where desirable or where conflict is possible.
   c. acquire and maintain the necessary resources to accomplish stated objectives.
   d. manage those resources effectively.
2. Improvement of managerial effectiveness normally is related to the accomplishment of individual objectives, on-the-job and external training, meaningful appraisals, salary reviews, and the manager's unwillingness to accept sub-standard or unsatisfactory performance.
3. All managers should use a "management by objectives program" throughout the year. Periodic reviews of these objectives, as compared to on-going progress over the year, is essential to the success of such a program.
4. All managers have enough resources to "manage by exception." Such management should allow the manager to identify his priorities and continually monitor and revise his basic plans and marketing policies.
5. The Debt-to-Equity Ratio should not exceed 1.50:1.
6. The current portion of long-term debt should not exceed the 1983 federal tax return covering depreciation.
7. Working Capital should be increased to $3,350,000.
8. The Quick Ratio should be not less than 1.25:1.
9. The Current Ratio should be not less than 2.25:1.
10. The year should end with a positive funds flow.

---

operations are usually more flexible in absorbing output shifts than large ones, still caused difficulty in balancing production facilities.
5. No size advantage in dealing with buyers and suppliers. The former are often so much larger that monopsony control often exists.
6. Diverse market demands, because buyers are also often fragmented—with some desiring special varieties of a product and willing to pay a premium rather than accepting a standardized product.
7. Captive manufacturing operations, owned by major firms who use plastic molded parts in their assembly processes.
8. Exit barriers exist, because marginal firms tend to stay in the industry longer than economically feasible.

In fact, industry trade publications indicated that marginal productivity was the general rule among those molders with 100 employees or less. While productivity rose as the size of the firm increased, profitability remained stubbornly below 5 percent for most of the firms in the industry.

STRATEGIC POSITIONING

The Dew family, as owner/manager of Diemolding, recognized that develop-ments in plastics technology had provided an increased number of applica-tions that had not even existed at the start of the last decade. A wider choice of resins and sizing compounds were now available and could be specifically designed to meet the needs of a broader cross-section of customers in the medical products, electronics, aerospace, and sports industries. However, these market opportunities were threatened by rising imports of finished goods, competition among various plastics for the same markets, and raw ma-terial price fluctuations (the latter caused, in large part, by the dumping of excess resins by U.S. firms in foreign spot markets).

Management believed that its emerging product development capability gave it a distinct market advantage. In order to encourage that competency, it had:

1. Adopted a more open management style, designed to promote this ca-pability by encouraging trial and error testing in a purposeful manner. Incentives and a relatively relaxed set of controls were adopted in an effort to generate the maximum number of ideas.
2. A new learning approach was adopted in order to more fully involve all functional areas in this development process.
3. Product development was also treated as a catalyst for change within the firm, as well as a generator of future revenue streams. Policy deci-sions were made which began to change the permutation of resources between custom and proprietary product lines.

Consequently, Diemolding management believed that its future growth and profitability were closely tied to its ability to capitalize on its perceived strengths: product development, process technologies, and market deploy-ment; i.e., changing its "mix" between custom and proprietary product lines. As a result, Diemolding management began a series of strategy sessions which were designed to assess each division's core capabilities, growth potential, quick response adaptability, and its raw staying power. The latter was viewed as a measure of a division's ability to sustain a protracted strike, competitive battle, or market decline.

Each division manager presented a detailed self-assessment on these spe-cific points. Each evaluation provided, in reality, a measure of the division's strategic adaptation profile. These evaluations became the basis for the firm's next series of strategic decisions—which again changed the structure and char-acter of the firm in the mid-1980s.

GENERAL MANAGEMENT PROBLEMS

As previously noted, attracting and retaining experienced division managers continued to be one of Diemolding's major problems. In 1983, the failure of several divisions to meet their profit goals acted to reinforce this point to top management. At that time, management turnover on the division leadership level was on the rise. Given plans to change the role then being played by one of the family members (the third generation), the two senior officers felt that managerial resources were becoming as important to the future of the firm as its capital resources.

During the 1979–1986 period, Diemolding's top management became painfully aware that its future success was a direct function of its ability to both hire and retain good general managers. The firm needed experienced managers on the division level and in key marketing and manufacturing positions. Rapid turnover in all of these levels had limited the firm's growth and affected its profitability.

When its policy of decentralization was initiated in 1979, by giving division managers broader authority and responsibility, the lack of depth of its managerial personnel became all too apparent. Given the number of much larger firms in the central New York area (who were also looking for good general managers) hiring on that level became one of Diemolding's competitive disadvantages. This was one of the reasons for top management's decision to abandon decentralization in favor of a more centralized operation.

During this same period, however, the firm was quite successful in hiring a number of experienced managers of a more specialized variety. A hostile takeover of Syracuse-based Carrier Corporation by United Technologies Corporation had changed the area's employment picture. While many Carrier managers left the area for greener pastures, others sought new jobs in the Upstate region. Low-cost housing, good school systems, and the generally high quality of worklife acted to constrain a decision to leave. Diemolding hired eight of these mangers to fill specific positions in various divisions.

However, its recruiting efforts for general managers was not improved by the situation at Carrier. Diemolding's size, the level and coverage of its compensation/fringe benefits packages, its private ownership, and its perceived commitment to a high-tech future all acted to reduce its attractiveness in the eyes of experienced general managers. Its inability to attract such individuals became a constraint on the firm's growth potential.

STRATEGIC ADAPTATION

While 1982 had been a breakeven year for the firm, 1983's results were a distinct improvement. Sales in the latter year exceeded the $20 million level for the first time. However, while in the prior year proprietary product sales had risen sharply and posted significant profit gains, 1983 sales in this segment were quite disappointing. The sales of custom products advanced across the board. Divisions which had done well in the former period did poorly in the latter—in spite of sales forecasts to the contrary. Thus, market identification, penetration, and consolidation problems continued as a major difficulty, along with division leadership and continuity.

The firm entered 1984 with 445 employees (an all-time high). Its six SBUs (the three molding divisions, one toolmaking and repair division, and two marketing divisions), given the growth and change which had taken place since the decentralization move in 1979, had become more difficult to manage. Family members had become fully attenuated with their respective managerial responsibilities. While each of the molding divisions continued to seek its respective market niche, concerns continued to surface because the output of the Canastota and Hubbard divisions continued to be sold by the two marketing divisions (DMC and DHD, respectively). Production and sales managers, although trying to coordinate their activities, continued to operate at cross-purposes in all too many instances.

An effort was made to come to grips with these problems in mid-1984. A major strategic management program was initiated, involving all division and corporate officers. The defined goals of this three-year program were to:

1. Critically examine the viability of the decentralized structure and decision-making capabilities of the firm.
2. Carefully analyze the basic markets and/or manufacturing capabilities for the future of the six SBUs.
3. Determine if these markets and/or manufacturing capabilities could meet divisional and corporate profit requirements.
4. Evaluate the present effectiveness of the management teams of each SBU, as related to its ability to meet both corporate management requirements and profit goals.
5. Forecast the human and financial resources necessary to support market and manufacturing requirements projected through 1987.
6. Consolidate the divisional profit projections into corporate statements and forecasts, and determine the acceptability of the resultant figures.
7. Determine the amount of debt acceptable to the shareholders, as measured by both total volume and the ratio of debt to net worth.
8. Determine the requirements for remaining privately owned, given the opportunity costs involved.
9. Begin to prepare for the succession transition resulting from either substantially reduced activity levels or from the retirement of the two senior officers.
10. Determine, based upon all of the above measures, the long-range objectives for 1986, 1987, and 1988.

At that time (year end, 1984), Diemolding's strategic assumptions for the next three-year period were:

1. The debt-to-equity ratio would be improved; ultimately to become 1:1 by the end of that period.
2. Long-term debt would be continuously worked down over the same period, at a 10 percent per year reduction (at least).
3. The funds flow for each division would average a positive balance over the period.

4. The firm would remain privately held.
5. Return on assets would be at least 24 percent of pre-tax profits, before any adjustments to the financial statements.
6. Profits on sales would average 10 percent (8–10 percent on custom molding sales and 10–12 percent on proprietary sales).

Although Diemolding's marketing problems continued to concern management, 1984 sales exceeded $24 million. However, operating and selling costs rose rapidly, reducing the firm's profitability relative to the previous year. As a result, a cost containment/reduction program was initiated in 1985. It proved to be relatively effective, as profit levels rose that year. However, sales lagged behind those in 1984. By this time, the board of directors (as reported by the firm's president to all salaried employees at year end) had become critical of management's failure to accomplish its business plans, either as a corporation on a consolidated basis, or on an individual division basis.

Top management believed that these concerns were warranted and resulted from its own unrealistic evaluation of both the strengths and weaknesses of the divisional managers. Considerable training and management development efforts had gone into improving competencies on that level. However, actual and planned divisional performance continued to fluctuate. As a result, the policy of decentralization continued to be scrutinized by both top management and the board of directors.

SUCCESSION MANAGEMENT

In a private, family owned-and-operated company, such as Diemolding Corporation, the normal route to organizational leadership is a generational progression. The owners, however, have a responsibility to other (than the family) constituencies for the successful operation of the firm. Employees, suppliers, customers, creditors, and the local community are all dependent, to one degree or another, upon the continuity of the corporation.

It is axiomatic to believe that the long-term health of any organization is primarily dependent upon the quality of the people who assume leadership positions. Yet few organizations develop a detailed description of the abilities, qualities, and competencies required for each senior position. The process by which individuals are developed and selected for most senior roles is relatively unplanned and, in large part, undefined. The fact that a manager is or is not producing well in his current position may be one of the least helpful pieces of information relative to "getting ahead." Success in the current position is not always an accurate measure of future potential. However, it is the one most often employed. In a firm such as Diemolding, with its difficulty in recruiting experienced general managers, it is one of the only measures available.

The stewardship of Donald F. and B. Jarvis Dew had brought continued growth and relative success to the firm. Don's son, Donald H., entered the business in 1966, and his managerial career had been shaped through a wide variety of line-management assignments since that time. Jarvis's son, Bruce—Donald H.'s junior by 10 years—had started with the firm on a part-time basis in 1981 and became a full-time employee upon his graduation from college in 1986.

In a small firm such as Diemolding, members of top management usually have to hold a broader variety of positions than would be the case in a much larger firm. Owner-managers are expected, as a matter of course, to have an intimate knowledge of all parts of their operations, markets, and products. While this may be honored as much in the breach as in the observance in some firms, general management experience is a normal part of the progression to the top.

At the start of the 1985 business year, Donald H. Dew was being programmed to take a "major role and/or complete responsibility for organizing and chairing quarterly and annual Directors' meetings." He had already successfully managed one of the divisions (Hubbard) and was in the process of taking over reporting/line responsibilities for other SBUs. His performance was being closely monitored by the senior family members and the "outside" members of the board of directors.

It was expected that both senior members of the family would be retired by the end of the current decade (Donald F. was—in 1987—62 years old and his brother Jarvis was 66). Before that time, the board expected that full succession would have been achieved, with Donald F. becoming president of the firm and Bruce becoming a division manager soon thereafter.

Another manager (not a family member) was also considered to be a key component of the succession plan. His career was somewhat reflective of the variety of roles which can be played in a firm of the size of Diemolding. Tom Gunnerman had been hired as the firm's comptroller. Within three years, he had become treasurer, and was also acting as the firm's chief financial officer (without that title). He had developed an interest in expanding the firm's proprietary business into the medical products area, and helped to initiate that operation. By 1984, he had become the general manager of the DHD Medical Products Division, while still acting as CFO.

Gunnerman developed a marketing capability which had certainly been unexpected when he joined the firm. While he lacked manufacturing experience, he was the principal force in "growing" the medical products initiative. As a result, he was considered as a key player in the future of the firm, and the only non-family member with any top management potential.

Personnel decisions were made which resulted in the 1986 sales year beginning with five of the six divisional managers being newly appointed to their positions. Thus, breaking-in and fine-tuning this new management team was considered a major priority for the year. The business plan which had been adopted was considered to be the most realistic and (possibly) conservative one developed over the past five years. Since the pre-tax corporate profit objective was 8 percent, the new team was faced with a real challenge.

Management believed that the firm was undercapitalized at this point,

EXHIBIT 4   DIEMOLDING CORPORATION: SUMMARY OF SALES AND INCOME BEFORE TAXES, 1984–1988 (AUDITED STATEMENT BASIS)

	1984		1985		1986		1987		1988	
	Sales	Before Tax	Sales	Before Tax	Sales	Before Tax	Sales	Before Tax	Sales	Before Tax
Canastota	9,960	448	8,744	(43)	12,196	274	12,307	629	11,927	85
DMC	948	(230)	858	(96)	1,073	(132)	—	—	—	—
Hubbard	6,772	92	6,312	92	7,822	225	7,583	360	11,504*	493*
DHD	3,739	(331)	4,249	404	5,261	398	6,653	546	—	—
Virginia	5,829	291	5,205	269	5,984	338	5,927	(200)	6,693	355
Dietooling	1,129	50	1,003	(101)	1,161	38	956	(18)	1,560	134
Other (Madison/TRG)	718	81	764	49	1,101	(108)	845	(49)	643	23
Inter-Company Sales	(4,483)	—	(3,926)	—	(5,481)	—	(4,874)	—	(1,664)	—
Corporate (O/H)	—	(389)	—	(250)	—	(23)	—	(230)	—	(291)
TOTAL	24,612	199	23,209	324	29,117	1,010	29,397	1,038	30,663	799
Total										602**
										1,401

Note: Amounts are given in thousands.
*Includes DHD—renamed the Medical Products Division.
**Gain on Virginia sale.

given the size of its operations. Rising sales during the year had stretched the firm's working capital needs. Long-term debt exceeded the $5 million level and the owners were concerned about being too heavily leveraged. Reinvestment in plant and equipment continued at the depreciation rate of about $850,000 annually. The point had been reached where increasing sales on low-profit product lines, in order to absorb overhead costs, no longer provided any advantage to the firm. Two of the three molding divisions were operating within their costing formula range of approximately 75 percent of utilization, while the other had yet to reach that objective.

The position taken by top management and the board of directors was that satisfactory profitability was necessary on the part of the firm's major divisions, if continued reinvestments were to continue in those divisions in the future. 1986 was considered to be a test year for this idea. If desired profits were not achieved, the possibility of downsizing the firm, to recapture a portion of the working capital utilized by some units, would have to be considered. Thus, higher profit levels, controlled capital expenditures, lower aging of receivables, and better inventory controls were the operating objectives for that year.

The books closed on a 1986 business year which registered a 25 percent increase in sales over the previous year. While pre-tax profits had more than doubled (from 1.4 percent to 3.4 percent), they were still well below the business plan (of 5.4%). The DHD Medical Products Division contributed the major share of these profits (see Exhibit 4). Its products were manufactured by Hubbard, making the two divisions interdependent. The same was true for DMC and Canastota. The former marketed the latter's output of both proprietary (a very small proportion) and custom products.

ORGANIZATIONAL REALIGNMENT

Top management had, in spite of the impressive sales increase, reached a decision that the firm had become too complicated, with too many divisions for a company doing only $29 million in business. Early in 1987, an effort was initiated to consolidate wherever possible. A focus strategy was adopted—to concentrate on specific markets and manufacturing/engineering specialities. Management recognized that its custom molding business was experiencing declining profit levels. On the other hand, both sales and profits were on the rise for proprietary medical products. An increasing proportion of Hubbard's capacity was now being devoted to those products. Basic decisions were needed relative to the desired proportion of proprietary versus custom business which should be produced by that division.

The DHD Medical Products Division and the DMC Technical Products Division had been originally created in order to (1) increase the sales of the manufacturing divisions (Hubbard and Canastota, respectively) that produced their products, and (2) to give the corporation some control over its own sales. Custom molding sales were a derived demand, while proprietary sales were directly related to the marketability of the firm's own products. The corporation's move into the proprietary arena was a diversification strategy which was designed to further distinguish Diemolding from its competitors.

By the end of fiscal 1986, 75 percent of Diemolding's total revenues were still being derived from custom molding operations, while the remaining 25 percent came from proprietary sales. In the Canastota Division, the five largest customers accounted for 75 percent of total volume (of which 88 percent was in the automotive industry). At the Virginia Division, the top five customers accounted for 76 percent of total volume; while the same number of customers only accounted for 46 percent of DHD's proprietary sales (and the latter's top ten accounts created only 64 percent of its total sales). Custom business was still based upon jobs where the customer usually owned the die used in the molding operation. While the Dietooling Division had the capability of rebuilding that die (or even making a new one), the customer was still in a position to take its die to a competing firm, when it decided to cancel its business with a molder like Diemolding.

It is the customer who designs the part to be molded. Once completed by a molder, that part is usually assembled with others into a final product bearing the customer's name. The ultimate success of that product is entirely dependent upon the customer's marketing and sales effectiveness. It was in an effort to break this dependence that the move to proprietary products had been initiated.

The Dietooling Division was, given its dual role of servicing the firm's in-house engineering needs and selling these same services to other firms, retooling its operations—in order to improve its overall delivery capability. A new general manager had been hired to accomplish that objective. It was his belief that his division would soon be well able to deliver the first part of its mission in good order, but had a long way to go in the effective marketing of its custom engineering services to outside clients.

He was also concerned that his division was barely able to price its services to other Diemolding units at a competitive level; i.e., equal to or below the cost of the same services which could be purchased from another vendor. He initiated a cost-reduction program as part of the general up-grading of the division's capital facilities. Delivery of a high-quality, cost-effective service thus became his first goal.

Dietooling's marketing capability could, at the time of the arrival of the new general manager, be best described as "limited." Management believed that the existence of a custom engineering capability gave it a distinct competitive advantage over the average "shoot-and-ship" molder—which usually lacked this capability. While Diemolding's customers indeed appreciated this service, it had not been promoted effectively to other manufacturers. It was in this area that new initiatives were needed.

The board of directors decided, in November 1986, as part of the new focus strategy, to merge the DMC Technical Products Division with the Canastota Division. The avowed purpose of this move was to reduce operating costs and to simplify the management of what had become a specialized proprietary business. The latter division was, however, still a matter of concern to top management in terms of (1) the ability of its general manager to deal effectively with all aspects of his responsibilities; (2) the lack of satisfactory cost controls over both custom and proprietary product output; and (3) the lack of methods improvement and increased automation which could substantially improve this division's productivity.

Early in 1987, the Virginia Division began to drop well behind its annual sales plan. Its lack of a broad customer base, very generalized thermoset markets, the aging of its capital base, and its apparent inability to add new customers with real growth potential were identified as its underlying problems. In addition, its distance from Diemolding management, difficulty in retaining management-level personnel in its rural Virginia location, and the effectiveness of its general manager were all causes of continuing concern. In a period when the rest of the corporation was moving toward specialized custom and proprietary markets, this division was experiencing difficulties of a "strategic fit" nature.

This division had experienced a continuous and often rapid turnover in its sales management and production management personnel. This form of instability led to an indeterminate strategic approach to the resolution of its basic market/product problems. It was the only one of the firm's three production divisions which had remained essentially as a "shoot-and-ship" operation. Its quality assurance program lacked consistency, creating customer relations problems of an on-going nature. It had also been unable to develop any proprietary products, in spite of efforts in the past to research and implement such a possibility.

Given its managerial turnover, Virginia's general manager often found himself wearing several hats, in terms of taking on a number of functional roles—in addition to his normal responsibilities. He was actually more comfortable in these familiar roles. In the period since he had assumed his division's leadership position, his managerial approach had remained one of a tactical, short-term variety—relative to the strategic perspective already adopted by Diemolding's other divisions. His actual-versus-planned sales/profits results varied widely from year to year. Although top management and the Canastota Division manager were spending more time at the Virginia location to support his efforts, progress was slow. During their absence, their own areas of responsibility were uncovered, due to the lack of any back-up capability.

As the 1987 business year progressed, top management and the board closely analyzed the growing interdependency between the DHD Medical Products Division and the Hubbard Division. Discussions centered around the possibility of further focusing the firm's operations by merging these two units. Anticipated advantages from such a move were expected to be (1) increased cost-saving opportunities, (2) elimination of some parochial attitudes which existed in these two SBUs, and (3) the enhanced capacity to design, develop, manufacture, and sell new products in a much faster and more efficient fashion.

The manager of the Canastota Division had started with the firm at age 17 as an hourly employee. He had, over his 35 years with the firm, developed into an outstanding manufacturing manager, who worked very well with many of the division's customers. However, after overseeing a major plant expansion, he appeared unable to effectively implement a viable cost containment program and to increase plant capacity (which was only 60 percent at the end of FY 1987). In addition, while he had the total respect of his employees, he could not come to grips with an increasing number of personnel problems awaiting resolution.

His situation appeared to be a classic "Peter Principle" case. However, he resisted any idea which would have either brought in someone to relieve him of some of these problem areas (an assistant division manager) or to return to the position of manufacturing manager of the division (with no payroll reduction). He also refused to consider the idea of developing a new position for him which would allow him to operate in those areas where he had already demonstrated his expertise.

His attitude appeared to be influenced by the presence of Dietooling's new manager, who had previously been in charge of manufacturing for one of Carrier Corporation's major units. That manager was understandably underemployed in his present assignment. Top management was seeking a new role for him with a broader range of responsibilities. Thus, all levels of management were sensitive to the leadership situation in the Canastota Division. However, it was a problem which required resolution early in the 1988 fiscal year.

1987 ended with Diemolding's pre-tax profit level much improved over the previous year. However, the Virginia Division had experienced a major loss—relative to its annual plan. This was offset by the performance of the Canastota and DHD Medical Products divisions. Thus, proprietary and specialized custom products were carrying the corporation, while its non-specialized thermoset markets were faltering.

In reviewing the 1987 results, the board agreed that 1988 would be a transitional year for the corporation. Decisions would have to be made across a broad range of problem areas, and all members understood that the resulting organization could be quite different from the one of 1987. The key decision areas were identified to be:

1. The advisability of either the divestiture or liquidation of the Virginia Division.
2. The possibility of the merger of the DHD Medical Products and Hubbard divisions, and the continued consolidation (centralization) of the firm's operations.
3. The completion of the corporation's succession management program.
4. The realignment of the management of the Canastota Division, given its current inability to improve its cost control operations and deal effectively with a number of sensitive personnel-related problems.
5. The need to reassess the Dietooling Division, in terms of improving its

ability to better service the firm's own manufacturing divisions and in marketing improved engineering services to other small manufacturing companies.

The resolution of this complex set of problems became the firm's managerial objective for 1988. Both top management and the board of directors believed them to be "doable"; yet were concerned about the timing of their effective implementation. There was some consensus that all of these problems could not be resolved during the coming calendar year, given their complexity and the "thin" management team available for their resolution.

At its December 1987 board meeting, the foregoing decision areas were prioritized and a three-year strategic management program was initiated. The first objective of this program was the divestiture of the Virginia Division. Efforts made that year to shore up that unit were expected to have a positive effect on its operations in 1988—especially in the sales area. Top management believed that its loss for that year (see Exhibit 4) could be reversed in 1988; thus improving the value of the division for divestiture purposes.

Several competing plastics manufacturers expressed interest in buying the Virginia Division, as did the current management team at that location. The latter acquisition offer was proposed in the form of a leveraged buy-out (LBO). As negotiations progressed during 1988, Virginia's sales volume recovered as expected. Its profitability also rebounded. This spurred that division's management to improve its buy-out offer—based upon a combination of local tax relief, financial support at the state level in the form of low-interest industrial revenue bonding (IRB), and, of course, its positive projections for the next few years.

Diemolding's top management closed the sale of the division to its own managers at the end of November 1988. The net effect of the sales transaction was treated as an extraordinary gain. By that time, the division had returned to profitability in good order (see Exhibit 4).

The second objective of the strategic management program was the approval of the merger of the Hubbard and DHD Medical Products divisions—to take place at the start of the 1988 calendar year and renamed the Medical Products Division. This merger process was expected to take at least two years; with a favorable financial impact not likely to occur until the second (1989) year.

Resistance to change, increased price competition in the markets for several key medical products, and the rising cost of raw materials slowed the effectiveness of the gains expected from this merger. The combined entity produced sales and profits in 1988 which were less than the sum for the individual divisions in both 1986 and 1987. As a result, management looked to 1989 to resolve some of the above problems and produce the planned gains expected as a result of the merger.

The third goal of the program was the completion of the succession management process. This step was initiated at the start of the 1989 calendar year (see Exhibit 2). Donald F. Dew's son, Donald H., assumed the position of president and CEO of the firm; with his father becoming chairman of the board. Jarvis Dew became vice chairman of the board and partially retired from the day-to-day operations of the firm. His son Bruce had, by that time, become head of the Dietooling Division. Bruce was being groomed to take over the financial reins of the firm within the next five years. It was still too early to determine how this third generation of the Dew family would fare in responding to the growing number of problems facing the firm.

This new management team was strengthened by a new head of the Canastota Division in May 1988. (That division was renamed the Automotive Division in early 1988, to reflect the focus strategy already adopted for the application of its manufacturing capabilities.) The division's performance fell far behind its 1987 record (see Exhibit 4) and serious cost-control problems were still unresolved by the end of that fiscal period. As a result, a number of corrective measures were planned for 1989 to control costs and raise the plant utilization rate much closer to the desired 80 percent level.

Given the nature of the foregoing problems, the Dietooling Division was not addressed in 1988. It was, among some other problem areas, simply put on hold for that period—to be more carefully reviewed in 1989, when management had hopefully resolved the foregoing set of problems.

PONTIAC DIVISION OF GENERAL MOTORS (A), (B), AND (C)

**PETER LAGENHORST
AND WILLIAM E.
FULMER**

"WE BUILD EXCITEMENT, PON-TI-AC!"

As he watched the sleek, sporty, black Firebird Trans Am and the fiery red Fiero in the new TV commercial, J. Michael Losh, the 40-year-old general manager of the Pontiac Division of General Motors, was convinced that Pontiac had returned to the tradition of a sporty image. According to Losh, "We're not going to be the low-priced division, we're not going to be selling luxury products, we're not going to have the broadest range of products. What we're going to sell are sporty and expressive cars." Although Pontiac's goals for 1987 were established—900,000 cars and 8.5 percent of the U.S. market—Losh needed to consider the direction Pontiac should take in the 1990s. Since GM's market share had dropped to 41 percent in 1986 and profits were expected to be under $3 billion, down more than $1 billion from 1985, new pressures were being felt at Losh's level. A significant pressure was Roger Smith's goal of reducing white-collar employment by 25 percent by 1990.

HISTORY OF PONTIAC IN GM

The beginnings of Pontiac were credited to a successful young businessman named Edward M. Murphy, who in 1893 started the Pontiac Buggy Company in Pontiac, Michigan.[1] In the next 10 years, Murphy became increasingly interested in the horseless carriages that began to appear around the streets of Pontiac. Sensing the automobile was here to stay and not just a rich man's novelty, he decided to enter the motor business by purchasing a two-cylinder

Source: **Prepared by Peter Lagenhorst under the direction of Professor William E. Fulmer, Harvard University, as a basis for classroom discussion and not to illustrate either effective or ineffective handling of administrative situations. © The Colgate Darden Graduate School Sponsors, University of Virginia, 1987, 1988.**

engine from a well-known engineer in the field of engine design, A. P. Brush. Four years later, in 1907, Murphy equipped a section of his buggy-making facility for car production and founded the Oakland Motor Car Company. With an initial investment of $200,000, Murphy produced the two-cylinder Oakland, and in 1908 he introduced a four-cylinder Model K, a more powerful and competitively priced vehicle. Production of the Model K was 278 in 1908 and 1,035 in 1909.

Because of its initial success, the company attracted the attention of another automobile entrepreneur, William C. Durant. Durant had already started to buy automobile companies to form the nucleus of what would become the General Motors Corporation. In 1909 the GM board of directors approved the purchase of a half-interest in the Oakland Motor Car Company. Oakland joined the emerging General Motors Company, which already included Buick and Oldsmobile car companies. (GM added Cadillac Motor Car Company in 1910 and Chevrolet Motor Car Company in 1918.)

Murphy, considered by Durant to be a potential future leader in GM, died in 1909 at the age of 45. GM then took full control of the Oakland company, and a longtime friend and associate of Murphy's, L. L. Dunlap, succeeded him as manager. (A complete list of all Pontiac general managers is in Exhibit 1.)

EXHIBIT 1　　PONTIAC DIVISION: GENERAL MANAGERS

OAKLAND MOTOR CAR COMPANY	1907–08	Edward M. Murphy
	1909–10	Lee Dunlap
	1911–14	George P. Daniels
	1916–20	Fred W. Warner
	1921–23	George H. Hannum
	1924–30	Alfred R. Glancy
	1931	Irving J. Reuter
PONTIAC DIVISION	1932–33	William S. Knudsen/F. O. Tanner
	1933–51	Harry J. Klinger
	1951–52	Arnold Lenz
	1952–56	Robert M. Critchfield
	1956–61	Semon E. Knudsen
	1961–65	Elliot M. Estes
	1965–69	John Z. DeLorean
	1969–72	F. James McDonald
	1972–75	Martin J. Caserio
	1975–78	Alex C. Mair
	1978–80	Robert C. Stempel
	1980–84	William E. Hoglund
	1984–	J. Michael Losh

Source: *Automotive News* (GM 75 Years Anniversary Issue, September 16, 1983).

In the following years, Oakland saw its production boom, even through tight financial times. It fast became a leader in ideas and products within the GM organization. The Model K grew to production of 4,639 vehicles in 1910. Following World War I, despite the warnings of skeptics, Oakland successfully put closed bodies on its light cars, and it pioneered a new, fast-drying Duco lacquer paint in 1923.

In 1926 Oakland introduced a new six-cylinder vehicle at the New York Auto Show. The Pontiac Six, or "Chief of the Sixes" as it was advertised, was named after Chief Pontiac of the Ottawas, who had ruled all Indian tribes bounded by the Great Lakes, the Alleghenies, and the Mississippi River. The new Pontiac, lighter than previous six-cylinder models, caught the public's favor, and 76,742 vehicles were sold in 1926.

Alfred P. Sloan, Jr., president of GM at the time, saw this entrant as another car to fill a slot in the wide range of automobile buyers' preferences. Backed by his famous statement, "A car for every purse and purpose," Sloan began to position the car divisions to meet that need, spanning the market with Chevrolet, Oldsmobile, Oakland, Buick Standard, Buick Master, and Cadillac. He had seen two gaps in the lineup, however, one between Chevrolet and Oldsmobile, and the other between Buick Master and Cadillac. The introduction of the new Pontiac Six filled the gap between Chevrolet and Oldsmobile, while the new LaSalle by Cadillac filled the other.

It was evident that production facilities were too small to accommodate both the new Pontiac and the existing Oakland car lines, so a new plant site was developed on 246 acres on the city's north side. Three assembly lines, an engine plant, a sheet metal plant, and a parts manufacturing plant were erected.

In the late 1920s, a shrinking automobile market and the onslaught of the Depression damaged the auto industry. While Pontiac's sales remained strong, Oakland's sales all but vanished, and with corporate cost cutting and consolidation, the Oakland Motor Car Company was terminated, as the Pontiac line became the new division, and was given a new name.

In 1933 Harry J. Klingler, then sales manager at Chevrolet, became general manager of Pontiac, the first to do so who was neither from engineering nor from manufacturing. GM felt Pontiac's engineering and manufacturing were satisfactory, so the concentration shifted to marketing. Klingler's first years were spent primarily on personnel changes, including bringing key marketing people from Chevrolet. The first two years of Klingler's management fell short of the long-range plan of 400,000 cars a year, but under Klingler, Pontiac made its greatest leap forward. In 1935 the first Pontiac engineered under his leadership was introduced. It had a distinctive silver streak on the radiator grille, which became the first identifying symbol of the Pontiac car. In 1935 sales hit 180,000 units, and production could not keep up with dealer orders. In 1941 Pontiac sold 330,061 units, becoming the largest producer in its price class ($3,000–$4,000) and the fifth largest in the nation.

Pontiac production ceased with the U.S. entrance into World War II, as auto facilities were converted to aid the war effort. Passenger-car manufacture

resumed in 1945, at which time an expansion program was launched to increase production of Pontiacs by 50 percent.

In 1951 Klingler was moved to vice president of Vehicle Production at
GM, and Arnold Lenz became general manager. Lenz's sudden death in 1952
led to R. M. Critchfield's taking over. Critchfield saw a need to expand and
modernize the Pontiac operation. A new car-finish building and a newly modernized V-8 engine plant were completed in 1954. A sales record of 581,860
cars was set one year later.

Semon E. (Bunkie) Knudsen, the son of a former GM president, took over
Pontiac in 1956. As the youngest GM general manager at the time (age 43), he
proceeded to refocus Pontiac's image away from big, boxy cars. Knudsen put
together a new engineering group headed by chief engineer Elliott (Pete) Estes
from Oldsmobile and John Z. DeLorean from Packard. The team methodically
went to work developing new models. An image of youthful cars emerged.

In three years the Knudsen/Estes/DeLorean team changed the product
lineup. In the fall of 1960, following intensive R&D and testing, Pontiac introduced a completely new car line, the Tempest series. Fresh in styling, the Tempest became an immediate success and was recognized by the corporation and
the media as the outstanding auto engineering achievement of the year.

When Knudsen became general manager of the Chevrolet Division in
1961, Estes was named the new general manager of Pontiac. He was credited
with many engineering innovations in Pontiac cars. One of the most popular
was the "wide track" principle, which supplied a car with a wider wheel base
than before for better road handling. In addition to his engineering innovations, Estes was successful in raising Pontiac to a third-place position in U.S.
sales, trailing only Chevrolet and Ford. Sales soared to nearly 700,000 units,
and U.S. market share rose to nearly 9 percent.

In 1965 Fisher Body plants and most assembly plants were combined into
the General Motors Assembly Division (GMAD) and a move was begun to standardize component parts among the five car lines. The same year, Estes followed Knudsen's footsteps to Chevrolet (and later became president of GM),
and DeLorean, then chief engineer, was named the new general manager. De-
Lorean, a prolific inventor in his own right, claimed credit for over 200 patents and applications, and had participated in such Pontiac innovations as the
wide track, the overhead cam engine, and the concealed windshield wipers. In
early 1967 Pontiac introduced its first car targeted towards the youthful,
sporty car market, the Firebird. In 1968 another sporty car was unveiled and
became an instant hit, the legendary GTO. With its rubber-like bumper, the
new GTO (the original version had been first introduced in 1964) attracted
nationwide attention and was named *Motor Trend's* "Car of the Year." Sales
records were shattered as 866,826 Pontiac cars were sold, an all-time high, and
Pontiac became a big name in auto racing. (See Exhibit 2 for Pontiac's historical model-year sales and Pontiac and GM domestic market shares.) For the
first time, sales of specialty cars—Tempest, Grand Prix, and Firebird—exceeded those of the traditional Pontiac line.

As his two predecessors had done, DeLorean became general manager of

GM DOMESTIC MARKET SHARES/ 1965-1985

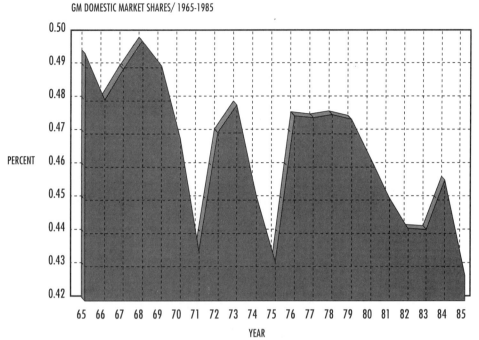

PONTIAC DOMESTIC MARKET SHARES/ 1965-1985

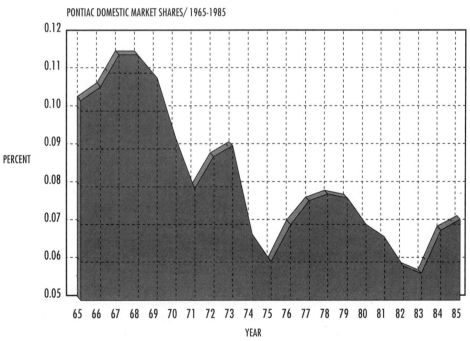

Source: Internal Pontiac Data Base.

EXHIBIT 2   (continued)

HISTORICAL MODEL YEAR (MY) SALES

YEAR	UNIT SALES			MARKET SHARE	
	Pontiac	*GM*	*U.S. Domestic*	*Pontiac*	*GM*
1965	609,674	2,898,346	5,865,998	10.4%	49.4%
1966	831,684	3,764,493	7,849,318	10.6%	48.0%
1967	833,224	3,559,541	7,275,073	11.5%	48.9%
1968	866,826	3,739,136	7,521,926	11.5%	49.7%
1969	843,610	3,827,010	7,809,535	10.8%	49.0%
1970	664,879	3,357,229	7,190,992	9.2%	46.7%
1971	576,021	3,130,180	7,197,407	8.0%	43.5%
1972	741,691	3,998,972	8,523,645	8.7%	46.8%
1973	854,343	4,444,716	9,328,487	9.2%	47.6%
1974	557,276	3,591,776	7,957,617	7.0%	45.1%
1975	465,410	3,350,434	7,734,662	6.0%	43.3%
1976	700,931	4,607,895	9,731,181	7.2%	47.4%
1977	811,904	5,092,331	10,758,739	7.5%	47.3%
1978	871,391	5,245,719	11,065,501	7.9%	47.4%
1979	828,603	5,119,078	10,812,885	7.7%	47.3%
1980	638,656	4,228,231	9,137,507	7.0%	46.3%
1981	601,218	4,032,727	8,951,056	6.7%	45.1%
1982	461,845	3,387,607	7,683,154	6.0%	44.1%
1983	513,239	3,876,006	8,796,364	5.8%	44.1%
1984	707,033	4,659,818	10,256,021	6.9%	45.4%
1985	785,617	4,694,979	10,994,475	7.1%	42.7%

Source: Internal Pontiac Data Base.

Chevrolet (he later left the corporation to develop the DeLorean Motor Car Company in Europe), and F. James McDonald became Pontiac's new general manager in 1969. McDonald, a manufacturing expert, continued the division's momentum by steering Pontiac into the compact market segment with a low-priced vehicle, the Ventura II. Other new additions to the division were a new administration building on the original plant site and a new engineering test facility. By 1971 Pontiac was holding on to the third-spot ranking in the indus-try sales race for the 10th time in 11 years—following only Chevrolet and Ford.

In 1972 Martin J. Caserio became general manager of Pontiac, following McDonald's move to the general manager's position at Chevrolet (and later to the presidency of GM). Caserio, who had been general manager of the Truck and Coach Division the previous six years, pushed Pontiac into the intermediate-car segment with a totally redesigned set of vehicles. These cars of the early 1970s were redesigned to be more luxurious.

In late 1973 and early 1974, when the oil crisis left many carmakers scrambling to increase fuel economy and efficiency, Pontiac was harder hit than most. With its "gas guzzler," or "muscle car" image, Pontiac sales dropped to 557,276 vehicles in 1974 and then to 465,410 vehicles in 1975. As in the other GM divisions, Pontiac struggled to refocus its cars. The product line was changed to reflect more fuel-efficient vehicles, and scrambling for survival, Pontiac abandoned the sporty, "muscle car" image. The race was on to build the lowest priced car, with the plushest interior and the softest velour trim. According to a Pontiac spokesman,

> During the mid to late '70s, we tried hard to respond. We joined everyone else in trying to build smaller, lighter, more fuel-efficient products. We chased the Chevrolet price leaders, tried to out-plush Buick, and out-Velour Oldsmobile.

In October 1975, Alex C. Mair was named the new general manager of Pontiac, as Caserio became group executive in charge of the Electrical Components Group. Pontiac's golden anniversary lineup in 1976 included a new sporty subcompact, the Sunbird, and a new platform for the Bonneville. These shorter and lighter weight vehicles were designed to meet the need for small and fuel-efficient automobiles, and helped increase sales in the short run.

When Mair was moved to the vice president's job of the Technical Staffs Group in 1978, Robert C. Stempel, then director of engineering at Chevrolet, became the new general manager of Pontiac. Considered one of the industry's leading engineering authorities, Stempel introduced a new lineup of vehicles that had major styling changes and engine updates to reflect even better fuel efficiency and handling than previously.

DEVELOPMENTS DURING THE 1980s

In August 1980, 45 year-old William E. Hoglund, formerly the corporate comptroller, became the new general manager of Pontiac. Hoglund was faced with a floundering division. Pontiac's market share and total sales were declining. As pressure rose from dealers and the corporation to reverse this trend, a group of concerned dealers met with GM's president, James McDonald, to discuss the future of Pontiac. Some dealers had sold or closed their Pontiac franchises, or added foreign car lines to help keep them afloat. The once successful image of sporty, youthful vehicles had been abandoned for a lineup that consisted of luxury vehicles—with wire wheels, whitewalls, and plenty of chrome—targeted for older car buyers. During the same time, other GM divisions had adopted strategies similar to Pontiac's; the result was a vehicle lineup that was almost parallel across all divisions. Except for some minor front and rear styling differences, the cars looked so similar that consumers had difficulty distinguishing among the divisions. By 1981 Pontiac had fallen to fifth position in U.S. industry sales, behind the third and fourth sister GM divisions, Buick and Oldsmobile, respectively.

NEW MISSION AND DIRECTION

In early 1981 Hoglund formed an "image team" consisting of key people from every Pontiac staff area, the advertising agency, and the Pontiac design staff. The task force met off-site at what is now referred to as the first Pontiac Image Conference, with its goal to determine Pontiac's overall direction for the 1980s. One of the key tools used at the two-and-a-half day conference was the perceptual map. With the results of extensive research at hand, the team plotted Pontiac's position in relation to the perceived images of other car manufacturers (Exhibit 3). The results showed that Pontiac was perceived as relatively neutral, an ordinary American car division. People just did not get excited about Pontiac or its cars, and the sales figures showed it. A change in strategy was clearly needed.

As a result of the Image Conference, an agreement was made by top Pontiac managers to regain the sporty, youthful image that Pontiac had built in the 1960s—the strategy that had once made the division successful. Pontiac would now distinguish itself from its sister divisions by emphasizing performance and handling in the design and manufacture of its vehicles.

Armed with these new directives, the managers were ready to bring in the entire Pontiac organization. A mission statement was issued to all employees:

> The mission of Pontiac is to be a car company known for innovative styling and engineering that results in products with outstanding performance and roadability.

A definition of the target market was formulated:

> Identified target market as a relatively young, better educated, higher income, 25 to 44 age group.

This group then represented 40 percent of the population but 55 percent of auto-buying power. By 1990 this group would compose 42 percent of the U.S. population and account for over one-half of all new car purchases. In 1981 the group's median household income was $32,000.

Results of focus-group discussions of the image were extremely positive. The results suggested that the upscale and/or luxury image fit more with Buick or Oldsmobile. Consumers remembered Pontiac as the excitement car of the 1960s and told management that's where they should be now.

Hoglund felt that consistent and continuous communication of Pontiac's new direction to all employees, the corporation, the dealer base, and the buying public was essential. He began working to instill a sense of teamwork in his staff. His personal dedication to change was viewed by many as the key to success. Meetings with corporate officials were frequent, because Pontiac wanted to identify the strategies it planned for the 1980s clearly, especially to gain top GM management support. These strategies had to fit into the overall corporate strategic direction of regaining lost market share and sales. The

EXHIBIT 3 PONTIAC DIVISION: PERCEPTUAL MAP, 1981

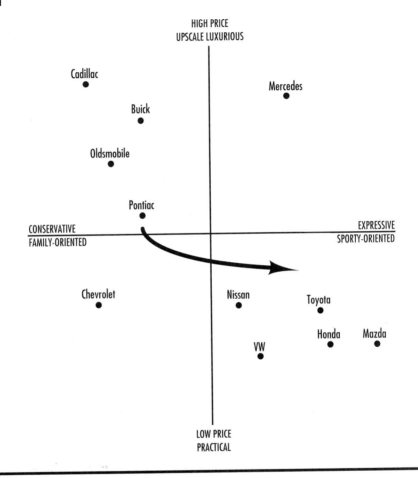

Note: Arrow indicates direction of Pontiac after Image Conference.

Source: Automotive News (September 15, 1986).

dealers were given an "image brochure" explaining the national marketing strategy so that they could begin implementing it on the local level.

Finally, and equally important, communication to the consumers through advertising played a key role. A clear and consistent advertising strategy was needed. As seen in Exhibit 4, this consistency began in 1982 with the slogan "Now the excitement begins." This base theme was the foundation for the 1983–1986 themes of "We build excitement." As the new vehicles began to be introduced throughout 1982–1985, consumers heard the same message relating Pontiac to excitement. To support the message, Pontiac started advertising on television and radio programs aimed at the young consumer.

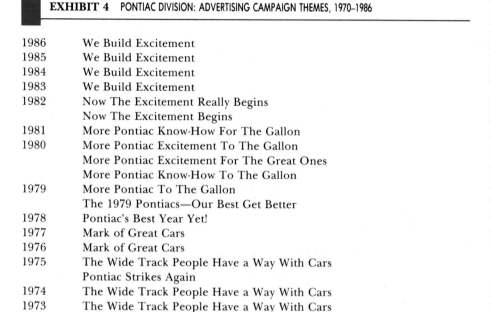

EXHIBIT 4   PONTIAC DIVISION: ADVERTISING CAMPAIGN THEMES, 1970–1986

1986	We Build Excitement
1985	We Build Excitement
1984	We Build Excitement
1983	We Build Excitement
1982	Now The Excitement Really Begins
	Now The Excitement Begins
1981	More Pontiac Know-How For The Gallon
1980	More Pontiac Excitement To The Gallon
	More Pontiac Excitement For The Great Ones
	More Pontiac Know-How To The Gallon
1979	More Pontiac To The Gallon
	The 1979 Pontiacs—Our Best Get Better
1978	Pontiac's Best Year Yet!
1977	Mark of Great Cars
1976	Mark of Great Cars
1975	The Wide Track People Have a Way With Cars
	Pontiac Strikes Again
1974	The Wide Track People Have a Way With Cars
1973	The Wide Track People Have a Way With Cars
1972	That's What Keeps Pontiac a Cut Above
1971	Pontiac . . . A Cut Above
	Pure Pontiac
1970	Wide Track (Above All It's a Wide Track Pontiac)
	This Is the Way It's Going to Be (We Take the Fun of Driving Seriously)

Source: Internal Pontiac document.

PRODUCTS UNDER THE NEW MISSION

The effort to reposition Pontiac to a more youthful market had to be accomplished first through the products. The redesigned sporty Firebird was introduced in 1982, but the first complete road car to be developed with the new mission and philosophy was the 1983 Pontiac 6000 STE. Although the midsize 6000 STEs shared GM's "A" chassis with the Chevrolet Celebrity, the Olds Cutlass Ciera, and the Buick Century, its design was differentiated from its GM counterparts. From the interior to the exterior, the ride and handling, the 6000 STE was distinguished from its competitors with its European style, its wide body side molding, and its sporty flare. The 6000 STE won positive reviews by auto magazines such as *Car and Driver* and was listed as one of its top 10 cars for several years. Of the cars Pontiac advertised heavily, it attracted the highest age group on average. Exhibit 5 shows some 1984 demographics of Pontiac buyers.

The introduction of the 6000 STE, the "touring sedan of the '80s," was the first of many product changes for the division. Other cars that followed the new philosophy were the Fiero, the Sunbird, and the 1985 Grand Am (built on the same "N" chassis as the Olds Calais and the Buick Somerset).

The Fiero's introduction helped Pontiac's effort to regain the sporty image. The Fiero was innovative in using all-plastic body panels, which won acclaim from engineering and manufacturing experts, as well as from auto magazines, as the wave of the future. The plastic body panels were mounted over a 250-piece steel "birdcage" chassis. According to *Business Week,*

> GM first assembles the chassis, largely using robots and automatic welders. Then it shoves the completed chassis into a huge "mill-and-drill" machine that shaves down its body-panel "locator pads" to proper height. Next, workers install the drivetrain and other equipment. Once the chassis' running gear is installed and tested, the body panels are added. The result: chip-free fenders and doors that always line up perfectly.
>
> GM refuses to say whether this year-old, experimental method is as cost-effective as the traditional approach of building a car body first and then equipping it. But the system offers a fast and cheap way to restyle a car. To change its shape, GM can just bolt new body panels onto the same chassis. Restyling conventional cars usually means extensive reengineering.[2]

In addition, the Fiero created dealer traffic, which helped sell all Pontiac carlines. On average, Fiero had the youngest buyers in Pontiac's line.

The introduction of Fiero had not been without problems, however. *Fortune* magazine reported,

> GM's sporty little Fiero illustrates why Detroit can stumble even when it makes its best efforts to catch up. Conceived before the quality philosophy caught hold, the Fiero was originally designed as a cheap commuter car. The project was killed and revived twice before it came to life as a jazzy, midengine two-seater. Along the way it acquired the Chevette's leaden steering system, which had no power boost in the Fiero because of the great distance between the engine and the front wheels. The car's ridiculous 10.2-gallon gas tank, designed with frugal commuting in mind, was the smallest made in the U.S. When the four-cylinder engine proved too unexciting for a sports car, Pontiac added a six-cylinder engine, but the engine fits so tightly that it takes a skilled mechanic to change the spark plugs. Worst of all, in the early models coolant from the radiator up front got so chilled by the time it reached the hot engine farther back that cracks developed in the engine block. Pontiac tried to assuage its customers by replacing engines free long after warranties had expired. For the most part these design errors have been or are being corrected, so the Fiero is now, in Harbour's [James E. Harbour, auto industry consultant] view, "a class vehicle."
>
> At the Pontiac, Michigan, plant where the car is assembled, managers, supervisors, and some line workers attend daily quality briefings that attest to Pontiac's desire to produce a fine car. A giant bulletin board on the plant floor keeps track of Fiero's quality. When it was first produced in 1984, Fiero scored 74 out of a possible 100, based on owner satisfaction surveys in GM's CAMIP (Continuous Automotive Marketing Information Process), conducted by Research Data Analysis. The bulletin board's most recent quarterly data show Fiero scoring 91, vs. 99 for Toyota's MR2, 97 for Mazda's RX7, and 89

EXHIBIT 5 PONTIAC DIVISION: DECISION MAKERS FOR PASSENGER CARS BOUGHT NEW, 1984

		DECISION MAKERS FOR CARS BOUGHT NEW				PONTIAC			
	Total U.S. '000	A '000	B % Down	C Across %	D Index	A '000	B % Down	C Across %	D Index
TOTAL ADULTS	167727	42666	100.0	25.4	100	2929	100.0	1.7	100
MALES	79263	23340	54.7	29.4	116	1379	47.1	1.7	100
FEMALES	88464	19326	45.3	21.8	86	1550	52.9	1.8	100
18-24	28671	4520	10.6	15.8	62	**361	12.3	1.3	72
25-34	39536	10669	25.0	27.0	106	680	23.2	1.7	98
35-44	28978	8416	19.7	29.0	114	733	25.0	2.5	145
45-54	22345	6417	15.0	28.7	113	489	16.7	2.2	125
55-64	22224	6552	15.4	29.5	116	*313	10.7	1.4	81
65 OR OLDER	25973	6093	14.3	23.5	92	352	12.0	1.4	78
18-34	68207	15189	35.6	22.3	88	1042	35.6	1.5	87
18-49	108058	26742	62.7	24.7	97	2038	69.6	1.9	108
25-54	90859	25502	59.8	28.1	110	1902	64.9	2.1	120
35-49	39851	11553	27.1	29.0	114	997	34.0	2.5	143
50 OR OLDER	59669	15924	37.3	26.7	105	891	30.4	1.5	86
GRADUATED COLLEGE	28091	11795	27.6	42.0	165	759	25.9	2.7	155
ATTENDED COLLEGE	28938	8414	19.7	29.1	114	671	22.9	2.3	133
GRADUATED HIGH SCHOOL	65503	16124	37.8	24.6	97	1243	42.4	1.9	109
DID NOT GRADUATE HIGH SCHOOL	45195	6334	14.8	14.0	55	*257	8.8	0.6	33
EMPLOYED MALES	56429	18081	42.4	32.0	126	1099	37.5	1.9	112
EMPLOYED FEMALES	43971	11895	27.9	27.1	106	959	32.7	2.2	125

EMPLOYED FULL-TIME	87773	27316	64.0	31.1	122	1787	61.0	2.0	117
EMPLOYED PART-TIME	12627	2660	6.2	21.1	83	**270	9.2	2.1	122
NOT EMPLOYED	67327	12690	29.7	18.8	74	871	29.7	1.3	74
PROFESSIONAL/MANAGER	25845	10693	25.1	41.4	163	671	22.9	2.6	149
TECH/CLERICAL/SALES	30895	9388	22.0	30.4	119	653	22.3	2.1	121
PRECISION/CRAFT	12629	3693	8.7	29.2	115	*281	9.6	2.2	127
OTHER EMPLOYED	31031	6203	14.5	20.0	79	*454	15.5	1.5	84
SINGLE	35557	8249	19.3	23.2	91	599	20.5	1.7	96
MARRIED	103585	22748	65.0	26.8	105	1913	65.3	1.8	106
DIVORCED/SEPARATED/WIDOWED	28585	6669	15.6	23.3	92	417	14.2	1.5	84
PARENTS	59295	14255	33.4	24.0	95	1217	41.6	2.1	118
WHITE	146081	38647	90.6	26.5	104	2681	91.5	1.8	105
BLACK	17974	3062	7.2	17.0	67	**244	8.3	1.4	78
OTHER	3672	957	2.2	26.1	102	**4	0.1	0.1	6
NORTHEAST-CENSUS	37005	9711	22.8	26.2	103	560	19.1	1.5	87
NORTH CENTRAL	42642	11104	26.0	26.0	102	1078	36.8	2.5	145
SOUTH	56777	13466	31.6	23.7	93	979	33.4	1.7	99
WEST	31303	8385	19.7	26.8	105	*313	10.7	1.0	57

A is the projected number of people, in thousands, in the cell defined by the heading and stub for the column and row concerned.

B is the result of percentaging this number "down" using the group defined by the heading as the base. For demographic stub items, this gives PROFILE.

C is the result of percentaging this number "across" using the group defined by the stub as the base. For demographic stub items, this gives PENETRATION.

D is an index of selectivity calculated by dividing C (Across %) by the across percent for the universe concerned (adults, males, females, etc.). Example: an index of 120 indicates that the group defined by the stub is 20% more likely to be in the group defined by the heading than is the total universe.

SIMMONS MARKET RESEARCH BUREAU, INC. 1984

*Projection relatively unstable because of sample base—use with caution

**Number of cases too small for reliability—shown for consistency only

Source: *Simmons Study of Media and Markets*, 1985

EXHIBIT 5 (continued)

	DECISION MAKERS FOR CARS BOUGHT NEW				PONTIAC			
	Total U.S. '000	A '000	B % Down	C Across %	D Index	A '000	B % Down	C Across %	D Index
NORTHEAST–MKTG.	38125	11000	25.8	28.9	113	623	21.3	1.6	94
EAST CENTRAL	24794	6209	14.6	25.0	98	587	20.0	2.4	136
WEST CENTRAL	28511	7288	17.1	25.6	100	648	22.1	2.3	130
SOUTH	48953	10897	25.5	22.3	88	850	29.0	1.7	99
PACIFIC	27344	7272	17.0	26.6	105	**221	7.5	0.8	46
COUNTY SIZE A	69301	18856	44.2	27.2	107	1284	43.8	1.9	106
COUNTY SIZE B	50633	12821	30.0	25.3	100	743	25.4	1.5	84
COUNTY SIZE C	26259	6333	14.8	24.1	95	*421	14.4	1.6	92
COUNTY SIZE D	21534	4656	10.9	21.6	85	*481	16.4	2.2	128
METRO CENTRAL CITY	50014	11516	27.0	23.0	91	528	18.0	1.1	60
METRO SUBURBAN	76832	21783	51.1	28.4	111	1638	55.9	2.1	122
NON METRO	40881	9367	22.0	22.9	90	763	26.0	1.9	107

TOP 5 ADI'S	39550	10912	25.6	27.6	108	648	22.1	1.6	94
TOP 10 ADI'S	54877	15118	35.4	27.5	108	960	32.8	1.7	100
TOP 20 ADI'S	77516	20932	49.1	27.0	106	1335	45.6	1.7	99
HSHLD INC. $50,000 OR MORE	17257	6665	15.6	38.6	152	*359	12.3	2.1	119
$40,000 OR MORE	33235	12188	28.6	36.7	144	837	28.6	2.5	144
$30,000 OR MORE	59693	20989	49.2	35.2	138	1456	49.7	2.4	140
$25,000 OR MORE	76275	26029	61.0	34.1	134	1806	61.7	2.4	136
$20,000–$24,999	18607	4666	10.9	25.1	99	*439	15.0	2.4	135
$15,000–$19,999	17175	3882	9.1	22.6	89	*242	8.3	1.4	81
$10,000–$14,999	24569	4429	10.4	18.0	71	*209	7.1	0.9	49
UNDER $10,000	31101	3660	8.6	11.8	46	*235	8.0	0.8	43
HOUSEHOLD OF 1 PERSON	19441	5563	13.0	28.6	112	457	15.6	2.4	135
2 PEOPLE	51803	14223	33.3	27.5	108	895	30.6	1.7	99
3 OR 4 PEOPLE	66933	16934	39.7	25.3	99	1039	35.5	1.6	89
5 OR MORE PEOPLE	29550	5947	13.9	20.1	79	*538	18.4	1.8	104
NO CHILD IN HOUSEHOLD	96587	26262	61.6	27.2	107	1591	54.3	1.6	94
CHILD(REN) UNDER 2 YEARS	10844	2525	5.9	23.3	92	**191	6.5	1.8	101
2–5 YEARS	26358	5688	13.3	21.6	85	*419	14.3	1.6	91
6–11 YEARS	30453	6517	15.3	21.4	84	*543	18.5	1.8	102
12–17 YEARS	36575	8389	19.7	22.9	90	762	26.0	2.1	119
RESIDENCE OWNED	117770	34002	79.7	28.9	113	2334	79.7	2.0	113
VALUE: $50,000 OR MORE	70166	23589	55.3	33.6	132	1583	54.0	2.3	129
VALUE: UNDER $50,000	47604	10413	24.4	21.9	86	751	25.6	1.6	90

for Nissan's Pulsar NX. Inside GM, Fiero looks good, since the company average CAMIP is 85.[3]

The shape and style of Fiero and the other new cars complemented the image the division was trying to regain. Pontiac's strategy of using image/specialty cars to sell other, lower-priced models was highly successful. While only accounting for a small portion of total sales, these image cars built a "halo" effect around the other Pontiac lines. For example, in 1986 the 6000 STE was the car most advertised, but the base 6000 was the most frequently purchased. As an image leader, the top-of-the-line STE was a performance-oriented vehicle with advanced technology in the powertrain, suspension, and steering. It also had an all-electronic dashboard and sporty trim packages. The base 6000 was more traditional, equipped with a standard engine and conventional dashboard, seats, and trim packages—a typical mid-size sedan. The base 6000 was $3,000–$4,000 less than the STE version.

CORPORATE REORGANIZATION

The GM North American Car Group, of which Pontiac was a part in 1984 (see Exhibit 6), had in the past encouraged its car divisions to produce vehicles in certain ranges for specific consumer segments. For example, when a person first entered the car market, a Chevrolet was the most likely choice; this division provided a wide range of products at entry-level prices. As the consumer grew older and also increased household income, he or she was thought to trade up to different divisions (in this case, Pontiac). The consumer would eventually pass through the entire GM chain (Chevrolet, Pontiac, Oldsmobile, Buick, and Cadillac). In practice, however, consumers were forsaking this chain for competitor car manufacturers. The Japanese and European car manufacturers were now major players in the market, and GM was faced with fierce competition. In order to meet the challenges these competitors brought to the industry, a restructuring was announced in early 1984.

The restructuring of the North American automotive operations created two car groups or profit centers: the Chevrolet-Pontiac-Canada Group (CPC) and the Buick-Oldsmobile-Cadillac Group (BOC). This restructuring came after a two-year, internal comprehensive study of the company, assisted by McKinsey and Company, to shape GM for the future, and was expected by some GM officials to take three to five years to put into effect. The reasons for the reorganization were: (1) to compete for market share, (2) to compete with manufacturers throughout the world, and (3) to compete in world-class quality, value, and customer satisfaction.[4] The reorganization sought to focus the production of small-car platforms in CPC, and the larger-car platforms in BOC so that the company could make better use of its resources and make each group totally responsible for the value-added chain (from initial design to final delivery). The Fisher Body and GMAD plants were divided between the two groups, which had complete engineering and operational responsibilities. Most product platforms would still be shared by several car-marketing divisions.

Although originally rumored that Chevrolet and Pontiac would market

EXHIBIT 6 PONTIAC DIVISION: ORGANIZATION CHARTS

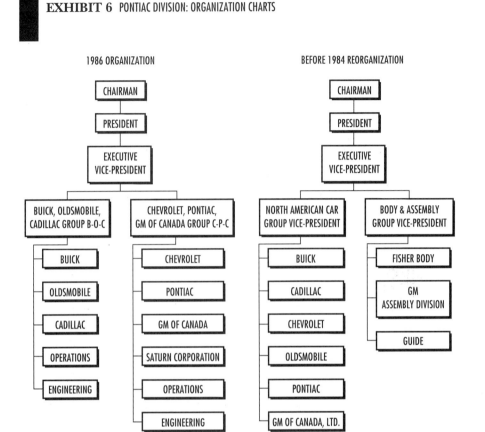

Note: These are partial organization charts.

Source: GM internal organization chart.

small, inexpensive cars and Olds, Buick, and Cadillac would market larger cars with more dual dealerships (most frequently linking Chevrolet and Oldsmobile for buyers favoring more traditional styling and Pontiac and Buick for more distinctive styling), the announcement stressed that each group would build vehicles for its own car divisions as well as the other group's divisions. Thus, it would still be possible, if market conditions warranted, for Pontiac to sell a large car and Buick a small car. Exhibit 6 shows the GM organization before and after the reorganization.

The general managers of the nameplate divisions no longer had operational responsibilities for the plants at their respective locations. For example, the general manager of Pontiac no longer had responsibility for the Pontiac complex, which included a foundry, an engine plant, a parts plant, and the Fiero plant. CPC now controlled these activities. However, the general managers did have to meet CPC goals such as the five-year business plan and criteria such as cost-control programs. The divisions were to focus attention on marketing and planning activities, and to avoid confusing the consumer.

Pontiac went through a reorganization of its own. The orientation changed from sales to consumer marketing. The actual organization shrunk from nearly 10,000 people to approximately 1,500, but the responsibility of departments reporting to Hoglund—sales and service, product planning, market planning (including strategic and business planning), finance, and personnel—increased. (Product engineering was consolidated at the group level with an informal reporting relationship to Hoglund.) Engineers that remained at Pontiac were charged primarily with developing distinctions for their version of shared platforms and articulating those needs to CPC. Marketing and planning people were increased from less than 20 to approximately 50. A team approach to planning among market planning, product planning, and product engineering, was initiated.

J. MICHAEL LOSH

In mid-1984 Hoglund became group executive of the Operating Staff Group (he was later named president of the Saturn Corporation and at the time of the case was BOC Group executive), and Mike Losh, then managing director of GM de Mexico, became the 14th general manager of Pontiac. At the age of 38, he was GM's youngest VP and general manager. He arrived on July 1, just before the beginning of the 1985 model year in September.

Born in 1946 in Dayton, Ohio, Losh began his career with General Motors as a GMI (General Motors Institute) student sponsored by the Inland Division. He graduated with a BS in mechanical engineering and an MBA from the Harvard Business School in 1970. Upon graduation, Losh became a staff assistant, then a senior analyst for Inland. Two years later he transferred to the GM central office in New York as a senior staff assistant in the treasurer's office. In 1974 he was promoted to director of Profit Analysis and Forecasts. In 1976 he moved to the Detroit central office as director of Product Programs for the financial staff. The following year he became director of finance at GM do Brasil in Sao Caetano do Sul. He joined GM de Mexico in early 1982 as deputy managing director and in December of that year was named president and managing director of GM de Mexico.

With the success of the Grand Am, Fiero, and 6000 STE, and the security of the stable Firebird and Sunbird, Losh seemed to have inherited a house in order. Sales were increasing, and Pontiac's market share for 1984 would be approximately 7 percent. With all its success, however, Pontiac faced many outside competitors who were making similar moves to target its specific market segment. The Europeans were already solid players, with their sporty vehicles. The Japanese were the most recent entrants with their technologically advanced cars—overhead cams, superior suspensions, and a tone of being generally sportier than U.S. cars. Losh believed the sporty, expressive market was going to become a battlefield for the world automakers. He predicted, "Sportiness and performance are emerging as major themes in a wide range of product segments for both import and domestic automakers."

In his first two years at the helm, Losh built on the changes initiated by Hoglund. In 1985 he initiated a series of annual marketing conferences, involving representatives from the total marketing process. A year later, three separate marketing conferences were held where, according to Losh,

> We established and developed the objectives and strategies for each 1987 car-line taking into account the carline's specific image, the market segment in which it competes, and its competitive strengths and weaknesses. For example, we are placing our major marketing efforts behind key image cars within each class.
>
> The purpose of this "impact strategy" is not only to promote specific cars within each class but also to accentuate the Pontiac image as the excitement builder. For 1987 our featured carline leaders include the Grand Am SE, Bonneville SE, Fiero GT, 6000 STE, Sunbird GT, and the Trans Am GTA.
>
> In addition, we've devised a new multi-line strategy where we promote one image carline with another—in this case, Fiero, Firebird, and Sunbird. The result is a more efficient and cost-effective way to promote our cars and image philosophy.
>
> Another major benefit of our 1987 marketing conferences is that we established key divisional objectives and prioritized marketing and communications challenges. We integrated all areas into a single marketing plan. This way, Merchandising, Dealer Marketing Groups, Public Relations, and National Advertising all came away with a clear understanding of their roles. The end result is that marketing conferences now play a key part in our total planning process and an even more important role in keeping us ahead of our competition.

Pontiac also borrowed from the Japanese the concept of "option grouping"—special versions of cars that carried a particular group of options, with only limited variations allowed. By the fall of 1986, the concept had been extended to all Pontiac models.

By late 1986 Pontiac's aggressiveness and clear image had become known throughout GM, especially because Pontiac was GM's number one "import fighter." The Fiero, Grand Am, and 6000 STE ranked 1, 3, and 5 among all domestic makes in attracting import buyers.

In addition, Pontiac was getting good press for its new products. Publications like *Car and Driver* and *Road & Track* had written positively about Pontiac's improved performance. The newest product change, to be introduced at the beginning of the 1987 model year, was the redesigned Bonneville, built on the same chassis as the Olds Delta 88 and the Buick LeSabre. Although there were some internal concerns about whether the car really fit the image of sporty expressive vehicles (Exhibit 7 shows the placement of the Bonneville on the perceptual map for 1987 Pontiac vehicles and major competitors), an October 1986 preview by *Motor Trend* reported:

> The new Pontiac Bonneville . . . is destined to be the benchmark against which cars in this class are compared. An essentially full-sized car without giving up intangibles like fun and driving comfort. The '87 Bonneville is as first-cabin as any automobile in its class on the world scene today.

In addition to the new Bonneville, a replacement for the 1000, the Le-Mans, was scheduled for introduction in the 1988 model year. This front-wheel-drive subcompact would be designed by GM's Adam Opel division in West Germany and built in South Korea by the new GM-Daewoo Motor Company joint venture. The LeMans would be the second platform Pontiac would not have to share with other divisions. Approximately 80,000 to 100,000 would be imported the first year. Such a method of introducing a new vehicle was considerably cheaper than the substantial investment required to bring out a totally new vehicle, which would take three to five years' lead time.

Another positive development was the improvement in Pontiac quality. Whereas in 1984 Pontiac's Customer Satisfaction Index ranked last among GM divisions, by 1986 it was about even with the other divisions. The lowest ratings were generally on older design models, with the 1000 receiving the lowest and the STE the highest. The ratings were also low for Pontiac dealerships that also handled competing GM makes. For example, the rating on a Pontiac 6000 was usually lower than its sister cars—Buick Century and Olds Cutlass Ciera—if the Pontiac was sold from the same dealership.

Fully aware of the objective of the "sporty division" in GM, dealers still wondered if Pontiac's comeback was for real. In a recent study of dealer attitudes toward brand franchises, however, Pontiac ranks a strong fifth, up from its previous ninth-place position. In fact, the Pontiac franchise ranked first among all American-built brands.

Losh still felt he needed to build confidence and support in the dealer network. He was especially concerned that one-third of the approximately 3,000 dealerships accounted for 80 percent of sales. (Pontiac was the chief line for 800 dealerships.) Losh believed that Pontiac needed to strengthen its franchises. "In some cases that means different locations with the same guy; in some cases, that means better facilities where he is; and in some cases, it means we need a new operator."

He hoped to have all Pontiac dealers wired into GM's computerized marketing network by fall of 1987. Although the information would be centralized, Pontiac had to decide whether to leave its local staffs in place or bring them into a single marketing center. Chevrolet was known to be favoring centralizing their "telemanagers."

Several other matters concerned Losh. To continue Pontiac's successful trends would require the division to become even more market-driven than it was. GM corporate parameters were starting to hamper that effort, however. As GM responded to its growing financial problems, capital reductions and program deletions were becoming a major concern for all GM managers. Not only was the widely reported all-plastic-body car project eliminated, which Pontiac had planned to use for some its 1990 models, but CPC was applying strict cost controls in an effort to reduce spending. If new products or changes in current products were needed, Losh would have to convince CPC to implement them in light of these spending restrictions.

Losh thought another major challenge facing him was a corporate program that white-collar employment be reduced by 25 percent by 1990. Al-

EXHIBIT 7 PONTIAC DIVISION: BONNEVILLE PERCEPTUAL MAP, 1987

THE NEW BONNEVILLE WITH THE 1987 PONTIAC LINEUP

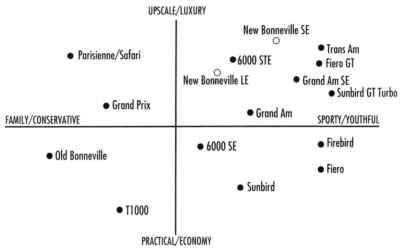

THE NEW BONNEVILLE VERSUS THE COMPETITION

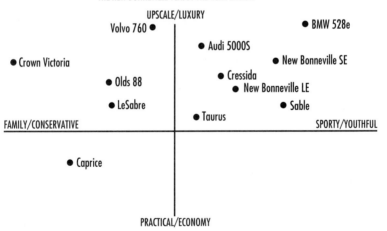

WHO THE NEW BONNEVILLE IS DESIGNED TO ATTRACT

CAR NAME	MEDIAN AGE	MEDIAN HH INCOME	EDUCATION
Traditional Pontiac	57	$38,000	High Sch./Coll.
New Bonneville	48	$42,000	College
Pontiac 6000	43	$41,000	College

though some of his senior managers soon would be eligible for early retirement and a few employees could be transferred to other parts of GM, perhaps as many as 250 people might have to be released. When and how he should handle the situation was of increasing concern to Losh.

Losh also wondered what effort could best be taken to achieve GM Chairman Roger Smith's long-range corporate plan to optimize the corporation's efforts to regain lost market share and simultaneously increase corporate profitability. Smith, who had initiated the corporate reorganization in 1984, was concerned about the success of all the GM divisions. From 1982 to 1985, Pontiac was the only GM division to boost its share of the $130 billion U.S. car market. Pontiac's market share was up 1.1 percentage point, compared to a total GM drop of 1.4 percentage points. With the success of the sporty, expressive car niche clear and in light of the others' poor performance, would Smith encourage or restrict the other divisions' moves into the segment? In short, one of Losh's biggest concerns was how much distinctiveness Pontiac would be able to maintain.

Losh also had operations concerns. Pontiac had only recently been able to produce enough manual transmissions to satisfy demand, and it did not begin providing the Fiero with five-speed transmissions until the summer of 1986. In addition, by mid-1986, Pontiac's share of GM's "N"-body production had increased to 50 percent, so that Grand Am production now took up the entire output of the Lansing plant, and Buick Somerset Regal and Oldsmobile Calais were sharing another plant. (See Exhibit 8 for a list of GM plants and platforms by product.) With the Grand Am expected to be Pontiac's number-one selling model in 1987, Losh was not sure one dedicated plant was enough. For the time being Losh thought the 1984 reorganization was working well:

> I don't know that we could have gotten the dedication and commitment out of the old organization that we've gotten today. And I don't know that we would have gotten the timely decisions on reallocating capacity under the old organization.
>
> Obviously, I'm influenced by the fact that things are going well for us in general, but the things that we need out of CPC are working. In many regards, perhaps it should be more difficult for us to deal with the reorganization than anybody else, because so many of our products are under the responsibility of BOC. [BOC's production accounted for more than half of Pontiac's sales.]

Expansion issues were also on Losh's mind. A recent Pontiac study indicated that by 1991, 144 nameplates would be on the marketplace, up from 111 in 1986. Although Pontiac's nine car lines were the most of any GM division, and there was growing corporate pressure to reduce the number of GM lines, Losh was considering introducing a minivan. There was a blurring of the market for vans and station wagons, and since 20 percent of such Pontiac lines as the 6000 and Parisienne were station wagons, Losh thought a minivan might soon be needed.

Losh was also concerned about the possibility of another energy crunch, and its effect on his sporty division and demographics. Also, how viable in the long term was this segment? The median age of a Pontiac buyer had dropped

EXHIBIT 8 PONTIAC DIVISION: GM PLATFORMS AND PLANTS

	CHEVROLET	PONTIAC	OLDSMOBILE	BUICK	CADILLAC
A	Celebrity	**6000**	Cutlass Ciera	Century	—
B	Caprice, Caprice Classic	**Parisienne**	Custom Cruiser Wagon	Electra Wagon LeSabre Wagon	—
B	—	—	Ninety-Eight	Electra/ Park Avenue	DeVille, Fleetwood Limousine, Funeral Coach
D	—	—	—	—	Fleetwood Brougham
E	—	—	Toronado	Riviera	Eldorado
F	Camaro	**Firebird**	—	—	—
G	Monte Carlo	**Grand Prix**	Cutlass Supreme	Regal	—
H	—	**Bonneville**	Delta 88	LeSabre	—
J	Cavalier	**Sunbird**	Firenza	Skyhawk	Cimarron
K	—	—	—	—	Seville
L	Corsica, Beretta	—	—	—	—
M	Sprint	—	—	—	—
N	—	**Grand Am**	Calais	Somerset/ Skylark	—
P	—	**Fiero, Fiero GT**	—	—	—
R	Spectrum	—	—	—	—
S	Nova	—	—	—	—
T	Chevette	**1000**	—	—	—
V	—	—	—	—	Allante
Y	Corvette	—	—	—	—

GENERAL MOTORS

Arlington, Tex. .... Monte Carlo, Cutlass Supreme
Bowling Green, Ky. .... Corvette
Detroit (Clark Ave.) .... Cadillac (rwd), Olds 88 (rwd), Caprice
Detroit-Hamtramck .. Toronto, Riviera, Eldorado, Seville
Doraville, Ga. .... Cutlass Ciera, Century
Fairfax, Kans. .... Chevrolet, Olds 88, LeSabre (rwd), Parisienne
Flint, Mich. .... LeSabre (fwd)
Flint (Buick City) .... Estate Wagons, Caprice Classic, Cutlass Supreme, Regal
Framingham, Mass. .... Celebrity, Cutlass Ciera
Janesville, Wis. .... Cavalier, Cimarron
Lake Orion, Mich .... Cadillac/ DeVille (rwd), Olds 98, Electra
Lakewood, Ga. .... Chevette, 1000, Acadian
Lansing .... Calais, Grand Am, Somerset
Leeds, Mo. .... Cavalier, Firenza, Skyhawk
Linden, N.J. .... GM-25 1987 models (fall 1986)
Lordstown, Ohio ...... Cavalier, Sunbird
Norwood, Ohio .... Camaro, Firebird
Oklahoma City .... Celebrity, Century
Pontiac .... Fiero
Pontiac (No. 8) .... Cutlass Supreme, Regal
Tarrytown, N.Y. .... 6000, Century
Van Nuys, Calif. .... Camaro, Firebird
Wentzville, Mo. .... Electra, Olds 98, Olds 88 (fwd)
Willow Run, Mich. .... Olds 88 (fwd)
Wilmington, Del. .... Caprice, GM-25 1987 models (fall 1986)

Source: *Automobile News* (October 27, 1986): E40; and *Automotive News*, 1986 Market Data Book Issue, p. 14.

639

from 42 in 1981 to 37 in 1985, and the proportion of Pontiac buyers in the key 25-to-44 age group had increased from 43 to 51 percent. Sales among the age group had increased 65 percent, and their median household income in 1985 was nearly $40,000. An internal GM study indicated that, although the current ratio of people aged 55 and under to the over-55 age was 4 to 1, by the year 2010, it would fall to 3 to 1, and by 2050, 2 to 1.[5]

By late 1986 Losh's earlier projection of record-breaking sales of 900,000 Pontiacs was clearly not going to be achieved—in spite of GM's aggressively low interest rates for new purchases and Pontiac advertising expenditures of approximately $70 million. In fact, the number would be approximately 840,000 or 7.5 percent of the U.S. market and 17.8 percent of all GM sales. Losh and his team were convinced that they could have sold more if they could have produced more. In addition, the Fiero, facing similar cars from Toyota, Ford, and Honda, had experienced a drop in sales of 21 percent from 1985. (See Exhibit 9 for sales figures for Pontiac cars.)

As he prepared to enter 1987, Losh's staff was proposing a 40 percent reduction in the number of options on the 1987 cars, which would make it a leader among GM divisions in making option cuts. He wondered how the dealers would react to further reductions, especially in light of his team's 1987 sales goal of 900,000:

Sunbird	110,000
Grand Am	235,000
6000	170,000
Fiero	75,000
Firebird	90,000
Bonneville	140,000
1000	11,000
Grand Prix	24,000
LeMans	30,000
Safari Wagons	15,000
	900,000

This was at a time when there was growing concern that the domestic auto industry's low interest rates in late 1986 and the changing tax laws would take business away from early 1987.

How he made his mark at Pontiac might well determine how far Losh would go at GM. Losh knew that many of the truly successful Pontiac general managers who had moved on to increasingly important positions at GM were those who, in some form or another, had implemented successful strategic moves in the divisions. Although Losh had been named "rookie of the year" in 1985 and "sales/marketing All-Star" in 1986 by *Automotive News,* he knew he couldn't let the division stand still. He had once commented to a group of GM managers, "I can tell you from firsthand experience, just when you think you're finished, you realize it's only the beginning." That seemed to be more true than ever in 1987.

EXHIBIT 9 PONTIAC DIVISION: ANNUAL CAR SALES BY LARGEST SELLING MODEL AND MAJOR CATEGORIES, 1980–1986

	1980	1981	1982	1983	1984	1985	1986
TOTAL ECONOMY SEGMENT	1416758	1821461	1550609	1610411	1596685	1724210	2063990
Ford Escort	0	284633	321952	323900	339209	410978	415521
Nissan Sentra/210	188695	161573	176678	212438	192186	212071	221012
Honda Civic	133111	158127	134054	139169	128494	146926	165677
Plymouth Horizon Sedan	77372	83950	48045	50861	74347	97508	101379
Chevrolet Spectrum	0	0	0	0	0	39624	93992
Volkswagen Domestic Golf/Rabbit	190220	159588	107396	83222	83084	83682	90056
Dodge Omni Sedan	61379	61018	40006	45843	65675	84575	88325
Mazda GLC	60784	70386	52260	55706	44387	49493	78450
Chevrolet Chevette	375396	376758	233858	183970	180341	135261	75761
Toyota Tercel	94503	115841	127329	150968	108889	102413	74330
Pontiac 1000	0	43097	52558	38286	28900	24180	20066
TOTAL SUBCOMPACT SEGMENT	837343	717153	666472	814313	1022800	1115239	1268521
Chevrolet Cavalier	0	43855	120587	216297	371836	422927	386258
Chevrolet/Nummi Nova (fwd)	0	0	0	0	0	16323	170661
Subaru	81094	104274	99856	109622	99706	153350	159888
Toyota Corolla	257812	209880	122995	117836	95753	131069	118486
Pontiac 2000 Sunbird	0	34424	59018	79509	123937	120207	109807
Volkswagen Jetta	8161	24773	21561	19157	36275	70502	97362
Buick Skyhawk (fwd)	0	0	32952	69946	116276	90700	77966
Nissan Stanza	66468	47242	55939	66030	47265	56844	69046
Oldsmobile Firenza	0	0	19562	43042	59490	52760	39212
Mitsubishi Tredia	0	0	0	11083	15079	10546	10346
TOTAL COMPACT SEGMENT	1627388	1730358	1249854	1158459	1292511	1665911	1967387
Honda Accord	176954	188044	180646	209567	256336	256255	296086
Ford Tempo	0	0	0	70986	255727	297656	251618
Pontiac Grand Am	0	0	0	0	26	98567	190994
Toyota Camry/Corona	37352	25549	6656	35054	85477	117539	144405
Plymouth Reliant	0	180103	151279	161757	141377	137074	131372
Oldsmobile Calais	0	0	0	0	29	113280	119740
Buick Somerset Regal	0	0	0	0	66	88103	113862
Dodge Aries	0	137066	112761	124650	110939	117742	104572
Mazda 626	50352	64867	58317	65672	70910	79889	95374
Chrysler LeBaron GTS	0	0	0	0	0	55740	71542

(continued)

EXHIBIT 9 (continued)

	1980	1981	1982	1983	1984	1985	1986
TOTAL MIDSIZE SEGMENT	1994295	1885261	1566210	2091446	2512523	2500540	2472094
Chevrolet Celebrity	0	0	67475	155953	307777	360167	395860
Oldsmobile Ciera	0	0	78542	169939	252669	315569	330572
Buick Century (fwd)	0	0	70778	134804	208745	239570	239278
Oldsmobile Supreme	269189	281390	175361	193305	201044	234242	202158
Pontiac 6000	0	0	36564	84816	124407	156994	196209
Ford Thunderbird	164795	80942	47903	99176	156583	169770	144577
Mercury Cougar Specialty	69572	34324	17732	63350	115546	130015	121972
Chevrolet Monte Carlo	177124	175155	105721	98865	127875	105568	117671
Buick Regal	192507	223992	148893	155906	134282	127386	82904
Pontiac Grand Prix/Bonneville	208258	215863	162876	169034	152470	117719	82478
Ford LTD	0	0	0	142817	198109	205889	50717
TOTAL REGULAR SEGMENT	964235	763567	677403	855614	1086663	1057901	948473
Oldsmobile Delta 88	156355	161766	168550	218604	259937	213833	241417
Chevrolet Caprice	307395	216630	205861	226750	264625	251693	228706
Ford LTD Crown Victoria	161537	120410	118527	124154	157068	173509	128280
Mercury Gran Marquis	58007	52552	69784	97341	131515	145242	112225
Buick LeSabre	94206	81244	102424	140812	161763	144684	104570
Pontiac Parisienne	119880	98955	12257	14459	55736	73109	72909
Chrysler New Yorker (fwd)	0	0	0	33494	56019	55831	59455
TOTAL LUXURY SEGMENT	326976	309839	397141	515811	577618	655147	703385
Cadillac DeVille (fwd)	0	0	0	0	46356	139718	164979
Lincoln Town Car	35845	31038	34620	59335	77475	116015	119180
Oldsmobile Regency 98	74497	83332	86338	113794	107335	118673	116615
Buick Electra 225	68890	59722	57704	75691	88397	90922	111245
Chrysler Fifth Avenue (rwd)	0	0	51757	77700	78399	112137	110639
Cadillac DeVille/Fleetwood (rwd)	147744	135747	145075	173086	151880	48883	60915
Lincoln Continental	0	0	21647	16205	27776	28799	19812
TOTAL SPORTS SEGMENT	1495091	1188208	1010813	2136718	1408466	1466628	1385355
TOTAL HIGHSPORT	124320	111693	101172	1180020	122444	160325	154729
Nissan 300/280Z	71594	64487	59853	68575	71617	67826	57187
Chevrolet Corvette	37471	33414	22086	25891	27986	37878	35969

Porsche 944/924	0	0	2567	12142	12716	14725	19871
Porsche 911	3226	3714	4403	5313	4513	4846	7533
Alfa Romeo Spider/Spyder Veloce	2749	1329	1486	1981	2461	4485	5103
Porsche 928	1427	1745	2136	2325	2332	2375	2673
Ferrari Italian Total	570	912	757	541	585	606	656
TOTAL MIDSPORT	623760	506380	535505	577467	842113	856983	790172
Chevrolet Camaro	131066	109707	148649	175004	207285	206082	173674
Toyota Celica	145485	103505	113599	119140	90784	72265	108725
Pontiac Firebird	95449	61460	83810	93378	105628	101797	96208
Honda Prelude	47041	49025	37137	35538	65694	72011	75409
Pontiac Fiero	0	0	0	2015	99705	90691	71283
Mazda RX7	46021	44053	46422	53402	53178	54656	53511
Nissan 200SX	86345	80748	54745	37189	51056	62595	49792
Dodge Daytona	0	0	0	802	42596	51299	40504
Chrysler Laser	0	0	0	925	52073	54758	31458
Toyota MR2	0	0	0	0	0	23812	30984
Isuzu Impulse	0	0	0	5720	13024	14955	11867
TOTAL LOWSPORT	747011	570135	374136	379231	443909	449320	440454
Ford Mustang	246008	173329	116804	116120	131762	159741	175598
Honda CRX	0	0	0	0	32625	53903	60782
Dodge Charger (fwd)	49329	50129	41534	45238	51799	49501	51695
Nissan Pulsar NX	0	0	0	43841	42319	45423	49458
Plymouth Turismo	57434	52959	38776	37079	47226	45385	47053
Toyota Corolla	0	44212	51714	24996	63570	37617	34006
Mercury Capri	67538	53491	29956	25500	19499	16829	13358
Mitsubishi Cordia	0	0	0	10422	14938	8662	5398
Renault Fuego	0	0	7613	13003	12528	5810	2480
Ford EXP	0	41601	43049	26471	24040	26450	626

ENDNOTES

1. Excerpts of the history of Pontiac were taken from *Automotive News* (GM 75th Anniversary Issue, September 16, 1983); *General Motors, The First 75 Years of Transportation Products,* from the editors of Automobile Quarterly; and *PMD Today,* an internal Pontiac newsletter.

2. "GM Moves Into a New Era," *Business Week* (July 16, 1984): 51.

3. Jeremy Main, "Detroit's Cars Really Are Getting Better," *Fortune* (February 2, 1987): 97.

4. Material Management, BOC Group—an internal GM document, p. 2.

5. Taken from the article "EAS Studies Designs to Aid Aging Drivers," in *GM Today,* a quarterly employee newsletter, October 23, 1986.

PONTIAC DIVISION OF GENERAL MOTORS (B)

Michael Losh, general manager of Pontiac, moved quickly to deal with the required 25 percent reduction in white-collar employment by 1990. By means of early retirements, some increase in turnover, transfers to other GM divisions, and use of a corporate buyout program, Losh was able to reduce the number of white-collar jobs from 1,000 in the fall of 1986 to 700 in the spring of 1987.

In conjunction with the white-collar reduction, Losh streamlined Pontiac's sales force by reducing the number of people involved and by reducing the number of geographical zones from 25 to 18. The sales force reshuffling was completed by June 1, 1987. Losh hoped such a move would both increase efficiency and create a better relationship with dealers.

Since dealers were such an important element to Losh's strategy for Pontiac, he moved to develop a more consultative relationship with dealers. One result of this program was to introduce a focused marketing effort in which advertising and dealer incentives could be tailored to the needs of dealers in different regions, rather than treating all dealers alike.

In June of 1987, the 1988 LeMans coupe and sedan were introduced. Its sporty European style (engineered by Opel) and Korean low-cost production (built by Daewoo Motor Company) made Pontiac management optimistic about its ability to replace the T1000. Pontiac was forecasting LeMans sales of 80,000 units for its first 14 months, ending August 1988.

Four major product changes also were ready for the 1988 model year—a newly designed Grand Prix, a restyled Sunbird, introduction of an uplevel Bonneville (the SSE), and the Fiero was given a new steering and suspension system and an upgraded engine performance package.

In September of 1987, Pontiac introduced a totally revised advertising tag line, with new print and television ads, to go with its new lineup of cars. The "Ride Pontiac Ride" theme, portrayed by new upbeat music, shots of young people, and exclusive use of uplevel image cars, had Pontiac management optimistic about future prospects for the division. Estimated total unit sales for model year 1988 were set at 817,000 units.

In October of 1987, Robert Stempel, a former Pontiac general manager, became president of GM. Not only was he the youngest GM president in 30 years, at age 53, but he had the reputation of being a solid "car man" who was not afraid to make hard decisions.

Perhaps the most exciting news for Pontiac came in January of 1988, when the new 1988 Grand Prix SE won the prestigious *Motor Trend* "Car of the Year" award. It was the fifth time Pontiac had won the award and the first since the 1968 GTO.

Not all was positive for Pontiac in 1987. The greatest concern was that both total unit sales and market share were below expectation. For example, where Pontiac had projected 1987 unit sales of 900,000, total sales were only 715,536:

	UNIT SALES		MARKET SHARE		
YEAR	*U.S. Domestic*	*GM*	*Pontiac*	*GM*	*Pontiac*
1986	11,167,289	4,713,898	840,865	42.2%	7.0%
1987	10,501,510	3,881,281	715,536	37.0%	6.8%

Furthermore, two specific Pontiac models were of special concern to Losh—the LeMans and Fiero.

By December 31, 1987, sales of the LeMans for its first seven months had reached a total of 27,000 units. The Daewoo Motor Company plant producing the LeMans had experienced two long strikes, during a period of national political unrest, and a three-week plant shutdown for expansion, thereby reducing the number of cars available for sale. With uncertain supplies, dealers were reluctant to promote the LeMans. By the end of February total sales had reached 33,000. There was growing concern that the LeMans might have trouble regaining its sales momentum.

The Fiero's 1987 model year sales were sharply down from the projection of 75,000. In January of 1987, GM cut back its Fiero production by 32 percent, resulting in the indefinite layoff of 1,241 of the Fiero plant's 2,350 employees. By the end of February GM had a 130-day supply of Fieros. In March, the rebates on Fieros were increased from $500 to $1,200. By late 1987 sales for the Fiero were running 41 percent behind the 1986 level. It was clear that there was increased competition in the two-seat, sporty car niche that Fiero had pioneered:

	1984	1985	1986	1987
Pontiac Fiero	93,485	90,303	68,340	41,830
Honda CRX	48,445	57,486	66,629	48,142
Mazda RX7	54,310	53,810	56,203	36,345
Toyota MR2	—	32,309	27,841	15,847

EXHIBIT 10   PONTIAC 1989 MODEL LINEUP

MODEL	PLATFORM	SEGMENT	BASE PRICE*
Bonneville	H	LARGE SEDANS	
SSE			$23,404
SE			17,704
LE			15,334
Grand Prix	W	MID COUPES	
SE			16,454
LE			15,304
Base			14,354
6000	A	MID SEDANS	
STE All Wheel Drive		New roof and rear deck lid.	23,049
S/E			15,849
LE			12,419
Station Wagon			14,219
Firebird	F	MID SPORT	
GTA			20,778
Trans Am			16,438
Formula			14,388
Firebird			12,438
Grand Am	N	COMPACT COUPE/SEDAN	
SE Coupe		New front/rear design.	14,024
LE Coupe			10,894
Sunbird	J	SMALL COUPE/SEDAN	
GT Coupe		New front design,	11,824
Convertible		IP/console.	17,324
SE Coupe			9,524
LE Coupe			9,274
LeMans	T	ECONOMY COUPE/SEDAN	
GSE		New for 1989.	9,464
SE Sedan			9,744
LE Sedan			8,314
LE Aerocoupe			8,014
Aerocoupe (Value Leader)			6,714
Safari	B	LARGE WAGONS	
Station Wagon		End Production at end of 1989 model year.	16,164
All Purpose Vehicle (APV)		VAN Introduction in 1990 MY	TBD

*Includes destination charges.

By early 1988, Losh's team had designed a new Fiero that they felt was a likely winner and that could be ready for introduction in 1990. There was, however, a growing feeling at corporate that the Fiero should be discontinued. Not only was the car unprofitable at current volumes, but GM had experienced difficulty achieving commercial success with niche marketing.

Losh also had to decide what to do about the minivan—a vehicle that GM classified as a truck. For some time he had wanted to introduce a Pontiac minivan to compensate for declining station wagon sales. There was, however, some concern from other GM product divisions as to the fit of such a vehicle in the Pontiac lineup.

Whatever position Losh took regarding the Fiero and the minivan, he knew he had to keep in mind the growing competitive pressures on GM and the resulting tightening of corporate resources.

PONTIAC DIVISION OF GENERAL MOTORS (C)

Losh announced in March 1988 that Pontiac would no longer produce the Fiero after the end of the 1988 model year (MY), which would occur August 31. Although the Fiero was the first car to generate enthusiasm in the two-seat market in 1984, by 1988 the market had fallen off to a point where it was unprofitable to produce the Fiero any longer.

Although the Fiero announcement was painful to Pontiac, the LeMans represented a more positive development. With an end to the current labor unrest in Korea, LeMans were being shipped on a regular basis, and sales were now running at approximately 6,000 units a month.

By mid-July 1988, sales for Pontiac were up. In fact, Pontiac's June sales had achieved the second highest monthly sales level ever with over 81,000 units sold for the month. Total sales for the model year to date ending June 30, 1988, were 574,051 units, compared to 530,818 units the previous year. The Grand Am, Bonneville, and the Grand Prix were leading the pack in sales. Pontiac had once again climbed to the third position in domestic industry sales behind Chevrolet and Ford respectively, while regaining the number two slot within GM.

In the July 18, 1988, issue of *Automotive News,* Losh was one of 25 industry executives and one of seven GM executives to be chosen an "All Star," and the only GM operating manager other than GM president Robert Stempel to receive this prestigious award. Losh was named Domestic Division Manager All Star.

As Pontiac prepared for the 1989 MY, Losh was especially optimistic about the new car lineup (Exhibit 10.) Leading the changes were the Grand Am with a newly designed front and rear appearance; a newly designed roof and rear deck lid for the 6000; a new, fresh design front end, instrument panel (IP), and console for the Sunbird; and a totally new uplevel LeMans, the GSE. Speaking to a group of Pontiac employees on July 25, Losh stated, "I wouldn't trade our current lineup for any other in the industry."

TOYS "R" US, 1989

CARON H. ST. JOHN

In 1948, Charles Lazarus began selling baby furniture in the back of his father's Washington, D.C., bicycle repair shop, located below the apartment where the Lazarus family lived. Within a few months, and in response to customer requests, he added a few toys to his line of baby furniture. Before long he realized parents who bought toys returned for more toys—but parents who bought furniture rarely came back. "When I realized that toys broke," he said, "I knew it was a good business."[1] Soon his entire business was focused on toys.

After the success of his first store, he opened his second store in Washington as a self-serve, cash-and-carry business. In 1958, he opened his third store—a 25,000-square-foot "baby supermarket" with discount prices and a large selection of products. Within a few years, a fourth supermarket-style store was opened. By 1966, the four stores in the Washington, D.C., area were achieving $12 million in annual sales.

In order to have the capital necessary for continued growth, Lazarus sold his four stores in 1966 to Interstate Stores, a retail discount chain, for $7 million. Lazarus stayed with Interstate and maintained operating control over the toy division. Between 1966 and 1974, the Toys "R" Us division of Interstate Stores grew from 4 to 47 stores through internal growth and a merger with Children's Bargain Town.

In 1974, the parent company, Interstate Stores, filed for bankruptcy. When Interstate completed reorganization and emerged from bankruptcy in 1978, the new company name was Toys "R" Us (TRU) and Charles Lazarus was chief executive officer. Since then, all but four of the Interstate Stores have been divested and all creditors have been paid.

Between January 1979 and January 1984, Toys "R" Us grew from 63 stores with sales of just under $350 million to 169 stores with sales of over $1.3 billion, for a compound annual growth rate of 30%. During the same years, profits increased from $17 million to $92 million for a compound annual

---

Source: **Prepared by Professor Caron H. St. John, Clemson University, as a basis for classroom discussion and not to illustrate either effective or ineffective handling of administrative situations. © Caron H. St. John, 1990.**

growth rate of 40%. TRU stock, which traded for $2 per share in 1978, split 3 for 2 for 4 years in a row and consistently traded above $40 per share. A $2 TRU stock investment made in 1978 was worth $200 in the spring of 1984.

After 1984, Toys "R" Us continued to grow and gain share of market in the toy retailing market. By 1988 sales had more than doubled to $3.14 billion with earnings of $204 million. At that time, Toys "R" Us operated 313 U.S. toy stores, 37 international toy stores, 74 Kids "R" Us clothing stores, and 4 department stores. As of 1988, Toys "R" Us was the largest toy retailer in the world with an estimated U.S. market share of greater than 21%.

Charles Lazarus has consistently been the motivating force behind the growth of Toys "R" Us. His vision is for Toys "R" Us to become the McDonald's of toy retailing: "We don't have golden arches, but we're getting there."[2] He credits his success in toy retailing to his love of the business. "What we do is the essence of America—making a business grow," he says. "If you're going to be a success in life you have to want it. I wanted it. I was poor. I wanted to be rich. . . . My ego now is in the growth of this company."[3]

TOY INDUSTRY

The U.S. toy industry saw the best of times and the worst of times during the decade of the eighties. Between 1980 and 1984, sales growth in the toy industry, fueled by electronic games and Cabbage Patch Kids, was very strong. Including electronic games, sales growth in those years exceeded 18% per year. Excluding the electronic games category, industry sales growth averaged 11%. While electronic games accounted for 18.4% of total U.S. toy sales in 1980, by 1982 they represented 30.9%—almost one-third—of total toy sales. During those same years, highly publicized toys such as Cabbage Patch Kid dolls, ET the Extra-Terrestrial toys, and the Trivial Pursuit board game accounted for 50% of non-electronic game sales. Traditional toys such as Slinky and Etch-A-Sketch accounted for the remaining 50%.

In 1984 and 1985, interest in electronic games fell sharply. This trend, combined with a dearth of blockbuster new toys of the caliber of Cabbage Patch Kids and Trivial Pursuit, resulted in relatively flat sales for the industry from 1985 to 1987. Total retail toy sales in 1988 were just over $13 billion.

TOY MANUFACTURING

During the slow growth years, many toy manufacturers suffered financially. Several companies posted losses in 1986 and 1987, and two large companies, Coleco and Worlds of Wonder, were forced into Chapter 11 bankruptcy.

By 1988, the industry had turned much of its energies toward cost control. Hasbro and Mattel closed facilities to reduce overhead costs and Tonka shifted much of its production to contract vendors in the Far East. Product development efforts focused on traditional favorites with considerably less emphasis on promotional games and toys, and licensed dolls and action figures (see

Exhibit 1). The movement toward traditional toys and cost containment was fueled by the bankruptcies of Coleco and Worlds of Wonder, the creator of the talking Teddy Ruxpin bear. The consensus in the industry was that both companies had become overly dependent on their promotional toys and had neglected cost controls.

TOY RETAILING

Until recently discount stores were the primary outlet for toy sales in the U.S. As shown in Exhibit 2, toy stores, particularly toy supermarkets such as Toys "R" Us and Lionel, have made major inroads into the retail toy market. Although all categories of retailers compete with each other, they use different approaches to appeal to customers. The national toy chains offer a large selection of products at low prices with a minimal level of in-store service. The discount stores frequently offer similar low prices and minimal service, but their selection is not as extensive as that of the toy chains. The small, independent toy stores provide personalized service and specialty items but ask higher prices. The larger department stores compete on the basis of convenience—the customer can purchase toys while shopping for other items. Toy depart-

EXHIBIT 1   TOY SHIPMENTS IN LEADING PRODUCT CATEGORIES (MILLIONS OF DOLLARS)

	1986	1987	% CHANGE
Plush			
(electronic, traditional)	$1,062	$1,174	10.5
Activity toys			
(educational, building sets, model kits, art)	850	1,092	28.5
Vehicles			
(remote control, battery, nonpower)	764	923	20.8
Dolls			
(baby, fashion)	1,663	920	(44.7)
Games & puzzles	760	861	13.3
Infant/preschool	816	840	2.9
Figures			
(action, robots)	1,105	702	(36.5)
Ride-on toys, except bicycles	288	570	97.9
Guns			
(weapons, accessories)	71	78	9.9
Other			
(playground, furniture, sports, audiovisual)	944	1,041	10.3
Total toy industry	$8,323	$8,201	(1.5%)

Source: Exstein, Michael B., "Toys "R" Us," *Shearson Lehman Hutton Investment Analysis* (August 19, 1988). (Original source: Toy Manufacturers of America, February 1988.)

EXHIBIT 2   U.S. TOY SALES BY TYPE OF STORE, PERCENT SHARE OF MARKET

	1982	1987
Toy, hobby, and game stores, including toy supermarkets	19	39
Discount	38	34
Other, including department stores	43	27

Source: Exstein, Michael B., "Toys "R" Us," *Shearson Lehman Hutton Investment Analysis* (August 19, 1988).

ments in the large department stores are small with minimum inventory and a limited product selection. Some large retailers such as J. C. Penney have dropped toy departments altogether.

There are approximately 85,000 retail toy outlets in the United States. With 313 U.S. outlets in 1988, Toys "R" Us is the largest national toy chain with 21.6% of total U.S. retail toy sales (see Exhibit 3). Child World, a division of Cole National, follows TRU with 6.0% of the market. Kay-Bee, a specialty toy retailer usually located in shopping malls, accounts for 4.9% of toy sales. Lionel Corporation, a large toy supermarket chain similar to Toys "R" Us, has 2.7% of the market. Between 1984 and 1986, Lionel was reorganizing under Chapter 11 of the Bankruptcy Act. When the company emerged from bankruptcy, it announced that it would attempt to grow and increase its share of the toy market by building 15 to 20 new stores per year.

Child World and Lionel have attempted to imitate Toys "R" Us by building similar warehouse-style stores. With few exceptions, TRU is the strongest competitor in those markets where the companies are in direct competition. Although all three competitors operate stores of similar size, TRU achieves an average of $8.4 million in sales a year per store compared to $4.4 million for Lionel and $4.9 million for Child World. In 1987, Child World attempted a price war that undercut the prices of TRU across several product categories.

EXHIBIT 3   MARKET SHARES OF MAJOR U.S. TOY RETAILERS IN 1987 (PERCENT)

Toys "R" Us (U.S. sales only)	21.6
Child World	6.0
Kay-Bee	4.9
Lionel	2.7
Circus World	1.1

Source: Exstein, Michael B., "Toys "R" Us," *Shearson Lehman Hutton Investment Analysis* (August 19, 1988).

The attack worked to increase sales at Child World stores at the expense of Toys "R" Us but profits were reduced so much at Child World that they are unlikely to try it again.

Toy retailing is a very seasonal business. Well over 50% of toy sales are reported in the fourth quarter—with much of those sales generated in the 6 weeks before Christmas. To balance the unevenness of toy sales, most toy stores sell other seasonal items such as swimming pool supplies and lawn furniture. The best selling toys, as of October 1988, are shown in Exhibit 4.

INDUSTRY TRENDS

Some demographic and industry trends that are expected to continue to influence demand for toys in the next several years are:

1. *Numbers of children.* The number of households headed by people aged 35 to 44 grew by 38% between 1980 and 1988. Since the late seventies, many of these members of the baby boom generation, who delayed having children while in their twenties, started having babies. Consequently, the 2-to-5-year-old age group has grown steadily for several years and may now be slowing down. Although the number of married couples of child-bearing age is expected to increase through 1990, by

---

EXHIBIT 4 TOP SELLING TOYS IN OCTOBER 1988

---

1. Nintendo Entertainment System (Nintendo)
2. Barbie (Mattel)
3. Micro Machines (Galoob)
4. Pictionary (Games Gang)
5. Real Ghostbusters (Tonka's Kenner)
6. G.I. Joe (Hasbro)
7. Win, Lose or Draw (Hasbro's Milton Bradley)
8. Hot Wheels (Mattel)
9. Starting Lineup (Tonka's Kenner)
10. Dolly Surprise (Hasbro's Playskool)
11. Teenage Mutant Ninja Turtles (Playmate)
12. Fun With Food (Fisher-Price)
13. Lil Miss Makeup (Mattel)
14. Kitchen (Fisher-Price)
15. Transformer (Hasbro)
16. Dyno-Rider (Tyco)
17. Super Mario Brothers, II (Nintendo)
18. Atari 2600 (Atari)
19. Sega Master System (Sega)
20. Koosh Ball (OddzOn)

Source: Pereira, Joseph, "Toy Makers Brace For a Blah Christmas," *Wall Street Journal* (November 22, 1988): B1.

2000 the number will have dropped precipitously as the baby bust generation replaces the baby boom.

2. *More money to spend on toys.* Many parents are having children after their households are formed and careers are established, so family incomes are higher. In many families, both parents are employed full-time. The higher family incomes mean there is more money for discretionary items such as toys.

3. *Broader market appeal of toy stores.* The toy market has joined with the video games and home electronics markets to form a broader category of "toys." The objective is to appeal to the teen and young adult market segment and draw this new group of buyers into the toy stores. While the industry was hurt badly by the decline in the video game market in 1984 and 1985, industry forecasters are predicting a resurgence of interest in the video game segment. The revival of the video game market is being led by a Japanese company, Nintendo, with 70% of the market. Analysts argue that companies are more technologically sophisticated and market-wise than they were in the early eighties and should be able to manage product demand.

4. *Licensing.* Licensing, or basing a product on a motion picture, television program, or comic strip character, accelerated in importance in the early eighties and is expected to continue to play a significant role in toy sales. According to manufacturers, toys based on popular characters appeal to an already established market. In recent years, however, toy retailers have criticized manufacturers for relying too heavily on licensed toys. They argue that there are too many licenses in the market and too large a variation in quality among them. Many retailers have cut back their stock of licensed products by as much as 10 to 30%, characterizing many licensed toys as "junk with stickers on it."

TOYS "R" US

The aim of Toys "R" Us is to be the customer's only place of purchase for toys and related products. Management says it is proud that TRU attracts the least-affluent purchasers because of the everyday discount prices and also attracts the most-affluent purchasers because of the extensive product selection. In order to provide total service to all customer segments, the company maintains tight operating procedures and a strong customer orientation.

RETAILING OPERATIONS

According to Charles Lazarus, "Nothing is done in the stores."[4] What he means is that all buying and pricing decisions are made at corporate headquarters in Rochelle Park, New Jersey. The corporate buying and pricing decisions are made using an elaborate computerized inventory control system where sales by item and sales by store are monitored daily. Those actual sales numbers are compared to forecasts, and when substantial differences exist, the slow items are marked down to get them out of the stores and the fast-selling items are reordered in larger quantities.

By closely following the buying habits of the consumer, TRU is able to pick up on trends before the crucial Christmas buying season and maintain more flexibility than competitors. In 1980, when sales of hand-held video games fell off sharply before Christmas, Toys "R" Us had been forewarned by its extensive monitoring system and had moved much of its stock of video games, at reduced prices, before the Christmas season. TRU was fully stocked with the big Christmas items that year—the Rubik's Cube and Strawberry Shortcake—unlike virtually all its competitors.

Toys "R" Us has gained a formidable reputation with toy manufacturers because of management's ability to predict the success or failure of new toys. Before the 1988 Christmas season, Toys "R" Us executives informed Hasbro that its $20 million new product, Nemo, aimed at the Nintendo market was dull and too expensive. Hasbro canceled the Nemo line and took a $10 million write-off. In August of 1988, TRU used its market-by-market sales data to show Ohio Arts Co. that its newly developed commercial for its new plastic building set was ineffective. Ohio Arts pulled the new commercial and substituted an older one that had been tried in Canada. Sales increased by 30%.

The TRU stores are regionally clustered with a warehouse within one day's driving distance of every store (see Exhibit 5). The company also owns a fleet of trucks to support its warehousing operations. The regional warehouses allow TRU to keep the stores well stocked and make it possible for TRU to order large quantities of merchandise early in the year, when manufacturers are eager to ship. Since most manufacturers will defer payments for 12 months on shipments made in the months immediately following Christmas, TRU is able to defer payment on about two-thirds of its inventory each year. TRU's competitors typically buy closer to Christmas, when buying terms are tighter.

All TRU stores have the same layout with the same items arranged on exactly the same shelves—according to blueprints sent from the corporate office. A TRU store is typically 43,000 square feet and is characterized by wide aisles and warehouse-style shelving stocked to the ceiling with over 18,000 different items. A substantial percent of the floor space is devoted to computers and computer-related products, and to non-toy items such as diapers, furniture, and clothing. However, toys, games, books, puzzles, and sports equipment are the major focus of the stores.

Each store is jointly managed by a merchandise manager and an operations manager. The merchandise manager has full responsibility for the merchandising effort in the store: content, stock level, and display. The operations manager is responsible for the building, personnel, cash control, customer service, and everything else that is not directly related to merchandise. Area supervisors oversee the total operations of three or four stores in a given area, and area general managers are responsible for the performance and profitability of all the TRU stores in a given market.

Toys "R" Us has little turnover among its middle and upper managers. In

EXHIBIT 5   TOYS "R" US STORES IN EACH OF THE COMPANY'S 22 U.S. REGIONS

WAREHOUSE/DISTRIBUTION REGION	NUMBER OF STORES
Washington, D.C., Virginia, Maryland	19
Southern California #1	13
Southern California #2	13
Northern California #1	9
Northern California #2	10
Illinois–Indiana	23
Wisconsin–Illinois	9
New York–New Jersey	30
Southern Texas–Louisiana	19
Michigan	19
New England	15
Northern Texas–Oklahoma	14
Pacific Northwest	11
Philadelphia	17
Northern Florida	9
Southern Florida	10
Georgia–Alabama–Tennessee	18
Western Ohio–Kentucky	18
Upstate New York	7
Carolinas	11
Cleveland–Pittsburgh	14
Phoenix	5

Source: Toys "R" Us, 1988 Form 10K.

the past 10 years, more than 40 employees have become millionaires through the company's employee stock option plan. According to TRU president, Norman Ricken, the company wants people who want to work. He says, "Toys "R" Us is not a 9-to-5 but an 8-to-faint job."[5]

MARKETING

As indicated earlier, each Toys "R" Us store carries over 18,000 items. Although toys represent, by far, the majority of the items stocked, other products include baby furniture, diapers, and children's clothing. The feeling at TRU is that the parent will go to the store to buy a necessity or nonseasonal item and will leave with at least one toy purchase. The average TRU customer spends over $40 per visit.

The product line at TRU includes home computers and software as well as traditional toys. This serves to broaden the company's customer base to include teenagers and adults, and to create add-on business at each retail unit. According to company statistics, products for these "older children" account for more than 15% of sales. TRU strongly feels this is not a change in its basic business—computers and software are toys for adults.

This strategy of carrying a wide selection of merchandise has benefited TRU in another way. The company has been successful in encouraging year-round buying at its stores. In 1980, 7.5% of profits were made in the nine months of January through September compared with 25% in fiscal year 1988.

TRU has a strong policy of year-round discount prices. Because TRU buys most of its merchandise during the off-season, when manufacturers are offering discounts, the company is able to pass the discounts on to the customer. TRU has a policy of not having store sales. Individual items will be marked down if they are not selling, but TRU does not have sales that are category-wide or store-wide.

Virtually all Toys "R" Us stores are located on an important traffic artery leading to a major shopping mall. A location of this type serves two purposes: it allows TRU to attract mall patrons without paying high mall rents, and it gives TRU the space to do business the way it wants to—as a large "supermarket" for toys, complete with grocery type shopping carts.

Other customer conveniences include the stock availability and return policies. Product availability is virtually guaranteed. Because of extensive inventory monitoring and attention to consumer buying habits, TRU rarely has a "stock out." Also, TRU boasts of a liberal return policy. The company claims it will accept all returns with no questions asked—even if a toy with no defect is broken by a child after several months of play.

Toys "R" Us does no national advertising. Before entering a new region, TRU promotes the opening of the new stores through heavy television and newspaper advertising. Once the stores are open, TRU may continue very limited television and newspaper advertising.

DOMESTIC AND FOREIGN EXPANSION

Toys "R" Us pursues a corporate objective of 18% expansion of retail space per year. In order to meet this objective, it has opened more than 35 new toy stores in the U.S. each year for several years (see Exhibit 6) and now has stores in 33 of the 50 states.

All of the expansions are made as a total entry into a new region. First, TRU builds a warehouse, then it clusters several stores within one day's driving distance of the warehouse so that prompt merchandise delivery is ensured. Typically, the warehouse and all the stores are up and running within the same fiscal year and in time for the Christmas season. Once TRU enters a local market with more than one store, it immediately becomes the low price leader in the area—forcing competitors to bring down their prices.

Charles Lazarus keeps a file of locations that have already been selected as potential sites for future U.S. stores. The regions are selected on the basis of demographic patterns and toy buying statistics. The individual store locations are decided after an analysis is completed of the area shopping malls, traffic patterns, and local retail toy competition. During fiscal 1988, TRU

EXHIBIT 6   NUMBER OF STORES AT YEAR-END

	1988	1987	1986	1985	1984	1983	1982	1981	1980
Toys "R" Us United States	313	271	233	198	169	144	120	101	85
Toys "R" Us International	37	24	13	5					
Kids "R" Us	74	43	23	10	2				

Source: Toys "R" Us, *1988 Annual Report.*

opened 42 new stores in the U.S. including five stores in a new market centered around Phoenix, Arizona. Long term plans call for regional expansion into Kansas City, Denver, Memphis, St. Louis, Minneapolis–St. Paul, and Salt Lake City. Charles Lazarus believes there is sufficient market demand for Toys "R" Us to build and operate a total of 700 stores in the United States.

In addition to domestic expansion, TRU is embarking on a plan of growth into the large non-U.S. toy market. The first Canadian and European stores were opened in late 1984. At the end of fiscal 1988, TRU operated 37 stores in Canada, Europe, and the Far East—13 more than in 1987. In 1989 TRU plans to build 15 more stores in Canada, West Germany, and the United Kingdom. (Company financial information is given in Exhibits 7 and 8.)

KIDS "R" US, TOO

TRU's only venture outside of toy retailing has been into children's clothing—a more than $6 billion industry in the United States alone. The corporate objective in creating Kids "R" Us was to "provide one stop shopping with an overwhelming selection of first quality, designer and brand name children's clothing in the season's latest styles at everyday prices. . . . We have taken the knowledge and systems we have refined for our toy stores over the past 30 years and applied some of these principles to our Kids "R" Us stores."[6]

In 1983, TRU opened its first two Kids "R" Us stores in the New York area. As of 1988 the company operated 74 Kids "R" Us stores in various markets in the U.S. with plans for 35 more stores in fiscal 1989. Each store offers a full assortment of first-quality, discount-priced clothing and accessories for children up to age twelve. The surroundings are spacious and well decorated with neon signs, color-coded departments, fitting rooms with platforms for small children, changing areas for infants, play areas for children, and color-coded store maps.

Some observers felt TRU would meet more resilient competition in children's clothing than it did in toys. Department and discount stores make more money on children's clothing than they do on toys and are not willing to give

EXHIBIT 7   TOYS "R" US, INC. AND SUBSIDIARIES: STATEMENTS OF CONSOLIDATED EARNINGS

	FISCAL YEAR ENDED		
	January 31 1988	*February 1 1987*	*February 2 1986*
(In thousands except per-share information)			
Net sales	$3,136,568	$2,444,903	$1,976,134
Costs and expenses:			
Cost of sales	2,157,017	1,668,209	1,322,942
Selling, advertising, general and administrative	584,120	458,528	408,438
Depreciation and amortization	43,716	33,288	26,074
Interest expense	13,849	7,890	6,999
Interest income	(8,056)	(7,229)	(8,093)
	2,790,646	2,160,686	1,756,360
Earnings before taxes on income	345,922	284,217	219,774
Taxes on income	142,000	132,000	100,000
Net earnings	$ 203,922	$ 152,217	$ 119,774
Net earnings per share	$1.56	$1.17	$.93

up that market easily. "Department stores fight when it comes to soft goods. That's their bread and butter, it's the guts of their business."[7] Some department store managers feel the purchase of children's clothing sets a family's buying patterns for years—so the implication of losing the children's department as a way to draw in families goes beyond the immediate loss of profits in that area.

After five years the Kids "R" Us move is finally beginning to show a profit. Kids "R" Us sells 85% of its clothing at a profit with 15% marked down to clear inventory. The industry average for markdowns is 22%. Kids "R" Us sales in fiscal 1987 were roughly $200 million with earnings of about $7 million.

COMPETITOR REACTION

TRU has an excellent reputation with consumers—a reputation that precedes the company into new market areas. Toys "R" Us also is feared and respected by its competitors. Examples of comments from competitors include:

- Toy store owner: "We were going, 'oh, nooo,' because they were coming in right across the street from us."[8]
- President of a buying guild about a children's store owner: "All I can tell you is his face turned white. You come up against a giant like this,

	FISCAL YEAR ENDED	
	January 31 *1988*	*February 1* *1987*
ASSETS		
Current Assets:		
Cash and short-term investments	$ 45,996	$ 84,379
Accounts and other receivables, less allowance for doubtful accounts		37,502
of $1,386 and $1,133	62,144	
Merchandise inventories	772,833	528,939
Prepaid expenses	5,050	3,566
Total Current Assets	886,023	654,386
Property and Equipment		
Real estate, net of accumulated depreciation of $31,238 and $22,400	762,082	600,747
Other, net of accumulated depreciation and amortization of $116,980		
and $86,207	351,037	240,218
Leased Property Under Capital Leases, net of accumulated depreciation of		
$16,840 and $15,797	11,397	12,440
Other Assets	16,520	15,175
	$2,027,059	$1,522,966
LIABILITIES AND STOCKHOLDERS' EQUITY		
Current Liabilities:		
Short-term notes payable to banks	$ 17,657	$ —
Accounts payable	403,105	305,705
Accrued expenses, taxes and other liabilities	167,280	118,260
Federal income taxes	71,003	73,059
Current portion:		
Long-term debt	876	973
Obligations under capital leases	1,071	968
Total Current Liabilities	660,992	498,965
Deferred Income Taxes	53,356	40,321
Long-Term Debt	159,788	63,966
Obligations Under Capital Leases	17,602	18,673
Commitments		
Stockholders' Equity		
Common stock par value $.10 per share:		
Authorized 200,000,000 shares		
Issued 130,530,467 and 127,110,608	13,053	12,711
Additional paid-in capital	252,493	239,721
Retained earnings	854,421	650,499
Foreign currency translation adjustments	23,586	8,449
Treasury shares, at cost	(5,929)	(5,571)
Receivable from exercise of stock options	(2,303)	(4,768)
	1,135,321	901,041
	$2,027,059	$1,522,966

Note: Figures are given in thousands.

with every major line discounted, and where do you go? If you're the average kiddy shop next door, do you take gas or cut your throat?"[9]

- Manufacturer about a buyer: "one department store buyer, arriving at the [TRU] store, said it caused her instant depression."[10]
- Atlanta toy retailers about TRU's entry into the Atlanta market:

I admire Toys "R" Us. They will own the town.
I hope they take the business from Zayre, Richway, Lionel and not us. We may have to start looking outside Atlanta for locations.
The new Toys "R" Us will saturate the market.[11]

- Michael Vastola, chairman of the board of Lionel Corporation: "They have paid a lot of attention to real estate and location, and it has paid off. You have got to say that they have a very disciplined, well-managed operation."[12]

ENDNOTES

1. Sherman, Stratford P., "Where the Dollars "R"," *Fortune* (June 1, 1981): 45–47.

2. Fesperman, Dan, "Toys "R" Us is a Giant in Kids' Business," *Miami Herald* (November 22, 1982).

3. Chakravarty, Subrata N., "Toys "R" Fun," *Forbes* (March 28, 1983): 58–60.

4. Sherman, "Where the Dollars "R"."

5. Pereira, Joseph, "Toys "R" Us, Big Kid on the Block, Won't Stop Growing," *Wall Street Journal* (August 11, 1988): B1.

6. "Kids "R" Us—The Children's Clothing Store Both Parents and Kids Will Choose," Press Release from Toys "R" Us, July 1983.

7. Ricci, Claudia, "Children's Wear Retailers Brace for Competition from Toys "R" Us," *Wall Street Journal* (August 25, 1983).

8. Fesperman, "Toys "R" Us is a Giant."

9. Ricci, "Children's Wear Retailers."

10. Ibid.

11. "A New Hat in Atlanta's Toy Ring," *Toys, Hobbies & Crafts* (May 1983): 5–8.

12. Kerr, Peter, "The New Game at Toys "R" Us," *New York Times* (July 4, 1983).

THE ELECTRONIC SPREADSHEET INDUSTRY: A COMPETITIVE ANALYSIS OF LOTUS AND ITS CHALLENGERS

**WILLIAM C. HOUSE AND
GARY D. WHITNEY**

INTRODUCTION

With sales of microcomputers increasing faster than sales of minicomputers and mainframes, sales of microcomputer software have been growing at a fairly rapid rate. The growth rate for microcomputer software was a respectable 24% in 1987 compared to 23% in 1986 and microcomputer software revenues are expected to increase by 27% in 1988.[1]

According to Dataquest,[2] worldwide shipments of personal computer units declined slightly from 15 million units in 1984 to 14.7 million units in 1985, but increased to 15.2 million units in 1986 and to 17.4 million units in 1987 (estimated). U.S. packaged software revenues have increased from 8.4 million in 1984 to 9.3 million in 1985, 11.0 million in 1986, and to 13.1 million in 1987.[3] U.S. Data Corporation has estimated that worldwide revenues of microcomputer software firms are growing three times faster than microcomputer hardware sales.[4] Revenues of the top 50 independent software companies increased from 1.9 million dollars in 1984 to 2.8 million in 1985, 3.6 million in 1986 and 5.2 in 1987.[5]

The microcomputer software industry has thousands of small independent suppliers with less than $1 million annual sales. The big three (Lotus, Ashton-Tate, and Microsoft), currently hold about 50% of the market as represented by revenues of the top 100 vendors. The gap between these three companies and other companies seems to be widening as a transition is made from a cottage industry to one dominated by a very few suppliers. Barriers to entry are increasing as the industry experiences intense competition, a high degree

Source: **Prepared by Professor William C. House and Gary D. Whitney, University of Arkansas, as a basis for classroom discussion and not to illustrate either effective or ineffective handling of administrative situations. © William C. House, 1989.**

of product similarity, and product changes geared to hardware innovations. Brand name recognition and increased marketing and product development/ implementation costs also discourage the entry of newly formed companies.

The "big three" also have large user bases, strong customer loyalty, and large, well developed research and development programs. These companies have sufficient financial resources to acquire competitors (e.g., Ashton-Tate's acquisition of Multimate), expand product bases, and to diversify into application areas not now covered. Ashton-Tate believes that price/performance, marketing and sales expertise, ease of use, product support, product line integration, and vendor financial strength are key factors in product success.[6] Although price competition has not been as important as brand name recognition and product improvements in product sales growth, an industry trend toward site licensing and volume discounts may make price more important in the future.

The electronic spreadsheet industry is growing less rapidly than other software industries and sales increases in recent years have not matched those of earlier years. Exhibit 1 shows the actual and expected unit sales of electronic spreadsheets from 1986 to 1990, according to one industry source. After levelling off in 1988, electronic spreadsheet sales are expected to grow at a slow but steady pace during the rest of decade. However, the timing and magnitude of the impact of OS/2 based hardware on spreadsheet demand is very uncertain at this point.

Spreadsheets and word processing programs are the most widely installed applications and represent slower growth, mature markets. Data base managers have somewhat more potential with modest growth possibilities. Graphics, CAD/CAM, project management, and desktop publishing applications represent the fastest growing markets with considerable room to develop without saturation. The Sierra Group in a recent poll of over 1,500 users found that 60% of users surveyed planned to buy word processing packages, 54% planned to buy data base managers, with 51% planning spreadsheet purchases and 35% expected to buy graphics presentation packages.[7]

EXHIBIT 1   ACTUAL AND ESTIMATED SALES OF ELECTRONIC SPREADSHEETS

YEAR	NUMBER
1986	1.20
1987	1.40
1988	1.50
1989	1.80
1990	2.00

Note: Data given in millions of units.

Source: IDC Corporation, *Computerworld* (December 21, 1987).

Exhibit 2 contains actual and estimated shipments of word processing, spreadsheet, graphics, communications, and data base management systems. With only modest sales growth expected from 1987 to 1988, for the period 1988 to 1992 spreadsheet sales are expected to increase at an average annual rate of 33% compared to 35% for word processing packages, 45% for graphics systems, 38% for communication packages, and 89% for data base managers.

LOTUS: COMPANY HISTORY AND DEVELOPMENT

Mitchell Kapor, a disk jockey with an interest in transcendental meditation, developed Lotus 1-2-3 in 1981 along with associate Todd Agulnick. At that time Kapor was president of Cambridge based Micro Finance Systems, a small New England software company. Several years earlier, Dan Bricklin, a Harvard University dropout, introduced the first electronic spreadsheet, Visicalc, which was designed for the Apple II computer.

Lotus has grown astronomically since its inception in 1983. In that first year, Lotus had sales of $53,000 and a staff of several dozen people. It has increased in size to the point that by 1987, revenues were just under 400 million and the number of employees has increased to 2,400. Jim Manzi, a former newspaper reporter and a Greek and Latin scholar, joined the firm in 1984 as sales and marketing manager. Kapor, an informal and undisciplined entrepreneur, came to rely increasingly on Manzi, who joined the company with a reputation as a hard headed businessman.

Kapor left the company in 1986 and Manzi became president. The brash, aggressive, and competitive former newspaper reporter very quickly made it clear he expected Lotus to continue to be the number one microcomputer software company in terms of size, sales, profits, and image. He is one of the highest paid chief executives in all industry, receiving more 26 million in sal-

EXHIBIT 2   SHIPMENTS OF APPLICATIONS SOFTWARE PACKAGES

	1987	1988*	1992*
Word processing	3.2	3.5	4.9
Spreadsheets	2.2	2.5	3.4
Graphics	1.4	1.8	3.3
Communications	2.1	2.5	3.8
Database management	1.0	1.4	5.0

Note: Data given in millions of units.

*Estimated

Source: Dataquest, *Personal Computing* (October 1988).

ary and stock options in 1987. Stock analysts have pointed out that Lotus's current president, unlike the chief executives of other major companies such as Microsoft, Ashton-Tate, and Borland, had no prior software company experience.

In 1987 as sales and profit growth began to level off, Manzi issued orders to staff members to exercise close control over costs. After a series of negative articles appeared in a New England newspaper in response to published reports of Manzi's salary and a series of insider stock sales shortly before announcement of further delays in introducing an updated version of Lotus, Manzi ordered company employees not to talk with the reporters of that newspaper. The order was later rescinded. Lotus claimed that officer salaries were not out of line with those of other industry leaders and justified the stock sales as necessary to cover income taxes on stock options granted to key executives. Concurrently with these developments, a number of key executives left the company and the stock price declined sharply.

Frank King, a 17 year IBM veteran involved in the development of the PC/3, became senior vice-president of software products in the spring of 1988. Due to his computer experience and engineering background, he has gained greater credibility with the Lotus staff than his predecessor. Outsiders say the more highly organized work environment contrasts highly with the informal, individualistic environment fostered by Kapor. However, morale appears to be better and annual turnover has declined to 15%, compared to an industry average of 20%.

PRODUCT DEVELOPMENT AND IMPLEMENTATION: SPREADSHEETS

Lotus's goal is to be number one in the microcomputer software industry in terms of sales, profits, size, and reputation. It relies heavily on one product, Lotus 1-2-3, which currently contributes 70% of its total revenues. Sales of its integrated package Symphony have been disappointing. The only new products introduced since 1984 have been add-ons or add-ins designed to speed up worksheet operation or to enhance such functions as data base management, word processing, and graphics display. Recently its sales and profits have lagged behind those of its number one competitor, Microsoft.

Lotus desires to improve 1-2-3 while still retaining the familiar look of the present version. Competitors such as Borland, Microsoft, Computer Associates, and Paperback Software are offering improved programs with added features at the same price as Lotus 1-2-3 or at even lower prices in some cases. The company has indicated an intention to develop versions of Lotus which will run on all types of computer hardware, including mainframes, minicomputers, and microcomputers. If this goal can be achieved, it would allow sharing of worksheets, files, and terminals while reducing training costs. However, achieving this objective is likely to be difficult. For example, writing one program which will work satisfactorily on the 8088, 80286, and 80386 micro-processor based hardware presents formidable challenges.

Since its introduction in 1983, Lotus has sold more than 3 million copies of its 1-2-3 program and holds 70–80% of the IBM-PC–compatible spreadsheet market. In its early years, the only serious competitors were Microsoft's Multi-plan and Sorcim's (now Computer Associates) Supercalc. Lotus sold 100,000 copies of 1-2-3 in its first year of operation and now sells that many copies in one month.

Paperback Software introduced VP-Planner as a Lotus clone during the mid-1980s for $99 and Borland in 1988 introduced a lower priced Lotus com-patible for $195 that has more features than 1-2-3 and can access all Lotus files and perform most Lotus functions. In addition, Borland has acquired the rights to Surpass from Sergio Rubenstein, the developer of Wordstar. Surpass is a higher priced Lotus compatible spreadsheet selling for $495 that has many advanced features. In 1987, Microsoft introduced an IBM-PC compatible ver-sion of its popular McIntosh spreadsheet Excel for $495 which has a graphical interface characterized by ease of use. During 1988, Lotus is expected to sell 1.2 million copies of 1-2-3, Borland is estimating sales of 150,000 copies of Quattro, and industry analysts expect Excel sales to be at least 120,000 units. VP-Planner and Supercalc sales should level off or even decline.

Lotus has about 76% of the IBM compatible market, Supercalc 4.1%, Mul-tiplan 3.2%, and other companies' spreadsheets about 16.7% in 1987. Micro-soft's Excel holds about 75% of the Apple McIntosh market with Lotus Jazz processing 17% of the market and others 8%. Lotus's introduction of 1-2-3 in the Apple market during 1988 was seen as negatively impacting sales of Jazz without having a significant effect on sales of Excel. As a result, Lotus announced plans to phase out Jazz soon after the 1-2-3 program for Apple was implemented.

Exhibit 3 contains spreadsheet sales in units for the major spreadsheet

EXHIBIT 3   SHIPMENTS OF MAJOR SPREADSHEET SUPPLIERS FOR 1985, 1986, AND 1987

	1985	1986	1987
Lotus 1-2-3	680	750	900
Multiplan	221	275	250
Excel-IBM	—	—	120
VP-Planner	—	100	60
Quattro	—	—	50
Supercalc	34	65	40

Note: Data given in thousands of units.

Source: Dataquest, *Personal Computing* (October 1986, 1987, 1988).

suppliers for 1985, 1986, and 1987. Lotus sales have continued to increase at a steady rate during this period while the sales of other spreadsheet companies have not kept pace. However, the effect of the introduction of two new competitors, Excel and Quattro, and revised versions of VP-Planner (Plus) and Supercalc (V) on Lotus sales cannot be determined at this point.

LOTUS 1-2-3

Lotus 1-2-3 is a relatively easy-to-use product with a broad user base. It is a familiar, proven package with established compatibility across company lines and with company divisions. Added power and utility come from Lotus add-ins such as HAL (natural language interface), Freelance Plus (graphics), and Manuscript (word processing). In comparison with competitors' spreadsheet products, Lotus has limited functions, poorer graphics, and a higher price in many cases. It has lost sales due to restrictive site licensing and copy protection provisions not attached to other spreadsheets. A lack of LAN support has caused some users to switch to other spreadsheets such as Supercalc.

Lotus competitors such as Supercalc, Multiplan, Excel, and Quattro can offer added features and ease of use along with function and file compatibility at the same or a lower price. However, other spreadsheets have the disadvantage that they must persuade buyers to undergo a retraining process for users and 1-2-3 file compatibility must be demonstrated before the alternative products become viable contenders.

Spreadsheet linking for 1-2-3 is cumbersome and multiple spreadsheets cannot be displayed on the same screen. Graphics capabilities are limited, and printing is often unwieldy and time consuming. Lotus's macro capability permits customization of the spreadsheet program to fit many different situations. Many users have invested a large amount of time, money, and effort in developing macros and templates for use with 1-2-3. This may inhibit switching to other products unless they are vastly superior to 1-2-3 and can clearly demonstrate file and macro compatibility.

To overcome some of its inherent limitations, Lotus has developed several add-ins to perform functions not available on its 2.0 or 2.1 version. Speedup increases the effective operating speed of Lotus by only recalculating cells affected by the previous command or command sequence. Learn gives Lotus the capability of memorizing keystrokes for macrogeneration without the need to use complex series of commands. HAL, a natural language interface, provides an easier to use command structure and permits easier linking of multiple spreadsheets than possible with the original product.

Lotus announced that after prolonged delay, release 3.0 of 1-2-3 would be made available during the fourth quarter of 1988. During the fourth quarter of 1988, a further postponement was announced, moving the target date for version 3.0 back to the second quarter of 1989. It is expected to add a number of performance features not possible with current versions of 1-2-3 such as the ability to link several worksheets, display up to three worksheets on the same screen, and to merge text and graphs in the same worksheet. Layered worksheets can be stored in main memory, faster recalculation of spreadsheet changes has been implemented, and the revised spreadsheet program can be automatically reconfigured to work with either DOS or OS/2 operating systems.

With all the new features added and an easier to use interface promised, the look and feel of version 3.0 may be considerably different than previous versions. If the new version requires considerable retraining, existing users of 1-2-3 may be reluctant to switch to the newer version or may even seriously consider adopting a competitive spreadsheet. Another problem is that version 3.0 will not run efficiently unless the user has the newer 286 or 386 microprocess based hardware. Lotus had originally claimed that the new version of 1-2-3 would perform satisfactorily on 8088 based systems if users had 640K of internal memory and a hard disk.

Lotus is striving to develop 1-2-3 versions that will run on both micros and mainframes, in distributed and nondistributed environments. New versions of 1-2-3 are being written in C language instead of Assembler to ensure high portability. As part of its plans to push 1-2-3 as an operating environment Lotus has announced a high level language for developing customized applications called Extended Applications Facility.

MICROSOFT—MULTIPLAN AND EXCEL

Multiplan has been a solid but nonspectacular software product with a slightly different formula and command structure than 1-2-3. It has data base capability with mouse support, runs under M/S Windows and on networks. Multiplan has 1-2-3 file read/write capability and can import files from DBase and RBase. Although the worksheet has no graphic capability, it can import graphs from Microsoft's Chart program.

Excel, a Microsoft worksheet program which proved popular on the Apple McIntosh, has a graphical interface and is more powerful than 1-2-3. It can operate on arrays, handle trend projection and optimization calculations, and display multiple spreadsheets on the same screen, linking them using a mouse or keystroke commands. The maximum spreadsheet size is two times that of Lotus and graphs can be printed from within the spreadsheet. The user may select from 42 different graph formats and numerous font, boldface, and italic sizes. Variable character heights, borders, shaded areas, and underlining are easy to implement. It is not copy protected and has flexible site licensing provisions.

Excel is designed for 286 or 386 personal computers with high resolution graphics, at least 640K of internal memory, and a hard disk. It is fully compatible with 1-2-3 files and has a help facility which automatically gives the Excel equivalent when a 1-2-3 sequence is entered. However, Excel is not keystroke compatible with 1-2-3 and is only 95% compatible with Lotus macros. It has a macro translator that translates 1-2-3 macros into Excel macros. Minimal recalculation is permitted and built in auditing and data base capabilities are also provided.

Microsoft is emphasizing high resolution graphics, mice, and an easy to use pull down menu system interface in a package which can only be run on 286 and 386 machines. It expects the windows interface and OS/2 presentation manager with which its program is compatible to become an industry standard. Excel is written in C language so portability is assured although it has no announced plans to make Excel available on the current generation of personal computers. Its greater appeal is still to McIntosh users.

BORLAND—QUATTRO AND SURPASS

Quattro, at $195, is less expensive and more functional than Lotus 1-2-3. It provides selective recalculation, more types of graphs, and a wide variety of screen display and printing options. Graphs can be printed from within the spreadsheet and the program takes full advantage of EGA and VGA graphics adapters. Quattro has full 1-2-3 file capability, improves macro development ability using a macro generator, and permits extensive customization of applications. For debugging purposes, individual commands within a macro sequence can be executed one at a time. It requires a minimum of 512K in internal memory and is not copy protected.

Surpass, at $495, will likely appeal to users who have reached the limit of Lotus 1-2-3 capabilities. A subset of Surpass can be used to implement all 1-2-3 keystrokes, files, macros, and formulas, making it unnecessary for complete retraining of former Lotus 1-2-3 users. It can handle multiple spreadsheets, align them in 3-D fashion, post changes from one spreadsheet to others automatically, and refer to a spreadsheet without requiring that it be in main memory. Dynamic links between spreadsheets are provided and a macro library contains command sequences which can be used on more than one spreadsheet. Multiple spreadsheets can be displayed on the screen, graphs may be displayed in 3-D format, and an undo command permits easy correction of mistakes. A built in file manager can perform many common DOS functions.

Borland has imitated Lotus by writing Quattro in assembly language, making it as fast and as compact as possible. Unlike Lotus, the company is opposed to using one product for multiple computer architectures. It prefers to develop a lower priced package that will make the fullest possible use of a given type of machine. For users who want a higher level Lotus look alike, the company can offer Surpass with more features than 1-2-3 at a comparable price.

SUPERCALC

Supercalc, acquired by Computer Associates when it absorbed Sorcim in the mid-1980s, permits use of larger spreadsheets than Lotus (i.e., about 2,000 additional rows) and is not copy protected. The command structure differs somewhat from Lotus but a careful reading of menus will allow users to accomplish most of the functions possible with Lotus. It reads and writes 1-2-3 files and can import or export Visicalc, DIF, and ASCII files. Graphics and data base modules are included in the program and as many as nine graphs per spreadsheet can be saved in memory. It permits macrorecording, providing more financial and logical functions than Lotus, and LAN support is also provided.

Version 5 of Supercalc permits faster retrieval of information from cells with similar names or codes than previously possible and is menu, macro, and file compatible with 1-2-3. An optional 1-2-3 interface facilitates user transition from 1-2-3 and macros can contain both 1-2-3 and Supercalc commands. Enhanced presentation graphics, a toggle on and off minimum recalculation feature, and an undo command for ease of use in correcting errors are provided. Macro-debugging and built in auditing capabilities are also included. A version of Sideways is thrown in as a bonus feature with each Supercalc purchase. Computer Associates has a volume discount and liberal site licensing policy for Supercalc.

VP-PLANNER

VP-Planner, developed by Alex Osborne's Paperback Software, is a low cost clone costing $99 that uses most Lotus commands plus a few new ones. It will read and write DBase files, record macros, and open up to six windows. While working on one spreadsheet, users can print another one. VP-Planner cannot run Lotus add-ins but some add-ons will work with this program (e.g., 1-2-3 Forecast, Ready to Run Accounting, Goal Seeker). VP-Planner has no built in graphics capabilities but can develop graphs using the separate VP-Graph program. Another drawback is that unlike other spreadsheet companies, it charges users for technical support.

The notoriety from the Lotus lawsuit charging copyright infringement based on the look alike, feel alike quality of VP-Planner has hurt sales. However, it is obvious that VP-Planner is more than just a Lotus clone. A new version, VP-Planner Plus carries a slightly higher price tag (i.e., $179.99) and provides twice as many financial and logical functions as Lotus, permits recalculation of selected cells, and is not copy protected. Graphics capabilities are only fair, not being in the same class as Quattro or Excel. An optional interface with pull down menus makes it easier to follow command sequences than possible with 1-2-3.

VP-Planner's database capability permits reading and writing DBase, VP-Info, and DIF files as well as viewing data in up to five dimensions. One obvious shortcoming of Paperback Software's marketing program is that it overstressed the value of VP-Planner as a low cost Lotus clone and did not emphasize its strong data base capability. In its most recent annual report, Paperback reported a net loss of $354,000 or 0.12 per share on sales of 4.7$ million compared to a net income of $77,000 or 0.02 per share on sales of 3.4$ million in the previous year.

ASHTON-TATE

Ashton-Tate, which gets 60% of its sales from DBase, its data base manager, is not an active player in the spreadsheet market although its does have an inte-

grated package named Framework. However, its competitive position is eroding because its current programs won't work on the new 386 machines and it
is facing intense competition in the data base market from Oracle, Borland,
and others. Both Lotus and Microsoft are moving into the data base market
with add-ins or built in capabilities as part of their spreadsheet programs.

PRODUCT DEVELOPMENT/IMPLEMENTATION— INTEGRATED SOFTWARE PACKAGES

Integrated software packages combine several functions such as word processing, spreadsheet, data base management, and communications all into one
package. The major advantage is that a user can perform a number of computer based functions with one program using a common command structure.
Not having to switch from one program to another each time a different function is performed saves time and effort. The disadvantage is that normally a
given integrated package will emphasize one or two functions such as spreadsheet or data base management and will provide only minimum capabilities
for others (e.g., word processing, graphics). Some users are reluctant to pay
the extra price for a package containing four or five functions when only one
or two will be used continually.

Many users desire a "core" product which can be used for data base,
spreadsheet, word processing, memo writing, desk calculating, scheduling, etc.
However, the market for individual applications (e.g., data base, word processing, spreadsheet) has grown faster than that for integrated software packages.
It is estimated that integrated package sales grew 4% in 1986 over 1985 while
sales of individual applications increased at a rate of 31%. Exhibit 4 shows
actual and estimated individual application package revenues compared to
those for integrated software packages for 1985 to 1989.

The major integrated software packages include Lotus Symphony which
has a strong spreadsheet, a fair data base, and a weak word processing capability, and Ashton-Tate's Framework, which has a strong database, a good word
processor, and a fair spreadsheet. Revenues from Symphony were estimated

EXHIBIT 4   REVENUES FOR INDIVIDUAL AND INTEGRATED SOFTWARE PACKAGES FOR 1985–1989

YEAR	INDIVIDUAL APPLICATIONS	INTEGRATED PACKAGES
1989	1.35 (bils) E	140 (mils) E
1988	1.15 (bils) E	130 (mils) E
1987	967 (mils) E	120 (mils)
1986	920 (mils)	107 (mils)
1985	625 (mils)	103 (mils)

Note: E = estimated

Source: PC Week (September 1987)

to be 39 million dollars in 1986 (36% market share) and Framework generated 26 million for a 26% share. The other major players were Innovative Software's Smartware which produced 14 million dollars in revenues for a 14% share of the market and the Enable Group's Enable package which captured 3% of the market with 4 million dollars in sales. More than 40 other competitors divided the remaining 22%.

At the lower end of the scale, Software Publishing Company introduced First Choice in August of 1986 and sold 70,000 units during the first six months of product life. It also sold 25,000 copies of its separate Professional Plan spreadsheet during 1986. It is estimated that SPC has sold 200,000 copies of First Choice at a list price of $195 through mid-1988. Version 2 of First Choice added graphics capabilities to other functions. Microsoft has converted its McIntosh integrated package Works for use on the IBM-PC and compatibles and is expected to be a strong competitor with a price comparable to First Choice. A recent entry by Spinnaker Software is its Better Working Eight-In-One program. At $59.95, it provides outlining, word processing, spelling checker, spreadsheet, data base, graphics, communications, and a desktop organizer with a memo pad, address book, and calendar.

REVENUE AND INCOME ANALYSIS

Exhibit 5 contains revenues for six companies that have developed and marketed electronic spreadsheets for the period 1984 to 1987. These companies include Ashton-Tate, Borland, Computer Associates, Lotus, Microsoft, and Software Publishing Company. Total spreadsheet industry revenues for the top six competitors have increased from 406.6 million dollars to 1.3 billion dollars or 329% (1984 = 100). The average annual increase in revenues for the period under consideration was 310.7 million or 76.2%.

Exhibit 6 shows net incomes for the period 1984 to 1987. Total industry income increased from 70.4 million to 216.9 million dollars, an increase of

EXHIBIT 5   ELECTRONIC SPREADSHEET COMPANY REVENUES

COMPANY	1984	1985	1986	1987
Ashton-Tate	$43.0	$82.0	$122.0	$211.0
Borland	1.1	11.6	29.7	38.1
Computer Associates	85.0	129.0	191.0	309.0
Lotus	157.0	226.0	283.0	396.0
Microsoft	97.0	140.0	198.0	346.0
Software Publ. Co.	23.5	37.2	23.7	38.6
Total revenues	$406.6	625.8	847.4	1,398.7

Note: Amounts are given in millions.

Source: Standard & Poor's Stock Reports, 1988.

EXHIBIT 6   ELECTRONIC SPREADSHEET COMPANY NET INCOMES

COMPANY	1984	1985	1986	1987
Ashton-Tate	$5.3	$6.5	$16.6	$30.1
Borland	0.1	0.9	0.9	1.3
Computer Associates	9.5	13.3	18.5	36.5
Lotus	36.0	38.2	48.3	72.0
Microsoft	15.9	24.1	39.3	71.9
Software Publ. Co.	3.6	5.8	0.7	5.2
Total income	$70.4	88.9	114.3	216.9

Note: Amounts are given in millions.

Source: Standard & Poor's Stock Reports, 1988.

146.5 million or 308% (1984 = 100). The average increase in net income for the period considered was 69.3%. Thus, total revenues increased 54% in 1985 over 1984, 35% in 1986 over 1985, and 59% for 1987 over 1986 while net income increased 26% for 1985 over 1984, 29% for 1986 over 1985, and 90% for 1987 over 1986.

Exhibit 7 shows total assets for the six spreadsheet companies for years 1984 to 1987. For the industry, assets increased from 329.5 million dollars to $1.3 billion or 390.3%, compared to a 329% increase in revenues and a 308% increase in net incomes. Assets increased 45% for 1985 over 1984, 57% for 1986 over 1985, and 71% for 1987 over 1986.

Exhibit 8 contains earnings per share for 1986 and 1987 as well as research and development expenditures as a percentage of sales revenues. Earnings per share increased at an average rate of 75% for the total industry compared to an average increase of 59% in total revenues and 90% in net income for

EXHIBIT 7   ELECTRONIC SPREADSHEET COMPANY ASSETS

COMPANY	1984	1985	1986	1987
Ashton-Tate	$31.0	$46.0	$88.0	$175.0
Borland	0.5	5.4	12.2	31.1
Computer Associates	118.0	148.0	245.0	439.0
Lotus	122.0	186.0	209.0	318.0
Microsoft	48.0	65.0	171.0	288.0
Software Publ. Co.	10.0	27.4	26.8	35.0
Total assets	$329.0	477.8	752.0	1,286.1

Note: Amounts are given in millions.

Source: Standard & Poor's Stock Reports, 1988.

EXHIBIT 8   ELECTRONIC SPREADSHEET EARNINGS PER SHARE, R&D OUTLAYS, ADVERTISING EXPENSES/SALES REVENUES, AND SALES PER EMPLOYEE

COMPANY	EPS		R&D EXPS/ SALES		ADV EXPS/ SALES	SALES/ EMPLOYEE	
	1986	1987	1986	1987	1986	1986	1987
Ashton-Tate	0.85	1.26	9.3	9.2	2.12	111	191
Borland	0.02	0.03	9.0	9.3	9.22	54	102
Comp. Assc.	0.42	0.74	18.0	13.0	0.73	49	160
Lotus	1.03	1.58	13.8	14.8	0.26	135	188
Microsoft	0.78	1.30	10.0	11.0	1.64	110	167
SW Publ Co.	0.10	0.69	24.9	19.9	4.81	100	162

Source: *Standard & Poor's Stock Reports; Software News* (October 1988); *Computer Industry Encyclopedia,* 1987.

1987 compared to 1986. Four of the six companies increased research and development expenditures as a percentage of sales slightly or not at all in 1987 while two companies (CAI and Software Publishing Company) significantly decreased their R&D outlays as a percentage of revenues. Also included in Exhibit 8 are advertising expenditures as a percent of sales revenues[8] and sales per employee which is sometimes used as a measure of productivity.

ENDNOTES

1. U.S. Department of Commerce, *Industrial Outlook* (Washington, D.C.: Government Printing Office: 1988).

2. *Time* (May 11, 1987).

3. *Standard & Poor's Industry Surveys,* May 1988.

4. Department of Commerce, *Industrial Outlook.*

5. *Software News* (May 1986, 1987, 1988).

6. *Standard & Poor's Industry Surveys,* May 1988.

7. *Computerworld* (May 9, 1988).

8. *Computer Industry Almanac,* 1987 (latest data available).

ADDITIONAL REFERENCES

Bulkeley, William. "After Years of Glory, Lotus is Stumbling in Software Market." *Wall Street Journal* (August 30, 1988).

Bryan, Marvin. "How Spreadsheets Add Up." *Personal Computing* (September 1987).

Hammons, Keith. "Teaching Discipline to Six Year Old Lotus." *Business Week* (July 4, 1988).

O'Reilly, Richard. "Computer File: Kahn, Microsoft Enter Competitive Spreadsheet Market." *Tulsa World* (January 24, 1988).

Radding, Alan. "Race of Power vs. Position." *Computerworld* (December 21, 1987).

"Lining Up Behind Three Visionaries" (Special Report). *Computerworld* (November 2, 1987).

Wilder, Clinton. "Lotus at Risk." *High Technology Business* (July 1988).

MICROSOFT (A): THE DECISION TO GO PUBLIC

ROBERT D. HAY AND
WILLIAM C. HOUSE

Microsoft Corporation, one of the largest companies in the rapidly growing microcomputer software industry, was founded by Bill Gates and Paul Allen in 1975. These two entrepreneurs wrote a version of the BASIC programming language to run on an early microcomputer. Spurred by the initial success of the program they developed, Gates dropped out of Harvard University after one year to devote full time to developing and selling software products. He and Allen formed a fledgling company known as Microsoft.

In 1980, IBM talked first to Gates and then to Digital Research Inc., developer of the CP/M operating system, about developing an operating system for its personal computer. When IBM could not make a deal with DRI, it came back to Microsoft and Gates for further discussion. Shortly thereafter, Gates purchased an operating system somewhat similar to CP/M from Seattle Computer Company for $50,000. He later offered it to IBM for a flat fee of $125,000 and they accepted.

The operating system became PC-DOS for IBM computers and was made available to IBM compatible computer manufacturers as MS-DOS (Microsoft Disk Operating System). By the end of 1983, Microsoft had generated $10 million in revenues from the sale of MS-DOS. Nearly 50% of business microcomputers in the United States (i.e., an estimated 8 million units) now use the MS-DOS operating system. Microsoft receives about $10 for each operating system purchased by a hardware manufacturer compared with $50 to $200 typically received by a software developer when it sells an application program to a distributor.

Source: **Prepared by Professors Robert D. Hay and William C. House, University of Arkansas, as a basis for classroom discussion and not to illustrate either effective or ineffective handling of administrative situations. Prepared from Microsoft Company and other published materials.** © **Robert D. Hay, 1989.**

PRODUCT LINES AND DISTRIBUTION CHANNELS

Microsoft has designed and developed more than 40 software systems and applications products. Its product lines include three operating systems, language products in six different computer languages, and six separate categories of applications software, including word processing, spreadsheet, file management, graphics, communications, and project management. A "mouse" interface device and several computer-oriented books are also marketed by the software firm.

The company has four primary distribution channels: Domestic OEM (31%), International OEM (13%), Domestic Retail (36%) and Microsoft Press (1%). The three major product groups include systems software (54% of revenues), application software (38% of revenues) and hardware books (8% of revenues).

Microsoft's Multiplan spreadsheet was introduced three years after Dan Bricklin and Visicorp initiated sales of Visicalc, the original electronic spreadsheet. A few months later, Lotus Corporation introduced 1-2-3, an integrated software package with many features not possessed by stand-alone spreadsheet packages. As a result, sales of Multiplan have ranked third in relation to 1-2-3 and Visicalc. Microsoft's WORD processing program was introduced in 1983 with an extensive sales promotion program, including demonstration disks inserted in *PC Magazine*. However, it has been criticized in some quarters as being difficult to use and has not been able to equal the sales of some other popular products like MicroPro's WORDSTAR. A promising new product, recently introduced after prolonged delays is Windows, an operating environment or program which allows users to split display screens, show the status of several applications at one time, and even share data among programs.

Chairman Gates feels that Microsoft may have concentrated too long on systems software and should pay more attention to applications software in the future. In his view, at least half the demand for personal computers in business environments will have been satisfied by the end of the 1980s. As a result, sales of hardware and operating systems will not grow as fast in the 1990s as they did during the 1980s, while demand for applications software should expand rapidly. Sales of systems software are expected to grow from about $33 million in 1984 to $900 million by 1988 while applications software sales are projected to increase from about $1 billion in 1984 to $6 billion in 1988.

Larger companies have an edge in the highly competitive personal computer software market. The top 10 companies had approximately 70% of all industry sales in 1985, up from 57% in 1984 (see Exhibit 1) and an estimated 30% in 1981. Twenty top-selling programs, many of them marketed by the top 10 companies accounted for 80% of all personal computer software sales. Info Corporation expects personal computer software sales to expand at only a 15% compound annual rate during the last half of the current decade compared to a 64% growth rate during the first half of the 1980s. As a result, the

EXHIBIT 1   ESTIMATED MARKET SHARES FOR MICROCOMPUTER SOFTWARE COMPANIES (1984)

Lotus	13%	Digital Research	3%
Microsoft	11%	(Private Company)	
IBM	8%	MicroPro	3%
Ashton-Tate	6%	Software Publishing	2%
Tandy Corporation	5%	Others	43%
Apple Computer	4%		

larger, more diversified companies with well-known product lines are likely to achieve larger sales and profit gains than smaller, single-product companies.

The microcomputer software industry has been subjected to rapid technological changes during the first half of the 1980s and a continuation of this trend is expected into the 1990s. As a result, large expenditures for product development are necessary to ensure market growth and penetration. In fiscal 1985, Microsoft spent 12% of total revenues on product development, compared to 11% in 1984. Lotus and Ashton-Tate, Microsoft's biggest rivals, spent approximately 9% of revenues on product development during 1985.

Exhibit 2 contains a comparison of financial data for Microsoft with four of its major competitors. Its sales and net income figures for 1985 rank second only to Lotus. Microsoft also has the highest profit margin of any of the five selected companies and its R&D expense as a percent of sales is second only to MicroPro. Thus, Microsoft compares favorably with its major competitors at the end of 1985 in terms of common measures of financial performance. The two largest competitors have year-end stock prices ranging from 21 to 23 and P/E ratios of 8 to 11.

EXHIBIT 2   COMPARATIVE FINANCIAL DATA FOR SELECTED MICROCOMPUTER SOFTWARE COMPANIES (1985)

	ASHTON-TATE	LOTUS	MICROSOFT	MICROPRO	SOFTWARE PUBLISHING
Sales (mils)	121.6	225.5	140.4	42.6	37.2
Net income	16.6	38.2	24.1	0.2	5.8
Net income (% of sales)	13.7	16.9	17.2	0.01	15.6
R&D expense (mils$)	11.3	21.2	17.1	8.3	6.0
R&D expense (% of sales)	9.3	9.4	12.2	19.6	16.1
Year-end stock price	23.0	21.25	N/A	2.06	7.50
P/E ratio	10.0	7.8	N/A	6.9	12.3
Estimated earnings (1986)	2.11	2.73	N/A	0.30	0.61

MANAGEMENT AND PERSONNEL: THIN BUT AGGRESSIVE

The chairman of Microsoft, Bill Gates, was a founder of the company along with Paul Allen. These two entrepreneurs had a partnership arrangement from 1975 to 1981. Gates is responsible for technical software development including product design and internal development and review. He is a hard-driving, hard-working executive who works 90 hours a week and expects his employees to follow suit. The loss of the services of Gates could significantly and adversely affect the company's position in the microcomputer software industry and its new product development efforts.

Steve Ballmer, a college classmate of Gates, shared major management responsibilities with him from 1980 to 1982. Ballmer worked as an assistant product manager for P&G for more than a year and spent one year at Stanford University. He is compatible with Gates in high speed information exchange despite his limited management background. Ballmer became vice president of marketing in 1984 and assumed the position of vice president of systems software in 1984.

James Towne was hired as president in 1982 from Textronix Corporation. During his short tenure at Microsoft he exhibited a very engaging personality and proved to be very good at delegating authority. However, he had very limited interaction with Gates and never seemed to mesh well with the organization.

Jon Shirley joined Microsoft as president and chief operating officer in 1983. He previously spent 25 years with Tandy Corporation, including the position of vice president of computer merchandising from 1978 to 1983. He was by all accounts a tough, efficient manager at Tandy, where he gained considerable experience in manufacturing and retailing operations. During his first five months at Microsoft, he cut manufacturing costs by 20% and helped reduce a large order backlog by scheduling production on the basis of 90-day projections instead of on an annual basis.

Frank Gaudette was hired as vice president, finance and administration, in 1984. He served in the same position at C3, Inc. from 1981 to 1983 and previously was with Informatics General Corporation. His past experience includes the management of three stock offerings for software and service companies.

Ida S. Cole joined Microsoft as vice president, applications software, in 1985. Previously she held the position of director of new product development at Apple Computer as well as director of marketing for the Apple II and III product lines.

The addition of outside personnel has strengthened the management team at Microsoft. However, responsibilities are still not clearly defined among key executives. Gates says that he is concerned with strategy, software development, relations with key customers and foreign countries, and personnel motivation. President Shirley is responsible for all other activities including marketing and production.

The philosophy of management of the organization is conservative financially but is middle of the road in many other respects. The management attitude in existence encourages participation in many organizational decisions as well as innovation in product development. Although key decisions are tightly controlled and coordinated at top levels, input from employees is encouraged before choices are made and implemented.

GOING PUBLIC: HOW MUCH IS THE FIRM WORTH?

In 1984, Gates promised to take the company public in 1986 if market conditions warranted. Assuming a price-earnings ratio of 20 times earnings, the total market value of the company in 1984 was estimated to be $240 million. Gates owned about one-half of the company's stock at that time and at least one-third of his workers also owned stock in the company. Microsoft watched carefully when Lotus and Ashton-Tate made public stock offerings in 1983 and did not fail to notice when three other software companies followed suit in 1984 and 1985. However, it was 1985 before the company tentatively decided to issue its first public offering of stock.

Several reasons were given for the delay in making the initial offering. Large cash reserves made immediate expansion unnecessary and with a sizeable personal fortune, Gates had no pressing need to increase the value of his holdings through the public sale of stock. He was also afraid that the process of going public, accompanied by intensive scrutiny of the financial community, would distract the company from its primary job of developing and marketing software.

In the first half of the decade of the 1980s, Gates had sold stock and granted stock options to a few individuals in order to attract and hold talented personnel. By its own calculations, the company estimated that by 1987 more than 500 people would own company stock. At that time, registration with the SEC would be mandatory. If the company had to register anyway, it might make sense to sell enough shares to ensure a liquid market for the company's stock.

One strategy would be to continue the company as a privately held organization, holding off on going public until the last possible minute in order to preserve the present corporation culture and operating control vested in a few select individuals, including Gates. However, as Jon Shirley, current president, pointed out, if the company was going to have to go public anyway, then it wanted to control the process, deciding when, with whom, and under what circumstances the public stock offering should be made.

Gates wanted to know how much the firm was worth. Once that value was determined, the total value of the company could be divided by the number of shares to be offered to determine the initial asking price of its stock.

Based on 1985 revenues of $140.4 million and an expected increase in capitalization of between $395 to $470 million, the new market value of the company would be between 2.4 and 2.9 times revenues compared with 1.7 and 1.3 for Ashton-Tate and Lotus, respectively. Microsoft's profit margin in 1985 was 17% compared to 16.9% for Lotus and 13.7% for Ashton-Tate. Microsoft has working capital of $58 million and no long-term debt as of the end of 1985. Exhibit 3 contains selected income statements and balance sheet data for Microsoft for the years 1982 to 1985.

Two possible adverse developments should be noted. One is an IRS claim

EXHIBIT 3   SELECTED CONSOLIDATED FINANCIAL DATA

	YEAR ENDED JUNE 30,				SIX MONTHS ENDED DECEMBER 31,	
	1982	1983	1984	1985	1984	1985
					(Unaudited)	
INCOME STATEMENT DATA						
Net revenues	$ 24,486	$ 50,065	$ 97,479	$140,417	$ 62,837	$ 85,050
Costs and expenses						
Cost of revenues	8,647	15,773	22,900	30,447	15,507	18,270
Research and development	3,597	7,021	10,665	17,108	7,414	8,720
Sales and marketing	4,009	11,916	26,027	42,512	18,268	24,429
General and administrative	3,037	4,698	8,784	9,443	3,831	6,980
Total costs and expenses	19,290	39,408	68,376	99,510	45,020	58,399
Income from operations	5,196	10,657	29,103	40,907	17,817	26,651
Nonoperating income (loss)	399	407	(1,073)	1,936	402	2,397
Income before income taxes	5,595	11,064	28,030	42,843	18,219	29,048
Provision for income taxes	2,088	4,577	12,150	18,742	8,223	11,930
Net income	$ 3,507	$ 6,487	$ 15,880	$ 24,101	$ 9,996	$ 17,118
Net income per share	$ .17	$ .29	$ .69	$ 1.04	$ .43	$ .72
Shares used in computing net income per share	21,240	22,681	22,947	23,260	23,253	23,936

	JUNE 30,				DECEMBER 31, 1985
	1982	1983	1984	1985	
					(Unaudited)
BALANCE SHEET DATA					
Working capital	$ 5,305	$ 9,952	$ 21,458	$ 41,442	$ 57,574
Total assets	14,784	24,328	47,637	65,064	94,438
Total long-term debt	—	—	705	650	—
Stockholders' equity	8,299	14,639	30,712	54,440	71,845

Note: Amounts given in thousands except per share.

that Microsoft is subject to the Personal Holding Company Tax, which could result in an additional assessment against the company of approximately $30 million plus interest. The other is an unpaid loan of $500,000 to one of its former directors, a Japanese computer designer, which the company regards as uncollectible. Neither of these two developments is expected to have a significant financial impact on the company.

REFERENCES

Bulkeley, William M. "Three Makers of Personal-Computer Software Are Good Bets for Further Growth, Many Say." *Wall Street Journal* (May 1986).

"Computers: High Tech Investors Should Play the Field to the Limit." *USA Today* (February 24, 1986).

Hillkirk, John. "Big 10 Crowd Others Off Software Field." *USA Today* (February 5, 1986).

"Major Leaguers Join the Fray Over Operating System." *Business Week* (April 16, 1984).

Miller, Michael W. "Microsoft Files with the SEC for Initial Offer." *Wall Street Journal* (February 4, 1986).

Prospectus, Microsoft, March 13, 1986.

Rebello, Kathy. "Microsoft Files to Go Public Next Month." *USA Today* (January 15, 1986).

———."Microsoft Stock No Short-Term Bargain." *USA Today* (March 14, 1986).

Shaeffer, Richard A. "Software Firms Going Public, Letting Investors in on Boom." *Wall Street Journal* (August 26, 1983).

Sherman, Stratford P. "Microsoft's Drive to Dominate Software." *Fortune* (January 23, 1984).

"Software: The Going Gets Rough." *Business Week* (March 24, 1986).

Uttal, Bro. "Inside the Deal that Made Bill Gates $350,000,000." *Fortune* (July 21, 1986).

Winslow, Ron. "Good Reviews are Heavenly in the Crowded Software Field." *Wall Street Journal* (March 8, 1985).

MICROSOFT (B): THE IMPLEMENTATION PROCESS

ROBERT D. HAY AND
WILLIAM C. HOUSE

Once a tentative decision was made to "go public," a series of related steps in the implementation process was set in motion. An examination of these steps yields insight into the processes involved in implementing the decision to go public. The steps involved in the process are presented here in sequential order of occurrence using a graphic format. A discussion of the factors involved in implementation of the decision is also contained in the following paragraphs.

Bill Gates, Jon Shirley, and David Marquette, an investor whose company owned slightly more than 6% of the stock, decided in April to consider an initial stock offering. However, Gates argued that they should wait until October. This would allow time for the company to introduce two new products and consummate an agreement with IBM concerned with program development. The delay would also give Gates time to discuss the offering possibility with key employees who owned stock or stock options and get their feedback. If the market conditions were not right or there was considerable employee opposition, the offering could be postponed a few months without endangering the company's long-term objectives. (See Exhibit 1.)

The CEO wanted to get the support of his employee-owners before he made the decision to go public. He needed a power base from which to implement the decision, including the support of his financial investors and backers, and the people who contributed their talents in exchange for a sizable portion of the outstanding common stock. Further, he needed the support of the venture capitalist who owned a large block of stock. He had to communicate with the stockholders who evidently gave him their blessing to go ahead.

In October the board of directors to "go public" and to select under-

Source: **Prepared by Professors Robert D. Hay and William C. House, University of Arkansas, as a basis for classroom discussion and not to illustrate either effective or ineffective handling of administrative situations. Prepared from Microsoft Company and other published materials. © Robert D. Hay, 1989.**

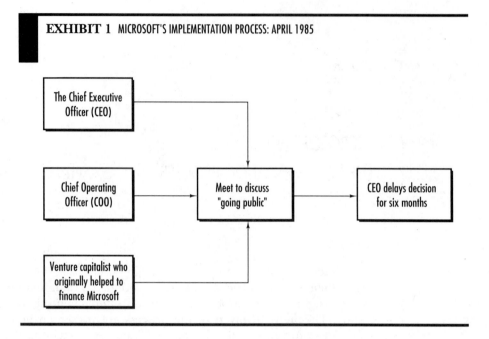

EXHIBIT 1 MICROSOFT'S IMPLEMENTATION PROCESS: APRIL 1985

writers for the proposed stock offering. The chief financial officer, Gaudette, was assigned the task. He argued that a first line Wall Street investment firm should be selected as the lead underwriter. Furthermore, he maintained that a firm that specializes in financing high technology companies should be selected as a comanager for the offering. The comanager was to assist the lead underwriters in making the initial offering by providing assistance and expertise based on its experience with previous stock offerings of high technology companies. After careful consideration, the list of lead underwriters was narrowed to the firms of Goldman, Sachs; Morgan Stanley; and Smith Barney with the possible addition of an underwriter in Microsoft's home state of Washington. Two New York firms and two companies from San Francisco that were specialists in high tech financing were placed on a separate list as cosponsors of the issue.

The chief financial officer was selected to be "the champion" of the strategy implementation process. He was delegated the responsibility and authority and accountability to carry out the project. He was committed to the project and had strong internal support from CEO and the board of directors. A series of joint decisions was made in selecting a tentative list of underwriters. (See Exhibit 2.)

All eight of the finalists (four specialists and four Wall Street firms) were contacted in November, and Gaudette asked to spend half a day with each candidate. He made a detailed list of questions to be asked each banker concerning the manner in which they planned to handle the issue. After all interviews were completed, Gaudette ranked the investment houses on a scale from

EXHIBIT 2 MICROSOFT'S IMPLEMENTATION PROCESS: OCTOBER AND EARLY NOVEMBER 1985

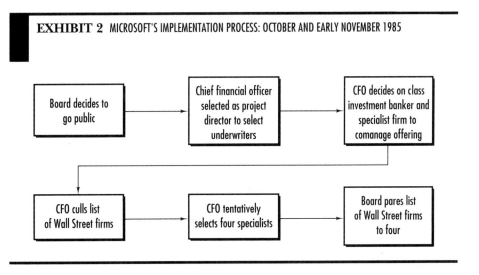

1 to 5 on 19 different categories. In his final assessment he stated that any of the eight firms could successfully handle the issue, but the final decision would hinge on how well the various candidates would mesh with Microsoft's corporate culture and management approach.

The internal organizational culture of Microsoft can best be described as consisting of complex tasks, participative leadership, both vertical and horizontal communication flows, career movements between departments, opinions sought from employees, a strong commitment among employees and managers, and new and developing projects—a rather organic internal culture. Microsoft's external environment is somewhat volatile and rapidly changing with a high degree of competition, shortage of resources, and changing technology. The basic product-market match strategy is best described as highly competitive, active, risky, volatile, and flexible.

Gaudette was especially impressed with Goldman, Sachs, noting that their underwriters were closely linked with their stock traders and that they closely monitored the behavior of large institutional buyers. He felt that they would maintain an orderly market in the face of stock sales by Microsoft employees.

In the meantime, Microsoft's law firm started the process of preparing a prospectus for the initial stock offering. During the process, the company's lawyers spelled out the strengths and weaknesses of the organization and tried to eliminate any contradictions in evaluations made. (See Exhibit 3.)

On December 4, after a conference with Gates and Shirley, Gaudette contacted Goldman, Sachs's San Francisco office and asked for a meeting to discuss a possible stock offering. After an initial dinner meeting, Gates gave a tentative O.K. The selection of a comanaging underwriter boiled down to a choice between Robertson, Colman, & Stephans, whom Gaudette preferred, and Alex. Brown, with which the company had a long-time relationship. After

EXHIBIT 3 MICROSOFT'S IMPLEMENTATION PROCESS: NOVEMBER 1985

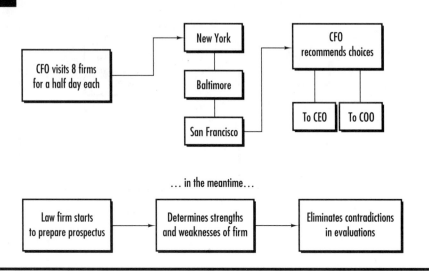

some discussion, Alex. Brown was selected on the basis of being better known at company headquarters. (See Exhibit 4.)

Communication at the dinner meeting played a significant role as each team of persons sounded out the other ones. Joint decision making again prevailed. The decision on the specialist comanager was made without a dinner meeting but on the basis of past relationships with the firm. The decision to go public was made through the formal organization structure, but the informal structure reinforced the formal decision-making process.

A more formal meeting was held at company headquarters on December 17 to completely discuss all aspects of the stock offering. A major consider-

EXHIBIT 4 MICROSOFT'S IMPLEMENTATION PROCESS: FIRST TWO WEEKS OF DECEMBER 1985

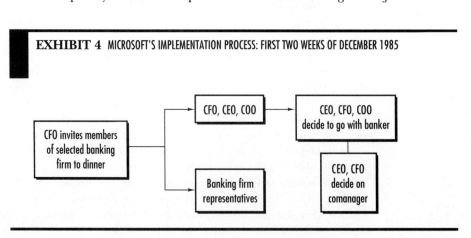

ation was to make the offering "jury proof" so no stockholder could make a legitimate case that he or she had been misled by statements made in the prospectus or by company officials during the offering process. At the meeting Gates announced that Microsoft was considering the sale of about two million shares at an assumed price of $15 to generate gross receipts of $30 million. Existing shareholders would be allowed to sell up to 10% of their holdings, for 600,000 or so shares, equivalent to about $10 million. If the underwriters exercised their customary options, another 300,000 shares would be sold in the public domain. All told, about 12% of Microsoft's stock would wind up in public hands, guaranteeing the long-desired liquid market.

Intense and careful consideration was given at that point to the initial offering price. Gates felt that Microsoft could command a higher price-earnings ratio than software companies like Lotus and Ashton-Tate but not as high a price multiple as mainframe software developers who had been in existence longer than Microsoft and had more stable earnings records. A price of $15, based on a price-earnings ratio of slightly more than 10 to 1 would place the offering midway between market prices of microcomputer software and mainframe software companies.

Two additional issues were also raised at the meeting. Concern was expressed by Gates and others as to whether and to what extent the stock offering would interfere with the company's normal business operations. Microsoft's lawyers also expressed concern about public statements from the company and suggested all official statements be reviewed by the legal staff during the offering period to avoid the appearance of trying to manipulate the stock to a higher level than circumstances would otherwise justify. (See Exhibit 5.)

Writing the prospectus was a tedious, time-consuming, and very important chore. In developing the prospectus, the writers had to express enough optimism to justify its use as a sales tool but not express such exaggerated claims as to invite charges of misrepresentation. The task took the entire month of January. The underwriters and security analysts involved grilled company officers so no office skeletons or surprise developments could surface to undermine the issue at the last minute. (See Exhibit 6.) Company employees generally took a more conservative and pessimistic view of the company's prospects than did the underwriters and security analysts.

Serious negotiations started to take place during this step in the implementation process. A management information system was in place at Microsoft to provide answers to any questions which might arise about the prospective issue and its effects on company finances, operations, resources, and strategies.

The final decision to be made was the price range for the initial offering. A price range of $17 to $20 was suggested by the underwriters. Gates argued intensely for a range of $16 to $19, since he felt it was unlikely the company would have to go any lower than the lower limit in order to sell shares. However, he felt uncomfortable about a price of $20. With the issue of the final price still unsettled, the final prospectus was proofed on February 1 and was sent to the SEC three days later. After the formal SEC registration, the officers

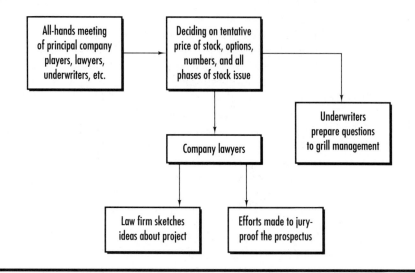

EXHIBIT 5 MICROSOFT'S IMPLEMENTATION PROCESS: LAST TWO WEEKS OF DECEMBER 1985

All-hands meeting of principal company players, lawyers, underwriters, etc.
Deciding on tentative price of stock, options, numbers, and all phases of stock issue
Underwriters prepare questions to grill management
Company lawyers
Law firm sketches ideas about project
Efforts made to jury-proof the prospectus

held meetings with investors and analysts in eight major cities including New York and London. The SEC temporarily delayed the offering to ensure that the offering would be widespread and not limited to a privileged few. (See Exhibit 7.)

The plan for issuing the stock was put in writing in the prospectus which plays a crucial role in going public. Coordination meetings with all the actors

EXHIBIT 6 MICROSOFT'S IMPLEMENTATION PROCESS: JANUARY – WHOLE MONTH 1986

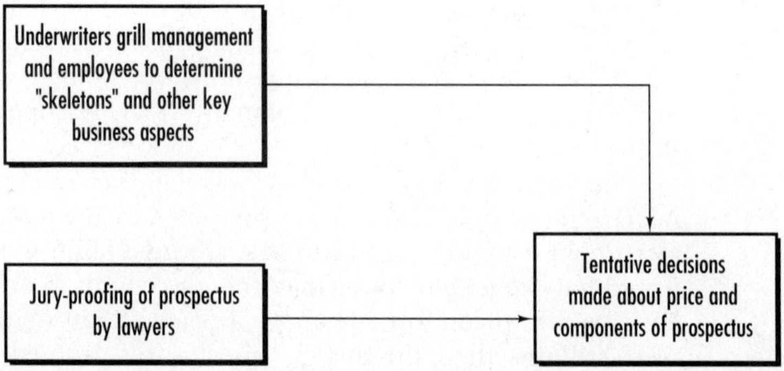

Underwriters grill management and employees to determine "skeletons" and other key business aspects
Jury-proofing of prospectus by lawyers
Tentative decisions made about price and components of prospectus

EXHIBIT 7 MICROSOFT'S IMPLEMENTATION PROCESS: FEBRUARY 1986

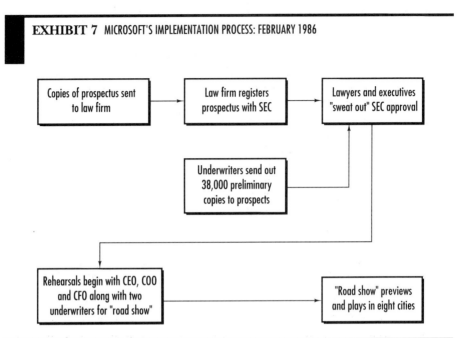

in the drama finally came to fruition. Ample time (i.e., approximately 11 months) was allowed to implement the strategy.

On March 6 the company law firm negotiated changes to the preliminary prospectus with the SEC. Once these negotiations were complete and necessary changes were made in the prospectus, the company could go ahead with the issue. (See Exhibit 8.)

After the SEC negotiation was complete, Gaudette lobbied to raise the price from its initial level. The underwriters noted that the initial response to the issue was very good and expected an opening price of about $25 a share. A survey of large investors indicated that a price of 20 to 21 would prove satisfactory. At this point, the underwriters expressed concern that a price of about 20 would cause the large investors to back out. Early indications from a survey of big investors seemed to confirm this fear.

EXHIBIT 8 MICROSOFT'S IMPLEMENTATION PROCESS: MARCH 1986

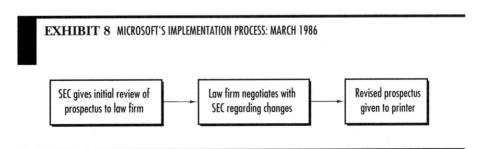

The final issue to be resolved was the underwriting discount or spread to cover underwriting expenses. Microsoft wanted the spread to remain low, no more than 6.5% of the stock price at the outside. After noting that Sun Microsystems negotiated a spread of 6.13% on an offering of $4 million, Microsoft decided to stand firm at that level or about $1.29 per share. Goldman Sachs maintained that the Sun Microsystems issue was an isolated case and stood fast for a spread of 6.5% or $1.36 per share.

The underwriting firm did indicate that it might go as low as $1.34. Gates said no, that $1.28 was the maximum acceptable fee. He felt that the underwriters would be able to sell more shares at the higher price and could make up any underwriting deficiency this way. Gaudette argued that the Microsoft issue would be easier to manage than the Sun Microsystems issue, thereby justifying a lower spread. Goldman, Sachs finally dropped its offer to $1.33 and Microsoft remained firm at $1.30. The argument was over less than $100,000 out of a total fee of $4 million. Finally, at the last possible minute, the two parties compromised at $1.31.

The SEC approved the deal and on March 13 the stock was publicly traded on the over-the-counter market at $25.75 a share. At the end of the day, 2.5 million shares had changed hands, with the stock trading at $27.75. Gates made $1.6 million for the shares he sold. In addition, the "going public" strategy and its implementation placed a market value of $350 million on the 45% share of the company that he owned.

REFERENCES

"Computers: High Tech Investors Should Play the Field to the Limit." *USA Today* (February 24, 1986).

Miller, Michael W. "Microsoft Files With the SEC for Initial Offer." *Wall Street Journal* (February 4, 1986).

Prospectus, Microsoft, March 13, 1986.

Rebello, Kathy. "Microsoft Files to Go Public Next Month." *USA Today* (January 15, 1986).

————. "Microsoft Stock No Short-Term Bargain." *USA Today* (March 14, 1986).

Shaeffer, Richard A. "Software Firms Going Public, Letting Investors in on Boom." *Wall Street Journal* (March 8, 1985).

Uttal, Bro. "Inside the Deal That Made Bill Gates $350,000,000." *Fortune* (July 21, 1986).

LAKESHORE, INC.

GEORGE S. VOZIKIS AND
TIMOTHY S. MESCON

INTRODUCTION

Lakeshore, Incorporated, once a tuberculosis sanatorium, has been operating as a rehabilitation facility since 1973 and offers rehabilitation of the whole person. Social and psychological needs are met as well as physical needs. The 50-acre Lakeshore campus, located near Birmingham, Alabama, was donated by the city of Homewood, a Birmingham suburb, and is the flagship facility for the comprehensive network of rehabilitation services. The 90-bed inpatient institution is part of a network which includes prosthetic and orthotic services, outpatient rehabilitation facilities, vocational training, a durable medical equipment company, a 36-bed transitional living unit, a sheltered workshop, and a specialized rehabilitation services unit for individuals injured in industrial accidents. The system is designed to provide continuing services and benefits for physically disabled individuals at every stage of the rehabilitation process.

Lakeshore's transitional living unit is the utopian dream of Dr. John Miller, a former medical director of Lakeshore, who has a vision of a complete rehabilitation process which includes the patient's reintegration into the community. The unit allows the patient to practice using facilities encountered in daily life such as the kitchen, bathroom, and bedroom. It is designed as an intermediate step between the hospital and the outside world. Rehabilitation services are designed to restore the disabled individuals, following disease or injury, to the highest physical, social, vocational, and economic usefulness of which they are capable. Rehabilitation can be viewed as the third phase of the medical care continuum, with the first being the prevention of illness, and the second the actual treatment of disease. This third phase involves rehabilita-

Source: **Prepared by Professor George S. Vozikis, The Citadel, and Professor Timothy S. Mescon, Kennesaw State College, as a basis for classroom discussion and not to illustrate either effective or ineffective handling of administrative situations.** © **George S. Vozikis, 1990.**

tion or a constructive system of treatment designed to enable individuals to attain their highest degree of functioning.

Comprehensive/specific services are provided for persons with the following conditions:

- Back pain
- Spinal cord injury
- Chronic and acute pain
- Industrial and sports injuries
- Circulatory problems
- Speech and language disorders
- Arthritis
- Orthopedic impediment
- Peripheral nerve injury
- Multiple sclerosis
- Cerebral palsy
- Musculoskeletal conditions
- Stroke
- Parkinson's disease
- Head injury
- Amputation
- Pediatric speech
- Hearing disorders

The following types of services are offered at the Lakeshore facilities:

- Physical therapy
- Functional evaluation
- Speech therapy
- Psycho-social counseling
- Work injury rehabilitation
- Sports injury
- Durable medical equipment
- Social work services
- Occupational therapy
- Language therapy
- Disability evaluation
- Community education programs
- Prosthetics and orthotics
- Patient education
- Family education
- Hearing assessment
- Rehabilitation
- Nutritional counseling
- Respiratory therapy

Lakeshore also houses the George C. Wallace Recreation Center. The concept of the recreation center was created by Lakeshore's present CEO, Michael

Stevens, who designed the barrier-free free center for "leisure therapy." The $1.2 million building has over 26,000 square feet and consists of a full-size gymnasium with a regulation-size basketball court which can also be used for volleyball and indoor racquet sports. The court is the home of the Birmingham Chariots wheelchair basketball team. Other organized activities at the facility include adapted training classes, team sports, Red Cross/YMCA programs, advanced lifesaving, personal safety courses, arts and crafts, and therapeutic exercises.

The facility also includes an indoor pool which has a transfer wall that allows a wheelchair patient to enter the pool from the height of the chair and re-enter the chair without the aid of a hoist. Lakeshore hopes to one day host the state competition, then the regional and national, and perhaps even the world handicapped Olympics in the pool. Paraplegic scuba diving is another of the planned activities.

Lakeshore has earned national respect because it is one of the few facilities which provides acute care and services all the way through job training in a single location. The vocational guidance and training facility, operated by the Alabama Vocational Rehabilitation Services, offers job placement counseling and opportunities in computer programming, dispatching, microfilming, switchboard operation, small engine repair, engraving, and driver education.

Referral to the Lakeshore Hospital can be made by any physician. Patients may be referred for a specific prescribed treatment or for an evaluation and therapy plan to be developed by the center's therapy management team. Referrals can also be made by discharge planners, insurance companies, industry representatives, and rehabilitation counselors. A patient may also be accepted without a referral following an evaluation by a staff physician.

The Lakeshore Mobile Rehabilitation Center is an outpatient facility that opened in the spring of 1986. The company has leased the entire first floor of the five-story Providence Hospital School of Nursing. The Lakeshore Center is Mobile's second comprehensive rehabilitation center, the other being Rotary Hospital, which provides inpatient and outpatient services. Lakeshore did a feasibility study and determined that more rehabilitation centers were needed in the Mobile area because of increased population in the area. The center, with its professional staff of 10 specialists, provides basically the same types of services as the main division in Homewood.

In the fall of 1985, the Huntsville Rehabilitation Center joined forces with Lakeshore to provide comprehensive outpatient services to the North Alabama area. Additionally, projected for completion in May 1987 are plans that include a 50-bed inpatient addition to Huntsville Hospital, which was based on a certificate of need awarded in 1984. The hospital will own the new wing but it will be managed by Lakeshore. The building design will allow the hospital to share many of its services with Lakeshore, such as radiology and medical specialities.

Lakeshore is a United Way agency, so keeping its costs down is an important factor. Patients referred by the Alabama Vocational Rehabilitation Service receive the vocational development portion of their services at no charge. The center is reimbursed by private insurance companies and Medicare, but those who do not have insurance are not turned away. Fees are adjusted on a sliding scale to ensure that health care services are available regardless of a person's level of income.

MAJOR ISSUES

One of the major issues that the rehabilitation industry will face in the future, due to changing demographic trends, will be an increase in the average age category. More disabled people will be in the 65-years-old-and-above category than in the less-than-44-years-old category. Studies have shown the younger age category to have decreased in number as much as 17% during the past decade.[1] The overall aging of the population is due to a decreasing birth rate. Currently, Lakeshore's concentration in their rehabilitation services is for the less-than-44-years-old category since statistics have shown that the highest percentage of disabled people is in that age category.[2]

The changing demographic trends indicate that Lakeshore will have to focus its services more toward the 65-years-old-and-above category. For example, Lakeshore currently gears its environment for the younger patients who are more likely to be interested in competitive sports and activities which help them to become rehabilitated sooner. In contrast, the focus in the future should be on psychological and sedentary activities.

Legislation now being studied would provide insurance for catastrophic illness to those who could not otherwise afford coverage. This will mean that a larger number of the elderly and poor will enter the market for rehabilitative services since they will no longer need to worry about making any kind of payment. Many of these patients do not seek out rehabilitative services now because they think they cannot afford it or because they are too proud to accept welfare assistance.

Another issue that Lakeshore might face in the future is a decrease in the percentage of physical impairments and disabilities in the state of Alabama. Currently, according to a survey sanctioned by the State Health Plan, Alabama has a higher percentage of physical impairments and disabilities than both the U.S. and the South and this prevalence rate is higher in the non-white population. According to statistics in the State Health Plan, 5% of all Alabamians, or 177,800 persons, are estimated to be disabled.[3] A small decrease in the prevalence rate could affect the continued growth of Lakeshore, Incorporated.

Another major issue that the rehabilitation industry may be forced to deal with is the reclassification of reimbursement procedures by the government. Until about four years ago, before Prospective Payment, hospitals were reimbursed by Medicare based on what it cost them to treat a disability such as a stroke or amputation. The Prospective Payment System implies that the facility is paid prospectively and health care administrators know beforehand how much per discharge will be paid based on the standard cost structure. The government then established a formula for reimbursement based on diagnostic related groups (DRGs). The formula tells a hospital exactly how much it will be reimbursed for a specific condition, regardless of how much the treatment actually costs. Rehabilitation units are exempt from DRGs and are reimbursed on what it actually costs them to treat a patient. What this means is that a rehabilitation center is in a better position to provide the kind of intensive therapy that disabled patients may require after being discharged from a hospital. A new Prospective Payment System is currently under study which would provide standard cost structures for rehabilitation facilities and remove this competitive advantage.

INDUSTRY COMPETITIVE STRUCTURE

A comprehensive rehabilitation center is a speciality hospital that deals specifically and exclusively with those disability conditions that result in permanent and long-term impairments. The Lakeshore Rehabilitation Complex is a privately held, specialty service system as are each of its two competitors in the state of Alabama. Each of these systems operates under a license granted to them under the State Health Plan. The licenses specify such operating characteristics as the number of beds that can be set up and staffed, the number of registered nurses and licensed practical nurses per patient, the number of other specialists per patient, the types of records that must be kept of programs operated by the facility.

Two other institutions operate in Alabama under the same type of license as Lakeshore: Spain Rehabilitation Center in Birmingham is a 78-bed state owned and operated rehabilitation center of University Hospital, and Rotary Rehabilitation Hospital in Mobile is a 50-bed private, non-profit hospital. Each of these facilities provides inpatient rehabilitative care in addition to outpatient services.

Spain Rehabilitation Center places major emphasis on teaching and research in addition to patient care. The center is one of seven regional spinal cord injury centers designated and funded by the National Institutes of Health. Its patients come from throughout the southeastern United States. Another special program at Spain is pulmonary rehabilitation and rheumatology.

Each of the three rehabilitation facilities in Alabama offers the following therapies or services: physical, occupational, respiratory, psychological, speech and hearing, rehabilitation nursing, drug-administered therapies, and social services, including discharge planning and follow-up services. Recreation therapy services are also provided at each of the three facilities. Custom prosthetic and orthotic devices are prepared by the Prosthetic Shop at Lakeshore Rehabilitation Complex. The Lakeshore Complex is the only one of the state's rehabilitative hospitals which provides custom orthotic and prosthetic services on-site. The other hospitals use the services of prosthetic and orthotic vendors located in the Birmingham area. The Lakeshore Prosthetic Shop was purchased from Spain Rehabilitation Hospital in 1980. Lakeshore also complements the rehabilitation process through the delivery of services of its transitional living unit, independent living unit, sheltered employment, and supportive resources for the patient within Alabama's comprehensive rehabilitative continuum of care. Vocational rehabilitation counseling is provided at both Spain and Lakeshore by employees of the Alabama Vocational Rehabilitation Service. The Lakeshore Complex also offers vocational evaluation and a range of other vocational rehabilitation services which would generally be utilized by patients in the transitional living unit or on an outpatient basis.

Discharge data from the Utilization Section of the *Annual Report for Hospitals and Related Facilities,* as submitted to the State Health Planning Agency, indicates that all the patients served by the three facilities can be grouped into one of six major disorder or disease classifications under the ICDA Code, 8th Revision. These are cerebrovascular disease, pulmonary disorders, arthritic disorders, neuromuscular disorders, spinal cord injuries, and amputations. This seems to indicate that the state's three inpatient rehabilitation hospitals are all serving basically the same type of customer needs.

STRENGTHS, WEAKNESSES, OPPORTUNITIES, AND THREATS

The rehabilitative health care industry in the state of Alabama is relatively young, and limited opportunities for growth exist. Of course, any additional beds will have to be approved by the State Health Board, upon formal submission of a certificate of need. As was mentioned earlier, Lakeshore has only been in existence for fourteen years, and four years ago, neither Lakeshore in Mobile nor Huntsville was in existence. Prior to this time, the patients in Alabama had to be served either by Spain Rehabilitation Hospital in Birmingham or by one of the outpatient systems, or they were forced to go out of state.

A major strength which results from being located in the Birmingham area is that it is possible to draw upon the resources of the University of Alabama Medical College, which is located less than five miles away. The major strength which Lakeshore has is the enormous resources available to it in a single location. Lakeshore is a fully integrated facility, which can offer the patient everything from prosthetics, to minor surgery, to participative sports for the handicapped, to job counseling and placement.

The weakest point appears to be its dependence on the State Health Agency, which rules over all health care services in the state. A minor consequences is the fact that the same agency also rules over every other health care facility in the state. A threat exists in the proposed government regulations, which could play a vital role if the Prospective Payment System should be modified to include the rehabilitation industry under the DRG system. Many opportunities exist for growth in the rehabilitation area if the corporation should strategically decide to pursue them. It has already committed to manage the facility in Huntsville, it is managing the Mobile facility, and it could possibly expand into other growth areas such as Dothan, Gadsden, or Tusca-loosa. Other potential growth could come in the way of patients from the border states of Tennessee, Florida, Georgia, and Mississippi. Lakeshore might also decide to expand its role as a vendor to supply prosthetic and orthotic devices to other rehabilitation units, either in or out of state. Currently eight such units are located in the Birmingham area alone; the general rule of thumb is one rehabilitation unit per 100,000 people.

GENERAL ORGANIZATION AND MANAGEMENT

Until the year 1984, the organization was structured much like any other not-for-profit hospital would be (Exhibit 1). The different functional groups, the Sheltered Opportunities Workshop, Rehabilitation Services, Transitional Living Unit, Medcore, System Services, and Lakeshore Hospital, each operated as separate entities; and Lakeshore, Incorporated, the parent holding company, was charged with responsibility for each of the operations.

In the latter part of 1984, immediately prior to the opening of the satellite facilities program, the strategic plan entailed in the reorganization of the for-profit and not-for-profit sections of the corporation was reorganized. Part of the organization remained a non-profit group, while the remainder became a for-profit group and was placed under Systems Services (Exhibit 2). This fundamental change was the result of long-range strategic thinking on the part

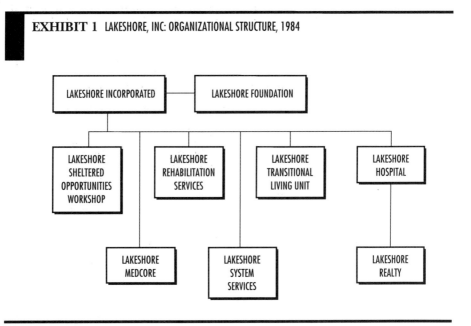

EXHIBIT 1 LAKESHORE, INC: ORGANIZATIONAL STRUCTURE, 1984

EXHIBIT 2 LAKESHORE, INC: ORGANIZATIONAL STRUCTURE, 1987

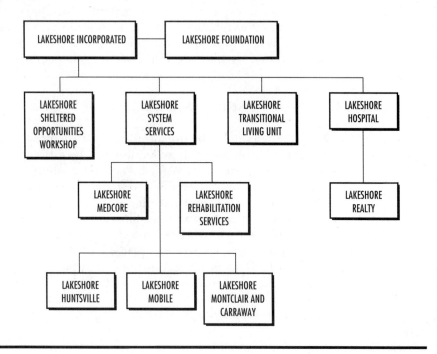

of the executive board and would allow the corporation to grow at a more controlled rate, as well as to benefit from the profits projected from the growth.

Lakeshore's board of directors is a volunteer group with 17 members. It is made up of bankers, lawyers, doctors, educators, and the mayor of Homewood. The board functions as most hospital boards do and is charged with guiding the overall direction of the company. The executive council functions independently of the board of directors. The executive council is charged with formulation and implementation of the strategic plan of the corporation. It is made up of nine people:

- Chief operating officer
- Chief executive officer
- Vice president of corporate finance
- Vice president of System Services
- Vice president of corporate development
- Regional medical director
- Corporate medical director
- Coordinator of medical services
- One other physician

The executive council meets on the second and last Fridays of each month. Meetings on the second Friday are held on the Lakeshore campus, and the last Friday meeting is held at a local state park in order to separate the council from the workplace and any interruptions that might occur. The meetings are based on a planned agenda, which must be approved by the president and chief executive officer. However, the council members can make additions to the agenda by submitting them to the president's office no later than the day before the meeting is to be held. The off-site meeting is held primarily as a strategy planning meeting and policy items discussed may include such things as new programs, new facilities, and financial decisions.

Lakeshore's chief executive officer, Michael Stevens, is a graduate of both Spain and Lakeshore rehabilitation centers. Stevens was injured in a diving accident in 1973 which left him paralyzed from the neck down. Following his discharge from Spain Rehabilitation Center, he was still not fully recovered and eventually entered Lakeshore as a patient. He has fully recovered now and a slight drag to his walk is the only evidence that remains of his accident. After his discharge, Stevens, who was employed in legal services at Prentice-Hall Publishing Company, decided to pursue his master's degree in hospital administration.

After he graduated, he did part of his residency at Lakeshore, and when the administrator resigned, he became the acting executive director. Stevens is a man who is driven by goals and objectives. He has led the corporation for 10 years now, and operations have improved as a result of his leadership. He has a keen business mind as well as a solid background in hospital administration, and he cares about people. This combination has helped to make him a winner.

The information system in place at Lakeshore includes the data-based office automation system recently purchased and installed. The system uses a Data General mainframe computer and handles everything from payroll functions, to patient data, to information management (including appointments, messages, electronic mail, word processing, etc.). The system has been in place for about one year and the corporation plans to have the entire system performing at its most efficient level within five years. The information services system is the responsibility of the vice president of corporate finance, because he happened to have a background in computers.

MARKETING

The market served by Lakeshore includes the entire state of Alabama, in addition to the border states of Florida, Tennessee, Georgia, and Mississippi; but its primary market includes the four-county area including Jefferson, Shelby, Walker, and Talladega. This four-county area makes up 76.6% of Lakeshore's patient base and is projected to have 2.2% growth rate between 1986 and 1990. The primary service area also contains 33% of Alabama's total population.[4]

Lakeshore is comprised of a group of interrelated services and products for the rehabilitation of the physically disabled. Among its services are a comprehensive rehabilitation hospital and outpatient facilities for patients who have completed their stay at Lakeshore Hospital or for those who do not require hospitalization. Through its Medcore Clinic, Lakeshore provides services for those individuals who are injured on the job. These services include not only rehabilitation, but also vocational evaluation, counseling, and case management as well.

Other related rehabilitation activities offered at Lakeshore include the fabrication and fitting of prosthetic and orthotic devices and the distribution and sale of durable medical equipment. Special services for the housing, vocational training, and employment of disabled individuals are provided. Also, for those who wish to participate, Lakeshore offers one of the finest handicapped athletic programs in the United States.

Although Lakeshore's main facility is located near Birmingham, it is affiliated with a growing network of inpatient and outpatient facilities. These include comprehensive rehabilitation hospitals designed to meet the needs of communities and cities beyond the greater Birmingham area. Lakeshore also offers management contracts and joint ventures to expand its quality programs to existing or new facilities.

These and other support programs offered through Lakeshore's network of rehabilitation services allow patients to be taken from the first stages of recovery through rehabilitation, job training, and employment to the point where they reach their full potential. The system is unique and provides a synergy of corporate services, based on the belief that to be successful rehabilitation must ensure that patients are equipped in every way to function in society.

The majority of Lakeshore's promotion and advertising is handled by an outside marketing agency. However, a director of public relations for the corporation has been hired recently. Her name is Dell Witcher, and she was employed as a news anchor for WBRC Channel 6 television station in Birmingham for several years prior to joining Lakeshore. Ms. Witcher's responsibility is to improve the image of the corporation through public relations, including speeches, video tapes, slide presentations, etc., which are made available to area doctors, educators, hospitals, and civic groups.

Lakeshore's pricing of its services is generally less than the average in the state of Alabama and the Southeast. Lakeshore's cost containment strategy requires the corporation to strive to remain a low-cost producer by carrying out aggressive cost containment strategies and by promoting increased productivity. Costs can be controlled further by keeping abreast of changes in medical education, technology, new practices, and knowledge through the establishment of new programs, acquisitions of new equipment, and changes in medical practice. Lakeshore will also consider participation in any multi-institutional sharing ventures that will enhance its ability to provide existing or new services in a more effective and efficient manner. These and other strategies will allow Lakeshore to reduce costs and improve both its price structure and its profits.

As evidence of Lakeshore's cost containment strategy, the following information is given in the State Health Plan: as of October 1, 1985, the per diem rate for Alabama's three comprehensive rehabilitation hospitals was $496.61 for Spain, $424.44 for Lakeshore, and $387.12 for Rotary.[5] This data is based on Medicaid cost reports.

PRODUCTION AND OPERATIONS

The major capital asset at Lakeshore, Incorporated, the hospital building and 50 acres on which the main campus is located, was donated to Lakeshore by the city of Homewood in 1973. Prior to that time, the building had been condemned by the city in 1970 after operating as a tuberculosis sanatorium for 50 years. The main building has since been remodeled and does not look like a 67-year-old structure; in fact, it looks like a very modern hospital. With the addition of the prosthetic and orthotic shop building in 1980 and the $1.2 million gymnasium and pool in 1981, the facility is an impressive one.

Lakeshore operates as a non-union shop employing about 400 people, mostly skilled professionals. Its business operations are separated into these nine different areas:

- Patient care services
- Business services
- Speech and hearing therapy
- Occupational therapy
- Recreation
- Clinical support services
- Financial services
- Psycho-social services
- Plant operations

For more detailed information on the organizational chart, see Exhibit 3.

Production capability in the orthotic and prosthetic shops has been in place since Lakeshore purchased the unit from Spain Rehabilitation Hospital in 1980. The shops employ seven technicians. Each technician is certified in either orthotics or prosthetics or both. Certification requires having a four-year college degree in addition to one year of training and successful completion of the certification exam. Presently eight other shops which fabricate orthotic and/or prosthetic devices are located in the Birmingham area.

The fabrication process begins with a psychological meeting with the client to assess his or her needs and develop a definitive prosthesis. The first step in the prosthetic process is to wrap the stump and produce a plaster casting. The casting will be used for analysis of stress points, nerves, muscle compositions, etc. Next the plaster casting is used to vacu-form a test socket

EXHIBIT 3 LAKESHORE, INC. HOSPITAL MANAGEMENT

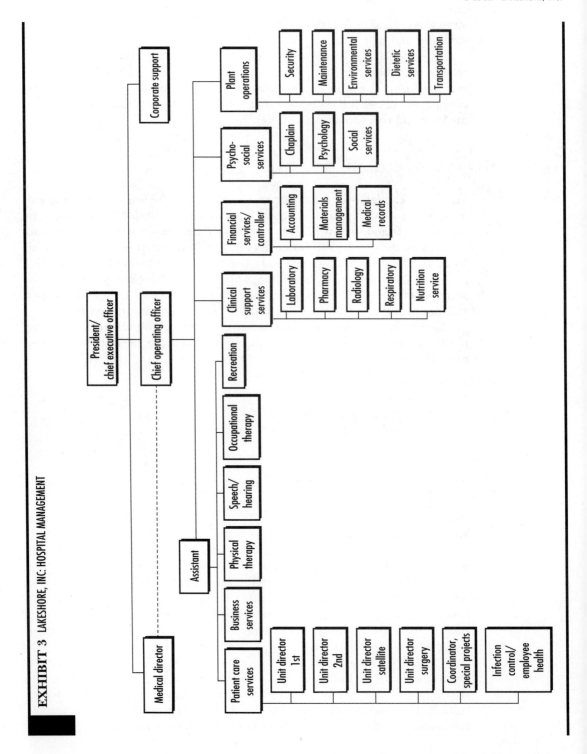

of thick plastic which is placed on the patient for static and dynamic alignment. The test socket and casting are then placed in a stand and built up with several layers of poly-felt material. The patient's skin color is then matched, the resin is mixed, and the limb is poured. Further alignment takes place at this point if necessary.

The fabrication of orthotic devices takes place here as well. The bracing is designed to assist those who only have partial control of their limbs or muscles, whether the result of defects, deformities, or injuries. The patient's needs are kept in mind at all times by the staff since they realize that motivation to learn to use the artificial limb or orthotic bracing is critical for it to be successfully used by the client. Follow-up is provided to the client in all cases.

Requirements for the quality of services provided by Lakeshore are spelled out in the State Health Plan, which requires all comprehensive rehabilitation hospitals to meet or exceed the certification requirements for the Medicare program. Lakeshore recognizes that in all levels of rehabilitation care, it is essential that the patient is exposed to the highest level of expertise and quality service available. It also realizes that the quality of care rendered is largely dependent on the qualifications of those rendering the services. To this end, Lakeshore strives to maintain a highly trained group of professionals and has a ratio of 60% registered nurses to 40% licensed practical nurses employed on its staff.

The cost of producing goods and services offered at Lakeshore is a major concern to management. Managers realize how important the sharing of services with other health care institutions and group purchasing arrangements are to effective cost containment. It has been demonstrated that the cooperative efforts of the Spain Complex and Lakeshore have resulted in the effective, efficient delivery of rehabilitative goods and services.

FINANCIAL INFORMATION

Lakeshore, Incorporated is a private institution and is not required to make public its financial data. The only information made available is the statement of income and expense contained in the certificate of need for Carraway Methodist Medical Center, as required by the State Health Planning Agency. This data covers the period from January 1985, through November 1986 and shows that Lakeshore Hospital incurred a $9,494 loss in 1985, a $10,652 profit in the first 11 months of 1986 and is projected to make profits of $59,557 in 1987 and $65,432 in 1988.

HUMAN RESOURCES

Lakeshore employs 400 people at its main campus in Birmingham, 120 at the Huntsville facility, and 10 in Mobile. None of the corporation's employees are represented by a labor union. Lakeshore recognizes that its human resources are its most valuable asset and treats its employees accordingly. Each of Lakeshore's employees is a guide in a way: a guide toward new hope, functioning minds and bodies rebuilt through rehabilitation, and attainable goals. New employees are given adequate time to become oriented to the Lakeshore way of helping people. They spend an entire day viewing videos, reviewing corporate policies and procedures, and getting to know their way around the campus so they will be able to give information or directions to anyone who asks. In this sense, they are guides and valuable marketing assets.

Turnover is the biggest personnel issue in the health care industry due to the high demand for skilled employees. Even though Lakeshore makes every attempt to promote from within its organization, it often resorts to the use of external sources to find the qualified personnel needed. Lakeshore accepts applications two days per week, conducts on-campus interviews, runs advertisements in newspapers and medical publications, and maintains personal contacts through various personnel associations. The result is a successful recruiting program.

Lakeshore's employee pay and benefits program is comparable to any in the area. This is due in part to the need to remain competitive in the labor segment of the health care industry. Different benefit packages are offered to the hourly employees, to the salaried non-exempt employees, to exempt salaried employees, and to top-level management. For example, salaried employees have their health care benefits paid for by the company; top-level managers receive increased levels of disability, health, and life insurance; and hourly employees receive paid sick leave and are allowed to accumulate any unused vacation or sick leave from one year to the next.

Lakeshore initiated a wellness program for its employees in January 1987. The program is open to participation by all employees and is designed to improve their physical conditioning. Employees participate in activities during their scheduled working hours, and awards are given to those who achieve their predetermined goal.

In keeping with its policy of requiring its employees to remain current on technology and education in the health care field, Lakeshore offers its employees leave of absence to continue their education. A job transfer policy also helps keep employees satisfied with the jobs they occupy. When a job becomes available, the opening is first communicated to the department managers who make their employees aware of the opening. Individuals may then bid for the job and the most qualified applicant will be awarded the job. An attempt is made to fill all jobs internally, where qualified applicants exist, before going to the outside for candidates.

Lakeshore has a formal salary administration program which is based on job descriptions and is reviewed annually. The present system has been in effect for three years and has been revised and improved each year. Individuals fit into a job family grade and salary range. The salary administration formula is based on the individual's experience and education and the job description. Salary levels are reviewed on an annual basis and as needed to maintain a competitive position in the Birmingham area health care industry.

The performance appraisal form rates the employee on job-based criteria to be as objective as possible, applying measurable goals and objectives which are set by the department head and communicated to the employees. The form is used for all but top management level employees. The performance appraisal form used for top management has some subjectivity built into it, which includes such immeasurable things as good will and granting interviews to students, etc.

The appraisal form is completed and discussed with the employee once a year. At this time the employee has the opportunity to write comments on the form and has the choice of signing it or protesting the appraisal to the department head. If not satisfied with the department head's response, the employee can protest to the director of human relations and finally to the chief operating officer. Once the form is completed and signed, the human resource department will review it, weighing the response and assigning points to the job criteria. Within two weeks the merit increase is granted based on total points, and the appraisal process is complete.

CONCLUSIONS

As a full service comprehensive rehabilitation institution, Lakeshore has developed a good relationship with area doctors and hospitals. Their system is designed to provide continuing services and benefits for physically disabled individuals at every stage of the rehabilitation process. The Lakeshore system is unique and provides a synergy of corporate services, based on the belief that to be successful rehabilitation must ensure that patients are equipped in every way to function in society. It is one of the few facilities in the country which provides acute care and services all the way through job training in a single location.

ENDNOTES

1. Saddler, Jeanne, "Low Pay, High Turnover Plague Day Care Industry," *Wall Street Journal* (February 19, 1987): 27.

2. Alabama State Health Planning Agency, "Alabama State Health Plan," mimeographed, 1986.

3. Ibid.

4. Alabama State Health Planning Agency, "Alabama Certificate of Need Application: Carraway Methodist Medical Center," mimeographed, 1986.

5. Alabama State Health Planning Agency, "Alabama State Health Plan."

ADDITIONAL REFERENCES

"Aiding Independence: Rehabilitation Center." *Huntsville Business* (First Quarter 1986): 16–26.

Caspell, Richard E., vice president of corporate services,

Lakeshore, Incorporated, Birmingham, Alabama. Interview (February 24, 1987).

Doremus, Harvey; Joseph, W. Benoy; and Zallocco, Ronald. "Strategic Market Planning For Hospitals." *Journal of Health Care Marketing* 4, no. 2 (Spring 1984); 19–28.

Elliott, Carolyn Payne, director of corporate relations, Lakeshore, Incorporated, Birmingham, Alabama. Interview (February 11, 1987).

Hart, Sylvia, "New Rehab Center Offers Service for Outpatients." *Mobile Register* (April 3, 1986): B2.

Jones, Alice, director of planning and development, Lakeshore, Incorporated, Birmingham, Alabama. Interview (February 11, 1987).

Kasten, Bernard L., Jr., M.D. *The Physician's DRG Handbook.* Cleveland: Lexi-Comp Inc., 1986.

Peters, Joseph P., and Webber, James. *Strategic Thinking, New Frontier for Hospital Management.* Chicago: American Hospital Association, 1985.

Russell, Ammy, staff administrative assistant, Lakeshore, Incorporated, Huntsville, Alabama. Interview. (February 4, 1987).

Swiers, Clark, prosthetic technician, Lakeshore, Incorporated, Birmingham, Alabama. Interview (February 24, 1987).

Vann, Lauralee. "Rehabilitation: Dealing With Human Life," *Birmingham News* (March 21, 1983): 19.

Watson, Eugene, vice president of corporate development. Lakeshore, Incorporated, Birmingham, Alabama. Interview (February 17, 1987).

Witcher, Dell, director of public relations, Lakeshore, Incorporated, Birmingham, Alabama. Interview (February 11, 1987).

TROUBLE IN TOYLAND: A NOTE
ON THE U.S. TOY INDUSTRY

DAVID W. GRIGSBY

The toy industry in America has been described as "free enterprise at its most untrammeled."[1] The intense competition among major toy producers has produced an amazing diversity of products. A typical large toy store, such as one of the Toys "R" Us outlets, stocks 18,000 different items. Toy sales in the late 1980s reached new all-time highs, but competition also had its drawbacks, and the latter part of the decade was marked by rising costs and severe financial troubles among some of the leading producers.

Much of the trouble the industry faced in 1988 has been attributed to the actions of the companies themselves. Toy manufacturers were criticized for overreacting to new markets with too many "fad" toys and engaging in destructive conflict over market share. The intensity of competition, coupled with the industry's severe seasonality (nearly half of all retail toy sales come in the last two months of each year), also made the industry a very difficult one to analyze.

Despite all of its problems and unpredictability, toy production in 1988 remained one of the few industries in which U.S. companies continued to lead the world. The problems of the 1980s, however, caused analysts to wonder if the U.S. toy industry would continue to thrive in the face of increasing internal and foreign competition. Although a number of mergers, consolidations, and most restructuring efforts by the larger firms promised to strengthen the industry, the future was very uncertain.

HISTORY OF THE INDUSTRY

As the first toy probably originated with the first child, the history of toys is as long as the history of mankind itself. Although it is sometimes difficult for

Source: **Prepared by Professor David W. Grigsby, Clemson University as a basis for classroom discussion and not to illustrate either effective or ineffective handling of administrative situations.** © **David W. Grigsby, 1989.**

archaeologists to trace the original use of artifacts, some findings suggest that prehistoric children were given modified household items for play. More readily identifiable toys have been found in the remains of all of the world's ancient civilizations, and often in astounding variety. The children of ancient Egypt, for example, were apparently well-provided with toys. Their brightly colored balls, dolls, tops, and pull-along animals dating from 1400 B.C. are on display in the British Museum. Ancient Greek vases and Roman reliefs depict children at play with their toys.[2] The first literary reference to toys is found in *The Clouds* of Aristophanes when Strepsiades, talking of his son, said that he built houses, boats, and little leather carts for play. In addition, Socrates is mentioned playing with his children on a hobby horse.[3]

Our knowledge of the evolution of toys from ancient to modern times comes primarily from the surviving toys of the children of rulers and the nobility. There are a number of very elaborate dolls, doll houses, and puppets from the Middle Ages and the Renaissance, but few common toys survive. A late–sixteenth-century print from France features what may be the first "fad" toy. A street scene shows both adults and children absorbed by the cup and ball skill game.[4] Until around the eighteenth century, toys for most children were still being made by hand from simple materials, usually by a member of the household.

Toy making as an industry first developed in eighteenth-century Germany. Under the very restrictive guild laws of the time, artisans were highly specialized and were forbidden to practice the crafts of other artisans. Toy making had emerged in the previous century as one of these specialties, and toys were produced in small family shops. Certain regions of Germany began to be identified as superior toy-making areas; the most noted of these was the Nuremberg area, where the toys were said to be the finest in the world. By the end of the eighteenth century, wholesale agents began to emerge to serve the growing commerce of Europe. Catalogs of toys appeared, listing the output of numerous small local artisans. Bestelmeir of Nuremberg, a wholesale toy dealer, listed over 1,200 entries.[5]

With the easing of guild restrictions in the late eighteenth and early nineteenth centuries, larger toy factories began to emerge, and agents were replaced by the companies' own sales forces. The first mass-produced toys, in the eighteenth century, were tin soldiers and simple dolls. Later, in the nineteenth century, the introduction of movable (wind-up) toys created a sensation, and more elaborate dolls were made widely available. As mechanization and standardization came about with the Industrial Revolution, toy making was transformed from a folk art into an enormous industry. By the beginning of the twentieth century, the toy industry was one of Germany's most important.

The toy industry in the United States developed very slowly through the eighteenth and nineteenth centuries. This was due, in part, to the widespread availability of toys from Europe. Although American-made tin and cast-iron toys were making their appearance by the mid-1800s, the toys of wealthy children came from Europe, especially from Germany and France. Meanwhile, the toys of children from more ordinary families were still being made at home or by local craftsmen. Mass manufacture of dolls did not begin in the U.S. until much later, although some outstanding handcrafted dolls were being produced in several places.[6]

The biggest boost to the U.S. toy industry came when German sources were cut off in World War I. Toy manufacturers expanded their lines to make up for the reduced inflow of expensive imports, and they discovered that they could produce innovative toys at competitive prices. They also benefited from a broadening market. As average incomes rose, more families began to buy ready-made toys. Innovations in retailing, such as Sears and Roebuck's mail order catalog and F. W. Woolworth's five-and-ten-cent stores, opened up new markets for manufactured toys. The 1903 issue of *Playthings,* the national magazine of the toy trade in the U.S., contained 18 pages; by 1914 it had expanded to 100 pages.[7] The U.S. toy industry continued to grow through the 1920s and 1930s and by World War II was firmly established as a major industry.

The Great Depression of the 1930s brought about some unexpected changes. Although sales were reduced significantly, lower costs of production enabled toy manufacturers to utilize new materials. Prior to the depression, most toys were made from scrap materials. Scrap from auto manufacturers went into steel toys, textile mill ends and scraps from garment makers were used in doll manufacturing, and wooden toys were made from the offall of lumber mills. With the demise of their traditional markets, sheet metal producers, lumber mills, and textile factories were happy to find new outlets, and the toy manufacturers were delighted to find themselves able to afford prime materials. Skilled labor also became more plentiful and more willing to work in the toy industry at rates of pay that had not attracted them before. The result was the manufacture of higher quality products, which further solidified the U.S. toy industry's reputation.[8]

The post–World War II era brought significant growth in the U.S. toy industry, as postwar affluence and sharp increases in birth rates combined to create a large and steadily rising demand for toys. Industry competition among the major producers was fueled by large national advertising budgets, especially for television. The rise of discount stores in the 1960s and the advent of large toy specialty retailers in the 1970s were factors that also contributed to industry growth. Technological advances, especially in electronic toys, continued to play a part in the competitive environment, and increased competition from new entrants in the industry worked to partially offset a trend toward consolidation through merger.

STRUCTURE OF THE U.S. TOY INDUSTRY

The U.S. toy industry in 1988 was dominated by large American-owned multinational corporations (MNCs). Five of these companies accounted for over one-third of all U.S. sales: Coleco, Fisher-Price, Hasbro, Mattel, and Tonka. All were independent, publicly held corporations with the exception of Fisher-Price, which was a subsidiary of Quaker Oats Corporation.

Since the manufacture of dolls, toys, and games was highly labor intensive, large companies manufactured little of their production domestically. They depended instead on either direct investment in foreign facilities or on contracting and licensing agreements with foreign companies. The primary toy producing countries for the large toy MNCs were Taiwan, Hong Kong, and South Korea.

Most domestic manufacturing was done by smaller firms that offered products in only one or two segments of the market. Because they depended on limited lines for all of their revenues, these second- and third-tier companies preferred to control their own production.

The Bureau of the Census estimated that only 32 percent of these smaller firms had over 20 employees.[9] According to the Bureau of Labor Statistics, overall employment in the U.S. toy industry stood at around 30,700.[10]

With the exception of Fisher-Price, which specialized in toys for infants and preschoolers, all five of the major companies produced full lines of toys and games for all age groups. Second-tier firms, however, tended to specialize in one or two lines of products. For example, Pressman Toy Company, a privately held company, specialized in board games and held a significant share of that market. Another example is the Tyco Company, which held a significant share of the market for model trains and automobile racing sets.

The existence of many small firms was evidence that barriers to entry were not high in the toy industry. It has been said that with a small investment in, for example, a plastics-forming machine and a good toy design, anyone could become a competitor in this industry, as the principal ingredient in a good-selling toy was imagination. Minimum investment in plant and equipment was around $3 million to $5 million.

More sophisticated entries also had been seen in the late 1980s. Worlds of Wonder, Inc. was formed in 1985 to produce and market high-tech innovations such as the Teddy Ruxpin talking bear and Lazer Tag. Its first-year sales reached $93 million.[11]

A number of large corporations looking for diversification opportunities had been attracted to the fast-paced competition of the toy industry. Rubbermaid's Lil Tykes division, acquired in 1984, had provided increased competition for Fisher-Price and for Hasbro's Playskool toys in the infants and preschool toy segment. American Greetings Corporation, the number-two producer of greeting cards, had become a top competitor in the plush toy segment and held a number of lucrative copyrights such as the Strawberry Shortcake characters.

MERGERS AND ACQUISITIONS

The U.S. toy industry was not immune to the 1980s "merger mania." Several large combinations had taken place prior to 1988. Most of these had been undertaken by companies attempting to become full-line producers to offset the instability inherent in the promotional toys market. A typical strategy was to acquire smaller companies with strong, stable products in traditional markets such as games and puzzles or infant and preschool toys. Hasbro's acquisition of both Milton-Bradley and Playskool Toys fit that pattern, as did Coleco's 1986 acquisition of both Selchow & Righter and Tomy Kogyo's subsidiaries in North America. The most aggressive merger move was the 1987 acquisition by Tonka Corporation of the larger Kenner-Parker Toys, itself the product of a former merger. Tonka's action moved the company from seventh place to third in overall market share and provided the company with well-balanced strengths across all significant segments of the industry.

INDUSTRY SALES AND SHIPMENTS

The size of the U.S. toy industry, as measured by manufacturers' shipments, had experienced phenomenal growth in the early 1980s, but increases had been sporadic and recent downturns had caused widespread concern. Shipment dollar value increased from $3.1 billion in 1976 to $8.8 billion in 1986, an average annual rate of 5.7 percent. Adjusted for inflation, the rate of increase was 4.8 percent. Though 1984 marked the industry's highest single-year increase, a phenomenal 51 percent in wholesale sales, later years had seen no significant growth. Wholesale shipments were expected to grow 5 to 8 percent in 1987, but the lack of hit toys, coupled with a number of individual company problems, caused shipments to slump to $8.2 billion, a one-year decrease of 6.8 percent.[12] (See Exhibit 1.)

Retail sales of toys had experienced similar growth over the decade, from $4.2 billion in 1976 to $12.5 billion in 1986. In 1987, retail sales achieved no growth but were stable at $12.5 billion.[13] The disparity between retail and wholesale sales levels in 1987 resulted from the reduction of large retail inventories that were carried over from 1986. Since 1984, the average markup, measured as the percentage difference between total manufacturers' shipments and total retail sales, had declined significantly (see Exhibit 2). Two trends in the industry may have been responsible for the profit squeeze. First, with the increasing dominance of the retail market by large chains such as Toys "R" Us, K-Mart, and Wal-Mart, wholesale buyers were exercising more influence over pricing. Second, stepped-up "copycatting" of successful new products resulted in shorter profit-taking periods and reduced margins for the originators of innovations.

INDUSTRY VOLATILITY

Analysts characterized the toy industry in the 1980s as extremely volatile. The rapid introduction and equally rapid decline in sales of products—that is, characteristically short product life cycles—were the rule rather than the exception in the industry. Video games, fad toys such as the Cabbage Patch Kids

EXHIBIT 1   U.S. TOY MANUFACTURER'S SHIPMENTS IN CURRENT AND CONSTANT DOLLARS, 1960-1987

YEAR	TOTAL SHIPMENTS IN CURRENT DOLLARS (MILLIONS)	% CHANGE	TOTAL SHIPMENTS IN (1967) DOLLARS* (MILLIONS)	% REAL CHANGE
1960	$ 838		$ 885	
1961	992	18.4%	1,040	17.5%
1962	1,100	10.9%	1,154	11.0%
1963	1,141	3.7%	1,195	3.5%
1964	1,213	6.3%	1,270	6.3%
1965	1,304	7.5%	1,343	5.7%
1966	1,420	8.9%	1,443	7.5%
1967	1,560	9.9%	1,560	8.1%
1968	1,824	16.9%	1,781	14.2%
1969	2,041	11.9%	1,938	8.8%
1970	2,259	10.7%	2,065	6.5%
1971	2,351	4.1%	2,088	1.1%
1972	2,652	12.8%	2,318	11.0%
1973	2,835	6.9%	2,405	3.7%
1974	3,005	6.0%	2,271	−5.5%
1975	3,089	2.8%	2,116	−6.9%
1976	3,105	0.5%	2,070	−2.2%
1977	3,392	9.2%	2,186	5.6%
1978	3,772	11.2%	2,311	5.8%
1979	4,255	12.8%	2,415	4.5%
1980	5,004	17.6%	2,520	4.3%
1981	5,922	18.3%	2,795	10.9%
1982	7,501	26.7%	3,386	21.2%
1983	7,506	0.1%	3,333	−1.6%
1984	8,270	10.2%	3,642	9.3%
1985	8,684	5.0%	3,751	3.0%
1986	8,810	1.5%	3,733	−0.5%
1987 (est.)	8,200	−6.9%	3,402	−8.9%

*Adjusted by Producer's Price Index (BLS).

Source: Toy Manufacturers of America.

line, and blockbuster board games such as Trivial Pursuit had all contributed to an atmosphere of unprecedented profits and high risks.

The Cabbage Patch Kids phenomenon is an extreme example of what a fad toy could do in the industry. Shortages of product occurred shortly after introduction, and long lines at retail outlets led to lengthy backorders and black market sales. In 1985, Cabbage Patch accounted for $600 million in sales for Coleco—over 77 percent of its net revenues.[14] Although fad toys were an unstabilizing force in the market, they were believed to generate additional

EXHIBIT 2 U.S. TOY INDUSTRY WHOLESALE AND RETAIL SALES, 1976-1987

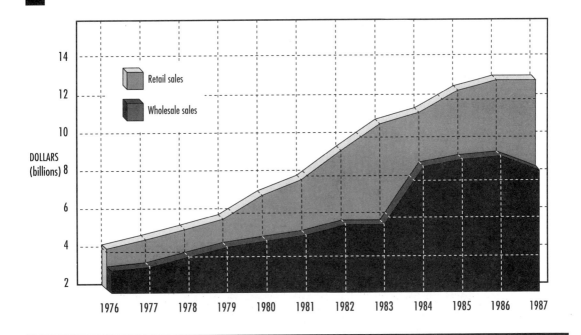

business for other toys. As customers sought out the fad toy in toy stores, they often encountered other toys and made impulse purchases.

Throughout the 1970s and 1980s, the emphasis on large profits from "hit" toys had caused most of the major toy manufacturers to concentrate their ef- forts on trendy toys, which often incorporated the latest technology, and to rely heavily on advertising to focus the public's attention on them. This trend led to escalating costs, which made the producer even more dependent on a "hit" in the marketplace. Consumers' tastes in toys were very unpredictable, however, and many predicted blockbusters ended up on the bargain dis- counters' shelves long before their break-even levels were reached. In seeking to alleviate the volatility in sales, toy manufacturers became more cautious, and many launched back-to-basics movements stressing dolls, cars, trucks, and stuffed animals. The extent to which the industry could control the fervor over blockbuster toys was considered to be a factor in determining stability in the future.

By 1988, the unpredictability of markets had caused toy industry leaders to reanalyze the basic ingredients of a successful toy. Traditional wisdom in the industry held that there were two approaches: "play value" and "collectible value." Play value simply meant that a child could do a variety of things with a toy. For example, Mattel's Barbie, which was still a best-selling toy after nearly thirty years, had play value because she could be dressed and played with in a wide variety of ways. A toy automobile with movable doors and driver had more play value than one without those features. Collectible value simply meant that people would buy the toy because they wanted to own it. Examples of toys with collectible value are the Madame Alexander line of costume dolls and Tonka's Willow figures.

Although the industry outlay for product research and development reached an estimated $240 million in 1987, companies often played hunches to come up with best-selling toy lines.[15] Hasbro, the largest U.S. toy manufacturer, spent close to $70 million on product development but actually relied more heavily on top management intuition than on market research to pick its winners. Stephen Hassenfeld, Hasbro's CEO, said he looked for three things in a new toy: play value, the toy's ability to be shared, and the toy's ability to stimulate the imagination.[16]

SEASONALITY

Because of the large volume of Christmas buying, disproportionate amounts of the toy industry's retail sales occur in the last quarter of each year. Toy manufacturers, therefore, must schedule their operations and distribution efforts on an annual basis, assuring an adequate supply of toys for this very important sales period. Most orders are placed early in the year, and deliveries for the Christmas season begin arriving in the stores by late summer or early fall (see Exhibit 3).

While this seasonal pattern has persisted, sales in the late 1980s indicated a trend toward greater off-season sales to offset the Christmas rush. Although Christmas sales had remained about the same, retail sales in the first three quarters had risen dramatically. In 1986, fourth-quarter sales accounted for about 60 percent of the annual retail volume, as opposed to about 70 percent in 1976.[17]

Year-round sales had been a long-sought-after goal in the toy industry, as more level patterns of purchases could alleviate high inventory carrying costs and difficult work scheduling and shipment problems. Industry analysts believed that the increasing percentage of non-Christmas sales reflected, in part, manufacturers' expansion of their product lines to include more toys for older teenagers and adults. Increased sales of toys for birthdays, graduations, and minor holidays had also been a boon to year-round sales, especially in the fast-growing plush toy segment. New retail distribution channels also had been instrumental in offsetting Christmas sales. Toys were now being sold in supermarkets, bookstores, greeting card shops, and other nontraditional outlets, where increased exposure had led to more impulse purchasing.

The advent of large toy superstores such as Toys "R" Us was also a factor. Major toy producers offered the superstores price breaks for early shipping dates, thereby offsetting the manufacturers' Christmas rush and clearing the warehouses early.

EXHIBIT 3 PERCENTAGE OF SALES ORDERED AND SHIPPED, BY MONTH

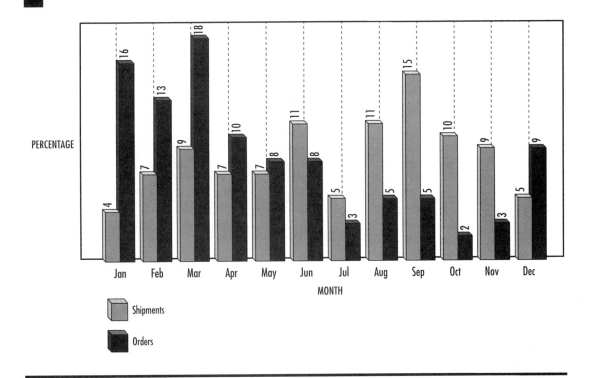

PERCENTAGE

MONTH

Shipments

Orders

ADVERTISING

Toy industry advertising expenditures, which were also heavily concentrated in the last quarter, reached three-quarters of a billion dollars for the first time in 1986 (see Exhibit 4). Since the 1950s, television had accounted for the majority of toy advertising volume. Most of the advertising budgets of major toy manufacturers went toward advertising a constantly changing mix of what were known in the trade as promotional toys. These toys typically had very short product life cycles and were often tied to licensing agreements with the entertainment industry. Toy retailers considered these heavily advertised toys a virtual necessity to stock because of the volume generated by the ads. Markups on heavily advertised toys tended to be modest, however. The average retail profit margin on television-advertised toys was about 15 to 25 percent, and the average for other toys was 35 and 40 percent. Several factors contributed to this difference. Retailers often used heavily promoted toys in their local advertising to price compete, offering these toys as loss leaders to build volume and generate increased store traffic. At the manufacturer's level, the

EXHIBIT 4   TOY INDUSTRY ADVERTISING EXPENDITURES, 1985–1987

MEDIUM	1985	1986	1987
Spot TV	$197,005,000	$208,415,300	$216,287,000
Network TV	129,792,900	125,261,000	119,108,500
Network Cable TV	7,779,200	10,376,400	12,475,400
Magazines	36,313,500	30,736,700	34,605,700
Newspaper Supplements	316,800	1,737,600	938,100
Outdoor	138,500	36,100	16,400
Network Radio	13,900	N/A	399,400
Totals	$371,359,800	$376,563,100	$383,830,500

high demand created by national TV ads allowed economies of scale that also lowered final consumer prices.[18]

In the promotional toys market, wholesale orders are dependent, to a degree, on the success of advertising programs. Toys first are shown to buyers at the annual Toy Fair in February. Ordering begins there and continues for several months. Shipments are made to distributors shortly after the orders are placed, and toys are transferred to retail outlets just as the new advertising campaigns begin, usually in late summer or early fall. If heavy initial demand is seen, distributors supplement their orders in the fall, and delivery of the additional volume is in place for the holiday season.

OVERSEAS PRODUCTION, IMPORTS, AND EXPORTS

All major U.S. toy companies make extensive use of overseas production. The largest sources of foreign production in 1988 were Taiwan, South Korea, and Hong Kong, together accounting for over 60 percent of all imports.[19] Long-standing arrangements in these countries had solidified the relationships between U.S. companies and the contracting firms, but changes were beginning to occur. South Korea and Taiwan were becoming increasingly affluent and could someday fail to offer comparatively favorable labor rates. The planned takeover of Hong Kong by the People's Republic of China in 1998 would likely require firms to alter their business practices there as well. Recent years had seen many new contracts going to companies in Thailand and the People's Republic of China, and these countries, along with countries in South America, were considered increasingly important sources for manufactured toys for the future.

For reporting purposes, all foreign manufacturing is counted as import, even though the products may have been created, manufactured, and marketed by a U.S. firm. In 1987, the total of all imports reached an all-time high of approximately $4.0 billion, a 29 percent increase over 1986.[20] Much of this figure reflected the overseas manufacture by American MNCs, but a growing part was due to the imports of foreign-based companies, particularly those in Japan, who were learning to cope with the rather stringent product safety requirements of the U.S. market.

Exports in 1987 totalled $231 million, an increase of about 25 percent over 1986. The three previous years had each seen a decline in U.S. exports.[21] (See Exhibit 5.) Stabilization of the dollar at a lower exchange rate had increased the competitiveness of American toys. As long as exchange rates remained low, U.S. firms were expected to improve their export levels, since the U.S. still dominated the world market in terms of toy design, innovation, and creativity. A continuing threat to this dominance was the relatively looser enforcement of patents and copyrights in many countries. U.S. toy manufacturers had begun to step up efforts to protect their markets, however, and had a number of infringement suits pending in Europe and the Far East.

EXHIBIT 5 TOY IMPORTS AND EXPORTS

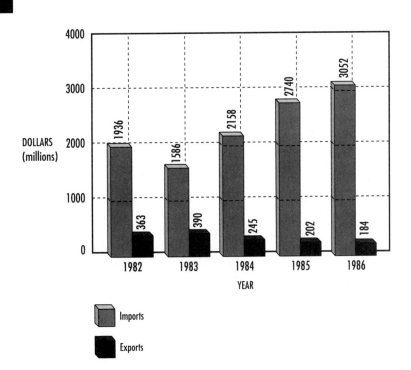

TOY MANUFACTURERS OF AMERICA, INC.

Toy Manufacturers of America, Inc. (TMA), founded in 1916, is recognized as the preeminent trade association for U.S. producers and importers of playthings. In 1988, its 250 members accounted for over 90 percent of the industry's total sales. TMA, formed to promote the interests of toy manufacturers, determined long ago that the best way to do that was to promote a strong sense of responsibility to the consuming public. The goal of providing "well-designed toys that are safe, sturdy, and stimulating—all at a competitive price" is an important one for both the association and its member firms. TMA's major activities include cooperating with government agencies in an ongoing toy safety assurance program, operating a credit information and collection service, compiling industry statistics, and providing consulting services. TMA also conducts a comprehensive public relations program and sponsors and maintains a Toy Industry Hall of Fame honoring individuals who have made contributions to the U.S. toy industry. TMA's most visible activity is the sponsorship of the American International Toy Fair, the most prestigious toy trade show in the world. Held each February in New York, the Toy Fair is best known to the public as the place where manufacturers' new toy designs are unveiled. The 1987 Toy Fair featured 1,045 exhibitors from around the world, with over 17,000 retail buyers in attendance.[22]

MARKET CATEGORIES

TMA tracks trends in twelve separate categories of toy products (see Exhibit 6). In 1988, sales in a few of these categories reflected recent dramatic shifts in heavily advertised toys. The large increase in the plush toy category in 1986, for instance, was due to large sales of the interactive talking animals, such as World of Wonder's Teddy Ruxpin and Ideal-Viewmaster's Talking Big Bird. Whole categories had also experienced recent shifts as consumers' tastes and preferences changed. Electronic games, for instance, showed large sales in 1982 from video arcade games sales, then tapered off, and rebounded in 1985 and 1986 with the introduction of VCR-based games and second-generation video arcade games. A few categories, such as riding toys, were relatively stable, reflecting the industry's continuing dependence on basic products. A large portion of toy sales still came from sales of traditional dolls, games, trucks, and stuffed animals, with many successful toy companies, especially the smaller ones, depending on this important core of the business.

DEMOGRAPHICS

Since children are the ultimate consumers of most toys, birth rates are watched closely by the toy industry. The number of births in the U.S. rose steadily from approximately 3.1 million births per year in 1975 to 3.7 million

EXHIBIT 6 ESTIMATED MANUFACTURERS SHIPMENTS BY PRODUCT CATEGORY

	1982	1983	1984	1985	1986
Action Figures/Dolls/Accessories	$882	$1,036	$2,446	$3,128	$2,193
Plush	281	360	544	585	1,062
Games/Puzzles	671	514	1,043	611	760
Totally Electronic Games	455	237	164	235	421
Infant/Preschool	459	508	739	824	860
Non-Riding Toy Vehicles	752	707	784	695	651
Sports/Outdoor Toys	348	328	419	457	515
Riding Toys	232	255	285	283	288
Arts/Crafts/Models	353	326	391	375	410
Role Playing Toys	144	170	269	255	261
Miscellaneous Activity Toys	215	247	275	290	356
Remaining Miscellaneous	613	658	891	946	1,033

Note: Amounts given in millions.

Source: TMA National Statistics Program based on manufacturers' prices at first billing value.

per year in 1985.[23] The country was experiencing what has been dubbed the baby boomlet, brought on when World War II baby boomers reached their childbearing years. This increase in toy consumers provided the industry with increased demand through the 1980s, and projections in 1988 indicated a fairly stable toy market through the early 1990s as the number of children between birth and age 14 was expected to increase about 8 percent. The baby boomlet was reaching its end, however. The number of births actually declined in 1986 to approximately 3,731,000 from 3,749,000 in 1985. Births were expected to stay above 3.7 million per year through the 1990s and then decline in the early 2000s.[24] (See Exhibit 7.)

Other long-range demographic trends provided a brighter outlook for the

EXHIBIT 7 CHILD POPULATION IN THE UNITED STATES—ESTIMATES AND PROJECTIONS

AGE	1980	1987	1994	2000
Under 5	18,128	18,866	18,823	17,626
5–9	17,291	17,511	19,281	18,758
10–14	16,564	16,139	18,552	19,519
Birth–14	52,073	52,516	56,656	55,953

Note: Amounts given in thousands.

Source: U.S. Department of Commerce, Bureau of the Census, *Population Estimates and Projections,* Series P-25, No. 952, No. 1000.

toy industry in 1988. Although the number of births was slowly declining, the percentage of first births was increasing and stood at about 42 percent.[25] Since the first child in a family typically receives more toys than later siblings, this trend was an encouraging one for the industry. Recent dramatic increases in the number of two-income families were also expected to translate into increased toy demand, since those families had more disposable income. Grandparents were living longer, and many of them had more money to buy toys than ever before. Increased divorce and remarriage rates also played a part in increasing toy demand, as children often had duplicate sets of toys, one at each parent's residence.

SOCIAL ISSUES AND THE REGULATORY ENVIRONMENT

The toy industry has long been the subject of much public scrutiny. Key areas of concern for organized consumer groups and regulatory agencies have been the industry's role in children's television through sponsorship, programming and licensing agreements, product safety concerns, and the potential social impact some toys may have in reinforcing antisocial behaviors or contributing to learned violence or sex-role stereotyping.

THE TOY INDUSTRY
AND CHILDREN'S TELEVISION

Major toy manufacturers have long depended on children's programs to introduce their products. These efforts have been especially visible on Saturday morning and in the growing after-school television market. Educators and consumer groups have taken the position that the children who are targeted by advertisers are often too impressionable and too unsophisticated to make critical judgments of the products and that ads on children's TV shows should therefore be heavily regulated. The result has been a number of restrictions placed on toy advertising by the Federal Trade Commission. By 1988 all ads for toys were required to depict realistic conditions for using the toys, without resorting to special effects that may be misinterpreted by the child. Toy advertisers also were required to show exactly which parts or components the toy contains and to state which parts must be bought separately. Voluntary guidelines on children's advertising had been adopted by all the major television networks, and most advertising firms subscribed to guidelines developed by the Better Business Bureau's Children's Advertising Review Unit, which went beyond the federal regulations.[26] In June 1988 Congress passed the Children's Television Practices Act, which limited the amount of commercial advertising on children's television to ten and one-half minutes per hour on weekends and twelve minutes per hour on weekdays.[27]

The close relationship between toy manufacturers and the advertising and entertainment industries is underscored by the heavy dependence on licensing agreements. "Hit-driven" companies attempt to obtain exclusive rights to motion picture and TV characters and story lines on which to base their toys. Multimillion-dollar contracts are signed in hopes that a forthcoming movie or TV show will generate the demand necessary to make the toy line profitable for the company. If they guess right, the results can be phenomenal. Kenner Corporations' Star Wars agreement in the 1970s returned extraordinary profits for over five years. The failure of the licensed toy line can be devastating, however, as the company that bought the exclusive rights to Howard the Duck can attest.

In a reversal of the licensing agreement idea, toy companies in 1988 began to create the toys first and then develop television programs around them. Examples are "Strawberry Shortcake," "Care Bears," and "Masters of the Universe" television shows. This innovation caused consumer groups to complain that the shows were nothing more than thirty-minute commercials and to call for regulations limiting them. The FCC agreed to study the issues and return a finding on the appropriateness of this innovation, but as of 1988, it had not specifically prohibited this type of product tie-in.

PRODUCT SAFETY

With product liability suits increasing, both in their frequency and in the levels of awards, safety concerns in 1988 were at an all-time high in the industry. All major companies spent heavily on safety testing, and several maintained permanent safety advisory boards consisting of safety consultants, parents, and educators.

The United States Consumer Product Safety Commission (CPSC) develops, issues, and enforces regulations concerning potentially harmful toys and games manufactured in the U.S. and carefully screens imports for safety flaws. Specific regulations cover such features as paint and other surface coatings, noise levels, electrical safety, chemistry set contents, test criteria for sharp edges and points, limitations on small parts, and requirements for use-and-abuse testing.[28]

In an attempt to head off potential problems before they become serious, TMA collaborates closely with the CPSC and other regulatory agencies. In 1976 a comprehensive voluntary safety standard was developed by TMA and published by the National Bureau of Standards. Now administered by the American Society of Testing and Materials and known as ASTM F963, the standards apply to all aspects of toy design, function, engineering, and production. Voluntary standards are under constant modification by TMA. By 1988, additions included standards for unsupported toy chest lids, passed in 1982, and the prohibition of the use of the chemical DEHP in vinyl pacifiers and teethers, passed in 1986.[29]

SOCIAL ISSUES AND REGULATION

Toys have long been recognized as powerful influences in the socialization of children. Through creative play, children learn behaviors that equip them to take on responsible adults roles in society. By 1988, a great deal of controversy had centered on some of the potentially harmful aspects of toys in the socialization process. War toys and toy guns had long been criticized for contributing to violence. A short story, "The Toys of Peace," written by "Saki" (H. H. Munro) in 1919 dealt satirically with the inevitability of war toys as playthings.[30] Although regulation had not addressed the violence-inducing issue, Congress considered legislation in 1988 to prohibit the sale of realistic toy guns that could be used as substitutes in armed robberies.[31]

Critics and parent groups had also argued that toy designs and marketing contribute to sex-role stereotyping, particularly in the doll sector. Ads traditionally had depicted girls acting in the role of mothers and housewives, while boys were shown as pilots, adventurers, and professionals. Although legislation had not addressed the potential of toys for enforcing stereotypes, manufacturers adopted voluntary guidelines to use fewer role-specific ads and to show both boys and girls using action toys.

MAJOR TOY MANUFACTURERS

Following the period of spectacular growth in 1984, toy industry sales had been relatively flat. Lack of sales growth had caused the major toy producers to increase their competitive moves, particularly in the search for "hit" toys. R&D costs had risen, as had licensing fees and advertising expenditures. These higher costs, combined with the lackluster sales, had produced few profits in the industry since 1985. Only Fisher-Price, a subsidiary of the giant Quaker Oats Corporation, increased its profits in 1987.[32] (See Exhibit 8.)

COLECO INDUSTRIES, INC.

Among the top five toy companies, Coleco had been the hardest hit by the recent market softness. Its dependence on blockbuster toys is demonstrated by the meteoric rise and fall of its Cabbage Patch Kids line. The company also invested heavily in the talking plush toy market, introducing a Talking Alf and a Touch and Talk Big Bird in 1986, neither of which performed as expected. Coleco's market share dropped to fifth in the industry in 1987. The company moved to lessen its dependence on "hit" toys in 1986 by acquiring both the Selchow & Righter Company, distributors of Trivial Pursuit, Scrabble, and Parcheesi, and the North American subsidiaries of Tomy Kogyo, which marketed a successful line of infant and preschool toys. The high cost of these acquisitions, coupled with an overall industry slump, resulted in back-to-back net losses of over $100 million each in 1986 and 1987.[33] Despite drastic cost reduction and corporate restructuring attempts in 1987, which included the layoffs of over 300 employees, the company filed for bankruptcy under Chapter 11 of the bankruptcy code on July 12, 1987, while continuing to operate.[34]

EXHIBIT 8 MAJOR TOY PRODUCERS: SALES AND NET INCOME 1985–1987

COMPANY	1985		1986		1987	
	Sales	*Net Inc*	*Sales*	*Net Inc.*	*Sales*	*Net Inc.*
Coleco Industries, Inc.	776,002	82,915	500,658	(111,249)	504,483	(105,351)
Fisher-Price Co.	442,400	47,308	485,300	50,956	596,700	65,040
Hasbro, Inc.	1,233,361	98,969	1,344,653	99,159	1,345,089	48,233
Mattel, Inc.	1,050,928	78,725	1,058,702	(8,251)	1,020,074	(92,495)
Tonka Corporation*	771,000	(68,900)	796,176	38,348	795,000	12,400

*Includes Kenner-Parker Toys, acquired by Tonka on October 16, 1987.

Source: 1987 annual reports.

FISHER-PRICE

The third-largest subsidiary of Quaker Oats Corporation, Fisher-Price had per-formed well for several years, moving from fifth to fourth in overall market share in 1987 while posting all-time-high profits. The company continued to stress its traditional strength in the infant and preschool toys segment, but had begun to diversify through internal growth, introducing a line of toys for older children in 1983 and a juvenile furnishings segment in 1984. Although Fisher-Price was not expected to compete heavily in the promotional toys mar-ket, its Puffalumps plush toy line was heavily advertised in 1987. F-P was also betting on the high-tech toy market with its PXL 2000, a $200 video camcorder for children introduced in 1987.[35]

HASBRO, INC.

From its start as a small family-owned toy company in the 1950s, Hasbro had grown to be the industry leader through aggressive product innovation and strategic acquisition. Although it also had suffered from the recent industry downturn, Hasbro managed to post profits each year. Corporate officials attri-bute the company's stability to two things: product choices that avoid depen-dence on "hit" toys and the company's broad base of stable products. Hasbro was the first of the major toy companies to diversify through acquisition, first acquiring Milton-Bradley, a leading manufacturer of games, and then acquir-ing Playskool Toys, with its substantial market share in the infant and pre-school toys segment. Hasbro's international operations were the largest in the industry, and its share of the world toy market had continued to increase an-nually. In 1987, the company made and sold 34 of the industry's top 100 prod-ucts, including the popular G.I. Joe, My Little Pony, and Transformers lines;

family favorites such as Mr. Potato Head and Tinkertoys; and the popular game A Question of Scruples.[36]

MATTEL, INC.

Although Mattel posted record losses in 1987, it continued to maintain its number-two position in market share with steady sales levels. Aggressive steps were taken to improve profit margins by restructuring Mattel's costs under new CEO John W. Amerman. The company's organization structure was simplified by reducing management levels, and 500 positions were eliminated. The company also reduced its worldwide manufacturing capacity by 40 percent. During the 1980s, Mattel depended on three of its long-standing product lines: Barbie Dolls, Hot Wheels, and the See 'N Say talking toys. Barbie, who would turn 30 in 1989, was still the largest selling doll on the market. In the past, expansion had come primarily through internal growth, although there were rumors in 1988 that the company was looking for a merger partner. An exclusive worldwide licensing agreement with Walt Disney Productions called for Mattel to design, develop, manufacture, and market Disney-branded infant and preschool toys.[37]

TONKA CORPORATION

In 1988 Tonka was the latest company to join the top five. Its acquisition of Kenner-Parker toys in 1987 was the largest toy company merger on record, making the combined company number three in market share with $795 in annual sales. Although the new company was constrained by high debt resulting from the acquisition process, it had a strong management team and a full line of proven products organized in three divisions. The Tonka division featured the company's traditional line of Tonka Tough toy vehicles as well as other products such as the popular Pound Puppy line. The Parker Brothers division had some of the best-selling games in the industry: Monopoly, Clue, Risk, and Sorry. The Kenner division had the stable products Nerf and Play-Doh and was tasked with developing new promotional lines. Tonka was also well positioned in the high-tech toy segment. Its Sega video system was one of the best of a new generation of home video units and was selling well.[38]

INDUSTRY OUTLOOK

In 1988, with analysts predicting that the U.S. economy would continue its modest growth well into the 1990s, rising levels of disposable income were expected to have a positive effect on toy sales. Although significant increases in the proportion of disposable personal income spent on toys (such as those of the early 1980s) were not predicted, toy purchases were expected to hold their own in Americans' spending patterns, especially during the all-important Christmas buying season. The result would be moderate overall increases.

Both retail sales and manufacturers' shipments were expected to increase an average of 1.3 percent through 1992.[39]

Demographic trends were expected to bring about some changes in emphasis across product lines. As the baby boomlet generation ages, toy makers will target older groups. Analysts look for an increased emphasis on toys for adolescents and young teens in the 1990s.

The 1988 caution concerning "hit" toys was expected to continue, and more toymakers were expected to shift their dependence away from them by solidifying their positions in basic toys and staple products. For most major toy producers, the strategy for long-term stable growth would be to use earnings from basic playthings to finance innovations and promotional toy efforts.

Import competition was also expected to increase, particularly in the doll segment, where it had already reached intense levels. Although American-based multinationals accounted for some of that increase through increased overseas production, toy companies from the Far East and Europe would continue to increase their shares in the U.S. market.

Continued restructuring of U.S. based firms was also expected. The top five toy companies, which held about one-third of the market, would likely increase their collective share by absorbing smaller toy makers and by continuing to penetrate the market. Besides being less dependent on the promotional markets, these broader-based companies should be more financially sound if they could avoid excessive acquisition-caused indebtedness. More dependable cash flows from basic toy lines would allow them to engage in better long-range financial planning as well.

Overall, the industry in 1988 seemed to be finding the solution to its past dependence on fad and fashion. While this development was expected to lead to more stability, questions remained about whether or not the new emphasis on staple product lines would enable the industry to maintain its world leadership, which had long been driven by the innovation and creativity of the American toymakers.

ENDNOTES

1. J. Adler, "Anything But Child's Play," *Newsweek* (March 5, 1984): 12.

2. A. P. Fraser, *The History of Toys* (London: Spring Books, 1972): 44.

3. Aristophanes, *The Clouds,* trans. R. H. Webb (Charlottesville: University of Virginia Press, 1960); 59.

4. Fraser, *History of Toys,* p. 81.

5. Ibid., p. 196.

6. Ibid., p. 177.

7. Ibid., p. 204.

8. Ibid., p. 222.

9. "Dolls, Toys, Games and Children's Vehicles," *U.S. Industrial Outlook* (Washington, D.C.: U.S. Department of Commerce, 1988): 47–8.

10. Ibid., p. 48-9.

11. "High-tech Toys in the Spotlight," *Standard & Poor's Industry Surveys* (March 26, 1987): L41.

12. *Toy Industry Fact Book* (New York: Toy Manufacturers of America, 1988): 3.

13. Ibid.

14. "High-tech Toys in the Spotlight," p. L43.

15. "R&D Scoreboard," *Business Week* (June 20, 1988): 151.

16. L. Therrian, "How Hasbro became King of the Toy Makers," *Business Week* (September 22, 1986): p. 90–93.

17. *Toy Industry Fact Book* (New York: Toy Manufacturers of America, 1987): 5..

18. Ibid., p. 14.

19. "Dolls, Toys, Games," p. 47–8.

20. Ibid., p. 48.

21. Ibid.

22. *Toy Industry Fact Book,* 1987, p. 2

23. U.S. Department of Commerce, Bureau of the Census, *Statistical Abstract of the United States* (Washington, D.C.: Government Printing Office, 1987): 57.

24. U.S. Department of Commerce, Bureau of the Census, *Population Estimates and Projections,* Series P-25 (Washington, D.C.: Government Printing Office, 1987): 35.

25. *Statistical Abstract of the United States,* p. 57.

26. *Toy Industry Fact Book,* 1987, p. 16.

27. "Limit on Kids' Television Ads Gets Strong Backing in House," *Congressional Quarterly Weekly Report* (June 11, 1988): 1600.

28. *Toy Industry Fact Book,* 1987, p. 8.

29. Ibid., p. 9.

30. H. H. Munro, *The Complete Works of "Saki"* (New York: Doubleday, 1976): 393–398.

31. "Cross Fire over Plastic Guns," *Time* (March 21, 1988): 33.

32. Quaker Oats Corporation, *1987 Annual Report.*

33. Coleco Industries, Inc., *1987 Annual Report.*

34. R. Mitchell and K. Kelly, "The Guys in the Dark Hats Coming to Coleco's Rescue," *Business Week* (August 1, 1988): 87.

35. Quaker Oats Corporation, *1987 Annual Report.*

36. Hasbro, Inc., *1987 Annual Report.*

37. Mattel, Inc., *1987 Annual Report.*

38. Tonka Corporation, *1987 Annual Report.*

39. *Toy Industry Fact Book,* 1988, p. 6.

HASBRO, INC.

DAVID W. GRIGSBY

In 1988, Hasbro, Inc. faced a number of critical decisions. Should the company continue to concentrate its efforts solely within the toy industry? If so, should it consider acquiring smaller second-tier toy producers or continue to build internally on its solid base of products? If not, what kinds of diversification should it explore?

Although Hasbro had maintained its number-one position in the toy industry for three consecutive years and posted respectable earnings, the industry itself was suffering through a prolonged period of declining sales and profits. Stephan and Alan Hassenfeld, the team of brothers who were the third generation of their family to run the company, had so far managed to avoid many of the problems that plagued other major toy producing firms. As the industry's problems deepened, however, their plans for the billion-dollar toy giant were the subject of much speculation within the industry.

HISTORY OF THE COMPANY

Hasbro, Inc. was founded in 1923 by the Hassenfeld brothers, three Polish immigrants who bought scraps of cloth from the textile mills near their Rhode Island home of Pawtucket. They used the cloth to make hat liners and cloth-covered pencil boxes. Soon the company began manufacturing its own pencils, an activity that was maintained until 1980. When the company was passed down to Merrill Hassenfeld, the son of a founder, he began manufacturing toys. The company's first toy products, in the 1940s, were nurse and doctor kits.

Under Merrill Hassenfeld, Hasbro grew steadily by implementing its strategy of internal expansion and careful product development. In the 1950s and

Source: **Prepared by Professor David W. Grigsby, Clemson University, as a basis for classroom discussion and not to illustrate either effective or ineffective handling of administrative situations. © David W. Grigsby, 1989.**

1960s, the company introduced several products that became perennial favorites, including Mr. Potato Head and G.I. Joe. In the industry, Hasbro was noted for its innovative approach to toy design and the high "play value" of its products. During the final years of his life, Hassenfeld turned the day-to-day operations of the company over to his sons, Stephen and Alan. In 1979, Stephen Hassenfeld, who was then 37, became the chairman and chief executive officer and Alan, who was 30, became president and chief operating officer.[1]

The Hassenfeld brothers began an aggressive expansion program. In 1983, Hasbro acquired Playskool Baby, Inc., one of the largest producers of toys for infants and preschool children. In 1984, Milton-Bradley Company, a leading maker of games and puzzles, was added to the company at a cost of $360 million. This acquisition made Hasbro the most comprehensive maker of toy products in the industry and set the stage for it to take over the number-one position in the industry.[2]

TOP MANAGEMENT AND ORGANIZATION

The Hassenfeld brothers have run the company with a rare blend of teamwork and careful separation of roles. Steven, the CEO, concentrates on finance, product development, and marketing. He personally directs all new product planning sessions and maintains a "hands-on" management style. Alan is in charge of domestic and international operations and serves as the company's representative within the toy industry. Both men grew up in the company and served long apprenticeships under their father. They were allowed a great deal of latitude in their earlier roles in the company and were encouraged to take risks by the older Hassenfeld. Stephen attributes his own success in running the company to this learning process.[3]

The top management team at Hasbro is relatively young. In 1988, its officers at the senior vice-president level and above averaged just over 46 years of age (see Exhibit 1). Although most top managers at Hasbro had been promoted through the ranks, several key positions were held by former Milton-Bradley executives. In all, seven of the top twenty-six officers were former Milton-Bradley executives. Other members of the Hassenfeld family have held executive positions within the company. Leonard Engle, an uncle, was vice-president for purchasing in 1988. Sylvia Hassenfeld, Stephen and Alan's mother, served as the vice-president for corporate affairs until 1987. The company's board of directors is composed of ten members: the Hassenfeld brothers, their mother, and seven outside directors.[4] As of 1988, the Hassenfeld family retained a 15-percent ownership share in the company.

Hasbro's top management is not without its detractors. A former Milton-Bradley officer was quoted by *Business Week* as saying, "They do little or no research. It's how everything feels in the gut. They're eventually going to run into a brick wall"; and a rival in the toy industry has said, "They're arrogant, very opportunistic, and very, very, aggressive."[5]

EXHIBIT 1 EXECUTIVE OFFICERS OF HASBRO, INC.

NAME	AGE	POSITION AND OFFICE PRESENTLY HELD	PERIOD SERVING IN CURRENT POSITION
Stephen D. Hassenfeld	46	Chairman of the board and CEO	1980
Alan G. Hassenfeld	39	President and COO	1984
Stephen A. Schwartz	38	Executive VP and marketing and product development	1987
Alfred J. Verecchia	45	Executive VP, finance and administration	1986
Barry J. Alperin	47	Senior VP, corporate	1985
Lawrence H. Bernstein	45	Senior VP, sales	1982
George R. Ditomassi, Jr.	53	Group vice-president	1984
Christopher P. Dona	37	Senior VP, human resources	1984
George A. Dunsay	44	Senior VP, conceptual design and technology	1987
Hugh C. Maxwell	59	Senior VP, engineering	1987
John T. O'Neill	43	Senior VP, finance	1987
Brian S. Prodger	51	Senior VP, Far Eastern operations	1987
Richard S. Thompson	56	Senior VP, international	1984
Norman C. Walker	49	Senior VP, European marketing	1987
Alfred C. Carosi, Jr.	42	VP, marketing services	1986
Nelson R. Chaffee	46	VP, management information systems	1986
William J. Daly	46	VP, industrial relations	1981
M. Leonard Engle	61	VP, purchasing	1971
Robert A. Finn	39	VP, operational planning	1985
Richard B. Holt	46	VP and controller	1987
William E. Lansing	68	VP, international marketing	1971
Donald M. Robbins	52	VP/general counsel and secretary	1974
Walter D. Slavens	35	VP and treasurer	1987
Phillip H. Waldoks	35	VP, corporate legal affairs	1985

Source: Hasbro, Inc., 1987 Form 10-K.

The organizational structure of Hasbro could be described as functional. Senior vice-presidents head up functional areas within the company and have responsibility for all product lines. Product specialization occurs only within the product development and marketing areas and begins below the vice-presidential level. Although the functional arrangement often creates significant communications problems, it allows the Hassenfeld brothers to maintain a tighter rein on key operating areas. As Stephen Hassenfeld recently told a reporter, "The passion would go out of the business if I had to be a CEO who only lobbies in Washington. Every single product has to go through a product development process and I never miss a meeting. That's the fun."[6]

CORPORATE CULTURE

The founding Hassenfeld brothers considered their employees part of a large extended family. Workers were often given extra money to take care of family emergencies and to meet unexpected expenses. They were invited to the Hassenfeld family's bar mitzvahs and weddings. In return, the workers responded with intense loyalty.

Maintaining this "family business" atmosphere continues to be a goal despite the company's growth to over 8,000 employees worldwide. As Stephen Hassenfeld said,

> It is difficult to retain many of the wonderful attributes we had as a family business. But even if you may lose some things as you grow and change, if you throw your hands up in the air and resign yourself to that fact, you lose a lot more, a lot faster. If you fight to keep some of the wonderful elements that come with people who know and care about one another, maybe you can retain a high percentage of those elements—the people, the feeling, the fun of it.[7]

Hasbro's devotion does not stop with paying lip service to good employee relations. The company's pay and benefits are among the best in the industry. Noncontributory pension plans cover all workers. Nonunion employees' pensions are based on years of service and their average pay during the five highest consecutive years. Unionized employees' pensions are based on a fixed amount for each year of service. Fully paid health care plans cover all employees and retirees and their families.

Stock options for key employees are an additional feature of the human resources management program. In 1988, over 2.4 million shares of common stock were reserved under the plan. A profit-sharing plan based on an annual discretionary contribution from the company covers all nonunion employees. In 1987, $1.8 million was distributed under the profit-sharing arrangement. Layoffs and work reductions have been used only rarely in recent years, despite lagging sales levels.

Alan Hassenfeld explains the legacy of caring within the company in this way: "My father and grandfather gave us the concept of being good people—not just good businessmen—whether it be in relationships with toy inventors, customers, or employees. One of the things we have that was passed on to Steve and me was really caring about people."[8]

This sense of caring extends beyond the business. In 1984, the Hassenfeld family established the Hasbro Children's Foundation to provide funding for innovative projects, research, and programs to improve the quality of children's lives. The foundation's funds have sponsored programs in health care for homeless children, research in AIDS and sickle cell disease, technological advances for hearing impaired and disabled children, reading and literacy programs, and a host of other projects.[9]

DIVISIONS

Hasbro's product lines extend across almost all sectors of the toy industry. With the addition of Milton-Bradley in 1984, the company became the first of the major toy producers to feature strong offerings in all of the best-selling segments: promotional toys, dolls, games and puzzles, and a full line of toys for infants and preschoolers. Products are developed and marketed through four divisions: Hasbro Toys, Milton-Bradley, Playskool, and International Operations.

HASBRO TOYS

Hasbro Toys, the company's promotional toys segment, features fashion dolls, miniature dolls, dress-up and role-playing products, and action and adventure toys. Toys in this segment are promoted heavily through advertising on children's television. Although the products generally carry more risk than those in other segments, there is a correspondingly higher opportunity for profits. Domestic sales of Hasbro-branded products accounted for 30 percent of the company's total revenues in 1987.

Leading the list of best sellers in this division is the popular G.I. Joe line of action-adventure toys. G.I. Joe, long the exclusive property of Hasbro, was retired in 1978. Convinced that the toy's popularity could be regained, Stephen Hassenfeld reintroduced the line in 1982, changing Joe's story line from "war hero" to "antiterrorist." Sales of G.I. Joe toys have increased every year since then.

My Little Pony and Transformers, also marketed through this division, have also been among the best-selling lines of toys in the industry. A new promotional toy, Pogo Bal, was introduced in 1987 and was among the industry's top five toys within six months.

The promotional doll segment has proved to be a problem in the past for Hasbro. The fashion doll Jem, introduced in 1986 to compete with Mattel's Barbie, did not perform as well as expected. The company has continued to pursue this market, however, and introduced Maxie, a more traditionally styled fashion doll, in 1988. The Maxie line also features her boyfriend Rob and a complete line of Barbie-like accessories.

MILTON-BRADLEY

According to the Retail Sales and Tracking Service, Hasbro's Milton-Bradley division led all games and puzzle makers in the industry in 1987.[10] This success is due to a combination of staple board games and puzzles that continue to sell well and some of the industry's best new game innovations. Leading the division in 1987 was the game A Question of Scruples, which sold over 3 million units in its first two years. Another new game that sold well was Win, Lose, or Draw, based on the popular television game show.

Scheduled for introduction in 1988 was the game Guess Who?, which has been a phenomenal success in Europe. Staple products for the M-B division are The Game of Life, Mousetrap, Operation, Electronic Battleship, and the Big Ben line of jigsaw puzzles. In 1987, sales of Milton-Bradley products accounted for approximately 18 percent of Hasbro's total revenues.

PLAYSKOOL

Acquired in 1983, Playskool is the company's division for infant and preschool toys and other related products. Playskool quickly became an important part of the corporation's activities shortly after the merger. A number of existing Hasbro products, such as its lines of plush toys, were moved under the Playskool umbrella and an all-out effort was made to compete with Fisher-Price with a complete line of toys for younger children. The result of that effort is evident in one of the company's stronger divisions. In 1987 Playskool products accounted for 21 percent of the company's total revenues.

Old favorites such as Tinkertoy, Mr. Potato Head, Weebles, and My Buddy and the Busy line of infant toys led sales in the Playskool division. Among the new products selling well were Pipeworks, a building set consisting of pipes and easy to assemble connectors, and the Nosy Bears line of plush toys.

In an effort to capitalize on the excellent reputation the Playskool label has among parents, the division has begun to develop and market nontoy products. For example, Baby Guards safety items help "childproof" cabinets and electrical outlets, and Playskool's new Deluxe Baby Monitor is a portable listening system for parents of infants.

INTERNATIONAL OPERATIONS

Hasbro has extensive international operations. It is the leading toy producer in both Canada and the United Kingdom, and its sales have continued to grow in Europe and in the Australian–New Zealand market. In 1987, 31 percent of the company's revenues were generated outside the United States, despite the fact that international sales in the industry reflected much the same relatively flat pattern as domestic sales, with little real growth overall.

Milton-Bradley products were Hasbro's best-performing international product line in 1987. The company offered a number of foreign language editions of its popular games overseas as well as new games developed through its U.K. product development unit.

International sales of infant and preschool products more than doubled in 1987. Although this increase came on a modest level of 1986 sales, Hasbro was optimistic about making significant inroads in this market, especially in Europe.

Hasbro-branded toys sold very well in international markets. G.I. Joe was reintroduced in Europe and the U.K. in 1987 and was already the number-one boy's line in France. Sales of My Little Pony and Transformers were also strong contributors to international sales totals. In 1988, Hasbro secured the rights to sell a new line of plush Disney figures throughout Europe.

PRODUCT RESEARCH AND DEVELOPMENT

Because a high percentage of sales in the industry tend to be fad toys, it has been estimated that, on the average, producers must replace approximately 60 percent of their volumes each year.[11] New product development has, therefore, become an essential part of any successful venture in the industry. Toy design is often a very secretive process. An inventor at Fisher-Price said, "We're an idea business, and all it takes is the kernel of an idea for another creative person to take the idea and make the product."[12]

At Hasbro, the idea people are not separated from the development people as they are at most other leading toy firms. Everyone in the research group is responsible both for new product ideas and for developing those ideas into viable products. The creative process for a product can take any-where from three to eighteen months as it develops from an idea to the fin-ished product stage, depending on the complexity of the design. Hasbro has the largest product design and development staff in the industry. Approxi-mately 550 employees work in the area, including designers, artists, model makers, and engineers. The company does not rely exclusively on in-house development, however. In 1986, Hasbro paid $3 million to Axlon, Inc. for the rights to electronic toys the smaller firm had developed.[13]

Although Hasbro spent over $69 million on research and product devel-opment in 1987,[14] making it the industry leader in R&D expenditures as a percentage of sales, final toy selection is still based largely on intuition. Stephen Hassenfeld prides himself on being able to spot eventual winners. He believes that too heavy a reliance on market research can stifle creativity. "If you're a leader," says Hassenfeld, "you're the one who creates what's signifi-cant. We're the trendsetters."[15]

MARKETING

The marketing effort at Hasbro is headed up by Stephen A. Schwartz, senior vice-president for marketing and product development. With a budget of over $200 million for advertising, promotion, and programming, his department is a significant force in the industry. In comparative terms, however, Hasbro is not a lavish spender on advertising. Its total advertising layout of 15.8 per-cent of total revenues in 1987 was below the industry average.

Much of the promotional budget went toward producing Hasbro's high-profile Saturday morning television shows, which are based on the company's dolls and action figures. Consumer advocates have criticized this form of promotion, claiming that the shows are really half-hour-long commercials and thus violate the ten-and-a-half-minute per hour limitation on advertising for children's television. The Federal Communications Commission had not responded to these complaints as of 1988, but possible limitations on this very successful form of promotion concerned the management at Hasbro.

In 1986, Hasbro produced and released to movie theaters two feature-length films based on its characters. The response was less than overwhelming, and the company eventually lost approximately $10 million on the venture.

The company's lines of products are sold through wholesalers, large retailers, chain stores, mail order houses, and catalog stores. Hasbro maintains its own sales force of 349 sales persons, who account for approximately 90 percent of sales. Hasbro also deals with 74 manufacturers' representative organizations, which account for the other 10 percent of sales. U.S. and Canadian customers number around 2,500, most of which are large chain stores, wholesalers, and distributors. Its largest customer is Toy "R" Us, Inc., which represented 11 percent of Hasbro's 1986 consolidated net revenue.[16]

PRODUCTION AND OPERATIONS

Hasbro, Inc. operates manufacturing facilities in Rhode Island, Massachusetts, Pennsylvania, New Jersey, New York, South Carolina, and Washington. Manufacturing processes consist of plastic injection molding, blow molding, printing, box making, and assembly. Foreign manufacturing facilities, which consist of much the same processes, are located in Canada, West Germany, Spain, Ireland, The Netherlands, France, and New Zealand.

In all, the company has 3.6 million square feet in owned buildings and 1.5 million square feet of leased space. The largest facility is located in East Longmeadow, Massachusetts, a 1.2 million-square-foot building that houses offices, warehouses, and a manufacturing plant. Corporate headquarters is located in Pawtucket, Rhode Island.

A number of components, accessories, and some finished goods are manufactured under contract by companies located in Hong Kong, Thailand, and Taiwan. For example, most plush toy manufacture and doll garment production is subcontracted to foreign suppliers. Totally finished foreign manufactured items account for approximately 52 percent of Hasbro's domestic net sales.

Most domestic production facilities are operated on a two-shift basis through most of the year, and molding facilities are operated on a three-shift basis. Of the company's 8,000 employees, approximately 5,800 are located in the United States. Approximately 2,700 employees are represented by labor unions in collective bargaining agreements.

Recent increases in the prices of certain types of plastic have increased manufacturing costs for Hasbro and other toy manufacturers. Further increases in raw plastics were expected in 1988.

COMPETITION

The U.S. toy industry underwent a roller-coaster-like pattern in the 1980s. The early part of the decade was characterized by phenomenal growth. Fad toys, electronic wizardry, and video games spurred rapid growth. Manufacturer's shipments rose an average of 21 percent annually in the first three years of the decade. Since 1985, sales have been relatively flat and actually declined in volume in 1987. The sluggishness in the industry has been attributed to the lack of imaginative innovations and to an overall increased cautiousness on the part of the toy companies.

The toy industry consists of a few very large companies and a multitude of smaller producers. Barriers to entry are not high, and start-up ventures are common. Despite this, the industry is dominated by the five largest companies: Hasbro, Coleco, Mattel, Tonka and Fisher-Price, who collectively hold over one-third of the market.

Most toy products are manufactured overseas, either by foreign subsidiaries of the major firms or through contract arrangements with foreign companies.

Hasbro has been number one in the industry since 1985. Not far behind is Mattel, the former industry leader, with sales in excess of $1 billion in 1987. In 1988 Mattel underwent significant cost restructuring under new top management, and by capitalizing on its perennial favorites, Barbie and Hot Wheels, could emerge as a serious challenger to Hasbro's leadership position.

Fisher-Price, a subsidiary of Quaker Oats Corporation, was one of the most profitable firms in the industry in 1987. Its traditional line of infant and preschool toys, which were Playskool's strongest competition, has been expanded to include toys for older children. Further expansions of the product line could result in Fisher-Price becoming a threat to Hasbro's leadership across the board.

Coleco, once number two in the industry, has fallen on hard times following its phenomenal success in 1985 with its Cabbage Patch Kids line. Its profits vanished in the 1986–1987 industry slump as the company tried in vain to replace the lost Cabbage Patch Sales. In 1987, the company filed for Chapter 11 bankruptcy.

Perhaps the most serious challenge to Hasbro's number-one position is the 1987 acquisition of Kenner-Parker, Inc. by Tonka Toys. The combination lifted Tonka immediately to the number-three position in the industry. The combined company has strengths in almost all of the industry's key markets, including promotional toys, games and puzzles, and infant and preschool toys. It also has an aggressive management team.

OPPORTUNITIES

As of 1988, the Hassenfeld brothers faced a number of options for the future. Within the toy industry, they could continue to expand Hasbro through further acquisitions of second-tier firms, or they could continue the company's growth through increased product development efforts. The recent softness of the market had caused widespread financial problems among smaller firms, many of whom had good product lines. Several of these were available for acquisition. With the five largest firms increasing their market shares, however, antitrust considerations could be a deciding factor.

(Financial data for Hasbro is given in Exhibits 2, 3, 4, and 5).

EXHIBIT 2   HASBRO, INC.: CONSOLIDATED STATEMENT OF EARNINGS

	1987	1986	1985
REVENUES			
Net sales	$1,326,140	1,329,631	1,220,352
Royalties	18,949	15,022	13,009
Total net revenues	1,345,089	1,344,653	1,233,361
Cost of sales	647,342	605,071	566,192
Gross profit	697,747	739,582	677,169
EXPENSES			
Research and product development	69,472	57,701	40,345
Advertising, promotion and programming	213,684	217,084	170,204
Selling, distribution, general and administrative	282,106	254,146	231,534
Total expenses	565,262	528,931	442,083
Operating profit	132,485	210,651	235,086
NONOPERATING (INCOME) EXPENSE			
Interest expense	33,021	29,619	37,661
Other (income) expense, net	(171)	(10,806)	2,510
Total nonoperating expense	32,850	18,813	40,171
Earnings before income taxes	99,635	191,838	194,915
Income taxes (note 7)	51,412	92,679	95,946
Net earnings	$ 48,223	99,159	98,969
EARNINGS PER COMMON SHARE			
Primary	$ .82	1.71	1.78
Fully diluted	$ .82	1.70	1.77
Cash dividends declared per common share	$ .0900	.0863	.0750

Note: Amounts given in thousands except per-share data.

Source: Hasbro, Inc., 1987 Form 10-K.

EXHIBIT 3   HASBRO, INC.: CONSOLIDATED BALANCE SHEETS

	1987	1986
ASSETS		
Current assets:		
Cash and cash equivalents	$129,728	$112,556
Marketable securities	32,042	3,505
Accounts receivable, less allowance for doubtful		
accounts of $19,700 and $17,700 in 1986	339,553	305,489
Inventories	133,585	122,902
Deferred income taxes	13,249	13,627
Prepaid expenses	44,472	43,383
Total current assets	692,629	601,462
Property, plant, and equipment, net	176,253	161,470
Other assets:		
Cost in excess of acquired net assets, less		
accumulated amortization of $15,931 in 1987		
and $11,424 in 1986	163,461	167,969
Other intangibles, less accumulated amortization		
of $12,666 in 1987 and $9,212 in 1986	37,358	43,116
Other	6,288	7,843
Total other assets	207,107	218,928
Total assets	$1,075,989	981,860
LIABILITIES AND SHAREHOLDERS' EQUITY		
Current liabilities:		
Short-term borrowings	$ 73,841	41,982
Current installments of long-term debt	556	493
Trade payables	88,239	91,142
Accrued liabilities	115,089	107,950
Income taxes	26,183	30,853
Total current liabilities	303,908	272,420
Long-term debt, excluding current installments	127,127	124,977
Deferred liabilities	3,414	4,191
Total liabilities	434,449	401,588
Shareholders' equity		
Preference stock of $2.50 par value. Authorized		
5,000,000 shares; issued 8% convertible series		
($25.00 stated value), 1,406,674 shares in 1987		
and 1,406,782 in 1986	3,517	3,517
Common stock of $.50 par value. Authorized		
75,000,000 shares; issued 52,582,809 shares		
in 1987 and 52,662,756 in 1986	26,426	26,331
Additional paid-in capital	286,985	286,083
Retained earnings	289,592	248,942
Cumulative translation adjustments	35,020	15,399
Total shareholders' equity	641,540	580,272
Commitments and contingencies		
Total liabilities and shareholders' equity	$1,075,989	981,860

Note: Amounts given in thousands except per-share data.

Source: Hasbro, Inc., 1987 Form 10-K.

EXHIBIT 4   HASBRO, INC.: CONSOLIDATED STATEMENTS OF CHANGES IN FINANCIAL POSITION

	1987	1986	1985
SOURCES OF WORKING CAPITAL			
Net earnings	$ 48,223	99,159	98,969
Items which do not use (provide) working capital:			
Depreciation and amortization of plant and equipment	52,077	34,009	19,467
Other amortization	11,667	9,853	9,358
Provision for deferred income taxes	(869)	1,757	(103)
Other	1,845	505	2,498
Total sources of working capital	$140,419	219,195	284,609
USES OF WORKING CAPITAL			
Additions to property, plant and equipment	$ 62,692	83,868	38,846
Reductions of long-term debt	1,875	62,708	56,591
Cash dividends declared	7,573	7,299	6,627
Translation effect on property, plant, and equipment and other assets	7,360	3,955	3,691
Redemption of redeemable preference stock	—	—	3,500
Purchase of product rights and licenses	—	17,861	2,780
Other	1,240	5,182	1,461
Increase in working capital	59,679	38,322	170,113
Total uses of working capital	$140,419	219,195	284,609
CHANGES IN COMPONENTS OF WORKING CAPITAL			
Increase (decrease) in current assets:			
Cash and cash equivalents	$ 17,172	15,573	44,402
Marketable securities	28,537	(81,897)	75,197
Accounts receivable	34,064	63,703	40,383
Inventories	10,683	55,046	(8,897)
Deferred income taxes	(378)	(2,821)	8,985
Prepaid expenses	1,089	21,424	6,271
	91,167	71,028	166,341
Increase (decrease) in current liabilities:			
Short-term borrowings	31,859	15,937	3,523
Current installments of long-term debt	63	(149)	(60,240)
Total payables	(2,903)	45,286	15,507
Accrued liabilities	7,139	(34,735)	36,943
Income taxes	(4,670)	6,367	495
	31,488	21,706	(3,772)
Increase in working capital	$ 59,679	38,322	170,113

Note: Amounts given in thousands.

Source: Hasbro, Inc., 1987 Form 10-K.

EXHIBIT 5 HASBRO, INC.: CONSOLIDATED STATEMENTS OF SHAREHOLDERS' EQUITY

	1987	1986	1985
CONVERTIBLE PREFERENCE STOCK			
Balance at beginning of year	$ 3,517	3,517	3,519
Shares converted into common stock	—	—	(2)
Balance at end of year	3,517	3,517	3,517
COMMON STOCK			
Balance at beginning of year	26,331	12,056	11,559
Stock option transactions	95	239	67
Stock split	—	13,149	—
Shares issued upon conversion of debentures	—	887	—
Shares issued in public offering	—	—	430
Balance at end of year	26,426	26,331	12,056
ADDITIONAL PAID-IN CAPITAL			
Balance at beginning of year	286,083	226,836	203,206
Stock option transactions	902	1,639	1,122
Shares issued upon conversion of debentures	—	57,608	—
Shares issued upon conversion of preference stock	—	—	2
Shares issued in public offering	—	—	22,506
Balance at end of year	286,985	286,083	226,836
RETAINED EARNINGS			
Balance at beginning of year	248,942	170,231	79,245
Net earnings	48,223	99,159	98,969
Stock split	—	(13,149)	—
Dividends declared	(7,573)	(7,299)	(6,627)
Accretion of redeemable preference stock	—	—	(96)
Redemption of redeemable preference stock	—	—	(1,260)
Balance at end of year	289,592	248,942	170,231
CUMULATIVE TRANSLATION ADJUSTMENTS			
Balance at beginning of year	15,399	5,293	(6,698)
Equity adjustments from foreign currency translation	19,621	10,106	11,991
Balance at end of year	35,020	15,399	5,293
Total shareholder's equity	$641,540	580,272	417,933

Note: Amounts given in thousands.

Source: Hasbro, Inc., 1987 Form 10-K.

Continued product development within the industry was almost a given for Hasbro, but the question remained as to how much to invest in this time of instability. An immediate decision facing the company in this area was whether or not to enter the second-generation video game market. Hasbro's decision not to acquire a first-generation system in 1980 had had mixed benefits. While it did not share in the large profits, it also avoided the down-side problem of dependence on video game revenues that characterized, for instance, Coleco. In 1988, the industry's projected profits from the new systems were tempting, and Tonka had already announced its entrance in the market with its Sega system.

Opportunities outside the industry also presented alternatives. New development efforts could be directed toward ventures outside the company's traditional markets. The Hassenfelds had been burned in earlier ventures outside the toy industry, however. Shortly after taking over as CEO in 1979, Stephen had opened a chain of day care centers and marketed a line of gourmet cookware. Both ventures had failed in short order, and the brothers have never strayed out of the toy box since. After three consecutive years of flat sales in the industry, however, it may be time to give the outside world another look.

One way to attempt to overcome the company's dependence on the fickle toy industry without getting into risky start-up ventures would be the acquisition of an unrelated business. Hasbro's debt structure is sound and may support a major acquisition effort if a suitable merger partner could be found.

With its leadership position in the industry secure, and these and other options available, the future for Hasbro, Inc. in 1988 looked optimistic despite the continuing trouble in the U.S. toy manufacturing industry.

ENDNOTES

1. L. Therrien, "How Hasbro Became King of the Toymakers," *Business Week* (September 22, 1986): 90.

2. Ibid., p. 91.

3. N. Gilbert, "Stephen Hassenfeld: More than a Family Affair," *Management Review* (September 1987): 19.

4. Hasbro Inc., *1987 Annual Report,* p. 47.

5. Therrien, "How Hasbro Became King," p. 92.

6. Gilbert, "Stephen Hassenfeld," p. 20.

7. Ibid.

8. Ibid.

9. Hasbro Inc., *1987 Annual Report,* pp. 24–27.

10. Ibid., p. 8.

11. Therrien, "How Hasbro Became King," p. 90.

12. A. Zusy, "The People Behind the Toys," *New York Times* (February 4, 1988): C6.

13. Therrien, "How Hasbro Became King," p. 91.

14. "R&D Scoreboard," *Business Week* (June 20, 1988): 151.

15. Therrien, "How Hasbro Became King," p. 92.

16. Hasbro, Inc., 1986 Form 10-K, p. 3.

MICHELE BOREN,
REGINA BRUCE,
BARRON GREEN,
VICTOR KHOO,
SEXTON ADAMS,
AND ADELAIDE GRIFFIN

DELTA AIR LINES, INC.

INTRODUCTION

It was 6:40 P.M. on August 2, 1985, and the first officer of cabin crew Flight 191 spotted lightning from a thunderstorm. The flight proceeded on into the thunderstorm and was caught by a sudden downburst of air which was blowing in the opposite direction. The cockpit voice recorder quoted the captain as saying "Push it up, push it way up," followed by "togo," which means to take up the plane at a higher altitude and go around the other direction.[1]

However, eight seconds later the aircraft struck a hill, emerged from the thunderstorm, and touched down on State Highway 114 and struck a vehicle. Then the plane burst into a ball of flames and collided with a water tower on the airport grounds. This was a flashback of Delta Air Lines Flight 191 as reported by the National Transportation Safety Board.[2] Ron Allen was glad that this unpleasant memory of Delta's worst aircrash in its history, which left 137 dead and 29 survivors, was almost over. But was it really over?

INDUSTRY OVERVIEW

We have not seen the total results of deregulation, by a long shot. The experiment in deregulation is not completed yet.[3]

Airports these days can be exciting places, especially if you happen to encounter an airline desk right after it has announced a flight cancellation. Riots, police, and arrests are not uncommon. The situation is becoming so bad that some of the major airlines are training their employees in crowd control.[4]

Source: **Prepared under the direction of Professor Sexton Adams, University of North Texas, and Professor Adelaide Griffin, Texas Woman's University, as a basis for classroom discussion and not to illustrate either effective or ineffective handling of administrative situations. © Sexton Adams and Adelaide Griffin, 1990.**

The airline industry had undergone tremendous changes since deregulation in 1978. Increased demand had caused serious problems for the industry in terms of service. In 1987, 126 million adults, 72% of the population, had flown at least once in their lives as compared to only 10% in 1967.[5] Fifty-three million adults made at least one airplane trip in 1986, as compared to 38 million in 1977.[6] As a result of this increase, congestion problems have been occurring.

There were several reasons for the congestion. Deregulation has made flying cheaper for the average citizen. According to the Air Transport Association, the average fare fell by 9.6% in 1986, the largest one year drop ever.[7] Combine the drop in general fares with the discount wars and a very attractive ticket was produced. Adding to this problem was the fact that airlines were changing their routes to a hub and spoke system. Hubbing means that several flights will converge on the same location at the same time, resulting in severe congestion.[8] When a delay occurs in the hub, the spoke location also will have a delay, causing a domino effect throughout the system.

GOVERNMENT REGULATION

The process of airline deregulation began in 1978 under President Jimmy Carter. Prior to deregulation, competition among airlines was limited by the Civil Aeronautics Board (CAB ceased to exist by 1985) in two of the three major areas of airline marketing—route authority and pricing—leaving only the amount of capacity (number of flights) up to the judgment of individual carriers. Also, there was tight control over the entrance of new airlines. The results were predictable: A fairly small number of major airlines—flying medium to large size jets—who served a broad network of large cities and small towns. In many cases, an airline's dealings with the CAB were more important than its dealings with customers. However, since the deregulation acts, customer service was viewed as a crucial element in an airline success story.

ECONOMIC FACTORS

The economy has clearly had a major impact on the airline industry. Many of the major airlines performed poorly during the recessionary period of 1980–1982. In 1985, the economy began to improve and oil prices reached record lows. These factors coupled with increased passengers led to record profits for some of the major carriers. But the profits of 1985 would be lowered in the following year due to the reduced prices brought on by the fare wars. Fares were being lowered while operating expenses were going up (see Exhibit 1).

During the first half of 1987, the economy continued to grow at a moderate pace. The Dow Jones Industrial Average had more than tripled since 1982. The energy and agricultural sectors had begun to regain strength. While the trade imbalance had improved slightly and the value of the dollar had begun

EXHIBIT 1 COMPOSITE INDUSTRY STATISTICS: AIR TRANSPORT INDUSTRY

	1987 (Est.)	1986	1985	1984
Revenues ($ mil)	45,800	42,405	45,826	42,059
Load factor	57.0%	57.7%	56.0%	58.2%
Operating margin	11.0%	10.8%	10.3%	11.6%
Depreciation	3320.0	3006.0	2881.8	2584.2
Net profit ($ mil)	525	143.9	584.7	913.3
Income tax rate	35.0%	—	40.6%	42.5%
Net profit margin	1.1%	0.3%	1.3%	2.2%
Long-term debt ($ mil)	19,000	17,593	15,452	12,173
Net worth ($ mil)	14,500	13,020	11,930	9,587.4
% Earned ttl. cap.	14.5%	2.5%	4.7%	7.0%
% Earned net worth	3.5%	32.0%	4.9%	9.5%

Source: Marilyn M. McKellin, "Air Transport Industry," *Value Line* (July 3,1987): 251.

to rise, economists were still concerned that the trade balance might worsen and that the value of the dollar would fall, pushing the U.S. into a recession. On October 19, 1987, the Dow Jones Industrial Average fell 508 points, 22.6% of market value.[9] The stock prices of several airline carriers were adversely affected. Were the predictions of recession coming true? What would the effects of a recession be on the airline industry?

FARE WARS

Prior to deregulation, the pricing of airline fares was controlled by the CAB with zero price competition among the airlines. Since deregulation, pricing strategies have become a very important factor in the airline strategy game. Deregulation has allowed many new entrants into the industry. Many of these new entrants had lower cost structures which allowed them to offer substantially discounted fares. The major carriers had to respond to these low fares in order to maintain their market shares. This resulted in the first fare war during the winter of 1982. Various approaches such as the frequent flier program and advance discount tickets were initiated.

Since most of the airline management teams were trained during the period of regulation, they did not have the experience to deal with these complex pricing strategies. Consequently, the prices of fares varied greatly within the industry and even within a given flight. Fare wars severely damaged many of the major carriers, who suffered decreased passenger revenues without a corresponding increase in the number of passengers.

With the advent of highly sophisticated computer systems, major carriers are currently tackling the pricing game much more effectively.[10]

INDUSTRY STRUCTURE

The airline industry was made up of three different leagues. They included major, national, and regional airlines. (See Exhibit 2.) This grouping was not set in stone and fluctuated considerably. The biggest example of this would be Braniff, dropping from a major airline to a national airline. The merger game was very prevalent in this time of deregulation. Since 1985, there have been more than eight major mergers which have decreased the number of major carriers from 20 to 8.[11] These acquisitions have not been cheap. The majors have spent or gone into debt for nearly $6 billion to buy each other.[12]

The number of independent major airlines was shrinking. Eight megacarriers existed and represented 91.7% of the nation's scheduled jet air travel.[13] This growth was coming at the expense of the national and regional lines. Many were either bought by larger airlines or made marketing agreements with them. In 1986, 75 airlines in this group were involved in code-sharing or other agreements with a larger airline.[14] The number of these lines has dropped by 59, from a high of 238 in 1981 to a low of 179 in 1985.[15]

The major airlines constituted most of the domestic flights between the large metropolitan areas as well as most of the international flights. They were by far the most expensive lines and recorded the most passenger miles and revenues. The national lines consisted mostly of domestic flights, concentrating upon the major metropolitan areas as well as the smaller hubs such as Cincinnati and Charlotte. The national price structure is lower than the majors, in general, with some airlines going strictly no-frills. The regional lines are the low-cost carriers of the industry. They usually operate only a few routes and act as feeders to the larger lines.

EXHIBIT 2   AIRLINE INDUSTRY LEAGUES

MAJOR AIRLINES	NATIONAL AIRLINES	REGIONAL AIRLINES
Texas Air	Southwest	Aspen Airways
United	American West	Metro Airways
American	Hawaiian	Florida Express
Delta	Alaska	SkyWest
Northwest	Midway	ASA
TWA	Braniff	Comair
Pan Am	Aloha	Business Express
USAir		

Source: James P. Woolsey, "Airlines Enjoy Modest Traffic, Financial Gains, Benefits of Lower Fuel Costs," *Air Transport World* (June 1987): 64.

FLIGHT SCHEDULES

> We will resist in every appropriate way any implication that Delta misleads the public.[16]

Competing with each other in flight schedules was nothing new to the airlines. Since deregulation, airlines were expanding their routes and increasing the frequency of flight schedules. This was achieved through acquiring additional aircraft for the company. As a result, several major airports' traffic was increasingly congested with more planes on their runways and terminals than they could accommodate. This problem triggered a new call for a possible reregulation on flight schedules at several major airports.

According to Department of Transportation (DOT) officials, there was an increasing trend in flight delay problems since December 1986. Delays at 22 airports were increased by 24.4 percent to 367,000 delays by 1986, and for the first three months of 1987, more than a third of customers' complaints against airlines were contributed by delays and cancellations.[17] The delay problems prompted the DOT to take some steps against flight scheduling at several major airports. The department chose Hartsfield Atlanta International Airport as the first of 13 airports to be investigated.

Upon investigation at Atlanta, Transportation Secretary Elizabeth Dole accused Delta of setting unrealistic flight schedules. The department said its investigation showed that more than 55 Delta flights to and from Atlanta arrived at least 15 minutes late 70 percent of the time during a 30-day sampling period. In addition, two Delta flights were late 100 percent of the time.[18]

Delta was "appalled" by Ms. Dole's accusation that it may be engaging in deceptive practices. The carrier maintained that its Atlanta schedules had not increased significantly since 1984. Delta said the transportation department was engaged in "a misguided effort to shift responsibility for airline delays away from the government's failure to staff and maintain an adequate air traffic control system."[19]

DELTA AIR LINES, INC.

MANAGEMENT

> The attitude of our people is unusual. Delta people pitch in where they are needed.[20]

Ron Allen was elected by the board of directors to become Delta's chairman of the board and chief executive officer on August 1, 1987. He was the successor of David Garrett, who reached mandatory retirement age after serving Delta for 41 years. Garrett exhibited strong leadership and nourished Delta through some bad times into a healthy, growing airline. His management style brought Delta through a time of uncertainty and changing environment caused by the Airline Deregulation Act of 1978. Delta encountered its first major net loss of $86.7 million in 1983, after 36 years of profitable operations.

Nevertheless, Delta was quick in responding to this crisis situation and bounced back in 1984 with a net income of $175.6 million, a $262.3 turn-around from 1983. According to Garrett, there were several factors contributing to this turnaround in profitability, which included an improvement in marketing strategy, increased computer application in travel agent programs by using DATAS II automated reservations system, significant fleet change, and dependence on commuter carriers in feeding passengers at Delta's major hubs. Garrett retired on July 31, 1987, but he plans to remain active as a member of the board and serve as chairman of the executive committee.

Allen, who was appointed as Delta's first-hand man, was a veteran in the airline business. He has been with Delta for 24 years, beginning his career in the Personnel Division and moving to the position of senior vice president for administration and personnel. By November 1983, he was promoted to president and chief operating officer, and after four years, he has become the new chief executive officer of Delta.[21]

Allen's successor was Hollis Harris, who was elected by the board as Delta's president and chief operating officer. Harris was a Delta veteran of 33 years. He worked his way up the corporate ladder from transportation agent in the Technical Operations, Operations, and Passenger Service divisions, to senior vice president of operations.

Delta's organization was set up with seven functional divisions—Finance, Marketing, Personnel, Technical Operations, Operations, Information Services and Properties, and General Counsel and Secretary. Each of these division is supervised by senior vice presidents and a chief financial officer who directly reports to the president and chief operating officer. Several subdivisions exist in each functional area, which are supervised by either vice presidents or assistant vice presidents.[22] An illustration of Delta's organization chart is shown in Exhibit 3.

Delta had always been very centralized. Ron Allen and his senior management group had always made the critical decisions. Even though the organization was very centralized, the senior management group was accessible to the rest of the company. Delta's management maintained an "open door" policy for its employees to discuss their problems and concerns.

In addition, Delta's management had generally maintained a policy of delegating the maximum degree of responsibility to its crew members. In September 1987, the FAA noted in its report that "this management style has worked well, and the airline has enjoyed an excellent reputation in the industry."[23]

OPERATIONS

> The competitive requirement today is to have a strong, high-frequency operation in major centers. You have to control a good deal of traffic in order to survive in a very volatile, competitive environment.[24]

Delta Air Lines, Inc. was the fourth largest air carrier providing scheduled air transportation for passengers, freight, and mail over a network of routes

EXHIBIT 3 ORGANIZATION CHART OF DELTA AIR LINES, INC.

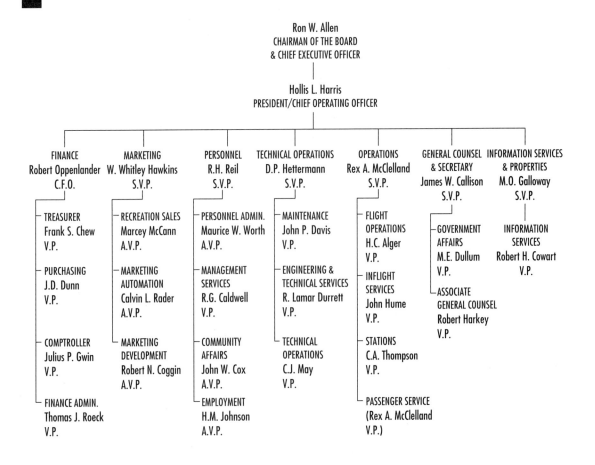

throughout the United States and overseas. Delta serves 132 domestic cities in 42 states, the District of Columbia, and Puerto Rico, and also operates flights to 20 international cities in 9 foreign countries.[25]

Expansion and Routes. Delta, in compliance with its strategic plan to become a major international airline, acquired Western Airlines in 1987. This acquisition increased Delta's presence in areas where it previously lacked strength. Forty-four new cities were added, including cities in Alaska, Hawaii, western Canada, and Mexico. New hubs were added at Salt Lake City and Los Angeles.

In addition to the new routes added by the merger with Western, Delta added new service from Atlanta through Portland, Oregon, to Tokyo, Japan, and Seoul, South Korea. New service was also added from Cincinnati to London.

The Cincinnati hub has undergone tremendous expansion and upgrade. Now Delta will compete head-on with other major carriers in the midwest. Delta more than doubled its daily flights to Cincinnati.[26]

Delta invented and currently operates under the hub and spoke system which has become the keystone of route development in the airline industry.[27] The hub and spoke system allows for fewer planes than if each regional base had to be connected with all the others by a direct flight.[28]

Major hubs for Delta are Dallas/Forth Worth, Atlanta, Salt Lake City, and Los Angeles. More than half of all Delta flights either begin or end at one of these cities.[29]

Delta uses four regional carriers to increase the efficiency of its hub operations: Atlantic Southeast Airlines, Comair, Business Express, and SkyWest. These carriers serve 93 cities and operate more than 1,400 flights per day.[30]

Cargo operations and mail carrier service continue to increase in 1987. Delta signed a new agreement with the United States Postal Service for the carriage of mail which is expected to increase the number of mail ton miles throughout 1988. Delta also continued its push into the special passenger markets such as conventions and groups, military and government, tour and cruise passengers, and family and senior citizen travelers.[31]

In an effort to support continued growth, Delta has expanded several facilities during 1987. Federal Inspection Service facilities were added in Atlanta and Dallas/Forth Worth and plans were made to add one to Cincinnati. Gate expansion occurred in Cincinnati, Dallas/Fort Worth, Portland, and Los Angeles. New terminal facilities were opened in Mobile and Fort Lauderdale.[32]

Aircraft.   In order to facilitate this expansion, Delta took delivery of 35 new aircraft in addition to 92 aircraft gained in the acquisition of Western.[33] The company now has use of 368 planes which consist of 132 B-727s, 36 DC-9s, 9 DC-10s, 12 DC-8s, 35 L-1011s, 22 B-767s, 86 B-737s, 28 B757s, and 8 MD-82/88s.[34] This represents over 59,000 passenger seats available to Delta.[35]

Delta has 63 aircraft on order and options on another 101 aircraft from 1988 through 1992.[36]

During 1987, Delta decreased its average cost per seat mile by 14%. This decrease along with a decline from the reduction in fuel prices and greater productivity from personnel helped Delta to decrease its unit cost and increase its operating revenues.[37]

Customer Service.   According to United States government records, Delta for the thirteenth consecutive year had the best customer service record. Delta was voted as the best airline by the readers of *Travel Holiday* magazine.[38] Delta was also one of the best airlines in not overbooking flights. Overbooking results in bumping some passengers from the flight, usually late arrivals. Delta did this to 1.3 passengers our of every 1,000 on an involuntary basis and 6.4

passengers our of 1,000 on a combined voluntary and involuntary basis. These numbers were second and first in the airline industry.[39]

Flight delays have continued to plague Delta. Delta has one of the worst records in overall percentage of reported flights arriving on time. In September of 1987, Delta only had 72.3% of reported flights that arrived on time. It ranked eleventh out of 13 airlines. Delta also had 4.7% of its regularly scheduled flights arriving late 70% of the time or more. This was the third worst percentage. Finally, Delta had 6 flights which arrived late 96% to 100% of the time. This was the most of any airline.[40]

COMPETITOR PROFILES

AMERICAN AIRLINES

American Airlines was the second largest domestic carrier. It had major hubs in Dallas/Fort Worth, Chicago, Nashville, Raleigh-Durham, and San Juan. American had international service to Canada, Mexico, the Caribbean, and Europe. American had been very profitable over the past four years, posting total profits of $1.09 billion.[41] In 1986, American purchased AirCal for $225 million. This was the major event of 1986 for the company and represented a new and stronger push into the west coast area.[42]

American filed suit this year against Texas Air Corporation claiming they illegally induced travel agencies to break contracts with American's Sabre reservation system. The suit seeks millions in actual claims that Texas Air used illegal methods to coerce travel agencies into using the Sabre system.[43]

Third quarter results for AMR, the parent company of American Airlines, showed a 27.8% drop in earnings. Revenues were up to $1,975.4 million while operating income was down $7.1 million.[44] Traffic increased almost 15%. Load factor, or percentage of seats filled, was unchanged at 66.0%.[45] American placed a large aircraft order in 1987, agreeing to take 15 767-300FRs from Boeing and 25 A300-600Rs from Airbus. Both deals were leases with easy-return provisions.[46] American was reportedly going to use the Airbus planes in the Caribbean and use the replaced jets for domestic expansion. The Boeing jets were to be placed in service in North America for European routes. The jets currently in that position had been used also for domestic purposes.

New routes have been established for 1987 to Zurich, Geneva, Paris, Frankfurt, and Tokyo.

UNITED AIRLINES

United Airlines was the largest single domestic airline in the United States. United had hubs in Chicago, Denver, San Francisco, and Washington, D.C., where flights serve North America as well as Europe, Mexico, and the Far East.

United Airlines' parent had changed its name from UAL, Inc. to Allegis Corporation and since that time it had also decided to divest the Hertz operations, the Westin and Hilton International hotel chains, and perhaps all or part of their computerized reservations system (CRS). The Hilton International hotel chain was sold to Ladbroke Group PLC of Britain for $1.07 billion.[47] Hertz was recently sold to a group including Ford Motor Co. and Hertz management for $1.2 billion.[48] The proceeds of the sale went to the shareholders. These moves were designed to protect the company from takeover by hostile entities.[49] The original plan was designed to give the company a full line of services which could meet all the needs of the passenger.

PAN AM CORPORATION

Pan Am was the seventh largest airline in the United States. The airline recently sold off its Pacific routes to United Airlines. It has concentrated its efforts upon the Atlantic and European routes. In 1987, Pan Am has shown relatively good growth with demand increasing from the Europeans due to the weaker dollar.[50] Improved feed systems to the JFK and Miami hubs has also helped increase growth. (Pan Am has made agreements with regional airlines which act as feeders to their main hubs of JFK and Miami.)[51]

Pan Am was determined to improve its future by decreasing labor costs.[52] Pan Am had tried to secure labor savings of $180 million over the time period 1985–1987.[53] Management feels that this is key to the long-term survival of the airline.[54]

A group of airline experts and a coalition of Pan Am's unions had negotiations on taking the company over. The airline experts, led by Kerk Kerkorian, were requiring greater concessions from the unions than current management. The situation was placed on hold until a more viable solution could be worked out.[55]

TEXAS AIR CORPORATION

Texas Air Corporation was ranked as the largest multi-airline corporation in the United States. The corporation was made up of Continental, Eastern, Frontier, People Express, New York Air, and Texas International. Texas Air's major hubs were in Houston, Denver, Atlanta, Miami, Kansas City, and Newark. The corporation serves primarily the domestic corridor. The massive growth that this company had undergone in the past year had caused several problems to occur. First, Texas Air is the owner of the most complained about airline—Continental.[56] Labor disagreements plague Eastern. Service and schedule disruptions, along with misplaced luggage had driven many passengers to other airlines.[57]

In 1987, Continental posted a passenger load drop to 56.2% from 60.4% in 1986.[58] Traffic increased 83.3%, which reflects Continental's merged operations with People Express and New York Air.[59] Eastern also reported a decline in traffic while reducing available seat miles. Eastern's load factor improved to 58.2% from 54.5% a year earlier.[60]

Continental reported that its September 1987 on-time performance was

80%, and that it completed 98.9% of flights, and transported 99.3% of its passenger bags to the right airport at the right time.[61]

NORTHWEST

By acquisition of Republic Airlines, Northwest Airlines had become the fifth largest airline company in the United States.[62] The carrier services all the major metropolitan areas in the United States and also serves the Far East and Canada.

Northwest is preparing to upgrade its fleet by ordering 100 Airbus A320s. The company will order up to 20 Airbus A340 widebodies in 1987, with delivery expected to occur in 1992.[63]

Northwest earned $76.9 million in 1986, up from 1985. Yields had increased with the integration of Republic and are thought to have had a good chance of increasing in 1987. Northwest appears to be in a good position with its marketing agreement with TWA, concerning its PARS computer reservation system. This will enable Northwest to have the travel agent leverage needed to compete with the other computer reservation system giants.[64]

USAIR

USAir was the ninth largest domestic carrier. USAir recently purchased PSA, which was a west coast carrier and owns 51% of Piedmont. These acquisitions give USAir a very competitive strategy.[65] USAir will enjoy a very strong west coast presence and with the addition of Piedmont, USAir's east coast network will be greatly enhanced.[66] When the acquisitions are completed, USAir will become the seventh largest domestic carrier.

In 1987, USAir was developing a new hub in Philadelphia and starting service to Atlanta, Jacksonville, Manchester, and Portland.

USAir increased its passenger boarding as well as load factors and revenues. USAir had to perform adequately in order to service its increased debt.[67]

TWA

Transworld Airlines was the sixth largest domestic airline. TWA services the continental United States, Europe, Mideast, India, and the Caribbean.

TWA owned Ozark Airways, which gave it a major hold in St. Louis. Since international service was very cyclical, Ozark gave TWA some stability in the domestic market.

TWA's flight attendants went on strike in March 1986, over wage cuts imposed by controlling owner Carl Icahn. Management eventually won by hiring new replacements, which cut costs by 10%.[68]

In spite of the labor union strike and the decreased international passenger mileage caused by anti-American terrorism, TWA still posted a net profit of $85 million in the fourth quarter of 1987, which reduced the overall deficit by $76 million.[69] This was good considering the losses in 1985 and 1986. With renewed interest in transatlantic travel, and a stronger position in the Mid-western market, TWA should continue on its rebound and improve profitability in the coming years.[70]

FINANCE/ACCOUNTING

> Financial strength is very important in a marketing war. It permits you to create an unprofitable price to fight off interlopers in a market.[71]

Delta's balance sheets and income statements are shown in Exhibits 4 and 5. For the fiscal year ending June 30, 1987, Delta had total operating revenues of $5,318,712,000. Net income was $263,729,000 compared with $47,286,000 in fiscal 1986. In addition, earnings per share of common stock was $5.90.[72]

Debt has long been used by Delta to finance its fleet expansion programs. As of June 30, 1983, Delta's long-term debt was in excess of $800 million. This debt generated approximately $62 million in interest expense for fiscal 1987.[73]

On December 18, 1986, Delta purchased all 61,331,334 outstanding shares of Western stock for $787 million by paying $384 million in cash and issuing 83 million shares of Delta stock for the balance. In addition, Delta assumed Western's long-term debt of $228 million, capital lease obligations totaling $199 million, and other non-current liabilities of $29 million.[74]

Delta's operating financial strength was demonstrated in the significant decrease in its unit cost during fiscal 1987. As shown in Exhibits 6 and 7, average cost per available seat mile was 7.12 cents, down 14% from the 8.30 cents average in fiscal 1986. The decline in seat mile cost is extremely important as airlines struggle to compete by providing the lowest fares to travelers.[75]

Delta continued to use lease financing to acquire new aircraft due to the fact that the company had a significant amount of investment tax credit and net operating loss carryovers. During fiscal 1987, all new aircraft acquired were sold and leased back from the purchaser using operating leases.[76]

MARKETING/SALES

> We have determined that much of Delta's future success will depend on the imagination and skill we bring to the use of fast-paced developments in the information management technologies.[77]

Delta had recently taken several actions to enhance its competitive situation for the future. The company's marketing plan called for expansion of the Dallas/Fort Worth and Cincinnati hubs. On July 30, 1986, Delta announced that it would double its operations at the Cincinnati airport by the end of the 1986 calendar year.[78]

In September 1987, Delta launched a new marketing campaign to counteract some of the negative press resulting from the crash of Flight 191 and the near mishaps earlier in 1987. The theme line "Delta: we love to fly and it shows" will replace Delta's two-year-old theme, "Delta gets you there." The company is expected to spend about $70 million on the new campaign.

Acquiring Western Airlines provided Delta with a significant improvement in its route system. Western added 44 cities to the 108 already served by Delta. Western's domestic operations were centered in the western half of the United States in areas were Delta did not have substantial operations.[79]

EXHIBIT 4 CONSOLIDATED BALANCE SHEETS, 1987 AND 1986

	JUNE 30	
	1987	1986
ASSETS		
Current Assets:		
Cash and temporary cash investments	$ 379,928	$ 61,315
Accounts receivable, net of allowance for uncollectible accounts	626,139	425,912
Refundable income taxes	—	10,485
Maintenance and operating supplies, at average cost	42,337	35,503
Prepaid expenses and other current assets	131,170	49,660
Total current assets	1,179,574	582,875
Property and Equipment:		
Flight equipment owned	4,485,898	4,174,632
Less: Accumulated depreciation	1,951,494	1,939,205
	2,534,404	2,235,427
Flight equipment under capital leases	221,811	—
Less: Accumulated amortization	16,307	—
	205,504	—
Ground property and equipment	1,078,185	965,980
Less: Accumulated depreciation	451,643	390,324
	626,542	575,656
Advance payments for new equipment	307,461	323,399
	3,673,911	3,134,482
Other Assets:		
Investments in associated companies	55,427	37,976
Cost in excess of net assets acquired, net of accumulated amortization of $5,529	371,756	—
Funds held by bond trustees	8,308	7,677
Other	53,407	22,452
	488,898	68,105
	$5,342,383	$3,785,462

(*continued*)

EXHIBIT 4   (continued)

| | JUNE 30 | |
	1987	1986
LIABILITIES AND STOCKHOLDERS' EQUITY		
Current Liabilities:		
Current maturities of long-term debt	$ 8,406	$ 10,921
Current obligations under capital leases	12,921	—
Short-term notes payable	11,000	9,000
Commercial paper outstanding	14,836	41,055
Accounts payable and miscellaneous accrued liabilities	455,686	270,445
Air traffic liability	506,669	286,579
Accrued vacation pay	110,835	88,595
Transportation tax payable	60,705	39,342
Total current liabilities	1,181,058	745,937
Non-Current Liabilities:		
Long-term debt	837,201	868,615
Capital leases	181.216	—
Other	80,320	38,949
	1,098,737	907,564
Deferred Credits:		
Deferred income taxes	590,876	427,339
Unamortized investment tax credits	98,525	150,594
Manufacturers credits	137,611	146,844
Deferred gain on sale and leaseback transactions	297,050	104,742
Other	614	496
	1,124,676	830,015
Commitments and Contingencies		
Stockholders' Equity:		
Common stock, par value $3.00 per share—		
Authorized 100,000,000 shares; outstanding 48,639,469 shares at June 30, 1987, and 40,116,383 shares at June 30, 1986	145,918	120,349
Additional paid-in capital	484,398	93,333
Reinvested earnings	1,307,596	1,088,264
	1,937,912	1,301,946
	$5,342,383	$3,785,462

Note: Amounts given in thousands.

Source: Delta Air Lines, Inc., *1987 Annual Report.*

EXHIBIT 5   DELTA AIR LINES, INC.: CONSOLIDATED STATEMENTS OF INCOME, 1987, 1986, AND 1985

	YEAR ENDED JUNE 30		
	1987	1986	1985
Operating Revenues:			
Passenger	$4,921,852	$4,132,284	$4,376,986
Cargo	280,271	240,115	235,199
Other, net	116,049	87,663	71,930
Total operating revenues	5,318,172	4,460,062	4,684,115
Operating Expenses:			
Salaries and related costs	2,228,814	1,963,575	1,856,243
Aircraft fuel	672,004	796,883	892,182
Aircraft maintenance materials and repairs	127,856	91,590	66,022
Aircraft rent	150,653	68,518	57,090
Other rent	145,473	109,778	92,839
Landing fees	89,519	65,879	60,908
Passenger service	219,834	180,409	170,163
Passenger commissions	432,066	359,299	350,690
Other cash costs	569,453	425,723	422,840
Depreciation and amortization	277,975	363,920	349,128
Total operating expenses	4,913,647	4,425,574	4,318,105
Operating Income	404,525	34,488	366,010
Other Income (Expense):			
Interest expense	(94,000)	(79,113)	(84,081)
Less: Interest capitalized	32,092	23,758	22,028
	(61,908)	(55,355)	(62,053)
Gain on disposition of aircraft	96,270	16,526	94,343
Miscellaneous income, net	8,312	7,775	6,863
	42,674	(31,054)	39,153
Income Before Income Taxes	447,199	3,434	405,163
Income Taxes (Provided) Credited	(219,715)	2,228	(186,624)
Amortization of Investment Tax Credits	36,245	41,624	40,914
Net Income	$ 263,729	47,286	$ 259,453
Net Income Per Common Share	$5.90	$1.18	$6.50

Note: Amounts given in thousands, except per-share data.

Source: Delta Air Lines, Inc., *1987 Annual Report.*

EXHIBIT 6   DELTA AIR LINES, INC.: OPERATING STATISTICS

	1987	1986	PERCENT CHANGE
Revenue plane miles (000)	407,773	311,347	+31%
Available seat miles (000)	69,013,669	53,336,135	+29
Available ton miles (000)	8,999,668	6,934,047	+30
Fuel gallons consumed (000)	1,435,801	1,126,876	+27
Avg. fuel price gallon	46.80	70.72	−34
Passenger load factor	55.66%	56.48%	− 1
Breakeven load factor	51.09%	56.01%	− 9
Cost per avail. seat mile	7.12	8.30	−14

Source: Delta Air Lines, Inc., *1987 Annual Report.*

Delta Air Lines signed a ten-year agreement to become the official airline of Walt Disney World. Many marketing opportunities will be provided as a result of the association with Walt Disney World such as: service personnel, on-site ticketing, etc.[80]

DELTA PROBLEMS

While we would like to put the series of safety incidents behind us, we will not and cannot allow ourselves to forget them, but rather we must learn from the experience.[81]

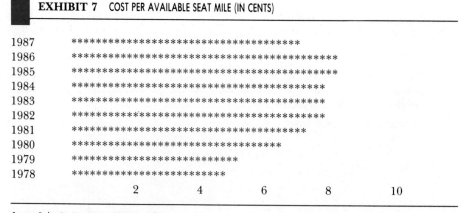

EXHIBIT 7   COST PER AVAILABLE SEAT MILE (IN CENTS)

```
1987    ************************************
1986    ******************************************
1985    ******************************************
1984    ****************************************
1983    ***************************************
1982    ***************************************
1981    **************************************
1980    *********************************
1979    **************************
1978    *************************
            2         4         6         8        10
```

Source: Delta Air Lines, Inc., *1987 Annual Report.*

According to the Federal Aviation Administration (FAA) investigation of Delta's training program on flight safety, numerous problems were uncovered with pilot-crew coordination, lapses in discipline, and poor cockpit communication. This investigation was triggered by a series of safety incidents at Delta in June and July of 1987. The report indicated the shortcomings as primarily due to a lack of clear-cut, definitive guidance from those responsible for developing and standardizing cockpit procedures. The inspection team also blamed the airline's management philosophy for the crew problems.[82]

Delta's management philosophy was to delegate a maximum degree of responsibility to its crew members. According to the FAA, this philosophy worked well in the past but there is a limit to this approach due to an increasingly complex and stressful environment. The report suggested that this philosophy caused crew members to work independently rather than functioning as team members.[83]

The series of safety incidents at Delta were recorded as follows:

- July 8, 1987. A Delta jumbo jet flying from London to Cincinnati strayed 60 miles off course and came within 100 feet of a Continental Airlines jet off the coast of Newfoundland.
- July 7, 1987. A Delta pilot heading for Lexington, Kentucky, mistakenly landed 20 miles away at Frankfort, Kentucky.
- June 30, 1987. The crew of a Delta jet accidentally turned off the engines while climbing over the Pacific Ocean after leaving Los Angeles. The pilot managed to restore power 600 feet above the ocean.
- June 18, 1987. A Delta jet had to abort its takeoff run as another jet passed 100 feet overhead while taking off in the opposite direction on the same runway.[84]

Delta was the brunt of much negative publicity due to the intense media coverage of the preceding events. Delta management identified breakdown in cockpit communication as the primary cause of the safety incidents. The firm has taken corrective action and individual disciplinary action in response to the incidents. While the negative coverage of these events was short-lived, Delta has been and continues to receive negative coverage in connection with the August 2, 1985, crash of Flight 191. The National Transportation Safety Board has reported the probable causes of the accident, which left 137 dead, as the flight crew's decision to initiate and continue the approach into a cumulonimbus cloud that they observed to contain lightning; the lack of specific guidelines, procedures, and training for avoiding and escaping low-altitude wind shear; and the lack of definitive, real-time wind shear hazard data.[85] Recent reports regarding the pre-trail events (a trial to determine liability in the accident is set for February 1, 1988) state that an expert witness for the plaintiffs, family of accident victims, will testify that the pilot, Captain Edward M. Connors, had been taking a prescription tranquilizer called Stelazine and that it affected his flying.[86] Delta spokesman Jim Lundy defended Connors by stating, "There is no indication that Connors was on medication at the time of the accident."[87] The National Transportation Safety Board said that if enough new evidence was revealed they might reopen the crash investigation.[88] Coverage of the Flight 191 accident will likely continue until all the lawsuits have been settled. Will such coverage cloud Delta's image?

ENDNOTES

1. James Ott, "Recorder Reveals Lightning Preceded Delta L-1011 Crash," *Aviation Week and Space Technology* (October 7, 1985): 26.

2. Ibid.

3. "Delta's Soft Landing," *Management Today* (July 1985): 71.

4. Jonathan Dahl, "Battling Crowds at the Airports," *Wall Street Journal* (October 19, 1987): 29.

5. Holman Jenkins, Jr., "Setting Course for Smoother Skies," *Insight* (October 26, 1987): 8.

6. Ibid.

7. Merger Myopia," *Wall Street Journal* (October 19, 1987): 27.

8. Jenkins, "Setting Course for Smoother Skies," p. 9.

9. Amy Stromberg, "How Panic Swept Wall Street," *Dallas Times Herald* (October 20, 1987): A7.

10. Kenneth Labich, "Winners and the Air Wars," *Fortune* (May 11, 1987): 74.

11. James P. Woolsey, "Airlines Enjoy Modest Traffic, Financial Gains, Benefits of Lower Fuel Cost," *Air Transport World* (June 1987): 64.

12. Ibid., p. 58.

13. Donald L. Pevsner, "Merger Mania is Putting Lower Air Fares in a Tailspin," *Dallas Morning News* (October 11, 1987): 10G.

14. Woolsey, "Airlines Enjoy Modest Traffic," p. 59.

15. Ibid.

16. Laurie McGinley, "U.S. Weighs Penalizing Delta, Eastern Over Scheduling at Airport in Atlanta," *Wall Street Journal* (April 10, 1987): 3.

17. James Ott, "Airlines View Flight Adjustments as Trend Toward Reregulation," *Aviation Week and Space Technology* (February 9, 1987): 34.

18. McGinley, "U.S. Weighs Penalizing Delta, Eastern," p. 3.

19. Ibid.

20. "Delta's Soft Landing," p. 70.

21. Delta Air Lines, Inc., *1987 Annual Report*, p. 10.

22. Ibid, p. 15.

23. David Tarrant, "FAA Faults Delta But Reports No Finable Offense," *Dallas Morning News* (September 19, 1987): 1.

24. Bruce A. Smith, "Delta Agrees to Acquire Western for $860 Million," *Aviation Week and Space Technology* (September 15, 1986): 31.

25. Delta Air Lines, Inc., *1987 Form 10-K*, p. 1.

26. Delta Air Lines, Inc. *1987 Annual Report*, p. 12.

27. Ibid., p. 4.

28. Jenkins, "Setting course for Smoother Skies," p. 9.

29. Delta Air Lines, Inc., *1987 Annual Report*, p. 12.

30. Ibid.

31. Ibid., p. 13.

32. Ibid., pp. 13–14.

33. Ibid., pp. 9–10.

34. Marilyn M. McKellin, "Air Transport Industry," *Value Line* (July 3, 1987): 259.

35. Delta Air Lines, Inc., *1987 Annual Report*, p. 10.

36. Ibid.

37. Ibid., p. 5.

38. Ibid.

39. Francis C. Brown III and Jonathan Dahl, "New Data on Airline Performance May End Up Misleading Travelers," *Wall Street Journal* (November 23, 1987): 25.

40. Laurie McGinley and Jonathan Dahl, "Delay Date: Airlines' Figures Hold Surprises—and Spark Controversy," *Wall Street Journal* (November 11, 1987): 22.

41. "U.S. Majors," p. 100.

42. Ibid., p. 110.

43. Dennis Fulton, "American Files Suit Against Texas Air," *Dallas Morning News* (October 16, 1987): 1D.

44. Dennis Fulton, "AMR Earnings Sag 27.8% in Quarter," *Dallas Morning News* (October 15, 1987): 6D.

45. "AMR's American Air Traffic," *Wall Street Journal* (October 12, 1987): 6.

46. "U.S. Majors," p. 100.

47. "Allegis Completes Hilton Sale," *Wall Street Journal* (October 15, 1987): 5.

48. James P. Miller, "Ford to Acquire U.S. Leasing for $68 a Share," *Wall Street Journal* (October 12, 1987): 2.

49. McKellin, "Air Transport Industry," p. 257.

50. Ibid., p. 265.

51. Ibid.

52. Ibid.

53. Ibid.

54. Ibid.

55. "Pan Am Proposal Requires Greater Worker Concessions," *Dallas Morning News* (October 15, 1987): 3D.

56. Laurie McGinley, "Consumer Gripes About Air Service Fell in September," *Wall Street Journal* (October 12, 1987): 29.

57. McKellin, "Air Transport Industry," p. 268.

58. Paulette Thomas, "Texas Air's Continental Unit Posts Drop in September Passenger Load to 56.2%," *Wall Street Journal* (October 7, 1987): 6.

59. Ibid.

60. Ibid.

61. Dennis Fulton, "Continental Reports September Performance," *Dallas Morning News* (October 16, 1987): 4D.

62. "U.S. Majors," p. 108.

63. Ibid.

64. Ibid.

65. McKellin, "Air Transport Industry," p. 271.

66. "U.S. Majors," p. 115.

67. Ibid.

68. Ibid.

69. Ibid.

70. McKellin, "Air Transport Industry," p. 270.

71. Delta's Soft Landing," p. 71.

72. Delta Air Lines, Inc. *1987 Annual Report,* p. 6.

73. Ibid., pp. 17–18.

74. Ibid., 8.

75. Ibid., p. 5.

76. Ibid., p. 4.

77. "Delta's Soft Landing," p. 69.

78. Delta Air Lines, Inc. *1986 Annual Report,* p. 2.

79. Delta Air Lines, Inc., *1987 Annual Report,* p. 12

80. Ibid., p. 13.

81. "FAA Faults Delta," p. 1A

82. Ibid., p. 1A.

83. Ibid., p. 28A.

84. Clemens P. Work, "The Gremlins in the Sky," *U.S. News and World Report* (July 20, 1987): 12–13.

85. "NTSB Documents Observations of Weather Prior to Delta Crash," *Aviation Week and Space Technology* (November 10, 1986): 89.

86. Ann Reeks, "Tranquilizer Affected Captain of Flight 191, Witness Contends," *Dallas Morning News* (December 9, 1987): 29A.

87. David Tarrant, "Delta 191 Pilot Used Tranquilizer," *Dallas Morning News* (November 15, 1987): 37A.

88. Ibid.

CASE 26

CLUB MED, INC.

ROBERT P. VICHAS

INTRODUCTION

Forbes magazine labeled it "Trouble in Paradise." Richard Phalon wrote in 1988, "Club Med, that once lusty purveyor of packaged sea, sand and sun vacations, is slipping into middle age bearing all the signs of an identity crisis. There are times when an income statement can be more unforgiving than a mirror."[1] Earnings per share had declined 6 percent despite a nearly 10 percent rise in sales; the equity market had become disenchanted with the stock; political and labor problems had caused temporary closings in Haiti and the Turks and Caicos Islands at the same time the popular Paradise Island (The Bahamas) resort was closed for renovations.

A year later in *Forbes,* Club Med responded, "I Am Sorry, We Have Changed."[2] Joshua Levine wrote in 1989, "With a new $12 million advertising campaign, Club Med, Inc. is shedding its old image as an endlessly partying, global singles bar. The playboy-playgirl image that Club Med has projected for the last 21 years is being rejected by much of the crucial U.S. market. An aging, more family-oriented U.S. has outgrown the Club Med of the 1970s."[3]

Does peace prevail anew in paradise? Club Med was restructured organizationally. It initiated a strategic shift from an international to a global concept. It refocused its North American marketing strategies. It developed a worldwide growth strategy for the 1990s. Revenues for Club Med, Inc. in 1989 rose 12 percent over 1988, while operating profits increased 128 percent during the same period.

Will Club Med's strategy for the 1990s steer the multinational corporation (MNC) through the straits of adversity, or did management build a castle of

Source: **Prepared by Professor Robert P. Vichas, Florida Atlantic University, as a basis for classroom discussion and not to illustrate either effective or ineffective handling of administrative situations. The author acknowledges the contributions of R. Carl Moor and the assistance of researchers Phil Breakwell, David Spencer, Mark Deary, and Luis Figuereido. © Robert P. Vichas, 1990.**

sand? Serge Trigano, chief executive officer (CEO) of Club Med, Inc., under-stood the challenge well. He said, "We are beginning 1990, the 40th year of the Club Med concept, with an aggressive strategy for growth. The challenge will be to execute this strategy effectively while rapidly adapting to changes in our markets."

HISTORY

A manager's life was not always filled with so many challenges at Club Med. One might have characterized it as idyllic, albeit primitive—a tranquil life on a Mediterranean island. Gerard Blitz, a Belgian, dreamed of providing war-weary continentals a vacation ambience, away from the afflictions and adver-sities found in a post–World War II Europe, which emphasized sports and love. Gilbert Trigano's family business sold army surplus tents—the ideal guest accommodations for communal bliss.

On the Spanish island Majorca, in Alcudia, Blitz established the first Club Méditerranée village in 1950, where guests helped cook meals and wash dishes and during balmy evenings, under the blue savannah of Mediterranean skies specked with white stars of universal love, discussed the harsh realities of cap-italism before snuggling down into sleeping bags. Despite its "escape from civilization" concept, Club Méditerranée was predestined for cascading changes and gushing growth from the day Blitz first approached Trigano, the tent seller, for his ideas.

A French Communist whose parents were Moroccan Jews, Gilbert Trigano fought in the communist resistance during World War II, became a reporter with the communist daily, *L'Humanité*, after liberation of France, then drifted into the family tent business.[4] After joining Club Med in 1954 as managing director (MD), Trigano became its gale-level force.

Nevertheless, not everything sailed smoothly for the newly embarked ven-ture. Although the firm had nearly run aground by the end of the decade, the threatening fog of financial distress dissipated in the sunshine of a new decade in 1961. A rescue ship, in the name of Groupe Edmond de Rothschild, took controlling interest in the sinking Club Med in exchange for a £1.0 million towline. Rothschild subsequently reduced its interest to 2.8 percent.

Transforming the back-to-nature dream of primitive paradise and eternal bliss (for a week or two) into a concept of uninhibited play in the sun, a romp in the sand, and discarding the cares, and clothes, of civilization, Trigano forged a highly profitable chain of resort-villages in France, Italy, Greece, and Africa. Polynesian-styled huts and bungalows replaced tents and sleeping bags. Today, pampered guests, in luxurious accommodations nestled on hilltops along the French Riviera, no longer need cook and wash dishes.

Chronologically, the firm opened its first straw hut village in 1954, its first ski resort in Leysin, Switzerland, in 1965, and in the American Zone its first village in 1968, and the first family "Mini-Club" in 1974. In 1976, the MNC acquired a 45 percent interest in Valtur, an Italian company, which had holiday villages in Italy, Greece, and Tunisia mainly for an Italian market. (Club Med either leased or operated many of its villages under management contract.) As an additional corporate activity, the MNC maintained time-sharing apartments and hotels. Although most members were French in the 1950s, by 1980 the proportion of French visitors had dropped to 45 percent of the total. From global headquarters in Paris (France), Club Méditerranée marketed its products worldwide.

In late 1981, when the firm again attempted decentralization, Serge Trigano, Gilbert's son, assumed leadership of the American Zone. It also began marketing its Rent-a-Village program that year to large corporations for meetings and market incentives.

Then, on May 17, 1984, the firm incorporated its American Zone in the Cayman Islands (B.W.I.) as Club Med, Inc. (CMI), a wholly owned subsidiary of Club Méditerranée S.A. It hoisted a new slogan: "The perfect climate for body and soul." To help Serge Trigano relocate from Paris to New York in 1984, the corporation loaned him $1.4 million, interest free[5]—a sufficient sum, even at Big Apple 1984 prices, for a capacious tent.

With Serge Trigano as its CEO, CMI was chartered to develop markets and operate in the United States and Canada, Mexico, The Bahamas and rest of the Caribbean, Southeast Asia, South Pacific, and parts of the Indian Ocean Basin; while Club Méditerranée, retaining responsibilities for marketing and operations in the rest of the world (Europe, Africa, and South America), mainly focused toward its European market. Worldwide, the organization maintained operations in 35 countries on 5 continents. CMI went public in September 1984. Its initial public offering in the U.S. of 3.4 million shares of common stock was oversubscribed at $17.00 per share. (Club Méditerranée shares traded on French, Luxembourg, and Belgian exchanges.) In the same month, CMI signed an agreement with the Seibu Saison Group, a Japanese retail and real estate firm, to develop resorts in Japan. A summer mountain resort and winter ski village, Club Med–Sahoro, opened on the island of Hokkaido in December 1987.

The original Trigano formula was to construct villages in exotic places and operate the business as a membership organization. What was Club Med's business? Some say it was the pleasure business. Club Med recently answered the question this way:

> What is Club Med? Quite simply, an inimitable style of vacation, based on some very simple ideas:
>   The first is to select the most beautiful locations in the world, and there build our leisurely vacation villages.
>   The next is to offer every activity imaginable to make your vacation ideal.

Then we carefully select a multinational, multilingual team of Gentils Organisateurs (G.O.s, or congenial hosts).

Finally, we give our villages a sense of complete freedom.[6]

In 1989, the New York office of Club Med circulated a "Club Med Fact Sheet." It stated that the world's largest vacation village organization (actually the eleventh-largest hotel chain) offered vacationers "unique, all-inclusive escapes from the stresses of daily life in some of the world's most exotic and scenic locations." Although the original concept remained intact throughout its 40 years of operations, product variations abounded.

For instance, Club Med entered the corporate meeting and incentive market with its Rent-a-Village. More than two dozen corporations, by the end of 1989, had rented parts of or an entire village. The MNC hosted several vacations for Sober Vacations International, a travel firm which specialized in vacations for recovering alcoholics and their families. Some villages added NAUI and PADI certification scuba diving programs as well as an English-style riding instructional workshop and lectures. In later years the organization cast off strictly sun and sand vacations and added ski, mountain, and other scenic settings to appeal to a diversity of tastes. (See Exhibit 1.)

June 1989 marked the opening of Club Med Opio, a 1,000-bed, 125-acre luxury village nestled in the hills behind Cannes on the French Riviera with a 360-degree view of the sea coast and mountains. The model for future Club Med villages, Opio offered luxury rooms, turkish baths, full convention and seminar facilities plus an 18-hole golf course and a 9-hole executive course designed by Cabell Robinson.

Brought online in 1989, the firm promoted a new Mini Club at St. Lucia for children. The Caribbean resort offered horseback riding for children ages 8 to 12 and flexi-vacations to encourage visitors to take long weekends at Club Med or combine a village stay with visits to nearby tourist attractions. An example of the new style village, Huatulco (Mexico), boasted five restaurants, larger rooms, and private terraces. Paradise Island (The Bahamas) and The Sandpiper (Florida) were repositioned as prime short-stay villages. Also, during the year, special honeymooners' packages were launched at Moorea, Bora, Caravelle, Huatulco, and Paradise Island, with an additional one planned for Club Med I.

In 1990, Club Med spread sail on luxury packages aboard the s/v Club Med I, the world's largest automated sailing vessel. The 617-foot ship, with five masts and seven passenger decks, would cruise the Mediterranean Sea during spring and summer months and the Caribbean in winter.

Besides the honeymoon specials and Mediterranean cruise package, Club Med introduced a professional golf academy at The Sandpiper, Culinary Week where renowned French chefs might even share culinary secrets with guests, flexi-vacations, and expanded sports programs.

With its broader line of products, added amenities in many villages to include locks on doors, ice machines, even occasional telephones and televisions,

EXHIBIT 1   THE AMERICAN WAY

"The pleasure of leisure is control," said Ron Paul, president of marketing consultant Technomic, Inc. of Chicago. "Consumers have lost control in recent years, not just over their careers but even over things like how long it takes to get somewhere by car or airplane."

People ages 18–29 prefer to spend leisure time away from home, unlike older baby boomers. Conservatives are more likely to prefer staying at home than liberals. Southerners are the biggest homebodies of all.

The *Wall Street Journal,* through the Roper Organization, asked more than 2,000 American adults to choose from a list of purchased entertainment experiences. Some results are summarized below. [*Source:* Meg Cox, "Staying at Home for Entertainment," *The American Way of Buying* (New York: Dow Jones & Company, 1990): 37–38.]

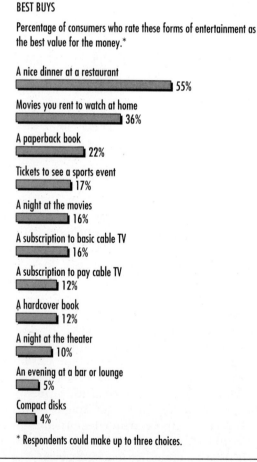

BEST BUYS

Percentage of consumers who rate these forms of entertainment as the best value for the money.*

A nice dinner at a restaurant
55%

Movies you rent to watch at home
36%

A paperback book
22%

Tickets to see a sports event
17%

A night at the movies
16%

A subscription to basic cable TV
16%

A subscription to pay cable TV
12%

A hardcover book
12%

A night at the theater
10%

An evening at a bar or lounge
5%

Compact disks
4%

* Respondents could make up to three choices.

Source: The Wall Street Journal Centennial Survey.

and someday perhaps telefax, plus 110 vacation villages located in 35 coun-tries, Club Med expected to appeal to a wider range of clientele: singles and couples, retired persons and children, organizations and businesses, profes-sionals and the wealthy, the adventurer and the timid. CMI, in 1990, owned, operated, or managed 26 vacation villages throughout its geographical area, 5 archeological villas in Mexico, 2 in Beijing, PRC, and retained the exclusive rights to sell vacation packages at resorts operated by Club Méditerranée. (See Exhibit 2.)

EXHIBIT 2   ONE FAMILY'S PERSPECTIVE

Kevin and Karin fit the U.S. member profile in terms of age, income, and professional status. They enjoyed year-round sports: skiing, diving, horseback riding, sailing, swim-ming. They had frequently visited Club Med villages in Europe, the Caribbean and U.S. They like the activities, security of no surprises and of what to expect from each visit. Besides being a vacationer, Kevin was also a potential investor. Therefore, he carefully observed the care and management of the properties with an eye on potential future growth and competition.

After several visits to the Martinique village in the Caribbean, they witnessed sig-nificant deterioration. Kevin said, "When we first started going to Club Martinique, most of the guests were professionals like ourselves. Then Club Med started running vacation specials from New York City. For an $18 an hour New Yorker who might be a street sweeper, the vacation special was cheap. They were noisy, partying all night. They got off the plane drunk. They were rowdy people who didn't fit with the tradi-tional Club Martinique visitor. We didn't need that kind of environment, so we stopped going there. We now go to Copper Mountain, Colorado [a Club Med ski vil-lage]." Kevin interpreted the changing character of Club Martinique as a signal of increasing competitive pressures.

Although Kevin and Karin had visited Copper Mountain twice and planned a return trip in winter 1991, they were unimpressed with the management of that village. "Every village has its local clown," explained Kevin, "but after a day on the slopes, we like to sip our drinks quietly in front the fireplace and meet new people. This clown is loud, doing nothing anyone really thinks is funny, and it's not the before-dinner environment we prefer. Besides, in American villages, they turn the children loose around six, before dinner, so the kids can eat with their parents. We don't care for the noise or children activity while enjoying a gourmet feast. By contrast, in Europe," Kevin continued, "the villages offer more hours of babysitting. Children eat together and join parents after dinner at 9 o'clock. It's a more sophisticated atmosphere."

Kevin did not like Club Med as an investment in 1990 any more than he did in 1985. "They seem to be growing for the sake of expansion. There's no quality growth, and I think village managers need more training and experience. Club Med is trying to be all things to all people, and I believe the increased competition, expecially in the U.S., has created some corporate panic."

Will Kevin and Karin return to a Club Med village? "We'll probably return to Copper Mountain. And I'm interested in the new sailing ship. We'll go back to Europe; we like it better," he added.

MARKETING

Typically, the firm marketed to its GMs (*gentils membres* or gentle members) an all-inclusive prepaid vacation package. It included transportation, lodging, three meals daily, wine and beer with meals, most sports and leisure activities, and evening entertainment. Additional fees for liquor, golfing, and horseback riding increased total vacation expenditures. Worldwide there were about 1.2 million GMs. The number of GMs visiting CMI villages rose from 383,600 in 1988 to 425,600 in 1989.

The key to success in the 1980s lay in the effective implementation of a carefully orchestrated marketing and ad campaign begun in 1980 to convey the message that Club Med was for everyone. The ad budget was raised from $8 million in 1983 to $10 million by 1985 to $12 by 1989 and $25 million for 1990. Management said that expanding penetration in the upscale vacation market was the goal of the firm's five new 30-second television ads. These presented vignettes of vacation possibilities available to singles, couples, and families. About three-fourths of the ad budget was assigned for television ads, the remainder for newspapers, primarily, and magazines, secondarily. Hard copy ads in newspapers and magazines featured testimonials from a variety of vacationers; this represented a new thrust for Club Med. Radio spots were aired during summer 1990. Nevertheless, the American Zone promotion budget exceeded that of its European counterpart about fourfold.

Paris had its own strategic decisions to make. Serge Trigano said, "We decided that we had three options: to remain a French company and lose markets elsewhere; to compete in each market; or to become European." The first option was inconsistent with the firm's global perspective. The second option would have led to catastrophic results. Trigano said, "If we had built a village just for, say, the German market, we would have had huge occupancy problems. The German market is at its peak in May and June and falls off in July and August." The third option meant acceptance of Europeanization. "In 1992, 1993, or whenever, we will all be Europe. So why not try to be European before Europe?" asked Trigano.[7]

The new brochure would market five levels of products. Level One would market a half-board holiday at a low basic price to overcome price resistance. Level Two would be the classical Club Med product. Level Three would appeal to those who travel business class, want a single room with telephone, and eat breakfast anytime before midday. Level Four consisted of a new product, packaged tours for people who wanted to explore a country. Serge Trigano said, "In the 1991 brochure we will introduce our own tour operator. The margins won't be high, but these tours will bring new customers, more traffic to airlines, and better occupancy in our hotels and villas." Level Five represented a combination of new products and new marketing. Gilbert Trigano envisioned a future, "maybe 50 years from now," when communications would be such that companies would not need working places, only meeting places.

CMI identified families as a fast growing market segment. About 40 percent of members were married, 40 percent had children, and 8 percent of its

EXHIBIT 3   1989 SURVEY OF NORTH AMERICAN MEMBERSHIP

Married members	40%
Single, divorced, or widowed	60%
Members with children	40%
Members who are children	8%
Membes between ages 25 and 44	71%
Members who are college graduates	72%
Percentage holding post-graduate degrees	28%
Professionals, executives, managers	68%
Proportion of repeat visitors	51%
Median age	35
Median household income (annual)	$60,000
Percent reporting incomes exceeding $75,000	36%
Percent reporting incomes exceeding $100,000	21%

Source: Club Med, Inc., "Club Med Facts," April 1989.

members were children. (See Exhibit 3 for a profile of the North American membership.) By late 1989, CMI had opened eight Mini Clubs and two Baby Clubs, which offered child care and activities up to 12 hours a day and one or two nurses 24 hours each day. The Baby Club, debuted in April 1985 at Club Med Fort Royal in Guadaloupe, was for infants and toddlers ages 4 to 23 months. Some units provided adjoining rooms for parents and their children. Management estimated that more than 100,000 children worldwide shared vacations with parents each year.

To develop a marketing style appropriate for the 1990s, management decided to be European rather than compete in each separate market. Seventeen villages were selected for an international flavor, where the MNC would guarantee to customers a welcome in their own language. Instead of a single package, several options surfaced during the 1980s to appeal to different customer segments. Forty new villages were planned for 1990–1995.

In Asia, the marketing slogan was "Absolutely Paradise." Occupancy in the Asian Zone was less subject to seasonal fluctuations: Australian and New Zealand markets have seasons reversed from Japan and the U.S. However, to improve occupancy in Asian Zone villages subject to seasonal fluctuations, Club Med maintained constant reduced off-season rates and raised in-season prices during 1989. It also opened a sales office in Taiwan.

The fastest growing Asian segment, the Japanese market, between 1984 and 1988 grew 200 percent. Links with Seibu Saison gave Club Med crucial distribution outlets through its stores. New destinations in Florida and The Bahamas were promoted to the Japanese during 1989. The firm advertised its Mexican villages to them in 1990.

Travel agents accounted for about 85 percent of vacation packages of

CMI. Typically they earned 10 percent commission on each package sold. By contrast, Club Méditerranée in Paris direct-booked about 70 percent of its business. The U.S. travel agent program embraced four- to five-day training sessions at clubs to acquaint agents with services. Following the on-site visit, agents would then receive a barrage of promotional materials, direct mail flyers, storefront decorations, mailing lists, newsletters, sales manuals, and a priority clearance for the next season. Despite implementation of this program, some travel agents claimed that Club Med's marketing efforts tended to neglect, even offend, them. Club Med responded by increasing its sales force from 7 regional managers and a 6-person "flying team" of troubleshooters to 23 regional and district sales managers with plans to double its sales force by the end of 1991.[8]

Two Florida travel agents interviewed in 1990 said that in the past Club Med had been reluctant to pay commissions. Now, they said, the MNC was increasing commissions (which could reach 18 percent on selected packages), and had improved communications regarding new tour offerings. A New Jersey travel agent, who sold many Club Med vacation packages in 1988, believed that the firm had difficulty selling itself to older clientele in an increasingly competitive market. The agent said, "The idea of free sex and a lot of drinking really turns off the older, more sophisticated people Club Med is trying to reach."[9]

PRICING

Club Med offered a variety of vacation packages: custom-tailored vacations, honeymoon specials, length-of-stay and transportation flexibility, sailing ship cruises, family villages, singles vacations, luxury packages, as well as standard ones. Children, ages 2 to 5, could stay free at selected locations and dates.

Advance booking, when confirmed, required a 25-percent prepayment per person plus membership fees: an initiation fee of $30 plus annual membership fee of $50 per family. Membership fees included illness and medical insurance coverage through a policy issued by Union des Assurances de Paris. Final payment for airfare, housing, meals, and entertainment was due 30 days prior to departure. Club Med earned additional income on the float. Although guests could settle accounts for beverages, sports equipment, and rentals when they checked out, not all villages accepted all credit cards for personal expenses, and none accepted personal checks.

The inclusive price did not cover costs of entry and exit visas or airport taxes, transfers, beverages after meal periods, snacks, beach towels, optional excursions, equipment rentals, horseback riding, and deep sea fishing. The strict 44-pound per person luggage allowance necessitated careful packing, because Club Med policy specifically excluded such carry-on items as garment bags and backpacks; extra charges were made for scuba gear and surfboards. Flight times, not guaranteed, were subject to change; other exceptions and caveats suggested careful perusal of the contract. Nevertheless, more than one-half of the firm's business derived from repeat customers, some of whom were frequent visitors. The following samples of prices represented published off-season rates for summer and fall 1990.

The Honeymoon Package at Caravelle (Guadaloupe) between May 5th and June 23rd, for two, was $1,998 from New York City and $1,898 from Miami. Double rooms were basic with shower and 220 voltage (adapters not furnished). The facility featured water sports, golf, tennis and archery, and a fitness center plus nightly entertainment and dancing, and even a video room with large-screen TV (no television in rooms). The "special honeymoon gift" for newlyweds included:

> a bottle of imported champagne on ice, 2 exclusive Club Med souvenir T-shirts, a basket of fruit, 2 complimentary packages of bar beads [i.e., Club Med money, prepaid with hard currency, used to settle the bar bill, and unused beads were nonrefundable], a private cocktail party for honeymooners only hosted by the Village Manager. Please ask for the honeymoon gift package at time of booking.[10]

Other off-season rates (usually May 5th to December 15th), per week, per person, double occupancy, payable only in U.S. dollars, from major U.S. cities—Chicago, Washington, D.C., Atlanta, New York City—follow (rates for children ages 6 to 11, if available, are in parentheses): Bora, Tahiti, $2,100 ($1,315); Opio, French Riviera, $1,625; St. Lucia, Caribbean, $1,200 ($1,100); Eleuthera, The Bahamas, $1,100 ($650); Huatulco ($1,000) or Ixtapa, Mexico, $1,200 ($700). (Prices are approximate since figures are rounded to simplify comparison.)

To compete with popular cruise ship and airline offers, independent tour operators, i.e., any person who could put together an affinity group of 20 or more persons, could earn discounts up to 15 percent. Those resorts which offered short-term stays charged an average $165 per day.

For more luxurious accommodations, Club Opio, 12 miles from Cannes (France), supplied air conditioned rooms with telephone, satellite television, bath with a tub, and hairdryer (guests still provided their own adaptors to convert the 220 volts to user-friendly currents). "Fashioned after a typical Provincial hamlet, [Club Opio] . . . unfolds on 125 acres of undulating countryside, in the midst of olive trees, pine forests, and flowering gardens, at an altitude of 990 feet. There are 5 restaurants, an outdoor and a heated indoor pool, piano bar, theatre, bridge room, movie and meeting room, and boutique. Opio welcomes ages 12 and over." All of this, for a week of fun, at summer rates, was offered for $1,850 from Los Angeles or $1,725 from Miami, double occupancy, of course.

After a week at Club Opio, one might depart from Pointe-a-Pitre (Cannes) aboard the 14,000 ton Club Med 1, of Bahamian registry, the fully automated 5-sail (sails could be raised or lowered in 90 seconds) ship, on a 19-day "The Big Blue" tour. Single rates varied from $3,420 on the Bali (lower) Deck to $6,150 for a suite on the Foca Deck. More modest weekly rates for the "Mediterranean Cruise" depended on the week chosen. Late June 1990, weekly rates ranged between $775 and $1,620 for singles, in contrast to mid-August rates of $2,490 to $4,620. Nevertheless, three persons to an outside cabin could sail a week on the blue Mediterranean for as little as $415 per person in late June or as much as $1,330 each in mid-August.

On the other (deck) hand, a "Caribbean Cruise" aboard the same ship between late September and mid-December cost a little more. Although three in an outside cabin (Bali Deck) could sail for low season rates of $1,075, or the week of November 17th for $1,330, singles on the Bali Deck must pay $2,010 and $2,490, respectively, or $3,780 and $4,620 for a Foca Deck suite. All Club Med 1 prices above excluded air fare.

Soft drinks, wine, and liquor, on board, cost $2 to $4 each. Medical services and duty-free items were also pricey, as well as laundry: "men's pajamas $5.40," "men's silk pajamas $6.40."[11]

The 442-passenger ship boasted 8 decks of Burmese teak and the latest maritime technology. Created by world-famous designer Alberto Pinto, its interior comprised a small casino operated by Casinos Austria, 197 guest quarters, "2 posh restaurants; 4 cocktail lounges; a nightclub; a large boutique with a duty-free shop; a health center with massage, sauna, and U.V. tanning machines; a beauty salon; and a multi-purpose hall for conferences, movies, shows, and special events."[12] Rooms measured about 188 square feet and suites 321 square feet, each with local and closed circuit television (mostly in French), radio, telephone, mini-bar, and private bathroom with hair dryer and bathrobe, plus 24 hour-a-day room service for a price (e.g., $4.50 for a chicken sandwich).

ORGANIZATION

Club Méditerranée began with a very simple and informal organizational structure: Gilbert Trigano appointed some friends and original vacationers, to manage different vacation spots in Europe. Gradually, a more complex, functional structure evolved and remained in place until 1971. Between 1971 and 1976, the organizational structure was modified. Area managers were named and had 10 to 15 village managers reporting to each. Because operationally it seemed as though several Club Meds had been created, management reverted to the pre-1971 structure after 1976.[13] The pre-1971 structure prevailed until the early 1980s, at which time management considered reorganization.

Five key goals dominated the organization:

1. Trigano wanted to double capacity every five years either by adding new villages or increasing the size of existing ones.
2. Innovation drove decisions to make Club Med different from other hotel chains and to respond to changing customer needs.
3. The firm sought to internationalize personnel and its strategy because the proportion of French customers was diminishing.

4. To remain price competitive, management sought ways to improve productivity and control rising costs by standardization of procedures.

5. Trigano insisted on retaining the original concept: protect the villages from the outside world and yet identify with each local environment as closely as possible.[14]

However, as markets changed, new products were introduced, and geographical diversification occurred, the organizational structure hindered more than facilitated efficient implementation of the corporate strategy. For instance, Serge Trigano, MD of operations, discovered that reporting to him were corporate managing directors, 16 country managers, 100 chiefs of village plus 8 product managers. The structure was too centralized: information overload; too much detail; difficult to adapt to the international character of customers; bottlenecks in assignments and supervision of personnel.

The corporation still recruited its GOs[15] from France, despite the fact that Americans accounted for 20 percent of business—which created a potential language and cultural barrier. Additionally, poor communications existed between marketing and operations.[16]

Consequently, the MNC was reorganized along the lines illustrated in Exhibits 4 and 5. Some aspects of the old structure remained the same, viz., the chief executive officer (CEO) and his managing directors (MDs) of financial affairs and new development. At the next level, titles of functional MDs were changed to joint MDs (JMDs) to suggest unity among various functional activities.

In another major structural change at the corporate level management combined the MDs of marketing and operations (M&O). The new MD participated both in operations and promotions of vacation programs, according to Jean Manre Darbouze, a CMI manager in New York City. Instead of assigning responsibilities for managing all product directors, country and village managers directly, a new level of managers, closer to actual areas of operation, now reported to the JMD of M&O.

Two regional JMDs of M&O assumed responsibility to internationalize these activities. The JMD for the American Zone controlled activities in North and South America, the Caribbean, and Tahiti. The JMD of the European Zone controlled activities in Europe, Australia, and the Far East. Geographical regions were subdivisionalized by country for each of which a country manager was appointed.

To avoid duplication, the MNC layered product directors between the corporate JMD of M&O and regional JMDs to facilitate global coordination of products through product directors at an upper management level, who could examine challenges worldwide instead of the more narrow country focus.

The villages, at the lowest level of the organizational chart in Exhibit 4, are illustrated in greater detail in Exhibit 5. The *Chef de Village*, (Chief of Village), at the heart of implementing Club Med's M&O strategies, dealt with daily operations, managed the many GOs, coordinated GO activities with the various programs, and was the direct link between customers and upper

EXHIBIT 4 CLUB MED, INC.: ORGANIZATIONAL STRUCTURE

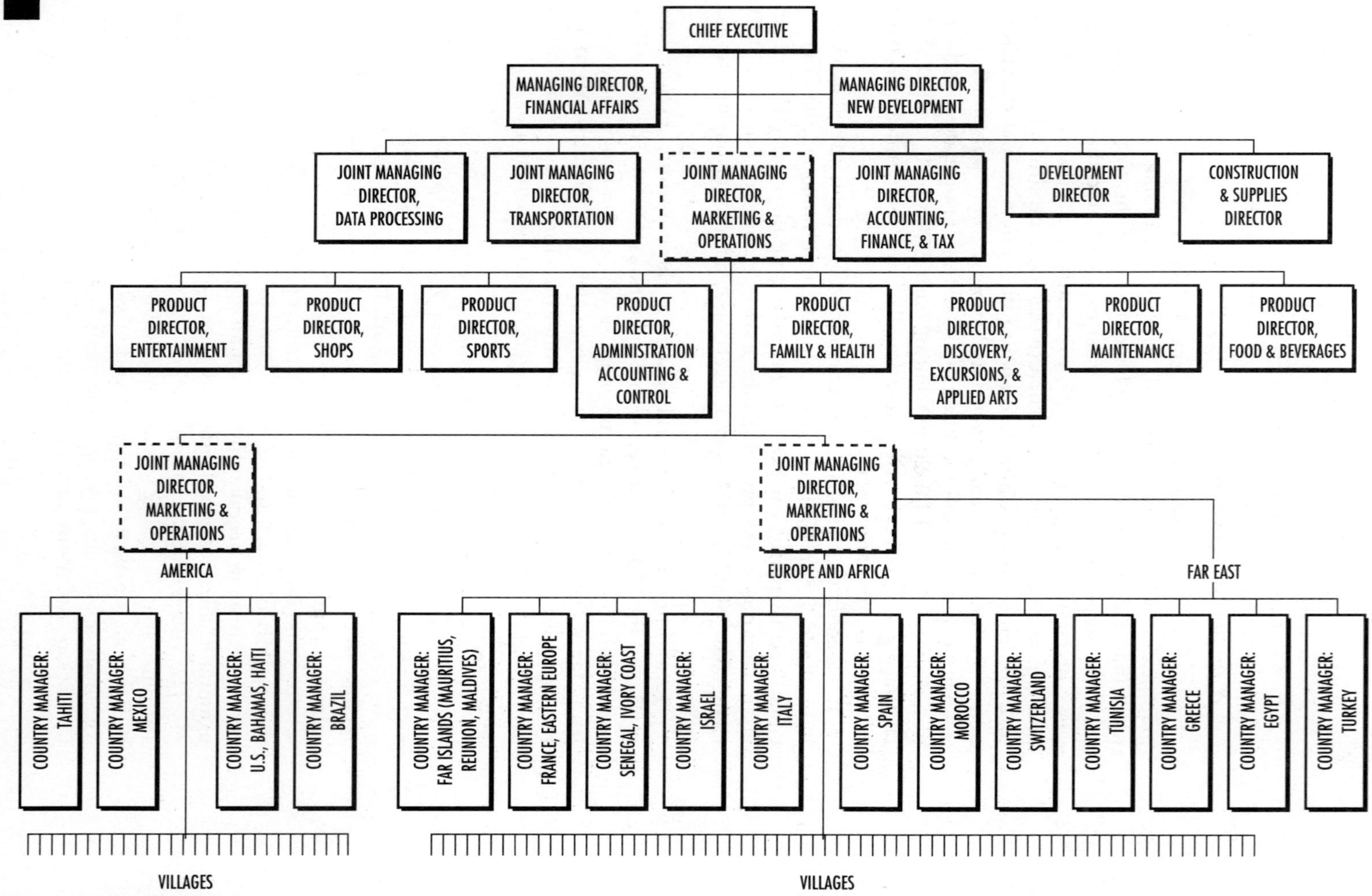

CHIEF EXECUTIVE

- MANAGING DIRECTOR, FINANCIAL AFFAIRS
- MANAGING DIRECTOR, NEW DEVELOPMENT
  - DEVELOPMENT DIRECTOR
  - CONSTRUCTION & SUPPLIES DIRECTOR

- JOINT MANAGING DIRECTOR, DATA PROCESSING
- JOINT MANAGING DIRECTOR, TRANSPORTATION
- JOINT MANAGING DIRECTOR, ACCOUNTING, FINANCE, & TAX
- JOINT MANAGING DIRECTOR, MARKETING & OPERATIONS

Product Directors:
- PRODUCT DIRECTOR, ENTERTAINMENT
- PRODUCT DIRECTOR, SHOPS
- PRODUCT DIRECTOR, SPORTS
- PRODUCT DIRECTOR, ADMINISTRATION ACCOUNTING & CONTROL
- PRODUCT DIRECTOR, FAMILY & HEALTH
- PRODUCT DIRECTOR, DISCOVERY, EXCURSIONS, & APPLIED ARTS
- PRODUCT DIRECTOR, MAINTENANCE
- PRODUCT DIRECTOR, FOOD & BEVERAGES

JOINT MANAGING DIRECTOR, MARKETING & OPERATIONS — AMERICA

VILLAGES
- COUNTRY MANAGER: TAHITI
- COUNTRY MANAGER: MEXICO
- COUNTRY MANAGER: U.S., BAHAMAS, HAITI
- COUNTRY MANAGER: BRAZIL

JOINT MANAGING DIRECTOR, MARKETING & OPERATIONS — EUROPE AND AFRICA / FAR EAST

VILLAGES
- COUNTRY MANAGER: FAR ISLANDS (MAURITIUS, REUNION, MALDIVES)
- COUNTRY MANAGER: FRANCE, EASTERN EUROPE
- COUNTRY MANAGER: SENEGAL, IVORY COAST
- COUNTRY MANAGER: ISRAEL
- COUNTRY MANAGER: ITALY
- COUNTRY MANAGER: SPAIN
- COUNTRY MANAGER: MOROCCO
- COUNTRY MANAGER: SWITZERLAND
- COUNTRY MANAGER: TUNISIA
- COUNTRY MANAGER: GREECE
- COUNTRY MANAGER: EGYPT
- COUNTRY MANAGER: TURKEY

EXHIBIT 5 CLUB MED, INC.: ORGANIZATIONAL STRUCTURE AT THE VILLAGE LEVEL

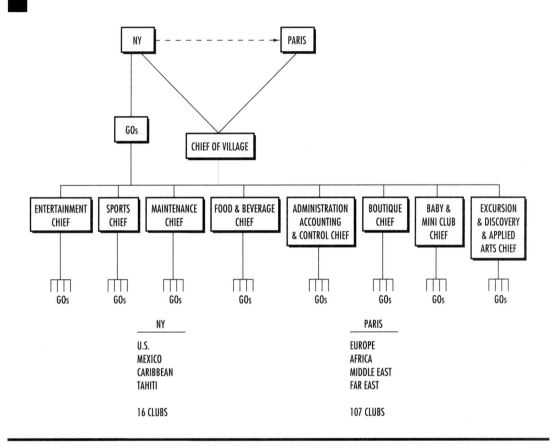

management. Through regionalization, problems surfaced at the village level were dealt with at a lower level in the new organizational hierarchy. Further, the *Chefs de Village* were now selected from many countries to make this element of operations truly multinational.

At the top of the organization, the Triganos remained firmly in charge. Gilbert Trigano, aged 69, long ago had left the Communist Party, although his sympathies lay with the political left. "The Communists saved my life," he said to a reporter in 1985. He was a long-time friend of socialist French president François Mitterand. In 1985, Mitterand named Trigano to head a project to train thousands of jobless persons to use computers.[17] Gilbert Trigano remained chairman of the board of CMI and chairman of the board, CEO, and MD of Club Méditerranée S.A.

His son, Serge Trigano, born in Paris, May 24, 1946, headed CMI as vice chairman of the board and CEO. Serge worked as a GO during college breaks from the Faculté de Droit et Science (Paris), where he earned a degree in economics. After serving as *Chef de Village* in six villages, he was considered executive material. In 1981, following some decentralization, Serge assumed leadership of the American Zone and became CEO in 1984 of the newly incorporated CMI. Between 1985 and 1987 he was also Club Méditerranée S.A.'s MD for development and operations of Europe and Africa. In 1987 he became its chief operating officer (COO), dividing time between world headquarters in Paris and offices and villages around the world. Serge concentrated mostly on operational matters, his father on strategic issues.

The president, COO, and chief financial officer (CFO) of CMI, Jean-Luc Oizan-Chapon, who had begun as a GO sports instructor with Club Méditerranée in its early years, later followed Serge Trigano to the American Zone. Other CMI corporate officers included: Alexis Agnello, executive vice president; Jacques Ganin, secretary; and Joseph J. Townsend, treasurer.

CMI board of directors included: Gilbert Trigano, chairman; Serge Trigano, vice chairman; Jacques Giraud, vice chairman; Alexis Agnello; Evan G. Galbraith, former U.S. Ambassador to France, now director international and senior advisor, Morgan Stanley & Co.; Harvey M. Krueger, MD, Shearson Lehman, Hutton Inc.; Stanley Komaroff, partner, Proskauer Rose Goetz & Mendelsohn; Richard A. Voell, president, CEO, The Rockefeller Group.

Stephen Wood described the global organization as too small, too French, with a management system characterized by worship of a 69-year-old guru and a product that was 40 years old.[18] President Jean-Luc Oizan-Chapon admitted that Americans and the French did not always get along well. Wood continued with his analysis, quoting from *Le Figaro:*

> Part of the uncertainty about Club Med's future is due to Trigano's dominant position within it. *Le Figaro* described as a 'delightful euphemism' the comment by a senior Club Med manager that 'the decision-making here is relatively centralized.' Yet, despite his age, to pose the question of Trigano's succession is, the newspaper noted, 'considered as sacreligious inside the club.'[19]

OPERATIONS

The basic operating unit, village or villa or comparable unit, was headed by a *Chef de Village*, who linked customers and JMDs. The life of a *Chef de Village* might be described in the name of Janyck Daudet, the youngest appointed *Chef* at age 26 in 1983. A native of Nîmes, France, he began as a ski instructor in Yugoslavia and worked in clubs from Morocco to Thailand as a GO. (Staff members were reassigned every six months not only to keep them motivated but also because some seasonal villages were closed part of each year.) Typically a GO earned less than minimum wages paid in most industrialized countries, plus room and board, was under age 30 and unmarried. A U.S. GO earned less than $500 a month in 1990. *Chefs* could earn salaries equivalent to a plant manager or possibly middle management. Daudet worked 18 hours a day but was on call 24 hours, 7 days a week, mingled with guests, performed in after-dinner shows, called midnight staff meetings, and maintained a high level of enthusiasm and energy. "It's impossible to do this too long," said Daudet. "It's fun, but you can't keep up this much energy forever."

For approximately every five GMs there was one GO; a GO for sports, dancing instruction, applied arts, excursions, food, bar, accounting, baby sitting, etc. After every season, or every six months, GOs would be moved from one village to another, with the exception of the chief of maintenance and local people hired as service personnel. Having remained firmly intact since inception, the GO concept afforded the firm a competitive advantage, according to management. Worldwide there were more than 8,000 GOs, from 32 countries, in 1990, 25 percent of whom were employed by CMI. About 3,000 new GOs were selected each year from an applicants' pool of 100,000. About one-half of the GOs were former GMs.

Toward the end of the 1980s, hiring French GOs was virtually halted as international teams were employed from the U.K., West Germany, and Italy plus cheaper talent discovered in some less developed countries. In early 1990 Club Méditerranée employed around 250 British GOs to service 17,000 British GMs in popular villages such as Marbella, Kos, Turkey, and Sardinia. Management also considered opening a London Club Med.

Nevertheless, despite this apparent shift in corporate policy, Shirley Slater and Harry Basch, aboard the newly launched Club Med I, wrote in 1990: "We would hope as more Americans travel aboard this elegantly designed ship, all of the Club Med G.O. staff, not just a few, will make necessary adjustments in language and attitude to welcome them."[20] Management said their objective was to achieve a 50-50 GM mix on the ship of Americans and Europeans, but did not indicate whether they intended to achieve a 50-50 GO mix as well.

The American Zone suffered its share of setbacks during fiscal year 1987–1988. Construction delays at Huatulco (1,000 beds) and Playa Blanca (580 beds) in Mexico resulted in lost revenue; openings delayed by a season or two gave competition an edge in these markets. Construction delays in The Bahamas postponed reopening of Paradise Island (670 beds) until February 1988. An adverse political environment resulted in the closing of Magic Isle (704 beds) in Haiti. Occupancy rates declined. (See Exhibit 6 for data on occupancy rates by geographical areas. Exhibit 7 lists worldwide operations.)

The following fiscal year witnessed more problems. Hurricane Gilbert shut down Cancun in September 1988; it reopened in April 1989. Then, in September 1989, Hurricane Hugo caused temporary closings of Caravelle on Guadeloupe and Turkoise in the Turks and Caicos Islands. Eleuthera, closed in May 1989 for renovations, reopened in December 1989. St. George's Cove in Bermuda ceased operations while a sale was negotiated.

On the upside, occupancy rates in the American Zone reached a new high of 66.3 percent; hotel days advanced from 2,000,000 in 1988 to 2,099,000 in 1989. The number of GMs from France and other European countries rose nearly 50 percent; and the number of GMs from Mexico, the Caribbean, and South America increased modestly. Inauguration of the newest 700-bed CMI

EXHIBIT 6   CMI OCCUPANCY AND CAPACITY, 1984–1989

ZONE	1989	1988	1987	1986
AMERICAN ZONE				
Number of Beds				
North America	1,032	1,032	1,030	470
Mexico-Caribbean	8,890	8,956	9,068	9,364
Occupancy (%)				
North America	74.6	68.5	56.5	65.4
Mexico-Caribbean	65.6	65.4	65.7	64.4
ASIAN ZONE				
Number of beds	3,330	3,330	3,250	2,550
Occupancy (%)	73.2	61.5	58.2	47.3
TOTAL AMERICAN AND ASIAN ZONES				
Number of Beds	13,252	13,318	13,348	12,384
Occupancy (%)	68.7	65.2	59.6	60.5

Note: Club Med employs a method significantly different from the lodging or hospitality industry, using beds rather than number of rooms. Therefore data are not comparable with the industry. It reports occupancy in terms of beds, based on two beds per room available for guests. It determines capacity on the basis of the average number of bed days available each year, i.e., the number of beds in each village multiplied by the number of days the village was open annually.

Source: CMI, *1988, 1989 Annual Report,* p. 22 (for both reports).

EXHIBIT 7   CLUB MED, INC. AND CLUB MÉDITERRANÉE: WORLDWIDE OPERATIONS

CLUB MED, INC. VILLAGES,
14,622 BEDS
American Zone

United States, 1,032 beds
Copper Mountain, Colorado
Sandpiper, Florida

Bermuda, 666 beds
St. George's Cove

Bahamas, 1,196 beds
Paradise Island
Eleuthera

Caribbean, 3,688 beds
Turks and Caicos Islands
Turkoise
Haiti
Magic Isle
Dominican Republic
Punta Cana

Guadeloupe
Caravelle
Martinique
Buccaneer's Creek
Saint Lucia
St. Lucia

Mexico, 3,928 beds
Sonora Bay
Playa Blanca
Ixtapa
Huatulco
Cancun
Archaeological villas
Teotihuacan
Cholula
Uxmal
Chichen Itzá
Coba

EXHIBIT 7 (continued)

Tahiti, 782 beds
Moorea
Bora Bora
Asian Zone
Japan, 200 beds
Sahoro
Thailand, 600 beds
Phuket
Malaysia, 600 beds
Cherating
Indonesia, 700 beds
Bali
Republic of Maldives, 250 beds
Farukolufushi
Mauritius, 370 beds
La Pointe aux Canonniers
New Caledonia, 550 beds
Chateau Royal
Villas
Republic of Maldives, 60 beds
Thulagiri
Reunion, 120 beds
Le Lagon**

CLUB MED, INC.
CORPORATE, DIRECT SALES,
AND REPRESENTATIVE OFFICES
North America
Canada
United States
Mexico
Asia
Japan
Taiwan
Hong Kong
Thailand
Malaysia
Singapore
Indonesia
Australia
New Zealand

CLUB MÉDITERRANÉE S.A.
VILLAGES, 50,437 BEDS*
Europe
Portugal, 1 village, 751 beds
Spain, 4 villages, 3,311 beds
France, 15 villages, 7,486 beds
Italy, 7 villages, 7,883 beds
Switzerland, 10 villages, 4,661 beds
Yugoslavia, 2 villages, 2,080 beds
Greece, 6 villages, 5,094 beds
Bulgaria, 1 village, 930 beds
Turkey, 5 villages, 4,164 beds
Africa and the Middle East
Israel, 2 villages, 1,114 beds
Egypt, 2 villages, 620 beds
2 Nile Cruise Ships, 143 beds**
Tunisia, 5 villages, 5,000 beds
Morocco, 7 villages, 4,703 beds
Senegal, 2 villages, 960 beds
Ivory Coast, 1 village, 380 beds
South America
Brazil, 2 villages, 1,300 beds

CLUB MÉDITERRANÉE S.A.
CORPORATE, DIRECT SALES,
AND REPRESENTATIVE OFFICES
Europe
United Kingdom
Spain
France
Italy
Belgium
The Netherlands
Switzerland
West Germany
Sweden
Turkey
South America
Venezuela
Brazil
Peru
Colombia
Argentina

---

*Club Méditerranée S.A. owns, operates, or manages 72 vacation villages and 2 villas (inns) in Europe, Africa, and South America.

**Not included in Club Med, Inc. bed and occupancy figures.

village, under construction on San Salvador (The Bahamas), was anticipated in 1992, in time for the 500th anniversary of Columbus' landing on that island.

Likewise, the Asian Zone in 1989 achieved new records. Occupancy rates attained 73.2 percent, and hotel days increased by 24.4 percent to 857,000. Exhibit 8 breaks down hotel days by zone and origin of business. Japan's market represented the jewel of the Pacific. The Japanese not only visited Sahoro—a winter ski resort and summer mountain resort—in record numbers (70.9 percent occupancy), but traveled in large numbers to locations throughout the Asian and American zones. The Tahitian villages of Moorea and Bora became more accessible via direct Air France flights between Tokyo and Papeete. (Bora had been closed for several months during 1989 for renovation but reopened in September.)

During 1990 CMI expected to increase aggregate bed capacity by nearly 500 at these villages: Sahoro (400 beds), Bali in Indonesia (800 beds) Phuket in Thailand (700 beds), and La Pointe aux Canonniers (440 beds). A new village in Vietnam was planned for the early part of the decade. On the other hand, the number of European visitors to Asia actually decreased from 1987 levels. The table in Exhibit 9 summarizes GMs by nationality groups from all regions of the world, who visited villages owned or managed by the company.

COMPETITION

Club Med had fashioned its worldwide profile during the 1950s. Because its style, and 40-year-old product, might not carry it through the century, management unfurled a strategy of market segmentation for implementation during

EXHIBIT 8   CMI: HOTEL DAYS BY ZONE, 1986–1989

ZONE	1989	1988	1987	1986
AMERICAN ZONE				
American & Canadian	1,480,000	1,510,000	1,495,000	1,574,000
Mexican & Caribbean	113,000	107,000	70,000	130,000
Asian/Pacific/Indian	78,000	71,000	69,000	48,000
French/Other European	394,000	280,000	229,000	211,000
South American	34,000	32,000	28,000	32,000
TOTAL	2,099,000	2,000,000	1,891,000	1,995,000
ASIAN ZONE				
American & Canadian	8,000	4,000	4,000	2,000
Asian/Pacific/Indian	607,000	500,000	429,000	306,000
French/Other European	242,000	185,000	183,000	94,000
TOTAL	857,000	689,000	616,000	402,000

Note: The above table shows the number of hotel days occupied by national groups from major world regions.

Source: CMI, *1988, 1989 Annual Report*, p. 23.

EXHIBIT 9   CMI: NUMBER OF GMs BY NATIONAL ORIGIN, 1986–1989

ZONE & NATIONAL ORIGIN	1989	1988	1987	1986
AMERICAN ZONE				
American & Canadian	215,100	218,100	210,800	220,000
Mexican & Caribbean	18,000	10,500	8,400	20,000
Asian/Pacific/Indian	13,200	12,700	12,500	6,100
French/Other European	38,200	25,500	18,900	17,200
South American	5,000	4,500	3,900	4,400
TOTAL	289,500	271,300	254,500	267,700
ASIAN ZONES				
American & Canadian	1,200	600	600	300
Asian/Pacific/Indian	113,500	94,300	71,100	55,000
French/Other European	21,400	17,400	24,200	9,500
TOTAL	136,100	112,300	95,900	64,800

Source: CMI, *1988, 1989 Annual Report*, p. 23 (for both reports).

the late 1980s and the 1990s. Consequently, the more diverse its products the more the number of new competitors it confronted. By the same token, aggressive competitors, as well as many imitators, also pursued strategies of product and market development, which eroded Club Med's dominant share of its specialty market. Accordingly, occupancy rates suffered.

Despite its global coverage, Club Med was still a small company, based on number of clients, compared with such European rivals as Thompson Travel and the German group, TUI. As a tour operator, Club Med fell from third to seventh place between 1984 and 1988. With growth in its home market of less than 3 percent annually, some 391,000 French clients in 1987–1988, the MNC faced rather limited potential in France.[21] Club Méditerranée was both innovator and imitator. When it launched its Europeanization program, the MNC selected 17 villages for conversion to an international flavor because its biggest competitor, Robinson, had 16 of them.

Trigano waxed philosophical on the changing markets:

When we started, 99 percent of the people in the Paris region had never seen the Mediterranean. I hadn't. Just to see the sea was a considerable emotional event. And in my first year we had a water-ski boat . . . and you could walk on the water. When the Club offered wonders like that, you didn't worry about the accommodation—in U.S. Army surplus tents. We were all together, sharing these wonderful experiences, so we became friends; and that friendship was a sort of powerful cement.

But the sense of discovery has gone now. People just want the best. Club Med can't be the same because life is not the same.

By the end of the 1980s, CMI had encountered customer price resistance, especially apparent in the winter 1988 season, when it raised prices 13 percent. Political unrest and labor problems, coupled with temporary closings, gave competitors an edge during 1988–1989.

Additionally, for many, Florida, with its own attractions, represented the gateway to the Caribbean. Because CMI was also in the vacation business, the term "vacation," which conjured up different images for vacationers, resulted in yet a broader definition of competition for CMI. (Exhibit 10 shows the way travelers perceive travel services.)

The Walt Disney Corporation, for example, attracted to Florida families and foreigners. With operations in California as well as France and Japan, it generated revenues approaching $5 billion and net income exceeding $700 million. It opened Disney/MGM Studios at Lake Buena Vista, Florida, to attract adults. Global revenues rose 150 percent during 1985–1989. Its image might best be summarized in an excerpt from an article in *Restaurants and Institutions:*

> You don't have to be a kid to love Disney's new image. You can be a business executive, for instance, booked into one of three new convention hotels opening next year at Disney World. Or you can be a teenager catching the curl on a boogie board at the new water park. Or a 'thirtysomething' baby boomer sitting in a TV kitchen eating a pot roast that would have done Donna Reed proud.[22]

Although Universal Studios' inauguration in June 1990 threatened direct competition to Disney's MGM, many competing attractions made central Florida even more interesting to vacationing families. With two working studios, the area was expected to become the east coast movie capital. Besides, long-term plans to make Orlando a giant international airline hub, with bullet train service to other Florida cities, could make it a destination city for Asians and Europeans alike. Bargain-basement airfares and tour packages, and a somewhat weaker U.S. dollar, enticed a flood of English and continental travelers to Florida during winter 1989.

Additionally, resorts, catering to an upscale business clientele, represented a lucrative segment of the lodging industry. Firms such as the Marriott Corporation, Holiday Inn, and Hyatt Regency, competing on a level with Club Med, created luxurious upscale resorts in different environmental settings. Conference centers, meeting rooms, quarters for executives, and getaway packages surfaced among American competitors.

EXHIBIT 10   TRAVEL INDUSTRY OUT OF TOUCH

A special *Wall Street Journal* survey, conducted by Peter D. Hart Research Associates, revealed that many believe travel companies often become fixated on services people do not care about, and ignore many services that people consider important. A survey of 403 of America's most frequent travelers (those who take 12 or more trips annually) found that many care little about in-room bars, computerized travel directions, or new

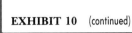

EXHIBIT 10   (continued)

gimmicks. What they do want are simple pleasures: quiet hotel rooms, clean rental cars, comfortable airplane seats.

Travelers like frequent flyer programs, good flight information, nonsmoking hotel rooms, and thick hotel room walls. They also see little real product differentiation among hotels, airlines, or car rentals.

"That's frightening," said John Nicolls, senior V.P. at Hyatt Hotels Corp. "We beat our heads against the wall trying to be different."

The chart below summarizes survey results. [*Source:* Jonathan Dahl, "Giving People What They Don't Want," *The American Way of Buying* (New York: Dow Jones & Company, 1990): 39–40.]

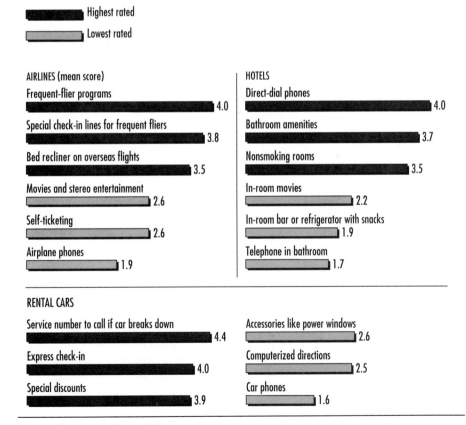

HOW TRAVEL SERVICES STACK UP
Frequent travelers were asked to rank the services that are most important to them in deciding which hotels, airlines, and rental car companies to use. With five being the top possible score, here are the highest and lowest rated services:

Highest rated
Lowest rated

AIRLINES (mean score)
Frequent-flier programs   4.0
Special check-in lines for frequent fliers   3.8
Bed recliner on overseas flights   3.5
Movies and stereo entertainment   2.6
Self-ticketing   2.6
Airplane phones   1.9

HOTELS
Direct-dial phones   4.0
Bathroom amenities   3.7
Nonsmoking rooms   3.5
In-room movies   2.2
In-room bar or refrigerator with snacks   1.9
Telephone in bathroom   1.7

RENTAL CARS
Service number to call if car breaks down   4.4
Express check-in   4.0
Special discounts   3.9

Accessories like power windows   2.6
Computerized directions   2.5
Car phones   1.6

Source: Wall Street Journal Centennial Survey

For instance, the Marriott Corporation, world's seventh-largest hotel chain with approximate 1988 revenues of $7.4 billion and net income of $2.4 million, established resorts in the same locations as Club Med; but these chains had a diversified customer base. Marriott entered new geographical markets, such as Warsaw, Poland, where it managed a 1,000-bed hotel. Similarly, Holiday Inn crated a new line of luxury hotels for executives and vacationers. Although the resort segment of the U.S. lodging industry had been growing steadily, larger national organizations had already set course for markets abroad.[23] Also, as the larger U.S. firms became more family oriented, they developed children programs in their resorts.[24] (See Exhibit 11 for resorts with children programs.) Other competitors, such as Hedonism II, Club Paradise, and Jack Tar Village, in imitation of Club Med, packaged lower priced vacations. Club Med judged these numerous copycat villages to be inconsequential competitors, struggling and second best. Nevertheless, Thomas J. Garzelli, vice president of Fly Fare Vacations, said, "There's no question that the people who are filling up these resorts are the right demographics to go to Club Med."[25] Most copycats, usually located in the Caribbean, were not global players; but they competed effectively in limited markets.

Similarly, in Japan, competition for the leisure yen was triggered by the success of Tokyo Disneyland: 15 million people had visited the theme park by March 31, 1990. Japanese corporations seeking to diversify mostly focused on the Japanese amusement park industry when industry revenues jumped from $1.4 billion (U.S. dollar equivalent) in 1982 to $2.5 billion anticipated for 1990.

EXHIBIT 11   RESORTS WITH PROGRAMS FOR CHILDREN

YEAR-ROUND
Marriott Mountain Shadows Resort, Scottsdale, Arizona
Marriott Tan Tar-a, Lake of the Ozarks, Osage Beach, Missouri
South Seas Plantation Resort and Yacht Harbor, Captiva Island, Florida
Sonesta Beach Hotel, Key Biscayne, Florida

SUMMER
Amelia Island Plantation, Amelia Island, Florida
Casa de Campo, La Romana, Dominican Republic
Dunfey Hyannis Resort, Hyannis, Massachusetts
Hyatt Hotel, Hilton Head Island, South Carolina
Hyatt Regency Cerromar Beach, Dorado, Puerto Rico
Mariner's Inn, Hilton Head, South Carolina
Marriott Grand Hotel, Point Clear, Alabama
Marriott Hilton Head Resort, South Carolina
Sagamore Hotel, Lake George, New York

Source: Iris Sanderson Jones, "Traveling with Kids," *Working Woman* (November 1986): 232.

For example, Nippon Steel's $200 million subsidiary, Space World Inc., created a lunar fantasy land, complete with Lucky and Vicky Rabbit, 500 miles southeast of Tokyo. By mid-1990, roughly 100 similar projects were in various stages of planning and construction—many in imitation of U.S. and European successes—some reminiscent of Club Med concepts, such as: a Mongolian tent village; an indoor wind-surfing pool; a pair of Spanish villas, and Scandinavian towns; or Madarao Bi-Lingual Land. However, with increasing competition, Yuji Nemoto, specialist with the Japan Development Bank, believed that some ventures would fail. He said, "After natural selection, the question is which ones will survive."[26] In September 1990, Matushita, a Japanese diversified manufacturer of electronic and other products with manufacturing plants worldwide including the United States, tendered an offer (subsequently accepted) to acquire Universal Studios in Florida.

Nevertheless, the newest and fastest growing wave of competitors, the cruise ship industry, which hoisted flags of many countries, generated all-inclusive trips and tours, not unlike Club Med's, and frequently traveled to the same exotic destinations. Multinational companies, such as Carnival Cruise Lines, Royal Viking, and Norwegian Caribbean, packaged multi-price level programs that appealed to young singles and marrieds, families, as well as leisure trips for retirees. By the end of 1987, it had grown to a $4 billion market in North America alone, and the lines made deep inroads into Club Med's Caribbean domain.

Robert H. Dickenson, vice president of sales and marketing for Carnival Cruise Lines, said, "Cruising was once the domain of the rich. Now cruising is open to everyone."[27]

FINANCES

Club Méditerranée, founded as a nonprofit sports organization in 1950, was incorporated as a *societé anonyme* (S.A.) in 1957 in France and went public in 1965. Effective November 1, 1983, via a formation agreement, most of Club Méditerranée villages, sales activities, related operations, investments, contracts, and commitments in the American Zone were transferred at book value. Incorporated in the Cayman Islands in 1984, CMI, a majority-owned (74 percent by October 31, 1989) subsidiary of Club Méditerranée S.A., sold 3,400,000 common shares through a public offering in the United States and 300,000 common shares in a private offering to certain club officers, directors, and employees. CMI maintained financial records in U.S. dollars prepared in conformity with generally accepted U.S. accounting principles.

With profits and dividends stagnating during 1987–1988, ownership of Club Méditerranée changed. For example, the Groupe Depots holding company increased its 2.1 percent interest in 1988 to about 9.0 percent by early 1990. The Japanese conglomerate, Seibu Saison, with its 3.0 percent stake, was joined in 1989 by Nippon Life and its 4.9 interest. Other players included Warburg Mercury with 4.5 percent and the Agnelli family with 2.9 percent. To

make a takeover bid more difficult, Club Méditerranée unsuccessfully negotiated interlocking shareholdings with Nouvelles Frontiéres, a tour operator
and air charter company. The joint venture would have boosted the MNC to
third place in the tour operators' league table.[28]

Summary financial data for CMI appear in Exhibit 12, stock prices and
share data in Exhibit 13, and detailed balance sheets in Exhibit 14 (on pages 784
and 785). Of property and equipment shown in the balance sheets, on the basis
of cost, less than 5 percent represented land value of the villages. Buildings, plus
building and leasehold improvements, accounted for the bulk of the value of
villages. Most properties were leased with an average lease of 15 years, ranging
from 1 to 27 years. Lease payments could be suspended in case of *force majeure*.
Seven leases required rentals based upon occupancy levels.

With international transactions conducted in several currencies, CMI had
suffered exchange rate losses. For several years it endured the negative impact
from net French franc-based costs and expenses. Despite a 10 percent worsen-
ing of the dollar in international markets, these losses stabilized in 1988 partly
due to a 35 percent increase in GMs from European countries who paid for
visits to American Zone villages with strong currencies. The firm also had
experienced the adverse effects of Mexico's decision to maintain a fixed exchange (below market) rate of pesos for dollars.

EXHIBIT 12   CMI: FINANCIAL HIGHLIGHTS, 1984–1989

	1989	1988	1987	1986	1985	1984
INCOME STATEMENT DATA						
Revenues	468.8	412.4	370.4	337.0	279.7	235.3
Gross profit	159.4	133.2	125.1	115.3	92.4	81.5
Depreciation	17.9	16.4	13.5	11.5	7.8	6.1
Operating income	25.4	11.2	20.0	19.8	16.0	15.1
Income before extraordinary items	20.4	8.7	16.8	17.4	14.2	11.5
Extraordinary items*	0.7	0.1	0.6	0.7	1.4	0.6
Net income	21.1	8.8	17.4	18.1	15.6	12.0
BALANCE SHEET DATA						
Working capital	27.5	42.5	4.6	30.9	31.9	34.6
Long-term debt	100.1	131.1	89.4	91.2	76.1	39.3
Shareholders' equity	207.6	189.4	184.2	159.0	142.5	129.5
Total assets	415.5	403.2	353.4	313.8	269.1	212.1

Note: Amounts given in millions of U.S. dollars.

   *The firm is taxed under many jurisdictions, some of which do not impose an income tax. Resulting from negotiated tax reductions for periods ranging
from 1991 to 2005, the firm received incentive concessions from the Dominican Republic, Turks and Caicos Islands, Haiti, Saint Lucia, Mauritius, Thailand,
and Indonesia. Also, the firm had net operating losses and various tax credit carryforwards, as well as tax loss carryforwards expiring mostly 1990 through
1994.

Sources: CMI, *1988 Annual Report, 1989 Annual Report.*

EXHIBIT 13 CMI: SHARE DATA, 1984–1990

	1989	1988	1987	1986	1985	1984
Net income/share	$1.50	$0.62	$1.23	$1.32	$1.14	$1.14
Weighted average shares outstanding (in millions)	14.1	14.1	14.1	13.7	13.7	10.6
Dividends* per share	$0.20	$0.20	$0.20	$0.20	n/a	n/a

*A semiannual dividend of $0.10 per share was paid in February 1990.

CMI: RANGE OF STOCK PRICES BY QUARTER, 1987–1989

	1989		1988		1987	
QUARTER ENDED	*High*	*Low*	*High*	*Low*	*High*	*Low*
January 31	16.875–12.625		15.000– 9.000		29.250–21.500	
April 30	19.875–15.750		16.250–11.750		29.000–25.000	
July 31	21.875–18.250		16.625–12.250		27.000–22.625	
October 31	20.625–17.375		15.750–13.250		24.750–12.250	

Sources: CMI, *1988 Annual Report, 1989 Annual Report.*

STRATEGY

Typically a firm begins as a domestic organization servicing its home market, then initiates international activities first with exports and later opens sales offices abroad and licenses foreign companies to manufacture its products. Subsequently, the multinational company establishes its own manufacturing and services subsidiaries. A few firms globalize operations. (Club Med's operations by market segment are shown in Exhibit 15 on page 786.)

Club Méditerranée began as an international firm with headquarters in Paris, operations in the Balearic Islands (about 120 miles southeast of Barcelona, Spain), and customers predominately, but not exclusively, French. As operations spread across the globe, management largely maintained the original strategies of Trigano with reactive modifications to those strategies as current conditions dictated.

President Oizan-Chapon said, "In business you take the risk; you cannot control everything." He mentioned two major factors that hurt Club Med in 1988: (1) political unrest, which precipitated closing its Magic Isle village in Haiti and negatively impacted occupancy rates in New Caledonia; (2) construction problems, which delayed opening of a big new village in Huatulco, Mexico. Richard Phalon estimated that the Mexican misadventure cost Club Med around $7 million (U.S.) in reimbursements and debits.[29]

Changing demographics and customer tastes could not be denied, although Oizan-Chapon insisted, "Only part of the market is maturing. Part of it is growing." He pointed out, "We are following a life cycle plan."

Product diversification efforts met with limited success. The North American market had encountered problems: west coast customers were less attuned to French culture than east coast ones. *Chef de Village* Jean-Luc Olivero thought that the problem was even more basic: Americans were puritanical. For instance, when Club Med bought the Sandpiper property in Florida from Hilton Hotels, management ordered removal of TVs and telephones from rooms. Americans preferred them. They were replaced in 1989.

EXHIBIT 14 CLUB MED, INC. CORPORATE BALANCE SHEETS, 1988–1989

YEAR ENDED OCTOBER 31 (IN THOUSANDS OF DOLLARS)	1989	1988
ASSETS		
Current assets		
Cash and cash equivalents	$ 56,881	$ 33,697
Marketable securities	15,506	35,000
Accounts receivable	24,488	19,568
Due from affiliates	6,108	4,846
Inventories	14,074	14,276
Prepaid advertising and marketing	8,259	9,571
Other prepaid expenses	6,564	4,668
Total current assets	131,880	121,626
Property and equipment		
Villages	307,633	291,222
Other	10,287	9,367
Construction in progress	6,289	12,588
	324,209	313,177
Less accumulated depreciation and amortization	(85,426)	(69,970)
Net property and equipment	238,783	243,207
Other assets:		
Investments in and advances to affiliates	9,767	6,778
Deposit on equity interest	4,778	4,778
Long-term investment	17,189	17,520
Other	13,115	9,326
Total other assets	44,849	38,402
	$415,512	$403,235

EXHIBIT 14 (continued)

YEAR ENDED OCTOBER 31 (IN THOUSANDS OF DOLLARS)	1989	1988
LIABILITIES AND SHAREHOLDERS' EQUITY		
Current liabilities:		
Due to banks	$ 418	$ 8,180
Accounts payable	13,133	10,249
Due to Club Méditerranée	6,393	4,107
Due to affiliates	—	220
Accrued expenses	42,120	27,373
Amounts received for future vacations	30,992	25,066
Current maturities of long-term debt		
Club Méditerranée	1,591	—
Other	9,716	3,956
Total current maturities of long-term debt	11,307	3,956
Total current liabilities	104,363	79,151
Long-term debt		
Club Méditerranée	—	1,501
Other	100,103	129,606
Total long-term debt	100,103	131,107
Minority interest and other	3,412	3,575
Commitments and contingencies		
Shareholders' equity		
Common shares, par value $1.00 per share, 20,000,000 shares authorized, 14,156,000 shares issued (14,146,000 in 1988), and 14,096,000 shares outstanding (14,087,000 in 1988)	14,096	14,087
Additional paid-in capital	115,036	14,921
Retained earnings	79,061	60,782
Foreign currency translation adjustment	(559)	(388)
Total shareholders' equity	207,634	189,402
	$415,512	$403,235

CMI developed a three-part growth strategy for the 1990s:

1. Broaden the appeal: increase market penetration of the core product, the Club Med village vacation.
2. Expand the reach: introduce the Club Med concept to countries with growing economies and desires for new vacation opportunities.
3. Widen the concept: develop new vacation products, particularly in the rapidly growing cruise market.[30]

EXHIBIT 15   CMI: OPERATING DATA BY MARKET SEGMENT, 1987–1989

REGIONS BY YEARS	CONSOLIDATED REGIONAL REVENUES	OPERATING INCOME (LOSS)	IDENTIFIABLE ASSETS
	1989		
North America	103.4	(8.4)	48.1
Mexico-Caribbean	175.4	10.8	264.5
Asia-Pacific	157.9	22.9	102.9
CONSOLIDATED	468.8	25.4	415.5
	1988		
North America	133.1	(11.7)	55.5
Mexico-Caribbean	151.6	8.2	241.6
Asia-Pacific	127.7	14.7	106.2
CONSOLIDATED	412.4	11.2	403.2
	1987		
North America	124.6	(1.6)	48.1
Mexico-Caribbean	143.6	12.0	223.3
Asia-Pacific	102.2	9.7	82.0
CONSOLIDATED	370.4	20.0	353.4

Note: Amounts given in millions of U.S. dollars. Consolidated revenues eliminate revenues between geographic areas and revenues originating in another area. Therefore ,although the North American area generated nearly twice the revenues shown above, these were spent in another region. By the same token, about 75 percent of revenues attributed to the Mexico-Caribbean region were generated elsewhere. In the Asia-Pacific area, most revenues generated there were spent in the region.

Source: CMI, *1989 Annual Report*, p. 41.

Of course, results for the 1990s would depend upon how effectively Club Med implemented its strategies.

ENDNOTES

1. Phalon, Richard, "Trouble in Paradise," *Forbes* (September 19, 1988): 56

2. Levine, Joshua, "I Am sorry, We Have Changed," *Forbes* (September 4, 1989): 136–137.

3. Ibid., p. 136.

4. Moskowitz, Milton, *The Global Marketplace* (New York: Macmillan, 1987).

5. Ibid., 148.

6. *Club Med,* Summer/Fall 1990 (sales brochure).

7. Wood, Stephen, "Club Med's Global Villages," *Business* (U.K.) (January 1990): 68–69.

8. Levine, "I Am Sorry, We Have Changed," pp. 136–137.

9. Phalon, "Trouble in Paradise," p. 61.

10. *Club Med,* Summer/Fall 1990 (promotional catalog).

11. Slater, Shirley, and Harry Basch, "Club Med I," *Cruise Travel* (July-August 1990): 25.

12. *Club Med,* Summer/Fall 1990 (promotional catalog).

13. Horovitz, Jacques, "Club Méditerranée [A]," in Leslie Rue and Phyllis Holland, *Strategic Management: Concepts and Experiences* (New York: McGraw-Hill, 1986): 645–646.

14. Ibid., pp. 648–649.

15. GOs, or *gentils organisateurs,* specialized by function, had the task of helping people make this vacation the best. They both organized and participated in events. Typically there were 80 to 100 GOs per village.

16. Horovitz, "Club Méditerranée [A]."

17. Moskowitz, *The Global Marketplace,* p. 147.

18. Wood, "Club Med's Global Villages," p.67.

19. Ibid.

20. Slater and Basch, "Club Med I," p. 25.

21. Wood, "Club Med's Global Villages," p. 66.

22. Quintan, Brian, "Disney's World Grows Up," *Restaurant and Institutions* (December 11, 1989): 50.

23. "New Club Med Wants an Antidote for Competition," *Business Week* (November 2, 1987): 120.

24. Jones, Iris Sanderson, "Traveling With Kids," *Working Woman* (November 1988): 231.

25. "Now Club Med Wants an Antidote," p. 120.

26. Ono, Yomick, "Theme Park Boom in Japan Spurs Investor Rush to Get on the Ride," *Asian Wall Street Journal Weekly* (August 13, 1990): 9.

27. "Now Club Med Wants an Antidote," p. 120.

28. Wood, "Club Med's Global Villages," pp. 66–67.

29. Phalon, "Trouble in Paradise," p. 61.

30. Club Med, Inc., *1989 Annual Report.*

LINCOLN ELECTRIC COMPANY, 1989   ARTHUR D. SHARPLIN

> People are our most valuable asset. They must feel secure, important, chal-
> lenged, in control of their destiny, confident in their leadership, be respon-
> sive to common goals, believe they are being treated fairly, have easy access
> to authority and open lines of communication in all possible directions. Per-
> haps the most important task Lincoln employees face today is that of estab-
> lishing an example for others in the Lincoln organization in other parts of
> the world. We need to maximize the benefits of cooperation and teamwork,
> fusing high technology with human talent, so that we here in the USA and all
> of our subsidiary and joint venture operations will be in a position to realize
> our full potential (George Willis, CEO, Lincoln Electric).

The Lincoln Electric Company is the world's largest manufacturer of arc-welding products and a leading producer of industrial electric motors. The firm
employs 2,400 workers in two U.S. factories near Cleveland and an equal number in eleven factories located in other countries. This does not include the
field sales force of more than 200. The company's U.S. market share (for arc-
welding products) is estimated at more than 40 percent.

The Lincoln incentive management plan has been well known for many
years. Many college management texts make reference to the Lincoln plan as
a model for achieving higher worker productivity. Certainly, the firm has been
successful according to the usual measures.

James F. Lincoln died in 1965 and there was some concern, even among
employees, that the management system would fall into disarray, that profits
would decline, and that year-end bonuses might be discontinued. Quite the
contrary, twenty-four years after Lincoln's death, the company appears as
strong as ever. Each year, except the recession years 1982 and 1983, has seen
high profits and bonuses. Employee morale and productivity remain very

---

Source: **Prepared by Professor Arthur D. Sharplin, McNeese State University, as a basis
for classroom discussion and not to illustrate either effective or ineffective handling
of administrative situations.** © Arthur D. Sharplin, 1990.

good. Employee turnover is almost nonexistent except for retirements. Lincoln's market share is stable. The historically high stock dividends continue.

A HISTORICAL SKETCH

In 1895, after being "frozen out" of the depression-ravaged Elliott-Lincoln Company, a maker of Lincoln-designed electric motors, John C. Lincoln took out his second patent and began to manufacture his improved motor. He opened his new business, unincorporated, with $200 he had earned redesigning a motor for young Herbert Henry Dow, who later founded the Dow Chemical Company.

Started during an economic depression and cursed by a major fire after only one year in business, the company grew, but hardly prospered, through its first quarter century. In 1906, John C. Lincoln incorporated the business and moved from his one-room, fourth-floor factory to a new three-story building he erected in east Cleveland. He expanded his work force to thirty and sales grew to over $50,000 a year. John preferred being an engineer and inventor rather than a manager, though, and it was to be left to another Lincoln to manage the company through its years of success.

In 1907, after a bout with typhoid fever forced him from Ohio State University in his senior year, James F. Lincoln, John's younger brother, joined the fledgling company. In 1914 he became active head of the firm, with the titles of general manager and vice-president. John remained president of the company for some years but became more involved in other business ventures and in his work as an inventor.

One of James Lincoln's early actions was to ask the employees to elect representatives to a committee which would advise him on company operations. This "Advisory Board" has met with the chief executive officer every two weeks since that time. This was only the first of a series of innovative personnel policies which have, over the years, distinguished Lincoln Electric from its contemporaries.

The first year the Advisory Board was in existence, working hours were reduced from fifty-five per week, then standard, to fifty hours a week. In 1915, the company gave each employee a paid-up life insurance policy. A welding school, which continues today, was begun in 1917. In 1918, an employee bonus plan was attempted. It was not continued, but the idea was to resurface later.

The Lincoln Electric Employees' Association was formed in 1919 to provide health benefits and social activities. This organization continues today and has assumed several additional functions over the years. In 1923, a piecework pay system was in effect, employees got two weeks paid vacation each year, and wages were adjusted for changes in the Consumer Price Index. Approximately 30 percent of the common stock was set aside for key employees in 1914. A stock purchase plan for all employees was begun in 1925.

The board of directors voted to start a suggestion system in 1929. The program is still in effect, but cash awards, a part of the early program, were discontinued several years ago. Now, suggestions are rewarded by additional "points," which affect year-end bonuses.

The legendary Lincoln bonus plan was proposed by the Advisory Board and accepted on a trial basis in 1934. The first annual bonus amounted to about 25 percent of wages. There has been a bonus every year since then. The bonus plan has been a cornerstone of the Lincoln management system and recent bonuses have approximated annual wages.

By 1944, Lincoln employees enjoyed a pension plan, a policy of promotion from within, and continuous employment. Base pay rates were determined by formal job evaluation and a merit rating system was in effect.

In the prologue of James F. Lincoln's last book, Charles G. Herbruck writes regarding the foregoing personnel innovations:

> They were not to buy good behavior. They were not efforts to increase profits. They were not antidotes to labor difficulties. They did not constitute a "do-gooder" program. They were expression of mutual respect for each person's importance to the job to be done. All of them reflect the leadership of James Lincoln, under whom they were nurtured and propagated.

During World War II, Lincoln prospered as never before. By the start of the war, the company was the world's largest manufacturer of arc-welding products. Sales of about $4 million in 1934 grew to $24 million by 1941. Productivity per employee more than doubled during the same period. The navy's Price Review Board challenged the high profits. And the Internal Revenue Service questioned the tax deductibility of employee bonuses, arguing they are not "ordinary and necessary" costs of doing business. But the forceful and articulate James Lincoln was able to overcome the objections.

Certainly since 1935 and probably for several years before that, Lincoln productivity has been well above the average for similar companies. The company claims levels of productivity more than twice those for other manufacturers from 1945 onward. Information available from outside sources tends to support these claims.

COMPANY PHILOSOPHY

James F. Lincoln was the son of a Congregational minister, and Christian principles were at the center of his business philosophy. The confidence that he had in the efficacy of Christ's teachings is illustrated by the following remark taken from one of his books:

> The Christian ethic should control our acts. If it did control our acts, the savings in cost of distribution would be tremendous. Advertising would be a contact of the expert consultant with the customer, in order to give the customer the best product available when all of the customer's needs are considered. Competition then would be in improving the quality of products and increasing efficiency in producing and distributing them; not in deception,

as is now too customary. Pricing would reflect efficiency of production; it would not be a selling dodge that the customer may well be sorry he accepted. It would be proper for all concerned and rewarding for the ability used in producing the product.

There is no indication that Lincoln attempted to evangelize his employees or customers—or the general public for that matter. Neither the chairman of the board and chief executive, George Willis, nor the president, Donald F. Hastings, mention the Christian gospel in their recent speeches and inter-views. The company motto, "The actual is limited, the possible is immense," is prominently displayed, but there is no display of religious slogans, and there is no company chapel.

ATTITUDE TOWARD THE CUSTOMER

James Lincoln saw the customer's needs as the *raison d'être* for every company. "When any company has achieved success so that it is attractive as an invest-ment," he wrote, "all money usually needed for expansion is supplied by the customer in retained earnings. It is obvious that the customer's interests, not the stockholder's, should come first." In 1947 he said, "Care should be taken . . . not to rivet attention on profit. Between 'How much do I get?' and 'How do I make this better, cheaper, more useful?' the difference is fundamental and decisive." Willis, too, ranks the customer as management's most important constituency. This is reflected in Lincoln's policy to "at all times price on the basis of cost and at all times keep pressure on our cost." Lincoln's goal, often stated, is "to build a better and better product at a lower and lower price." "It is obvious," James Lincoln said, "that the customer's interests should be the first goal of industry."

ATTITUDE TOWARD STOCKHOLDERS

Stockholders are given last priority at Lincoln. This is a continuation of James Lincoln's philosophy: "The last group to be considered is the stockholders who own stock because they think it will be more profitable than investing money in any other way." Concerning division of the largess produced by incentive management, he wrote, "The absentee stockholder also will get his share, even if undeserved, out of the greatly increased profit that the efficiency produces."

ATTITUDE TOWARD UNIONISM

There has never been a serious effort to organize Lincoln employees. While James Lincoln criticized the labor movement for "selfishly attempting to bet-ter its position at the expense of the people it must serve," he still has kind words for union members. He excused abuses of union power as "the natural reactions of human beings to the abuses to which management has subjected them." Lincoln's idea of the correct relationship between workers and managers is shown by this comment: "Labor and management are properly not warring camps; they are parts of one organization in which they must and should cooperate fully and happily."

BELIEFS AND ASSUMPTIONS ABOUT EMPLOYEES

If fulfilling customer needs is the desired goal of business, then employee performance and productivity are the means by which this goal can best be achieved. It is the Lincoln attitude toward employees, reflected in the following comments by James Lincoln, which is credited by many with creating the success the company has experienced:

> The greatest fear of the worker, which is the same as the greatest fear of the industrialist in operating a company, is the lack of income. . . . The industrial manager is very conscious of his company's need of uninterrupted income. He is completely oblivious, evidently, of the fact that the worker has the same need.

> He is just as eager as any manager is to be part of a team that is properly organized and working for the advancement of our economy. . . . He has no desire to make profits for those who do not hold up their end in production, as is true of absentee stockholders and inactive people in the company.

> If money is to be used as an incentive, the program must provide that what is paid to the worker is what he has earned. The earnings of each must be in accordance with accomplishment.

> Status is of great importance in all human relationships. The greatest incentive that money has, usually, is that it is a symbol of success. . . . The resulting status is the real incentive. . . . Money alone can be an incentive to the miser only.

> There must be complete honesty and understanding between the hourly worker and management if high efficiency is to be obtained.

LINCOLN'S BUSINESS

Arc-welding has been the standard joining method in shipbuilding for decades. It is the predominant way of connecting steel in the construction industry. Most industrial plants have their own welding shops for maintenance and construction. Manufacturers of tractors and all kinds of heavy equipment use arc-welding extensively in the manufacturing process. Many hobbyists have their own welding machines and use them for making metal items such as patio furniture and barbecue pits. The popularity of welded sculpture as an art form is growing.

While advances in welding technology have been frequent, arc-welding products, in the main, have hardly changed. Lincoln's Innershield process is a notable exception. This process, described later, lowers welding cost and improves quality and speed in many applications. The most widely used Lincoln electrode, the Fleetweld 5P, has been virtually the same since the 1930s. The most popular engine-driven welder in the world, the Lincoln SA-200, has been a gray-colored assembly including a four-cylinder continental "Red Seal" engine and a 200 ampere direct-current generator with two current-control knobs for at least four decades. A 1989 model SA-200 even weighs almost the same as the 1950 model, and it certainly is little changed in appearance.

The company's share of the U.S. arc-welding products market appears to have been about 40 percent for many years. The welding products market has grown somewhat faster than the level of industry in general. The market is highly price-competitive, with variations in prices of standard items normally amounting to only a percent or two. Lincoln's products are sold directly by its engineering-oriented sales force and indirectly though its distributor organization. Advertising expenditures amount to less than three-fourths of a percent of sales. Research and development expenditures typically range from $10 million to $12 million, considerably more than competitors.

The other major welding process, flame-welding, has not been competitive with arc-welding since the 1930s. However, plasma-arc-welding, a relatively new process which uses a conducting stream of super heated gas (plasma) to confine the welding current to a small area, has made some inroads, especially in metal tubing manufacturing, in recent years. Major advances in technology which will produce an alternative superior to arc-welding within the next decade or so appear unlikely. Also, it seems likely that changes in the machines and techniques used in arc-welding will be evolutionary rather than revolutionary.

PRODUCTS

The company is primarily engaged in the manufacture and sale of arc-welding products—electric welding machines and metal electrodes. Lincoln also produces electric motors ranging from $\frac{1}{2}$ horsepower to 200 horsepower. Motors constitute about 8 to 10 percent of total sales. Several million dollars has recently been invested in automated equipment that will double Lincoln's manufacturing capacity for $\frac{1}{2}$ to 20 horsepower electric motors.

The electric welding machines, some consisting of a transformer or motor and generator arrangement powered by commercial electricity and others consisting of an internal combustion engine and generator, are designed to produce 30 to 1,500 amperes of electrical power. This electrical current is used to melt a consumable metal electrode with the molten metal being transferred in super hot spray to the metal joint being welded. Very high temperatures and hot sparks are produced, and operators usually must wear special eye and face protection and leather gloves, often along with leather aprons and sleeves.

Lincoln and its competitors now market a wide range of general purpose and specialty electrodes for welding mild steel, aluminum, cast iron, and stainless and special steels. Most of these electrodes are designed to meet the standards of the American Welding Society, a trade association. They are thus essentially the same as to size and composition from one manufacturer to another. Every electrode manufacturer has a limited number of unique products, but these typically constitute only a small percentage of total sales.

Welding electrodes are of two basic types: (1) Coated "stick" electrodes, usually fourteen inches long and smaller than a pencil in diameter, which are held in a special insulated holder by the operator, who must manipulate the electrode in order to maintain a proper arc-width and pattern of deposition of the metal being transferred. Stick electrodes are packaged in six- to fifty-pound boxes. (2) Coiled wire, ranging in diameter from .035″ to 0.219″, which is designed to be fed continuously to the welding arc through a "gun" held by the operator or positioned by automatic positioning equipment. The wire is packaged in coils, reels, and drums weighing from fourteen to 1,000 pounds and may be solid or flux-cored.

MANUFACTURING PROCESSES

The main plant is in Euclid, Ohio, a suburb on Cleveland's east side. The layout of this plant is shown in Exhibit 1. There are no warehouses. Materials flow from the half-mile-long dock on the north side of the plant through the production lines to a very limited storage and loading area on the south side. Materials used on each work station are stored as close as possible to the work station. The administrative offices, near the center of the factory, are entirely functional. A corridor below the main level provides access to the factory floor

EXHIBIT 1 MAIN FACTORY LAYOUT

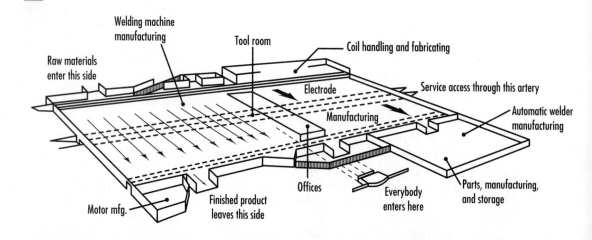

from the main entrance near the center of the plan. *Fortune* magazine recently declared the Euclid facility one of America's ten best-managed factories, and compared it with a General Electric plant also on the list:

> Stepping into GE's spanking new dishwasher plant, an awed supplier said, is like stepping "into the Hyatt Regency." By comparison, stepping into Lincoln Electric's 33-year-old, cavernous, dimly lit factory is like stumbling into a dingy big-city YMCA. It's only when one starts looking at how these factories do things that similarities become apparent. They have found ways to merge design with manufacturing, build in quality, make wise choices about automation, get close to customers, and handle their work forces.

A new Lincoln plant, in Mentor, Ohio, houses some of the electrode production operations, which were moved from the main plant.

Electrode manufacturing is highly capital intensive. Metal rods purchased from steel producers are drawn down to smaller diameters, cut to length and coated with pressed-powder "flux" for stick electrodes or plated with copper (for conductivity) and put into coils or spools for wire. Lincoln's Innershield wire is hollow and filled with a material similar to that used to coat stick electrodes. As mentioned earlier, this represented a major innovation in welding technology when it was introduced. The company is highly secretive about its electrode production processes, and outsiders are not given access to the details of those processes.

Lincoln welding machines and electric motors are made on a series of assembly lines. Gasoline and diesel engines are purchased partially assembled but practically all other components are made from basic industrial products, e.g., steel bars and sheets and bar copper conductor wire.

Individual components, such as gasoline tanks for engine-driven welders and steel shafts for motors and generators, are made by numerous small "factories within a factory." The shaft for a certain generator, for example, is made from raw steel bar by one operator who uses five large machines, all running continuously. A saw cuts the bar to length, a digital lathe machines different sections to varying diameters, a special milling machine cuts a slot for the keyway, and so forth, until a finished shaft is produced. The operator moves the shafts from machine to machine and makes necessary adjustments.

Another operator punches, shapes, and paints sheetmetal cowling parts. One assembles steel laminations onto a rotor shaft, then winds, insulates, and tests the rotors. Finished components are moved by crane operators to the nearby assembly lines.

WORKER PERFORMANCE AND ATTITUDES

Exceptional worker performance at Lincoln is a matter of record. The typical Lincoln employee earns about twice as much as other factory workers in the Cleveland area. Yet the company's labor cost per sales dollar in 1989, twenty-six cents, is well below industry averages. Worker turnover is practically non-existent except for retirements and departures by new employees.

Sales per Lincoln factory employee currently exceed $150,000. An observer at the factory quickly sees why this figure is so high. Each worker is proceeding busily and thoughtfully about the task at hand. There is no idle chatter. Most workers take no coffee breaks. Many operate several machines and make a substantial component unaided. The supervisors are busy with planning and record keeping duties and hardly glance at the people they "supervise." The manufacturing procedures appear efficient—no unnecessary steps, no wasted motions, no wasted materials. Finished components move smoothly to subsequent work stations.

Appendix A includes summaries of interviews with employees.

ORGANIZATION STRUCTURE

Lincoln has never allowed development of a formal organization chart. The objective of this policy is to insure maximum flexibility. An open door policy is practiced throughout the company, and personnel are encouraged to take problems to the persons most capable of resolving them. Once, Harvard Business School researchers prepared an organization chart reflecting the implied relationships at Lincoln. The chart became available within the company, and present management feels that had a disruptive effect. Therefore, no organizational chart appears in this report.

Perhaps because of the quality and enthusiasm of the Lincoln workforce, routine supervision is almost nonexistent. A typical production foreman, for example, supervises as many as 100 workers, a span-of-control which does not allow more than infrequent worker-supervisor interaction.

Position titles and traditional flows of authority do imply something of an organizational structure, however. For example, the vice-president, sales, and the vice-president, Electrode Division, report to the president, as do various staff assistants such as the personnel director and the director of purchasing. Using such implied relationships, it has been determined that production workers have two or, at most, three levels of supervision between themselves and the president.

PERSONNEL POLICIES

As mentioned earlier, it is Lincoln's remarkable personnel practices which are credited by many with the company's success.

RECRUITMENT AND SELECTION

Every job opening is advertised internally on company bulletin boards and any employee can apply for any job so advertised. External hiring is permitted only for entry level positions. Selection for these jobs is done on the basis of personal interviews—there is no aptitude or psychological testing. Not even a high school diploma is required—except for engineering and sales positions, which are filled by graduate engineers. A committee consisting of vice-presidents and supervisors interviews candidates initially cleared by the personnel department. Final selection is made by the supervisor who has a job opening. Out of over 3,500 applicants interviewed by the personnel department during a recent period fewer than 300 were hired.

JOB SECURITY

In 1958 Lincoln formalized its guaranteed continuous employment policy, which had already been in effect for many years. There have been no layoffs since World War II. Since 1958, every worker with over two years' longevity has been guaranteed at least thirty hours per week, forty-nine weeks per year.

The policy has never been so severely tested as during the 1981–1983 recession. As a manufacturer of capital goods, Lincoln's business is highly cyclical. In previous recessions the company was able to avoid major sales declines. However, sales plummeted 32 percent in 1982 and another 16 percent the next year. Few companies could withstand such a revenue collapse and remain profitable. Yet, Lincoln not only earned profits, but no employee was laid off and year-end incentive bonuses continued. To weather the storm, management cut most of the nonsalaried workers back to 30 hours a week for varying periods of time. Many employees were reassigned and the total workforce was slightly reduced through normal attrition and restricted hiring. Many employees grumbled at their unexpected misfortune, probably to the surprise and dismay of some Lincoln managers. However, sales and profits—and employee bonuses—soon rebounded and all was well again.

PERFORMANCE EVALUATIONS

Each supervisor formally evaluates subordinates twice a year using the cards shown in Exhibit 2. The employee performance criteria, "quality," "dependability," "ideas and cooperation," and "output," are considered to be independent of each other. Marks on the cards are converted to numerical scores which are forced to average 100 for each evaluating supervisor. Individual merit rating scores normally range from 80 to 110. Any score over 110 requires a special letter to top management. These scores (over 110) are not considered in computing the required 100 point average for each evaluating supervisor. Suggestions for improvements often result in recommendations for exceptionally high performance scores. Supervisors discuss individual performance marks with the employees concerned. Each warranty claim is traced to the individual employee whose work caused the defect. The employee's performance score may be reduced, or the worker may be required to repay the cost of servicing the warranty claim by working without pay.

COMPENSATION

Basic wage levels for jobs at Lincoln are determined by a wage survey of similar jobs in the Cleveland area. These rates are adjusted quarterly in accordance

EXHIBIT 2   MERIT RATING CARDS

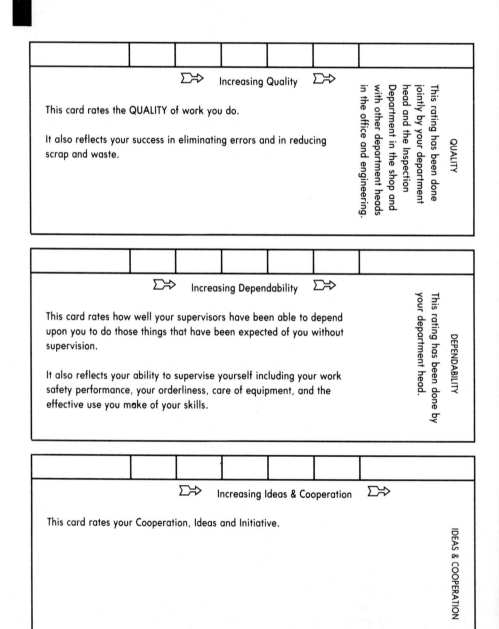

⎯⇨   Increasing Quality   ⎯⇨

This card rates the QUALITY of work you do.

It also reflects your success in eliminating errors and in reducing scrap and waste.

QUALITY

This rating has been done jointly by your department head and the Inspection Department in the shop and with other department heads in the office and engineering.

⎯⇨   Increasing Dependability   ⎯⇨

This card rates how well your supervisors have been able to depend upon you to do those things that have been expected of you without supervision.

It also reflects your ability to supervise yourself including your work safety performance, your orderliness, care of equipment, and the effective use you make of your skills.

DEPENDABILITY

This rating has been done by your department head.

⎯⇨   Increasing Ideas & Cooperation   ⎯⇨

This card rates your Cooperation, Ideas and Initiative.

IDEAS & COOPERATION

EXHIBIT 2 (continued)

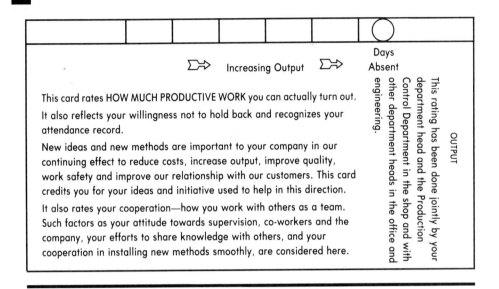

Increasing Output

Days Absent

This card rates HOW MUCH PRODUCTIVE WORK you can actually turn out. It also reflects your willingness not to hold back and recognizes your attendance record.

New ideas and new methods are important to your company in our continuing effect to reduce costs, increase output, improve quality, work safety and improve our relationship with our customers. This card credits you for your ideas and initiative used to help in this direction.

It also rates your cooperation—how you work with others as a team. Such factors as your attitude towards supervision, co-workers and the company, your efforts to share knowledge with others, and your cooperation in installing new methods smoothly, are considered here.

OUTPUT

This rating has been done jointly by your department head and the Production Control Department in the shop and with other department heads in the office and engineering.

with changes in the Cleveland area wage index. Insofar as possible, base wage rates are translated into piece rates. Practically all production workers and many others—for example, some forklift operators—are paid by piece rate. Once established, piece rates are never changed unless a substantive change in the way a job is done results from a source other than the worker doing the job.

In December of each year, a portion of annual profits is distributed to employees as bonuses. Incentive bonuses since 1934 have averaged about 90 percent of annual wages and somewhat more than after-tax profits. The average bonus for 1988 has $21,258. Even for the recession years 1982 and 1983, bonuses had averaged $13,998 and $8,557, respectively. Individual bonuses are proportional to merit-rating scores. For example, assume the amount set aside for bonuses is 80 percent of total wages paid to eligible employees. A person whose performance score is 95 will receive a bonus of 76 percent (0.80 × 0.95) of annual wages.

VACATIONS

The company is shut down for two weeks in August and two weeks during the Christmas season. Vacations are taken during these periods. For employees with over twenty-five years of service, a fifth week of vacation may be taken at a time acceptable to superiors.

WORK ASSIGNMENT

Management has authority to transfer workers and to switch between overtime and short time as required. Supervisors have undisputed authority to assign specific parts to individual workmen, who may have their own preferences due to variations in piece rates. During the 1982–1983 recession, fifty factory workers volunteered to join sales teams and fanned out across the country to sell a new welder designed for automobile body shops and small machine shops. The result—$10 million in sales and a hot new product.

EMPLOYEE PARTICIPATION IN DECISION MAKING

Thinking of participative management usually evokes a vision of a relaxed, nonauthoritarian atmosphere. This is not the case at Lincoln. Formal authority is quite strong. "We're very authoritarian around here," says Willis. James F. Lincoln placed a good deal of stress on protecting management's authority. "Management in all successful departments of industry must have complete power," he said. "Management is the coach who must be obeyed. The men, however, are the players who alone can win the game." Despite this attitude, there are several ways in which employees participate in management at Lincoln.

Richard Sabo, assistant to the chief executive officer, relates job enlargement/enrichment to participation. He said, "The most important participative technique that we use is giving more responsibility to employees. We give a high school graduate more responsibility than other companies give their foremen." Management puts limits on the degree of participation which is allowed, however. In Sabo's words:

> When you use "participation," put quotes around it. Because we believe that each person should participate only in those decisions he is most knowledgeable about. I don't think production employees should control the decisions of the chairman. They don't know as much as he does about the decisions he is involved in.

The Advisory Board, elected by the workers, meets with the chairman and the president every two weeks to discuss ways of improving operations. As noted earlier, this board has been in existence since 1914 and has contributed to many innovations. The incentive bonuses, for example, were first recommended by this committee. Every employee has access to Advisory Board members, and answers to all Advisory Board suggestions are promised by the following meeting. Both Willis and Hastings are quick to point out, though, that the Advisory Board only recommends actions. "They do not have direct authority," Willis says. "And when they bring up something that management thinks is not to the benefit of the company, it will be rejected."

Under the early suggestion program, employees were awarded one-half of the first year's savings attributable to their suggestions. Now, however, the value of suggestions is reflected in performance evaluation scores, which determine individual incentive bonus amounts.

TRAINING AND EDUCATION

Production workers are given a short period of on-the-job training and then placed on a piecework pay system. Lincoln does not pay for off-site education, unless very specific company needs are identified. The idea behind this latter policy, according to Sabo, is that everyone cannot take advantage of such a program, and it is unfair to expend company funds for an advantage to which there is unequal access. Recruits for sales jobs, already college graduates, are given on-the-job training in the plant followed by a period of work and training at one of the regional sales offices.

FRINGE BENEFITS AND EXECUTIVE PERQUISITES

A medical plan and a company-paid retirement program have been in effect for many years. A plant cafeteria, operated on a break-even basis, serves meals at about 60 percent of usual costs. The Employee Association, to which the company does not contribute, provides disability insurance and social and athletic activities. The employee stock ownership program has resulted in employee ownership of about 50 percent of the common stock. Under this program, each employee with more than two years of service may purchase stock in the corporation. The price of these shares is established at book value. Stock purchased through this plan may be held by employees only. Dividends and voting rights are the same as for stock which is owned outside the plan. Approximately 75 percent of the employees own Lincoln stock.

As to executive perquisites, there are none—crowded, austere offices, no executive washrooms or lunchrooms, and no reserved parking spaces. Even the top executives pay for their own meals and eat in the employee cafeteria. On one recent day, Willis arrived at work late due to a breakfast speaking engagement and had to park far away from the factory entrance.

FINANCIAL POLICIES

James F. Lincoln felt strongly that financing for company growth should come from within the company—through initial cash investment by the founders, through retention of earnings, and through stock purchases by those who work in the business. He saw the following advantages of this approach:

1. Ownership of stock by employees strengthens team spirit. "If they are mutually anxious to make is succeed, the future of the company is bright."
2. Ownership of stock provides individual incentive because employees feel that they will benefit from company profitability.
3. "Ownership is educational." Owners-employees "will know how profits are made and lost; how success is won and lost. . . . There are few socialists in the list of stockholders of the nation's industries."

4. "Capital available from within controls expansion." Unwarranted expansion would not occur, Lincoln believed, under his financing plan.
5. "The greatest advantage would be the development of the individual worker. Under the incentive of ownership, he would become a greater man."
6. "Stock ownership is one of the steps that can be taken that will make the worker feel that there is less of a gulf between him and the boss. . . . Stock ownership will help the worker to recognize his responsibility in the game and the importance of victory."

Until 1980, Lincoln Electric borrowed no money. Even now, the company's liabilities consist mainly of accounts payable and short-term accruals.

The unusual pricing policy at Lincoln is succinctly stated by Willis: "At all times price on the basis of cost and at all times keep pressure on our cost." This policy resulted in the price for the most popular welding electrode then in use going from 16 cents a pound in 1929 to 4.7 cents in 1938. More recently, the SA-200 Welder, Lincoln's largest selling portable machine, decreased in price from 1958 through 1965. According to Dr. C. Jackson Grayson of the American Productivity Center in Houston, Texas, Lincoln's prices increased only one-fifth as fast as the Consumer Price Index from 1934 to about 1970. This resulted in a welding products market in which Lincoln became the undisputed price leader for the products it manufactures. Not even the major Japanese manufacturers, such as Nippon Steel for welding electrodes and Osaka Transformer for welding machines, were able to penetrate this market.

Substantial cash balances are accumulated each year preparatory to paying the year-end bonuses. The bonuses totaled $54 million for 1988. The money is invested in short-term U.S. government securities and certificates of deposit until needed. Financial statements are shown in Exhibit 3. Exhibit 4 shows how company revenue was distributed in the late 1980s.

HOW WELL DOES LINCOLN SERVE ITS STAKEHOLDERS?

Lincoln Electric differs from most other companies in the importance it assigns to each of the groups it serves. Willis identifies these groups, in the order of priority ascribed to them, as (1) customers, (2) employees, and (3) stockholders.

Certainly the firm's customers have fared well over the years. Lincoln prices for welding machines and welding electrodes are acknowledged to be the lowest in the marketplace. Quality has consistently been high. The cost of field failures for Lincoln products was recently determined to be a remarkable 0.04 percent of revenues. The Fleetweld electrodes and SA-200 welders have been the standard in the pipeline and refinery construction industry, where price is hardly a criterion, for decades. A Lincoln distributor in Monroe, Louisiana, says that he has sold several hundred of the popular AC-225 welders, which are warranted for one year, but has never handled a warranty claim.

Perhaps best-served of all management constituencies have been the employees. Not the least of their benefits, of course, are the year-end bonuses, which effectively double an already average compensation level. The foregoing description of the personnel program and the comments in Appendix A further illustrate the desirability of a Lincoln job.

While stockholders were relegated to an inferior status by James F. Lincoln, they have done very well indeed. Recent dividends have exceeded $11 a share and earnings per share have approached $30. In January 1980, the price of restricted stock, committed to employees, was $117 a share. By 1989, the

EXHIBIT 3 LINCOLN ELECTRIC: CONDENSED COMPARATIVE FINANCIAL STATEMENTS

BALANCE SHEETS

	1979	1980	1981	1982	1983	1984	1985	1986	1987
ASSETS									
Cash	2	1	4	1	2	4	2	1	7
Bonds & CDs	38	47	63	72	78	57	55	45	41
N/R & A/R	42	42	42	26	31	34	38	36	43
Inventories	38	36	46	38	31	37	34	26	40
Prepayments	1	3	4	5	5	5	7	8	7
Total CA	121	129	157	143	146	138	135	116	137
Other assets**	24	24	26	30	30	29	29	33	40
Land	1	1	1	1	1	1	1	1	1
Net buildings	22	23	25	23	22	21	20	18	17
Net M&E	21	25	27	27	27	28	27	29	33
Total FA	44	49	53	51	50	50	48	48	50
Total assets	189	202	236	224	227	217	213	197	227
CLAIMS									
A/P	17	16	15	12	16	15	13	11	20
Accrued wages	1	2	5	4	3	4	5	5	4
Accrued taxes	10	6	15	5	7	4	6	5	9
Accrued div.	6	6	7	7	7	6	7	6	7
Total CL	33	29	42	28	33	30	31	27	40
LT debt		4	5	6	8	10	11	8	8
Total debt	33	33	47	34	41	40	42	35	48
Common stock	4	3	1	2	0	0	0	0	2
Ret. earnings	152	167	189	188	186	176	171	161	177
Total SH equity	156	170	190	190	186	176	171	161	179
Total claims	189	202	236	224	227	217	213	197	227

(*continued*)

EXHIBIT 3   (continued)

INCOME STATEMENTS

	1979	1980	1981	1982	1983	1984	1985	1986	1987
New sales	374	387	450	311	263	322	333	318	368
Other income	11	14	18	18	13	12	11	8	9
Income	385	401	469	329	277	334	344	326	377
CGS	244	261	293	213	180	223	221	216	239
Selling, G&A**	41	46	51	45	45	47	48	49	51
Incentive bonus	44	43	56	37	22	33	38	33	39
IBT	56	51	69	35	30	31	36	27	48
Income taxes	26	23	31	16	13	14	16	12	21
Net income	30	28	37	19	17	17	20	15	27

Note: Amounts are given in millions of dollars. Column totals may not check and amounts less than $500,000 (0.5) are shown as zero, due to rounding.
   *Includes investment in foreign subsidiaries, $29 million in 1987.
   **Includes pension expense and payroll taxes on incentive bonus.

stated value, at which the company will repurchase the stock if tendered, was
$201. A check with the New York office of Merrill Lynch, Pierce, Fenner and
Smith at that time revealed an estimated price on Lincoln stock of $270 a
share, with none being offered for sale. Technically, this price applies only to

EXHIBIT 4   LINCOLN ELECTRIC: REVENUE DISTRIBUTION

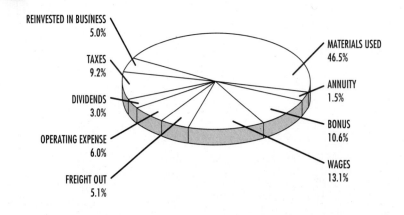

REINVESTED IN BUSINESS
5.0%

TAXES
9.2%

DIVIDENDS
3.0%

OPERATING EXPENSE
6.0%

FREIGHT OUT
5.1%

MATERIALS USED
46.5%

ANNUITY
1.5%

BONUS
10.6%

WAGES
13.1%

the unrestricted stock owned by the Lincoln family, a few other major holders, and employees who have purchased it on the open market. Risk associated with Lincoln stock, a major determinant of stock value, is minimal because of the small amount of debt in the capital structure, because of an extremely stable earnings record, and because of Lincoln's practice of purchasing the restricted stock whenever employees offer it for sale.

A CONCLUDING COMMENT

It is easy to believe that the reason for Lincoln's success is the excellent attitude of the employees and their willingness to work harder, faster, and more intelligently than other industrial workers. However, Sabo suggests that appropriate credit be given to Lincoln executives, whom he credits with carrying out the following policies:

1. Management has limited research, development, and manufacturing to a standard product line designed to meet the major needs of the welding industry.
2. New products must be reviewed by manufacturing and all producing costs verified before being approved by management.
3. Purchasing is challenged to not only procure materials at the lowest cost, but also to work closely with engineering and manufacturing to assure that the latest innovations are implemented.
4. Manufacturing supervision and all personnel are held accountable for reduction of scrap, energy conservation, and maintenance of product quality.
5. Production control, material handling, and methods engineering are closely supervised by top management.
6. Management has made cost reduction a way of life at Lincoln, and definite programs are established in many areas, including traffic and shipping, where tremendous savings can result.
7. Management has established a sales department that is technically trained to reduce customer welding costs. This sales approach and other real customer services have eliminated nonessential frills and resulted in long-term benefits to all concerned.
8. Management has encouraged education, technical publishing, and long range programs that have resulted in industry growth, thereby assuring market potential for the Lincoln Electric Company.

Sabo writes, "It is in a very real sense a personal and group experience in faith—a belief that together we can achieve results which alone would not be possible. It is not a perfect system and it is not easy. It requires tremendous dedication and hard work. However, it does work and the results are worth the effort."

APPENDIX A

Employee Interviews

Typical questions and answers from employee interviews are presented below. In order to maintain each employee's personal privacy, fictitious names are given to the interviewees.

INTERVIEW 1

Betty Stewart, a 52-year-old high school graduate who had been with Lincoln thirteen years and who was working as a cost accounting clerk at the time of the interview.

Q: What jobs have you held here besides the one you have now?
A: I worked in payroll for a while, and then this job came open and I took it.
Q: How much money did you make last year, including your bonus?
A: I would say roughly around $25,000, but I was off for back surgery for a while.
Q: You weren't paid while you were off for back surgery?
A: No.
Q: Did the Employees Association help out?
A: Yes. The company doesn't furnish that, though. We pay $8 a month into the Employee Association. I think my check from them was $130.00 a week.
Q: How was your performance rating last year?
A: It was around 100 points, but I lost some points for attendance for my back problem.
Q: How did you get your job at Lincoln?

A: I was bored silly where I was working, and I had heard that Lincoln kept their people busy. So I applied and got the job the next day.

Q: Do you think you make more money than similar workers in Cleveland?

A: I know I do.

Q: What have you done with your money?

A: We have purchased a better home. Also, my son is going to the University of Chicago, which costs $13,000 a year. I buy the Lincoln stock which is offered each year, and I have a little bit of gold.

Q: Have you ever visited with any of the senior executives, like Mr. Willis or Mr. Hastings?

A: I have known Mr. Willis for a long time.

Q: Does he call you by name?

A: Yes. In fact he was very instrumental in my going to the doctor that I am going to with my back. He knows the director of the clinic.

Q: Do you know Mr. Hastings?

A: I know him to speak to him, and he always speaks, always. But I have known Mr. Willis for a good many years. When I did Plant Two accounting I did not understand how the plant operated. Of course you are not allowed in Plant Two, because that's the Electrode Division. I told my boss about the problem one day and the next thing I knew Mr. Willis came by and said, "Come on, Betty, we're going to Plant Two." He spent an hour and a half showing me the plant.

Q: Do you think Lincoln employees produce more than those in other companies?

A: I think with the incentive program the way that it is, if you want to work and achieve, then you will do it. If you don't want to work and achieve, you will not do it no matter where you are. Just because you are merit rated and have a bonus, if you really don't want to work hard, then you're not going to. You will accept your ninety points or ninety-two or eighty-five because, even with that you make more money than people on the outside.

Q: Do you think Lincoln employees will ever join a union?

A: I don't know why they would.

Q: So you say that money is a very major advantage?

A: Money is a major advantage, but it's not just the money. It's the fact that having the incentive, you do wish to work a little harder. I'm sure that there are a lot of men here who, if they worked some other place, would not work as hard as they do here. Not that they are overworked—I don't mean that—but I'm sure they wouldn't push.

Q: Is there anything that you would like to add?

A: I do like working here. I am better off being pushed mentally. In another company if you pushed too hard you would feel a little bit of pressure, and someone might say, "Hey, slow down; don't try so hard." But here you are encouraged, not discouraged.

INTERVIEW 2

Ed Sanderson, a 23-year-old high school graduate who had been with Lincoln four years and who was a machine operator in the Electrode Division at the time of the interview.

Q: How did you happen to get this job?

A: My wife was pregnant, and I was making three bucks an hour and one day I came here and applied. That was it. I kept calling to let them know I was still interested.

Q: Roughly what were your earnings last year including your bonus?

A: $45,000

Q: What have you done with your money since you have been here?

A: Well, we've lived pretty well and we bought a condominium.

Q: Have you paid for the condominium?

A: No, but I could.

Q: Have you bought your Lincoln stock this year?

A: No, I haven't bought any Lincoln stock yet.

Q: Do you get the feeling that the executives here are pretty well thought of?

A: I think they are. To get where they are today, they had to really work.

Q: Wouldn't that be true anywhere?

A: I think more so here because seniority really doesn't mean anything. If you work with a guy who has twenty years here, and you have two months and you're doing a better job, you will get advanced before he will.

Q: Are you paid on a piece rate basis?

A: My gang does. There are nine of us who make the bare electrode, and the whole group gets paid based on how much electrode we make.

Q: Do you think you work harder than workers in other factories in the Cleveland area?

A: Yes, I would say I probably work harder.

Q: Do you think it hurts anybody?

A: No, a little hard work never hurts anybody.

Q: If you could choose, do you think you would be as happy earning a little less money and being able to slow down a little?

A: No, it doesn't bother me. If it bothered me, I wouldn't do it.

Q: Why do you think Lincoln employees produce more than workers in other plants?

A: That's the way the company is set up. The more you put out, the more you're going to make.

Q: Do you think it's the piece rate and bonus together?

A: I don't think people would work here if they didn't know that they would be rewarded at the end of the year.

Q: Do you think Lincoln employees will ever join a union?
A: No.
Q: What are the major advantages of working for Lincoln?
A: Money.
Q: Are there any other advantages?
A: Yes, we don't have a union shop. I don't think I could work in a
    union shop.
Q: Do you think you are a career man with Lincoln at this time?
A: Yes.

INTERVIEW 3

Roger Lewis, a 23-year-old Purdue graduate in mechanical engineering who
had been in the Lincoln sales program for fifteen months and who was working in the Cleveland sales office at the time of the interview.

Q: How did you get your job at Lincoln?
Q: I saw that Lincoln was interviewing on campus at Purdue, and I went
    by. I later came to Cleveland for a plant tour and was offered a job.
Q: Do you know any of the senior executives? Would they know you by
    name?
A: Yes, I know all of them—Mr. Hastings, Mr. Willis, Mr. Sabo.
Q: Do you think Lincoln salesmen work harder than those in other
    companies?
A: Yes. I don't think there are many salesmen for other companies who
    are putting in fifty- to sixty-hour weeks. Everybody here works
    harder. You can go out in the plant, or you can go upstairs, and
    there's nobody sitting around.
Q: Do you see any real disadvantage of working at Lincoln?
A: I don't know if it's a disadvantage but Lincoln is a spartan company,
    a very thrifty company. I like that. The sales offices are functional,
    not fancy.
Q: Why do you think Lincoln employees have such high productivity?
A: Piecework has a lot to do with it. Lincoln is smaller than many
    plants, too; you can stand in one place and see the materials come
    in one side and the product go out the other. You feel a part of the
    company. The chance to get ahead is important, too. They have a
    strict policy of promoting from within, so you know you have a
    chance. I think in a lot of other places you may not get as fair a
    shake as you do here. The sales offices are on a smaller scale, too. I
    like that. I tell someone that we have two people in the Baltimore
    office, and they say, "You've got to be kidding." It's smaller and more
    personal. Pay is the most important thing. I have heard that this is
    the highest paying factory in the world.

INTERVIEW 4

Jimmy Roberts, a 47-year-old high school graduate who had been with Lincoln seventeen years and who was working as a multiple-drill press operator at the time of the interview.

Q: What jobs have you had at Lincoln?
A: I started out cleaning the men's locker room in 1967. After about a year I got a job in the flux department, where we make the coating for welding rods. I worked there for seven or eight years and then got my present job.
Q: Do you make one particular part?
A: No, there are a variety of parts I make—at least twenty-five.
Q: Each one has a different piece rate attached to it?
A: Yes.
Q: Are some piece rates better than others?
A: Yes.
Q: How do you determine which ones you are going to do?
A: You don't. Your supervisor assigns them.
Q: How much money did you make last year?
A: $53,000.
Q: Have you ever received any kind of award or citation?
A: No.
Q: Was your rating ever over 110?
A: Yes. For the past five years, probably, I made over 110 points.
Q: Is there any attempt to let the others know . . . ?
A: The kind of points I get? No.
Q: Do you know what they are making?
A: No. There are some who might not be too happy with their points and they might make it known. The majority, though, do not make it a point of telling other employees.
Q: Would you be just as happy earning a little less money and working a little slower?
A: I don't think I would—not at this point. I have done piecework all these years, and the fast pace doesn't really bother me.
Q: Why do you think Lincoln productivity is so high?
A: The incentive thing—the bonus distribution. I think that would be the main reason. The pay check you get every two weeks is important too.
Q: Do you think Lincoln employees would ever join a union?
A: I don't think so. I have never heard anyone mention it.
Q: What is the most important advantage of working here?
A: Amount of money you make. I don't think I could make this type of money anywhere else, especially with only a high school education.
Q: As a black person, do you feel that Lincoln discriminates in any way against blacks?

A: No. I don't think any more so than any other job. Naturally, there is a certain amount of discrimination, regardless of where you are.

INTERVIEW 5

Joe Trahan, 58-year-old high school graduate who had been with Lincoln thirty-nine years and who was employed as a working supervisor in the tool room at the time of the interview.

Q: Roughly what was your pay last year?
A: Over $56,000; salary, bonus, stock dividends.
Q: How much was your bonus?
A: About $26,000.
Q: Have you ever gotten a special award of any kind?
A: Not really.
Q: What have you done with your money?
A: My house is paid for—and my two cars. I also have some bonds and the Lincoln stock.
Q: What do you think of the executives at Lincoln?
A: They're really top notch.
Q: What is the major disadvantage of working at Lincoln Electric?
A: I don't know of any disadvantage at all.
Q: Do you think you produce more than most people in similar jobs with other companies?
A: I do believe that.
Q: Why is that? Why do you believe that?
A: We are on the incentive system. Everything we do, we try to improve to make a better product with a minimum of outlay. We try to improve the bonus.
Q: Would you be just as happy making a little less money and not working quite so hard?
A: I don't think so.
Q: Do you think Lincoln employees would ever join a union?
A: I don't think they would ever consider it.
Q: What is the most important advantage of working at Lincoln?
A: Compensation.
Q: Tell me something about Mr. James Lincoln, who died in 1965.
A: You are talking about Jimmy Sr. He always strolled through the shop in his shirt sleeves. Big fellow. Always looked distinguished. Gray hair. Friendly sort of guy. I was a member of the advisory board one year. He was there each time.
Q: Did he strike you as really caring?
A: I think he always cared for people.
Q: Did you get any sensation of a religious nature from him?
A: No, not really.

Q: And religion is not part of the program now?
A: No.
Q: Do you think Mr. Lincoln was a very intelligent man, or was he just a nice guy?
A: I would say he was pretty well educated. A great talker—always right off the top of his head. He knew what he was talking about all the time.
Q: When were bonuses for beneficial suggestions done away with?
A: About eighteen years ago.
Q: Did that hurt very much?
A: I don't think so, because suggestions are still rewarded through the merit rating system.
Q: Is there anything you would like to add?
A: It's a good place to work. The union kind of ties other places down. At other places, electricians only do electrical work, carpenters only do carpenter work. At Lincoln Electric we all pitch in and do whatever needs to be done.
Q: So a major advantage is not having a union?
A: That's right.

POLAROID CORPORATION/ INNER CITY, INC.

JOHN A. SEEGER
AND MARIE ROCK

Bill Skelley, manager of Polaroid Corporation's Inner City subsidiary, gazed intently across his circular conference table, emphasizing his concerns with the company's future:

> We are a forty million dollar company, just as responsible for its operations as any other profit-center firm. We assemble parts for Polaroid's cameras . . . we package film . . . we do silk screen printing. At the same time, we help people who have never before succeeded at work to develop the skills they need, to hold a job anywhere. When we finish training somebody to be productive, we place them in a mainstream job with some other employer, to make room for a new trainee here.
>
> We're held responsible for the bottom line. Since 1978, we've returned more than our budgeted contribution to Polaroid headquarters. [Exhibit 1 shows Inner City's financial statements for 1985 and 1986.]
>
> Now, though, the whole economy is changing, with serious implications for us. Our history and skills lie in the manufacturing area, but all the economic growth is in the service sector: that's where the entry-level jobs are. To give our graduates a chance, we have to change the work we train them to do. We have to decide what work Inner City should take on—what new business we should go into.
>
> And the low unemployment rate here in Massachusetts makes it hard to attract new trainees. Our waiting list for employment used to have a thousand to fifteen hundred names; now there is virtually no waiting list at all. A skeptic might say our whole reason for existing is obsolete.

Source: **Prepared by Professor John A. Seeger and Marie Rock, Bentley College, as a basis for class discussion. Distributed by the North American Case Research Association.** © **John A. Seeger, 1988.**

POLAROID CORPORATION

Polaroid Corporation was founded in 1937 by Edwin H. Land, who continued to lead the firm until his retirement in 1980. Through those years the company was based entirely on the products of Dr. Land's inventive genius—polarized filters and instant photography. Polaroid experienced rapid growth in sales, employment, and profitability until 1978, when sales grew 30 percent over the previous year, reaching $1.4 billion with a return on equity of 13.8 percent. In 1979, however, several factors—including Kodak's penetration of the instant photography market, the failure of Polaroid's instant motion picture system, and an oil-starved economic recession—put an end to the growth. (Exhibit 2 on page 816 shows ten years' operating results for Polaroid.)

From its inception, Polaroid Corporation reflected the values of its founder. The company was an innovator in participative management systems and responsiveness to community needs. In the late 1960s, autonomous worker teams were introduced in Polaroid's film manufacturing plant. When public criticism in 1970 focused on the use of instant photography in South Africa's apartheid identification pass program, Polaroid sent an employee team to investigate; supporting that group's analysis, the company refused to

EXHIBIT 1   INNER CITY, INC. STATEMENT OF OPERATIONS

| | YEAR ENDING DECEMBER 31, | | | |
| | 1985 | | 1986 | |
	Budget	*Actual*	*Budget*	*Actual*
Sales	$44,576	$38,457	$30,407	$35,401
Cost of Sales				
Direct Material	42,078	35,857	27,666	32,595
Direct Labor	490	610	536	621
	42,568	36,467	28,202	33,216
Gross Margin	2008	1,990	2,205	2,185
Other Direct Costs	0	0	113	154
Other Income	0	16	0	2
Subtotal	2,008	2,006	2,092	2,033
Operating Costs				
Indirect Labor[1]	646	655	860	693
Staff Labor[2]	798	793	840	746
Overhead	564	499	392	496
Subtotal	2008	1,947	2,092	1,935
Surplus from Operations[3]	$ 0	$ 59	$ 0	$ 98

EXHIBIT 1   (continued)

STATEMENT OF FINANCIAL CONDITION

	DECEMBER 31,	
	1985	*1986*
ASSETS		
Cash	$ 6	$ 44
Accounts Receivable		
Polaroid	558	480
Trade-Net	64	36
Other	3	5
Inventories	544	904
Prepaid Expenses	4	1
Total Current Assets	1,179	1,470
Plant and Equipment, Net	99	98
Total Assets	$1,278	$1,568
LIABILITIES AND OWNERS' EQUITY		
Accounts Payable	$ 7	$ 30
Accrued Expenses	16	42
Total Current Liabilities	23	72
Advance from Parent, Net	2,778	3,019
Total Liabilities	2,801	3,091
Capital Stock	1	1
Paid in Surplus	24	24
Retained Earnings (Deficit)	(1,548)	(1,548)
Total Liabilities and Owner's Equity	$1,278	$1,568

Note: Amounts given in thousands.
  [1]Inner City, Inc. staff.
  [2]Polaroid Corporation staff.
  [3]Redistributed to Parent Corporation.

supply film to the government there. In 1978, Polaroid discontinued *all* sales in South Africa.

Richard Lawson, director of corporate materials management and services for Polaroid and president of Inner City, Inc., commented:

> Dr. Land believed in helping people to grow and attain their limits. He created the Polaroid philosophy, recognizing that it takes people to produce a quality product and that everyone, even the sweeper, had good ideas. Here, the sweeper has a chance to become a lab technician.

EXHIBIT 2   POLAROID CORPORATION AND SUBSIDIARY COMPANIES—TEN-YEAR FINANCIAL SUMMARY

	1986	1985	1984	1983	1982	1981	1980	1979	1978	1977
CONSOLIDATED STATEMENT OF EARNINGS										
Net sales										
United States	$964.3	$779.3	$743.5	$730.1	$752.5	$817.8	$791.8	$757.2	$817.4	$645.8
International	664.9	515.9	528.0	524.4	541.4	601.8	659.0	604.3	559.2	416.1
Total Net Sales	1629.2	1295.2	1271.5	1254.5	1293.9	1419.6	1450.8	1361.5	1376.6	1061.9
Cost of Goods Sold	921.7	756.0	735.2	698.3	769.6	855.4	831.1	876.8	778.3	575.7
Marketing, Research, Engineering and Administrative Expense	571.8	505.6	492.6	462.1	472.6	520.8	483.9	449.4	418.2	337.3
Total Costs	1493.5	1261.6	1227.8	1160.4	1242.2	1376.2	1315.0	1326.2	1196.5	913.0
Profit from Operations	135.7	33.6	43.7	94.1	51.7	43.4	135.8	35.3	180.1	148.9
Other Income	18.1	28.9	39.5	32.5	45.5	49.2	25.4	13.3	20.3	19.0
Interest Expense	18.6	22.3	20.9	26.5	35.5	29.9	17.0	12.8	5.9	6.4
Earnings Before Income Taxes	135.2	40.2	62.3	100.1	61.7	62.7	144.2	35.8	194.5	161.5
Federal, State, Foreign Income Taxes	31.7	3.3	36.6	50.4	38.2	31.6	58.8	(3)	76.1	69.2
Net Earnings	$103.5	$36.9	$25.7	$49.7	$23.5	$31.1	$85.4	$36.1	$118.4	$92.3
Earnings Per Share	3.34	1.19	.83	1.61	.73	.95	2.60	1.10	3.60	2.81
Cash Dividends Per Share	1.00	1.00	1.00	1.00	1.00	1.00	1.00	1.00	.90	.65
SELECTED BALANCE SHEET INFORMATION										
Working Capital	$637.0	$697.8	$734.2	$769.0	$745.4	$749.5	$721.9	$525.9	$609.5	$589.6
Net Property, Plant and Equipment	357.7	349.0	306.6	227.0	281.8	332.9	362.2	371.6	294.8	225.9
Total Assets	1479.2	1384.7	1346.0	1319.1	1323.6	1434.7	1404.0	1253.7	1276.0	1076.7
Long-Term Debt	—	124.6	124.5	124.4	124.3	124.2	124.1	—	—	—
Stockholders' Equity	994.7	922.2	916.3	921.6	902.9	958.2	960.0	907.5	904.3	815.5
OTHER STATISTICAL DATA										
Additions to Property, Plant and Equipment	$82.9	$104.5	$82.7	$51.8	$31.5	$42.5	$68.1	$134.6	$115.0	$68.7
Number of Employees	14,765	12,932	13,402	13,871	14,540	16,784	17,454	18,416	20,884	16,394
Return on Stockholders' Equity	10.8%	4.0%	2.0%	5.4%	2.5%	3.2%	9.1%	4.0%	13.8%	11.8%

Note: Unaudited. Years ended December 31. Dollars in millions, except per-share data.

Our first goal is to build a company that makes a quality product we can all feel proud of. Hand in hand with this is a belief that we have to be good community members.

INNER CITY, INC.

Inner City, Inc. was a subcontract manufacturing firm, processing materials or assembling parts for Polaroid or other companies. Bill Skelley described his operation:

We tell prospective customers, "We'd like to work for you. Send us your raw materials inventory. We'll process it and send it back to you. We're located on Columbus Avenue in Roxbury, and our work force is 95 percent minority."

If we had to tell the whole story, we might add, "Most of our people are unskilled. They've been with us, on average, only a couple of months. Most have no previous work history, or they've had problems at earlier jobs. Some have served time. We hire from the bottom of the labor force; our incoming trainees don't attach any importance to timeclocks or absenteeism or discipline or dress. Most just don't know what real work is, or how an employer expects them to behave."

When you ask prospective customers to send their work into Roxbury, all sorts of perceptions start running through their minds. But when they come to visit, they find our trainees obviously working hard, and they're surprised. They say, "Wow, you guys have a very efficient, neat, well-organized and clean operation! How do you do it?" We say, "That's what we expect. You can't run a place like this unless that's the order of business."

THE ENVIRONMENT

Inner City occupied the top four floors of a freshly painted, six-story brick and concrete building in Roxbury, a poor, predominantly black neighborhood of Boston. The building was flanked on two sides by vacant lots awaiting urban redevelopment; behind it were nineteenth century brick row houses, deteriorated by time and characteristic of much of historical Boston. Many houses were boarded up and abandoned, symbolizing the area's chronic unemployment—three times higher than that of surrounding neighborhoods. Across the street, bustling, dusty construction work continued on a new rapid transit line, spearhead of a major redevelopment program. According to plans for urban development, the area surrounding Inner City would eventually boast of cobblestone streets, brick walkways, and new housing.

When Inner City was incorporated in 1968 as a subsidiary of Polaroid Corporation, the city of Boston, along with the rest of the nation, was experiencing great social unrest. Only four years earlier, the first federal civil rights laws had been enacted. Equal employment opportunity had not yet been legislated; discrimination was commonplace in employment, housing, voting, education, transportation, and in the daily lives of many Americans. Organizations which had represented the black community since 1910 were joined by college students to protest social injustices. Often, demonstrations intended to be non-violent broke into rioting and destruction—sometimes initiated by law enforcement personnel, sometimes by extremists among the protesters. Press and television coverage brought the violent encounters into public consciousness.

Reacting to spreading social unrest and violence, President Johnson launched a number of projects, including the War on Poverty in 1964, designed to derail the accelerating problems of the nation's youth and unemployed. Antipoverty programs, including training programs conducted by public agencies and private corporations, sprang up around the country. Still, social upheaval continued. In the mid- to late 1960s, several civil rights leaders and activists were assassinated, sparking even more social dissension across the country. Protesters against racism, against the Vietnam War, and against "the Establishment" marched through city streets and across college campuses, including those in Boston.

Riots erupted in major U.S. cities. Large areas of Rochester burned, as did Washington's black neighborhood. In Los Angeles, the vast area called Watts burned for days as snipers prevented fire fighters from entering and looters vandalized those stores still standing; 35 died in the riot, as 833 others were injured and 3,600 more were arrested. In May of 1970, National Guard troops opened fire on students at Kent State University, killing 4 and wounding 10. Across the country, colleges closed until the following September, in sympathy with the slain students and to prevent further violence on their own campuses. Nervous civic leaders in Boston eyed the Roxbury ghetto, anticipating the worst.

THE FOUNDING OF INNER CITY, INC.

Governments, businesses, and civic minded groups of minorities and whites attempted to cope at the local level with the nationwide illnesses of racism and unemployment. At Polaroid Corporation, black employees and the Management Executive Committee focused on the issues. Richard Lawson, a member of the original planning team, recalled its formation:

> We had formed a "Volunteer Committee," where we shared ideas related to company business. At first we met on our own time. Then Polaroid let us meet on company time, and allowed us to do more and more. As the Volunteer Committee grew in size, its running became a full time job held by elected officials who represented to management Polaroid's black employee viewpoint.
>
> At this same time a movement was taking place in Washington which called for private enterprise to respond to the problem of hard-core unemployment in the nation's inner cities. We came up with the idea of establishing a small manufacturing plant in Boston's inner city, that would be a stepping stone for people coming to work at Polaroid or elsewhere.
>
> I worked at Inner City during its first year, and then went back to Polaroid. From there I went to the Harvard Business School. About a year after I returned to Polaroid, Inner City was in financial turmoil. Community leaders

felt the troubles resulted from mismanagement, and because I was a recent Harvard graduate, I was made manager of Inner City in 1973. Nowadays, assignments to Inner City are voluntary. Mine in '73, was not.

Inner City was losing $700,000 to $800,000 a year with no apparent end in sight, and turning out only about fifty graduates a year. It was costing us $9,000 to train a single graduate, far more than it would cost to send them to college. Inner City's operating systems duplicated all the overhead of the parent corporation; by simplifying things, I got the average cost down to $3,000 per graduate.

For the life of me, I couldn't run a business to see it lose money. And I didn't think it was right for a successful business to carry a losing business. Now we run Inner City like any business in the United States. It makes money. If it doesn't, it had better answer why. Inner City now has to answer questions like, "What did you do?," and "What do you plan to do?" [Exhibit 3 summarizes operating results for ten years, ending in 1986.]

ORGANIZATION

In 1987, Richard Lawson served as president and chairman of the board of directors of Inner City, Inc. Twelve other Polaroid executives, four of them

EXHIBIT 3 SURPLUS (DEFICIT) FROM OPERATIONS

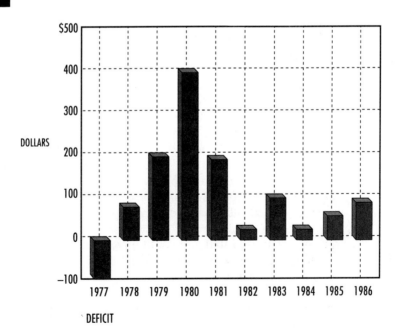

members of the firm's executive committee, served as members of the Inner City board.

Inner City's own staff numbered about thirty, of whom seventeen were Polaroid employees on loan to the subsidiary. The balance were specialists in counseling, training, and placement areas, where skills were more plentiful in the open employment market than in Polaroid's staff. Some of these "Inner City staff" members were graduate students or interns from local universities.

Although small, the organization provided room for advancement for its people. One production supervisor had recently become a company planner, and several positions were held by former trainees. (Exhibit 4 shows the 1987 organization chart.)

MANUFACTURING OPERATIONS

Inner City's various material products included film and camera products, silk screen and offset printing products, and special products. Typically, Inner City purchased raw materials from its customer, processed them, and then sold the finished product back to the customer. According to Bill Skelley,

> Polaroid was reluctant at first to give us some of their work, as you can imagine, but we proved that we could package film worth many millions of dollars. Some of the products we manufacture are essential to Polaroid. If we couldn't make the production and delivery schedule, whole divisions could be shut down or wouldn't be able to build their final products. Camera drive trains are an example.

Inner City's manufacturing operations occupied the top four floors of the Roxbury building, receiving raw materials by truck from Polaroid locations in Needham, Norwood, and Waltham. The work day began at 7 A.M. and continued until 3:30 P.M., with trainees allowed one-half hour for lunch. Primary demand for Polaroid's products determined the number of trainees, which varied between 70 and 130 people. Bill Skelley had attempted to develop work from sources other than the parent company, but the jobs had not provided the kind of challenging work he felt was appropriate for the trainees.

Film packing operations were located on the sixth floor and occupied some 25 to 50 workers (of a total work force numbering 100 people.) Packs of film for the Sun 600 camera and the Spectra line arrived by pallet loads, totaling 30,000 to 80,000 packs per day, depending on the schedule. Inner City's people packaged this film into groups of two, three, four, and five packs. The work involved little skill and could be expanded quickly as demand changed.

On the fifth floor, another ten to fifteen trainees worked at assembling a portion of the "hard body" for the Sun camera, applying the lens panel, trim button and retainer, and decorative stripe. Approximately 7 to 10,000 bodies per day were shipped to the Norwood plant. Photocopying and silk screening operations—the only department to serve a significant number of outside customers—employed eight trainees on the fourth floor.

EXHIBIT 4 THE INNER CITY ORGANIZATION: POLAROID STAFF MEMBERS

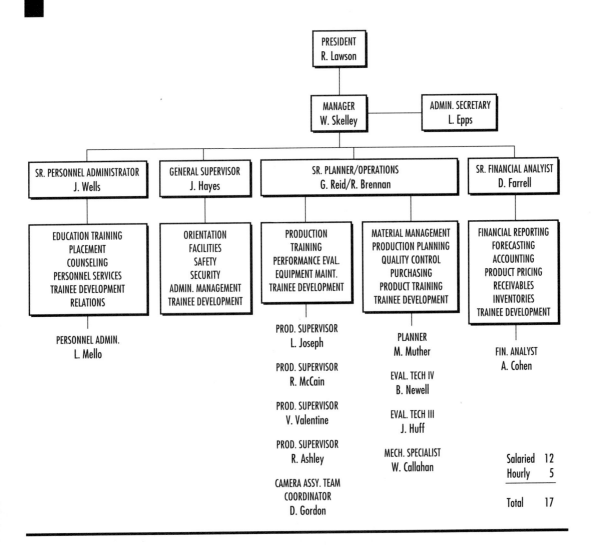

The most complex jobs in the Inner City involved the drive assembly for the Sun camera. Some thirty-five to forty trainees on the third floor worked at the task, handling twenty-six intricate parts to build the drives. Five to six of these people, two of whom were Polaroid staff members, worked on quality control. Drive production remained relatively constant at 3,600 per day; the long learning times involved made it difficult to scale up operations quickly. Bill Skelley discussed quality control:

We can't afford to have the slightest quality control problem. People will quickly take the work away from us. The standards that are applied to an operation like this versus the standards that are applied in the mainstream are really different. If you have 2 percent rejection, somehow the 2 percent looks like 25 perent because you are going to be held to a higher standard.

COMPETITION

Competition for Inner City existed in both training and manufacturing. In training, government manpower development programs attempted similar goals but rarely achieved them; the "hard-core unemployed" were considered beyond reach. In manufacturing, the chief competition was with Polaroid's own internal production operations. Bill Skelley commented:

> I don't think there is anyone that quite does what we do, but we do have competitors. I have to convince managers within Polaroid to allow us to quote on increasing our subcontracting load. If we can't competitively quote and produce scheduled quality work, then we won't get that product. We have lost a number of lines because our quotes weren't competitive with internal costs. However, in some cases we run a more efficient shop than Polaroid.
>
> There's also the offshore competition that the whole country is going through now. A lot of the type of work we do here, which is basic light hand assembly, is what America is sending offshore.
>
> If you're looking from the training point of view, I guess our competition comes from those companies that offer entry level employment at low wages and with no future, like some segments of the fast-food industry. They take people off the street and employ them a while. It takes people some time to realize that they're not going anywhere.
>
> And there are competitors in the manufacturing arena such as small sub-contractors that still tend to run on a sweatshop mentality, pay slightly above minimum wages with no benefits packages, offer people somewhat steady employment, yet no opportunity for career advancement.

At one time, Inner City competed with workshop-training programs contracted by various charities and state rehabilitation commissions. According to Bill Skelley, Inner City had moved away from that sort of work:

> Workshops are no longer competitors of ours and I think that's a significant transition. Years ago we did the same kind of work—basic stuffing, putting components into a package. I think we've taken a significant step up: now we are focused on more intricate assembly, which is stepping into the high-tech arena, but requires much more in the way of quality control.

MANPOWER DEVELOPMENT OPERATIONS

In the 1960s, the federal government encouraged private industry to set up manpower training programs by paying companies to hire and train otherwise unqualified people. Jim Wells, senior personnel administrator, commented:

It was the thing to do, to take federal money and set up a nice program. But we didn't want bureaucrats coming in saying, "Hey, Jim Wells, tomorrow we want you to do this." The next year they take half your budget and say, "Well, sorry, but we need to put the money somewhere else!"

To our conscious knowledge, we did not borrow any program ideas from anyone. The program evolved. We didn't have a blueprint; we just built some things and they worked, so we expanded on them.

There has always been a tremendous difference between how the people were treated here, versus how they were dealt with in the federally funded city and state programs. I think it's the expectation levels we have here. Things are accepted in other programs that we just don't accept here.

PROGRAM DESIGN

The program began with a four- to eight-hour orientation session where applicants heard in detail what would be expected of them. Those who decided to go ahead were hired into the first of the program's three phases, as the minimum wage of $3.55/hour.

During their first week of Phase I, trainees were introduced to the program, the staff, and all the products which were manufactured at Inner City. Trainees were moved through different tasks to find the area that best suited their skills. Here they were told the quality and production standards that would be expected. Prominently displayed on the factory walls were easy-to-read charts tracking each trainee's attendance record and hourly production (for individuals) or daily output for groups.

After a month's demonstration of a cooperative attitude, good attendance, and work record, trainees were promoted to Phase II. Their pay was increased to $3.80 per hour. Trainees also attended required seminars on job performance, health and hygiene, and job seeking skills. (Exhibit 5 shows the content of these seminars and lists the other seminars available.)

Each month, Inner City selected one of its trainees for the "Employee of the Month" award. Eligible people were at least six weeks into Phase II, had perfect attendance records, and had demonstrated an ability to get along with others. Supervisors recommended trainees to a rotating committee of staff members who picked the monthly winners. "Recruiters from other companies love to pick up our Employees of the Month," said Bill Skelley.

Production workers at Inner City were permitted to develop their own preferred methods of accomplishing the work. Millie Muther, production supervisor, commented:

We'll show them how to run a machine, but if they have a better way of doing it, and if the quality is as good, then they can do it their own way. There's no set way that a trainee must work.

I'm a firm believer: the person that's building the product, really knows how to do it better than anyone else. They'll try to get the most done. They're being paid for it.

EXHIBIT 5   INNER CITY SEMINARS

SEMINAR SUBJECTS

1. Health and Hygiene	10. Emotions and Behavior
2. Job Performance	11. Preparing your taxes
3. Transition Group	12. Understanding the Judicial System
4. Financial Literacy	13. Jobs for the 80's
5. Educational and Vocational Choices for Adults	14. The Black Contribution
6. Planned Parenthood	15. Consumer Education
7. Nutrition and Budgeting	16. Orientation to Computers
8. Child Development	17. Polaroid Photography
9. The Job Entry Phase	18. Jobs in the Service Industry
	19. Housing Resources

MANDATORY SEMINAR: JOB PERFORMANCE
8 hours total (4 hours Inner City time)

- Why People Work
- Components of Good Job Performance
- Importance of Quality
- Value of Performance Evaluations
- Criteria for Evaluating Performance
- Hierarchical Structure of Companies
- Jobs for the 80s
- How to be Successful on the Job
- Communicating Effectively with Supervisors
- Understanding the Supervisor's Job
- Job Benefits
- Job Postings
- Upward Mobility
- Resignations

MANDATORY SEMINAR: HEALTH AND HYGIENE
6 hours total (3 hours Inner City time)

- Proper Nutrition
- Preventive Medicine
- Care of the Body
- Hair Care
- Skin Care
- Nail Care
- Dental Care
- Health Clinics
- Patients' Rights
- The Physical Exam
- Birth Control
- Venereal Disease
- Sickle Cell Trait
- Hypertension

MANDATORY SEMINAR: TRANSITION GROUP, JOB-SEEKING SKILLS
26 hours total (14 hours Inner City time)

- Self-Assessment
- Motivation
- Getting What You Want
- Job Applications
- Resume Preparation
- Interviewing Techniques
- Role Play Interviews
- In-House Interviews
- Off-Site Interviews
- Stress Management
- Fitting In
- Adjustments to a New Job

TRAINEES

Although trainees joined the program in small groups, they completed it individually, depending on whether and when they were ready to work elsewhere. That decision was made by a group of Inner City staff, usually at the suggestion of the trainee's immediate supervisor. A trainee could be placed in an outside job in as little as four months or as long as nine months.

Other than a minimum age of eighteen, there were no eligibility requirements for Inner City trainees. Anyone could apply. Selection was on a first-come, first-served basis. Most trainees were in their early twenties. The oldest recruit was a man in his sixties; on occasion, the parent of a graduate became a trainee. Word-of-mouth communication was the program's only advertising up until 1985, when the thriving economy of Massachusetts had reduced the overall unemployment rate to just over 3 percent. At that time, Inner City began to use radio advertising to attract trainees.

Bill Skelley summed up the plight of many trainees:

> We have a lot of people in here who are really very bright, very sharp. But when it comes to work, they've had problems. Maybe because of social factors, maybe because of not knowing how to go about getting a job or maybe because the places they apply to have certain criteria that exclude them because of color or some other factor. In any event, they have less than desirable work histories.
>
> We take a couple of approaches to you as a trainee: we make you feel good about yourself initially; we tell you we expect an awful lot out of you; and we're not going to accept anything less. We say, "That's what you've got to do to be successful; now we'll help you with it. Are you willing to pay the price? That's the key question; if you are, you will be successful. If you're not, you'll probably wind up being terminated."

Trainee Gene Lang straddled a chair and chomped on a candy bar, hungry after working a full shift at Inner City, Inc.:

> Before I came to Inner City, I only got jobs for one thing: quick cold cash, then I'd split. But this place really turned my head around. This is a place that wants you to work, to be on time and to learn. They said to me, "You'll learn about holding on to a job by being here on time, by following the rules and by taking pride in yourself and your work." Well, that sounded like so much crap to me. But you get here, man, and you see the other trainees. They been here a few weeks and so you see that they really work together. And that's the key, it's family. I mean, you might have some family scraps once in a while, but everyone starts to care about each other.
>
> We all start to believe in each other, that we can make it through the program and graduate so that we can work in a permanent job someplace else. There *are* exceptions, the ones who don't want to be family; they usually goof off and get canned.
>
> And it's tough here. They want you to know that you can make it through the program, but it's up to you to show your supervisor that you're serious about it, 'cause they sure as hell are.

PLACEMENT

Inner City placed approximately 100 trainees per year in a variety of manufacturing and service settings. Since 1968 over 1,600 program graduates had been placed in 53 Boston-area companies, ranging from high technology to education to service. For the first ten years, the firm's trainees were placed with the parent company when their skills were sufficiently developed. In the business downturn of 1978, Polaroid's hiring policy changed; after that time, all graduates were placed with other Boston-area employers.

An important pre-placement activity was the "mock interview," with Inner City staff members playing the role of the potential employer. Millie Muther described the trainee's view of this experience:

> One of my people had his first mock interview just today; that's his suit hanging there in the corner. He worked until 1:00, then changed into his suit and tie in the men's room. He says, "Are you sure I look all right?" Well, his collar was folded up, so he let me fix it. He says, "Can you see me shaking? Do you know how nervous I am? Is he going to say hello first or do I say it first to him?" He just got caught up, and so nervous. They're very proud to be all dressed up and going for their first interview. Even if it's only a mock interview, it's very important to them. He went downstairs and did a super job.

Brian Stebbins, a college senior in a management internship program, served as an assistant supervisor to Millie Muther and described the progress of a former trainee who had experienced a successful placement.

> You hear from former trainees every once in a while. I'm thinking of one who came back here to visit; he had had a really tough life before he came here and he had a tough beginning here, too. He was finally placed after a while. When he came back, he showed us his new bank book to show us his savings, and he wanted us to look out the window to see the car he just bought. But I remember that he had some very tough problems while he was here. We just kept telling him: "Willie, if you just keep working and do well here, you'll get a good job and you'll see a big turnaround." He came into our office one day and just broke down and started crying. He's over forty, but he broke down trying to tell us that he was a man and he wanted a job. That was heartbreaking. We kept encouraging him. We said there would be a change, but I don't think that he believed us completely until he went out and got the job.

Bill Skelley pointed out another placement potential for some trainees—promotion to Inner City staff positions:

> One trainee was just made a supervisor. We found after she came here, she had graduated from college in North Carolina; she's done very well. Another former trainee handles our whole payroll system; she's taking college courses at Northeastern now. Another former trainee is doing a fine job as a crew chief on the production floor. It really helps to see someone who works beside you go up the ladder. These people are excellent role models.

RETENTION

Typically, about one-quarter of the trainees entering Inner City's program graduated to "regular" full-time employment. Some 30 percent—referred to as "negative results" by the staff—were either fired or quit in the face of termination. Another large group left after a few months' training, to take other, higher-paying jobs. Non-graduates, Bill Skelley pointed out, benefited from their training while employed in the program, even though they chose not to finish it. By year, the numbers of people hired and placed are shown in the first part of Exhibit 6.

Retention rates for Inner City graduates in their first jobs were tracked from 1982 to 1984 and indicated a substantial success during the graduates' first several months at work. The second part of Exhibit 6 shows that, of the total of 183 graduates covered by surveys, 158 or 85 percent stayed with their original employers for at least ninety days after placement. By the six-month point, retention had dropped only slightly to 140 or 77 percent. By year of placement, retention rates were measured as shown in Exhibit 6.

TRAINING POLICIES

Inner City emphasized its commitment to preparing people for long-term employment by implementing policies that might be considered stringent in many businesses.

SUSPENSIONS

Unruly and disruptive behavior or refusal to work was controlled through the use of suspensions. Millie Muther described handling a trainee's refusal to cooperate—a situation which might warrant a suspension:

> You say to yourself, "Why is that person doing that today? He is usually pretty good and has never refused to do a job." So you talk to that person and you

EXHIBIT 6 INDIVIDUALS HIRED AND PLACED

	1982	1983	1984	1985	1986
Number hired	248	426	479	511	460
Number placed	62	94	130	106	102

RETENTION RATES: 1984 STUDY GROUP

YEAR PLACED	SURVEY TOTAL	EMPLOYEES STILL ON THE JOB AT			
		3 Mo.	6 Mo.	12 Mo.	18 Mo.
1982	57	50 (88%)	44 (77%)	42 (74%)	38 (67%)
1983	85	75 (90%)	68 (82%)	43 (52%)	17 (21%)
1984	41*	33 (80%)	28 (68%)	*	*

*Small sample; first quarter placements only; this group not on job long enough to measure beyond six months.

get to the core of the problem and you solve it. It's usually a misunderstanding with someone else or a problem at home. But, if something like that continues, or is done more than once, we usually suspend them for three days because you can't refuse to do a job. You may not like to do it, but you can't refuse.

An example might be a trainee—Eddie—who has just been placed. He started out really well—had no problems at all. Then all at once he changed. He came in one day with a certain attitude; it just wasn't him. He still came in on time, but he wouldn't communicate. You can't place people with an attitude like that. We talked about his behavior to get at the source of his problem.

We had put up bars on all the sixth floor windows—kids were breaking in from the roof to steal film. The first day of the bars was when we saw the change in Eddie. It hadn't occurred to me that the bars would affect anyone. But Eddie had spent time in jail, and the bars had a special meaning for him. Knowing the problem helped me work with him. It made me feel pretty good when he finally did get a job—and it's a job he wants.

There are different ways to deal with problems. I've had people refuse to do a job, and when I've talked to them, it's because they've had this back problem, or they've had this operation, and they can't help it. If they don't speak up or communicate in the correct manner, they could wind up getting terminated. So it's another lesson for them.

TERMINATIONS

Continued disruptive behavior is usually a way of testing the supervisor and can lead to termination early in the program. Millie Muther described some of the tactics used by trainees, and their results:

They're brand new, so naturally they're going to put me through the test first. If there is a change in supervision, then they're going to put the new supervisor through the test to see if they can get away with more.

They test you by coming back from lunch or breaks late. They're supposed to punch in for morning, at lunch, at when they leave for the day, but not for breaks. So if they are late from break, the first time I usually ignore it, but after that I'll talk to them. And I'll say, "I saw you the other day when you were late. I didn't say anything because I was hoping it was just a mistake on your part."

I try to put the ownership back on them, and to make sure they realize that I'm not out to get them, that I want to help them. After that, they'll go on warning and then they could be terminated if their behavior doesn't improve. You stress to them that no matter where they work, they have to come back on time, not one or two minutes late, or they're not going to keep their job. They learn eventually.

We terminated a man on the spot, a couple of weeks ago. He put four packs of film underneath his hat. A lot of people saw that, so you can't let him get away with it. At first, we were going to wait—to catch him red-handed leaving the floor. But we've tried that before; you get interrupted for a few seconds, and the thief is gone. So we talked it over and said he's got it under his hat, and it shouldn't be there, so let's get rid of him now. A legal department in some big company would say the film doesn't cost you much; a lawsuit would cost a lot. But this is a training program. It's different. And even this guy has a right to appeal.

Trainees know up front that I'm not here to fire them. I don't fire people; I never have. I've signed the termination papers, but they've done the firing to themselves. They'll say, "I don't know why you fired me, I don't know what I did." And so you show them the record, and point out that they didn't learn by going on warning or by being talked to. There are only so many breaks I can give them.

There was no specific rule at Inner City regarding the number of warnings prior to termination from the program. Rules were well defined, however, regarding processes for reinstatement of trainees.

APPEALS BOARD

Not all terminations were permanent; Inner City gave its trainees a second chance. The terminated trainee received an appeals letter with his or her final check. The letter stated an appeal date, typically two weeks from the termination date, and a meeting time of 3:30 P.M. According to Millie Muther, punctuality was considered to be an important indicator of a trainee's willingness to continue with the program.

They have to be prompt and be here by 3:30. If they're a minute late, we don't see them because it proves that they really don't want their job. Ninety-nine percent of them are here before 3:30. Right now, I have twenty-eight people on my floor; six of them have gone through the appeal process. When they come back, many of them seem to be okay for a while. Then all of a sudden some of them slip back again, and they end up being terminated. In the second termination, there is no appeal.

MEETING A CHANGING ENVIRONMENT

Long-term corporate commitment by Polaroid was essential to Inner City's ability to meet the challenges of an ever-changing environment.

CORPORATE COMMITMENT

The commitment of Polaroid to Inner City's survival had been evident since its inception. Bill Skelley addressed this issue:

When the parent company experiences difficult times—which we have gone through—it is forced to look at all facets of the company. Look at Inner City. Is it a cost or a drain on the company? If we lost a million dollars, there would be a lot of people sitting in Polaroid headquarters questioning the validity of this program. That could happen very quickly. Unemployment is 3.7 percent in this state; the lowest since sliced bread came on the board. Jobs are going begging; you have to bus people in from Timbuktu.

It would be easy to ask. "Why do you need Inner City any more?" The people who make those decisions must have an in-depth understanding of what is happening in the real world. Polaroid, went through a 30 percent reduction in personnel, beginning in '78 or '79. Today the company is down to about 9,000 employees, domestically—some 14,000 worldwide. It really tested the corporate commitment to have products built by temporary people at Inner City, while full-time Polaroid employees were losing their jobs.

Now the corporation is staying lean. Like most big companies, it hires *only* temporary people for entry-level manufacturing work. Last year they hired over 2,000 temps, and many of them came right out of Inner City's ranks. Say you were working here at $3.50 an hour, and you got a note saying, "Come to work at Polaroid and you can make $7 an hour." You'd say, "When do I report?" We told our people those were only temporary jobs; they'd be let go in three to six months, and they couldn't come back here if they left. Some held on there longer than we'd expected; others were back on the streets within three weeks. But such is life.

CURRENT PROBLEMS AND ALTERNATIVES

Bill Skelley summarized some of the current problems and alternatives for Inner City:

For the first time in our history, the people we hire have options in their lives. Virtually *anyone* can get a job. Historically, our people had only us as a viable option.

How do we motivate people to go through training when they can go out and get a job on their own, even though it's a dead-ended job? That's what we're struggling with—trying to convince younger people today to do some long-range planning. Long-range career planning for many of them is based on next Saturday night's party. Planning for six to nine months, never mind the next couple of years, is difficult.

Do we have to pay them more? Then, how do we price our products competitively? And if we pay more, we create another problem: people won't want to leave here. This is an environment geared to making them feel good about themselves, and we're also convenient to their homes. So, if we raise their pay by "X" cents per hour, whatever that may be, we reduce their incentive for leaving.

Also, for the first time in our history, the majority of our 1986 placements were in the service sector. Now "service sector" means a lot of things. For us, it *doesn't* mean flipping hamburgers—because we won't do that. But it *could* mean working in a bank as a teller. It could mean working in a hotel as a telephone operator or a receptionist or a bell captain or a housekeeper.

The skill levels needed for service sector jobs are higher than for entry-level manufacturing jobs. Which means that our people have to be better prepared. To go and sit on the production line at an electronics firm as an entry-level manufacturing person is pretty basic—it's just putting the piece parts together. To go and do a comparable job in a hotel requires a lot more from you. For instance, one of our women in a housekeeping function at a major hotel has to interface with a computer five or six times a day. She's got to go to the computer and punch numbers in to find out where her next assignment is, how many towels and bars of soap she needs. And this is in an entry-level job. We have to do a better job of preparing our people.

We're finding a population more in need at the same time that the jobs are more demanding. There's a widening gap. The schools are at an all-time low on preparing people for the world of work. There's a 47 percent noncompletion rate in the city's schools, and even those that *do* complete aren't prepared to get a job on their own.

We're trying now to tailor our training program to the service sector. I think 56 percent of our graduates last year went into service sector jobs; two years ago it was 14 percent. The advantage of service sector jobs is that they are mostly in Boston; we don't run into the transportation problem we normally have. See, our people don't drive; 99 percent of them don't own a car. And if you get jobs out on Route 128 or in some distant suburb, you are limited by a transportation problem.

We're trying to expand our silk screening business with a new machine that more than quadruples our capacity. It teaches a specific skill. Hopefully we can place somebody in that type of business.

We have to look at other service-related alternatives. For example, the fulfillment business is a multi-billion dollar industry. Let's say that you buy five six-packs of a soft drink and send the labels in and you get a free digital watch. Who sends you the watch? Companies don't do it themselves. We tried to do it once, but we got out of it because we weren't doing it right. Now we're looking at doing it again.

We're also looking at data entry. What if we set up a data entry business here? That sounds good but changes the way we approach things: it would require a higher skilled person. It means that we would have to keep people longer. Rather than turning people over in six months it means that they're going to be here for two or three years. And if that happens, then you've got to pay them a competitive market wage. You've got to add a benefits package and you can't serve as many people. Our costs skyrocket. How do you offset those costs?

Another idea is an "externship" kind of program, where we place our temporary employees in a Polaroid production operation and we supervise them there. Hopefully it will be a good training tool for us. We're doing it now on a limited basis. We provide the supervisors, so we've got to make money at it.

We're still doing camera assembly, but some of it may be automated through robotics over the next few years, so I'm looking at products we can bring in for 1989. What happens if some of that gets automated? Then we switch to the service sector.

We've gone through our period of rapid growth. We're plateauing now, and looking at a redirection; new growth will come out of that. Redirection could mean that we'll be out of this building in a few years; I believe we'll have a new place to reside. There's going to be a *change* in direction. The world is changing around us. If we don't change with it, we limit what we can do.

MORTON THIOKOL, INC.

JYOTI N. PRASAD

On May 7, 1987, the *Wall Street Journal* reported what Morton Thiokol had all along been apprehensive of. The report said that Jane Smith, widow of Challenger co-pilot Michael Smith, filed a $1.5 billion lawsuit against the U.S. government, Morton Thiokol, Inc. and former space agency engineer Lawrence Mulloy, who supervised the shuttle-booster rocket program at the time of the January 28, 1986, disaster which caused a massive dent in the U.S. space program. All seven crew members, including teacher Christa McAuliffe, were killed in the accident.

The suit, filed in U.S. District Court in Orlando, Florida, sought $500 million in damage jointly from the three defendants, accusing them of negligence in the shuttle accident. The suit asked for an additional $1 billion in punitive damages from Thiokol, manufacturer of the shuttle's booster rockets. The complaint alleged that Thiokol's behavior was "willful, wanton, malicious" and showed a "reckless disregard for human life." The suit also demanded to bar Thiokol from further shuttle work. It asserted that Thiokol was wrong in telling NASA that the rocket defect could be fixed. "The fact is," the complaint said, "that these joints are so fundamentally and basically unsound that it is impossible for them to be fixed."

While the families of four astronauts reached a settlement with the Justice Department and Thiokol late in 1986, giving up the right to file future claims in return for at least $750,000 each, survivors of another astronaut, Ronald McNair, filed a suit against Thiokol. In addition, Roger Boisjoly, a Thiokol engineer who argued against the shuttle launch, had filed two suits against his former employer.

In its *1986 Annual Report,* Morton Thiokol reported that:

Along with other business enterprises, the Company has experienced, effective April 1, 1986, substantial increases in insurance premiums and sub-

Source: **Prepared by Professor Jyoti Prasad, Eastern Illinois University, as a basis for classroom discussion and not to illustrate either effective or ineffective handling of administrative situations.** © **Jyoti N. Prasad, 1989.**

stantial decreases in the risks covered. With respect to the Company's aircraft products liability insurance, the policy limits remain the same, but the extent of the coverage has been reduced to exclude certain property damage, most significantly property damage to or losses (including loss of use) of satellites or space launch vehicles or their cargoes. This creates an exposure to the Company for satellite placement motors previously delivered but unflown or under contract for delivery to customers. In both cases, the Company has warned its customers of the situation and is seeking to negotiate an appropriate allocation of risk exposure, limiting the Company's exposure to an acceptable dollar amount such as the replacement cost of the particular motor involved in any accident. If such negotiations are not successful, if there is a loss and if the Company's liability were determined by a court in a particular situation not to be so limited, the resultant damages could have a material adverse effect on the financial condition of the Company. (Morton Thiokol, Inc., *1986 Annual Report*, p. 27).

BUSINESS AND PRODUCTS

Morton Thiokol operates in three business segments: specialty chemicals, aerospace, and salt manufacturing, and markets a wide range of products for industrial, government, and consumer use, both in the U.S. and internationally.

AEROSPACE

The aerospace segment consists of propulsion and ordinance products and services performed principally under contracts and subcontracts with various U.S. government agencies and aerospace prime contractors.

Propulsion includes research, development, and production of solid rocket motor systems which is used for: space vehicles such as the Space Shuttle, to position satellites in orbit, for strategic missiles such as the Trident (submarine-launched), for tactical missiles such as the Maverick, Sidewinder, and MX missiles. This propulsion technology has been applied by Morton Thiokol in the manufacturing of gas generators for use in automobiles' passive restraint systems.

Development and production of gas generators for automobile airbag inflation systems dramatically increased as the 100,000th production unit was delivered to Mercedes Benz. Additionally, Morton Thiokol was selected by Chrysler late in fiscal 1986 to be its airbag production source. Both domestic and foreign auto manufacturers are investigating airbag installation resulting from the Mercedes initiative and the Department of Transportation ruling to require passive restraint systems for 10% of all model cars sold in the U.S.

Services of the aerospace segment include the launch and recovery operations for the Space Shuttle. The loss of the Challenger shuttle flight resulted in the suspension of production of Space Shuttle solid rocket motors and the redirection of resources to the failure investigation and redesign of the field and nozzle joints of the motors. Approval of the motor redesign will be followed by requalification and certification of the motors leading to resumption of production of motors for shuttle flights, which are currently scheduled to commence in fiscal 1988.

Morton Thiokol has numerous patents in the aerospace field, most of which relate to solid propulsion. These demonstrate the technical inventiveness of the aerospace segment's staff and are useful in furthering the company's business relationship with its customers. The U.S. government has a royalty-free license under each patent for an invention developed at its expense. Since the government provides, directly and indirectly, the majority of this segment's business, the possible loss of all such business would have a materially adverse effect on Morton Thiokol's operations.

The aerospace segment had 1986 fiscal sales of $933 million, an increase of 8% over fiscal 1985. Profits also rose 6% to $96 million. (See Exhibit 1.) It is the largest producer of solid rocket propulsion systems for the U.S. market, representing approximately 40% thereof. Principal competitive factors are technical performance, quality, reliability, price, depth, and capabilities of personnel and adequacy of facilities. Space sales, which account for 18% of Morton Thiokol's total sales, were down 7%, largely stemming from standdown of shuttle flights.

EXHIBIT 1 MORTON THIOKOL, INC.: OPERATIONS IN DIFFERENT BUSINESSES

SALES AND PROFIT	SALES[1]			PROFIT[2]		
	1986	1985	1984	1986	1985	1984
Aerospace	$ 933.1	864.5	733.8	96.3	91.2	71.5
Specialty Chemicals	651.8	615.8	646.2	87.4	789.7	82.9
Salt	365.0	352.0	355.0	74.3	57.6	50.7
Business Totals	$1,949.9	1,832.3	1,735.0	258.0	238.5	205.1
General corporate expense—net				(32.8)	(33.4)	(37.9)
Consolidated net sales and pretax income	$1,949.9	1,832.3	1,735.0	225.2	205.1	167.2

[1]Aerospace Group sales encompass propulsion and ordnance products and services performed principally under contracts and subcontracts with various United States government agencies and aerospace prime contractors. Net sales under United States government contracts and subcontracts amounted to $888, $835, and $702 million for 1986, 1985, and 1984, respectively, or 46%, 46%, and 40%, respectively, of the company's net sales; export sales from the United States were less than 10% of sales to unaffiliated customers; and intersegment and intergeographic area sales and transfers were insignificant.

[2]Business segment profit is before income taxes, interest income, interest expense, and allocation of certain corporate administrative expenses, but includes foreign exchange gains and (losses) of $3.8, ($.3) and ($.5) million in 1986, 1985, and 1984, respectively.

Sources: Moody's Industrial Manual, 1986, pp. 3288–95. Morton Thiokol, Inc., 1986 Annual Report, pp. 22–23.

The solid propulsion facilities are located at Elkton, Maryland; Huntsville, Alabama; Carson City, Nevada; and near Brigham City, Utah. The Elkton and Carson City land and buildings are owned by the company. Those in Huntsville are substantially owned by the U.S. government, and those in Utah are partly company-owned, partly government-owned, and partly leased.

SPECIALTY CHEMICALS

Morton Thiokol manufactures high technology chemical products for a wide variety of customer applications. The largest product group consists of laminating adhesives and coatings designed primarily for use in the manufacturing of food packaging materials from paper, film, and foil. The second largest group consists of chemicals for the electronics market, including principally dry film photoresists and curable screen resists used as part of a process to imprint circuit patterns onto printed circuit boards and semiconductors (silicon chips).

Morton Thiokol also manufactures customized performance coatings principally for use on plastic substrates in the automotive, consumer electronics, appliance, and business machines markets, and liquid dyes to color petroleum products for identification purposes. Other dyes and coloring products are used in printing and writing inks, plastics, foods, drugs, and cosmetics. Specialty chemicals products are marketed throughout the world directly to customers and indirectly through distributors and agents.

Morton Thiokol has always considered it important to acquire domestic and foreign patent protection for the numerous proprietary products and processes of the specialty chemicals segment deemed valuable to the business. Accordingly, such protection has usually been obtained whenever possible. Patent protection currently extends for various periods up to the year 2004. Patents in the electronic chemicals, packaging, adhesives and coatings, biocides, and heat stabilizer product lines considerably contribute to the company's market position.

The majority of this segment's business, including the two largest product groups, is highly competitive. There is substantial competition from a variety of alternative materials. The company had over 90% of world capacity to produce sodium borhydride (used principally as a bleaching chemical in paper manufacturing), and also had a majority share of the markets for biocides to incorporate into plastics, inorganic research chemicals, hydride chemicals, and specialty metal powders. Principal methods of competition include technical service for specialized customer requirements, price, and quality.

The specialty chemical group achieved 1986 fiscal year sales of $652 million, a gain of 6% over the prior year. Operating profit, however, showed a decline of 3% to $87 million. (See Exhibit 1.)

The worldwide electronics industry recession affected Morton Thiokol in the second half of fiscal 1985 and worsened throughout fiscal 1986. Considered by many to be the most severe ever experienced by the industry, this recession detracted significantly from the specialty chemicals' sales growth and was responsible for the operating profit decrease.

Specialty chemical products are manufactured at 25 locations in the United States (some of which are operated through divisions or wholly owned subsidiaries); by wholly owned subsidiaries in Canada, Mexico, France, the United Kingdom, Italy, the Netherlands, Singapore, and West Germany; and by three joint venture corporations in Japan.

SALT

Morton Thiokol produces and sells salt principally in the U.S. and Canada for human and animal consumption, water conditioning, and highway ice melt-ing, as well as for industrial and chemical uses. Sales of Morton brand table salt in the U.S. are approximately equal to the aggregate of all other table salt sales. Salt for water conditioning is sold principally for residential use mostly in packages. Salt for industrial and chemical use is sold in bulk and in pack-ages, and is used for food and meat processing and in a wide variety of chemi-cal applications. Salt for ice melting on streets and highways is sold mostly in bulk form to government agencies, with some ice melting salt being sold in packages under the Safe-T-Salt brand.

Sales of salt are made through the company sales forces, as well as through independent distributors, agents, and brokers. Regional sales offices and cus-tomer services facilities are maintained throughout the U.S.

Total salt production by Morton Thiokol was about 9.8 million tons in fiscal 1986. Rock salt brine well reserves have sufficient reserves to satisfy an-ticipated production requirements for the foreseeable future. Sales of highway ice control salt are quite seasonal, and vary with winter weather conditions in areas of its use. Ice control salt is stockpiled by both the company and by its customers.

All areas in which the salt segment operates are highly competitive. Its market share varies widely depending on the geographic area and the type of product involved. This segment uses price, service, product performance, and technical, advertising, and promotional support as its principal methods of competition.

Sales increased 4% to $365 million and earnings were at $74 million (See Exhibit 1.) However, new product national introductions for Morton Seasoned Salt and Morton garlic salt brands offset the increase in this business segment.

ACQUISITIONS

In 1982 Morton-Norwich was searching for an acquisition that would help it expand in specialty chemicals. (See Exhibit 2 for a history of the company.) It had just sold its pharmaceuticals division to Procter & Gamble and was willing

EXHIBIT 2 MORTON THIOKOL, INC.: HISTORY

1969	April 25	Title of Morton-Norwich adopted and plan of merger with Morton International.
	September 2	Incorporated in Delaware.
	November 30	Merged with Morton International.
1971		Morton International, Norwich Pharmaceutical, and Texize Chemical, Inc. merged and became operating divisions thereof.
1982	June	Company sold Norwich-Eaton Pharmaceuticals Division to Procter & Gamble for $371 million.
	August	Acquired assets of Specialty Chemicals Group of Phillip Morris Industries, Inc.
	September	Merged with Thiokol Corporation and corporate name changed to Morton Thiokol.
1984		Sold Southwest Chemical Services, Inc.
1985		Sold Texize Division to Dow Chemical Co. for $131 million cash and 1.4 million shares of company stock.
1986	January 28	Space Shuttle tragedy occurred and seven astronauts were killed. Failure of booster rockets designed and manufactured by Morton Thiokol were blamed for the tragedy.
1987	May 7	A $1.5 billion suit was filed against Thiokol by the widow of one of the astronauts who perished in Challenger disaster.
	May 28	Thiokol successfully staged a full-scale test of a redesigned and improved booster rocket. NASA has set the next shuttle flight for June 1988.

to pay $540 million to acquire 49.5% of Thiokol common stock. This acquisition boosted its stake in the fast growing chemical market as well as put Morton into the space and defense business. Morton's plan was to nurture the specialties area with funds from its "cash cow," Morton Salt. For Morton-Norwich the marriage with Thiokol was expected to offset some revenue loss suffered in the sale of its pharmaceutical division.

Morton engaged in an aggressive expansion in late 1985 when an agreement was finalized for the purchase of the powder coatings assets and business of Polymer Corporation, a subsidiary of Cheeseborough-Ponds, Inc. This acquisition was expected to further Morton's growth in the specialty chemicals area and improve its business portfolio. It had about $95.5 million in cash and short-term investments with a low debt to equity ratio to use in expansion at the end of 1986. Even in 1987 Morton Thiokol does not appear to be done with its acquisitions. However, Morton does not plan to dilute earnings with costly acquisitions just for the sake of expanding. (The company's financial data are given in Exhibits 3 and 4.)

EXHIBIT 3 MORTON THIOKOL, INC.: CONSOLIDATED BALANCE SHEETS

	1986	1985	AS OF JUNE 30 1984	1983	1982	1981
ASSETS						
Current Assets:						
Cash and short-term investments	$ 46.1	93.5	92.8	15.8	307.1	47.2
Receivables	316.6	275.3	282.4	222.7	101.9	142.6
Inventories	221.5	200.9	187.6	195.4	86.2	126.0
Prepaid expenses	12.4	13.1	11.4	14.0	20.6	18.1
Total Current Assets	$ 596.6	582.8	574.2	447.9	515.8	333.9
Other Assets						
Cost in excess of net assets of acquisitions, less amortization	192.0	194.3	146.8	148.5	4.9	6.7
Non-current assets of discontinued operations	—	—	—	—	—	33.5
Miscellaneous	34.5	30.4	51.1	32.0	19.4	44.3
Property, Plant & Equipment:	890.1	798.8	756.3	718.4	367.1	472.8
Less allowances for depreciation	296.2	238.1	229.6	195.5	160.3	194.7
Net property, plant & Equipment:	593.9	560.7	526.7	522.9	206.8	278.1
TOTAL ASSETS	$1,417.0	1,368.2	1,298.8	1,151.3	746.9	696.5

(continued)

LIABILITIES & STOCKHOLDERS' EQUITY

Current Liabilities						
Notes payable and current portion of long-term debt	$ 26.5	15.7	12.4	13.0	12.8	32.7
Accounts payable	128.9	131.0	144.5	108.3	46.8	67.2
Accrued salaries and other expenses	140.6	140.8	134.3	134.6	77.7	44.6
Income taxes	57.0	29.5	94.5	70.9	99.9	20.1
Total Current Liabilities	$ 353.0	317.0	385.7	326.8	237.2	164.6
Non-Current Liabilities						
Long-term Debt, less current portion	31.7	152.7	149.5	149.9	69.1	98.9
Deferred Income Taxes	161.7	139.5	83.2	78.8	35.8	45.5
Other Non-Current Liabilities	48.7	54.2	44.1	45.8	20.9	5.3
Stockholders' Equity						
Common stock	51.1	51.1	16.9	16.8	13.7	13.7
Additional paid-in capital	75.8	76.1	70.6	59.8	59.2	59.3
Retained earnings	799.3	698.7	565.5	484.6	429.7	313.8
Foreign currency translation adjustments	(7.9)	(22.0)	(16.7)	(10.7)	(9.5)	—
Less cost of common stock in Treasury	(96.4)	(99.1)	—	—	(9.5)	—
Net Stockholders' Equity	821.9	704.8	636.3	550.5	383.9	382.2
TOTAL LIABILITIES & STOCKHOLDERS' EQUITY	$1,417.0	1,368.2	1,298.8	1,151.3	746.9	696.5

Note: Amounts given in millions.

Sources: Moody's Industrial Manual, 1986, pp. 3288–95. Morton Thiokol, Inc., *1986 Annual Report.*

EXHIBIT 4 MORTON THIOKOL, INC.: CONSOLIDATED STATEMENTS OF INCOME AND RETAINED EARNINGS

YEAR ENDED JUNE 30

	1986	1985	1984	1983	1982	1981
Net sales	$1,949.9	1,832.3	1,735.0	1,270.4	534.7	486.0
Interest, royalties, and sundry income	16.2	14.9	10.2	17.4	17.5	11.3
	1,966.1	1,847.2	1,745.2	1,287.8	552.2	497.3
Deductions from income:						
Cost of products sold	1,476.0	1,398.3	1,334.9	976.7	383.6	351.0
Selling, admin. and general expense	203.6	186.0	192.8	158.7	95.8	88.6
Research and development expense	37.7	33.7	28.0	20.9	6.6	6.0
Interest expense	23.6	24.1	22.3	24.3	16.4	13.2
Total deductions from income:	1,740.9	1,642.1	1,578.0	1,180.6	502.4	458.8

(continued)

Income from continuing operations before income taxes	225.2	205.1	167.2	107.2	49.8	38.5
Income taxes	92.3	85.6	70.1	42.0	14.9	11.9
Income from continuing operations	132.9	119.5	97.1	65.2	34.9	26.6
Income from discontinued operations	—	31.3	12.7	13.3	21.8	26.4
Gain on disposition of discontinued operations		75.1			79.8	
Net Income	132.9	197.9	109.8	78.5	136.5	53.0
Retained earnings at beginning of year	698.7	565.5	484.6	429.7	373.8	280.9
	831.6	763.4	594.4	508.2	510.3	333.9
Less:						
Cash dividends paid	32.3	30.7	28.9	23.6	20.6	20.1
Common stock split effected in a dividend		34.0				
Retained earnings at end of year	$ 799.3	698.7	565.5	484.6	429.7	313.8
SHARE DATA						
Income per common and equivalent share:						
Income from continuing operations	$ 2.80	2.44	1.92	1.43	.86	.65
Income from discontinued operations	—	.06	.25	.29	.54	.65
Gain on disposal of discont. operations		1.51			1.98	
Net income	$ 2.80	$ 4.01	$ 2.17	$ 1.72	$ 1.40	$ 1.30
Cash dividends per share	$ .685	.627	.574	.527	.507	.497

Note: Amounts given in millions, except per-share data.

Sources: Moody's Industrial Manual, 1986, pp. 3288–95. Morton Thiokol, Inc., *1986 Annual Report.*

POISON PILL ANTI-TAKEOVER PLAN

Morton Thiokol adopted a "poison pill" anti-takeover measure which was designed to make a hostile takeover very costly for any company. This was in light of the perceived takeover attempt by Dow Chemical in November of 1984. Dow had held 8% of Morton's common stock and was seeking to increase it to as much as 15%, stating that its only interest in Morton was as an investment. To stop the takeover Morton Thiokol agreed to sell the Texize part of its operation to Dow for $131 million in cash and got back 1.4 million of its shares that Dow held. Morton also received an agreement from Dow not to buy any additional shares for the next decade. Giving up Texize provided cash without a negative impact on earnings and also gave Morton a chance to retire some of its stock. The Texize business accounted for about 13% of Morton Thiokol's sales and about 12% of its earnings.

EFFECTS OF THE SHUTTLE DISASTER

When the orbiter Challenger was destroyed and its seven crew-member's killed in an explosion 73 seconds after liftoff on January 28, 1986, investigation of the disaster was focused on the booster's O-rings as the probable cause of the loss of shuttle's mission. These O-rings were produced by Morton Thiokol and were used to seal the booster segments. The immediate effects of the disaster on Morton Thiokol resulted in the layoffs of about 200 workers and placement of 1,400 others on a four-day week. The unit also instituted overhead cost restraints in all areas of its organization. The layoffs were the first in 20 years at the Morton Thiokol facility.

The company experienced other related problems as well. Although the company's aerospace program was a big money-maker during the early 1980s, its growth in that sector had begun to mature even before the explosion. The whole business grew at 50% in sales, but slower development was expected for the second half of the 1980s because the aerospace program simply could not continue at the same rate. The total loss of the shuttle business would be a large negative, but in fact the growth-rate had already started to slow down even before the disaster. The company had $1.83 billion in sales for the fiscal year ending June 1985 and the Space Shuttle program accounted for about 15% of its profit from continuing operations. Each launch earned for the company between $10 million and $20 million in revenues and in 1987 it was still under contract with NASA for a total of 35 shuttle launches. At the time of the Challenger disaster there had been only 25 shuttle launches.

Morton Thiokol faced heavy criticism after the disaster occurred. Although Morton recommended that the launch be postponed during a telephone conference between company representatives in Utah and NASA and company representatives at Kennedy Space Center January 27, four Morton Thiokol managers reversed the decision later the same day because, they said, the data on which the engineers based their fears was uncertain and inconclusive. Company engineers continued to protest that the launch was unsafe. Morton Thiokol managers were criticized as being worried more about the company's pocketbook than flight safety. The month before the January 28 launch, NASA had taken the first step toward finding a second supplier for the booster rockets.

Morton has been the space agency's only supplier since 1973, when it was chosen over three competitors to develop and produce the booster rockets. In the past two years, four companies—Hercules Inc., United Technologies Corporation's Chemical System Division, Aerojet Strategic Propulsion Company, and Atlantic Research Corporation—have expressed strong interest in making booster rockets for NASA. NASA also said that it plans to purchase at least 50% of its rockets from Thiokol and to require a second supplier to buy the nozzles for the rockets from Thiokol which would drive down the cost and enhance national security. However, NASA does not believe they can afford to spend $100 million or so in certification costs for a rocket produced by a new supplier. Potential suppliers also are reluctant to spend the money. In addition, one industry source says that NASA clearly wants to keep Morton Thiokol's skilled corps of engineers from being broken up and that Morton is still the best supplier of solid-fuel rockets.

The investigation commission report stated that Thiokol management changed its position to go ahead with the launch to accommodate a "major customer." One senator contended the managers who overrode their engineers to give the go-ahead for the Challenger launch were saying, "Let's get our pocketbook and forget about safety." But two Thiokol engineers publicly testified that they argued against the ill-fated launch. Morton Thiokol was accused of taking punitive steps against the engineers after they testified that they opposed the launch but were overruled by Thiokol superiors under pressure from NASA. Thiokol denied allegations from both men, saying that their job responsibilities had changed progressively in the accident's aftermath, owing to the shift from production to investigative work and redesign studies.

The report did stress that top NASA officials who gave the final approval for the Challenger launch did not realize the seriousness of the joint problem and did not know that Thiokol had initially advised against launching. But the commission report also found that a briefing at NASA headquarters last August provided enough evidence to warrant "corrective action" before subsequent shuttle flights.

FUTURE OUTLOOK

As of late in 1987 it appeared that Morton Thiokol's specialty chemicals might contribute about 40% of the company's operating profits in fiscal 1987. Late in the year this segment was the company's top profit center, helped by redeployment of assets earlier in the year. Meanwhile, it was expected that Morton Thiokol's electronic chemicals business might improve in coming months, aided by a modest rebound in the depressed electronics industry. The weaker dollar was also helping with exports and the currency translations of foreign earnings.

Until the shuttle launches resume, Morton Thiokol's shuttle work would consist primarily of redesign and testing of the booster rockets. Morton Thiokol was expected to continue to be the best supplier of solid rocket fuels into the 1990s and probably would remain a key space shuttle contractor for the following several years because of its agreements with NASA and its expertise in advanced booster rocket technology. However, space division revenues may fall about 10% with profits falling by a greater percentage.

Looking further ahead, Morton's specialty chemical business might probably become still stronger with the help of additional small acquisitions. These gains would, probably, more than offset declines in space shuttle and salt businesses.

REFERENCES

Chemical and Engineering News (1982). "Merger Would Be Big in Electronics Chemicals." July 26, p. 7

Chemical and Engineering News (1984). "Dow Increases Holding of Morton Thiokol." April 16, p. 47.

Chemical Week (1982). "A Merger to Create a Huge Specialties Firm." July 28, p. 12.

Chemical Week (1983). "A Fast Takeoff for Morton Thiokol." December 7, p. 41.

Chemical Week (1984). "Greenmail Gambit?" November 21, p. 14.

Investment News and Views (1984). "Explosive Growth." January 11, pp. 47–51.

James, Frank E. (1986). "Analysts See No Severe Impact on Morton if Rocket is Faulted in Shuttle Disaster." *Wall Street Journal*. February, p. 2.

Kolcum, Edward H. (1986). "Morton Thiokol Engineers Testify NASA Rejected Warnings on Launch." *Aviation Week & Space Technology*. March 3, pp. 18–19.

Levin, Doron P. (1984). "Dow Chemical Will Buy Unit From Thiokol." *Wall Street Journal*. November 16, p. 8.

McGinley, Laura (1986). "NASA to Prove Transfers of Engineers at Thiokol After Damaging Testimony." *Wall Street Journal*. May 14, p. 5.

Mills, David (1985). "Morton Thiokol, Inc. Wants to Increase Its Acquisitions in a Drive for Growth." *Wall Street Journal*. May 20, p. 12.

Moody's Industrial Manual (1986). "Morton Thiokol, Inc." Pp. 3288–95.

Stevenson, Gelvin (1984). "Morton Thiokol Heads Dow off at the Pass." *Business Week*. December 3, p. 37.

Treehitt, Jeffery (1985). "Morton Thiokol: A Fit in Specialty Chemicals." *Chemical Week*. October 20, p. 27.

Value Line (1987). "Morton Thiokol." July 17, p. 514.

Wall Street Journal (1984). "Dow Chemical Agrees to Stop Buying Shares in Thiokol for 10 Years." November 19, p. 20.

Wall Street Journal (1985). "Morton Thiokol, Inc. Adopts a Poison Pill Anti-Takeover Plan." March 29, p. 48.

Wall Street Journal (1987). "U.S., Thiokol Sued by Widow of a Pilot on Challenger." May 7, p. 6.

Wall Street Journal (1987). "Morton Thiokol Successfully Staged a Full-scale Test of a Space Shuttle Booster Rocket . . ." May 28, p. 1.

MANVILLE CORPORATION, 1989   ARTHUR D. SHARPLIN

- Manville chief attorney, 1934: "[I]t is only within a comparatively recent time that asbestosis has been recognized by the medical and scientific professions as a disease—in fact one of our principal defenses in actions against the company on the common law theory of negligence has been that the scientific and medical knowledge has been insufficient until a very recent period to place on the owners of plants or factories the burden or duty of taking special precautions against the possible onset of the disease in their employees."

- Editor, Asbestos magazine, 1935: "Always you have requested that for certain obvious reasons, we publish nothing, and, naturally your wishes have been respected."

- Manville vice president, 1935: "I quite agree that our interests are best served by having asbestosis receive the minimum of publicity."

- Manville chief executive, 1982: "Not until 1964 was it known that excessive exposure to asbestos fiber released from asbestos-containing insulation products can sometimes cause certain lung diseases."

- Former Manville chief executive, 1987: "The suggestion that the chapter 11 filing was for the benefit of officers is laughable."

- Manville chief executive, 1988: "[Manville's bankruptcy choice was] the most courageous and most ethical decision ever made by a Fortune 500 company."

- Manville annual report, 1989: "In essence, the [bankruptcy] plan created a new Manville able to operate free from direct involvement in the asbestos claim procedures and asbestos-related lawsuits."

Asbestos is a natural fiber, extracted by crushing asbestos-containing rock, mainly from open-pit mines, and sifting and blowing away the unwanted mate-

Source: **Prepared by Professor Arthur D. Sharplin, McNeese State University, as a basis for classroom discussion. The author appreciates the assistance and encouragement of the Center for Business Ethics at Bentley College, of which he is a fellow.** © **Arthur D. Sharplin, 1990.**

rial. Asbestos is impervious to most acids, to human body fluids, and to oxygen. As the material is worked or disturbed, it exudes dust made up of microscopic pieces of the fiber. The dust is almost impossible to filter out of air. Ingested, asbestos inflicts mechanical injury, especially in the lungs, where the constant motion causes tissue to be penetrated and cut by the fibers. This leads to progressive and irreversible scarring, thickening, and calcification of the lungs and their linings (the pleura), a condition called asbestosis. A rare and always-fatal cancer of the pleura (sometimes also affects the peritoneum, the lining of the abdomen), mesothelioma, is strongly connected with asbestos exposure, as are increased incidence and severity of lung cancer and many other respiratory ailments. The first symptoms of asbestos disease typically appear ten to thirty years after exposure begins. But early damage is easily detectable by x-rays and some cancers and respiratory deficiencies show up after only a year or two. Cigarette smokers are several times more susceptable to respiratory diseases, including those related to asbestos, than are non-smokers.

Use of asbestos in the U.S. rose from around 200,000 metric tons a year in the 1930s to a plateau of about 700,000 during the 1950s, 1960s, and early 1970s. Then it dropped sharply, to just over 100,000 metric tons by 1985.[1] The following description of asbestos was written by columnist Bruce Porter in 1973, just as the dangers of breathing asbestos dust were becoming widely recognized by the general public:

> Perhaps no other mineral is so woven into the fabric of American life as is asbestos. Impervious to heat and fibrous—it is the only mineral that can be woven into cloth—asbestos is spun into fireproof clothing and theater curtains, as well as into such household items as noncombustible drapes, rugs, pot holders, and ironing-board covers. Mixed into slurry, asbestos is sprayed onto girders and walls to provide new buildings with fireproof insulation. It is used in floor tiles, roofing felts, and in most plasterboards and wallboards. Asbestos is also an ingredient of plaster and stucco and of many paints and putties. This "mineral of a thousand uses"—an obsolete nickname: the present count stands at around 3,000 uses—is probably present in some form or other in every home, school, office building, and factory in this country. Used in brake linings and clutch facings, in mufflers and gaskets, in sealants and caulking, and extensively used in ships, asbestos is also a component of every modern vehicle, including space ships.

Worldwide, asbestos production plateaued at about 4.6 million metric tons a year in the mid 1970s. Through 1986, world production dropped only a little, apparently because increased shipments to developing countries offset declining usage elsewhere.[2] Canada, the world's dominant marketer of asbestos in the late 1980s, sold an estimated 42 percent of its output to Asia in 1988, up from just 16 percent in 1979. Other leading producers were Russia, Zimbabwe, and Brazil.[3]

From about the turn of the century, Manville Corporation (Johns-Manville Corporation until 1981) was the world's leading asbestos company, involved in mining and sale of the raw fibers as well as development, manufacture, and marketing of intermediate and finished asbestos products. Manville executives and their cohorts in other asbestos companies knew the dangers of breathing asbestos dust during the 1930s. They took many actions to suppress research and publicity about the problem and continued into the 1980s to disclaim their early knowledge. Manville was the main target of a trickle of asbestos-health (A-H) lawsuits in the 1920s and early thirties which would become a flood by the 1980s.

With the asbestos riches to fund its defense, Manville paid little to A-H victims. But it was not able to replace the asbestos profits as they collapsed in the seventies. Despite aggressive attempts to diversify, the company saw declining earnings after 1978 and a loss for the first half of 1982. The A-H judgments were skyrocketing, in amount and number; Manville's bonds were downgraded; and the company's auditor qualified its opinion on the 1981 financial statements. On the evening of August 25, 1982, the board of directors was briefed on bankruptcy reorganization. A petition for protection from creditors under chapter 11 of the U.S. Bankruptcy Code had already been prepared. It was approved by the board that night and filed the next day.

It would be more than six years before a plan to emerge from court protection would be final. Many of the asbestos victims would die in the meantime. And the tens of thousands who had been held off by the bankruptcy court during those years would find their claims shunted to a separate trust (the A-H Trust) and effectively subordinated to those of commercial creditors as well as to other interests.

Within months after paying its first claim, the A-H Trust would run short of funds. Petitions by uncompensated victims to preserve funds for their claims would be rejected. And the bankruptcy judge would reaffirm his earlier ruling that no A-H victim could ever again seek recompense from Manville, its executives, or its insurers.

In the meantime, the third generation of Manville top managers would serve out their tenures and retire, many with large termination bonuses. Others would leave as co-owners or managers of millions in divested assets, assets originally purchased mainly with asbestos profits but freed of asbestos claims by the bankruptcy court. And a fourth generation of executives would take over. With a billion dollars in cash and credit at their disposal, immune from income taxes by virtue of $600 million in loss carryforwards, and forever free of the nettlesome asbestos lawsuits, they would begin to expand fiberglass and forest products production, then Manville's main businesses, and to look for technologies and divisions to purchase from other companies.

COMPANY BACKGROUND

In 1898, Manville founder Henry Ward Johns, who had invented many uses for asbestos, died of scarring of the lungs, assumedly asbestosis.[4] His company survived and became a success by the usual standards. Manville saw consistent growth in sales and profits until the seventies. Dividends were paid every year except for the war years of 1915–1916 and the depths of the Depression in 1933–1934. Manville was one of the "Dow-Jones Industrial Thirty" for many years.

The same year Johns died, a British factory inspector described the illness suffered by asbestos textile workers: "In the majority of cases the evil is very insidious. . . . The worker falls into ill-health and sinks away out of sight in no sudden or sensational manner."[5] And in 1918, Prudential Insurance Company's chief actuary wrote, "[I]n the practice of American and Canadian life insurance companies asbestos workers are generally declined on account of the assumed health injurious conditions of the industry."[6] Studies reported in the medical literature in 1924, 1928, and in 1930 began to show more fully the nature of the asbestos-health problem. The 1930 research revealed 26.3 percent of the workers studied had fairly serious asbestosis, a name given to the disease in 1927.[7]

By 1929, Manville was defending lawsuits for asbestos deaths. In court, the company claimed employees assumed the risks of employment, knew or should have known the dangers, and were contributorily negligent. Legal documents in these cases bore the signatures of senior Manville officials who would remain with the company until the late 1960s. In 1930, Dr. A. J. Lanza, of Metropolitan Life Insurance Company (Manville insurer), began a four-year study on the "Effects of Inhalation of Asbestos Dust upon the Lungs of Asbestos Workers."[8] His preliminary report, written the next year, showed 87 percent of the workers with over fifteen years exposure and 43 percent of those with under five years of exposure had x-ray signs of fibrosis.[9] The report was reviewed by officials of various asbestos companies, including Manville, and would be published in a form they approved four years later.

In 1934, Manville's chief attorney wrote to the company:

> [I]t is only within a comparatively recent time that asbestosis has been recognized by the medical and scientific professions as a disease—in fact one of our principal defenses in actions against the company on the common law theory of negligence has been that the scientific and medical knowledge has been insufficient until a very recent period to place on the owners of plants or factories the burden or duty of taking special precautions against the possible onset of the disease in their employees.[10]

That same year, Manville vice president and corporate secretary Vandiver Brown reviewed a draft of Dr. Lanza's report and wrote him,

> All we ask is that all of the favorable aspects of the survey be included and that none of the unfavorable be unintentionally pictured in darker terms than the circumstances justify. I feel confident that we can depend upon you and Dr. McConnel to give us this "break." . . . [11]

The next year, Brown wrote another industry executive, Sumner Simpson, "I quite agree that our interests are best served by having asbestosis receive the minimum of publicity."[12] He was commenting on Simpson's response to a letter by Anne Rossiter (editor of the industry journal *Asbestos*) in which she had written,

You may recall that we have written you on several occasions concerning the publishing of information, or discussion of, asbestosis.... Always you have requested that for certain obvious reasons, we publish nothing, and, naturally your wishes have been respected.[13]

In 1936, Brown and Simpson convinced nine other asbestos companies to provide a total of $5,000 per year for the industry's own three-year study of the effects of asbestos dust on guinea pigs and rabbits by Dr. LeRoy U. Gardner. Brown wrote Gardner, "In the event it is deemed desirable that the results be made public, the manuscript of your study will be submitted to us for approval prior to publication."[14] Gardner would later tell the companies of "significant changes in guinea pigs' lungs within a period of one year" and "fibrosis" produced by long fibers and "chronic inflammation" caused by short fibers.[15] He would make several requests for additional funding but would die in 1946 without reporting final results.

The A-H lawsuits increased in number through the 1930s, but Manville continued to successfully defend or settle them, using the same defenses as in the 1920s but adding a statute-of-limitations defense, made possible by the long latency period of asbestos diseases. The asbestos companies continued to be able to prevent significant publicity about asbestos and health.

World War II brought Manville spiralling sales and profits, as thousands of tons of asbestos were used in building war machines, mainly ships—resulting in exposure of hundreds of thousands of shipyard workers and seamen, many of whom would die of asbestos diseases decades later.

In 1947, a study by the Industrial Hygiene Foundation of America found that from 3 to 20 percent of asbestos plant workers already had asbestosis and a Manville plant employing 300 was producing "5 or 6 cases annually that the physician believes show early changes due to asbestos."[16]

In 1950, Dr. Kenneth W. Smith, Manville chief physician, gave superiors a report showing that of 708 workers he studied only four had "essentially normal and healthy lungs" and 534 had "fibrosis extending beyond the lung roots," "advanced fibrosis," or "early asbestosis."[17] Concerning the more serious cases he wrote, "The fibrosis of this disease is irreversible and permanent so that eventually compensation will be paid to each of these men but as long as the man is not disabled it is felt that he should not be told of his condition so that he can live and work in peace and the company can benefit from his many years of experience."[18]

By 1952, John A. McKinney, Fred L. Pundsack, Chester E. Shepperly, Monroe Harris, and Chester J. Sulewski had all joined the company in various capacities. They would be Manville's top five officers as it prepared to seek bankruptcy court protection thirty years later.

Dr. Smith later said he tried to convince senior Manville managers to authorize caution labelling for asbestos in 1953. In a 1976 deposition, he characterized their response: "We recognize the potential hazard that you mentioned, the suggested use of a caution label. We will discuss it among ourselves and make a decision." Asked why he was overruled, Smith said, "[A]pplication of a caution label identifying a product as hazardous would cut out sales."[19]

In 1956, the board of governors of the Asbestos Textile Institute (made up of Manville and other asbestos companies) met to discuss the increasing publicity about asbestos and cancer and agreed that "[E]very effort should be made to disassociate this relationship until such a time that there is sufficient and authoritative information to substantiate such to be a fact."

The next year, the Asbestos Textile Institute rejected a proposal by the Industrial Health Foundation that asbestos companies fund a study on asbestos and cancer. Institute minutes reported, "There is a feeling among certain members that such an investigation would stir up a hornet's nest and put the whole industry under suspicion."[20]

An increasing number of articles connecting asbestos with various diseases appeared in medical journals over the next few years. And in 1963 Dr. I. J. Selikoff, of Mt. Sinai Medical Center in New York, read a report of his study of asbestos insulation workers before the American Medical Association meeting. Like the earlier research, the Selikoff study implicated asbestos ingestion as the causal factor in many thousands of deaths and injuries. Selikoff would soon estimate that at least 100,000 more Americans would die of asbestos diseases before the year 2000. The study and the articles, news stories, and academic papers which followed focused public attention on the asbestos and health issue. An estimated 100 articles on asbestos-related diseases appeared in 1964 alone.

In later congressional testimony, Selikoff told of one group of 632 insulation workers he had followed from 1942 through 1962:

> During these years, 27 men have died of asbestosis, of a total of 367 deaths. ... [I]n addition,] while we would have expected approximately six or seven deaths due to lung cancer among these men, there were 45. While we would have expected nine or ten cancers of the stomach or colon, there were 29. ... Incidentally, since 1963 the figures have been, if anything, even worse. While we would have expected approximately 50 of the remainder of these men to have died in the past five years, there have been 113 deaths. And while we would have expected 3 to have died of cancer of the lungs or pleura, 28 have died of this disease.[21]

Incredibly, Manville officials claimed Selikoff's 1964 report was their first knowledge of the danger, a fabrication they would persistently repeat over the next two decades. For example, on August 27, 1982, McKinney would blazon,

> Here's the bottom line. *Not until 1964 was it known that excessive exposure to asbestos fiber released from asbestos-containing insulation products can sometimes cause certain lung diseases.*[22]

And the *1982 Annual Report and Form 10-K* would state, "[T]he Company has maintained that there was no basis for product warnings or hazard controls until the results of scientific studies linking pulmonary disease in asbestos insulation workers with asbestos exposure were made public in 1964."[23]

In 1964, Manville agreed to place the first caution labels on *some* asbestos products. In carefully crafted understatement, the labels read, "Inhalation of asbestos in excessive quantities over long periods of time may be harmful" and suggested that users avoid breathing the dust and wear masks if "adequate ventilation control is not possible." The company's most profitable—and deadly—product, bags of asbestos fiber for distribution to other manufacturers and insulators throughout the world, would not be caution labeled for another five years.

In the decades before 1970, Manville's sales grew somewhat slower than the Gross National Product. But the company benefited from relatively low fixed costs, due to a largely depleted and depreciated capital base and the total absence of long-term debt in the capital structure. With low operating and financial leverage, the firm was able to adapt to sales downturns in 1957, 1960, 1967, and 1970 and still earn profits in each of those years. By 1970, Manville had about $400 million ($1.2 billion in 1989 dollars) in book value net worth, garnered almost entirely from the mining, manufacture, and sale of asbestos products, for which Manville still held a dominant market position.

During the 1960s, a number of the senior officials who had been with Manville since the 1930s died or retired. Compared to just the 1966 board of directors, the 1970 board had a majority of new members. In 1970, departing from a tradition of promoting from within, the board of directors installed an outsider, psychologist Richard Goodwin, as president. Thus began a prolonged effort to diversify Manville away from asbestos and to change its image. At the same time, scattered efforts were made to protect Manville employees. Goodwin later said, "We closed a couple of carding mills—not here, overseas—because of dust. You couldn't even see across the floor. That's bad news."[24]

But the focus was on the grand scheme. Goodwin arranged to move the corporate headquarters from its old Madison Avenue brick building to the Denver countryside. There, he purchased the 10,000 acre Ken Caryl Ranch and planned a luxurious "world headquarters," the first phase of which was to cost $60 million. He also led the company through more than twenty small acquisitions—in lighting systems, golf carts, irrigation sprinklers, and other products. He arranged several major real estate deals, which he would later claim[25] kept Manville from collapsing in 1978–1980. In the process, Manville's long-term debt was escalated from zero to $196 million and fixed costs increased several fold. A short, steep recession in 1975 cut Manville's profits in half, back to 1970 levels. U.S. asbestos consumption had begun its decline, which was to accelerate and total more than 50 percent by 1982.

And Manville was suffering reverses in its fight against the A-H lawsuits. In 1972, Manville and five other asbestos companies lost the landmark Clarence Borel asbestos tort lawsuit, which, according to a later news report, "triggered the greatest avalanche of toxic tort litigation in the history of American jurisprudence."[26] The appeals court in that case wrote, "The evidence . . . tended to establish that none of the defendants ever tested its product to determine its effect on industrial insulation workers. . . . The unpalatable facts are that in the twenties and thirties the hazards of working with asbestos were recognized."[27] Goodwin later said, "I kept telling [legal chief John A.] McKinney to settle asbestos cases. . . . He was back every two weeks wanting to change the strategy to one of confrontation. . . . He's a combative guy."[28]

McKinney soon had additional ammunition. Not only did profits turn down in 1985, as stated earlier, but in an April 1976 deposition, Dr. Kenneth Smith, former Manville medical director, told of his knowledge of asbestos dangers during the 1940s. He also revealed his 1950 finding that the lungs of 704 of the 708 Manville asbestos workers he studied showed asbestos damage. He went on to describe his unsuccessful efforts to get caution labels put on Manville asbestos products.[29]

Five months after the Smith deposition, the nine outside directors of Manville demanded the resignation of Richard Goodwin. According to Goodwin, the three directors who transmitted the demand refused to explain their action.[30] A later Manville chief executive would claim Goodwin had been a womanizer and an alcoholic,[31] a claim Goodwin would vehemently deny.

McKinney—who had joined the company before 1950—took over as chief executive. He divested many of the Goodwin acquisitions and turned his attention to "aggressive defense" of the asbestos lawsuits and the search for a "substantial acquisition." McKinney also made plans for a $200 million expansion in the company's fiberglass operations. In the 1977 "Presidents Review," he wrote, "[W]e do not expect asbestos fiber to dominate J-M earnings to the extent it has in the past."[32]

Then, in April 1977, the "Raybestos-Manhattan Correspondence" was discovered by asbestos plaintiff attorneys. Included were many letters and memoranda among Manville officials and other asbestos industry executives. Most were written during the 1930s. A South Carolina judge hearing an asbestos case wrote,

> The Raybestos-Manhattan Correspondence very arguably shows a pattern of denial of disease and attempts at suppression of information which is highly probative [and] reflects a conscious effort by the industry in the 1930s to downplay, or arguably suppress, the dissemination of information to employees and the public. . . . [33]

The asbestos lawsuits were not mentioned in the 1977 annual report, issued at the end of March 1978. However, the 1977 Form 10-K described 623 "current" A-H lawsuits against the company and 94 cases which had been settled. Many of the suits involved multiple plaintiffs asking as much as $4 million each.[34]

Confronted with the new and damning evidence, a growing number of juries would award punitive damages against Manville during 1981 and 1982, as much as a million dollars per claimant. And many suits would name current and former Manville executives as defendants.[35] By August of 1982, asbestos-health claims against the company would number 20,000 with new suits being filed at the rate of three an hour every business day.[36] The average cost per case, according to company officials, would be "sharply higher" than in prior years, averaging $40,000 per claim.[37]

The managers at Manville were particularly vulnerable to charges of conspiring to hide past sins of the company, if not for committing them. The top five executives had each been with the firm since 1952 or before. All had been senior officials since at least the early seventies.[38]

The outside directors were eminent in their respective fields, but they too could hardly claim noninvolvement. Among them were the deans of the School of Architecture at Princeton and the Graduate School of Business Administration at New York University. The latter had previously been chief executive of American Can Company. Also included were the chief executive of Ideal Basic Industries, Inc., who had earlier been elected three times as governor of Colorado; the head of Phelps Dodge Corporation; and the top managers of three other companies.[39] The average tenure of the eleven directors was seventeen years, and all but two had been directors over ten years. Six had joined the board in the sixties and two others, the inside directors, had worked for Manville since about 1950.[40]

Ideal Basic Industries (IBI), a major producer of potash and portland cement, spurned a Manville buyout initiative in early 1978. It may have been important that the chief executive of IBI, John A. Love, was on the Manville board of directors and knew the nature of Manville's need. Next, Manville began a takeover battle (with Texas Eastern Corporation) for Olinkraft Corporation, a wood products company concentrated in paperboard and paper. Olinkraft's main assets were about 600,000 acres of prime southern timberland and several paper mills.

Manville won the contest and closed the deal in the last half of 1978. The purchase price was $595 million, 2.24 times book value and over twice recent market value. About half was paid in cash and the rest was represented by a new issue of cumulative preferred stock which was required to be repurchased beginning in 1987. As the merger was being negotiated, Manville's share price fell markedly.

The directors and officers were guaranteed indemnification by Manville, a contract they had the company reaffirm in 1981.[41] There was tangible evidence they needed such protection. For example, there were many attacks by asbestos victims against the estate of Vandiver Brown, Manville vice president and secretary during the 1930s, attacks which would continue into the mid-1980s.[42]

But ordinary business problems after 1978 imperiled the managers' indemnity and rendered even their jobs insecure, not to mention the professional embarrassment failure might bring such illustrious directors and executives. That year, the company began what seemed an irreversible downward slide. Revenues (in 1986 dollars) fell from $2.74 billion in 1978 to a $2.18 billion annual rate for the first half of 1982, a 20-percent drop. And earnings available to common stock (also in 1986 dollars) simply evaporated, going from $198 million to an $85 million annual-rate *loss*.[43] Earnings available to common stock, of course, excluded dividends on the debt-equivalent preferred stock issued in the Olinkraft acquisition. Despite its acquisitions, Manville remained intensely concentrated in construction-dependent businesses, which all suffered from the construction industry recession that began in 1979.

Manville's auditor, Coopers and Lybrand, qualified its opinion on the company's 1980 and 1981 annual reports.[44] Of course, Standard and Poor's and Moody's downgraded Manville's debt.[45] And Manville's insurers gave the executives little solace; they stopped paying for most of the asbestos claims by 1981,[46] and generally could not pay punitive damages anyway. The firms which insured Manville during the 1970s and 1980s, when many asbestos-health problems manifested, argued the claims should be paid by those which insured the company when most 1980s claimants were exposed, during the 1930s, 1940s, and 1950s. The insurers from the earlier period took the reverse position. This "manifestations versus exposure" debate gave the insurers a rationale for refusing to pay claims, without confronting the issue of Manville's culpability, which some of the insurers, especially Metropolitan Life Insurance Company, clearly shared.[47] Manville sued its insurers for refusing to pay and eventually reached out-of-court settlements with most of them.

The small amounts Manville actually paid for "asbestos health costs," $13 million in 1981 and $16 million in 1982,[48] could hardly be blamed for the financial collapse. Those costs never amounted to even 1 percent of sales. But loss of asbestos profits was clearly a major factor. Until at least 1978, the immensely profitable asbestos trade had been the company's mainstay. Sales of the raw fiber alone had produced 41 percent of Manville's operating profit as late as 1976, though accounting for only 12 percent of revenues that year.[49] Further, many of the company's manufactured products had been asbestos based, including asbestos felts, papers, textiles, asbestos-cement shingles, asbestos-cement water and sewer pipe, and asbestos paper and millboard.[50]

Public awareness of asbestos-health dangers continued to increase and U.S. purchases of the substance had fallen by 36 percent in 1980 alone.[51] The directors voted to reorganize the company in 1981, placing the non-asbestos operations in separate corporations under the parent Manville. Some thought this was a brazen attempt to shield the non-asbestos assets from asbestos claims, an effort which was given little chance of success under common law and the Uniform Commercial Code. But lawyer McKinney and his cohorts surely knew the rules might be different under bankruptcy law.

By 1982, Manville's asbestos-fiber revenues were at half the 1976 level. An estimated 60 percent of the fiber was sold internationally, mainly in western Europe.[52] And each dollar of fiber sales produced markedly less operating profit, 18 cents versus 33 cents in 1976.[53] A special committee of the board of directors was formed to study the asbestos mess. The 1982 annual report would describe the results of that study:

> On the basis of epidemiological and statistical reports, using conservative assumptions favorable to Manville, Manville Corporation projected that more than 32,000 additional asbestos-health related lawsuits would be filed against one or more of the Debtor Corporations by the year 2000.... If the disposition cost (including legal fees) of the A-H Claims were to average approxi-

mately $40,000 per claim as projected, the aggregate cost of disposing of the A-H Claims through conventional tort litigation would be at least $1.9 billion.[54]

Researchers of the Environmental Sciences Laboratory at Mt. Sinai School of Medicine, home base of Dr. I. J. Selikoff, found many faults with the Manville-sponsored study and concluded it provided "a serious underestimate of disease associated with past asbestos exposure."[55]

The stock market reflected Manville's deteriorating situation. By mid-August 1982, the company's common stock price had dropped below $8, less than one-fourth its 1977 high. Exhibits 1, 2, and 3 provide comparative financial information for the several years before August 1982.

IN FULL READINESS FOR CHAPTER 11

The company was well-prepared for a chapter 11 filing. Manville was still able to pay its bills; but the 1978 bankruptcy act had removed insolvency as a requirement for filing. The Olinkraft purchase had been structured so half the cost would not come due until 1987 and later. Filing would stay that obligation. The 1981 reorganization had segregated the asbestos assets in separate corporations. Each corporation could file its own chapter 11 petition. They could submit separate or joint reorganization plans. Management could decide which.

EXHIBIT 1   COMPARATIVE INCOME STATEMENTS, 1976–JUNE 1982

	1982 6 MOS.	1981	1980	1979	1978	1977	1976
Net sales	$ 949	$2,186	$2,267	$2,276	$1,649	$1,461	$1,309
Cost of sales	784	1,731	1,771	1,747	1,190	1,066	983
Sell, G&A	143	271	263	239	193	174	166
R&D & engineering	16	34	35	31	33	28	25
Operating income	6	151	197	259	232	193	135
Other income	1	35	26	21	28	2	1
Interest exp.	35	73	65	62	22	20	15
Income before tax	(28)	112	157	218	238	175	121
Income tax	(2)	53	77	103	116	89	48
Net income	(25)	60	81	115	122	86	73
Prfrd. stock div.	12	25	25	24	—	—	—
Net income for CS	$ (37)	$ 35	$ 55	$ 91	$ 122	$ 86	$ 73

Note: Dollar amounts are given in millions. Totals may not check, due to rounding.

EXHIBIT 2   COMPARATIVE BUSINESS SEGMENT INFORMATION, 1976–1981

	1981	1980	1979	1978	1977	1976
Revenues						
Fiberglass products	$ 625	$ 610	$ 573	$ 514	$ 407	$ 358
Forest products	555	508	497	—	—	—
Nonfiberglass insulation	258	279	268	231	195	159
Roofing products	209	250	273	254	204	171
Pipe products & systems	199	220	305	303	274	218
Asbestos fiber	138	159	168	157	161	155
Industrial & specialty products	320	341	309	291	301	309
Corp. rev. net	12	9	11	20	12	(22)
Intersegment sales	(95)	(84)	(106)	(94)	(74)	(56)
Total	$2,221	$2,292	$2,297	$1,677	$1,480	$1,291
Income from Operations						
Fiberglass products	$ 90	$ 91	$ 96	$ 107	$ 82	$ 60
Forest products	39	37	50	—	—	—
Nonfiberglass insulation	20	27	27	35	28	18
Roofing products	(17)	9	14	23	14	8
Pipe products & systems	0	(5)	18	26	24	(3)
Asbestos fiber	37	35	56	55	60	60
Industrial & specialty products	50	55	43	36	25	19
Corp exp., net	(23)	(38)	(23)	(23)	(24)	(49)
Elim. & adj.	3	11	2)	1	3	2
Total	$ 198	$ 223	$ 280	$ 260	$ 212	$ 116

Note: Dollar amounts are given in millions. Totals may not check, due to rounding.

Manville had ready access to top consultants and attorneys. For fifty years, the firm had been close to Morgan Stanley and Company and Davis Polk and Wardwell. Morgan Stanley was a leading investment banker, Davis Polk a top New York law firm.

And there were no rebels on the management team. Eight of the eleven directors had been with Manville since the fifties and sixties. After Goodwin took over in 1970, no senior manager came in from outside. In fact, the top five executives in 1982 each had at least thirty years tenure. Only one, president Fred Pundsack, would voice dissent, and he would shortly abandon ship.

Best yet, almost none of the company's $1.1 billion debt was secured. Mc-Kinney would soon boast of "nearly $2 billion in unencumbered assets." That would prove to be a real advantage in bankruptcy. Unsecured creditors normally have no claim on or control over any particular assets, so there is usually a very real threat their claims can be wholly or partly discharged under a reorganization plan. Another leading asbestos producer, UNR Industries, Inc.,

EXHIBIT 3　COMPARATIVE BALANCE SHEETS, DECEMBER 1976–JUNE 1982

	JUNE 30 1982	DECEMBER 31					
		1981	1980	1979	1978	1977	1976
ASSETS							
Cash	$ 10	$ 14	$ 20	$ 19	$ 28	$ 39	$ 25
Marketable securities	17	12	12	10	38	121	66
AR & NR	348	327	350	362	328	263	239
Inventories	182	211	217	229	219	149	144
Prepayments	$ 19	19	20	31	32	30	26
Total CA	$ 576	$ 583	$ 619	$ 650	$ 645	$ 601	$ 501
Land & imp.	—	119	118	114	99	64	64
Buildings	—	363	357	352	321	264	259
Mach. & equip.	—	1,202	1,204	1,161	1,043	642	598
		$1,685	$1,679	$1,627	$1,462	$ 970	$ 921
Ac depr. & depl.	—	(525)	(484)	(430)	(374)	(337)	(327)
		$1,160	$1,195	$1,197	$1,088	$ 633	$ 594
Timber & timberland	—	406	407	368	372	0	0
Total PP&E	$1,523	$1,566	$1,602	$1,565	$1,460	$ 633	$ 594
Other assets	148	149	117	110	113	99	93
	$2,247	$2,298	$2,338	$2,324	$2,217	$1,334	$1,188
LIABILITIES & STOCKHOLDERS' EQUITY							
ST debt	$ 0	$ 29	$ 22	$ 32	$ 23	$ 18	$ 20
AP	191	120	126	143	114	69	58
Ac compensation & benefits	0	77	80	54	45	37	32
Income tax	0	30	22	51	84	57	32
Other liab.	149	58	61	50	63	54	48
Total CL	$ 340	$ 316	$ 310	$ 329	$ 329	$ 235	$ 189
LT debt	499	508	519	532	543	203	208
Other non-current liab.	93	86	75	73	60	23	11
Defrd. income tax	186	185	211	195	150	130	108
Total liab.	$1,116	$1,095	$1,116	$1,129	$1,083	$ 591	$ 516
Preferred stock	$ 301	$ 301	$ 300	$ 299	$ 299	$ —	$ —
Common stock	60	59	58	56	55	54	54
Capital above par	178	174	164	152	142	134	134
Ret. earnings	642	695	705	692	643	561	492
Curr. trans. adj.	(47)	(22)	0	0	0	0	0
Treas. stock	(3)	(3)	(4)	(4)	(6)	(7)	(9)
Total SE	$1,131	$1,203	$1,222	$1,196	$1,134	$ 742	$ 672
	$2,247	$2,298	$2,338	$2,324	$2,217	$1,334	$1,188

Note: Dollar amounts are given in millions. Totals may not check, due to rounding.

had filed a chapter 11 petition in July 1982. So decisions in that case would help Manville avoid pitfalls in its own.

The Appendix gives an overview of the chapter 11 process.

THE BANKRUPTCY REORGANIZATION

Manville filed its chapter 11 bankruptcy petition on August 26, 1982. The common stock fell from $7.875 the day before the filing to $4.625 a few days later. All legal actions against the company, including the asbestos tort lawsuits, were automatically stayed under provisions of the bankruptcy law. There were immediate calls for liquidation of the company, which by best estimates would have produced about $2-2.4 billion in cash.[56] Liquidation could have been accomplished through orderly sale of subsidiaries or individual assets under chapter 11 or chapter 7 (the chapter of the Bankruptcy Code under which debtors are simply liquidated, often, but not necessarily, through a "hammer sale," and the proceeds applied to claims).

The company's largest division, Manville Forest Products Corporation (MFP), emerged from chapter 11 protection March 26, 1984. Under the court order confirming its plan, MFP was obligated to pay its commercial debt, but was free of asbestos claims.[57] Various other units, notably the main asbestos fiber subsidiaries and certain asbestos-cement pipe operations, were sold that year, also free of Manville's asbestos liabilities.[58]

A reorganization plan for the remaining divisions was filed by Manville management in 1986. The bankruptcy judge in the case issued a confirmation order December 22, 1986, but full implementation of the plan was held up pending the outcome of two appeals from the order.[59]

The plan provided for essentially full payment of $472 million of unsecured commercial creditor claims which had not been paid earlier. Secured obligations were to be either paid in full or reinstated with payment of accrued interest. Common stockholders were to be practically dispossessed through issuance of additional shares and rights. Preferred stockholders were to receive a mixture of common and "preference" shares worth an estimated 15 percent of the face value of their preferred shares.

A trust (the A-H trust), set up to pay asbestos-health claims, was to receive the following assets: (1) $615 million in expected insurance settlement proceeds, partly deferred and all contingent on the plan surviving all appeals; (2) $111 million estimated confirmation-date value in cash and receivables; (3) a zero-coupon bond worth an estimated $249 million[60]—in an October 1987 debate at the National Conference on Business Ethics, Manville's new chief executive, W. Thomas Stephens, said the value of the bond was $350 million; (4) other debt securities valued at about $45 million; (5) 50 percent of Manville's common stock, which was to be required to be voted for management's choices for directors for at least four years after plan consummation—sale of the stock was to be restricted for at least five years after consummation; and (6) contingent claims on 20 percent of corporate earnings beginning the fourth fiscal year after consummation and on a new issue of convertible preferred stock.[61]

After the publicity surrounding the Manville bankruptcy, hundreds of property-damage (PD) claims began to be filed. They were mainly claims for estimated costs of cleaning asbestos out of the thousands of schools and government and commercial buildings where it had been used as insulation or fire proofing. By 1986, the PD claims totaled over $70 billion. Manville's plan provided that a PD trust would be set up to pay these claims. It would be initially funded with $100 million from Manville and $25 million from the A-H trust. The PD trust was also supposed to get certain extra funds the A-H trust might have.

The A-H claimants committee, consisting of nineteen lawyers and one asbestos victim, endorsed the Manville plan, emphasizing the $2.5 billion nominal value of the A-H trust. However, one expert used discounted cash flow analysis to calculate the value of the proposed trust assets at only $572 million.[62]

HOW THE MANAGERS FARED UNDER CHAPTER 11

Compared to the chaos which imperiled the executives' fortunes and jobs in the months before August 1982, the situation which existed thereafter must have seemed sublime. Chapter 11 brought the executives a lightened management load, improved pay and benefits, munificent retirement for those who desired it, and bonuses and "golden parachutes" for others. The pre-filing executives and directors even arranged to continue their power over the corporation after its emergence from bankruptcy court protection. Finally, some of the pre-filing managers were able to control, or even own, company assets freed of asbestos claims long before the chapter 11 case was settled. Manville chief McKinney later wrote, "The suggestion that the chapter 11 filing was for the benefit of officers is laughable. . . . The filing preserved the position of the victims as equal creditors (virtually all unsecured) in the event of a financial calamity."[63]

LIGHTENED MANAGEMENT LOAD

When Manville filed its chapter 11 petition, the management burden was lightened by a surplus of cash and the ability to avoid substantial interest expenditures. Payment terms on accounts and notes receivable are not affected by bankruptcy; so they flowed in. But $627 million in unsecured liabilities were frozen under the "automatic stay" of the Bankruptcy Code, most to be paid only after conclusion of the chapter 11 proceedings.[64] The company was not required to pay this debt, nor to even accrue interest on it after the filing. Consequently, Manville's cash and marketable securities balance mushroomed, varying from a little over $200 million in December 1982 to $716 million September 30, 1988—compared to $27 million on June 30, 1982, shortly before the filing.[65]

The impact of the automatic stay on profitability was substantial. The pre-filing unsecured debt, including accounts payable and other accrued liabilities, was down to $490 million by December 1986.[66] But if the avoided interest on even that amount had been accrued yearly, Manville would have suffered an overall loss for the five years 1982–1986 instead of the $92 million total net profit it reported.

Further, the managers were undoubtedly more comfortable in the legal/administrative milieu of the bankruptcy court than in the economic one of competitive business. Chairman John A. McKinney and four more of the eleven directors in 1982 were attorneys (although one, chief outside lawyer William D. Tucker, Jr., had just joined the board that year). The company had been involved in asbestos-tort litigation since the 1920s. The litigation and related public affairs matters had been a dominant concern since the early 1970s. This proposition is further buttressed by the contrast between Manville's success in staving off the asbestos-health claims until the 1980s, on one hand, and its inability to reverse the economic downslide which began in 1979, on the other.

IMPROVED PAY AND BENEFITS

The directors and top executives of Manville, mostly unchanged after the sixties, increased their pay and improved their benefits while in bankruptcy. For example, chief executive John McKinney's reported cash compensation went from $408,750 in early 1982 to $638,005 in 1985, his last full year of employment. Senior vice president Chester Sulewski's increased by 88 percent from 1982 to 1986. The cash compensation of W. Thomas Stephens, who became president in September 1986, was 39 percent higher that year than in 1985, the first year he appeared in the company's Compensation Table.[67] By the time Manville emerged from chapter 11, Stephens' cash compensation grew by another 50 percent, to $682,925.[68]

The annual cash compensation of the thirty-two officers and directors of Manville was reported as $3.9 million in March 1982.[69] It was $5.5 million for just the twenty-five executive officers during 1986.[70]

SECURE RETIREMENT, "GOLDEN PARACHUTES," AND BONUSES

And the most senior pre-filing managers were able to retire in economic security, shielded by the bankruptcy court and indemnified by Manville against the asbestos liabilities. The Manville reorganization plan provided that the A-H trust would be responsible for defending and paying any future asbestos claims against the company, its insurers, or the executives and directors. Mc-Kinney's severance agreement, effective September 1, 1986, granted him cash payments totalling $1.3 million, two extra years of fringe benefits, and two extra years of longevity for retirement purposes. Two other managers were given severance agreements at the same time providing for payments totalling $1,030,000 and certain other benefits.

By December 1986, four of the five most highly paid executives shown in the *1982 Proxy Statement* had left the company. J. T. Hulce resigned as president in 1986, allegedly under pressure from the asbestos victims' committee, and was authorized $530,000 in severance pay.[71] G. Earl Parker, Manville's legal chief under McKinney, retired in March 1987. His severance agreement, approved by the bankruptcy court in September 1987, provided for payments of $430,000 a year through 1989, a total of $1.2 million, counting from March 1987, when he stepped down.[72] These were all specially approved payments in addition to retirement and other benefits. The board of directors remained mostly unchanged from the 1982 board, with only one of the nine outside directors having departed.

The executives left behind were also reassured of large termination payments upon choosing or being asked to leave and probable bonuses in the meantime. At a special board meeting in New York held on October 11, 1985, McKinney discussed "Confidential Minute Number 13," which was said to address severance pay of up to two times annual salary for officers and other "key managerial personnel" upon any termination of employment. It was specifically agreed that the special pay would even apply to persons terminated after any assignment of a trustee in the bankruptcy case.[73]

In mid-July 1987, Manville obtained court approval for a new executive bonus plan for that year increasing the possible bonuses for certain managers from 57.5 percent of annual salaries to 97.1 percent. The allowable bonuses for achieving less than 80 percent of goals were reduced.[74] In 1986–1988, $2.8 million in bonuses were paid to the top five officers of Manville; W. Thomas Stephens got $980,331 of that.[75]

POST-CONSUMMATION POWER

The power of the pre-filing directors and replacement senior managers promised to remain firm for at least four years after plan consummation. Two new directors were appointed at the insistence of a group of preferred shareholders in 1984,[76] but no other new outside director appeared on the 1987 board.[77] A third new director, Randall Smith, a limited partner in Bear Stearns & Co., had served briefly. Smith was appointed after Bear Stearns accumulated a large holding of Manville common stock.[78] Smith resigned his directorship in late 1985. Despite repeated petitions by shareholders for annual and special meetings, at which new directors might have been elected, none were permitted after the bankruptcy filing.[79]

Further, the Manville reorganization plan provided that at least half of all common shares, those held by the A-H Trust, would be voted for management's nominees to the board of directors for four years after the consummation date.[80] While the initial post-consummation board of directors included seven new outside members, six of the pre-filing directors remained, as did chief executive W. Thomas Stephens, assuring pre-consummation management of at least a stalemate in event of any dispute.[81]

CONTROL OF ASSETS FREE OF ASBESTOS CLAIMS

Some of the executives who left the company were able to remain in control of substantial assets, assets then free and clear of asbestos claims against Manville. For example, the group which bought Manville's Canadian asbestos division on July 1, 1983, was headed by the chief executive officer of Johns-Manville Canada.[82] Aside from about $47 million apparently borrowed on the asbestos assets and remitted to Manville, the $117 million to $150 million (Canadian) selling price was payable "out of 85.5% of available future cash flows from asbestos fiber operations."[83] Those cash flows were so great the bill was paid in just four years. In 1989, Peter Kyle, president of the Canadian company, said, "As far as leveraged buy-outs go, I don't think there are any as good as this one."[84] The other divisions sold in 1983, notably certain asbestos-cement pipe operations, were presumably transferred with management in place.

After leaving Manville in 1986, former president Hulce and another former Manville executive helped form a company, BMZ Materials, Inc., which purchased several Manville plants with annual sales of $17.5 million. The purchase price was $5.5 million in cash and a $1.5 million promissory note.[85]

Several other sales of Manville assets were approved by the bankruptcy court.[86] In all these cases, the assets involved were placed beyond the reach of the asbestos victims.

Even some of the managers who stayed with Manville, those in Manville Forest Products Corporation, controlled assets not subject to asbestos claims as early as 1984. That subsidiary accounted for more than a third of Manville's assets in 1986.[87] As previously mentioned, it emerged from bankruptcy court protection in 1984.

BENEFITS FOR ATTORNEYS AND CONSULTANTS

The Manville executives and directors found themselves able to distribute much of the largesse produced by decades of asbestos production to a host of consultants and attorneys and to mediate the distribution of millions more. For example, Davis Polk and Wardwell, a New York law firm which had represented Manville since 1928, was co-counsel for the chapter 11 proceedings and charged over $200,000 a month at first.[88] By 1989, the firm would receive about $13 million and co-counsel Levin & Weintraub & Crames about $6 million.[89] First Boston Corporation was authorized $100,000 a month in late 1984 to serve as financial adviser to certain creditor groups and eventually received over $5 million.[90] These figures do not include millions in expenses, which were generally paid in full.

Leon Silverman, the "Legal Representative for Future Claimants" appointed by the bankruptcy court, submitted bills for $2.3 million for August 1, 1984, through December 31, 1986.[91] Dr. Frederick W. Kilbourne was paid $73,550 for work as Manville's actuarial expert during November 1983 through April 1984.[92]

The pattern continued. For the first six months of 1987, 22 law firms submitted bills in the Manville chapter 11 proceeding for $5,733,983.[93] The "Provisional" trust budget for January–August 1987 provided $4.6 million to administer the A-H trust, including $194,000 for executive searches, $840,000 to pay Smith and three assistants, and $257,000 for the six trustees, who were scheduled to meet seven times.[94] The trust rented 32,038 square feet of office space in Washington, D.C., at an annual cost of $849,007.[95] In addition to their $30,000 annual compensation, each trustee was to get $1,000 a day for meetings, intercontinental travel, and other work performed for the trust. The executive director of the Association of Trial Lawyers of America, Marianna S. Smith, was hired as chief executive officer of the A-H trust at $250,000 a year.

The managing trustee was authorized $1,500 for each day his part-time trust duties were to occupy over half his time. The trust budget for the ten months September 1987 through June 1988 was 9.6 million, including $2.9 million for salaries and benefits. Adequate funding for such expenses was assured by the transfer of $150 million from Manville to the trust and was approved by the bankruptcy judge November 25, 1987, two years before the trust paid its first asbestos claim.[96]

Through 1986, Manville had dispensed $64 million in chapter 11 costs.[97] The billings for fees alone totaled $106 million by November 1988, plus millions more in expenses.[98]

In addition, the asbestos victims' attorneys were to generally get a third or more of all payments to victims from the A-H trust. For example, the firm of Stanley J. Levy, who represented 1,500 victims, was expected to receive $13 million.[99] If settlements over time were to total as much as $2 billion, as promised, plaintiff lawyers might claim $600 million.

Of course, Manville and its executives had standing in the bankruptcy court to approve or contest all of the payments mentioned above, standing they often, but selectively exercised.[100]

THE PLIGHT OF THE ASBESTOS VICTIMS

By 1988, an estimated 41,500 new A-H claims were waiting to be filed against Manville[101] and, of course, many of the 20,000 1982 claimants had died. Total A-H claims filed in the United States by mid-1987 against all companies were estimated at 70,000.[102] In July 1987, the A-H trustees estimated payments from the trust could begin during the spring of 1988,[103] nearly six years after Manville's bankruptcy filing. By January 1988, it seemed clear the bankruptcy judge's confirmation order would be appealed to the U.S. Supreme Court unless overturned by the Second Circuit U.S. Court of Appeals.[104] The estimate of when payments could begin was moved back to "April to November 1988."[105] But in March 1988 the appeals court was still mulling one of the appeals.[106]

In a letter dated July 22, 1988,[107] Nillar T. Clark expressed her desperation to Judge Lifland:

> ... February 28, 1985, three years, five months ago, my husband, Vernon Clark, died from malignant mesothelioma due to asbestosis.... Sir, what I am asking of you is, will you please advise me as to the status of *when* and *if* this will *ever* be cleared so that I can receive some help.... My husband left very little insurance and I am working as a medical transcriptionist at the Veterans Administration Medical Center, Augusta. I am struggling to hold onto our home. I have a daughter, a juvenile diabetic, of college age, and desperately need help. . . .

Judge Lifland wrote in reply he was "in deep sympathy" with her plight, blamed the delay on appeals from his orders, and, by copy of his letter, asked the attorney for the victims committee to give her "further details."[108]

In addition to the delay, the asbestos victims had other reasons to despair. First, A-H representatives in the bankruptcy court had been effectively preempted, apparently because of Manville's threat to contest their contingent fee contracts with victims. Second, the victims were to have little control over Manville or the A-H trust for years after consummation. Third, the Manville plan provided for effective subordination of A-H claims to commercial debt, even that which was unsecured. Fourth, many of Manville's pre-filing assets had already been irrevocably insulated from potential claims against them by A-H victims. Finally, the prospective payments to the A-H trust provided for in the plan seemed substantially uncertain as well as inadequate. In fact, the trust would report inability to pay claims in the last half of 1989, having committed all its available funds to judgments and settlements from 1975 to 1982 and before.[109] At that time, the names of 1985 claimants like Mrs. Nillar T. Clark would still be thousands down on the list of claims being processed.

CONCERN THAT CONSUMMATION MIGHT NOT OCCUR OR MIGHT BE REVERSED

Some A-H victims were convinced the Manville plan offered their best hope for compensation. Heather Bechtel, head of Asbestos Victims of America, wrote in 1986, "Victims are well aware that they hold no power in this reorganization process and they resent it. Some are holding the slim hope that just maybe by some accident some money will come before they die."[110] As it turned out, the plan was eventually consummated, but in early 1988 there were at least two reasons for such victims as Bechtel described to worry that might not occur.

First, there was evidence the A-H trustees were concerned Manville had made inadequate disclosure of incriminating evidence during reorganization. The head of the Asbestos Victims of America said attorneys had told her the inadequate disclosure might necessitate a new vote on the plan by stockholders, creditors, and claimants. A news service reported some attorneys believed Manville and the A-H trust were anxious to avoid later claims that the full extent of the company's knowledge was hidden during the reorganization.[111] And a person familiar with the case said certain A-H trustees became concerned about such concealment after reading a court-ordered summary of evidence in a Washington claims court case, mentioned below.

There was some more objective evidence of the concern. One of Manville's attorneys wrote Judge Lifland that questions had been raised about the "breadth of the restraining provisions" which protected the A-H trustees and others involved in the trust from legal attack. Judge Lifland issued a new order on March 18, 1987, barring any action concerning "administration, enforcement or settlement of accounts" related to the trust in any court except the bankruptcy court.[112] And $20 million of the trust assets were later set aside to indemnify the trustees.[113] Also in March 1988, Manville and the A-H trust announced the creation of a depository for asbestos-related documents, mainly those produced from 1983–1987 in Manville's California lawsuit against its insurance carriers and a Washington, D.C., claims court case the company had filed against the government. The California lawsuit had led to the insurance settlements which were to provide most early funding for the A-H trust. The depository, located near Manville's Denver headquarters, was opened in April 1988 and, according to Manville, was to contain over 44 million pages. It was available to "those involved in resolving health claims against the company."[114]

Second, court rulings in late 1987 and early 1988 seemed to suggest criminal indictments of Manville or its officials were possible. Such indictments could void Judge Lifland's ability to protect the company and its managers, in part because bankruptcy courts cannot try criminal matters. In two Delaware cases Raymark Corporation (formerly Raybestos-Manhattan Corporation) was found liable for civil conspiracy[115] with Manville to conceal or misrepresent the health hazards of asbestos. And a court in Washington state ruled Manville and Raymark engaged in "concert of action" to each market asbestos-containing products without warning of their potential dangers.[116] Concerning the Delaware cases, the court later ruled the standard of proof required in civil conspiracy was "preponderance of evidence," not the "clear and convincing" test Raymark wished to impose. The court did not address whether the stronger test had been met, only that it was not required. The judge wrote, "I find no basis for singling out this type of intentional tort, or intentional torts in general, which involve a greater level of culpability than that involved in negligent conduct, for favored treatment in the proof of the wrongdoing."[117] While the Manville plan would weather the early storm of conspiracy rulings and be confirmed, filings in a Rhode Island case in 1988 would provide new impetus to the effort to prove Manville the leader in an extensive, decades-long conspiracy to suppress research, evidence, and publicity about asbestos dangers.[118]

A-H REPRESENTATIVES PREEMPTED
IN BANKRUPTCY COURT

After 1984, the asbestos victims were essentially powerless to affect the outcome of the chapter 11 process, in part because Manville management was apparently able to neutralize their committee in the bankruptcy court. The committee consisted of nineteen contingent-fee attorneys and one asbestos victim, who suffered a stroke and was temporarily disabled early in the proceedings. Until early 1984, the committee had aggressively confronted Manville management. For example, during September 1983 through January 1984, the committee asked the bankruptcy court to dismiss the bankruptcy filing,[119] rejected management's proposed reorganization plan,[120] requested that Manville's top management be replaced with a trustee,[121] and even petitioned the court to cut the managers' salaries.[122] But in January 1984, Manville obtained a hearing date on its motion to void the A-H attorneys' contingent-fee agreements, which generally gave the attorneys a third or more of any settlement or judgment proceeds.[123] Manville had called the fee arrangements "completely unconscionable."[124] There seemed a high likelihood Manville could have prevailed had it continued to press the matter; Judge Lifland opposed the contingent fees and later expressed dismay that A-H claimants were not informed of ways to contest them.[125]

But the A-H committee fell into line and in March 1984 withdrew its motion to decrease management salaries.[126] And Manville management relaxed its effort to void the contingent-fee arrangements. For the ensuing two years, the *Asbestos Litigation Reporter,* which reported legal news and filings in asbestos cases,[127] revealed no actions by the A-H committee to contest the authority or benefits of Manville management or to remove the company from bankruptcy court protection.[128] By July 1984, Manville was predicting quick agreement to its reorganization plan by all parties, including the A-H committee.[129] Leading asbestos attorney, and member of the A-H committee, Ronald Motley later wrote, "[The] intimation that there is some relationship between Manville's withdrawal of its objection to contingency fees in exchange for the AH Committee's not opposing certain management decisions is both false and insulting."[130] Motley's indignation may be somewhat understandable, since he later became aggressive outside the bankruptcy court in showing that Manville had led other asbestos companies in a conspiracy to deprive the public of information about asbestos and health.[131]

The A-H committee became a strong management ally in seeking approval of the plan. For example, the committee sponsored promotional brochures for inclusion in the 100,000 information packets and ballots on the plan mailed in September 1986 to persons who provided evidence they had asbestos-related disease.[132] The brochures stated, "The Asbestos Victims Committee urges you to vote in favor of the Plan.... Vote yes on the Manville Reorganization Plan."[133] Despite the promotional activity, including a nationwide multimedia campaign, one of the two national organizations of asbestos victims opposed the plan and the other refused to endorse it.[134] But many A-H victims had long before given their voting proxies to the attorneys they chose to represent them. A-H attorneys throughout America apparently acted en masse in voting the asbestos victims' proxies for the plan. And tens of thousands of persons were allowed to vote as asbestos victims though they had never submitted an actual claim. In any case, the results were reminiscent of elections of party bosses in communists countries: Manville claimed its plan received an incredible 96 percent of the 52,440 A-H votes cast.[135] Of course, the unsecured creditors, for whom the plan generally provided for full payment, voted yes.

Bankruptcy Judge Lifland further weakened any active opposition to the Manville plan by asbestos victims in late 1987, when he approved the transfer of $150 million into the A-H trust. Victims' hopes were undoubtedly raised because the money was not excluded from eventually being used to pay A-H claims. But the court order approving the transfer provided that if the plan failed to survive all appeals, unspent funds would go first to pay property damage claims and then to "charitable purposes."[136] So if opposition to the Manville plan from any quarter were to prove successful, an additional $150 million of Manville's assets, in this case cash, would be unavailable to pay A-H claims. Besides, much of the money would be consumed by trust administrative expenses, then running about $1 million a month.[137]

LITTLE CONTROL OVER MANVILLE
AFTER CONSUMMATION

Even after plan consummation, if and when that were to occur, the A-H claimants would have little power over Manville or the A-H trust. As previously mentioned, six of the pre-1982 directors were to remain on the post-consummation board, as was chief executive W. Thomas Stephens assuring management of at least a stalemate in any dispute. The trust would own 50 percent or more of Manville's common stock. But sale of the stock was to be restricted for five years and the stock was to be required to be voted for management's choices for directors for at least four years after consummation.[138] As it turned out, the trust ran short of money in 1989 and seemed likely to sell some of its Manville stock to get more.[139] That would diminish the voting power the trust could exercise, even after the four years. In addition, the trustees seemed inclined to relinquish the rights of control it did have. For example, Manville's 1989 proxy statement reported, "The Trust has elected not to exercise its right to approve two nominees for Director for the 1989 Annual Meeting."[140]

Even if the trust had retained control over management, that would not have assured the victims of influence. The A-H trustees, including an investment banker, four lawyers, and a business consultant, were to have lifetime tenures. Vacancies were to be filled by the remaining trustees, after consultation with Manville and selected asbestos counsel.[141]

A-H CLAIMS SUBORDINATED TO THOSE
OF COMMERCIAL CREDITORS

The plan would effectively subordinate the A-H claims to those of commercial creditors, even unsecured ones. For example, an estimated $473 million in cash was to be distributed by Manville soon after the plan's effective date.[142] *But only $55 million of this was to go to the victims' trust* (technically, the trust would get $80 million but would have to give $25 million of that to the property damage trust).[143] In contrast, the general unsecured creditors would get $248 million in cash.[144] The rest of the unsecured creditors' principal, with interest, would be paid within four and one-half years.[145] All this was turning out pretty much as planned through mid 1989, except the A-H trust received $150 million from Manville in December 1987 so it could operate even before plan consummation. It passed almost unnoticed that this money allowed trust operations to become a fait accompli, devastating any remaining opposition to the Manville plan.

Much of Manville's pre-filing commercial debt had already been reinstated or paid, as divisions were reorganized or sold free and clear of asbestos claims during the lengthy chapter 11 process. As a result, the liabilities subject to chapter 11 proceedings reported on Manville's balance sheet declined by $161 million from 1982–1986.[146]

The plan prohibited interest on asbestos-health claims.[147] But unsecured creditors were allowed 12 percent interest.[148] And the creditors were granted $114 million in debentures for interest while Manville was in bankruptcy.[149] Further, the plan provided that Manville's ability to pledge assets to the victims' trust would be limited until the unsecured creditors were paid in full.[150] Finally, as discussed below, most payments to the A-H trust would be made from future earnings of the company, earnings which were far from certain. In contrast, general unsecured creditors were paid from the pool of liquid assets available upon plan confirmation and within four and one-half years thereafter. As the A-H trust was running short of money in 1989, Manville reported cash and marketable securities balances exceeding $270 million, providing assurance unsecured creditors could be paid.[151]

MANVILLE ASSETS SHIELDED FROM A-H CLAIMS

The reorganization of Manville Forest Products corporation in 1983 forever insulated that division's $870 million in assets[152] from victims' claims. Another $301 million in pre-filing assets were shielded from the asbestos liabilities through the sale of Manville's U.S. pipe operations in 1982 and the asbestos fiber operations in 1983.[153] In each case, commercial creditors of the affected divisions either were paid in full or had their claims reinstated. Manville's Denver headquarters and a number of other assets were sold in 1987 and 1988, all protected from asbestos claims by the bankruptcy court. In fact, Manville retained responsibility for cleaning up asbestos residue on certain of the transferred property, further increasing the property's value.[154]

PAYMENTS TO A-H TRUST UNCERTAIN

The major promised source of long-term funding for the A-H trust was an unsecured, zero-interest Manville bond (promoted as a "$1.65 billion bond"). The bond would provide for semi-annual payments of $37.5 million in the fourth through the twenty-fifth fiscal years after consummation.[155]

Aside from Manville's ability to pay the bond installments in the long run, there was reason for concern about the purchasing power they would represent. Using Manville's inflation assumption of 5.2 percent,[156] those payments would each be worth $29 million (consummation-year dollars) in the fifth year, $23 million in the tenth year, $17.5 million in the fifteenth year, and $14 million in the twentieth year. If inflation were to average, say, 3 percent higher than Manville anticipated, the installments in the twentieth year would each be worth only $8 million. Further, there was a provision for the payments to be reduced under certain circumstances after the thirteenth fiscal year following consummation.[157]

Further, Manville's ability to pay its obligations to the A-H trust seemed problematical at best. The company estimated a $473 million payout under its plan upon consummation, most to commercial creditors, and another $546 million during the ensuing five years. A capital spending program was projected to consume another $800 million over those five years.[158] These amounts total $1.8 billion, compared to Manville's estimated liquidation value for all its assets of $2-2.4 billion.[159] So after paying out over 80 percent of its asset value—over twice its reported net worth[160]—in just five years, Manville promised to honor its further obligations under the plan. These further payments would average $108 million a year for years six, seven, and eight, including the two annual payments of $37.5 million to the A-H trust.[161] In addition, Manville had retained responsibility for asbestos cleanup of properties it had sold free of asbestos claims. In 1989, the company estimated the cost of cleaning those and other sites would be $85 million, but admitted, "[I]t is not possible to determine with certainty what the ultimate cost will be. . . ."[162]

In proving feasibility of the plan, Manville and its investment banker, Morgan Stanley and Company, "projected" the company's cash flows forward through 1991.[163] These figures were then "extrapolated" through 2011.[164] Exhibit 4 shows Manville's historical sales and net earnings for 1978–1986[165] and the projections for 1987–1991. Also listed are the interest expense amounts for each of those years. As the table illustrates, Manville's net earnings declined from $121 million in 1978 to $60 million in 1981. Then, from 1982–1986 net earnings averaged only $16 million a year. Manville would have lost money for the 1982–1986 period except for two non-recurring advantages. First, the company avoided at least $50 million a year in average interest charges on liabilities subject to chapter 11 proceedings.[166] The unsecured portions of these liabilities varied from $627 million in 1982 to $490 million in 1986. Interest expense was projected to average $85 million a year more in 1987–1991 than in 1982–1986. Second, other income averaged $52 million in 1982–1986.[167] It was put at only $14 million a year for 1987–1991.[168]

EXHIBIT 4   ACTUAL AND PROJECTED SALES, NET EARNINGS, AND INTEREST

YEAR	NET SALES	NET EARNINGS	INTEREST
Historical			
1978	$1,648	$121	$ 22
1979	2,276	115	62
1980	2,267	81	65
1981	1,895	60	72
1982	1,685	(98)	52
1983	1,729	67	26
1984	1,814	77	21
1985	1,880	(45)	23
1986	1,920	81	20
Projected			
1987	2,043	108	112
1988	2,239	86	114
1989	2,411	108	116
1990	2,636	118	115
1991	2,480	47	106

Note: Dollar amounts given in millions.

EXHIBIT 5   COMPARATIVE INCOME STATEMENTS, 1982–1988

	1988	1987	1986	1985	1984	1983	1982
Net sales	$2,062	$1,935	$1,803	$1,880	$1,814	$1,729	$1,685
Cost of sales	1,545	1,440	1,368	1,473	1,400	1,370	1,329
Sell, G&A	203	206	213	246	238	224	256
R&D & eng.	36	32	35	35	36	35	28
Restructuring costs	139	(3)	47	153	2	—	—
Other income (loss)	69	50	39	63	61	61	32
Income from operations	207	310	180	36	200	161	104
Interest expense	40	25	20	23	21	26	52
Ch. 11 & A·H cost	12	15	28	61	43	39	18
Disposition of assets	—	—	—	—	—	(3)	46
Income tax	66	113	54	(2)	58	40	8
Income, cont. ops.	89	157	78	(45)	77	60	(21)
Income disc. ops.	7	7	4	—	—	7	(77)
Extraordinary charge	96	164	81	(45)	77	67	(98)
Acctg. change	(1,288)	(91)	0	0	0	0	0
Net Income	(107)	0	0	0	0	0	0
	$(1,299)	$ 73	$ 81	$ (45)	$ 77	$ 67	$ (98)

Note: Dollar amounts given in millions. Totals may not check, due to rounding.

The projections promised an annual average of $93 million in net earnings for the five years after 1986, compared to $16 million average for the preceding 5 years—this despite the projected payment of $85 million a year more interest than in 1982–1986 and the loss of $38 million a year in other income.

In arriving at this remarkable result, Manville and Morgan Stanley claimed income from operations would reach $370 million in 1990. They estimated it would *average* $283.4 million annually for the five years 1987–1991.[169] That is almost exactly double the $145 million average for the preceding five years and more than Manville had ever earned in any single year.[170]

Manville issued extensive disclaimers for itself and Morgan Stanley concerning the projections. For example, the company reported, "NO REPRESENTATIONS CAN BE MADE WITH RESPECT TO THE ACCURACY OF THE PROJECTIONS OR THE ABILITY TO ACHIEVE THE PROJECTED RESULTS ... the above pro forma and projected financial statements are unaudited ... Morgan Stanley did not independently verify the information considered in its reviews of [the assumptions upon which the projections were

EXHIBIT 6   COMPARATIVE BUSINESS SEGMENT INFORMATION, 1982–1988

	1988	1987	1986	1985	1984	1983	1982
*Revenues**							
Fiberglass products	937	877	809	803	780	720	609
Forest products	678	596	541	459	451	427	436
Specialty products	501	506	494	674	254	248	285
Nonfiberglass insulation	—	—	—	—	203	209	232
Roofing products	—	—	—	—	190	228	211
Corp. & elmntns	15	6	−2	8	—	—	—
Corp. rev. net	—	—	—	—	39	35	14
Intersegment sales	—	—	8	—	(43)	(76)	(69)
Total	$2,131	$1,985	$1,842	$1,943	$1,873	$1,791	$1,717
Income from Operations							
Fiberglass products	$ 123	$ 151	$ 120	$ 69	115	$ 97	$ 75
Forest products	127	100	62	34	63	53	48
Specialty products	38	36	27	(38)	22	18	28
Nonfiberglass insulation	—	—	—	—	16	9	11
Roofing products	—	—	—	—	(11)	(10)	(6)
Corp. & elmntns	(81)	23	(29)	(28)	—	—	—
Corp. exp. net	—	—	—	—	(4)	(6)	(22)
Elim & adj.	—	—	—	—	—	1	7
Total	$ 207	$ 310	$ 180	$ 36	$ 200	$ 161	$ 141

Note: Dollar amounts given in millions. Totals may not check, due to rounding.

*Includes net sales and other income, net.

EXHIBIT 7   COMPARATIVE BALANCE SHEETS, 1982–1988

	DECEMBER 31						
	1988	1987	1986	1985	1984	1983	1982
ASSETS							
Cash and equiv.	$ 219	$ 210	$ 137	$ 7	$ 9	$ 19	$ 11
Marketable securities	54	385	307	314	276	240	206
AR & NR	298	309	292	314	285	277	310
Inventories	146	160	153	153	164	141	152
Prepmts	14	27	24	29	17	22	17
Total CA	731	1,091	914	817	752	700	696
Land & imp.	95	97	99	95	96	97	108
Buildings	253	261	312	304	308	303	332
Mach & Equip	1,366	1,330	1,234	1,156	1,121	1,056	1,090
Ac depr & depl	(645)	(597)	(586)	(538)	(513)	(472)	(547)
Timber & timberland	357	367	376	385	392	395	402
PP&E, net	1,427	1,458	1,434	1,402	1,405	1,379	1,385
Other assets	235	204	165	174	182	174	154
	$2,393	$2,753	$2,513	$2,393	$2,339	$2,253	$2,236
LIABILITY & STOCKHOLDERS' EQUITY							
ST debt	$ 77	$ 21	$ 30	$ 26	$ 20	$ 14	$ 12
AP	103	104	93	84	102	94	86
Ac compensation & benefits	97	101	103	94	81	65	63
Income tax	31	14	16	12	18	10	32
Other accrued liab.	113	73	62	69	35	26	29
Total CL	421	312	304	286	256	208	221
LT debt	869	223	80	92	84	4	12
Liab. subj. to ch. 11	0	547	575	578	574	713	736
Other non-cur. liab.	208	101	118	115	67	61	60
Deferred income tax	97	198	161	144	162	136	140
Total liab.	1,595	1,381	1,239	1,214	1,142	1,122	1,170
Preferred stock	$ 418	$ 301	$ 301	$ 301	$ 301	$ 301	$ 301
Preference stock	89	—	—	—	—	—	—
Common stock	0	60	60	60	60	60	60
Capital above par	761	178	178	178	178	178	178
Ret. earnings	(479)	821	749	667	713	635	568
Curr. trans. adj.	8	12	(11)	(26)	(53)	(41)	(39)
Treas. stock	0	(2)	(2)	(2)	(2)	(2)	(2)
Net worth	798	1,370	1,275	1,178	1,197	1,131	1,066
	$2,393	$2,753	$2,513	$2,393	$2,339	$2,253	$2,236

Note: Dollar amounts given in millions. Totals may not check, due to rounding.

based] and for purposes of its reviews relied upon the accuracy and complete-ness of all such information. . . . [Under certain] PESSIMISTIC ASSUMP-TIONS MANVILLE WOULD NOT GENERATE THROUGH ITS OPERA-TIONS SUFFICIENT CASH TO MEET ALL OF ITS OBLIGATIONS UNDER THE PLAN DURING THE PERIODS ANALYZED."[171] Yet, the presentations were accepted by the bankruptcy court as providing plan feasibility.

Exhibits 5, 6, and 7 summarize Manville's financial statements for the several years following August 1982.

CONCLUSION

On October 16, 1987, Manville chief executive W. Thomas Stephens appeared in a debate with management professor Arthur Sharplin before the National Conference on Business Ethics. Stephens generally described past company managers as well intentioned but misinformed. He mentioned certain lessons he had learned: (1) Chapter 11 was the right decision. (2) "Today, its 'Let the seller beware' and it's as it should be." (3) The industry did not tell employees and customers enough about the dangers of asbestos.[172]

On the broad question of toxic waste, Stephens said, "I think the companies and the officers of those companies should be held totally accountable for their actions. . . . Some horrible mistakes have been made in the past. . . . But I think the emphasis should be on solving the problem, learning the lessons from the past, and not bashing the guys that screwed up."[173]

Later Stephens said the advantage of the victims owning stock through the A-H trust was that they would be long-term investors looking for long-term results, not just a boost in one quarter's earnings. He expressed his hope that Manville would experience a rebirth, "like the Phoenix," when it emerged from chapter 11.

The cover story in the November 1987 issue of *Corporate Finance* was entitled "Miracle at Manville: How Tom Stephens Raised the Bread to Overcome Bankruptcy." The article said many considered the Manville bankruptcy "the ultimate management cop-out of all time." It continued, "Soon these critics will have to eat their words."[174]

In a January 1988 *Financier* article, Stephens wrote, "We have set a goal: That the new Manville will be the model of ethical corporate behavior. We have demonstrated what we can and will do. I'm proud of our record."[175]

In March 1988, Stephens took questions from a University of Montana business ethics class. He told the students he thought Manville's bankruptcy choice was "the most courageous and most ethical decision ever made by a Fortune 500 company."[176]

On March 30, 1988, the Second Circuit U.S. Court of Appeals issued its long-awaited decision on the remaining appeal from the Manville confirmation order. The other appeal had been rejected earlier and a petition for a rehearing was also rejected, setting the stage for a further appeal to the U.S. Supreme Court. Ninety days were allowed to seek review by the Supreme

Court. A spokesperson for the A-H trust said if the Supreme Court refused to hear the appeals, consummation of the plan could occur sometime in the fall and payments to victims could begin by year end.

The Supreme Court did refuse and the reorganization plan was finally confirmed October 28, 1988. Manville's plan was consummated on November 28 that year. The A-H trust had not paid a single claim but had expended $15 million since its establishment in January 1987. The six trustees had been paid $440,555 plus expenses.[177] *Asbestos Watch,* the newsletter of the White Lung Association, observed,

> The Manville Corporation and its officers are facing a bright future. The picture is not so rosy for their hundreds of thousands of victims. The company which murdered so many of its workers is looking forward to emerging from bankruptcy as a viable and healthy company. . . . [178]

Many settlements had already been agreed upon. Actual payments had to await various audits and completion of "settlement documents," which had been completed for only about 20 percent of the "settled" claims by mid-October 1988.[179] Essentially all of these settlements were for awards won by victims before August 26, 1982, and stayed by the bankruptcy filing. The first checks were mailed to victims near the start of 1989, the seventh new year after the asbestos claims were frozen. By march 15, 1989, the A-H trust reported it had settled 14,339 claims with an average promised payment of $37,832.[180]

The trust had committed all of its available funds, to pay an estimated 15 percent of the total claims.[181] Executive director Marianna Smith suggested unpaid claimants might be offered installment payments, but an A-H attorney said, "Nobody wants an IOU." In the alternative, Smith suggested, the trust might have to sell some of its 24 million shares of Manville common stock, then trading just above $7 a share, or convert its preferred stock into as many as 72 million common shares, which could also be sold.[182] There were numerous press reports about the problems the trust was having.

John A. McKinney, two years retired in 1989, wrote,

> Shareholders were wiped out in order to provide funding to: 1) pay lawyers several hundred million dollars; 2) pay shipyard workers without ever taking testimony as to whether the government caused their injuries, as numerous trial courts and juries have held; 3) pay whatever money remained to property-damage claimants who have yet to produce a single person made ill by occupying a building containing asbestos.[183]

McKinney noted that his resistance to the compromise which produced the final reorganization plan was considered stubbornness and remarked, "In this context, I am proud to be called stubborn."[184]

Leon Silverman, a New York attorney who represented future victims in the bankruptcy court and helped craft the Manville plan, said, "This recent flurry of publicity should not lead to disquiet. All of these problems were anticipated in the original plan and should not result in diminution of payments to claimants."[185] And trust executive director Smith said, "Based on current projections over the life of the trust, there will be enough money to pay all the claimants, although there will be temporary cash shortfalls."[186]

Manville's glossy 1988 annual report, packed with full-color pictures of smiling employees and executives, proudly announced, "In essence, the plan created a new Manville able to operate free from direct involvement in the asbestos claim procedures and asbestos-related lawsuits."[187] And CEO Thomas Stephens wrote of the $1 billion he had available to finance growth plans, promising, "For starters, we"ll continue to upgrade our manufacturing technologies. Secondly, we're aggressively seeking acquisitions and joint ventures that take full advantage of our existing strengths."[188] In their letter to shareholders, Stephens and chairman of the board George C. Dillon, who had been a Manville director since 1969, wrote, "Now that a solution to the asbestos tragedy has been implemented, we will build on our strengths and continue to be a world-class organization."[189]

As the Manville plan became more certain of confirmation, the firm began an extensive effort to improve the image of "the new Manville." For example, Stephens poses as Jesus for the cover picture on the November 1987 issue of *Corporate Finance.* The caption reads, "Miracle at Manville." Stephens sit on a huge stone surrounded by loaves of bread and a basket of fishes.[190] Inside, the article expresses wonder at Stephen's "miracle."

In the October 17, 1988, *Business Week,* a glowing Stephens cuddles his shotgun and hunting dog in a woodsy scene. The accompanying article emphasizes the strain Manville might experience in paying its obligations to the asbestos-health trust and cautions victims not to "kill the golden goose."

The January 2, 1989, *Fortune* magazine lists Stephens among 1988's "25 most fascinating business people." Stephens, who *Fortune* says is "gleeful," is shown sitting on a bundle of Manville lumber, while the accompanying article proclaims, "Free at Last." The writer asserts, "Asbestos victims will benefit [from Manville's profitability under Stephens]."

Manville chief financial officer John Roach looks out from the cover of the July 1989 *CFO* magazine. One hand is on a huge world globe, the other curled to a fist under his chin. In big letters above his head: "REDEEMING MANVILLE." The article tells what a bad reputation Manville had and states, "Manville is out to redress past wrongs—by growing big enough to repay its victims." The article contains a number of artful misrepresentations, such as the suggestion that major banks lost millions in the bankruptcy—and that, therefore, the banks' willingness to finance Manville's new growth plans is remarkable.

ENDNOTES

1. Barry I. Castleman, *Asbestos: Medical and Legal Aspects* (Clifton, N.J.: Prentice-Hall Law and Business, 1987), 614.

2. Ibid., 636–7.

3. Alan Freeman, "Canadian Asbestos Mining Enjoys a Modest Recovery," *Wall Street Journal,* March 10, 1989, B2.

4. David Ozonoff, "Failed Warnings: Asbestos-Related

Disease and Industrial Medicine," in Ronald Bayer, ed., *The Health and Safety of Workers: Case Studies in the Politics of Professional Responsibility* (Oxford: Oxford University Press, 1988), 151.

5. Quoted in Ibid., 155–6.

6. Quoted in Ibid., 157.

7. Ibid., 155, 167.

8. Vandiver Brown to A. J. Lanza, December 10, 1934.

9. Ozonoff, "Failed Warnings," 167.

10. George S. Hobart to Vandiver Brown, December 15, 1934.

11. Vandiver Brown to A. J. Lanza, December 21, 1934.

12. Vandiver Brown to S. Simpson, October 3, 1935.

13. Anne Rossiter to Sumner Simpson, president of Raybestos-Manhattan, Inc., September 25, 1935.

14. Vandiver Brown to LeRoy U. Gardner, November 20, 1936.

15. LeRoy U. Gardner, M.D., "Interim Report on Experimental Asbestosis at the Saranac Laboratory," enclosure to letter from Vandiver Brown to Sumner Simpson, December 26, 1939.

16. W.C.L. Henderson, "Industrial Hygiene Foundation of America, Inc.: Report of Preliminary Dust Investigation for Asbestos Textile Institute," June 18, 1947, 2, 15.

17. Kenneth W. Smith, "Industrial Hygiene—Survey of Men in Dusty Areas," enclosure to memorandum marked *"Confidential"* from A. R. Fisher (Manville president) to Vandiver Brown, February 3, 1949, 2.

18. Ibid., 3.

19. Dr. Kenneth W. Smith, Discovery deposition, Louisville Trust Company, Administrator of the estate of William Virgil Sampson, v. Johns-Manville Corporation, File no. 164-122, (Court of Common Pleas, Jefferson County, Kentucky, April 21, 1976). A Manville attorney later claimed Smith was an alcoholic.

20. David A. Shaw, "Memorandum in Opposition to Motions for Summary Judgment Filed by the Wellington Defendants and Defendant Raymark Industries," reprinted in *Asbestos Litigation Reporter,* November 18, 1988, 18051.

21. Irving J. Selikoff, testimony before House of Representatives, Select Committee on Labor, Committee on Education and Labor, U.S. Congress, March 7, 1968.

22. Manville Corporation, "Beleaguered by Asbestos Lawsuits Manville Files for Reorganization," news release, August 27, 1982.

23. Manville Corporation, *1982 Annual Report and Form 10-K,* December 31, 1982, 49.

24. Richard Goodwin, telephone interview, May 3, 1988.

25. Ibid.

26. "Arkansas Plane Crash Kills Marlin Thompson, Robin Steele, Four Others," *Asbestos Litigation Reporter,* December 2, 1988, 18086–7.

27. Clarence Borel v. Fibreboard Paper Products Corporation, et al., 493 F. 2d. 1076–1109 (5th Cir. 1973).

28. Richard Goodwin, telephone interview, April 22, 1988.

29. Dr. Kenneth W. Smith, Discovery deposition, Louisville Trust Company, Administrator of the estate of William Virgil Sampson, v. Johns-Manville Corporation, File no. 164-122, (Court of Common Pleas, Jefferson County, Kentucky, April 21, 1976). A Manville attorney later claimed Smith was an alcoholic.

30. Herbert E. Meyer, "Shootout at the Johns-Manville Corral," *Fortune,* October 1976, 146–54.

31. W. Thomas Stephens, conversation with author, October 16, 1987.

32. Manville Corporation, *1977 Annual Report,* December 31, 1977, 2.

33. Amended Order (Survival and Wrongful Death Actions), Bennie M. Barnett, Administrator, for Gordon Luther Barnett, deceased, v. Owens-Corning Fiberglass Corp., et al. (Court of Common Pleas, Greenville County, South Carolina, August 23, 1978), 10 and 5.

34. Johns-Manville Corporation, *U.S. Securities and Exchange Commission Form 10-K* for year ended December 31, 1977, 26–7.

35. Ronald L. Motley (leading asbestos plaintiff attorney), telephone conversation with author, October 9, 1987. Also see Manville Corporation, *U.S. Securities and Exchange Commission Form 10-Q,* June 30, 1982, II-8 (discussion of Louisiana cases).

36. G. Earl Parker, "The Manville Decision," Paper presented at the symposium "Bankruptcy Proceedings—The Effect on Product Liability," conducted by Andrews Publications, Inc., Miami, March 1983, 3.

37. Manville Corporation, "Manville Files for Reorganization," news release, August 26, 1982, 2.

38. Manville Corporation, *1982 Proxy Statement,* March 25, 1982, 12; *Moody's Industrial Manual,* 2 (New York: Moody's Investor Service, 1971), 1424; (1972), 3222; (1973), 2907–8; and (1974), 2040.

39. Manville Corporation, *1982 Proxy Statement,* March 25, 1982, 4–7.

40. Ibid., 4–7.

41. Manville Corporation, *1981 Proxy Statement,* September 11, 1981, Exhibit 2, 5–7.

42. "Stay Sought for Lawsuits Against Estate of Vandiver

Brown," *Stockholders & Creditors News Re. Johns-Manville Corp., et al.*, November 5, 1984, 3082.

43. Manville Corporation, *1982 Annual Report and Form 10-K*, December 31, 1982, 7; and *U.S. Securities and Exchange Commission Form 10-Q*, June 30, 1982, I-2. Also, Johns-Manville Corporation, *1978 Annual Report*, 36. U.S. Consumer Price Index figures were obtained from Ibbotson Associates, *Stocks, Bonds, Bills, and Inflation: 1987 Yearbook* (Chicago: Ibbotson Associates, 1987), 30.

44. Manville Corporation, *1980 Annual Report*, 21; and *1981 Annual Report*, 15.

45. See, for example, "Manville Ratings Cut by Standard and Poor's," *Wall Street Journal*, June 11, 1982, 36.

46. Manville Corporation, *U.S. Securities and Exchange Commission Form 10-Q*, June 30, 1982, II-11–II-14.

47. An excellent argument for the conspiracy theory is found in David A. Shaw, "Memorandum in Opposition to Motions for Summary Judgment Filed by the Wellington Defendants and Defendant Raymark Industries," reprinted in *Asbestos Litigation Reporter*, November 18, 1988, 18048–53.

48. Manville Corporation, *1982 Annual Report and Form 10-K*, 7.

49. Manville Corporation, *1977 Annual Report*, 1.

50. Johns-Manville Corporation, *1977 Annual Report*, 8, 10, and 13.

51. Raymond A. Joseph, "Problems Have Long Plagued Asbestos Firms," *Wall Street Journal*, August 30, 1982, 15. (U.S. Interior Department figures in thousands of metric tons for 1976–1981 are given as 659, 610, 619, 561, 359, and 350, respectively.)

52. Manville Corporation, *1982 Annual Report and Form 10-K*, 18 and 30; and Johns-Manville Corporation, *1977 Annual Report*, 1.

53. Ibid.

54. Manville Corporation, *1982 Annual Report and Form 10-K*, 9.

55. William J. Nicholson, "Comments on 'Projections of Asbestos Disease, 1980–2000—A. M. Walker,'" January 30, 1983, reprinted in *Asbestos Litigation Reporter*, March 11, 1983, 6355–64.

56. Manville Corporation, *First Amended Disclosure Statement, Second Amended and Restated Plan of Reorganization, and Related Documents*, August 22, 1986, M-399.

57. Manville Corporation, *1983 Annual Report and Form 10K*, 13.

58. Ibid., 15.

59. See, for example, "Appeals Consolidated in 2nd Circuit, Possible Hearing in October," *Stockholders and Credi-*

tors News Service Re. Johns-Manville Corp., et al., September 21, 1987, 6953.

60. Arthur Sharplin, "Liquidation versus 'The Plan,'" reprinted in *Asbestos Litigation Reporter*, November 21, 1986), 13636–40.

61. Ibid.

62. Ibid.

63. John A. McKinney to Arthur Sharplin, May 11, 1987.

64. Manville Corporation, *1982 Annual Report and Form 10-K*, December 31, 1982, 6 and 11.

65. Ibid., 6; Manville Corporation, *1986 Annual Report and Form 10-K*, 39; *U.S. Securities and Exchange Commission Form 10-Q*, for the quarter ended September 30, 1988, I-2; and *U.S. Securities and Exchange Commission Form 10-Q*, for the quarter ended June 30, 1982, I-3.

66. Manville Corporation, *1986 Annual Report and Form 10K*, December 31, 1986, 45.

67. Manville Corporation, *1982 Proxy Statement*, 10; *1985 Annual Report and Form 10-K*, 79; and *1986 Annual Report and Form 10-K*, 63.

68. Manville Corporation, *1989 Proxy Statement*, April 14, 1989, 8.

69. Manville Corporation, *1982 Proxy Statement*, March 22, 1982, 10.

70. Manville Corporation, *1986 Annual Report and Form 10-K*, December 31, 1986, 63.

71. Cynthia F. Mitchell, "Manville to Pay Large Severance to 2 Executives," *Wall Street Journal*, June 24, 1986, 3 and 5. Also see Cynthia F. Mitchell, "Manville President Quits After Dispute with Asbestos Plaintiff over Top Posts," *Wall Street Journal*, April 30, 1986, 34.

72. Sharplin, "Liquidation versus 'The Plan.'" Also see Johns-Manville Corporation, et al., "Application for an Order Approving Severance Pay Agreements," reprinted in *Stockholders and Creditors News Service*, September 8, 1986, 5569–5572; and "Judge Approves Severance Pay for G. Earl Parker," *Stockholders and Creditors News Service*, October 5, 1987, 6988–6989.

73. "Key Manville Officers Allowed Severance in Event of Termination by Trustee," *Stockholders and Creditors New Service*, April 7, 1986, 4995.

74. "New Bonus Plan for Executives Approved by Court," *Stockholders and Creditors News Service*, August 10, 1987, 6778–9.

75. Manville Corporation, *1989 Proxy Statement*, April 14, 1989, 8.

76. "Manville Adds 3 to Board to Increase Shareholder Input," *Wall Street Journal*, August 3, 1984, 4.

77. Manville Corporation, *1986 Annual Report and Form 10-K*, 56–59.

78. See Dean Rotbart and Jonathan Dahl, "Manville's Common Stockholders May Have Potent Ally as Bear Stearns Bolsters Holdings," *Wall Street Journal*, July 25, 1984, 51.

79. See, for example, Manville Corporation, *1986 Annual Report and Form 10-K*, 33.

80. Manville Corporation, *First Amended Disclosure Statement, Second Amended and Restated Plan of Reorganization, and Related Documents*, August 22, 1986, 41.

81. Manville Corporation, *1986 Annual Report and Form 10-K*, 56–61.

82. "Hearing on Sale of J-M Canada Scheduled for August 30," *Stockholders and Creditors News Service*, August 15, 1983, 1315.

83. Ibid.

84. Alan Freeman, "Canadian Asbestos Mining Enjoys a Modest Recovery," *Wall Street Journal*, March 10, 1989, B2.

85. "3 Manville Manufacturing Plants Sold to Former President Hulce," *Denver Post*, January 5, 1988, 2C; and "Manville Sells Three Plants for $7 million," *Stockholders and Creditors News Service*, January 11, 1988, 7, 261–2.

86. See, for example, "Court Approves Sale by Manville of 100 Acres for $22 Million," "Court Approves Sale of 14 Acres to Manville Joint Venture," and "Order Authorizing Sale of Manville, NJ Property," *Stockholders and Creditors News Service*, January 11, 1988, 7261, 7262, and 7264, respectively.

87. Manville Corporation, *1986 Annual Report and Form 10K*, 53.

88. "Four Law Firms Submit Bills Totaling $1.8 Million as of December 31, 1982," *Stockholders and Creditors News Service*, March 14, 1983, 794.

89. "Total Fees Included $18.8 million for Bankruptcy Counsel," *Stockholders and Creditors News Re. Johns-Manville Corp., et al.*, January 23, 1989, 8438.

90. "In re Johns-Manville Corporation, et al., Debtors, Third Supplemental Order Approving Expanded Retention and Reduced Compensation of Investment Banker, 82 B 11656-76 (BRL) (SD NY November 16, 1984)," reprinted in *Stockholders and Creditors News Service*, December 10, 1984, 3184; also, "In re Johns-Manville Corporation, et al., Order Determining Applications for Allowance of Final Compensation and Section 503(b) Applications," reprinted in *Stockholders and Creditors News Service*, January 23, 1989, 8443–7.

91. "In re Johns-Manville Corporation, et al., Debtors, Statement of Compensation of the Legal Representative for Future Claimants and His Counsel," [82 B 11656-62

and 82 B 11664-76 (BRL) (SD NY August 14, 1987)] reprinted in *Stockholders and Creditors News Service*, September 7, 1987, 6945.

92. "Affidavit of J. Thomas Beckett in Support of the Motion of the Committee of Unsecured Creditors for an Order Authorizing and Directing Final Payment to Actuarial Experts, 82 B 11656-76 (HCB) (SD NY August 3, 1987)," in *Stockholders and Creditors News Service*, August 24, 1987, 6819.

93. "Firms Seek $5.7 Million in Legal Fees for Six Months Ending June 30," *Stockholders and Creditors New Service*, September 7, 1987, 6905.

94. "Manville Personal Injury Settlement Trust Provisional Budget/Expense Estimates (January through August 1987)," *Stockholders and Creditors News Service*, August 10, 1987, 6800.

95. "Terms of Lease for Personal Injury Trust Quarters Approved," *Stockholders and Creditors News Service*, December 7, 1987, 7193.

96. "Manville Trust Forms Being Printed; $9.2 million (sic) Interim Budget," *Stockholders and Creditors News Service*, January 25, 1988, 7295.

97. Manville Corporation, *1986 Annual Report and Form 10-K*, 40; and *1983 Annual Report and Form 10-K*, 6.

98. "$106 Million in Fees Sought for Manville Chapter 11 Work," *Stockholders and Creditors News Re. Johns-Manville, et al.*, December 5, 1988, 8233.

99. Ibid.

100. See, for example, ibid., 8233–4.

101. "Plan Protects Manville, Shortchanges Victims," *Asbestos Watch*, 4:1 (Fall 1986), 1.

102. "JM Trust to Accept Claims in January, Negotiate Even Before Consummation," *Stockholders and Creditors News Service*, July 6, 1987, 6681

103. Ibid., 6680

104. Marianna S. Smith (executive director, Manville Personal Injury Settlement Trust), "Memorandum to Attorneys with Pre-petition Cases," January 27, 1988, reprinted in *Asbestos Litigation Reporter*, February 5, 1988, 16503.

105. Ibid.

106. "2nd Circuit's Delay in Kane Appeal Causes Speculation," *Stockholders and Creditors News Service*, March 7, 1988, 7417.

107. Nillar T. Clark to Honorable Burton Lifland, July 22, 1988, reprinted in *Stockholders and Creditors News Re. Johns-Manville et al.*, April 10, 1989, 8749.

108. Burton Lifland to Mrs. Nillar T. Clark, July 27, 1988, reprinted in *Stockholders and Creditors News Re. Johns-Manville, et al.*, April 10, 1989, 8750.

109. "Mississippi Workers Seek to Enjoin Payments by Trust," *Stockholders and Creditors News Service,* April 24, 1989, 8754.

110. Heather Bechtel, quoted in *Asbestos Litigation Reporter,* November 21, 1986, 13584.

111. "All Manville Documents to Be Available at Repository in Denver," *Asbestos Litigation Reporter,* March 4, 1988, 16657.

112. "Judge Lifland Bars Any Actions Relating to Administration of PI Trust," *Asbestos Litigation Reporter,* April 8, 1988, 16798.

113. "'Omnibus (sic) Decision' Reinforces Ban on Suits Against Manville," *Stockholders and Creditors News Re. Johns-Manville Corp., et al.,* March 20, 1989, 8670.

114. "All Manville Documents to Be Available at Repository in Denver," *Stockholders and Creditors News Service,* March 7, 1988, 7415.

115. *Black's Law Dictionary* defines *civil conspiracy* as "a combination of two or more persons who, by concerted action, seek to accomplish an unlawful purpose or to accomplish some purpose, not in itself unlawful, by unlawful means."

116. "Delaware Jury Awards $75 Million in Punitive Damages Against Raymark," *Stockholders and Creditors News Service,* November 23, 1987, 7171-2; "Delaware Jury Awards $22 Million in Punitive Damages Against Raymark," *Asbestos Litigation Reporter,* March 18, 1988, 16723; and "Washington Judge Finds Concert of Action by Raymark and J-M," *Asbestos Litigation Reporter,* March 18, 1988, 16724. *Black's Law Dictionary* defines *concerted action* as "action that has been planned, arranged, adjusted, agreed on and settled between parties acting together pursuant to some design or scheme."

117. "DE Judge: Conspiracy Requires Only 'Preponderance of Evidence' Proof," *Asbestos Litigation Reporter,* March 4, 1988, 16665.

118. David A. Shaw, "Memorandum in Opposition to Motions for Summary Judgment Filed by the Wellington Defendants and Defendant Raymark Industries," reprinted in *Asbestos Litigation Reporter,* November 18, 1988, 18048-53.

119. "Committee of Asbestos Related Litigants Again Asks Bankruptcy Court to Dismiss Johns-Manville Bankruptcy," *Asbestos Litigation Reporter,* September 23, 1983, 7148.

120. "Asbestos Claimants Committee Rejects Plan," *Asbestos Litigation Reporter,* November 25, 1983, 7416.

121. "Asbestos-Related Litigants Move to Have Bankruptcy Court Appoint Trustee," *Asbestos Litigation Reporter,* January 6, 1984, 7625.

122. "Committee of Asbestos-Related Litigants and/or Creditors Withdraws Its Motion to Reduce Salaries of Manville Officers," *Asbestos Litigation Reporter,* March 16, 1984, 7999.

123. "Hearing Set on Replacement for Plaintiff Contingency Fee Arrangements," *Asbestos Litigation Reporter,* February 3, 1984, 7785.

124. "Johns-Manville Asks Court to Void Asbestos-Claimants Attorney Fees," *Asbestos Litigation Reporter,* November 25, 1983, 7411.

125. "Judge Lifland Refuses to Stop Trust Payments to Claimants," *Stockholders and Creditors News Re. Johns-Manville Corp., et al.,* May 8, 1989, 8799.

126. "Committee of Asbestos-Related Litigants and/or Creditors Withdraws Its Motion to Reduce Salaries of Manville Officers," *Asbestos Litigation Reporter,* March 16, 1984, 7999.

127. Published by Andrews Publications, Edgemont, PA 19028.

128. "In re Johns-Manville Corp.," *Asbestos Litigation Reporter: Eight-Year Cumulative Index, February 1979–July 1987,* August 1987, 37-8.

129. "Essentials of Consensual Plan Should Be Soon," *Asbestos Litigation Reporter,* July 20, 1984, 8687.

130. Ronald L. Motley to Arthur Sharplin, April 1, 1988.

131. Ronald L. Motley, "Plaintiff's Supplemental Reply to Defendants's Motion for Summary Judgment" (filed in U.S. District Court for South Carolina, Civil Action No. 85-819 and others), October 2, 1987.

132. "100,000 Ballots and Information Packets Being Mailed This Week," *Stockholders and Creditors News Service,* September 8, 1986, 5513.

133. The Committee of Asbestos-Related Litigants and/or Creditors Representing Asbestos-Health Claimants of Manville Corporation, "Questions and Answers on Asbestos-Health Claims and the Manville Reorganization Plan" and "A Very Important Message for People With Asbestos-Related Diseases," undated, distributed in August–October 1986.

134. Continuing correspondence between Arthur Sharplin and Heather R. Maurer, executive director of Asbestos Victims of America, and Paul Safchuck, president of the White Lung Association, 1984–1989.

135. "Manville Says Overwhelming Majority of Voters Accepted Plan," *Asbestos Litigation Reporter,* December 5, 1986, 13677.

136. "Manville Pays First $150 Million to Settlement Trust Mostly for Claims," *Stockholders and Creditors News Service,* December 21, 1987, 7231.

137. "Manville Trust Claims Forms Being Printed; $9.2 Million (sic) Interim Budget," *Stockholders and Creditors News Service,* January 25, 1988, 7295. The budget authorized $9.6 million for the ten months September 1987 through June 1988.

138. Manville Corporation, *First Amended Disclosure Statement, Second Amended and Restated Plan of Reorganization, and Related Documents,* August 22, 1986, M-41.

139. "Mississippi Ship Workers Seek to Enjoin Payments by Trust," *Stockholders and Creditors News Re. Johns-Manville Corp., et al.,* April 24, 1989, 8754.

140. Manville Corporation, *1989 Proxy Statement,* April 14, 1989, 13.

141. Manville Corporation, *First Amended Disclosure Statement, Second Amended and Restated Plan of Reorganization, and Related Documents,* August 22, 1986, M-65.

142. Ibid., M-402 and M-407.

143. Ibid., M-72 and M-180.

144. Ibid., M-47.

145. Ibid., M-60.

146. Manville Corporation, annual reports, respective years.

147. Manville Corporation, *First Amended Disclosure Statement, Second Amended and Restated Plan of Reorganization, and Related Documents,* August 22, 1986, M-46.

148. Ibid., M-46 and M-47.

149. Ibid., M-48.

150. Ibid., M-300 and M-343.

151. Manville Corporation, *U.S. Securities and Exchange Commission Form 10-K,* for the fiscal year ended December 31, 1988, 33.

152. Manville Corporation, *First Amended Disclosure Statement, Second Amended and Restated Plan of Reorganization, and Related Documents,* August 22, 1986, M-431.

153. Manville Corporation, *1983 Annual Report and Form 10-K,* 17 and 18.

154. For example, see "Court Approves Sale by Manville of 100 Acres for $22 million," *Stockholders and Creditors News Service,* January 11, 1988, 7261.

155. Manville Corporation, *First Amended Disclosure Statement, Second Amended and Restated Plan of Reorganization, and Related Documents,* August 22, 1986, M-67, M-68, and M-278.

156. Ibid., M-76.

157. Ibid., M-67 and M-68.

158. Ibid., M-519.

159. Ibid., M-399.

160. Ibid., M-418.

161. Ibid., M-519.

162. Manville Corporation, *Quarterly Report of Securities and Exchange Form 10-Q,* March 31, 1989, II-2.

163. Manville Corporation, *First Amended Disclosure Statement, Second Amended and Restated Plan of Reorganization, and Related Documents,* August 22, 1986, M-405.

164. Ibid., M-86 and M-87.

165. Manville Corporation, annual reports for respective years.

166. Ibid.

167. Ibid.

168. Manville Corporation, *First Amended Disclosure Statement, Second Amended and Restated Plan of Reorganization, and Related Documents,* August 22, 1986, M-405.

169. Ibid., M-405.

170. Manville Corporation, annual reports for respective years.

171. Manville Corporation, *First Amended Disclosure Statement, Second Amended and Restated Plan of Reorganization, and Related Documents,* August 22, 1986, M-75 and M-77.

172. "Ethical Dilemmas of Chapter 11 Reorganization," transcript of session at the National Conference on Business Ethics, October 16, 1987. Reprinted in *Stockholders and Creditors News Re. Johns-Manville Corp., et al.,* December 7, 1987, 7196–7216.

173. Ibid., 7215.

174. Stephen W. Quickel, "Miracle at Manville: How Tom Stephens Raised the Bread to Overcome Bankruptcy," *Corporate Finance,* November 1987 (no page numbers; reprint of article provided by Manville Corporation).

175. W. Thomas Stephens, "Manville-Asbestos Ethical Issues Shaping Business Practice: *Financier,* January 1988, 33–36.

176. Patricia Sullivan, "The High Cost of Ethics: Manville Chief Defends Bankruptcy Decision," *The Missoulan* (Missoula, Montana, newspaper), March 10, 1988, 2.

177. "Manville Personal Injury Settlement Trust Financial Statements," *Stockholders and Creditors News Re. Johns-Manville, et al.,* March 6, 1989, 8639–55.

178. "Healthy Manville Immune from Suits—Victims' Trust Works to Solve Payment Problems," *Asbestos Watch,* 6:2 (November–December 1988), 1, 3–4.

179. "Interim Report to the Court by the Trustees of the Manville Personal Injury Settlement Trust," *Stockholders and Creditors News Re. Johns-Manville, et al.,* December 5, 1989, 8242.

180. "Bankruptcy Court Approves PIST Interim Report," *Stockholders and Creditors News Re. Johns-Manville Corp., et al.,* April 10, 1989, 8714–15.

181. "Mississippi Ship Workers Seek to Enjoin Payments by Trust," *Stockholders and Creditors News Re. Johns-Manville, et al.,* April 24, 1989, 8754.

182. Stacy Adler, "Payouts Do Not Imperil Manville Trust: Director," *Business Insurance,* February 13, 1989, 2 and 33.

183. John A. McKinney to editor, *Business Month,* February 1989, 5.

184. Ibid.

185. Adler, "Payouts Do Not Imperil Manville Trust: Director," 2.

186. Ibid.

187. Manville Corporation, "A Historic Year: Manville Looks to the Future," *Summary Annual Report: MvL,* April 1989, 15.

188. Manville Corporation, "The New Manville: Off and Running," *Summary Annual Report: MvL,* April 1989, 32.

189. Tom Stephens and George C. Dillon, "To Our Shareholders," in Manville Corporation, *Summary Annual Report: MvL,* April 1989, 13.

190. The story of Jesus's miracle of the loaves and fishes is told in Matthew 14: 15–21.

APPENDIX A

Chapter 11 Bankruptcy

The U.S. Bankruptcy Code took effect October 1, 1979, and was amended in 1984, 1986, and 1988. Chapter 11 of this law replaced various business reorganization provisions contained in chapters X, XI, and XII of the 1898 Bankruptcy Act, which provisions dated generally from the 1938 Chandler Amendment to that act (*Bankruptcy Code, Rules and Forms* 1989, 290–294). The number of business reorganization filings under bankruptcy law went from about 6,000 in 1980 to an average of over 20,000 annually late in the decade (*Annual Report of the Director of the Administrative Office of the United States Courts*, various years).

BANKRUPTCY REORGANIZATION GAINS RESPECTABILITY

Before about 1982, few large or respected firms resorted to bankruptcy and virtually all which did were insolvent. Hambrick and D'Aveni (1988) studied 45 bankruptcies among the 2,500 largest firms in the United States during 1972–1981 and concluded all involved actual or imminent insolvency. But in 1982 Braniff Airlines, Wickes, Addressograph-Multigraph, Revere Copper and Brass, and Manville Corporation all filed chapter 11 petitions. By January 1989, the list of companies which had filed also included Texaco, LTV, Wheeling-Pittsburg Steel, Allegheny International, A. H. Robins, Continental Airlines, and a host of similarly well-known corporations. Several of these companies, most notably Texaco, Manville, and A. H. Robins, were far from insolvency, at least in the cash flow sense (inability to pay maturing obligations) if not in the bankruptcy sense (debts greater than assets at fair valuation) when they filed.

Not only were bigger, more prestigious companies filing, but many firms were doing so for new reasons. Hambrick and D'Aveni (1988, 6) noted that a "wave" of bankruptcies after 1981 was due to "attempts to escape onerous contracts." Morse and Shaw (1988, 1193) made a similar observation. Bankruptcy was used by Continental Airlines to abrogate a labor contract, by A. H. Robins and Manville to cope with massive toxic tort liabilities, by Texaco to delay and renegotiate a $12 billion court judgment, and by Public Service Company of New Hampshire to bring pressure for utility rate increases and regulatory restructuring.

Chapter 11 had clearly lost much of its stigma, to the extent such stigma ever existed. The stigma thesis is open to question because the primary research which concluded chapter 11 is a discrediting label (Sutton and Callahan 1987) failed to discriminate between the effects of filing and those of the presumable mismanagement or misfortune which may have necessitated the filing. In some measure, chapter 11 had become merely a strategy, another way of managing the demands of various stakeholders.

THE NATURE AND PURPOSE OF BANKRUPTCY LAW FOR CORPORATIONS

At its core, bankruptcy law is debt collection law (Jackson 1986, 3). It is designed to solve the common pool (Friedman 1971; Hardin 1968; Libecap and Wiggins 1984; and Jackson 1986, 11–12) and equitable problems which accompany creditor perceptions of actual or impending insolvency of a debtor. Jackson (1986) argued that boundedly rational, self-interested creditors whose debtor appears insolvent will exercise their rights under the "grab" provisions of the Uniform Commercial Code. Those provisions generally follow a "first-come, first-served" principle and hold the first creditor acquiring and publicizing an interest in a particular asset of a debtor may be first, and fully, paid out of that asset (Jackson 1986, 7–19). Only publicized interests are recognized because of a long-standing provision of Anglo-American law that secret interests in property held by another are void (Baird 1983, 53–54). Bankruptcy law respects that principle.

Because of grabbing from the common pool which occurs outside of chapter 11, assets which are worth more together or in certain hands are separated or put in other hands; that is, the assets are not deployed to maximize their value. Thus, an insolvent debtor's owners (taken to include all holders of claims, including creditors) as a group suffer. An equitable problem exists because the first creditors in line might strip the debtor carcass bare, leaving nothing for equally deserving creditors further back; that is, the assets are not distributed fairly. To avoid either result, bankruptcy law aims to substitute a process which will assure the pool of debtor assets are *deployed* so as to maximize their value, and that such value is *distributed* to owners according to the relative values of their prebankruptcy rights (Jackson 1986, 22).

It is probably not a purpose—although it may often be a result—of bankruptcy law to provide a "fresh start" for corporations. This argument is most cogently made by Jackson (1986, 225–252), who points out that the discharge of prebankruptcy debts, so necessary for a financial fresh start, does not even exist for corporate debtors under chapter 7 (liquidation). Still, the fresh start

ideal for individual debtors dates at least from the "jubilee year" tradition of
the Old Testament whereby all debts were forgiven every fiftieth year (*Leviticus*
25:8–55). And the analogy between corporate and personal bunkruptcies cannot be totally escaped.

THE CHAPTER 11 PROCESS

A federal bankruptcy judge assumes oversight of any firm which petitions for
"reorganization" under chapter 11. As Yacos, later judge in the landmark Public Service Company of New Hampshire bankruptcy case, pointed out, all a
firm needs is "the filing fee and a petition saying [the firm] wants relief"
(quoted in Casey, McGee, and Stickney 1986, 250n). It does not have to be
insolvent.

According to former Wickes Companies chairman Sanford Sigoloff, the
judge acts as a "super CEO," for each chapter 11 company. Each bankruptcy
judge acts under the supervision of a federal district court, to which bankruptcy court rulings are easily appealable. In fact, cognizant district judges
sometimes take charge of certain aspects of bankruptcy cases, or whole cases,
themselves. This arrangement is intended to protect the bankruptcy judges,
who do not have the lifetime tenures and salary protection afforded other
federal judges, from political influence (Ferriell 1989).

Upon filing for chapter 11 protection, the firm becomes the "debtor in
possession" (DIP) with essentially all the rights, powers, and duties of a trustee
in bankruptcy (*Bankruptcy Code, Rules and Forms* 1989, 307–308). A trustee or
examiner may be appointed to, respectively, replace or supervise the DIP. The
petition itself acts to impose an automatic stay of all prefiling claims against
the debtor (*Bankruptcy Code, Rules and Forms* 1989, 91). The prefiling managers
continue to operate the company in "the ordinary course of business" while
a plan to emerge from court protection is being formulated, approved, and
confirmed. A U.S. Trustee, often an experienced bankruptcy attorney, helps
in the administration of cases under the bankruptcy court's jurisdiction. Reorganization is accomplished through the formulation and implementation of a
written plan.

A committee of unsecured creditors is appointed by the U.S. Trustee to
represent that stakeholder group. A committee of equity security holders may
also be appointed, and usually is. Committees or advocates may be established
to represent other stakeholder groups. In the Manville Corporation case, for
example, a committee was set up for asbestos tort claimants and an individual
was appointed as an advocate for future claimants. In the A. H. Robins case,
a committee was formed to represent women who had used the company's
Dalkon Shield intrauterine device. The committees are authorized to consult
with the DIP in the administration of the case and to participate in the formulation of a plan of reorganization.

For the first 120 days after filing, only the DIP—or the trustee, if appointed—can submit a reorganization plan. If a plan is not submitted within

120 days and accepted by claimant groups within 180 days, any party in interest, even an individual shareholder or creditor, may file a plan. But both time
limits may be extended or shortened for cause by the bankruptcy court. For
example, Manville Corporation was given more than five years to prepare its
plan and seek approval of it. On the other hand, Worlds of Wonder, Inc. filed
for chapter 11 protection in December 1987 and a plan submitted by the company's banks and unsecured creditors was approved by the bankruptcy court
in March 1988.

Here are the main requirements for confirmation of a plan by the court:
First, the plan must be proposed in "good faith" and the proponent must
disclose certain specified information. Second, each holder of a claim or interest who has not accepted the plan must be allowed at least as much value, as
of the plan's effective date, as chapter 7 liquidation would provide. Third,
each class of claims or interests which is "impaired" under the plan must have
accepted the plan unless the judge rules the plan "does not discriminate un-
fairly and is fair and equitable with respect to the class." The terms *impaired*
and *accepted* deserve further explanation. A class of claims or interests is unim-
paired if reinstated and the holders compensated for damages or if paid in
cash. Acceptance of a plan by a creditor class requires approval by over half
in number and at least two-thirds in amount of allowed claims in the class.
Classes of interests, such as shareholders, must approve by at least two-thirds
in amount of such interests actually voted. The final requirement is that confirmation of the plan must not be deemed likely to be followed by the need
for further financial reorganization or liquidation.

As mentioned above, all prefiling claims are automatically stayed by the
simple filing of the petition. The judge may lift the stay with regard to particular claims. Otherwise it remains in effect until a plan is consummated.

Executory contracts, except financial accommodations (such as agreements to lend money), may be assigned, assumed, or rejected by the debtor.
"Executory" means neither party has completed its legal obligations under the
contract. The rejection of executory contracts may create allowable claims,
which are usually treated as prefiling, unsecured claims.

Administrative costs of the proceeding and any post-filing obligations are
given priority for payment. Ideally, any remaining value will be distributed to
the claimant and interest groups in order of their nonbankruptcy entitlements
(Jackson 1986, 20–33). Thus, the allowed prefiling claims on the debtor estate
may be satisfied in this sequence: (1) secured debt (up to the value of respective collateral as of the effective date of the plan), (2) unsecured debt (including nominally secured debt above the value of respective collateral), and (3)
equity interests in order of preference (e.g., preferred, then common). Claimants within each group, again ideally, share pro rata according to the value of
their respective claims. The "value" may be distributed as cash, securities, or
other real or personal property.

Negotiation among stakeholder representatives and court intervention
often result in departures from such an "ideal" distribution. With very limited
exceptions, any claim not provided for in the final reorganization plan or the

order confirming it is discharged. However, the court may approve a written waiver of discharge executed by the debtor *after* the confirmation order.

MANAGERIAL STAKEHOLDERS IN CHAPTER 11

As noted above, upon filing management becomes the "debtor in possession," with the rights and obligations of a bankruptcy trustee. In a broad sense, the debtor in possession is charged with preserving and enhancing the bankrupt estate and developing a reorganization plan which will equitably allocate the value of the estate among competing interests. Invariably, mangers of bankrupt firms are bombarded with powerful, conflicting demands. Employees want their jobs assured at the same or higher pay levels. Stockholders oppose dilution of their interests and want share price to be propped up and dividends to be reinstated at the earliest possible time. Creditors seek payment or special considerations, such as extra collateral, authority to "perfect" existing claims, or higher interests rates. The typical bankruptcy judge wants decorum and consensus to prevail and rapid progress to be made toward consummation of a workable plan, usually with a strong preference for a consensual one. And the community at large may fear company retrenchment and the loss of jobs, corporate giving, and economic and social activity that may bring.

The traditional Theory of the Firm, implying as it does shareholder wealth maximization as a managerial goal, provides little guidance for the managers. In fact, acting as agents for shareholders would be incompatible with the managers' new fiduciary duty—as an impartial trustee. Shareholders are usually represented by a committee in the bankruptcy court. Putting management on their side would prejudice the interests of other claimants. Besides, little or no owner's equity may be left in the debtor firm, so the court may rule there is no shareholder interest to protect. Shareholders may even be disenfranchised. For example, the judge in the six-years-long Manville case turned down several petitions to require management to conduct annual and special stockholder meetings. He even disbanded the shareholders' committee in the bankruptcy court.

Faced with such an ambiguous charter and imbued with awesome power as debtor in possession, managers may be tempted to neglect the interests of stakeholders other than themselves. Doing that implies certain strategies, some of which can be initiated before filing and others of which may follow filing. Compared to outright liquidation or austere survival without court protection, bankruptcy reorganization can lead to improved pay and benefits, lengthened careers, lowered job demands, and heightened respectability for the managers. Sigoloff noted that boards of directors should play a central role in chapter 11 reorganizations. In fact, it may be the board which should ultimately be viewed as the "debtor in possession." Assuming majority outside membership, the board may meet minimal standards for a "disinterested" fiduciary or trustee.

REFERENCES

Baird, D. G. (1983) Notice filing and problem of ostensible ownership. *Journal of Legal Studies,* 12(1), 53–67.

Bankruptcy Code, Rules and Forms (1989). St. Paul, Minn.: West.

Casey, C. J., McGee, V. E., and Stickney, C. P. (1986) Discriminating between reorganized and liquidated firms in bankruptcy. *Accounting Review,* 61(2), 249–262.

Ferriell, J. T. (1989) Constitutionality of the Bankruptcy Amendments and Federal Judgeship Act of 1984. *American Bankruptcy Law Journal,* 63 (Spring 1989), 109–198.

Freidman, A. E. (1971) The economics of the common pool: Property rights in exhaustible resources. *UCLA Law Review, 18, 855–887.*

Hambrick, D. C., and D'Aveni, R. A. (1988) Large corporate failures as downward spirals. *Administrative Science Quarterly,* 33, 1–23.

Hardin, G. (1968) The tragedy of the commons. *Science,* 162, 1243–1248.

Jackson, T. H. (1986) *The Logic and Limits of Bankruptcy Law.* Cambridge, Minn.: Harvard.

Libecap, G. D., and Wiggins, S. N. (1984) Contractual responses to the common pool: Prorationing of crude oil production. *American Economic Review,* 74, 87–98.

Morse, D., and Shaw, W. (1988) Investing in bankrupt firms. *Journal of Finance,* 43(5), 1193–1206.

Sutton, R. I., and Callahan, A. L. (1987) The stigma of bankruptcy: Spoiled organizational image and its management. *Academy of Management Journal,* 30(3), 405–436.

XIAN DINNER THEATRE: THE TANG DYNASTY

PAUL W. BEAMISH
AND
JOHN KAI-CHUN WU

In early January 1986, Wilson Siu and Manlo Cheng, partners in Cultural Tours (CT), a travel agency and tour organizer headquartered in Honolulu, Hawaii, received the consultants report on their proposed joint venture in China. The consultants report raised a wide range of issues including the wisdom of proceeding with the investment if certain points could not first be satisfactorily resolved.

The joint venture (JV) agreement, for an elaborate dinner-theatre complex in Xian, China, had been signed in March 1985. Since then considerable further negotiations had occurred. The partners in Cultural Tours were aware that there were far more joint venture agreements signed in China than were ever actually implemented. In their case, although few financial resources had been committed, their inclination was to proceed unless there were compelling reasons to stop.

BACKGROUND

In October 1984 on one of his routine group tour assignments to Xian, China, Mr. Wilson Siu was frowning on his inability to organize some evening activities for his group. He expressed his problem to Yu Chao Ming, a local tour guide and good friend of Mr. Siu. As an experienced guide, Mr. Yu fully understood the problem and confirmed that there was no suitable evening activity for the tourist group, at least none available which could be booked and

Source: **Prepared by Associate Professor Paul W. Beamish and John Kai-Chun Wu, University of Western Ontario, as a basis for classroom discussion. Financial assistance from the Canada-China Management Program is gratefully acknowledged.** © **1989, the University of Western Ontario.**

planned in advance. The entrepreneurially spirited Mr. Yu then suggested the dinner-theatre concept. Mr. Siu thought it was a good solution and felt other tour operators might also be interested.

The principals of CT realized that they did not have the needed resources to do the project alone so they decided to seek a partner. An ideal candidate would be an individual or group from China which could complement CT. Mr. Siu asked Mr. Yu, who worked for China International Travel Service, Xian Branch (CITS), to take the idea to his boss, Zhang Xiaoke. The idea was received by Mr. Zhang with equal enthusiasm. CT and CITS very quickly agreed to form the joint venture. The two groups had extensive previous dealings and had built a good rapport between them. By March 1985, a JV contract was signed. Shortly thereafter it was approved by the Chinese government. The JV contract called for a project with a budget of US$3 million. The dinner-theatre—to be called the Tang Dynasty (Tang)—would be built from the ground up and take an estimated 12 months to complete. The Tang would consist of a theatre restaurant, banquet hall, V.I.P. rooms, coffee shop, cocktail lounge, and gift and souvenir shop. The Tang would have a total seating capacity of 500 to 800. The cuisine served in the Tang, its decor and entertainment would be authentic to the Tang Dynasty era.

TOURISM IN CHINA

With 5,000 years of civilization, China was steeped in history and culture. Yet given China's previous self-induced isolation, most foreigners had little first hand knowledge about the vast country. Since China's open door policy in 1979, China had attracted a wave of tourists intent on exploring the country.

In the process of attracting tourists, China had earned badly needed foreign currency. To better accommodate the tourists and to further exploit the profit potential, a significant portion of foreign investment was in international standard hotels. More and better accommodations would bring China an increasing number of tourists. Exhibit 1 shows the yearly (1980–1985) tourist arrivals and foreign exchange earnings.

Of the 1.4 million non-Chinese visitors (tourists, business people, and other) in China in 1985, 190,836 visited Xian. About 161,373 were on organized tours and stayed an average of 2.1 days. Foreign arrivals in Xian had increased by 40% between 1984 and 1985.

Xian is a 3,000-year-old city with a rich cultural history. There were numerous museums, archaeological remains, and historical monuments for tourists to explore. Xian had been the capital of China for many dynasties including the most notable of all, the Tang Dynasty (618–907 A.D.). Xian had as much, if not more, history than Athens or Rome, and was by far the most visited city in China by organized tours.

The biggest draw in Xian was its Terra Cotta Warriors. These were life-sized and intricately detailed porcelain figures arranged in battle formation.

EXHIBIT 1   TOURISM IN CHINA

	1980	1981	1982	1983	1984	1985
Arrivals (in millions), total	5.7	7.8	7.9	9.5	12.9	17.8
Overseas Chinese + resident of Hong Kong, Macau, and Taiwan	5.2	7.1	7.2	8.6	11.7	16.4
Other	0.5	0.7	0.7	0.9	1.2	1.4
Foreign exchange earned (in US$ billions)	0.6	0.8	0.8	0.9	1.1	1.3

Source: State Statistical Bureau, *Statistical Yearbook of China.*

There were believed to be over 7,000 individually detailed figures. Only about 1,000 had been unearthed so far because of a lack of funds and concern about their deterioration in open air. (After these figures were first unearthed, their color faded completely.)

Currently, most tourist activities involved sightseeing, but these sight-seeing activities were limited to daylight hours. The number of activities available to tourists in the evening was extremely limited.

Tang's targeted customers were the organized tourists from foreign countries. They would be brought to the Tang to conclude their days' activities. The JV partners wished to bring the Tang to an international standard of excellence such that it would become the second most visited spot in Xian after the Terra Cotta Warriors.

The planned size of the Tang was justified on the basis of the current and expected increase in number of tourists. The number of organized tourists arriving in Xian was expected to increase by at least 20% per year. The large size of the stage (7,000 square feet) would allow for artistic freedom for the dance troupe. Given the size of the stage, it did not make economic sense to have a theatre restaurant with only small seating capacity. If the Tang wanted to project an image that it was grand and fit for a king, then they did not want to crowd the guests. Architecturally, it would be very hard to create the feeling of a grand palace in a small area. Also it would be difficult and expensive to add capacity later.

The Tang would create a brand new night activity available to the tour organizer for inclusion in the tour package. Its many advantages would include:

1. not a competing day activity, available at night;
2. combined two distinct night activities into one, dinner and show;
3. available all the time—easy to plan and book ahead;
4. could be a strong selling feature of the tour package;

5. high benefit to cost ratio, a lot of enjoyment but very little extra cost;
6. the facility would be first class and guests would feel comfortable in it.

There was currently no direct competition. The indirect competition included restaurants away from the major hotels, and stage shows which were not marketed directly to tourists.

The need for transportation would be reduced if dinner and show were in one location. The Tang would offer a much better facility than other potential competitors. It would also offer food that was different, but make available Western cuisine.

The economics of the project were good; three parties benefited directly; CT, CITS, and China. From the projections (see Exhibit 2), China would be the biggest winner. In addition to the initial investment of US$3 million, the project would generate another US$64 million in badly needed foreign currency over a 10-year period. Only about US$10 million of that would leave the country as interest, debt repayment, and profit.

The Chinese government's various direct tax and other receipts would total over US$11 million. CITS's share of the profit over the 10 years was expected to be US$3.53 million after tax, plus all profit from the Tang after the first 10 years. CT's own share of profits was expected to be about US$3.3 million after tax.

THE PLANNED OPERATION

The daily operation of the Tang would be modelled after a Las Vegas show. The guests would first feast on an authentic Tang period multi-course dinner banquet (see Exhibit 3 for sample menu) served by staff wearing traditional Tang outfits/costumes. After dinner, tourists would see authentic Tang period music and folk dances accurately recreated by the renowned Shaanxi Provincial song and Dance Troupe. The purpose of such careful attention to detail was to take the guests back in time and let them experience the Tang era. The Dance Troupe would be under contract to the Tang.

The Tang was expected to employ 200–250 people. Initially key staff would be brought in from Hong Kong, however the majority of staff would be hired locally. One of the most important tasks for the staff from Hong Kong would be to train local employees.

THE FOREIGN JOINT VENTURE PARTNER

From its head office in Honolulu, CT had branch offices in Los Angeles, Vancouver, Toronto, Hong Kong, and London, England. The principals of CT were Mr. Wilson Siu, managing director of the United States and Mr. Manlo Cheng, managing director of Canada. Mr. Cheng and Mr. Siu were both

EXHIBIT 2 TANG DINNER THEATRE: TEN YEARS PROJECTION

Annual Tourist Count (1st year)	150,000 people
Annual Price and Expense Increase	5%
Annual Tourist Count Increase	5%
Cost of Good Sold Percentage	60%
Tourist Share—Dinner Show	80%
Tourist Share—Lunch Show	90%
Comm/Ind Tax (% of gross income)	5%
Total Construction Cost (000)	US$3,000
Contract Period	10 years
Interest Rate	12%

DESCRIPTIONS	YEAR 1	YEAR 2	YEAR 3	YEAR 4	YEAR 5	YEAR 6	YEAR 7	YEAR 8	YEAR 9	YEAR 10	TOTAL
Dinner Show (guest/day)	329	345	362	331	400	420	441	463	486	510	
Lunch Show (guest/day)	370	388	408	428	450	472	496	520	546	574	
Restaurant-Dinner show (guest/day)	200	210	221	232	243	255	268	281	295	310	
Restaurant-Lunch Show (guest/day)	100	105	110	116	122	128	134	141	148	155	
Coffee Shop (guest/day)	40	42	44	46	49	51	54	56	59	62	
Gift Shop and Misc. (guest/day)	100	105	110	116	122	128	134	141	148	155	
Dinner Show (US$ per guest)	20.00	21.00	22.05	23.15	24.31	25.53	26.80	28.14	29.55	31.03	
Lunch Show (US$ per guest)	4.00	4.20	4.41	4.63	4.86	5.11	5.36	5.63	5.91	6.21	
Restaurant-Dinner (US$ per guest)	10.00	10.50	11.03	11.58	12.16	12.76	13.40	14.07	14.77	15.51	
Restaurant-Lunch (US$ per guest)	5.00	5.25	5.51	5.79	6.08	6.38	6.70	7.04	7.39	7.76	
Coffee Shop (US$ per guest)	3.00	3.15	3.31	3.47	3.65	3.83	4.02	4.22	4.43	4.65	
Gift Shop and Misc. (US$ per guest)	2.00	2.10	2.21	2.32	2.43	2.55	2.68	2.81	2.95	3.10	
Loan Repayment Percentage	10%	10%	15%	30%	35%	0%					
Loan balance at beginning of year (000)	3,000	2,700	2,400	1,950	1,050	0	0	0	0	0	
Financial Projection (in 000 US$)											
Dinner Show	2,400	2,646	2,917	3,216	3,546	3,909	4,310	4,752	5,239	5,776	38,711
Lunch Show	540	595	656	724	798	880	970	1,069	1,179	1,300	8,710
Restaurant-Dinner Show	730	805	887	978	1,079	1,189	1,311	1,445	1,593	1,757	11,775
Restaurant-Lunch Show	183	201	222	245	270	297	328	361	398	439	2,944
Coffee Shop	44	48	53	59	65	71	79	87	96	105	706
Gift Shop and Misc.	73	80	89	98	108	119	131	145	159	176	1,177
Total Annual Gross Income	3,969	4,376	4,825	5,319	5,864	6,466	7,128	7,859	8,664	9,553	64,024

											Total
Direct Operating Expenses	2,382	2,626	2,895	3,192	3,519	3,879	4,277	4,715	5,199	5,732	38,414
Commercial/Ind Tax	198	219	241	266	293	323	356	393	433	478	3,201
Building Tax (1.2% Const. Cost)	36	36	36	36	36	36	36	36	36	36	360
Land Use Charge (Lease Rent)	82	82	82	82	82	82	82	82	82	82	820
Insurance (Const. Cost*7%/10yr)	21	21	21	21	21	21	21	21	21	21	210
Total Operating Expense	2,719	2,983	3,275	3,597	3,951	4,342	4,772	5,247	5,771	6,348	43,005
Net Operating Income	1,250	1,393	1,550	1,723	1,914	2,124	2,356	2,612	2,894	3,204	21,018
Depreciation (Straight Line)	300	300	300	300	300	300	300	300	300	300	3,000
Interest Expense	360	324	288	234	126	0	0	0	0	0	1,332
Net Taxable Income	590	769	962	1,189	1,488	1,824	2,056	2,312	2,594	2,904	16,686
Chinese's Share of Profit	30%	30%	30%	30%	30%	50%	50%	50%	50%	50%	
Chinese Business Tax Percentage	0%	0%	55%	55%	55%	55%	55%	55%	55%	55%	
Chinese Profit Before Tax	177	231	288	357	446	912	1,028	1,156	1,297	1,452	7,344
Chinese Business Tax	0	0	159	196	245	502	565	636	713	799	3,815
Chinese Profit After Tax	177	231	130	160	201	410	463	520	584	653	3,529
Overseas Business Tax Percentage	0%	0%	20%	20%	20%	40%	40%	40%	40%	40%	
Overseas Local Tax Percentage	10%	10%	10%	10%	10%	10%	10%	10%	10%	10%	
Overseas Profit Before Tax	413	538	673	832	1,041	912	1,028	1,156	1,297	1,452	9,343
Overseas Business Tax	0	0	135	166	208	365	411	462	519	581	2,847
Overseas Local Tax	41	54	67	83	104	91	103	116	130	145	934
Overseas Profit After Tax	372	484	471	582	729	456	514	578	648	726	5,561
Overseas Cash Flow Before Debt Payment	672	734	771	882	1,029	756	814	878	948	1,026	8,561
Loan Principal Payment	300	300	450	900	1,050	0	0	0	0	0	3,000
Overseas Cash Flow After Debt Payment	372	484	321	(18)	(21)	756	814	878	948	1,026	5,561
Investor's Share Percentage	67%	67%	67%	67%	67%	33%	33%	33%	33%	33%	
Investor's Net Cash Flow	248	323	214	(12)	(14)	252	271	293	316	342	2,233
Cultural Travel's Net Cash Flow	124	161	107	(6)	(7)	504	543	585	632	684	3,328
Government Total Tax Collection	276	309	633	748	887	1,317	1,472	1,643	1,831	2,038	11,158
Cumulative Cash Flow—CITS	177	408	537	698	899	1,309	1,772	2,292	2,875	3,529	
Cumulative Cash Flow—Government	276	584	1,222	1,970	2,857	4,174	5,646	7,288	9,119	11,158	
Cumulative Cash Flow—Investors	249	571	785	773	759	1,011	1,282	1,575	1,891	2,233	
Cumulative Cash Flow—Cultural	124	285	392	397	330	834	1,426	2,011	2,644	3,328	

EXHIBIT 3   XIAN DINNER THEATRE: SAMPLE MENU

MENU

LA PERLE DE CATHY
des coquilles Saint-Jacques enrobées de purée de
taro sautées avec une garniture de légumes du jardin dans
de la sauce aux huitres

LE MARIAGE ROYAL
les délicieux raviolis qui accompagnent notre célèbre
consommé au bain-marie avec champignons noirs
sont préparés selon des recettes authentiques des régions
sud et nord du Pays du Dragon

L'EPINGLE DE LA PRINCESSE
un filet de boeuf légèrement sauté à la perfection avec des
oignons — un plat royal dans le palais des Tang

LA CHALEUR DU ROI DRAGON
des bouquets servis avec des noix glacées au miel une
création de notre chef hautement recommandée

LA FEE DES LOTUS
un plat de riz sauté préparé de façon aussi singulière
ne peut que vous surprendre

LA MELODIE DES SAULES
un dessert exquis censé être le favori de l'impératrice Tang

DELICES D'APRES-DINER
fruit de saison
thé au jasmin

菜 谱·メニュー

春色滿園
パール・オブ・キャシー
ヘースト代のタロイモと帆立て貝のフライ、オイスター・ソース風味の
野菜添え

翡翠草蓋　紛黃仙君
ロイヤル・マリッジ
中國南北の地方独特の調理法で作られた、椎茸と水ギョーザ入りスープ

暖宮艷彩
プリンセスのピン
テンダーロイン肉と玉ねぎの炒め ── 唐時代の貴族の優雅な料理

龍取綱川
ヒート・オブ・ザ・キング・ドラゴン
大蝦と甘みのあるクルミの炒め、バリバリ風味
当レストラン・シェフが自慢の自製の料理

茜蓉香飯
ロータス・フェアリー
し豚を珍らしせ作しい調理法

花朝甘露
ウィローのメロディー
唐の皇后が好んで食したといわれるデザート

臨壇峰火　茉莉花香
お食事の後には
季節のフルーツ
ジャスミン茶

MENU

PEARL OF CATHY
taro pasted sea scallops deep-fried to golden brown garnished
with garden green in oyster sauce

THE ROYAL MARRIAGE
the dumpling delicacies accompanying our famous
double-boiled consomme with black mushrooms are prepared
from authentic recipes originated from the southern and
northern parts of the Land of the Dragon

THE PRINCESS' PIN
tenderloin of beef slightly fried to perfection with onion —
a royal concoction in the Tang Palace

HEAT OF THE KING DRAGON
crispy king prawns served with honey glazed walnut —
our chef's own creation and is highly recommended

LOTUS FAIRY
a fried rice dish so uncommonly prepared would
definitely surprise you

THE WILLOW'S MELODY
a delightful dessert reputed to be the favourite
of the Tang Empress

AFTER DINNER DELIGHT
seasonal fruit
jasmine tea

---

considered to be overseas Chinese by the Chinese government. Along with two other private investors from Hong Kong (HK), they had formed the Golden Field Investment, Ltd. This investment company, incorporated in Hong Kong, would be the legal foreign participant in the JV. The company was registered in HK to take advantage of the relatively low corporation tax rate of 17%. This flat rate compared favorably to the rates in Canada or the United States. In practice, CT and its principals would be the major players on the foreign JV partner side. (For simplicity, hereafter CT will be referred to as the foreign partner of the JV.)

CT had been in the travel business for many years, having organized numerous tours to China and other parts of the world. However, their main expertise was in organizing tours to the Orient. From CIT's point of view, CT was one of the top five tour operators in the world in terms of good relationships. As a consequence, CT could organize a tour to Xian, China with the CITS much faster than the six to nine months that was normally required.

This good relationship had helped CT to negotiate a JV with the CITS in a relatively short time.

THE CHINESE JV PARTNER

CITS, China Travel Service (CTS), and China Youth Travel Service (CYTS) were the three central travel agency units that were responsible for all organized tourists' arrivals into China. Each of the three had branches in major cities in China. CTS's responsibility included foreigners (not their main thrust), overseas Chinese, and local tourists. CYTS's responsibility was similar to CTS's but their group of tourists was youths. CITS was responsible for only foreign tourists.

The Xian branch of the CITS was the legal participant in the JV. CITS allowed tour organizers all over the world to book activities in the Xian area. They also had information on all possible tourist activities in Xian. To avoid possible congestion, they scheduled activities in Xian and allowed tour organizers to book and plan out the activities of the tour. They also supplied local tour guides. It would be impossible for a tour organizer to bypass the CITS.

CITS's unique position as the only booking agent in Xian for tour operators all over the world gave CT a strong reason to enter into a JV with CITS. The proposed dinner theatre would cater mainly to the foreign tourists for which CITS had almost total responsibility.

Mr. Yu and Mr. Zhang were the key persons in the CITS attempting to spearhead CITS's entry into the JV. Their commitment, determination, and innovativeness to get the Tang off the ground were evident from the beginning. As well they enjoyed a cordial relationship with the principals of CT.

THE ORIGINAL NEGOTIATION

The original negotiation went quickly by most standards, which is not to say that there were no problems. One of the major reasons for such a speedy negotiation was because CT had good previous dealings with CITS. CT was able to go to CITS directly.

Both partners felt that the dinner-theatre appeared feasible. Both saw the profit potential and felt the risk of the project was relatively low.

CT had a need for CITS and vice-versa. Each JV partner believed in friendship and informal dealings and figured that minor disagreements on the contract terms could be worked out easily between them later on. The most important thing in the minds of the partners during negotiations was to get the JV project going as soon as possible. They knew the JV contract would be subjected to lengthy approval processes, therefore they felt that they could iron out any differences then. Appendix A contains an overview of the Chinese-Foreign JV Law. Translated excerpts from the original JV contract are in Appendix B. Subsequent to the signing of the original contract, there were a number of amendments to the contract.

CT'S INVESTMENT

The major investment made by CT in the JV was in the form of foreign currency. The capital investment by CT was budgeted at US$3.0 million. The money was to be used primarily to finance the cost of building, furnishing, and equipping the theatre-restaurant. In addition, CT was expected to provide the necessary management and coordination in the construction and setup stage. CT would also provide competent foreign management to operate the Tang. CT would have full authority in operating the Tang during the 10-year JV contract period. However, CITS would also provide some appointees to assist in the management of the Tang. Within the contract period CT would transfer management and other skills needed to operate the Tang to CIT's appointees and other local people.

CT would also contribute substantial investment in terms of time, money, and efforts into the JV. As far as the JV was concerned, these types of investments would not be recorded or be reimbursed by the JV directly. CT would actively promote the Tang, and be a good customer of it.

CIT'S INVESTMENT

Compared to CT, CITS would make a much lower monetary investment in the JV. It was estimated that CITS would send about US$0.7 million to prepare the land that the Tang would occupy. The money would be spent for the relocation of the families then living on the land and for various utility upgrades. CITS was slated to spend most of the money anyway because it had planned to use the land for its own staff residence. CITS would spend about US$1.5 million on the building cost of its staff residence. Since CITS staff residence would now be built as an extension of the Tang Complex, there would be some savings to CITS.

CITS planned to continue its effort to help the foreign partner and the JV overcome the excessive amount of bureaucracy that existed in China. The greatest contribution that CITS would bring to the JV was the captive market. CITS also indicated that they would provide loans or loan guarantees to the JV if needed.

CHINA'S INVESTMENT

An oft-heard argument was that China makes a significant investment in any JV by contributing cheap and readily available manpower and resources. A similar business venture in the West would require more capital and labor. However, increasingly such arguments were countered with the view that there were added burdens such as low productivity, poor quality, special taxes, and low skill levels which resulted in incremental costs in other areas.

FINANCING

Originally, the plan was to finance the Tang project by equity. CT had planned to issue 300,000 shares at US$10 per share to raise the estimated US$3.0 million required. In view of other options and the difficulty and cost of raising US$3.0 million in equity, this plan was dropped. The foreign partner wished to minimize their actual cash outlay so decided that debt financing would be used extensively.

PROBLEMS ENCOUNTERED

One of the problems that faced both CT and CITS was the difficulty in finding a suitable site on which to build the Tang. To find a large site with easy access for tourists was difficult. All the land in China was state owned and could not be bought or sold. Therefore it was not possible for the JV to pay a premium for a suitable piece of land even if they wanted to. It happened that CITS owned the right to use a piece of land just opposite to their office. Originally the land was slated to be used for the building of residences for the staff of CITS. But due to a shortage of funds, CITS had not yet used it. In order for the JV to use the land the JV would have to first clear the land. The land was currently occupied by about 30 families and CITS would have to bear the cost of relocation (estimated to be US$0.25 million).

Another requirement was that the JV would assist CITS in building their staff residence. Each operating unit (or company) in China must provide a residence for its staff so the JV itself would also need to build a residence for its staff. The JV would still be required to pay a land use fee to the government.

After the signing of the JV contract the JV progressed slowly. The initial excitement of the project had begun to wear off—serious and determined efforts were needed to push the JV ahead. The principals of CT were busy with their own other business thus leaving them little time to deal with the JV. They also encountered difficulty in finding both equity and debt financing in their respective home countries and had to resort to finding financing in China and Hong Kong.

THE MANAGEMENT

As set forth by the JV contract, CT would be responsible for the operation of the Tang and CT would appoint the general manager. Since CT did not have the needed management, it would look for suitable candidates in HK. The general manager would require experience in preparing and implementing a complete and detailed business plan that would be in line with CT's goals and the goals of the JV. It would be quite important for the Tang to begin operation as smoothly and as quickly as possible because the JV contract would only last for 10 years. During this period CT would need to recover their capital

EXHIBIT 4   XIAN DINNER THEATRE: ARCHITECT'S MEMO, 1985

DANCE COMPANY

I think we should start negotiating with the dance troupes. If we have a better idea of their charges and availabilities, we will have a better idea of how much the ticket price is going to be and therefore our income.

We should establish a contract with the best dance troupe in town.

DETERMINE INCOME STREAM FOR THE PROJECT

My gut feeling is that the major income producer in this project is the theatre restaurant. The income per head is high, it is in foreign currency, it could be pre-collected. The income per head in the banquet room or the coffee shop is rather low but it costs the same amount per square foot for construction. As the other larger hotels in Xian get built, the affluent locals will be attracted to the larger restaurants and the tourists will dine in their hotels rather than be bused to the Tang Restaurant.

My vote would be to eliminate the whole second floor and the kitchen to go with it. It means lower construction cost, a shorter construction period, less financing, and better profit margin.

BUDGETING AND ACCOUNTING

The budget for this project is very, very tight, 3 million dollars US. Cost of construction is comparatively low in China, a similar project in the United States, for the podium only, will cost around 15 million US for development and construction.

We should immediately find out accurately how much we have spent as of today so that we know where we are on the development budget.

CHINESE TAX

The Chinese tax always come as an unpleasant surprise to development projects. To avoid this from happening to our project, I suggest we should insist CITS and/or BOC list all taxation in writing so that there will be no misunderstanding in the future. Our budget is so tight, we cannot afford surprises!

RESTAURANT OPERATION AND THE OPERATOR

An experienced operator needs to be found. His/her input on seating arrangement can mean reconfiguration of the dining area, his/her determination on the menu to be served can mean enlargement or reduction of the kitchens.

For the operation of the project, we have the options of running it ourselves or to lease it out to a restaurant group.

CONTRACTOR AND CONSTRUCTION MANAGER

In the selection of building contractor, we have several options. The first is if we carry the risk of being our own general contractor, and subcontract the work out. If we have three separate contractors, someone has to coordinate the work of these people, this is the work of a construction manager. The second option is to invite general contractors to bid on the whole job, the successful bidder will be responsible for all the subcontractors.

The advantage of the first option is that there may be some savings, since we are carrying the risks of whatever might happen during construction. In the case of having a general contractor, we don't have to worry if the subcontractors are doing their jobs properly. The general is responsible for that.

My vote to this subject is to take the second option, the reason being that we are

EXHIBIT 4   (continued)

not experienced nor qualified enough to be a general contractor for a project of this size.

LOANS AND FINANCING
We should list what is outstanding to close the loan. Everything hinges upon its approval. This is of first priority, we must get it done as soon as possible.

DEVELOPMENT SCHEDULE
We should go back to conventional construction scheduling to ensure that the budget will stay within 3 million. We need to pay off the consultants so that they will continue to finish the drawings and specifications.

MARKETING AND PRESALE
Due to the tight budget, it's likely that we might be short on money towards the end of construction. Any extra money we can bring in through presale would be helpful. There are bound to be more large hotels built in the next few years, and these hotels could very well have theatre restaurants in them. How can we prevent ourselves from becoming obsolete in the future? Securing the best dance troupe can help. What else? What is it that we can offer that the other "biggies" cannot?

AMENDMENTS TO CIT'S CONTRACT
There are a lot of things that we have brief verbal understandings with CITS which are not in the written contract. How are we going to divide the professional fees? How much of the foundation cost are they going to be responsible for? How are we going to divide the maintenance costs for the building in the future? It's better to figure out our differences now than later.

and make a return. Therefore there was little room for error or experimentation. The Tang was relatively large, therefore a competent and experienced manager was required. Officially, the general manager was to report to the board of directors of the JV but unofficially, the general manager most likely would represent CT in the Tang.

Initial success would depend on the Tang's ability to sell itself to tour organizers. Although the average cost for tours was high, there was little room for the tour operator to earn profits. Hotel and air fare costs were about 70% of the tour price. The 30% left over was for everything else. A higher commission or a larger rebate offered by Tang would be looked upon favorably by the tour organizer.

CONCLUSION

At the end of 1985, Charles Lau, a Chinese-American architect, outlined in a long memo to all partners the items that required immediate attention. Mr.

Lau had been retained by CT from the beginning to act as an architect and consultant for the Tang project. Exhibit 4 contains some excerpts from this memo. He expected to call a meeting of all partners to discuss the issues which needed to be addressed before the JV project could proceed.

A P P E N D I X A

The Chinese Foreign JV Law

In July, 1979, the National People's Congress (NPC), the supreme governing body of the Peoples Republic of China (PRC), promulgated the first law on Chinese-foreign joint ventures. Various areas in China were designated as Special Economic Zones (SEZ) where foreigners were encouraged to locate their investment. For the next five years, 14 more coastal cities were opened for foreign investment. However foreign investments were by no means restricted only to these areas.

The JV Law was intended to encourage foreign businessmen, overseas Chinese, as well as Chinese compatriots from Hong Kong, Macao, and Taiwan to enter into a JV or other form of cooperation with PRC institutions. Wholly foreign owned ventures were also welcome. After only five and a half years, PRC's new policy had attracted nearly US$9 billion in foreign investments including projects in energy, transportation, crop raising and animal husbandry, electronics, machinery building, raw and packaging materials, rubber products, textiles, agriculture, hotels, leasing, food, furniture, and wine.

Since 1979, other laws and regulations were also put into place, including the Income Tax Law (for companies and individuals), Foreign Exchange Control Law, Trademark and Patent Law, and Contract Law. The PRC have put these laws in place to better manage the large influx of foreign investments. These laws were intended to protect the interest of the Chinese people as well as the foreign investors and workers. Foreigners had to abide by these and other laws in China and were in turn protected by them.

A large number of sectors were open for foreign investments. There seemed to be no hard policy governing where in China the JVs were to be located but certain areas such as the SEZs were encouraged. JVs located in the SEZs had a greater number of options in terms of line of businesses allowed. Also there were some extra benefits (such as tax holidays and/or tax reduction) to the JV if it was to locate in the SEZs.

A Chinese-foreign JV was defined as consisting of one or more foreign investors and one or more Chinese investors entering into a JV contract. After signing of the contract the JV contract still needed to be approved by the Chinese government. The JV would be run by both of the participants and had many distinctive features. Chinese and foreign JV partners would share responsibilities, rights, and interests according to their respective share contribution. The actual investment of each partner could take many forms but it was converted to one kind of currency for the calculation of the share contribution. The JV would be set up as a limited liability company and its liability would be limited to the extent of the total assets. Each JV partner's liability was limited to its share of the registered capital and each was not responsible for the debt of other partners. The JV had full right of independent operation and could handle its own imports and exports directly. Chinese law did not require control of a JV by the Chinese partner but did require foreign partners to have at least a 25% share in the JV. The term of the JV was generally expected to be between 10 to 30 years; a longer term was possible if the situation called for it (i.e., large investment with long construction period and low profit). At least six months before the expiration of the initial term, if the JV partners agreed to continue the JV, then the JV could make an application to the appropriate government agency to renew the JV contract.

APPENDIX B

Excerpts from the Original JV Agreement

- CT's investment is budgeted to be US$3.0 million.
- CITS will provide the use of the serviced land and all utilities. CITS will be responsible to make application with various government agencies in regard to the construction. CT will be responsible to pay all fees incurred from the construction and any other fee incurred prior to the opening of the business.
- The Tang will be operated by CT for a period of 10 years. CITS will provide assistance. On expiration of the term, CT must conclude all its financial obligations to others, for no compensation whatsoever. CT must forfeit any future profit and hand over all assets of the Tang in good working condition subject to the normal wear and tear. Then the JV contract will conclude.
- CT will be in charge of the allocation and the proper disbursement of various expenses during construction and the normal business operating period. The net profit after tax will be divided 7:3 in the first five years and equally in the remaining five years with CT getting the bigger share. However, if the US$3.0 million capital investment was not repaid after the initial five years, then the net profit will remain divided in a 7:3 ratio for an extra year and can continue to the end of the contracted 10 year term.
- After the Tang opens, CT will pay CITS a land use fee of US$35 for every square meter the Tang occupies. The fee is to be paid in foreign currency.
- For construction disbursement if it were payable within China, then it must go through the Bank of China and if it were payable elsewhere, then payment must be supervised by a Bank of China appointed foreign bank.
- CITS will help CT to secure guarantees from the Bank of China on any foreign loan that CT might have.
- The JV will be managed by a board of five directors, two from CITS and

three from CT. The chairman of the board will be one of the two CITS directors while the vice-chairman will be one of the three CT directors.

- The board is responsible to see to it that the JV will abide by China's laws and regulations.
- The board will meet twice a year or can meet if situations call for it. The decision of the board will be based on the majority.
- The board will set up a construction project management team to oversee the construction of the Tang. The team will answer to the board. CT will appoint the team leader and CITS will appoint the second in command.
- The project management team's duties included on-going supervision and reporting to the board and various government agencies; make the necessary registration for the Tang; look after custom requirements; assist the needed foreign construction workers in obtaining work permits and look after their living accommodations; and meet the budget.
- If quality and price are the same, then the source of the material needed for construction should be from China.
- On materials acquisition, the project management team will assign someone in China to be responsible if the materials are from China. Someone in Hong Kong will be assigned the responsibility if the materials are from elsewhere.
- CITS will make the necessary applications to have materials brought in duty-free.
- CT will be responsible for the design of the Tang but will have input from China Northwest Building Design Institute. CT will reimburse the institute for any cost incurred.
- CITS will assist in getting design approval from government agencies.
- The building should withstand an earthquake that measures 8.0 in the Ritcher Scale.
- Subject to CT and CITS's agreement, the building foundation is to be done by the Third Construction Engineering Company of Xian. The main contractor will be from Hong Kong.
- The construction of the Tang is expected to be completed in 12 months.
- The final inspection of Tang's construction will be performed by the project management team and the appropriate government departments.
- For daily operations of the Tang, CT can appoint a management team from Hong Kong to manage the Tang in CT's place. This team will answer to the board.
- CT will appoint the general manager (GM) and CITS will appoint the assistant general manager. On important matters, the management team must get approval from the board.
- The general manager will select the needed department heads. To facilitate the Chinese to advance its management skill, the general manager will train suitable candidates for such positions.
- The GM will formulate suitable operating procedures and plans. CITS

will assist in hiring and training. All plans of operation including employee training plans are subject to approval from the board.

- CT and CITS will abide by the law of the PRC and fulfil their obligations. Both foreign and domestic workers will do the same.

- The Tang will make application to the government to have its taxes or duties reduced as currently allowed by the government.

- All the accounting methods and principles used by the Tang should conform to Chinese and International Standard. Once the board approved the financial statements, net profit can then be distributed to the JVers. CT's share of the profit should first be used to repay principal and interest. Based on China's regulations, the board must appoint a recognized accounting firm to look after Tang's books. Tang's books can be audited by the government.

- CITS will help the Tang to get approval from the government on using the straight line method of depreciation thus allowing CT to repay the principal.

- PRC's law will allow CT, the Tang, and its foreign employees to remit funds abroad.

- The Tang will be insured by the Chinese People Insurance Company against property loss. If the Chinese People Insurance Company will not insure the Tang, then the Tang can seek an insurance company elsewhere. Trade payable will be the first beneficiary in the case of loss.

- The Tang will pay for all insurance costs. Beside property insurance, personal insurance and investment insurance will be paid by the Tang.

- If possible, disputes resulting from the JV should be settled by the JV partners. If it can't be resolved, then the matter can be brought to the Chinese International Industry and Commerce's appointed committee. Further action can be taken to the International Commerce organization in Sweden. The resolution of the arbitrator-board will be final and the losing party will be responsible for all costs.

- The JV contract comes into effect once the Chinese government approves it.

- Any breach of contract by either party that results in damages will be paid by the party that caused the breach to the party that was harmed by the breach.

- If PRC changes its laws and regulations so that the foreign JVer may be harmed by it, then both parties will try to do what they can to ensure that the foreign JVer receives the benefits they are entitled to get.

KNP, N.V. (ROYAL DUTCH PAPERMILLS)

ALAN BAUERSCHMIDT
AND DANIEL SULLIVAN

Koninklijke Nederlandse Paperfabrieken N.V. (KNP), or Royal Dutch Papermills, specializes in the production and sale of paper and board products to serve the printing and packaging industries throughout the world. The firm originated in 1850 as a small papermill on the Maas River in the Province of Limburg in The Netherlands, and this location in the city of Maastricht continues to be the site of one of the three modern Dutch papermaking mills operated by the firm. Another papermill containing two papermaking machines is located across the Maas in Belgium, while the firm also produces packaging materials at various European locations and has investments in paper merchant operations in a number of countries.

These activities reflect a progressive expansion of the firm that requires a degree of centralized control, and the corporate headquarters for the management of the domestic and international activities of the firm occupies a modern office building located at Erasmusdomein 50, in a newer portion of the ancient and historic city of Maastricht. It is here that Mr. Wilmer Zetteler, the commercial director of KNP België, considers his response to an interviewer's questions concerning the emerging international business strategy of KNP and the decisions that will be necessary to meet the challenges faced by the firm he represents. Mr. Zetteler appreciates that any reply he might make must be understood in the context of the emerging position of his firm in the paper industry and the European Community.

KNP AND THE WORLD PAPER INDUSTRY

The evolution of the papermaking industry and the emergence of the modern European economic system has shaped the development of KNP. In the year

Source: **Prepared by Professor Alan Bauerschmidt and Daniel Sullivan, University of South Carolina, as a basis for classroom discussion and not to illustrate either effective or ineffective handling of administrative situations. © Alan Bauerschmidt and Daniel Sullivan, 1987.**

immediately following World War II, the relatively undamaged but depreciated plant at Maastricht produced only 10,000 tons of paper, but by 1950 the firm had begun its pioneering effort in the production of coated paper and became the first European producer of such papers, using technology obtained under a license from the Consolidated Paper Company in the United States. A companion plant, also producing the top grade coated paper used in the printing of brochures, art books, and catalogues is located at Nijmegen on the Waal river, the extension of the Rhine in the Gelderland province of the Netherlands. Another mill at Meerssen, a town outside the city limits of Maastricht, produces uncoated papers that are world renowned in the markets for colored and watermarked paper, although the overall demand for such traditional forms of paper remains small and the capacity of the three paper-making machines at this plant only total 27,000 tons per year.

The oil price shock of 1973 led the firm to reconsider its fundamental strategy and further specialize in the production of high-grade coated papers to gain prominence in international markets. This is a field of activity in which the firm was already well known and it has expanded that position in the specialized grades of paper it now produces. A mill was constructed at Lanaken, across the Maas in Belgium, just north of the Albert Canal, to further advance this niche strategy in the area of lightweight coated paper. The products of this plant, incorporated as KNP België, are used mainly in the printing of magazines, brochures, catalogues, and promotional material. This plant became the site for the addition of a second papermaking machine in 1986, increasing the capacity of the plant by 175,000 tons of paper each year. The original Fourdrinier machine at this location has an annual capacity of 145,000 tons, and the combined capacity of the four mills operated by KNP in the two countries is approximately 700,000 tons per year, with a total of six papermaking machines in addition to the three small machines at the Meerssen plant.

The separate packaging division of KNP has nine plants that produce various forms of carton board for the packaging industry and other industrial applications. These products include solid, folding, corrugated, and other board products for the converted manufacture of boxes. In addition the plants at Oude-Pekela and Sappemeer produce a greyboard used in the manufacture of files, jigsaw puzzles, books, and various types of deluxe packaging. This product of KNP's *Verpakkingsgroep* is exported to manufacturers in 35 countries under the Kappa board trade name, and the firm is one of the world's largest manufacturers of this product.

The plant at Oude-Pekela in The Netherlands' northern Province of Groningen also produces the solid board that is used in the manufacture of boxes that are necessary for the export of packaged products, as well as some typical products such as flowers, vegetables, and fruit. This board product is manufactured on machines similar to those used in the manufacture of paper, but the board machines of KNP use purchased waste paper, rather than virgin pulp as a raw material in the manufacturing process. The firm owns and operates eight waste paper collection firms that have a capacity to provide 250,000 tons of this raw material each year. Some 30,000 tons of this capacity was added during 1986, with the acquisition of two firms.

A factory in the Dutch town of Eerbeek produces folding box board. This product consists of thin layers of board used mainly for boxes and packaging, and the pharmaceutical and food industries create a heavy demand for this product of KNP. Again, as with all the carton board manufacturing conducted by KNP, waste paper is the raw material used in the manufacture of this product. Overall, KNP process 500,000 tons of waste paper in the course of a year's operation, and there is strong price competition due to financial aid from nearby firms in West Germany for this essential raw material.

In 1986, KNP acquired the German firm of *Herzberger Papierfabrik Ludwig Osthushenrich* GmbH and Co. KG that manufactures boxes in four locations in West Germany. The Oberstrot plant gained in the Herzberger acquisition also produces liner and corrugated board used in the manufacture of boxes and other packaging applications. The Herzberg and Oberau plants that were acquired also produce the corrugated materials used in box converting operations, while the Herzberg location joins the Eerbeek plant in The Netherlands in producing the folding board used in the manufacture of boxes. These acquisitions increased the capacity of the packaging division of KNP by 60 percent, and the Herzberger plants draw on the board stocks of KNP for a portion of their required raw materials. It might be noted that the Herzberger operations convert 70 percent of their board output into boxes.

In addition to the four German packaging plants gained in this recent acquisition, KNP has ownership positions in box making operations in The Netherlands, Italy, and Spain, and each of these are supplied with board stock manufactured by other divisions of the firm. KNP is also a partner in a joint venture with Buhrmann-Tetterode N.V. in the operation of a mill at Roermond, on the Maas river just north of Maastricht, which is capable of producing 350,000 tons of paper by using waste paper as raw material for use in the manufacture of corrugated board. With the addition of a fourth machine at the mill in 1986, this joint venture has become one of the principal suppliers of packaging paper for the European market.

The third organizational component of KNP resulted from a series of acquisitions of paper merchants beginning in the late 1970s that served to complete the forward integration of the value chain associated with paper making, converting, and distribution. Each of these acquisitions involved a defensive strategy to prevent competitors from capturing existing channels of distribution for KNP products. At the present time KNP conducts a paper merchant operation in Belgium, France, and the U.K. In addition, the firm owns an approximate 35 percent interest in Proost en Brandt, one of the two largest paper merchants in The Netherlands, located in Amsterdam, and 51 percent in Scaldia Papier B.V., located in Nijmegen.

Exhibit 1 displays the group structure of KNP, while Exhibits 2 and 3 summarize the plant capacity of the principle divisions of the company. Exhibits 4 and 5 provide a financial summary of the activities of the firm as drawn from the current annual reports. Exhibit 6 shows the locations of the facilities of the firm in The Netherlands.

EXHIBIT 1 KNP N.V.: GROUP AND DIVISIONAL ORGANIZATION

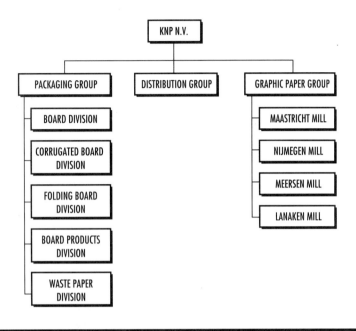

EXHIBIT 2 KNP N.V.: PLANT CAPACITIES OF PACKAGING GROUP

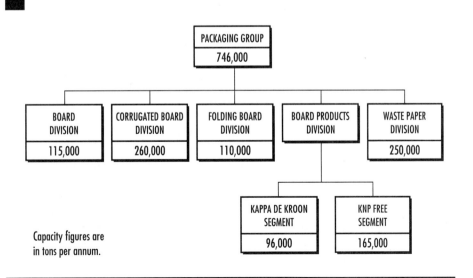

Capacity figures are
in tons per annum.

EXHIBIT 3 KNP N.V.: PLANT CAPACITIES OF GRAPHIC PAPER GROUP

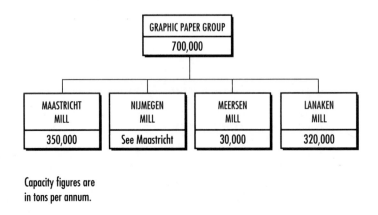

Capacity figures are
in tons per annum.

INTERNATIONALIZATION OF THE FIRM

The extension of KNP's activities outside of its home country is not surprising; along with most other Dutch manufacturers, the firm has always been an exporter and maintained an international perspective. The market for paper in the Netherlands is insufficient to support a plant dedicated to that market, and any firm manufacturing paper in The Netherlands must visualize a market that extends beyond the borders of its home country. Europe is KNP's principal market, and in 1986, 75 percent of its paper product and 45 percent of its packaging materials were sold outside The Netherlands.

In fact all of the products produced by the firm are manufactured for the larger European market, as there is no distinct market for paper in The Netherlands. The portion of the total product of the firm sold outside the European market consisted of output similar to that produced for the primary market, although the firm is willing to meet the specifications of purchasers in every market that is within the capability of the firm. Therefore, it is impossible for anyone in the firm to recall the first sale of any product in a foreign country; however, the location of the original mill on the Maas between Belgium and Germany would lead to the belief that sales of paper products to printers in each of these nations must date from the origin of the firm.

The portion of Belgium immediately adjacent to the Province of Limburg is included in the Belgian Province of Limburg, and the people of that province are largely Flemish, with close ethnic and cultural ties to the Dutch. A similar situation exists to the east where there are relatively strong cultural links with the inhabitants of those portions of Germany adjacent to the Dutch border, as no natural barriers divide the two nations in this portion of the

EXHIBIT 4 KNP N.V.: BALANCE SHEET

	1986	1985	1984	1983	1982	1981	1980	1979	1978	1977
ASSETS										
Tangible Fixed Assets	1156529	606237	433024	397588	384692	382035	341651	332083	323274	334550
Financial Fixed Assets	51848	55252	43826	7337	17752	20067	18603	19720	43716	54239
Inventories	289363	201059	203194	182381	178384	185376	163377	157340	130188	117327
Accounts Receivable	418355	260556	267031	227434	203701	199923	162865	162105	123938	116868
Cash	185307	195864	10938	8311					5471	9572
	2101402	1318968	958013	823051	784529	787401	686496	671248	626587	632556
LIABILITIES AND EQUITY										
Issued Share Capital	82810	74180	70943	70943	59185	56909	56909	56909	56909	56909
Share Premium Account	103691	58784	41644	41644	31420	33696	33696	33696	33696	33696
Other Reserves	421543	330634	255009	206545	173966	168820	165382	165322	168871	164501
Shareholders Equity	608044	463598	367596	319132	264571	259425	255987	255927	259476	255106
Minority Interests in Group Companies	104918	70786	2215	123	123	140	106	103	103	103
Equalization Fund (Subsidiaries)	180434	70858	61451	47677	39464	34135	22325	10037	3894	
Group Equity	893396	605242	431262	366932	304158	293700	278418	266067	263473	255209
Provisions	198743	102802	105403	92809	118259	117348	109842	114348	112826	118911
Long Term Liabilities	535398	271398	137988	147820	166002	147535	110017	121448	130684	108578
Current Liabilities	473865	339526	283360	215490	196110	228854	188219	169385	119604	149858
	2101402	1318968	958013	823051	784529	787437	686496	671248	626587	632556

Note: Figures are given in thousands of Dutch guilders.

EXHIBIT 5 KNP N.V.: PROFIT AND LOSS STATEMENT

	1986	1985	1984	1983	1982	1981	1980	1979	1978	1977
Net Sales	1581491	1616344	1496887	1213461	1174308	1164384	1065293	950886	816592	717514
Changes in Inventories	4079	11301	3587	-9165	8870	8387	4326	11504	5439	2762
Own Work Capitalized	7191	6573	4077	5274	5609	5782	5214	3573	2879	1263
Other Operating Income	8672	2583	475	796	2241	1331	652	2318	1949	529
	1601433	1636801	1505026	1210366	1191028	1179884	1075485	968281	826859	722068
Raw Materials and Consumables	855784	917468	944217	717926	722904	742812	627443	524025	419638	411239
Work Subcontracted and Other External Costs	89073	82489	63485	59173	52316	51036	53421	50912	42925	33238
Labor Costs	316833	314731	288278	283633	290399	287311	289270	273932	250956	205788
Depreciation of Tangible Fixed Assets	74809	71547	55113	54758	52836	51524	51290	50132	47685	44675
Other Operating Costs	69786	59666	49572	42649	38245	39891	39842	36867	32136	25563
Total Operating Costs	1406285	1445901	1400665	1158139	1156700	1172574	1061266	935868	793340	720503
Operating Results	195148	190900	104361	52227	34328	7310	14219	32413	33519	1565
Profit on Financial Fixed Assets	131	167	201	0	0	0	0	0	0	900
Interest Income	5101	11558	3437	2139	2609	2527	1478	1351	1297	784
Interest Expense	13871	27624	18443	17603	22236	19854	15716	14200	12226	6564
Results on Ordinary Operations Before Taxes	186509	175001	89956	36763	14701	-10017	-19	19564	22590	-3315
Taxes Thereon	68720	66140	27643	10457	4014	-5959	-143	10284	9637	-3245
	117789	108861	61913	26306	10687	-4058	124	9280	12953	-70
Share on Results of Partly-Owned Companies	15103	8397	1481	-1672	-2070	-2128	55	1813	920	1446
Results on Ordinary Operations After Taxes	132892	117258	63394	24634	8617	-6186	179	11093	13873	1376
Extraordinary Income (Expense) Net	0	0	0	11764	-97	0	-14443	0	0	0
	132892	117258	63394	36398	8520	-6186	-14264	11093	13873	1376
Minority Interests	297	-21	-16	0	0	0	0	0	0	0
	132595	117279	63410	36398	8520	-6186	-14264	11093	13873	1376

Note: Figures are given in thousands of Dutch guilders.

EXHIBIT 6 KNP N.V.: PLANT LOCATIONS

Rhine lowlands that fringe on the Ardennes. The history of these two portions of Europe include a strong common link that is connected with the defensive positions held by the Romans on the Rhine and Charlemagne's capital in Aachen, immediately to the east of Maastrict.

Because of these demographic and geographic features, KNP identifies Europe and the European Community as its principal market. The modern manufacture of paper products depends upon sufficient demand to permit capacity operation of large volume paper machines. Each of the paper machines operated by KNP reflect state-of-the-art technology, and the firm has made a great effort and investment in the greenfield development of modern plants or the rebuilding of existing machinery to permit it to effectively compete in its specialized niches. The Netherlands has a population of approximately 15 million. This is a woefully inadequate number to provide enough demand to absorb the capacity of a single modern paper machine manufacturing lightweight coated paper for the printing trades, which is the premier product of the firm. On the other hand the European Community has a population of approximately 275 million and a modern economy that can easily support a number of competing firms manufacturing the types of paper products produced by KNP. Exhibit 7 shows the makeup of the European Community.

It should be understood that in most European countries paper is traditionally marketed through paper merchants who serve to distribute the various products of paper mills to converters and printers. These merchants serve national or sub-national markets. Although the original relationship of KNP with a foreign market is lost in history, its typical pattern of market development has been to establish a relationship with paper merchants in the various national markets it chooses to serve.

Sometimes this pattern of market development is not quite as straightforward. When the demand for light-weight mechanical machine coated paper in the U.S. emerged, KNP already maintained a relationship with a paper merchant on each coast to serve the U.S. market for the other products of the firm, but the light-weight coated product required a more direct approach to the printing customer. KNP skirted the traditional distributors and developed an exclusive relationship with the Wilcox-Walter-Furlong Paper Company, a paper merchant in Philadelphia, to stock and sell KNP's product in the eastern portion of the United States. The firm followed a somewhat different but equally effective route to the burgeoning market for light-weight coated paper in the western portions of the U.S.; there it markets the product to printers through the offices of MacMillan Bloedel, a firm that holds a 30 percent stock interest in KNP, and whose chairman and director of international operations both serve on the supervisory board of KNP.

The firm has progressively increased the capacity of its plants to meet increased demand in its committed markets. KNP makes a commitment to a market when it contains the potential for a continuing demand for the specialized products of the firm. Such demand can only exist in a nation or an integrated group of nations with a modern and sophisticated economy. The European Community is an example of such a market, and the emergence of the community in the years following World War II paralleled the development of KNP's international ventures.

The foreign activities of KNP can be divided basically into two segments and two stages. The first stage included a segment that existed since the beginnings of the firm in the 19th century, with the transport of the products of the firm to immediately adjacent localities that by force of political circumstances happened to be in other nations. At the same time the special products of the firm were entering into the more extensive foreign trade that are historically typical of firms in The Netherlands. There is no clear separation of these two segments of the initial foreign trade of this firm.

The second stage of the international business activity of the firm was a

EXHIBIT 7 THE EUROPEAN COMMUNITY

simple elaboration of the trade conducted across national political boundaries. This was the broader cross-national trade permitted by the development of the European Community. Thus the international business activity of KNP can be divided into a pre- and post-WWII period, with the more worldwide export activity of the firm overlapping these two periods.

As indicated previously, the establishment of the European Community appears as the most important factor in the development of KNP. The history of growth and development of KNP following WWII is not untypical of other manufacturers throughout the various industries of Europe. However, this apparent motivation for the expansion of international activity does not account for the management knowledge and skill that had to be present to permit the firm to grasp the opportunity provided by the reconstruction of the European economy under the new economic confederation.

The operating capacity of modern paper making mills is the key factor in the extension of markets. The trend has been toward larger and larger capacity as the technology of paper making has evolved. One can only speculate as to the course of actions that firms would take if technological developments advanced an opportunity for mini-mills such as has occurred in the steel industry. Papermaking is only one example of an industry that requires a highly developed economy to absorb efficient production.

The European Community is a unique design to overcome the various barriers that prevent the extension of economic activity to permit efficient production. As the community emerged, firms in the paper industry (among others) used skilled sales agents that were proficient in dealing with the new market. At the same time, firms that were extending their activities throughout the growing market became expert in meeting the different needs of the various component national economies. Language provides no barrier to a firm such as KNP where executives typically speak a number of the European languages. It is also apparent that residual difference in the cultures of the various nations that make up the European Community provide a negligible barrier to the international business of firms in the papermaking industry.

As far as the extra-continental trade of KNP is concerned, it exported its specialized products to Africa and the Middle East initially. After the beginning of the present decade it began exporting its products to Australia and the Far East, along with an emerging export activity to the U.S. and Canada. These new locations for trade presented no special problems and the penetration of new markets depends more on the level of economic development of the country than any other factor. For example, language barriers are unimportant as managers in the firm have the necessary language skills, and the firm is accustomed from its earliest days to the language necessities and cultural appreciations associated with foreign export.

The inclusion of the U.K. in the European Community provides insight on the way in which KNP goes about extending its international market. The firm considered its traditional markets as including France and Germany, in addition to the Benelux countries, and it was committed to this combination of markets. It then began to develop a similar long-term commitment to the paper market in the U.K., which began with the unusual measure of first working through a sales agent to reach the outlets to the printing trades. At a later point the firm established a more permanent position in the U.K. by having Contract Papers Limited, a large English paper merchant, distribute its paper products. KNP now owns a 45 percent interest in this company.

As indicated previously, KNP moved to the acquisition of paper merchants in many of its committed markets under the pressure of competitive actions that threaten to control such channels of distribution. This has occurred in The Netherlands, Belgium, France, and the U.K. It has not taken place in Germany, which represents the other major national market of KNP in the European Community. While competitive pressures have not induced such an extension of the firm in the German market, KNP is monitoring this situation very carefully.

KNP is now one of Europe's largest producers of coated paper as well as one of the leading producers of board. Both of these activities are highly specialized and internationally oriented fields, and it should be noted that The Netherlands imports over half its total paper requirement while exporting 60 percent of its total paper and board production. This notice is reinforced by an examination of KNP's 1986 Annual Report, which shows that 31 percent of sales were in The Netherlands, 55 percent elsewhere in the European Community, and 14 percent elsewhere in the world.

GLOBALIZATION OF THE FIRM

KNP has not reached a stage of globalization characterized by intermediate production in various localities and final production in the specific markets served. While the specialized paper products of KNP are global products their manufacture does not lend itself to the global integrated strategy as described by Yves Doz and other theorists of international business. Therefore, KNP would be best described as following a multifocal international business strategy.

Following the theoretical distinction made between the concepts of internationalization and globalization, it might be noted that the paper industries in Europe and North America have different configurations. American firms tend to be more fully integrated vertically and horizontally in respect to the full range of forest products. European firms, with the exception of the Scandinavians, have little opportunity to integrate backward and acquire extensive woodlands in their home countries. Because North American firms can command woodlands adequate to supply the raw materials for paper production and have a large domestic or regional market for their products, globalization of production is generally a moot point and of only theoretical interest in strategic planning. Because European paper manufacturers lack a wider forest products orientation, there is little inclination to consider the opportunities to exploit comparative advantage in many global manufacturing locations. Globalization, therefore, is oriented toward forward integration of distribution activities. The Swedes and Finns, on the other hand, have forest resources but are handicapped by lack of a domestic market for finished paper products and face firm competitors in the markets for paper products in developed nations where high value-added products might be sold.

KNP appears among those European firms on the leading edge of globalization of distribution activities in the paper industry. As indicated previously,

KNP has seen fit to acquire foreign paper merchants that are involved in the warehousing of paper products for sale to converters and printers in various domestic markets. At present KNP owns Papeteries Libert S.A. in Paris; the firm also has a 51 percent interest in Scaldia Papier N.V. in Wilrijk, Belgium and a 45 percent interest in Contract Papers (Holdings) Ltd. in London. At home the firm holds a 35 percent interest in Proost en Brandt, N.V. in Amsterdam, acquired in the early 1970s, and a 51 percent interest in Scaldia Papier B.V. in Nijmegen.

These acquisitions took place during 1978 and 1979 as a defensive move to protect vital channels of distribution in the European Community from competitors, and Mr. Zetteler denies that the firm was principally interested in capturing profits from distribution or promoting growth through constraints on channels. Competitors began acquiring paper merchants that sold KNP products and threatened to promote the stock of goods manufactured by their own firms. The paper merchants acquired by KNP continue to stock a full range of goods, including those produced by competitors.

Paper merchants are the traditional extension of the distribution system in the paper and board industry. Paper manufacturers receive orders from paper merchants for the range of common products that are intermediate goods used by final producers. They also may enter into various forms of cutting and sheeting operations as an adjunct to distribution. Occasionally a paper manufacturer will sell directly to the larger printing and converting firms, but the operation of direct sales offices can be considered as the more modern development. Nevertheless, all three of these arrangements are extant and viable methods of distribution.

Paper merchants serve national markets through a fleet of trucks that transport the warehoused products to printers and manufacturers of converted paper products, who either distribute products to final consumers or supply manufacturers producing products with a paper or board component. Generally paper merchants cater to the needs of users in their own country, and the paper merchant operations of KNP are each national firms with wide distribution in their respective nations.

No distinct figures exist in published reports as to the results of KNP's foreign ventures in distribution channels. Overall, distribution provided 7.9 percent of operation revenues of the firm and 2.0 percent of operating results, while the paper group provided 62.9 percent of operating revenues and 71.7 percent of operating results and the packaging group produced 29.2 percent of operating revenue and 26.3 percent of operating results. These figures ignore the influence of internal transfers, which made up 8.2 percent of the total operating activity of the firm and may have had an important part to play in the reported results in respect to distribution.

OTHER ASPECTS OF GLOBALIZATION

While the acquisition of an ownership position in paper merchant operations is a major thrust of the international marketing strategy of KNP, it does not mark the initial globalization of the activities of the firm. The purchase of shares in Celupal S.A., a manufacturer of paper products for the packaging industry in Spain, took place some 20 years ago. The global connotations associated with the construction of the Lanaken plant can can also be debated.

In many respects the creation of KNP België N.V. in Lanaken is a prime example of the establishment of a greenfield manufacturing operation in a foreign country. The Lanaken paper manufacturing operation was established at the point when the business strategy of the firm shifted toward the production of special grades of coated paper for the printing trades. This decision, just before the energy crisis in the early 1970s has let the firm exploit those grades of specialty paper that had a higher value added in manufacture. It was largely distinct from the move to acquire paper merchant operations outside the country, although the two strategic moves took place during the same decade and generally support the strategy of focusing on a segment of the overall line of products in the paper industry. The creation of the greenfield operation at Lanaken was in support of an offensive European niche strategy, while the acquisition of paper merchants in France, Belgium, and the U.K. was a defensive maneuver to prevent erosion of existing channels of distribution that supported the more extensive range of products produced by KNP.

Some portion of the lightweight coated paper produced at Lanaken is shipped to The Netherlands; however, it is obvious that the Lanaken plant was established to serve the European market that is the principal focus of the firm. Nevertheless, it is clear that the plant might have served the same purpose if located in The Netherlands, and although the Belgian government did provide certain assistance and cooperation during the establishment of the plant this was not a prime consideration in the location of the new mill.

It can be supposed that the plant that was finally constructed at Lanaken would have had to be located somewhere in the heavy industrial triangle of north-west Europe to minimize the transportation costs of final distribution to key European markets. The Liege-Limburg-Aachen area is close to the heart of this triangle and is well served by the infrastructure necessary for paper production. The location of Lanaken adjacent to the Albert Canal provides direct access to the facilities of the port of Antwerp and pulp shipments from worldwide sources. It, therefore, is likely that any other decision to locate this plant would have been close to the actual location, and the actual site is quite ideal. The Lanaken plant does draw a small portion of its coating material requirements from the Maastricht plant, producing some economies of scale in this aspect of the operation, but otherwise the papermaking plants are self-sufficent and completely independent.

The situation is somewhat different in respect to the packaging materials operations of KNP in Germany, Italy and Spain. The packaging converters of the firm draw on the packaging board manufactured by KNP in The Netherlands and Germany to fulfill or supplement their raw material requirements, and economies of scale in the production of packaging paper and board is the principal reason for the production of these intermediate products at central locations. It is necessary that such locations be strategically situated to minimize transportation costs, and the firm is contemplating some restructuring of activities at a later point in time to rationalize production at the acquired packaging plants.

Although the paper production facilities of KNP are largely free-standing in each of the two national operations, distribution of paper products remains in part dependent on owned paper merchants and sales offices in host country locations. The packaging material production facilities of KNP depend upon multinational operations of specialized components of the manufacturing value chain. The company, therefore, provides an illustration of the use of two types of global strategy.

FUTURE GLOBALIZATION OF ACTIVITIES

Given the past strategic development of KNP it is obvious that the firm will adopt the form of global production and distribution strategy dictated by the present state-of-the-art at any point in time. The firm is somewhat more judgmental about the degree to which it would internationalize its activity. For example, KNP will not seek to enter the American market on a short-term basis simply because a temporary short-fall in supply exists in this market and existing capacity of the firm is temporarily underutilized. It must be ready to make a long-term commitment of capacity to this market before it would consider exporting any product.

It also appears that KNP has no intention of specializing production components in various part of the world to capture the benefits of comparative advantage in various locations, but this is more likely the result of the nature of the integrated operation of paper manufacturing; the industry is limited in the amount of global specialization that can be practiced. On the other hand the firm does specialize in the production of board and its conversion into packaging materials in separate national locations.

A more important question is whether KNP would ever consider entering into the upstream, extractive portion of the paper business that would provide for the globalization of the firm, given the limited opportunity to manufacture pulp in The Netherlands. American observers have the example of the major papermakers in their countries being backwardly integrated into the extractive portion of the business and consider it a competitive advantage. Some American and Japanese firms have been enticed into participation with foreign governments in the development and harvest of forest resources to obtain sure sources of supply for pulp.

Theorists suggest from empirical evidence provided by certain industries that the evolution of globalization and internationalization includes the backward and forward integration of the firm into global arrangements. The previous example of some American and Japanese firms integrating backward into the forests of less developed nations to gain assured sources of cheap raw materials for paper manufacture is one instance of an evolutionary development in globalization. Other examples of globalization include the shipment of antiquated paper machines or converting equipment to less developed countries where they can be operated in a somewhat economic fashion with lost cost labor or energy resources.

FUTURE STRATEGIC DEVELOPMENTS

There is no doubt that the top management team of KNP is aware of these developing features of the worldwide paper industry, and it is somewhat obvious that Mr. Zetteler will take these features into account as he contributes to the decisions that will shape the future of KNP. It is already apparent within his own division of the firm that technological developments at hand will shortly begin to modify the marketing and production strategies of the firm and the industry. For example, early in 1987 the firm started a 70,000 ton capacity chemi-thermomechanical pulp line in integrated operation with the new Paper Machine 8 at the Lanaken mill. This marks the first integrated paper production operation for KNP, using softwood drawn from the Ardennes, and replacing the chemical pulp purchased in international commodity markets. The firm contemplates doubling this integrated capacity with a second pulp line in the next couple of years. It is rumored that chemical-thermomechanical pulp (CTMP) operations of this sort have the potential to permit reduction of the minimal efficient scale (M.E.S.) of production of high value-added paper products such as light-weight machine coated papers that are produced in bulk in the around-the-clock operation of high-speed paper machines.

The emergence of KNP and firms that follow its lead as an integrated European producer of special papers for the printing trades would undoubtedly enhance the opportunity to compete in various world markets. The United States has already witnessed the penetration of its domestic markets for printing papers as a result of the declining value of the dollar and the superior quality of certain paper products that has been the result of innovations in production by European firms. However, any firm that wished to make a committed entry into the U.S. market would have to consider the costs of transportation of finished paper goods and the comparative advantage of U.S. producers resulting from available forest resources.

CASE 33

CATERPILLAR, INC., IN LATIN AMERICA

ROBERT P. VICHAS
AND TOMASZ
MROCZKOWSKI

Although Caterpillar's presence in Latin America dated to 1914, when the U.S.-based multinational corporation opened its first dealership in Panama, manufacturing in Latin America did not commence until 1960, when the company initiated assembly operations in Brazil, its fourth largest national market.

A giant in the global construction equipment industry, Caterpillar was challenged in the early 1980s by Komatsu Ltd., a Japanese multinational corporation. Having grown from a weak rival one-tenth the size of Caterpillar in 1961 to the world's second largest supplier of construction equipment, Komatsu confronted Caterpillar on the latter's home turf in the U.S. as Caterpillar had done 20 years earlier in Japan.

In 1988 Komatsu renewed its assault by forming a strategic alliance with Dresser Industries of Dallas, Texas. The Komatsu-Dresser joint venture presented the latest threat to Caterpillar's Latin American markets. Although Caterpillar, with a strategy of competitive renewal and its "plant with a future," had successfully defended itself from Komatsu's strategic thrusts in the 1980s, the U.S. MNC would face a new set of challenges in the 1990s.

CATERPILLAR, INC.

A U.S. multinational corporation headquartered in Peoria, Illinois, Caterpillar could trace its origins to two inventors who, in the late 1800s, independently had developed leading-edge technology of that era. Their inventions led to automation of agricultural production in the state of California. Subsequently the two formed the Caterpillar Tractor Co.

Source: Prepared by Professor Robert P. Vichas, Florida Atlantic University, and Professor Tomasz Mroczkowski, American University, as a basis for classroom discussion and not to illustrate either effective or ineffective handling of administrative situations. © Robert P. Vichas, 1990.

Although the company for years had exported its products from the United States, globalization began in 1950 when the firm announced formation of its first foreign subsidiary in the United Kingdom. By the end of the 1950s, it had established manufacturing subsidiaries in the United Kingdom, Australia, and Brazil. Before the end of the 1960s, the MNC had expanded operations into France, Belgium, South Africa, and Mexico with sales subsidiaries in Europe and the Far East to service those dealerships.

Historically, Caterpillar had led the global construction equipment industry with a strategy of broad and deep market penetration within two main categories of heavy equipment: (1) earthmoving, construction, and materials handling machinery, and (2) engines. Several subsidiaries serviced the Latin American markets.

CATERPILLAR AMERICAS CO.

To support its 34 dealers who sold Caterpillar machines, engines, lift trucks, paving products, parts, and repair service in Latin America and the Caribbean, Caterpillar Americas Co. (also headquartered in Peoria, Illinois) controlled four district offices.

Two of these district offices were located in Plantation, Florida. The Northern District Office supported dealers in Colombia (1985), Ecuador (1925), French Guiana (1973), Guyana (1975), Netherland Antilles (1987), Suriname (1941), and Venezuela (1927). (Numbers in parentheses represent year dealership was established.) The Caribbean/Central America District Office serviced 16 dealers, the first of whom was appointed in Panama (1914), the most recent in Jamaica (1987).

In Santiago, Chile, a third district office served dealers in Argentina (1971), Bolivia (1969), Chile (1940), Paraguay (1951), Peru (1942), and Uruguay (1927). Located in Houston, Texas, the fourth district office assisted customers and dealers in Mexico.

CATERPILLAR AMERICAS EXPORTING COMPANY (CAMEC)

Yet another subsidiary, CAMEC, called Florida home. The Miami Lakes operation exported Caterpillar parts on behalf of its Latin American and Caribbean dealers. These replacement parts and components might have been manufactured in Latin America, shipped to the United States, and then reexported to still another Latin American country.

CATERPILLAR WORLD TRADING CORPORATION

Another subsidiary, Caterpillar World Trading Corporation, arranged for the acquisition of Caterpillar products through countertrade or barter for a variety of products. This type of trade permitted Caterpillar to penetrate markets where inconvertibility of foreign currency remained a problem.

Of its 15 manufacturing plants outside of the United States, both Brazilian and Mexican subsidiaries were wholly owned. The only other Latin American manufacturing plant, an independent manufacturer in Argentina, produced under a licensing agreement with Caterpillar. Altogether, the MNC marketed over 100 models of earthmoving, construction, and materials-handling machines; 40 paving/compaction products; 80 lift truck models; and 25 basic engine models.

Brazil. Caterpillar Brasil S.A. (CBSA) opened a parts distribution center in 1954 in Santo Amaro. To support Brazilian exports, it initiated assembly operations in 1960. Inaugurated in 1976 in Piracicaba, a second plant manufactured tracktype tractors, motor graders, wheel loaders, and scrapers. Brazil represented the MNC's fourth largest national market.[1]

To maintain market dominance, Caterpillar Brasil strengthened its manufacturing presence during the latter 1970s in response to competitive challenges of Komatsu, Dresser Industries, Case, Fiatallis, VME, and TEREX. Caterpillar expanded both manufacturing capacity and product lines. In 1973, it had purchased nearly 1,000 acres of land, about one-half of the new industrial park, Unidade Industrial Unileste, north of Piracicaba, which was the largest land acquisition Caterpillar had ever made outside of the United States.

By 1989, the firm had enlarged the Piracicaba operation to almost 1 million square feet with ambitions nearly to double the physical size again by 1992, at which time it planned to close the Santo Amaro plant. Altogether the two facilities in Brazil employed about 5,000 persons.[2]

Not only had CBSA management to cope with the competitive thrusts of Komatsu and Dresser but also with various constraints imposed by Brazilian government policies and regulations, such as local content laws. In order to obtain more duty- and tax-free import privileges, which benefits its competitors were already receiving, CBSA signed an accord with the government in 1980. CBSA agreed to export $2.0 billion worth of equipment between 1980 and 1990. (Note: All monetary values are stated in U.S. dollars.) The commitment was predicated on projections that domestic and export demand for the 1980s would at least be equal to or better than the 1970s,

However, demand declined. CBSA project manager Bill Cook said that the world market for construction equipment collapsed after Caterpillar had entered into the agreement. "Both the export market and the domestic market declined. So we couldn't export what we said we would, nor did we need to import what we thought."

Of the 1980 export pact, CBSA vice president Don Coonan said, "There was a very real threat there. We had a contractual agreement that we weren't meeting. In fact, it looked like we would only get about 40 percent of that amount. We agreed we ought to have a strategy for CBSA."

Facing a potential penalty of $335 million for not meeting the export target, management had to reevaluate its goals and strategy. Of its several short and long term goals, the following ranked highest:

1. Become more cost effective.
2. Increase management effectiveness.
3. Emphasize quality in the production processes.
4. Develop a more export driven organization.
5. Comply with local content laws.
6. Meet aggressive market challenges of Komatsu and Dresser.

Several task forces were created. Coonan headed an export task force. Its objective was to increase exports from Brazil. Another group focused on a new strategy for CBSA. They found that CBSA had noncurrent product, volatile demand, complex operations, deteriorating manufacturing facilities, and excess costs.

During the mid-1980s, corporate headquarters had compiled an in-depth study and evaluation of Komatsu. Management reevaluated its Latin American presence. Caterpillar had realized a 16-percent gain for all of Latin America during 1986; much of that headway was attributable to the Brazilian operations. In 1987, corporate headquarters opted to strengthen its commitment in Brazil and support changes required by CBSA.

The new strategy embraced several significant elements. First, the new strategy called for renegotiation of the contract with the Brazilian government. CBSA management succeeded in renegotiating export requirements from $2 billion down to $816 million.

Second, to meet the goal of making CBSA a more export driven organization, Brazil would become the new world source for scraper bowls (except elevating scrapers). A new motor grader series, as well as the D4H along with a newer model of the track-type tractor, would be dual-sourced with Brazil designated as one of two manufacturing sites. Also, CBSA would manufacture the 3116 engine and countershaft transmission for use in Brazilian-built machines. Over the long term CBSA wanted its exports to account for 35 percent of total sales.

Third, modernization to achieve better cost and quality control became part of the manufacturing plan. Consolidation included expansion of the Piracicaba plant to accommodate increased production. Chuck Gladson, technical director, said, "We upgraded and simplified our processes through use of technology and layout."

Factories were reorganized to improve materials handling. Cook said, "We positioned ourselves with new manufacturing philosophies."

Fourth, because cost effectiveness was essential to remain competitive, CBSA planned to reduce the number of different models it built. At that time CBSA built two distinct versions of each model: one for the domestic market that complied with local content requirements, another version for export.

Fifth, in order to increase the allowable volume of products for domestic sale, CBSA intended to improve supplier capabilities in Brazil. Cook said, "We explained to our suppliers that we're looking at things from a world class perspective—that means higher volumes, lower costs and high expectations for quality and reliability from them." Reaching its local content goal would permit CBSA to expand Brazilian sales. Without greater domestic sales, CBSA's earning power would be considerably restricted.

Sixth, to meet efficiency goals, CBSA management reorganized its reporting structure in 1988 to implement consolidation of the two-plant operations. The departments of manufacturing, industrial relations, quality control, and materials at each plant were merged under one department head, who held simultaneous responsibility for the departments in both plants. Management created the new organizational structure in Exhibit 1 to improve accountability and efficiency.

Implementation of the new strategy, consolidation, modernization, and new product programs were scheduled over a five-year period. However, CBSA faced a number of environmental challenges:

1. A volatile Brazilian market.
2. Inflation of 1,000 percent a year.
3. Price controls that limited prices of final outputs but not necessarily the cost of raw material inputs and labor.
4. Government-owned and protected industries.
5. Brazilian debt crisis that restricted availability of foreign exchange for imports and profit repatriation.
6. Local content regulations.
7. A massive governmental bureaucracy.
8. Political uncertainty and capital flight.
9. An aggressive foreign competitor, Komatsu.

On the positive side, Brazil, the world's seventh largest economy with abundant natural resources, offered potential opportunities in mining, agri-

EXHIBIT 1   PARTIAL ORGANIZATION CHART OF CBSA, 1988

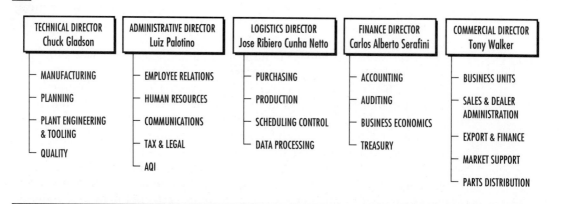

TECHNICAL DIRECTOR Chuck Gladson	ADMINISTRATIVE DIRECTOR Luiz Palotino	LOGISTICS DIRECTOR Jose Ribiero Cunha Netto	FINANCE DIRECTOR Carlos Alberto Serafini	COMMERCIAL DIRECTOR Tony Walker
MANUFACTURING	EMPLOYEE RELATIONS	PURCHASING	ACCOUNTING	BUSINESS UNITS
PLANNING	HUMAN RESOURCES	PRODUCTION	AUDITING	SALES & DEALER ADMINISTRATION
PLANT ENGINEERING & TOOLING	COMMUNICATIONS	SCHEDULING CONTROL	BUSINESS ECONOMICS	EXPORT & FINANCE
QUALITY	TAX & LEGAL	DATA PROCESSING	TREASURY	MARKET SUPPORT
	AQI			PARTS DISTRIBUTION

Source: "A Letter for Caterpillar Management," April 1989, p. 3.

cultural, and construction markets, as well as growing infrastructure needs. Brazil had the highest developed industrial structure in South America; many MNCs considered it a potentially attractive investment; and should Brazil resolve its political and fiscal problems, established companies would have first crack at newly emerging opportunities. However, even from a perspective of late 1988, realization of market projections were subject to considerable variance. Since uncertainties continued into 1989 for Brazil, Mexico seemed to offer greater promise.

Mexico.   During the early part of the decade of the 1980s, the U.S. MNC suffered a precipitous decline in Mexican sales due in part to lower oil prices. (Mexico was a net exporter of petroleum, an important generator of foreign exchange.) Caterpillar blamed a challenging economic environment, high foreign debt, and high interest rates in the U.S. for its problems in Latin America.

Despite operating losses, Caterpillar preserved a strong relationship with its Mexican dealers in Chihuahua (1945), Monterrey (1981), Ciudad Obregon (1929), Mexico City (1926), and Guadalajara (1974). This established dealership network was costly to sustain. Caterpillar typically turned around requests for parts within 48 hours—an important consideration in the purchase of heavy equipment—and service that competitors could not always match. In addition to its dealerships, the firm maintained manufacturing facilities in Monterrey.

Of Caterpillar's seven wholly owned foreign subsidiaries, two of them were located in Latin America: one in Brazil, the other, Conek SA de CV, in Mexico. For the first time in company history Caterpillar had accepted a minority interest of 49 percent in a joint venture formed in 1981 with the Mexican chemical producer, CYDSA, which owned the other 51 percent of Conek. The name, Conek, derived from the two words: construction plus equipment. Caterpillar believed that a partnership with CYDSA was a good match; CYDSA had operations throughout Mexico, and Mexican law required a local partner.

Caterpillar had decided to locate the plant in Monterrey, Nuevo Leon, for several reasons.

1. CYDSA recommended the location.
2. Monterrey was the second largest industrial city in Mexico.
3. It was near raw material sources: natural gas, steel, and trained labor and technical people educated at Monterrey Institute of Technology.
4. There was stability of state and local governments.
5. Fewer labor problems arose here than in some border areas where organized labor had disrupted work.
6. The work ethic and business philosophy seemed more akin to the U.S.

With the crash of the Mexican economy in 1982, CYDSA found itself under financial constraints due to its U.S. dollar-denominated debts and wanted to divest its interest in Conek. Caterpillar searched for a new Mexican partner. Partners which Caterpillar preferred had insufficient capital; those who came forward with sufficient capital Caterpillar did not want. Consequently, in December 1983, Caterpillar requested exemption from Mexican law and permission from the government for 100 percent ownership of the subsidiary. (Note: Current Mexican law allows 100 percent foreign ownership; however for foreign investments exceeding $100 million, the foreign investor must have a Mexican partner.)

In August 1984 the government gave its permission for the company to assume 100 percent ownership of its Mexican subsidiary. In November 1984 Caterpillar completed the transaction and acquired CYDSA's interest in Conek; in that month Conek became a wholly owned subsidiary of Caterpillar, Inc. in Peoria, Illinois. Until that point in time, Conek's operations had been essentially an assembly plant. Beginning in early 1985, the subsidiary began full-scale manufacturing to produce components and parts primarily for sale to the United States.

Conek shipped its output to corporate headquarters in Illinois or to other Caterpillar sales companies in the United States for reexport. By mid-1989, export production at Conek was about 40 percent finished products and 40 percent components and replacement parts; the remaining 20 percent of manufacture was destined for production of lift trucks and parts for the Mexican market. Local content varied according to the product; heavy manufactures requiring substantial steel usage might have 99 percent local content.

Products were transported by truck to Texas. Ing. Adan J. Peña Guerrero, treasury manager at Conek, said that by clearing customs in Monterrey prior to shipment, the paperwork required about 24 hours versus three days at the Texas border. He also said that with anticipated construction of the Colombia Bridge between Nuevo Leon and Texas, built exclusively for the expedient movement of exports and imports, the new 10-mile bridge near Laredo would save the firm considerable time and money. Currently, strong labor unions required expensive and delaying off-loading and reloading to cross the border. Additionally, the Mexican government sought private investors to construct a 15-mile toll highway direct to the bridge to bypass Nuevo Laredo.

Caterpillar maintained three industrial locations near Monterrey. Nearly 3.3 million square feet, the main manufacturing plant sat on 272 acres of industrial land. A second location, used for parts warehousing and some electronics manufacture, comprised almost 100 acres, plus a third site at Santa Catarina about half that size.

With a 1989 total of 1,700 office and plant workers (whose average age was 23 years) on a three-shift schedule, Conek operated at full capacity. Ing. Peña Guerrero proudly pointed out that office workers followed the American system of 8:00 to 5:00 with a 30-minute lunch break in the plant cafeteria. He said, "Most office employees usually arrive 15 or 20 minutes before 8 and do not leave until 10 or 15 minutes after 5." This contrasted sharply with Mexico City where the work day traditionally might begin at 9:00, with a two-hour mid-afternoon lunch, and end at 7:00 P.M.

Although Ing. Peña Guerrero was born in Monterrey, he preferred the efficiency of a U.S.-styled system. He had earned his M.S. degree in engineering at the Monterrey Institute of Technology (ITSEM), a private university, and an M.B.A. from the University of Wisconsin at Milwaukee. At age 31, he managed five supervisors and a total of 42 employees over whom he kept a watchful eye. He reported directly to another Mexican, Juan Gamez, finance manager, who, in turn, reported to the general manager, Jim Palmer.

Conek paid plant workers slightly above market rates and generated employee loyalty and cooperation by:

1. using a complaint and suggestion book to which management usually reacted within one week;
2. publishing a monthly employee newsletter, titled "Conexion";
3. holding periodic one-hour plant-wide meetings to inform employees of news, progress, and events;
4. maintaining close supervision over all employees;
5. creating an intense training program to improve quality and productivity;
6. offering free bus service to employees from the city to the plant.

Because the manufacturing facility was some distance from urban Monterrey, a daily bus picked up employees at designated points and times. Several advantages derived from this program:

1. Employee costs for transportation were reduced.
2. People arrived at work on time.
3. Riders could either rest or develop friendships during the ride.
4. Employees were less likely to talk casually with unionized workers from other plants.

The training program helped achieve corporate goals of greater productivity (lower costs of production) and higher quality. For example, welders must be adept at using a technique not employed in typical manufacturing. Conek required a six-week intense training course. Peña said that Conek had sent some employees to Texas for special welding training. After two weeks the welding school had sent them back to Mexico, because Conek had already trained them better for specific tasks than the school could. Peña added, "Conek also pays employees for college courses and for M.B.A. degrees."

Conek used Just-in-Time (JIT) inventory control and Duran Quality Control techniques. To resolve minor problems at the shop level, small quality control (QC) circles were activated. For larger problems Conek employed an annual quality improvement program (QIP), which, according to Peña, excelled over QC. Functioning like a task force, QIP focused on specific problems and on how to save money. All of this effort had paid off for the manufacturer. Peña said, "Conek has had no delivery or quality problems [since 1986]."

In Mexico, Caterpillar's chief competitor, Komatsu, was number two in the construction equipment market. Clark Equipment ranked as an unimportant third-place competitor; and all remaining competitors together represented only a minor threat to Caterpillar.

Conek and its parent had many strengths: It was well established in the market. It maintained a costly dealership network. It had built an international reputation. Its trademark, CAT, and the distinct yellow color of its equipment were instantly recognizable. Conek, as one of several sourcing points for components in a world-wide network, was assured of continued demand for its manufactures. Additionally, in its manufacture of finished products and components, Conek:

1. used a high grade heavy steel, from a Mexican source, not readily available everywhere;
2. maintained very good relations with its local steel supplier and had experienced no sourcing problems;
3. manufactured high quality products which required less refabrication, and, therefore, lowered overall costs;
4. tested all equipment thoroughly at the plant site and before shipment;
5. maintained careful quality control in its highly integrated operations;
6. insisted upon quality workmanship (e.g., welding) not necessarily found in all competing products;
7. achieved good cost control and continued to strive for higher productivity to maintain price competitiveness.

Financially the operation had not achieved payback of investment due to large start-up costs. A typical payback period in this industry would be on the order of 10 to 15 years. CYDSA, Conek's former partner, used payback projections of 18 years. By taking advantage of its experience curve, training employees for quality and productivity, and achieving a careful mix of exports and imports, Caterpillar expected to shorten the payback period of its Mexican subsidiary.

To test possibilities of diversification, Conek modestly invested in a small plant to assemble tractor electronics. The project had not been financially successful, due, in part, to sourcing problems for electronic chips. Its foreign source provided chips only twice yearly, which generated an inventory problem between overinvesting in inventory or a stock-out which would shut down the production line. The chip manufacturer needed longer production runs to bring down its costs. Since Conek was not a major purchaser, it had little influence on the supplier.

Peter Donis, president of Caterpillar, in early 1989, had said that profitability was constrained by higher material costs, higher start-up costs incurred by the factory modernization program, and higher-than-expected short term interest rates to finance working capital needs.

Nevertheless, with a turnaround expected by 1990 in the Mexican economy, Caterpillar anticipated an increase in sales of construction machinery. The new president of Mexico seemed to have considerable popular support for his economic development strategy, which was to: (a) open the economy to foreign competition, (b) privatize most public enterprises, (c) move toward creating a market economy, (d) encourage foreign direct investment, and (e) inter alia. Despite Caterpillar's aggressive stance, Komatsu's yellow (in imitation of CAT products) bulldozers could be seen excavating sites for construction of new commercial buildings in the heart of Monterrey, not many miles from Caterpillar's production facilities.

KOMATSU, LTD.

Caterpillar's chief competitor was the Japanese multinational corporation, Komatsu Ltd. Within most Latin American markets, Caterpillar and Komatsu's other competitors were frequently a distant number three or four in a particular country, often market spoilers; but altogether they did account for a respectable volume of business. Not only had Komatsu to concern itself with Caterpillar but also with those competitors whose presence in individual markets was most threatening to the Japanese firm.

Originating as the Takeuchi Mining Factory in 1894, Komatsu Ltd. manufactured and marketed a full line of construction equipment, industrial presses, and machinery such as robots and laser machines to customers in over 150 countries. The parent organization of the Komatsu Group, comprised of 60 affiliated companies, Komatsu Ltd., maintained world headquarters in Tokyo, Japan.

Komatsu had faced a major crisis in 1961 when Caterpillar announced a joint venture in Japan with Mitsubushi Heavy Industries Ltd. With one-tenth the sales of Caterpillar, Komatsu recognized that survival was problematic unless prices and quality of its products were competitive. Komatsu signed a license agreement with Cummins Engine, Inc. (U.S.) to manufacture and sell diesel engines, and subsequently entered into several other joint venture agreements with U.S. firms (which were later terminated).

Nevertheless, Komatsu did not establish its first foreign subsidiary until 1967: N.V. Komatsu Europe S.A. in Belgium. Global expansion began in earnest with creation of Komatsu America Corp. and the establishment of Brazilian and German subsidiaries. Bulldozer production commenced at Komatsu do Brasil in 1975, at Dina Komatsu Nacional S.A. in Mexico in 1976, and at P.T. Komatsu Indonesia in 1983.

BRAZIL

Formed in 1970 in São Paulo, Komatsu do Brasil initialized the first overseas bulldozer production in 1975. In those early years the Brazilian operation neither figured prominently in Komatsu's corporate global plans nor had it been successful financially. Because corporate net income in 1983 had declined about 20 percent from 1982, management blamed the Brazilian subsidiary for a significant share of those corporate losses and attributed them to unfavorable economic conditions in Brazil.

Of Third World countries, Shoji Nogawa (president of Komatsu) wrote: "Developing countries, also important markets for the industry, generally experienced economic difficulties, with their burdens of extensive debt further aggravated by the high level of U.S. interest rates."[3] (The Middle East had been Komatsu's most important foreign market.)

Corporate management said, in 1985, "Internationalization for Komatsu means not only establishing more efficient corporate management in overseas marketplaces but, more importantly, pursuing more effective customer-focused operations as the Company continues to expand its worldwide customer portfolio."[4] Despite management's stated commitment to globalization, the firm continued to manufacture principally in Japan for export to its foreign markets. Even as late as 1986, foreign manufacturing represented only 5 percent of company total, while 95 percent of manufacturing was still done in Japan.

Then, in 1987, under leadership of Komatsu's new corporate president, Masao Tanaka, the company sped up globalization of its operations. Setting a new target, management wanted foreign manufacturing to account for 35 percent of total production and pushed to integrate its manufacturing bases in Brazil, Mexico, and Indonesia into a framework of strategically defined roles.

MEXICO

Komatsu's Mexican subsidiary, Dina Komatsu Nacional, S.A. de C.V., also experienced a change during 1987 when the Japanese MNC's share in this joint venture rose from 40 to 68 percent ownership.[5] Dina Komatsu Nacional, a joint venture with Nacional Financiera, the government-owned Mexican development bank, began to manufacture bulldozers in 1976; but it produced no profit in its nearly 13-year history. The Mexican government, under President Salinas de Gotari, had been trying to privatize much of the public sector and divest itself of unprofitable joint ventures. Although the government's investment in Komatsu had been on the sale block since early 1988, potential private investors showed little interest in the offer.

Primarily, Komatsu's global strategy had been one of export development. The Mexican venture figured in a defensive move to counter Caterpillar in Mexico. Perceiving the Mexican market as a subunit of the larger North and South American market, Komatsu chose to do battle on U.S. soil and in 1988 sought to strengthen its presence in the Americas' market with a joint venture (JV).

THE UNITED STATES

Management of the world's second largest integrated maker of construction machinery stated that competitive strength "lies in its versatile technological base and its tradition of quality first."[6] Entry into the U.S. construction equipment market was a cornerstone in Komatsu's global market penetration strategy.[7]

When Komatsu opened its manufacturing facility in Chattanooga, Tennessee in 1985, it had an 8-percent share of the U.S. market, which it had hoped to double. Nobuo Murai, president of Komatsu America Corp., said, "Our goal is a market share of 15 percent in the near term and 20 to 25 percent in the long term."[8] Komatsu faced increasing obstacles in its exports to the United States due to the depreciated value of the dollar coupled with trade conflict issues between the U.S. and Japan.

Masao Tanaka (corporate president) in 1988 wrote: "Strategically, we are committed to establish a competitive operational system on a global scale, by setting up a worldwide manufacturing/sales network capable of flexibly and effectively responding to changes in the economic climate."[9]

To strengthen its competitive position in both North and South America, Komatsu and Texas-based Dresser Industries, Inc. announced in February 1988 the formation of a strategic alliance in which the two companies would combine their construction equipment manufacturing and engineering facilities in the U.S., Canada, and Latin America. Operationalized September 1, 1988, the 50–50 joint venture, Komatsu Dresser Company, constituted an initial capitalization of $200 million for machinery and automation plus $50 million to refurbish manufacturing plants. Sales for 1989 were projected at $1.5 billion. The strategic alliance also called for the creation of Komatsu Dresser Finance Division to finance sales both to wholesale and retail customers.[10]

Essential elements of the agreement were: Komatsu and Dresser would share equally in the management of Komatsu Dresser, which had exclusive manufacturing and marketing rights for North, Central, and South America. The joint venture also would distribute replacement parts, engage in engineering, and establish training and test centers as well as sales and administrative offices.[11]

The new alliance also required consolidation of three foreign subsidiaries—Komatsu America Corp., Komatsu America Manufacturing Corp., and Komatsu do Brasil—together with Dresser's Construction Equipment and Haulpak divisions and Dresser's manufacturing subsidiary in Brazil. Of this 1988 joint venture, Komatsu management wrote:

> The venture clearly symbolizes one successful outcome of Komatsu's internationalization strategy to establish the three-core comprehensive operations in Japan, the U.S. and Europe. It also advances Komatsu's commitment to further promote international cooperation with other firms for mutual business expansion as an equal partner.[12]

Based in Libertyville, Illinois, a Chicago suburb, Komatsu Dresser Company began operations in late 1988 with 5,000 workers employed at eight plants in the United States, Canada, and Brazil. It had more than 3.5 million square feet of factory space. One of these plants, the Haulpak Division (which produced mining trucks), was only 22 blocks down Adams Street from Caterpillar's Peoria, Illinois, corporate headquarters.

The new strategic alliance allowed Komatsu to shift much final assembly from Japan to the Americas and fight the battle for Brazil and the rest of Latin America right in Illinois. The new company would become number two in the Americas in the construction equipment industry.

FIGHTING FOR MARKET DOMINANCE

When battle lines between the two firms were drawn in 1961, Komatsu developed Total Quality Control (TQC) to become competitive in price and quality, broadened its product offerings to match Caterpillar's, reduced manufacturing costs, increased exports, and, by 1980, became recognized as the world's second largest manufacturer of construction machinery. It dominated the Japanese market with a 60 percent share.

Generally, in every country-market the Japanese had entered in recent decades, they applied a market-share pricing strategy, which meant using a low entry price to build market share and, in the long run, dominate the targeted market. However, shifts in exchange rates and the debt-laden economies of Brazil and Mexico dampened that success pattern for Komatsu.

Komatsu's exports to the U.S. had doubled in 1983. Its world market share rose to around 20 percent; and its U.S. market share had been expanded to 8 percent by the mid-1980s. The Japanese firm had managed to boost volume by 40 percent with very little escalation in employment by the heavy application of robotics. Management was spending $80 million a year alone on automation while continuing to diversify products in order to become a major producer of automated production systems and robots. By 1985, the firm had erected three large R & D laboratories, established five foreign production facilities—including a plant in the United States and in the United Kingdom—and added plastics, electronics, robots, metal presses, and other products to its line.

Prior to 1985 a high dollar exchange rate and price-cutting strategy gave Komatsu a 40 percent price advantage over Caterpillar. Its export ratio was 64 percent. But environmental factors swung against Komatsu. The dollar-yen relationship turned in favor of the dollar. Due to the strong yen, export-oriented Komatsu had to raise prices by 18 percent in 1986, while Caterpillar raised their prices an average 3 percent, the first increase since 1984; Komatsu lost 2 percent market share to Caterpillar. Komatsu's 1986 profits plummeted by 33 percent, exports fell nearly 5 percent, and in 1987 its president, Shoji Nogawa, resigned in the midst of unfavorable rumors. Komatsu's battle cry had been *MARU 'C'* (or "encircle CAT") to put Caterpillar in a defensive position.

However, Caterpillar maintained a solid financial position, held significant leadership in many areas of construction equipment technology, and by its size and global network was well positioned to take an offensive, rather than a defensive, position. Management initiated a strategic analysis.

Asked to assess strengths and weaknesses of Caterpillar and Komatsu, middle managers from various functional activities developed a comparative competitive analysis between Japan and the U.S. By rating the two firms on a seven-point scale, they developed comparative analysis on 17 factors. Professors Tomasz Mroczkowski and Marek Wermus tabulated the summary of responses appearing in Exhibit 2. On the seven-point scale, a rating of 1 was most favorable to Komatsu, a rating of 7 most favorable to Caterpillar. The

EXHIBIT 2 KOMATSU VS. CATERPILLAR: COMPETITIVE ADVANTAGES AS PERCEIVED BY U.S. EXECUTIVES (SUMMARY OF RESPONSES)

| | ADVANTAGE/SAMPLE MEAN | | | | | | | ADDITIONAL STATS | | |
| | KOMATSU | | | | CATERPILLAR | | | | | |
AREA	1	2	3	4	5	6	7	$S_{\bar{x}}$	Mc	Mo
1. Cooperative labor-management relations	1.52							.16	1.25	1.00 (18)
2. Cooperative business-government relations	1.59							.15	1.34	1.00 (16)
3. Labor costs	1.82							.26	1.34	1.00 (16)
4. Workforce trained in stat & quality control		2.07						.17	2.05	2.00 (10)
5. Strong organizational culture		2.22						.25	1.02	1.00 (11)
6. Pressure of management for short-term profit		2.64						.26	2.43	2.00 (7)
7. Better trained blue-collar			2.92					.32	3.69	4.00 (8)
8. Capital charges			3.32					.27	3.68	4.00 (11)
9. Responses to international markets				3.65				.29	3.79	4.00 (7)
10. Better trained white-collar				3.67				.32	3.60	4.00 (8)
11. Overall management				4.04				.25	4.06	4.00 (8)
12. Superior marketing intelligence				4.52				.36	4.63	4.00 (6)
13. Modern equipment & machinery				4.78				.21	4.71	4.00 (7)
14. Advanced manufacturing technology					5.15			.28	5.64	6.00 (17)
15. Product research & development					5.78			.19	5.94	6.00 (17)
16. Technologically more advanced products						5.96		.16	6.03	6.00 (16)
17. Superior design & product development capabilities						6.00		.21	6.13	6.00 (12)

Source: Tomasz Mroczkowski and Marek Wermus, "Improving Competitiveness Survey."

arithmetic mean represented the management group's averages. Additional statistics are included in the table.

Caterpillar's managers perceived Komatsu as operating in a lower labor cost environment and enjoying access to lower cost capital, a cooperative industry-government relationship, a cooperative labor force that had extensive skills in statistical process control, and that Komatsu's managers were not under pressures to produce short term profits.

Caterpillar's managers saw their own superiority in design and product development, R&D, technological level of products, and a world-wide reputation for quality products supported by a dealer network.

To counteract Komatsu's drive, Caterpillar reduced production capacity 25 percent, cut inventories 37 percent, slimmed down its labor force, and closed plants. With plant closures Caterpillar was no longer a vertically integrated company. It defended market share with deep price discounts, and offered smaller machines to smaller sized contractors. The heart of the turnaround decision was to (a) cut operating costs by 22 percent, (b) give more price authority to local managers, and (c) diversify into other product areas.

PLANT WITH A FUTURE

In October 1986, Caterpillar president Peter Donis said:

> Although we've reduced costs by more than 20 percent, we're not stopping there. We've returned to profitability, but we expect cost and price pressures to continue. Our costs are still 15 to 20 percent higher than our foreign competitor's, and in spite of the dollar weakening, transaction prices for our products are about the same now that they were in 1981. So, Caterpillar's long-term profitability will not be secure until we do, in fact, become the industry's low cost producer. We've developed a strategy for achieving the additional cost reduction. We call it our Plant with a Future.[13]

For Caterpillar, the Plant with a Future (PWAF) concept portrayed in Exhibit 3 embraced all elements of manufacturing as well as product design, supplier relationships, and logistics. Although this new manufacturing strategy went beyond simple cost cutting, its implementation and integration of facilities would continue for the rest of this century. At the heart of PWAF was automation, new factory layouts, and continuous work flow. Caterpillar executive vice president, Pierre Gueridon, said, "We believe computer-integrated manufacturing is our supreme weapon for cost reduction. It's the area where we have the largest long term advantage over the Japanese."

Based on a cell manufacturing concept, plants and equipment were arranged to process families of components from start to finish. For example, machining, welding, heat treating, and painting might all be functions within a single cell. Work flow was continuous. Since all cells fed the assembly line just-in-time, it required JIT delivery to the cells. Immediate objectives were to simplify and integrate.

EXHIBIT 3 PWAF AND ITS THREE BASIC COMPONENTS

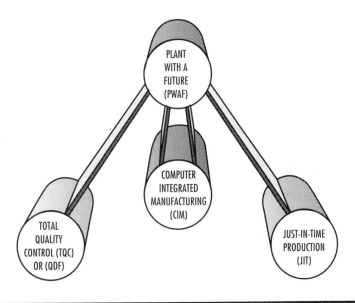

Computer integrated manufacturing (CIM) linked self-contained manufacturing cells (i.e., independent islands of automation) to a material, tooling, and information network to allow for electronic communication between engineering, logistics, and the factory floor. By the next decade, interplant communication would be routine through a corporate information center coupled with global marketing and financial data bases. With complete implementation of the strategy and integration of operations, all systems, from the plant's host computer to personal computers on the shop floor, could communicate to result in unprecedented coordination and optimization of all manufacturing functions: supplier delivery, scheduling of equipment, tooling, quality control, maintenance, and troubleshooting.

Gueridon said, "At our Gosselies [Belgium] plant, for example, we expect PWAF changes to result in a 22 percent reduction in material costs and a 31 percent reduction in labor costs by 1990."

Conek, the Mexican subsidiary, exemplified successful execution of this new strategy. Management implemented JIT and Duran quality control techniques, small QC circles at the shop level, and an annual QIP to resolve bigger challenges. Critical to success at Monterrey were cost and quality control.

On the other hand, CBSA, the Brazilian subsidiary, best reflected "gradualism": Caterpillar's chief approach to automation and implementation of the PWAF. PWAF automation was conceived as a self-financing program with highest priorities for capital investments. Funds generated from reduced inventories and improvement in efficiencies would finance these investments. Caterpillar management expected its manufacturing plants to migrate from present systems to a hybrid system and to end up with PWAF, a purely customer-driven manufacturing philosophy.

RETURN TO PROFITABILITY AND A NEW CHALLENGE

The Japanese invader was not invincible. Komatsu's exports decreased because most were dollar denominated; and the dollar was overpriced in terms of yen. Its profits fell by a third in 1986.

On the other hand, Caterpillar's competitive position sharply improved. Profits in 1986 were $76 million ($0.77 per share), and, in 1987, $350 million ($3.51 per share). Sales were up; employment at Caterpillar increased by 732 persons in 1987; and market share rose. Exhibit 4 depicts global market shares in 1987.

Caterpillar still had the most recognizable and respected name in the construction equipment industry. Its products commanded a price premium. It had a world-wide dealership and parts distribution network. Project teams were working on quality improvement projects. A massive program of statistical process control training had been successfully launched to transfer the responsibility for quality control to employees. The PWAF strategy, now in

EXHIBIT 4 SHARES OF WORLD CONSTRUCTION MACHINERY SALES, 1987

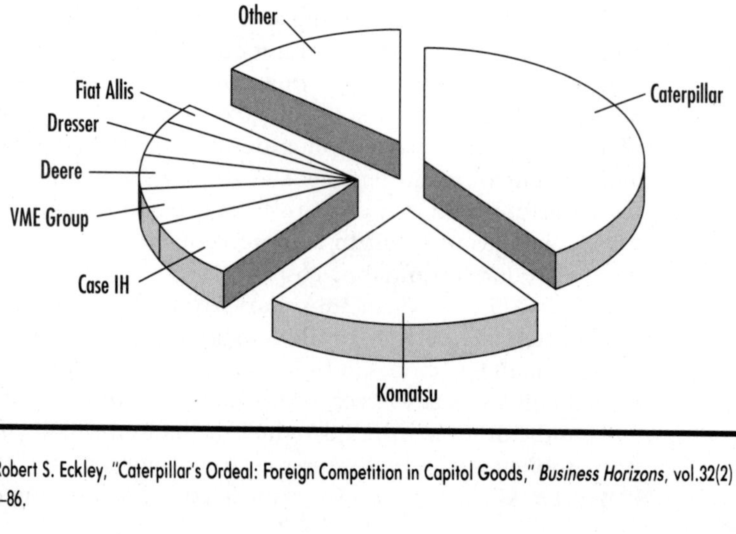

Source: Robert S. Eckley, "Caterpillar's Ordeal: Foreign Competition in Capitol Goods," *Business Horizons,* vol.32(2) (March/April, 1989): 80–86.

place, seemed to function well. Certainly 1988 would be a good and trouble-free year.

A banner year, 1988, not only witnessed a 25 percent rise in revenue but also a 76 percent leap in profits. (See Exhibit 5 for summary financial data and other statistics.) Alexander Blanton, of Merrill Lynch, said, "I estimate the company's earnings power at between $8 and $10 per share by 1990." Exhibit 6 graphically illustrates quarterly changes in net income during the decade.

Komatsu had not been especially successful in Latin America. Its Mexican joint venture had never produced a profit. Brazilian losses severely affected corporate profitability. It did not have the dealership network that Caterpillar had long ago established throughout Central and South America as well as the Caribbean.

Nevertheless, the Komatsu-Dresser strategic alliance presented a serious challenge to Caterpillar in Latin America. With both Komatsu and Dresser, along with Caterpillar, having a strong manufacturing presence in Brazil, this market might become the strategic battleground for Latin America. Although all companies had older, less efficient manufacturing facilities, Caterpillar had already initiated its program of modernization to cut costs, improve quality, and consolidate product line—the PWAF strategy.

In its 1988 JV agreement, Komatsu would give up to $300 million to Dresser to upgrade factories, which, prior to the agreement had been running at 50 percent capacity. Although both Komatsu and Dresser continued to introduce new products, they maintained separate, yet competing, dealerships.

By July 1989, Caterpillar had registered strong gains in sales outside of the U.S.; approximately 52 percent of business now derived from foreign sources. (See data in Exhibit 7 for foreign versus domestic sales, 1984–1988.) Global revenues of $5.7 billion marked a 15 percent increase over the comparable six-month period in 1988. Net income for the first half on 1989 of $282 million resulted in $2.78 profit per share of common stock compared to $2.60 per share the first six months of 1988. Employment rose to 60,881.[14]

Early 1989 recorded no further major changes in the Latin American environments for either MNC. Considerable uncertainty reined in most key Latin American markets. Argentina experienced yet another economic crisis as a new president was about to assume office. Peru's hyperinflation and communist terrorism produced a chaotic situation as the country entered a campaign year for the presidency. Brazil's economic condition continued to deteriorate; national elections were scheduled for late 1989. The most stable economies appeared to be Chile, which had successfully implemented a program partially consistent with free market philosophy, and Mexico, which was trying to move toward a market economy. Chile would elect a new president by year's end; and Mexico's president was still in the first half of his term.

Caterpillar had parried Komatsu's strategic thrust but not without difficulties. For instance, for the three-year 1986–1988 period, decreases in production costs fell short of the targeted 5-percent annual rate of reduction. Part of the problem could be attributed to translation losses due to unfavorable swings in foreign exchange rates. During 1989 the PWAF program experi-

EXHIBIT 5   CATERPILLAR, INC.: CONSOLIDATED FINANCIAL POSITION AT DECEMBER 31, 19____

	1980	1981	1982	1983	1984	1985	1986	1987	1988
Current assets	2933	3544	3433	3383	2915	2982	3363	4006	5317
Intangible assets	—	147	117	99	96	77	60	47	71
Other fixed assets	3165	3594	3651	3486	3212	2957	2865	3578	4298
TOTAL ASSETS	6098	7285	7201	6968	6223	6016	6288	7631	9686
Current liabilities	1711	2369	1197	1576	1939	1742	2180	2758	3435
Long term debt	955	1059	2508	2055	1432	1206	959	1308	2138
Equity	3432	3857	3496	3337	2852	3068	3149	3565	4113
TOTAL DEBT/EQUITY	6098	7285	7201	6968	6223	6016	6288	7631	9686

CONSOLIDATED INCOME STATEMENT AT DECEMBER 31, 19____

	1980	1981	1982	1983	1984	1985	1986	1987	1988
Revenue	8598	9154	6469	5424	6576	6725	7321	8180	10255
Operating profit	831	903	(253)	(310)	(339)	233	137	498	924
Net profit (loss)	565	579	(180)	(345)	(428)	198	76	350	616
Dividends per share of common stock ($)	2.325	2.40	2.40	1.50	1.25	0.50	0.50	0.50	0.75
Average number of employees	86,350	83,455	73,249	58,402	61,624	53,616	53,731	54,463	60,558

Note: Figures given in millions of U.S. dollars.

Sources: Figures derived from annual reports.

EXHIBIT 6 CATERPILLAR QUARTERLY NET INCOME

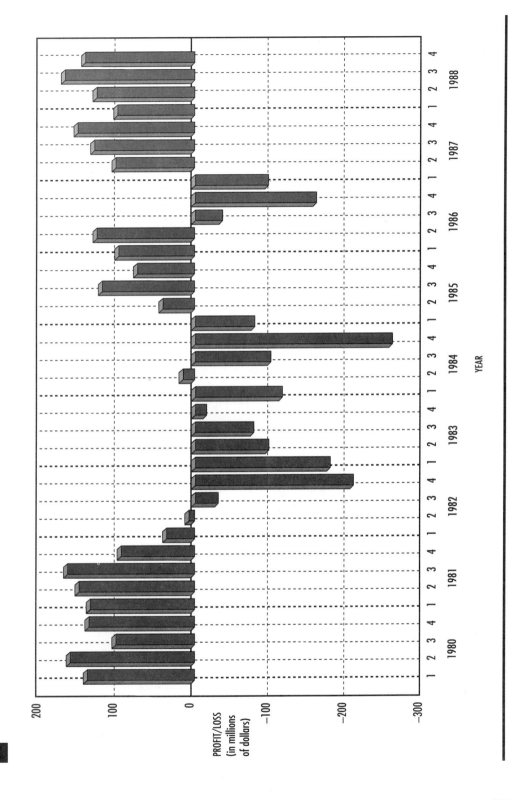

EXHIBIT 7 CATERPILLAR, INC.: FOREIGN AND DOMESTIC SALES

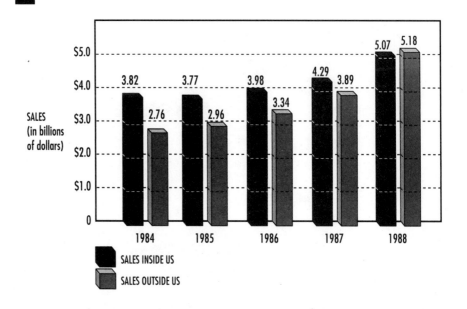

enced cost overruns exceeding $300 million. Uncertainty still characterized Latin American markets. A new competitor, Komatsu Dresser Company, was in training for yet another round. In early 1989, the Strategic Planning Committee, comprised of senior managers from various functional areas, was charged with the task of evaluating strategic options for the 1990s. The challenge to Caterpillar continued.

ENDNOTES

1. "A Letter for Caterpillar Management," April 1989 (internal document):4.

2. "Cat Unit Merges Brazilian Facilities," *Journal Star* (Peoria, Ill.), (December 10, 1988): 2.

3. Komatsu, *1983 Annual Report*, p. 3.

4. Komatsu, *1984 Annual Report*, p. 10.

5. "Komatsu Raises Stake in Mexico Venture," *Japanese Economic Journal,* 25 (August 29, 1987): 13.

6. "A Letter for Caterpillar Management," cover.

7. "Komatsu Digs Deeper into the U.S.," *Business Week* (October 1, 1984): 53.

8. Farnsworth, Clyde, "Chattanooga Reviving Itself with Foreign Capital," *Chattanooga Times* (October 10, 1985).

9. Komatsu, *[Quarterly] Financial Report* (March 31, 1988): 2.

10. *Wall Street Journal* (August 17, 1988): 32.

11. "Dresser, Komatsu Form Joint Venture," *Pit & Quarry* (March 1988): 12.

12. Komatsu, *1987 Annual Report* p. 8.

13. Speech by Peter Donis at the General Electric/Northwestern University Executive Dialog Series, October 14, 1986.

14. Caterpillar 1989 quarterly financial reports.

NEC CORPORATION'S ENTRY INTO EUROPEAN MICROCOMPUTERS

MICHAEL HERGERT
AND ROBIN HERGERT

In April 1985, nearly five years after the introduction of its first personal computer to the European market, NEC Corporation (formerly Nippon Electric Company, Ltd.) had not yet established a significant presence in Europe. Despite the vast commercial potential of microcomputers, and despite NEC's widely recognized technological leadership and considerable financial resources, the company had not transferred its phenomenal success in Japan, where it had captured 55 percent of the personal computer market, to Europe. The time had come for NEC to reevaluate its strategy for entry into the rapidly evolving European microcomputer market, to review its current position, and to consider its options for the future.

EVOLUTION OF NEC CORPORATION

From its modest beginnings in 1899 as an importer and then manufacturer of telephone equipment. NEC, with 1984 sales of $8 billion, and net income of nearly $200 million, had become a leading international force in telecommunications, the world's third largest vendor of microchips, and Japan's number two computer maker (behind Fujitsu). Expanding from a single plant in Tokyo, NEC became a multinational corporation, manufacturing 15,000 products in 71 plants scattered throughout Japan and 11 other countries, supplying these products to over 140 nations through its 21 marketing and service organizations in 13 countries, and employing 78,000 people worldwide. Expertise in the three major areas of the information industry—telecommunications, semiconductors, and computers—placed NEC in a unique and enviable posi-

Source: **Prepared by Professors Michael Hergert and Robin Hergert, San Diego State University, as a basis for classroom discussion. © Michael Hergert and Robin Hergert, 1990.**

tion to challenge its rivals both at home and abroad. Claimed Tadahiro Sekimoto, NEC's president, "IBM may be ahead in computers, AT&T has good
capacity in communications, and Texas Instruments is strong in semiconductors. But no company has such a combination of businesses in all three areas."

Until only 25 years ago, however, NEC's primary line of business was making telecommunications equipment for the domestic market. Set up in 1899
by American Telephone and Telegraph's (AT&T) Western Electric subsidiary,
NEC became Japan's first joint venture company. During these early years,
Western Electric furnished all the product designs for its minority partner. In
1925 NEC passed into the hands of International Telephone and Telegraph
(ITT), which sold off the last of its shares in 1978.

Natural disasters and human catastrophes played a major role in shaping
the course of NEC's evolution. A major earthquake in 1923 destroyed a large
proportion of Japan's wired communications system, prompting the Ministry
of Communications not only to rebuild the network, but also to supplement
it with a radio broadcasting system, which would not be as vulnerable to seis-
mological activity. NEC thus moved into the field of radio, borrowing Western
Electric technology to produce its first vacuum tubes in 1928. World War II
precipitated the destruction of nearly 80 percent of the telephone installations
in Japan. Japanese authorities once again sought desperately to replace the
communications infrastructure, and this time it appeared that microwave
technology would provide the answer. NEC thus entered the field of microwave communications. In 1985 it claimed world leadership in microwave, with
over 30 percent of "uncommitted" (those that do not favor local suppliers)
world markets. Ironically, NEC also licensed its technology for microwave devices made of gallium arsenide to its former joint venture partner, Western
Electric.

The postwar years also witnessed the creation of a climate favorable to
NEC's development in other directions. Reconstruction of the telecommunications system stimulated the demand for equipment, and the network was to be
administered by the newly created Nippon Telegraph and Telephone Public
Corporation (NTT). NEC, whose former president became first president of
NTT, was NTT's largest supplier, although NTT had not been increasing investment levels and was beginning to bow to strong political pressure to purchase some equipment from the United States.

During the years immediately following the war, Japanese authorities
eased restrictions on consumer radio use, thus accelerating the growth of a
consumer segment. In response, NEC created a wholly owned subsidiary in
1953, New Nippon Electric, Ltd. (NNE), to take responsibility for the production and sales of electric household appliances. At one time NEC's second
most important business after communications, accounting for 20 percent of
NEC's sales, consumer products dwindled to 8 percent of sales in the early
1970s.

It was also during the postwar period that NEC began researching solid-
state technology. In 1949 the company turned its investigative efforts toward
semiconductors, a more reliable and higher-quality alternative to vacuum

tubes. Soon after transistors became commercially available in the early 1950s. NEC launched an all-out campaign to catch up with the United States. It began volume production of transistors in 1958, and in 1964 its efforts were rewarded by a major contract in Australia. More recently, NEC's rapid growth in computer sales had provided a large in-house market for its semiconductor division. Rather than depend exclusively on its captive market, however, the company had spent heavily to expand into the merchant market, becoming Japan's largest chip maker in the process. NEC boasted that its Kumamoto plant on Kyushu—Japan's "silicon island"—was the largest factory in the world producing memory chips. According to an industry expert, "NEC is the leader because it was the first Japanese company to understand that semiconductors are big business in itself (sic)."

Although "buy domestic" policies currently represented an ever-increasing threat to NEC's penetration of American and European markets, protectionist attitudes at home during the 1930s provided the catalyst for research that would eventually lead NEC into such advanced technologies as fiber optics. At that time, most of the patents, parts, and materials for telecommunications equipment originated outside Japan, eliciting a wave of sentiment for domestic technology. The search began for an alternative to Bell Laboratories' "loaded" cable for long-distance transmission. The solution was found in 1937 with the completion of a "nonloaded" cable carrier transmission system. One of the engineers working on this all-Japanese project was Dr. Koji Kobayashi, NEC's chairman and chief executive officer. Short, stocky, and still domineering enough at the age of 78 to frighten his colleagues, Kobayashi had been the principal architect of NEC's success in the last 20 years. NEC's continued involvement in transmission technology led to the development of a system capable of carrying digital signals in 1962. Six years later, following investigation into the possibility of using light to transmit information, NEC produced SELFOC, its first optical fiber.

NEC's pioneering role in microwave transmission enabled the company to carve a distinctive international niche and to apply its expertise to the field of satellite communications. After watching the first television show to be relayed by Telestar 1, Dr. Kobayashi personally orchestrated NEC's entry into this emerging industry. Traveling to Hughes Aircraft Company headquarters in Los Angeles, he arranged a joint venture with Hughes to develop a synchronous communications satellite. The successful product of this collaborative effort was Relay I, whose first transmission was the shocking announcement of President John F. Kennedy's assassination. By 1985 NEC had established a dominant position in satellite communications and was the only company to supply the entire system, including the satellite itself.

It was also telecommunications research that provided NEC's springboard into data processing. Company engineers, seeking a faster way to design filters for transmission lines, developed the world's first solid-state computer. NEC licensed Honeywell technology from 1962 to 1979, and, following a suggestion from MITI in 1971, elected to produce mainframe computers that were not compatible with those of IBM. This decision contributed to NEC's limited presence in world data-processing markets; meanwhile archrivals Fujitsu and Hitachi, also under MITI's direction, built up a significant international business in the so-called IBM plug-compatible computers, designed to be plugged into IBM installations as replacements for IBM machines. Nevertheless, at home NEC had captured 16 percent of the thriving mainframe market, and it dominated the markets for printers, displays, and other peripherals. NEC's personal computers had raced to the front of the pack in Japan since their introduction in 1979.

To its competitors outside Japan, NEC was known and respected primarily as a supplier of microchips and telecommunications equipment. Although the company had been involved in several ventures in the Far East during the first 20 years of its existence, it was not until the early 1960s, an era of falling trade restrictions and resultant growth in world trade, that NEC emerged as a multinational corporation. Its first overseas manufacturing facility, a joint venture in telecommunications, was set up in Taiwan in 1958. Other plants followed in neighboring Asian countries, Latin America, and the United States, where NEC incorporated its first North American subsidiary, Nippon Electric New York, Inc., in 1963. Its first European plant, for assembly of microchips, was opened in Ireland in 1975. A second, bigger chip factory in Scotland became operational in late 1982. Representing only 10 percent of sales in 1965, international sales accounted for 35 percent of NEC's revenues in 1984. Over half of these overseas sales were attributable to communications, a market NEC had exploited particularly successfully in the United States and Brazil. The corporation supplied equipment to five of the seven regional Bell operating companies formed after the breakup of AT&T and held 80 percent of the Brazilian microwave market. NEC's stock is currently listed on the Amsterdam, Frankfurt, London, Basel, Zurich, and Geneva exchanges. Financial data for NEC appears in Exhibit 1.

PRODUCT AREAS

NEC is divided into four separate divisions for its main businesses: communications, computers and industrial electronic systems, electric components, and home electronics. Summaries of the company's performance by product area follow with analyses of the major factors that characterize the respective markets and a list of NEC's major products.

COMMUNICATIONS

Sales of communications systems and equipment in fiscal 1984 rose to $2.55 billion and had been growing at a compounded annual rate of 15.3 percent since 1980. NEC is the largest Japanese telecommunications company and has had considerable success in export markets, including selling its digital public telephone exchange in 28 countries. The company is also the world's largest supplier of satellite earth stations and microwave communications equipment,

EXHIBIT 1   NEC INCOME STATEMENT AND BALANCE SHEET DATA, 1984

	1984	PERCENT CHANGE 1983–1984
Income Statement Data (in thousands, except per share figures):		
Sales and other income..	$8,017,862	23%
Net sales	7,830,489	22
Communications..	2,546,031	9
Computers and industrial electronic systems	2,391,107	34
Electron devices	1,889,231	35
Home electronics..	754,693	14
Other...	249,427	1
Income before income taxes	384,578	36
Income taxes	213,671	29
Net income	170,907	35
Per share of common stock		
Net income..	0.166	30
Cash dividends	0.034	19
Balance Sheet Data (in millions):		
Assets:		
Cash and securities	$1,894	
Accounts receivable	3,299	
Inventories..	1,572	
Gross fixed assets...	3,773	
Accumulated depreciation (loss)	(1,780)	
Other assets..	485	
Total assets	$9,243	
Liabilities and net worth:		
Short-term debt...	$2,091	
Accounts payable..	2,010	
Other current liabilities......................................	1,089	
Long-term debt..	1,579	
Other long-term liabilities..................................	657	
Stockholders' equity..	1,171	
Retained earnings...	646	
Total liabilities and net worth	$9,243	

Source: NEC annual report.

having captured 50 percent and 33 percent, respectively, of these world markets.

NEC's product offerings in this area are very broad. The major products are electronic telephone-switching systems, digital data-switching systems, telephone sets, teleconference systems, facsimile equipment, carrier-transmission equipment, submarine cable repeaters, fiber-optic communication systems, microwave and satellite communications systems, laser communications equipment, mobile radio equipment, pagers, broadcast equipment, satellites, radio application equipment, and defense electronic systems.

Although just under one third of NEC's sales are in communications, profit margins in this area have been squeezed as the company makes the transfer from analog to digital communications. International markets for telecommunications have become intensely competitive as companies struggle to maintain a presence in an overcrowded market. Sustained growth in computer sales has helped to reduce NEC's dependence on communications from 44 percent of sales in 1974 to 32 percent in 1984.

As the volume of NEC's business with its major customer, NNT, did not grow significantly in 1984, NEC is looking to the private sector and overseas markets for future growth. The company projects that the world telecommunications market will grow more rapidly in the latter half of the decade than it has over the past five years. NEC is keen to enter the newly liberalized U.K. market; it intends to build a plant in the United Kingdom and has recently won a major order to supply British Telecom and Securicor with mobile radios for their joint cellular radio mobile telephone network.

COMPUTERS AND INDUSTRIAL
ELECTRONIC SYSTEMS

Computer and industrial electronic systems recorded sales of $2.39 billion in fiscal 1984, sustaining a compounded annual growth rate of 26.7 percent since 1980. The division has an extensive product list. The major products are super computers, general-purpose ACOS series computers, minicomputers, control computers, personal computers and software, data communications equipment and software, peripheral and terminal equipment, magnetic memory equipment, distributed data-processing systems, office-automation systems, word processors, industrial telemetering systems, postal automation systems, numerical control equipment, medical electronic equipment, speech recognizers, industrial and communications control systems, robots, and CAD/CAM systems.

Although within Japan, NEC still lags behind Fujitsu and IBM in overall computer sales, the company leads the Japanese market in sales of personal computers with a 55 percent share. It was also the only major computer maker between 1974 and 1981 to increase its share of the Japanese market, both in cumulative value and number of machines installed. As a result, computers now account for 31 percent of revenues, up from 20 percent in 1974. According to Takeshi Kawashi, head of radio communications, the major reason for this success lies in NEC's strength in semiconductors.

Although NEC is looking to overseas data-processing markets for growth, its penetration of international markets for computers is very limited. The Japanese company has garnered only a tiny share of the personal computer market in the United States, the single largest of NEC's foreign markets. The

16-bit Advanced Personal Computer (APC) made its marketing debut in Europe in fiscal 1984, following its introduction in Australia and the United States the year before. In March 1984, NEC entered into an agreement with the United States–based Honeywell Information Systems, Inc., granting Honeywell distribution and manufacturing rights for NEC's large computers. The link with Honeywell gives NEC a strong marketing arm and access to a customer base in the United States. It also gives Honeywell an extension to its range of computers it could not have afforded to develop itself. In years past NEC had licensed technology from Honeywell.

Industry analysts attribute NEC's lack of significant international presence in computers in foreign markets to the company's refusal to produce IBM-compatible mainframes. Observers note that IBM's more aggressive stance and its dominance of the mainframe market has made it very hard for other companies to succeed with different systems. NEC counters that companies that seek to poach IBM's customers by offering technically compatible machines expose themselves to the threat of crippling retaliation by IBM. Yukio Mizuno, senior vice president in charge of the computer division, intimates that the battle with the U.S. giant is undergoing a shift in emphasis: "IBM's profits will come increasingly from software, maintenance, and system communications rather than from the computer hardware itself. So we have to compete with IBM in software rather than hardware."

Though NEC is putting huge resources into improving the production of its software—it has 13 wholly owned software subsidiaries and employs some 8,500 programmers—senior vice president Tomihiro Matsumura believes that Japan's social and educational system may be a handicap. By emphasizing highly organized group activity, he thinks it discourages the individualism that often sparks off innovation. The company aims to fill the gap by tapping outside talent. It has already commissioned American software houses to write programs for it, notably for its personal computers. It plans to set up its own software centers in the United States and recruit American programmers to staff them.

Although NEC management predicts that demand for computers and industrial electronic systems will continue to rise as harsh conditions force companies to rationalize and upgrade their operations, it also admits that competition is certain to mount as computer manufacturers around the world move to capitalize on the wealth of opportunity at hand. Industry observers are less than completely enthusiastic about NEC's ability to capitalize on these international opportunities. Says Frederic G. Withington, vice president for information systems at Arthur D. Little, "While they've done fine with the Spinwriter [high-quality printer] and [semiconductor] components, in computers they aren't strong enough."

ELECTRONIC COMPONENTS

NEC's sales of electronic devices reached $1.89 billion in fiscal 1984 and had been growing at a compounded annual rate of 23.1 percent since 1980. The company leads the increasingly successful Japanese assault on the world's semiconductor markets, and it ranks among the globe's top four microchip suppliers, along with Texas Instruments, National Semiconductor, and Motorola of the United States. A sustained global shortage of memory and other devices has contributed heavily to this performance. NEC's chip business currently accounts for 24 percent of revenues, up from 16 percent in 1975, and it is the most profitable of its product lines.

The company produces a wide range of electronic devices. The major products are integrated circuits (ICs), circuits for large-scale integration (LSIs), circuits for very-large-scale integration (VLSIs), microprocessors, transistors, diodes, gallium arsenide field-effect transistors; gate arrays, electron tubes, color picture tubes, display tubes, plasma display panels, lasers, laser application devices, circuit components, rectifiers, bubble memories, and vacuum equipment.

While Texas Instruments, the world's biggest chip maker, is laying off workers in anticipation of a weaker semiconductor market, NEC is pressing ahead with the construction of new plants and the expansion of existing facilities, both at home and abroad. The Japanese multinational insists that demand for its chips still outstrips supply, and it is vying for top position in the chipmakers' league by year's end. According to preliminary estimates by the California market research firm Dataquest, NEC's semiconductor sales will grow by about 60 percent in 1985, allowing it to overtake Motorola and to close the gap on TI.

NEC can apparently withstand the slower market growth more easily than its American rivals because Japanese demand for chips has been less volatile than demand across the Pacific. The four top Japanese chip makers—NEC, Fujitsu, Hitachi, and Toshiba—are also four of the biggest chip consumers. This makes demand easier to forecast and moderates the industry's boom-bust cycles. There is thus no need for chip users to overbook to ensure deliveries when demand is rising.

Another factor in NEC's favor is its strength in both memory chips and microprocessors. Prices for the latter tend to be more stable than prices for memory chips. The firm has also invested heavily in the mass production of cheap memory chips. NEC's main microchip plant in Kumamoto, southern Japan, is the largest and most efficient in the world.

HOME ELECTRONICS

The fourth main area of NEC's business is home electronics. This division posted sales of $755 million in fiscal 1984 and has grown at a compounded annual rate of 11 percent since 1980. It is an area of NEC's activities that is easily overlooked because it only represents 10 percent of revenues, down from 14 percent in 1981, and is fairly insignificant alongside the leading producers of consumer electronics in Japan such as Matsushita, Sony, Sanyo, JVC, and Hitachi.

The NEC-brand product line is extensive, and the major products include television sets, video recorders, portable video cameras, television projectors, radio receivers, transceivers, tape recorders, hi-fi audio systems, compact disk digital audio systems, personal computers, lighting products, refrigerators, microwave ovens, kitchen appliances, and air conditioners. NEC does not manufacture the whole range, but concentrates on producing consumer electronic products while rebranding the nonelectronic appliances.

Despite the firm's modest showing in consumer electronics, NEC believes that the division, and particularly the personal computer, is potentially highly important. NEC's president explains, "In 10 or 20 years' time, consumer products will be the largest single part of [our strategy]."

NEC STRATEGY

NEC sees itself as a tree whose roots are firmly embedded in high technology. One product recently developed by the Tokyo-based company is an automatic software-development system that makes productivity 5 to 50 times more efficient than previous manual work. Known as SEA/I, the system is designed for automation of software development, which was chiefly a manual process until now. SEA/I is among the most advanced systems of its kind in the world. Yet management thinks it could do better, committing over 10 percent of consolidated sales to research, development, and engineering activities.

NEC's competitors are beginning to run out of adjectives to describe such relentless striving for higher performance. The Japanese multinational, however, harbors still bolder ambitions. It has set its sights on the twin goals of increasing sales at an annual pace of 18–20 percent for the rest of the decade and of becoming a world leader in the creation of the high-technology information society of tomorrow. To reach these overall growth objectives, NEC plans to raise overseas contribution to sales from 35 percent to 40 percent, half of it manufactured outside Japan.

If NEC's targets are bold, its operational style is even riskier. While archrivals Fujitsu Ltd. and Hitachi Ltd. have set up partnerships with computer manufacturers in the United States and Europe to assure a sizable penetration of the information-processing markets, NEC has generally shunned such shortcuts in favor of developing its brand name. Explains Dr. Kobayashi, NEC's chairman, "Our intention is simple: walking on our own feet." The company's president, Dr. Tadahiro Sekimoto, elaborates on this point: "We aim to establish real companies abroad that can design, make, and maintain the products that they sell on their own." He is convinced that this policy of decentralization is the most effective way to secure NEC's future in an increasingly volatile and treacherous business climate. Indeed, growing fears of a trade war with the United States and the European Economic Community (EEC) have heightened the sense of urgency.

As a result of this go-it-alone approach, coupled with the decision not to make computers that are compatible with those made by IBM, NEC's machines have not yet achieved significant penetration in the West. To compensate,

NEC has resorted to aggressive marketing and ruthless price cutting. "NEC uses its profits in other areas to allow it to cut prices in computers," says Tamizo Kimura, an analyst at Yamaichi Research Institute. A strategy based on price competition, however, is not totally without risk. In a suit brought by U.S. rivals Aydin Corporation and MCL, Inc., the Commerce Department in 1982 found Nippon Electric guilty of dumping $3 million worth of microwave communications components on the U.S. market.

As NEC has also discovered, establishing offshore manufacturing operations can cause other kinds of headaches as well. Neither Electronic Arrays, a small California chip maker bought in 1978, nor its telecommunications plant opened the same year in Dallas, Texas, was judged to be up to Japanese quality standards in 1982. Executives were appalled by the conditions they found when they took over Electronic Arrays. Workers at NEC's Kumamoto plant must change into special protective garments and pass through a forced-air "shower" before entering the ultra-clean section where the most delicate part of the chipmaking process is performed. "But in California, people were wandering in wearing street clothes," according to one NEC manager. A good deal of management effort has been devoted to bringing the plants up to snuff.

Although NEC departed from the firm's policy of developing largely through internal growth when it acquired Electronic Arrays, executives say there are no plans to bolster international marketing operations through the purchase of other companies with strong marketing organizations. However, Dr. Sekimoto does not rule out this possibility categorically. An enthusiast of American futurologist Alvin Toffler, the president quips, "After all, this is the Age of Drastic Change."

NEC's second driving ambition is symbolized in its slogan "C&C," standing for the convergence of computer and communications technologies that lies at the heart of the revolution in electronic information handling. Since Dr. Kobayashi first publicly coined the term at the International Telecommunications Exposition in Atlanta in 1977, NEC's patriarch has been actively promoting C&C within his entire organization. This theme dominates NEC management and activities to an almost obsessive degree. No document, no conversation—whether formal or informal—is complete without some reference to C&C.

This convergence of computer and communications technologies is, of course, widely recognized by electronics companies throughout the world, bringing computer companies such as IBM into telecommunications and communications companies such as AT&T into data processing. Few companies, however, have made this convergence into such a pervasive management theme, and fewer still actually straddle these worlds quite as comprehensively as NEC. The concept is made tangible in the so-called decision room at corporate headquarters in Tokyo, where top management regularly meets. An elegant wood-paneled chamber, it is equipped with a panoply of sophisticated systems permitting two-way video communications with distant offices and instantaneous retrieval and display of massive amounts of information.

Despite NEC's technical achievements and strongly held belief in the convergence of computers and communications, the company has a long way to go in coordinating its communications, computer, semiconductor, and consumer electronics divisions. Says Dr. Sekimoto, "I think they will remain separate forever. For instance, the communications business will always be there . . . the telephone will never disappear. In the same way the stand-alone computer will never disappear. However, C&C will create new fields and will become very much bigger."

The enhance cooperation, the company has set up occasional project teams that span the different divisions, such as for automatic broadcasting equipment and some defense projects. In addition, the marketing and sales organization, which is separate from the manufacturing divisions, has a team devoted to the promotion of C&C products such as office and factory automation.

THE EUROPEAN MICROCOMPUTER INDUSTRY

In 1985 the microcomputer industry in Europe displayed many features typical of emerging markets. Great technological uncertainty, buyer confusion, and unclear market segments created an environment where strategy formulation was difficult at best. Current events left many industry observers puzzled; spectacular successes and failures were the norm, and some of the world's mightiest multinationals had proven unable to establish viable competitive positions. Among this group was NEC, whose European microcomputers had failed to capture a significant market share, even after five years of attempts.

In this market, even a precise product description is controversial. Microcomputers span the range from simple machines costing a few hundred dollars and primarily used for playing games to sophisticated desktop units capable of supporting several hundred users simultaneously. For the following discussion, the main emphasis is on products selling for $1,000 to $10,000 and designed for individual use. A typical microcomputer setup has the components described below.

SYSTEM UNIT

The system unit is the heart of a microcomputer. It contains the microprocessor, which is the semiconductor chip where numerical operations actually take place. The microprocessor size is an important determinant of the speed and power of the computer. First-generation microcomputers, such as the Apple II, relied on an 8-bit microprocessor, meaning that information is processed for computations in blocks of 8 units. An 8-bit microprocessor is quite adequate for many applications, and is still used in a large number of products.

IBM ushered in the second generation of microcomputers in August 1981 when it introduced the PC. The PC uses the Intel 8088 microprocessor, which processes 16 bits of information at a time. This permits the IBM PC and other second-generation products to run more powerful software and handle larger problems. It also creates the possibility of making the microcomputer a multitasking machine (i.e., capable of handling more than one job at a time) and a multiuser machine (i.e., capable of handling more than one user at a time).

More recently, even larger microprocessors have become common. The IBM AT, introduced in August 1984, is a 16–24 bit product, and the Apple Macintosh, also introduced in 1984, has a 32-bit processor. Although the technology of large microprocessors was well established by 1985, limited availability and high costs have made many microcomputer producers wary of committing to advanced technology.

In addition to a central processing unit, a microcomputer must have internal memory. Internal memory consists of RAM (Random Access Memory) and ROM (Read Only Memory). Both RAM and ROM are made up of memory chips installed inside the system unit. ROM consists of instructions permanently stored in the machine that cannot be modified by the user. ROM memory often contains essential software to control the operation of the machine and increasingly is used to provide applications packages, such as word processing or spreadsheet software. RAM memory is addressable by the user, meaning that he can write his own data and programs to memory for temporary storage and can modify the contents at will. The amount of internal memory in a microcomputer plays a large role in determining the size of the problem that can be handled. Memory is measured in kilobytes (K). Most microcomputers have at least 64K of RAM. Larger machines may be expanded to 640K or more.

EXTERNAL MEMORY

In addition to internal memory, microcomputers generally provide some form of external storage medium for permanent storage. Early microcomputers stored data on audio cassettes, but this proved to be slow and unreliable. In 1978 Apple began using floppy diskettes for external storage, which quickly became adopted as the standard system. Floppy diskettes are inexpensive disks of magnetic storage film that are capable of recording 160–2400K of data. Individual diskettes sell for under $2.50. The disk drive used to store data onto diskettes sells for $150 to $500, depending on size and storage capacity. A typical microcomputer system will have one or two disk drives, which can be mounted inside the system unit or in separate expansion cabinets. During 1984 and 1985, the use of hard disks as a storage medium increased dramatically. Hard disks, also known as Winchester disks or fixed disks, are similar in size to floppy disks, but are capable of holding far greater amounts of information. Hard disks for microcomputers typically hold 10–20 megabytes of data (1 megabyte = 1000 kilobytes), and are available up to 100 megabytes or more. Prices for hard disks have fallen drastically during the last two years, and they are now available for as little as $500. Exotic mass storage devices of even greater capacity should be available in the near future. In 1985, 3M announced a laser optical disk capable of holding 450 megabytes of information on a 5.25-inch disk. Industry analysts expect the disk drive to sell for under $1,500 within a few years.

VIDEO DISPLAY

Microcomputers display information on several forms of video devices. Early microcomputers were often hooked into television sets for display. Current computers typically have a dedicated cathode ray tube (CRT) device, which can display output in multiple colors and screen formats. In order to increase the portability of microcomputers, extensive research is being done on LCD, plasma, and other flat-screen technologies. In late 1984, Data General announced a notebook-sized computer with a fold-up, full-sized (25 lines by 80 characters) display.

PRINTERS

To create a physical record of microcomputer output, it is necessary to use some form of printing device. The most popular printer technology is the dot matrix. Dot-matrix printers are inexpensive ($200 and up) and relatively fast (as many as 400 characters per second). The main drawback of dot-matrix printers is that they are unable to provide high-quality output and are viewed by many people as unsuitable for business correspondence. For letter-quality printing, daisy wheel printers are more common. Daisy wheel printers work on the same principle as many office typewriters and are able to provide very high-quality output. A daisy wheel printer intended for office use will usually sell for at least $1,000.

New printing technologies are also emerging. In 1984 Hewlett Packard introduced its LaserJet printer, which is based on the xerographic process used in copier machines. Laser printers are fast, very high quality, capable of producing any form of graphics output (unlike daisy wheel printers), and are extremely quiet. Similar printers had been available previously from Xerox and others, but at prices of $25,000 to $400,000. The HP LaserJet sells for approximately $3,000.

MODEMS

Modems (or modulator-demodulators) are devices that allow a microcomputer to access another computer over telephone lines. This is very useful for accessing data provided by an outside information vendor, or for accessing data stored in a central location within a company. Modems also allow microcomputers to function as computer terminals for use with a larger computer to run jobs beyond the capability of the microcomputer. This linkage is viewed as an important first step in office automation.

SOFTWARE

Most microcomputer users view their machines as a black box capable of running specific applications. Software is the complementary product that makes this possible. The two main categories of software are operating system software and applications software.

Operating systems software does the housekeeping of a microcomputer. It manages files and controls the operations of other programs, such as applications software. Because this function is central to the operation of a microcomputer, the operating system determines the extent to which data and programs can be shared between two microcomputers. Generally, two microcomputers that share the same operating system are compatible, although different versions of the same system can lead to problems. Because the operating system controls the microprocessor, the software is somewhat specific to the chip and architecture of the individual product.

For the first generation of 8-bit microcomputers, CP/M, developed by Digital Research Corporation, was the most widely used operating system. However, since the advent of 16-bit microprocessors, the operating system used by IBM, MS DOS, has emerged as the de facto industry standard. The choice of which operating system to employ is a crucial one to the strategy of a firm. The choice of operating system will determine which applications programs will run on a given computer. If a firm chooses to follow IBM's lead and uses MS DOS, this provides the advantage of immediate access to a large number of software programs available in the market. Unfortunately, it also creates a stigma of copying IBM's product and being viewed as a "me-too" producer. Alternatively, a firm can choose to provide a proprietary operating system. This has the advantage of allowing a firm to differentiate itself and provide the only applications software capable of being used on the machine. It also creates the risk that the new operating system and software will not be viewed as sufficiently superior to the industry standard products to warrant switching systems. Apple has followed this latter approach in developing specialized software for its Macintosh line of products.

Applications software provides functional capability to a microcomputer. The main uses for applications software are word processing, spreadsheet analysis, database management, graphics, communications between computers, and games. In addition, language compilers, such as BASIC and FORTRAN, allow users to run specific programs written in those languages. Some of the most popular software packages and their prices are shown in Exhibit 2.

A cottage industry supplying software for microcomputers has emerged in the United States and Europe. For example, the DataPro Directory of Microcomputer Software lists over 1,000 firms in the United States in which PC software is included in their principal line of business. Early analysts of the microcomputer industry predicted that a typical user would spend at least as much on software as on hardware. Recent events have led these analysts to reconsider their positions. Many microcomputer producers have adopted the practice of bundling software with their hardware and pricing the package very aggressively. For example, in early 1985, the Sanyo MBC 555, an IBM-compatible microcomputer with 128K of RAM and two floppy disk drives, was available for under $1,000. This price included several popular software packages, such as MS DOS, Easywriter, Wordstar, Calcstar, Spellstar, Mailmerge, and Infostar, which if bought separately would cost over $1,000. For many users, this is all the software they would ever need.

EXHIBIT 2   POPULAR MICROCOMPUTER SOFTWARE PACKAGES

PRODUCT	RETAIL PRICE	MAIL-ORDER PRICE	APPLICATION
dBase III	$695	$339	Database
Framework	695	339	Integrated multifunction
Multiplan	195	115	Spreadsheet
Sidekick	55	35	Utility
1-2-3	495	289	Integrated multifunction
Symphony	695	409	Integrated multifunction
Wordstar 2000	495	239	Word processing
VisiCalc 4	250	159	Spreadsheet
Volkswriter Deluxe	395	149	Word processing
rBase: 4000	495	269	Database
Microsoft Word	375	235	Word processing
TK Solver!	399	265	Modeling/simulation
SuperCalc III	395	245	Spreadsheet
Perfect Writer	349	179	Word processing
Crosstalk XVI	195	99	Communications
Prokey	130	79	Utility

Source: PC World, March 1985.

MARKET SIZE AND SEGMENTATION

The European microcomputer industry is not a unified market of standard products or users. Rather, it is composed of many national markets, each with different requirements, levels of sophistication, and distribution channels. As a result, it is dangerous to generalize about competitive requirements for success using the whole of Europe as a reference point.

Many industry observers believe that the evolution of the European market will parallel the development of the American market. In the 1970s, this seemed to be the case, as European markets were dominated by American multinationals exporting products they were already selling in the United States. A brief summary of key events in the evolution of the microcomputer industry appears in Exhibit 3.

The largest market in Europe is the United Kingdom, with approximately 24 percent of the $2 billion industry in 1983. As shown in Exhibit 4, Germany is a close second, and the four largest markets (United Kingdom, Germany, France, and Italy) account for 76 percent of European sales.

The major market segments are as follows:

- The home user/hobbyist whose demand is oriented toward smaller micros and leisure applications. This segment was especially well developed in England by Sinclair. A strong position in the home market is

EXHIBIT 3   EVOLUTION OF MICROCOMPUTER INDUSTRY

1974	Intel announces the 8080 microprocessor
	Motorola announces the 8600 microprocessor
1975	Early microcomputer kits appear on market
	Dick Heiser opens first retail computer store in Santa Monica
1976	Zilog announces Z80 microprocessor
	Steve Wozniak designs Apple 1; Apple founded by Wozniak and Steve Jobs
	Steve Leninger joins Radio Shack to design a computer
	100 companies active in field by year-end
	132 computer clubs in existence by year-end
1977	Apple II announced
	Radio Shack TRS-80 announced
	Microsoft begins to market BASIC and FORTRAN for microcomputers
	First Computerland franchise store opened in Morristown, New Jersey; 24 stores open by year-end
	Over 200 active manufacturers by year-end
1978	Atari announces the 400 and 800 computers
	Apple and Radio Shack begin using 5¼″ disk drives
	Dan Bricklin and Bob Frankston write VisiCalc
1979	Texas Instruments introduces 99/4 home computer
	Radio Shack announces Model II business computer
	Micropro announces Wordstar
	NEC demonstrates the 8000 computer at Hannover, West Germany, trade show
1980	Sinclair ZX80 introduces first computer under $200
	Apple introduces the Apple III
	Epson announces the MX-80 printer
	Microsoft agrees to work with IBM to design software
	Xerox, DEC, and Intel announce Ethernet Local Area Network
1981	Osborne introduces the first transportable computer
	IBM announces the PC
	Microsoft produces MS-DOS (PC-DOS) for IBM PC
1982	Commodore 64 announced
	DEC announces Rainbow 100
	Apple begins selling "user friendly" LISA in United States
	Franklin introduces Apple-compatible ACE 100
	NEC announces 16-bit Advanced Personal Computer
	NEC introduces the 8800 series in Europe
	Seven IBM-compatible computers appear on the market
1983	IBM introduces PCjr and PC XT
	Radio Shack announces Model 100 notebook computer; NEC announces 8201
	Timex introduces Timex/Sinclair 2000, but withdraws from market eight months later
	Texas Instruments withdraws 99/4A
	Osborne Computer files for bankruptcy

EXHIBIT 3   (continued)

	NEC begins selling 8201 notebook computer in Europe
	IBM lookalikes flood the market
1984	Apple announces Macintosh, Apple IIc
	Hewlett-Packard introduces Model 110 notebook portable, similar in power to desktop machines
	Mattel, Timex, Specta-Video, Victor, Actrix, and Computer Devices leave market or sell out
	Warner sells Atari to Jack Tramiel after losses of $539 million
	NEC sells over 1 million personal computers in Japan
	First national TV advertising for software (Lotus Symphony and Ashton-Tate Framework); number of software manufacturers tops 500

Source: Creative Computing, November 1984.

EXHIBIT 4   EUROPEAN NATIONAL MARKETS, 1983

	REVENUES	PERCENTAGE OF EUROPEAN MARKET
United Kingdom	$480 million	24%
Germany	460	23
France	360	18
Italy	220	11
Scandinavia	160	8
Benelux countries	140	7
Spain/Portugal	100	5
Switzerland/Austria	80	4
Total (approximately 300,000 units)	$2 billion	100%

EUROPEAN USER SEGMENTS BY SIZE

	PERCENTAGE OF TOTAL MARKET	
	UNITS	VALUE
Home	61%	12%
Business	26	63
Education	7	3
Scientific	6	22

Source: International Data Corporation.

thought to provide a basis for creating customer loyalty that can be exploited in trade-ups to larger products.

- The educational institution that purchases microcomputers to teach computer literacy. This segment has not proven very lucrative for producers because government purchasers are price sensitive and may use their purchasing power to promote a national champion. This segment has been used as a loss leader by some manufacturers to create brand visibility and preferences. For example, Apple has created an educational consortium of major universities that receive Macintosh computers at deep discounts.
- The scientist who uses the microcomputer instead of a mainframe to perform very specific applications. Scientific applications typically require powerful microcomputers with specialized software.
- The business user who relies on a microcomputer for word processing, data analysis, terminal emulation, or a variety of other administrative tasks. As shown in Exhibit 4, this is the largest segment in Europe, accounting for nearly two thirds of all microcomputer revenues.

DISTRIBUTION

Microcomputers in Europe are sold through a variety of channels. Although distribution networks differ somewhat across countries, the following channels generally exist to some extent in all European nations. A summary of the distribution channels for Europe appears in Exhibit 5.

DIRECT SALES FORCE

For large accounts, direct sales calls are common. Companies with an existing position in a related field, such as telecommunications, large computers, or office products, are most likely to emphasize this channel. This provides the advantage of being able to sell a bundle of related products as a customized system to corporate clients. The ability to provide such systems is thought to be a crucial capability for future success in large accounts.

RETAIL STORES

Retail computer stores are the single most important channel of distribution, accounting for over one third of all sales in Europe, and as much as 45 percent in the United Kingdom. This category includes company-owned stores, such as those used by Tandy as its exclusive form of distribution, mass merchandisers who sell a wide variety of consumer products in addition to microcomputers, independent retailers, and franchise chains, of which Computerland and Entre are the largest. As of 1984, Computerland operated 791 stores worldwide and generated sales of $1.4 billion. Computer franchise stores, which originally appeared in the United States and are well established in

EXHIBIT 5   EUROPEAN DISTRIBUTION NETWORKS FOR MICROCOMPUTERS PRICED $1,000 AND ABOVE

	RETAIL OUTLETS	SYSTEM HOUSES	TOTAL NETWORK
United Kingdom	832	350	1,182
Germany	672	250	922
France	620	250	870
Italy	580	100	680
Belgium	144	100	244
Netherlands	145	70	215
Spain	130	70	200

DISTRIBUTION NETWORK BY TYPE OF OUTLET (PERCENTAGES BASED ON 1983 VOLUMES)

	MASS OUTLETS	COMPUTER STORES	OFFICE EQUIPMENT STORES	SYSTEM HOUSES	DIRECT SALES
United Kingdom	7–10%	42–45%	2–4%	23–25%	20–22%
Germany	3–4	26–29	22–24	24–26	20–22
France	<1	38–40	4–5	32–34	22–25
Italy	—	31–35	19–21	28–32	16–18
Spain	4–6	33–35	16–18	29–31	13–15
Belgium	3–5	38–40	8–10	24–28	21–23
Netherlands	2–4	33–35	12–14	18–20	30–32
USA	28	33	6	13	15

Source: Electronics Business and Electronics Intelligence.

that market, have yet to make a similar impact in Europe. Nonetheless, both Computerland and Entre have announced aggressive plans to expand their European networks.

PRODUCTION

Manufacturing microcomputers is a relatively easy task. Components and sub-assemblies are readily available on world markets, and many producers have adopted policies of purchasing nearly all inputs externally and simply assembling the product and attaching their brand name. Even IBM, with its great potential for vertical integration, has chosen to rely on outside vendors for nearly all of the components of the PC. As shown in Exhibit 6, approximately 73 percent of the manufacturing cost of the IBM PC comes from components purchased from Asian producers. Exhibit 7 summarizes the manufacturing strategies of several major microcomputer producers.

EXHIBIT 6   IBM PC MANUFACTURING SOURCES

ELEMENT	IBM	OTHER	
Video display	—	Korea	$ 85
Printer	—	Japan	160
Floppy disks	$ 25	Singapore	165
Keyboard	—	Japan	50
Semiconductors	105	Japan	105
Power supply	—	Japan	60
Case and final assembly	105		—
Total cost	$235		$625

Source: Business Week, March 11, 1985.

BASES FOR COMPETITIVE ADVANTAGE

In choosing a competitive strategy in microcomputers, there are numerous bases for competitive advantage. The strategies of many competitors are derived from their strategies in related markets. Because the microcomputer is at the intersection of several technologies, firms have been attracted to the industry from many directions. This pattern of gateways is summarized in Exhibit 8. For example, as producers of typewriters, such as Olivetti and Triumph-Adler, saw their products increasingly being replaced by word processors, they were induced into offering their own microcomputers. Similarly, as microcomputers became more powerful and better substitutes for larger computers, integrated computer companies were motivated to introduce their own products. On the technology side, the trend toward a convergence of data processing and telecommunications brought the entry of AT&T, ITT, and NEC. Similarly, consumer electronics companies (Panasonic, Sharp, Tandy), toy producers (Atari, Mattel, Coleco), and start-ups (Apple, Fortune) all entered the market with distinctive motivations, resources, and ways of doing business.

This variety of perspectives has manifested itself in different competitive postures. It is possible to strive for competitive advantage in any of the following (not necessarily mutually exclusive) ways.

COST LEADERSHIP

In its announcements and in its actions IBM has indicated that it intends to be the low-cost producer of microcomputers. It has even deviated substantially from corporate tradition to attain this goal. For example, despite its strong existing capabilities in many aspects of microcomputer technology, IBM has

EXHIBIT 7 MICROCOMPUTER MANUFACTURING STRATEGIES

COMPANY	MAJOR MODELS	MAIN UNIT	KEYBOARD	MONITOR	DISK DRIVE	PRINTER	SOFTWARE
Apple	IIe, Lisa	MF	OS	OS	OS	OS	MF
Atari	400, 800	MF	OS	N/A	OS	OS	MF
Commodore	VIC-20, 64	MF	OS	OS	OS	OS	MF
DEC	Rainbow	MF	MF	MF	MF	MF	OS/MF
Hewlett-Packard	75C, HP-86, 87, 150	MF	OS	MF	MF	MF	MF
IBM	PC, XT	OS/MF	OS	OS	OS	OS	OS/MF
Tandy	Model III, Model XVI, Color Computer	MF	OS	MF	OS	OS	MF
Texas Instruments	Professional	MF	MF	OS	MF	MF	MF

Abbreviations: MF = manufactured in-house; OS = bought from outside supplier

EXHIBIT 8 MICROCOMPUTER ENTRY GATEWAYS

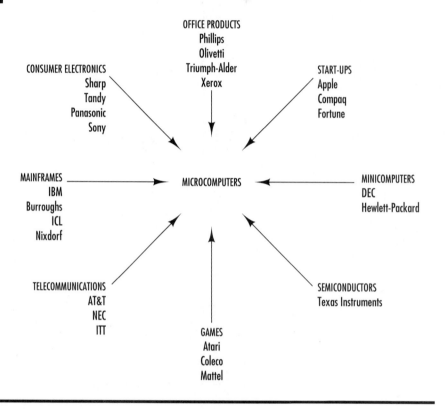

declined to vertically integrate for fear of increasing its costs. In the case of printers, which IBM purchases from Epson, the IBM printer-manufacturing division was invited to submit a bid for supplying dot-matrix printers. The bid was higher than Epson's, and thus was refused, despite tremendous internal politicking to push it through. IBM's large market share allows it to receive volume purchasing discounts and scale economies in assembly and marketing. Although it has yet to occur, industry analysts look to Asia for significant future challengers to IBM's cost position.

FULL-LINE COMPLEMENTARITY

Another strategic approach is to view the microcomputer not as a stand-alone product but as part of an office system. Producers who sell a full line of office products, such as PABXs, local area networks, telex machines, terminals, large computers, and word processors, can sell their microcomputers as part of an integrated system. This overcomes the problems of incompatibility between individual products supplied by different vendors. DEC and Xerox have been leaders in pursuing this strategy.

PROPRIETARY CLOSED SYSTEM

As an alternative to conforming to industry standards in hardware and software, a microcomputer producer may elect to introduce its own unique computer architecture and operating system. As mentioned earlier, the benefits of differentiation must be weighed against the risk of the market not accepting the new system.

Microcomputers exist in multiple configurations of processor speed, memory size, machine size, and other special features. It is possible for a manufacturer to specialize in one hardware segment of the market and attempt to build an image as the industry leader. For example, Compaq recorded the all-time largest volume of sales in the first year of operation for a company (over $100 million) by dominating the market for "transportable" microcomputers. These products weigh approximately 30 pounds and are self-contained for relatively easy movement.

"ME-TOO"

The single most common competitive strategy in microcomputers is to offer a clone or look-alike product that emulates the industry standard (generally IBM). There are currently hundreds of companies that produce microcomputers that are physical and electronic copies of IBM's PC. Such products generally sell for discounts of 15–40 percent off the IBM price. This strategy is not limited to small firms: ITT, Siemens, Ericsson, Olivetti, and Tandy have joined ranks with the many start-up firms that offer products with little or no enhancement to the basic IBM model. Indeed, this has led many observers to speculate that the microcomputer may be entering a stage of evolution resembling a commodity.

NATIONAL MARKET SEGMENTATION

European national markets for microcomputers demonstrate some differentiating characteristics that create the possibility of national market segmentation. Local governments have a long history of preferential purchasing of large computers, and this has continued into the realm of microcomputers as well. Different languages and cultures also create possible advantages for a local supplier. For example, no foreign producer has succeeded in capturing any significant share of the Japanese market. IBM failed to reach the company target of 120,000 PCs sold in Japan in 1984 despite a reorganization and new product design to push the microcomputer. Attempts by Sinclair, Tandy, Commodore, and Apple have been similarly frustrated. Early product offerings by all these companies were simply exports of existing machines and were unable to use kana and kanji characters. Today, NEC has over 50 percent of the Japanese microcomputer market, and its chief rivals are all Japanese firms.

TECHNOLOGICAL LEADERSHIP

Another method for strategic differentiation is to strive for leadership in the underlying technology of microcomputers. The current standard microcomputer, as exemplified by the IBM PC, is a modest machine relative to state-of-the-art possibilities. Faster microprocessors, higher density storage, more advanced memory chips, better fundamental architecture, and more sophisticated operating systems are all currently possible. However, packaging these components into a high-powered microcomputer creates significant risks: lack of software, high costs, risks of supply interruptions, and general lack of customer acceptance in the same way as a proprietary closed system.

COMPETITOR PROFILES

In 1985 the European microcomputer market was crowded with several hundred firms, ranging from small start-ups working out of a garage to some of the world's largest corporations. Exhibit 9 provides a financial overview of some of the most significant competitors. Strategic profiles appear in the following paragraphs.

IBM

IBM is the world leader in microcomputers. IBM began selling microcomputers in the United States in August 1981 and started exports to Europe in January 1983. Today, IBM dominates both markets. In 1984 it is estimated that IBM sold over 2 million PCs in the United States alone. IBM's market share is especially high in the corporate market. In early 1985 it was estimated that 76 percent of all desktop computers in Fortune 500 companies are made by IBM. To serve this market, IBM relies on its direct selling staff of 6,000 to 7,000 people, compared to 60 for Apple, the second largest supplier.

In the European market, IBM attained a market share of 16 percent in its first year. This figure would have been higher if not for chronic parts shortages at its Greenock, Scotland, plant. By 1984 IBM had captured over 30 percent of the market and seemed destined to replay its American success.

IBM's strategy was based on several key elements. As mentioned earlier, IBM is dedicated to low-cost production, even if this implies reliance on outside vendors. Low costs have been translated into aggressive pricing. As shown in Exhibit 10, IBM has cut the price of the PC by over 62 percent since its introduction. This has kept tremendous pressure on "me-too" producers to keep their prices low.

IBM has also blanketed the microcomputer market with a full line of products. At the low end, IBM introduced the PCjr in late 1983 at a price of $699.

EXHIBIT 9 COMPETITOR PROFILES

APPLE COMPUTER (1983)

Income statement data	(millions)	*Sales by activity*	
Net sales	$983	Microcomputers	100%
COGS	484		
Depreciation	22		
R&D	60	*Sales by area*	
Marketing	230	United States	78%
G&A	57	Europe	13
EBIT	130	Other	9
Net income	77		
Dividends	0		

Balance sheet data			
Cash	$143	Accounts payable	$ 53
Accounts receivable	136	Notes payable	0
Inventory	142	Other current liabilities	76
Other current assets	48	Long-term debt	0
Fixed assets	67	Other liabilities	50
Other noncurrent assets	21	Shareholders' equity	378
		Preferred stock	0

IBM (1983)

Income statement data	(millions)	*Sales by activity*	
Net sales	$23,274	Processors	23%
Other income	16,906	Peripherals	15
COGS	13,033	Office systems	14
Depreciation	3,362	Program products	6
R&D	2,514	Other sales	6
Engineering expense	1,068	Rentals	23
SG&A	10,614	Maintenance	11
Operating profit	9,589	Other services	2
Other income	741		
EBIT	10,330	*Sales by area*	
Net income	5,485	United States	58%
Dividends	2,251	Europe	27
		Americas/Far East	15

Balance sheet data			
Cash	$ 5,336	Accounts payable	$ 1,253
Accounts receivable	6,380	Notes payable	532
Inventory	4,381	Other current liabilities	7,722
Other current assets	973	Long-term debt	2,674
Net fixed assets	16,142	Other liabilities	1,843
Other noncurrent assets	3,831	Shareholders's equity	23,019
		Preferred stock	0

(*continued*)

EXHIBIT 9   (continued)

COMMODORE INTERNATIONAL (1983)

Income statement data	(millions)	Sales by activity	
Net sales	$681	Home computers	45%
COGS	346	Business and educational systems	23
Depreciation	14	Peripherals	19
R&D	37	Software	9
Marketing	139	Office equipment	4
SG&A	24		
EBIT	121	Sales by area	
Extraordinary item	4	United States	58%
Net income	92	Canada	16
Dividends	0	Europe	23
		Other	3
Balance sheet data			
Cash	$ 23	Accounts payable	$246
Accounts receivable	180	Notes payable	21
Inventory	327	Other current liabilities	61
Fixed assets	81	Long-term debt	92
Other noncurrent assets	4	Other liabilities	4
		Shareholders' equity	191
		Preferred stock	0

TANDY CORPORATION (1983)

Income statement data	(millions)	Sales by activity	
Net sales	$2,475	Microcomputers	35%
Other income	38	Stereos	18
COGS	1,008	Radios and TVs	14
Depreciation	39	Components	13
R&D	N/A	Calculators and toys	12
SG&A	930	Telephones	8
EBIT	536		
Net income	279	Sales by area	
Dividends	0	United States	84%
		Canada	8
		Europe	5
		Other	3
Balance sheet data			
Cash	$280	Accounts payable	$ 65
Accounts receivable	107	Notes payable	56
Inventory	844	Other current liabilities	165
Other current assets	32	Long-term debt	138
Fixed assets	258	Other liabilities	37
Other noncurrent assets	61	Shareholders' equity	1,121
		Preferred stock	0

EXHIBIT 9   (continued)

OLIVETTI (1983)

Income Statement data	(billions of lire)	*Sales by activity*	
Net sales	L3,736	Typewriters and word processors	23%
COGS	1,824	Terminals	24
Depreciation	226	Computers	21
R&D	187	Telecommunications	5
SG&A	1,031	Other office equipment	27
Operating profit	468		
Other expenses	173		
Net income	295	*Sales by area*	
Dividends	84	United States	7%
		Europe	76
		Latin America	5
		Other	12

Balance sheet data			
Cash	L1,381	Accounts payable	L 797
Accounts receivable	1,546	Notes payable	715
Inventory	808	Other current liabilities	603
Other current assets	105	Long-term debt	1,391
Fixed assets	1,034	Other liabilities	373
Other noncurrent assets	247	Shareholders' equity	1,242

HEWLETT PACKARD (1983)

Income statement data	(millions)	*Sales by activity*	
Net sales	$4,710	Computers	60%
COGS	2,195	Test equipment	26
R&D	493	Medical instruments	9
Marketing	771	Analytical	5
SG&A	523		
Net income	296	*Sales by area*	
Dividends	432	United States	59%
	0	Europe	29
		Other	12

Balance sheet data			
Cash	$ 880	Accounts payable	$ 351
Accounts receivable	951	Other current liabilities	569
Inventory	798	Long-term debt	71
Other current assets	151	Other liabilities	283
Fixed assets	1,431	Shareholders' equity	2,937

EXHIBIT 10 IBM PRICING STRATEGY FOR THE PC

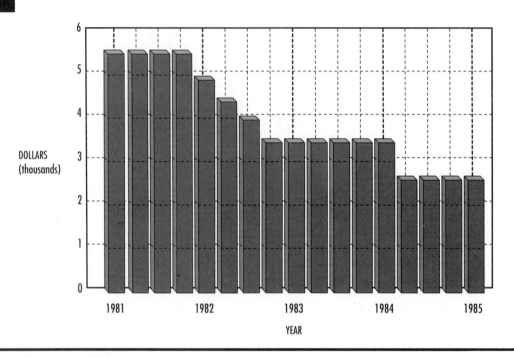

Source: Business Week, March 25, 1985.

The PCjr was targeted at the home user and was capable of running much of the software written for the PC. IBM's first venture into the home market was backed up with extensive advertising. According to IBM sources, during the period from August 1 to December 31, 1984, 98 percent of the American public saw at least 30 PCjr advertising messages. At the high end, IBM announced the PC AT in August 1984 as the flagship of its microcomputer line. The AT is based on a sophisticated microprocessor that facilitates multitasking and multiuser systems. Along with the AT, IBM introduced a local area network capable of supporting up to 72 users simultaneously.

IBM's strategy has also capitalized on its strengths in related markets. As the world's largest computer maker, IBM has a worldwide distribution network and an unequaled reputation for service. In 1982 the U.S. Justice Department dropped a 13-year antitrust suit against IBM, and since that date IBM has moved aggressively into new markets and technologies. IBM has acquired Rolm Corporation, a leading producer of telecommunications products, and has purchased a minority interest in Intel, the supplier of microprocessors for the PC. IBM has also experienced antitrust problems in Europe. The European Commission of the European Economic Community filed suit against IBM in late 1980 accusing the company of abusing its leadership position and restricting competition. For IBM, the stakes in Europe are high. IBM operates 15 factories and nine research laboratories in Europe, employing over 100,000 people.

APPLE COMPUTER

Apple is one of the legends of microcomputing. In 1976 Steve Jobs and Steve Wozniak quit their jobs in Silicon Valley and began experimenting with the use of microprocessors. After designing a crude computer system, Jobs and Wozniak sold their van and calculator to raise $1,300 in seed money. The machine was an instant success, and Apple began to grow explosively. From these humble beginnings, Apple Computer grew to $1.9 billion in annual sales by 1985 and took its place in the Fortune 500.

Apple's early success was based on its ability to innovate and to make computers less threatening to large segments of the population, many of whom had never used a computer before. Apple's early leadership gave it extensive distribution in hobby and specialist shops and a large market share in small businesses and the home. Apple entered the European market in 1978 and proceeded to attain a very strong position. However, increased competition has led to an erosion in Apple's position in both the United States and Europe. In 1984 Apple pinned its hopes on the Macintosh, a machine designed to make computers as friendly and as easy to use as possible. Apple claimed that a new user could begin to perform productive work within 30 minutes of using the Macintosh for the first time. This is in stark contrast to the esoteric and complex languages associated with most microcomputer applications. Priced at $2,495, the Macintosh was placed in direct competition with IBM's PC.

TANDY

One of Apple's earliest competitors in microcomputers was Tandy Corporation. Tandy built a strong position in the early stages of market development on the basis of its strong retail store network. In 1985 Tandy sold computers out of approximately 1,350 Radio Shack stores worldwide. Until 1984 Tandy had maintained a proprietary operating system. However, more recent products are IBM compatible. Tandy is particularly strong in the "notebook" (under 10 pounds) segment, where it has the largest share of any producer.

COMMODORE

Commodore was another early entrant into the microcomputer business. In the United States, Commodore focused on the low end of the market and built a strong position in inexpensive machines used for game playing and computer literacy. Commodate entered the European market in 1977 and was somewhat more successful in penetrating the small-business segment. By 1983 Commodore had the largest installed base of microcomputers (in terms of units) of any manufacturer in Europe. In 1984 Commodore introduced a line of IBM-compatible machines targeted at the corporate market.

EUROPEAN COMPETITORS

The leading European producers of microcomputers were Oliveti of Italy, Triumph-Adler of Germany, Applied Computer Technologies of the United Kingdom, Bull-Micral and SMT-Goupil of France, and L. M. Ericsson of Sweden. Although each of these firms had captured roughly 10 percent of their home markets, none had succeeded in developing significant exports. In addition to the leading firms in each national market, many small companies had emerged. For example, in France alone, there were over 90 small firms offering 170 different machines. These small competitors were joined by nearly every large European firm that had previously sold large computers, telecommunications equipment, consumer electronics, office products, or other related goods. The list of competitors includes such firms as Rank Xerox, Siemens, Philips, ICL, Nixdorf, and Thomson. In 1984 AT&T bought 25 percent of Olivetti and began a program of reciprocal product distribution. This exchange was intended to strengthen Olivetti's position in telecommunications products and AT&T's position in small computers. Like most of the competitors mentioned, Olivetti's strategy was to offer an IBM compatible machine at a lower price.

JAPANESE COMPETITORS

Although often discussed, the Japanese threat in microcomputers had failed to materialize in either American or Europe. As shown in Exhibit 11, many Japanese firms exported their products. However, none had attained an overall share of 5 percent or more outside of Japan. The failure of the Japanese to penetrate the United States or Europe was attributed to the following factors:

Inadequate Distribution. The landslide of entrants into microcomputers left many firms scrambling for distribution. Japanese firms generally lacked established channels of their own and were slow to break into other means of distribution. The problem was particularly severe in Europe, where most dealers would handle only three brands at a time. This meant that available shelf space was often captured by IBM, Apple, and a local producer.

Poor Software. Early Japanese products were offered with little software for applications. The first generation of Japanese products were late to adopt the popular CP/M operating system, thus leaving users confused as to what software was available. More recently, the Japanese products have usually followed the IBM standard and have access to the large published base of programs. However, critics often complain that the Japanese products do not offer any advantages over the IBM machine or its look-alikes.

Poor Documentation. In the rush to bring products to the market, many user guides were translated quickly and were poorly produced. This gave the Japanese products a reputation for being hard to use.

EXHIBIT 11   JAPANESE MICROCOMPUTERS FOR EXPORT

COMPANY		PRODUCT	RAM	MICROPROCESSOR	FORMAT	SOFTWARE BUNDLE
Canon		X-07	8K–24K	8 bit	P	No
		AS-100	64K–512K	16 bit	D	No
Casio		FP-200	8K	8 bit	P	Yes
Epson		HX-20	16K–32K	8 bit	P	No
		QX-10	16K–256K	8 bit	D	Yes
Fujitsu		16s	128K–1Mb	8 bit	D	No
NEC		APC	128K–640K	16 bit	D	No
		APC III	128K–640K	16 bit	D	No
		PC-6000	16K–32K	8 bit	D	No
		PC-8800	128K	8 bit	D	No
		PC-8200	16K	8 bit	P	Yes
		PC-8401	64K	8 bit	P	Yes
Panasonic		Sr. Partner	128K–512K	16 bit	T	Yes
Ricoh	(OEM)	Monroe 2000	128K–640K	16 bit	D	No
Sanyo	MBC	550/555	128K–256K	16 bit	D	Yes
	MBC	1100/1150	64K	8 bit	D	Yes
	MBC	4000/4050	128K–512K	16 bit	D	Yes
Seiko		8600 XP	256K	16 bit	D	Yes
Sharp		PC-5000	128K–256K	16 bit	P	Yes
Sony		SMC-70	64K	8 bit	D	No
Sord		IS-11	32K–64K	8 bit	P	Yes
		M23P	128K	8 bit	D	Yes
		M68	256K–1Mb	16/32 bit	D	No
Toshiba		T300	192K–512K	16 bit	D	No

Abbreviations: P = portable; D = desk top; T = transportable.

Source: Creative Computing, August 1984.

Despite the poor start by Japanese firms, the presence of these companies gave many competitors cause for concern. Memories of the Japanese success in televisions, VCRs, stereo equipment, cameras, and other similar products were painfully fresh for microcomputer firms who had competed with the Japanese in these markets previously.

NEC'S ENTRY INTO THE EUROPEAN MICROCOMPUTER MARKET

In 1985 NEC was struggling to find a way to transfer its success in the Japanese microcomputer market to Europe. At home, NEC enjoyed a market share of over 55 percent in personal computers. In addition to systems, NEC offered a full line of peripherals such as printers, screens, and modems. NEC's position in the Japanese market was similar to the role of IBM in America and Europe. A majority of personal computer software developed in Japan was written for NEC machines.

NEC first tested the European market in 1979 when it displayed the PC 8000 at the annual industrial fair in Hannover, West Germany. The PC 8000 was an 8-bit machine with 32K of RAM, expandable to 64K. As a result of a mediocre response at Hannover, NEC delayed the entry of the PC 8000 until the following year. By 1981 NEC was selling microcomputers in Germany, The Netherlands, France, Spain, and Italy. Sales grew slowly, but steadily, and in late 1982 NEC launched the PC 8800, an upgraded machine with a 8-bit processor, 64K memory, and excellent color graphics. These two machines were the mainstays of NEC's product line for the next two years.

NEC continued to expand into both smaller and large machines. In 1983 NEC introduced the 8201, a notebook computer weighing only four pounds. Despite its small size, the 8201 featured an 8-bit processor and 16–64K of RAM, with three software packages built in. In 1985 the 8401 was introduced and offered more memory, a bigger screen, more software, and a built-in modem, all for under $1,000. As they have done in mainframes, NEC has declined to conform to the IBM standard in microcomputers.

During this period, NEC began to develop distribution channels throughout Europe. Some observers felt that this process was inhibited by NEC's complex organizational structure. Small computers were administered through two independent divisions: NEC Home Electronics, headquartered in Neuss, West Germany, and NEC Business Systems, headquartered in London, England. NEC Home Electronics was responsible for distributing 8-bit computers, such as the 8000 and 8800 series, and the supporting peripherals. NEC Business Systems handled 16-bit computers, such as the APC and APC III, introduced in 1984, as well as office-automation equipment. The two divisions operated independently and were responsible for developing their own marketing strategy and distribution channels. For most countries, NEC worked through an exclusive national distributor who specialized in NEC products and sought retail distributors. For example, in France, NEC worked through Omnium Promotion, who had secured retail distribution for NEC in 80 stores throughout France.

NEC was best known in Europe for its computer peripherals. Obtaining distribution for microcomputers was extremely difficult as a result of the practice of handling only three brands in each store. For peripherals, however, distribution was far easier for NEC to obtain. NEC's Spinwriter series of printers was extremely popular and in great demand by retail store operators. In France, the Spinwriters are sold through over 350 outlets. In addition, competition in peripherals was less intense. Although it was widely suspected that few microcomputer companies were making a profit on their computers, NEC acknowledged that the peripherals business was very lucrative.

NEC produced all of its microcomputers in Japan. The freight to Europe was approximately 10 percent of the product's cost, and an additional 5.4 percent duty was paid on entry. NEC stated that it would continue to produce exclusively in Japan as long as delivered costs were minimized. If volume in Europe became sufficient, or EEC policy dictated import penalties, NEC would consider local production.

RECENT EVENTS

As NEC contemplated its strategy for the European market in early 1985, recent events gave the company cause for concern. Persistent rumors of an imminent shake-out made NEC executives wonder if the time for a major commitment to this market had already passed. Several smaller firms, such as Osborne and Gavilan, had already gone bankrupt, and even the industry leaders were beginning to feel the pinch. In March 1985 IBM announced that the PCjr had not met expectations and would be discontinued. Similarly, Apple suffered a number of setbacks. Sales for the Macintosh dropped 45 percent in the first quarter of 1985, and Apple was forced to shut down four factories to work off unsold inventories. Continued sluggish sales of the higher-priced LISA finally led Apple to discontinue the product. Meanwhile, DEC stopped production of its Rainbow, and Xerox was rumored to be getting out of the microcomputer business entirely. NEC management felt that its outstanding technological skills in microcomputers and related markets and its competitive cost structure should provide the basis for success. However, making the concept of C&C a reality was proving far more elusive than NEC had anticipated.

A P P E N D I X

fisCAL Software

INTRODUCTION

Accompanying *Strategic Management for Decision Making* is the financial analysis software package fisCAL, a product of the Halcyon Group. The most comprehensive microcomputer-based program of its type available, fisCAL is widely used by financial analysts, investors, and strategic decision makers. fisCAL provides an interactive financial decision-making environment, producing a wide variety of analyses and reports and is capable of multi-period analysis. Using its data base of industry statistics, fisCAL generates comparisons between the firm and competitors in its industry. The following list contains reports generated by fisCAL.

- Breakeven analysis
- Financial ratio analysis
- Industry comparisons by dollar value
- Industry comparisons by percentage
- Operating capital analysis
- Cash market value analysis (5 methods)
- Trends analysis, including z-score bankruptcy predictor
- Cash flow analysis
- Operating ratio analysis
- Dupont strategic profit model
- Index of sustainable growth model
- Gross margin return on inventory investment model
- Statistical anlysis
- Pro forma income statements, 5 years
- Pro forma balance sheets, 5 years
- Projected cash flow analysis, 5 years

Despite its sophistication, fisCAL is easy to use. All instructions may be selected from easy-to-understand menus, and the reports generated by fisCAL are clear and easy to read. To guide the user through the analyses and to avoid "information overload," each investigation is accompanied by a report summary written in both a quantitative and a narrative format.

Eight cases from *Strategic Management for Decision Making* have been prepared for use with fisCAL. They range in complexity from single period breakeven analysis in the Pizza Delights case to sophisticated considerations of financial expansion and merger in the Eastman Kodak case. Table 1 contains a listing of the fisCAL cases along with the strategic financial factors addressed in each case.

Using the order of cases suggested here, the student is gradually introduced to increasingly more complex financial analyses. Starting with single-period analysis and simple financial procedures such as breakeven analysis in the first fisCAL case, students can work at their own speed to discover how the program works. By the fifth case, Sonoco Products Company, students will be able to utilize multiperiod data to compare statements and financial ratios with data from industry competitors, analyze trends in balance sheet and income statement accounts, interpret Dupont strategic profit models, generate

TABLE 1   fisCAL CASES

CASE NUMBER	CASE	STRATEGIC FINANCIAL FACTORS
5	Pizza Delights	Growth Profit sustainability
34	NEC Corporation's Entry into European Microcomputers	Industry Comparisons Downside Risk
18	Toys "R" Us, 1989	Expansion in Slow-Growth Industry Multiyear Analysis
25	Delta Air Lines	Downside Risk Price Wars Expansion
9	Sonoco Products Company	High Growth Rate Heavy Debt Risk Factors
27	Lincoln Electric Company, 1989	Controlled Expansion Controlled Costs Stock Value
33	Caterpillar, Inc., of Latin America	Market Competition Profitability Cost Reduction
14	Eastman Kodak Co.	Expansion Merger Cost of Capital

pro forma statements, do "what-if" analysis, and use a wide range of other procedures and models available with fisCAL. Students who have had previous experience with advanced financial analysis concepts may opt to start with one of the later cases.

The following is a case-by-case summary of the strategic financial issues and applicable reports generated by fisCAL. Instructions for installing and starting the program on your computer are contained in the fisCAL package.

Case 5: PIZZA DELIGHTS

Financial considerations in the Pizza Delights case center around profitability concerns and the future growth of the enterprise. Reports are for single-period analysis only, making this a good case to use as an introduction to fisCAL.

The following reports are applicable to the investigation of the strategic financial issues in the Pizza Delights case: breakeven analysis, comparison of financial statement accounts to industry norms, and financial ratios comparisons. These reports will reveal a number of areas of concern to Pizza Delights management, including the necessity to engage in cost cutting. Since cost containment is a primary consideration in the case, special attention also should be given to the firm's breakeven analysis report.

If the student is just beginning to use fisCAL, more advanced analyses might best be omitted for now. Growth considerations, however, are an important topic in the case. Therefore the fisCAL index of sustainable growth report, which compares profits, dividends, and payout ratios to industry norms, might prove interesting. Although several additional reports are also generated by fisCAL for Pizza Delights (including operating capital analysis, cash market value analysis, and Dupont strategic profit model) these should be studied only to get an idea of their utility, since these analyses do not bear directly on the issues in the case.

Case 34: NEC CORPORATION'S ENTRY INTO EUROPEAN MICROCOMPUTERS

The NEC case is an excellent one for the introduction of multiple-firm analysis using fisCAL. In addition to the 1984 results for NEC, financial data for six competitors has also been coded. Included are the 1983 figures for Apple Computer, Commodore International, Hewlett-Packard, IBM, Olivetti, and Tandy. To standardize the data, figures for Olivetti were converted to dollars at the rate of 1,000 Italian lira per dollar and entered as millions of dollars. All analyses are for single period results only. Therefore, trends analysis and pro forma results are not applicable in the NEC case.

Breakeven analysis, industry comparison of balance sheet and income statement items, financial ratio analysis, and operating capital analysis are all relevant in the NEC case. Given the availability of these reports for all seven

TABLE 2 APPLICABLE REPORTS BY CASE

	PIZZA	NEC (1)	TOYS	DELTA	SONOCO	LINCOLN	CATERPILLAR	EASTMAN
Single Period								
Summary	X	X	X	X	X	X	X	X
Breakeven	X	X	X	X	X	X		
Industry comparisons	X	X						X
Financial ratios	X	X		X	X			X
Operating capital		X		X	X			
Cash market value						X (2)		X
Trends								
Analysis		X	X	X	X		X	X
Cash flow			X	X	X			X
Operating ratios			X	X				
samSON								
Dupont model		X		X	X	X	X	X
Index of sustainable growth	X	X	X		X	X	X	X
Growth model ROII								
proFOR								
Statistical analysis (3)	X		X	X	X	X	X	X
Future position			X	X	X	X	X	X

Notes:

(1) For the NEC case, reports listed are also available for six competitors: Apple Computer, Commodore, Hewlett-Packard, IBM, Olivetti, and Tandy.

(2) In the Lincoln case, students should convert cash market value to per share stock value manually.

(3) To obtain statistical analysis of past trends, students should <PRINT SCREEN> when the statistical analysis is shown in proFOR.

979

firms, students should be able to obtain a clear picture of the dynamics of competition in the European microcomputer industry.

Recent events described at the end of the case pose the direct threat of market deterioration. Therefore, downside risk considerations should be a primary concern in the financial analysis of NEC and its competitors. NEC's Dupont strategic growth model and its index of sustainable growth should provide some insight into the likelihood of NEC surviving in case of restricted market conditions. Comparing these anlayses with those of the six other competitors might also lend some insight into predicting the outcome of a market shakeout.

Case 18: TOYS "R" US, 1989

The Toys "R" Us case provides the first opportunity to do multiple-year analysis. Data for 1987 and 1988 are coded for fisCAL analysis. The principal financial strategic issue for this industry-leading company is maintaining its expansion program in a slow-growth industry.

Trends, cash flow, and operating ratio analyses should be carefully studied. Although the comparisons are based on only two years of data, significant tendencies are highlighted. Given the company's strategy of rapid growth, the index of sustainable growth report also should be interpreted carefully.

Given the size and dominance of Toys "R" Us, industry comparisons generated by fisCAL should be taken lightly and should not be a primary focus of study. Considering TRU's high fixed costs and expansion plans, however, breakeven analysis is important.

Pro forma statements are available in the Toys "R" Us case. These are especially helpful in analyzing potential problems associated with the company's ambitious growth strategy.

Case 25: DELTA AIR LINES

The principal strategic financial issues in the Delta Air Lines case are

(1) Effects of the industry-wide price wars on the firm's profitability
(2) Provision of the financial resources for the company's planned expansion
(3) Downside risk associated with predictions of decreased industry profits in the future

fisCAL analysis may be used to address each of these issues, either one at a time or simultaneously.

Relevant single-period fisCAL reports in the Delta case are breakeven analysis, financial ratio analysis, and operating capital analysis. Since the passenger airline industry is undergoing a severe but temporary "shock wave," industry comparisons should be interpreted cautiously. A cash market value analysis may also generated for Delta, but as there are no merger, acquisition, or divestiture issues in the case, it is not relevant for decision-making purposes.

Trends analyses generated by fisCAL are helpful in the Delta case. Two years of data, 1986 and 1987, have been coded for analysis. Trends analysis reports, cash flow analysis, and operating ratios should all be studied for relevant decision issues. Given the questions surrounding future profitability and planned expansion, the Dupont analysis of the composition of net profits and the five-year projected statements generated by the proFOR routine are very useful in assisting strategic decision making in the case.

Case 9: SONOCO PRODUCTS, INC.

Sonoco is a high growth rate company that has recently acquired a sizable new subsidiary by financing the acquisition with debt. Strategic financial issues therefore revolve around the effects of this acquisition and the accompanying debt load on future profitability and subsequent growth of the enterprise. Two years of financial data, 1987 and 1988, have been coded for analysis.

Breakeven analysis, financial ratio comparisons, and an analysis of operating capital are all relevant in the Sonoco case, since each of these can shed light on the effects of the acquisition. fisCAL multi-year analyses are also relevant. Trends in balance sheet and income statement accounts and in ratios are essential to understanding the strategic financial situation in which the company has placed itself. Cash flow analysis, which highlights cash flows from operations versus investing and financing activities, should be studied in light of the recent merger.

Considering Sonoco's stated policy of sustained rapid growth, both the Dupont analysis of the composition of net profit margin and the index of sustainable growth analysis should be considered relevant to decision makers. Pro forma statements should also be studied.

Case 27: LINCOLN ELECTRIC COMPANY, 1989

Lincoln Electric, in contrast to Sonoco, is a firm with the stated policy of internal growth through the retention of earnings and stock purchases of employees rather than through the use of debt. fisCAL financial analysis should therefore center on whether Lincoln's policies of slow, controlled expansion, close control over costs, and managing for enhanced stock value are adequate to provide for the company's capital needs.

Relevant single period fisCAL analyses for the Lincoln Electric case are the breakeven analysis, which highlights cost factors, and the cash market value analysis, which indicates how the employee/owners' investments are performing. (Note that the cash market value analysis must be manually converted to per share data to be relevant to that issue.)

Nine years of historical data provide the basis for trends analysis. Although most balance sheet and income statement trends are not significant, trends in ratios, most of which are positive, lend support to the company's very careful financial management policies. Cash flow analysis is not relevant in this case but the Dupont strategic profit model is. Given Lincoln Electric's policy of using very little financial leverage, the index of sustainable growth model should be studied in terms of the options that the policy foregoes.

Case 33: CATERPILLAR, INC., IN LATIN AMERICA

Strategic financial factors in the Caterpillar case include intense market competition, profitability, and cost reduction. Caterpillar faces a severe challenge to its Latin American markets from Komatsu, supported by a powerful Komatsu-Dresser joint venture in the United States. The company has recently adopted a new competitive strategy that includes significant improvements in cost effectiveness and a large-scale plant modernization program. fisCAL analysis should therefore focus on projections of long-run performance in light of these goals.

Since much of the detail for individual balance sheet and income statement accounts is omitted in this case, in-depth industry comparisons and financial ratio analysis are not available. Summary data have been coded for nine years, however, and these provide a good basis for establishing trends. The fisCAL trend analysis report reveals that, while the company is correct in choosing cost effectiveness as one of its major objectives, its recent performance—cost trend vs. revenue—can certainly be improved.

Although the company's most immediate concerns are controlling costs and meeting the Komatsu challenge in Latin America, long-run growth goals should also be assessed. Both the Dupont strategic profit model and the index of sustainable growth analysis are therefore relevant.

Pro forma analysis is perhaps the most important area for analyzing the Caterpillar case. The five-year financial statement projections and cash flow analysis, which can be altered by changing the assumptions to fit various competitive scenarios, should be thoroughly studied.

Case 14: EASTMAN KODAK COMPANY: THE STERLING DRUG ACQUISITION

The Eastman Kodak case provides an opportunity for more sophisticated financial analysis. Strategic issues in the case that may be analyzed with fisCAL are the effects of a large recent merger and future expansion plans of the company.

Eastman is facing possible obsolescence of its main product lines and has recently embarked on a program of diversification. The recent acquisition of Sterling Drug Company, which dramatically increased the company's revenues, has also created a significant increase in its debt position. Eight years of data have been coded for fisCAL analysis.

Relevant single period analyses include industry comparisons, financial ratio analysis, and cash market value analysis. Note that 1988 data are for the newly merged entity and should therefore be critical in assessing Eastman's ability to assimilate its acquisition of Sterling Drug.

Trends in financial statement accounts and ratios as compared to industry standards reveal a number of strong and weak points in the case that should be noted. Multi-year cash flow analysis is useful for separating the cash flow from operations from the effects of financing the Sterling merger. The Dupont strategic profit model, which analyzes the sources of Eastman's high rates of returns, should also be studied. The index of sustainable growth, which shows a very high growth rate for the company, should be used as well.

fisCAL pro forma statistical analysis and five-year projections for Eastman are perhaps the most important reports in this case. Assumptions about sales growth rates and costs should be altered and "what-if" analysis run. The company's program of expansion will require significant earnings in the future, so the analysis should try to determine the company's sensitivity to downturns in revenue and possible increases in both fixed and variable costs.

NAME INDEX

Key
f = figure
t = table
b = box

A

Adams, Sexton, 494–524, 739–757
Ader, Lauren, 494–524
Aidiff, Alan, 324–339
Airbus Industries, 80
Akers, John, 27
Albanese, Robert, 186
Alcoa, 10–11
American Airlines, 95
American Express, 127*t*
American Home Products, 89
American Hospital Supply Company, 95
American Management Association, 179
American Motors, 28
American Society for Quality Control, 136
Amit, R, 93*f*
Anderson, Robert L, 549–559
Andrews, KR, 10
Anheuser Busch, 55, 86, 114, 115*t*
Apex, 127*t*
Apple Computer Company, 11, 52, 81
Arthur Anderson, 127*t*
Arthur D Little, 127*t*
Asp, Peter, 340–367
Athena Group, 127*t*

Avis, 95–96
Avishai, B, 127

B

B Altman & Co, 70
Bain, 82–83
Baker, JC, 14*t*
Bank of America, 28, 127*t*
Banker's Trust of South Carolina, 59
Barman, S, 151
Barney, JB, 95–96*b*
Bauerschmidt, Alan, 906–921
Beamish, Paul W, 888–905
Bear, Stearns & Co, 127*t*
Beecham PLC, 161
Bettis, 14, 56–57
Bizzell, Bobby G, 549–559
BMW, 83
Boardman, AE, 73
Boeing Aircraft Company, 80, 83, 86
Boron, Michele, 739–757
Boston Consulting Group (BCG), 37–39
Boulton, WR, 53–54*b*
Bower, J, 209, 211*f*

SUBJECT INDEX

Key
f = figure
t = table
b = box